ENCYCLOPEDIA OF

Latter-day Saint
HISTORY

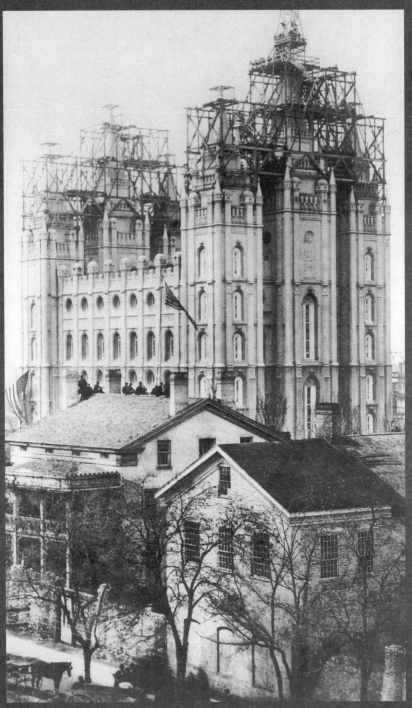

Salt Lake Temple capstone-laying ceremony, 6 April 1892.

ENCYCLOPEDIA OF

Latter-day Saint
HISTORY

EDITED BY
ARNOLD K. GARR
DONALD Q. CANNON
RICHARD O. COWAN

PHOTOGRAPHIC EDITOR
RICHARD NEITZEL HOLZAPFEL

DESERET BOOK COMPANY
SALT LAKE CITY, UTAH

Library of Congress Cataloging-in-Publication Data

Encyclopedia of Latter-day Saint history / edited by Arnold K. Garr, Donald Q. Cannon, Richard O. Cowan.
      p. cm.
    Includes bibliographical references.
    ISBN1-57345-822-8 (hb)
    1. Church of Jesus Christ of Latter-day Saints—History—Encyclopedias. I. Garr, Arnold K. 1944– II. Cannon, Donald Q., 1936– III. Cowan, Richard O., 1934–

BX8611.E53 2000
289.3'09—dc21

00-59618

Printed in the United States of America   18961-6410

10   9   8   7   6   5   4   3   2   1

CONTENTS

PREFACE

As TEACHERS OF HISTORY of The Church of Jesus Christ of Latter-day Saints, we have recognized the need for a convenient, one-volume reference work. Our objective has been to present accurate, concise, and readable articles on a wide variety of Church history topics. These range from items dealing with the Restoration and its early days to articles on current topics. In all, this encyclopedia contains more than 1,400 entries.

More than 350 authors have contributed to this work. Of them, about 50 are colleagues in Religious Education at Brigham Young University and an additional 50 come from other colleges and departments within Brigham Young University. Our authors live in 26 states and approximately 20 nations. In many cases, these authors are the recognized authorities on the topics they treat.

Entries in the encyclopedia discuss a variety of topics. Some describe places that are the sites of specific events, while others present the Church's history in all 50 states, all Canadian provinces, and more than 200 other countries, territories, and political entities. More than 450 entries are biographies, including essays on all who have served in the First Presidency and the Quorum of the Twelve Apostles, other selected general authorities, and many local pioneers in the international Church. Other entries treat key events—both in and out of the Church—that have affected the direction of Latter-day Saint history. Still other entries discuss organizations, issues, and other themes.

A typical entry begins with a topic sentence that identifies in a few words the significance of the subject being treated. The body of the article then presents a succinct discussion. A list of sources includes places where you can turn for additional information on the subject.

The encyclopedia includes numerous cross-references to help you find the information you are seeking. Words in bold type indicate a cross-reference to another article. To conserve space, we often use the phrase "the Church" in referring to The Church of Jesus Christ of Latter-day Saints.

We have tried diligently to provide the most accurate information, but sometimes sources present conflicting data or no information at all. In some instances we chose to include only the information we felt was most reliable; in a few other cases we listed alternative dates when conflicting sources appeared to be equally credible.

We acknowledge assistance given by many others. We are grateful for the contributions from our numerous authors and for the assistance of those who have reviewed portions of our text. We express our thanks particularly to Lisa Kurki and Richard D. McClellan, who as student editors made refinements in form and style and checked sources for accuracy. We also appreciate Matthew Green, Bryan Rasmussen, Sarah Barnham, Leah Call, Rebecca Jackson, Matthew Willden, Sydney Hughes, Rachel Wilkins, and Michele Daetwyler, who have helped us shepherd the entries through the various stages of manuscript preparation. We are grateful to Religious Education at BYU for providing funds to make this help available. We particularly appreciate the support and encouragement given by Dean Robert L. Millet and our department chairs, Raymond S. Wright and Paul H. Peterson. We are also grateful for the support our families gave us during the many hours we were away from them while working on this project. Finally, we express our thanks to the people at Deseret Book who gave appreciated refinement to our manuscript and prepared this work for publication: Deseret Book imprint director Cory Maxwell; senior editor Suzanne Brady and her editorial colleagues; art director Richard Erickson; and typographer Laurie Cook.

It is our conviction that The Church of Jesus Christ of Latter-day Saints is God's restored kingdom on earth, that it has a divine destiny, and that it is led by inspiration. We have sought to be fair, scholarly, and responsible in our treatment of the subjects we have included in this book. We hope not only that you will find the facts you are seeking but also that you will gain a greater appreciation for the accomplishments of the Church and its people.

ENCYCLOPEDIA OF
LATTER-DAY SAINT HISTORY

AUSTRALIA. The first branch of the Church on the Australian continent was established in 1844; in 1904 the first meetinghouse, Gibbon Street Chapel, was erected in Brisbane.

AARONIC PRIESTHOOD. The Aaronic Priesthood, a lesser **priesthood** or "appendage" to the **Melchizedek Priesthood**, was restored 15 May 1829 by **John the Baptist** to **Joseph Smith** and **Oliver Cowdery**. This priesthood provides authority to baptize and carry out other responsibilities. Early **revelations** (D&C 20; 84; 107) identify four Aaronic Priesthood offices—**deacon**, **teacher**, **priest** and **bishop**—and the duties of each. Priests are to preach, teach, expound, exhort, baptize, and administer the **sacrament**; visit members in their homes and teach them to pray and fulfill **family** duties; conduct **meetings** and **ordain** priests, teachers and deacons. Teachers are to watch over Church members: prevent iniquity, lying, backbiting, and evil speaking; see that members attend meetings and do their duties; conduct meetings; and expound, exhort, teach, and invite souls to come unto **Christ**. Deacons are to assist teachers in their duties as occasion requires. Each office is to have a **quorum** (a deacons quorum has 12 deacons; teachers, 24; and priests, 48) and a quorum presidency. A bishop is president of the Aaronic Priesthood in his **ward**. Through most of the nineteenth century, male adults filled the Aaronic Priesthood offices, assisted by a few youths. Latter-day Saint Aaronic Priesthood history has passed through four distinct periods:

1. Before the **endowment** was received and before wards were organized (1829–1845). Aaronic Priesthood bearers were adults (except for a few outstanding youths). Their primary duty was to visit members in their homes. Their quorums were **stake** quorums.

2. Acting priesthood bearers with stake quorums (1846–1877). After the temple endowment was broadly introduced in 1845, men called on missions or marrying for eternity had to receive their endowments, a prerequisite for which was Melchizedek Priesthood ordination. That left few adult males to serve in Aaronic Priesthood offices. To fill the ranks, Melchizedek Priesthood bearers were called to serve as acting priests, teachers, and deacons. Some boys received priesthood ordinations.

Deacon, teacher, and priest quorums were stake units. In Utah, wards became the main local units and ward bishops the primary local officer, aided by a corps of acting teachers and priests called block or ward teachers. Deacons served as ward meetinghouse custodians.

3. Acting and ordained priesthood bearers with ward quorums (1877–1908). In 1877 the **First Presidency** instructed that every worthy young man receive priesthood ordination. Soon boys from ages 11 to 18 received the priesthood; most became deacons and stayed such until becoming elders. Few boys blessed or passed the sacrament or did what is now called **home teaching**.

4. Age groups of youth with ward quorums (1908–present). In 1908 the First Presidency restructured the Aaronic Priesthood to be a priesthood for boys. They approved that worthy boys be ordained at set ages and advance through each office: deacons at age 12, teachers at 15, priests at 18, and elders at 21. Church headquarters produced lesson manuals and assigned duties geared to these age levels. For ward teaching, ordained teachers and priests served as junior companion-apprentices to Melchizedek Priesthood holders. In the 1930s the Church began an adult Aaronic Priesthood program for converts and less-active adult men.

In 1928 the ages of 12, 15 and 18 were changed to 12, 15 and 17, respectively, with the elders' age set at 20. That age was reduced to 18 in October 1934, but by December it was raised to 19. In 1954 the teachers' age became 14, and the priests' age was changed to 16, so the ages became 12, 14, and 16, and elders were ordained at age 20 (now 18).

Since the 1920s, stakes and wards have held annual programs and activities commemorating the **restoration** of the Aaronic Priesthood. **Monuments** on **Temple Square** (1958) and by the **Susquehanna River** (1960) honor the restoration of the Aaronic Priesthood.

From the earliest days until 1977, the **presiding bishop** was considered the overall president of the Aaronic Priesthood. That supervisory work is now shared by the presiding bishopric, First Presidency, and the Twelve.

SOURCES

"Authorized Ages for Ordination to Offices in the Aaronic Priesthood." *Improvement Era* 38 (January 1935): 40.

Hartley, William G. "From Men to Boys: LDS Aaronic Priesthood Offices, 1829–1996." *Journal of Mormon History* 22 (Spring 1996): 80–136.

Marrott, Robert L. "History and Functions of the Aaronic Priesthood and the Offices of Priest, Teacher and Deacon . . . 1829–1844." Master's thesis, Brigham Young University, 1970.

"Melchizedek Priesthood." *Improvement Era* 38 (March 1935): 162.

Palmer, Lee A. *Aaronic Priesthood through the Ages.* Salt Lake City: Deseret Book, 1964.

Widtsoe, John A. *Priesthood and Church Government.* Rev. ed. Salt Lake City: Deseret Book, 1965.

WILLIAM G. HARTLEY

ABEL, ELIJAH.

Elijah Abel, an early **black** convert, faithful pioneer, and missionary, was born 25 July 1810 in Frederick, **Maryland**. He was baptized during September 1832 by Ezekiel Roberts in **Kirtland, Ohio**, and ordained an **elder** on 3 March 1836. **Zebedee Coltrin** ordained Elijah a **seventy** in the third **quorum** on 20 December that same year.

Elijah Abel was a carpenter by trade, but in **Nauvoo** he served as the undertaker. He was a member of the **Kirtland Safety Society**, signing his name to the articles of agreement whereby the firm would be managed. In 1853 he and his wife arrived in **Utah**, where they managed the Farmham Hotel. In 1883 he served a mission to **Canada**. He died 25 December 1884 in **Salt Lake City**, just two weeks after his return from the mission field.

SOURCES

Bringhurst, Newell G. "Elijah Abel and the Changing Status of Blacks within Mormonism." *Dialogue* 12 (Summer 1979): 22–36.

Jenson, Andrew. *Latter-day Saint Biographical Encyclopedia.* 4 vols. 1901–36. Reprint, Salt Lake City: Western Epics, 1971. 3:577.

"Journal History." LDS Church Historical Department, Salt Lake City. 20 December 1836. 1, 2 January 1837. 2–3.

Lee, Harold B. *Doing the Right Things for the Right Reason.* Brigham Young University Speeches of the Year. Provo, Utah, 19 April 1961.

CALVIN R. STEPHENS

ABRAHAM, BOOK OF. See BOOK OF ABRAHAM

ABREA, ANGEL.

Angel Abrea was the first **general authority** from Argentina. Born 13 September 1933 in Buenos Aires, **Argentina**, to Edealo and Zulema Estrada Abrea, he was converted to the Church at age 13. He married Maria Victoria Chiapparino on 4 July 1957. The marriage was solemnized in 1966 in the **Salt Lake Temple**. They became the parents of three children.

Angel Abrea graduated from the University of Buenos Aires and worked as a certified public accountant. He served as secretary of the treasury in the city of San Miguel. Before his call to the Seventy, he served as **stake president** of the Buenos Aires **Stake**, **regional representative**, and president of the Argentina Rosario **Mission** and the Buenos Aires Argentina **Temple**. He was called 4 April 1981 to the First Quorum of the **Seventy**.

SOURCES

"First Latin American General Authority." *Church News,* 11 April 1981, 3.
1999–2000 Church Almanac. Salt Lake City: Deseret News, 1998. 25.

BRIAN M. HAUGLID

ACADEMIES. The Church has always fostered the **education** of its people. In **Kirtland** Joseph Smith established the **School of the Prophets** and in **Nauvoo** chartered a university. In **Winter Quarters** and on the trek across the plains, small Church and family schools proliferated. When the pioneers arrived in the valleys of the West, this pattern intensified, especially in the absence of public education and the presence of competing schools from other religious denominations. Between 1875, when the **Brigham Young Academy** was established, and 1910, the Church School System developed and operated thirty-three stake academies in seven states, **Mexico**, and **Canada**; all of these institutions began as elementary schools emphasizing vocational and cultural course work. Gradually, especially after 1900, courses were upgraded to include secondary and teacher-training courses, with some even offering college-level course work. As cultural centers encouraging music, drama, and sports within their respective communities, the academies were well respected and highly regarded educationally.

With the Utah Free School Act of 1890, the widespread rise of public schools throughout the West, and the Panic of 1903, which seriously impaired the finances of the Church, the academies went into an irreversible decline. By 1903 only twenty-three still functioned, and by 1927 the Church had closed or turned over to the state all but eight of them. By 1934, at the low point of the **great depression**, only the Juárez Stake Academy in **Colonia Juárez, Mexico**, remained as an academy. Three former academies, though still under Church jurisdiction, had expanded their curriculum: Brigham Young Academy had become **Brigham Young University**, Salt Lake Stake Academy had become **LDS Business College**, and Bannock Stake Academy had become **Ricks College**. Prominent among those turned over to the state were **St. George** Stake Academy (later **Dixie State College**), Sanpete Stake Academy in Ephraim, Utah (Snow College), Weber Stake Academy in **Ogden, Utah** (**Weber State University**), and St. Joseph Stake Academy (Gila Junior College, then Eastern Arizona College).

Although the demise of the academies was a disappointment to many, the **Church Educational System** continued operating Brigham Young University in **Provo, Utah**; Ricks College (later BYU–Idaho) in **Rexburg, Idaho**; LDS Business College in **Salt Lake City, Utah**; and a myriad of **seminaries**, **institutes**, and other educational programs instructing hundreds of thousands of high school and university students around the world.

SOURCES

Bennion, Milton Lynn. *Mormonism and Education.* Salt Lake City: [LDS Church] Department of Education, 1939.
Clark, James R. "Church and State Relationships in Education in Utah." Ed.D. diss., Utah State University, 1958.
Wilkinson, Ernest L., ed. *Brigham Young University: The First One Hundred Years.* 4 vols. Provo, Utah: Brigham Young University Press, 1975–76.

RICHARD E. BENNETT

ACTIVITIES COMMITTEES. Church leaders have always emphasized wholesome participation in cultural and physical activities for members of all ages. **Pioneers** sang, danced, and participated in games while crossing the plains. Among the first structures to be erected in the Great **Salt Lake Valley** was the Old Bowery, where the **Saints** participated in **music, drama, dance**, and other social activities.

As the Church became established in the West, provisions were made for social and recreational interaction through the various auxiliary organizations in which the Saints had the opportunity to develop their talents. From 1935 to 1971, all-church tournaments were held in **Salt Lake City**, and representative teams from many areas competed for Church championships in basketball, softball, tennis, and golf. In 1972 service and activities committees were established in most **wards** and **stakes** as part of the **Aaronic Priesthood Mutual Improvement Association**.

In January 1977, under the direction of the **First Presidency**, a General Activities Committee was called to work under **priesthood** leadership to foster and promote cultural arts and physical activities among Church members worldwide. The executive committee consisted of Keith M. Engar, chair; Pat L. Davis, cultural arts specialist; and Clark T. Thorstenson, physical activities specialist. Additional committee members were later chosen as activity specialists. In the fall of 1977, the *Activities Committee Guidelines* was first published, outlining the organizational structure and operational format for wards and stakes. By 1986, seventeen additional manuals, **pamphlets**, or filmstrips were available for use by activities committees.

In 1984, by conservative estimate, some 1,556,400 members throughout the world participated in Church-sponsored activities. By 1986, when the General Activities Committee was discontinued, ward and stake activities committees had been well established throughout the Church.

SOURCES

Kimball, Spencer W. Regional Representatives Seminar. Salt Lake City, 31 March 1977.

Shields, Shirley H. "History of the General Activities Committee of The Church of Jesus Christ of Latter-day Saints." Ph.D. diss., Brigham Young University, 1986.

Thorstenson, Clark T. *Activities Sponsored by the Church.* Pamphlet, 1984. A compilation of cultural arts and physical activities statistics from responding Church units.

CLARK T. THORSTENSON

ADAM. As "first man of all men" on the earth (Moses 1:34), father of the human **family** (D&C 27:11; 138:38), **prophet** (Moses 5:10), and first president of the higher or **Melchizedek Priesthood** (*TPJS*, 157), **Adam** plays a significant role in the plan of salvation and is thus a prominent figure in the **revelations** of the **Restoration**. The Prophet **Joseph Smith** spoke much about him. Adam stands next to **Jesus Christ** in priesthood authority and "presides over the spirits of all men" (*TPJS*, 157). Whenever the keys of the **priesthood** are revealed to mortals on earth, it is by Adam's authority. The revelations given through the Prophet Joseph Smith identify other names and roles by which Adam is known: Michael (D&C 27:11), the archangel (D&C 88:112), and the Ancient of Days (D&C 138:38).

In premortal life, Adam, known as Michael, participated in the earth's creation. His actions in the Garden of Eden brought about the Fall, resulting in the birth of the human family and the introduction of death into the world (2 Ne. 2:22–25; Moses 6:48, 59). Three years before his own death, Adam summoned his righteous posterity to **Adam-ondi-Ahman**, where he bestowed on them his final blessing (D&C 107:53) and prophesied what would befall them "unto the latest generation" (D&C 107:56). As the Ancient of Days, Adam will return to Adam-ondi-Ahman to visit his people before the second coming of Jesus Christ (D&C 116). At the end of the Millennium, he will lead the hosts of the righteous against the wicked in a final great battle and will overcome the devil and his followers (D&C 88:111–15).

SOURCES

Smith, Joseph. *Teachings of the Prophet Joseph Smith.* Selected by Joseph Fielding Smith. Salt Lake City: Deseret Book, 1976. 157–58.

ANDREW C. SKINNER

ADAM-ONDI-AHMAN. The location known as Adam-ondi-Ahman has significance in ancient times, in Latter-day Saint history, and in the future. On 19 May 1838, while visiting **Lyman Wight** at Spring Hill, **Daviess County, Missouri**, the **Prophet Joseph Smith** revealed that the area was anciently the homeland of **Adam** and his posterity and was known as Adam-ondi-Ahman (D&C 78:15; 116; 107:53–56).

A few Latter-day Saint settlers had moved into Daviess County in 1837, but most came during the summer and fall of 1838. On 28 June of that year, a **stake** was created with **John Smith**, the Prophet's uncle, as president and **Reynolds Cahoon** and Lyman Wight as **counselors**. Vinson Knight was appointed **bishop**. A **temple** site at Adam-ondi-Ahman (frequently called Diahman) was dedicated. The exact site is not known, but presumably the **Saints** intended to build the temple on the public square in the center of the community.

By mid 1838, Diahman had become the main **Latter-day Saint** settlement in Daviess County, as well as the most populated community, numbering about 600 to 750 settlers. The hostilities that erupted in mid-October forced many Saints living in outlying areas to move to Diahman for protection. At this time with the arrival of Kirtland Camp the settlement's population may have swelled to as many as 1,500. After the surrender to **Missouri** authorities in November, the Saints were forced to evacuate, and most of them temporarily relocated in **Caldwell County** before making their way out of the state in early 1839. With the departure of the Mormons, Adam-ondi-Ahman became known as Cravensville, after John Cravens. By the early 1870s most inhabitants had moved away, and the community ceased to exist.

During the later twentieth century, the LDS Church made several purchases of land totaling approximately 3,500 acres, including the original settlement site of Adam-ondi-Ahman. Church labor missionaries also live and work there year-round, beautifying and improving the property.

On 19 May 1838, Joseph Smith indicated in his "Scriptory Book" (a personal journal) that "the remains of an old Nephitish Alter an[d] Tower" were discovered. A 1980 excavation uncovered what appears to be a Native American burial mound. Several of Joseph Smith's contemporaries indicated that during visits to the area during the summer and fall of 1838, the Prophet identified Tower Hill as being the location of an ancient altar constructed by Adam, where he offered sacrifices. In short, Tower Hill is both the location of some Indian remains and the general location of Adam's altar.

Significantly, Latter-day Saints believe that before the Lord makes his final appearance to the nations of the earth, he will make a special appearance at Adam-ondi-Ahman. **Elder Bruce R. McConkie** wrote: "He will come in private to his prophet and to the apostles then living. Those who have held keys and powers and authorities in all ages from Adam to the present will also be present. And further, all the faithful members of the Church then living and all the faithful saints of all the ages past will be present. It will be the greatest congregation of faithful saints ever assembled on planet earth. It will be a **sacrament** meeting. It will be a day of judgment for the faithful of all the ages. And it will take place in Daviess County, Missouri, at a place called Adam-ondi-Ahman."

SOURCES

Gentry, Leland H. "Adam-ondi-Ahman: A Brief Historical Survey." *BYU Studies* 13 (Summer 1973): 553–76.

———. "The Land Question at Adam-ondi-Ahman." *BYU Studies* 26 (Spring 1986): 45–56.

———. "Was a Temple Site Ever Dedicated at Adam-ondi-Ahman?" *Ensign* 4 (April 1974): 16.

Jessee, Dean C., ed. *The Papers of Joseph Smith.* Vol. 2. Salt Lake City: Deseret Book, 1992. 244–45.

Matthews, Robert J. "Adam-ondi-Ahman." *BYU Studies* 13 (Autumn 1972): 27–35.

McConkie, Bruce R. *The Millennial Messiah.* Salt Lake City: Deseret Book, 1982. 578–79.

Smith, Joseph. *History of The Church of Jesus Christ of Latter-day Saints.* Edited by B. H. Roberts. 2d ed. rev. 7 vols. Salt Lake City: The Church of Jesus Christ of Latter-day Saints, 1932–51. 3:34–35.

ALEXANDER L. BAUGH

ADAMS, GEORGE J. George J. Adams was a successful missionary in the early 1840s who was later excommunicated from the Church and affiliated for a time with **James J. Strang** and his movement. Born in 1811 at Oxford, **New Jersey**, Adams was an accomplished 29-year-old Shakespearean actor living in **New York** when he joined the Church in 1840. He used his animated preaching and debating style to gain hundreds of converts and the attention of news correspondents. In 1841 he left on a mission to **England**, where he stayed for about a year and then returned to the **United States**. Adams was living in **Illinois** at the time of the **martyrdom** of the **Prophet Joseph Smith**.

In April 1845 Adams was excommunicated from the Church for scandal. From 1846 to 1851 he affiliated with James J. Strang. He was viceroy in Strang's Beaver Island Kingdom when it was established on 8 July 1850. In October of that year there were implications of adultery, theft, and apostasy which led to his excommunication by the Beaver Islanders on 16 September 1851. In 1861 he founded the Church of the Messiah in New England and in 1866 moved to the Holy Land; Mark Twain described his encounter with the imperiled colony in his book *Innocents Abroad.* Adams eventually returned to the United States and died at Philadelphia in May 1880.

───────

SOURCES

Amann, Peter. "Prophet in Zion: The Saga of George J. Adams." *New England Quarterly* 37 (1967): 477–500.
Holmes, Reed M., and G. J. Adams. *The Forerunners.* Independence, Mo.: Herald House, 1981. 19–53.

JOHN HAJICEK

ADOPTION, LAW OF. An early interpretation of the doctrine of **family** exaltation, the law of adoption was the practice of Church members being sealed to prominent Church leaders. Most Latter-day **Saints** today are well aware of such sacred **temple ordinances** as **baptism for the dead** and eternal **marriage** for both the living and the dead. These are ordinances that can seal husband, wife, and children together in eternal family units as well as link ancestral families together intergenerationally. Lesser known, however, is how these doctrines and practices developed over time, "line upon line, precept upon precept."

Aware that there could be no salvation of the family outside the priesthood, many early Latter-day Saints were directed by **Brigham Young** and other Church leaders to be "adopted" or sealed to faithful Church leaders instead of to their own parents, many of whom had either roundly rejected the gospel or clung to their own religious beliefs. Consequently, thousands were "adopted" into the families of Brigham Young, **John Taylor, Wilford Woodruff, Willard Richards**, and other early **apostles** and prominent leaders. This practice, begun in **Nauvoo**, continued throughout the **exodus** period and characterized early temple work in the West.

Gradually the practice of adoption gave way to the more natural principle of being sealed to one's own family—for several reasons. It was seldom convenient for Church leaders to be in attendance, as required, for temple adoptions. Furthermore, some leaders fell away from the Church, leaving confusion and dismay in the minds of their adopted families. More important, the emerging understanding of the doctrine that "all who have died without a knowledge of this gospel, who would have received it if they had been permitted to tarry, shall be heirs of the celestial kingdom" (D&C 137:7) gave renewed hope for all ancestors, regardless of their faith and condition in this life. Finally, Wilford Woodruff, as president of the Church, announced a revelation in April 1894 that discontinued the practice and called upon members everywhere "from this time to trace their genealogies as far as they can, and to be sealed to their fathers and mothers" (*Deseret Weekly*, 541–44).

SOURCES

Bennett, Richard E. *Mormons at the Missouri, 1846–1852: "And Should We Die."* Norman, Okla.: The University of Oklahoma Press, 1987. 187–94.

Deseret Weekly 48 (1894): 541–44.

Irving, Gordon. "The Law of Adoption: One Phase of the Development of the Mormon Concept of Salvation, 1830–1900." *BYU Studies*. 14 (Spring 1974): 291–314.

Woodruff, Wilford. "The Law of Adoption." *Utah Genealogical and Historical Magazine* (October 1922): 145–59.

RICHARD E. BENNETT

ADULT AARONIC PROGRAM. See PROSPECTIVE ELDERS.

AFRICA.

The immense and complex continent of Africa covers one-fifth of the world's land mass and is four times larger than the **United States**, with twice as many people divided into 2,000 tribes and ethnic groups.

The history of the Church in Africa is unique. Although Latter-day Saint missionaries arrived in Africa in 1853, Africa was isolated by its great distance from the center of the Church. One full century passed from the time the missionaries arrived in **South Africa** until a **general authority** visited the **Saints** there—President **David O. McKay** in 1954. Africa is also the only continent in which nearly all of the vast population waited for up to 125 years before missionaries were sent to teach them, as well as the last continent to receive a temple (Johannesburg, South Africa, in 1985).

In August 1852, just five years after the **pioneers** entered the **Salt Lake Valley**, Jesse Haven, Leonard L. Smith, and William H. Walker were called to establish the Church in the Cape of Good Hope on the southern tip of the continent of Africa, which is now part of South Africa. They traveled without purse or scrip and arrived 18 April 1853, seven months after their departure from **Salt Lake City**.

They immediately began proselyting, but mobs interrupted their **meetings** and pelted them with rocks and eggs. Ministers urged their congregations not to feed the missionaries or listen to them but to starve them out of Africa. Through their dedicated service and divine intervention, the work eventually began to move forward. Two months after their arrival, the missionaries baptized their first convert. Two years later there were 176 members in six small **branches** of the Church. Between 1865 and 1904, however, no full-time missionaries were called to Africa, and in 1918 Church membership was only 339, many converts having gathered to **Utah**. After **World War II**, when missionary numbers increased, the South Africa government imposed a quota on Latter-day Saint missionaries, allowing only 65 to be in the country at one time (Letter).

The first **stake** on the continent was organized in Johannesburg, South Africa, in 1970, with Louis P. Hefer as president. In 1972 the **Book of Mormon** was translated into Afrikaans, which accelerated **missionary work**. That same year the **seminary** and **institute** programs were established in southern Africa by E. Dale LeBaron.

In 1978 monumental changes occurred that affected the Church in Africa more than anything since the arrival of the missionaries 125 years earlier. In June the **First Presidency** and the Twelve received the **revelation** in the **Salt Lake Temple** granting all worthy males the **priesthood** (**Official Declaration 2**). In August 1978, following negotiations with Church leaders, the South African government revoked its policy limiting the number of foreign missionaries.

The revelation allowing all worthy men to receive the priesthood, coupled with this change in governmental policy, opened the way for "one of the most spectacular events in the history of The Church of Jesus Christ of Latter-day Saints: the beginning of missionary work in Black Africa" (Morrison, 3). Unlike any other time in Church history, thousands of Africans—primarily from **Nigeria** and **Ghana**—had been converted to the gospel during the three decades before the 1978 revelation without the aid of missionaries and without receiving baptism. After studying the Book of Mormon and other Church **literature**, many wrote to Church headquarters requesting information and even baptism. During this period there were more letters coming from these unbaptized Africans than all of the rest of the world combined. Literature was sent, but because the country did not have any priesthood holders, these people were asked to wait for baptism. Undaunted, they formed congregations so they could worship together and share their message with others. Many of the congregations bore the name of the Church, and most were independent from each other. By the mid-1960s, more than 60 congregations existed in Nigeria and Ghana, and more than 16,000 followers were pleading and praying for membership in the Church. Some enterprising converts even established LDS bookstores.

Soon after the 1978 revelation on the priesthood, Rendell and Rachel Mabey and Ted and Janath Cannon were sent to Nigeria and Ghana as the first missionaries to black Africa. Many of the unbaptized pioneer converts, who had waited for up to 14 years, joined the Church with their congregations. These included **Joseph B. Johnson, Priscilla Sampson-Davis, Anthony Obinna, David W. Eka, William Paul Daniel**, and **Moses Mahlangu**. Within one year there were 1,700 members in 35 **branches**. **Growth** and training local leaders became the greatest challenges for the Church in Africa.

Within ten years the number of missions increased from one in all of Africa to four missions in southern Africa and four in West Africa. In October 1978, less than five months after the revelation on the priesthood, a South Africa **area conference** was held in Johannesburg, presided over by President **Spencer W. Kimball**. Although this was the second visit by a Church president to South Africa, it was the first time that more than one **general authority** had been in South Africa at the same time—a total of five were at the conference.

The first **temple** in Africa was dedicated at Johannesburg 25 August 1985 by President **Gordon B. Hinckley**, a **counselor** in the First Presidency. The first president and matron for this temple were Harlan W. and Geraldine Merkley Clark.

On 15 May 1988, after less than ten years of proselyting, the first stake in which all priesthood leaders were black was organized in Aba, Nigeria. Regarding the uniqueness of the occasion, Elder Neal A. Maxwell noted that this was a historic day for the Church "in this dispensation, and in any dispensation" (*Church News*). In October 1990 the sub-Saharan African nations were organized as the Africa Area.

Historically, Africans have suffered much from famine and disease, and the Church has made considerable efforts to provide relief. In 1985 the First Presidency called upon Church members in **Canada** and the United States to join in two special fasts and to contribute generously to the fast offering fund to help victims of famine in Africa and other areas. Nearly 11 million dollars were contributed, much of which was used to aid suffering in 17 African countries.

In February 1998 President Gordon B. Hinckley became the first Church president to visit the Saints in black Africa, holding meetings in Ghana, Nigeria, **Kenya**, and the cities of Johannesburg, Durban, and Cape Town, South Africa. While in Ghana, President Hinckley announced plans for the Church to build a temple in the capital city, Accra.

By the end of 1998, the Church was registered in 48 sub-Saharan African nations and established in 27. Of the 1,243 full-time missionaries serving in Africa in 1998, 43% (537) were from Africa. In October 1998 the Africa Area was divided into the Africa West Area and the Africa Southeast Area.

Since the revelation in 1978, Church growth in sub-Saharan Africa has been phenomenal. From 1853 to 1978 (125 years), membership had grown to only 7,712 in southern Africa with one **stake** and one mission. In contrast, from 1978 to 2000 (22 years) membership soared to 136,872 in 30 stakes and 12 missions.

SOURCES

Allen, James B., and Glen M. Leonard. *The Story of the Latter-day Saints.* 2d ed. Salt Lake City: Deseret Book, 1992.

Ferguson, Isaac C. "Freely Given." *Ensign* 18 (August 1988): 10–15.

LeBaron, E. Dale, ed. *All Are Alike unto God.* Orem, Utah: Granite Publishing, 1998. 116–38.

Letter from the South African Government, August 1978. In possession of E. Dale LeBaron.

Mabey, Rendell N., and Gordon T. Allred. *Brother to Brother.* Salt Lake City: Bookcraft, 1984.

Middleton, John, ed. *Encyclopedia of Africa South of the Sahara.* 4 vols. New York: Macmillan Library Reference USA, 1997.

Monson, Farrell Ray. "History of the South African Mission of The Church of Jesus

Christ of Latter-day Saints, 1853–1970." Master's thesis, Brigham Young University, 1971.

Morrison, Alexander B. *The Dawning of a Brighter Day.* Salt Lake City: Deseret Book, 1990.

"Nigeria Marks Twin Milestones." *Church News,* 21 May 1998, 6.

"Nigeria Stake: An Alliance of Faith, Work." *Church News,* 21 May 1988. 6–7.

1999–2000 Church Almanac. Salt Lake City: Deseret News, 1998.

Oral histories of early Church converts collected by E. Dale LeBaron. Copies at BYU Library, Provo, Utah; LDS Church Historical Library, Salt Lake City, Utah.

"Red Cross Thanks Church for Hunger-Fund Donation." *Church News,* 9 April 1988, 23.

E. DALE LEBARON

AFRICAN-AMERICANS. See BLACKS.

AGENT. The **law of consecration** required the **bishop** to accept consecrations, assign stewardships, and take care of the storehouse. Agents such as **Algernon Sidney Gilbert** were called to help the bishop carry out these weighty temporal tasks (D&C 53:4; 57:6). Although the law of consecration was later suspended and the formal office of "agent" was no longer needed, this title was sometimes given to such Church members as **Oliver Granger**, **William W. Phelps**, **William Clayton**, **Willard Richards**, and James Sloan, who were called upon to assist the Church in buying land, getting out of debt, and so forth. Today, **counselors**, executive secretaries, and **ward** clerks assist bishops with their more varied responsibilities.

SOURCES

Black, Susan Easton. *Who's Who in the Doctrine and Covenants.* Salt Lake City, Utah: Bookcraft, 1997.

Cowan, Richard O. *Answers to Your Questions about the Doctrine and Covenants.* Salt Lake City: Deseret Book, 1996. 68.

The Doctrine and Covenants Student Manual. Salt Lake City: The Church of Jesus Christ of Latter-day Saints, 1981.

EMILY C. ZEIGLER

AGRICULTURAL MISSIONARIES. See WELFARE SERVICES MISSIONARIES.

ALABAMA. Early Latter-day Saint missionaries arrived in Alabama from **Nauvoo, Illinois**, in 1842, and the first **branch** of the Church was organized that year in Tuscaloosa County. Moderate growth has continued in the state, except during the **Civil War**. When hostilities abated and proselyting resumed, Alabama was included in the **Southern States Mission** (1876).

Early Latter-day Saint converts from Alabama joined with others from **Georgia** and **Mississippi** to make up the **pioneer** company called the **Mississippi Saints**. They left northern Mississippi in 1846, wintered at **Pueblo, Colorado**, and entered the **Salt Lake Valley** within days of the first pioneer company in July 1847. Later, Alabama emigrants helped to colonize a Latter-day Saint community in Kelsey, **Texas**.

At the beginning of the year 2000, Alabama was home to 27,680 **Saints**; 6 **stakes**, located in Bessemer, Birmingham, Dothan, Huntsville, Mobile, and Montgomery; and one full-time **mission**, headquartered in Birmingham. In September 2000 the Church dedicated a temple in Birmingham, Alabama.

SOURCES

Berrett, LeMar C. "History of the Southern States Mission, 1831–1961." Master's thesis, Brigham Young University, 1960.

Jenson, Andrew. *Encyclopedic History of The Church of Jesus Christ of Latter-day Saints.* Salt Lake City: Deseret News, 1941.

1999–2000 Church Almanac. Salt Lake City: Deseret News, 1998. 170–71.

DAVID F. BOONE

ALASKA. Latter-day Saints were among those drawn to Alaska by a gold rush at the end of the nineteenth century.

The first known baptism in Alaska occurred 25 June 1902, when Edward G. Cannon baptized K. N. Winnie in the Bering Sea near Nome. **Elders** of the Northwestern States Mission assessed conditions in 1913 and preached widely during the summer of 1928, but no missionaries labored year-round before 1940. **World War II** suspended **missionary work** but also drew **Saints** to area military posts.

Alaska's first branch was established in Fairbanks on 10 July 1938; the first **stake** was organized in Anchorage on 13 August 1961. In 1974 the Alaska Anchorage Mission was formed. The first Church-built meetinghouse was dedicated in Anchorage in 1958, and distinctive log **meetinghouses** dotted remote areas after 1978. In 1997 President **Gordon B. Hinckley** announced plans to build the Anchorage Temple, one of the first three "small **temples**." It was dedicated in January 1999. At the beginning of the year 2000, Alaska had 25,340 Church members living in 6 **stakes** and 65 **wards** and **branches**.

SOURCES

Jasper, Patricia B., and Beverly M. Blasongame, eds. *A Gathering of Saints in Alaska.* Salt Lake City: Hiller Industries, 1983.
1999–2000 Church Almanac. Salt Lake City: Deseret News, 1998. 171–72.

JOHN THOMAS

ALBANIA. Located on the Balkan Peninsula, Albania was the last previously Communist-ruled nation in Eastern **Europe** to grant proselyting status to the LDS Church and missionaries. Between 1967 and 1990, the Communists banned all religious worship. Thereafter the three traditional religions—**Muslim**, Orthodox, and Roman Catholic—were reestablished.

The first Latter-day Saint contacts were for **humanitarian aid**: couple missionaries serving as doctors, nurses, and educators were invited into the country in 1992, following visits by Latter-day Saint **general authorities.** In that same year, young adult missionaries began proselyting activities under the **Austria** Vienna East Mission. Following government recognition, the Albania Tirana Mission was opened in July 1996.

Church membership grew rapidly to 500, and 6 branches were organized. After weeks of economic and political unrest, 31 missionaries were evacuated in March 1997, but many returned in September. Due to continuing civil strife, the remaining 24 missionaries were reassigned to other **missions** in August 1998.

At the beginning of the year 2000, Albania had 789 members in 7 branches.

SOURCES

"Church Reassigns Missionaries Serving in Albania." *Church News,* 29 August 1998, 5.
Mehr, Kahlile. "Frontier in the East." Manuscript history, Albania.
1999–2000 Church Almanac. Salt Lake City: Deseret News, 1998. 267.

EDWIN B. MORRELL

ALBERTA TEMPLE. See CARDSTON ALBERTA TEMPLE.

ALBERTA, CANADA. The province of Alberta has become the "**Utah**" of **Canada** for the Latter-day **Saints**. **Pioneers** arriving in wagon trains established communities and bred a progeny that, combined with convert growth, vitalized Church and country. At the suggestion of President **John Taylor** in 1887, **Cache Valley Stake President Charles Ora Card** and several others sought refuge beneath the British flag from arrest under ambitious enforcement of **antipolygamy** laws. A visit by the **First Presidency** of the Church in 1889 affirmed the colonization effort and also resulted in the later release of President Card from his Cache Valley presidency and in his call as Canadian **Mission president**.

Economic opportunity brought additional Latter-day Saint pioneers to Alberta as homestead prospects encouraged many. Card encouraged naturalization to qualify for land grants. Church funding of land purchases and leases helped establish business and agricultural interests. By 1890, Richard Pilling was irrigating with a water wheel on St. Mary's River. Member participation at agricultural conventions and fairs spread interest in **irrigation**.

A cooperative called the Cardston Company Limited, as well as a cheese factory, sawmill, and other businesses, further certified economic prospects. Rail and telephone lines by the mid-1890s afforded access for the Saints between Utah and Alberta. In 1895 the Alberta **Stake** was organized with Charles Ora Card as president.

The Northwest Coal and Navigation Company of Lethbridge proposed a major irrigation project using Latter-day Saint laborers and British capital, creating access to land and water. A contract was signed with Church leaders in 1898. Advertising and mission calls brought many; the towns of Magrath and Stirling sprouted as a direct result. Raymond was established as a result of the sugar beet investment by Latter-day Saint magnate **Jesse Knight**. By 1903 the Taylor Stake (named after **apostle John W. Taylor**) was created for these towns.

Purchase and subdivision of the Cochrane ranch in 1906 provided additional economic opportunities, eventuating the establishment of Glenwood, Hartley, and Hillspring.

The 1912 announcement of the **Cardston Alberta Temple** cemented Church establishment. Members could be endowed and sealed for themselves and their dead after its 1923 dedication. Continued immigration resulted in the 1921 creation of the Lethbridge Stake (which covered the rest of the province for many years). Migration to larger Alberta cities began on a larger scale around **WWII**. The desire for advanced education, government service, completion of military obligations, missionary work, and business opportunity in a buoyant economy produced a groundswell of Church development. **Hugh B. Brown** and N. **Eldon Tanner**, who later served in the **First Presidency**, were prominent during the 1940s and 1950s.

The Western Canadian **Mission** was organized in Edmonton in 1941. The Canada Edmonton Mission was organized in July 1998, and the Edmonton Cardston Alberta Temple was dedicated 11 and 12 December 1999. At the beginning of the year 2000, the province had 63,866 members living in 21 stakes and 192 **wards** and **branches**.

Sources

Card, Brigham Young. et al., eds. *The Mormon Presence in Canada*. Edmonton: University of Alberta Press, 1990.

Tagg, Melvin S. *A History of the Mormon Church in Canada*. Lethbridge, Alberta: 1968.

John P. Livingstone

ALCOHOL. See WORD OF WISDOM.

ALLEN, AMANDA INEZ KNIGHT.

Amanda Inez Knight and **Lucy Jane Brimhall** and were set apart as the Church's first official single sister missionaries on 1 April 1898, called to labor in **Great Britain**. Amanda was born 8 September 1876 in Payson, **Utah**, to millionaire **Jesse Knight** and Amanda McEwan Knight. She attended **Brigham Young Academy** from 1889 to 1896. She served in **Great Britain**, tracting, street preaching, and gospel teaching until 19 May 1900. She became the Brigham Young Academy dean of **women** for two years and married Robert Eugene Allen 11 June 1902. They had five sons. A philanthropist, active in civic and political affairs, she also served as the **Utah Stake Relief Society** president from 1918 to 1924. Afterwards she was a Relief Society general board member from 1927 until her death on 5 June 1937 in **Provo**, Utah.

Sources

Kunz, Calvin S. "A History of Female Missionary Activity in The Church of Jesus Christ of Latter-day Saints, 1830–1898." Master's thesis, Brigham Young University, 1976.

Mangum, Diane L. "The First Sister Missionaries." *Ensign* 10 (July 1980): 62–65.

"Mourned: Mrs. Allen." *Deseret News*, 7 June 1937, 11.

William G. Hartley

ALLEN, JAMES. James Allen, an Army officer who organized the **Mormon Battalion** for service in the **Mexican War** in 1846, was born on 15 February 1806 in **Ohio**. He graduated from **West Point Military Academy** in 1829 and served in both the infantry and cavalry at various posts in **Michigan**, **Illinois**, **Kansas**, and **Iowa**. Church members initially viewed Allen's request for 500 volunteers with suspicion, but his polite and honest manner quickly won him the confidence of the **Saints**. After recruiting the battalion, he served as its commanding officer from 16 July to 23 August 1846, when he died of "conjestive fever" at **Fort Leavenworth**, Kansas (Yurtinus, 98).

SOURCES

Cullum, George Washington. Biographical register of the officers and graduates of the U.S. Military Academy at West Point, N. Y. Vol. 1. Boston: Houghton, Mifflin, 1891. 442–43.

Stevenson, C. Stanley. "Expeditions into Dakota." South Dakota Historical Collections. 9:347–48.

Yurtinus, John F. "A Ram in the Thicket: The Mormon Battalion in the Mexican War." Ph.D. diss., Brigham Young University, 1975.

ANDREW H. HEDGES

ALMANACS. Early Latter-day **Saints** had a rich New England heritage that included the publishing of almanacs, which were used as calendars and sources of agricultural information. These publications included other useful information such as common medical cures, history, and astronomy. The **Mormons** began publishing their own almanacs at an early point in their history.

Although the **Literary Firm** in **Kirtland, Ohio,** had planned to issue an almanac in the 1830s, the first one actually published by a Latter-day Saint was **Orson Pratt's** *Prophetic Almanac for 1845*. It borrowed heavily from the standard American almanacs of the day, with a calendar and astronomical data along with the birth and death dates of secular leaders and prominent individuals. **Elder** Pratt also included some of his own doctrinal teachings, as well as those of his brother Parley and of **Joseph Smith**.

Orson Pratt's second effort, the *Prophetic Almanac for 1846,* was more distinctly Mormon with its exclusion of secular names and dates and the inclusion of dates of Latter-day Saint interest. In this issue he continued his missionary vent with doctrinal pieces and information. His intention was to publish the almanac annually, but these were the only two. He prepared one for 1849 at **Winter Quarters**, but there was no way to publish it.

W. W. Phelps published the *Deseret Almanac* between 1851 and 1866 in **Salt Lake City**. From 1859 to 1864 it was called the *Almanac*. The 14 issues again borrowed from standard almanacs of the day, with the inclusion of religious and cultural articles uniquely pertaining to Latter-day Saints. He also included items of medical, agricultural, and social information.

The first edition of the ***Deseret News Church Almanac*** was published in 1974 by the staff of the *Church News* in cooperation with the **Historical Department** of the Church. It was issued annually until 1983, after which time it became a biennial publication containing facts and statistics of the Church. This soft-bound publication includes biographical sketches of past and present **general authorities** and chronologies of both the history of the Church and of events during the previous two years. It also contains the geographical and population information of the Church and its units throughout the world.

SOURCES

1999–2000 Church Almanac. Salt Lake City: Deseret News, 1998.

Whittaker, David J. "Almanacs in the New England Heritage of Mormonism." *BYU Studies* 4 (Fall 1989): 89–113.

GUY L. DORIUS

AMADO, CARLOS H. Carlos Humberto Amado, the first **general authority** from **Guatemala**, was born 25 September 1944 in Guatemala City. His **family** joined the Church when he was nine years old; young Carlos was skeptical of the religion at first but was soon persuaded when he learned about **Boy Scouts**. He married Mayavel Pineda in 1971, and they became the parents of six children. **Elder** Amado was the area director of the **Church Educational System** in Guatemala and served as a **bishop, stake president, mission president**, and **regional representative** before being called as one of the first members of the Second **Quorum** of **Seventy** in April 1989 at age 44. Three years later he was sustained to the First Quorum of Seventy.

SOURCES

"New Calls: Second Quorum of the Seventy Created; 12 New General Authorities Sustained." *Church News,* 8 April 1989, 5.

"News of the Church." *Ensign* 19 (May 1989): 92.

DAVID KENISON

AMERICA. Scriptural pronouncements declare America to be "a land which is choice above all other lands" (Ether 2:10; 1 Ne. 13:30); a land consecrated to those whom the Lord brings to it (2 Ne. 1:7); a land in which peoples are personally established by the Lord himself to fulfil the covenant that he made with Israel and where the powers of heaven are manifested (3 Ne. 20:22); a land of liberty and guaranteed protection against all other nations, providing its inhabitants are righteous (2 Ne. 1:7); a land whose citizens must "serve the God of the land, who is **Jesus Christ**" or "be swept off" the face of it (Ether 2:10,12); and the land upon which the **New Jerusalem** will be established (3 Ne. 20:22). Modern **apostles** and **prophets** have taught that "the Lord prepared America as the site for the restoration of his Church in the latter days, laying a groundwork for it over a period of nearly two thousand years" (Petersen, 7). President **N. Eldon Tanner** of the **First Presidency** declared that the discovery of America was not an accident. "The event had been foreordained in the eternal councils. The prophets of old had it in view" (Benson, 48).

The **Book of Mormon** powerfully confirms that God's hand has been intimately involved in the history of America. The first group of people to be led to this continent by the Lord were the Jaredites, who came during the building of the tower of Babel (Ether 1:33–43). They knew of the choice status of the land and the divine decree that its inhabitants must live in righteousness in order to possess it (Ether 2:9–12). But they became wicked, and, thus all were destroyed in fulfilment of the Lord's promises and warnings (Ether 15:29, 33).

Another important group of people to be led to America by the Lord was the family of Lehi, six hundred years before the coming of the Messiah in mortality. The Lord revealed to them that he was keeping America hidden from other nations in order to fulfill his purposes. He again promised that those inhabitants of America who would keep the commandments would prosper and possess the land "unto themselves" (2 Ne 1:8–9).

The prophet Nephi saw in **vision** events that would transpire in American history. He "beheld a man among the **Gentiles**" upon whom the Spirit of God rested in order to guide him in his discovery of the Western Hemisphere (1 Ne. 13:12). Modern prophets have identified this person as **Christopher Columbus**. Furthermore, Nephi beheld many other multitudes of Gentiles that the Lord guided as they settled the American continent. And he saw how the Lord delivered them "out of the hands of all other nations," giving these American colonists ultimate victory against their "mother Gentiles" in the American Revolution (1 Ne. 13:13–19).

All of this was accomplished in preparation for the restoration of The Church of Jesus Christ of Latter-day Saints, which was organized in the United States of America on **6 April 1830** (D&C 20:1). To the Prophet **Joseph Smith** the Lord revealed that he had "established the Constitution of this land, by the hands of wise men whom I raised up unto this very purpose, and redeemed the land by the shedding of blood" (D&C 101:80). Apostle and future Church president **Ezra Taft Benson** said: "Every Latter-day Saint should love the inspired **Constitution of the United States**—a nation with a spiritual foundation and a prophetic history—which nation the Lord has declared to be his base of operations in these latter days" (Benson, 91). In 1787 the Constitution of the United States was drafted and went into effect two years later with the election of **George Washington**, the first president of the new nation. He vehemently squelched any effort to have himself or any other person made king in America. In fulfillment of Book of Mormon prophecy, America would have no kings: "This shall be a land of liberty unto the Gentiles, and there shall be no kings upon the land, who shall raise up unto the Gentiles" (2 Ne. 10:11).

Modern prophets have testified of the greatness of America's founding fathers. In 1877 the signers of the **Declaration of Independence** appeared to **Wilford Woodruff** in a vision in the **St. George Temple**, asking that baptisms be performed in their behalf. President Woodruff testified "that those men who laid the foundation of this American Government . . . were the *best spirits* the God of Heaven could find on the face of the earth. . . . General Washington and all the men that labored for the purpose were inspired of the Lord" (Woodruff, 89).

Church members have always been encouraged to support the laws of the land and work within the system of government to effect change, even though in the nineteenth century the United States federal government was not always supportive of the Saints in their **petitions for redress** stemming from violent persecutions and other wrongs. Perhaps the most famous example of the lack of support is U.S. President **Martin Van Buren**. When asked by the Church to protect and defend the rights of its members after they were expelled from Missouri because the state's governor had issued an **extermination** order, Van Buren replied, "Your cause is just, but I can do nothing for you" [*HC*, 4:40, 80]).

America is a land with not only a prophetic destiny and sacred history but a tremendous responsibility to serve as a beacon of hope to the oppressed (*JD*, 6:368). It must stand for and teach principles of liberty and righteousness in all the world.

SOURCES

Benson, Ezra Taft. "The Constitution—A Glorious Standard." *Ensign* 6 (May 1976): 91–93.

Journal of Discourses [JD]. 26 vols. London: Latter-day Saints' Book Depot, 1854–86.

Petersen, Mark E. *The Great Prologue*. Salt Lake City: Deseret Book, 1975.

Smith, Joseph. *History of The Church of Jesus Christ of Latter-day Saints*. Edited by B. H. Roberts. 2d ed. rev. 7 vols. Salt Lake City: The Church of Jesus Christ of Latter-day Saints, 1932–51.

Woodruff, Wilford. Conference Report (April 1898): 89.

ANDREW C. SKINNER

AMERICAN INDIAN. See LAMANITES and NATIVE AMERICANS.

AMERICAN PARTY.

The American Party was an anti-Mormon organization founded in 1904 by a group of **Utah** citizens including **Frank S. Cannon** and **Thomas Kearns** (both of whom had served in the U.S. Senate). The party ran several candidates in the 1904 Utah State election but was soundly defeated in a tri-party race. Cannon and Kearns then devoted all their energies to the 1905 **Salt Lake City** municipal election. In that contest the American Party candidates won the race for mayor and a majority of the seats on the city council. The party dominated Salt Lake City government from 1905 to 1911. It elected Ezra Thompson as mayor in 1905. He was followed by John S. Bransford for the next two terms. The American Party was finally swept out of office in 1911 when a nonpartisan, commission form of government was brought into being.

SOURCES

Alexander, Thomas G., and James A. Allen. *Mormons and Gentiles: A History of Salt Lake City*. Boulder, Colo.: Pruett Publishing, 1984.

Roberts, B. H. *A Comprehensive History of The Church of Jesus Christ of Latter-day Saints, Century One*. 6 vols. Salt Lake City: The Church of Jesus Christ of Latter-day Saints, 1930.

ARNOLD K. GARR

AMERICAN SAMOA. See SAMOA.

AMERICA'S WITNESS FOR CHRIST. See **PAGEANTS.**

AMHERST, OHIO. Amherst, Ohio, the site of an early **branch** of the Church, is primarily known as the location of the formation of the **First Presidency. Joseph Smith** was sustained as president of the High Priesthood at the 25 January 1832 Amherst conference, at which **Doctrine and Covenants** 75 was revealed. The Amherst area in northern Ohio, thirty miles west of Cleveland, became a pocket of enthusiastic new converts to the Church. **Parley P. Pratt** settled there in December 1826. **Sidney Rigdon** established a **Campbellite** congregation in 1829, and Parley enthusiastically joined and became a Campbellite preacher in the area. After Parley moved to **New York**, he returned as a missionary of the Church and was arrested on a frivolous charge. In a humorous account, he told of escaping with the infamous bulldog, Stu-boy, chasing him. **Lorenzo Snow** attended college in nearby Oberlin. The long-misrepresented **Spaulding manuscript** is presently housed in the college library there. A branch of the Church was also established in adjoining Brownhelm, where **Levi Hancock** baptized seventy-one people one spring day in 1831. Such well-known **Saints** as the Carters, Barneses, Barneys, and Andruses, along with Joel Johnson, **Sylvester Smith**, Warren and Amanda Smith, and **John E. Page** were converted in the Amherst area.

SOURCES

Backman, Milton V., Jr. *The Heavens Resound: A History of the Latter-day Saints in Ohio, 1830–1838.* Salt Lake City: Deseret Book, 1983. 62, 106, 241.

Pratt, Parley P. *Autobiography of Parley P. Pratt.* Edited by Parley P. Pratt Jr. Salt Lake City: Deseret Book, 1985. 9–18, 36–39.

KARL RICKS ANDERSON

ANCESTRAL FILE. Ancestral File is a computerized collection of genealogies, primarily containing records submitted to the **Family History** Department since 1979. Individuals and **family** organizations have submitted their pedigrees and family group records to make available lineage-linked genealogies showing ancestors and descendants, to help reduce duplication of genealogical research effort, and to help coordinate and preserve compiled genealogies.

Ancestral File is one of several files in **FamilySearch**™, an automated system of programs and databases, and contains more than 35 million names of persons from throughout the world. Most of the names are lineage-linked, although the data have not been verified by the Family History Department. Source documentation is not shown; however, the file does give names and addresses of those who contributed, as well as of other interested researchers.

Ancestral File is available in two versions, both of which may be found at the **Family History Library**™ and **Brigham Young University's** Harold B. Lee Library:

(1) As part of FamilySearch™, Ancestral File is available on compact discs (on network at some locations) where names of living and deceased individuals are shown; Latter-day Saint **temple ordinance** information is shown for many deceased individuals (however, the Ordinance Index is the official index for temple dates). This version is found at **Family History Centers** as well as at some public and private libraries. It is also available for use at home. Users may download information, correct information where necessary, or contribute new information to the file.

(2) Ancestral File may be found on the Internet at FamilySearch™ Internet Genealogy Service (www.familysearch.org), which may be searched at no cost. Names of living individuals are not shown on this version of Ancestral File, nor are Latter-day Saint temple ordinance dates. The Internet version may not be corrected nor added to.

Kip Sperry

ANDERSON, JOSEPH. Joseph Anderson, the longest living **general authority** in this dispensation, was born 20 November 1889 in **Salt Lake City.** He graduated from **Weber Academy** at the age of 15 and then went on a mission to **Germany** and **Switzerland.** He began serving as personal secretary to **Heber J. Grant** in 1922. Upon President Grant's death, **Elder** Anderson was made secretary to the **First Presidency** and remained in that capacity through the administrations of Presidents **George Albert Smith, David O. McKay,** and **Joseph Fielding Smith.** On 6 April 1970 at the age of 80, he became an **assistant to the Twelve,** the oldest man ever to be called as a **general authority.** Six years later he was sustained to the First **Quorum** of the **Seventy.** From 1972 to 1977 he was assistant, associate, and managing director of the **Church Historical Department.** He became an **emeritus general authority** in September 1978 and passed away 13 March 1992 in Salt Lake City at age 102.

Sources

Flake, Lawrence R. *Mighty Men of Zion.* Salt Lake City: Karl D. Butler, 1974. 353.

Wells, Elayne. "Friend to Seven Prophets Turns 100." *Church News,* 18 November 1989, 14.

Lawrence R. Flake

ANDERSON, MAY. Mary Jane Anderson (May), the second general president of the **Primary**, was born in **Liverpool, England**, 8 June 1864. She was promised as a young girl that someday she would write for the children of the Church. As the first editor of the *Children's Friend,* May spent 38 years writing for children. A gifted teacher, she helped formulate a progressive curriculum for the Primary as secretary, counselor, and then as the general president. Her administration, spanning the years 1925–39, refined class divisions, introduced the Trail Builder and Home Builder groups, began the annual Penny Parade, and proposed building a larger facility for **Primary Children's Hospital**. May Anderson died 10 June 1846 in **Salt Lake City**. Though May never gave birth, President **David O. McKay** said at her funeral: "I call her a mother. . . . Motherhood consists of caring, loving, and rearing children" ("Tribute," 349).

Sources

"A Tribute to May Anderson." *Children's Friend* 45 (August 1946): 349.

Harward, Conrad A. "A History of the Growth and Development of the Primary Association of the LDS Church from 1878 to 1928." Master's thesis, Brigham Young University, 1976.

Madsen, Carol Cornwall, and Susan Staker Oman. *Sisters and Little Saints: One Hundred Years of Primary.* Salt Lake City: Deseret Book, 1978.

Peterson, Janet, and LaRene Gaunt. *The Children's Friends: Presidents of the Primary and Their Lives of Service.* Salt Lake City: Deseret Book, 1996.

Janet Peterson

ANDORRA. A small principality in the Pyrenees mountains between **France** and **Spain**, Andorra's approximately 65,000 inhabitants speak Catalan, French, and Spanish. It is part of the Spain Barcelona Mission. The first convert was baptized in 1992, and a **branch** was organized the following year. At the beginning of 2000, there were 64 Church members in one branch.

Source

1999–2000 Church Almanac. Salt Lake City: Deseret News, 1998. 268.

Richard O. Cowan

ANDRUS, MILO. Pioneer, patriarch, stake president, and missionary, Milo Andrus was born on 6 March 1814 in Wilmington, **New York.** A teenage convert in **Kirtland**, he helped build the **Kirtland Temple** and marched in **Zion's Camp**. In February 1835, when barely in his twenties, he was called to the First **Quorum** of **Seventy**. He led the Florence, **Ohio**, branch to **Missouri**. He was part of the Church's successful missionary effort in **England**. In **Nauvoo**, he served as **bishop**. At **St. Louis**, he served as a stake president for about nine months and led a wagon train to **Utah** at the conclusion of his assignment there. Nicknamed "The Eloquent Expounder" he preached sermons that led hundreds, including a noted intellectual, Carl Eyring, to the Church (Barrett, back cover).

In **Utah**, Milo was ordained a patriarch in 1884. The husband of 11 wives and father of 57 children, he built roads, railroads, and canals throughout Utah and southern **Idaho** and was involved in early Utah politics. He served as a major in the **Utah War** and chaplain of the state legislature. Andrus died in Oxford, Idaho, on 19 June 1893. His Pony Express station and hotel are preserved in Pioneer Heritage State Park in **Salt Lake City**.

SOURCE

Barrett, Ivan J. *Trumpeter of God.* American Fork, Utah: Covenant Communications, 1992.

WILLIAM E. HOMER

ANGELL, TRUMAN O. Truman Osborn Angell Sr.'s acceptance of demanding tasks given him by **Joseph Smith** and **Brigham Young**, distinguished this otherwise ordinary artisan. A descendant of Roger Williams, Truman was born 5 June 1810 in Providence, **Rhode Island**. His parents, Phebe Morton and James W. Angell, did not get along with each other, and his father was absent most of his youth. At 17 Truman was apprenticed to a joiner and shortly thereafter moved with his mother to upstate **New York**. There he met and married Polly Johnson; together they joined the Church in 1833. Angell experienced **missions**, service on the **Kirtland Temple**, cruelties of the **extermination order** in Missouri, a supervisory role on the **Nauvoo Temple**, and exodus to the **Salt Lake Valley**. There Truman performed his most noted work as Church architect: the **Salt Lake Temple**. In 1856 Brigham Young sent Truman to **Europe** with a blessing and admonition to "comprehend the architectural designs" observable there (quoted in Brown, 130). On return, Truman himself intimately managed construction. His resignation as architect in 1861 was reversed by the voice of **general conference** in 1867: he responded by spending his remaining years inching the granite walls heavenward. He died 16 October 1887 in Salt Lake City. The Salt Lake Temple stands as an enduring monument to him.

SOURCES

Ashton, Wendell J. *Theirs Is the Kingdom.* Salt Lake City: Bookcraft, 1945.

Brown, Archie Leon. *141 Years of Mormon Heritage.* Oakland, Calif.: Archie Leon Brown, 1973.

STEVEN C. HARPER

ANGELS. The **scriptures** as well as modern **prophets** confirm the reality of angels. This is one of the glorious truths restored to an unbelieving world through the Prophet **Joseph Smith.** Angels are messengers who help to carry out the Lord's work, especially watching over the earth and ministering to its mortal inhabitants. The **Doctrine and Covenants** teaches that all angels who minister to this earth are individuals "who do belong or have belonged to it" (D&C 130:5). **Elder Bruce R. McConkie** wrote, "These messengers, agents, angels of the Almighty, are chosen from among his offspring and are themselves pressing forward along the course of progression and salvation, all in their respective spheres" (McConkie, 35). **Parley P. Pratt** affirmed, "Gods, angels and men are all of one species, one race, one great family" (Pratt, 21). Thus, contrary to some artistic representations, angels do not have wings (Smith, 162). The scriptures indicate that wings are merely symbolic representations of angels' power (D&C 77:4). Joseph Smith gave a detailed description of the angel **Moroni** as to leave no doubt that he is human in form, though in a glorified state (JS–H 1:30–33).

Angels played a significant role in the restoration of the gospel and early history of the Church in this dispensation, bringing back to earth **priesthood** keys and educating the Lord's anointed. Besides Moroni, the Prophet Joseph Smith made mention of other specific angels as well as their assigned roles and responsibilities: **John the Baptist,** restoring the **Aaronic Priesthood** (D&C 13); **Peter, James, and John,** restoring the higher priesthood (D&C 27:13); **Moses, Elias,** and **Elijah,** bestowing keys of the priesthood (D&C 110:11–16); Michael, the archangel (a title connoting leadership); Gabriel, Raphael, and "divers angels, from Michael or **Adam** down to the present time, all declaring their dispensation, their rights, their keys, their honors, their majesty and glory, and the power of their priesthood; giving line upon line, precept upon precept; here a little, and there a little; giving us consolation by holding forth that which is to come, confirming our hope" (D&C 128:21).

Angels are individuals who are sent by the Lord as messengers, or ministers. They may be unembodied spirits, disembodied spirits, or translated and resurrected beings. Unembodied spirits are individuals who have not yet taken a physical body through birth. Disembodied spirits are those who, having died, await resurrection in the postmortal spirit world (D&C 129:6). Translated and resurrected beings possess physical bodies different from those of earthly mortals.

Angels conferring keys possess physical bodies, either resurrected or translated. In one of the most valuable instructions ever given on the nature of angels, Joseph Smith explained that righteous spirits can convey information but do not perform tasks requiring physical contact so as not to deceive mortals (D&C 129:1–9). All righteous angels are subject to the will and command of Jesus Christ (Moro.7:30).

The scriptures of the **Restoration** teach that **Satan** also has his angels (D&C 29:37) and that without the redemption and resurrection made possible by **Jesus Christ** all humankind would have become angels to a devil (2 Ne. 9:9). In addition, because of the restoration of the Aaronic Priesthood, the children of God may, according to the purposes of God, enjoy the ministering of angels in mortality (D&C 13).

SOURCES

McConkie, Bruce R. *Mormon Doctrine.* 2d ed. Salt Lake City: Bookcraft, 1966. 35–37.
McConkie, Oscar W. *Angels.* Salt Lake City: Deseret Book, 1975, 1997.
Pratt, Parley P. *Key to the Science of Theology.* Salt Lake City: Deseret Book, 1979. 21.
Smith, Joseph. *Teachings of the Prophet Joseph Smith.* Selected by Joseph Fielding Smith. Salt Lake City: Deseret Book, 1976. 162, 325–26.

ANDREW C. SKINNER

ANGOLA. The People's Republic of Angola is located on the southwest coast of **Africa**. The nation's official language is Portuguese, but most Angolans live in rural areas and speak an African dialect. About 90% of the country's 11 million people are Christians, with Catholicism being the dominant faith. In recent decades Angola has been ravished by **war** and famine.

Angola granted the Church official recognition in 1993, and the first

branch was established three years later with Tshaka Mbenza Vuamina, a professor at the University of Angola, as president. From 1980 to 1996, approximately 400 Angolans joined the Church outside of their homeland, primarily in **Portugal** and **France**. Many returned to Angola and helped to establish the Church there. Several of these Saints met in homes and functioned as a group before becoming a branch. At the beginning of the year 2000, there were 502 Church members living in two branches.

SOURCES

"First Branch Formed in Angola after Years of Strife." *Church News,* 7 September 1996. 5.
Johnson, Lisa A. "The Secret of His Success." *New Era* 22 (May 1992): 20–25.
1999–2000 Church Almanac. Salt Lake City: Deseret News, 1998. 268.

E. DALE LEBARON

ANTHON, CHARLES. Along with **Samuel L. Mitchell**, Charles Anthon was one of the **New York City** scholars **Martin Harris** consulted in 1828 regarding a small sample of **Book of Mormon** engravings and a translation thereof, which he had obtained from **Joseph Smith**. Born 19 November 1797 in New York City, Anthon became a professor of Greek and Latin studies at Columbia College (now Columbia University) and was among the leading classical scholars of his day. Harris had made a wise choice.

Just how much Anthon knew about the **Egyptian** or Reformed Egyptian languages is highly debatable. He did say, however, according to Martin Harris, that "the translation was correct, more so than any he had before seen translated from the Egyptian" and gave Harris "a certificate . . . that they were true characters." Later in the interview Anthon made his now famous statement, "I cannot read a sealed book" (quoted in Roberts, 101–2)—a direct fulfillment of prophecy (Isa. 29: 10–11; 2 Ne. 27:6–10).

Anthon most likely was showing off to Harris and later destroyed the certificate he had offered. The real importance of Anthon is not how much he knew of the Egyptian language but that Harris returned home convinced of the truth of the Book of Mormon, supporting Joseph Smith financially and as a scribe. Charles Anthon died in 1867.

SOURCES

Kimball, Stanley B. "I Cannot Read a Sealed Book." *Improvement Era* 60 (February 1957): 80–82, 104, 106.

————. "Charles Anthon and the Egyptian Language." *Improvement Era* 63 (October 1960): 708–10, 765.

————. "The Anthon Transcript: People, Primary Sources, and Problems." *BYU Studies* 10 (Spring 1970): 325–52.

Roberts, B. H. *A Comprehensive History of The Church of Jesus Christ of Latter-day Saints, Century One.* 6 vols. Salt Lake City: The Church of Jesus Christ of Latter-day Saints, 1930. Vol. 1.

STANLEY B. KIMBALL

ANTIGUA AND BARBUDA.

ANTIGUA AND BARBUDA. Antigua and Barbuda form an English-speaking constitutional monarchy where most of the 100,000 residents are members of the Church of England. Latter-day Saint missionary work began in this Caribbean nation at its capital, St. John's, in May 1984. The first missionaries were **Elder** Ralph and Sister Aileen Tate. Evelyn Shaw was the first person baptized in Antigua, 15 September 1984. The first to receive the **Aaronic Priesthood** was Ezzard Weston, 2 December 1984. The St. John's **Branch** was organized 6 January 1985 with Elder Rex B. Blake as president. At the beginning of the year 2000, the country had 115 members and one branch.

SOURCE

1999–2000 Church Almanac. Salt Lake City: Deseret News, 1998. 269.

TODD KRUEGER

ANTI-MORMONISM.

ANTI-MORMONISM. The existence of vigorous and widespread anti-Mormonism—beginning even before the **organization of The Church** of **Jesus Christ** of Latter-day **Saints** and lasting to the present day—is distressing, but not surprising, to most **Mormons.** The audacious claim of being "the only true and living Church upon the face of the whole earth"(D&C 1:30), restored and directed by God himself, is seen by some as an open invitation to attack. For Mormons the very existence of this constant barrage of invectives against the Church provides evidence of the truthfulness of that claim—because the Church is true and so important, **Satan** is determined to destroy it. Were it merely a man-made organization, there would be little or no opposition.

Anti-Mormonism takes many forms—from physical attacks, to the long line of legal (or often illegal) edicts and maneuvers. The most common and tangible form of anti-Mormonism is found in the literally thousands of newspaper and **magazine** articles, **pamphlets,** and books that have circulated widely wherever the Church has moved throughout the world. This arsenal of printed propaganda has been enhanced over the past century by various forms of electronic media, including movies, tape recordings, videos, and the Internet. While the intensity and frequency of the attacks have quickened with the phenomenal **growth** of the Church, the basic themes have remained the same—impugning the character and call of **Joseph Smith** and his successors, denouncing the **Book of Mormon**, rejecting the possibility of modern-day **revelation**, and quarreling with the doctrinal differences between Mormonism and "orthodox Christianity," such as **plural marriage** and the standing of **blacks** in the Church.

Many religious leaders view the Church's ubiquitous missionaries and extensive proselytizing program as a threat and thus target the Latter-day Saints. Scores of professional anti-Mormon organizations and "ministries" have come and gone over the past century and a half.

Over the years, the most vociferous and vicious of the Church's critics have been former members, who often seem motivated by a desire to capitalize on their supposed status as experts on the subject. From **John C. Bennett** of **Nauvoo** to **Ann Eliza Young** and other so-called victims of **polygamy** to others during the twentieth century—all have basically the same message: they have been saved out of Mormonism and now have selflessly devoted their efforts to helping others "escape" as well. In truth, they experience so little success in the endeavor to draw people out of the Church that their real objective becomes to prevent "innocent victims" from coming into the Church, to keep them from getting *Trapped by the Mormons* (a 1922 film made in **England**). Their success in this latter objective cannot be measured, but the **First Presidency** of the Church noted in 1983, during the heyday of a widely viewed anti-Mormon film: "This opposition may be in itself an opportunity. Among the continuing challenges faced by our missionaries is a lack of interest in religious matters and in our message. These criticisms create such an interest in the Church that questions and inquiries come to individual members and to local leaders. This provides an opportunity to present the truth to those whose attention is thus directed toward us. We have evidence to indicate that in areas where opposition has been particularly intense, the growth of the Church has actually been hastened rather than retarded" (quoted in "Leaders," 2).

While during the first century of the Church's existence it sometimes responded publicly to defamation, the position of the Church during much of the twentieth century was generally to ignore anti-Mormon attacks and concentrate its efforts and resources on proclaiming the gospel and perfecting the Saints in positive ways.

SOURCES

"Leaders Urge Positive Reply to Critics." *Church News,* 18 December 1983, 2.

Nelson, William O. "Anti-Mormon Publications." *Encyclopedia of Mormonism.* Edited by Daniel H. Ludlow. 4 vols. New York: Macmillan, 1992. 1:45–52.

Nibley, Hugh W. *Sounding Brass.* Salt Lake City: Bookcraft, 1963.

LAWRENCE R. FLAKE

ANTIPOLYGAMY MOVEMENT. Building upon a broader long-standing national suspicion of **Latter-day Saints**, an antipolygamy campaign appeared in the late 1800s. Many politicians made names for themselves by promising to rid the nation of Mormon practices. Americans often viewed the Saints as disloyal, in part because of their strong allegiance to a **prophet.** The **Utah War** of 1857–58 and the **Mountain Meadows Massacre** seemed to confirm these suspicions in the national mind. Once the **Republican Party** came into existence, its presidential candidates ran every four years on platforms stressing the need to eradicate **polygamy,** one of the "**twin relics of barbarism**" along with **slavery.** The Saints' economic cooperation, especially in the late 1800s, was viewed as alien and threatening to many. But the practice of polygamy was an easy rallying point around which various anti-Mormon sentiments could assemble.

In 1862 Congress began to legislate against Latter-day **Saint** interests. On 1 July 1862, Congress passed the Morrill Anti-Bigamy Act, which made the practice of polygamy a felony. The act was completely ineffective, in part because the Latter-day Saint-dominated territorial legislature had vested the probate courts with criminal jurisdiction, ensuring that there would be no prosecutions under the Morrill Act.

The completion of the transcontinental **railroad** in 1869 ended the isolation which had long protected Latter-day Saint society. Congress tried to reach them again in 1874 with the **Poland** Act, which sharply limited the jurisdiction of the territorial probate courts and placed polygamy prosecutions in the **United States** District Courts. There the judges and prosecutors were federal appointees, many of them political hacks, while probate court officers were elected by territorial residents.

An 1875 First Amendment freedom of religion test case was orchestrated with **George Reynolds**, a secretary to **Brigham Young**, as the defendant. His eventual conviction was affirmed in 1879 by the Supreme Court, which found that freedom of religion did not protect religiously motivated plural marriage. In rejecting Reynolds's appeal, the Supreme Court compared polygamy to human sacrifice. It was the first time the Supreme Court had considered any constitutional freedom of religion question. Reynolds was sentenced to two years hard labor and fined $500.

But the Saints remained defiant, and federal prosecutors found it almost impossible to prove actual marriages. Brigham Young's 1877 death led to **John Taylor**'s becoming president of the Church in 1880, and he was equally defiant.

In 1882 Congress tried again with the Edmunds Act, which established the new crime of unlawful cohabitation, carrying a six-month prison sentence per count. It established a **Utah** commission modeled after post–**Civil War** reconstruction government in the old Confederacy to run the affairs of the territory. It also removed Latter-day Saints from public office and juries and took away the voting rights of many.

Unlawful cohabitation did not require proof of a marriage, only that men held themselves out to the community as being married to more than one woman. The federal courts affirmed convictions on such proof as providing groceries for plural families or repairing their homes, ensuring convictions by mostly non-Mormon juries. Some **women** were jailed for refusing to testify against their husbands.

Future **apostle Rudger Clawson** was convicted of polygamy and unlawful cohabitation in October 1884. He was sentenced to four years at hard labor, the longest sentence ever handed down. In 1885 Salt Lake **Stake** president **Angus Munn Cannon** was convicted of unlawful cohabitation and appealed to the Supreme Court in an important test case. When the Supreme Court affirmed his conviction in December 1885, federal prosecutions began in earnest.

Over the next several years, more than 1,300 Saints were imprisoned under the Edmunds Act, and many others were fined. Some of those imprisoned served their time in the Utah Territorial Prison in the Sugar House area of Salt Lake. Others served their sentences in **Michigan** and **Nebraska**. Polygamists were also prosecuted in **Idaho**, **Arizona**, and other territories.

At this point the Mormon "**underground**" was established to hide the men and some women federal prosecutors pursued. A few defendants agreed to abandon plural marriage and their plural families in exchange for suspended sentences, but most went defiantly to prison. An 1887

Supreme Court decision involving the multiple convictions of apostle **Lorenzo Snow** limited the sentences of most Latter-day Saint defendants to six months. Most defendants then declined to fight conviction and viewed their sentences as a sign of their religious commitment.

In 1887 Congress passed the most draconian legislation of all, the Edmunds-Tucker Act. It repealed the right of Utah women to vote, which the territorial legislature had established in 1870; directed prosecutors to seize all LDS Church holdings valued at more than $50,000—a devastating blow, because the Church was so involved with the territory's economic development; and declared the children of polygamous marriages to be illegitimate.

While these prosecutions unfolded, the national media seized on the Mormon world as fodder for lurid novels and salacious exposes of life in plural families. These had much more to do with entertainment than reality. Various religious denominations sent missionaries to save the lost souls in Utah Territory but met with little success. Among these were **Joseph Smith III** and other missionaries from the **Reorganized Church of Jesus Christ of Latter Day Saints**.

The **1890 Manifesto** suspending plural marriage came soon after a Supreme Court decision that authorized the federal seizure of $3 million of Church-held property under the Edmunds-Tucker Act, about $45 to $50 million in modern dollars. By that point the campaigns had totally disrupted Mormon society.

These events were not simply the result of the practice of plural marriage. The Latter-day Saints were caught up in an anti-immigrant mood at a time when most converts were from **Europe**, and they were often lumped together with Catholics, who were also unpopular. Latter-day Saints tended to vote as a block, and they rejected allegiance to the two major national political parties. The Church's economic policies that encouraged agriculture and cooperation while discouraging mining gained them enemies who saw Utah Territory as a lost mining opportunity.

SOURCES

Allen, James B., and Glen M. Leonard. *The Story of the Latter-day Saints.* 2d ed. Salt Lake City: Deseret Book, 1992. 297–434.

Firmage, Edwin Brown, and Richard Collin Mangrum. *Zion in the Courts: A Legal History of the Church of Jesus Christ of Latter-day Saints, 1830–1900.* Urbana: University of Illinois Press, 1988.

Larson, Gustive O. *The "Americanization" of Utah for Statehood.* San Marino, Calif.: Huntington Library, 1971.

KENNETH DRIGGS

APOSTASY. See RESTORATION.

APOSTLE. Though the term *apostle* (from Greek *apostellein*) literally means "one sent forth as an agent or representative," in the Church it almost always refers to one ordained to that specific office in the **Melchizedek Priesthood.** Apostles are special witnesses of the name of Christ—his divinity and reality—in all the world (D&C 107:23). The Church of **Jesus Christ** in this last dispensation includes a **quorum** of twelve apostles, as did the ancient Church, for which Jesus chose from among his disciples twelve whom he named apostles (Luke 6:13) and sent forth to be his witnesses and leaders after his ascension (Acts 1:2–6). This body regulates the affairs of God's kingdom on earth under the direction of three presiding **high priests,** also ordained apostles, who form the **First Presidency.** As they did in Jesus' day, the modern apostles and the First Presidency hold the keys of the priesthood—the controlling authority of the Church delegated by God to men on earth (D&C 107:33, 35; compare John 15:16). President **Brigham Young** said of this authority: "The keys of the eternal Priesthood, which is after the order of the Son of God, are comprehended by being an apostle. All the Priesthood, all the keys, all the gifts, all the **endowments,** and everything preparatory to entering into the presence of the Father and of the Son, are in, composed of, circumscribed by, or I might say incorporated within the circumference of, the Apostleship" (*JD,* 1:134–35).

The senior apostle is the president of the Church, the only individual authorized to exercise all priesthood keys at any time (D&C 132:7). He and two counselors form the First Presidency, the supreme governing body or presiding quorum over the whole Church. It is separate and apart from the Quorum of the Twelve Apostles, though the latter is designated as a body or quorum equal in authority and power to the First Presidency (D&C 107:22–24). This means that when the First Presidency is dissolved at the death of the president of the Church, the Twelve "then exercise all of the power and authority previously reserved to the Presidency" (McConkie, 49).

Anciently, **Peter, James, and John** served as the chief apostles and were therefore privileged to receive special instructions as well as witness special events according to the Lord's own choosing, including his transfiguration (Matt. 17:1–9) and his agony in Gethsemane (Mark 14:32–33). The first apostles in our dispensation were ordained under the hands of these three ancient apostles (D&C 27:12–13; 128:20). President **Joseph**

Fielding Smith explained that the keys given to Peter, James, and John (D&C 7:7) "constituted the authority of Presidency of the Church in their dispensation. . . . These keys were given at the transfiguration to these Apostles, and they in turn gave them to Joseph Smith and **Oliver Cowdery** in this dispensation" (Smith, 1:49). Brigham Young testified that "Joseph Smith, Oliver Cowdery, and **David Whitmer** were the first Apostles of this dispensation" (*JD*, 6:320). **Heber C. Kimball** indicated that **Martin Harris** was also ordained at some point (*JD*, 6:29). Subsequently, the **Three Witnesses to the Book of Mormon** were commissioned to select and ordain twelve other men to form the first Quorum of the Twelve Apostles in these latter days (D&C 18:26–30, 37–40; *JD*, 6:29; McConkie, 47). This quorum was organized in February 1835.

Today, as in ancient times, others besides the members of the Quorum of the Twelve may be ordained apostles; however, the Lord has indicated that the number of official members of the Quorum of the Twelve Apostles should be maintained by filling any vacancies that might arise (D&C 118:1). This fits exactly the inspired pattern established in the first-century Church (Acts 1:15–26).

When the Savior visited the Nephites in the New World after his resurrection, he chose twelve special disciples to lead his Church and administer his ordinances in the Americas (3 Ne. 12:1). The **Prophet Joseph Smith** indicated that these men were apostles (*HC*, 4:538). The twelve Nephite leaders were to judge their own people, and they, in turn, would be judged by the twelve apostles Jesus had chosen during his mortal ministry. These original twelve apostles would also judge the rest of the twelve tribes of Israel (Mormon 3:18–19; D&C 29:12).

Sources

Journal of Discourses [JD]. 26 vols. London: Latter-day Saints' Book Depot, 1854–86. 1:134–135; 6:29, 320.

McConkie, Bruce R. *Mormon Doctrine*. 2d ed. Salt Lake City: Bookcraft, 1966. 46–47, 49–50.

Ogden, D. Kelly, and Andrew C. Skinner. *New Testament Apostles Testify of Christ: A Guide for Acts through Revelation*. Salt Lake City: Deseret Book, 1998.

Smith, Joseph. *History of The Church of Jesus Christ of Latter-day Saints [HC]*. Edited by B. H. Roberts. 2d ed. rev. 7 vols. Salt Lake City: The Church of Jesus Christ of Latter-day Saints, 1932–51.

Smith, Joseph Fielding. *Church History and Modern Revelation*. 2 vols. Salt Lake City: The Council of the Twelve Apostles, 1953. 1:49.

Andrew C. Skinner

APRIL 6. April 6 is significant to Latter-day **Saints** as the date in 1830 when **Joseph Smith** officially organized the Church at the **Peter Whitmer** Farm in **Fayette, New York**. This date was divinely appointed in **revelation** as the day for the Church to be restored (D&C 20:1). One hundred and fifty years later, when President **Spencer W. Kimball** dedicated the restored log house on the **Whitmer farm**, he proclaimed 6 April to be the day **Jesus Christ** was born. The **Book of Mormon** (3 Ne. 1:12–19; 2:8; 8:5) and the New Testament (Matt. 26:2) together date the death of Jesus Christ to shortly after the Jewish Passover, sometime in late March or early April. Because Joseph Smith's **first vision** took place "early in the spring" of 1820 (JS–H 1:14), this event may also have occurred on 6 April. Over the years the annual **general conference** of the Church has been scheduled on or near this date.

SOURCES

Anderson, Richard Lloyd. *Guide to the Life of Christ.* Provo, Utah: Richard Lloyd Anderson, 1992.

Kimball, Spencer W. "Remarks and Dedication of the Fayette, New York, Buildings." *Ensign* 10 (May 1980): 54.

Lefgren, John. *April Sixth.* Salt Lake City: Bookcraft, 1980.

JED L. WOODWORTH

ARCHITECTURE. The **Kirtland Temple**, dedicated in 1836, marked the beginning of Latter-day Saint Church architecture and what would become a hierarchy of building types, including **temples, tabernacles, meetinghouse**s, and auxiliary buildings. Each building type is a material manifestation of deeply held religious beliefs. Church architecture, regardless of building type and style, is directly subject to the president of the Church and his appointed builders and architects.

Developments within Latter-day Saint architecture can largely be grouped into five major periods: 1) 1836–47, 2) 1847–69, 3) 1869–90, 4) 1890–1920, and 5) 1920 to present. The first, 1836–47, was marked by the temple-meetinghouse and the **priesthood** hall. Though the temple remains the most important building type within the Church, it began essentially as a meetinghouse. The Kirtland Temple (1836) was in form essentially a double-hall meetinghouse (D&C 95:13–17). The later **Nauvoo Temple** (1846) had the added function of a baptismal font in the basement and facilities for endowments and sealings in the attic. With the introduction of the temple **endowment** at Nauvoo, temples would function within the exclusive domain of sacred space, other functions being accommodated in distinct building types.

Following the **Saints**' arrival in **Utah**, the pioneer period between 1847 and 1869 saw a proliferation in building types within the Church. Because subsequent temples no longer functioned as meetinghouses, two new building types were devised to satisfy the general liturgical and administrative needs of the Saints. The first was the tabernacle and the second the meetinghouse.

The tabernacle, as a building type, was conceived earlier but not fully implemented until the pioneer period. It was specifically designed to meet the congregational needs of a **stake**, a larger ecclesiastical unit composed of several **wards**. As a building type, a tabernacle was second in hierarchical importance to temples. In fact, only temples lent more prestige to a community. The importance accorded a tabernacle is reflected in its size and elaborate design; whereas, a meetinghouse is simpler and designed to accommodate the needs of the smaller ward. Some tabernacles also functioned as the meetinghouse for the local ward.

A number of specialized buildings appeared during this period. One was **Relief Society** halls, which were built for the women's auxiliary of the Church. They were commonly associated with the upper floor of a coop-store and used by the sisters for the improvement of themselves and those within the Church. Other types were **tithing** offices, which were used as collecting points for monetary and in-kind donations from the Saints. Relief Society halls and tithing offices were used into the early part of the twentieth century. The priesthood hall, as a building type, was abandoned soon after the Saints' arrival in Utah.

The completion of the transcontinental railroad in 1869 marked the end of the pioneer period and beginning of a new era in Church architecture. The period between 1869 and 1890 saw an increase in building to satisfy the growing population of the Church. Building types remained constant but were often larger and more elaborate in design. This was due in part to a new generation of builder–architects, followed by a small cadre of professional architects who were more conscious of contemporary trends in architecture. The transformation was most noticeable in the late 1870s and 1880s, particularly in the larger communities.

The period between 1890 and 1920 saw a new level of architectural achievement and sophistication. It was also a period that saw a decline in building types. Relief Society halls and tithing offices were abandoned because of societal changes, a shift toward monetary donations, and a new generation of tabernacle and meetinghouse designs, which accommodated the spatial needs of the priesthood and Relief Society.

The style of temples, tabernacles, and meetinghouses became more reflective of current architectural trends. Buildings varied in style from Parish Gothic to the Prairie style of Frank Lloyd Wright. The complexities of diversification in style and the financial demands on the membership to support such diversification, however, eventually led to standard planning. This was done in an effort to more efficiently use Church funds while keeping up with the constant demand for new and more adequate places of worship.

Standard planning, beginning in the 1920s, affected the design of meetinghouses more than tabernacles, for the latter continued to maintain a more individualized appearance. The Church abandoned the tabernacle form in the 1960s for the less pretentious stake center. The stake center, as a new form, was little more than an enlarged meetinghouse.

The urgent need for places of worship following **World War II** led to the **Labor Missionary Program** in the 1950s. The program, which began in **New Zealand**, soon spread through the **Pacific** and to the **United States**, **England**, and **Europe** in an effort to maximize the number of buildings constructed for the amount of money expended. The result was simplified standardized designs for meetinghouses, stake centers, and even temples, which could be built by apprenticed laborers under experienced construction supervisors. The accelerated pace of building paralleled the escalating growth of the Church. With the demise of the Labor Missionary Program in the 1970s as well as the energy crisis, a new generation of generic, energy saving, standard designs appeared. They were replaced in the 1980s and 1990s by more appealing standard designs derived from a postmodernist palette of past styles. The most significant change came in temple design. The late 1990s saw the introduction of smaller, less expensive structures that would bring the benefits of the temple to more people.

The paring down of a relatively complex hierarchy of building types to essentially two—temples and stake/meetinghouses—is indicative of the seriousness with which the Church accepts its mission of taking the gospel to people of the world in the most efficient way possible.

SOURCES

Bradley, Martha Sonntag. "Mormon Standard Plan Architecture: Form Versus Function." Master's thesis, Brigham Young University, 1980.

Hamilton, C. Mark. *Nineteenth-Century Mormon Architecture and City Planning*. New York: Oxford University Press, 1995.

C. MARK HAMILTON

AREA. In 1984 the **First Presidency** announced the organization of 13 geographical "areas" in the world to help manage the growing challenge of directing the worldwide Church. Each area was presided over by an area presidency called from the First **Quorum** of **Seventy**. The presidency, assisted by **regional representatives**, was responsible for providing training and counsel to **stake** and **mission presidents** and directing the affairs of the Church in their assigned area. Initially, there were seven areas in the **United States** and **Canada** and six covering the rest of the world.

In 1995 regional representatives were released, and area authorities were called instead to assist the area presidency. By 1999 the number of areas had grown to 28, with presidencies called from the First and Second Quorums of Seventy, as well as **area authority seventies**.

SOURCES

"Area Presidencies Called as Church Modifies Geographical Administration." *Ensign* 14 (August 1984): 75.

Cunningham, Perry H. "Area, Area Presidency." *Encyclopedia of Mormonism.* Edited by Daniel H. Ludlow. 4 vols. New York: Macmillan, 1992. 1:65–66.

Hinckley, Gordon B. "The Sustaining of Church Officers." *Ensign* 15 (May 1985): 6.

DAVID KENISON

AREA AUTHORITY SEVENTY. In the April 1995 **conference** of the Church, President **Gordon B. Hinckley** released the **regional representatives** who were currently serving and announced a major administrative change in the **priesthood**. Effective 15 August 1995, a new local officer known as an **area** authority would be called to work administratively with the area Presidencies in the Church. This was the first step in the creation of the area authority seventy. Referring to the large number of regional representatives who had been serving, President Hinckley explained that the new area authorities would be fewer in number and, like the regional representatives, would reside in their home areas. They were to be called from the ranks of faithful **high priests** who had previous or present leadership experience and would retain their employment and serve for a period of time, generally six years. As precedence for the change, President Hinckley quoted the **Doctrine and Covenants**, which states: "Whereas other officers of the church, who belong not unto the Twelve, neither to the **Seventy**, are not under the responsibility to travel among all nations, but are to travel as their circumstances shall allow, notwithstanding they may hold as high and responsible offices in the church" (D&C 107:98).

In the April 1997 conference, President Hinckley again announced an adjustment to the administrative ranks of the Church by presenting the names of the area authorities to be **ordained** seventies. They would be known as area authority seventies and would serve for a period of years in a voluntary capacity in the area in which they lived. They were to retain their employment and reside in their homes.

A major difference created by this change was that area authority seventies became officers of the Church with specific ties to a **quorum**. Now those living in **Europe, Africa, Asia, Australia**, and the **Pacific** belong to the Third Quorum of Seventy. Those in **Mexico, Central America**, and **South America** belong to the Fourth Quorum. Those in the **United States** and **Canada** belong to the Fifth Quorum.

Because of their ordination as seventies, area authority seventies are called to preach the gospel and be especial witnesses of the Lord **Jesus Christ**. Unlike the First and Second Quorum of Seventy, who serve as **general authorities**, these brethren serve as area authorities. Much like their brethren in the First and Second Quorums, these officers of the Church may be assigned to preside at **stake conferences**, create or reorganize **stakes** and set apart stake presidencies, and serve in area presidencies. Upon their release as area authority seventies, they return to their home stake high priest quorum.

According to President Hinckley, this change in administration with the service of area authority seventies and area presidencies allows for unlimited growth of the Church across the world.

SOURCES

Hinckley, Gordon B. "May We Be Faithful and True." *Ensign* 27 (May 1997): 4–6.
———. "This Work Is Concerned with People." *Ensign* 25 (May 1995): 51–53.

GUY L. DORIUS

AREA CONFERENCES. In response to worldwide Church growth, area conferences were established in various locations around the world "to take the conferences to the people" (Kimball, 107). Those residing within specified geographical boundaries were invited to gather together for spiritual and temporal guidance and to meet face to face with **general authorities**.

The main purposes of these conferences were to "take the gospel to the people in their own environment and in their own language, encourage the **Saints** in their duties, increase their faith and devotion, and raise the voice of warning" (Tanner, 80).

The first area conference occurred in **Manchester, England**, 27–29 August 1971. From 1971 through 1980 they were held in approximately 50 cities in various countries.

SOURCES

"First Presidency Issues Statement on Conference." *Church News*, 27 February 1971, 3.

Fyans, J. Thomas. "Making Conferences Turning Points in Our Lives." *Ensign* 4 (November 1974): 63–65.

Kimball, Spencer W. "Why Do We Continue to Tolerate Sin?" *Ensign* 5 (May 1975): 107.

Tanner, N. Eldon. "The Purpose of Conferences." *Ensign* 6 (November 1976): 80–83.

LARRY R. SKIDMORE

ARGENTINA. Argentina, one of the largest countries in **South America**, gained its independence from **Spain** in 1816. The first Latter-day **Saints** in the country were German immigrants who arrived following the close of **World War I**. Wilhelm Friedrichs and Emile Hoppe were eager to share the gospel with the German community in their new homeland. They published newspaper articles, held meetings in their homes, and soon had a number of people interested in the Church. They reported their efforts to the **general authorities** in **Utah** and requested that **elders** be sent to baptize these converts.

In the fall of 1925 the **First Presidency** sent **Elder Melvin J. Ballard** to open **missionary work** in Argentina. He was accompanied by two members of the **First Council of the Seventy: Elder Rulon S. Wells**, who spoke fluent German, and **Elder Rey L. Pratt**, whose knowledge of Spanish and of Latin American customs would prove essential. They arrived in Buenos Aires on 6 December. Six days later, the first converts in Argentina, six Germans, were baptized in the Rio de la Plata. Early on Christmas morning a group assembled in the 3 de Febrero Park on the banks of the same river, where Elder Ballard dedicated "all these South American nations" for the preaching of the gospel (Moss, 175). He anticipated that as a result of this mission many European immigrants would accept the gospel but believed that the greatest success would ultimately come from among the indigenous **Lamanites**. In June 1926 Reinhold

Stoof, a German convert, arrived to take charge of the South American Mission. Before Elder Ballard left for home, he prophesied that "the work will grow slowly at first just as an oak grows slowly," but eventually "the South American Mission is to be a power in the church" ("Argentina," 37).

In 1930 Rosario became the second Argentine city to receive the gospel. By this time the emphasis was shifting from the German-speaking minority to the Spanish-speaking majority. When President Stoof was released in 1935, the South American Mission was divided, with separate Argentine and Brazilian missions being created. In that year there were 192 Church members in Argentina. With the coming of **World War II**, missionaries were not evacuated all at once as had been the case in **Europe**, but as their missions ended they were not replaced. Local Argentine Saints, though new in the Church, assumed responsibilities of leadership.

In postwar years the Church grew rapidly in Argentina. By 1950 there were 1135 members. In 1954 **David O. McKay** became the first president of the Church to visit Argentina. The country's president, Juan Peron, personally arranged for the Saints to hold their conference in the prestigious thousand-seat Cervantes Theater. Church growth was reflected in the 1966 organization of the first Argentine **stake** at Buenos Aires. In 1981 **Elder Angel Abrea**, a native of Argentina, became the first general authority called from **South America**.

Growth has continued in Argentina at an increasing pace. The mission has been divided several times, stakes have multiplied, and the Latter-day Saints have become a significant force for good in the country. At the beginning of the year 2000, there were 288,865 members located in 64 stakes and in 801 wards or branches.

SOURCES:

Moss, James R., et al. *The International Church.* Provo, Utah: BYU Publications, 1982.
Olsen, Judy C. "Argentina's Bright and Joyous Day." *Ensign* (February 1998): 36–43.

RICHARD O. COWAN

ARIZONA. Since the days of Arizona's beginnings as a territory, Latter-day Saints have made significant contributions to the rise and development of this state. Located immediately south of **Utah**, Arizona was a natural target for **Mormon colonization** during the last half of the nineteenth century. The earliest Latter-day Saint to enter the desert territory was

Jacob Hamblin, coming in 1854 as a missionary to the **Indians**. In 1873 President **Brigham Young** instructed Horton D. Haight to assemble the first party of **Saints** to colonize in Arizona. Although this first venture was largely a failure, it paved the way for others who would follow.

In 1876, four companies of Latter-day Saints were sent to Arizona under the leadership of **Lot Smith**, Jessie O. Ballenger, George Lake, and William C. Allen. This group of 200 pioneers established the first permanent Latter-day Saint settlement in Arizona, along the drainage of the Little Colorado River. Over succeeding years, other pioneers journeyed further south to the Salt Lake River Valley in central Arizona and to the Gila Valley. Obstacles to the settlement of these regions included tensions with Indians, drought, recurrent flooding, and conflicts with various groups of non-Latter-day Saint settlers. In spite of the challenges, these hardy **pioneers** established approximately 35 communities throughout the state.

The earliest settlements were established specifically to practice the united order. Some were named after Church leaders. Among these were Brigham City, Joseph City, **Snowflake**, Taylor, and Wilford. Others, such as **Mesa** and Sunset, reflected the natural beauty of the area. The first **stake**, organized in 1887, was the Little Colorado Stake. Other stakes followed as Church membership began to expand. During its territorial days, Mormon pioneers provided leadership in areas such as agriculture, the cattle industry, and government. In the early 1880s, a branch of **ZCMI**, organized as the Arizona Cooperative Mercantile Institution (ZCMI), was established in Northern Arizona.

In spite of the contributions of the Latter-day Saints, disagreements emerged with their non-Mormon neighbors, generally having to do with water rights, land use, and political influence. During the mid-1880s, a handful of polygamist leaders were rounded up, tried, and sentenced to prison for the federally banned practice of polygamy. Fear of further prosecutions caused a number of families to flee Arizona and establish **Mexican colonies** further south. After the 1890 **Manifesto** announced the end of plural marriages, a spirit of renewal returned to Mormon communities in the territory; Arizona entered the new century, and Church growth once again flourished. The Latter-day Saints were influential in Arizona's drive for statehood, a goal which was accomplished in 1912.

In 1927 a **temple** was dedicated at Mesa. By 1930 Church membership in the "Copper State" had jumped to 18,732. Over the years since that time, Church membership has multiplied. At the beginning of the year 2000, the state had 305,034 members living in 71 stakes and 623

wards and **branches**. In the April 2000 general conference **President Hinckley** announced that the Church would build a temple in Snowflake.

Arizona has a rich heritage of Church leaders. Although not born there, **Spencer W. Kimball**, twelfth president of the Church, lived in south-central Arizona until his call as an **apostle** in 1943. Another influential leader was **Elder Delbert L. Stapley**, a member of the Twelve from 1950 until 1978, who was born in Mesa. In recent years Latter-day Saints have played prominent roles in Arizona agriculture, government, professional sports, and industry.

SOURCES

Allen, James B., and Glen M. Leonard. *The Story of the Latter-day Saints.* 2d ed. Salt Lake City: Deseret Book, 1992. 372–75, 393.

McClintock, James H. *Mormon Settlement in Arizona.* Tucson, Ariz.: University of Arizona Press, 1985.

1997–1998 Church Almanac. Salt Lake City: Deseret News, 1996. 190–93.

ROBERT C. FREEMAN

ARIZONA TEMPLE. The Mesa Arizona Temple stands as a symbol of the strength and commitment of local **pioneers**. From the early days of the **Mormon** settlement in **Arizona**, Latter-day **Saints** longed for the day when a temple would be built in their desert home. Like the **Hawaii** and **Cardston Alberta Temples**, which were built in the same era, this structure was designed without towers. Announced in 1919, work on this neoclassical temple began in 1922 and took five years to complete at a cost of approximately $500,000. The temple was dedicated 23 October 1927 by President **Heber J. Grant**, becoming the seventh temple built after the **exodus** to the West. Nearly 50 years later, at the conclusion of a major renovation, it became the first latter-day temple to be rededicated. In the dedicatory prayer, President **Spencer W. Kimball** emphasized the special role of the Arizona Temple in blessing the lives of the **Lamanite** people. One of the few temples to have a **visitors' center**, it has provided Christmas visitors with a beautiful display of lights and music. Additionally, each spring an Easter **pageant** is performed on the grounds, which is attended by large audiences.

SOURCES

Cowan, Richard O. *Temples to Dot the Earth.* Springville, Utah: Cedar Fort, 1997.

———. "The Arizona Temple and the Lamanites." In *Arizona.* Edited by H. Dean

Garrett and Clark V. Johnson. *Regional Studies in Latter-day Saint Church History* series. Provo, Utah: Brigham Young University, 1989.

ROBERT C. FREEMAN

ARKANSAS. As early as 1835, **Elders Wilford Woodruff** and Henry Brown arrived as missionaries in Arkansas. Three years later **Abraham O. Smoot** labored in the state. These elders experienced some success, helping to establish the Church permanently.

In 1857 **apostle Parley P. Pratt** was assassinated near Van Buren, Arkansas. This later contributed to tensions resulting in the **Mountain Meadows Massacre** in **Utah**, when travelers from Arkansas boasted that Pratt had been killed in their state.

For several years little **missionary work** occurred in Arkansas. In 1875, however, Elders Henry G. Boyle and J. D. H. McAllister baptized between 80 and 90 people in Des Arc. In 1876 the state was included in the original **Southern States Mission**, where it remained until it was transferred to the Southwestern States Mission (1895), later renamed the Central States Mission (1904).

The Church's numerical strength in Arkansas was dramatically affected by emigration. During the 1870s and 80s, Latter-day **Saints** from the state went west to bolster Church settlements there. These relocated Saints helped establish communities in **Arizona**, **New Mexico**, and Utah. The twentieth century, however, brought new growth. The first **stake** in Arkansas was organized at Little Rock in 1969.

At the beginning of the year 2000, there were 20,077 members and 4 stakes with 52 **wards** and **branches** located in Little Rock, Fort Smith, Jacksonville, and Rogers. A mission was headquartered in Little Rock.

SOURCES

Berrett, LaMar C. "History of the Southern States Mission, 1831–1861." Master's thesis, Brigham Young University, 1960.

Jenson, Andrew. *Encyclopedic History of The Church of Jesus Christ of Latter-day Saints.* Salt Lake City: Deseret News, 1941.

1999–2000 Church Almanac. Salt Lake City: Deseret News, 1998. 175–77.

DAVID F. BOONE

ARMENIA. Latter-day **missionary work** in the **Middle East** began with the Turkish mission in 1884 when Mr. Vartooguian, an Armenian living in Constantinople, requested that the Church send missionaries to

Turkey. In response, **Elder Jacob Spori** arrived in Constantinople on 30 December 1884. He taught and baptized Mr. Vartooguian, along with his wife and two children, who became the first members of the Church from Armenia. In 1888 Ferdinand F. Hintze, "Father of the Armenian Mission," had great success preaching to thousands in the Armenian communities of Turkey and baptizing seven people.

Following the Turkish massacre of hundreds of thousands of Armenians during **World War I**, the Church held a special fast on 23 January 1920, raising $115,000 to help the many homeless and starving Armenian children. **Joseph Wilford Booth**, who served as president of the Turkish (Armenian) Mission for more than 12 years, delivered the money in 1921 by request of the **First Presidency**.

Because of continued governmental problems in the late 1920s and early 1930s, the Church slowed missionary activities in the Middle East and recommended that the **Saints** there emigrate to **Utah**. For half a century the Church had little influence in Armenia. Nevertheless, one week after a massive earthquake killed more than 50,000 and left half a million people homeless, **Elder Russell M. Nelson** delivered a check for $100,000 from the Church to the people of Armenia. In 1989 **Jon M. Huntsman** and Armand Hammer arranged to build a $13 million concrete plant in Armenia to provide the means for Armenians to rebuild their homes.

On 24 June 1991, Elders Russell M. Nelson and **Dallin H. Oaks** dedicated the Republic of Armenia for the preaching of the gospel. Since then the Church has grown steadily in Armenia. At the beginning of the year 2000, the country had 656 members organized into one **district** and five **branches**.

SOURCES

Clark, James R., comp. *Messages of the First Presidency of The Church of Jesus Christ of Latter-day Saints.* 6 vols. Salt Lake City: Bookcraft, 1965–75. 5:188.

Frandsen, Russell M. "The Character of Ferdinand F. Hintze and the Armenian Mission." Manuscript. LDS Church Historical Department, Salt Lake City.

Jenson, Andrew. *Church Chronology: A Record of Important Events.* 2d ed. rev. Salt Lake City: Deseret News, 1899. 117.

McKay, David O. *Gospel Ideals.* Salt Lake City: Improvement Era, 1953. 572.

1999–2000 Church Almanac. Salt Lake City: Deseret News, 1999. 272.

"Two Republics in USSR Are Dedicated." *Church News,* 28 September 1991, 3.

CLINTON D. CHRISTENSEN

ARRINGTON, LEONARD J.

ARRINGTON, LEONARD J. In addition to serving as Church historian (1972–82), Leonard James Arrington taught at **North Carolina** State

College (1941–42); at **Utah** State University (1946–72); and at **Brigham Young University**, where he was Lemuel Hardison Redd Jr. Professor of Western American History (1972–87) and director of the Charles Redd Center for Western Studies (1972–80) and the **Joseph Fielding Smith Institute for Church History** (1980–87). He is the prize-winning author of several books and articles on economics and history, including *Great Basin Kingdom: An Economic History of the Latter-day Saints, 1830–1900* (1958) and *Brigham Young: American Moses* (1985).

Born near Twin Falls, **Idaho**, 2 July 1917, Arrington studied at the University of Idaho (B.A., 1939) and the University of North Carolina (Ph.D., 1950). During **World War II**, he served in the military in North **Africa** and **Italy**. He taught in Italy (1958–59) and at the University of **California** in **Los Angeles** (1966). The founding president of the **Mormon History Association**, he also presided over the Western History Association (1968–69) and the Agricultural History Society (1969–70).

In 1972 he was called as Church historian and head of the newly organized History Division. The only Church historian who was not a **general authority**, Arrington served until 1982. He and his first wife, Grace Fort (d. 1982), were the parents of three children. In 1983 he married Harriet Horne. Leonard Arrington died 11 February 1999 in **Salt Lake City**.

SOURCE

Arrington, Leonard J. *Adventures of a Church Historian.* Urbana: University of Illinois Press, 1998.

THOMAS G. ALEXANDER

ART. **Mormon** art is the aesthetic visual history of the Church since 1820. Within this tradition can be found expressions of faith, religious commitment, and historical experience, portrayed through a wide variety of styles, forms, and mediums.

Linda Jones Gibbs explains that although Latter-day Saint artists from the mid-nineteenth century have "forged no new artistic pathways, their art is nevertheless worthy of consideration" (Gibbs, 1). She suggests that "at times subject matter is unique in regards to the treatment of Latter-day Saint religious and historical themes and in the depiction of regional landscape," and that individually "these works of art are . . . very often comparable to works by more famous contemporary artists" (Gibbs, 1).

She further comments that "collectively, they serve as an artistic barometer, reflecting the aesthetic tastes and temperament of the times" (Gibbs, 1).

In early Church history, Latter-day Saint art consisted of personally commissioned portraits of early Church leaders. Many of these paintings later appeared in the **Kirtland Temple**. In **Nauvoo** artists such as Sutcliffe Maudsley and William Major painted several more portraits, and some of the **Saints** also began working with sculpture and documentary art. After the **Martyrdom** and the move west, the Saints began to recognize the epic nature of their history. Historical paintings became the major focus of several emigrant artists in **Utah**, providing visual documents of daily life. Important artists of this movement include C.C.A. **Christensen**, George Ottinger, and Dan Weggeland. At the same time, the dramatic natural landscapes of the new **Zion** became prime subjects for the British emigrant artists, including Alfred Lambourne, John Tullidge, Reuben Kirkham, and H. L. A. Culmer. Members of these two groups created portraiture and helped paint murals in **meetinghouses**, **tabernacles**, **temples**, and homes, with Dan Weggeland being the most active.

As the **Salt Lake Temple** neared completion, the Church sent several artists, such as John Hafen, Edwin Evans, Lorus Pratt, and John B. Fairbanks, to Paris to acquire the skills to paint murals in the temple. These artists returned with the new impressionistic style and influenced a whole generation of Latter-day Saint artists. Such later Utah artists as James Harwood, Alma Wright, Lee Greene Richards, and J. Leo Fairbanks focused on landscape painting and portraiture; some also studied sculpture (Cyrus Dallin, **Mahonri Young**, **Avard Fairbanks**, Torlief Knaphus). The result was a proliferation of classically inspired monuments celebrating significant events in Church history.

After **World War I**, Latter-day Saint artists received most of their training in **New York City** (LeConte Stewart, Waldo Midgley, **Minerva Teichert**). This change led many to focus their work on American settings, and they began to produce art with strong Latter-day Saint overtones. The Mormon **pioneer** landscape with barns, villages, and rows of poplar trees frequently appeared as visual evidence of a people applying faith in a desert and making the region blossom as a rose.

During the early 1900s, some of the most skilled Latter-day Saint artists also had the opportunity to create temple murals. After these paintings were eliminated from most of the temples in the second half of the century, this important aspect of Latter-day art ceased. Over the years, however, many paintings on canvas have been used in the temples to create a feeling of reverence and faith.

Since 1960 **Brigham Young University** has developed as a center for Mormon art. Together, teachers and students (Dennis Smith, Gary Smith, Trevor Southey, Valoy Eaton) generated a Mormon Arts Festival, which encouraged artists to define and create art that addressed their time, culture, doctrine, and testimony.

Most Church-related art is created as a personal visual expression of the artist's beliefs (Wulf Barsch, Lee Bennion, Brian Kerschisnik, Al Rounds, Peter Fillerup). It is not created to be a part of worship; works of art are not used as objects of religious devotion. The benchmarks for this artistic tradition are faith, commitment, and religious understanding in depicting Latter-day Saint experience and history.

SOURCES

Gibbs, Linda Jones. *Masterworks*. Salt Lake City: The Church of Jesus Christ of Latter-day Saints, 1984.

Oman, Richard G., and Robert O. Davis. *Images of Faith: Art of the Latter-day Saints*. Museum of Church History and Art. Salt Lake City: Deseret Book, 1995. 1–3.

Swanson, Vern G., Robert S. Olpin, and William C. Seifrit. *Utah Art*. Salt Lake City: Peregrine Smith Book, 1991.

Wheelwright, Lorin F., and Lael J. Woodbury. *Mormon Arts*. Vol. 1. Provo, Utah: Brigham Young University Press, 1972.

RICHARD G. OMAN AND DAVID ERICSON

ARTICLES AND COVENANTS, THE. Now known as sections 20 and 22 of the **Doctrine and Covenants**, the Articles and Covenants were significant to the early Church in three ways: (1) as a "Constitution of the Church," the Articles and Covenants set forth fundamental procedures. (2) As a declaration of basic doctrines, they served the same function as creeds commonly issued by other Churches during the nineteenth century, clearly stating doctrinal platforms. (3) As a forerunner to future compilations of revelations, the Articles and Covenants were often cited in those later revelations (D&C 33:14; 42:13; and 107:89, for example). The relationship of subject matter in sections 20 and 68 (the latter received shortly after the decision to publish the **Book of Commandments**) suggests that the Articles and Covenants were an important step in the process leading to the current Doctrine and Covenants.

In 1959 Virginia Ryder Watters, great-great-granddaughter of **Symonds Ryder**, donated an original rough draft of the Articles and

Covenants to the **Historical Department** via a Latter-day Saint high school student her husband knew. The document is titled "A commandment from God unto Oliver how he should build up his Church & the manner thereof." It concludes "A true copy of the Articles of the Church of Christ. O.C. [Oliver Cowdery]" ("Historical," 287, 290).

Although sections 20 and 22 were dated April 1830 and were read and unanimously accepted at the first regular **conference** of the Church two months later, it appears from Cowdery's draft that **Joseph Smith** and Oliver Cowdery were formulating the document throughout 1829.

SOURCES

Cowan, Richard O. *Doctrine & Covenants: Our Modern Scripture.* Provo, Utah: Brigham Young University, 1978.

Woodford, Robert J. "The Articles and Covenants of the Church of Christ and the Book of Mormon." *Doctrines for Exaltation: The 1989 Sperry Symposium on the Doctrine and Covenants.* Salt Lake City: Deseret Book, 1989. 262–73.

———. "The Historical Development of the Doctrine and Covenants." 2 vols. Ph.D. diss., Brigham Young University, 1974. 1:286–301.

RICHARD D. MCCLELLAN

ARTICLES OF FAITH, THE. Joseph Smith explained the beliefs of Latter-day **Saints** in 13 statements that became known as the Articles of Faith. Today they are part of the Latter-day Saint **scriptures** in the **Pearl of Great Price.** They are not considered a comprehensive statement of belief but rather a convenient summary of some of the most important and distinctive tenets of the Church.

In March 1842, John Wentworth, editor of the *Chicago Democrat,* wrote a letter to the **Prophet** asking for a history of the rise of Mormonism. In response Joseph Smith sent what is called the **Wentworth Letter** (Smith, 4:535–41) in which the Prophet reviewed significant events of the rise of the Church and added a summary of the Latter-day Saint faith, expressed in 13 statements beginning with the phrase "we believe" or "we claim" (#11).

Several earlier lists of the beliefs of the Church were prepared by Joseph Smith and others that may have influenced the list in the Wentworth Letter. The revelation in section 20 of the **Doctrine and Covenants** (1830) was originally entitled the "Articles and Covenants of the Church" and contained many of its most significant beliefs. **Oliver Cowdery** listed 8 "principles" in the *LDS Messenger and Advocate* (Oct.

1834); **Parley P. Pratt** listed 18 "principles and doctrines" in *Late Persecution of the Church of Jesus Christ of Latter-day Saints* (1840); and **Orson Pratt** listed 19 paragraphs of "faith and doctrine" in his *Interesting Account of Several Remarkable Visions* (1840), many of which begin with the phrase "we believe." The order of the paragraphs in Orson Pratt's **pamphlet** is very similar to the list of 13 in the Wentworth Letter.

The 13 statements from the Wentworth letter were printed and circulated among the members of the Church in the *Times and Seasons* (1842) and among nonmembers in several publications about the Church. **Franklin D. Richards** printed the articles from the *Times and Seasons* in his collection of texts for the Saints in **England** that he entitled *The Pearl of Great Price* (1851). **Elder** Richards did not give a title to the articles, but when Orson Pratt revised the Pearl of Great Price in 1878, he entitled them "Articles of Our Faith." In October **conference** 1880, the Pearl of Great Price was presented to the membership of the Church and accepted as part of the **standard works**; thus the Articles of Faith became canonized scripture. In October conference 1890, Elder Franklin D. Richards specifically presented the Articles of Faith to the membership of the Church "as the rule of faith and conduct for Latter-day Saints," and the membership again accepted and sustained them. Minor alterations were made in the wording and punctuation of the Articles of Faith in 1902 and 1981. In the revised edition of the Pearl of Great Price prepared by **James E. Talmage** in 1902, they were given the title "The Articles of Faith of The Church of Jesus Christ of Latter-day Saints"—the title by which they are still known.

The first article describes the Latter-day Saint belief in the three members of the Godhead. The next two affirm that men will not be punished for **Adam**'s sins but that through Christ's atonement they can receive remission for their own sins if they are obedient to gospel principles and ordinances, which are outlined in the fourth article.

Articles 5 and 6 describe the order and organization of the Church. Articles 7–10 describe belief in the continuation of spiritual gifts, in the **Bible** and **Book of Mormon** as **scripture**, in modern revelation, and in **Zion** being built preparatory to the second coming of Christ.

Article 11 affirms the Church's commitment to religious freedom, while Article 12 pronounces belief in being subject to governments and law. Finally, Article 13 sets forth the Saints' commitment to basic Christian virtues.

The Articles of Faith have been used to teach the beliefs of the Church to members and nonmembers throughout its history. As early as

1850 the Articles were printed as broadsides. In modern times missionaries often distribute wallet-size cards containing the Articles of Faith.
Over the years, children and adults have been encouraged to memorize
the Articles of Faith as a demonstration of their mastery of gospel beliefs.
Two important works have been written using the 13 articles of faith as a
framework for their comprehensive presentation and discussion of the
doctrines and theology of the Church: James E. Talmage's *The Articles of
Faith* (1899) and **Bruce R. McConkie**'s *A New Witness for the Articles of
Faith* (1985).

SOURCES

Brandt, Edward J. "The Origin and Importance of the Articles of Faith." In *The Pearl
    of Great Price.* Edited by Robert L. Millet and Kent P. Jackson. Vol. 2 of Studies in
    Scripture series. Salt Lake City: Randall Book, 1985.

McConkie, Bruce R. *A New Witness for the Articles of Faith.* Salt Lake City: Deseret
    Book, 1985.

Smith, Joseph. *History of The Church of Jesus Christ of Latter-day Saints.* Edited by
    B. H. Roberts. 2d ed. rev. 7 vols. Salt Lake City: The Church of Jesus Christ of
    Latter-day Saints, 1932–51.

Talmage, James E. *The Articles of Faith.* Salt Lake City: Deseret News, 1899.

Whittaker, David J. "Articles of Faith." *Encyclopedia of Mormonism.* Edited by Daniel
    H. Ludlow. 4 vols. New York: Macmillan, 1992. 1:67–69.

"'The Articles of Faith' in Early Mormon Literature and Thought." *New Views of
    Mormon History: A Collection of Essays in Honor of Leonard J. Arrington.* Edited by
    D. Bitton and M. Beecher. Salt Lake City: University of Utah Press, 1987. 63–92.

DAVID ROLPH SEELY

ARTICLES OF FAITH, THE (BOOK). *The Articles of Faith,* written
by **James E. Talmage** in 1899, is subtitled "a consideration of the principal
doctrines of The Church of Jesus Christ of Latter-day **Saints**." In this
volume Talmage presents the doctrines and beliefs of the Church within
the framework of the 13 **Articles of Faith**. The **First Presidency** commissioned Talmage in 1891 to prepare a text to be used in the Church
schools and religion classes. Talmage developed the 24 chapters of his
book through a series of lectures on the doctrine of the Church that he
originally presented to his class on theology from 1893 to 1894 and that
were published in serial form in the *Juvenile Instructor*. Talmage
completed his manuscript in 1898; his text was reviewed and approved
by the First Presidency and published by the Church in 1899. Major
revisions appeared in the twelfth edition, published in 1924. Since its
publication it has been widely distributed in many editions and various
translations and remains in print to the present day, the copyright being

held by the First Presidency of the Church. It has served through the years as a standard reference work for Latter-day Saints on **Mormon** doctrine, and it is one of the books approved for reading by full-time missionaries.

SOURCE

Talmage, James E. *The Articles of Faith.* Salt Lake City: Deseret News, 1899.

DAVID ROLPH SEELY

ARUBA. Like neighboring **Bonaire** and **Curacao**, the small island of Aruba is an autonomous territory of the **Netherlands** off the coast of **Venezuela**. Its 69,000 inhabitants are largely of African decent. The local creole language of Papiamento reflects Portuguese, Spanish and Dutch influences. The first Latter-day Saint **branch** was organized there on 13 August 1986, and missionaries arrived early the next year. Selections of the **Book of Mormon** were translated into Papiamento soon thereafter. At the beginning of the year 2000, there were 230 Church members in one **branch**.

SOURCE

1999–2000 Church Almanac. Salt Lake City: Deseret News, 1998. 361.

EMILY C. ZEIGLER

ASHLEY, WILLIAM H. William H. Ashley, a fur trapper in the **Utah** area before the coming of the **Latter-day Saints**, was born in Chesterfield County, **Virginia**, in 1778, 1782, or 1785. He and his partner, Andrew Henry, formed the Henry-Ashley Company, which attempted to establish trade on the upper **Missouri River** in 1822. Repeated losses of men and supplies in that area caused the company's operations to be moved to **Wyoming** and northern Utah.

Although active in the fur trade for only a short time, Ashley made it possible for other giants of the fur trade to get their start, bringing with him such "enterprising young men" as James Clyman, William Sublette, David Jackson, Thomas Fitzpatrick, **Jed Smith**, **Jim Bridger**, and Joe Meek. With men in the mountains year-round, he established a system that became the legacy of the mountain trade—the **fur trade rendezvous**. He died at St. Louis, Missouri, in June 1838.

SOURCES

Carter, Harvey L. "William H. Ashley." *The Mountain Men and the Fur Trade of the Far*

West. Edited by LeRoy Hafen. 10 vols. Glendale, Calif.: Arthur H. Clark, 1965–72. 7:23–24.

Gowans, Fred R. *Rocky Mountain Rendezvous: A History of the Fur Trade Rendezvous, 1825–1840.* Layton, Utah: Peregrine Smith Books, 1985.

Morgan, Dale L. *The West of William H. Ashley.* Denver: Old West Publishing, 1964.

FRED R. GOWANS AND JAMES WIRSHBORN

ASHTON, MARVIN J. At the death of **Elder** Marvin Jeremy Ashton, a member of the **Quorum** of the Twelve **Apostles**, President **Thomas S. Monson** wrote, "'Here and there and now and then, God places a giant among men.' And I saw this giant of a man growing weak and frail, and I thanked God in a silent prayer for the sweet association I had with Marvin J. Ashton" (quoted in Avant, 4).

Born 6 May 1915 in **Salt Lake City**, Elder Ashton spent his younger years working in his father's lumber business. After graduating with honors in business administration from the **University of Utah**, he served a full-time mission in **Great Britain** (1937–39) under President **Hugh B. Brown**. Upon his return, he married Norma Berntson. Elder Ashton had great rapport with and compassion for the youth of the Church and served many years in the **scouting** program and as a member of the YMMIA general board. As managing director of Church **Social Services**, he made great contributions to helping those involved in serious problems.

On 3 October 1969, he was called as an **assistant to the Twelve**. His call to the apostleship came 2 December 1971 when he was 56 years old. He served for 22 years in that **Quorum** until his death on 25 February 1994 in Salt Lake City at the age of 78.

SOURCES

Avant, Gerry. "Focus on the Apostles: Hourglass in Apostle's Office Symbolizes Challenge with Time." *Church News,* 18 August 1985, 4.

England, Breck. "Elder Marvin J. Ashton: Friend to Prisoners and Prophets." *Ensign* 16 (July 1986): 6–11.

Flake, Lawrence R. *Prophets and Apostles of the Last Dispensation.* Provo, Utah: Religious Studies Center, Brigham Young University, 2001. 509.

LAWRENCE R. FLAKE

ASIA. More than one-third of the earth's people inhabit Asia, the largest and most populous landmass in the world. Almost every geographical feature is found here: large deserts, the world's highest mountains, lush temperate farmlands, tropical rice fields, cool grasslands, and so on. Many nations of peoples with highly varied complexions and features inhabit these lands. All of the great world religions were born in Asia.

Latter-day Saint interest in Asia began in **India**, **Burma**, Siam, **Thailand**, and **Hong Kong** in the 1850s. Failing to establish a foothold at that time, almost 50 years passed before the Church established the Japanese Mission in 1901, with **Elder Heber J. Grant** as its first president. With its closing in 1924, Asia was again without a Latter-day Saint mission.

At the turn of the millennium, Latter-day Saint growth in Asia was essentially only 50 years old. Following **World War II**, Church expansion came fairly rapidly in Asia. The Japanese Mission was reopened in 1948. Missionaries were sent to Hong Kong in 1949 (discontinued 1953), and with the rise of the **Korean War** in 1950, thousands of Latter-day Saint service personnel were organized into groups in **Japan**, **Korea**, **Taiwan**, the **Philippines**, and elsewhere in Asia. The role of devoted Latter-day Saint servicemen and their families has been important in the establishment and sustenance of the Church in most of the countries of East and Southeast Asia. In 1955 Elder **Joseph Fielding Smith** divided the Far East Mission with headquarters in Tokyo, Japan, into the Northern Far East Mission (Japan and South Korea), with headquarters in Japan, and the Southern Far East Mission (all of the remaining nations around **China** to **Pakistan**), with headquarters in Hong Kong. Missionaries were sent from Japan to South Korea in 1956. Missionary work began in the Philippines in 1961. Latter-day Saint servicemen and women and other Church members entered **Thailand** that same year and **Vietnam** in 1962. The Church has had a presence in India since 1964; **Singapore**, **Indonesia**, and **Malaysia** since the late 1960s; Sri Lanka since the late 1970s; and **Cambodia**, **Mongolia**, Nepal, and Pakistan since the 1990s.

Asia's Latter-day Saint population was 631,000 in 1997. The largest memberships were in the Philippines (389,000); Japan (108,000); South Korea (69,000); Taiwan (22,000); and Hong Kong (19,000).

Unlike the peoples of the **Pacific**, who are almost entirely Christian, only the Philippines in Asia is predominantly Christian (93%). Although the population of Asia outnumbers that of the Pacific by around two billion, doing missionary work in Asian nations has been much more challenging than in Christian nations. Some of the reasons for greater difficulty in bringing converts into the Church are: The nations of Asia are ancient civilizations with grand artistic, literary, philosophical, religious,

political, and governmental traditions. While the nations of Western
Europe were barbaric, the nations of Asia had generally highly developed
civilizations. The religions of South, Southeast, and East Asia are generally quite relativistic, preferring pluralism to ideas of religious certainty.
Religious relativity and tolerance have been used to twist Latter-day
Saints' belief in the veracity of their message into a negative. The dominant idea is that the truth claims of all religions must be considered equal
and of similar worth. Most Asians believe it is impossible to have the full
truth and consider those who have such certainty to be either unwise or
intolerant. Asian ideas of toleration do not allow for religious certainty.
Most Asian religions and philosophies (e.g., Hinduism, Buddhism,
Confucianism, Taoism, and Shinto) are more ancient than Christianity
and the restored gospel, thus conferring an element of seniority and supe-
riority upon them in the eyes of their believers.

In some parts of Asia, particularly India and the People's Republic of
China, Roman Catholicism and Protestantism have been associated with
"gunboat diplomacy," colonialism, and imperialism. Though Latter-day
Saints were not involved in such affairs, they have been somewhat tainted
by these problems. In the post–World War II era, some Asian nations
have maintained fears that Christian missionaries will once again use
political, military, or religious power to dominate their nations and societies. Trust in the altruistic purposes of missionaries is low. These fears
have made doing Latter-day Saint missionary work more difficult than in
Christian parts of the world.

In addition, four other challenges face the Church in Asia: materialism;
lack of religiosity; cultural differences; and languages and cross-cultural
communications. Many Asians have made wealth their religion; work and
the accumulation of wealth are a principal focus for many. Organized religion and communal worship are not as important in Japan and some
other parts of Asia as they are in the **United States**. Cultural and language
differences continue to make communication difficult between representatives of different cultures. For speakers of English, learning the
languages of Asia has presented a much more difficult challenge than
learning European languages.

In spite of these problems, many thousands of Filipinos, Japanese,
Chinese, Thais, and others have joyfully accepted the restored gospel.
Temples have been dedicated in Tokyo, Japan (1980); Taipei, Taiwan
(1984); Manila, Philippines (1984); Seoul, Korea (1985); Hong Kong,
China (1996), and Fukuoka, Japan (2000). At the beginning of the year
2000, there were 37 **missions**, 130 **stakes**, 131 **districts**, 774 **wards**, and

1,060 **branches** of the Church in Asia with Church membership reaching 710,772.

SOURCES

Britsch, R. Lanier. *From the East: The History of the Latter-day Saints in Asia, 1851–1996.* Salt Lake City: Deseret Book, 1998.
1999–2000 Church Almanac. Salt Lake City: Deseret News, 1998.

R. LANIER BRITSCH

ASSISTANT PRESIDENT. The term assistant president applies to the **First Presidency** of the Church and is also found in Church documents referring to temple presidencies, Seventies presidencies, and mission presidencies. In the case of the First Presidency, the assistant president, sometimes called "Second President" or "Associate President," stood in authority above the counselors.

Oliver Cowdery was ordained assistant president of the Church 5 December 1834, and **Hyrum Smith** replaced him on 24 January 1841 (D&C 124:91–96).

The office of assistant president also fulfilled the law of witnesses (2 Corinthians 3:1). Oliver Cowdery had been present when the Aaronic and Melchizedek Priesthoods and the keys were restored, so he was the second witness to these events. By revelation, Hyrum Smith replaced Oliver Cowdery in this role, so the two **martyrs** at Carthage sealed their testimonies with their blood (Hebrews 9:16–17). Since then, no one has been called to this position.

SOURCES

Clark, James R., comp. *Messages of the First Presidency of The Church of Jesus Christ of Latter-day Saints.* 6 vols. Salt Lake City: Bookcraft, 1965–75. 2:304–5.
McConkie, Bruce R. *Mormon Doctrine.* 2d ed. Salt Lake City: Bookcraft, 1966. 55.
———. *The Promised Messiah.* Salt Lake City: Deseret Book, 1978. 592.
Smith, Joseph Fielding. *Doctrines of Salvation.* Compiled by Bruce R. McConkie. 3 vols. Salt Lake City: Bookcraft, 1954–56. 1:211–13.

ROBERT L. MARROTT

ASSISTANTS TO THE TWELVE. President **J. Reuben Clark** Jr., first counselor in the **First Presidency**, announced the calling of assistants to the Twelve at the April 1941 **general conference**. He explained that "the rapid growth of the Church in recent times, the constantly increasing establishment of new **Wards** and **Stakes**, the ever widening geographical area covered by Wards and Stakes, the steadily pressing necessity for increasing our missions in number and efficiency that the Gospel may be brought to all men, the continual multiplying of Church interests and activities calling for more rigid and frequent observation, supervision, and direction—all have built up an apostolic service of the greatest magnitude" (Clark, 94–95).

President Clark stated that the assistants would be **high priests** who would serve under the direction of the **First Presidency** and the **Quorum** of the Twelve **Apostles**. Their number would be determined by the need of the Church. **Marion G. Romney**, **Thomas E. McKay**, Clifford E. Young, Alma Sonne, and **Nicholas G. Smith** were then sustained.

Thirty-eight men held the position of Assistant to the Twelve from April 1941 until October 1976, at which time President **Spencer W. Kimball** called the Assistants to serve in the First Quorum of the **Seventy**, which had been organized in October 1975.

SOURCES

Clark, J. Reuben, Jr. Conference Report (April 1941): 94–95.

Kimball, Spencer W. "The Reconstitution of the First Quorum of the Seventy." *Ensign* 6 (November 1976): 9.

1997–1998 Church Almanac. Salt Lake City: Deseret News, 1996.

CALVIN R. STEPHENS

ASSOCIATE PRESIDENT. See ASSISTANT PRESIDENT.

ATCHISON, DAVID.

David Rice Atchison, U.S. Senator, attorney, and friend of the **Latter-day Saints**, was born 11 August 1807 at Frogtown, **Kentucky**. David studied law at an early age before moving to Liberty, **Missouri**, in 1830. Following the expulsion of the Latter-day **Saints** from **Jackson County, Missouri**, in 1833, and again during the Mormon conflict in northern Missouri in 1838–39, the Saints employed Atchison's law office, including partners **Alexander Doniphan**, Amos Rees, and William T. Wood, as their legal counsel.

When armed conflict between the Latter-day Saints and the Missourians erupted during the summer and fall of 1838, Atchison was the ranking militia officer in northern Missouri and acted to quell the disturbances. Because of the fairness and impartiality he exhibited toward the Saints, in late October, at the height of the Mormon conflict, Missouri Governor **Lilburn W. Boggs** relieved Atchison of his command.

Atchison enjoyed a distinguished political career serving as a member of the state House of Representatives (1834–40) and as a U.S. Senator (1843–55). A staunch Democrat, he played a prominent role in pro-slavery issues in **Kansas** and supported the Confederacy during the **Civil War**. Following the war he retired from public service, spending the last 20 years of his life on a farm in Clinton County. He died 6 January 1886 and was buried in Plattsburg, Missouri.

SOURCES

Anderson, Richard Lloyd. "Atchison's Letters and the Causes of Mormon Expulsion from Missouri." *BYU Studies* 26 (Summer 1986): 3–47.

Miller, David B. "David Rice Atchison: Pro-Slave Missourian." *Missouri Folk Heroes of the 19th Century.* Edited by F. Mark McKiernan and Roger D. Launius. Independence, Mo.: Herald Publishing, 1989. 85–112.

Parrish, William E. *David Rice Atchison of Missouri: Border Politician.* Columbia: University of Missouri Press, 1961.

———. "David Rice Atchison, Frontier Politician." *Missouri Historical Review* 50 (July 1956): 339–54.

ALEXANDER L. BAUGH

ATHLETES AND SPORTS. The **Prophet Joseph Smith** shaped the Church's attitude toward sports by frequently engaging in athletic contests. He enjoyed wrestling, pulling sticks, shooting marbles, fishing, and shooting at a mark.

The Church's dedication to sports is demonstrated by the long-standing practice of building gymnasiums inside **meetinghouses**. Nearly all chapels constructed in North **America** in the last half of the twentieth century have included a full-court basketball/multipurpose playing surface as part of the cultural hall. Many wards and stakes sponsor teams in a variety of sports for **young men** and **young women** ages 12–18, as well as for adult men and women. **Ward** teams typically play other teams within their **stake**. For many years, the Church sponsored "All-Church" tournaments in **Salt Lake City**, which were considered some of the largest athletic tournaments in the world. In order to be invited to play in Salt Lake City, ward teams had to advance through stake, regional, and **area** competitions. All-Church tournaments were discontinued in the early 1970s.

The first Latter-day Saint athlete to achieve international notoriety was Alma Richards, who won a gold medal in the high jump at the 1912 Olympic Games in Stockholm, **Sweden**. Creed Haymond, a sprinter for the University of **Pennsylvania**, won the 100- and 220-yard dashes at the Intercollegiate Association of Amateur Athletics of America in 1919. Other prominent Latter-day Saint track and field athletes include Jay Silvester, world record holder in the discus; Olympians Henry Marsh, Ed Eyestone, Clarence Robison, Paul Cummings, and Doug Padilla; two-time NCAA heptathlon champion and world-record hurdler Tiffany Lott; American hammer record holder Amy Palmer; and Olympic distance runner Julie Jenkins.

Perhaps the most famous Latter-day Saint athlete of the first half of the twentieth century was boxer Jack Dempsey, who became World Heavyweight Champion. Other Latter-day Saint world champion boxers were Gene Fullmer (middleweight) and Danny Lopez (featherweight).

In baseball, pitcher Vernon Law won the Cy Young Award in 1961 with the Pittsburgh Pirates. Dennis Eckersley was 1992's American League Cy Young Award winner and MVP (most valuable player). **Dale Murphy** was a two-time National League Most Valuable Player (1982–83) with the Atlanta Braves. Harmon Killebrew, a home run king for the Minnesota Twins, was inducted into baseball's Hall of Fame. Ken Hubbs earned National League Rookie of the Year honors in 1962 with the Chicago Cubs. Other prominent Latter-day Saint major leaguers include all-stars Vance Law, Wally Joyner, Jack Morris, Cory Snyder, and Bruce Hurst. Dane Iorg was a World Series hero in 1982 with the St. Louis Cardinals and again in 1986 with the Kansas City Royals.

Many Latter-day Saint athletes have made their mark on the gridiron. **Steve Young** was named Most Valuable Player in the National Football League in 1992 and 1994. He was also MVP of Super Bowl XXIX. Other Latter-day Saint players earning all-pro distinction include Merlin Olsen, Todd Christensen, Vai Sikahema, and Bart Oates. In college football, Ty Detmer won the Heisman Trophy in 1990. Merlin Olsen, Jason Buck, and Mohamed Elewonibi won the Outland Trophy. Merlin Olsen, Gifford Nielsen, Marc Wilson, and Danny White are inductees in the College Football Hall of Fame. Junior Ah You earned All-America distinction at Arizona State and was later inducted into the Canadian Football League Hall of Fame. **LaVell Edwards** is one of the winningest coaches in college football history, leading BYU to the national championship in 1984.

Former **Brigham Young University** basketball coach **Stan Watts** and BYU All-American **Kresimir Cosic** were inducted into the Naismith Memorial Basketball Hall of Fame. Danny Ainge, winner of college basketball's Eastman and Wooden Awards as the nation's outstanding player, won several championships with the Boston Celtics and later became a successful National Basketball Association coach. Other Latter-day Saint coaches and players of prominence include Dick Motta, Tom Chambers, Fred Roberts, Greg Kite, Mel Hutchins, and Shawn Bradley. The BYU men's basketball team won the National Invitational Tournament in 1951 and 1965, and the **University of Utah**, led by All-American Arnie Ferrin, won the 1944 NCAA Tournament. BYU's women's basketball player Tina Gunn Robison was named the outstanding player in the nation and led the nation in scoring, as did Tresa Spaulding. Julie Kroemenhoek received All-America honors playing basketball for the University of Utah and was the career scoring leader in the Western Athletic Conference.

In golf, Johnny Miller won the U.S. and British Opens before being inducted into golf's Hall of Fame and moving into the television booth as a broadcaster with NBC. Billy Casper was victorious twice in the U.S. Open and also won the Master's. John Fought was U.S. Amateur champion in 1977 and PGA Rookie of the Year in 1979. Keith Clearwater was PGA Rookie of the Year in 1987. Mike Reid enjoyed a lengthy career on the PGA tour with several victories. Bruce Summerhays began a successful stint on the Senior PGA Tour at the age of 50. The BYU golf team won the NCAA championship in 1981.

Other prominent Latter-day Saint athletes include 1984 Olympic Gold Medal gymnast Peter Vidmar; all-around rodeo world champion cowboy Lewis Field; volleyball players Dylann Duncan and Amy Steele Gant; BYU volleyball coach Elaine Michaelis; swimmer Lelie Fonoimoana; national champion divers Keith Russell, Courtney Nelson, and Vanessa Bergman; race car driver Ab Jenkins; and Olympic Gold Medalist and world champion wrestler Mark Schultz.

VAL HALE

AUSTRALIA. English immigrants William Barratt (1840) and Andrew Anderson (1841) first introduced the gospel to Australia. Barratt baptized Robert Beauchamp, who later served as president of the Australia Mission (1869–74), and Anderson established the first **branch** of the Church in

1844 near Wellington, New South **Wales**. The first American missionaries, **John Murdock** and Charles Wandall, arrived in Sydney 30 October 1851.

Establishment of the Church in Australia progressed slowly. Early missionaries struggled with vast distances and a lack of printed materials; they competed with people's preoccupation with "the gold fever" and often had to put their **missionary work** on hold while they earned money to support themselves. A monthly periodical, *The Zion's Watchman* (1853–56), was published in an effort to counteract false statements in the press and to defend Church policies.

Many of the early converts eagerly worked towards emigration to **Zion**. During the nineteenth century, an estimated 45% to 55% of the Australian **Saints** participated in the gathering (Newton, 134). Noteworthy among the Australian immigrants was a company of 28 Saints who set sail on the ship *Julia Ann* for **San Francisco** 7 September 1855. Twenty-six days into the voyage the ship struck a reef off the Society Islands and broke apart. Stranded on a small island for 60 days, the survivors were miraculously rescued.

Those who remained behind provided the nucleus for Church growth in Australia. The first chapel was built in 1904 on Gibbons Street, Brisbane. Eighteen years later the second chapel was built in Melbourne, facilitating the Victorian government's decision to recognize Latter-day Saint **marriage**s—the first Australian state to do so. Between 1929 and 1958, the *Austral Star* provided members with Church news and instruction. The first Australian **stakes** were created in Sydney, Melbourne, and Brisbane during 1960. Nine years later, the first international **seminary** and **institute** program was organized in Brisbane.

At the beginning of the year 2000, the Church in Australia had grown to include 99,121 members in 31 **stakes** and 7 missions. While Church meetings are predominantly conducted in English, there were also **wards** and **branches** that catered to speakers of other languages: Spanish, Tongan, Samoan, Vietnamese, Chinese (Mandarin), and Filipino (Tagalog). The first aboriginal meetinghouse was dedicated in Elliott, Northern Territory, in 1984. That same year Australia's first temple was dedicated in Sydney on 20 September. In 1998 the Church announced plans to build a temple in Brisbane, and by the year 2000, the Church had begun construction on temples in Adelaide, Melbourne, and Perth.

Prominent Australian members of the Church include Joseph Harris Ridges, builder of the original **Tabernacle** organ; William Fowler, author of the hymn "We Thank Thee, O God, for a Prophet"; and Robert E. Sackley, a member of the **Quorum**s of **Seventy** (1988–93).

SOURCES

Eggington, William G. "The Church in Australia." *Encyclopedia of Mormonism.* Edited by Daniel H. Ludlow. 4 vols. New York: Macmillan, 1992. 1:86–88.

Newton, Marjorie. *Southern Cross Saints: The Mormons in Australia.* Mormons in the Pacific series. Laie, Hawaii: Institute for Polynesian Studies, 1991.

———. "Pioneering the Gospel in Australia." *Ensign* 16 (October 1986): 32–41.

Smith, John Devitry. "The Wreck of the *Julia Ann.*" *BYU Studies* 29 (Spring 1989): 5–29.

GAYE STRATHEARN

AUSTRIA. In 1841 **Elder Orson Hyde**, on his way to the **Holy Land**, was the first to bring the restored gospel to the land that presently constitutes Austria. But it was not until 1865 that missionaries were directed to enter what was at the time the Austrian-Hungarian monarchy. Elder **Orson Pratt** and William W. Ritter arrived in Vienna that year and began preaching the gospel. Religious intolerance, however, prevented the work from taking hold at that time, and Elders Pratt and Ritter soon returned to London.

A second attempt began in 1883 when two missionaries, Paul E. B. Hammer and Thomas Biesinger, were sent from the Swiss-German **Mission** to Vienna. Elder Hammer baptized Paul Haslinger that year, the first baptism to take place on Austrian soil. Religious persecution made missionary work difficult, however, with few baptisms in Austria proper, though there was some success in other areas of the monarchy. It took another 18 years for the first **branch**, Haag am Hausruck in Upper Austria, to be organized. With the beginning of hostilities in 1914, the missionaries were withdrawn from **Europe**.

Following **World War I** and the breakup of the Austrian-Hungarian monarchy, the Church again sent missionaries to Europe. Austria, reduced to its present size, seemed a fertile ground for the gospel message, and the Church began to prosper. Greater religious tolerance also contributed to this **growth**. The Vienna **District** was organized in 1920, with branches established in Linz in 1921 and Salzburg in 1928. Members in Haag am Hausruck constructed the first Austrian Latter-day Saint **meetinghouse** in 1937.

Missionary work again came to a halt with the outbreak of **World War II**. Many male members of the Church were drafted into the German military, which left most branches without adequate **priesthood** leadership. Priesthood holders who were too old to be drafted tried to visit the branches and members to administer the **sacrament**.

After the **War**, Austria was occupied by the Allied powers, and Latter-day Saint missionaries returned to preach the gospel. In 1955 the four Allied powers signed a peace treaty with Austria and withdrew their armed forces, leaving the Republic to manage its own destiny. In the same year, The Church of **Jesus Christ** of Latter-day **Saints** was recognized by the new Republic as an official religion, perhaps the first such national government recognition of the Church in Europe. Yet despite increased baptisms, emigration kept the Church from growing substantially in the first 15 years following the war.

By 1960 branches had been organized in Graz, Innsbruck, Dornbirn, Klagenfurt, and other smaller cities. The Vienna Austria Stake was organized in 1980, followed by the Salzburg Austria **Stake** in 1997. At the beginning of the year 2000, there were 3,889 members of the Church in Austria in 22 **wards** and **branches** and 14 dedicated buildings. Before and after the collapse of the Communist governments, Austria played a key role in carrying the gospel to the lands of Eastern Europe.

SOURCES

"1955–1995, 40 Jahre Staatsvertrag, 40 Jahre staatliche Anerkennung der Kirche Jesu Christi der Heiligen der Letzten Tage in Osterreich." N.p.: The Church of Jesus Christ of Latter-day Saints, n.d.

Temply, Heinrich Marion. *Das Licht Scheint in der Finsternis, Geschichte der Kirche Jesu Christi der Heiligen der Letzten Tage in Osterreich.* Typescript. N.p., n.d.

PAUL Y. HOSKISSON

AUXILIARIES.

AUXILIARIES. Auxiliaries are organizations designed to assist and complement the **priesthood**, and have been part of the Church since the **Nauvoo** era. At the end of 1999 the auxiliaries of the Church were **Relief Society** (women 18 years and older), **Sunday School** (all members 12 and over), **Young Women** (12 through 18), **Young Men** (12 through 18), and **Primary** (children 18 months to 11 years of age). The Relief Society is the oldest Church auxiliary, having been founded in Nauvoo in 1842. The Sunday School had its origins in earlier decades but became Church-wide in the 1860s. The Cooperative Retrenchment Association began in 1869 (forerunner of the Young Women). The Young Mens' **Mutual Improvement Association** began in 1875 (forerunner of the Young Men). The Primary began in 1878. The **Religion Class** Association, organized in 1890 to provide religious instruction for elementary children, was assimilated by the Primary in 1929. While each auxiliary has particular tasks, in general they provide gospel instruction, social development, and recreational opportunities.

SOURCE

Erickson, Irene Hewette. "Auxiliary Organizations." *Encyclopedia of Mormonism.* Edited by Daniel H. Ludlow. 4 vols. New York: Macmillan, 1992. 1:89–90.

DONALD Q. CANNON

AVARD, SAMPSON. Sampson Avard is best known as the leader of the infamous **Danites**. He was born in October 1803 at Guernsey, St. Peter's Parish, **England**. He emigrated to the **United States** in 1835 and settled in Freedom, Beaver County, **Pennsylvania**. While serving as a **Campbellite** preacher he became acquainted with the **Saints** early in 1835 and was baptized by Elder **Orson Pratt** the following October (Gentry, 425). A well-educated surgeon, Avard organized the **Danites**—a troublesome Mormon military group—once he arrived in **Far West, Missouri**, in 1838 (*Correspondence*, 97).

Avard is most remembered for his false testimony against the **First Presidency** of the Church sworn before Judge Austin A. King's Court of Inquiry held in November 1838. He was the first of the apostates to testify, and his testimony more than any other did damage to the First Presidency and others. Euphorically in a letter to Governor **Lilburn W. Boggs**, General John B. Clark, commander of the state militia forces wrote: "I will here remark, but for the capture of Sampson Avard, a leading **Mormon** . . . I do not believe I could have obtained any useful facts. No one disclosed any useful matter until he was captured and brought in" (*Correspondence*, 90). Avard's false testimony allowed Judge King to confine the First Presidency and others in prison in **Richmond** and **Liberty, Missouri**, to await trial (*Correspondence*, 97–103). Excommunicated in 1839, he became a practicing physician in Madison County, Illinois, where he died in 1869.

SOURCES

Cannon, Donald Q., and Lyndon W. Cook, eds. *Far West Record: Minutes of The Church of Jesus Christ of Latter-day Saints, 1830–1844.* Salt Lake City: Deseret Book, 1983.

Document Containing the Correspondence, Orders &c. in Relation to the Disturbances with the Mormons; and the Evidence Given before the Hon. Austin A. King, Judge of the Fifth Judicial Circuit of the State of Missouri. Published by Order of the General Assembly, Fayette, Mo.: *Boon's Lick Democrat,* 1841.

Gentry, Leland H. "The Danite Band of 1838." *BYU Studies* 14 (Summer 1974): 421–50.

CLARK V. JOHNSON

BOOK OF MORMON. After the revelation on priesthood in 1978, missionary work expanded rapidly in many areas of the world; here, an African convert prepares to use copies of the Book of Mormon to share his testimony with others.

BABBITT, ALMON W. Almon Babbitt, president of the **Kirtland Stake**, was born in Cheshire, Massachusetts, on 1 October 1812. Soon after his baptism in 1833, he participated in **Zion's Camp**. In **Nauvoo** he served as a postmaster attorney and member of the **Council of Fifty**. In 1845, he was one of three **agents** designated to dispose of Church assets in Illinois after the **exodus** to the Salt Lake Valley. Babbitt experienced recurrent difficulties with Church leadership. He was disciplined on several occasions and rebuked in the Doctrine and Covenants (124:84). He died in a skirmish with **Indians** somewhere between Fort Kearny and Fort Leavenworth on 7 September 1856.

SOURCES

Black, Susan Easton. *Who's Who in the Doctrine and Covenants.* Salt Lake City: Bookcraft, 1997. 2–5.
Knight, Gregory R. "Journal of Thomas Bullock." *BYU Studies* 31 (Winter 1991): 24n.

ROBERT C. FREEMAN

BACKENSTOS, JACOB B. Non-Mormon Jacob B. Backenstos, whom **Orson Spencer** called a "noble-hearted patriot," was a loyal friend to **Joseph Smith** and the **Nauvoo Saints**. Backenstos defended the **Latter-day Saints** on numerous occasions, sometimes at the peril of his own life. As the **Illinois** legislature considered the repeal of the **Nauvoo Charter**, Representative Backenstos "pleaded like an **apostle** for the rights of his constituents" (Smith, 7:363). As county sheriff during the tense fall of 1845, he made several declarations to mob factions, ordering them to "disperse, desist, and forthwith go to their homes" (*Roberts*, 493).

SOURCES

Roberts, B. H. *A Comprehensive History of The Church of Jesus Christ of Latter-day*

Saints, Century One. 6 vols. Salt Lake City: The Church of Jesus Christ of Latter-day Saints, 1930. 2:493.

Smith, Joseph. *History of The Church of Jesus Christ of Latter-day Saints.* Edited by B. H. Roberts. 2d ed. rev. 7 vols. Salt Lake City: The Church of Jesus Christ of Latter-day Saints, 1932–51.

KIM C AVERETT

BAHAMAS. The Bahamas consist of a chain of nearly 800 islands and lie north of Cuba. The inhabitants speak English and French Creole. During 1979 Latter-day Saint families moved to the islands and requested that missionaries be sent. These were the families of Larry and Marge McCombs and Albert and Karen Ballard. Full-time missionaries arrived during the latter part of 1979. One of the first converts was Alexandre Paul, the Haitian consul general to the Bahamas. The first **branch** was organized in 1981. As with those on other Caribbean islands, missionaries in the Bahamas were limited for a time, and visas were difficult to obtain.

By 1988 there were two branches in the Bahamas—the English-speaking Nassau Branch (80 members), and the French Creole-speaking Soldier Road Branch (60 members). On 8 May 1988 the first **meeting-house** in the Bahamas was dedicated on Nassau's New Providence Island; it served both branches. At the beginning of the year 2000 there were 503 members on the islands in two branches.

SOURCES

Crockett, David R. *Church History in the Bahamas.* LDS Gems archives.

"From around the World." *Church News,* 19 March 1988. 10.

Millett, Richard L. "*The Work Spreads to the Other Islands of the Caribbean.*" Manuscript.

1999–2000 Church Almanac. Salt Lake City: Deseret News, 1998. 275.

DAVID R. CROCKETT

BAHRAIN. See MIDDLE EAST and MUSLIMS.

BALLANTYNE, RICHARD. An early Scottish convert, Richard Ballantyne is known in the Church as the founder of the **Sunday School**. Born in Whiteridgebog, **Scotland**, on 26 August 1817, Ballantyne was involved with Presbyterian Sunday School classes in his youth. He was baptized in 1842 and emigrated to **Nauvoo** the following year. He and his **family** suffered persecution with many of the early **Saints**. In 1846, Ballantyne was kidnapped and held hostage for two weeks before being released. During the exodus from Nauvoo, he met Huldah Meriah Clark, and they were married upon their arrival at **Winter Quarters** in February 1847.

In December 1849 Ballantyne called some 50 children to his home in **Salt Lake City** and held the first Sunday School. The meetings included singing, prayers, lessons, recitations, catechisms, and even examination days to assure the material was properly learned. Soon other schools were begun in **Utah**, and the organization was later formalized. A monument at First West and Third South Streets in Salt Lake City marks the spot of those early cabin **meetings**.

In 1852 Ballantyne was called to assist in opening **missionary work** in **India**. He sailed from **San Francisco** with a group of other missionaries but was afflicted with smallpox only five days out of port. Fervent faith and prayer by the little group of **elders** resulted in a miraculous **healing**. Ballantyne labored for 15 months in India, publishing several pamphlets and a periodical. Returning via **England**, he presided over a company of Saints crossing the ocean and then led a wagon train across the plains in 1855.

Ballantyne later married two other wives and was father of 22 children. He lived in **Ogden** in his later years and died in that city on 8 November 1898.

SOURCES

Ballantyne, Richard. Journals. 9 vols. Historical Department, The Church of Jesus Christ of Latter-day Saints, Salt Lake City.

Jenson, Andrew. *Latter-day Saint Biographical Encyclopedia.* 4 vols. 1901–36. Reprint, Salt Lake City: Western Epics, 1971. 1:703–6.

Sonne, Conway B. *Knight of the Kingdom: The Story of Richard Ballantyne.* Salt Lake City: Deseret Book, 1989.

DAVID KENISON

BALLARD, M. RUSSELL.

Melvin Russell Ballard Jr., **apostle**, missionary, and businessman, was born 8 October 1928 in **Salt Lake City** to Melvin R. and Geraldine Smith Ballard. From a distinguished heritage, M. Russell Ballard is the grandson of **elders Melvin J. Ballard** and **Hyrum Mack Smith**, both of the Council of the Twelve. Elder Ballard's service in the **British Mission** (1948–1950) proved to be one of the greatest growing periods of his life. He attended the **University of Utah** where he met Barbara Bowen. They were married 28 August 1951 in the **Salt Lake Temple** and became the parents of seven children. Elder Ballard was a businessman with a varied career in mining, automotive sales, real estate, and investments. He has been an active participant in community organizations.

In 1974 Elder Ballard was called as the president of the **Canada Toronto Mission**. While serving in this position, he was sustained to the First **Quorum** of **Seventy** on 3 April 1976 and was called to the presidency of the Seventy on 21 February 1980. On 6 October 1985 Elder Ballard was sustained as a member of the Quorum of the Twelve Apostles and was ordained an apostle 10 October 1985 at age 57.

Sources

Lubeck, Kathleen, "Elder M. Russell Ballard: True to the Faith." *Ensign* 16 (March 1986): 6–11.
1999–2000 Church Almanac. Salt Lake City: Deseret News, 1998. 21.

Matthew O. Richardson

BALLARD, MELVIN J. Melvin Joseph Ballard, **apostle** and missionary, was born 9 February 1873 in **Logan, Utah**. As a boy he received a special blessing from **patriarch Zebedee Coltrin**. He married Martha A. Jones three weeks before his departure in 1896 for a **mission** in the East. When he returned, he was called on another mission—this time to the Boise Valley, where he organized a **branch** that soon mushroomed into one of the strongholds among the **stakes** of **Zion**.

In 1909 he was set apart as president of the Northwestern States Mission. On 7 January 1919, at age 45, he became one of the Twelve Apostles. While in that **quorum**, he traveled to **South America**, where he offered a prayer dedicating that continent to the spreading of the gospel. He served on the **music** committee of the Church, prepared and issued the Latter-day Saint **hymnbook**, and was instrumental in establishing and developing the **Boy Scout** program in the Church. When he died 30 July 1939 in Salt Lake City of leukemia, he left as one of his greatest legacies his personal witness of the **Savior**, which he had shared with thousands.

Sources

Flake, Lawrence R. *Prophets and Apostles of the Last Dispensation.* Provo, Utah. Religious Studies Center, Brigham Young University, 2001. 447.

Hinckley, Bryant S. "Melvin J. Ballard." *Improvement Era* 35 (October 1932): 712–15, 735.

Lyman, Richard R. "Melvin J. Ballard: A Beloved Apostle Departs." *Improvement Era* 42 (September 1939): 522–72.

LAWRENCE R. FLAKE

BANCROFT, HUBERT HOWE. Hubert Howe Bancroft, a book collector and historian in **California**, wrote one of the first histories of the Latter-day Saints written by a sympathetic non-Mormon. Published in 1889 in **San Francisco**, Bancroft's *History of Utah* includes an even-handed treatment of the **Joseph Smith**, **Brigham Young**, and **John Taylor** periods of Church history. Born 5 May 1832 in Granville, **Ohio**, Bancroft moved to California in 1852, opened a bookstore in San Francisco in 1856, and began writing a multivolume history of the west coast and intermountain region—which included *History of Utah*—in 1870. Bancroft died 2 March 1918 at Walnut Creek, California, having sold his personal library (the famous "Bancroft Library") to the University of California in 1905.

SOURCES

Bancroft, Hubert Howe. *History of Utah.* San Francisco: The History Company, 1889.

Caughey, John Walton. *Hubert Howe Bancroft, Historian of the West.* Berkeley and Los Angeles: University of California Press, 1946.

ANDREW H. HEDGES

BANGLADESH. Bangladesh is located on the north coast of the Bay of Bengal and is home to more than 129 million people. The earliest members of the Church in the country may have been Kenneth and Beatrice Nielsen, who worked in Bangladesh for the Canadian government from 1985 to 1986. Other Canadian members, including Norman and Olive Arbuckle, followed the Nielsens in 1986, at which time a branch was organized in Dhaka. Bono Barua, who had worked as the Nielsen's cook, and his **family** were baptized at this time, as was Roseline Gomes, who later served in the **Canada** Winnipeg **Mission**. At the end of 1998 the country had less than 100 members (mostly expatriates) living in one **branch**.

SOURCE

"Expatriate Serves Mission." *Church News,* 15 May 1993, 7.

1999–2000 Church Almanac. Salt Lake City: Deseret News, 1998. 275–76.

ANDREW H. HEDGES

BAPTISM FOR THE DEAD. The Lord himself declared that baptism is a requirement for entering the **kingdom of God** (John 3:5). Baptism for the dead is a sacred **ordinance** performed by proxy in Latter-day Saint **temples** whereby worthy, living members of the Church are baptized in water on behalf of persons who died without the benefit of baptism by proper authority. **Joseph Smith** learned that this ordinance "was instituted from before the foundation of the world" (D&C 124:33). The Prophet referred to the doctrine of baptism for the dead as "glad tidings" and part of the plan of salvation available to all (Millet, 65).

The history of the doctrine and practice of baptism for the dead in the ancient Church of **Jesus Christ** is better documented than some might think, though such history is not well known among many present-day Christians, or admitted to by others. Paul preached the doctrine of baptism for the dead as a substantiating argument in favor of a universal resurrection when he instructed the Corinthian Saints as recorded in a straightforward biblical passage: "Else what shall they do which are baptized for the dead, if the dead rise not at all? Why are they then baptized for the dead?" (1 Cor. 15:29). The early Church Father and apologist Tertullian (circa A.D. 160–230) verified that the practice was, in fact, taught by the **apostle** Paul and carried out by early Christians.

In this dispensation the first public mention of baptism for the dead was, according to the Prophet Joseph Smith's own declaration, made during the Prophet's sermon at the funeral of Seymour Brunson on 15 August 1840. (It seems apparent that he had been contemplating the subject for a time.) After the funeral service, a widow named Jane Nyman, to whom the Prophet had referred in his sermon, was baptized vicariously for her deceased son in the **Mississippi River**—the first occasion of the performance of the ordinance in modern times. In early days proxies were baptized for individuals regardless of gender (*JD*, 5:85), but now females stand as proxies only for females, and males only for males. On 19 January 1841 the Prophet received the **revelation** known as **Doctrine and Covenants** 124 in which the Lord put the ordinance of baptism for the dead in the context of restored knowledge and power associated with the fulness of the **priesthood** and commanded that the ordinance be performed in the house of the Lord (D&C 124:28–42).

Baptisms are performed for the dead in much the same way as they are for the living. The language of the baptismal prayer is identical to the prayer pronounced for the living, except that the proxy is baptized for and in behalf of the deceased person. As with baptism for the living, witnesses are present at the baptism for the dead, and a record of the ordinance is kept in Church archives (D&C 128:3, 8). The ordinance of **confirmation** and giving the gift of the Holy Ghost by proxy follows baptism for the dead as it does baptism for the living. Those residing in the spirit world, who are given the benefit and service of proxy ordinances performed in this world, have their agency to accept or reject those ordinances. In the Church today any worthy member age twelve and over may enter the temple and be baptized and confirmed for the dead.

SOURCES

Journal of Discourses [JD]. 26 vols. London: Latter-day Saints' Book Depot, 1854–86.

Millet, Robert L. *Life After Death: Insights from Latter-day Revelation.* Salt Lake City: Deseret Book, 1999. 57–74.

ANDREW C. SKINNER

BARBADOS. Barbados is the easternmost Caribbean island and a sovereign state of **Great Britain**, with English-speaking inhabitants. Before the arrival of missionaries, Greg Young shared the gospel with a former classmate, John Naime. He and his wife and children were the first to be baptized in Barbados, 16 April 1978.

In 1979 the first full-time missionaries arrived and experienced immediate success. On 20 October 1979 the Christ Church **Branch** was organized with John Naime as president.

This missionary success soon attracted strong opposition in the local media. The government started to require that missionaries obtain expensive work permits. With the help of J. Willard Marriott Jr., the restrictions were lifted, allowing more missionaries to enter the country. In 1983 the **West Indies Mission** was created with headquarters in Barbados. The government again restricted missionary work in 1988, and many missionaries had to leave. At the beginning of the year 2000, there were 568 church members living in three branches.

SOURCES

Crockett, David R. *Church History in the Barbados.* LDS Gems archives.

1999–2000 Church Almanac. Salt Lake City: Deseret News, 1998. 276.

DAVID R. CROCKETT

BATEMAN, MERRILL J. On 1 January 1996, Merrill J. Bateman, who had been serving as the **presiding bishop** of the Church, became the president of **Brigham Young University** and the first BYU president to serve simultaneously as a **general authority**. He was called as a member of the First Quorum of the **Seventy** at the time of his appointment at BYU. Born 19 June 1936 in Lehi, **Utah**, he married his high school sweetheart, Marilyn Scholes, in the **Salt Lake Temple** on 23 March 1959 following a **mission** in **England**. He received his B.S. in economics from the **University of Utah** in 1960 and his Ph.D. in economics from the **Massachusetts** Institute of Technology in 1965.

Elder Bateman held a number of business, university, and Church positions prior to his call as a general authority. He served as dean of the Graduate School of Management and the College of Business at BYU from 1975 to 1979 after four years as director of commodity research and vice president at Mars, Inc. Following his years as dean, he was the owner-manager of two companies—a commodities-consulting firm and a management and investment service firm. In the Church, Bateman served as a **bishop**, high councilor, **stake president**, and **regional representative**. On 3 October 1992 he was sustained as a member of the Second Quorum of the Seventy. He became presiding bishop on 2 April 1994 and a member of the First Quorum of the Seventy on 2 November 1995.

As president at BYU he focused on serving more students through expanded enrollment and the use of technology to facilitate the sharing of BYU courses with Church members throughout the world, as well as to enhance on-campus teaching. He also emphasized the importance of educating both minds and spirits at BYU.

SOURCE

Bell, James P. "Merrill J. Bateman: Breadth and Depth." *BYU Magazine* 50 (March 1996): 19–27.

ALAN L. WILKINS

BATTLE OF NAUVOO. See NAUVOO, BATTLE OF.

BEAN, WILLARD. Willard Washington Bean was a long-time missionary in **Palmyra, New York**. He was born 16 May 1868 in Provo, **Utah**.

During the height of anti**polygamy** persecution in Utah (1886), several **general authorities** went on extended missions to avoid arrest, and Willard was selected as driver and camp-hand for the delegation. They traveled through Utah, **Arizona**, and **Mexico**, holding **conferences** and encouraging the beleaguered **Saints**.

Called on a second **mission** (1890) to serve in the newly completed **Manti Temple**, Willard participated in temple **ordinances**, slept and ate in the **temple**, and assisted the aging president, **Daniel H. Wells**, until his death in 1891.

A third assignment came when Willard was called to serve a proselyting mission (1893), during which he presided over the Middle **Tennessee** Conference of the **Southern States Mission**. His final assignment during this mission (1895) was to return to the scene of the **Cane Creek Massacre** (1884) and report his findings to Church authorities. The people were still hostile toward the Church, and Bean believed his life was in danger.

Between missionary assignments, Bean married Rebecca Peterson (1914) and together they were called (1915) to live "for five years or longer" in **Manchester, New York**, and improve the image of the Church. They resided in the **Joseph Smith home** and experienced great opposition. Through persistence, civic involvement, and tenacity, they gained respect for and reestablished the Church where the **Restoration** began. After 24 years the Beans returned to **Salt Lake City**, where they served as guides on **Temple Square**. Willard died on 13 October 1949 in Salt Lake City and Rebecca on 25 June 1976 in Provo, Utah.

SOURCE

Zimmerman, Vicki Bean. *Willard Bean: The Fighting Parson.* Utah: s.n., 1981.

DAVID F. BOONE

BEAR RIVER MASSACRE. On 29 January 1863, federal troops under the command of Colonel **Patrick E. Connor** attacked a sleeping **Shoshoni** village encamped northwest of Franklin, **Idaho**, slaughtering nearly 300 men, women, and children. Connor initiated the brutal military action hoping to eradicate **Native Americans** who had been implicated in a number of raids on emigrant wagons traveling the **California** and **Oregon trails** during the previous three years. He believed that some of the perpetrators were encamped with their families at the wintering site. Resident **apostle Ezra T. Benson** and **Cache Valley bishop Peter Maughan** were sickened by reports brought back from witnesses to the carnage but hoped that the action would end years of thefts and other altercations between the Indians, who considered Cache Valley their homeland, and the Latter-day Saints, who had begun to establish communities there in 1856. Some of the survivors of the decimated bands led by Sagwitch and Sanpitch joined the Church in the 1870s and eventually settled at Washakie, a Church-sponsored farm in Box Elder County, Utah.

SOURCE

Madsen, Brigham D. *The Shoshoni Frontier and the Bear River Massacre.* Salt Lake City: University of Utah Press, 1985.

SCOTT R. CHRISTENSEN

BECKHAM, JANETTE HALES. Janette Callister Hales Beckham, the tenth general president of the Young Women, was born 7 June 1933 in Springville, Utah. Following her 1955 marriage to Robert H. Hales and in addition to rearing her family of five children, Janette was actively involved in community and Church service. A member of the Primary general board, she received a call in 1990 as the second counselor in the Young Women general presidency. Two years later, she was called to be the general president. During her administration, from 1992 until 1997, the Young Women introduced a new camp manual that emphasized service, spirituality, and the Young Women Values; the organization also celebrated the 125th anniversary of the Young Women program. After her first husband died, Janette married Raymond E. Beckham in 1995.

SOURCES

"New Young Women General Presidency Called." *Ensign* 22 (May 1992): 106.
Peterson, Janet, and LaRene Gaunt. *Keepers of the Flame: General Presidents of the Young Women.* Salt Lake City: Deseret Book, 1993.

JANET PETERSON

BEEHIVE CLASS. The Beehive Class, a program developed for young women ages 12 to 13, was organized in 1913 to replace the Junior Class in the Young Lady's Mutual Improvement Association. Established guidelines required the "young ladies" to accomplish goals to "sleep outside or with wide open windows; refrain from candy, chewing gum, sundaes, and sodas for at least two months; and, know the proper use of hot and cold baths" (quoted in Peterson and Gaunt, 28).

Later the Young Women program initiated a Personal Progress

Program, and in 1985 the general presidency established the Young Women Values. Under these programs, a Beehive received the Recognition of Truth award by accomplishing such activities as writing a personal history, participating in regular **scripture** study, attending Church **meetings**, and completing two experiences in each of the seven Young Women Value areas.

SOURCES

M.I.A. Handbook. Salt Lake City: The Church of Jesus Christ of Latter-day Saints, 1928.

Peterson, Janet, and LaRene Gaunt. *Keepers of the Flame: General Presidents of the Young Women.* Salt Lake City: Deseret Book, 1993. 28.

MAREN M. MOURITSEN

BEEHIVE HOUSE. The Beehive House in **Salt Lake City**, noted for the sculpted beehive on its roof, was built 1853 to 1855 as the primary residence of **Brigham Young**. Two of President Young's wives, Mary Ann Angel and later Lucy Decker Young, and their families occupied the structure. In 1888 his son **John W. Young** acquired the Beehive House. He razed the rear section, including the **family** store, and replaced it with a large Victorian addition.

Church presidents **Lorenzo Snow** and **Joseph F. Smith** lived in the Beehive House during their terms as president of the Church. After serving as a residence for young women from 1920 to 1959, the Beehive House was renovated and opened as a museum in 1961.

SOURCES

Spencer, Clarissa Young. *Brigham Young at Home.* Salt Lake City: Deseret Book, 1974.

Taylor, Rachel G. "The Beehive House." *Relief Society Magazine* 30 (September 1943): 535–39, 556.

W. RANDALL DIXON

BELARUS. LDS Church efforts in Belarus began in January 1993 when Karl and Hanna Borcherding, a German couple, were called to serve in Minsk. Under the leadership of **mission president** Howard L. Biddulph of the **Ukraine** Kiev **Mission**, the next year saw steady progress for the Church in Belarus. Full-time **elders** arrived in March 1993. In May **Elder Russell M. Nelson** of the Quorum of the Twelve **Apostles** arrived to dedicate Belarus for the preaching of the gospel. A year later, in January

1994, the Church was officially registered with the government. A **television** broadcast on the day of registration featured area, mission, and local Church leaders and gave the Church an opportunity to expose millions in Belarus to its message. Belarus is now part of the **Lithuania** Vilnius Mission. At the beginning of the year 2000, the Church had 372 members in Belarus attending one **branch**.

SOURCES

Biddulph, Howard L. *The Morning Breaks: Stories of Conversion and Faith in the Former Soviet Union.* Salt Lake City: Deseret Book, 1996.
1999–2000 Church Almanac. Salt Lake City: Deseret News, 1998. 276.

SCOTT BRADSHAW

BELGIUM. The tiny kingdom of Belgium was artificially created in 1830 as a buffer state between the surrounding countries of **France**, **Germany**, and the **Netherlands**. The northern part, Flanders, is Dutch-speaking and in 1999 composed 58% of the population of ten million. The southern part, Wallonia, is French-speaking and includes 32% of the population; Brussels, the bilingual capital, accounted for 10%. This situation explains some of the shifts in Latter-day Saint missionary activity over the years.

The first reported missionary to Belgium was Gustave Chaprix, who arrived in Brussels on 5 June 1861, sent by French **Mission President Louis Bertrand**. No record of his work has been found, however. In 1868 the Swiss **Mission** sent Octave Ursenbach, who spent two months in Flanders (Antwerp) and Wallonia (Liege) and concluded that nothing could be done. Twenty years later, in 1888, **Mischa Markow** obtained some baptismal success in Antwerp among German-speaking people. More missionaries from the Swiss-German Mission were sent, resulting in some 80 converts. In 1891 responsibility for Belgium was given to the Netherlands Mission. Some of its missionaries, fluent in French, then crossed the lingual border to the thriving industrial region of Liege in French-speaking Wallonia. In 1892 President Timothy Mets organized branches in Antwerp, Brussels, and Liege.

WALLONIA AND BRUSSELS

By 1905 there were a hundred members in the Brussels and Liege conferences. In 1912 a total of 179 members, 26 children under 8, and 14 traveling missionaries were recorded. This relative strength of

French-speaking members contributed to the 1912 reopening of the French Mission, which had been closed since 1864. The Liege Conference became the flagship of that mission, but the outbreak of **World War I** resulted in the conference reverting temporarily to the Netherlands Mission.

Anti-Mormon sentiment seems to have been rare, although the Netherlands Mission history reports an incident on 30 November 1896 in Liege, when a group manifested anger in front of the home of a newly converted **family** named Creuiwel. A legend developed that a mob of 500 people stormed the home and tried to kill the missionaries. No trace of such an incident can be found in the local newspapers or police reports, however, so the incident must have been minor. It seems **missionary work** and meetings were never otherwise thwarted.

After World War I the French Mission, which included Belgium, was reopened in 1923 with headquarters in Geneva, **Switzerland**. The industrial area of Liege kept its early tradition as a **Latter-day Saint** center. By 1930 two chapels had been built, and membership stood at 344. In 1937 **Heber J. Grant** visited Liege and dedicated a new chapel in nearby Herstal. The Latter-day Saints also gained much visibility through a basketball team of missionaries.

During **World War II**, when missionaries were withdrawn, local leaders were able to keep all branches organized and functioning. Proselyting also continued, which resulted in 50 new converts. The positive trend continued after the **war**, again with a very successful basketball team of missionaries. In 1963 the Franco-Belgian Mission was created with headquarters in Brussels. The Brussels Belgium **Stake** was organized in 1977. It covered most of French-speaking Belgium, with the exception of Liege, which in 1998 was still a mission **district**.

FLANDERS AND BRUSSELS

The first recorded Latter-day Saint baptism in Belgium occurred in Antwerp in 1888. Until the First World War, missionary efforts continued sporadically in Flanders but with little success. After the war and until 1947, missionary activity was French-speaking with no efforts towards the millions living in the north. But on 30 November 1947, President Cornelius Zappey of the Netherlands Mission sent four Dutch-speaking missionaries to Antwerp. The years that followed saw a slow but steady growth, resulting in small branches in Antwerp, Brussels, Ghent, and Mechelen as part of the Antwerp district. In the early 1970s a number of new cities were opened and two districts organized.

Pleading from members resulted in the opening of the Antwerp Belgium Mission in 1975, but it was not maintained for financial reasons, and Flanders reverted to the Netherlands Mission in 1982. The mission was reopened in 1990 and closed again in 1994 for the same reason. The Antwerp Belgium Stake was organized in 1994, covering all of Flanders and some units in the south of the Netherlands.

BELGIUM IN PERSPECTIVE

Generally speaking, the free and democratic structure of Belgium, including absolute freedom of religion, has never impeded Latter-day Saint missionary work. Strong familial ties to ideological traditions, mainly Catholic, made conversions more difficult, however. According to a 1983 inquiry among members, missionary success was more likely to occur among people with socialist backgrounds or among those estranged from the Catholic Church (Decoo, 61–77).

In 1996 the Belgian Parliament instituted an Investigation Commission on Sects, as a consequence of media publicized killings and alleged misconduct among some cults. The state police conducted an investigation to list all the "sects" in Belgium. The Latter-day Saints were included and succinctly investigated, but they were not harassed. The report of the Investigation Commission, published in 1997, hardly paid any attention to the Mormons but still listed the Church as a sect.

At the beginning of the year 2000, Belgium had two stakes, 29 wards and branches, and 5,771 members of the Church.

SOURCES

Burvenich, An. "Het ontstaan van de Kerk van Jezus Christus van de Heiligen der Laatste Dagen in Belgie, 1861–1914." Master's thesis, State University of Ghent, 1999.

Chard, Gary Ray. "A History of the French Mission of The Church of Jesus Christ of Latter-day Saints, 1850–1960." Master's thesis, Utah State University, 1965.

Decoo, Wilfried. "Mormonism in a European Catholic Region: A Contribution to the Social Psychology of LDS Converts." *BYU Studies* 24 (Winter 1984): 61–77.

Liege Conference History.

Markow, Mischa (1854–1934). Reminiscences [n.d.]. LDS Church Archives, The Church of Jesus Christ of Latter-day Saints, Salt Lake City.

Netherlands Mission History Record.

AN BURVENICH AND WILFRIED DECOO

BELIZE. Belize is located on the east coast of **Central America**. Formerly known as British Honduras, it received its independence in 1981.

During May 1980 the first missionaries arrived. Ernesto Alay was their first convert, baptized 1 June 1980. One of the early members in 1981 was Harold Smith, who later became a leader of the Church in Belize. When he and his wife first attended **meetings** in Belize City, there were only about 12 members attending. The Belize **District** was organized on 17 April 1983 with Harold Smith as president. On 7 December 1992 Belize was dedicated (by **Elder Russell M. Nelson**) for the preaching of the gospel. About 36 members gathered for the service.

On 13 November 1997 the **Saints** in Belize were delighted to receive a visit from President **Gordon B. Hinckley**. About 1,200 members gathered to hear the **prophet**. By the beginning of the year 2000, there were 2,605 Belizian Church members living in 16 **branches**.

SOURCE

1999–2000 Church Almanac. Salt Lake City: Deseret News, 1998. 277.
"Tiny Nation of Belize Is Dedicated." *Church News,* 19 December 1992, 3.

DAVID R. CROCKETT

BELL, TERREL H. Latter-day Saint and distinguished educator Terrel H. Bell served nationally during the administrations of **United States** presidents Nixon, Ford, and Reagan. Born 11 November 1921 in Hot Spring, **Idaho**, Bell was left fatherless at age eight. After high school, Terrel attended Albion Normal School, where he graduated in education. Early in his career, Bell was a superintendent of schools in both Idaho and **Wyoming**. Later he was appointed **Utah** state superintendent of public instruction. In 1970 Terrel Bell worked as assistant U.S. commissioner of education, then as acting commissioner, and finally in 1974 as **commissioner of education**. In 1976 he returned to Utah as commissioner of higher education. In 1980 Bell was named U.S. secretary of education. Four years later he returned to Utah to teach at the **University of Utah**. He died 22 June 1996.

SOURCES

Bell, Terrel H. *The Thirteenth Man.* New York: Free Press, 1988.
Knight, Hal. "T. H. Bell Faces Big Challenge in Cabinet." *Church News,* 31 January 1981, 3.

ROBERT C. FREEMAN

BENBOW, JOHN. John Benbow, a wealthy farmer in Herefordshire, was born 1 April 1800 at Grendon Warren, Herefordshire, **England**. He made possible the publication of 3,000 copies of the **Book of Mormon** and the first Latter-day Saint **hymnbook** in England by a generous financial contribution. In this regard he has been compared with **Martin Harris**, who financed the publication of the first edition of the Book of Mormon in **America**. Benbow's contribution was £250 (about $16,000 in today's money). John and his wife, Jane, were members of the **United Brethren** when **Wilford Woodruff** came to their farm. They were among the first six of the group to be baptized, 6 March 1840, only two days after hearing the gospel. He was ordained a **teacher** in the **Aaronic Priesthood** on 22 April of that year, the same day he was introduced to **Brigham Young** and **Willard Richards**.

Since a large room in the Benbow mansion was licensed for preaching, they made it freely available to **Elder** Woodruff. On 8 September 1840, John and his wife emigrated to the United States with 50 fellow **Saints**, many of whom were converts from the United Brethren. John paid the passage for 40 of them. The day before the ship sailed, he signed an agreement relinquishing all claim to the money provided for the publication of the Book of Mormon.

He died in South Cottonwood, Salt Lake County, **Utah**, in 1874 at age 74.

SOURCES

Allen, James B., Ronald K. Esplin, and David J. Whittaker. *Men with a Mission: The Quorum of the Twelve Apostles in the British Isles, 1837–1841*. Salt Lake City: Deseret Book, 1992.

Black, Susan Easton. "A Profile of a British Saint, 1837–1848." In *British Isles*. Edited by Donald Q. Cannon. Regional Studies in Latter-day Saint Church History series. Provo, Utah: Brigham Young University, 1990. 103–14.

Bloxham, V. Ben, James R. Moss, and Larry C. Porter, eds. *Truth Will Prevail: The Rise of The Church of Jesus Christ of Latter-day Saints in the British Isles, 1837–1997*. Cambridge: Cambridge University Press, 1987.

DAVID COOK

BENNET, JAMES ARLINGTON. Joseph Smith's first choice as a vice presidential running mate in the 1844 U.S. presidential election, James Arlington Bennet was born in **New York** in 1788. Evidently **John C. Bennett** (not related; note difference in spelling) introduced James to the Church in 1841 and arranged for him to be appointed inspector general of the **Nauvoo Legion** the following year. James was baptized a member of the Church in 1843. When Joseph asked him to be his vice presidential running mate, Bennet declined. After the **martyrdom** of the **Prophet** in 1844, he left the Church. A year later, however, he visited **Nauvoo** and declared his intentions to go west with the **Saints**. He aspired to be leader of the Nauvoo Legion, but when **Brigham Young** turned him down, Bennet disassociated himself from the Saints and spent the rest of his life in the eastern **United States**. Bennet died in 1865.

SOURCES

Cook, Lyndon W. "James Arlington Bennet and the Mormons." *BYU Studies* 19 (Winter 1979): 247–49.

Jessee, Dean C., ed. *The Papers of Joseph Smith.* Vol. 2. Salt Lake City: Deseret Book, 1992. 525.

ARNOLD K. GARR

BENNETT, ARCHIBALD F. Archibald Fowler Bennett, the man who set the standard of excellence in **genealogy** for the Church, was born 17 March 1896 in Dingle, **Idaho**. He married Ella Milner in 1921. Bennett became the secretary (1928) and librarian (1929) of the **Genealogical Society of Utah**, which in effect made him the general manager of the Church's genealogical activities from 1928 to 1961. Under his leadership, the society embarked on its worldwide microfilming program, and in 1964 he became supervisor of the new branch library system designed to share those films with the world.

He was not only an inspired administrator but an inspiring teacher. In the early 1950s, Bennett wrote *A Guide for Genealogical Research,* which was one of the first scholarly works designed for "earnest" researchers. During this same time frame, he helped set up adult education courses through the extension services of **Brigham Young University** and began to teach genealogy in the **institute** program at the **University of Utah** and as a part-time faculty member of Religious Education at BYU. In 1954 Bennett pioneered the use of **television** as an educational tool for genealogy.

His professional success was acknowledged in 1961 when he became a fellow of the American Society of Genealogists and posthumously in 1994 when he was named a member of the National Genealogy Hall of Fame. Spiritually, he never lost sight of the real reason for the Church's emphasis on family history, as can be seen in his hymn, "Holy Temples on Mount Zion," which closes with the stirring reminder: "For the prisoners shall go free." Archibald Bennett died in American Fork, **Utah**, on 28 August 1965.

SOURCES

Allen, James B., Jessie L. Embry, and Kahlile B. Mehr. *Hearts Turned to the Fathers.* Provo, Utah: *BYU Studies,* 1994–95.
"Archibald Fowler Bennett, 1896–1965." Arlington, Va.: National Genealogy Hall of Fame, 1994.
Hymns of The Church of Jesus Christ of Latter-day Saints. Salt Lake City: The Church of Jesus Christ of Latter-day Saints, 1985. No. 289.

DAVID H. PRATT

BENNETT, JOHN C. John Cook Bennett, a friend and associate of the **Prophet Joseph Smith** in **Nauvoo**, quickly rose to a position of great importance in the Church, only to leave it 13 months later and help bring about the Prophet's **martyrdom** in 1844. Bennett was born in Fairhaven, **Massachusetts**, on 3 August 1804. He moved to **Ohio** with his parents in 1808, received a good education in classical languages and mathematics, studied medicine with his uncle, Dr. Samuel Hildreth, and was licensed by and became a member of Ohio's Twelfth Medical District in 1825. He married a young woman from Massachusetts and practiced medicine in several states. He came to hold several professorships, including one in gynecology at Willoughby University, Ohio. He preached on occasion as a Methodist minister between 1825 and 1830. In 1830 Bennett became a disciple of Alexander Campbell and met **Sidney Rigdon** before the latter converted to Mormonism that same year. In the decade that followed, Bennett became involved in enterprises that later earned him the reputation of being a huckster. He also began to foster the image of a military man. Soon after migrating to **Illinois** in 1838 he was given a high office in a division of the Illinois militia (though no one knows exactly why), and in July 1840 was appointed quartermaster general of the militia of the state of Illinois by Governor Thomas Carlin.

Bennett probably first came in contact with the Church in 1834 while Joseph Smith and Sidney Rigdon were at **Kirtland, Ohio**, only four miles from Willoughby University. After an exchange of correspondence in 1840, Joseph Smith issued a general invitation to Bennett to join with the **Saints** in **Nauvoo**, which he did in September 1840. John C. Bennett's meteoric rise to power was again seen as he entered Nauvoo civil and religious affairs. By 4 February 1841 he had been elevated to three of the highest leadership posts in the city: mayor, chancellor of the university, and major general of the **Nauvoo Legion**. During the April 1841 **general conference** he was sustained as an additional counselor to Joseph Smith.

Bennett's problems began in earnest in June 1841 when **Hyrum Smith** and **William Law** confirmed that Bennett, who had been presenting himself as an eligible bachelor, already had a wife and children back in Ohio. When confronted, Bennett admitted the truth of his situation and subsequently tried unsuccessfully to commit suicide. The circumstances surrounding Bennett's moral turpitude in Nauvoo seem to have been the doctrine of **plural marriage**, which he tried to pervert. Bennett took advantage of his profession as a gynecologist, sought to have illicit relationships with women, and told them they were married to him spiritually and that the Prophet approved this (he later admitted such was a lie). The relationship between the Church and John C. Bennett deteriorated until Joseph Smith initiated Church disciplinary proceedings on 15 May 1842. By June 1842 Bennett had resigned his leadership positions in Nauvoo, removed his name from Church records, and left the city. He became an ardent foe of the Prophet Joseph Smith and stirred up great persecution against the Church, helping to create a volatile atmosphere in which the murders of Joseph and Hyrum Smith could occur. In November 1842 his work, *The History of the Saints; or, An Expose of Joe Smith and Mormonism,* was published in Boston.

After the death of Joseph Smith, Bennett aligned himself with Sidney Rigdon and then became chief advisor to **James J. Strang** in 1846. After he fell from grace among the Strangites, Bennett moved around the country promoting his enterprises. He died in Polk City, **Iowa**, in 1867. Tragically, John C. Bennett seems to have not realized the great blessings promised to him by the Lord in **Doctrine and Covenants** 124:16–17, where it states that the Lord would "crown him with blessings and great glory."

SOURCES

Skinner, Andrew C. "John C. Bennett: For Prophet or Profit." In *Illinois*. Edited by H. Dean Garrett. Regional Studies in Latter-day Saint Church History series. Provo, Utah: Brigham Young University, 1995. 249–65.

Smith, Andrew F. *The Saintly Scoundrel: The Life and Times of Dr. John Cook Bennett.* Urbana: University of Illinois Press, 1997.

ANDREW C. SKINNER

BENNION, ADAM S.

BENNION, ADAM S. Adam Samuel Bennion was ordained a member of the Quorum of the Twelve **Apostles** 9 April 1953. His service in the

Church included **Deseret Sunday School** board member from 1915 to 1953, superintendent of Church schools from 1919 to 1928, and member of the Church Board of **Education** from 1915 to 1935. He wrote several books while serving in the **Sunday School**, including the first teacher training manual. Published in 1957, his book *The Candle of the Lord* is still quoted.

Born 2 December 1886 in Taylorsville, Salt Lake County, **Utah**, Bennion married Minerva Richards Young on 14 September 1911 in the **Salt Lake Temple**. They were blessed with five children. Receiving his B.S. at the **University of Utah** in 1908, Bennion went on to complete an M.A. at Columbia in 1912 and a Ph.D. at the University of **California** at Berkeley in 1923. He was a distinguished educator in public and Church sectors. As the principal at Granite High School, Bennion was instrumental in beginning the first Church **seminary**. In 1927 he became an executive with the Utah Power and Light Company. As a successful businessman, he made contributions in Utah's civic affairs. He died in **Salt Lake City** 11 February 1958.

SOURCES

Bell, Kenneth G. "Adam S. Bennion: Superintendent of L.D.S. Education, 1915–1928." Master's thesis, Brigham Young University, 1969.

Braithwaite, John A. "Adam Samuel Bennion: Educator, Businessman, and Apostle." Master's thesis, Brigham Young University, 1965.

MARY JANE WOODGER

BENNION, LOWELL L. Lowell Lindsey Bennion, renowned teacher, counselor, and humanitarian, was born in **Salt Lake City**, 26 July 1908. He was the fifth child of Cora Lindsey Bennion and Milton Bennion. After his graduation from the **University of Utah** in 1928, Lowell married Lela Merle Colton and left for the Swiss-German Mission. Two and a half years later, Merle joined him for a Ph.D. program at the University of Strasbourg, **France**. After he returned to Utah, Lowell founded the Church's fourth **institute of religion**, at the University of Utah.

Lowell taught and counseled a generation of Latter-day Saint youth from 1935 to 1962. For 27 years he directed the Teton Valley Boys Ranch, which he founded, while serving as **bishop** of his ward. For 16 years, he directed the Community Services Council, transforming it into a volunteer organization for the needy. He also founded the Utah food bank and the first homeless shelter. He wrote 20 Latter-day Saint manuals and 16 other books.

In 1992 the Utah legislature honored Bennion with a joint resolution, and the Caring Institution in Washington, D.C., cited him as one of the most caring souls in all humanity (Halamandaris, 158). His response to these ever-increasing honors: "If you publicly give credit for good things done, it diminishes the act of kindness" (Bradford, 349). Today, two institutions bear his name: The Lowell Bennion Center for Community Service at the University of Utah, and the Lowell L. and Merle Colton Bennion Community Services Building in Salt Lake City. Lowell Bennion died 22 February 1996 of Parkinson's disease.

SOURCES

Bennion, Lowell L. *How Can I Help? Final Selections by the Legendary Writer, Teacher, Humanitarian.* Salt Lake City: Aspen Books, 1996.

Bradford, Mary Lythgoe. *Lowell L. Bennion: Teacher, Counselor, Humanitarian.* Salt Lake City: The Dialogue Foundation, 1995. 349.

———. "Lowell Bennion and the Raspberry Cure." *This People* (Fall 1997): 70–80.

England, Eugene, ed. *The Best of Lowell L. Bennion: Selected Writings 1928–1988.* Salt Lake City: Deseret Book, 1988.

———. "The Legacy of Lowell L. Bennion." *Sunstone 19* (September 1996): 27–44.

Halamandaris, Val J., ed. *Faces of Caring: A Search for the 100 Most Caring People in History.* Washington: Caring Publishing, 1992. 158.

MARY LYTHGOE BRADFORD

BENNION, MILTON. Milton Bennion, superintendent of the Latter-day Saint **Sunday Schools** (1943–49), was born 7 June 1870 in Taylorsville, **Utah**, to John Bennion and Mary Turpin. He married Cora Lindsey 22 June 1898 in the **Salt Lake Temple**, and they became the parents of 10 children.

Deeply interested in **education**, Milton received a B.S. from the **University of Utah** and an M.A. from Columbia University. He received an honorary Ed.D. from the University of Utah, where he became a professor of philosophy. He also served as chairman of a committee on character education for the National Council of Education. Bennion died 5 April 1953 in **Salt Lake City**.

SOURCES

Jenson, Andrew. *Latter-day Saint Biographical Encyclopedia.* 4 vols. 1901–36. Reprint, Salt Lake City: Western Epics, 1971. 4:205–6.

1999–2000 Church Almanac. Salt Lake City: Deseret News, 1996. 93.

BRIAN M. HAUGLID

BENNION, SAMUEL O. Samuel Otis Bennion was a member of the First Council of **Seventy** from 14 April 1933 to 8 March 1945. He was born 9 June 1874 in Taylorsville, **Utah**. From 1906 to 1907 he was a missionary in the **Central States Mission**, then from 1908 to 1933 he served as president of that **mission**. Highlights of his 27 years in **Missouri** include accompanying **George Albert Smith** and **Anthony Ivins** to **Far West** and there rediscovering the **temple** site in August 1908. He also moved mission headquarters from Kansas City to **Independence**. President Bennion witnessed the exhumation of Joseph and **Hyrum** Smith's bodies from their burial site in **Nauvoo** in 1928. Of this experience he wrote, "I could hardly keep back the tears" (Letter).

Bennion was sustained as one of the Seven Presidents of the Seventy on **6 April** 1933. In 1934 he was named vice president and general manager of the *Deseret News* and chairman of the Utah **Pioneer** Trails and Landmarks Association. Bennion died of a heart attack on 8 March 1945 in **Salt Lake City** at age 70. Of his death Harry S. Truman, then vice president of the **United States**, wrote, "I have lost a friend and Utah has lost one of her great men" ("Samuel," 183).

SOURCES

Bennion, Samuel O. Letter to President Heber J. Grant and counselors, 21 January 1928, written from Independence, Missouri.

Green, Forace, comp. *Testimonies of our Leaders*. Salt Lake City: Bookcraft, 1958. 296–98.

"Samuel O. Bennion of the First Council of the Seventy." *Improvement Era* 48 (April 1945): 183.

SUSAN EASTON BLACK

BENSON, EZRA T. Ezra Taft Benson, **apostle, pioneer,** and colonizer, was born 22 February 1811 at Mendon, Worcester, **Massachusetts**. He was baptized near **Quincy, Illinois,** 19 July 1840. In March 1841 he moved to **Nauvoo**, where he lived until 1846.

Benson figured prominently in the western **exodus**. While crossing Iowa in 1846, he was called to the presidency at **Garden Grove** and later at **Mount Pisgah**. In July, while encamped at Pisgah, he was chosen as a member of the **Quorum** of the Twelve. He was ordained an apostle by **Brigham Young** at **Council Bluffs, Iowa,** 16 July 1846. Later he was selected captain of one of the five emigrating companies and was also a member of the original 1847 pioneer vanguard company (D&C 136:12). During the fall of 1847, he returned to Iowa, where along with **Orson**

Hyde and **George A. Smith** he presided over the **Saints** until July 1849, when he immigrated to **Utah**.

From 1850 to 1860, Elder Benson figured prominently in the settlement of Tooele County. In 1860 he was called to preside over the Saints in **Cache Valley**. He died unexpectedly on 3 September 1869 in **Ogden, Utah**, at age 58.

His great-grandson **Ezra Taft Benson** (1899–1994) became the thirteenth president of the Church.

———

SOURCE

Evans, John Henry, and Minnie Egan Anderson. *Ezra T. Benson: Pioneer, Statesman, Saint.* Salt Lake City: Deseret News, 1947.

ALEXANDER L. BAUGH

BENSON, EZRA TAFT. Ezra Taft Benson, thirteenth president of The Church of Jesus Christ of Latter-day **Saints**, was born 4 August 1899 in Whitney, **Idaho**. He was the eldest of George Taft Benson Jr. and Sarah Ballif Dunkley's 11 children. His great-grandfather **Ezra T. Benson**, after whom he was named, was the first **apostle** called after the death of **Joseph Smith**.

Ezra Taft, or "T" as he was called, spent his early years living and working on the **family** farm in Whitney. He took on increased responsibility when as a young man his father was called away to serve a mission. Ezra's reading included the scriptures, particularly the **Book of Mormon**, Horatio Alger' s motivational youth stories, and a set of books entitled *Little Visits with Great Americans*. He attended the Oneida Stake Academy and later the **Utah** State Agriculture College.

He served in the military service during **World War I** and was a missionary for the Church in **England**, presiding in the Newcastle area in 1923.

After his mission he attended **Brigham Young University**, where he received his bachelor's degree with honors and was named in the yearbook as "the most popular man."

He married Flora Smith Amussen 23 September 1926 in the **Salt Lake Temple** following her mission to **Hawaii**. Her father, Carl Christian Amussen, was a prominent Utah **pioneer** jeweler who served several **missions** for the Church. Flora attended college in **Logan**, where she was the student body vice-president, won the women's single tennis championship, and took the lead in a Shakespearean play. Of his wife, **Elder** Benson said that she had more faith in him than he had in himself.

Ezra began participating in the **Boy Scout** movement as an assistant Scoutmaster and eventually was named to its national executive board. Through the years, he received Scouting's Silver Beaver, Antelope, and Buffalo awards, as well as international Scouting's highest honor—the Silver Wolf.

Obtaining his master's degree in agricultural science from **Iowa** State College in 1927, he did additional graduate work at the University of California at Berkeley.

He served as the farm agent for Franklin County, Idaho, and then as the extension specialist for the University of Idaho with offices in **Boise.** His work in promoting farm cooperatives brought him to **Washington, D.C.,** where he was the executive secretary of the National Council of Farmer Cooperatives—one of the major farm organizations in **America.** He served on a four-man National Agricultural Advisory Committee to President Franklin D. Roosevelt during **World War II.**

Ezra's Church service included being a stake president in Boise, Idaho, and then the first **stake president** in the nation's capital, from which he would be called to the Quorum of the Twelve Apostles. He and **Spencer W. Kimball** were ordained apostles 7 October 1943.

He served as the **European Mission** president in 1946 on an epic assignment to those **war**-torn countries. His exceptional organizational skills and government "know how" resulted in the widespread distribution of food and clothing to the devastated **Saints.** He lifted their spirits, organized them, and reopened the doors for missionary work. This account is well told in the books *On Wings of Faith* and *A Labor of Love.*

In 1953 Elder Benson was sworn in to serve in the cabinet of President Dwight D. Eisenhower as the United States Secretary of Agriculture—the highest office in government to be held by a member of the Church up to that time. Through his encouragement, prayer was inaugurated in all cabinet meetings. He soon became known for his moral courage in standing for principles in spite of intense opposition. These principles were spelled out in his books *Farmers at the Crossroads* and *Freedom to Farm.* His fight for these principles before congressional committees, and as he traversed the country holding hundreds of press conferences and delivering countless speeches, is revealed in his autobiography *Crossfire: My Eight Years with Eisenhower.* His work brought the first major legislative victory in the Eisenhower administration. Those eight years in the cabinet resulted in widespread and favorable coverage for the Church. Twice he was featured on the cover of *Time* magazine, and his family's portrayal of a Mormon **family home evening** on Ed Morrow's popular national weekly television show, "Person to Person," resulted in the most fan mail ever received for that program. Universities across the country, from **Maine** to Hawaii, extended to him honorary doctoral degrees. President **David O. McKay** said that Secretary Benson's work in Washington, D.C., would "stand for all time—as a credit to the Church and the nation."

In 1973 Elder Benson became the president of the Quorum of the Twelve Apostles. The unity he instilled, along with his administrative skills and his standard of "what's best for the kingdom," moved the work in a monumental way.

In 1975 Brigham Young University established the Ezra Taft Benson Agriculture and Food Institute and later named a science building after him, as did **Ricks College**.

On 10 November 1985 Ezra Taft Benson became the president of the Church, selecting **Gordon B. Hinckley** and **Thomas S. Monson** as his counselors. His first address at the **general conference** in which he was sustained as Church president was entitled "Cleansing the Inner Vessel." This discourse established one of the major themes of his ministry—the moving forward of the Book of Mormon. His talk "The Book of Mormon Is the Word of God" was delivered in more than 20 regional conferences. The Saints responded to his challenge of getting the Church out from under condemnation for having treated the Book of Mormon lightly (D&C 84:54–57) by distributing more copies of the Book of Mormon during the next six years than all the previous years combined of this dispensation. Some of his most powerful Book of Mormon discourses are contained in his book *A Witness and a Warning*.

As president of the Church, he delivered eight major addresses to the Saints at their various ages and stages—to the children, **young men** and **young women**, **single adult** brothers and sisters, the fathers, the mothers, and the elderly. These talks are compiled in the book *Come, Listen to a Prophet's Voice*. His landmark discourse "Beware of Pride" is considered a classic.

During President Benson's ministry the Church published the **pamphlet** *For the Strength of Youth*, and **temples** in North and **South America**, **Europe**, and **Asia** were dedicated, as was the BYU **Jerusalem Center for Near Eastern Studies**. Sheri Dew wrote his official biography, and *The Teachings of Ezra Taft Benson* was published. Earlier compilations of his words are found in *So Shall Ye Reap* and *God, Family, Country*.

His voice of warning over many years in the cause of freedom can be found in hundreds of his speeches and in his books, including *The Red Carpet, The Title of Liberty, This Nation Shall Endure,* and *An Enemy Hath Done This.* On the two-hundredth anniversary of the signing of the **Constitution of the United States,** President Thomas S. Monson reflected: "I think it is no small coincidence—in fact, I think it is the inspiration of the Almighty God—that at this particular time we have serving as president of The Church of Jesus Christ of Latter-day Saints, President Ezra Taft Benson, one of the greatest advocates of freedom, and one of those who loves most the Constitution" (quoted in Baird, 7).

His worldwide contact with government leaders, including heads of state, opened more doors for the gospel, and during his administration missionary work expanded into 50 additional countries whose combined population exceeded 834 million. His final book was entitled *Missionaries to Match Our Message.*

President and Sister Benson had six children—two sons and four daughters. He performed the **marriage** of each of his children in the Salt Lake Temple. He believed that salvation is a family affair and to that end he was an obedient son, exemplary brother, faithful husband, and loving father. A family goal for which he worked hard was to have "no empty chairs in the next life," a theme based on a line of poetry he cherished: "We're all here, father, mother, sister, brother, all who hold each other dear, each chair is filled, we're all back home."

On President Benson's ninetieth birthday, the president of the United States, George Bush, honored him with the Presidential Medal, citing his service to God, family, and country—mankind's three great loyalties. True to remembering and honoring those loyalties to the end, it seemed fitting that President Benson died on Memorial Day, 30 May 1994, in Salt Lake City. He was buried in Whitney, Idaho. He served as a great **prophet** (for God), **patriarch** (for family), and **patriot** (for country).

SOURCES

Baird, Judith L. "LDS Youth Give Musical Tribute in Nation's Capital." *Church News,* 26 September 1987, 7.

Dew, Sheri L. *Ezra Taft Benson: A Biography.* Salt Lake City: Deseret Book, 1987.

REED A. BENSON

BENTLEY, JOSEPH T. Joseph Taylor Bentley, superintendent of the **Young Men's Mutual Improvement Association** from 1958 until 1962, was born 6 March 1906 in **Colonia Juárez, Chihuahua, Mexico,** (where he spent his early years) to Joseph C. Bentley and Maud Mary Taylor. The small settlement was caught up in the Mexican Revolution of 1910.

Joseph was educated at the Juárez Stake **Academy** and **Brigham Young University.** After working briefly in **New York City** (1927), he held positions as a teacher, accountant, and school administrator in both **Mexico** and **Utah.** In 1953 Bentley began teaching in the accounting department at Brigham Young University and soon after became an assistant to university president **Ernest L. Wilkinson** and to Harvey Taylor, Administrator of Church Schools.

Brother Bentley served in numerous callings in the Church, including several stake presidencies, a **temple** presidency, as a **stake president, mission president,** YMMIA superintendent, general manager of the *Improvement Era,* and **mission representative** to **Hungary** (1976–78). He and his wife, Kathleen, were the parents of six children. President Bentley died 15 June 1993 in **Provo, Utah.**

JOSEPH C. BENTLEY

BERMUDA. Bermuda is a dependency of the **United Kingdom,** located in the Atlantic Ocean, 580 miles east of **North Carolina.** Most of the estimated population of 62,000 are Protestant. Latter-day Saints serving in the **United States** Air Force and Navy and their families created the first Latter-day Saint presence in Bermuda. **Sacrament** meetings and **Sunday School** classes were held beginning 8 October 1961 among the military personnel. The Bermuda **Branch** was organized 25 June 1966 by **mission president W. Jay Eldredge.** The first Bermudan **priesthood** holder was Vernon Every. **Seminary** classes began in Bermuda in 1994. At the beginning of the year 2000, there were 101 members living in one branch.

SOURCE

1999–2000 Church Almanac. Salt Lake City: Deseret News, 1998. 403.

TODD KRUEGER

BERNHISEL, JOHN M. John Milton Bernhisel, **Utah** territory's first congressional delegate, was born 23 June 1799 in Tyrone Township, Cumberland County, **Pennsylvania.** A physician by profession, John graduated with a medical degree from the University of Pennsylvania in 1827. He was practicing medicine in **New York City** when he joined the

Church. The exact date of his conversion is not known, but he was ordained a **bishop** in that city on 15 April 1841.

He moved to **Nauvoo** in 1843, where he lived for a time in the **Mansion House** with **Joseph Smith** and his **family**. John was with the **Prophet** in 1844 when Joseph decided to surrender to the authorities in **Carthage**, an event that ultimately led to the **Martyrdom**. On this occasion, it was to Bernhisel that Joseph Smith made the prophetic statement: "I am going as a lamb to the slaughter" (*Utah Historical Quarterly*, 151).

A year after the death of the Prophet, John married Julia Ann Van Orden. In 1847–48 he crossed the plains to **Salt Lake City**. On 6 January 1849 Bernhisel was sent to **Washington, D.C.**, to petition Congress for territorial status. Then on 4 August 1851, the Utah territory elected John as its first congressional delegate, an office he held for ten years (1851–59, 1861–63). After serving in Congress, Bernhisel resumed his medical practice in Salt Lake City, where he died 28 September 1881.

SOURCES

Barrett, Gwynn W. "John M. Bernhisel: Mormon Elder in Congress." *Utah Historical Quarterly* 36 (Spring 1968): 143–67.

———. "John M. Bernhisel: Mormon Elder in Congress." Ph.D. diss., Brigham Young University, 1968.

ARNOLD K. GARR

BERRETT, WILLIAM E. William E. Berrett, Latter-day Saint educator and administrator, served as vice president of **Brigham Young University** (1953–63) and vice administrator of Church schools in charge of religious **education** (**seminaries** and institutes). He served in a dual capacity until 1963 when he was named administrator of seminaries and **institutes of religion**.

Born 2 June 1902 in Union, **Utah**, William attended Union Elementary School, Jordan High School, and the **University of Utah**. He lettered on the University of Utah debate team five years and graduated with high honors in 1924. William married Eleanor Louise Callister (1903–89) in the **Salt Lake Temple**, 2 June 1926. They had four children: Verne, Sharon, Richard, and William Brian (Bill). A member of Phi Kappa Phi, he received his LL.B. degree in 1933 and juris doctorate from the University of Utah in 1966. He was also awarded an honorary doctor of laws degree from Brigham Young University in 1965.

William taught in the Latter-day Saint seminaries at Roosevelt, Utah (1925–27); Rigby, **Idaho** (1927–32); Kanab, Utah (1932–34); Salt Lake

Granite School District (1934–37); and Salt Lake West High School (1937–46). From 1936 to 1943 he served on the administrative staff as editor, and from 1936 to 1946 he and **J. Wylie Sessions** taught all the training classes at the Latter-day Saint mission home. A member of the general board of the **Deseret Sunday School Union** (1937–46 and 1947–54), he was also a professor of religion at Brigham Young University (1949–53). From 1971 until his death, he served as **patriarch** in the Edgemont North **Stake** in **Provo, Utah**. He wrote two books for use in the Church schools: *The Restored Church* and *Doctrines of the Restored Church*. Other books include: *Teachings of the Book of Mormon* (1952), *Teachings of the Doctrine and Covenants* (1954), *Readings in LDS Church History* (3 vols., cowritten with Alma P. Burton, 1952, 1954, 1958). He also wrote many courses of study for various Church auxiliary organizations, including the **Melchizedek Priesthood** course of study for 1962. He retired in 1970 and died 30 November 1993 in Provo, Utah.

Richard Berrett

BERTRAND, LOUIS A. Louis Alphonse Bertrand was a brilliant writer, French revolutionary, and advocate of the gospel in a war-torn, unlistening country. He was born 8 January 1808 near Marseilles, **France**, under the name John Francis Elias Flandin. Originally intended for the ministry, he went into trade at an early age and lived in the **United States**, **South America, China**, and **India**. Upon his return to Paris he became steeped in political affairs and was chosen a member of the Revolutionary Committee of 1848, resulting in three months' prison time. It was likely during this time that he changed his name to protect his wife and two young boys. After the revolution, Bertrand remained in Paris, where he served for a time as the political editor of *Le Populaire*—a prominent and influential communist periodical run by the **Icarians** (a small branch of whom had settled at **Nauvoo, Illinois**, after the **Saints' exodus**). In September 1850 he was contacted by **John Taylor**, then the French Mission president, who baptized him three months later on 1 December.

A skilled writer and editor in both French and English, Bertrand was instrumental in completing the translation of the **Book of Mormon** into French; he also translated the **Doctrine and Covenants** and several other Latter-day Saint works and helped establish the Church **periodical** *L'etoile du Deseret*. In 1853 Bertrand, as a missionary, taught Victor Hugo and other revolutionary refugees on the Island of Jersey; they "listened with attention at the time, but their heads were too full of revolution to think much about the gospel of Jesus Christ" (Manuscript, 1853:133).

After spending four years in the **Salt Lake Valley**, where he received numerous awards for his agricultural produce, Bertrand was called back to France as the **mission president** in 1859. There he worked tirelessly, publishing articles and books on Mormonism, fighting both his own political history and the oppressive political and intellectual currents of the time, and seeking permission to preach in France. He formally petitioned Louis Napoleon III, who read Bertrand's request, laughed, and tore it to pieces. Bertrand returned to Utah in 1864, leaving behind his family, who refused to accept his faith.

A close friend to **Brigham Young** ever since his first stay in **Utah** when he lived in the president's home, Bertrand briefly oversaw the prophet's cocoonery, bringing it to its peak production of 800,000 silkworms. For the remainder of his life, Bertrand acted as a correspondent for the *Deseret News* and was often consulted as an expert in both viniculture and sericulture. He died 21 March 1875.

――――――

SOURCES

Bertrand, Louis A. *Memoires d'un Mormon*. Paris: E. Dentu, Libraire, Palais-Royal, ca. 1862.

Manuscript History of the Church. LDS Church Historical Department, Salt Lake City.

McClellan, Richard D. "Louis A. Bertrand: One of the Most Singular and Romantic Figures of the Age." Honor's thesis, Brigham Young University, 2000.

RICHARD D. MCCLELLAN

BIBLE. As a foundation of the Lord's true Church in these latter days, the Bible was a major factor leading to the restoration of the gospel. As a result of his personal reading of a passage in the epistle of James, **Joseph Smith** was prompted to ask God which of all the Christian denominations he should join (JS–H 1:11–14). In his adult years, as the mature prophet of the **Restoration**, he taught that the Bible was the inspired word of God, that every person of common intelligence could see God's "own handwriting" in the Bible, and that "he who reads it oftenest will like it the best, and he who is acquainted with it, will know the hand wherever he can see it" (Smith, 56). Joseph Smith frequently used the Bible in his sermons and "much of the Prophet's teaching focused on passages from the Bible, which was frequently his tool for explaining doctrine" (Jackson, x).

The version that Joseph Smith used was the King James (Authorized)

Version, which remains the official English language version of the Church. The **First Presidency** statement in 1992 on the Bible declared: "While other Bible versions may be easier to read than the King James Version, in doctrinal matters latter-day **revelation** supports the King James Version in preference to other English translations. All of the presidents of the Church, beginning with the Prophet Joseph Smith, have supported the King James Version by encouraging its continued use in the Church" ("First Presidency," 80).

Notwithstanding the great value Joseph Smith placed on the Bible, he also acknowledged the errors it contained. In February 1832 he stated "that many important points touching the salvation of men, had been taken from the Bible, or lost before it was compiled" (Smith, 10–11). Consequently, when asked in 1842 about the history of the Church and its beliefs by Mr. John **Wentworth**, editor and proprietor of the *Chicago Democrat,* Joseph included in statement number eight on the list now called the **Articles of Faith**: "We believe the Bible to be the word of God as far as it is translated correctly." In October 1843 the Prophet somewhat expanded that statement: "I believe the Bible as it read when it came from the pen of the original writers. Ignorant translators, careless transcribers, or designing and corrupt priests have committed many errors" (Smith, 327). This statement complements ancient prophetic declarations in the Book of Mormon that warned of "many plain and precious things taken away" from the Bible before it went forth "unto all nations of the **Gentiles**" (1 Ne. 13:26–29).

Because the King James Version of the Bible was not free of error, Joseph Smith undertook the study of biblical languages to better understand the text. He observed, for example, that "our latitude and longitude can be determined in the original Hebrew with far greater accuracy than in the English version. There is a grand distinction between the actual meaning of the prophets and the present translation" (Smith, 290–91). The Prophet was also commanded by the Lord to undertake, through inspiration, a new translation of the Bible, now known as the **Joseph Smith Translation**. Of this enterprise the Lord said, "The scriptures shall be given, even as they are in mine own bosom, to the salvation of mine own elect" (D&C 35:20).

Still it is important to remember that the Church honors and reveres the Bible; it is one of the **standard works** of the faith. Members of the Church in this day are commanded to teach the principles of the gospel, "which are in the Bible" (D&C 42:12). President **Heber J. Grant**, seventh president of the Church (1918–45), relates the appropriate attitude of the faithful regarding the Bible: "All my life I have been finding additional evidences that the Bible is the Book of books, and that the Book of Mormon is the greatest witness for the truth of the Bible that has ever been published" (Grant, 660). The **First Presidency** noted in 1992: "The most reliable way to measure the accuracy of any biblical passage is not by comparing different texts, but by comparison with the Book of Mormon and modern-day **revelation**" ("First Presidency," 80).

SOURCES

"First Presidency Statement on the King James Version of the Bible." *Ensign* 22 (August 1992): 80.

Grant, Heber J. "Concerning the Bible." *Improvement Era* 39 (November 1936): 660.

Jackson, Kent P., comp. and ed. *Joseph Smith's Commentary on the Bible.* Salt Lake City: Deseret Book, 1994. ix-xvi.

Smith, Joseph. *Teachings of the Prophet Joseph Smith.* Selected by Joseph Fielding Smith. Salt Lake City: Deseret Book, 1970. 10–11, 56, 290–91, 327.

ANDREW C. SKINNER

BIBLE, REVISION OF. See JOSEPH SMITH TRANSLATION OF THE BIBLE.

BIDAMON, LEWIS C.

BIDAMON, LEWIS C. On 23 December 1847, about three and a half years after the death of Joseph Smith, the Prophet's widow, **Emma Hale Smith**, married Lewis Crum Bidamon. Bidamon was born 16 January 1804 in Smithville, **Virginia**, and when he was 14 his family moved to **Ohio**. Major Bidamon served as commanding officer for **Abraham Lincoln** in the Black Hawk **Indian** War. He became the stepfather of the **Prophet's** five children. Before he married Emma, he had been married twice and was the father of two daughters. Lewis was known for his profanity, drinking, and infidelity, but Emma expressed affection for him and accepted his shortcomings. Bidamon died 11 February 1891 in **Nauvoo, Illinois**.

SOURCES

Avery, Valene Tibbits, and Linda King Newell. "Lewis C. Bidamon, Stepchild of Mormondom." *BYU Studies* 19 (Spring 1979): 375–82.

Jenson, Andrew. *Latter-day Saint Biographical Encyclopedia.* 4 vols. 1901–36. Reprint, Salt Lake City: Western Epics, 1971.

Youngreen, Buddy. *Reflections of Emma, Joseph Smith's Wife.* Orem, Utah: Grandin Book. 39–42.

BRIAN L. SMITH

BIDWELL-BARTLESON PARTY. The first wagons to travel through the area of **Utah** were part of a **California**-bound party led by John Bidwell and John Bartleson in 1841. They traveled with a party guided by Thomas Fitzpatrick as far as Soda Springs, from where the Bidwell-Bartleson group continued toward California. The other group, with Fitzpatrick as guide, followed the **Oregon Trail** to their destination among the Oregon **Indian** tribes. The new party of 32 men, one woman, and one child set out on 11 August with vague directions to find the Humboldt and follow it, then push west. The journey in northern Utah and country north of the Great Salt Lake was arduous, but the desert of western Utah and **Nevada** proved more difficult, as the party lost its way and abandoned its wagons. They arrived in California in November, the first emigrant party to cross the **Great Basin** and the Sierra Nevada.

SOURCES

Durham, Michael S. *Desert between the Mountains: Mormons, Miners, Padres, Mountain Men, and the Opening of the Great Basin, 1772–1869.* New York: Henry Holt and Company, 1997. 73–76.

Goetzmann, William. *Exploration and Empire.* New York: Alfred A. Knopf, 1966. 169–71.

Poll, Richard, ed. *Utah's History.* Provo, Utah: Brigham Young University Press, 1978. 71–72.

FRED R. GOWANS AND LINDA WHITE

BIGLER, HENRY W. Henry William Bigler was a nineteenth-century Latter-day Saint who during January 1848 recorded in his journal the discovery of gold at Sutter's Mill. Noted **California** historian Hubert Howe Bancroft described Bigler as "a cool, clear-headed methodical man" (Bancroft, 32n). Born 28 August 1815 in Shinnston, **West Virginia**, Bigler was present at Sutter's Mill as a result of his service with the **Mormon Battalion** (1846–47). Following his release from the battalion, he was called on a proselyting **mission** to the **Sandwich Islands** from 1850 to 1854. He served a second mission to the islands from 1855 to 1858. During this subsequent assignment, he was the **mission president**.

During the last quarter of the nineteenth century, Bigler labored as an ordinance worker at the **St. George Temple**. He believed that this service in the **temple** far exceeded in significance either his trek west with the Mormon Battalion or his presence at the gold discovery. About 20 years after Bigler's death, assistant Church historian **Andrew Jenson** praised him as "an unassuming, humble, useful man, beloved by everyone who knew him" (quoted in Bishop, 159). Bigler died 24 November 1900 in **St. George, Utah.**

SOURCES

Bancroft, Hubert H. *History of California.* 7 vols. San Francisco: History Book Company, 1884–90. 6:32.

Bishop, M. Guy. *Henry William Bigler: Soldier, Gold Miner, Missionary, Chronicler, 1815–1900.* Logan, Utah: Utah State University Press, 1998.

M. GUY BISHOP

BISHOP, OFFICE OF. The calling of bishop is an office in the **Aaronic Priesthood** that was restored in 1831. A **presiding bishop** serves at the general level, while **ward** bishops serve locally. A bishop and two **counselors** compose a bishopric. Historically, a ward bishop's main duties have included being a judge and disciplinarian; a president of the Aaronic Priesthood and supervisor of ward youth; presiding **high priest**, spiritual leader, counselor, and father of the ward; superintendent of **ordinances** performed at the ward level (i.e. baptisms, **confirmations**, blessings of babies, the **sacrament**, **settings apart** to ward callings, and **priesthood** ordinations); administrator in "all temporal things," including tithes, offerings, ward finances, record keeping, and **meetinghouses**; and ensure that needy members are assisted (D&C 20:67; 41:9; 42:30–39; 58:17; 72:5; 107:15, 68, 119).

During the 1830s **Edward Partridge** and **Newel K. Whitney** served as regional bishops in **Missouri** and **Ohio**, handling finances (including consecration properties) and supervising Aaronic Priesthood **quorums**. After tithing was introduced (1838), bishops received and disbursed **tithing**. In **Nauvoo** high priests ordained as bishops were assigned to each municipal ward. This was the Church's first use of wards as local units. During the trek west, **Winter Quarters** and **Kanesville** had wards and ward bishops. In 1849 **Salt Lake City** was divided into 19 "bishop's wards," and since then wards have been a basic local Church unit. As wards built meetinghouses, bishops began conducting ward sacrament **meetings**. To manage "in kind" tithing (cash was scarce), bishops operated tithing storehouses and corrals. A bishopric and corps of teachers (block or ward teachers) were the main **pioneer**-era ward officers. Research shows that the average length of service for nineteenth-century Utah bishops was 11 years. Bishops were not only Church but also civic leaders in their communities.

During the twentieth century, several developments changed the workload of ward bishops. Chapels became larger, more functional, and more comfortable. In 1908 separate ward priesthood quorums began meeting at the same hour in a ward priesthood meeting conducted by the bishopric, and bishops became directors of ward teaching. Bishops' involvement with Aaronic Priesthood work expanded after 1908 when priesthood holders were organized by distinct age groupings and assignments. Tithing changed from "in kind" to cash by 1910, easing the bishop's workload. Since the 1930s, bishops have fostered ward projects within the **Welfare Program** and have used LDS **Social Services** as a counseling resource for ward members. In the 1960s, **Melchizedek Priesthood** quorums took over responsibility from bishoprics for ward teaching—newly designed as **home teaching**. In the 1970s and 1980s, bishops' terms were reduced to a "norm" of about 5 years and average ward sizes went from 600 or more members to 400 or 500. In the 1980s the combined block meeting plan simplified bishops' schedules, and Church tithes began funding wards, freeing bishops from annually soliciting ward budget donations from members. Computerization of membership and financial records simplified bishops' record-keeping tasks. **Church court** procedures were also modified, giving bishops wider latitude when judging members' misconduct.

SOURCES

Beecher, Dale F. "The Office of Bishop." *Dialogue* 15 (Winter 1982): 103–15.

Pace, Donald G. "Community Leadership on the Mormon Frontier: Mormon Bishops and the Political, Economic, and Social Development before Statehood." Ph.D. diss., Ohio State University, 1983.

Palmer, Lee A. *Aaronic Priesthood through the Centuries.* Salt Lake City: Deseret Book, 1964.

Widtsoe, John A. *Priesthood and Church Government.* Salt Lake City: Deseret Book, 1939.

WILLIAM G. HARTLEY

BISHOP, PRESIDING. See PRESIDING BISHOPRIC.

BISHOPS' STOREHOUSE. See WELFARE PROGRAM.

BLACK HAWK. Originally named Antonga, Black Hawk was already an important **Ute** Indian chief when the Latter-day **Saints** first settled in the **Utah** area. Undoubtedly because of his outspoken resistance to their settlement, the **Latter-day Saints** renamed him Black Hawk after the most famous champion of **Native American** rights in the Saints' former homeland in the Midwest. During the 1850 conflict at Fort Utah, Black Hawk was forced by the residents of **Provo** to assist them in attacks against his own people. After viewing firsthand the resulting carnage, for the next two decades Black Hawk was among the most vigorous and violent challengers to Mormon settlement.

Black Hawk is best known for his leadership in the Mormon-Indian conflict called the **Black Hawk War.** In 1865 Black Hawk put together an imposing Native American war machine that put Mormon Utah virtually in a state of siege for more than half a decade. He enlisted individuals from various bands of Utes, **Shoshones**, Piautes, **Navajos**, Apaches, and Hopis as well as white and Hispanic cattle thieves and directed scores of raids in which thousands of Mormon-owned cattle were stolen and marketed as far away as Santa Fe, **New Mexico**. Killing Latter-day Saints was secondary to the goal of obtaining cattle and driving back the line of Mormon settlement. Black Hawk was seriously wounded in the Battle of Gravelly Ford near Salina, Utah, in 1866 and died in 1870.

SOURCE

Peterson, John A. "Black Hawk War." *Utah History Encyclopedia*. Edited by Allan Kent Powell. Salt Lake City: University of Utah Press, 1994. 43–44.

JOHN A. PETERSON

BLACK HAWK WAR. The Black Hawk War, which took place from 1865 to 1872, was the longest and most serious physical conflict in **Mormon** history. The primary complaint the Ute chief **Black Hawk** had with the Latter-day **Saints** was the hunger, frustration and death produced among his people by the creation of Mormon settlements on sites that for generations had been essential components of **Native American** subsistence systems. In April 1865 Black Hawk and a few dozen other **Utes** commenced the seven-year war by driving off a large herd of Mormon-owned cattle, killing five Latter-day Saints in the process.

Hundreds of hungry Indians turned to Black Hawk for leadership, and he quickly crafted a loose confederacy of various Native American groups bent on feeding themselves on Mormon cattle and driving back the line of Latter-day Saint expansion. Eventually diverse groups from a huge section of the country, now comprising parts of seven large western states, joined Black Hawk in his raids on the Mormons. The Saints responded by building scores of forts and by deploying the **Nauvoo Legion**. In the course of the conflict, about 70 Latter-day Saints were killed and perhaps twice that many Indians. Brigham Young used the scriptures as a handbook on how to direct the war, especially the **Book of Mormon**'s war chapters and Section 98 of the **Doctrine and Covenants**. The Black Hawk War thus provides a unique case study of the application of revealed principles regarding warfare by a modern **prophet**.

SOURCE

Peterson, John A. "Black Hawk War." *Utah History Encyclopedia.* Edited by Allan Kent Powell. Salt Lake City: University of Utah Press, 1994. 43–44.

JOHN A. PETERSON

BLACKS. For reasons we do not know, blacks were denied **priesthood** and **temple** blessings until 1978. **Missionary work** and conversions in places throughout the world, especially in Latin **America** and **Africa**, were thereby somewhat limited. Like other New Englanders, early Latter-day **Saints** generally opposed slavery. Although at least two black men— **Elijah Abel** and Walker Lewis—were ordained during Joseph Smith's lifetime, sometime in the 1840s Church leaders announced that blacks could not hold the priesthood. Nevertheless, black Latter-day Saints were among the first **pioneers** who went to **Utah** in 1847. A few blacks throughout the United States and in such countries as Brazil continued to join the Church and remained faithful.

Church leaders, however, did not issue an official public statement on this priesthood restriction until 1949, when they explained that the restrictions on priesthood were "not a matter of the declaration of a policy but of direct commandment from the Lord" (Bringhurst, 230). In 1963 the Church issued a statement that attempted to separate priesthood exclusion from the **civil rights** movement, but African-Americans still publicly attacked the Church. In 1969 the **First Presidency** issued another statement confirming priesthood restriction.

Nine years later, in June 1978, Church president **Spencer W. Kimball** announced the revelation providing that all worthy men "may be ordained to the priesthood without regard for race or color" (**Official Declaration 2**). Before this revelation, during the nineteenth and early twentieth century, Church leaders had advised missionaries not to teach blacks. For example, the first missionaries to Brazil worked mainly with German immigrants. No missionaries were sent to Africa, and in the United States they generally stayed out of African-American neighborhoods and rarely taught blacks unless approached. But as early as 1946, blacks in **Nigeria** had asked for missionaries, even organizing churches on their own and using the **Book of Mormon** to teach one another. During the 1960s and 1970s the Church had experienced tremendous growth in Brazil, and determining who was black was a sensitive issue in the racially mixed country. Construction of a temple there in the mid 1970s focused attention on this delicate matter.

Following the 1978 revelation, the Church opened missions in Africa. Ten years later leaders organized the first stake in black Africa in Nigeria. Missionaries throughout the world, including the United States, started working in black neighborhoods. Because Church records do not list race or color, it is impossible to determine how many blacks have been baptized except in some parts of Africa. It is clear, however, that blacks have joined the Church in increasing numbers. They have received temple blessings and served as missionaries and ward and stake leaders. Brazilian **Helvecio Martins** served as a member of the Second **Quorum of Seventy** from 1990 to 1995.

SOURCES

Bringhurst, Newell G. *Saints, Slaves, and Blacks: The Changing Place of Black People within Mormonism.* Westport, Conn.: Greenwood Press, 1981. 230.

Embry, Jessie L. *Black Saints in a White Church: Contemporary African-American Mormons.* Salt Lake City: Signature Books, 1994.

JESSIE L. EMBRY

BOGART, SAMUEL. Samuel Bogart, an itinerant Methodist preacher and company captain in the Ray County militia, actively operated against the **Latter-day Saints** during the 1838 **Missouri** conflict. His most famous encounter occurred 25 October when his company attacked a Mormon contingent led by **apostle David W. Patten** at **Crooked River**. Later, following the Saints' surrender at Far West, Bogart was assigned to apprehend members of the Church charged with participating in the battle at Crooked River.

Shortly after the **Saints** were expelled from Missouri, Bogart took up residence in **Caldwell County**. In November 1839 he was elected judge in that county. On the day of his election, however, he became engaged in a bitter argument and shot and killed his opponent's nephew. He escaped without being apprehended and settled in **Texas**, where his **family** later joined him.

SOURCE

Baugh, Alexander L. "Samuel Bogart's 1839 Letter about the Mormons to the Quincy Postmaster." *Nauvoo Journal* 7 (Fall 1995): 52–56.

ALEXANDER L. BAUGH

BOGGS, LILBURN W. Lilburn W. Boggs, governor of **Missouri**, issued the **Extermination Order** demanding that Latter-day Saints be removed from the state. He was born 14 December 1796 in Lexington, **Kentucky**. Boggs eventually settled in **Independence**, **Missouri**, where he operated a mercantile business. An ardent Jacksonian Democrat, he was also active in Missouri politics, being elected three times, as a state senator (1826–32, 1842–46), lieutenant governor (1832–36), and governor (1836–40).

During his four years as the state's chief executive, he spearheaded the chartering of the state bank, established the University of Missouri at Columbia, organized the public school system, and procured funding for the construction of a new state capitol building. In spite of his achievements, however, his administration was not a popular one. He was highly criticized for many of his actions, including the 1838 **Mormon War** and his infamous Extermination Order.

On 6 May 1842, an unknown assailant shot the former governor at his home in Independence. Although his wounds were severe, after a time he fully recovered. Blame for the attack soon focused on **Orrin Porter Rockwell**, with **Joseph Smith** being charged as an accessory to the crime. Eventually the Prophet was tried in an **Illinois** court and acquitted. Rockwell was not as fortunate. On 5 March 1843 he was arrested in connection with the Boggs incident while in **St. Louis**. He was jailed in Independence and Liberty until 11 December, when Fifth Circuit Court judge Austin King finally released him.

In 1846 Boggs left Missouri and journeyed to northern **California**,

eventually settling in Napa, where he died 14 March 1860 at age 63. He
was buried in the Tulocay Cemetery.

SOURCES

Baugh, Alexander L. "Missouri Governor Lilburn W. Boggs and the Mormons." *John Whitmer Historical Association Journal* 18 (1998): 111–32.

Gayler, George R. "The Attempts of the State of Missouri to Extradite Joseph Smith, 1841–1843." *Missouri Historical Review* 58 (October 1963): 21–36.

Gordon, Joseph F. "The Political Career of Lilburn W. Boggs." *Missouri Historical Review* 52 (January 1958): 111–22.

McLaws, Monte B. "The Attempted Assassination of Missouri's Ex-Governor, Lilburn W. Boggs." *Missouri Historical Review* 60 (October 1965): 50–62.

Marriott, L. Dean. "Lilburn W. Boggs: Interaction with Mormons Following Their Expulsion from Missouri." Ed.D. diss., Brigham Young University, 1979.

ALEXANDER L. BAUGH

BOLIVIA. Bolivia is located in the center of **South America**. Its population speaks Spanish, Quechua, and Aymara and is 95% Roman Catholic.

The first missionaries that entered the country came from the Andes
Mission on 24 November 1964, and within two years **branches** were
opened in Oruro and Santa Cruz. In 1968 Carlos Pedraja—the first missionary called from Bolivia—was called to the Andes South Mission. He
later became a **stake** and **mission president**. The Bolivia Santa Cruz
Mission was organized in 1977 and was later renamed the Bolivia
Cochabamba Mission. On 3 March 1977 President **Spencer W. Kimball**
visited an **area conference** in La Paz that was attended by about 4,373
members.

On 14 January 1979 the first stake in Bolivia was organized with
Noriharu Ishigaki Haraguichi as president. The Church began sponsor-
ing humanitarian aid projects to help members and non-Mormons
throughout the country learn to improve health conditions. In 1989, after
the assassination of two **elders** from **Utah**, the **First Presidency** decided
to decrease the number of nonnative missionaries sent to Bolivia. In 1990
membership was 64,000 in the country. Ten years later at the beginning
of the year 2000, there were 112,222 members living in 21 stakes and 232
wards and branches in Bolivia. On 30 April 2000 the Church dedicated
the Cochabamba Bolivia Temple.

SOURCES

Hart, John L. "Prophet Breaks Ground for New Temples." *Church News*, 23 November 1996, 3.

"Helping Villagers Help Themselves." *Church News,* 24 February 1990, 8.
Litster, Allen. "Pioneering in the Andes." *Ensign* 27 (January 1997): 16–22.
1999–2000 Church Almanac. Salt Lake City: Deseret News, 1998. 278.
"200,000 in Six Nations Hear Prophet." *Church News,* 23 November 1996, 8.

Rebecca Jackson

BONAIRE. Like Curacao and Aruba, Bonaire is an autonomous island territory of the Netherlands just off the coast of Venezuela. Its 11,000 inhabitants are largely of African decent. The local creole language of Papiamento reflects Portuguese, Spanish, and Dutch influences; selections from the **Book of Mormon** were translated in Papiamento in 1987. At the beginning of the year 2000, there were 80 Latter-day **Saints** and one **branch** there.

Richard O. Cowan

BONNEVILLE, BENJAMIN L. E. Under the direction of Benjamin Louis Eulalie Bonneville, **Joseph Walker** explored the **Salt Lake Valley** before the coming of the **Mormon pioneers**. Born 14 April 1796 in Paris, **France**, Bonneville entered West Point Military Academy at age 17. His assignment to the Seventh Infantry was the beginning of his association with the trans-**Mississippi** frontier, which would last his entire lifetime. Requesting a leave of absence from the army in 1831, he formulated plans to explore the Rocky Mountains as a private venture. Bonneville was the first to take wagons over **South Pass** in 1832—the route he followed along the **Platte River** would be followed by future westward emigrations. Shrewd competition in the fur trade business led to failure of his endeavor. He established Fort Bonneville (Fort Nonsense) near the confluence of Horse Creek and Green River. Bonneville had two goals in mind for his venture: (1) to build a trading post on the Columbia River, and (2) to explore the Great Salt Lake, whose tributaries would yield many furs. Bonneville was responsible for Joseph Walker blazing a trail across the **Great Basin** through the Sierras and into **California**. Upon reentry in the U.S. Army, Bonneville was assigned command of Fort Kearny on the **Oregon Trail**. He tried to publish his western travel narratives, but failing at this he sold the manuscript to Washington Irving for $1,000. Irving later published *The Adventures of Captain Bonneville.* In the 1870s, geological surveyor G. K. Gilbert named Lake Bonneville—a prehistoric body of water that once extended over most of northwestern

Utah and into Nevada and Idaho (the Great Salt Lake is all that remains)—in honor of Captain Bonneville. Benjamin Bonneville died 12 June 1878 in Fort Smith, **Arkansas**.

SOURCES

Hafen, LeRoy R., ed. *The Mountain Men and the Fur Trade of the Far West.* Edited by LeRoy Hafen. 10 vols. Glendale, Calif.: Arthur H. Clark, 1966–72. Vol. 5.
Irving, Washington. *The Adventures of Captain Bonneville.* Norman, Okla.: University of Oklahoma Press, 1986.
———. *A Tour on the Prairies.* Alexandria, Va.: Time-Life Books, 1983.

FRED R. GOWANS AND VERN GORZITZE

BONNEVILLE INTERNATIONAL CORPORATION. Bonneville International Corporation (BIC), organized in 1964, is the parent company of Church-owned commercial **broadcasting** operations. BIC is under the umbrella of Deseret Management Corporation. The broadcast group grew out of the **KSL** operation in **Salt Lake City**, which first began radio broadcasting in 1922.

The founding president of BIC was Arch L. Madsen. Dr. Rodney H. Brady was president and CEO from 1985 to 1996. On 7 June 1996, Bruce T. Reese was named president and CEO. President **Gordon B. Hinckley** was one of Bonneville's founding directors. He served as chairman of the BIC board of directors until 1996, when he was succeeded by James B. Jacobson.

Bonneville owned or acquired stations in Salt Lake City (1964), Seattle (1964, 1995), **New York City** (1966), Kansas City (1967, 1991, 1993), **Los Angeles** (1969, 1998), Chicago (1969, 1997), **San Francisco** (1976, 1983, 1997), Dallas (1978, 1995), Phoenix (1991), **Washington, D.C.** (1996), Houston (1997), and Cedar City, **Utah** (1997). In addition, BIC owns and operates a number of nonbroadcast support companies. During the 1990s Bonneville responded to a changing broadcast industry environment by concentrating activities in five major cities, with primary emphasis on radio broadcasting.

In 1999 Bonneville's holdings included 17 radio and television stations and 6 communication support companies: KZLA-FM, Los Angeles; WLUP-FM, WNND-FM, WTMX-FM, Chicago; KOIT-AM, KDFC-FM, KOIT-FM, KZQZ-FM, San Francisco; WTOP-AM, WXTR-AM, WGMS-FM, WTOP-FM, WWVZ-FM, WWZZ-FM, Washington, D.C.; KSL-AM, KSL-TV, Salt Lake City; KCSG-TV, Cedar City, Utah;

Bonneville Communications, Salt Lake City; Bonneville LDS Radio Network, Salt Lake City; Bonneville Satellite Company, Salt Lake City; Bonneville Washington News Bureau, Washington, D.C.; Bonneville Worldwide Entertainment, Salt Lake City; Video West Productions, Salt Lake City.

Positive messages produced by Bonneville companies are heard in virtually every city in **America** and hundreds of locations throughout the world.

Ownership of broadcast capabilities came about in recognition of the tremendous power of the broadcast media to reach wide audiences and to have a positive influence. The company's goal is to make certain every community in which Bonneville operates is a better community because Bonneville is there. BIC's slogan is: "A Values-driven Company Composed of Values-Driven People."

SOURCES

"Bonneville International Corporation." Brochure. Salt Lake City, 1989.

Wolsey, Heber G. "The History of Radio Station KSL from 1922 to Television." Ph.D. diss., Michigan State University, 1967.

RODNEY H. BRADY

BOOK OF ABRAHAM. The book of Abraham in the **Pearl of Great Price** records some of the events in Abraham's life and several revelations of God to Abraham, including an account of the creation. **Joseph Smith** translated the book from an ancient **Egyptian** papyrus that belonged to a collection of at least three other papyri and four mummies that the Church purchased from **Michael Chandler** in **Kirtland, Ohio**, in July 1835 (Peterson, 42). These Egyptian antiquities were part of a larger collection that had been discovered in **Egypt** by **Antonio Lebolo** sometime between 1817 and 1821. After Lebolo's death, the mummies were sent to **New York** for sale, where Chandler acquired them in late 1832 or early 1833 (Peterson, 38–41).

Soon after the purchase of the papyri, Joseph Smith began translating the book of Abraham. On 5 July 1835 he stated that he had "commenced the translation of the characters or hieroglyphics, and much to our joy found that one of the rolls contained the writings of Abraham" (Smith, 236). The book of Abraham was first published in three issues of the *Times and Seasons* on 1 March, 15 March, and 16 May 1842. These installments contained all of the book of Abraham as we now have it, including the three facsimiles. In February 1843 an editorial in the *Times and Seasons* stated that Joseph Smith had promised more installments of the book of Abraham (95), but because of continued persecution and the press of other duties, these were never published.

In 1851 **Elder Franklin D. Richards**, then serving as president of the **British Mission**, gathered together several of the revelations of Joseph Smith, including the book of Abraham, for the use of the British **Saints**, and published them as the Pearl of Great Price. This volume was accepted as **scripture** in October conference 1880 and became part of the standard works of the Church.

In the first two chapters of the book of Abraham, there are many important details of Abraham's early life not found in the **Bible**. Among these is an account of Abraham's near-death at the hand of Pharaoh's idolatrous priest, along with the method of his escape (Abr. 1:7–20). This book also clarifies several important doctrines of the Church. These include a concise explanation of the Abrahamic Covenant (Abr. 2:6–11); an account of the vastness of God's creations, including the order by which the various planets and stars of his kingdom are governed (Abr. 3:1–13); the doctrine of the premortal existence of man and his eternal nature (Abr. 3:18–22); the doctrine of foreordination (Abr. 3:23); and the concept of the earth as a testing ground for God's children (Abr. 3:24–26). The last two chapters of the book of Abraham add much to our knowledge of the earth's creation. This account tells us that the earth was organized out of already existing materials rather than created out of nothing (Abr. 3:24), that a plurality of gods participated in the creation (Abr. 4), and that the creation itself was carefully planned in a heavenly council before it was carried out (Abr. 5:1–3).

SOURCES

Smith, Joseph. *History of The Church of Jesus Christ of Latter-day Saints.* Edited by B. H. Roberts. 2d ed. rev. 7 vols. Salt Lake City: The Church of Jesus Christ of Latter-day Saints, 1932–51. 2:236.

Times and Seasons, 1 February 1843, 95.

Peterson, H. Donl. *The Pearl of Great Price: A History and Commentary.* Salt Lake City: Deseret Book, 1987. 38–41.

MICHAEL D. RHODES

BOOK OF COMMANDMENTS. In 1830 the **Prophet Joseph Smith** began assembling a collection of early **revelations** which he had received. This collection was to be assembled in a book known as the Book of

Commandments, for the Government of the Church of Christ. At a special **conference** on 1–2 November 1831, it was decided that 10,000 copies would be printed. Eventually the number of copies was reduced to 3,000, and the printing was assigned to **W. W. Phelps**, a publisher who had joined the Church in June 1831. The revelations were separated into chapters and verses, and by 1833 Phelps had completed five 32-page signatures containing 65 revelations. On 20 July 1833 the printing facility in **Independence, Missouri**, was destroyed by a mob of some 300 to 500 people. Most of the uncut printed pages were thrown into the street, but before they could be burned, two young members, **Mary Elizabeth Rollins** and her sister Caroline, risked their lives and salvaged some of the printed pages. These pages were eventually bound into about a hundred copies bearing the title the Book of Commandments. Very few original copies are known to exist at present date. In 1835 the contents of the Book of Commandments were included in the **Doctrine and Covenants**.

SOURCES

Smith, Joseph. *History of The Church of Jesus Christ of Latter-day Saints.* Edited by B. H. Roberts. 2d ed. rev. 7 vols. Salt Lake City: The Church of Jesus Christ of Latter-day Saints, 1932–51. 1:222–37, 390–93.

Woodford, Robert J. "The Historical Development of the Doctrine and Covenants." Vol. 1. Ph.D. diss., Brigham Young University, 1974.

MATTHEW O. RICHARDSON

BOOK OF JOSEPH. Writings found on one of at least two papyrus rolls purchased by the **Saints** in **Kirtland, Ohio**, in 1835 are known as the book or record of Joseph—the great-grandson of Abraham—who was taken to **Egypt** and later revered as a great patriarch in the **family** of Israel. **Joseph Smith's** history indicates that **Michael H. Chandler** came to Kirtland on 3 July 1835 to exhibit four Egyptian mummies with some papyrus rolls containing hieroglyphic figures. Soon afterward the mummies and papyrus were purchased by the Saints for $2,400, a significant sum in those days. With **W. W. Phelps** and **Oliver Cowdery** acting as scribes, Joseph began translating some of the hieroglyphic characters. The **Prophet** recorded that "much to our joy [we] found that one of the rolls contained the writings of Abraham, another the writings of Joseph of Egypt, etc.,—a more full account of which will appear in its place" (Smith, 2:236).

Because Joseph Smith did not completely translate or publish the contents of Joseph's record, perhaps the best source of information about them is found in a letter Oliver Cowdery wrote to William Frye in 1835. Among the ideas that he said it contained were matters relating to the Fall, including a representation of a walking serpent standing near a female figure, the writings of Enoch, and a portrayal of the Judgment. He described the latter as a scene depicting the Savior seated upon his throne, crowned, with the twelve tribes of Israel assembled before him, as well as the nations and kingdoms of the earth over which **Satan** reigns, with Michael the archangel holding the keys to the bottomless pit, and the devil being chained. He concluded, "I am certain that it cannot be viewed without filling the mind with awe" (Hunter, 37).

Why the Prophet Joseph Smith did not translate and publish the Book of Joseph as he did the **book of Abraham** is unknown. The **Book of Mormon** states that Joseph of old left records which were preserved on the Brass Plates. Lehi quoted from those records when bestowing a blessing on his own son, also named Joseph (2 Ne. 3:3–10).

SOURCES

Hunter, Milton R. *Pearl of Great Price Commentary.* Salt Lake City: Bookcraft, 1963.

Smith, Joseph. *History of the Church of Jesus Christ of Latter-day Saints.* Edited by B. H. Roberts. 2d ed. rev. 7 vols. Salt Lake City: The Church of Jesus Christ of Latter-day Saints, 1932–51. 2:235–36.

ANDREW C. SKINNER

BOOK OF MORMON. Published in 1830 in western **New York**, the Book of Mormon came forth as a translation of religious records written mainly by two groups of people (the Nephites and the Jaredites) who came from the ancient Near East and inhabited the Americas centuries ago. Accepted as Christian revelation by The Church of Jesus Christ of Latter-day **Saints**, this **scripture** contains significant historical accounts from antiquity and, at the same time, has filled important roles in modern Latter-day Saint history.

COMING FORTH OF THE BOOK OF MORMON

God ministered to **Joseph Smith** "by an holy **angel**" and gave him "power from on high, by the means which were before prepared, to translate the Book of Mormon" (D&C 20:6, 8). Beginning in September 1823, the angel **Moroni** often visited and instructed the young **Prophet**, who received the plates of Mormon and the Nephite interpreters in 1827 from

Moroni at the **Hill Cumorah**, near **Palmyra, New York**. Joseph was strictly charged to protect the plates, for "strenuous exertions" would soon be made to get them from him (JS–H 1:60). In December 1827, Joseph moved from his parents' home in **Manchester** township, New York, to the home of the parents of his wife, **Emma Hale**. Soon the young couple bought their own home nearby. There, in **Harmony, Pennsylvania**, he began translating the book of Lehi into English, with Emma and Reuben Hale acting as scribes.

It was important to early Saints that the coming forth of the Book of Mormon fulfilled several biblical prophecies (Ezekiel 37:16; John 10:16), especially Isaiah 29:11–12 when **Martin Harris** presented some characters from the plates to the learned **Charles Anthon** and other scholars in **New York City**. Harris reported that Anthon withdrew his initial endorsement after Harris told him that the record was "a sealed book" (JS–H 1:65), although Anthon later tried to disassociate himself from Harris's account of their encounter.

After the translated pages became lost, the translation process recommenced in earnest on 7 April 1829, with **Oliver Cowdery** serving as scribe. In 1832 Joseph Smith wrote that Cowdery, a young school teacher, had been directed by God in a **vision** to serve in this calling. The two men met for the first time on Sunday evening, 5 April.

Virtually the entire Book of Mormon as it is known today was dictated, line upon line, by Joseph Smith and transcribed by Oliver Cowdery at an amazing pace. The work pressed forward hour after hour, producing a finished copy of the first draft, without the benefit of any research books, notes, or editorial revisions. In spite of several interruptions (including such things as a trip to **Colesville** on or about 10 May, the restoration of the **Aaronic Priesthood** by **John the Baptist** on 15 May, the receipt of several **revelations** now contained in the **Doctrine and Covenants**, and a move in early June by buckboard one hundred miles north to **Fayette, New York**), the original manuscript was completed by the end of June, within about ten weeks. At that time, near the **Peter Whitmer** home in Fayette, New York, the angel Moroni appeared to the **Three Witnesses** and showed them the plates. Soon thereafter in **Manchester, New York**, the **Eight Witnesses** also saw the plates and left their testimony of the divinity of the work.

On 11 June 1829, the copyright for the Book of Mormon was secured. The application, filed in the federal Northern District of New York, used the Title Page of the Book of Mormon as the book's description. On 25 August 1829, Martin Harris mortgaged his farm to provide financing for the publication. Oliver Cowdery labored for eight months to supply the printer, E. B. Grandin, with a printer's manuscript. Printing and binding were finished, and the book was offered for sale on 26 March 1830.

In the first edition, 5,000 copies were printed in Palmyra, New York. Between 3,000 and 5,000 copies were published in **Kirtland, Ohio** (1837), with very minor changes. For example, in the 1830 edition, Joseph Smith had identified himself as "author and proprietor," consistent with the language of the 1790 federal copyright law pertaining to any person claiming to be an "author or proprietor." Translators of the Bible in that era sometimes listed themselves as "authors." Averting this confusion, Joseph changed the word "author" to "translator" in the 1837 edition. In 1840, 2,000 more copies were printed in Cincinnati (generally called the **Nauvoo Illinois** edition). Most of the books in these editions were sold or given away by Mormon missionaries traveling through those regions and abroad.

THE BOOK OF MORMON AS HISTORY

The volume contains 15 books. Covered in most detail are three historical periods: (1) the period of migration of an Israelite prophet named Lehi and his family from Jerusalem to the New World around 590 B.C.; (2) the 158 years from the time of King Benjamin's farewell address down to the appearances of the resurrected Christ among the Nephites at the **temple** of Bountiful in A.D. 34; and (3) the time of the Nephite demise in the late fourth century after Christ, reported by **Mormon** and his son Moroni. One of the final books, the book of Ether, gives a largely retrospective account of the history of the Jaredites, who had arrived in the Western Hemisphere much earlier and eventually had perished in battle around 200 B.C. Several other groups, notably the **Lamanites**, figure in the main account; their descendants are believed by Latter-day Saints to be scattered among the **Native Americans** of North and **South America**.

The volume was organized by the prophet and military commander Mormon, who compiled and abridged numerous records written by many authors spanning the one thousand-year history of the Nephite people. Historiographically, the Book of Mormon is complex. In addition to reporting various political, military, legal, economic, personal, literary, and social developments, the record contains many prophetic and sacred teachings about **Jesus Christ**, accounts of visions and spiritual experiences, and admonitions regarding religious practices and moral behavior.

THE BOOK OF MORMON AS TESTIMONY

The book quickly became a touchstone for conversion and belief among early Latter-day Saints. For these adherents, the book dramatically demonstrated that **God** speaks to all people, remembers and delights in his covenant peoples, and holds **America** as a promised land. The book thus stood from the time of its first appearance as a second witness of the word of God contained in the **Bible** and of the realization that God was still a God of miracles.

In the first fifty years of Church history, copies of the Book of Mormon were relatively scarce, making it difficult for many members to use it regularly in daily religious life or to know its text in depth. Elders **Parley P. Pratt** and **William E. McLellin** used the book often in their missionary work, but in this regard they appear to have been exceptional.

In the **pioneer** era, the Book of Mormon stood, especially, as an important evidence of the prophetic calling of Joseph Smith. **Brigham Young**, for example, rarely discoursed on the contents of the book; more often he commented on such things as how the forces of evil opposed it, or how scientific evidence and witnesses demonstrate its truthfulness.

At the opening of the twentieth century, Church members characteristically drew from the Book of Mormon as a source of stories or teachings peculiar to the **Restoration**. **Elder B. H. Roberts**, for example, saw the book as a philosophical masterstroke of pure thought on such doctrines as opposition in all things, agency, the plan of salvation, and the atonement of Jesus Christ and declared the "prayers perfect" for administering the **sacrament** (Moro. 4–5).

Turning away from a rising tide of secularism, the educational programs of the Church began teaching distinct classes on the Book of Mormon in the late 1930s and 1940s. In the mid-twentieth century, scholars, especially at Brigham Young University, began to examine the book carefully as history for its own sake. **Sidney Sperry** and others emphasized form and textual criticism and biblical backgrounds of the Nephite scriptures. **Hugh Nibley** and others saw relevance for the Book of Mormon in Arabic, Egyptian, and broad historical typologies. Archaeologists, including John L. Sorenson, focused on Mesoamerican studies and anthropology.

In the closing decades of the twentieth century, printings of the book began to carry the subtitle, "Another Testament of Jesus Christ." Motivated by strong counsel from **President Ezra Taft Benson**, the Church placed extensive emphasis on the Book of Mormon, as has been documented through the dramatic increase in the number of references to the book that began at that time in conference talks, teaching curricula, scholarly publications, and personal study programs. In this era, the Book of Mormon has been mainly seen as a tool for inviting all to come unto Christ and "partake of his goodness" (2 Ne. 26:33), for "the convincing of the **Jew** and **Gentile** that Jesus is the Christ" (Book of Mormon, Title Page).

SOURCES

Benson, Ezra Taft. *A Witness and a Warning.* Salt Lake City: Deseret Book, 1988.

"Book of Mormon." *Encyclopedia of Mormonism.* Edited by Daniel H. Ludlow. 4 vols. New York: Macmillan, 1992. 1:139–216.

Nibley, Hugh W. *The Collected Works of Hugh Nibley.* Salt Lake City: Deseret Book and FARMS, 1987–89. Vols. 5–9.

Reynolds, Noel B. "The Coming Forth of the Book of Mormon in the Twentieth Century." *BYU Studies* 38 (Spring 1999): 7–47.

Sorenson, John L. *An Ancient American Setting for the Book of Mormon.* Salt Lake City: Deseret Book and FARMS, 1985.

Welch, John W. *Illuminating the Sermon at the Temple and the Sermon on the Mount.* Provo, Utah: FARMS, 1999. 179–98.

JOHN W. WELCH

BOOK OF MORMON, MANUSCRIPTS AND EDITIONS. The earliest text of the **Book of Mormon** is preserved in two manuscripts— the original and the printer's—as well as in the first published edition, 1830, **Palmyra, New York**. The scribes wrote down the text of the original manuscript as **Joseph Smith** dictated. The first 116 pages (called the book of Lehi) were lost in 1828 by **Martin Harris**, Joseph's first scribe. Thereafter, **Oliver Cowdery** was the major scribe for the portion of the text dictated in the spring and early summer of 1829.

In preparing the manuscript for publication, Joseph Smith had Oliver Cowdery and other scribes make a copy of the original—the printer's manuscript—to take to the **Grandin printing shop**. This second manuscript was not produced all at once but as the printer needed copy. About three-fourths of the way through, the scribes apparently fell behind in their copy work, so for about 15% of the text (Hel. 13–Morm. 9) they let the printer use the original manuscript to set the type for the 1830 edition. Nonetheless, the printer's manuscript was completed.

In 1841 Joseph Smith placed the original manuscript in the cornerstone of the **Nauvoo House**. In 1882, **Lewis Bidamon** (**Emma Smith's** second husband) removed it from the cornerstone. Unfortunately, water seepage and mold had destroyed most of the manuscript but about 28% is still extant. The LDS Church owns most of the remaining leaves. The printer's manuscript, owned by the **RLDS Church**, is in good condition and is missing only about three lines of text.

The original manuscript does have a few errors (mostly due to mishearing by the scribe). Its accuracy depended on Joseph Smith and his scribes carefully checking their work. There is evidence that Joseph spelled out difficult words (such as the unfamiliar Book of Mormon names) to his scribe.

Copying the text from the original manuscript into the printer's manuscript introduced some minor errors, but overall the copy work was accurate. Similarly, the 1830 edition also introduced some minor errors, but only a small proportion of these changes make any difference in meaning. The original text is very consistent in usage. The language appears to be a mixture of early modern English (the biblical style), upstate **New York** dialect, and occasional Hebrew-like phraseology.

The 1830 typesetter (**John H. Gilbert**) frequently marked up his copy text with punctuation and paragraph marks but made very few editing changes as he set the text. For the second edition (1837, **Kirtland, Ohio**), Joseph Smith made many grammatical changes (in dark heavy ink) in the printer's manuscript, basically converting his original upstate New York dialect to more standard English. Joseph also made a few more changes for the third edition (1840, Cincinnati, Ohio). Other significant Latter-day Saint editions (notably 1879, 1920, and 1981) have involved grammatical editing, restoring of earlier readings, and changes in format.

ROYAL SKOUSEN

BOOK OF MOSES. The Book of Moses is the first part of the **Pearl of Great Price**. It begins with an account of several **visions** given to **Moses**, then extends through the early chapters of Genesis to Noah. It is an extract from the **Prophet Joseph Smith**'s revelatory translation of the Bible and differs from all other versions of Genesis in that it restores many unique doctrinal and historical concepts.

Notable among the contributions are extensive clarifications about God's eternal purposes in the creation of man and the earth (1:27–40); the spirit creation of all things (3:4–7); a premortal council in which the Redeemer was appointed and **Satan** rebelled (4:1–6); the effects of the fall (5:9–12; 6:47–56); the introduction of the gospel among fallen man (5:4–15, 58–59); the baptism of **Adam** (6:53–68); the wickedness of Cain (5:16–41); the intelligence of Adam and his righteous posterity, having a pure language, both spoken and written (6:5–6); the seeric ministry of Enoch (6:24–8:1); and the ministry of Noah (8:8–32).

The Book of Moses is theologically rich. Perhaps best known is 1:39, wherein the Lord declares: "This is my work and my glory—to bring to pass the immortality and eternal life of man." Another informative passage is 5:7, in which an angel explains to Adam that animal sacrifice "is a similitude of the sacrifice of the Only Begotten of the Father." Yet another, 6:54, "the Son of God hath atoned for original guilt, wherein . . . children . . . are whole from the foundation of the world." Cain's secret league with Satan is described in 5:31, with Cain's boast: "I am Mahan, the master of this great secret, that I may murder and get gain." And Enoch's people are characterized in 7:18 as Zion, "because they were of one heart and one mind, and dwelt in righteousness; and there was no poor among them."

The Moses material was revealed to Joseph Smith in 1830–31. Portions were published in early Church magazines, *The Evening and the Morning Star* and *Times and Seasons*, as well as in the "Lectures on Faith." Extracts in unconnected form were included in the 1851 Pearl of Great Price, without a unifying title. In the 1878 edition, the first chapter was labeled "Visions of Moses," and the remainder (placed in chronological order) was labeled "The Writings of Moses." In 1902 the title "Book of Moses" was applied by Elder James Talmage and remained so until 1981, when it was changed to "Selections from the Book of Moses."

The Moses material was canonized in 1880 as part of the Pearl of Great Price. It was true revelation from the day it was revealed 50 years earlier. Canonizing did not increase its truth or worth but did make it official Church literature.

SOURCES

Matthews, Robert J. "How We Got the Book of Moses." *Ensign* 16 (1986): 43–49.

———. "A Plainer Translation." *Joseph Smith's Translation of the Bible.* Provo, Utah: Brigham Young University Press, 1975. 68–72, 219–29.

ROBERT J. MATTHEWS

BOOK OF REMEMBRANCE. Chapter 6 of Moses records that a book of remembrance was kept in the days of Adam: "And a book of remembrance was kept, in the which was recorded, in the language of Adam, for it was given unto as many as called upon God to write by the spirit of inspiration . . . and a genealogy was kept of the children of God. And this was the book of the generations of Adam" (vv. 5, 8).

Since the early days of the LDS Church, members have kept **family** records, **journals** and diaries, family **Bibles**, photograph albums, and other records. During the twentieth century, many Church members have combined pedigree charts, family group records, photographs, personal histories, and other memorabilia into a book of remembrance, sometimes kept in a legal-size binder. By the end of the twentieth century, many individuals were using computer genealogy programs, such as **Personal Ancestral File**, to record their genealogies in a letter-sized binder.

Kip Sperry

BOOTH, EZRA. Ezra Booth was a gifted Methodist preacher from Mantua, **Ohio**, who joined the Church in the **Hiram, Ohio,** vicinity around May 1831. He witnessed **Joseph Smith**'s miraculous healing of Elsa Johnson's rheumatic arm, which influenced him to join the Church. **Lyman Wight** ordained Ezra Booth a **high priest** 3 June 1831.

Booth accompanied **Isaac Morley** on a trip from Ohio to **Jackson County, Missouri,** in the summer of 1831. While there he witnessed a disagreement between Joseph Smith and **Edward Partridge** over Church matters in Missouri. Booth later reported this incident in his **anti-Mormon** literature. He soon apostatized after this incident, and fellowship was withdrawn from him 6 September 1831. He formally denounced Mormonism on 12 September 1831. Ezra Booth was one of the first apostates from the Church to publish anti-Mormon literature.

Sources

Cook, Lyndon W. *The Revelations of the Prophet Joseph Smith.* Salt Lake City: Deseret Book, 1985. 72

Roberts, B. H. *A Comprehensive History of The Church of Jesus Christ of Latter-day Saints, Century One.* 6 vols. Salt Lake City: The Church of Jesus Christ of Latter-day Saints, 1930. 1:265–67.

Smith, Joseph. *History of The Church of Jesus Christ of Latter-day Saints.* Edited by B. H. Roberts. 2d ed. rev. 7 vols. Salt Lake City: The Church of Jesus Christ of Latter-day Saints, 1932–51. 1:215–17, 260nn.

Robert L. Marrott

BOOTH, J. WILFORD. Joseph Wilford Booth was an educator and longtime **mission president** in the Near East. Born 14 August 1866 in Alpine, **Utah,** He married Mary R. Moyle in 1890 and completed his education at **Brigham Young Academy** in 1896. After teaching school for a few years, he was called on a **mission** to **Turkey** from 1898 to 1902. He subsequently served as mission president in the **Middle East** from 1904 to 1909 and then from 1921 to 1928. His greatest efforts concentrated among the Armenian population in what are today Turkey and **Syria**, although some success was also realized among Greeks and Arabs.

While presiding in the Middle East, Booth established a place of settlement for Latter-day **Saints** in that region. He was also able to assist converts to emigrate from the Middle East and aid others in obtaining jobs, homes, skills, and a measure of protection during an era of international conflict that culminated in widespread Armenian genocide.

On 5 December 1928, President Booth died in Aleppo, Syria, from a heart attack at the age of 62 while still presiding over the mission. Because of quarantines and exorbitant shipping costs, Church leaders in consultation with Sister Booth determined to bury him in Syria near the people he loved and served, as a tribute to his untiring efforts in that region. In 1933 President **John A. Widtsoe** dedicated a monument to Booth for his service. The monument became his tombstone.

SOURCES

Lindsay, Rao H. "A History of the Missionary Activities of the Church of Jesus Christ of Latter Day Saints in the Near East, 1884–1929." Master's thesis, Brigham Young University, 1958.

Jenson, Andrew. *Encyclopedic History of The Church of Jesus Christ of Latter-day Saints.* Salt Lake City: Deseret News, 1941. 888–90.

DAVID F. BOONE

BORGLUM, GUTZOM. See SCULPTORS.

BOTSWANA. Botswana is a parliamentary democracy located northwest of **South Africa**. Its population is only 15% Christian, the majority following indigenous religions. English and Setswana, an African dialect, are the main languages of the people.

The Church in Botswana had its beginnings through two returned missionary Peace Corps workers: Patricia Lutz of Levittown, Pennsylvania, who was assigned to Molepolole, and Javotte Pickering of Enterprise, **Utah**, working in Kang. They were later joined by the Maurice Mzwinila and Anthony Mogare families from Botswana, who joined the Church while studying in the **United States**.

Formal **missionary work** commenced in Botswana in 1990 under the direction of President R. J. Snow of the South Africa Johannesburg Mission. **Elder** Bruce Midgley and his wife, Patricia, were the first missionaries assigned to Botswana, and a group was organized in Gabarone on 24 June 1990 with Midgley as the presiding elder.

In September 1990 Kwasi Agyare Dwomoh, an architect from Ghana working for the Botswana government, along with his wife and **family**, joined the Church. Brother Dwomoh became Botswana's first **branch** president in August 1991 when the Church was officially registered. By March 1992 the branch was divided, and Brother Dwomoh was called as the first **district** president. He and his wife were the first members from Botswana to be sealed in the Johannesburg South Africa **Temple**. By the beginning of the year 2000, membership had grown to approximately 700 **Saints** living in 2 wards and a branch that are part of the Roodeport South Africa **Stake**.

SOURCES

1999–2000 Church Almanac. Salt Lake City: Deseret News, 1998. 279.

Oral histories of early Church converts collected by E. Dale LeBaron. Copies at BYU Library, Provo, Utah; LDS Church Historical Library, Salt Lake City, Utah.

E. DALE LEBARON

BOWEN, ALBERT E. Albert Ernest Bowen, twentieth-century **apostle** and attorney, was born 31 October 1875 in Henderson Creek, **Idaho**. He married Aletha Reeder in 1902 and soon thereafter was called to leave his wife behind and accept a two-year **mission** call to **Switzerland** and **Germany**. Later, while employed as a faculty member at **Brigham Young University**, he met with a tragic loss. His lovely young wife died in childbirth, leaving in his care two newborn infants. These twin boys were the only children ever born to him.

Brother Bowen received a law degree from the University of Chicago and married Emma Lucy Gates. He practiced law successfully in **Logan** and **Salt Lake City**. He served for 12 years on the general board of the **Deseret Sunday School Union**, became the general superintendent of the **YMMIA**, and on 8 April 1937 was chosen to be a member of the Quorum of the Twelve. In this capacity he served the Church valiantly, making particular contributions to the **welfare program** and the **Church**

Educational System, as well as in business and legal matters of the Church. **Elder** Bowen died 15 July 1953 at age 77 in Salt Lake City.

SOURCES

Evans, Richards L. "Albert E. Bowen: A Lesson from One Man's Life." *Improvement Era* 55 (November 1952): 792–95, 845–46.

Flake, Lawrence R. *Prophets and Apostles of the Last Dispensation*. Provo, Utah: Religious Studies Center, Brigham Young University, 2001. 469.

Quinney, Joseph. "Albert E. Bowen of the Council of the Twelve." *Improvement Era* 40 (May 1937): 278–81, 311.

LAWRENCE R. FLAKE

BOY SCOUTS. The Church's long association with the scouting movement as an activity program for young men is based on shared values of duty to God, service to others and personal achievement. In 1911 **Elder Anthony W. Ivins** initiated the Church's first scouting program. At a meeting of the general board of the **Young Men's** Mutual Improvement Association (YMMIA), he proposed a program called **MIA** Scouts for all young men between ages 12 and 18. Soon scouting activities were part of the regular MIA youth meetings throughout the Church.

In 1913 the national organization of the Boy Scouts of America chartered the Church's MIA Scouts as members. The success of the program prompted Church leaders to name scouting as the official activity program of the **Aaronic Priesthood** in 1928. In 1952 the Church officially adopted **cub** scouting as part of its **Primary** program for boys ages 8 through 10 and later the Blazer patrol for 11-year-old scouts. In the years that followed, the Exploring program was added as an Aaronic Priesthood activity for young men ages 16 to 18 (1959) and the Varsity program for boys ages 14 and 15 (1972).

Scouting remains important as the Church fulfills its international mission. In areas outside North America, the Church provides an Aaronic Priesthood scouting program that is usually not affiliated with local community Boy Scout organizations.

SOURCES

Benson, Ezra Taft. *Teachings of Ezra Taft Benson*. Salt Lake City: Bookcraft, 1988.

"M.I.A. Scouts." *Improvement Era* 15 (March 1912): 287–88.

The Story of Scouting in The Church of Jesus Christ of Latter-day Saints. Salt Lake City. n.d.

Strong, Leon M. "A History of the Young Men's Mutual Improvement Association 1875–1938." Master's thesis, Brigham Young University, 1939.

Williams, John Kent. "A History of the Young Men's Mutual Improvement Association 1939–1974." Master's thesis, Brigham University, 1976.

DENNIS A. WRIGHT

BOYNTON, JOHN F. John Farnham Boynton, **ordained an apostle** 15 February 1835, became a noted scientist and inventor after being excommunicated from the Church 12 April 1838. Born 20 September 1811 in Bradford, **Massachusetts**, Boynton served **missions** to **Pennsylvania** and **Maine** following his baptism in 1832. Financial reverses after his mission with the Twelve to the eastern states turned Boynton against the **Prophet Joseph Smith** in 1837, when he and others attempted to seize control of the **Kirtland Temple**. Following his excommunication and two years in **California**, Boynton moved to Syracuse, **New York**. Married twice and the father of five children, Boynton died at Syracuse 20 October 1890.

SOURCES

Black, Susan Easton, comp. *Membership of The Church of Jesus Christ of Latter-day Saints, 1830–1848.* 50 vols. Provo, Utah: Religious Studies Center, Brigham Young University, 1984–88. 6:425–27.

———. *Who's Who in the Doctrine and Covenants.* Salt Lake City: Bookcraft, 1997. 32–35.

Jenson, Andrew. *Latter-day Saint Biographical Encyclopedia.* 4 vols. 1901–36. Reprint, Salt Lake City: Western Epics, 1971. 1:91.

ANDREW H. HEDGES

BRANCH. A small ecclesiastical unit of the Church is called a *branch*. While there is no minimum number of members required to form a branch, its size usually ranges from a few Latter-day **Saints** to about 200 members.

Soon after the **organization of the Church** on 6 April 1830, the first branch was created in **Colesville**, Broome County, **New York**, at **Joseph Knight's** farm. With the establishment of **wards** in the early 1840s in **Nauvoo**, branches took on a secondary role, serving primarily to establish new congregations in outlying areas.

Today branches are organized under two circumstances. In **mission** areas, all congregations are called branches, several of which compose a **district**. Where **stakes** and wards exist, branches are formed where Church membership is small. In addition, branches are sometimes organized to meet language or other special needs of members.

Branches function in essentially the same capacity as wards. Each is presided over by a branch president and two counselors, who perform roles similar to those of a **bishop** and his counselors in a ward. The branch president must hold the office of **elder** in the **Melchizedek Priesthood**; however, he need not be a **high priest**.

SOURCES

Cowan, Richard O. "Branch, Branch President." *Encyclopedia of Mormonism.* Edited by Daniel H. Ludlow. 4 vols. New York: Macmillan, 1992. 1:219.

Jenson, Andrew. "Colesville Branch." *Encyclopedic History of The Church of Jesus Christ of Latter-day Saints.* Salt Lake City: Deseret News, 1941. 152.

McConkie, Bruce R. *Mormon Doctrine.* 2d ed. Salt Lake City: Bookcraft, 1966. 102.

RUSSELL C. RASMUSSEN

BRANNAN, SAMUEL. Samuel Brannan was one of the most colorful and controversial of the early **Saints**. He was born 2 March 1819 in Saco, **Maine**, where missionaries **Orson Hyde** and **Samuel Smith** visited his **family** in 1832. Brannan moved to **Kirtland, Ohio**, with his sister in 1833, joined the Saints, apprenticed in the Church's printing office, and enjoyed a close relationship with the **Smith family**.

By 1837 Brannan ended his apprenticeship and spent five years as a tramp printer, visiting "most of the States." He rejoined the Saints about 1842 and was soon serving a mission in **New York City**. He published the *Prophet,* the official Latter-day Saint newspaper there, and served briefly as "President of the Saints in the East." Brannan was excommunicated for an unauthorized **plural marriage** performed by **William Smith**, but he soon regained his membership with the support of **Parley P. Pratt**.

In 1845, as Church leaders in **Nauvoo** planned the westward **exodus**, they directed Brannan and the New York Saints to travel by sea to **California**, from which point they could meet the main body of the Saints in the West. Brannan sought the aid of adventurer **Lansford Hastings**, politician Amos Kendall, and entrepreneurs A. W. and A. G. Benson, who were interested in conquering the Mexican province of California. Some 230 Latter-day Saints sailed from New York under Brannan's leadership aboard the ship *Brooklyn* on 4 February 1846—the same day the first wagons crossed the **Mississippi River** from Nauvoo.

Brannan settled in Yerba Buena (later **San Francisco**) and established the first settlement in the San Joaquin Valley at New Hope, anticipating that the main body of the Church would settle there. He crossed the

Great Basin in 1847 and attempted unsuccessfully to persuade **Brigham Young** to continue to California. Brannan returned as "President of the Saints in California" and sought to manage Church affairs until the discovery of gold, but by 1849 his apostasy was complete. In 1851 Parley P. Pratt excommunicated him for unbelief and also for his involvement in the vigilante movement—not, as is often charged, for his alleged appropriation of Church funds. Brannan built an enormous fortune during the gold rush, but hard living and a divorce reduced him to poverty by 1880. Land speculation later took him to **Mexico** and **Arizona**. He died in Escondido, California, on 5 May 1889, largely forgotten.

SOURCES

Bagley, Will. "'Every Thing Is Favourable! And God Is on Our Side': Samuel Brannan and the Conquest of California." *Journal of Mormon History* 23 (Fall 1997): 185–209.

———, ed. *Scoundrel's Tale: The Samuel Brannan Papers.* Spokane, Wash.: Arthur H. Clark, 1999.

Bringhurst, Newell G. "Samuel Brannan and His Forgotten Final Years." *Southern California Quarterly* 79 (Summer 1997): 139–60.

WILL BAGLEY

BRAZIL. Brazil is the fifth-largest country in the world, encompassing an area larger than the continental United States, or about as large as the European subcontinent. The total population in 1998 was estimated to be about 162 million.

The first Latter-day **Saints** in Brazil were German immigrants who arrived in the southern region in the early years of the twentieth century. The South American mission, then headquartered in **Argentina**, officially sent the first full-time missionaries to work among the German-speaking colonies in southern Brazil around 1927. From that time until the organization of the Brazilian mission on 25 May 1935, **missionary work** was restricted to the German colonies. Because of strong nationalistic pressures imposed by the Brazilian government, which saw the cultural isolation of the German colonies as a potential threat to national security, the **Church** abolished the use of German language in church meetings in 1939. In 1942, the Church officially adopted Portuguese as the proselytizing language.

At first the work progressed rather slowly: by the time of the dedication of the **São Paulo Temple** in 1978 there were only 15 organized stakes and about 54,000 members in the whole country. After the completion of the temple (which happened a few months after the Church's announcement of the revelation that extended the **priesthood** to all worthy males) the work progressed at a phenomenal rate. In the next 12 years, 41 new stakes were organized, embracing more than 300,000 members in the country—the third largest concentration of Church members in the world, surpassed only by the **United States** and **Mexico**.

In 1994 Church units could be found in only 362 cities across Brazil—less than 10% of the total number of cities in the country. Half of the Brazilian cities in which the Church was then present had populations with more than 100,000 inhabitants.

The Church began construction on additional temples in Recife (1996), Campinas (1998), and Porto Alegre (1998). By the beginning of the year 2000 there were 26 missions, 186 stakes, 1,879 units, and 743,182 members in Brazil. The largest concentrations of members were then found in the states of Sao Paulo, Rio Grande do Sul, Parana, Rio de Janeiro, Minas Gerais, Pernambuco, and Santa Catarina.

Four Brazilians have served as **general authorities**: Elders **Helio de Rocha Camargo**, **Helvecio Martins**, Claudio Roberto Mendes Costa, and Athos Marques Amorim. All served in the Second **Quorum** of the **Seventy**, and Elder Camargo also served in the First Quorum.

SOURCES

Grover, Mark L. "Mormonism in Brazil: Religion and Dependency in Latin America." Ph.D. diss., Indiana University, 1985.

Martins, Marcus H. "The Oak Tree Revisited: Brazilian LDS Leaders' Insights on the Growth of the Church in Brazil." Ph.D. diss., Brigham Young University, 1996.

MARCUS H. MARTINS

BREASTPLATE. See URIM AND THUMMIM.

BRETHREN, THE.

A term of respect often used by Latter-day **Saints** in referring to **general authorities**.

RICHARD O. COWAN

BRIDGER, JIM.

Jim Bridger was a celebrated mountain man, trader, and guide to western explorations who figured in the **Saints'** early **Great Basin** experience. Born in Richmond, **Virginia**, on 17 March 1804 and raised on the frontier, he signed on with **William H. Ashley**'s expedition of 1822 and spent most of five decades in the Rocky Mountain regions.

In search of beaver, Bridger was an early explorer of the **Salt Lake Valley** and is widely credited with being one of the early discoverers of the Great Salt Lake during the winter of 1824–25. Exploration by Bridger and other mountain men helped open the emigrant trails. With a declining fur trade, Bridger tried to capitalize on surging emigrant traffic by establishing **Fort Bridger** and the **Oregon Trail** in the early 1840s. **Brigham Young**'s emigrant party of 1847 met and consulted with Bridger near his trading post, deciding to proceed to Salt Lake Valley despite Bridger's concerns.

Latter-day Saint apprehensions about his dealings with local **Indians** forced Bridger to abandon his post temporarily in 1853; the post was eventually sold to the Mormons and consequently burned during the so-called "**Utah War**" of 1857–58.

Bridger continued to serve as guide to Western expeditions and died in Washington, **Missouri**, on 17 July 1881.

SOURCES

Alter, J. Cecil. *Jim Bridger.* Norman, Okla.: University of Oklahoma Press, 1962.

Gowans, Frederick R., and Eugene E. Campbell. *Fort Bridger: Island and the Wilderness.* Provo, Utah: Brigham Young University Press, 1975.

Ismert, Cornelius M. "James Bridger." *The Mountain Men and the Fur Trade of the Far West.* Edited by LeRoy Hafen. 10 vols. Glendale, Calif.: Arthur H. Clark, 1966–72. 6:85–104.

Vestal, Stanley. *Jim Bridger: Mountain Man.* New York: William Morrow, 1946.

SCOTT ELDREDGE AND FRED R. GOWANS

BRIGGS, JASON W. See REORGANIZED CHURCH OF JESUS CHRIST OF LATTER DAY SAINTS.

BRIGHAM CITY, UTAH. Located in Box Elder County, **Utah**, Brigham City became home to one of the Church's most successful nineteenth-century economic cooperatives. Settlement began in the spring of 1851 when William Davis, James Brooks, and Thomas Pierce brought their families to a site along Box Elder Creek. They established Davis Fort by building a row of adjoining log rooms surrounded by a log palisade. By 1852 the village contained about 139 people. In the next two years, several hundred recent emigrants joined the community, many from **Scandinavia** and **Wales**.

During the Church's **general conference** in October 1853, **Brigham Young** asked **Elder Lorenzo Snow** to take charge of the new settlement which had informally become known as Youngsville. Elder Snow moved his **family** there in 1854, and by 1855 had renamed the settlement Brigham City in honor of Brigham Young.

Under Snow's direction, a cooperative store was established there in 1864, followed by a tannery in 1866. The success of these enterprises and a desire for a more encompassing **Mormon** cooperative economy led to the incorporation in 1870 of the Brigham City Mercantile and Manufacturing Association. This venture functioned as a joint stock enterprise, offering stock or goods in exchange for labor and raw materials. The cooperative proved to be economically vigorous. After just a few years, the association included nearly forty departments, including a woolen factory, dairy, butcher shop, sawmill, tailor shop, molasses mill, furniture and cabinet shop, blacksmith shop, rope factory, pottery shop, cooperage, tin shop, broom factory, and a shingle, lath, and picket mill.

A devastating fire at the woolen factory in 1877, followed by an onerous federal tax assessment on the coop scrip in 1879 caused the association to fail. Most of its departments were sold to private owners over the next few years.

In 1865, Latter-day **Saints** in Brigham City began construction of the Box Elder **Stake Tabernacle**. It was dedicated October 1890 by **Wilford Woodruff**. Heavily damaged by fire in 1896, it was then rebuilt and rededicated in 1897. It remains in use today, one of the architectural masterpieces of the Church.

In 1999 Brigham City, the seat of Box Elder County, had five stakes and twenty-eight **wards**, and boasted a population (1996) of 16,398 people.

SOURCES

Huchel, Frederick M. *A History of Box Elder County*. Salt Lake City: Utah State Historical Society and Box Elder County Commission, 1999.

Nielsen, Vaughn J. *The History of Box Elder Stake*. Brigham City, Utah: Pat's Print Shop, 1977.

SCOTT R. CHRISTENSEN

BRIGHAM YOUNG ACADEMY. See **BRIGHAM YOUNG UNIVERSITY.**

BRIGHAM YOUNG COLLEGE. Founded in **Logan, Utah** on 24 July 1877, Brigham Young College (BYC) served nearly 40,000 students during its 49-year history (1877–1926). When Church president **Brigham Young** established the college he deeded nearly 10,000 acres of his personal property as an endowment to help maintain the school. He wanted the curriculum to emphasize three basic areas: 1) A liberal and scientific education; 2) A trade such as carpentry or farming; and 3) Classes in religious education. The history of BYC can be divided into three general periods of time. From 1877 to 1894 it operated basically as a normal school—preparing students to become elementary school teachers. From 1894 to 1909 it began offering college courses and granted bachelors degrees. From 1909 to 1926 the school changed its status to function as both a high school and junior college. The Church discontinued Brigham Young College in 1926 because other educational institutions, which were established after BYC, began duplicating the school's course work—Utah State Agricultural College (1888) developed classes in **teacher training**; the public schools (1890) offered a secondary education course; and the Latter-day Saint **seminary** program (1912) taught religion classes. Three of BYC's presidents/principals went on to serve as president of Utah State Agricultural College: Joshua H. Paul, **Joseph M. Tanner**, and William J. Kerr. Joseph Tanner also became superintendent of Church Schools. Four of BYC's most distinguished alumni were called to serve in the **Quorum** of Twelve **Apostles**: **Richard R. Lyman, Melvin J. Ballard, John A. Widtsoe**, and **Albert E. Bowen**.

SOURCES

Garr, Arnold K. "Brigham Young College." *Encyclopedia of Mormonism.* Edited by Daniel H. Ludlow. 4 vols. New York: Macmillan, 1992. 2:219–20.

Garr, Arnold K. "A History of Brigham Young College, Logan, Utah." Master's thesis, Utah State University, 1973.

ARNOLD K. GARR

BRIGHAM YOUNG MONUMENT. In the center of the most significant intersection in downtown **Salt Lake City** is a large granite monument with a heroic-sized **Brigham Young** at the top, flanked by a sitting **Indian** who represents the first inhabitants of the valley, and a sitting fur trapper, representing the first white inhabitants of the area. **Wilford Woodruff** selected Cyrus Dallin (1861–1944) as the artist in 1891 after he had completed the Angel **Moroni** Statue for the **Salt Lake Temple**.

The bronze figure of Brigham Young was first displayed in front of the **Utah** Building at the 1893 Chicago World's Fair. Later it was unveiled on **Temple Square** during the 1897 Pioneer Jubilee, before being placed on the completed monument in 1900.

The artist grew up in Springville, Utah. He became Utah's first artist to achieve a national reputation. After studying in Paris, Dallin settled in Boston, where he received commissions for the Paul Revere monument at Old North Church, Governor Bradford monument on the Boston Commons, and Chief Massosoit monument at Plymouth Rock.

SOURCE

Francais, Rell G. *Cyrus G. Dallin: Let Justice Be Done.* Springville, Utah: Springville Art Museum and the Utah American Revolution Bicentennial Commission, 1976.

RICHARD G. OMAN

BRIGHAM YOUNG UNIVERSITY.

BRIGHAM YOUNG UNIVERSITY. Brigham Young University in **Provo, Utah**, is America's largest Church-sponsored institution of higher learning, owned and operated by The Church of **Jesus Christ** of Latter-day **Saints**. Well-known for its high academic standards, its honor code of personal conduct, a beautiful campus, and successful athletic programs, Brigham Young University began in less auspicious circumstances, barely surviving several early challenges.

Precedent for such a unique school was established in 1840 when **Joseph Smith** formed the short-lived University of **Nauvoo** in **Illinois**. Later, after Brigham Young had led the **Mormon exodus** west to the Rocky Mountains, he and other **pioneer** leaders established the University of Deseret in 1850, the forerunner of the **University of Utah**. As Latter-day Saint populations grew in the **Great Basin**, public schools multiplied while other religious denominations established schools of their own to "convert" Mormon school children. Toward the end of his life Brigham Young sought to establish a school for his people possessing the academic and religious-based qualities similar to those of a small Provo school operated by Warren and Wilson Dusenberry since 1863 but closed because of financial exigencies.

Subsequently, President Young willed four acres of land and other monetary provisions to inaugurate a new school. Under the terms of his deed of trust, Brigham Young Academy was incorporated 16 October 1875, and the first term began with 29 very young "scholars" (mostly elementary and high school students) in January 1876. Brigham Young handpicked the German-born educator and Latter-day Saint convert, **Karl G.**

Maeser, to supervise the new school (a post he would hold for 17 years) and to infuse the teachings of the Church into virtually every aspect of secular learning. "Teach not even the alphabet and the multiplication tables without the Spirit of the Lord," he instructed Maeser. Further, in Maeser's own words, "No book shall be used that misrepresents, or speaks lightly of the Divine mission of our Savior, or of the **Prophet Joseph Smith**, or in any manner advances ideas antagonistic to the principles of the Gospel" (Wilkinson, 1:178).

Despite every good intention, the little Provo school barely survived. Funding was inadequate due to a host of reasons. There was much wrangling over the probate of Brigham Young's estate. Low tuition receipts, a tragic fire in 1884, diminished Church support during the **antipolygamy** "raids" of the 1880s, and a depressed agrarian economy exacerbated by the Panic of 1893—all held the school back. Without the unwavering support of such early financiers as **Abraham O. Smoot**, Harvey H. Cluff, and later **Jesse Knight**, as well as the sacrifices of a chronically underpaid, yet patient faculty, the school would surely have foundered. Only after the Church finally decided against the organization of a church university in **Salt Lake City**, and instead made of the Academy *the* normal school for teacher education in the Church, was the school's future assured.

Under the capable direction of **Benjamin Cluff**, Maeser's young successor, new and larger facilities were secured, the curriculum was upgraded, and the school's name was changed to Brigham Young University. Not the least of his accomplishments was the thwarting of a state-sponsored effort to make the university part of the University of Utah. After Cluff's resignation in 1903, **George H. Brimhall**, pushed expansion of the school north and east onto "temple hill" supervising the construction of the Karl G. Maeser Memorial Building in 1911. The famous white-painted "Y" on the mountainside east of the campus, symbolizing the growing vitality and student spirit of the school, appeared in 1906, the same year that bachelor degrees were first conferred.

Only gradually did the school shed its high school image and become more of a true university. In fact, it was not until 1928, under President Franklin S. Harris, an internationally-acclaimed agricultural scientist and educator, that the school finally gained accreditation status by the Association of American Universities. Meanwhile, BYU survived yet another series of crises when the Church, for financial and political reasons, relinquished control to the state of most of its other schools and academies in the early 1920s and 1930s. Choosing to retain BYU primarily to train future Church teachers and educators, Church leaders such as **David O. McKay, Stephen L Richards, J. Reuben Clark**, and others pledged the Church's full financial backing along with a Church-appointed Board of Trustees to supervise the school. These critically important decisions finally set the school on a path of financial security and potential growth that allowed it to flourish even during the dark days of the Depression.

After 24 years of service, Harris, beloved by his faculty and student body, stepped down in 1944 and was succeeded by Howard S. McDonald. Following McDonald's comparatively short term in office—distinguished by postwar campus planning, improved faculty pay, and the beginning of a sizeable capital campaign—**Ernest L. Wilkinson**, an early BYU alumnus and a successful Washington lawyer, was appointed the sixth president of the University in 1951. With the full support of President David O. Mckay, an educator himself by profession, the tireless, indomitable, and conservatively minded Wilkinson embarked on a remarkable, if sometimes controversial, 20-year program of campus expansion. He increased student enrollment from 5,000 to 25,000, upgraded and diversified academic offerings in a score of new colleges and departments, strengthened the faculty, and ensured the character and integrity of the university as a truly religious-oriented, Latter-day Saint school. One of his self-admitted most significant accomplishments was the establishment of student **ward** and **stake** church organizations for the rapidly growing student body.

Succeeding presidents have built wisely on these earlier foundations and successes in the hope of building a "Zion University." Both **Dallin H. Oaks**, who served from 1971 to 1980, and his successor, **Jeffrey R. Holland**, who served from 1980 to 1989, have since become members of the **Quorum** of the Twelve **Apostles**. **Rex E. Lee**, former solicitor general of the **United States** and founding dean of the J. Reuben Clark Law School presided over the university from 1989 to 1995. **Elder Merrill J. Bateman**, economist, businessman, and former **presiding bishop** of the Church, as a concurrent member of the First Quorum of **Seventy**, was the first sitting **general authority** to preside over the school. Under his direction, BYU moved further toward faith-based learning, excellence in teaching as well as research, and a capital development endowment fund numbering in the hundreds of millions of dollars.

Of the many successful "semester abroad" educational programs, perhaps the most successful was that in Jerusalem, an effort that has since grown into the **Jerusalem Center for Near Eastern Studies**, instituted in 1968. Today the Center's beautiful facilities, located on the northern half of the Mt. of Olives and overlooking the ancient city, are a Jerusalem landmark. Offering a wide variety of academic programs, the Center has overcome resolute opposition from certain religious groups and has become a place of religious harmony and interfaith understanding.

On the other side of the world, the **BYU–Hawaii campus**, an outgrowth of the former Church College of Hawaii, covers 6,000 acres near **Laie, Hawaii**. This four-year liberal arts college serves a cosmopolitan student body of more than 2,000 students from all over the **Pacific** Rim.

The "spirit" of BYU continues to be seen perhaps best of all in its remarkable student body. Composed of young men and women from all across the country and from 107 countries worldwide, most are Latter-day Saints and more than 50% have served **missions** for the Church and speak foreign languages. Admission standards are among the highest in America. Nominated in 1999 as America's most "cold sober" student body, the school's 32,731 part-time and full-time students (a full time equivalent of 29,693) live by the Honor Code of ethical and moral behavior, revere their "Cougar" football, basketball, and other sports teams, worship in wards held in campus facilities, and travel the world in touring song and dance troupes as young ambassadors for the school and the Church. Where once the tiny Academy sought hard to recruit a few hundred students, today thousands more apply from all over the world than can possibly be admitted.

At the end of the twentieth century Brigham Young University remained the "flagship" of the Church's educational system, boasting 1,515 full-time faculty and an alumni of more than 340,000. Several graduate degrees were offered in such colleges as Fine Arts and Communications, Biology and Agriculture, **Education**, Engineering and Technology, **Family**, Home and Social Sciences, Humanities, Nursing, Physical and Mathematical Sciences, Physical Education, Law, and the School of Business. While research is a priority of its faculty, Brigham Young University remains a teaching university primarily committed to providing the best undergraduate education possible for as many as possible. Although an ever-decreasing percentage of Latter-day Saint students could attend BYU because of the exponential growth in worldwide Church membership, through expanding its off-campus extension services via mail and the Internet, it was preparing to teach hundreds of thousands of young Latter-day Saints all over the world.

Yet, regardless of unlimited Church growth on the one hand and limited enrollment ceilings on the other, BYU will remain in the forefront of Church Education. As President Holland aptly said, BYU will continue because it is a vital part of Latter-day Saint theology, because it fulfills prophecy, because there must be an alternative to the intellectual one-sidedness of secular learning at the university level, and because there remains a distinctly Latter-day Saint balanced approach to higher education (Holland). Wedded to the high ideals and principles of the Church, Brigham Young University is a profoundly religious school, an ideal, and an experiment in modern educational history, with an unyielding commitment to character development, spiritual growth, and higher learning in both the things of the world and the things of **God**.

SOURCES

Holland, Jeffrey R. "A School in Zion." *Educating Zion.* Edited by John W. Welch and Don E. Norton. Provo, Utah: Brigham Young University Press, 1996.
Wilkinson, Ernest L., ed. *Brigham Young University: The First One Hundred Years.* 4 vols. Provo, Utah: Brigham Young University Press, 1975–76.

RICHARD E. BENNETT

BRIGHAM YOUNG UNIVERSITY–HAWAII CAMPUS. Brigham Young University–Hawaii Campus is a fully accredited regional university in **Laie, Hawaii**, made up of approximately 2,200 students from 60 nations of the world. Emphasizing the **arts** and **sciences**, business, and teacher **education**, the university offers programs leading to bachelor's degrees in 30 academic majors.

Envisioned by **David O. McKay** as early as 1921, the campus grounds were dedicated by President McKay as Church College of Hawaii on 12 February 1955, with Dr. Reuben D. Law as its first president. A **Pacific** Board of Education had oversight for the college until 1974, when it became **Brigham Young** University—Hawaii Campus.

From its beginning, the campus has provided educational opportunities for Latter-day **Saint** students from the Pacific and Asian Rim countries. In the early 1960s, the **Polynesian Cultural Center** was conceived and built to provide employment for such students. It has since become an extension of the campus, providing practical training for nearly a third of the student body, plus substantial funding for scholarships.

Known for its intimate multicultural environment, the University is respected for its academic programs. It publishes two major journals, *Pacific Studies* and *TESL Reporter.*

One of President McKay's prophetic statements at the dedication of the campus has become the guiding light for BYU–Hawaii students: "From this school . . . will go men and women whose influence will be felt for good towards the establishment of peace internationally" (Law, 67).

SOURCES

Britsch, R. Lanier. *Moramona: The Mormons in Hawaii.* Laie, Hawaii: Institute for Polynesian Studies, 1989.

Law, Reuben D. *The Founding and Early Development of The Church College of Hawaii.* St. George, Utah: Dixie College Press, 1972.

ERIC B. SHUMWAY

BRIGHAM YOUNG UNIVERSITY–IDAHO. See RICKS COLLEGE.

BRIGHAM YOUNG UNIVERSITY STUDIES. See BYU STUDIES.

BRIMHALL, GEORGE H. President of **Brigham Young University** from 1900 to 1921, George Henry Brimhall was responsible for expanding the institution's physical plant and upgrading its academic curriculum. Born 9 December 1852 in **Salt Lake City**, Brimhall married Alsina Elizabeth Wilkins in 1874, with whom he had six children; he also married Flora Robertson, with whom he had nine children.

After graduating in 1877 from Brigham Young Academy, Brimhall commenced his career in education administration, serving first as principal of Spanish Fork schools and then as superintendent of **Provo** community schools. In 1890 he began his long association with Brigham Young Academy/University, serving as head of the intermediate department and preparatory school, and then as principal of the normal department. In 1900 he was appointed president of the school and soon purchased 74 acres of land on "Temple Hill," where the upper campus was later built. During his presidency, five new buildings were constructed. Brimhall also sought to improve the quality of instruction, hiring four LDS professors trained at Harvard, University of Chicago, Cornell, and the University of **California**. This action precipitated the so-called Modernist Controversy over the methods the four used in teaching, and ultimately the four were dismissed or forced to resign in 1911.

Brimhall stepped down as BYU president in 1921 but remained as head of the school's Department of Theology and Religion. After enduring a long period of deteriorating health, he died in Provo, **Utah**, 29 July 1932.

SOURCES

Bergera, Gary James, and Ronald Priddis. *Brigham Young University: A House of Faith.* Salt Lake City: Signature Books, 1985.

Wilkinson, Ernest L., ed. *Brigham Young University: The First One Hundred Years.* 4 vols. Provo, Utah: Brigham Young University Press, 1975–76.

NEWELL G. BRINGHURST

BRIMHALL, LUCY. See KNIGHT, LUCY BRIMHALL.

BRITISH COLUMBIA, CANADA. Vancouver Island, off the coast of British Columbia, **Canada**, was identified early by **Brigham Young** and British missionary leaders as a potential haven for westward-bound **pioneers**. In 1886 **Charles O. Card** and comrades explored this westernmost province but ultimately settled in **Cardston, Alberta**. In 1902 British Columbia became part of the Northwestern States **Mission**. Not until 1911 was a Vancouver **branch** established, with Edward Neill as president. Members met in homes and halls until 1925 when a tall, narrow chapel was purchased on a lofty corner lot. Vancouver became a **ward** of the Seattle **Stake** in 1938. Later it was reorganized as a branch, becoming the hub of the Vancouver **District**. Branches sprung up in New Westminster and Vancouver Island (Victoria and Nanaimo). By 1952 there were six branches with North Vancouver, Nanaimo, and White Rock added. The Vancouver Stake and Alcan (now Canada Vancouver) Mission were organized in 1960. By the year 2000 there were 27,564 members living in 8 stakes and 80 wards and branches.

SOURCES

Anderson, Charles P., Tirthanker Bose, and Joseph I. Richardson, eds. *Circle of Voices.* Lantville, British Columbia: Oolichan Books, 1983. 136–48.

McCue, Robert J. "The Church of Jesus Christ of Latter-day Saints and Vancouver Island: the establishment and growth of the Mormon community." *BC Studies* 42 (Summer 1979): 51–64.

Tagg, Melvin S. *A History of the Mormon Church in Canada.* Lethbridge, Alberta: Lethbridge Herald, 1968.

JOHN P. LIVINGSTONE

BRITISH ISLES. See ENGLAND, IRELAND, SCOTLAND, and WALES.

BRITISH MISSION. In 1837 **Joseph Smith** declared that the Lord told him "something new must be done for the salvation of His Church" (Smith, 2:489). This "something new" was sending missionaries to Great Britain. **Heber C. Kimball** and **Orson Hyde** of the **Quorum** of the Twelve **Apostles**, accompanied by five other missionaries, arrived in **Liverpool** 20 July 1837. Three days later they were able to commence their work at Preston where Reverend **James Fielding**, a brother of one of the missionaries, invited them to preach to his congregation. During the next eight months more than 1500 people joined the Church.

This was followed two years later by a mission during which 9 of the 12 apostles, under the direction of **Brigham Young**, went to Great Britain. President Young later summarized the apostles' accomplishments during their year in Britain: "We landed in the spring of 1840, as strangers in a strange land and penniless, but through the mercy of God we have gained many friends, established churches in almost every noted town and city in the kingdom of Great Britain, baptized between seven and eight thousand, printed 5000 Books of Mormon, 3000 Hymn Books, 2500 volumes of the *Millennial Star,* and 50,000 tracts, and emigrated to Zion 1000 souls" (quoted in Bloxham, 162).

The British Mission quickly became a major source of converts to the Church and the source of more immigrants to **Nauvoo** (and later **Utah**) than any other non-American country. As a vast and well-organized Church **emigration** program was conducted, Liverpool was also the point of embarkation for most of the emigration from other parts of **Europe**. Approximately 89,500 **Mormon** emigrants bound for **America** departed from the Liverpool docks between 1840 and 1868. The British Mission also became a major publishing and distribution center for the Church. One of its publications, the *Millennial Star,* served the **Saints** in Britain and elsewhere from 1840 until it was discontinued in 1970.

For about 90 years the presidents of the British Mission, who were generally members of the Quorum of the Twelve Apostles, supervised not only the work in Britain but the missions on the continent of **Europe** as well. This continued until 1929 when the British Mission, with its own president, was separated from the administration of the European Mission.

One of the problems facing the British Mission during its first century was migration to America; by the time of the mission's centennial celebration in 1937 there were still only 6300 British Latter-day Saints in their native land. **Missionary work** was seriously disrupted during **World War I** and **World War II**, and there was a slight decline in membership.

The years following World War II, however, saw more rapid growth with an especially large number of baptisms in the early 1960s. This was partly because Church leaders were encouraging the Saints to stay and build up the kingdom in their own lands and partly because missionaries sometimes baptized large numbers of youth without their families, which resulted in a serious problem of retaining membership. The late 1960s began a period of consolidation, with emphasis on baptizing families. The result was better retention, stronger Church programs, and eventually a dramatic increase in the number of young men from the British Isles called on full-time missions

Two especially significant events marked the maturity of the Church in the British Isles. One was the dedication of the **London Temple** in 1958. The other was the creation of the first British **Stake** in 1960, a sign that the British Church had attained sufficient strength and local leadership had matured to the point that the British Saints could fully take over the affairs of the Church in the areas involved. Significantly, it was at this point that the British Mission began to break up. With the exception of the short-lived Welch Mission (1845–1854), the British Mission had retained its original boundaries until 1960, when the North British Mission was created. More subdivisions over the next four years led to a total of nine missions in the area in 1964. By 1982 all of the original British mission, with the exception of the Republic of **Ireland**, was covered by stakes. By 1998 there were almost 175,000 members in 45 stakes and 388 **wards** and **branches** in the **United Kingdom** and Ireland.

SOURCES

Bloxham, V. Ben, James R. Moss, and Larry C. Porter, eds. *Truth Will Prevail: The Rise of The Church of Jesus Christ of Latter-day Saints in the British Isles, 1837–1997.* Cambridge: Cambridge University Press, 1987.

Cowan, Richard O. "The Church Comes of Age in Britain." In *British Isles.* Edited by Donald Q. Cannon. Regional Studies in Latter-day Saint History series. Provo, Utah: Brigham Young University, 1990. 193–214.

Cuthbert, Derek A. *The Second Century: Latter-day Saints in Great Britain, Volume 1, 1937–1987.* Cambridge: Cambridge University Press, 1987.

———. "Church Growth in the British Isles, 1937–1987." *BYU Studies* 27 (Spring 1987): 13–26.

Evans, Richard L. *A Century of Mormonism in Great Britain.* Salt Lake City: Deseret News, 1937.

Grant, Bryan J. "British Isles, The Church in." *Encyclopedia of Mormonism.* Edited by Daniel H. Ludlow. 4 vols. New York: Macmillan, 1992.. 1:227–32.

Jensen, Richard L., and Malcolm R. Thorp, eds. *Mormonism in Early Victorian Britain.* Salt Lake City: University of Utah Press, 1989.

Jenson, Andrew. "British Mission." *Encyclopedic History of The Church of Jesus Christ of Latter-day Saints.* Salt Lake City: Deseret News, 1941. 92–94.

Smith, Joseph. *History of The Church of Jesus Christ of Latter-day Saints.* Edited by B. H. Roberts. 2d ed. rev. 7 vols. Salt Lake City: The Church of Jesus Christ of Latter-day Saints, 1932–51.

JAMES B. ALLEN

BROADCASTING. Broadcasting is transmitting electromagnetic signals from a single point of origin to widely dispersed receivers. It is an inexpensive, highly effective means of communicating to a mass audience. The term refers to AM, FM, and short-wave radio as well as television signals. Related broadcasting activities include telecasting, cable casting, and direct broadcast satellites (DBS).

The power of broadcasting to communicate the gospel of **Jesus Christ** was apparent to Church leaders at the start of the radio age. From initial ownership and experimentation in radio technology in the 1920s, the Church expanded its reach through the electromagnetic spectrum to include ownership of radio and television stations, **satellite** transponders, and media production facilities. In 1999 the Church held licenses for one radio station in **Los Angeles**, three in Chicago, three in **San Francisco**, five in **Washington, DC**, two in **Salt Lake City**, and one in **Rexburg, Idaho**. The Church also owned three television stations—two in Salt Lake City and one in Cedar City, **Utah**. Operation of these stations was primarily the responsibility of **Bonneville International Corporation**, but **Brigham Young University** held licenses for and operated one educational radio and one television station, and **Ricks College** operated one educational radio station.

Church development and use of DBS began in the 1980s. At the end of the twentieth century, the Church delivered satellite signals directly to **stake** centers across North **America**, with additional satellite capability that offered more limited DBS services to **Europe**, **South America**, **Africa**, the **Pacific**, and **Asia**. Most DBS transmissions involved **general conference**, various training videos, and occasional fireside addresses.

The Church also added the Internet to its technological outreach, using the newest computer capabilities to enhance its reach through broadcast and satellite services.

SOURCES

Christensen, Bruce L. "Broadcasting." *Encyclopedia of Mormonism.* Edited by Daniel H. Ludlow. 4 vols. New York: Macmillan, 1992. 232–34.

Esplin, Fred C. "The Church As Broadcaster." *Dialogue* 10 (Spring 1977): 25–45.

Hollstein, Milton. "The Church as Media Proprietor." *Dialogue* 10 (Spring 1977): 21–24.

BRUCE L. CHRISTENSEN

BROCCHUS, PERRY. See RUNAWAY OFFICIALS

BRODIE, FAWN M. In 1945 Alfred A. Knopf published a psycho-biographical study of the life of **Joseph Smith** titled *No Man Knows My History.* The book's author, Fawn McKay Brodie, was officially excommunicated from the Church six months later for heresy—a charge she admitted was true. When interviewed by Shirley E. Stephenson, Brodie stated that she "was convinced before [she] ever began writing the book that Joseph Smith was not a true **prophet**" (quoted in "Dissident Historian," 279). Thus, her book did not find a receptive audience among faithful Latter-day **Saints**.

Though praised for its literary style, Brodie's book was condemned by many historians as seriously flawed. Yet it continues to be widely read. Brodie has been called Mormonism's best-known rebel, and she has been regarded as a historian of distinction.

Born 15 September 1915 at Huntsville, **Utah**, Fawn Brodie was educated at **Weber College**, the **University of Utah**, and the University of Chicago. The daughter of **general authority Thomas E. McKay** and the niece of President **David O. McKay**, Brodie taught history at UCLA, and in 1959 she received the Commonwealth Club of **California's** Literature Award. In 1975 Brodie was designated by the *Los Angeles Times* as woman of the year. Fawn Brodie died 10 January 1981 in Santa Monica, **California**.

SOURCES

Bringhurst, Newell G. "Fawn McKay Brodie: Dissident Historian and Quintessential Critics of Mormondom." *Differing Visions: Dissenters in Mormon History.* Edited by Rodger D. Launius and Linda Thatcher. Chicago: University of Illinois Press, 1994. 278–300.

Bringhurst, Newell G., ed. *Reconsidering No Man Knows My History: Fawn M. Brodie and Joseph Smith in Retrospect.* Logan, Utah: Utah State University Press, 1996.

KENNETH W. GODFREY

BROOKLYN (SHIP). As 1845 concluded, the eastern **Saints** were warned "to flee Babylon, either by land or by sea" (Smith, 7:516). Many faithful Saints responded to the call and under the leadership of **Elder Samuel Brannan** successfully sailed to the West Coast, becoming the first group of Church members to arrive there. Coincidentally, on 4 February

1846, as they left **New York** Harbor to cross the oceans, the first company of **Nauvoo** exiles were crossing the **Mississippi River** and heading west.

These seafaring Saints were led by Captain Abel W. Richardson and his crew of two mates, a steward, a cook, and a dozen sailors. Although statistics vary somewhat, careful research suggests that the passengers consisted of 70 men, 63 women, and 101 children, including about a dozen nonmembers. Before setting sail, adult passengers were charged $75 each; children were charged half price. There were 11 passengers who died en route and two children born during the voyage, appropriately named Atlantic and Pacific. After a long voyage around Cape Horn and with stops at the Juan Fernandez and **Sandwich Islands**, they eventually reached Yerba Buena (**San Francisco**) Bay on 31 July 1846.

Sources

Church History in the Fulness of Times. Salt Lake City: The Church of Jesus Christ of Latter-day Saints, 1993. 326–28.

Hansen, Lorin K. "Voyage of the Brooklyn." *Dialogue* 21 (Fall 1988): 47–72.

Smith, Joseph. *History of The Church of Jesus Christ of Latter-day Saints.* Edited by B. H. Roberts. 2d ed. rev. 7 vols. Salt Lake City: The Church of Jesus Christ of Latter-day Saints, 1932–51. 7:516.

Fred E. Woods

BROOKS, JUANITA. Juanita Brooks was born 15 January 1898 in Bunkerville, **Nevada**, the oldest of 11 children. Recognized by scholars as one of Mormondom's outstanding historians, she received her education from **Dixie College**, **Brigham Young University**, and Columbia University.

She is best known for her treatment of the massacre at **Mountain Meadows** and its participants. Her honesty in interpretation of facts was important to the way she wrote Mormon history. Such statements as "nothing but the truth is good enough for the church to which I belong" and "truth suppressed is its own kind of lie" helped establish her reputation.

Juanita taught at Dixie College for many years, wrote 12 books, edited eight others, and wrote many articles that were published throughout the west. This led to a position with the State of **Utah** in the Historical Records Survey during the **great depression** and later to a position with Huntington Library where she made the collection of original diaries available for research by scholars.

Juanita was given an award by the **Mormon History Association** in

1978 for her lifetime of research and writing about the Latter-day Saint past. She died 26 August 1989.

SOURCE

Peterson, Levi S. *Juanita Brooks: Mormon Woman Historian.* Salt Lake City: University of Utah Press, 1988.

KARL F. BROOKS

BROWN, HUGH B. Hugh Brown Brown, **counselor** in the **First Presidency**, was born 24 October 1883 in Granger, **Utah**, to Homer Manly Brown and Lydia Jane Brown. He was raised in **Alberta, Canada**, where tending cattle and farming left little time for formal **education**. Hugh took it upon himself to attain the best education possible and was known as an avid reader. He served a **mission** to **England** in 1904, and upon his return, he married Zina Card in the **Salt Lake Temple** in 1908. They were the parents of nine children.

A veteran of **World War I**, Hugh B. Brown served in Canada's Thirteenth Overseas Mounted Rifles. Following his military service, he studied law at the Law Society of Alberta, finished a five-year apprenticeship, and was admitted to the bar in 1921. His first law practice was in Lethbridge, Alberta, Canada. In 1927 he moved to **Salt Lake City** to practice law with **J. Reuben Clark Jr.** **Elder** Brown left his law practice and taught religion courses at **Brigham Young University** from 1946 until 1950. He then returned to Canada as president of an oil development firm in Alberta.

Hugh B. Brown was the first **stake president** of the Lethbridge **Stake** in Canada and then called as the Granite, Utah Stake president in 1930. He was president of the **British Mission** in 1937 until **World War II** began in 1939. During the **war**, the First Presidency called him to serve as coordinator for all Latter-day Saint servicemen stationed in **Europe** (100,000 **Mormon** men). Following the war, he returned to **London** as the British Mission president. In 1946, President Brown was stricken with tic douloureux, a painful disease of the nervous system. An operation to relieve the pain left the right side of his face partially paralyzed. Elder Brown was called as an **assistant to the Twelve** on 4 October 1953. On 10 April 1958, he was **ordained** an **apostle** in the **Quorum** of the Twelve. Elder Brown became an additional counselor in the First Presidency to **David O. McKay** on 22 June 1961. He then became President McKay's second counselor on 12 October of the same year. He served as first counselor from 4 October 1963 to 18 January 1970. He died 2 December 1975 in Salt Lake City, Utah, at age 92.

SOURCES

Brown, Hugh B. *An Abundant Life: The Memoirs of Hugh B. Brown.* Edited by Edwin B. Firmage. Salt Lake City: Signature Books, 1988.
Campbell, Eugene E. *Hugh B. Brown, His Life and Thought.* Salt Lake City: Bookcraft, 1975.

MATTHEW O. RICHARDSON

BROWN, JAMES. Captain James Brown, a well-traveled missionary, soldier, and founder of the city of **Ogden, Utah**, was born in Rowan County, **North Carolina**, on 30 September 1801.

Baptized in **Illinois** in 1838 and a **Nauvoo** resident, he also preached in the southern states. In 1846 he joined the **Mormon Battalion**, wintered with sick soldiers in Pueblo, then led them into the **Salt Lake Valley** on 29 July 1847. Later that year he purchased, from Miles Goodyear, a plot of land and a fort on the Weber River. In January 1848, he moved onto that land, and since that time he has been considered the first citizen of what became the city of **Ogden**. After a short mission to British Guiana in 1852, he aided the 1853–54 Mormon migration from **St. Louis**. While living in Ogden, he served on the city council from 1855 until his death in 30 September 1863.

SOURCES

Black, Susan Easton, comp. *Membership of The Church of Jesus Christ of Latter-day Saints, 1830–1848.* 50 vols. Provo, Utah: Religious Studies Center, Brigham Young University, 1984–88.
Jenson, Andrew. *Latter-day Saint Biographical Encyclopedia.* 4 vols. 1901–36. Reprint, Salt Lake City: Western Epics, 1971. 2:283–84.

JOHN THOMAS

BROWN, JAMES S. James Stephens Brown, a missionary, **pioneer**, soldier, and lecturer, was born 4 July 1828 in Davidson, **North Carolina**. He was baptized in **Missouri** on 7 July 1844 and volunteered for the **Mormon Battalion** two years later. He was also at Sutter's Mill when gold was discovered.

Brown served a mission to the Society Islands in 1849, and in **England** a decade later; he also preached and worked in **Wyoming** and other frontier areas. He returned to the Society Islands as mission president from 1892 to 1893. During his lifetime Brown married four times and fathered 30 children. Although he later lost a leg in an accident, he continued to be active until his death in **Salt Lake City** in 1902.

SOURCES

Black, Susan Easton, comp. *Membership of The Church of Jesus Christ of Latter-day Saints, 1830–1848*. 50 vols. Provo, Utah: Religious Studies Center, Brigham Young University, 1984–88.

Brown, James S. *Life of a Pioneer: Being the Autobiography of James Stephens Brown*. Salt Lake City: George Q. Cannon and Sons, 1900.

JOHN THOMAS

BROWN, JOHN. John Brown, leader of the **Mississippi Saints**, was born in Sumner County, **Tennessee**, on 23 October 1820 to Martha and John Brown. He was the twelfth of 14 children. He joined the Church in 1841 and soon thereafter served in the **Southern States Mission**. In 1844 he met and married Elizabeth Crosby.

In 1846 he led 14 families from the South to **Fort Laramie, Wyoming**, but when he learned that the **pioneers** had stopped at **Council Bluffs** for the winter, he took the **Mississippi** Saints to **Pueblo, Colorado**. Leaving them there, John returned east and joined his **family** at **Winter Quarters**.

The following spring he headed west with the pioneer company. On 19 July 1847, he and **Orson Pratt** ascended Big Mountain and were the first of the group to see the Great **Salt Lake Valley**. In August he returned east and brought his family back to the valley in 1848.

John served as **bishop** at Pleasant Grove in Utah Valley for 29 years, and also as a **stake patriarch**, member of the **Utah** territorial legislature, justice of the peace in nearby Lehi, and mayor of Pleasant Grove from 1863 to 1883. He died at his home in Pleasant Grove on 4 November 1896.

SOURCES

Carter, Kate B. *Our Pioneer Heritage*. Vol. 2. Salt Lake City: Daughters of the Utah Pioneers, 1959.

Brown, John Zimmerman. *Autobiography of Pioneer John Brown, 1820–1896*. Salt Lake City: Stevens & Wallis, 1941.

CLARK V. JOHNSON

BROWN, VICTOR L. Victor Lee Brown was called in April 1972 as **presiding bishop** of the Church, and he served in that capacity until 1985. He first entered the ranks of the **general authorities** in 1961 when presiding bishop **John H. Vandenberg** selected Bishop Brown as his second counselor. During his ten years in that position, he made an outstanding contribution as head of the new Church Distribution and Translating Department, which provided materials in many languages for members of the Church all over the world. On **6 April** 1985, he was called to the First Quorum of the **Seventy**, where he served until becoming an **emeritus general authority** on 1 October 1989.

Born in **Cardston, Alberta, Canada**, on 31 July 1914, Victor moved with his mother and father to **Salt Lake City** in 1930, where he attended the **University of Utah** and **LDS Business College**. In 1940 he began a career as an executive for United Airlines and held positions in Salt Lake City, **Washington, D.C.**, Denver, and Chicago. He married Lois Kjar of Salt Lake City. **Elder** Brown died 26 March 1996 in Salt Lake City.

SOURCES

Flake, Lawrence R. *Mighty Men of Zion*. Salt Lake City: Karl D. Butler, 1974. 486.

Zobell, Albert L. "Victor Lee Brown of the Presiding Bishopric." *Improvement Era* 64 (December 1961): 913.

LAWRENCE R. FLAKE

BROWNING, JONATHAN. Jonathan Browning was a Latter-day Saint gunsmith who invented the repeating rifle and a six-shot repeater. He was born 22 October 1805 in Brushy Fork, Sumner, **Tennessee**, and opened his first gunshop there in 1825. The business closed in 1834, when Browning moved to **Quincy, Illinois**. Here he learned about Mormonism. Conversations with **Joseph Smith** led to his baptism and removal to **Nauvoo**. Browning left Nauvoo in 1846, and settled in **Council Bluffs, Iowa**, before migrating to the **Salt Lake Valley** in 1852 and later to **Ogden, Utah**. At each location he continued his work as a gunsmith. Browning died 21 June 1879 at age 73.

SOURCES

Black, Susan Easton. "Jonathan Browning, Mormon Gunsmith." *Muzzle Blasts* 30 (July 1997): 11–14.

Gentry, Curt, and John Browning. *John M. Browning, American Gunmaker: An*

Illustrated Biography of the Man and his Guns. Garden City, New York: Doubleday and Co., 1964.

A History of Browning Guns from 1831. St. Louis, Mo.: Browning Arms Co., 1942.

SUSAN EASTON BLACK

BUCHANAN, JAMES. James Buchanan, best known in **Mormon** history as the president who sent **Johnston's Army** to **Utah,** was born 23 April 1791 near Mercersberg, **Pennsylvania.** Soon after being elected fifteenth president of the **United States** in 1856, James Buchanan became aware of the difficulties of federal officers assigned to Utah Territory. Their reports to **Washington** indicated their inability to work with local leaders and their limited understanding of or sympathy for **Mormon** beliefs. Associate Justice **W.W.** **Drummond** labeled his own attempts to administer government in Utah as "noonday madness and folly" and suggested sending a non-Mormon governor to the area with "sufficient military aid" to remedy the situation (Roberts, 205). As a result of such reports, in May 1857 Buchanan issued an order that provided for a 2,500-man force to accompany newly appointed governor **Alfred Cumming** to Utah.

The government appropriated more than a million dollars for thousands of wagons, oxen, horses, and mules to transport supplies for the huge Utah Expedition (see **Utah War**). While in a forced winter encampment near **Fort Bridger**, arbitrators negotiated a peaceful settlement. In June the troops marched into **Salt Lake City** and on to Cedar Valley where they established **Camp Floyd**. Buchanan's reluctance to terminate the expensive and unpopular expedition, and his failure to send peace negotiators until after the troops arrived in Utah Territory, led some to refer to the expedition as Buchanan's Blunder.

President Buchanan died 1 June 1868 in Lancaster, Pennsylvania.

SOURCES

Furniss, Norman F. *The Mormon Conflict, 1850–1859.* New Haven: Yale University Press, 1960.

Roberts, B. H. *A Comprehensive History of The Church of Jesus Christ of Latter-day Saints, Century One.* 6 vols. Salt Lake City: The Church of Jesus Christ of Latter-day Saints, 1930. 4:205.

AUDREY M. GODFREY

BUILDING MISSIONARIES. Ever since **Joseph Smith** received a commandment to "establish a house" of learning and worship in 1832

(D&C 88:119), Latter-day Saints have struggled to provide appropriate buildings. In the 1950s the Church's worldwide growth demanded methodological changes to meet building needs. Short of capital and skilled labor, the Tonga Mission president called local young Mormon men to building missions. They consecrated their time and labor and received technical training. The Church provided housing and skilled contractors to teach and manage. By 1952 missionaries finished the Liahona School in Tonga and began work in New Zealand.

In 1955, under the direction of Wendell B. Mendenhall, new chairman of the Church Building Committee, building missionaries were institutionalized. Now skilled supervisors were also called. They left contracting firms to serve; they took their families and received a subsistence stipend. This combination of leaders and laborers constructed the Church College of Hawaii, the New Zealand Temple, and, as the program spread to Europe in 1960 and the Far East, Latin America, and North America in 1962, more than 2,000 buildings throughout the Church, before being phased out by the 1970s.

Some difficulties arose because of pride, an occasional delinquent missionary, or cultural differences between North American supervisors and less affluent local members; also, the destruction of American materials by the climate of the South Pacific proved costly. Most agree, however, that the gains of cooperation and consecration overwhelm the losses. In fact, one supervisor called in 1963, Norman Hammond, left a new home and prospering firm to accept his assignment. "It was the greatest experience of my life," he affirmed. Having never recovered his temporal losses, Hammond is content knowing "the Lord [does not] take things from you without giving blessings" (Interview).

Sources

Allen, James B., and Glen M. Leonard. *The Story of the Latter-day Saints.* 2d ed. Salt Lake City: Deseret Book, 1992.

Anderson, Paul L., and Richard W. Jackson. "Building Program." *Encyclopedia of Mormonism.* Edited by Daniel H. Ludlow. 4 vols. New York: Macmillan, 1992. 1:236–38.

Britsch, R. Lanier. *Unto the Islands of the Sea: A History of the Latter-day Saints in the South Pacific.* Salt Lake City: Deseret Book, 1986.

Cowan, Richard O. *The Church in the Twentieth Century.* Salt Lake City: Bookcraft, 1985.

Cummings, David W. *Mighty Missionary of the Pacific.* Salt Lake City: Bookcraft, 1961.

Hammond, Norman. Interview by Steven C. Harper, 9 July 1999.

Newton, Marjorie. *Southern Cross Saints: The Mormons in Australia.* Laie, Hawaii: Institute for Polynesian Studies, 1991.

Steven C. Harper

BULGARIA. Mormonism was first preached in Bulgaria by Hungarian-born **Mischa Markow**. He proselytized briefly in Bulgaria in the summer of 1900 before being expelled from the country. For the following 90 years, the Church did not have a presence in Bulgaria, but in 1980 selections from the **Book of Mormon** were published in Bulgarian. As a result, a small number of Bulgarians living outside their country joined the Church.

On 13 February 1990, **Elder Russell M. Nelson** dedicated Bulgaria for **missionary work**, and on 10 September of that year, six missionaries (under direction of the **Austria** Vienna East Mission) entered the country. All six missionaries taught English classes. On 24 November 1990, the first baptismal service in Bulgaria was conducted for six converts: Emil and Diana Christov, their two sons, and Ventizlav and Marela Lazarov.

In June 1991, the Church was formally recognized by the Bulgarian government. That same month, the Mladost and Central **branches** were formed. On 1 July 1991, the Bulgaria Sofia Mission was created with Kiril P. Kiriakov as president.

By the beginning of the year 2000, twelve branches and one **district** were functioning in Bulgaria, with 1,367 Church members.

Sources

Kehr, William Hale. "Missionary to the Balkans, Mischa Markow." *Ensign* 10 (June 1980): 29–32.
"Mission to Be Created in Bulgaria." *Church News,* 18 May 1991, 3.

Scott R. Christensen

BULLOCK, THOMAS. Thomas Bullock, a clerk for **Joseph Smith** and **Brigham Young**, distinguished himself as a prominent pioneer diarist. He was born 23 December 1816 in Leek, Staffordshire, **England**. Even though Thomas was an excellent student, he quit school at age 13 to take a job as a clerk in a law office, laying the foundation for his life's work. He married Henrietta Rushton in 1838, and they were baptized members of the Church in 1841.

Two years later they emigrated to **Nauvoo**, where Thomas became a clerk to Joseph Smith. He recorded several of the Prophet's sermons, including the "**King Follett Discourse**." When most of the **Saints** left Nauvoo in 1846, Thomas stayed behind at Brigham Young's request to chronicle the non-Mormon takeover of the city. In 1847, Bullock was clerk for the vanguard pioneer company on its journey to the **Salt Lake Valley**.

In **Utah**, Thomas was chief clerk for the House of Representatives and secretary to the **First Presidency**. As chief clerk in the Church Historian's Office, he compiled much of what would become the seven-volume *History of the Church*. He spent the last years of his life in Summit County and died in Coalville on 10 February 1885. Bullock's work as a diarist, clerk, and scribe made a significant contribution to Church history.

SOURCES

Bagley, Will, ed. *The Pioneer Camp of the Saints: The 1846 and 1847 Mormon Trail Journals of Thomas Bullock.* Spokane, Wash.: Arthur H. Clark, 1997. 25–38.

Despain, C. Ward. "Thomas Bullock, Early Mormon Pioneer." Master's thesis, BYU, 1956.

Simon, Jerald F. "Thomas Bullock as an Early Mormon Historian." *BYU Studies* 30 (Winter 1990): 71–88.

ARNOLD K. GARR

BUREAU OF INFORMATION. See TEMPLE SQUARE.

BURKHARDT, HENRY. Johannes Henry Burkhardt was an important Church leader in Eastern **Germany** after **World War II**. He was born in Chimnitz, Germany, in 1930. From 1945 (when East Germany came under the communist system of government) until 1989 (the opening of the Berlin wall), the many thousands of Latter-day **Saints** behind the "Iron Curtain" were essentially cut off from regular contact with **general authorities** and the **mission president**, whose office was generally located in West Berlin. Henry Burkhardt, a third-generation member was called in 1952 to be a **counselor** to the mission president presiding over eastern Germany, the German Democratic Republic (GDR).

During these years, and especially after the Berlin wall was erected in 1961, Henry Burkhardt was recognized by the **communist** government in the GDR as the official spokesman for the Church in that country, and as such he had major responsibilities in representing the Church to his own government as well as to the general authorities and mission presidents outside the GDR. He served in this office until 1984, by which time two **stakes** had been formed inside the GDR and a **temple** was being constructed. Henry Burkhardt was then called as president of the **Freiberg Germany Temple,** which was dedicated in 1985. In 1989 the Berlin Wall came down, and in 1991 Henry Burkhardt was appointed manager of the **family history** and genealogical center in Frankfurt.

SOURCE

Burkhardt, Henry. Interview by Matthew K. Heiss. James Moyle Oral History
    Program, LDS Church Historical Department, Salt Lake City. 24 October 1991.

GAROLD N. DAVIS

BURNED-OVER DISTRICT. The **Prophet Joseph Smith** wrote, "there was in the place we lived [Palmyra/Manchester, Ontario County, New York] an unusual excitement on the subject of religion" (JS–H 1:5). This "unusual excitement" was part of what historians call the second **great awakening,** which occurred throughout frontier **America** between 1816 and 1837. The religious revivalism was so constant in western New York that the area west of the Catskill and Adirondack Mountains between Albany and Buffalo was termed the "Burned-Over District." Spontaneous religious camp meetings inspired religious excitement such as revivals, quickenings, and awakenings conducted by Methodist circuit riders, Baptist farm preachers, Presbyterian ministers, Episcopal priests, and other Protestant **missionaries.** Joseph's quest for religious understanding was sparked in the fires of the Burned-Over District.

SOURCES

Backman, Milton V., Jr. *Joseph Smith's First Vision.* Salt Lake City: Bookcraft, 1971.
    53–89.
Cross, Whitney R. *The Burned-Over District.* Ithaca, N.Y.: Cornell University Press,
    1950.

W. SIDNEY YOUNG

BURTON, H. DAVID. H. David Burton was called on 27 December 1995 and sustained on 6 April 1996 to replace **Merrill J. Bateman** as the **presiding bishop** of the Church. Before this, he had served as first counselor to Bishop **Robert D. Hales** (1992–1994) and to Bishop Bateman (1994–1995). His experience with the presiding bishopric had actually begun earlier when he served as its executive secretary for 14 years. Bishop Burton's previous Church callings included a mission to **Australia**, bishop's counselor, **bishop**, **high councilor**, **stake president**, and **temple** sealer.

A native of **Salt Lake City**, Bishop Burton was born 26 April 1938. He received a bachelor's degree in economics from the **University of Utah** and a master's degree in business administration from the University of **Michigan**. Prior to his call as a general authority, he was assistant Church budget officer and also worked for Kennecott Copper and the Utah State Tax Commission. He and his wife, Barbara Matheson Burton, became the parents of five children.

SOURCES

"New Presiding Bishopric Called." *Church News*, 30 December 1995. 3.
"New Presiding Bishop, Counselors Called." *Ensign* 26 (March 1996): 74.
1999–2000 Church Almanac. Salt Lake City: Deseret News, 1998. 46.

GUY L. DORIUS

BURTON, RICHARD. Sir Richard Burton (1821–90), British explorer, writer, and scholar, visited **Utah** during the summer of 1860. He later published a book (1862) about his experiences, entitled *The City of the Saints*. While in general his book deals with western **America**, most of its chapters are about the **Mormons**. He wrote about the geography and statistics of the Utah Territory, included a chapter on **Brigham Young**, and had extensive material on the LDS Church. Burton was positive about the Saints, stating that "their faith has not succumbed to the most violent persecution inflicted upon any people in modern times" (Roberts, 530). **B. H. Roberts** asserted that *The City of the Saints* was the best book about the Mormons written by a non-Latter-day Saint author during the first century of the Church. Burton died 2 October 1890 in Trieste, **Italy**.

SOURCES

Brodie, Fawn McKay. *The Devil Drives: A Life of Sir Richard Burton*. New York: W. W. Norton, 1967.
Burton, Sir Richard Francis. *The City of the Saints*. Niwot, Colorado: The University Press of Colorado, 1990.
Roberts, B. H. *A Comprehensive History of The Church of Jesus Christ of Latter-day Saints, Century One*. 6 vols. Salt Lake City: The Church of Jesus Christ of Latter-day Saints, 1930. Vol. 4.

DONALD Q. CANNON

BURTON, ROBERT T. Indian fighter, musician, marshal, tax collector, and **general authority** are only a few of the many titles that describe Robert Taylor Burton. The tenth of 14 children, Robert was born 25 October 1821 and reared in **Ontario, Canada**. He served four **missions** for the Church and was a member of the **Nauvoo Legion** as well as of the **Nauvoo** choir and brass band. In **Utah** he was a member of the relief party that rescued the snowbound **handcart** companies in the fall of 1856. Among Brother Burton's numerous civil positions were sheriff, constable, **United States** deputy marshal, city councilman, territorial legislator, and regent of the **University of Deseret**. He was called as second counselor to **presiding bishop Edward Hunter** in 1874 and ten years later as first counselor to Bishop **William B. Preston**, serving in that position until his death on 11 November 1907 in **Salt Lake City**.

SOURCES

"Bishop Robert Taylor Burton." *Improvement Era* 11 (January 1908): 159.

Burton, Janet Seegmiller. *Be Kind to the Poor: The Life Story of Robert Taylor Burton.* N.p.: Robert Taylor Burton Family Organization, 1988.

Flake, Lawrence R. *Mighty Men of Zion.* Salt Lake City: Karl D. Butler, 1974. 495.

LAWRENCE R. FLAKE

BURTON, THEODORE M. Chemistry professor Theodore Moyle Burton became a **general authority** in 1960. He was born 27 March 1907 in **Salt Lake City, Utah**. He served a Swiss-German **Mission** from 1927 to 1930 and then returned to earn his bachelor's degree at the **University of Utah** in 1932. He married Minnie Susan Preece in the **Salt Lake Temple** in 1933 and earned his master's degree at the University of Utah the following year. Brother Burton worked in **Europe** for several years as a technical assistant to the U.S. treasury attaché, first in Vienna and then in Berlin. He began teaching at Carbon College (now College of Eastern Utah) in 1941 and became a chemistry professor at Utah State University in 1943. He interrupted his teaching career to earn a Ph.D. at Purdue University in 1951. The Church called him to serve as president of the West German Mission in 1957, **assistant to the Twelve** in 1960, and a member of the First **Quorum** of **Seventy** in 1976. As a general authority he served as president of the **European Mission**, managing director of the Genealogical Department, and area supervisor in Europe. He was named

emeritus general authority on 1 October 1989 and died later that year on 22 December in Salt Lake City.

SOURCES

"Elder Burton Hailed as a Godly Man." *Church News,* 30 December 1989, 12–13.
"Elder Theodore M. Burton Dies." *Ensign* 20 (March 1990): 76–77.

ARNOLD K. GARR

BURUNDI. The republic of Burundi, located in East Central Africa, has French as its official language. More than 60% of the people are Roman Catholic, and 32% follow indigenous beliefs.

In 1992, when Burundi adopted a new constitution, the Church organized a **branch** in Bujumbura and placed it under the direction of President Homer M. LeBaron of the **Zaire** Kinshasa Mission. Egide Nzojibwami, who had joined the Church in Liege, Belgium, while attending university, was set apart as the first branch president on 27 November 1992. At the time of his call, he was dean of the school of Geological Engineering at the University of Burundi.

In October 1993 a destructive civil **war** erupted in Burundi. The missionaries were soon removed for security reasons, and President Nzojibwami also exited the country, leaving members without any formal organization. Because of the country's political and civil instability, Burundi was transferred from the Zaire Kinshasa Mission to the Africa West Area in 1998. By the year 2000 there were 28 members living in the country, attending one branch.

SOURCES

1999–2000 Church Almanac. Salt Lake City: Deseret News, 1998. 287.
Oral histories of early Church converts collected by E. Dale LeBaron. Copies at BYU Library, Provo, Utah; LDS Church Historical Library, Salt Lake City, Utah.

E. DALE LEBARON

BUSINESSES. The Church's involvement in business ventures over the years has primarily been to satisfy public needs and to further the building of the **kingdom of God** on earth. The Church's earliest businesses met territorial **Utah**'s needs for basic services where private enterprises were either unable or unwilling to do so. For example, the Church and its leaders established the *Deseret News* and the Deseret Telegraph to extend communications throughout the territory; they built the Utah Central and other **railroads** to assist transportation; and they organized **Zion's** and other banks to provide financial support. The Church's business ventures also extended into manufacturing, textiles, irrigation, merchandising, and other ventures.

Although some of the early business enterprises were successful or later sold by the Church for a profit, many were not. Indeed, some companies were organized with the knowledge that the Church would probably lose more money than it would earn by providing essential services. What is more, many early Latter-day **Saint** entrepreneurs saw their financial contributions in some companies more as a sacrifice for building the kingdom than money-making investments. By the beginning of the twentieth century, however, a number of Church-owned companies had become financially viable.

President **Joseph F. Smith** explained that the Church "had always tried to 'help establish home industries and to aid in setting certain business enterprises on their feet,' in order to provide employment and 'to develop the material resources of the country, that the people and the land may prosper'" (Alexander, 76). As more private enterprises were created in Utah and the new state moved into the twentieth century, the Church began to divest itself of companies that came into direct conflict with established businesses or proved to be too time-consuming or burdensome for the **general authorities**. This slow divestiture of businesses continued throughout the twentieth century.

By 1923 the Church's financial ventures had become so complex that Church leadership and legal advisors decided to separate its holdings into two distinct categories. The Corporation of the President was organized to hold ecclesiastical property, while Zion's Securities Corporation was created to administer all taxable and nonecclesiastical property. This financial arm of the Church was later restructured, and Deseret Management Corporation became the parent or holding company for most of the Church's for-profit companies. Under this umbrella were Zion's Securities Corporation (which henceforth became specifically responsible for real estate and property management), Beneficial Development Company, and Proprietary Holding. These three entities focused on the Church's real estate businesses, which included Deseret Ranches of **Florida**—the largest cattle operation in the **United States**—and Deseret Farms of **California**—the largest producer of nuts in the agriculturally rich San Joaquin Valley (Ostling and Ostling, 121). Also under this same umbrella were insurance, hotel, and communications enterprises. Beneficial Life Insurance and its several subsidiaries provided insurance for members and nonmembers alike. Hotel **Temple Square** Corporation managed the Inn at Temple Square and other hotel and catering businesses in **Salt Lake City**.

At the end of the twentieth century, some of the most significant of the Church's business enterprises were those involved with communications. Deseret News Publishing produced the daily *Deseret News* with a circulation of more than 70,000 and had a half interest in Newspaper Agency Corporation. **Deseret Book Company** was involved in publishing, wholesaling, and retailing, with stores in Utah and other parts of the western United States. Deseret Book and its subsidiary, Shadow Mountain Press, were also involved in the production and distribution of music and software libraries on compact disc. In 1999 Deseret Management Company acquired the independent publishing firm Bookcraft, Inc., which was merged with Deseret Book.

Bonneville International Corporation became the broadcast arm of the Church. It acquired more than a dozen radio and two television stations located in several major markets from coast to coast. It also owned several support companies. Many of Bonneville's programs reached an international audience.

Other taxable enterprises the Church either owned or had interest in included World Media Inc., the Magnolia Management Corporation, Deseret Trust of California, Property Reserve of **Arizona**, K2H Farms, Columbia Ridge Farms, and Bonneville Holding Company. The Church continued to have significant interest in formerly owned companies such as Zion's Bancorp. For many years, the Church held controlling interest in **ZCMI** (Zion's Cooperative Mercantile Institution), a chain of department stores throughout Utah. Nevertheless, in keeping with the Church's efforts to divest itself of unnecessary businesses, ZCMI was sold in 1999 to the May Company.

Even more significantly, in 1996 President **Gordon B. Hinckley** asked general authorities to resign from all private and public boards of directors. This departure from corporate positions by Church leadership was the result of the ecclesiastical burden brought on by unprecedented membership growth.

Among the corporations that furthered the goals of the Church or were used to help both members and nonmembers were Deseret Mutual Insurance Corporation (which provided insurance for Church employees), Deseret Trust, Foreign Lands Corporation, LDS **Social Services**, LDS Foundation, Deseret International Charities, **Nauvoo Restoration Inc.**,

Polynesian Cultural Center, Ricks College (later BYU–Idaho), and **Brigham Young University**. Most of these corporations were nontaxable. Other nontaxable Church corporations used to assist the needs of members were the ones directly under the authority of the Corporation of the **Presiding Bishop**. These companies included Beehive Clothing and Deseret Transportation, which shipped products for welfare services.

Latter-day Saint businesses have evolved from numerous companies created to provide services for pioneer communities to an intricate network of corporations that serve the needs of Church members and strive to further the spreading of the gospel.

Sources

Alexander, Thomas G. *Mormonism in Transition: A History of the Latter-day Saints, 1890–1930*. Urbana: University of Illinois Press, 1986. 74–76, 89–96.

Brady, Rodney H. "Church Participation in Business." *Encyclopedia of Mormonism.* Edited by Daniel H. Ludlow. 4 vols. New York: Macmillan, 1992. 1: 240–43.

"LDS Financial Empire Puts Church at Fortune 500 Level." *The Salt Lake Tribune,* 30 June 1991.

Ostling, Richard N., and Joan K. Ostling. *The Power and Promise: Mormon America.* New York: Harper San Francisco, 1999. 113–29.

Craig L. Foster

BYU STUDIES. Established in 1959, *BYU Studies* has become a highly respected voice for the community of Latter-day Saint scholars. Published sporadically until 1968, it has appeared quarterly since then, containing many significant articles on Church history topics. The journal publishes annual indexes and in 1991 published a 32-year index. In addition to publishing articles on Church history, it has also recently published full-length historical documents jointly with respected university presses, including *The William E. McLellen Journals* with the University of **Illinois** Press in 1994.

Charles Tate

CANADA. Joseph F. Smith and others at the dedication of the temple site in Cardston, Alberta, Canada, on 27 July 1913. This temple was the first outside the United States.

CACHE VALLEY. Located 70 miles north of **Salt Lake City**, Cache Valley is divided by the present **Utah/Idaho** state line. It was first inhabited by **Native American** bands as they wandered through the area. The valley was used as a place for "caching," or storing, furs and other goods by early American trappers such as **William Ashley**, Michel Bourdon, **Peter Skene Ogden**, and **Jim Bridger**. When the **Mormons** met Jim Bridger in 1847, he informed them that they might consider settling in Cache Valley, because it was the only green valley he had seen in the basin. The leaders of the Church took this counsel to heart, and by the summer of 1855, **Erastus Snow** had visited the valley and given a glowing report. The decision was made to establish a ranch in the valley, and the Utah territorial legislature granted **Brigham Young** 9,500 acres south of **Logan** for a herd ground. The Elkhorn Ranch, later called the Church Farm, was established. The first permanent settlement was founded 15 September 1856 by a group sent by Brigham Young under the leadership of **Peter Maughan**. The settlement became known as Maughan's Fort (later named Wellsville). From this beginning, other settlements spread throughout the valley. The first community in what became Idaho Territory in 1863 was Franklin, established in April 1860.

Cache Valley's fertile valley floor supported an agricultural community that became known for its grain and dairy products. A branch of the **railroad** connected it to the outside world in 1873, and other commercial endeavors gave the valley an economical base. Logan became the county seat. The founding of Utah State Agricultural College (later Utah State University) in 1888 set the capstone of a strong educational focus by the citizens of the area.

Cache Valley developed into a stronghold of the Church. The settlers were committed to building the **Kingdom of God**. **Wards** and **stakes** filled the valley as the population expanded. **Tabernacles** were built in many of the communities, and in 1877, under the direction of Brigham

Young, **Orson Pratt** dedicated a site on the east bench of Logan for the building of a **temple**. The Saints needed seven years to complete the **Logan Temple**, which was dedicated 17 May 1884 by President **John Taylor** and has been the spiritual focal point of the valley. From the northern end of the valley have come two presidents of the Church: **Harold B. Lee**, from Clifton, Idaho, and **Ezra Taft Benson**, raised in Whitney, Idaho.

SOURCES

Peterson, F. Ross. *A History of Cache County*. Salt Lake City: Utah State Historical Society, 1997.

Ricks, Joel E., ed. *The History of a Valley: Cache Valley Utah-Idaho*. Logan, Utah: Cache Valley Centennial Commission, 1956.

Van Cott, John W. *Utah Place Names: A Comprehensive Guide to the Origins of Geographic Names*. Salt Lake City: University of Utah Press, 1990.

H. DEAN GARRETT

CAHOON, REYNOLDS.

Reynolds Cahoon was a man who held many leadership positions in the early Church and was a close friend of **Joseph Smith**. Cahoon was born 30 April 1790 in Cambridge, **New York**. He lived in the **Kirtland, Ohio**, area when **Parley P. Pratt** preached there. Pratt baptized him 11 October 1830. Shortly thereafter he was ordained an **elder** by **Sidney Rigdon**. Joseph Smith ordained him a high priest 3 June 1831.

In June 1831, Reynolds Cahoon and **Samuel Smith** were called to travel to **Jackson County, Missouri**. Cahoon returned to Kirtland in September. On 11 October 1831 he was appointed to raise funds to enable Joseph to complete his translation of the **Bible**. He was set apart as first counselor to **Bishop Newel K. Whitney** 10 February 1832. Cahoon was a member of the three-man **Kirtland Temple** Committee; he also served as a counselor in a **stake** presidency with President **John Smith** in **Adam-ondi-Ahman, Missouri**, and in an **Iowa** stake.

On 10 August 1835, Joseph Smith Jr. charged Reynolds Cahoon with failing to correct his children. Cahoon admitted his error.

In 1844 Cahoon delivered the letter to Joseph from **Emma Smith**, entreating Joseph to return from Iowa and face the mobs in **Illinois**. He accused Joseph Smith of cowardice for leaving the **Saints**. Nevertheless, Reynolds remained active in the Church and eventually made the trek across the plains to settle with the Saints in the **Salt Lake Valley**. He died 29 April 1861 in South Cottonwood, Salt Lake County, **Utah**.

SOURCES

Cook, Lyndon W. *The Revelations of the Prophet Joseph Smith.* Salt Lake City: Deseret Book, 1985. 73, 96–97.

Smith, Joseph. *History of The Church of Jesus Christ of Latter-day Saints [HC].* Edited by B. H. Roberts. 2d ed. rev. 7 vols. Salt Lake City: The Church of Jesus Christ of Latter-day Saints, 1932–51.

Smith, Joseph. *Teachings of the Prophet Joseph Smith.* Selected by Joseph Fielding Smith. Salt Lake City: Deseret Book, 1970. 376–80.

ROBERT L. MARROTT

CALDWELL COUNTY, MISSOURI. Caldwell County, created chiefly for the Latter-day **Saints** in **Missouri** in the mid-1830s, was the center of the Church for a brief period of time. Following the expulsion of the Mormons from **Jackson County, Missouri**, in 1833, most Church members relocated in **Clay County**. Although Clay's residents were much more open and fair-minded than Jackson's old-time settlers, by June 1836 continued Mormon **immigration** caused local residents to feel that the Saints' stay in Clay County had lasted long enough. Rather than resorting to further physical violence, Clay's citizenry opted to allow the Latter-day **Saints** to relocate peacefully.

As early as 1834, Mormon families had begun moving north and east from Clay County into the more sparsely populated areas in neighboring Ray County. In March 1836, Church leaders in Missouri began searching out possible sites for permanent settlement in some of the more uninhabited regions of that county. After making extensive explorations, the Church purchased a one-mile square plot situated near Shoal Creek on 8 August 1836. The site was subsequently named **Far West**.

As the Saints' numbers began to increase in the new region, some believed that the Mormon problem might be solved if a county was created exclusively for the Latter-day Saints. **Alexander Doniphan**, Clay County's representative to the state legislature and a Mormon sympathizer, spearheaded the bill to create the new county. Initially, it was proposed that the county be 24 miles square, encompassing 16 townships, each being 6 miles square, with the southern boundary line lying between the 53rd and 54th township lines. Non-Mormon settlers living in the six-mile strip bordering the 54th township protested being placed in the Mormon county and signed a petition against the proposition. To appease the settlers in the disputed territory, the proposal was modified to keep the six-mile tract in Ray County and make the new county only 18 by 24 miles. While this benefited the non-Mormons living in the contested area, a number of Latter-day Saint families living there remained outside the Mormon county. Passage of Doniphan's bill came on 29 December 1836, with Far West being designated as the county seat. The county was named Caldwell in honor of Matthew Caldwell of **Kentucky**, a friend, **Indian** scout, and fellow soldier with Joseph Doniphan, the father of Alexander Doniphan.

While Far West was the largest community in the county, smaller Latter-day Saint settlements were established on or near Shoal, Log, Bush, Mill, Panther, Mud, and Plum Creeks and **Crooked River**. Settlements bearing the name of some of the original founders or inhabitants included: Allred Settlement (William, William M., and Wiley Allred), Curtis Settlement (Jeremiah Curtis), Carter Settlement (Simeon and Orlando Carter), Durfey Settlement (James and Perry Durfey), Free Settlement (Absalom and Joseph Free), Lyon Settlement, also called Salem (Aaron C. Lyon), Myers Settlement (Jacob Myers), Plumb Settlement (Merlin Plumb), Stevens Settlement (Roswell Stevens), and **Haun's Mill** Settlement (Jacob Haun). These sites were abandoned at the time the Saints were expelled from the state in 1839.

By late 1838, the population in and around Far West numbered in the vicinity of 4,000 to 5,000, making it the largest community in northwestern Missouri. Conservative figures put the total county population in Caldwell around 8,000, although it may have been as high as 10,000. After agreeing to leave the state in 1838, most of the Latter-day Saints sold their lands and homes to buyers at substantially reduced prices or abandoned their property altogether. In 1843 a new county seat was established at Kingston, named after Judge Austin A. King, the circuit court judge who presided over the trials associated with the Mormons in 1838 and 1839.

Since 1909 the LDS Church has made several land purchases in Caldwell County in the vicinity of Far West and currently owns approximately 582 acres, part of which includes the original **temple** site.

SOURCES

Baugh, Alexander L. "A Call to Arms: The 1838 Mormon Defense of Northern Missouri." Ph.D. diss., Brigham Young University, 1996.

History of Caldwell and Livingston Counties, Missouri. St. Louis: National Historical Company, 1886.

Jenson, Andrew. "Caldwell County, Missouri." *Historical Record* 8 (January 1889): 685–732.

ALEXANDER L. BAUGH

CALHOUN, JOHN C. John Caldwell Calhoun, one of the foremost statesmen in the **United States**, was born 19 March 1782 in Abberville, **South Carolina**. From his election to the Senate in 1810 until his death in 1850, Calhoun, along with **Henry Clay** and Daniel Webster, dominated the Senate. A member of the Senate Committee on Foreign Affairs during the **War** of 1812, Calhoun later served as secretary of war, vice president, and again as **South Carolina**'s senator from 1832 to 1843, when he resigned to campaign for the presidency. When Calhoun recognized he would not secure the **Democratic** nomination, he retired from politics, only to be appointed secretary of state in 1844 and to return to the Senate in 1845.

Seeking redress for **Mormon** property losses in **Missouri**, **Joseph Smith** met with Calhoun in 1840. Calhoun insisted the case was beyond the purview of federal authorities. During Calhoun's bid for the presidency, Smith wrote to him, inquiring whether he would support the Mormons in their fight for redress if elected. Calhoun reiterated that he would not intervene because "the case does not come within the jurisdiction of the Federal Government" (Smith, 156). Joseph responded tartly that "Congress, with the President as Executor, is as almighty in its sphere as Jehovah is in his" (*HC*, 160). John C. Calhoun died 31 March 1850 in Columbia, South Carolina.

SOURCES

John C. Calhoun. 3 vols. New York: Russell and Russell, 1944–51.

Smith, Joseph. *History of The Church of Jesus Christ of Latter-day Saints.* Edited by B. H. Roberts. 2d ed. rev. 7 vols. Salt Lake City: The Church of Jesus Christ of Latter-day Saints, 1932–51. 6:156, 160.

BRIAN Q. CANNON

CALIFORNIA. The Church and California have maintained a mutually beneficial relationship for more than 150 years since the time of the Church's first colony in the American West at **San Francisco**. In 1999 California had the largest Church population in the United States outside **Utah**.

California Church history began in 1845, when a group of **Saints** in the Eastern **United States** were directed to hire a ship and sail to the bay of "St. Francisco," where they expected the main body of the Church to join them. On 4 February 1846 (the same day the Saints left **Nauvoo**) nearly 300 boarded the ship *Brooklyn* under the leadership of 26-year-old **Samuel Brannan**. They left **New York City** and began a 24,000-mile voyage via **Hawaii** to San Francisco Bay, where they arrived on 31 July 1846, three weeks after California became United States territory and a year before the first Saints reached the **Salt Lake Valley**. They were California's first large group of United States settlers, creating an instant city out of a tiny wind-swept village.

In January 1847, the 400-plus men, women, and children of the **Mormon Battalion** arrived in **San Diego**. With the *Brooklyn* Saints they erected some of California's first permanent structures, including a sawmill on the American River, where they were working when gold was discovered. Latter-day Saint **pioneers** in California developed the mining of gold, the raising of grain, vegetables, fruits, and seeds, and the breeding of cattle—all of which greatly benefited both the Church and the state.

In the spring of 1847, after Saints had helped rescue the survivors of the **Donner Party**, Brannan traveled east across **Nevada** and Utah and found the vanguard company of the Saints on the trail in **Wyoming**. When **Brigham Young** informed him that they would be settling in the Salt Lake Valley rather than California, the disenchanted Brannan went back to California and dropped his leadership role in Church affairs. In 1848 other Saints decided to leave for Utah, carving out the first wagon road from northern California to **Salt Lake City**, a road that hundreds of thousands later traveled during the California **gold** rush.

When California applied for statehood in 1850, U.S. president **James Polk**, Brigham Young, and others supported the idea of merging California and "Deseret" (Utah) into one state, but the messenger carrying the proposal arrived in California too late. The local legislature had already decided California's eastern border would be where it is today.

In 1851, approximately 450 Church pioneers arrived from Utah to found the city and county of **San Bernardino** and California's first **stake**. Over the next several years, thriving branches were organized. Nevertheless, in 1857, the Church withdrew because of the **Utah War** and remained absent for 35 years.

When the Church's practice of **plural marriage** became a heated national issue and the Church was disenfranchised, California sheltered

Church exiles, while its politicians lobbied the United States Congress for tolerance and acceptance. Their efforts helped reestablish the Church, secure Utah's **statehood**, and reintroduce the Church into California.

Since 1892, when Church branches were formed again in Oakland and Sacramento, the Church has enjoyed steady, sometimes spectacular, growth throughout the state—more than 25 times that for the state population as a whole.

In the 1920s an exceptional immigration of talented Church members flowed into California. Many of these people became noted leaders. Included are two California governors and a Church president, as well as nationally and internationally recognized figures in science, business, education, sports, and the arts.

During these years the state also became a "proving ground" for stake **welfare**, **seminary** and **institute**, **single adult**, and **family home evening** programs that have since been adopted worldwide.

Since the migration of the 1920s, nearly 10% of the Church has lived in California. In the year 2000 Church membership was 740,236, and since 1967 the entire state has been blanketed by stakes, which in the year 2000 numbered 160, with 1,311 wards and branches. There were also 17 missions and 4 **temples: Los Angeles** (1954), **Oakland** (1964), San Diego (1993), and Fresno (2000).

In California, the Church also has a strong ethnic presence. In the state's largest cities, there is no ethnic majority. Church members come from every ethnic and socioeconomic background. There are more than 200 Church ethnic units, including half a dozen ethnic stakes.

The Church's influence among California's 30 million-plus inhabitants is strong. A recent Church-sponsored poll showed that virtually every Californian knows at least one Latter-day Saint, with more than a third describing their relationship as "close." The futures of both the state and the Church look bright. The influence of each throughout the world is increasing as they continue their long symbiotic relationship.

SOURCE

Cowan, Richard O., and William E Homer. *California Saints*. Provo, Utah: Religious Studies Center, Brigham Young University, 1996.

WILLIAM E. HOMER

CALIFORNIA VOLUNTEERS. The Third California Volunteers was a force dispatched from **California** to **Utah** in late 1862, ostensibly to guard the overland mail and telegraph routes. Led by Colonel **Patrick Edward Connor**, it numbered around 700 men. The soldiers' presence was a source of discomfort among the Latter-day Saints, particularly because **Brigham Young** had offered to guard the routes with local men. Many of the **Saints** believed that the volunteers had been sent to the territory for surveillance of **Mormon** activity and considered the soldiers' presence to be an affront to the Saints' national loyalty.

The volunteers established **Fort Douglas** directly east of **Salt Lake City** on 20 October 1862 and were involved in the early development of mining in the territory. They remained until the end of the **Civil War**, after which Fort Douglas continued to be used as a military installation for the **United States** government.

SOURCES

Allen, James B., and Glen M. Leonard. *The Story of the Latter-day Saints.* 2d ed. Salt Lake City: Deseret Book, 1992.

Madsen, Brigham D. *Glory Hunter: A Biography of Patrick Edward Connor.* Salt Lake City: University of Utah Press, 1990.

Roberts, B. H. *A Comprehensive History of The Church of Jesus Christ of Latter-day Saints, Century One.* 6 vols. Salt Lake City: The Church of Jesus Christ of Latter-day Saints, 1930. 5:15–18, 61–70.

MATTHEW P. WILLDEN

CALL, ANSON. Anson Call was a close associate of **Joseph Smith** and **Brigham Young**, an early **pioneer**, a rescuer of **handcart** companies, a defender against **Johnston's Army**, and a noted colonizer of the West. Born 13 May 1810 in Fletcher, **Vermont**, to Cyril Call and Sally Tiffany, Anson was baptized in 1836. He gathered with the **Saints** in **Kirtland, Ohio**, and suffered the persecutions of **Missouri** and **Illinois**. As a captain of 20 wagons, Anson arrived in the **Salt Lake Valley** in 1848, settled in Bountiful, **Utah**, and fulfilled a prophecy of Joseph Smith that he would be a great colonizer in the Rocky Mountains as the **Saints** gathered there. He helped colonize Davis, Iron, Millard, Tooele, and Box Elder Counties in Utah as well as **Carson Valley, Nevada**, and Callville, **Arizona**—now covered by Lake Mead.

Call served as **bishop, counselor** in the Davis **stake presidency**, judge, deputy marshal, territorial legislator, and president of agricultural, irrigation, and silk-producing companies. A husband of 6 wives, he fathered 23 children and adopted 2 **Indian** children before he died in Bountiful, Utah, 31 August 1890 at the age of 80.

———

SOURCES

Call, Anson. *The Life and Record of Anson Call.* Manuscript. LDS Church Historian's Office, Salt Lake City.

Call, Duane D. "Anson Call and His Contribution toward Latter-day Saint Colonization." Master's thesis, Brigham Young University, 1956.

Carlisle, Howard M. *Colonist Fathers, Corporate Sons: A Selective History of the Call Family.* Salt Lake City: Calls Trust, 1996.

KENNETH REY CALL

CALLIS, CHARLES A. Charles Albert Callis, **mission president** and member of the Quorum of the Twelve **Apostles**, was born 4 May 1865 in Dublin, **Ireland**. His father died at a young age, leaving Charles's mother to provide the best she could for their four young children. She moved to **Liverpool, England**, where she encountered the restored gospel, which changed her family's life forever. They immigrated to **America** with assistance from the **Perpetual Emigrating Fund** and settled successively in Bountiful, Farmington, and Coalville, **Utah**. Because of the necessity of providing a livelihood for the family, there was little time or funding for formal schooling.

Largely self-taught in law, "Charlie" began to pull himself out of a destitute and deprived childhood. His rise to prominence continued as he was elected Summit County's representative to the state legislature and later the county attorney. His political career was short lived in Utah because he accepted a series of **mission** calls from the Church: first to **Wyoming**, then to his native **Great Britain**, and finally, soon after his marriage to Grace Elizabeth Pack, to the **Southern States Mission**. His call to the South was for two years, but after a short stay he was selected to be the mission president and remained for more than 28 years. Pursuing his interest in law, President Callis passed the bar exams in three different states: Utah, **South Carolina**, and **Florida**. While he had little time to practice law, the stature of his accomplishments gave him respectability in social and legal circles. This helped him find friends for the Church. He was also able to legally defend several of his missionaries.

In 1933 he became an apostle, but he continued in his responsibilities in the South until a replacement could be called. Known Churchwide for his powerful and persuasive oratory, he gave a series of radio broadcasts on the tenets of the gospel.

A longtime dream was realized in January 1947 when **Elder** Callis organized the first **stake** in the southeastern United States at Jacksonville, Florida. What made the organization even more noteworthy was that it was completely staffed by local leaders. Remaining in Jacksonville, following the organization, he took care of ordinations, training, and other administrative responsibilities. While there, Elder Callis suffered a massive heart attack and died on 21 January 1947.

SOURCES

Flake, Lawrence R. *Prophets and Apostles of the Last Dispensation*. Provo, Utah: Religious Studies Center, Brigham Young University, 2001. 461.

Larsen, Kathleen Callis. *A Biography of Charles Albert Callis and Grace Elizabeth Park Callis*. Utah: s.n., 1974.

DAVID F. BOONE

CAMARGO, HELIO R. Helio da Rocha Camargo—formerly a captain in the Brazilian army, a banker, and a Methodist pastor—served in both the First and the Second **Quorums** of **Seventy**. Born 1 February 1926 in Rio de Janeiro, Helio entered a military academy at 17. While a soldier, he married Nair Belmira de Bouvea—with whom he had six children. Despite a debilitating gunshot wound, he achieved the rank of captain before his early retirement.

The Camargo family moved to São Paulo, where Helio began a banking career and entered the Methodist seminary. About three years into his studies, Reverend Camargo—now an ordained minister—invited two Mormon **missionaries** to explain their doctrines to his classmates during a course on the beliefs of other religions. Later, after he and two other students had been expelled for not conforming to the doctrine of infant baptism, Brother Camargo read the literature left with him by the missionaries, and his entire family eventually joined the Church.

Brother Camargo served as a **bishop, stake president, mission president in Brazil**—as did both of the other two students expelled from the seminary—and as a **regional representative**. Elder Camargo was sustained to the First Quorum of the Seventy 6 April 1985, and to the Second Quorum when it was created. During this time he served in the **South America** North **Area** presidency under **Elder F. Burton Howard**. He was released 6 October 1990.

SOURCES

Hart, John L. "New Callings: First Quorum of the Seventy." *Church News*, 16 June 1985. 4, 13.

1999–2000 Church Almanac. Salt Lake City: Deseret News, 1998. 77.

RICHARD D. MCCLELLAN

CAMBODIA. In the 1970s and 1980s, many Cambodian political refugees fled to **Thailand** and other countries of final resort. Latter-day Saint missionaries were called to teach the restored gospel among this population in the **United States** and elsewhere. In 1993, when political conditions allowed, President Larry R. White of the Thailand Bangkok **Mission**, in concert with **area** president John K. Carmack, made arrangements for **Welfare Services missionaries** to work in Phnom Penh, the capital city of Cambodia. Vichit Ith, a Cambodian member living in Bangkok, helped make the arrangements that led to official recognition of the Church, which came early in 1994. On 23 March 1994, missionaries Sharlene and Donald C. Dobson, who were transferred from the **India** Bangalore Mission, arrived in Phnom Penh with President White to begin humanitarian projects. Four days later they officially opened **missionary work**.

On 8 August 1994, four Cambodian-speaking **elders**—Richard W. Henderson, Jamie T. Hipwell, John T. Smith, and Brian W. Strong (all from different U.S. missions)—were transferred to Phnom Penh and immediately began teaching the gospel. Since that time, with the exception of a period of political turmoil in 1997, the Church has grown relatively rapidly. Cambodia became a mission in 1997, with Leland D. White as president. At the dawn of the year 2000 there were 1,018 members residing in five branches.

The most important event in Cambodian Church history was the visit of President **Gordon B. Hinckley** to Phnom Penh on 28–29 May 1996 and his dedication of the country for the preaching of the gospel.

SOURCES

Britsch, R. Lanier. *From the East: The History of the Latter-day Saints in Asia, 1851–1996.* Salt Lake City: Deseret Book, 1998. 407–13.
1999–2000 Church Almanac. Salt Lake City: Deseret News, 1998. 287.

R. LANIER BRITSCH

CAMEROON. The Republic of Cameroon is located on the western coast of **Africa** on the Gulf of Guinea, and its official languages are

French and English. Half of the population follows traditional religions; one-third of the people are Christian.

Prior to 1990, only a few Church members ever lived in Cameroon. Two couples from Canada were serving as missionaries in the country when the Church received legal recognition in September 1993. At this time about 30 people had already been baptized, and approximately 60 others were investigating the Church.

The Cameroon Yaounde **Mission** was created on 1 July 1992, with Robert L. Mercer as its first president. Mission headquarters were moved to Abidjan, **Ivory Coast**, on 18 May 1993. That same year **seminary** classes began for the youth in Cameroon. In 1996 a Church group was organized in Duoala. As of the year 2000 there were 194 members living in one **branch**.

SOURCES

1999–2000 Church Almanac. Salt Lake City: Deseret News, 1998. 287–88.

Oral histories of early Church converts collected by E. Dale LeBaron. Copies at BYU Library, Provo, Utah; LDS Church Historical Library, Salt Lake City, Utah.

E. DALE LEBARON

CAMPAIGN FOR THE PRESIDENCY, JOSEPH SMITH'S 1844. See PRESIDENTIAL CAMPAIGN OF JOSEPH SMITH.

CAMPBELLITES. The Campbellite ideology was a **restorationist** movement in the early nineteenth century that looked forward to the reestablishment of the ancient Christian church. It prepared many of the people in northern Ohio for the teachings of Mormonism. Their founder, Alexander Campbell, not only rejected all existing churches but denounced their creeds as being of human (not biblical) origins. His only creed was the **Bible**. Although Campbell believed that congregations who patterned their beliefs and worship after the New Testament church could refer to themselves as "churches of Christ," he suggested that his new restorationist movement could properly be called "Disciples of Christ." He vehemently opposed the use of the name "Campbellites" to identify the restoration movement he was leading. He insisted that true Christians should not be identified by names of human leaders.

Although **Sidney Rigdon** was influenced by Campbell in the 1820s, and his congregation in Mentor, Ohio, was one of the first groups to be expelled from a Baptist alliance for embracing Campbell's views, Rigdon refused to support Campbell in 1830 when he initiated a new quest to restore ancient Christianity. The two men disagreed on a number of key issues, such as employment of communal societies and gifts of the spirit. Instead of uniting with the Disciples, in November 1830 Rigdon joined a new movement led by Joseph Smith; soon after many other Campbellites converted to Mormonism in Mentor and **Kirtland, Ohio.**

SOURCES

Backman, Milton V., Jr. *Christian Churches of America: Origins and Beliefs.* New York: Charles Scribner's Sons, 1983.

———. "The Quest for a Restoration: The Birth of Mormonism in Ohio." *BYU Studies* 12 (Summer 1972): 346–64.

MILTON V. BACKMAN JR.

CAMP DOUGLAS, UTAH. See FORT DOUGLAS.

CAMP FLOYD, UTAH.

In the summer of 1858, several thousand federal soldiers established Camp Floyd in Cedar Valley, west of Utah Lake. A year earlier the men had been sent from **Fort Leavenworth** by President **James Buchanan** to put down a reported rebellion of **Mormons** in **Utah** Territory. After a peace treaty rendered their presence unnecessary, they were posted to Cedar Valley to build and guard emigrant roads and keep peace with **Native Americans**. The camp differed from most forts of the time in that it was linear in layout rather than rectangular, enclosing a central square. The post was also the headquarters for the army's Department of Utah. In 1860, a reassignment of the troops began as men were called into service in the **Civil War**. By the end of 1861, the post stood empty. All that is left is the military cemetery and a restored commissary building housing a modest museum.

SOURCES

Godfrey, Audrey M. "A Social History of Camp Floyd, Utah Territory, 1858–1861." Master's thesis, Utah State University, 1989.

Moorman, Donald R. *Camp Floyd and the Mormons: The Utah War.* Salt Lake City: University of Utah Press, 1992.

AUDREY M. GODFREY

CAMP OF ISRAEL. See PIONEERS.

CANADA. Canada was the first country outside the United States to hear the message of the **Restoration.** Missionaries first preached in British North **America** (what is now Canada) within a year of the **organization of the Church.** In the summer of 1832, missionaries to Upper Canada (**Ontario**) included Phineas Young, Eleazer Miller, Enos Curtis, and Elial Strong. **Joseph Smith** himself visited Mt. Pleasant, Brantford, and other areas west of Toronto in 1833 and said of his visit there, "We hope that great good may yet be done in Canada which O Lord grant for thy name's sake" (journal). Two of the most successful of these early missionaries were **John E. Page**, who baptized almost 1,000 people in the upper Rideau Canada/Lanark County regions in 1836 and 1837, and **Parley P. Pratt.** **Elder** Pratt was instrumental in the conversion of British-born **John Taylor** and **Joseph Fielding** and his sisters, Mary and Mercy, and in doing so opened "an effectual door" for **missionary work** in the **British Isles.**

Missionaries also sought out friends, **family**, and listeners in the southern townships of Lower Canada (**Quebec**) and in the maritime provinces of **Nova Scotia**, **New Brunswick**, and **Prince Edward Island**, where several small **branches** were organized in the 1840s.

With the call to gather with the Church, the **Mormon** presence dwindled dramatically in eastern Canada such that by 1861 the official Canadian census counted only 74 Latter-day **Saints** in all of Ontario. Over the next several years, Church membership in Eastern Canada lapsed into near oblivion.

Meanwhile, shortly after the constitutional birth of the country in 1867, President John Taylor dispatched **Charles Ora Card** to western Canada in 1886 and 1887 to establish a new settlement free from the **antipolygamy** raids in **Utah** and **anti-Mormon** hysteria of the time. Card successfully formed a small Mormon colony on Lee's Creek, some 125 miles south of Calgary. The Mormon presence soon flourished from a few hundred settlers near **Cardston** to almost 10,000 in 1911, living in nearby southern **Alberta** "Mormon towns" such as Raymond, Stirling, Taber, Glenwood, and Kimball. Alberta missionaries fanned out from Cardston to **Saskatchewan** and **Manitoba** in the east and to **British Columbia** in the west. Gradually Latter-day Saints became well respected for their hard work and industry in building an economy based on ranching, **sugar** beet farming, and canal building. The Church established the Canadian Mission in 1919, and President **Heber J. Grant** dedicated the **Cardston Alberta Temple** in 1923.

The Canadian west became a marvelous nursery of leadership and inspiration as second and third generation Alberta Saints pursued their careers in Canadian cities from coast to coast. A symbol of this more recent growth was the dedication of a second Canadian temple in Toronto, Ontario, in 1990. Several prominent Canadians have served the Church, including N. **Eldon Tanner**, **Hugh B. Brown**, **Ardeth G. Kapp**, **Elaine L. Jack**, **Victor L. Brown**, and Alexander B. Morrison.

At the beginning of the year 2000, in this benevolent country of wide cultural and linguistic diversities and a population of more than 30 million, the Church counted 156,575 members and 44 **stakes** (19 in Alberta), with 454 wards and branches. Whether in Yellowstone, Northwest Territories, in Sudbury, Ontario, or in Cranbrook, **Newfoundland**, the Canadian Saint is a study in faith, tolerance, loyalty, and courage, meeting the challenges of sparse membership, vast distances, extremes in climate, and religious misunderstanding. In 1999 the Church dedicated temples in Halifax, Regina, and Edmonton, and the following year one in Montreal.

Sources

Bennett, Richard E. "A Study of The Church of Jesus Christ of Latter-day Saints in Upper Canada, 1830–1850." Master's thesis, Brigham Young University, 1975.

Card, Brigham Young. et al., eds. *The Mormon Presence in Canada*. Edmonton: University of Alberta Press, 1990.

Smith, Joseph, Jr. Journal. 17–22 October 1833. LDS Church Historical Department, Salt Lake City.

Tagg, Melvin S. "A History of The Church of Jesus Christ of Latter-day Saints in Canada, 1830–1963." Ph.D. diss., Brigham Young University, 1963.

RICHARD E. BENNETT

CANARY ISLANDS. See SPAIN.

CANE CREEK MASSACRE. On Sunday 10 August 1884 at Cane Creek, **Tennessee**, a mob attacked the home of James Condor, killing two missionaries and two members of the Condor family. James Condor's son, Martin, and stepson, James Hudson, were killed while trying to defend Elders John H. Gibbs and William S. Berry, who were also killed. James Condor's wife was shot through the hip, crippling her for life. Six days later Elder **B. H. Roberts**, the assistant president of the mission, risked his life by going to Cane Creek in disguise and retrieving the bodies of the deceased missionaries. The bodies were then sent to **Utah** for burial.

The massacre was the result of a false report of a purported Mormon

Bishop West speaking treason against the United States in an article entitled "Red Hot address" that was published in the *Salt Lake Tribune* 15 March 1884 and circulated throughout the nation.

SOURCES

Roberts, B. H. *A Comprehensive History of The Church of Jesus Christ of Latter-day Saints, Century One.* 6 vols. Salt Lake City: The Church of Jesus Christ of Latter-day Saints, 1930.

The Tennessee Massacre and Its Causes; or The Utah Conspiracy, A Lecture by John Nicholson. Salt Lake City: Juvenile Instructors Office, 1884.

CALVIN R. STEPHENS

CANNON, ABRAHAM H.

Though his life was short, Abraham Hoagland Cannon became an influential member of the **Quorum** of the Twelve **Apostles**. He was born 12 March 1859 while his father, **Elder George Q. Cannon**, was absent from **Salt Lake City** on a mission to the eastern states. At age 21 Abraham served as a missionary in **England**, **Germany**, and **Switzerland**. Following his return to **Utah**, he was sustained 8 October 1882, at the age of 23, as a member of the First Council of the **Seventy** and seven years later, 7 October 1889, as one of the Twelve Apostles.

Elder Cannon was closely associated with the operation and publication of the *Juvenile Instructor* and *Contributor* **magazines** and also with the *Deseret News.* Thousands of readers enjoyed his articles.

Elder Cannon's sudden death on 19 July 1896 (age 37) in Salt Lake City was a shock to the citizens of Utah and to the **Saints** everywhere. President **Wilford Woodruff** received a special manifestation that Elder Cannon had been called to perform a great mission in the spirit world. He recorded: "The Spirit of God rested upon me at the close of this manifestation in a powerful manner and bore testimony to me of the truth of the revelation to me concerning Abraham H. Cannon" (quoted in Cowley, 579).

SOURCES

Cowley, Matthias F. *Wilford Woodruff: History of His Life and Labors.* Salt Lake City: Bookcraft, 1964.

Flake, Lawrence R. *Prophets and Apostles of the Last Dispensation.* Provo, Utah: Religious Studies Center, Brigham Young University, 2001. 415.

Jenson, Andrew. *Latter-day Saint Biographical Encyclopedia.* 4 vols 1901–36. Reprint, Salt Lake City. Western Epics, 1971. 1:167.

LAWRENCE R. FLAKE

CANNON, ANGUS M. As Salt Lake **Stake president** for 28 years, Angus Munn Cannon had a profound impact on the Church, the community, and his **family**. The second son and fourth child of George Cannon and Ann Quayle, he was born in **Liverpool, England**, 17 May 1834. **Elder John Taylor**, who had married Leonora, Angus's aunt, converted the family and baptized them on 11 February 1840. The family sailed from Liverpool in September 1842. After six weeks his mother died and was buried at sea. When his father also died in 1844, Angus lived with his sister, Mary Alice, and her husband, Charles Lambert, after arriving in **Nauvoo**. As one of the last to leave Nauvoo, Angus experienced the **miracle of the quail**. At **Winter Quarters** he helped build a house to provide shelter for the family. They arrived in **Salt Lake City** in early 1849.

At first Angus worked as a farmer and woodcutter but later supported his family through ranching and mining. In 1854 Angus received a **mission** call to serve in the eastern **United States**. As a consequence of the **Utah War**, he was called home in 1858. Later that summer he married two sisters he had met in **Delaware**, Ann Amanda and Sarah Maria Mousley. He was called to the "**Cotton Mission**" and thereby helped settle **St. George**. He returned to Salt Lake in 1867 because of ill health. Ten years later he was called as president of the Salt Lake Stake, which then included Salt Lake, Tooele, Davis, Morgan, Summit, and Wasatch Counties. His presidency established many significant precedents for Church policy. Angus married four more wives in the 1870s and 1880s: Clarissa Cordelia Moses Mason, Martha Hughes, Maria Bennion, and Johanna Danielsen. As a polygamist he was convicted of unlawful cohabitation and served six months in the penitentiary.

In 1904 Angus was released as stake president and called as **patriarch**. He died 7 June 1915 in Salt Lake City, and his funeral services were held in the Assembly Hall on **Temple Square**, a building he had helped to erect.

Sources

"Angus M. Cannon: Frustrated Mormon Miner." *Utah Historical Quarterly* 57 (Winter 1989): 36–45.

Cannon, Donald Q. "Angus M. Cannon: Pioneer, President, Patriarch." *Supporting Saints: Life Stories of Nineteenth-Century Mormons.* Edited by Donald Q. Cannon and David Whittaker. Provo, Utah: Brigham Young University, 1985. 369–401.

Donald Q. Cannon

CANNON, ELAINE A. Elaine Anderson Cannon, general president of the **Young Women** organization from 1978 to 1984, was born 9 April 1922 in **Salt Lake City**. She served on the Church **Correlation** Committee and worked extensively with college-age adults as a leader in the **Latter-day Saints Student Association** and in organizing the Church's sorority, **Lambda Delta Sigma**. She was also a catalyst in moving forward Church programs for youth.

Soon after her marriage to D. James Cannon in 1943, Elaine was women's editor of the *Deseret News,* as well as a daily columnist. While rearing her six children, she continued to write. She was a newspaper reporter, wrote for a weekly television program in 1949, and did freelance work for such national magazines as *Seventeen* and *Better Homes and Gardens.* In 1959 she became an associate editor for "Era of Youth," a section of the *Improvement Era* that finally led to the publication of the *New Era* in 1971. Remaining active in writing and public speaking, she published more than 50 books.

Sister Cannon's service as general president of the Young Women is remembered as a time of simplification. The general board became smaller, and the Church's consolidated Sunday meeting schedule led to a more spiritual focus in the Young Women's lessons.

SOURCE

Peterson, Janet, and LaRene Gaunt. *Keepers of the Flame: General Presidents of the Young Women.* Salt Lake City: Deseret Book, 1993.

CYNTHIA DOXEY

CANNON, FRANK J. Frank J. Cannon, son of **George Q. Cannon** of the **First Presidency**, was a prominent newspaper editor, a founder of Utah's **Republican Party**, the state's first senator, and a popular speaker. He became the state's **Democratic Party** chair, and in his later life, founder of the **anti-Mormon American Party**. He also wrote two widely read books criticizing the Church.

Cannon was born in **Salt Lake City** on 25 January 1859, the same year his father became a member of the **Quorum** of the Twelve **Apostles**. He was a good student who, though timid as a youth, developed fine oratorical skills. After graduating from the **University of Deseret**, he moved to **Ogden** and secured employment in the Weber County Recorders Office. Discovering that he possessed writing skills, he worked at the *Juvenile Instructor's* office, edited the *Logan Journal,* was a reporter for the

San Francisco Chronicle, and after the turn of the twentieth century, edited the *Salt Lake Tribune.* Active in politics, he was the **Utah** territorial delegate to Congress in the 1890s. His service was rewarded when **statehood** came to Utah, inasmuch as he was elected, along with Arthur Brown, to the **United States** Senate.

After the death of his father, Frank began to write articles critical of **Joseph F. Smith** and other Church leaders. After reading these, William G. Rachlon filed charges against Cannon, who was tried before a Church court and excommunicated on 15 March 1905. Moving to Denver, Cannon lectured against the Church and wrote anti-Mormon literature, including *Under the Prophet in Utah* and *Brigham Young and His Mormon Empire.* He died 25 July 1933 in Denver, and his body was brought back to Utah and buried in the Ogden Cemetery 30 July.

SOURCE

Godfrey, Kenneth W. "Frank J. Cannon: Declension in the Mormon Kingdom." *Differing Visions: Dissenters in Mormon History.* Edited by Roger D. Launius and Linda Thatcher. Urbana: University of Illinois Press, 1994. 241–61.

KENNETH W. GODFREY

CANNON, GEORGE Q. George Quayle Cannon, **counselor** in the **First Presidency**, missionary, statesman, author, and business magnate, was eulogized by newspapers across the nation as second only to **Brigham Young** in having an impact in the transformation of **Utah** from a sage-covered prairie to a prosperous state of the Union (*Missionary Years,* 6).

President Cannon was born 11 January 1827 in **Liverpool, England**, where his **family** was converted to the gospel when he was 12. Immigrating to **Nauvoo**, George lived through the drama of the persecutions and **martyrdom** of **Joseph Smith** and moved to the West with the first large company of **Saints** in 1847. On this journey he met 12-year-old Elizabeth Hoagland, whom he later married. In 1849 Brigham Young called him to accompany a group of missionaries to **California** to obtain much-needed funds for the Church by digging gold. From **San Francisco** he set sail to **Hawaii** to fulfill the second of five **missions**, which would last a total of 15 years.

After a five-year absence, Elder Cannon returned to **Salt Lake Valley** and married his sweetheart. They then left on another mission to San Francisco, this time to publish the *Western Standard,* a newspaper defending Mormonism. A few weeks after his return, Brother Cannon was called to serve a mission in the East and became the chief executive in the Church's mammoth emigration operation. It was during this eastern mission that he learned of his calling to the **Quorum** of the Twelve **Apostles**. He was ordained an apostle upon his return to **Salt Lake City**, 26 August 1860. He served his fifth mission in **Great Britain** as president of the **European Mission**, returning to Utah in 1864 and serving as private secretary to Brigham Young for three years. In the winter of 1864–65, he devoted his outstanding executive talents to the organization of the **Sunday School**, the far-reaching influence of which is incalculable. In connection with this endeavor, he began the publication of the *Juvenile Instructor*. He also edited the *Deseret News*. During the period from 1867 to 1882, Elder Cannon was engaged in various political activities, including many trips to **Washington, D.C.**, in pursuit of **statehood** for Utah. He also served five terms as a U.S. Congressman. His political career ended in 1882 when his seat in the House of Representatives was denied him because of his acceptance and practice of **plural marriage**. Elder Cannon served as counselor to four presidents of the Church: Brigham Young (1873–77), **John Taylor** (1880–87), **Wilford Woodruff** (1889–98), and **Lorenzo Snow** (1898–1901). He died 12 April 1901 in Monterey, California.

SOURCES

Bitton, Davis. *George Q. Cannon: A Biography.* Salt Lake City: Deseret Book, 1999.

Cannon, Donald Q. "George Q. Cannon and the British Mission." *BYU Studies* 27 (Winter 1987): 97–112.

Flake, Lawrence R. *George Q. Cannon: His Missionary Years.* Salt Lake City: Bookcraft, 1998.

———. *Prophets and Apostles of the Last Dispensation.* Provo, Utah: Brigham Young University, 2001. 181.

LAWRENCE R. FLAKE

CANNON, HUGH J. Hugh Jenne Cannon, a long-serving local ecclesiastical leader in **Utah** who also ministered around the globe, was born in **Salt Lake City** 19 January 1870 to President **George Q. Cannon** and Sarah Jenne Cannon.

Cannon's first mission to **Germany** ended when he escorted the remains of his brother, David, home to Utah. He later returned as president of the German Mission from 1901 to 1905 and again presided over the Swiss-German Mission from 1925 to 1928. In Salt Lake, he served

27 years on the **Sunday School** general board and presided over the Liberty Utah Stake for 20 years (1905–25).

A manager of his father's publishing company, he edited the *Juvenile Instructor* and then served as managing editor of the *Improvement Era* from 1928 until his death. From 1920 to 1921, he accompanied Elder **David O. McKay** on an unprecedented tour of world missions, which was marked by miraculous experiences. Hugh J. Cannon died in Salt Lake City 6 October 1931.

SOURCES

Cannon, Hugh J. "Around-the-World Travels of David O. McKay and Hugh J. Cannon." Manuscript. LDS Church Archives, Salt Lake City. 1925.

Jenson, Andrew. *Latter-day Saint Biographical Encyclopedia.* 4 vols. 1901–36. Reprint, Salt Lake City: Western Epics, 1971. 4:233, 507.

JOHN THOMAS

CANNON, LUCY G. As president of the **Young Women**'s Mutual Improvement Association from 1937 to 1948, Lucy Grant Cannon implemented programs which organized young women into age groups; introduced new manuals, incentive programs, and annual themes; and increased young women's participation in recreational activities. She had previously served in the YWMIA presidency as first counselor to **Ruth May Fox** (1923–29) and second counselor to **Martha Horne Tingey** (1929–37). Born 22 October 1880 in **Salt Lake City** to **Heber J. Grant** and Lucy Stringham, she served a mission to the Western States in 1901 and married George Jenkins Cannon 26 June 1902. They had seven children. Lucy died 27 May 1966 in Salt Lake City.

SOURCES

Evans, Joyce O., et al. *A Century of Sisterhood, 1869–1969.* Salt Lake City: Deseret Book, 1970.

Jenson, Andrew. *Latter-day Saint Biographical Encyclopedia.* 4 vols. 1901–36. Reprint, Salt Lake City: Western Epics, 1971. 4:256.

Josephson, Marba C. *History of YWMIA.* Salt Lake City: Deseret Book, 1956.

MARY JANE WOODGER

CANNON, MARTHA HUGHES. Martha Maria Hughes Cannon, a physician and the first female elected state senator in the **United States**, was born near Llandudno, **Wales**, 1 July 1857. The daughter of converts Peter and Elizabeth Evans Hughes, "Mattie" accompanied her parents to **Utah** in 1861.

After earning degrees from the **University of Deseret** (1875), the University of **Michigan** (M.D., 1880), and the University of **Pennsylvania** (1882), Cannon served as resident physician at the **Deseret Hospital** from 1882 to 1886. On 6 October 1884, she married Salt Lake **Stake president Angus M. Cannon**, the fourth of his six plural wives. They had three children: Elizabeth, James, and Gwendolyn.

As a young woman, Mattie served as secretary of the Tenth **Ward Retrenchment** Society and the **Sunday School. Mary Isabelle Horne** described her as a faithful member of the Church throughout her life.

On 3 November 1896, Mattie was one of five "at large" **Democratic** candidates elected to the state senate from Salt Lake County. The race attracted national attention because she defeated her husband, Angus, who was one of the **Republican** candidates. In her two terms she concentrated on public health and safety issues.

After leaving political life, she divided her time between Utah and **California**. She died in **Los Angeles** 10 July 1932. A statue of Cannon was unveiled in the Utah State Capitol rotunda 24 July 1996.

SOURCES

Cannon, Janath. "Taking the Great Plan Into Consideration: Martha Hughes Cannon." *Heroines of the Restoration*. Edited by Barbara B. Smith and Blythe Darlyn Thatcher. Salt Lake City: Bookcraft, 1997. 242–58.

Leiber, Constance L., and John Sillito, eds. *Letters from Exile: The Correspondence of Martha Hughes and Angus M. Cannon*. Salt Lake City: Signature Books, 1989.

White, Jean Bickmore. "Dr. Martha Hughes Cannon: Doctor, Wife, Legislator, Exile." *Sister Saints*. Edited by Vicky Burgess-Olson. Provo, Utah: Brigham Young University Press, 1978. 383–95

CONSTANCE L. LIEBER AND JOHN SILLITO

CANNON, SYLVESTER QUAYLE. Before his call as an **apostle** in 1938, Sylvester Quayle Cannon served as **Salt Lake City** engineer (1913–25), **stake president** (1917–25), **presiding bishop** (1925–38), and associate to the Quorum of the Twelve **Apostles** (1938–39).

Born in Salt Lake City 10 June 1877 to George Q. and Elizabeth Hoagland Cannon, Sylvester earned a degree in mining engineering from **Massachusetts** Institute of Technology (1899). He served a mission in **Belgium** (1899) and two terms as president of the Netherlands-Belgium

Mission (1900–02 and 1907–09). Cannon worked as a mining engineer from 1902 to 1905, principally on Cannon **family** properties. During the following years, he supervised hydrographic and irrigation surveys of the Weber River system for the **Utah** State Engineers office (1905–07). After returning from **Holland** in 1909, he resumed the practice of hydraulic and irrigation engineering. Following service as Salt Lake City's water supply engineer (1912–13), he was hired as city engineer.

In this capacity, he supervised improvements such as streets, waterworks, and sewers, and he played a pivotal role in the development of a zoning system and in the control of air pollution. His service as presiding bishop coincided with the boom days of the late 1920s and the stock market crash and partial economic revival of the **great depression**. He worked with stake presidents, the **Relief Society** general presidency, and state and local governments in providing relief to Latter-day **Saints** and other Utah citizens. In 1930 he chaired a state committee to investigate the cause of recurrent flooding on the Wasatch Front. He died in Salt Lake City, 29 May 1943.

SOURCES

Alexander, Thomas G. "Sylvester Q. Cannon and the Revival of Environmental Consciousness in the Mormon Community." *Environmental History.* 3 (October 1998): 448–507.

Cannon, Sylvester Q. *Torrential Floods in Northern Utah, 1930.* Agricultural Experiment Station Circular 92. Logan, Utah: Utah State Agricultural College, 1931.

Cannon, Winfield Q. Oral history interview by Thomas G. Alexander, 25 April 1995.

Lyman, Richard R., R. A. Hart, and R. K. Brown. "American Society of Civil Engineers, Memoir, Sylvester Quayle Cannon." Photocopy in author's possession.

1997–1998 Church Almanac. Salt Lake City: Deseret News, 1997.

THOMAS G. ALEXANDER

CAPE VERDE. Cape Verde is a collection of volcanic islands in the Atlantic Ocean, several hundred miles off the west coast of **Africa**. They were heavily forested (verde) and uninhabited when the Portuguese and their **black** African slaves settled there in the 1400s. These islands are now dry, barren, wind swept, and economically depressed. The people, language, and culture blend aspects of **Portugal** and West Africa. The first Latter-day Saint missionaries to Cape Verde came from the **Spain** Las Palmas **Mission** in January 1989. In September 1994 **Elder Dallin H. Oaks** dedicated Cape Verde for the preaching of the gospel. President **Gordon B. Hinckley** visited the **Saints** of this region in February 1998.

In addition to the many people who have joined the Church on the islands, many Cape Verdeans have joined the Church in places to which they have immigrated, principally the **United States** and Portugal. By the beginning of the year 2000 the country had about 3,893 members in 19 **branches**.

SOURCES

"Cape Verde Dedicated." *Church News*, 24 September 1994, 3, 5.
"President Hinckley Uplifts Members in Nova Scotia, Africa, Northern Mexico." *Ensign* 28 (February 1998): 113–14.

MARJORIE DRAPER CONDER

CARD, CHARLES O. Charles Ora Card, often called "Canada's **Brigham Young**" for his efforts in the Latter-day Saint colonization of southern Alberta (Godfrey, title), was born 5 November 1839 in Ossian Township, Allegany County, **New York**. Growing up in New York and **Michigan**, he was baptized 12 April 1856, just before his **family** moved to **Salt Lake City**.

Card moved to **Logan, Utah**, in 1859, where he worked as a miller, built roads and canals, served as a selectman, and supervised the building of the Logan **Tabernacle** and **Logan Temple**. He was called to serve as the Cache Stake president in 1884.

After being arrested in 1885 for practicing **polygamy**, Card was called by President **John Taylor** to colonize southern **Alberta, Canada**. The town of **Cardston, Alberta**, was named in his honor. From 1886 to 1903, Card served as **stake** president of the Alberta Stake, supervising the building of roads, communities, and an extensive irrigation canal system. In addition, he established ties for the Church with numerous influential political and business dignitaries and made fast friends with leaders on the nearby Blood **Indian** Reservation.

Card was married to Sarah Jane "Sally" Birdneau (later divorced), Sarah Jane Painter, Zina Young Williams, and Lavinia Clark Rigby. When his health failed, he moved back to Utah, where he died in Logan 9 September 1906.

SOURCES

Card, Brigham Y., and Donald G. Godfrey. *The Diaries of Charles Ora Card: The Canadian Years, 1886–1903*. Salt Lake City: University of Utah Press, 1993.
Godfrey, Donald G. "Canada's 'Brigham Young': Charles Ora Card, Southern Alberta Pioneer." *American Review of Canadian Studies* 17 (1988): 223–38.

Hudson, A. James. *Charles Ora Card: Pioneer and Colonizer.* Master's thesis, Brigham Young University, 1961.

Laura D.L. Card

CARDSTON, ALBERTA. Fleeing **plural marriage** prosecution in **Utah**, 47-year-old **Charles Ora Card** founded the southern **Alberta**, Canada, town of Cardston in June 1887. With wife Zina Young Williams, Card and eight other families built log homes and dugouts on Lee's Creek, two miles southwest of its mouth on the St. Mary's River and immediately south of ground reserved for the Blood **Indian** Band of the Blackfoot Confederacy. Card had initially dedicated some land south between the Waterton and Belly Rivers during an earlier scouting mission. On returning with his vanguard group he discovered that their original site was unavailable. Being informed by locals of a site on Lee's Creek forfeited by a leaseholder, they found good soil, healthy grass, as well as a nearby coal vein, and soon substantiated their settler's claim on the property with government officials in Lethbridge.

The Cardston **stake** was organized 9 June 1895 as the 35th stake in the Church, with C. O. Card as president. A second stake in Cardston proper would not be organized until 1983.

The **pioneers** brought unique irrigation and cooperative experience that did not go unnoticed. Though early united order efforts were not successful, agricultural and business ventures prospered. In 1898, Church leaders at **Salt Lake City** contracted to build a large irrigation canal, which encouraged immigration and stimulated the development of additional **Mormon** communities.

The 1923 dedication of the **Cardston Alberta Temple**, the first outside the **United States**, identified Cardston as the spiritual hub for **Latter-day Saints** in Western **Canada**. In spite of its seminal place in Latter-day Saint history, Cardston retains a modest agricultural and educational economy, exporting youth to larger Canadian cities to further business, education, and professional opportunities.

Sources

Bates, Jane E. W. *Founding of Cardston and Vicinity: Pioneer Problems.* Compiled by Zine Woolf Hickman. Salt Lake City: William L. Woolf, 1960.

Rosenvall, Lynn A. "The Transfer of Mormon Culture to Alberta." *Essays on the Historical Geography of the Canadian West.* Edited by Lynn A. Rosenvall and S. M. Evans. Calgary, Alberta: University of Clagary, 1987. 122–44.

Tagg, Melvin S. *A History of the Mormon Church in Canada.* Lethbridge, Alberta.: 1968.

John P. Livingstone

CARDSTON ALBERTA TEMPLE. Located in **Cardston, Alberta, Canada**, the Cardston Alberta Temple was the first Latter-day Saint temple built outside of the **United States**. On 8 October 1888, one year after **Mormon** settlers had founded Cardston, Elder **John W. Taylor** prophesied a temple on the low western hill.

The **First Presidency** directed that this **temple** would depart from traditional design, having no towers. Architects Hyrum Pope and Harold Burton were strongly influenced by Frank Lloyd Wright. Adorned with beautiful woods, the four endowment lecture rooms form the arms of a Maltese cross projecting outward from the elevated central celestial room. The building measures 165 feet square by 110 feet high. President **Joseph F. Smith** dedicated the site 27 July 1913, and ground was broken the following 9 November. The temple was dedicated 26 August 1923 by President **Heber J. Grant**.

Remarkable spiritual experiences during the 25-year administration of Edward G. Wood, the first temple president, have become well known. "Automobile caravans" to the temple strengthened **Saints** throughout the Northwest.

Subsequent additions expanded the temple's capacity and enhanced its efficiency. Following extensive renovations, the temple was rededicated 22 June 1991 by President **Gordon B. Hinckley**.

In 1995, the **Cardston Alberta Temple** was officially named a Canadian Historic Site. The commemorative plaque recognized the temple as "the first consciously modern building in the province of Alberta."

SOURCES

Cowan, Richard O. *Temples to Dot the Earth*. Springville, Utah: Cedar Fort, 1997. 121–26, 262.

Wood, V. A. *The Alberta Temple: Centre and Symbol of Faith*. Calgary: Detselig Enterprises, 1989.

RICHARD O. COWAN

CARELESS, GEORGE. George Edward Percy Careless (1839–1932), a musical pioneer in the early days of the Church, was given the title "Chief Musician of the Church" by President **Brigham Young** in 1865. Born in London, **England**, 24 September 1839, George was a child musical prodigy, self-taught on the violin and possessing a clear soprano voice. He joined the Church in 1850 at age 11. In 1859 he began formal studies at the Royal Academy of Music in London, completing their four-year course in only three years. In 1862 he began playing professionally in the London area under many great conductors. He also led the Goswell Branch choir for the Church.

George emigrated to the **Salt Lake Valley**, arriving 3 November 1864. In addition to his 11 years as director of the **Tabernacle Choir** (1869–80), he brought professional status to the **Salt Lake Theater** Orchestra and founded both the Careless Concert Orchestra in 1879 and the Careless Opera Company in 1885. To the **Saints** in the **Salt Lake Valley**, he introduced the music of Haydn, Rossini, and Weber; brought the first performance of Handel's *Messiah* (1875); and presented some of the first full-scale productions of the new operettas of Gilbert and Sullivan. During his lifetime he composed more than 80 hymn settings, nine of which were used in the 1985 Latter-day Saint hymnbook. George Careless died on 16 December 1932 in **Salt Lake City**.

SOURCES

Davidson, Karen Lynn. *Our Latter-day Saint Hymns: The Stories and the Messages.* Salt Lake City: Deseret Book, 1988. 353.

Jenson, Andrew. *Latter-day Saint Biographical Encyclopedia.* 4 vols. 1901–36. Reprint, Salt Lake City: Western Epics, 1971. 1:738–39.

Maxwell, David. "'The Morning Breaks': George Careless, Musical Pioneer." *Ensign* 14 (February 1984): 47–50.

GERALD L. HOMER

CARRINGTON, ALBERT. Albert Carrington, **apostle** and **counselor** to **Brigham Young**, was born 8 January 1813, at Royalton, **Vermont**, only a few miles from the birthplace of **Joseph Smith**, but he did not meet the **Prophet** until 1844, shortly before the Prophet's **martyrdom**. Albert was baptized in July 1841 while living in Wiota, **Wisconsin**. Brother Carrington went west with the **Saints** and was elected city clerk, historian, and postmaster in Salt Lake City. A graduate of Dartmouth College and trained in law, he chaired the committee that drafted the constitution for the provisional **State of Deseret**, served in the legislature of **Utah** Territory, helped survey the Great Salt Lake, and worked as editor of the *Deseret News* for eight years.

Elder Carrington rendered valuable service to the Church in Utah and abroad as a member of the **Quorum** of the Twelve (1870–73, 1877–85) and as an additional counselor to President Brigham Young (1873–77). Four times during the period from 1868 to 1882 he served two-year terms as president of the **European Mission**. In 1872 he journeyed throughout **Europe** and **Asia Minor** with **George A. Smith** of the

First Presidency, apostle **Lorenzo Snow**, and others under assignment from President Brigham Young.

In November 1885 he was tried by his fellow apostles, found guilty of transgression, and excommunicated. In 1887 he was rebaptized and two years later, on 19 September 1889, he died in Salt Lake City.

SOURCES

"Albert Carrington." *Encyclopedia of Mormonism.* Edited by Daniel H. Ludlow. 4 vols. New York: Macmillan, 1992. 4:1634.

Flake, Lawrence R. *Prophets and Apostles of the Last Dispensation.* Provo, Utah: Religious Studies Center, Brigham Young University, 2001. 293.

Jenson, Andrew. *Latter-day Saint Biographical Encyclopedia.* 4 vols. 1901–36. Reprint, Salt Lake City: Western Epics, 1971. 1:126.

LAWRENCE R. FLAKE

CARROLL COUNTY, MISSOURI. See DEWITT, MISSOURI.

CARSON, KIT. One of the best-known trappers of the Rocky Mountains, Kit Carson began trapping out of Santa Fe in 1826. In the 1830s he moved into the northern and central Rockies, and he spent the winter of 1833 to 1834 near what is now Ouray, **Utah**. His trapping routes covered most of the western states, and from 1838 to 1841 he spent considerable time in the vicinity of Brown's Hole and the Uintah Basin. He was the guide for **John C. Frémont** from 1843 to 1844, during which time he explored the Great Salt Lake. It was from Frémont's reports that Carson was catapulted into national fame.

SOURCES

Carter, Harvey L. "Kit Carson." *The Mountain Men and the Fur Trade of the Far West.* Edited by LeRoy Hafen. 10 vols. Glendale, Calif.: Arthur H. Clark, 1966–72. 105–31.

Quaife, Milo M. *Kit Carson's Autobiography.* Lincoln: University of Nebraska Press, 1965.

FRED R. GOWANS AND KERRY OMAN

CARSON VALLEY, NEVADA. Carson Valley, a fertile grassland oasis at the foot of the Carson Range, became the site of the first white settlement in what is now the state of **Nevada**. In 1849 Hampton Beatie and six other Latter-day **Saints** traveling with a company of **gold**-seekers from

Salt Lake City to California opted to remain in the Carson Valley, building a trading post there for other California-bound pioneers. Beatie's one-story log cabin was the first known structure built in what became Nevada. Beatie brought merchandise and cattle from Placerville, California, and sold the supplies to travelers preparing to cross the Sierra Nevada mountains. He sold the post after three months to Stephen Moore and returned to the Salt Lake Valley. There, he shared his experiences with his new employer, John Reese, who set out for Carson Valley with 19 other men and 10 to 12 wagon loads of goods, arriving in the summer of 1851. Reese purchased the site from Moore for $20 and paid the neighboring Washoe tribe two sacks of flour for land rights. The Carson Valley Post became known as Mormon Station.

The population grew as families from Utah were called to settle the area. In 1854 the Utah territorial legislature organized Carson County. Brigham Young appointed apostle Orson Hyde to serve as the probate judge and create the Carson Stake of Zion. Because the Carson Valley and Mountain Range reminded Elder Hyde of Genoa, Italy, when the township of Mormon Station was surveyed its name was changed to Genoa. Approximately 65 families were settled in the Valley in 1856.

The following year, Brigham Young called many of the Saints back to the Salt Lake Valley in preparation for the approach of Johnston's Army. About 450 Saints from Genoa responded, leaving approximately 200 members in the Carson Valley. The exodus left the region without an effective government. In 1861, the U.S. Congress created the territory of Nevada, which included the Carson Valley.

Genoa is the oldest town in the state of Nevada. It remained the county seat until 1915. The Nevada State Division of State Parks has reconstructed the county courthouse into a museum and the original site of Mormon Station is a state historic park.

SOURCES

Jenson, Andrew. *Latter-day Saint Biographical Encyclopedia.* 4 vols. 1901–36. Reprint, Salt Lake City: Western Epics, 1971. 3:577.

Nevada State Parks. "Mormon Station State Historic Park." Pamphlet. Carson City, Nevada.

W. SIDNEY YOUNG

CARSON VALLEY (NEVADA) MISSION.

A group of California-bound, gold-seeking Mormons led by Joseph DeMont, Hampton Sidney Beatie, and Abner Blackburn established a trading post known as

"Mormon Station" in Carson Valley (now in **Nevada**) in June 1850. The group soon sold its interests and returned to **Utah**. There Beatie told John Reese, Church member and merchant, about the potentially lucrative merchandising location. In 1851 Reese set up a store and ranch at Mormon Station to supply miners flocking to California gold fields. Other Mormons soon settled in the area.

Carson County was created by Utah Territory's legislature on 12 January 1854 but was not fully organized until 1855. **Apostle Orson Hyde** was appointed to serve as county probate judge. He renamed Mormon Station "Genoa" (after **Columbus**'s birthplace, in Italy), and the town was designated as county seat.

In 1855 and 1856, Church officials issued calls to members in Utah to serve as colonizing missionaries primarily in the Carson, Eagle, and Washoe Valleys. A **stake** was organized in Eagle Valley 4 October 1856. By the following April, LDS Church membership had reached 287. Sporadic disagreements arose between the predominant Mormons and the non-Mormon miners, who resented being controlled by decisions of Utah officials and outnumbered electorally.

The missionaries were summoned to return immediately to Utah in early September 1857 because of the advance of **Johnston's Army** and were forced to sell their property at distressed prices. Church funds were used to purchase guns and ammunition in **San Francisco**, California; the munitions were freighted to Utah by the colonists as they abandoned their settlements in late September, thus ending the Carson Valley Mission.

SOURCES

Arrington, Leonard J. *The Mormons in Nevada*. Las Vegas: Las Vegas Sun, 1979.

Bagley, Will, ed. *Frontiersman Abner Blackburn's Narrative*. Salt Lake City: University of Utah Press, 1992.

Owens, Kenneth N. *Archaeological and Historical Investigation of the Mormon-Carson Emigrant Trail, Eldorado and Toiyabe National Forests*. Vol. 2. Placerville, Calif.: U.S. Forest Service, 1990.

JAY G. BURRUP

CARTHAGE JAIL. Located in the southwest corner of Carthage, **Illinois**, Carthage Jail was the site of the **martyrdom** of Joseph and Hyrum Smith on 27 June 1844. Because of this event, Carthage Jail is one of the most frequently visited historic sites in Illinois.

On 22 March 1839, the **Hancock County** Commission ordered that the county clerk issue a call for bids for the construction of the county's first jail. Yellow limestone, quarried about four miles northeast of town, was used in constructing the prison. The walls were three feet thick at the base and two feet thick at the upper level. The doors were made from white walnut, and the 22-inch-wide window frames from black walnut. The jail originally had six rooms; later, a small kitchen was added on the east side.

A narrow winding staircase led to two attic rooms with low ceilings. The cell room had one barred window on the west and two small openings on the north used for ventilation. The large room near the stair's landing, where the Martyrdom occurred, was the jailer's bedroom. The cost of constructing the jail was $4,105. **Joseph Smith**, while incarcerated, spent time in the debtor's cell on the ground floor, in the prisoner's cell on the second floor, and in the front upstairs bedroom.

The prisoners received water for washing and a towel for drying each morning. The jailer's wife washed prisoners' clothes weekly, but those being held were expected to provide their own candles for lighting. The Carthage Jail had a few beds and a small library. Clergymen provided a Sunday service.

The jail was used for about 25 years and then became one of the nicest homes in the county. Under the direction of President **Joseph F. Smith**, the Church purchased the building and property in 1903 for $4,000. In 1938, the structure was renovated. The Church restored the jail to prepare for the commemoration of the 1994 sesquicentennial of the Prophet's martyrdom. The restoration made the jail more closely resemble its appearance at the time of Joseph and Hyrum's death.

Sources

McRae, Joseph A., and Eunice McRae. "Carthage Jail: A Physical Description of an Historical Structure." *Improvement Era* 45 (June 1942): 372–73, 391.

———. *Historical Facts Regarding the Liberty and Carthage Jails.* Salt Lake City: Utah Printing, 1954.

Kenneth W. Godfrey

CATTARAUGUS INDIANS.

The Cattaraugus Indians were located in the western part of **New York** state. When the **Lamanite missionaries of 1830 to 1831** traveled to **Missouri**, they "called upon an Indian nation at or near Buffalo" (Pratt, 47). They spent part of a day teaching the Indians about their forefathers. Upon departure, the missionaries left two copies of the **Book of Mormon**. It appears that these Indians were living

on the Buffalo Creek Reservation, which was dissolved in 1846. A footnote in the **History of the Church** identifies these Native Americans as
members of the Cattaraugus tribe (Smith, 121).

SOURCES

Pratt, Parley P. *Autobiography of Parley P. Pratt.* Edited by Parley P. Pratt Jr. Salt Lake
    City: Deseret Book, 1985.
Smith, Joseph. *History of The Church of Jesus Christ of Latter-day Saints [HC].* Edited
    by B. H. Roberts. 2d ed. rev. 7 vols. Salt Lake City: The Church of Jesus Christ of
    Latter-day Saints, 1932–51. 1:121.

H. DEAN GARRETT

CAYMAN ISLANDS. Located in the Caribbean Sea south of Cuba, the
Cayman Islands, a popular tourist attraction, are a British dependancy. A
branch was established 25 November 1981, with **missionary** work opening there four years later. At the beginning of the year 2000, there were
87 Latter-day **Saints** in one branch.

SOURCE

1999–2000 Church Almanac. Salt Lake City: Deseret News, 1998. 403.

EMILY C. ZEIGLER

CELESTIAL MARRIAGE. See **MARRIAGE** and **PLURAL
MARRIAGE.**

CENTRAL AFRICA REPUBLIC. Located north of the Democratic
Republic of Congo (formerly **Zaire**), the inhabitants of the Central Africa
Republic speak French and local dialects. Approximately half of the
population is Christian.

   Carol Forrest, the first Latter-day Saint known to be living in the
country, arrived in June 1991 to serve in the U.S. Peace Corps. A returned
missionary, she actively shared the gospel, and three months after her
arrival she was set apart as a district missionary in the **Cameroon
Yaounde Mission.** A year later, 20 converts were baptized and two
branches were organized. Celestin N'Gakondou was called to preside
over the Bangui First Branch and Gaspard Lapet became president of the
Bangui Second Branch. In 1993 Raymond and Christianne Fourtina, a
missionary couple from **France**, arrived in the country. A **seminary**

program for the youth began in 1995. At the beginning of the year 2000 there were 135 Church members living in one branch.

SOURCE

1999–2000 Church Almanac. Salt Lake City: Deseret News, 1998. 298.

E. DALE LEBARON

CENTRAL AMERICA. Central America is the narrow stretch of land between North and **South America**, including **Guatemala**, **El Salvador**, **Honduras**, **Nicaragua**, **Costa Rica**, **Panama**, and **Belize**. Although this region has been characterized by political instability and economic difficulty, it experienced significant Church **growth** during the second half of the twentieth century. The first missionaries to Central America reached Guatemala in 1947, and five years later **Elder Spencer W. Kimball** of the **Quorum** of the Twelve **Apostles** organized the Central America **Mission** with headquarters in Guatemala City, dedicating the nations of Central America for the preaching of the gospel. **Missionary work** began almost simultaneously in the neighboring countries of El Salvador and Honduras and soon followed in Nicaragua (1953), Panama (1965), and Belize (1980). By 1967 the Church had created a **stake** in Guatemala City, and the first Central American **temple** was announced for that city the following year. Dedicated in December 1984, the Guatemala City Temple served **Saints** from all of Central America.

Between 1970 and 1990, Church membership in this region grew from 29,000 to 200,000, surpassing all predictions. In 1990 the **First Presidency** created the Central America **Area** from the Mexico-Central America Area. This change allowed Central American Saints to have more contact with Church leaders, particularly **general authorities**. Headquarters were in Guatemala City, and Elder Ted E. Brewerton of the **Seventy** served as the area's first president. Central America reached another milestone at this time when **Carlos H. Amado** was called as a **counselor** in the area presidency, becoming the first Guatemalan to serve as a general authority.

Many Central American Saints have joined the Church at great sacrifice, often giving up friends and business opportunities as they accept gospel teachings. Church members typically walk long distances to attend Sunday **meetings**, and many also suffer from educational, medical, and economic hardships. But Saints from this region have accepted such challenges, serving missions and fulfilling leadership positions. Most of those serving full-time missions in Central America come from these countries, and many have returned home to strengthen their wards and branches. In January 1997 thousands gathered in various locations to meet with President **Gordon B. Hinckley** during his ten-day tour of Central America. By the beginning of the year 2000, the region had 454,944 members with 89 stakes and 12 missions.

SOURCES

Hart, John L. "Central America: Work Is Booming As Members Eagerly Share Their Testimonies with Friends." *Church News*, 16 February 1991, 8.
1999–2000 Church Almanac. Salt Lake City: Deseret News, 1998. 12, 163.

LISA KURKI

CENTRAL PACIFIC MISSION. See **JAPANESE/CENTRAL PACIFIC MISSION IN HAWAII.**

CERTIFICATES. See **LICENSES.**

CEYLON. See **SRI LANKA.**

CHAD. See **MIDDLE EAST** and **MUSLIMS.**

CHANDLER, MICHAEL H. During the last part of June and early July 1835, Michael H. Chandler, an Irish immigrant, was in the Cleveland-**Kirtland, Ohio**, area displaying four **Egyptian** mummies. They were part of a collection that originally included 11 mummies and papyri. In the spring of 1833, he had begun displaying the collection in cities that included **New York**, Philadelphia, Baltimore, Lancaster, and Pittsburgh.

The **Prophet Joseph Smith** became interested in the papyri records once he discovered they contained some of the writings of Abraham and Joseph. Chandler wanted to sell the mummies with these documents, but Joseph was only interested in the papyri. Because Chandler would not sell them separately, the **Saints** purchased the collection for $2,400. It is believed that Chandler was acting as an agent for a shipping company in Philadelphia. While working with the papyri over the next seven years,

Joseph received what would become the **book of Abraham**, now in the **Pearl of Great Price**.

In 1836, Chandler and his wife, Frances, bought a farm approximately 40 miles southeast of Kirtland, near Parkman, Ohio, where Chandler died in 1866. Along with several family members, he is buried in the West Farmington Cemetery several miles east of their farm.

SOURCES

Peterson, H. Donl. *The Story of the Book of Abraham.* Salt Lake City: Deseret Book, 1995. 86–102.

Smith, Brian L. "A Book of Abraham Research Update." *Religious Studies Center Newsletter.* Brigham Young University, May 1997. 5–8.

Smith, Joseph. *History of The Church of Jesus Christ of Latter-day Saints.* Edited by B. H. Roberts. 2d ed. rev. 7 vols. Salt Lake City: The Church of Jesus Christ of Latter-day Saints, 1932–51. 2:348–349.

BRIAN L. SMITH

CHAPLAINS. Through the years members of The Church of **Jesus Christ** of Latter-day **Saints** have functioned as chaplains in numerous settings, including the military, **hospitals**, prisons, legislative bodies, scouting, industry, law enforcement agencies, fire departments, and service organizations.

The title of chaplain as it relates to the Church is institutional and not ecclesiastical. As an **apostle**, **Spencer W. Kimball** taught that in the Church individuals should not be addressed as Doctor, Colonel, or Judge but as **Elder**, Brother, or Sister. The title of chaplain fits in the same category. It is a secular title, not an office in the **priesthood**. When sacred **ordinances** were performed by men serving as chaplains, it was by virtue of the priesthood they held and not because of their role as chaplain.

From the Church's early history, its leaders have designated men to serve as chaplains in such undertakings as **Zion's Camp**, the **Nauvoo Legion**, **pioneer** companies crossing the plains, the **Mormon Battalion**, **colonization** expeditions, the **Utah War**, and territorial—and later state—legislatures. Numerous **general authorities** have served in these capacities.

The most frequent involvement of Church members as chaplains has been in the **United States** military—including active duty, reserve, and National Guard components. Evidence indicates that Elias S. Kimball may have been the first federally commissioned Latter-day Saint to serve as a chaplain. Before his appointment to serve with American forces in the **Spanish-American War** in 1898, he was serving as the president of the **Southern States Mission**.

During **World War I**, the Church was authorized 20 chaplain positions in the armed forces, but due principally to a strong anti-Mormon lobby, only three of those positions were filled. The most prominent of the three men who served was **Elder B. H. Roberts**, who was a member of the First Council of the **Seventy**. He had been serving with the **Utah** National Guard and began his active duty tour at the age of 60. He is often referred to as the dean of LDS chaplains.

During **World War II**, 46 Latter-day Saint men served as chaplains, 44 during the 1950s, 63 in the Vietnam era, and 104 between 1975 and 1999.

The Church inaugurated the practice of setting apart Latter-day Saint chaplains as "special missionaries" with the advent of the Korean War. Beginning in the mid-1960s, they were given the same ministerial certificates authorized for and carried by full-time proselyting missionaries, though their work did not involve formally sharing the gospel except by personal invitation. Their service as commissioned officers meant that their income came as federal employees and not from Church funds. Their work had the elements of both a chosen vocation and a Church calling.

Although their responsibilities have been as varied as their assignments, the chaplains' basic duties have been somewhat constant. They include conducting worship services for multidenominational and at times multifaith congregations, religious **education** programs, and presentations on the subject of morality and ethics. They engage in many facets of counseling and visit hospitals, homes, disciplinary facilities, work centers, and duty locations, including combat areas. They perform **marriages** and also conduct funeral, memorial, and graveside services. A principal responsibility and opportunity is that of being a constant reminder to those who wear the uniform, and to their families, of the Lord's interest in their lives.

SOURCES

Boone, Joseph F. *The Roles of The Church of Jesus Christ of Latter-day Saints in Relation to the United States Military, 1900–1975.* Ph.D. diss., Brigham Young University, 1975.

Kimball, Edward L., and Andrew E. Kimball. *Spencer W. Kimball.* Salt Lake City: Bookcraft, 1977. 284.

JOSEPH F. BOONE

CHIEF LITTLE SOLDIER. See LITTLE SOLDIER, CHIEF.

CHIEF WALKER. See WALKARA.

CHIHUAHUA, MEXICO. See MEXICAN COLONIES.

CHILDREN'S FRIEND. At the turn of the century, the **Primary** general board felt an urgent need for continual communication with Primary officers and teachers throughout the Church. The answer was the *Children's Friend,* developed chiefly by **Louie B. Felt**, general Primary president, and **May Anderson**, who served as editor for 37 years. The **magazine** first appeared in 1902 as the Primary's official periodical.

Early issues emphasized weekly Primary lessons. Later, departments for parents, officers, and **teacher training** were added. In the second decade, the focus changed to Primary children themselves, evidenced by the addition of the "Just for Fun" page in 1913. Other features included stories, riddles, pictures, games, as well as contributions from Primary children throughout the Church. To appeal to young readers, the magazine's page size was doubled in 1923, and the type and pictures were enlarged. In January 1971, the *Children's Friend* was replaced by the *Friend* magazine.

SOURCES

Kerr, Marion Belnap. "The Children's Friend for Fifty Years." *Children's Friend,* (January–February 1952): 29, 76.

1997–1998 Church Almanac. Salt Lake City: Deseret News, 1996. 484.

KRISTIN B. GERDY

CHILE. The first Latter-day **Saints** to arrive in Chile were **Elder Parley P. Pratt**, his wife Phebe, and Elder Rufus C. Allen. Because of revolutionary conditions and the missionaries' inability to learn Spanish, they remained only a few months. On 2 March 1852, Elder Pratt left Chile "without a sufficiency of the language to turn the keys of the Gospel as yet" (Pratt, 397). The next Latter-day Saint presence did not come until the early 1950s, when the **family** of William Fotheringham moved to Santiago. President **David O. McKay** visited them there in 1954. In 1956 Chile became part of the Argentine **mission**. In June of that year, Elders Joseph C.

Bentley and Verle Allred arrived from **Argentina**, and on 25 November they baptized Ricardo García and others. The first **branch** was organized at Santiago on 5 June 1956 (later known as the Ñuñoa Branch). There were about 450 members in Chile in 1959 when the country became part of the new Andes Mission.

The Chilean Mission, with Delbert Palmer as president, was organized 8 October 1961 with 1,100 members. By 1972 there were 20,000 members in the country, and on 19 November Elder **Gordon B. Hinckley** organized the first **stake** at Santiago, with Carlos Cifuentes as president. That same year the **Church Educational System** began the **seminary** program in Chile and for a time operated a school in Santiago.

On 27 February 1977, President **Spencer W. Kimball** addressed an audience of more than 7,000. On this occasion, Elder **Bruce R. McConkie** prophesied that the Church would become the most powerful influence in the nation. He predicted that the existing seven stakes would become seventy times seven. The Santiago **Temple** was dedicated by President Hinckley in 10 sessions 15–17 September 1983. In 1996 the Chile Area was organized with F. Melvin Hammond as president and Jerald Lynn Taylor and Eduardo Lamartine as counselors. The following year the 100th stake was organized at Puerto Varas, Chile, becoming one of four nations to have 100 or more stakes. This came only 25 years after the first stake had been organized.

On 23 August 1998, the land of Chile was officially dedicated by Elder **M. Russell Ballard**, grandson of Elder **Melvin J. Ballard**, who had dedicated the continent of **South America** three-quarters of a century earlier. On 26 April 1999, President Hinckley presided at a **conference** attended by about 57,500 in a large stadium in the nation's capital. At the beginning of the year 2000 there were 502,153 members in Chile living in 186 stakes and 1,879 **wards** and branches. Church members represent more than 3% of the population—the highest ratio of Latter-day Saints of any country in the world outside of **Polynesia**.

SOURCES

1997–1998 Church Almanac. Salt Lake City: Deseret News, 1996. 308–11.

Palmer, A. Delbert. "Establishing the LDS Church in Chile." Master's thesis, Brigham Young University, 1979.

Pratt, Parley P. *Autobiography of Parley P. Pratt.* Edited by Parley P. Pratt Jr. Salt Lake City: Deseret Book, 1966. 371–403.

EDUARDO LAMARTINE

CHINA, PEOPLE'S REPUBLIC OF. The Church has never had much presence in China, before or since communist rule, but the situation is changing. In 1853 there was a short-lived attempt to plant the gospel in China by **Hosea Stout** and two companions, James Lewis and Chapman Duncan. These efforts lasted but a few weeks, cut short largely because of the great Taiping Rebellion. Then in 1921, within the palace compound of the Forbidden City in Peking, **Elder David O. McKay** dedicated China for the preaching of the gospel. There was no follow-up, however, because of the country's turmoil of warlordism, civil **war**, and foreign invasions.

United States recognition of China came in December 1979, followed by the "opening" of China in the 1980s. Significantly, President **Spencer W. Kimball** had drawn special attention to China in an historic September 1978 seminar for regional representatives as well as in March 1979. It was clear that the challenge for the Church in China was on his mind and that the Lord's hand was in the matter. In recent years many important activities have helped prepare China to receive the restored gospel. Latter-day Saint professionals, mainly businessmen, lawyers, teachers, journalists, and diplomats, along with their families, have contributed immeasurably by projecting a positive image as **Latter-day Saints** and by assisting with official contacts between the Church and Chinese government officials. Important in this latter connection is Elder Chia Chu-jen, an **area authority seventy**, and Tim Stratford, a lawyer and long-time resident of Beijing. Many of the Latter-day Saint professionals in China formerly served as missionaries in **Taiwan** and **Hong Kong**.

Another important influence for the Church has been the tours of **Brigham Young University** performing groups that have gained wide notoriety in China. Launched by BYU president **Dallin H. Oaks** in 1979, a BYU group was the first cultural exchange group to perform under China's new "open door" policy. These tours have continued yearly and have been seen by many millions of Chinese. At the same time, hundreds of graduate students have come from China to BYU, and a number of them have joined the Church. An additional noteworthy influence has been the BYU China Teacher's Program. To date some 400 teachers have been placed in dozens of Chinese universities, mainly to teach English.

As of 1998 Chinese nationals were forbidden by law to attend Latter-day Saint religious **meetings**. A series of **general authorities** have met with officials of the Chinese government over the years for the purpose of improving the Church's position. The process of obtaining permission for Chinese nationals baptized overseas to attend Church services once they return to China is still underway. No proselyting activities of any kind are allowed or carried out by the Church or its members in China.

Government policy has changed over time from a dogmatic suppression of all "superstition" (religion) to a pragmatic view that some religions have "socially redeemable" qualities that may be useful in a new modernized China. Chinese officials have acknowledged that the LDS Church is seen as a legitimate religion, not as an undesirable cult.

In 1998 three regular expatriate **branches** of the Church in Beijing, Shanghai, and Guangzhou were established with the tacit approval of the Chinese authorities. Other smaller groups exist in various places, all falling within the jurisdiction of the "China International **District**." The regular attendance of the largest branch, Beijing, averaged well over 150 members.

PAUL HYER AND JEFFREY RINGER

CHRIST. See JESUS CHRIST.

CHRISTENSEN, C. C. A. The most famous work of Carl Christian Anton Christensen (1831–1912) is the "**Mormon** Panorama," a series of 23 murals that tells the early history of the Church from "The **First Vision**" to "The Entry of the **Pioneers** into the **Salt Lake Valley**." Christensen presented a Church history lecture along with the "Mormon Panorama" display throughout the territory. He wanted to make the young people who had experienced neither the trials of **Missouri** and **Illinois** nor the crossing of the plains aware of the divine providence of the Lord and the sacrifices of their parents in bringing forth the **restoration** of the gospel and the gathering of the **Saints** to **Zion**.

Born 28 November 1831 in Copenhagen, Denmark, Christensen studied at the Royal Academy of Art in that city. An early Danish convert, he pulled a handcart across the plains in 1856. In **Utah** he became a farmer, poet, newspaper editor, stake **patriarch**, and painter of murals in the **Manti Temple**. After serving four **missions** to **Scandinavia**, his last years were spent in the Church **Historical Department** compiling the early history of that mission. Christensen died 3 July 1912 in Ephraim, Utah.

SOURCE

Jensen, Richard L., and Richard G. Oman. *C. C. A. Christensen 1831–1912: Mormon Immigrant Artist*. Salt Lake City: Museum of Church History and Art, 1984.

RICHARD G. OMAN

CHRISTIAN CHURCHES IN AMERICA AND MORMONISM.

A relative newcomer on the American religious landscape, Mormonism emerged at the time of the Second **Great Awakening** and the **Restorationist** movement that swept the country from the beginning of the nineteenth century until the **Civil War**.

The first Christian denomination to arrive on American shores was the Roman Catholic Church. Spanish explorers were accompanied by Franciscan missionaries, who established missions throughout the Southwest. French explorers in **Canada** and the **Mississippi** valley were followed by Jesuits. The first settlers in the American colonies either came for religious reasons, as did the Congregationalists (Plymouth and **Massachusetts**) and the Quakers (**Pennsylvania**), or for economic reasons, as did the Anglicans (**Virginia** and the colonies to its south) and Catholics (**Maryland**). Other people (Presbyterians and Lutherans) came seeking cheap land and brought their religion with them. By 1776 the largest denominations were the Congregationalists, the Presbyterians, the Baptists, and the Episcopalians (Anglicans).

The first half of the nineteenth century saw a radical shift in denominational alignment. The Methodist and Baptist religions grew enormously due to missionary efforts on the frontier. The number of Catholics grew through immigration. Thus, by 1850 the largest denominations in the country were Methodists, Baptists, Catholics, and Presbyterians (Finke and Stark, 55).

During this period, the Restorationist movement appeared as an attempt to restore New Testament Christianity, which the movement's leaders believed had been lost. Restorationism was strongly present in New England, Virginia, **North Carolina**, **Ohio**, and **Kentucky**, with Barton Stone and Thomas and Alexander Campbell playing leading roles in the latter two states. As adherents to the **Campbellite** movement, **Sidney Rigdon** and **Parley P. Pratt** did not question the need for a restoration. When they encountered The Church of **Jesus Christ** of Latter-day **Saints**, with its unique claim to **priesthood** authority, they embraced it.

Since its beginnings The Church of Jesus Christ of Latter-day Saints has grown steadily. By the end of the twentieth century, the Church was the fifth largest denomination in the **United States**, exceeded only by the Roman Catholics, Southern Baptists, United Methodists, and the Evangelical Lutheran Church in America (Noll, 465).

SOURCES

Finke, Roger, and Rodney Stark. *The Churching of America, 1776–1990: Winners and*

    Losers in Our Religious Economy. New Brunswick, N.J.: Rutgers University Press,
    1992.
Noll, Mark A. *A History of Christianity in the United States and Canada.* Grand Rapids,
    Mich.: William B. Eerdmans, 1992.

ROGER R. KELLER

CHRISTIAN HISTORY AND THE GOSPEL. Events of Christian
history played a vital role in the restoration of the gospel of **Jesus Christ**
and paved the way for the founding of the Church. Indeed, the story of
the **Restoration** through **Joseph Smith** actually began with the pure
Christianity established by Jesus himself almost 2000 years previously in
the **Holy Land.**

From a Latter-day Saint perspective, the historical **apostasy** and subsequent loss of divine authority began in the New Testament period and
spread in the ensuing centuries. During **Joseph Smith's First Vision**
(1820), Christ told the Prophet that all existing churches had gone astray,
both in their teachings and in their practices, although they had "a form
of godliness." Thus, it was necessary for a restoration of the gospel to take
place.

Although Christian history saw a number of minor reform movements in its first 15 centuries, the time wasn't ripe for a major reformation in **Europe** until the 16th century. Martin Luther had no intention of
breaking with traditional Roman Catholicism; he wanted only to purify
the church and return it to the original teachings of New Testament
Christianity as he understood them. Latter-day **Saints** regard the
Protestant Reformation as a preparation for the more complete restoration of the gospel. The Reformers were men of deep religious faith and
unquestioning trust in God, and they made an important contribution to
the Restoration. But without direct revelation from heaven, they could
not restore the true gospel of Jesus Christ. This was the mission of the
Prophet Joseph Smith.

The Church of Jesus Christ of Latter-day Saints is fundamentally
American by birth. The religious environment in the United States during
the early nineteenth century was predominantly Protestant, which
allowed for religious differences and resulted in many rival churches.
This Protestant American society provided a religious and political atmosphere that made it possible for the gospel to be restored.

The Bible used by Joseph Smith was the King James Version of 1611.
The Prophet's reading of that Bible, particularly James 1:5–6, led to his

personal encounter with God the Father and his Son Jesus Christ and to the eventual restoration of the gospel.

SOURCES

Allen, James B., and Glen B. Leonard. *The Story of the Latter-day Saints.* 2d ed. Salt Lake City: Deseret Book, 1992. 7–35.

Lindberg, Carter. *The European Reformations.* Oxford: Blackwell Publishers, 1996.

Richards, LeGrand. *A Marvelous Work and a Wonder.* Salt Lake City: Deseret Book, 1961. 25–33.

DONG SULL CHOI

CHRISTIANS, MORMONS ARE. Because Latter-day **Saints** profess **Jesus Christ** as their personal Lord and Savior, they stand within the parameters that identify persons as "Christians," as defined by other Christian denominations.

It has always been confusing to Latter-day Saints when they are told that they are not really Christians. They ask, "How can one belong to The *Church of Jesus Christ* of Latter-day Saints and not be recognized as Christian?" for they have always assumed that Christians are persons who profess faith in and follow the Lord Jesus Christ to the best of their abilities, albeit imperfectly. But perhaps other definitions of *Christian* preclude Latter-day Saints. We will look briefly at definitions of *Christian* in the most recent *Catechism of the Roman Catholic Church* and in the *1989–90 Book of Order of the Presbyterian Church (U.S.A.).*

The most concise definition of a Christian in the *Catechism* is as follows: "All who have been justified by faith in Baptism are incorporated into Christ; they therefore have a right to be called Christians, and with good reason are accepted as brothers in the Lord by the children of the Catholic Church" (Sec. 818). The Roman Catholic criterion for efficacious baptism is that it be done in the name of the Father, the Son, and the Holy Ghost. Since Latter-day Saint baptism is carried out in this manner, it is valid, and Mormons have a right to the title Christian by the above definition.

Similarly, the Presbyterian *Book of Order* states that "the church universal consists of all persons in every nation, together with their children, who profess faith in Jesus Christ as Lord and Savior and commit themselves to live in a fellowship under his rule" (G-4.0101). This aptly describes Mormon belief.

Beliefs distinct to Roman Catholic Christians, Presbyterian Christians, and Mormon Christians make each body unique. At the center of the faith, however, stands Jesus Christ, the common Lord, who calls all to his service as Christians—his followers.

SOURCES

Catechism of the Catholic Church. New York: Doubleday, 1994.

The Constitution of the Presbyterian Church (U.S.A.), Part II: Book of Order. Louisville, Ky.: Office of the General Assembly, 1989.

ROGER R. KELLER

CHURCH, NAMES OF. The Church's name was specified by revelation and is a statement of its true identity. The Savior instructed the Nephites that his Church should bear his name (3 Ne. 27:8). Hence, following the 1830 organization of the Church, it was commonly known as "The Church of Christ." By 1834 Church members were frequently ridiculed as "Mormons" or "Mormonites." In that year a Church council approved the designation "Latter-day Saints" as a preferred alternative. Members of the New Testament Church were called "**Saints**" (see, for example, Rom. 1:7; 1 Cor. 1:2; Eph. 1:1). Even though the word *saint* comes from the same Latin root as "sanctify" and refers to one who is holy, this term may also apply to those who are still striving for perfection (Eph. 4:12). In the mid-1830s, the title "Church of the Latter-day Saints" was frequently used. A revelation in 1838, however, specified that the Church's proper name should be "The Church of Jesus Christ of Latter-day Saints" (D&C 115:4).

Beginning with the capitalized definite article "The," the Church's name affirms its unique status as "the only true and living church upon the face of the whole earth" (D&C 1:30). In 1995 the Church adopted a new logo with the words *Jesus Christ* rendered most prominent (*Church News*). The new emphasis acknowledges whose Church it truly is.

SOURCES

Church News, 23 December 1995, 3.

Cowan, Richard O. *Answers to Your Questions about the Doctrine and Covenants.* Salt Lake City: Deseret Book, 1996. 132–33.

RICHARD O. COWAN

CHURCH AND STATE. See **POLITICS.**

CHURCH BUILDING COMMITTEE. See **BUILDING PROGRAM.**

CHURCH COLLEGE OF HAWAII. See **BRIGHAM YOUNG UNIVERSITY–HAWAII CAMPUS.**

CHURCH COURTS. See **DISCIPLINARY COUNCILS.**

CHURCH EDUCATION. See **EDUCATION.**

CHURCH EDUCATIONAL SYSTEM (CES). Known by various names during its long history, the Church's educational system began as early as the **School of the Prophets** in the 1830s and expanded with the creation of **academies** in the 1870s and 1880s. In 1888 a general Church Board of Education was created to promote and coordinate these schools. Since the appointment of **Karl G. Maeser** as general superintendent of Church schools that same year, educational administrators have met the needs of youth, developed programs, provided professional training, produced and distributed curriculum, and overseen physical facilities.

The **First Presidency** appoints its members and presides over the Board of Education, which consists of members selected from the **Quorum** of Twelve **Apostles** plus other general officers, including the presidents of the **Relief Society** and **Young Women**. Under their direction, the commissioner of Church Education presides over the entire system. Members of the Board of Education also form the boards of trustees for **Brigham Young University, Ricks College** (later BYU–Idaho), and **LDS Business College**, whose presidents report to the commissioner. Also reporting to the commissioner is the CES administrator for **seminaries, institutes**, and other Church schools (particularly elementary and secondary schools in the **Pacific** and **Latin America**). Assisting the commissioner are several zone administrators, who compose the Church Educational Executive Council.

Locally, seminaries and institutes are administered by area or country directors assigned to geographical locations throughout the world, who are assisted by coordinators, institute directors, seminary principals, and instructors. Most of the instructors throughout the world are local Church members who are appointed to teach seminary. In 1999, 35,824 volunteer teachers and 3,390 professional religious educators taught seminary or institute in 144 different countries. **Stake** and local Church leaders also assist in administration, especially in identification, enrollment, and registration of youth in their stakes.

Sources

Bennion, Milton Lynn. *Mormonism and Education*. Salt Lake City: Deseret Book, 1939.

Berrett, William E. *A Miracle in Weekday Religious Education.* Salt Lake City: Salt Lake Printing Center, 1988.

Encyclopedia of Mormonism. Edited by Daniel H. Ludlow. 4 vols. New York: Macmillan, 1992.

Craig K. Manscill

CHURCH ORGANIZATION. See ORGANIZATION OF THE CHURCH.

CHURCH HISTORIAN'S OFFICE. See HISTORIAN, CHURCH.

CHURCHILL, WINSTON. Winston Churchill (1874–1965), the son of an American mother and a British nobleman, served as home secretary in the British government from 1911 to 1915. During his tenure a wave of unparalleled attacks against the **Mormons** peaked in 1911. Many false stories circulated in the newspapers accusing Mormon **elders** of flattering thousands of English girls into joining their polygamous harems in **Utah.** These stories, plus an **anti-Mormon** rally and several novels misrepresenting the Church, all fueled widespread prejudice against the **Saints.** Complaints reached the Home Office, and Churchill reported: "No ground for action [against the Mormons] has been found. I am informed that polygamy is now forbidden by the rules of the Mormon Church" (quoted in Bloxham, Moss, and Porter, 227–28). So strong were the anti-Mormon feelings during this period that the British parliament debated whether or not to expel all Latter-day Saints from **England.** Young Churchill courageously defended the right of religious freedom, thus helping the Church's cause. No expulsion occurred. Churchill went on to become the prime minister of Britain, leading the country to victory during **World War II.**

SOURCES

Bloxham, V. Ben, James R. Moss, and Larry C. Porter, eds. *Truth Will Prevail: The Rise of The Church of Jesus Christ of Latter-day Saints in the British Isles, 1837–1997.* Cambridge: Cambridge University Press, 1987.

Church History in the Fulness of Times. Salt Lake City: The Church of Jesus Christ of Latter-day Saints, 1993.

David Cook

CHURCH NEWS. In April 1931 the *Church News* was launched as a tabloid-size weekly supplement to the *Deseret News,* Salt Lake City's daily newspaper owned by The Church of **Jesus Christ** of Latter-day **Saints**. Its purpose is to inform, instruct, motivate, and strengthen the membership of the Church. In 1943, while remaining a supplement to the newspaper, the *Church News* began to be mailed separately to subscribers outside the *Deseret News* circulation area. While primarily located in the **United States**, subscribers in the late twentieth century could be found in many areas of the world. In fact, at a 50th anniversary dinner of the *Church News* in 1981, President **Gordon B. Hinckley** said that the sun never sets on the *Church News*.

The *Church News* not only provides a window to happenings at Church headquarters but also publishes news and features of the Church and its members from around the globe, giving it an international flavor reflective of the Church's worldwide membership. In 1995 the publication extended its reach to the World Wide Web, providing coverage of the Church electronically to a global audience. The *Church News* also biennially publishes the *Deseret News Church Almanac,* a book of facts and information about the Church.

SOURCE

Smart, William B. "Half a Century of Worldwide Growth Reflected in 'News.'" *Church News,* 19 September 1981. 2.

DELL VAN ORDEN

CHURCH OFFICE BUILDINGS. There have been five structures known as "the Church office building," ranging from the first building of 216 square feet to the current general Church Office Building of 683,000 square feet. By definition the Church office building is the structure that houses the offices of the president of the Church, other **general authorities**, and some Church departments. From time to time, various departments and general authorities have been housed in numerous buildings due to the growth of Church membership and administrative needs.

The first two offices that housed the president of the Church, not included in the five structures just spoken of, were in buildings that had been designated primarily for other purposes: the **Kirtland Temple** in Ohio and a mercantile establishment known as the **Red Brick Store** in **Nauvoo**. From these two offices the **Prophet Joseph Smith** administered the affairs of the Church.

After the **Saints** had moved west, the first Church Office Building, measuring 18 feet by 12 feet, was built in 1848 by **Daniel H. Wells**. The exact site of the building is not known, but it served the Church for two years.

From 1850 to 1852 the headquarters of the Church were located in the home of President **Brigham Young**, known as the White House or the **Mansion House**. It was located on East South Temple Street where the Elks Club building now stands, one block east of the present Church Administration Building.

Headquarters were next located in the President's Office, which was built in 1852 by **Truman O. Angell**, the Church architect. It connected the Beehive and **Lion Houses** on South Temple Street and served the First Presidency through the administrations of Presidents Brigham Young, **John Taylor**, **Wilford Woodruff**, **Lorenzo Snow**, and **Joseph F. Smith**, a total of 65 years. During this period the **Gardo House** was also used occasionally.

The fourth building, now known as the Church Administration Building, was completed in 1917 and measures 140 feet by 75 feet with four floors. Originally this building housed all the general authorities and most of the departments of the Church. Currently this building houses the **First Presidency**, the Quorum of the Twelve **Apostles**, and some of the **Seventy**.

As the Church population increased and the Church administration grew proportionally, the departments originally located in the Administration Building were relocated in nearby office buildings. In 1972 a 28-story building, known today as the Church Office Building, was completed. Still the tallest building in **Salt Lake City**, this fifth office building of the Church houses most Church departments and the offices of the **presiding bishopric**. This impressive building—with its sculptured gardens, fountain, and huge oil mural on canvas depicting **Jesus** shortly before his ascension—is toured by thousands of visitors each year.

SOURCE

"The New General Church Office Building." *Ensign* 3 (January 1973): 139–43.

CRAIG K. MANSCILL

CHURCH UNIVERSITY, THE. See UNIVERSITY OF THE CHURCH OF JESUS CHRIST OF LATTER-DAY SAINTS, THE.

CITY OF JOSEPH. See NAUVOO

CITY PLANNING. Joseph Smith consistently emphasized the importance of Church members residing in communities, and in 1833 he sent the **Saints** in **Jackson County** a plan for building the City of **Zion**. This plan proposed a community based on a uniform grid pattern, oriented to the cardinal points of the compass with three large central blocks for **temples**, schools, and other public buildings. Additionally, the city included 46 ten-acre blocks with 20 lots per block, wide streets (132 feet), specified building materials (brick or stone), uniform setback of homes, landscaping and gardens on the lot, farms located around the town, and an optimal area and population for the community (one square mile for 15,000 to 20,000 inhabitants). Two months after sending his first plan, the Prophet sent a revision (August 1833). This second plan included a larger size of two square miles (and presumably a proportionate increase in community population), 132 half-acre blocks, and a reduction in size and number of the central "temple blocks."

Kirtland, Ohio, which was surveyed shortly after the City of Zion plan was proposed, is most similar to the plan. Kirtland's differences are in the city size and in the number and size of blocks for temples, but otherwise it is very similar to Joseph's second plan. Other settlements established under the direction of the Prophet Joseph diverged more recognizably from his plans, suggesting that the concept of the City of Zion was more important than the details of city layout, or that none of the cities established was seen by the Prophet as replacing the City of Zion for Jackson County. Nauvoo, for example, had streets less than one-half the size (50 feet) of the original City of Zion, and blocks that were smaller, with only four lots per block. Communities established in the **Great Basin** under the direction of **Brigham Young** included some of the City of Zion characteristics, most notably wide streets, large lots, and large blocks. The importance of the Prophet Joseph's City of Zion plan in the development of Latter-day Saint communities in the Midwest and the Great Basin was recognized by the American Institute of Certified Planners, who selected Smith and the City of Zion plan as the second recipient of the National Planning Landmarks Award in 1996.

SOURCES

Jackson, Richard. "The Mormon Village: Genesis and Antecedents of the City of Zion Plan." *BYU Studies* 17 (Winter 1977): 223–40.

Romig, Ronald E., and John H. Siebert. "Jackson County, 1831–1833: A Look at the Development of Zion." *Restoration Studies* 3 (1986): 286–304.

RICHARD H. JACKSON

CIVIL RIGHTS. Latter-day Saints have been affected by civil rights issues throughout their history. In the **United States** these rights are statutory protections and guarantees provided by the Constitution, including freedom of the press, religion, speech, assembly, due process, and equal protection under the law. While claiming these rights for themselves and supporting such rights for others, Latter-day Saints have not consistently enjoyed these privileges. For example, the **Saints'** difficulties in **Missouri** during the 1830s resulted in the significant loss of civil protections for Latter-day Saints, including property and due process. Consequently, while praising the Constitution as a "glorious standard" and a "heavenly banner," the **Prophet Joseph Smith** declared that the Constitution "is not broad enough to cover the whole ground" (Smith, 3:304–5; 6:56–57). The circumstances surrounding the death of the Prophet and the departure of the Saints from **Illinois** also involved grave absence of constitutional protection. Later in the century, Latter-day Saints saw, as a serious erosion of First Amendment privileges, the passage of the **Morrill Anti-Bigamy Act of 1862**, followed by its 1879 validation in *Reynolds v. United States* and the crippling legislation it unleashed.

A major issue facing Latter-day Saints in the twentieth century was connected to Church denial of priesthood to **blacks**. This was popularly linked to the modern civil rights movement, which included the 1954 Supreme Court decision in *Brown v. Board of Education* and the comprehensive Civil Rights Acts of 1964 and 1968, along with the Voting Rights Act of 1965. These prohibited discrimination in public accommodation, schools, housing, voting, and employment for reasons of color, race, religion, or national origin. The Church was fully supportive of these developments, but at the same time it experienced increased pressure to lift the priesthood restriction. Church leaders responded to the growing criticism with several statements summarizing the Church's position on blacks in both society and the Church. The declarations (1) decried the evils of discrimination; (2) repeated support for full civil rights for blacks and other minorities; (3) explained that the restrictions on granting the priesthood to blacks were a matter of faith and that the reasons had not been revealed; and (4) expressed the expectation that someday the full blessings of the gospel would be available to all people (see, for example, Brown, 91; The **First Presidency**, 70–71; Lee, 117–18). While some disapproval continued, the harsh condemnation of the Church over this issue began to diminish following the 1978 revelation granting the priesthood to all worthy males (**Official Declaration 2**).

SOURCES

Brown, Hugh B. Conference Report (October 1963): 91–95.

Hall, Kermit L., ed. *The Oxford Companion to the Supreme Court of the United States.* New York: Oxford University Press, 1992.

Lee, Harold B. Conference Report (April 1972): 115–19.

"Letter of First Presidency Clarifies Church's Position on the Negro." *Improvement Era* 73 (February 1970): 70–71.

Mauss, Armand L. "Mormonism and the Negro: Faith, Folklore, and Civil Rights." *Dialogue* 2 (Winter 1967): 19–39.

Riggs, Robert E. "Civil Rights." *Encyclopedia of Mormonism.* Edited by Daniel H. Ludlow. 4 vols. New York: Macmillan, 1992. 1:286–87.

Smith, Joseph. *History of The Church of Jesus Christ of Latter-day Saints.* Edited by B. H. Roberts. 2d ed. rev. 7 vols. Salt Lake City: The Church of Jesus Christ of Latter-day Saints, 1932–51.

DALE C. MOURITSEN

CIVIL WAR. In 1832 the **Prophet Joseph Smith** foretold a great rebellion, beginning in **South Carolina**, which would divide the nation, pit the southern states against the northern states, and end up causing the death and misery of many people (D&C 87:1–5; 130:12–13). Latter-day Saints regard this prophecy as unequivocally being fulfilled in the American **Civil War** which began, as predicted, when South Carolina seceded from the Union 20 December 1860 and Confederate forces fired on the federal installation of Fort Sumter located in Charleston Harbor, South Carolina, 12 April 1861. The carnage ended four years later in May 1865 and cost the lives of some 618,000 men as well as causing immeasurable misery—again as prophesied.

Because the main body of Saints had already moved west to the Great **Salt Lake Valley**, the outbreak of the Civil War did not have a significant effect on the Church. Governor **Cumming** of the **Utah** Territory was from **Georgia**, so he retired from his post in 1861, feeling duty bound to return to his home state like many southerners at the outbreak of the war. **Johnston's Army**, which had been in Utah for three years, was recalled to the East on account of the war, abandoning **Camp Floyd** in 1861. Believing in the inspired nature of the **Constitution**, Church members generally supported the cause of keeping the Union together; however, they also supported the notion of local sovereignty because of their own experience with the federal government and, thus, were not totally unsympathetic to the views of the Confederacy.

When the transcontinental **telegraph** was completed in 1861, President **Brigham Young** sent a message to the president of the telegraph company stating that Utah had not seceded from the Union but stood firmly by the Constitution. Acting governor Frank Fuller also wired President **Abraham Lincoln** at that same time, confirming the loyalty of Utah's citizens to the cause of the Union. In 1862, because all available Union troops were committed to the war effort, President Lincoln wired **Brigham Young** and authorized him to empower a company of cavalry to guard the unprotected overland mail and telegraph services.

The Church continued to send out missionaries during the Civil War years. Most of them went to European countries.

SOURCES

Allen, James B., and Glen M. Leonard. *The Story of the Latter-day Saints.* 2d ed. Salt Lake City: Deseret Book, 1992. 317–23.

Matloff, Maurice, ed. *American Military History.* Washington, D.C.: Office of the Chief of Military History, 1973. 184–280.

ANDREW C. SKINNER

CLARK, J. REUBEN, JR. Joshua Reuben Clark Jr., influential statesman and **counselor** to three Church presidents, was born 1 September 1871 in Grantsville, **Utah**. A scholar from his youth, Reuben graduated first in his class from the **University of Utah**, where he had served as student body president and secretary to university president **James E. Talmage.** Reuben married Luacine Annetta Savage on 14 September 1898 in the **Salt Lake Temple.**

At age 32, Reuben enrolled at the Columbia College of Law. Three months after graduation in 1906, he was appointed to the State Department, where he served as assistant solicitor and later as solicitor. Reuben left the State Department in 1913 to practice municipal and international law. During **World War I**, he was instrumental in preparing the original Selective Service regulations.

Reuben again served his country in 1928 when President Calvin Coolidge appointed him undersecretary of the State Department. In 1930 he was named ambassador to **Mexico**, a position he held until 1933.

In 1931 Reuben received a letter from President **Heber J. Grant,** asking him to be his second counselor. Because of Brother Clark's responsibilities as ambassador, the appointment was not announced until 1933, when he was sustained on **6 April**. He was sustained as first counselor to President Grant on 6 October 1934; he was ordained an **apostle** one week later.

Unlike many of his predecessors, President Clark did not have extensive experience in Church administration, his prior service being limited to teaching **Sunday School**. Yet he carefully researched any assignment that crossed his desk and offered thoughtful solutions. In 1940 his recommendation that **general conference** be carried over closed-circuit radio initiated media coverage outside the Wasatch Front. He was also instrumental in developing the Church welfare system.

Even while in the **First Presidency**, President Clark filled government assignments and civic obligations. He was a delegate to international conferences and served on the Republican National Committee and the Foreign Bondholders' Protective Council.

President Clark was sustained as first counselor to President **George Albert Smith** on 21 May 1945. He became second counselor to President **David O. McKay** on 9 April 1951 and first counselor on 12 June 1959—a position he held until his death on 6 October 1961 in Salt Lake City. His 28-year tenure in the First Presidency is the longest in Church history.

A prolific speaker, President Clark's most memorable addresses discussed the Savior, financial matters, and the pioneering spirit.

SOURCES

Fox, Frank W. *J. Reuben Clark: The Public Years.* Provo, Utah: Brigham Young University Press, 1980.

Quinn, D. Michael. *J. Reuben Clark: The Church Years.* Provo, Utah: Brigham Young University Press, 1983.

Yarn, David H., Jr. "A Glimpse of J. Reuben Clark, Jr." BYU Forum Address, 5 August 1975. Reprinted for the dedication of the J. Reuben Clark College of Law. Provo, Utah: Brigham Young University, 1975.

KRISTIN B. GERDY

CLAWSON, RUDGER. Rudger Clawson, president of the **Quorum** of the Twelve **Apostles** and a courageous missionary, was born 12 March 1857 in **Salt Lake City**. When he was only 18 years old, he served as a secretary to apostle **John W. Young**. A few years later, Rudger was called on a **mission** to the southern **United States**. On 9 July 1879, while serving in **Georgia**, Elder Clawson and his companion, **Joseph Standing**, were accosted by a vicious **anti-Mormon** mob. They shot Elder Standing, killing him in front of his horrified companion, and then turned their guns on Elder Clawson. Instead of running, the missionary folded his arms across his chest and calmly said, "Shoot!" This display of courage unnerved the mob, and they left him alone. This act was symbolic of the valor he would display in his Church service throughout his life.

In 1887 he was called to settle in **Brigham City** and preside over the **stake** there. In this assignment he had occasion to participate with apostle **Lorenzo Snow** in restoring the life of Ella Jensen, a teenage member of the stake who had been dead for several hours. On 10 October 1898, he was called to the Quorum of the Twelve; three years later he was chosen as second counselor in the **First Presidency** to **Lorenzo Snow**. Elder Clawson was never set apart to this position, however, because President Snow passed away just four days after general conference. Returning to the Quorum, Elder Clawson served a total of 45 years as an apostle, including 22 years as President of the Twelve. He died in Salt Lake City on 21 June 1943.

Sources

Flake, Lawrence R. *Prophets and Apostles of the Last Dispensation.* Provo, Utah: Religious Studies Center, Brigham Young University, 2001. 259.

Jenson, Andrew. *Latter-day Saint Biographical Encyclopedia.* 4 vols. 1901–36. Reprint, Salt Lake City: Western Epics, 1971. 1:174.

"Rudger Clawson." *Encyclopedia of Mormonism.* Edited by Daniel H. Ludlow. 4 vols. New York: Macmillan, 1992. 4:1634.

Lawrence R. Flake

CLAY, HENRY. Henry Clay, noted for his abilities as a lawyer, public speaker, congressman, and compromiser, crossed paths with the Latter-day Saints as a U.S. presidential candidate in 1844 and as architect of the **Compromise of 1850**. Born 12 April 1777 in Hanover County, **Virginia**, Clay entered the House of Representatives from **Kentucky** in 1811, from which post he, as Speaker, agitated for war with **England** in 1812, helped negotiate the Treaty of Ghent and the **Missouri Compromise**, and promoted a series of measures designed to foster domestic agriculture, industry, and markets.

Failing in his bid for the presidency in 1824 and 1832, Clay ran again in 1844, prompting **Joseph Smith** to ask him what his course of action would be relative to the **Saints'** efforts to obtain **redress** for their

Missouri losses. Clay responded that he could "make no promises, [and] give no pledge to any particular portion of the people of the **United States**" (Smith, 376). When other candidates replied similarly or not at all, Joseph began his own **presidential campaign**.

Clay drafted the Compromise of 1850 six years later, repudiating the Saints' petition for statehood by creating the **Utah** Territory instead. He died 29 June 1852 in **Washington, D.C.**

SOURCES

Remini, Robert V. *Henry Clay: Statesman for the Union.* New York: W. W. Norton, 1991.

Smith, Joseph. *History of The Church of Jesus Christ of Latter-day Saints.* Edited by B. H. Roberts. 2d ed. rev. 7 vols. Salt Lake City: The Church of Jesus Christ of Latter-day Saints, 1932–51. 6:64–65, 376.

ANDREW H. HEDGES

CLAY COUNTY, MISSOURI. The Latter-day Saints settled in Clay County, **Missouri**, as a temporary place of refuge after they were driven from **Jackson County** in 1833. The residents of Clay County generally received the **Mormons** with friendship while the **Saints** lived there, largely in an impoverished condition. Meanwhile, Church leaders in exile negotiated unsuccessfully with the **Jackson County** authorities for redress for their past suffering and failed also in their extensive pursuit for justice in the courts.

By **revelation, Joseph Smith** organized **Zion's Camp** in **Kirtland, Ohio,** to help the Saints in Missouri. The **Prophet** intended this armed paramilitary relief party to escort his people back to Jackson County (D&C 103). As misunderstandings about the Camp arose, however, hundreds of fearful citizens in Missouri's western counties mobilized for war. When he arrived at Clay County in June 1834, Joseph Smith, in response to divine revelation (D&C 105), promptly disbanded Zion's Camp to avoid a bloody conflict. Before returning to Ohio, he formed a **stake** organization among the exiles, appointing **David Whitmer** as president, with **William W. Phelps** and **John Whitmer** as **counselors**.

Later at Kirtland, Joseph Smith advanced a program of heavy emigration from the East to Clay County. He anticipated that a large "united effort" would soon enable the Saints to cross the **Missouri River** and redeem **Zion** in Jackson County (Smith, 2:145).

By June 1836, the gathering to Clay County and some Latter-day Saint religious beliefs alarmed the residents, who feared the growing

Mormon dominance and reminded the Saints of their original intention of living in the county only temporarily. Chaotic public meetings at the courthouse in **Liberty**, the county seat, and private meetings elsewhere cemented animosity against the Saints. Mobs forcefully stopped Mormon immigration at the county's eastern border and brutally attacked one of their settlements near the residence of Isaac Morley, southwest of Fishing River. Foreseeing further bloodshed and desiring to live "in a covenant of peace" with the citizens, the Mormons were willing to move from the county (Smith, 2:453). Church leaders scouted for a new gathering place, and in September 1836 the Saints began to move to **Caldwell County** in northern Missouri.

SOURCES

Parkin, Max H. "Latter-day Saint Conflict in Clay County." In *Missouri*. Edited by Arnold K. Garr and Clark V. Johnson. Regional Studies in Latter-day Saint Church History series. Provo, Utah: Brigham Young University, 1994. 241–60.

Smith, Joseph. *History of The Church of Jesus Christ of Latter-day Saints*. Edited by B. H. Roberts. 2d ed. rev. 7 vols. Salt Lake City: The Church of Jesus Christ of Latter-day Saints, 1932–51. 2:36–146, 448–66.

MAX H. PARKIN

CLAYTON, WILLIAM. Best known for his **hymn "Come, Come, Ye Saints,"** William Clayton also made many other contributions to early **Mormon** history. Born 17 July 1814 in Penwortham, **England**, in 1837 he became one of the earliest British converts to the Church. He served in the **British Mission** presidency from 1838 to 1840, during which time he quit his work as a factory clerk and devoted all of his time to missionary activity, mostly in **Manchester, England**. In 1840 he emigrated to **America** with his wife, two children, and several in-laws. Arriving in Commerce (soon renamed **Nauvoo**), **Illinois**, on 24 November, he was advised to settle across the **Mississippi River** in the Mormon settlement of **Zarahemla, Iowa**. After a year, however, he found himself unable to make a living, and he was grossly disappointed with the failure of the settlement. Nevertheless, Clayton was deeply devoted to the **Prophet Joseph Smith**, and never letting any of his own disappointments affect that devotion, he spent the rest of his life bearing fervent testimony of the divinity of Joseph Smith's mission. In June 1842 he succeeded **Willard Richards** as a clerk to the Prophet and soon became one of his closest associates and confidants. Clayton recorded the **revelation** on **plural marriage** when it was dictated by Joseph Smith in 1843, and he ultimately became the husband of nine additional wives (three of whom left him).

A meticulous record keeper, Clayton kept several important Church records and helped prepare Joseph Smith's official history. In addition, he was recorder and clerk of the Nauvoo City Council, secretary *pro tem* of the Nauvoo Masonic Lodge, an officer in the Nauvoo **Music** Association, and a member of the politically significant **Council of Fifty**.

Clayton and his **family** were among the first Mormons to leave Nauvoo in the winter **exodus** of 1846. On 15 April, while camped on the plains of Iowa, he penned the words to "Come, Come, Ye Saints," one of Mormonism's best-loved hymns. He was at **Winter Quarters, Nebraska,** during the following winter and headed west in 1847 with the vanguard company that selected the site for the new Mormon settlement in the **Salt Lake Valley**. His **journal**, published in 1921, provided the best-known account of that journey. He also prepared and published *The Latter-day Saints' Emigrants' Guide,* which became an important guide not only for later Mormon migrants but also for **pioneers** on their way to **California** and **Oregon**.

His Utah activities included more record keeping for the Church and a number of important civic positions, including territorial auditor and territorial recorder of marks and brands. He also served as treasurer of the **Deseret Telegraph** Company and secretary of the Church-owned department store **ZCMI**. He also tried, at various times, a debt-collection business, filing land claims, money lending, and legal work. He died 4 December 1877 in **Salt Lake City**.

SOURCES

Allen, James B. *Trials of Discipleship: The Story of William Clayton, a Mormon.* Urbana: University of Illinois Press, 1987.

Clayton, William. *An Intimate Chronicle: The Journals of William Clayton.* Edited by George D. Smith. Salt Lake City: Signature Books and Smith Research Associations, 1972.

Clayton, William. *Manchester Mormons: The Journal of William Clayton, 1840–1842.* Edited by James B. Allen and Thomas G. Alexander. Santa Barbara, Calif.: Peregrine Smith, 1974.

Clayton, William. *William Clayton's Journal.* Salt Lake City: The Clayton Family Association, 1921.

JAMES B. ALLEN

CLEVELAND, GROVER. Grover Cleveland, president of the **United States** from 1885 to 1889 and again from 1893 to 1897, was involved in several events that had a significant impact on **Mormon** history. Born 18 March 1837 in Caldwell, **New Jersey**, to Richard and Ann Neal Cleveland, Grover moved with his family to Fayetteville, **New York**, when he was only four years old. When Grover was about 12 years old, the **family** moved to Clinton, New York, where he attended high school.

Cleveland practiced law in Buffalo, where he was elected mayor (1881–82). He served as governor of New York from 1883 to 1885 and was then elected president of the United States. He was the first **Democrat** to be elected to that office since **James Buchanan** in 1856, almost three decades earlier. He was also the first U.S. president who was friendly toward the Mormons since **Abraham Lincoln** (1861–65), who had served 20 years before.

Two years after Cleveland became president, Congress passed the **Edmunds-Tucker Act** of 1887, the most severe of all antipolygamy legislation. Cleveland refused to sign the bill, but it became law without his signature. Taking this position preserved his political future but also indicated sympathy toward the Mormons. Later that same year Cleveland pardoned **Rudger Clawson**, a prominent Latter-day Saint who had served three years of a four-year jail sentence for polygamous cohabitation.

After the Mormons stopped practicing **plural marriage** in 1890, President **Benjamin Harrison** waited three years before he granted amnesty to polygamists, and it was restricted to **Saints** who had abided by the law since 1890. After Grover Cleveland came back into office, he extended a more general amnesty on 25 September 1894. Earlier that year, on 16 July, Cleveland also signed the Enabling Act, which paved the way for **Utah** to become a state. On 4 January 1896 President Cleveland signed the proclamation stating that Utah had officially become a state, thus ending a half-century of antagonistic federal domination in the territory. Grover Cleveland will always be remembered as one who was fair-minded toward the Latter-day Saints. He died in Princeton, New Jersey, 24 June 1908.

SOURCES

Larson, Gustive O. *The Americanization of Utah for Statehood.* San Marino, Calif.: The Huntington Library, 1971.

Nevins, Allen. *Grover Cleveland: A Study in Courage.* New York: Dodd, Mead, 1932.

Roberts, B. H. *A Comprehensive History of The Church of Jesus Christ of Latter-day Saints, Century One.* 6 vols. Salt Lake City: The Church of Jesus Christ of Latter-day Saints, 1930. Vol. 6.

ARNOLD K. GARR

CLOTHING. The Saints' clothing was like that worn by the common people of the day. Even **Joseph Smith** chose to wear ordinary, unpretentious clothing rather than the unique attire worn by other religious leaders. In light of his example, the pattern did not develop of presiding officers in Latter-day Saint meetings wearing formal collars or other distinctly ministerial clothing. Although an 1831 **revelation** directed "let all thy garments be plain, and their beauty the beauty of the work of thine own hands" (D&C 42:40), many Saints in **Kirtland** sought to keep up with the latest Eastern fashions. In **Nauvoo** the **Prophet** chastised Church members for giving more attention to fine clothing than to the poor.

Burial clothing was the first to develop a distinctive Latter-day Saint style. White, the color of innocence, was commonly used for the burial of children, but most adults in Europe and America were buried in black. Beginning in Nauvoo, however, white also became popular for adult burials. Some members of the **Mormon Battalion** and **pioneers** on the plains were buried in **temple** clothing. Within a few decades this practice became standard.

In pioneer **Utah**, Church leaders emphasized the 1831 revelation on clothing to promote home manufacturing. The Saints were also encouraged during that period to develop their own fashions. Rejecting the tightly corseted, dirt-dragging dresses of their day, some Latter-day Saint women, in 1852, sought to develop a fashion based on the ideas of New Yorker Amelia Bloomer. **Eliza R. Snow** led this movement, with other women contributing ideas and sewing talents. The emphasis on homemade plain clothing reached a high point in the 1870s in such experimental communities as **Orderville**. These communities disbanded during the 1880s, however, due in part to the derision by outsiders of old-fashioned clothing styles, homemade shoes, straw hats, and gray jeans. Surviving dresses suggest that during the 1890s the editors of the *Young Woman's Journal* successfully influenced their young readers to choose darker colors and more conservative styles as symbols of modesty.

During the twentieth century, attention was given to clothing worn by those participating in priesthood **ordinances**. By the 1940s white clothing was worn almost universally by the baptismal candidate and the baptizer. In 1957 the presiding bishopric instructed young men to wear white shirts and appropriate ties while administering the sacrament. This standard has never become universal but remains widespread.

From the beginning of the **Restoration**, missionaries attempted to dress their best. Over the years, each **mission** developed its own standards based on local tradition. Some required dark brown suits; others, dark swallowtail jackets and striped pants; most required a business suit of some kind. Almost all missionaries were required to wear hats, with the derby becoming standard. In the 1950s, however, after the wearing of hats had become generally less fashionable, the requirement was gradually removed at the discretion of individual mission presidents. By 1960 few missionaries wore hats. Attention then shifted to hair length, which was set to meet standards of respectability. The most distinctive variations in missionary clothing developed in the **Pacific** Islands. In some areas, missionaries, like most members, wore white suits or jackets and straw hats. As indigenous members began proselyting in **Tonga**, wraparound skirts (*lava lavas*) and a traditional knitted apron (*tavalu*) became standard missionary dress, typically worn with the usual white shirt and tie.

At the close of the twentieth century, standard missionary dress had become a dark suit, white shirt, and tie for men and conservative dresses for women. This is also the standard Latter-day Saint fashion for worship services, with many variations in some non-Western areas, such as tropical regions.

SOURCES

Anderson, Carma DeJong. "A Historical Overview of the Mormons and Their Clothing, 1840–1850." Ph.D. diss., Brigham Young University, 1992.

Walkup, Fairfax Proudfit. "The General Trends and Characteristics of Utah Pioneer Dress from 1847 to 1875." Master's thesis, Utah State Agricultural College, 1947.

MARK L. STAKER

CLUFF, BENJAMIN, JR.

Toward the end of the nineteenth century, educator Benjamin Cluff Jr. propelled the **Brigham Young Academy** of **Provo** into national academic respectability while managing to preserve the unique spiritual mission charted by its pioneer founder. Cluff was born in Provo, Utah, on 7 February 1858 and later studied mathematics, English, and pedagogy at the University of Michigan (B.S. 1890; M.S. 1894). In 1892 he succeeded **Karl G. Maeser** as principal (later president) of Brigham Young Academy, a position he held for 12 years.

Academic and extracurricular innovations during Cluff's administration were numerous. The academy broadened curriculum, lengthened class time, awarded degrees, published journals, founded laboratories, instituted missionary training, convened athletic competitions, and invited professors from outside **Utah** to lecture. A collegiate department was created in 1896, the same year the Church absorbed the school's liabilities and formally agreed to provide large-scale financial subsidy.

The crowning achievement of Cluff's administration came in October 1903, when the name Brigham Young Academy was officially changed to **Brigham Young University**. Two months later Cluff resigned as president of the institution to become superintendent of the Utah-Mexican Rubber Plantation.

Cluff died in Redondo Beach, **California**, on 14 June 1948.

SOURCES

Roberts, Eugene L., and Eldon Reed Cluff. "Benjamin Cluff Jr.: Scholar, Educational Administrator, and Explorer." Manuscript. Special Collections and Manuscripts, Brigham Young University Library, Provo, Utah. 1947.

Wilkinson, Ernest L., ed. *Brigham Young University: The First One Hundred Years.* 4 vols. Provo, Utah: Brigham Young University Press, 1975–76.

JED L. WOODWORTH

COBB, CAMILLA. Founder of the first **Utah** kindergarten, Camilla Clara Meith Cobb was born 24 May 1843 in Dresden, Saxony, **Germany**. She joined the Church at age 13 and emigrated to Utah with her sister Anna and Anna's husband, **Karl G. Maeser**. Upon arrival in Utah, she taught with Maeser in several ward schools. She married James T. Cobb on 14 November 1864; they had 6 children. She received kindergarten training in **New Jersey** and in 1874 opened the first kindergarten for her own and **Brigham Young's** children and grandchildren. She served Utah children for most of her adult life—both as a teacher and a Primary worker. Camilla passed away on 19 October 1933 in **Salt Lake City**.

SOURCE

Britsch, Catherine L. "Camilla C. Cobb: Founder of the Kindergarten in Utah." Ed.D. diss., Brigham Young University, 1997.

CATHERINE BRITSCH FRANTZ

COFFEE. See **WORD OF WISDOM.**

COLE, ABNER. Editor of the **Palmyra** weekly newspaper, *The Reflector,* Abner Cole, under the pseudonym of Obadiah Dogberry, violated **Joseph Smith's** copyright on the **Book of Mormon** by publishing extracts from 1 Nephi and Alma between 2 January 1830 and 22 January 1830. Reportedly a former justice of the peace, Cole stopped his illegal activities only after the Prophet confronted him. Cole initially reported to his readers that he had found nothing "treasonable" in the Book of Mormon (Bushman, 108). He nevertheless ridiculed the book and the Prophet in later editions of his paper, even after the Church had moved to **Kirtland**. Abner Cole died in Rochester, New York, 13 July 1835.

SOURCES

Bushman, Richard L. *Joseph Smith and the Beginnings of Mormonism*. Urbana: University of Illinois Press, 1988. 108, 120–24.

Rich, Russell R. "The Dogberry Papers and the Book of Mormon." *BYU Studies* 10 (Spring 1970): 315–20.

Smith, Lucy Mack. *History of Joseph Smith by His Mother*. Edited by Preston Nibley. Revised edition edited by Scot Facer and Maurine Jensen Proctor. Salt Lake City: Bookcraft, 1996. 215–22.

ANDREW H. HEDGES

COLESVILLE, NEW YORK. Formed from Windsor Township on 2 April 1821, Colesville Township is located 12 miles east of Binghamton in the northeastern part of Broome County, **New York**. The township is named after Nathaniel Cole Sr., a Revolutionary War veteran who settled on what became Cole's Hill in 1795.

Joseph Knight Sr. owned a 142-acre farm in the township of Colesville on the east side of the **Susquehanna River**, opposite the village of Nineveh. **Joseph Smith Jr.** was employed by Joseph Knight in 1826 and allowed to take Knight's "cutter" (sleigh) down the Susquehanna to court Miss **Emma Hale** of **Harmony, Pennsylvania**. Knight later supplied the Prophet and Oliver Cowdery with writing materials and other provisions while the **Book of Mormon** was being translated at Harmony, Pennsylvania, in April and May 1829. After the **organization of the** Church on **6 April** 1830 at **Fayette**, the **Prophet** immediately continued his proselyting in Colesville. The "first miracle of the Church" was performed there by the Prophet when he cast an evil spirit out of **Newel Knight**. With other missionaries, Joseph Smith was successful in converting some 68 members of Knight's extended **family** and friends during 1830 and 1831. Joseph Knight Sr., his wife Polly Peck, Emma Hale Smith, and some others were baptized in the millrace at the Knight farm on 28 June 1830. At the confirmation services for these new converts, Joseph Smith was arrested by a constable on a warrant charging him with being a "disorderly person" and taken to the village of **South Bainbridge** in adjoining Chenango County. Joseph Knight Sr. enlisted the services of

James Davidson and John S. Reid as legal counsel. The Prophet was acquitted of the charge at South Bainbridge and also gained acquittal on a similar charge in a second trial that convened in Colesville, Broome County. Commencing in October 1830, **Hyrum Smith**, brother of the Prophet, presided over the Colesville **Branch**. Newel Knight succeeded him when Hyrum was called to **Ohio** in March 1831. It was Joseph Knight Sr. who drove the Prophet and Emma in his sleigh from New York to **Kirtland, Ohio**, leaving in late January and arriving at Kirtland on 1 February 1831. The Colesville Branch was obedient to the call to gather given at the 2 January 1831 **conference** of the Church in Fayette (D&C 38). In April 1831 Newel Knight led the exodus of the Colesville Branch in their move from Broome and Chenango Counties to Kirtland, Ohio, via Cayuga Lake, the **Erie Canal**, and Lake Erie. This Colesville branch stayed together and played a key role in early Latter-day Saint history, both in Ohio and **Missouri**.

SOURCES

Hartley, William G. *Stand by My Servant Joseph: A History of the Joseph Knight Family and the Restoration.* Salt Lake City: Deseret Book, 2001.

Jacob, Leone R. *Famines, Fires, & Festivals: A History of Colesville 1785–1978.* Tunnel, New York: Town of Colesville, 1978.

Porter, Larry C. "A Study of the Origins of The Church of Jesus Christ of Latter-day Saints in the States of New York and Pennsylvania, 1816–1831." Ph.D. diss., Brigham Young University, 1971. 172–98, 296–311.

Smith, Joseph. *History of The Church of Jesus Christ of Latter-day Saints [HC].* Edited by B. H. Roberts. 2d ed. rev. 7 vols. Salt Lake City: The Church of Jesus Christ of Latter-day Saints, 1932–51. 1:81–96; 6:392–97.

LARRY C. PORTER

COLOMBIA. The first missionaries to Colombia arrived in May 1966 as part of the Andes Mission. Antonio Vela and Aura Ivars were among the first converts to be baptized. On 1 July 1971, the capital city, Bogotá, became the headquarters for a new mission that included the entire nation. Continued growth has brought the formation of four **missions** and the call of a native Colombian, Julio Davila, as a member of the Second Quorum of the **Seventy** (1991–96). Strife within the country required the temporary removal of North American missionaries in 1988. Later they were allowed to return.

Church members faithfully united to provide for the needs of others following two major earthquakes, in Popayan (1983) and Armenia

(1999). At the beginning of the year 2000 there were 129,105 members of the Church living in 23 **stakes** and 309 **wards** and **branches** within the country. A significant milestone was met when the Bogotá Colombia **Temple** was dedicated 24 to 26 April 1999.

SOURCE

1999–2000 Church Almanac. Salt Lake City: Deseret News, 1998. 305–6.

CRAIG J. OSTLER

COLONIA JUÁREZ. See MEXICAN COLONIES.

COLONIZATION. During the nineteenth and early twentieth centuries, the Church promoted settlement programs to develop living places for **Saints** gathering to **Zion** and for new generations of members. Through it the Saints colonized, or created specifically Latter-day Saint settlements, throughout the Intermountain West—**Utah**, **Idaho**, **Nevada**, **Arizona**, **Colorado**, **Wyoming**—and in **California**, **Canada**, and **Mexico**.

During **Brigham Young**'s presidency, some 350 Latter-day Saint settlements were created in the West, earning him the title "The Colonizer." Three principles guided his colonizing efforts: (1) to gather thousands of believers into one geographic area, Saints needed to quickly claim and develop all the available, productive land, resources, and main travel routes possible; (2) to operate a **Mormon** society properly, temporally and spiritually, the people must live in cities, towns, and villages modeled after **Joseph Smith**'s unique "City of Zion" layout plans, under Church leadership; (3) for the good of the whole, people must subordinate themselves to the group's best religious, economic, and political interests as determined by Church authorities responsible for imposing policy and systems.

In general, members of the Twelve or other tested leaders led the colonizing ventures, and members were called on missions to go with them and establish core settlements. Then, clusters of satellite settlements developed around these, either through Church direction or, more often, through individual members' initiatives. Most Latter-day Saint settlements were agricultural villages. Several were founded near **Native American** settlements in order to teach their inhabitants agriculture and the gospel. A number were established to develop particular resources, such as coal, iron, lead, or cotton. A handful of settlements served as outposts at entry points into the **Great Basin**. President Young paid regular visits to the settlements to know firsthand how they were developing. Many **pioneer** families helped establish not just one but several colonies during their lifetimes. A major part of the Church's energy during the latter half of the nineteenth century was devoted to the colonization of North American settlements.

INTERMOUNTAIN WEST

Colonizing within the Intermountain West regions occurred in three distinct phases:

Phase 1: 1847 to 1857. Within two years of their arrival, Saints had settled the Great **Salt Lake Valley**, the Tooele Valley, **Provo, Ogden**, and places in between. "We wish to have a chain of Settlements," President Young said in 1849, "extending from this place to the coast as well as all other good locations within the Limits of our State," which then included present Nevada (Letter). That year **apostle Parley P. Pratt** led an exploring party to central and southern Utah. His report determined sites for 25 towns between Great **Salt Lake City** and **St. George** and identified resources to develop, including iron ore near present Cedar City. In 1851 colonizing ventures led by various apostles and other leaders established dozens of families in the Cedar City area (to produce iron) and in **Fillmore**, Tooele, Sanpete County, Box Elder County, and Nephi. These became permanent settlements. Church leaders founded two **Indian** mission colonies, at Moab in Utah and **Fort Limhi** in Idaho, a lead mining mission in **Las Vegas**, and entry-point colonies at **Carson Valley**, Nevada, and the **Fort Bridger** area of Wyoming. A large California colony existed briefly in **San Bernardino**. When the **Utah War** threatened, leaders closed down distant colonies and called the Saints home. These colonies did not reopen.

Phase 2: 1858 to 1869: Colonists were sent into **Cache Valley**, the Bear Lake area, southeastern Idaho, and the Sevier and Sanpete areas. In the April 1861 **general conference**, Brigham Young announced the names of people he had selected to colonize southern Utah's "Dixie" region. With St. George as the hub settlement, they grew crops adapted to the hot climate—mainly cotton.

Phase 3: 1869 to 1877: During this period of time, new colonizing regions were opened in the **Uintah Basin**, Arizona, the San Luis Valley in Colorado, and southern Nevada.

CANADA AND MEXICO

In the 1880s mounting **antipolygamy** prosecutions caused Church leaders to create Latter-day Saint colonies outside the **United States**. Starting with **Colonia Juárez** in 1885, the Church opened seven colonies in **Chihuahua** (Juárez, Diaz, Dublan, Pacheco, Chuichupa, Garcia, and Cave Valley) and two in Sonora (Oaxaca and Morelos). The Juárez **Stake** (1895) governed the **wards** and **branches**, and the Juárez Stake Academy became the colonies' main school. In 1912 Saints evacuated because of the Mexican Revolution, and only Colonia Juárez and Colonia Dublan were resettled and continue today as predominantly Latter-day Saint towns.

In 1886 President **John Taylor** instructed Cache **Stake president Charles Ora Card** to find settlement sites in southern **Alberta, Canada,** and a year later Saints from Utah established **Cardston**, 15 miles north of the U.S. border. By 1900 13 more Latter-day Saint settlements were added. The Alberta Stake was organized in 1895 and continues to be a Latter-day Saint stronghold.

BIG HORN BASIN

In 1893 a company of Saints, mostly from eastern Utah, went to the Big Horn country in northern Wyoming and founded Burlington. In 1900 **Elder Abraham O. Woodruff** of the Twelve organized a Latter-day Saint emigration there, which founded Byron, Cowley, Leavitt, and other settlements. In 1901 the Big Horn Stake was organized.

By 1900, an estimated 500 Mormon colonies had been established in the Intermountain West, Canada, and Mexico. Of these, about 80 have ceased to exist. As the twentieth century opened, the Church ceased to directly promote colonizing ventures.

SOURCES

Arrington, Leonard J. *Great Basin Kingdom.* Lincoln: University of Nebraska Press, 1958.

Brown, S. Kent, Donald Q. Cannon, and Richard H. Jackson, eds. *Historical Atlas of Mormonism.* New York: Simon & Schuster, 1994.

Campbell, Eugene E. *Establishing Zion: The Mormon Church in the American West, 1847–69.* Salt Lake City: Signature Books, 1988.

Hunter, Milton R. *Brigham Young the Colonizer.* Salt Lake City: Deseret News, 1940.

Larson, Andrew Karl. "I Was Called to Dixie." Salt Lake City: Deseret News, 1961.

Young, Brigham. Letter to Amasa Lyman, 30 September 1849.

WILLIAM G. HARTLEY

COLORADO. The first permanent Latter-day **Saint** settlers in Colorado were converts to the Church from the southern **United States** who established a colony in the San Luis Valley in 1878. They were preceded by Latter-day Saints from **Mississippi** who stopped temporarily in the region in 1846, wintering at the present-day site of **Pueblo** before continuing on to the **Salt Lake Valley,** which they reached in July 1847. The first **stake** of the Church in Colorado was organized among the convert colonizers in 1883 at Manassa and was named the San Luis Stake. Manassa's most famous Latter-day Saint native son was Jack Dempsey (1895–1983), the one-time world heavyweight boxing champion who earned the nickname "the Manassa Mauler." As the number of **Mormon** settlers increased in southern Colorado (especially at Fort Lewis Mesa), the Young Stake was organized in 1913, encompassing Montezuma and La Plata Counties.

By far the largest Church growth after 1900 occurred through proselyting efforts along the eastern slope of the Rocky Mountains, particularly in Denver, where the Western States **Mission** was headquartered. The Colorado Mission (later renamed) had been created in 1896, and a year later the Denver **Branch** was organized. Future Church president **Harold B. Lee** served there from 1920 to 1922. In November 1911 the **Tabernacle Choir** gave a concert in the city. It was not until 1940 that the Denver Stake was created, which stretched from Laramie, **Wyoming,** in the north to Pueblo, Colorado, in the south and was presided over by Edward E. Drury. Two future **presiding bishops** of the Church at one time also served in the Denver Stake presidency: **John H. Vandenberg** and **Victor L. Brown.**

Church membership in Colorado reached almost 70,000 by 1980. In 1982 plans were announced to build the Denver **Temple,** which was completed and dedicated in 1986. Following the temple's dedication, the Church continued to grow in membership and increase in public recognition. The state's governor—Roy Romer—addressed a special Church fireside following the 1990 inauguration of the state's released-time **seminary** program. Latter-day Saint volunteers assisted Catholics with the visit of Pope John Paul II to the Denver area in 1993. At the beginning of the year 2000 there were approximately 112,232 members in 28 stakes and 238 **wards** and branches in the state. By 1999 two **missions** were headquartered in the state: Colorado Denver North and Colorado Denver South.

SOURCES

Bird, Twila. *Build unto My Holy Name: The Story of the Denver Temple.* Denver: Denver Colorado Area Public Relations Council, 1987.

Jenson, Andrew. "The Founding of Mormon Settlements in the San Luis Valley, Colorado." *Colorado Magazine* 17 (1940): 174–80.

ANDREW C. SKINNER

COLTRIN, ZEBEDEE. Zebedee Coltrin, a participant in many early Church history events, was born 7 September 1804 at Ovid, **New York**. At the age of ten he moved with his family to **Ohio**, where he was converted and baptized 9 January 1831.

Zebedee was a member of the **School of the Prophets** held in the **Newel K. Whitney store** between 24 January and the middle of April 1833. He was present in the school when the **Word of Wisdom** was revealed and the **First Presidency** was set apart. He was also an eyewitness to the appearance of the Father and the Son. He marched in **Zion's Camp** in 1834.

When the First **Quorum** of the **Seventy** was organized on 28 February 1835, Zebedee was called to be one of the seven presidents of that quorum. He spent 16 years doing missionary work. He was a member of the Kirtland Hebrew School in 1836 and participated in the dedication of the **Kirtland** and **Nauvoo Temples**.

Zebedee was a member of the original **pioneer** company that entered the **Salt Lake Valley** July 1847 and was later called to settle Spanish Fork. He was ordained a **patriarch** by **John Taylor** in 1873 and gave more than one thousand blessings prior to his death 21 July 1887 in Spanish Fork, **Utah**.

SOURCE

Stephens, Calvin R. "The Life and Contributions of Zebedee Coltrin." Master's thesis, Brigham Young University, 1974.

CALVIN R. STEPHENS

COLUMBUS, CHRISTOPHER. Not only was Christopher Columbus a great navigator and explorer, but Latter-day **Saint apostles** and **prophets** have regularly taught that his first voyage to **America** was a fulfillment of **Book of Mormon** prophecy and that he served as a forerunner to the **restoration** of the gospel. Columbus was born in Genoa (now part of **Italy**) between 25 August and 31 October, probably in the year 1451. He made four voyages to the Americas between 1492 and 1503 and died 20 May 1506 in Valladolid, **Spain**.

Six hundred years before the birth of **Christ**, the Book of Mormon prophet Nephi declared: "I looked and beheld a man among the **Gentiles**, who was separated from the seed of my brethren by the many waters; and I beheld the Spirit of **God**, that it came down and wrought upon the man; and he went forth upon the many waters, even unto the seed of my brethren, who were in the promised land" (1 Ne. 13:12). President **Gordon B. Hinckley** affirmed: "We interpret that to refer to Columbus. It is interesting to note that the spirit of God wrought upon him" (Hinckley, 52). Columbus himself wrote: "With a hand that could be felt, the Lord opened my mind to the fact that it would be possible to sail . . . and he opened my will to desire to accomplish the project. This was the fire that burned within me. . . . Who can doubt that this fire was not merely mine, but also of the Holy Spirit?" (West and Kling, 105).

George Q. Cannon taught that Columbus's discovery of America "was a preparatory work for the establishment of the **kingdom of God**. This Church and kingdom could not have been established on the earth if [Columbus's] work had not been performed" (*JD*, 14:155).

Columbus was one of the men for whom **Wilford Woodruff** performed **ordinances** in the **St. George Temple** (*JD*, 19:229).

SOURCES

Garr, Arnold K. *Christopher Columbus: A Latter-day Saint Perspective.* Provo, Utah: Brigham Young University, 1992.

Hinckley, Gordon B. "Building Your Tabernacle." *Ensign* 22 (November 1992): 50–52.

Journal of Discourses [JD]. 26 vols. London: Latter-day Saints' Book Depot, 1854–86. 14:55; 19:229.

West, Delno C., and August Kling. *The* Libro de las profecias *of Christopher Columbus.* Gainesville: University of Florida Press, 1991.

ARNOLD K. GARR

"COME, COME, YE SAINTS." In April 1846, **William Clayton** and most of his **family** camped in the mud at Locust Creek. He worried about his wife Diantha, who was still in **Nauvoo** awaiting the birth of her first child. The slow progress of the company and the burdens of caring for his large family disheartened him. When he received word that Diantha had given birth to a healthy baby boy, he penned the words of a song of praise, which he called "All Is Well." The song became an anthem for later groups of **Saints** and continues to give hope to members today.

SOURCE

Church History in the Fulness of Times. Salt Lake City: The Church of Jesus Christ of Latter-day Saints, 1989. 313.

AUDREY M. GODFREY

COMMERCE, ILLINOIS. See **NAUVOO, ILLINOIS.**

COMMISSIONER OF EDUCATION. See **CHURCH EDUCATIONAL SYSTEM**

COMMUNISM. Communism is a system of collective ownership and central economic control based on the teachings of Karl Marx (1818–83) and Friedrich Engels (1820–95). Soviet communism became a frequently discussed point of controversy following the Bolshevik revolution of 1917. In 1930 Latter-day **Saints** joined members of other faiths in protesting religious intolerance in **Russia**. The official recognition of the Soviet Union by the **United States** government in November 1933 sparked further debate. Finally, during the **great depression**, a few Latter-day Saints advocated communism as the means of solving the world's economic problems and of reestablishing the **law of consecration**, or the **united order**. In 1936 the **First Presidency** distinguished between atheistic communism, based on force, and consecration revealed by the Lord, based on voluntary action. They therefore insisted that communism could not bring about the united order. In following decades, Elder **Ezra Taft Benson** became a vocal critic of what he called "godless communism."

As communism gained control of Eastern **Europe** and Southeast **Asia**, Church growth in these areas was severely impeded. Although a few of these governments permitted limited Church activity, the fall of communist regimes in Eastern Europe during the last two decades of the twentieth century paved the way for accelerated Church growth in many countries. President **Spencer W. Kimball's** 1977 prayer of dedication in **Poland** and the 1985 dedication of the **Freiberg Temple** in East **Germany** contributed to the Church's remarkable expansion in these areas.

SOURCES

Benson, Ezra Taft. *The Threat of Communism.* Salt Lake City: Deseret Book, 1960.
Clark, James R., comp. *Messages of the First Presidency of The Church of Jesus Christ of Latter-day Saints.* 6 vols. Salt Lake City: Bookcraft, 1965–75. 6:17–18.

RICHARD O. COWAN

COMMUNITY OF CHRIST. See **REORGANIZED CHURCH OF JESUS CHRIST OF LATTER DAY SAINTS.**

COMPREHENSIVE HISTORY OF THE CHURCH, A. The six-volume *A Comprehensive History of The Church of Jesus Christ of*

Latter-day Saints, though published in 1930, is still one of the most valuable sources for those who seek to understand **Mormon** history.

Brigham H. Roberts, one of the seven presidents of the **Seventy** and one of the Church's most gifted writers, noted early in the twentieth century that the *Salt Lake Tribune* was publishing a series of articles attacking the origin of the **Book of Mormon**. Roberts wrote to the editor and requested an opportunity to write a refutation to the author's arguments. He was told the articles were reprints written by a former Salt Lake City attorney, Theodore Schroeder, and were taken from the *New York Historical Magazine*. Roberts wrote to the magazine's editor, repeating his request, and was told that if his rebuttal met the magazine's standards it would be published. His articles, four in number, were so good that the editor asked that he write a detailed history of the Church, which would be published serially. Roberts accepted the offer, and for six years his history appeared in each month's issue of the magazine, renamed *The Americana*. Each article was about 42 pages in length.

In 1928, when a Church committee began making preparations to celebrate the centennial of the Church's organization, Roberts suggested that a chronology of the Church's history be prepared. **Elder George Albert Smith** recommended that Roberts's own *Americana* series be updated and published in book form. The motion passed, and Roberts went to work. Finally, on **6 April** 1930, at the Church's **general conference**, Roberts presented his completed six-volume, 3,400-page history to the Church. He called it a sermon.

When published, *A Comprehensive History of the Church* was the most complete, most accurate, and by far the best history of Mormonism in existence. Roberts probed problems and analyzed the causes of events, his prose bearing testimony that God's hand had often guided Church leaders and members alike. Though he was not a professional historian, his account of the rise of the Church, the Saints' sojourns in **Kirtland**, **Missouri**, and **Nauvoo**, the **pioneer trek** of 1847, and the building of a religious kingdom in the **Great Basin** is a monument not only to the Church but to Roberts, the self-made historian.

SOURCES

Bergera, Gary James, ed. *The Autobiography of B. H. Roberts.* Salt Lake City: Signature Books, 1990. 225–29.

Madsen, Truman G. *B. H. Roberts: Defender of the Faith.* Salt Lake City: Bookcraft, 1980. 357–66.

KENNETH W. GODFREY

COMPROMISE OF 1850. The Compromise of 1850 resolved five slavery-related issues dividing the North and South and also rejected the Utah Saints' first petition for statehood. In 1849, the Saints petitioned Congress for the creation of the "State of Deseret," which included in its boundaries all or parts of present-day Utah, Nevada, Idaho, Wyoming, Colorado, New Mexico, Arizona, Oregon, and California. Under the Compromise, California was admitted to the Union as a free state. As a concession to southerners, Congress created two territorial governments —Utah and New Mexico—and left the slavery question for the people living in those territories to decide. Both these moves considerably reduced the size of the Saints' envisioned state, the last one effectively rejecting the Saints' bid for statehood. The Compromise also solved a boundary dispute between Texas and New Mexico, abolished the slave trade in the District of Columbia, and allowed for the passage of a new fugitive slave law.

SOURCE

Hamilton, Holman. *Prologue to Conflict: The Crisis and Conflict of 1850.* Lexington: University of Kentucky Press, 1964.

ANDREW H. HEDGES

CONDIE, RICHARD P. Richard P. Condie, a tenor soloist and music educator, is best known as the director of the Tabernacle Choir from 1957 to 1974. Born 5 July 1898 in Springville, Utah, Condie earned music degrees from Brigham Young University (1923) and the New England Conservatory of Music (1928). He later studied conducting with Robert Shaw and F. Melius Christiansen. After appearing in operatic roles with companies in Europe, North Africa, and New York, Condie returned to Utah, where in succeeding decades he taught at the McCune School of Music, Utah State University, Brigham Young University, and the University of Utah. He became the assistant director of the Tabernacle Choir in 1937 and, upon Spencer Cornwall's retirement 20 years later, became the choir's regular conductor. During his 17 years as conductor, he completely redefined the choir's sound, rejecting the sedate, vibrato-free singing that Cornwall preferred in favor of an operatic tone—lush, romantic, and dynamically expressive. Immediately after being appointed conductor, Condie began a long-term collaboration with Eugene Ormandy and the Philadelphia Orchestra, with whom the choir made a series of records for the Columbia label, including the Grammy

Award–winning "Battle Hymn of the Republic" (1958). Under Condie's direction the choir also began its weekly television show, performed its first **satellite** broadcast, and mounted its most elaborate international tours thus far. Richard Condie died 22 December 1985 in **Salt Lake City**.

SOURCES

Calman, Charles Jeffrey, and William I. Kaufman. *The Mormon Tabernacle Choir.* New York: Harper & Row, 1979.

Hicks, Michael. *Mormonism and Music: A History.* Urbana: University of Illinois Press, 1989.

MICHAEL HICKS

CONFER. Defined as giving or bestowing something from God to man, *conferring* divine gifts is accomplished through **priesthood** authority by the laying on of hands. Thus the priesthood, keys of the priesthood, and the **Holy Ghost** are all *conferred* or bestowed upon an individual. Although usage has changed over the years since the early days of the Church, the term *confer* in reference to the priesthood is now distinguished from *ordain*, which refers to bestowing a specific priesthood office.

MATTHEW O. RICHARDSON

CONFERENCE (MEETING). About 30 Latter-day **Saints** gathered for their first conference on 9 June 1830, fulfilling a command of the Lord to meet every three months or from time to time (D&C 20:61). They administered "emblems of the body and blood of . . . Christ," and the Holy Ghost was poured out in a "miraculous manner" (Jenson, 4). Exhortation and instructions were given, many prophesied, and hearts were filled with "joy unspeakable," thus setting a pattern for future Church conferences and **meetings**. Subsequent conferences, often lasting several days, recorded such events as the renunciation of **Hiram Page's seerstone**, the ordination of the first **high priests**, and the organization of the first conference (**Jackson County, Missouri**, 4 August 1831). On 1 November 1831, at a special conference in **Hiram, Ohio**, the **Saints** agreed to publish what the Lord referred to as "the book of my commandments" (D&C 1:6). During the **Nauvoo** period, "general" conferences were regularly established as annual and semiannual gatherings.

After the Saints settled in **Utah, stakes** began to multiply, and quarterly stake conferences were instituted. These meetings allowed **general authorities** to visit and counsel local members. Such conferences continued the tradition of instruction and exhortation, leadership training, and admonition. In 1971 the Church began holding **area conferences**. The first was held in **Manchester, England**, and was presided over by President **Joseph Fielding Smith**.

SOURCES

Jenson, Andrew. *Church Chronology: A Record of Important Events Pertaining to the History of The Church of Jesus Christ of Latter-day Saints.* Salt Lake City: Deseret News, 1899. 4–7.

Roberts, B. H. *Outlines of Ecclesiastical History: A Text Book.* Salt Lake City: Deseret Book, 1902. 328.

Smith, Joseph. *History of The Church of Jesus Christ of Latter-day Saints.* Edited by B. H. Roberts. 2d ed. rev. 7 vols. Salt Lake City: The Church of Jesus Christ of Latter-day Saints, 1932–51. 1:84–85.

KIM C AVERETT

CONFERENCE (UNIT). When considered as a location, a conference is "a geographical area of specified boundaries constituting a territorial unit in a Mission," which encompasses branches (Talmage, 216). Latter-day Saint use of this term can be traced back to May 1835 (Smith, 2:222–23).

Since 1927 the term "**district**" has been used instead of "conference" (Talmage, 216) and has the same meaning.

SOURCES

Ellsworth, S. George. "A History of Mormon Missions in the United States and Canada, 1830–1860." Ph.D. diss., University of California, 1951. 147–70.

Smith, Joseph. *History of The Church of Jesus Christ of Latter-day Saints.* Edited by B. H. Roberts. 2d ed. rev. 7 vols. Salt Lake City: The Church of Jesus Christ of Latter-day Saints, 1932–51. 2:222–25, 238, 241, 253.

Talmage, James E. "Districts and Conferences." *Millennial Star* 89 (7 April 1927): 216.

LARRY R. SKIDMORE

CONFERENCE CENTER. The Conference Center, located on the block north of **Temple Square**, was built to replace the **Tabernacle** as the site of **general conference** sessions and other **meetings**, programs, and **pageants**. President **Gordon B. Hinckley** broke ground on 24 July 1997, and the building was ready in April 2000 for the first general conference of the new millennium. The Conference Center seats 21,000 (nearly 3.5 times the capacity of the Tabernacle). The mammoth structure was built to the highest seismic codes, using the latest in architectural and engineering skills, and with state-of-the-art **broadcasting** capabilities. The building features granite exterior facing—the same kind of stone used for the **Salt Lake Temple**—rooftop gardens, fountains, plazas, and marble-lined walking paths. President Hinckley said of the Conference Center in the last session of general conference held in the Tabernacle (October 1999): "It is not of the same design as this Tabernacle, but it is also of a unique and wonderful kind. . . . It is a very large and a truly magnificent structure. . . . It is a bold step we are taking. But this boldness is in harmony with the tremendous outreach of the Church across the world. We have no desire to outdo **Brigham Young** or his architects. . . . We wish only to build on the tremendous foundation which President Young laid in pioneering this marvelous work here in the valleys of the West" (Hinckley, 117).

SOURCE

Hinckley, Gordon B. Conference Report (October 1999): 116–17.

LLOYD D. NEWELL

CONFERENCE REPORTS. The official reports of the **general conferences** of the Church are published as Conference Reports. Printed regularly since 1898, Conference Reports include remarks and commentary provided by the conducting general authorities, conference addresses, music of the conference, and any other important editorial commentary. Conference Reports are distributed as booklets to Church leaders, Church employees, and libraries. Because of the limited distribution of Conference Reports, the *Improvement Era* began publishing conference proceedings in 1942. In 1971, the *Ensign* replaced the *Era* in reporting conference proceedings, typically printing them in the May and November issues. With this combined distribution, the general audience of the Church and other interested parties have ready access to conference proceedings, which by 1999 were also made available on the Internet.

SOURCE

Tate, Charles. "Conference Reports." *Encyclopedia of Mormonism.* Edited by Daniel H. Ludlow. 4 vols. New York: Macmillan, 1992. 1:305–6.

MATTHEW O. RICHARDSON

CONFIRMATION. The **ordinance** of confirmation, also known as bestowal of the gift of the Holy Ghost, has been performed since the **organization of the Church.** The New Testament practice was reiterated to the **Prophet Joseph Smith** during the translation of the **Book of Mormon** (Acts 8:14–20, 19:1–7; Moro. 2:1–2). At the **meeting** when the Church was organized, **6 April** 1830, the Prophet stated, "We . . . laid our hands on each individual member of the Church present [apparently those previously baptized and those baptized that day], that they might receive the gift of the Holy Ghost, and be confirmed members of the Church of **Christ**" (Smith, 1:77–78). The practice continues in the Church today after a candidate has been baptized by immersion.

SOURCES

First Presidency. Circular Letters, 23 January 1998. LDS Church Archives, The Church of Jesus Christ of Latter-day Saints, Salt Lake City.

Smith, Joseph. *History of The Church of Jesus Christ of Latter-day Saints.* Edited by B. H. Roberts. 2d ed. rev. 7 vols. Salt Lake City: The Church of Jesus Christ of Latter-day Saints, 1932–51.

RONALD O. BARNEY

CONGO. Located on the west central coast of **Africa** on the northern border of **Zaire** (Democratic Republic of Congo), the Republic of Congo (formerly known as French Equatorial Africa) has a population of about three million. In 1999 most of the people spoke French and Kongo. About half of the country was Christian, and most of the remaining population followed tribal religions.

One of the first citizens of Congo to join the Church was Jean Patrice Milembolo, who was baptized while attending a university in **France** in 1986. He eventually became a **district** president and supervisor of the **Church Educational System** for Congo.

In 1991 a military uprising in Zaire made it necessary to move the headquarters of the Zaire Kinshasa **Mission** north across the Congo River to Brazzaville, the capital city of Congo. On 23 December of that year, the Congo government granted formal recognition to the Church. The following year, a third nation, **Burundi**, was added to the mission. In January 1994, due to devastating uprisings in all three countries, the mission was closed for six months, and the Church was left in the hands of local leaders.

By the beginning of the year 2000 there were approximately 1,600 Church members in Congo in six **branches** and one district.

SOURCES

"Congo Grants Formal Status to the Church." *Church News,* 28 December 1991, 3.

Middleton, John, ed. *Encyclopedia of Africa South of the Sahara.* 4 vols. New York: Macmillan Library Reference USA, 1997. 1:362–69.

1999–2000 Church Almanac. Salt Lake City: Deseret News, 1998. 306.

Oral histories of early Church converts collected by E. Dale LeBaron. Copies at BYU Library, Provo, Utah; LDS Church Historical Library, Salt Lake City, Utah.

E. DALE LEBARON

CONGO, DEMOCRATIC REPUBLIC OF. See DEMOCRATIC REPUBLIC OF CONGO.

CONNECTICUT. Although they had no converts, **Elders Samuel H. Smith** and **Orson Hyde** proselyted in Connecticut as early as 1832. The first converts came in 1837, when **Wilford Woodruff** shared the gospel with his **family**. He baptized three members of his family as well as three others and later set up a small **branch**. In 1839 the **Eastern States Mission** was created and two more branches were organized in Connecticut. The Church experienced little **growth** in the state at this time, and in the 1850s most members left. By 1930 there were three branches but only 198 members. In 1937 the New England Mission was created, and over the next 10 years leaders began to see significant **growth** in Connecticut. Between 1955 and 1959 membership doubled. In 1966 the Hartford **Stake**, which included much of Connecticut and parts of **Massachusetts**, was created. A year after the Connecticut Hartford Mission was created in 1979, membership was 6,300. In 1992 a **temple** was announced for Hartford, but three years later the Church decided to build two temples instead—one in Boston and another in the **New York City** suburbs. By the beginning of the year 2000 there were 12,163 members living in Connecticut in 3 stakes and 34 **wards** and branches.

SOURCES

Alexander, Thomas G. *Things in Heaven and Earth: The Life and Times of Wilford Woodruff, a Mormon Prophet.* Salt Lake City: Signature Books, 1991. 58.

Berrett, LaMar C., ed. *New England and Eastern Canada.* Vol. 1 of *Sacred Places.* Salt Lake City: Bookcraft, 1999. 52–56.

Jenson, Andrew. *Encyclopedic History of The Church of Jesus Christ of Latter-day Saints.* Salt Lake City: Deseret News, 1941. 157.

1999–2000 Church Almanac. Salt Lake City: Deseret News, 1998. 186–87.

Rebecca Jackson

CONNOR, PATRICK E.

CONNOR, PATRICK E. Patrick Edward O'Connor (later changed to Connor), known as the father of **Utah** mining and the "first Gentile in Utah," was born in Kerry, **Ireland**, 17 March 1820. Historical documents conflict on the specific day of his birth, but O'Connor insisted that he was born on St. Patrick's Day in 1820. At the age of twelve he immigrated to **New York City** with his family. In 1839 he joined the U.S. Army to fight in the **Mexican War**, at which time he abbreviated his surname to Connor. After his discharge he followed the Gold Rush to **California**, where he married Johanna Connor (she had the same last name) on 14 August 1854.

With the outbreak of the **Civil War** Connor volunteered his skilled leadership in support of the Union. He was assigned to lead the **California volunteers,** with instructions to guard the western mail lines from **Indian** attacks. In October 1862 he established **Fort Douglas** east of **Salt Lake City**. After the war he remained in Utah to mine claims he had staked, some of which were located in what is now Bingham Canyon. To promote his mining ventures he created the *Daily Union Vedette*—an **anti-**Mormon newspaper that Connor used to draw a large **Gentile** population to Utah. His declared goal was to politically overwhelm the **Mormons**, whom he considered to be disloyal to the **United States** government.

In July 1870 Connor founded the **Liberal Party** to counter the political influence of the Latter-day **Saints** in Utah. He was unsuccessful in his efforts to win any major political office. In his later years he began to suffer financially and, after losing his most valuable mines, died 16 December 1891 in Salt Lake City. He was buried at the Fort Douglas cemetery.

SOURCES

Madsen, Brigham D. *Glory Hunter: A Biography of Patrick Edward Connor.* Salt Lake City: University of Utah Press, 1990.

Powell, Allan Kent, ed. *Utah History Encyclopedia.* Salt Lake City: University of Utah Press, 1994. 112–13.

Roberts, B. H. *A Comprehensive History of The Church of Jesus Christ of Latter-day Saints, Century One.* 6 vols. Salt Lake City: The Church of Jesus Christ of Latter-day Saints, 1930. 5:15–18, 61–70.

Matthew P. Willden

CONSECRATION, LAW OF. The practice of consecration was commanded by revelation early in 1831 (D&C 42:30–42). During **Joseph Smith**'s lifetime it helped meet the economic needs of a rapidly growing church and its poor members and echoed the economic practice set forth in the New Testament (Acts 2:44) and in Enoch's city of **Zion** (Moses 7:18–19), recognizing that ultimately everything belongs to God (Psalm 24:1). Consecration—the act of setting apart or devoting oneself and possessions for sacred purposes—became a law of the Church in 1831 and passed through four phases during the **Prophet**'s lifetime.

PHASE 1: 1831 TO 1833

Mormon consecration was actually a hybrid combining individualism and communitarianism. While the program required total consecration of all possessions as well as yearly donation to the Church of all surplus profits, it also encouraged individual freedom and initiative in the management of stewardships. The individual deeded all of his property to the **bishop** and received from him a stewardship, which he would continue to own unless he left the Church. Furthermore, individuals could negotiate with the bishop for what they needed for their "support" and "comfort." The Prophet believed that large surpluses of the **Saints'** own products, placed in the bishop's storehouse, would not only eradicate poverty but would also raise the living standard across the board—providing incentives for producing a surplus. The property in the storehouse, known as the "residue" or common property, was derived from initial consecrations and from annual surpluses; although held by the bishop, it was understood to be jointly owned by all of the stewards.

The first attempt to implement the law of consecration was in the **Kirtland, Ohio**, area in the spring of 1831. This program failed and was terminated within 30 days. The second attempt was in **Jackson County, Missouri**, later that same year. Phase I ended in 1833 largely because of misunderstanding, inexperience, and human selfishness. The *coup de grace* came in the spring of that year when a court upheld a Mr. Bates's petition to recover property that he had earlier consecrated. In retrospect, the failure of the 1831 economic law of the Church is not surprising. First, it seemed to run counter to conventional notions of private property. Second, the members of the Church in **Missouri** were by and large poor before they entered the consecration system—redistribution of property thus resulted in a leveling down rather than a leveling up of the stewards' living standard.

PHASE 2: 1833

Two significant modifications were made to remedy the problems resulting from the Bates case: (1) The stewardships or "inheritances" became the private property of the stewards. (2) The bishop's authority to unilaterally designate or "appoint" a stewardship was softened. Phase 2 was hardly implemented before the Mormons were expelled from Jackson County, Missouri, in late 1833 and early 1834. Thereafter, in Clay and adjacent counties, the consecration law was applied and practiced unevenly among the scattered Saints.

PHASE 3: 1837 TO 1838

As the Missouri Saints began migrating north into **Caldwell** and **Daviess Counties**, there was little to consecrate other than the labor of their hands and a willing heart. The bishopric in Missouri, in December 1837, asked members to voluntarily contribute 2% of their net worth; this initial contribution was to be followed by yearly inventory with the bishop. Although this voluntary contribution initiative was never implemented, it did serve as a prelude to a new economic system revealed in July 1838. This new law of consecration required all of a member's surplus in addition to 10% of his annual interest or net profits (D&C 119). Most of the Saints, however, had little or no surplus at all. Threatened with the possibility of financial collapse, the Saints in Caldwell County quickly resorted to communal cooperation.

PHASE 4: 1838 TO 1844

During the expulsion of the Mormons from Missouri in 1838 and 1839, makeshift economic programs, some sponsored by the Church, were created to assist the poor in their exodus. Although these welfare programs were temporary, they were generally communal in theory and practice, being administered by committees. Once the Saints had settled at **Nauvoo, Illinois**, and surrounding areas, some thought to implement earlier aspects of consecration, which they still accepted as a law of the Church. The quantity of the consecration was now the decision of the donor. Rather than setting specific percentages, the Prophet emphasized true generosity in giving and freedom from all taint of self-interest as the Saints fed the hungry, clothed the naked, and comforted the afflicted, regardless of religious affiliation. During the remainder of Joseph Smith's lifetime, contributions and donations were obtained by regular encouragement from the pulpit and by general epistles. The Saints were still expected to make a sacrifice of their time, talents, and property.

Beyond this general call for voluntary contributions, in 1842 Joseph Smith sought to perfect a program of sacrifice and consecration among those whom he believed to be faithful and loyal. He proposed to accomplish this by placing a few (and later many) of the Saints under explicit covenants of obedience while at the same time teaching them exalting keys of knowledge and power. The sacred ritual which encompassed these covenants and ordinances was known as the ancient order of the **priesthood** or the **temple** endowment. The covenant of consecration became a vital part of the process by which they could become joint heirs with **Christ** in receiving the powers, knowledge, and glory of the Father by consecrating their energy and resources to the Church and by sacrificing all things for the advancement of God's work on the earth.

Thus, the implementation of specific economic programs from 1831 to 1844 changed significantly in practice though not in principle. The possessions, skills, and time of the Saints were essential components in building the **kingdom of God** on the earth. Each economic program given to the Saints during these early years was designed to bring them to this realization. Unfortunately, however, none of these economic programs worked exceptionally well, and Joseph Smith increasingly emphasized freedom in economic activity. While in 1831 there had been rigid managerial control based on formal deeds, by 1844 Joseph Smith taught that spiritual commitment and love were higher expressions of consecration than legal stewardship agreements. During this time (1838), tithing had also become established as a minimum standard of economic consecration for the faithful.

SOURCES

Arrington, Leonard J., Feramorz Y. Fox, and Dean L. May. *Building the City of God: Community and Cooperation among the Mormons.* Salt Lake City: Deseret Book, 1976.

Cook, Lyndon W. *Joseph Smith and the Law of Consecration.* Orem, Utah: Keepsake Paperbacks, 1991.

LYNDON W. COOK

CONSTITUTION OF THE UNITED STATES.

A **revelation** recorded in the **Doctrine and Covenants** declares that the Constitution of the United States is God-given and inspired: "I established the Constitution of this land, by the hands of wise men whom I raised up unto this very purpose" (D&C 101:80). All Church presidents have made statements concerning the Constitution of the **United States**, attesting to its prominent place in **Mormon** culture. **Joseph Smith** was particularly vocal on the subject of the Constitution. At least 52 quotations on this subject have been attributed to him. He called the Constitution "a glorious standard" and claimed to be "the greatest advocate of the Constitution of the United States there is on the earth" (Cannon, 4, 8).

Among recent Church presidents, **Ezra Taft Benson** had the most to say regarding the Constitution. More than 120 quotations on this subject are attributed to him. His love for that document is captured in this statement: "I testify that America is a choice land. God raised up the founding fathers of the United States of America and established the inspired Constitution. This was the required prologue for the restoration of the gospel. America will be a blessed land unto the righteous forever, and is the base from which God will continue to direct the worldwide latter-day operations of his kingdom" (Cannon, 210).

One interesting theme that has caught the attention of both Church leaders and members is the idea that the Constitution will become so endangered that it will "hang by a thread," only to be rescued by the faithful **elders** of the Church. This idea had its origin with Joseph Smith. While no direct quotation has been found, there are several indirect references. For example, **Eliza R. Snow** recalled: "I heard him [Joseph Smith] say that the time would come when this nation would so far depart from its original purity, its glory, and its love for freedom and its protection of civil rights and religious rights, that the Constitution of our country would hang as it were by a thread. He said, also, that this people, the sons of **Zion**, would rise up and save the Constitution and bear it off triumphantly" (Cannon, 13).

Veneration of the Constitution has caused Latter-day **Saints**, especially those living in the United States of America, to take seriously their political obligations. Thus, most Latter-day Saints strive to take part in governmental procedures such as elections. Likewise, they seek to be good citizens and responsible members of the communities where they reside. For them, beliefs concerning the Constitution have been translated into action.

SOURCES

Cannon, Donald Q. *Latter-day Prophets and the United States Constitution*. Provo, Utah: Religious Studies Center, Brigham Young University, 1991.

Hancock, Ralph C. "Constitution of the United States of America." *Encyclopedia of Mormonism*. Edited by Daniel H. Ludlow. 4 vols. New York: Macmillan, 1992. 1:317–19.

Donald Q. Cannon

CONTRIBUTOR. In October 1879 **Junius F. Wells** launched a literary magazine to encourage young writers and to support the programs of cultural education in the **Young Men's** and **Young Ladies' National Mutual Improvement Associations**. Consisting of 17 volumes, the monthly *Contributor* published short articles from youth and their leaders on Latter-day Saint history, beliefs, **scriptures**, and values, plus uplifting short stories, poetry, and music. The illustrated magazine also encouraged topics such as health and science, home arts, travel, biography, education, religion, and government. Major contributors included Edward H. Anderson, Augusta Joyce Crocheron, **George Reynolds**, B. H. **Roberts**, Josephine Spencer, **James E. Talmage**, **Emmeline B. Wells**, **Junius F. Wells**, and **Orson F. Whitney**. The *Contributor* was succeeded in 1897 by the *Improvement Era*.

SOURCES

Contributor. 17 vols. Salt Lake City: Junius F. Wells, October 1879–September 1885; Salt Lake City: The Contributor Co., January 1886–October 1896.

Whitney, Orson F. "Home Literature." *Contributor* 9 (June 1888): 297–302.

Glen M. Leonard

COOKE, PHILIP ST. GEORGE. Philip St. George Cooke, commanding officer of the **Mormon Battalion** from Santa Fe to **California** and commander of the cavalry in **Johnston's Army**, was born in **Virginia** 13 June 1809. Cooke graduated from the **West Point** Military Academy in 1827 and had been assigned to various posts in the West before serving with, and against, the **Mormons**. Known for his discipline and honor, Cooke reportedly doffed his hat in respect when Johnston's Army traveled through **Salt Lake City**. Cooke served in the Union Army during the **Civil War** and died in **Michigan** 20 March 1895.

SOURCES

Cooke, Philip St. George. *Exploring Southwestern Trails, 1846–1854*. Edited by Ralph P. Bieber and Averam B. Bender. Glendale, Calif.: Arthur H. Clark, 1938. 17–30.

McHenry, Robert. *Webster's American Military Biographies.* Springfield, Mass.: G & C Merriam, 1978. 79–80.

Spiller, Roger J., ed. *Dictionary of American Military Biography.* 3 vols. Westport: Greenwood Press, 1984. 1:205–8.

ANDREW H. HEDGES

COOK ISLANDS (RAROTONGA). The Cook Islands, located west of **French Polynesia**, were first visited by **Elder** Noah Rogers in May and June 1845. On 23 May 1899, Daniel C. Miller in **Tahiti** sent Elders Osborne J. P. Widtsoe and Marvin W. Davis to Avarua, Rarotonga, to commence **missionary work**. The queen discouraged her London Missionary Society populace from attending Latter-day Saint **meetings**, and missionary efforts closed in November 1903 without any conversions.

Missionary work recommenced in May 1942 under member Fritz Bunge-Kruger. By 1946 there were almost 40 Latter-day **Saints**. Elder **Matthew Cowley** dedicated the Cook Islands on 1 July 1947. The first full-time missionaries were Elder and Sister Trevor Hamon, and then Elders Donlon DeLaMar and John L. Sorenson, in 1947. Although the Cook Islands have been administered by several **missions**, work has been continuous since 1947. Highlights were the visit of President **David O. McKay** in 1955 and the construction of five chapels by the **building missionary** program. In the year 2000 there were 880 members in six **branches** under one **district** administered by the **New Zealand** Auckland Mission. The **Book of Mormon** was published in Cook Island Maori in 1966.

SOURCES

Britsch, R. Lanier. *Unto the Islands of the Sea: A History of the Latter-day Saints in the Pacific.* Salt Lake City: Deseret Book, 1986. 10, 34–35, 332–36.

1999–2000 Church Almanac. Salt Lake City: Deseret News, 1998. 306–7.

R. LANIER BRITSCH

COOPERATIVE MOVEMENT OF THE 1860s. As the economic landscape shifted in **Utah** during the 1860s, **Brigham Young** set in motion measures he hoped would maintain and enhance the Latter-day Saint covenant community. These measures included the reorganization of the **Relief Society**, the reestablishment of the **School of the Prophets**, and a renewal in economic cooperation.

Earlier, the **Saints** had cooperated in digging canals and building fences, roads, and public buildings. The cooperative movement of the 1860s expanded these efforts in unprecedented ways. It began when **Lorenzo Snow** established the successful **Brigham City** Cooperative Association in 1864. Brigham Young called for similar efforts throughout the territory four years later. In **Salt Lake City**, he and other businessmen established Zion's Cooperative Mercantile Institution (**ZCMI**), which acted as the central wholesaler to local cooperatives being established in every settlement. The scale of the undertaking in Utah was unprecedented; no other endeavor, even in **England**, could compare with the Latter-day Saints' effort.

This new economic cooperation engendered opposition from most non-Mormon businessmen in the region. Even some wealthy **Mormons** opposed the effort and established a protest movement known as the **Godbeites**.

The cooperative movement was motivated by both practical and religious concerns. Economically, Church leaders wanted to control prices in the region, so that all businesses operated with the public interest in mind. They also wanted to maintain independence from the "merchants of Babylon" who were often vocal critics of the Church but nevertheless reaped inordinately high profits from their business dealings with the Saints. Furthermore, they wanted to off-set some possible negative impacts of the transcontinental **railroad**, which was quickly reaching **Zion**'s borders. Particularly, this new transportation highway would flood Utah with inexpensive goods, destroying the local economy and immediately integrating the area into the national market economy. Local residents would ultimately only supply raw materials to the East and then, out of necessity, be compelled to repurchase the finished products at great disadvantage.

The religious motivation was most fundamental—Brigham Young was inspired by the principles of **consecration** revealed through **Joseph Smith**. These principles would need to be lived by the Saints in order to truly establish Zion as **Enoch** had done (Moses 7:18–19). Brigham Young stated that the cooperative movement of the 1860s "was only a stepping stone to what is called the Order of Enoch, but which is in reality the order of Heaven" (Young).

Sources

Alexander, Thomas G. *Utah, the Right Place: The Official Centennial History.* Salt Lake City: Gibbs Smith, 1995. 153–55.

Allen, James B., and Glen M. Leonard. *The Story of the Latter-day Saints.* 2d ed. Salt Lake City: Deseret Book, 1992. 335–43.

Arrington, Leonard J., Feramorz Y. Fox, and Dean L. May. *Building the City of God: Community and Cooperation among the Mormons.* Salt Lake City: Deseret Book, 1976. 79–133.

Young, Brigham. *Deseret News,* 2 June 1869. 199.

RICHARD NEITZEL HOLZAPFEL

COPLEY, LEMAN. Leman Copley, a controversial member of the Church in the early days, figures prominently in two sections of the **Doctrine and Covenants.** Born 1781 in **Connecticut** and a member of the **Shaker** community in North Union, **Ohio**, Leman was baptized and ordained an **elder** in the Church in 1831. He owned 759 acres of land in **Thompson, Ohio**, and invited the **Colesville, New York, Saints** to settle and improve upon the land he had purchased (D&C 51). In May 1831 he asked for and received a **revelation** on the Shakers (D&C 49), which resulted in an unsuccessful **mission** to that group in North Union. Soon Copley broke his covenant of consecration and apostatized (D&C 54). On 1 April 1836 Leman asked **Joseph Smith's** forgiveness and was rebaptized. He stayed in the Madison/Thompson area, where he died and was buried in 1862 in the Thompson Evergreen Cemetery.

SOURCES

Smith, Joseph. *History of The Church of Jesus Christ of Latter-day Saints.* Edited by B. H. Roberts. 2d ed. rev. 7 vols. Salt Lake City: The Church of Jesus Christ of Latter-day Saints, 1932–51. 1:167–69, 180–81; 2:433.

KEITH W. PERKINS

CORAY, MARTHA. Martha Jane Knowlton, friend of the **Prophet Joseph Smith** and early **Mormon** scribe, was born 3 June 1822 in Covington, Kenton County, **Kentucky.** She joined the Church in Bear Creek, **Hancock County, Illinois,** in February 1840 and married Howard Coray there on 6 February 1841. Living mostly in **Nauvoo** until May 1846, the Corays arrived in **Utah** in 1850.

Sister Coray made three significant contributions to Church history: (1) she recorded talks given by the **Prophet Joseph Smith** in Nauvoo "when no one else was acting as clerk"; (2) she acted as amanuensis (stenographer) to **Lucy Mack Smith** when she dictated her remembrances of her son, the Prophet Joseph Smith; and (3) she served as the only woman on **Brigham Young Academy**'s (BYU) original board of trustees, from 1875 to 1881.

Her husband said that she "became well acquainted with the Prophet; and as such greatly venerated him. I have frequently heard her say, that he himself was the greatest miracle to her she had ever seen; and that she valued her acquaintance with him above everything else" (Journal, 11). Martha died 14 December 1881 in **Provo, Utah**.

SOURCE

Howard Coray Journal. Brigham Young University Library. Provo, Utah.

CHARLES TATE

CORNWALL, J. SPENCER. J. Spencer Cornwall, conductor of the Mormon **Tabernacle Choir** for 23 years, transformed the choir from a local ensemble to an internationally known musical organization. During his tenure (1935–57) the weekly choir broadcast became an award-winning radio program, and the choir was voted one of the three finest in **America**. It also issued its first LP recording and made its first European concert tour. Cornwall increased the choir's repertoire from a hundred to more than a thousand numbers, presented dramatized and concert versions of several oratorios, and ushered the choir into the world of film and television as a featured musical organization in documentaries and television specials. He also established a sound system that enabled the choir to sing on tune in the acoustically difficult **Tabernacle**.

Born in Millcreek, **Utah**, 23 February 1888, Cornwall married Mary Alice Haigh in June 1913. He received his music education from Northwestern University, the Chicago Music College, and the Christian School of Music in Chambersburg, **Pennsylvania**.

He was supervisor of music in the Granite and Salt Lake school districts, originating the annual school music festivals. He was associated with several **Salt Lake City** choral groups, including the Civic Opera and Oratorio Society, and guest conducted and adjudicated choirs throughout the United States.

Cornwall was on the YMMIA general board and was a member of the general Church Music Committee, for which he taught courses in choral conducting. He composed several operettas and arranged numerous Latter-day Saint **hymns**, including the popular "**Come, Come, Ye Saints**." He wrote three books: *Fundamentals of Conducting, A Century of Singing,* and *Stories of Our Mormon Hymns*. He died 26 February 1983 in Salt Lake City at age 95.

SOURCES

Cornwall, J. Spencer. *A Century of Singing*. Salt Lake City: Deseret Book, 1958.

Gregory, Fern Denise. "J. Spencer Cornwall: The Great Salt Lake Mormon Tabernacle Choir Years, 1935–1957." Ph.D. diss., University of Missouri-Kansas City, 1984.

———. Oral History. Interview by Carol Cornwall Madsen, 1981. James Moyle Oral History Program, LDS Church Historical Department, Salt Lake City.

CAROL CORNWALL MADSEN

CORPORATION OF THE PRESIDENT. See BUSINESSES.

CORRELATION. Elder Harold B. Lee, who played a key role in the movement, explained that "correlation means merely to place the **priesthood** of God where the Lord said it was to be—as the center and core of the Church and **kingdom of God**—and to see that the Latter-day Saint homes also have their place in the divine plan of saving souls" (*Genealogical*). Over the years, Church leaders have taken several steps to see that priesthood **quorums**, auxiliary organizations, and other facets of Church activity are working harmoniously to accomplish this aim.

In 1960, the **First Presidency** felt a need to correlate the studies and review the jurisdiction of each of the auxiliaries and directed the General Priesthood Committee, headed by Elder Lee, to prayerfully study this matter and make recommendations to them. The result was the organization of correlation committees on Church-wide (1961), ward (1964), and stake levels (1967).

Priesthood correlation was responsible for further developments in helping the Latter-day Saint **family** to have its "place in the divine plan of saving souls" through such practices as introducing **home teaching** (1964), strengthening the **family home evening** program by providing a manual with helpful instructional aids (1965), clearing Monday evenings of other Church activities to help the parents provide for family-related activities (1970), and encouraging gospel study in the home using the new editions of all the **standard works** (1979–81).

Curriculum offerings were also restructured into three age groups: children (birth to age 12), youth (12 to 18), and adults (18 and older). The various priesthood and auxiliary organizations no longer developed their own curriculum but were assigned to carry out that which was developed by general church curriculum committees. The magazines of the various organizations were replaced by three new publications (1971) aligned with the curriculum age groupings: the *Friend* for children, the *New Era* for youth, and the *Ensign* for adults.

Another change was having a unified Church year (beginning 1967), in which Church programs had the same age groupings and began and ended at the same time. A consolidated meeting schedule (1980) grouped various meetings into a three-hour block on Sundays.

President N. Eldon Tanner testified: "Priesthood Correlation is the closest blueprint yet in mortality to the plan presented in the Grand Council of Heaven before the world was created and is the most effective utilization thus far of special keys given to the Prophet Joseph Smith in the Kirtland Temple. . . . Priesthood Correlation is asking the priesthood leadership to 'Put on the strength of the priesthood,' and to assume full responsibility with the 'power' at their disposal to build up the Church and, eventually, the Kingdom of God here upon the earth" (*Minutes*).

SOURCES

Cowan, Richard O. *The Latter-day Saint Century.* Salt Lake City: Bookcraft, 1999. 194–203.

Genealogical Devotional Addresses 1968. Talk given August 16, 1968. 55.

Minutes of the Priesthood Genealogy Committee Training Session, December 1963.

"Top 10 Stories of the 20th Century." *1999–2000 Church Almanac.* Salt Lake City: Deseret News, 1998. 117–25.

DANIEL H. LUDLOW

CORRILL, JOHN. John Corrill was a **counselor** to **Bishop Edward Partridge** in the early days of the Church but was later excommunicated. John was born 17 September 1794 near Barre, **Massachusetts** and baptized into the Church 10 January 1831 in **Kirtland, Ohio**. On 3 June 1831 he was one of the first men ordained to the office of **high priest**. That same day he was called as second counselor to Bishop Edward Partridge. During that year he took up residence in **Jackson County, Missouri**. Following the expulsion of the **Saints** from Jackson, he moved to **Clay County**. At the request of Church leaders, he returned to Kirtland in the fall of 1834, where he remained until after the dedication of the **Kirtland Temple**, then returned to Missouri in the spring of 1836.

Throughout the entire Missouri period, Corrill defended the interests of the **Saints**, frequently acting as a negotiator for the Church. In August

1838 he was elected as the first representative from **Caldwell County** to the Missouri legislature, but his service in this capacity was short-lived. Following the 1838–39 session, Corrill left the state and moved to **Illinois**. At the time of his departure from Missouri, he had become disaffected from the Church and was subsequently excommunicated on 17 March 1839. He died in 1843.

───────

SOURCES

Corrill, John. *A Brief History of the Church of Jesus Christ of Latter-day Saints (Commonly Called Mormons), Including an Account of Their Doctrine and Discipline; with Reasons of the Author for Leaving the Church*. St. Louis: John Corrill, 1839.

Winn, Kenneth H. "'Such Republicanism as This': John Corrill's Rejection of Prophetic Rule." *Differing Visions: Dissenters in Mormon History*. Edited by Roger D. Launius and Linda Thatcher. Chicago: University of Illinois Press, 1994. 45–75.

ALEXANDER L. BAUGH

CORSICA. A large island belonging to **France**, Corsica is located in the Mediterranean Sea between **Spain** and **Italy**. At the beginning of the year 2000, there were 49 Latter-day **Saints** in one **branch**.

EMILY C. ZEIGLER

COSIC, KRESIMIR. The history of the Church in Yugoslavia (now **Croatia**, **Slovenia**, Bosnia, **Serbia**, and Montenegro) started with one man, Kresimir Cosic. "Kreso" was born in Zagreb 26 November 1948. He grew up in Zadar and on a nearby Dalmatian island, where his grandparents lived. Reaching a height of 6' 11" in his teens, he was a natural to play basketball. He was recruited by **Brigham Young University**, where he was soon a favorite, known for his antics and good humor on the court, and nicknamed the "Gentle Giant." During this time he learned English, read the **Book of Mormon**, and joined the Church.

Cosic was offered two NBA contracts but declined both and returned to Yugoslavia to establish the Church there. While playing and coaching in **Italy**, **Greece**, and Yugoslavia, he participated in four Olympics, winning the gold medal and most valuable player award when Yugoslavia defeated **Russia** in 1980. He also began and then supervised translation and publication of the Book of Mormon in Serbo-Croatian. He helped to establish official recognition of the Church and located and renovated a spacious apartment in Zagreb, which became Yugoslavia's first Latter-day Saint chapel. He taught his friends and teammates the gospel, and several were baptized.

He and his wife, Ljerka, were the parents of three children. At his untimely death of cancer on 27 May 1995, he was deputy ambassador for Croatia in **Washington, D.C.**, working tirelessly for peace in his troubled homeland.

SOURCE

Mehr, Kahlile. "Kresimir Cosic of Yugoslavia: Basketball Superstar, Gospel Hero." *Pioneers in Every Land.* Edited by Bruce A. Van Orden, D. Brent Smith, and Everett Smith Jr. Salt Lake City: Bookcraft, 1997. 22–38.

ANN N. MADSEN

COSTA RICA. Under the direction of the **First Presidency**, Arwell Pierce, president of the Mexican Mission, visited Costa Rica in 1946 to investigate conditions for introducing the gospel. The following year the Church received official recognition, and the first two missionaries arrived. A **conference** was held in June 1950, and two months later the first **branch** was organized in San José. The first missionaries from Costa Rica were Sisters Alicia Arrendondo and Cristina Peralta, called in 1952, and **Elder** Manuel Arias Sandoval, called in 1953. The latter opened **missionary work** in **Nicaragua**. The first chapel, located in the Los Yoses neighborhood of San José, was dedicated in 1964.

In subsequent years, missionary success has led to the organization of additional branches and the construction of more chapels. Representatives from **Salt Lake City** and other areas have given training to local Church leaders. As members strove to live the standards of the gospel more completely, larger groups of young men and women have fulfilled missions throughout the Americas and **Europe**.

In 1952 Costa Rica became part of the new Central American **Mission**, but a separate Costa Rica Mission was organized in 1974. The first **stake** in Costa Rica was established in 1977. The first excursion to the **Arizona Temple** in Mesa was conducted in 1976, requiring a round trip of 15 days. Similar trips followed in successive years, and in 1984 an air excursion was conducted to the **Mexico City Temple**. With the dedication of the **temple** in **Guatemala** City, trips to the temple became more frequent. In 1999 construction began on the San José Costa Rica Temple.

By the beginning of the year 2000, there were 30,118 members, 5 stakes, 78 **wards** and branches, 1 mission, and 6 **districts**.

SOURCE

1999–2000 Church Almanac. Salt Lake City: Deseret News, 1998. 307.

MARIO JAVIER JIMÉNEZ SANDÍ

COTTON INDUSTRY. See TEXTILES.

COTTON MISSION. Because of the potential to grow cotton in Southern **Utah**, 28 families were called in 1857 to settle the town of Washington, **Utah**. Early experiments proved to be only moderately successful, but the outbreak of the **Civil War** made cotton from the South unavailable. During a **general conference** in 1861, 300 names were read; these people were to move to **St. George** to raise cotton. The first year's crop was small, but the second year the **Saints** had such a surplus that they hauled 74,000 pounds to the **Mississippi River** markets.

A cotton factory was completed for use in 1867, and by 1870 a second story and better equipment were added. The new equipment would handle wool, cotton, or combinations of both. The factory became the largest west of the Mississippi.

With the close of the Civil War and the coming of the **railroad**, the cotton industry in Utah was doomed. It limped along until 1910, when the factory was closed, and the whole venture became history.

SOURCES

Larson, Andrew Karl. *I Was Called to Dixie*. St. George, Utah: Dixie College Foundation, 1992.

Mortensen, A. R., ed. *Utah's Dixie: The Cotton Mission*. Salt Lake City: Utah State Historical Society, 1961.

KARL F. BROOKS

COUNCIL BLUFFS, IOWA. Council Bluffs, located across the **Missouri River** from Omaha, **Nebraska**, took its name from an 1803 meeting of explorers Meriwether Lewis and William Clark with the Oto Missouri **Indians**. It was a focal point of Latter-day Saint activity between 1846 and 1853.

The **Saints** initially applied the name "Council Bluff(s)" to a district on both sides of the river. The cohesion of the Saints at this time facilitated the 1846 recruiting of the **Mormon Battalion** to fight in the **Mexican War**. That same year, the Saints built scores of no-tax roads, bridges, and ferries, including three over the Missouri River.

Church authorities governed some 90 temporary settlements near Council Bluffs, including Grand Encampment, **Iowa**; Cold Spring Camp, Cutler's Park, and **Winter Quarters**, Nebraska; and Kanesville, Iowa. Ecclesiastical law prevailed here until counties were organized (1848–51) in southwestern Iowa. Through U.S. Indian agents, the Saints interacted with the Pottawattamie, Ottawa, and Chippewa tribes of southwestern Iowa and the Oto/Missouri and Omaha Indians of eastern Nebraska. In December 1847, the town of Kanesville (named for **Thomas L. Kane**) was laid out near the bluffs on the east bank of the Missouri. Here the First Presidency was sustained in a newly built "log **tabernacle**" on 27 December 1847. Church headquarters had been established at Winter Quarters on the west bank, but when government officials asked the Saints to leave Indian lands early the next year, the main settlement was moved to Kanesville.

Perhaps as many as 25,000 acres of farming, plus myriad small Latter-day Saint businesses, branches of the Church, tuition schools, courts, justices of the peace, newspapers, and cultural groups were found in the city of Kanesville and the surrounding territory during the years 1846 to 1853. After 1852, probably more California migrants crossed the Missouri River here than at all other points combined.

Kanesville was also a key point in Latter-day Saint migration; many migrants landed at New Orleans and traveled by steamboat up the Mississippi and Missouri Rivers to this point. **Elder Orson Hyde** was assigned to remain here and give direction to the Saints there. He published the *Frontier Guardian* from 1849 to 1852. By 1853, an estimated 31,600 Saints had migrated from there to the **Great Basin**. Although the last major migration occurred in 1853, some Saints stayed on before moving west.

In 1853, after most of the Saints had left, the name Kanesville was changed to Council Bluffs. From this time onward, this name referred specifically to the town rather than to the broader district.

SOURCES

Holmes, Gail G. "A Prophet Who Followed, Fulfilled, and Magnified." *Lion of the*

Lord: Essays on the Life and Service of Brigham Young. Edited by Susan E. Black and Larry C. Porter. Salt Lake City: Deseret Book, 1995. 128–53.

Hyde, Orson, ed. *Frontier Guardian.* Kanesville, Iowa, 1849–52.

GAIL HOLMES

COUNCIL OF FIFTY. On 7 April 1842 **Joseph Smith** received a **revelation** titled "The **Kingdom of God** and His Laws With the Keys and Power Thereof, and Judgement in the Hands of His Servants, Ahman Christ" (Quinn, 166–67), which called for the organization of a special council. This council, popularly known as the Council of Fifty because of its approximate number of members, was formally organized by Joseph Smith on 11 March 1844. Latter-day **Saints** believed that the gospel was restored, at least in part, to prepare the world for the second coming of the Messiah, **Jesus Christ**. The Council of Fifty, according to one **historian**, was designed "to bring about the political transformation of the world, just as the church was intended to change the world religiously" (Hansen, 11). Another historian wrote that "the primary role of the Council of Fifty was to symbolize the otherworldly world order that would be established during the millennial reign of Christ on earth" (Quinn, 163).

The Council of Fifty played a role in preparing some Latter-day Saint males to function as a sort of legislature in the Kingdom of God (Ehat, 260–61). A few non-Mormons were also invited to participate in the Council, symbolizing the millennial condition of members and non-members working together in harmony as Christ ruled as King of Kings.

Following the organization of the council, Joseph Smith told them that he had received its constitution by direct revelation. The **Prophet** was told, "Ye are my Constitution and I am your God and ye are my spokesmen" (quoted in Ehat, 259). In other words, God, through his prophet, would direct the Council of Fifty by means of revelation.

Several rules of procedure were adopted at a meeting held on 18 April 1844. For example, the president of the Church served as standing chairman of the council, and except for the chair, the members sat according to age. Decisions of the council had to be unanimous, and "no member [was] to be absent . . . unless sick or on Council business" (quoted in Ehat, 261).

Joseph Smith frequently taught council members the meaning of the **Constitution of the United States** and how it could be applied "to the Latter-day saints in the world and during the millennium" (Quinn, 164).

Members of the council were also involved in Joseph Smith's **presidential campaign**, helped to direct affairs in **Nauvoo**, and assisted in planning the move west.

Following the murder of Joseph Smith, **Brigham Young** presided over the Council of Fifty and used it as the Saints moved west and settled in the **Great Basin**. **John Taylor** revitalized the Fifty, and they met annually during his administration so members could receive instruction regarding political matters (Quinn, 173). Since that time the Council of Fifty has not played an active role in Latter-day Saint history.

SOURCES

Clark, James R. "The Kingdom of God, the Council of Fifty, and the Star of Deseret." *Utah Historical Quarterly* 26 (April 1958): 130–48.

Ehat, Andrew F. "'It Seems Like Heaven Began on Earth': Joseph Smith and the Constitution of the Kingdom of God." *BYU Studies* 20 (Spring 1980): 253–79.

Hansen, Klaus J. *Quest for Empire*. Lincoln: University of Nebraska Press, 1967.

Quinn, D. Michael. "The Council of Fifty and Its Members, 1844 to 1945." *BYU Studies* 20 (Winter 1980): 163–97.

KENNETH W. GODFREY

COUNCIL OF TWELVE APOSTLES. See APOSTLES.

COUNCILS. President **Stephen L Richards** taught that "the genius of our Church government is government through councils." He added, "I have no hesitancy in giving you the assurance, if you will confer in council as you are expected to do, God will give you solutions to the problems that confront you" (*Richards*, 86). Councils have been an important part of Church administration in any dispensation. Elder **M. Russell Ballard** explained that "God called a grand council in the premortal world to present His glorious plan for our eternal welfare. The Lord's Church is organized with councils at every level, beginning with the Council of the **First Presidency** and the **Quorum** of the Twelve **Apostles** and extending to **stake**, **ward**, **quorum**, **auxiliary**, and **family** councils" (Ballard, 102). All **priesthood** quorums in the Church are, in essence, councils (D&C 107:85–89; Widtsoe, 140).

In the early part of this last dispensation, the Lord revealed that the Twelve Apostles are a traveling, presiding, **high council** (D&C 107:33). There were two standing high councils in the early part of this dispensation: one in **Kirtland, Ohio**, organized 17 February 1834; and the other in

Clay County, Missouri, organized 3 July 1834 (D&C 107:36). **Joseph Smith** said that the pattern for the first high council as set forth in section 102 is an example or pattern for all high councils of the Church. The Lord has revealed the necessity and purpose of these high councils, declaring that such assemblies are "appointed by **revelation** for the purpose of settling important difficulties which might arise in the Church, which could not be settled by the church or the bishop's council to the satisfaction of the parties" (D&C 102:2). Additionally, Church councils are administrative assemblies called together in an atmosphere of mutual understanding to render consultation on matters relating to Church discipline, disposition of lands, receiving revelation pertaining to their own jurisdiction, and any other issues relating to the blessing of the lives of Church members.

SOURCES

Ballard, M. Russell. Conference Report (October 1993): 102–6.

Richards, Stephen L. Conference Report (October 1953): 85–87.

Widtsoe, John A. *Priesthood and Church Government*. Salt Lake City: Deseret Book, 1939. 306.

C. ROBERT LINE

COUNSELOR. As members of a presidency, counselors share responsibility and act as advisors to the president. The **Doctrine and Covenants** states that to be assisted by a counselor is a privilege (102:10). A revelation given to the **Prophet Joseph Smith** summarized the duties of a counselor: "I . . . will bless . . . thee, inasmuch as thou art faithful in counsel, . . . in prayer always, vocally and in thy heart, in public and in private, also in thy ministry in proclaiming the gospel . . . among thy brethren. And in doing these things thou wilt do the greatest good unto thy fellow beings, and wilt promote the glory of him who is your Lord. Wherefore, be faithful . . . succor the weak, lift up the hands which hang down, and strengthen the feeble knees" (D&C 81:3–5).

SOURCE

Hinckley, Gordon B. "In . . . Counselors There Is Safety." *Ensign* 20 (November 1990): 48–51.

MARCUS H. MARTINS

COURTS, CHURCH. See DISCIPLINARY COUNCILS.

COVE FORT, UTAH. Located northeast of the junction of I-15 and I-70, Cove Fort is situated in the southeast corner of Millard County, Utah. The abandonment of Fort Willden at that same general location in 1865 left travelers without a sanctuary from the elements or protection from hostile **Indians** during the **Black Hawk War**. **Brigham Young** called on **Ira Nathaniel Hinckley** to build a substantial fort on Cove Creek. Ira arrived at the site of Cove Fort, in company with President Young, on 29 April 1867. Other craftsmen, including Ira's brother Arza, were soon assembled. The walls of the extant fort are constructed in the form of a square, 100 feet on each side. These walls are mainly composed of black volcanic rock and dark limestone laid up in lime mortar; they stand 18 feet high. On 21 August 1919, President **Heber J. Grant** sold the fort and ranch to the William H. Kesler **family**, who had occupied the land from 1903. On 13 August 1988, ceremonies were conducted at the fort, returning the structure to the LDS Church for restoration as a historic site.

SOURCES

Porter, Larry C. "A Historical Analysis of Cove Fort, Utah." Master's thesis, Brigham Young University, 1966.

———. "Cove Fort." *Utah History Encyclopedia.* Edited by Allan Kent Powell. Salt Lake City: University of Utah Press, 1994. 119–20.

LARRY C. PORTER

COVEY, STEPHEN R. Known for his impact on business environments, Stephen R. Covey, together with Hyrum Smith, was co-founder of the Franklin Covey Company, one of the largest management and leadership development organizations in the world. Stephen was born 24 October 1932 in **Salt Lake City**, Utah, and married Sandra Merrill. He is perhaps best known as the author of *The 7 Habits of Highly Effective People,* which was ranked as a number one best-seller by the *New York Times,* having sold more than 12 million copies in 32 languages and 75 countries throughout the world.

Dr. Covey received his undergraduate degree from the **University of Utah** and his MBA from Harvard; he completed his doctorate at **Brigham Young University**. While at BYU he served as assistant to the president and was also a professor of business management and organizational behavior.

Brother Covey served a **mission** for the Church to **Great Britain** and has served as **bishop, high councilor, mission president** to **Ireland**, and **regional representative**. He is the author of numerous religious articles and books, including *Spiritual Roots of Human Relations, How to Succeed with People, The Divine Center,* and *Marriage and Family: Gospel Insights,* which was cowritten with Truman G. Madsen.

MAREN M. MOURITSEN

COWDERY, OLIVER. Oliver Cowdery, one of the Three **Witnesses of the Book of Mormon,** was **Joseph Smith**'s assistant in translating and publishing that ancient record, as well as his companion in receiving the **priesthood** and keys from biblical prophets authorizing the reestablishment and latter-day work of Christ's Church; he also served as the **assistant** (or associate) **president of the Church.**

Oliver was born in Wells, **Vermont,** on 3 October 1806. His older brothers were well educated, and Oliver followed them to **New York,** coming into contact with the **Smith family** as a teacher boarding in their home during the Winter of 1828 and 1829. The Prophet's mother describes how Oliver's initial curiosity about the discovery of the **Book of Mormon** matured into conviction. The Prophet said Oliver was given confirmation by a divine **vision** and by the Spirit's witness (Jessee, 10; D&C 6:22–24).

Joseph Smith was then a young husband, cultivating his small farm in upper **Pennsylvania.** After Martin Harris lost the 116-page Book of Lehi transcribed in 1828, the Prophet expected that the Lord would send another scribe (D&C 5:34). This promise was fulfilled when Oliver's school term finished, and he volunteered to write while the Prophet translated the present Book of Mormon from April through June 1829.

Joseph Smith "dictated by the inspiration of heaven" (Jessee, 29). He and Oliver were impressed by the Savior's discourse on baptism given during his American ministry (Jessee, 30; 3 Ne. 11), and they knelt in prayer 15 May 1829 to inquire of God near the **Susquehanna River.** Here **John the Baptist** appeared in glory and ordained them to the Aaronic Priesthood, commanding them to baptize and ordain each other (JS–H 1:68–71). This messenger explained that the Melchizedek Priesthood, which would authorize them to lay on hands to give the gift of the Holy Ghost, would be "**conferred**" on them (Jessee, 290; *HC,* 1:39–40). The ancient **apostles Peter, James, and John** afterward appeared and bestowed the **Melchizedek Priesthood** and its keys on Joseph and Oliver (JS–H 1:72; D&C 27:12–13). This event preceded Church organization, since the power of confirmation was used by the two leading elders at formal incorporation on **6 April** 1830 (Jessee, 303; *HC,* 1:77–78).

In June 1829 Oliver and two others were promised a view of the **gold plates** and sacred Nephite objects (D&C 17). The **angel** appeared to Joseph Smith and the Three Witnesses and showed them the plates, while God's voice declared the translation correct (Jessee, 296–98; *HC*, 1:52–57).

Oliver became assistant or associate president of the Church on 5 December 1834; after his excommunication in 1838, this position was given to **Hyrum Smith** (D&C 124:91–96). In 1836 Oliver participated in the spiritual outpouring surrounding the **Kirtland Temple** dedication (27 March), and the crowning event came on 3 April, when heavenly beings appeared to Joseph and Oliver there. The Savior first accepted the **temple**, and then **Moses, Elias** (D&C 27:6–7), and **Elijah** transmitted to them the keys necessary for preaching the gospel to the world and performing temple **ordinances** (D&C 110).

Oliver's life is consistent with the extraordinary visitations outlined above. He vigorously furthered the expanding movement of the Church, leading the **Lamanite mission of 1830 to 1831**, which established a Church presence in **Missouri** after bringing in more than a hundred dedicated converts in the **Kirtland** area. This was the beginning of a rich harvest in northern **Ohio**, which became the administrative center of the Church from 1831 through 1837. Forced to leave Missouri in 1833, Oliver then edited several Church publications in Ohio and was Joseph Smith's chief assistant for publishing the first **Doctrine and Covenants** (1835). Oliver was appointed to the Kirtland **high council** and then formally taken into the **First Presidency**, ranking second to Joseph Smith for a time (Jessee, 20–25). He also served as a secretary and traveled extensively in the East and Midwest on Church business. In writing and speaking, he reiterated his personal witness that angels restored the Nephite record and the Aaronic and Melchizedek priesthoods.

Oliver was estranged from the Prophet by late 1837, a year of severe testing. In January the value of **Kirtland Safety Society** paper money dropped, and the hard times of a national depression soon followed. Economic discouragement became the seedbed for doubting certain doctrines and even the Prophet's position as sole revelator for the Church (D&C 21:1–5). Oliver was excommunicated from the Church on 12 April 1838 in **Far West, Missouri**. His written resignation expressed regret at differences, which he confined to "the outward government of this Church" (*HC*, 3:18, note).

The former "second elder" (D&C 20:3) spent the next decade in non-Mormon society. During this time he succeeded as a respected attorney in Ohio and **Wisconsin**, staying active in politics and occasionally editing a **Democratic** newspaper. His private letters in this period show that his inner convictions about the Church never changed.

Oliver married Elizabeth Ann Whitmer, David's sister, in 1832, and their first child, Maria Louise, lived a long life, dying without having had children only two days after her mother died in 1892. The five other children of Oliver and Elizabeth Ann died in early childhood (Gunn, 219).

In declining health and convinced that he belonged with the Church, Oliver sold out in Elkhorn, Wisconsin, and in late 1848 traveled to **Council Bluffs, Iowa**, where he testified of seeing the Book of Mormon plates and of receiving the Aaronic and Melchizedek priesthoods from angels. He planned to migrate west but settled temporarily with the Whitmer **family** in **Richmond, Missouri**, where chronic lung disease took his life on 3 March 1850.

Oliver Cowdery's final letter indicates he accepted the assignment of the Twelve to lobby in **Washington, D.C.**, for Mormon interests. His immediate family and several relatives were present at his deathbed, and several wrote that Oliver's final words expressed love for the Savior and his conviction of the truth of the Book of Mormon and the restoration of the priesthood.

SOURCES

Anderson, Richard Lloyd. *Investigating the Book of Mormon Witnesses.* Salt Lake City: Deseret Book, 1981.

Gunn, Stanley R. *Oliver Cowdery.* Salt Lake City: Bookcraft, 1962.

Jessee, Dean C. *The Papers of Joseph Smith,* Vol. 1. Salt Lake City: Deseret Book, 1989.

Smith, Joseph. *History of The Church of Jesus Christ of Latter-day Saints [HC].* Edited by B. H. Roberts. 2d ed. rev. 7 vols. Salt Lake City: The Church of Jesus Christ of Latter-day Saints, 1932–51.

Smith, Lucy Mack. *Biographical Sketches of Joseph Smith.* Reprint of the 1853 edition, Provo, Utah: Grandin Book, 1995.

RICHARD LLOYD ANDERSON

COWLEY, MATTHEW. Matthew Cowley, 20th-century apostle and missionary, was born 2 August 1897 in Preston, **Idaho**, to **Matthias Foss Cowley** and Abbie Hyde Cowley. When he turned 17 he received a mission call to **New Zealand**. He was blessed to learn and speak the Maori language fluently. At the conclusion of his three-year mission, **President Joseph F. Smith** gave him a special assignment to remain in New Zealand

and translate the **Doctrine & Covenants** and **Pearl of Great Price** into the Maori language, as well as revise the translation of the **Book of Mormon**.

In 1919, at age 22, Matthew returned home. He had not graduated from high school, but with the assistance of **University of Utah** faculty he began his law studies. After two years, he was admitted to George Washington University in **Washington, D.C.** He was employed as Senator **Reed Smoot's** executive secretary and as an assistant to the Senate Finance Committee.

In 1922, Matthew Cowley married Elva Eleanor Taylor. During his 12 years of law practice, he served for two years as the Salt Lake county attorney.

In 1938, Cowley was called to preside over the New Zealand Mission. In October 1940, the full-time American and Canadian missionaries were called home because of **World War II**. The Cowleys stayed in New Zealand for another five years until the war was over. During their mission, they adopted a son.

In September 1945, the Cowleys returned home. Three weeks later, Brother Cowley was sustained as an **apostle** and served in that capacity for just over eight years. He died in **Los Angeles** 13 December 1953, at age 56.

SOURCES

Cowley, Matthew. *Matthew Cowley Speaks.* Salt Lake City: Deseret Book, 1954. vii-ix.

Smith, Henry A. *Matthew Cowley: Man of Faith.* Salt Lake City: Bookcraft, 1954. 63, 65, 168.

GLEN L. RUDD

COWLEY, MATTHIAS F. Matthias Foss Cowley, missionary, colonizer, and **apostle**, lost his place in the **Quorum** of the Twelve **Apostles** because of his persistent advocacy of **plural marriage**. He was born 25 August 1858 in **Salt Lake City** and served two **missions** to the southern states over a four-and-a-half-year period, during which time he led two companies of **Saints** from the South to **Colorado**. Upon his return to Utah, he worked for the *Contributor,* served as a chaplain in the territorial legislature, and married Abbie Hyde on 21 May 1884. He was second counselor in the Oneida, **Idaho,** stake presidency at the time of his apostolic call in 1897.

As an apostle he organized the Northwestern States Mission, met U.S. president William McKinley, and frequently visited the Saints in

Mexico. He continued to teach and administer polygamy after the Church issued the **Manifesto of 1890**. His refusal, with **John W. Taylor**, to testify at the Smoot hearings about his involvement in plural marriage brought heavy criticism of the Church and eventually resulted in their resignations from the Quorum of the Twelve on 28 October 1905. He edited the journals of **Wilford Woodruff** for publication in 1909. His **priesthood** was suspended in 1911 but was restored on 3 April 1936. He died in Salt Lake City on 15 June 1940.

Sources

Jenson, Andrew. *Latter-day Saint Biographical Encyclopedia.* 4 vols. 1901–36. Reprint, Salt Lake City: Western Epics, 1971. 1:168–72.
Jorgensen, Victor, and B. Carmon Hardy. "The Taylor-Cowley Affair and the Watershed of Mormon History." *Utah Historical Quarterly* 48 (Winter 1980): 4–36.
1997–1998 Church Almanac. Salt Lake City: Deseret News, 1996.

John Thomas

CRICKETS, PLAGUE OF. See SEAGULLS, MIRACLE OF.

CROATIA. In 1889 one missionary entered what would later become Yugoslavia, but the restored gospel did not go forward significantly among these peoples until the 1970s, when Yugoslav citizens who were converted elsewhere (**Switzerland, Germany, Austria**, and **America**) returned home. The leading **pioneer** was **Kresimir Cosic**, a Croatian from Dalmatia who was converted in 1971 while playing basketball at **Brigham Young University**. He returned to proselyte in Zadar and Zagreb, Croatia, and arranged for the translation (beginning 1974) and publication (1979) of the **Book of Mormon** in Croatian (Serbo-Croatian in the Latin alphabet).

As **district** president, Cosic, along with various Austria Vienna **mission presidents**, sought recognition for the Church in Croatia and **Serbia**. The Yugoslav Mission was opened in 1975 but closed the following year. Young adult missionaries were allowed to quietly proselyte from 1978 to 1981, and several couples carried on from 1981 under the Austrian and East European (eventually the Austria Vienna East) **missions**.

The long-sought-for registration of the Church in Yugoslavia came in 1985, and then only in Croatia. It was granted after the first **branch** chapel facility was constructed in a Zagreb apartment building. The following year, young missionaries returned, and membership grew.

Croatians declared their independence from Yugoslavia in 1991 and fought the Serbians periodically until 1996. Throughout the conflict the Church widely distributed **humanitarian aid**. Missionaries have continued to serve in Croatia since 1996 under the Austria Vienna South Mission. By the year 2000 the Croatian **district** had increased to some 299 members in four branches.

SOURCES

Mehr, Kahlile. "Frontier in the East." Manuscript history Yugoslavia and Croatia.

Mehr, Kahlile. "Kresimir Cosic of Yugoslavia: Basketball Superstar, Gospel Hero." *Pioneers in Every Land.* Edited by Bruce A. Van Orden, D. Brent Smith, and Everett Smith Jr. Salt Lake City: Bookcraft, 1997. 22–38.

1999–2000 Church Almanac. Salt Lake City: Deseret News, 1998. 308.

EDWIN B. MORRELL

CROOKED RIVER, BATTLE OF. During the early morning hours of 25 October 1838, a contingent of **Mormon** militia from **Caldwell County, Missouri**, engaged in armed conflict with a company of state militia from Ray County under the command of Captain **Samuel Bogart** at Crooked River in northern Ray County. The event was precipitated when word reached **Far West** that Bogart's men had taken three Mormon men prisoners and threatened to kill them. **Elias Higbee**, a Caldwell County judge, issued a call for volunteers to rescue the prisoners, appointing **David W. Patten**, an LDS **apostle**, to lead the company. Although the Caldwell militia succeeded in routing Bogart's troops and in rescuing the Mormon prisoners, a number of casualties resulted on both sides. Seven members from the Caldwell company were wounded— Eli Chase, James Hendricks, Curtis Hodge, Joseph Holbrook, Arthur Milliken, William Seeley, and Norman Shearer. Three were killed— Gideon Carter, Patrick O'Banion (a non-Mormon who had been asked to guide them to Bogart's camp), and David W. Patten. The Ray militia suffered one casualty, Moses Rowland, and half a dozen wounded. On 27 October, two days after the battle, Governor **Lilburn W. Boggs** received word of the conflict. The report led him to perceive not only that the Mormons had perpetrated the conflict but that they were coming out in open rebellion against the state of **Missouri** by deliberately attacking state militia. The governor took immediate and decisive action and issued his infamous **extermination order,** calling for the removal of the Saints from Missouri.

SOURCES

Baugh, Alexander L. "A Call to Arms: The 1838 Mormon Defense of Northern Missouri." Ph.D. diss., Brigham Young University, 1996.
———. "The Battle between Mormon and Missouri Militia at Crooked River." In *Missouri.* Edited by Arnold K. Garr and Clark V. Johnson. Regional Studies in Latter-day Saint Church History series. Provo, Utah: Brigham Young University, 1994. 85–103.
Le Sueur, Stephen C. *The 1838 Mormon War in Missouri.* Columbia, Mo.: University of Missouri Press, 1987. 131–42.

ALEXANDER L. BAUGH

CROSBY, WILLIAM. William Crosby, noted emigrant, colonizer, and Church leader, was born 19 September 1808 in Knox County, **Indiana**. He joined the Church and became a prominent leader in **Mississippi**. In 1844, following the **martyrdom** of **Joseph Smith**, he traveled to **Nauvoo**, but soon afterwards he returned to Mississippi to prepare the **Saints** to gather. He was appointed captain of an emigration party called the **Mississippi Saints** and traveled more than 1,600 miles to **Pueblo, Colorado**. During the winter he and others returned to Mississippi to bring their own families, and they arrived in **Salt Lake City** in October 1848. In 1850 Crosby assisted **Brigham Young** in implementing the **Perpetual Emigrating Fund**. In 1851 he again moved his **family**, this time to **California** to colonize **San Bernardino**. In 1857 they returned to Utah when the Saints abandoned the settlement due to the **Utah War**. The Crosbys settled in Kanab, Utah, where William died in 1882.

SOURCES

Carter, Kate B., comp. *Heart Throbs of the West.* 3 vols. Salt Lake City: Daughters of Utah Pioneers, 1947–48.

DAVID F. BOONE

CUB SCOUTS. See BOY SCOUTS.

CUMMING, ALFRED. Alfred Cumming, the first non-Mormon governor of the territory of **Utah**, was born in 1807 in Augusta, Georgia. He was escorted from the East by **Johnston's Army** in 1857. Appointed by President **James Buchanan**, he faced the task of gaining the support of a wary constituency. He gained the respect of and maintained cordial relations with **Mormon** leaders by acting as a buffer between them and federal judges and the army. He found that all court records of the territory were accounted for and in order and made practical suggestions for handling many of the concerns of the legislators. In May 1861 Cumming returned to his native state of **Georgia** with the good will of the people of Utah. He died 9 October 1873 in Augusta, Georgia.

SOURCES

Furniss, Norman F. *The Mormon Conflict, 1850–1859.* New Haven: Yale University Press, 1960.

Roberts, B. H. *A Comprehensive History of The Church of Jesus Christ of Latter-day Saints, Century One.* 6 vols. Salt Lake City: The Church of Jesus Christ of Latter-day Saints, 1930. 4:473–74, 545.

AUDREY M. GODFREY

CUMORAH. See HILL CUMORAH.

CURAÇAO. Like the neighboring islands of **Bonaire** and **Aruba**, Curaçao is an autonomous territory of the **Netherlands** just off the coast of **Venezuela**. Its 170,000 inhabitants are largely of African descent. The local creole language of Papiamento reflects Portuguese, Spanish, and Dutch influences; selections of the **Book of Mormon** were translated into Papiamento in 1987. At the beginning of the year 2000, there were 348 Latter-day **Saints** in one **branch** there.

EMILY C. ZEIGLER

CURTIS, ELBERT R. Elbert Raine Curtis, general superintendent of the **Young Men's Mutual Improvement Association** from October 1948 to April 1958, was born 24 April 1901 in **Salt Lake City**. Prior to this calling, he served as president of the Western States **Mission** from October 1941 to April 1945. He was also president of the Sugar House **Stake** from April 1947 to April 1949. He and his wife, Luceal Rockwood, had three children. Elbert R. Curtis died 20 May 1975 in Salt Lake City.

GUY L. DORIUS

CUTLER, ALPHEUS. Alpheus John Cutler, a faithful Latter-day Saint during the life of **Joseph Smith**, later left the Church and formed an apostate **schismatic group**. Born 29 February 1784 in Plainfield, New Hampshire, Cutler converted to Mormonism in 1833. He moved his **family** from **New York** to **Ohio**, where as a master stonemason he helped build the **Kirtland Temple**. In 1839 he assisted in laying the cornerstones of the temple at **Far West, Missouri**, and in **Nauvoo** he again worked as a **temple** builder and also served on the Nauvoo **high council** and the **Council of Fifty**. During the **exodus** from Nauvoo, his campsite at **Winter Quarters** was named Cutler's Park in his honor.

About this time Cutler became convinced that **Brigham Young**, in moving the Church west, was surrendering the doctrines of establishing **Zion** at **Independence, Missouri**, and of redeeming the **Indian**. Bowing to pressure from supporters such as Chauncey Whiting, Luman H. Caulkins, and Edmund Fisher, the 62-year-old leader reluctantly quit the **Saints** and moved his followers eastward, eventually settling in Manti, Fremont County, **Iowa**, where he oversaw the formation of The Church of Jesus Christ (the "Cutlerites") in 1853. After some relatively unsuccessful **missions** to the **Delaware** and other tribes in the early 1850s, Cutler died of tuberculosis in Manti, Iowa, on 10 August 1864. A handful of followers of his church still remain in Independence, Missouri, and northern **Minnesota**.

SOURCES

Bennett, Richard E. "Lamanism, Lymanism and Cornfields." *Journal of Mormon History* 13 (1986–87): 45–60.

Fletcher, Rupert J., and Daisy W. Fletcher. *Alpheus Cutler and the Church of Jesus Christ*. Independence, Mo.: Church of Jesus Christ, 1974.

Jorgensen, Danny L. "Building the Kingdom of God: Alpheus Cutler and the Second Mormon Mission to the Lamanites, 1846–1853." *Kansas History* 15 (Autumn 1992): 192–209.

———. "The Old Fox: Alpheus Cutler, Priestly Keys to the Kingdom and the Early Church of Jesus Christ." *Differing Visions: Dissenters in Mormon History*. Edited by Roger D. Launius and Linda Thatcher. Urbana: University of Illinois Press, 1994.

RICHARD E. BENNETT

CYPRUS. Cyprus is an island in the Mediterranean Sea off the coast of **Turkey** and **Syria** that received the gospel through the **apostle** Paul during his first missionary journey. In 1962 a group of Latter-day Saint families were in Cyprus on U.S. government assignments. They were organized into the Nicosia **Branch**, which has been dissolved and reorganized several times over the years.

On 15 September 1993, **Elder Joseph B. Wirthlin** dedicated Cyprus for the preaching of the gospel. At that time there were 26 members in the branch. On this occasion Elder Wirthlin prayed: "May these marvelous **Saints** who are gathered here this morning, who are few in number, be magnified because of their faith, their love, and their obedience to thee. Let them be a catalyst around which strong units of thy Church will be established. Let thy Spirit be poured out upon the inhabitants of this land" ("Elder Wirthlin," 3).

At the beginning of the year 2000 there were 99 members in three branches on Cyprus. The island is part of the **Greece** Athens **Mission**.

SOURCES

"Elder Wirthlin Dedicates the Island of Cyprus for the Preaching of Gospel." *Church News*, 27 November 1993, 3.

1999–2000 Church Almanac. Salt Lake City: Deseret News, 1998. 308.

DAVID R. CROCKETT

CZECH REPUBLIC. Brief missionary visits to Prague in 1884 and 1928 and the pleadings of the Brodilová **family** resulted in the founding of the Czechoslovak Mission in 1929. Thus began the first sustained proselyting among the Slavic peoples of Central and Eastern **Europe**. Missionaries served in Czechoslovakia until 1939, then between 1946 and 1950, and again since 1990.

During the 1930s the membership increased to 150. The Church was registered and functioned publicly in the Czech provinces of Bohemia and Moravia. The **Book of Mormon** was published in Czech in 1933, and the **Pearl of Great Price** in 1938. A total of 57 missionaries labored in some 15 cities with branches established in several of them.

From 1939 to 1945, during the Nazi occupation, the Church continued to function under faithful local **priesthood** leaders and added a few members. The missionaries returned in 1946. A total of 39 were granted residence visas, the last arriving in 1948. They served in many of the prewar cities, established new branches, and added 135 members.

But by 1950, two years after the communist takeover of Czechoslovakia, all of the missionaries had been expelled and the Church had been banned. Despite ongoing Czech police interrogations, the members continued to inconspicuously visit each other in their homes. They continued to take the **sacrament** and to pay **tithing**. During the Prague Spring Liberalization in 1968, local leaders petitioned for recognition but were refused. The **Saints** were visited quietly from year to year by nearby European Church leaders, by former Czech missionaries, and even by **general authorities** and officers, all as tourists. By 1972 the members began to meet weekly in homes in Prague and Brno under the direction of the **district** president. After 1981 the Czech District became part of the East European Mission (from 1987, the **Austria** Vienna East) and were visited more often.

In the 1980s the Saints were supplied with a pocket-size Czech edition of the Book of Mormon and a similar combined edition of the Pearl of Great Price and **Doctrine and Covenants**. They also received monthly **First Presidency** messages in Czech. Dozens of converts were privately prepared and secretly baptized through a unique fellowshipping program involving numerous Czechs. These participated in the Moravian members' public fitness program of exercising, nutrition, and counseling about positive, but not openly religious, living. Those who responded spiritually were introduced to the Book of Mormon.

In 1990, following the collapse of Communist rule, the reestablished constitutional government in Prague granted full Church recognition to the Latter-day Saints and proselyting status to the Czechoslovak Mission (the Czech Prague Mission after 1993). The missionaries served in as many as 25 Bohemian and Moravian cities, as well as in four western Slovak cities. Since 1985 the members have been privileged to visit the Freiberg **Temple** regularly. Many young Czech members have served **missions** in other countries. Since 1997 the Saints have received the full text of **general conference** addresses, published twice yearly in the quarterly *Liahona*. By the beginning of the year 2000 there were about 1,654 members organized in four **districts** and 19 **branches**.

SOURCES

Gardner, Marvin K. "Jiri and Olga Snederfler: A Closer Look at Two Czech Pioneers." *Liahona* (English) 21 (September 1997): 16–24.

Mehr, Kahlile. "Czech Saints: A Brighter Day." *Liahona* (English) 21 (September 1997): 10–15.

———. "Frontier in the East." Manuscript history, Czechoslovakia and the Czech Republic.

1999–2000 Church Almanac. Salt Lake City: Deseret News, 1998. 309.

EDWIN B. MORRELL

DESERET ALPHABET. The publication of 1 and 2 Nephi in the Deseret Alphabet in 1869 was part of the Church's effort to create a phonetic way of writing the English language.

DANCE. Dance played a significant role in the early years of the Church. Presidents **Joseph Smith** and **Brigham Young** stressed that temporal and physical welfare were the basis for spiritual welfare. Dance served this objective well. It included men and women of all ages, including boys and girls, and provided physical exercise, easy social entry, and uplifting expression. Converts to the Church, who gathered from many parts of the world, brought with them their cultural dances, which they shared, thereby unifying and enriching the **Saints**. On most occasions of celebration and recreation, and even in times of desperation and trial, dance was used as a means of socialization and interaction. After the **pioneers** had pitched camp on 1 March 1846 during their trek across **Iowa**, for example, Brigham Young had them out dancing to the music of **William Pitt**'s brass band. Some spectators were surprised at this behavior and observed:

"A dance! How could they? Indeed, the Iowans who gathered round could scarcely believe their eyes. The men cleared away the snow in a sheltered place. Warmed and lighted by the blazing logs of their fire, fifty couples, old and young, stepped out in the dance" (Cameron, 92).

Dance was widely used as personal and social edification by all members of the Church. Richard F. Burton observed: "Dancing seems to be considered an edifying exercise. The **Prophet** dances, the **Apostles** dance, the **Bishops** dance" (Burton, 280). Nevertheless, Brigham Young affirmed: "I want it distinctly understood that fiddling and dancing are no part of our worship. The question may be asked, What are they for, then? I answer, that my body may keep pace with my mind" (Widtsoe, 373). Brigham Young clarified that dance should be pursued only as an uplifting activity. "Those who cannot serve God with a pure heart in the dance should not dance" (Widtsoe, 375).

The tradition of dance has continued in the Church through to the present. The **Mutual Improvement Association** sponsored local dances as well as regional and Church-wide dance festivals. President **Boyd K.**

Packer has counseled: "Go to, then, you who are gifted; cultivate your gift. Develop it in any of the arts and in every worthy example of them. . . . Never express your gift unworthily. Increase our spiritual heritage in **music**, in **art**, in **literature**, in dance, in **drama**" (65).

SOURCES

Burton, Richard F. *The City of the Saints.* New York: Harper and Brothers, 1861.
Cameron, Marguerite. *This Is the Place.* Caldwell, Idaho: Caxton, 1975.
Packer, Boyd K. "The Arts and the Spirit of the Lord." *Ensign* 6 (August 1976): 60–65.
Young, Brigham. *The Discourses of Brigham Young.* Compiled by John A. Widtsoe. Salt Lake City: Deseret Book, 1941.

SARAH LEE GIBB

DANIELS, WILLIAM P. William Paul Daniels was one of the first people of African descent to receive the gospel in **Africa**. He was born 28 August 1864 in Stellenbosch, **South Africa**, and served for 16 years as a deacon in the Dutch Reformed Church before being taught by the missionaries in 1913. Deeply impressed with the gospel message, he traveled with two of his sons to Utah in 1915 to observe Church members and more thoroughly study the gospel. During this eight-month visit, Brother Daniels was baptized. Prior to returning to South Africa, he received counsel from **Elder David O. McKay** of the Quorum of the Twelve **Apostles**, who told him: "Don't worry, Brother Daniels. If you don't hold the priesthood on earth, you will hold it in heaven" (quoted in LeBaron, 215). He also received a blessing from President **Joseph F. Smith**, which meant a great deal to him throughout his life.

After Brother Daniels returned home he lived as a faithful Latter-day Saint, but the social atmosphere at the time made it difficult for his family to participate in Church **meetings** or activities. They usually held church in their home, and each Monday evening they studied Elder John A. Widtsoe's book *Jesus the Christ.* They called their family gatherings the "Branch of Love."

Brother Daniels died 13 October 1936 in Stellenbosch. On his deathbed, he bore his testimony of the Church to his family and laid his hands on his children and blessed them.

SOURCES

LeBaron, E. Dale, ed. *All Are Alike unto God.* Orem, Utah: Granite Publishing, 1998.
Oral histories of early Church converts collected by E. Dale LeBaron. Copies at BYU Library, Provo, Utah; LDS Church Historical Library, Salt Lake City, Utah.

E. DALE LEBARON

DANITES. The Danites were a **defensive** paramilitary organization sanctioned neither by the state nor by the Church. They operated in northern Missouri during the summer and fall of 1838. There were essentially two Danite groups, both composed primarily of Mormons. The larger group was organized at **Far West** in **Caldwell County** in June; a second, somewhat smaller, unit was established in mid-July at **Adam-ondi-Ahman** in **Daviess County**.

The entire organization, both in Caldwell and Daviess Counties, was led by **Sampson Avard**, who instituted initiation rites and secret oaths of loyalty and encouraged subversive activities. Avard worked principally with the Caldwell County group; **Lyman Wight** was the acknowledged leader in Daviess County. Danite influence in the military activities in predominantly Mormon Caldwell County was less pronounced because the defense operations there were primarily conducted by the regular state militia. Mormon defenders residing in non-Mormon Daviess County were not part of the county or state militia and conducted their operations under Danite leadership.

During June 1838, Danites intimidated several key Mormon dissidents, forcing them to flee Far West. They also attempted to coerce reluctant **Saints** into consecrating their surplus money and property to the Church. Finally, they sought to influence the political outcome of the August county elections in favor of the Latter-day Saints.

Joseph Smith did not have any affiliation or connection with the Danite organization. Although he was aware of the Danites' existence, he was not told of Sampson Avard's insurgent teachings. He did take part in the civil conflict in northern Missouri but not in concert with the Danites.

SOURCES

Gentry, Leland H. "The Danite Band of 1838." *BYU Studies* 14 (Summer 1974): 421–50.

Whittaker, David J. "The 'Danites' in Mormon History." *By Study and Also By Faith.* Edited by John M. Lundquist and Stephen D. Ricks. 2 vols. Salt Lake City and Provo: Deseret Book and the Foundation for Ancient Research and Mormon Studies, 1990. 1:166–74.

ALEXANDER L. BAUGH

DAUGHTERS OF UTAH PIONEERS. Daughters of Utah Pioneers (DUP), an honorific organization, was founded with the intent of keeping alive the memories of the **Utah pioneers** and their accomplishments for their posterity and others as an inspiration and guide. An outgrowth of the Pioneer Jubilee in 1897, DUP was founded in 1901 with 46 charter members. At first only descendants of Utah pioneers up to 1850 were admitted as full members. Membership was expanded to include descendants of pioneers from the **handcart** era, up to 1858, and still later to descendants of any pioneers who arrived before the coming of the railroad in 1869. DUP was incorporated by the State of Utah in April 1925. The organization has been a major force in preserving the heritage of the Utah pioneers. Its original small displays of pioneer artifacts has grown to fill a substantial museum at 300 North Main Street in **Salt Lake City** as well as numerous DUP museums throughout the **Mormon** West. DUP promoted the Utah state flag and have placed numerous markers commemorating pioneer era achievements. They continue an ambitious program of research and publication about the pioneers of the Mormon West.

SOURCE

Winn, Norma B., and Emma R. Olsen, comps. *Daughters of Utah Pioneers through the Years*. Salt Lake City: Daughters of Utah Pioneers, 1990.

MARJORIE DRAPER CONDER

DAVIESS COUNTY, MISSOURI.

On 29 December 1836 the **Missouri** legislature passed the bill creating Caldwell and Daviess Counties in northwestern Missouri. **Alexander W. Doniphan**, Clay County's representative in the state legislature and a **Mormon** sympathizer, sponsored the bill. Daviess County was nearly 24 miles square and situated to the north of **Caldwell County**. It was named after Colonel Joseph H. Daviess, a commander killed at the battle of Tippecanoe in **Indiana** in 1811 and a friend of Doniphan's father. **Gallatin** was established as the county seat.

A few Latter-day **Saints** began settling Daviess County in 1837, but most came in 1838. One of the most prominent Mormon settlers in Daviess County was **Lyman Wight**. In February 1838 he purchased a farm and established a ferry on the Grand River in the area known as Spring Hill. On 19 May 1838, while visiting Wight, **Joseph Smith** received a **revelation** indicating that Spring Hill was anciently known as **Adam-ondi-Ahman**, and was the former homeland of **Adam** and his posterity (D&C 107:53–56; 116).

During the summer of 1838, a major LDS settlement was established at Adam-ondi-Ahman (Diahman for short), which soon became the largest settlement in the county. On 28 June 1838, Joseph Smith organized the Adam-ondi-Ahman **Stake**, with **John Smith** as president and **Reynolds Cahoon** and Lyman Wight as **counselors**. Vinson Knight was appointed **bishop**. A **temple** site at Adam-ondi-Ahman was also dedicated. Besides Diahman, Mormon settlers also lived in the Marrowbone (also called Ambrosia), Honeycreek, Lickfork, and Grindstone Forks settlements. In October 1838, the Mormon population in Daviess County approximated 1,500 but may have been as high as 2,000, including **Kirtland Camp.**

A number of conflicts between the Mormons and Missourians broke out in Daviess County beginning 6 August 1838 with an election-day skirmish at Gallatin. Outbreaks between both parties in September led to the call-out of the state militia to quell the fighting. Fearing additional reprisals, during the month of October, Mormon defenders under the leadership of Lyman Wight took control of the region, forcing the non-Mormon inhabitants to leave the county. While the Saints surrendered to the state militia at **Far West** on 1 November, a second surrender also occurred at Diahman nine days later. Following the surrender, most Saints living in Daviess County abandoned their homes and property and temporarily moved into Caldwell County before leaving the state during the first few months of 1839.

SOURCES

Baugh, Alexander L. "A Call to Arms: The 1838 Mormon Defense of Northern Missouri." Ph.D. diss., Brigham Young University, 1996.

History of Daviess County: Missouri, An Encyclopedia of Useful Information, and a Compendium of Actual Facts. Kansas City: Birdsall & Dean, 1882.

Jenson, Andrew. "Daviess County, Missouri." *Historical Record* 9 (January 1889): 724–32.

ALEXANDER L. BAUGH

DEACON. The office of deacon is an office in the **Aaronic Priesthood.** A deacon is a "standing minister" assigned to assist **teachers** to "watch over the church" and also to warn, expound, exhort, teach, and bring members to **Christ** (D&C 20:57; 84:30, 111). The Church's first deacons were Titus Billings, Serenes Burnett, and John Burk, ordained some time before 15 October 1831.

For four decades deacons were usually adults, and the 12-member deacons **quorums** were **stake** entities. Deacons helped the poor and cared for the **meetinghouses**—providing coal and wood for heat and oil for lamps, dusting seats, sweeping floors, and opening windows on hot days. By the 1870s deacons quorums were becoming **ward** entities. An 1877 directive said that all Latter- day Saint boys should receive at least one Aaronic Priesthood office before adulthood. In response, boys ages 11 to 20 became deacons, and most remained in this office until they were ordained **elders**. By the 1870s deacons helped collect fast offerings, which were mostly food rather than money. Few passed the **sacrament**. In 1908 the Church set ordination ages at 12 for deacons, 15 for **teachers**, and 18 for **priests**, and leaders began to advance boys from one office to the next. Since 1908 deacons' main duties have been to pass the sacrament, collect fast offerings, help keep chapels clean, and do projects to help the needy. Deacons today are ages 12 and 13.

SOURCES

Hartley, William G. "Deacon Power." *New Era* 5 (May 1975): 6–10.

———. "From Men to Boys: LDS Aaronic Priesthood Offices, 1829–1996." *Journal of Mormon History* 22 (Spring 1996): 80–136.

Palmer, Lee A. *Aaronic Priesthood through the Centuries.* Salt Lake City: Deseret Book, 1964.

WILLIAM G. HARTLEY

DEAD, REDEEMING THE. **Joseph** Smith learned in 1823 that the fourth chapter of Malachi prophesied **Elijah** would return to reveal the **priesthood** and "plant in the hearts of the children the promises made to the fathers, and the hearts of the children shall turn to their fathers" (Smith, 1:12). **Doctrine and Covenants** 110, received 3 April 1836, documents the return of Elijah and the **restoration** of the power to seal on earth and in heaven. In Doctrine and Covenants 128, Latter-day **Saints** learned that the turning of hearts involved baptism for the dead. The promises made to the fathers—**Adam**, Noah, Abraham, and all of their descendants—included the opportunity for exaltation and the promise of resurrection through **Jesus Christ**: "All who have died without a knowledge of this gospel, who would have received it if they had been permitted to tarry, shall be heirs of the celestial **kingdom of God**; also all that shall die henceforth without a knowledge of it, who would have received it . . . shall be heirs of that kingdom" (D&C 137:7–8). Christ promised: "The hour is coming, and now is, when the dead shall hear the voice of the Son of God: and they that hear shall live" (John 5:25). The **apostle** Peter wrote: "For this cause was the gospel preached also to them that are dead, that they might be judged according to men in the flesh, but live according to God in the spirit" (1 Peter 4:6), and Paul taught about **baptism for the dead**: "Else what shall they do which are baptized for the dead, if the dead rise not at all? why are they then baptized for the dead?" (1 Cor. 15:29).

By the time of his **martyrdom** in 1844, Joseph Smith had established the pattern for providing the dead with baptisms, **confirmations, endowments, marriage** vows, and **family sealings** that were to be valid in the postmortal world. The **Nauvoo Temple** was the first in which baptismal ordinances for the dead were a regular part of **temple** worship. Today, in temples that dot the globe, living proxies receive the ordinances of the gospel of Jesus Christ in behalf of millions who have died without these blessings. President **Joseph F. Smith** foresaw "the great work to be done in the temples of the Lord . . . for the redemption of the dead, and the sealing of the children to their parents . . . [he] beheld the faithful elders of this dispensation, when they depart from mortal life . . . preaching of the gospel . . . in the great world of the spirits of the dead. The dead who repent will be redeemed, through obedience to the ordinances of the house of God" (D&C 138:48, 57–59). How many of the dead will accept these ordinances? President **Wilford Woodruff** taught: "There will be very few, if any, who will not accept the gospel" (Durham, 157).

SOURCES

Woodruff, Wilford. *The Discourses of Wilford Woodruff.* Compiled by G. Homer Durham. Salt Lake City: Bookcraft, 1946.

Smith, Joseph. *History of the Church of Jesus Christ of Latter-day Saints.* Edited by B. H. Roberts. 2d ed. rev. 7 vols. Salt Lake City: The Church of Jesus Christ of Latter-day Saints, 1932–51.

RAYMOND S. WRIGHT

DECLARATION OF INDEPENDENCE. Members of The Church of Jesus Christ of Latter-day Saints have respected and revered the United States Declaration of Independence as a sacred document, written by inspired men, which exhorts eternal truths. The Declaration of Independence was drafted in 1776 by Thomas Jefferson and others and signed on 4 July when 56 representatives from the 13 united American colonies met in Philadelphia to declare themselves independent and free from the rule of **Great Britain**. Latter-day prophets have declared that God raised up these men for this very purpose (D&C 101:80). **Brigham Young** taught that the signers of the document "were inspired from on high to do that work" (quoted in Widtsoe, 550). The signers appeared to **Wilford Woodruff** in the **St. George Temple** in 1877, requiring that he vicariously perform temple **ordinances** on their behalf. Woodruff declared that "Every one of those men that signed the Declaration of Independence, with General [George] Washington, called upon me as an **apostle** of the Lord **Jesus Christ**, in the temple at **St. George**, two consecutive nights, and demanded at my hands that I should go forth and attend to the ordinances of the House of God for them" (Woodruff, 89–90).

The statement that "all men are created equal; that they are endowed by their Creator with certain inalienable rights; that among these are life, liberty, and the pursuit of happiness" is consistent with principles found in the **Doctrine and Covenants** that outline the responsibilities righteous people have in governing free republics (D&C 134:5).

Historically, the Church has seen the Declaration of Independence as a potential source of protection of an individual's right to worship. When the **Saints** suffered persecution in **Ohio**, **Missouri**, and **Illinois**, as United States citizens they asked for redress, in part, by virtue of the freedoms listed in the Declaration. The coming forth of this document, with its guarantees of freedom, is seen as part of the divine preparation of a promised land, choice above other lands (1 Ne. 13:30) as the setting for the latter-day restoration of the gospel.

─────────

SOURCES

Benson, Ezra Taft. *The Teachings of Ezra Taft Benson*. Salt Lake City: Bookcraft, 1988.

Woodruff, Wilford. *The Discourses of Wilford Woodruff*. Compiled by G. Homer Durham. Salt Lake City: Bookcraft, 1946.

McConkie, Bruce R. *Mormon Doctrine*. 2d ed. rev. Salt Lake City: Bookcraft, 1966. 377.

Widtsoe, John A., ed. *Discourses of Brigham Young*. Salt Lake City: Deseret Book, 1925. 550.

Woodruff, Wilford. Conference Report (April 1898): 89–90.

MARY JANE WOODGER

DECLARATIONS. See PROCLAMATIONS.

DELAWARE.

DELAWARE. Early Latter-day Saint missionaries introduced the Church into Delaware in 1837. For years Wilmington was the center for Latter-day Saint growth in the state, but branches were also created in Dover, Salisbury, and Elkton. Early converts were encouraged to migrate west, adversely affecting Church growth in the state. The first organization beyond the **branch** level occurred in 1960, when three Delaware units became part of the Philadelphia **Stake**. The Wilmington Stake (1974) was made possible with an influx of Latter-day **Saints** attracted by employment opportunities. At the beginning of the year 2000 there were 3,730 members residing in one stake and 7 **wards** and a branch.

SOURCES

Jenson, Andrew. *Encyclopedic History of The Church of Jesus Christ of Latter-day Saints.* Salt Lake City: Deseret News, 1941. 178–79.
1999–2000 Church Almanac. Salt Lake City: Deseret News, 1998. 187–88.

DAVID F. BOONE

DELAWARE INDIANS. The Delaware Indians inhabited the Delaware Valley and were probably the first Native Americans to come into contact with Europeans. They signed the first treaty with the **United States** on 17 September 1778, leading to a series of moves from the Delaware Valley to **New Jersey, Pennsylvania, Ohio, Indiana,** and then **Missouri.** Eventually, a reservation in **Kansas** was established, and they made their final move to the Indian Territory in 1866.

The missionaries to the Lamanites in 1830 and 1831 visited the Delaware tribe in Kansas Territory in 1831. For several days they taught Chief William Anderson Kithtilhund about the restored gospel. Because they had no written permission from the Indian agency, the missionaries were removed from the reservation. No other formal contact was made with this tribe at that time.

SOURCE

Pratt, Parley P. *Autobiography of Parley P. Pratt.* Edited by Parley P. Pratt Jr. Salt Lake City: Deseret Book, 1973. 53–57.

H. DEAN GARRETT

DELTA PHI KAPPA. Delta Phi Kappa (DPK) was first a university debating society (1869–1900) and then a fraternity for returned missionaries (1920–78). It had chapters at **Brigham Young University, Utah** State University, the **University of Utah, Idaho** State University, **Weber State** University, **Arizona** State University, and Southern Utah State College at Cedar City. Four chapters had chapter houses. Although not Church-sponsored, Delta Phi Kappa had Church approval. Six **general**

authorities served as DPK national presidents: **Elders John A. Widtsoe, Matthew Cowley, Milton R. Hunter,** Henry D. Taylor, **Paul H. Dunn,** and **Marion D. Hanks.** Unpaid national executives oversaw chapter operations. Part fraternity, part religious club, DPK chapters had rituals and sponsored socials, elected DPK Dream Girls, and performed service projects. Delta Phi Kappa choruses were popular. In 1978 DPK merged with **Sigma Gamma Chi,** the Church's college fraternity.

SOURCE

Hartley, William G. *Delta Phi Kappa Fraternity: A History, 1869–1978.* Salt Lake City: Delta Phi Kappa Holding Corp., 1991.

WILLIAM G. HARTLEY

DEMOCRATIC PARTY. The relationship between the **Mormon** Church and the Democratic Party has a checkered history. In the early days of the Church, essentially the **Nauvoo** period, Church members switched support back and forth between the Whigs and the Democrats, owing allegiance to neither party.

During the early years in **Utah,** politics tended to divide along religious lines, with the Mormon **People's Party** on one side and the **Gentile Liberal Party** on the other. In order to achieve statehood, Church leaders encouraged the **Saints** to affiliate with both the national Democratic and **Republican** Parties. Support for these two parties by Latter-day Saints was fairly evenly divided for about one decade.

Mormon support for the Democratic Party waned after 1900 because of the rise of Republican **Reed Smoot** and the national political alliances he formed. There were exceptions, however, such as the election of a democrat, William H. King, to the U.S. Senate. The Democrats were strengthened by the emergence of Franklin D. Roosevelt on the national political stage. For example, in 1932, Democrat Elbert D. Thomas defeated Reed Smoot for the U.S. Senate, and later Democrat Herbert B. Maw was elected governor of Utah.

In the last half of the twentieth century the Democratic Party in Utah was relatively weak. Most Congressional delegates were Republican. A notable exception was the election of such Democratic governors as Calvin L. Rampton and Scott M. Matheson.

Looking beyond Utah, there were proportionately more Democrats among Church members. In fact, one study indicated that nationwide,

Latter-day Saints tend to be moderate in their political preference, as opposed to conservative in the Mountain West.

SOURCES

Mauss, Armand. "Moderation in All Things: Political and Social Outlooks of Modern Urban Mormons." *Dialogue* 7 (Spring 1972): 57–69.

Sillito, John. "Democratic Party." *Utah History Encyclopedia.* Edited by Allan Kent Powell. Salt Lake City: University of Utah Press, 1994. 133–34.

DONALD Q. CANNON

DEMOCRATIC REPUBLIC OF CONGO. Zaire gained its independence from **Belgium** in 1960 and was known as the Belgian Congo until 1971, when it was named Zaire. Following a revolution in 1997, Zaire's name was changed to Democratic Republic of Congo. This nation, which is as large as the **United States** east of the **Mississippi River,** has French as its official language, and 80% of its people are Christian.

Among the earliest Church converts from Zaire were Banza Mutombo and his wife, Regine. They had been given scholarships by their church to study in **Switzerland,** and while there they were introduced to The Church of Jesus Christ of Latter-day Saints. They were baptized 2 October 1979 and then returned to Zaire to fulfill obligations to their previous church. They kept in contact with the LDS Church's **International Mission** and met with Latter-day Saint expatriates until the Church was organized in Zaire. Their two sons, Banza Jr. and Philippe Muchioko, were the first to be baptized in Zaire.

Mbuyi Nkitabungi of Zaire was baptized in 1980 while attending school in Belgium. Less than two years later he was serving a **mission** in **England.** In 1985 Mbuyi returned to Zaire and was immediately called to serve in Church leadership positions, including **branch** president.

Through the efforts of **David M. Kennedy,** a special representative of the **First Presidency,** the Church was granted legal status in Zaire in February 1986, and in September of that year the Church began meeting in its first building, a remodeled villa that seated 200. On 1 July 1987 the Zaire Kinshasa Mission was established, with R. Bay Hutchings and his wife, Jean, presiding. On 30 August **Elder Marvin J. Ashton** of the **Quorum** of the Twelve **Apostles** dedicated Zaire for missionary work.

Following a military uprising in 1991, mission headquarters were moved for about two years from Kinshasa, Zaire, to neighboring Brazzaville, **Congo. Burundi** became part of the mission a year later. During this time, despite the absence of full-time missionaries, the local

members carried on the work to the extent that a second stake was organized, in Lubumbashi. In January 1994, due to devastating uprisings in
all three countries, the mission was closed for six months. Beginning in
1995, President Roberto Tavella rebuilt the mission by calling four local,
single elders. That number grew to 100 Congolese missionaries in 1999.
By the year 2000, membership had grown to 8,197 with three stakes and
33 **wards** and branches. This remarkable growth is happening through
the efforts of local missionaries in the midst of political upheaval that
continues to plague the region.

SOURCES

LeBaron, E. Dale, ed. *All Are Alike unto God.* Orem, Utah: Granite Publishing, 1998.
  103–15.

Middleton, John, ed. *Encyclopedia of Africa South of the Sahara. 4 vols.* New York:
  Macmillan Library Reference USA, 1997. 4:396–407.

1999–2000 Church Almanac. Salt Lake City: Deseret News, 1998. 309–10.

Wright, David E. "Orderly Growth Marks Church in Zaire." *Ensign* 21 (April 1991):
  76–77.

"Zaire's People—Thirsty for Gospel." *Church News,* 18 July 1987, 3.

E. DALE LEBARON

DENMARK. At the October **general conference** of 1849, President
Brigham Young called **Elder Erastus Snow** of the **Quorum** of the Twelve
Apostles to open the work of the gospel in the lands of **Scandinavia.** He
was to be accompanied by Elders Peter O. Hansen, John E. Forsgren, and
George P. Dykes. Hansen's sailor brother had joined the Church in Boston
and wrote to Peter, who was still in Denmark, of his conversion. With no
Latter-day **Saints** at the time in Denmark to teach him the restored
gospel, Peter traveled to **America** and was baptized in **Nauvoo.** Later in
Nauvoo, Peter was assigned by Brigham Young to work on a Danish
translation of the **Book of Mormon.** Forsgren, from **Sweden,** had also
joined the Church in the East and moved to Nauvoo to be with the
Saints. He was called to labor in Sweden. Dykes had been a missionary
in the **Wisconsin** territory among Norwegian immigrants. Many were
converted, and a **branch** was established. Because Dykes knew the language and the customs of the people, he was called to labor in **Norway.**

Elder Snow and his companions arrived in Denmark on 14 June
1850 (Peter Hansen had arrived in Copenhagen a month earlier) and
dedicated the lands of Denmark, Sweden, and Norway for the preaching
of the gospel. Although the Danish parliament had passed a freedom of
religion law in 1849, the early missionaries and converts faced considerable opposition. Despite severe persecution, the first baptisms occurred

in August 1850, and the first branch was established 15 September 1850. Several other branches were subsequently established in various parts of the country.

In 1851 the Book of Mormon was published in Danish—the first foreign language edition. Many other tracts and publications were also published in Danish that assisted in **missionary work** and bolstered the faith of the Danish converts. In 1852 the first group of Danish converts emigrated to America. With the encouragement of the Church leadership and the financial assistance of the **Perpetual Emigrating Fund**, about 14,000 Danish Saints eventually gathered with the Church in **Utah**. The 1860s saw unparalleled growth in Church membership in Scandinavia generally, and Denmark specifically, despite continuing persecution.

In 1905 the Scandinavian Mission was divided to become the Swedish Mission and the Danish-Norwegian Mission. In 1920 the Danish Mission was created (now called the Denmark Copenhagen Mission). During **World War I** and again in **World War II**, virtually all American missionaries were called home. Missionary work continued, however, through the faithful service of full-time Danish missionaries and local Saints. After the wars, missionaries were again called to Denmark, and the work resumed. Although convert baptisms in the country were relatively few—from 50 to 200 a year—the Church grew spiritually, and members increased in faithfulness. On 16 June 1974, the Copenhagen Denmark **Stake** was created by President **Ezra Taft Benson**. It was the first stake not only in Denmark but in all of Scandinavia. In 1978 a second stake was formed in Denmark—the Aarhus Denmark Stake. In 1999 construction began on a temple in Copenhagen, which would serve the Saints and bless the Church in Denmark and southern Sweden. By the beginning of the year 2000 the country had 4,527 members and 25 **wards** and branches.

SOURCES

Christensen, Marius A. "A History of the Danish Mission of The Church of Jesus Christ of Latter-day Saints, 1850–1965." Master's thesis, Brigham Young University, 1966.

Jenson, Andrew. *History of the Scandinavian Mission.* Salt Lake City: Deseret News Press, 1927.

Mulder, William. *Homeward to Zion: The Mormon Migration from Scandinavia.* Minneapolis: University of Minnesota Press, 1957.

Van Orden, Bruce A. *Building Zion: The Latter-day Saints in Europe.* Salt Lake City: Deseret Book, 1996.

BRENT L. TOP

DEPRESSION, GREAT. The economic disaster of the 1930s, called the **great depression**, was caused by a wave of speculative buying, which drove prices up, followed by a wave of selling on the stock market, which caused its collapse on 29 October 1929—known as "Black Tuesday." Investors were ruined, businesses and banks failed, and millions of individuals were thrown out of work. Many people had no money even for necessities. Utah, where most of the Church members resided, was hit especially hard because of its ties to the agricultural and mining industries, which were devastated. Unemployment in the state reached 35% in 1932, compared to the national average of about 25%. The Church was affected significantly as the dollar amount of tithes and offerings decreased dramatically (though the number of donors dipped only slightly, which was viewed by Church leaders as a mark of the faithfulness and commitment of the members). Improvements and repairs to Church facilities were postponed, new construction projects canceled, and many members had to put off missionary service. Nevertheless, the Church as an institution remained financially solvent by cutting expenditures taken from **tithing** receipts (from $4 million in 1927 to $2.4 million in 1933). Church members throughout the world were gravely affected by the economic and social devastation of the **great depression**.

While American president Franklin D. Roosevelt and other government officials responded to the economic crisis by inaugurating the programs of the "New Deal" beginning in 1933, Church leaders set about instituting their own program. As early as 1930 the **presiding bishop** began urging members to care for one another based on principles of welfare service found in the **scriptures**; welfare projects in various local areas were begun. In 1935 **Harold B. Lee** was called by the **First Presidency** to formulate the Church-wide **welfare program**, which was announced a year later at April **general conference**. In 1937 President **J. Reuben Clark Jr.** encouraged all Church members to store, where possible, a year's supply of food, clothing, and other necessities. The Cooperative Securities Corporation was also formed to coordinate welfare projects. In 1938 **Deseret Industries** was created. Though the **great depression** severely taxed the Church, the welfare program that came out of it affirmed to members the inspired leadership by which the Church is guided.

Sources

Allen, James B., and Glen M. Leonard. *The Story of the Latter-day Saints.* 2d ed. Salt Lake City: Deseret Book, 1992. 517–25.

Cowan, Richard O. *The Latter-day Saint Century.* Salt Lake City: Bookcraft, 1999. 181.

Andrew C. Skinner

DER STERN. On 21 December 1868, **Karl G. Maeser**, president of the Swiss-German Mission, received a letter from **Brigham Young** directing him to begin a **periodical** for the German-speaking Latter-day **Saints**. In response, the first issue of *Der Stern* ("The Star") was published 1 January 1869. *Der Stern* has been published since that time, except during **World War II**. During **World War I**, few German-speaking Latter-day Saints living in the **United States** received issues of *Der Stern* because French officials, suspicious of material printed in German, confiscated the periodicals as they passed through that country.

Der Stern, though retaining its original name, was consolidated under the **Unified Magazine** program (1967)—later renamed **International Magazines** (1974–2000)—and contained articles similar to those that appeared in the *Ensign, New Era,* and *Friend,* with additional sections devoted to unique concerns of German Latter-day Saints. By January 2000, the titles of all international Church periodicals, including *Der Stern,* had been changed to *Liahona.*

SOURCES

Draper, Larry W. "Publications." *Encyclopedia of Mormonism.* Edited by Daniel H. Ludlow. 4 vols. New York: Macmillan, 1992. 3:1173–77.

Jenson, Andrew. *Encyclopedic History of The Church of Jesus Christ of Latter-day Saints.* Salt Lake City: Deseret News, 1941. 836–37.

Maeser, Reinhard. *Karl G. Maeser: A Biography.* Provo, Utah: Brigham Young University, 1928. 57.

JEFFREY L. ANDERSON

DESERET, STATE OF. A little more than two years after the **Saints** entered the **Salt Lake Valley**, Church leaders recognized a need for political organization because of immigrants passing through to **California** and **Oregon**. Consequently, the **Council of Fifty**, or General Council, decided to hold a state convention to draft a constitution for the proposed state of Deseret. The constitution was accepted on 10 March 1849. Two days later an election was held with only one slate of candidates. Those elected were **Brigham Young**, governor; **Willard Richards**, secretary of state; **Newel K. Whitney**, treasurer; **Heber C. Kimball**, chief justice; **John Taylor** and Newel K. Whitney, associate justices; and **Daniel H. Wells**, attorney general.

The proposed state of Deseret covered about 490,000 square miles, extending from the Sierra Nevada mountains on the west to the Rocky Mountains on the east. It included present-day **Utah**, **Nevada**, and parts of **California**, **Arizona**, **New Mexico**, **Colorado**, **Wyoming**, and **Idaho**. The inclusion of southern California offered ports of entry for immigration and goods needed by Deseret citizens.

During 1849 and 1850, officers organized counties, incorporated cities, and passed laws regulating political, social, economic, and military affairs of the state; they also organized the **Perpetual Emigrating Fund** to help the poor immigrate to **Zion** from their countries of origin.

The State of Deseret officially ended when Congress passed the Compromise of 1850, which made California a state and created the territories of Utah and New Mexico. The Deseret Assembly was dissolved on 5 April 1851, although the Council of Fifty continued to meet sporadically as a "ghost government" for the next two decades.

SOURCES

Larson, Gustive O. *The Americanization of Utah for Statehood.* San Marino, Calif.: Huntington Library, 1971.
Morgan, Dale L. *The State of Deseret.* Logan, Utah: Utah State University Press, 1987.

CLARK V. JOHNSON

DESERET, UNIVERSITY OF. See UNIVERSITY OF UTAH.

DESERET ALPHABET. Intending to create a phonetic way of writing the English language, **Brigham Young** conceived the Deseret Alphabet as early as 1845, when he attended some phonographic (shorthand) classes instructed by **George D. Watt**. In 1852 President Young spoke on the reform of the language and later gave instruction to the board of regents at the **University of Deseret** to reform the written language. Later, Watt helped to devise the symbols now known as the Deseret Alphabet.

The board promoted the alphabet by holding meetings among many influential segments of the population and by publishing articles in the *Deseret News.* Brigham Young even had his clerks record his history and also a financial ledger in Deseret. It was not until 1868 that the board published the first two primers in Deseret. A year later they published part of the **Book of Mormon**, followed by the entire Book of Mormon. The books were never widely distributed. With President Young's death, the board discontinued its attempt to reform the written language.

SOURCES

Alder, Douglas D., Paula J. Goodfellow, and Ronald G. Watt. "Creating a New

Alphabet for Zion: The Origin of the Deseret Alphabet." *Utah Historical Quarterly* 52 (Summer 1984): 275–86.

New, Douglas Allen. "History of the Deseret Alphabet and Other Attempts to Reform English Orthography." Ed.D. diss., Utah State University, 1985.

RONALD G. WATT

DESERET BOOK COMPANY.

In 1866, **Elder George Q. Cannon**, a member of the **Quorum** of the Twelve **Apostles**, was concerned about books coming into the **Utah** territory that were having a "pernicious influence on those who read them." He established George Q. Cannon and Sons as a privately owned commercial bookstore in **Salt Lake City**. Then in 1871, the printers of the *Deseret News* began printing, binding, and selling books. The two companies merged in 1900. This organization united with the Deseret Sunday School Union bookstore in 1919 to form Deseret Book Company.

In 1979 Deseret Book published an extensively cross-referenced Latter-day Saint edition of the **Bible** and in 1981 a new edition of the Triple Combination, along with the Topical Guide and Bible Dictionary appendices. Deseret Book has also published many important doctrinal books of interest to Latter-day Saint readers and, in more recent years, a number of inspirational, self-help, and fictional books as well as music products.

In the year 2000 the company, headquartered in Salt Lake City, operated four imprints: Deseret Book, Bookcraft, Shadow Mountain, and **Eagle Gate**. Wholly owned by the Church, Deseret Book Company transacted business in the **United States** and many foreign countries through its own network of retail stores, a wholesale division, and various direct sales outlets.

SOURCE

Knowles, Eleanor. *Deseret Book Company: 125 Years of Inspiration, Information, and Ideas.* Salt Lake City: Deseret Book Company, 1991.

RICHARD G. PETERSON

DESERET CLUB.

First established at UCLA in 1932, the Deseret Club functioned as a campus organization for gospel instruction and social activities among Latter-day **Saint** students. Local lawyer Preston D. Richards and UCLA dean of graduate study Dr. Vern O. Knudson initiated the club. A constitution was framed, and other clubs spawned, primarily throughout **California** and the western states. Local **priesthood** leaders recommended Latter-day Saint faculty advisors, which allowed students to use on-campus facilities. Often these clubs fostered the development of **institutes of religion**. In 1971 Deseret Clubs were discontinued as Church leaders established the **Latter-day Saints Student Association**.

SOURCES

Anderson, A. Gary. "A Historical Survey of the Full-Time Institutes of Religion of The Church of Jesus Christ of Latter-day Saints, 1926–1966." Ph.D. diss., Brigham Young University, 1968.
Berrett, William E. *A Miracle in Weekday Religious Education.* Salt Lake City: Salt Lake Printing Center, 1988.

JOHN P. LIVINGSTONE

DESERET HOSPITAL. See **HOSPITALS**.

DESERET INDUSTRIES. A year after the Church **Welfare Program** was announced, Salt Lake businessman Stewart Eccles was sent to **Los Angeles** to study Goodwill Industries. Upon his return, he submitted a proposal that the Church establish a similar operation. On 12 August 1938, in an old post office building, the first Deseret Industries store opened in **Salt Lake City**, Utah, with 13 employees. Within a week, donated goods were received, processed, sold, and distributed. **Stakes** and **wards** in the **Salt Lake Valley** were encouraged in a letter from the **First Presidency** and **presiding bishopric** to cooperate fully in stimulating an interest in this new aspect of the Welfare Program. The first organized collection drives were conducted in the Ensign and Liberty Stakes, followed shortly thereafter by many others.

Deseret Industries was set up to be a nonprofit retail business operated as part of the welfare services of the Church. Its objective is to provide work, training, and job placement for members with special needs, such as individuals with physical or mental disabilities, those of advanced age, and members who are otherwise unable to find gainful employment.

In 1940, a second store was opened in the Sugarhouse area of Salt Lake City. During the ensuing six decades, the success and growth of the company has been a tremendous blessing to tens of thousands of people. As of 1998, Deseret Industries operated 47 stores, a manufacturing plant for mattresses and furniture, and the Humanitarian Service Center, where clothing, medical supplies, and educational materials were processed to be distributed to people in need worldwide.

SOURCE

Rudd, Glen L. *Pure Religion: The Story of Church Welfare Since 1930.* Salt Lake City: The Church of Jesus Christ of Latter-day Saints, 1995. 124–26.

GLEN L. RUDD

DESERET NATIONAL BANK. The Deseret National Bank, "the only **Mormon** commercial bank in **Utah**" for a number of years, was established in 1871 (Carter 15:9). Originally known as Hooper, Eldredge & Co., the bank was reorganized, enlarged, and founded by seven of Utah's most prominent **pioneer** leaders, including **Brigham Young**, who was elected the new bank's first president.

By 1872 the bank had received a national charter and had a capital of $200,000. By 1880 that capital had risen to about $1,000,000. The bank continued to experience success throughout its existence. In fact, **Zion's Bank** had its beginnings as an offshoot of Deseret National Bank.

Deseret National continued its close association with the LDS Church and was Utah's leading bank well into the 20th century. In 1932 Deseret National Bank was merged into what eventually became First Security Corporation. At the end of the 20th century, First Security Corporation was a major banking institution throughout the western **United States**.

SOURCES

Arrington, Leonard J. *David Eccles: Pioneer Western Industrialist.* Logan, Utah: Utah State University Press, 1975. 256–57.
Carter, Kate B., ed. *Our Pioneer Heritage.* Salt Lake City: Daughters of Utah Pioneers, 1967–72. 10:326–28; 15:8–10.

CRAIG L. FOSTER

DESERET NEWS. The *Deseret News*, owned by the Church, is one of the most influential newspapers in the Intermountain West. It began publication in **Salt Lake City** on 15 June 1850 under the direction of **Brigham Young**. It was published as a weekly periodical from 1850 to 1898 and, besides, as a semiweekly from 1865 to 1922. The *Deseret Evening News*, a daily, began publication in 1867 and changed its name to the *Deseret News* in 1920.

The *Deseret News* has editorially taken a conservative to moderate position with special attention to high moral values. **Willard Richards** was the first editor of the *Deseret News* (1850–54). Other **general authorities** who have served as editors include: **Albert Carrington** (1854–59), **George Q. Cannon** (1867–73, 1877–79), and **Charles W. Penrose** (1880–92, 1899–1907). **Mark E. Petersen** worked as a reporter, news editor, and manager before becoming editor of the *News* in 1946.

In 1952, **Elder** Petersen brought the *News* into an agency arrangement with the *Salt Lake Tribune,* which combined printing, circulation, and advertising departments while keeping editorial and news departments separate. Under the new arrangement, **Thomas S. Monson** became the assistant classified advertising manager. Elder Monson served as an officer, director, and chairman of the **periodical** before stepping down in 1996 after 49 years of service. In 1997, President Monson dedicated a new nine-story Deseret News Building in Salt Lake City.

The *Deseret News* has published a special weekly supplement entitled *Church News* in its Saturday editions since 1931. This section enables readers to keep current on news of the Church worldwide.

SOURCES

Ashton, Wendell J. *Voice of the West: Biography of a Pioneer Newspaper.* New York: Duell, Sloan & Pearce, 1950.

Lloyd, R. Scott. "New Home for Pioneer Newspaper." *Church News,* 31 May 1997, 3–4.

McLaws, Monte Burr. *Spokesman for the Kingdom: Early Mormon Journalism and the Deseret News, 1830–1898.* Provo, Utah: Brigham Young University Press, 1977.

J. MICHAEL HUNTER

DESERET SUNDAY SCHOOL UNION. See SUNDAY SCHOOLS.

DESERET TELEGRAPH. At the height of its success, the Deseret Telegraph, a Church-owned and operated business, provided telegraphic service to communities from **Idaho** to **Arizona**, as well as mining towns in southeastern **Nevada**.

During the winter of 1856 and 1857, telegraphic training was provided and cash collected throughout **Utah** Territory to purchase the necessary equipment. All communities were expected to treat the telegraph as a provided assistance in this cooperative venture. After a year of preparation and stringing the line, the telegraph was ready for operation in February 1867.

The Deseret Telegraph Company was established 18 January 1867. In 1876 news of Custer's massacre at Little Big Horn reached the world through the Deseret Telegraph. The telegraph continued to be a tithing-subsidized, Church-operated service throughout its existence. In 1900 it was sold to Western Union for $10,000.

SOURCES

Arrington, Leonard J. "The Deseret Telegraph—A Church-Owned Public Utility." *Journal of Economic History* 11 (1951): 117–39.

———. *Great Basin Kingdom: Economic History of the Latter-day Saints, 1830–1900.* Lincoln: University of Nebraska Press, 1958. 228–31, 407.

CRAIG L. FOSTER

DEVIL. See SATAN.

DE VOTO, BERNARD. Bernard De Voto, one of Utah's finest writers, was born 11 January 1897 in Ogden, Utah, and was raised by a Latter-day Saint mother and a Roman Catholic father. De Voto was educated at the University of Utah and at Harvard before pursuing a career as a writer and author. He began as a novelist, writing five novels, including *The Life of Jonathan Dyer,* a story of his maternal pioneer heritage, and *Chariot of Fire,* a story of growing up in a mountain community. As a journalist and critic, he wrote for *Saturday Review* and later for *Harper's* magazine, wherein his column, "The Easy Chair," ran for almost 20 years.

De Voto is best remembered as a literary historian. His award-winning trilogy, *The Year of Decision* (1943), *Across the Wide Missouri* (1947), and *The Course of Empire* (1952), tell of his beloved West—the explorations of Lewis and Clark, the fur trade, and of Manifest Destiny and the American migrations westward in 1846 and 1847. They remain masterpieces of literature as well as history, a panoramic sweep through America's past. For De Voto, American history was not in the argument, the monograph, and the intellectualization but in the well-written story that made up the majesty of the country's past.

Yet De Voto was possessed of a lifelong ambivalence, a love-hate relationship that characterized and tormented him. As much as he loved America and the West—its mountains, rivers, climate, and pioneer history—he disliked the dominant religion and culture of his Utah home. An "articulate antagonist," born critic, and natural dissenter, he distrusted religious absolutes as well as political extremes of any kind

(Hacker, 235). Although he came to regret his youthful sarcasm and brash criticism of everything Mormon and eventually even came to admire **Brigham Young** as one of America's greatest leaders, he was always offended by Mormon theology. Yet few writers have told of the Mormon exodus to the **Salt Lake Valley** with such passion, conviction and respect for the pioneers' suffering and faith.

Late in his life he became an ardent conservationist, a crusader for preserving the West against land grabbers and dam builders. A tireless worker and heavy smoker, De Voto died of a heart attack 13 November 1955 in **New York City** at the age of 58.

SOURCES

Fetzer, Leland A. "Bernard De Voto and the Mormon Tradition." *Dialogue* 6 (February 1971): 23–38.

Hacker, Peter R. "Shooting the Sheriff: A Look at Bernard De Voto, Historian." *Utah Historical Quarterly* 58 (Summer 1990): 232–43.

Stegner, Wallace. *The Uneasy Chair—A Biography of Bernard De Voto.* Garden City, N.Y.: Doubleday, 1974.

RICHARD E. BENNETT

DE WITT, MISSOURI. In June 1838, Church leaders in **Far West, Missouri,** negotiated with Henry Root and David Thomas, both land speculators, to acquire nearly one-half of the town lots in the settlement community of De Witt, situated approximately 70 miles from Far West in the lower southeastern section of Carroll County. Following the purchase, a number of **Latter-day Saint** families began relocating there. The establishment of the Mormons in the community was immediately opposed, and county regulators used a number of means to coerce the Mormons into moving. Beginning 1 October, several hundred local citizens laid siege to the settlement. For several days the Saints succeeded in defending the community but finally capitulated on 10 October. Following the surrender, approximately 400 Latter-day **Saints** abandoned their homes and property and moved to **Caldwell County**. The siege of De Witt marked the first sustained confrontation against the Mormons in the 1838 Mormon-Missouri conflict.

SOURCE

Baugh, Alexander L. "A Call to Arms: The 1838 Mormon Defense of Northern Missouri." Ph.D. diss., Brigham Young University, 1996.

ALEXANDER L. BAUGH

DIARIES. See JOURNALS.

DIBBLE, PHILO. Philo Dibble, a close friend of the **Prophet Joseph Smith**, experienced and recorded many interesting events in **Ohio**, **Missouri**, and **Illinois**. Born 6 June 1806 in Peru, **Massachusetts**, Dibble was baptized by **Parley P. Pratt** 16 October 1830 in **Kirtland, Ohio**. Present when Joseph Smith and **Sidney Rigdon** saw the **Vision of the Three Degrees of Glory**, Dibble noted how Joseph appeared "strong as a lion" after receiving the vision, while Sidney seemed "weak as water" (Dibble, 81). Having moved from Kirtland to **Missouri** in 1832, Dibble was shot by a mob when the **Saints** were expelled from **Jackson County**. He recovered fully after a blessing from **Newel Knight**. After living in **Clay County, Caldwell County, Quincy**, and **Nauvoo**, Dibble followed **Brigham Young** to Utah. He married three times and became a father of eight, served as director of a co-op store in Centerville, Utah, and died 11 June 1895 in Springville, Utah, where he is buried.

SOURCES

Black, Susan Easton, comp. *Membership of The Church of Jesus Christ of Latter-day Saints, 1830–1848.* 50 vols. Provo, Utah: Religious Studies Center, Brigham Young University, 1984–88. 14:1–5.

Dibble, Philo. "Philo Dibble's Narrative." *Early Scenes in Church History.* Salt Lake City: Juvenile Instructor, 1882. 74–96.

"Recollections of the Prophet Joseph Smith." *Juvenile Instructor* 27 (1892): 22–23, 303–4, 345.

ANDREW H. HEDGES

DIDIER, CHARLES. Charles Didier, a member of the First **Quorum** of the **Seventy**, became a **general authority** in 1975, the first to be appointed from outside the **United States**. In 1999 he continued to be the only general authority called from a Francophone country.

Elder Didier was born 5 October 1935 in Ixelles, **Belgium**, and joined the Church in 1957. He earned a bachelor's degree in economics at the University of Liège in Belgium and served as an officer in the Belgian Air Force Reserve. He married Lucie Lodomez, and they became the parents of two sons.

Prior to his call as a general authority, Elder Didier, who spoke five languages, was employed by the Church as European manager for translation and distribution in Frankfurt, **Germany**. After his call as a general authority,

Elder Didier served in leadership positions throughout the world. Between 1992 and 1995 he served as a member of the presidency of the Seventy.

SOURCE

1997–1998 Church Almanac. Salt Lake City: Deseret News, 1996. 25.

CRAIG L. FOSTER

DISCIPLES OF CHRIST. See CAMPBELLITES.

DISCIPLINARY COUNCILS. Most institutions have mechanisms for disciplining or expelling members. **Doctrine and Covenants** sections 42, 58, 102, and 107 assign such responsibilities to the **bishop's** and **stake high council** courts, with ultimate appeal to the **First Presidency**. Successive issues of the *General Handbook of Instructions* elaborate and regularize procedures.

The earlier phrase "church courts" was changed to "disciplinary councils" to emphasize discipline as a positive force aiding repentance, not a punitive measure to purge iniquity in the Church.

The bishop's disciplinary council has plenary jurisdiction over all local Church members, except for excommunication of a **Melchizedek Priesthood** holder. The high council court, however, has full powers and also considers appeal from the bishop's disciplinary council.

Procedures are intended to be fair but informal. Decision is by the bishop or stake president, with other members of the court sustaining the decision. Permissible results now include exoneration, informal probation, formal probation, disfellowshipment, and excommunication.

Publicity by open confession or by announcement of disfellowshipment or excommunication in Church meetings has been replaced by informing only Church leaders who need to know the information, except in the case of heresy or predatory behavior.

SOURCES

Bush, Lester E., Jr. "Excommunication and Church Courts: A Note from the *General Handbook of Instructions.*" *Dialogue* 14 (Summer 1981): 74.

Kimball, Edward L. "Confession in LDS Doctrine and Practice." *BYU Studies* 36 (1996–97): 1.

———. "The History of LDS Temple Admission Standards." *Journal of Mormon History* 24 (Spring 1998): 135.

EDWARD L. KIMBALL

DISPENSATION OF THE FULNESS OF TIMES. A dispensation is a period of time in which the fulness of the **gospel** of **Jesus Christ** is enjoyed by men and women on earth. That fulness includes saving ordinances, doctrines concerning God and his **plan of salvation**, **priesthood** or divine authority, and the organization of the Church and **kingdom of God**. Exactly how many dispensations there have been from the beginning is unknown, although Latter-day Saints often speak of seven major dispensations. Dispensation heads include such prophet leaders as **Adam**, **Enoch**, **Noah**, **Abraham**, **Moses**, and **Jesus Christ**. **Joseph Smith Jr.** was called to preside over this, the final dispensation. The dispensation of the fulness of times is the dispensation of dispensations, the means whereby all of the doctrinal streams of the past flow into the great reservoir of revealed truth, by which all things are eventually gathered together in Christ (Eph. 1:10; D&C 112:30–31).

"Many great and important things pertaining to the Kingdom of God" (Articles of Faith 9) have been revealed since the call of Joseph Smith, and other matters are yet to be made known. These include sacred truths and powers that have been a part of past dispensations, as well as "things which have been kept hid from before the foundation of the world, things that pertain to the dispensation of the fulness of times" (D&C 124:41; compare 121:26; 128:18). This is the last great dispensation, and with it has come the assurance that there will never again be an apostasy from the true Church and priesthood of God. The Church of Jesus Christ of Latter-day Saints will be on the earth, fully operational and among all nations (JS–M 1:31), at the time the Savior returns in glory to inaugurate his millennial reign.

Robert L. Millet

DISTRICT. Where **stakes** are not organized, proselyting **missions** are divided by geographical boundaries into segments called districts, which include all branches within their territorial limits. A district president presides over each district. With sufficient member growth, districts are organized into stakes with **wards**.

Temple districts are geographical areas within which members are expected to attend a specific temple.

Larry R. Skidmore

DISTRICT OF COLUMBIA. See **WASHINGTON, D.C.**

DIXIE COLLEGE. Originally called **St. George** Stake Academy, Dixie College was founded in 1911 after two earlier attempts: one in 1875, and the other between 1895 and 1899. **Stake** leaders finally succeeded in winning both local and Church headquarters' support for an academy, similar to some 25 existing elsewhere in the Church. The people of Washington County donated funds and labor to match an appropriation from Church headquarters, enabling the hiring of seven faculty members and the construction of a building on the southeast corner of the town square.

In 1917 the Church established a curriculum on campus to prepare teachers. As a result, the school became known as Dixie College. While the school remained at this site, both high school and college courses were taught, and the college became the center for community cultural and athletic activities. In an attempt to cut Church expenses in the middle of the **great depression**, the Church ended its sponsorship of Dixie College in 1933. A committee of local citizens took up an effort urging the **Utah** legislature to sponsor the college. State leaders finally agreed to do so if the local citizens would fund the college for the first two years.

The joint high school and college curriculum ended in 1963 when the college moved to a new campus on the east edge of the city. The move contributed to major enrollment growth from the 355 students who transferred with the college. By 1970 there were 1,204 students; 1,790 by 1980. The continued expansion of buildings and curriculum filled the 100-acre campus by 1998 with an enrollment of more than 5,000. Extensive vocational and preprofessional programs were added. In the late 1990s general education and transfer courses still attracted most students. Four-year college programs were also offered through a Southern Utah University cooperative program on the Dixie campus. In the fall of 2000 Dixie College became Dixie State College, offering three four-year programs.

SOURCES

Colvin, Lloyd. "The Rise, Progress and Development of Dixie Junior College." Master's thesis, University of Utah, 1962.

Gregerson, Edna J. *Dixie College: Monument to the Industry of a Dedicated People.* Salt Lake City: Franklin Quest, 1993.

Moss, Robert Hafen. "An Historical Study of the Factors Influencing the Organization of Education in Washington County, 1852–1915." Master's thesis, Brigham Young University, 1961.

DOUGLAS D. ALDER

DOCTRINAL EXPOSITIONS. Pursuant to their calling as **prophets, seers, and revelators**, **apostles** have issued formal statements, labeled as official declarations, **proclamations**, epistles, and doctrinal expositions. All official declarations are given with the intent to regulate the affairs of the Church, clarify doctrines, or testify to the world. The more formal announcements given to the general public from time to time are often labeled proclamations. All official pronouncements for the Church are given by the **First Presidency** and sometimes the **Quorum** of the Twelve.

A series of doctrinal expositions of deep significance were given by the Prophet **Joseph Smith** during the last five years of his life. These included discussions on the first principles of the gospel, the resurrection, the first and second comforters (Smith, 3:379–81), the **priesthood** (Smith, 3:385–91), **baptism for the dead** (Smith, 4:424–26; 5:142–53), the **Articles of Faith** (Smith, 4:535–41), reproof of wickedness (Smith, 4:588), the gift of the Holy Ghost (Smith, 5:26–32), the greatness of **John the Baptist** (Smith, 5:260–62), the Second Coming (Smith, 5:336–37), explanations of Daniel and the book of **Revelation** (Smith, 5:339–45), and salvation through knowledge (Smith, 5:387–90). Doctrinal expositions given after the Prophet Joseph Smith include clarifications on doctrinal topics such as the origin of man (1909), **evolution** (1925), and the use of the term *father* in **scripture** (1916).

Early in the 20th century, in response to Darwin's theories, the First Presidency issued a statement firmly testifying of the divine origin of man. They explained that man's origin lay within the heavenly realms instead of the earthly depths and that man began life as a human being in the likeness of a Heavenly Father. Through divine revelation Latter-day **Saints** know that "man is the child of God, formed in the divine image and endowed with divine attributes, and even as the infant son of an earthly father and mother is capable in due time of becoming a man, so the undeveloped offspring of celestial parentage is capable, by experience through ages and aeons, of evolving into a God" (Clark, 206). A second doctrinal exposition entitled "Mormon View of Evolution" was given in 1925, reemphasizing the 1909 exposition (Ludlow, 1669–70).

In June 1916, the First Presidency and the Council of the Twelve Apostles gave a detailed statement on the distinctive roles of **God the Father** and his Son **Jesus Christ**. The exposition relates how the term *father* can be applied differently in the scriptural text. First, father can be used by one who is a literal parent. We are literally spirit children of Heavenly Father. Jesus Christ is a literal child of Heavenly Father. Second, one can be called "Father" when referred to as one who has created or organized something. Under the direction of Heavenly Father, Christ created many heavens and worlds (Ether 4:7). Because his creations are eternal, Christ can be addressed as the "everlasting Father" (Isa. 9:6). Third, Christ can be called "Father" by those who accept his gospel and become heirs of eternal life. All those who gain eternal life become sons and daughters of Christ in the distinctive sense (D&C 25:1; 39:1–4; 1 Jn. 3:8–10). Fourth, the title "Father" may be applied to Christ because of divine investiture of authority: "Thus, the Father placed His name upon the Son; and Jesus Christ spoke and ministered in and through the Father's name; and so far as power, authority, and Godship are concerned His words and acts were and are those of the Father" (Ludlow, 1670–77).

SOURCES

Clark, James R., comp. *Messages of the First Presidency of The Church of Jesus Christ of Latter-day Saints.* 6 vols. Salt Lake City: Bookcraft, 1965–75. Vol. 4.

Ludlow, Daniel. "Doctrinal Expositions of the First Presidency, Appendix 4." *Encyclopedia of Mormonism.* Edited by Daniel H. Ludlow. 4 vols. New York: Macmillan, 1992. 4:1665–77.

Smith, Joseph. *History of The Church of Jesus Christ of Latter-day Saints.* Edited by B. H. Roberts. 2d ed. rev. 7 vols. Salt Lake City: The Church of Jesus Christ of Latter-day Saints, 1932–51.

BRIAN L. SMITH

DOCTRINE AND COVENANTS. The Doctrine and Covenants is a collection of **revelations** and declarations received through **Joseph Smith** and other latter-day **prophets** of God. It exists for the establishment and direction of The Church of Jesus Christ of Latter-day **Saints** and its members. It consists of 138 sections and two declarations, along with an explanatory introduction. All but seven of these items were received through the Prophet Joseph Smith.

The Doctrine and Covenants is the only book that contains a preface revealed by the Lord himself (D&C 1). In the Preface, the Lord declares that this book is to be a voice of warning to members of the Church and to the people of the world (1:1–10). It declares that those who study these revelations will come to an understanding, be corrected if they err, be instructed if they seek wisdom, and be chastened if they sin (1:24–28). The Lord bears testimony of the truthfulness of the book's content and promises that what is prophesied therein will all come to pass (1:37–39).

Most of the revelations were received in response to a problem or a question that required the Prophet to approach the Lord for guidance.

Joseph dictated the revelation to a scribe, who made a manuscript of the revelation.

During the summer of 1830, the Prophet Joseph Smith began to prepare for publication the revelations received to that point. A conference of **elders** held in **Hiram, Ohio**, during the first week of November 1831 decided to publish the revelations in what would be called the **Book of Commandments**. Because of mob activities against members of the Church in **Jackson County, Missouri**, the publication of the Book of Commandments was thwarted. Efforts continued, and an expanded compilation was completed in **Kirtland, Ohio**, in August 1835. The book contained 102 sections of revelations, along with the *Lectures on Faith,* warranting a change of name. The new title was "Doctrine and Covenants"—representing the doctrine, as reflected in the *Lectures on Faith,* and the revelations, referred to as the covenants. The compilation was presented to the membership of the Church, and it was accepted as one of the **standard works**.

Since the first version of the Doctrine and Covenants, several editions have been published, each including additional sections of revelations and official declarations. By 1876 the Doctrine and Covenants contained 136 sections. The 1921 edition included the same 136 sections. The *Lectures on Faith,* however, being judged as important teachings but not revelations, were removed from the publication. This edition also contained the "Official Declaration," or "**Manifesto**," which announced the cessation of **plural marriage**. The 1921 edition also featured new headings and footnotes. This edition remained in place until 1981, when two additional sections, 137 and 138, were added, along with a second Official Declaration, a report of the revelation giving the **priesthood** to all worthy male members. New and improved headings and footnotes replaced those found in the 1921 edition.

The Doctrine and Covenants reflects the various ways in which revelation is given. The words of angels are found in sections 2, 13, and 27. Inspired prayers are recorded in sections 65 and 109. **Visions** are recorded in sections 76, 137, and 138, and an account of a personal appearance of heavenly beings is found in section 110. Section 102 contains minutes of the organizing meeting of the first **high council** of the Church. Several revelations were received through the **Urim and Thummim** used by Joseph Smith to translate the **Book of Mormon**. Many others were received through the Holy Ghost alone. Some of the revelations were given for the benefit of individuals, and others were given in response to problems most members of the Church faced. These revelations have application today to the entire Church and to individual members.

The Doctrine and Covenants contains the foundation for many of the doctrines of the Church, including the coming forth of the Book of Mormon and its role in the Restoration (sections 3, 5–6, 8–10, 17), the organization of the Church (sections 20, 22, 41, 124), the restoration of the priesthood and its doctrines (sections 2, 13, 20, 84, 88, 107, 121), the knowledge of the postmortal life (sections 76, 131, 137–138), the nature of the **family** and eternal **marriage** (sections 68, 131–132), and information concerning the second coming of Christ, the resurrection, and the eternal nature of the body (sections 45, 88, 133).

It is evident that the foundation of the Church is contained in the Doctrine and Covenants. These revelations and declarations proclaim the restoration of the gospel of **Jesus Christ** and the **organization of the Church** in the **dispensation of the fulness of times**. This book stands as evidence of the power of revelation that is active in the Church today, testifying that the heavens are open and that God reveals his will in this time and age. While Joseph Smith referred to the Book of Mormon as the "keystone" of our religion, President **Ezra Taft Benson** identified the Doctrine and Covenants as the "capstone."

SOURCES

Cowan, Richard O. *Answers to Your Questions about the Doctrine and Covenants.* Salt Lake City: Deseret Book, 1996.

Garrett, H. Dean. *Great Teachings from the Doctrine and Covenants.* Salt Lake City: Bookcraft, 1992.

Millet, Robert L., and Larry E. Dahl., eds. *Insights into the Doctrine and Covenants: The Capstone of Our Religion.* Salt Lake City: Bookcraft, 1989.

H. DEAN GARRETT

DOGBERRY, OBADIAH. See COLE, ABNER.

DOMINICAN REPUBLIC. During the 1960s, two or three Latter-day Saint families temporarily lived in the Dominican Republic to assist in reestablishing the government after many years of dictatorship. In 1968, a Church member from **Mexico**, Flavia Salazar Gomez, and her nonmember husband from the Dominican Republic lived in Santiago. She contacted the **mission president** in Orlando, **Florida**, about receiving a priesthood blessing and having her new baby receive a name and a blessing. President Glen L. Rudd and one of the missionaries stopped in the Dominican Republic on their way to **Puerto Rico**, found Sister Gomez, and gave her a blessing and restoration of health. She and her husband stayed in the country for a short while thereafter.

The first permanent members of the Church in the Dominican Republic were Eddie and Mercedes Amparo and their family, who arrived in the country on 9 June 1978, the same month the revelation was announced that all worthy men could hold the priesthood. John and Nancy Rappleye also arrived. The two families met together and began a missionary effort. In August 1978, Rudolfo Bodden became the first member to be baptized in the country.

In November 1978, **President Richard Millet** of the Fort Lauderdale **Mission** sent ten Spanish-speaking missionaries into the Dominican Republic, marking the real beginning of the vigorous missionary program there.

The Dominican Republic Santo Domingo Mission was organized 1 January 1981, with a membership of 2,500. **President Spencer W. Kimball** visited the **Saints** there in March 1981.

In 1996 construction began on the Santo Domingo **Temple**—the first temple in the Caribbean. By the beginning of the year 2000, the Dominican Republic had 69,466 members with 11 **stakes** and 171 **wards** and **branches**.

SOURCES

1999–2000 Church Almanac. Salt Lake City: Deseret News, 1998. 311–13.

Rudd, Glen L. "Keeping the Gospel Simple." *Ensign* 19 (January 1989): 71–72.

GLEN L. RUDD

DONIPHAN, ALEXANDER.

Alexander Doniphan, an attorney and friend of the **Mormons** in **Missouri**, was born 8 July 1808 in Mason County, **Kentucky**. He achieved remarkable success as a state politician and as commander of the First Missouri Volunteers during the **Mexican War**. When not yet 21 years old, he was admitted to the bars in both Kentucky and **Ohio**, but like so many other young men of the period, Doniphan moved westward, arriving in Missouri in 1830. Within three years he achieved fame by serving as the legal counsel for Mormons expelled from their homes in western Missouri.

Doniphan began legal action to place the Saints back on their land and to obtain damages for losses resulting from **anti-Mormon** violence in the autumn of 1833. He also filed criminal charges against those accused of mob actions. He did not have much success, and in the end the Saints were unable to return to **Jackson County**. In early 1838, however, Doniphan sponsored legislation in the Missouri State Assembly to create **Caldwell County** in western Missouri as a haven for the Mormons.

The **Saints** did not enjoy peace there for very long. On 27 October 1838, Missouri governor **Lilburn W. Boggs** issued the infamous **extermination order** against the Mormons. Major General **Samuel D. Lucas** went to **Far West** to enforce the order and, on 31 October he arrested **Joseph Smith** and several other Church officers.

The next day General Lucas convened a court-martial, found Joseph Smith and other Mormon leaders guilty of treason, and ordered their execution by firing squad. Doniphan, apparently the only lawyer present, protested that the court-martial had been "illegal as hell" because civilians were not subject to military law and the judges sitting for the court-martial were not all members of the military. In spite of this, on the morning of 2 November, Doniphan, a brigadier general in the Missouri state militia, received orders to execute the prisoners. He refused to carry out this order and wrote to General Lucas: "It is cold-blooded murder. I will not obey your order. My brigade shall march for Liberty tomorrow morning, at 8 o'clock; and if you execute these men, I will hold you responsible before an earthly tribunal, so help me God" (Smith, 3:190n).

Doniphan's stand prompted Lucas to take the prisoners to Independence and then to **Richmond** for trial during the week of 12 November 1838. Once again, Doniphan served as the Mormons' legal counsel. After a preliminary court of inquiry, most of the prisoners were released, but Joseph Smith and a few other leaders were placed in the **Liberty Jail** over the winter of 1838 and 1839 to await trial. Eventually, Doniphan was able to get a change of venue for them from Daviess to Boone County. En route to the county seat at Columbia, they were allowed to escape and leave the state.

The Saints parted company with Doniphan, moving on to **Illinois** and **Utah**. Doniphan became a commander in the U.S. Army, distinguishing himself through service in the Mexican War and later through his political and legal career. When he visited **Salt Lake City** in 1874, the Saints received him warmly. He died 8 August 1887 at his home in Richmond, Missouri.

SOURCES

Dawson, Joseph G. *Doniphan's Epic March: The 1st Missouri Volunteers in the Mexican War.* Lawrence, Kans.: University Press of Kansas, 1999.

Duchateau, Andre Paul. "Missouri Colossus: Alexander W. Doniphan, 1808–1887." Ph.D. diss., University of Oklahoma, 1973.

Launius, Roger D. *Alexander William Doniphan: Portrait of a Missouri Moderate.* Columbia, Mo.: University of Missouri Press, 1997.

LeSueur, Stephen C. *The 1838 Mormon War in Missouri.* Columbia, Mo.: University of Missouri Press, 1987.

Maynard, Gregory P. "Alexander W. Doniphan: Man of Justice." *BYU Studies* 13 (Summer 1973): 462–72.

Smith, Joseph. *History of The Church of Jesus Christ of Latter-day Saints.* Edited by B. H. Roberts. 2d ed. rev. 7 vols. Salt Lake City: The Church of Jesus Christ of Latter-day Saints, 1932–51.

ROGER D. LAUNIUS

DONNER-REED PARTY. The ill-fated Donner-Reed party of westbound travelers is well known for its 1846 demise in the Sierra **Nevada** mountains, where early snows and starvation with accompanying cannibalism took a heavy toll. Early Latter-day **Saints** were connected to this group of immigrants in at least four important ways.

First, traveling in the Donner-Reed Party was a Latter-day Saint family headed by a widow named Lavina Murphy. Another Latter-day Saint family, that of Thomas Rhoads, met and traveled with the Donner-Reed Party for a time but chose to part company with them, a decision that saved their lives—they arrived safely in Sacramento in September 1846.

Second, as rescue efforts were organized to save the survivors of the party, John and Daniel Rhoads, sons of Thomas, became key players. **Samuel Brannan**, leader of the Saints in **San Francisco**, also used his newspaper to aid in the rescue.

A third Latter-day Saint connection with the party was made by returning **Mormon Battalion** members who discovered and buried the remains of the dead in the mountains.

The final involvement was less direct. In 1847 the vanguard **pioneer** company was benefited by the trail cut by the Donner Party into the **Salt Lake Valley** the year before.

SOURCES

Dorius, Guy L. "Crossroads in the West: The Intersections of the Donner Party and the Mormons." *Nauvoo Journal* 9 (1997): 17–27.

McGlashan, C. F. *History of the Donner Party: A Tragedy of the Sierra.* San Francisco: Wohlbruck, 1934.

GUY L. DORIUS

DOUGLAS, STEPHEN A. Stephen Arnold Douglas, an important figure in American history, was one of only a few prominent politicians who befriended **Joseph Smith** and the **Latter-day Saint** people when they came as refugees to **Illinois** in 1839. Douglas was born 23 April 1813 in Brandon, Vermont, and was only 26 years old when the Latter-day **Saints** arrived in **Quincy**. He was the recognized leader of the **Democratic Party** in western Illinois. He quickly gained the confidence of Joseph Smith and assisted in the passage of the **Nauvoo Charter**. As a member of the Illinois Supreme Court, he visited **Nauvoo** during the spring of 1841 and in a public address praised the Saints for their enterprise and industry.

Early that summer the **Prophet** was arrested on the charge of being a **Missouri** fugitive. Judge Douglas issued him a writ of habeas corpus and agreed to hear the case in Monmouth, where the circuit court was scheduled to meet. When Joseph's lawyer, Orville Browning, recounted the Saints' suffering in Missouri, Douglas and others shed tears. On the day following Browning's moving defense, Douglas dismissed the case and was accused by the state's Whig newspapers of courting the Mormon vote.

In December 1842, when another warrant for the Prophet's arrest was issued, Joseph sought advice from Douglas before he was again tried in district court and released. Six months later, 18 May 1843, the Prophet, on his way back to Nauvoo from **Ramus**, stopped in Carthage and had dinner with Douglas. The judge asked Joseph to relate for him the history of the Missouri persecutions. As the Prophet concluded his recital he said, "Judge, you will aspire to the presidency of the **United States**; and if ever you turn your hand against me or the Latter-day Saints, you will feel the weight of the hand of Almighty [God] upon you; and you will live to see and know that I have testified the truth to you; for the conversation of this day will stick to you through life" (Smith, 394).

After the murders of Joseph and **Hyrum Smith**, Douglas, now a Congressman, encouraged **Brigham Young** and the Twelve to accept a peace settlement and leave Illinois in the spring of 1846, something the Saints were planning to do anyway.

Following the **Compromise of 1850**, Douglas wrote the territory bills for **New Mexico** and **Utah** and helped see that they were passed. He is also credited with naming the region Utah. In 1851 Douglas softened feelings toward the Mormons after the territorial "**runaway officials**" came east and spoke out against Brigham Young and his people. Douglas's influence helped Brigham Young to remain the territory's governor.

In May 1857, Douglas was asked by an Illinois grand jury to express his views regarding Kansas, the Dred Scott decision, and conditions in Utah. Swept up in the tide of denuniciation that then existed, he denounced the Mormon people, uttering words that he knew were not true. He was particularly harsh with regard to plural marriage. Later Douglas sought the United States presidency in 1856 and 1860, but each time he ran he was defeated. Stephen Douglas died 3 June 1861 in Chicago, Illinois, at age 48.

SOURCES

Johannsen, Robert W. *Stephen A. Douglas.* New York: Oxford University, 1973.

Smith, Joseph. *History of The Church of Jesus Christ of Latter-day Saints.* Edited by B. H. Roberts. 2d ed. rev. 7 vols. Salt Lake City: The Church of Jesus Christ of Latter-day Saints, 1932–51.

_____. *Times and Seasons* 2 (15 May 1841): 417–18.

Van Orden, Bruce A. "Stephen A. Douglas and the Mormons." In *Illinois.* Edited by H. Dean Garrett. Regional Studies in Latter-day Saint History series. Provo, Utah: Brigham Young University, 1995. 359–78.

KENNETH W. GODFREY

DRAMA. "**Mormons** and the theatre have long been intimately associated." The **Saints** established a theatre in their city of **Nauvoo, Illinois**, where **Joseph Smith** fostered drama. Joseph taught members of the Church to seek after all things "virtuous, lovely, or of good report or praiseworthy." The arts, therefore, especially drama and theatre, were highly prized. The production of plays did not cease in Nauvoo until the city was abandoned in 1846.

Drama continued to flourish after the Saints arrived in the **Salt Lake Valley** in 1847, and the first Bowery was erected at that time. A second and third Bowery were constructed in 1849, and Brigham Young requested that the "Deseret Musical and Dramatic Society" be organized for the performing of plays in the Bowery. In 1853 the more expanded **Social Hall** was erected, and finally in 1862 one of the finest theatres in the country was dedicated in **Salt Lake City**. At the dedication of the **Salt Lake Theatre**, **Brigham Young** said: "Upon the stage of a theater can be represented in character, evil and its consequences, good and its happy results and rewards; the weakness and the follies of man, the magnanimity of virtue and the greatness of truth. The stage can be made to aid the pulpit in impressing upon the minds of a community an enlightened sense of a virtuous life, also a proper horror of the enormity of sin and a just dread of its consequences. The path of sin with its thorns and pitfalls, its gins and snares can be revealed, and how to shun it" (Young, 243).

Dramatic writing and theatrical performance have continued to flourish in the Church. The Promised Valley Playhouse in Salt Lake City was dedicated in 1972. Standard plays and new works by Church members such as Ralph Rodgers Jr., Pat Davis, Newell Dayley, and Charles Whitman were performed. When this playhouse was closed in 1997, the Bountiful Regional Center (formerly The Valley Music Hall, purchased by the Church in 1986) was remodeled for the staging of the original musical-drama *Barefoot to Zion,* by Orson Scott Card and Arlen Card.

Church-sponsored schools, including **BYU**, **Ricks College** (later BYU–Idaho), and **BYU–Hawaii** teach playwriting, acting, directing, and design courses, and the dramatic works developed are staged by the theater departments. Works by such Latter-day Saint playwrights as Clinton Larson, Thomas Rogers, Tim Slover, Carol Lynn Pearson, Doug Stewart, Eric Samuelsen, and Randy Booth have been produced.

In the 1950s the LDS Motion Picture Studio in **Provo, Utah**, under the direction of Judge Whittaker, began filming original screenplays by Latter-day Saint writers. To this day, new screenplays are being produced for the Church as well as student-written screenplays from the BYU theatre and media arts program.

SOURCES

Maughan, Ila Fisher. *Pioneer Theatre in the Desert.* Salt Lake City: Deseret Book, 1961.

Young, Brigham. *Discourses of Brigham Young.* Compiled by John A. Widtsoe. Salt Lake City: Deseret Book, 1941. 243.

———. "Happiness and Social Enjoyment." *Brigham Young.* Teachings of Presidents of the Church series. Salt Lake City: The Church of Jesus Christ of Latter-day Saints, 1997. 183–91.

CHARLES METTEN

DRESDEN MISSION. See GERMANY DRESDEN MISSION.

DRUMMOND, WILLIAM W. Historians of the **Utah War** (1857–58) find a trigger for conflict in William Wormer (W. W.) Drummond, a federally appointed judge who served on the **Utah** Supreme Court from 1854 until his voluntary resignation three years later.

Drummond's resignation letter of 30 March 1857, addressed to U.S. attorney general Jeremiah S. Black, alleged that "the chief executives of the nation, both living and dead, [are] slandered and abused from the masses, as well as from all the leading members of the Church, in the most vulgar, loathsome, and wicked manner that evil passions of men can possibly conceive" (U.S. House, 213). Drummond called for a non-Latter-day-Saint governor and recommended that this appointee be "supported with a *sufficient* military aid." Two months later, President **James Buchanan** ordered 2,500 troops stationed at **Fort Leavenworth, Kansas**, led by Colonel Albert Sidney Johnston, to accompany Governor **Brigham Young's** replacement, **Alfred Cumming**, to Utah.

SOURCES

Furniss, Norman F. *The Mormon Conflict, 1850–1859.* New Haven: Yale University Press, 1960.

U.S. House. *Exec. Doc.* 71, 35th Congress, 1st Session. 10, 212–14.

JED L. WOODWORTH

DURHAM, G. HOMER. As a member of the First Quorum of the **Seventy** from 1977 to 1985, G. Homer Durham served as managing director of the Church Historical Department. Previous to this appointment, his Church positions included member of the **Sunday School** executive committee (1971–73), **regional representative** (1976–77), and president of the Salt Lake Central **Stake** (1973–76). He was born in Parowan, **Utah**, on 4 February 1911 to George Henry and Mary Ellen Marsden Durham. He married Eudora Widtsoe (daughter of **John A. Widtsoe**) on 20 June 1936. Trained as an educator, he received a Ph.D. from the University of **California** at **Los Angeles** in 1939. Before his call to the First Quorum of the Seventy, he had a long and distinguished career as an educator; he served as president of **Arizona** State University from 1960 to 1969 and as Utah's first commissioner of higher **education** from 1969 to 1976. A gifted writer, he was a contributing editor for the *Improvement Era* (1946–70) and wrote *Joseph Smith: Prophet Statesman* (1944). He died 10 January 1985 at **Salt Lake City**.

SOURCE

Sabine, Gordon. *G. Homer: President, Arizona State University 1960–69.* Tempe: Arizona State University Libraries, 1992.

MARY JANE WOODGER

DYER, ALVIN R. Alvin Rulon Dyer, **counselor** to President **David O. McKay**, was born 1 January 1903 in **Salt Lake City**. A talented musician and athlete, he served in the **Eastern States Mission** from 1922 to 1924. While he was serving his sixth year as **bishop** of the Monument Park **Ward** in Salt Lake City, he received a call to preside over the Central States Mission. In 1958 he served as a counselor in the general superintendency of the **YMMIA** and that same year was called to serve as an **assistant to the Twelve**. Though not a member of the Quorum of the Twelve, he was ordained an **apostle** by President David O. McKay in 1967; in April 1968 he became an additional counselor in the **First Presidency**. At the death of President McKay, the Quorum of the First Presidency was dissolved, and **Elder** Dyer returned to his position as an assistant to the Twelve and served as managing director of the Church **Historical Department** from 1972 to 1975. He later became a member of the First Quorum of the **Seventy** when the assistants to the Twelve were moved into that body. Elder Dyer passed away 6 March 1977 in Salt Lake City at the age of 74.

SOURCES

Flake, Lawrence R. *Prophets and Apostles of the Last Dispensation.* Provo, Utah: Religious Studies Center, Brigham Young University, 2001. 301–3.
"Services Pay Tribute to Elder Alvin Dyer." *Church News,* 12 March 1977, 4.

LAWRENCE R. FLAKE

THE EVENING AND THE MORNING STAR.

| Vol. I. | Independence, Mo. March, 1833. | No. 10. |

THE CHURCH OF CHRIST.

HE that is Alpha and Omega, the beginning and the end, even Jesus Christ, is the head of the church, and the gates of hell cannot prevail against it.—Adam was the first member of the church of Christ on earth, and the first high priest after the order of the Son of God.

In order to show the rise of the church in the first days, we take an extract from the words of Enoch.

And Enoch continued his speech, saying, The Lord which spake with me, the same is the God of heaven, and he is my God, and your God, and ye are my brethren, and why counsel ye yourselves, and deny the God of heaven?

The heavens hath he made: the earth is his footstool; and the foundation thereof is his.

Behold he hath laid it, an host of men hath he brought in upon the face thereof.

And death hath come upon our fathers: nevertheless we know them, and cannot deny, and even the first of all we know, even Adam:

For a book of remembrance we have written, among us, according to the pattern given by the finger of God:

And it is given in our own language.

And as Enoch spake forth the words of God, the people trembled, and could not stand before his presence:

And he saith unto them, because that Adam fell we are; and by his fall came death; and we are made partakers of misery and wo.

Behold satan hath come among the children of men, and tempteth them to worship him:

And men have become carnal, sensual and devilish, and are shut out from the presence of God.

But God hath made known unto my fathers, that all men must repent.

And he called upon our father Adam, by his own voice, saying, I am God; I made the world, and men before they were.

And he also said unto him, If thou wilt turn unto me, and hearken unto my voice, and believe, and repent of all thy transgressions, and be baptized, even by water, in the name of mine only begotten Son, which is full of grace and truth, which is Jesus Christ, the only name which shall be given under heaven, whereby salvation shall come unto the children of men:

And ye shall ask all things in his name; and whatsoever ye shall ask, it shall be given.

And our father Adam spake unto the Lord, and said, Why is it that men must repent and be baptized in water?

And the Lord said unto Adam, Behold I have forgiven thee thy transgressions in the garden of Eden.

Thence came the saying abroad among the people, That Christ hath atoned for original guilt, wherein the sins of the parents cannot be answered upon the heads of the children, for they are whole from the foundation of the world.

And the Lord spake unto Adam, saying, Inasmuch as thy children are conceived in sin, even so when they begin to grow up, sin conceiveth in their hearts, and they taste the bitter, that they may know to prize the good.

And it is given unto them to know good from evil: wherefore they are agents unto themselves, and I have given unto you another law and commandment:

Wherefore teach it unto your children, that all men, every where, must repent, or they can in no wise inherit the kingdom of God:

For no unclean thing can dwell there, or dwell in his presence:

For in the language of Adam, Man of Holiness is his name; and the name of his only Begotten, is the Son of Man, even Jesus Christ, a righteous Judge which shall come.

I give unto you a commandment to teach these things freely unto your children, saying,

That, inasmuch as they were born into the world, by the fall which bringeth death, by water and blood and the Spirit, which I have made, and so become of dust a living soul, even so ye must be born again of water and the Spirit, and cleansed by blood, even the blood of mine only Begotten into the mysteries of the kingdom of heaven; that ye may be sanctified from all sin, and enjoy the words of eternal life in this world, and eternal life in the world to come, even immortal glory:

For by the water ye keep the commandment; by the Spirit ye are justified, and by the blood ye are sanctified, that in you is given the record of heaven, the Comforter, the peaceable things of immortal glory.

The truth of all things; that which quickeneth all things, which maketh alive all things; that which knoweth all things, and hath all power according to wisdom, mercy, truth, justice, and judgment.

And now, behold I say unto you, this is the plan of salvation unto all men: the blood of mine only Begotten which shall come in the meridian of time:

And behold all things have his likeness, and all things are created and made to bear record of me, both things which are temporal, and things which are Spiritual; things which are in the heavens above, and things which are on the earth, and things which are in the earth, and things which are under the earth, both above and beneath: all things bear record of me.

And it came to pass when the Lord had spoken with Adam, our father, that Adam cried unto the Lord, and he was caught away by the Spirit of the Lord, and was carried down into the water, and was laid under the water, and was brought forth out of the water.

And thus he was baptized, and the Spirit of God descended upon him; and thus he was born of the Spirit, and became quickened in the inner man:

And he heard a voice out of heaven saying, Thou art baptized with fire, and with the Holy Ghost:

This is the record of the Father, and the Son, from henceforth and forever: and thou art after the order of him who was without beginning of days or end of years, from all eternity to all eternity. Behold thou art one in me, a son of God; and thus may all become my sons. Amen.

In addition to this, we make a further extract from the words of Enoch, as published in the Star of August last. It shows to what a state of purity the church had arrived in its day, besides being a good example for every disciple to follow, that means to do the will of God, in our day, in order to abide a celestial glory in his presence. It reads thus:—"And the Lord came and dwelt with his people, and they dwelt in righteousness. The fear of the Lord was upon all nations, so great was the glory of the Lord, which was upon his people: And the Lord blessed the land, and they were blessed upon the mountains, and upon the high places, and did flourish.

And the Lord called his people Zion, because they were of one heart and of one mind, and dwelt in righteousness; and there was no poor among them: and Enoch continued his preaching in righteousness unto the people of God. And it came to pass in his days, that he built a city that was called the city of holiness, even Zion."

As before said, Christ is the head of his church, and from him comes every good and perfect gift. And for the perfecting of the saints and so forth, he has bestowed offices and ordinances, with order, for the benefit of the whole church.—The high priesthood, of which order is he, the Son of God, or this priesthood being a type of his order, is set forth as follows, by Alma:

"And again: my brethren, I would cite your minds forward to the time which the Lord God gave these commandments unto his children; and I would that ye should remember that the Lord God ordained priests, after his holy order, which was after the order of his Son, to teach these things unto the people; and those priests were ordained after the order of his Son, in a manner that thereby the people might know in what manner to look forward to his Son for redemption.

And this is the manner after which they were ordained: being called and prepared from the foundation of the world, according to the foreknowledge of God, on account of their exceeding faith and good works; in the first place being left to choose good or evil; therefore they having chosen good, and exercising exceeding great faith, are called with a holy calling, yea, with that holy calling which was prepared with and according to a preparatory redemption for such.

And thus they having been called to this holy calling on account of their faith, while others would reject the Spirit of God on account of the hardness of their hearts and the blindness of their minds, while, if it had not been for this, they might had as great privilege as their brethren.

Or in fine: in the first place they were on the same standing with their brethren, thus this holy calling being prepared from the foundation of the world for such as would not harden their hearts, being in and through the atonement of the only begotten Son, which was prepared:

And thus being called with this holy calling, and ordained unto the high priesthood of the holy order of God, to teach his commandments unto the children of men, that they also might enter into his rest. This high priesthood being after the order of his Son, which order was from the foundation of the world; or in other words, being without beginning of days or end of years, being prepared from all eternity to all eternity, according to his foreknowledge of all things. Now they were ordained after this manner: being called with a holy calling, and ordained with a holy ordinance, and taking upon them the high priesthood of the holy order, which calling and ordinance and high priesthood, is without beginning or end; thus they become high priests forever, after the order of the Son, the only begotten of the Father, which is without beginning of days or end of years, which is full of grace, equity and truth. And thus it is. Amen.

Now as I said concerning the holy order of this high priesthood: there were many which were ordained and became high priests of God; and it was on account of their exceeding faith and repentance, and their righteousness before God, they choosing to repent and work righteousness, rather than to perish; therefore they were called after his holy order, and were sanctified, and their garments were washed white, through the blood of the Lamb.

Now they, after being sanctified by his Holy Ghost, having their garments made white, being pure and spotless before God, could not look upon sin, save it were with abhorrence; and there were many, exceeding great many, which were made pure, and entered into the rest of the Lord their God.

And now, my brethren, I would that ye should humble yourselves before God, and bring forth fruit meet for repentance, that ye may also enter into that rest."

EVENING AND THE MORNING STAR. Published in Independence, Missouri, from June 1832 through July 1833, *The Evening and the Morning Star* was the first newspaper of the Church.

EAGLE GATE. Eagle Gate, a landmark of **Salt Lake City**, was erected in 1859 and served as a gateway to **Brigham Young**'s farmlands. The original gate was 22 feet wide and adorned with a 4,000-pound bronze eagle created by Ralph Ramsay. It eventually became a toll gate to maintain public roads. In 1890, Eagle Gate was removed to accommodate electric trolley transportation. A public outcry caused the gate to be reconstructed on 5 October 1891. In an April 1960 traffic accident, the narrow gate was knocked over. The new Eagle Gate became an all-metal construction, expanded to 76 feet in width. Grant Fairbanks sculpted a new eagle with a wingspan of more than 20 feet resting atop a beehive 36 feet above the ground. A capsule with time-related objects is located inside the gate. It was dedicated 1 November 1963 and is considered a monument to the **pioneer** spirit.

SOURCE

"Eagle Gate Dedication Services." Salt Lake City: Utah State Department of Highways Reproduction Department, 1 November 1963.

MATTHEW O. RICHARDSON

EASTERN STATES MISSION. The Eastern States Mission was the oldest mission in the Church (after the **British Mission**), holding within its boundaries the earliest historical sites of the **Restoration**. The mission began with the calling of its first permanent president, **John P. Greene**, who on 6 May 1839 was appointed by **Joseph Smith** to "go to the City of **New York**, and preside over the **Saints** in that place and in the regions round about" (Smith, 3:347). The mission was temporarily discontinued from 1850 to 1854; from 1858 to 1865; and from 1869 to 1893. In 1974 it became the New York New York Mission.

The Eastern States Mission used early Church history sites to teach the Restoration story. Church leaders purchased and then memorialized land where Joseph Smith Jr. was born and had his **First Vision**, where he was first visited by the angel **Moroni**, and where the **Book of Mormon** plates were buried. On one of these sites, the **Hill Cumorah**, the mission sponsored an annual **pageant** called *America's Witness for Christ*, which began in 1937. Sometimes 20,000 or more people attended a pageant performance. Most of the attendees were not Latter-day Saints. After 1964 the pageant continued under the direction of the Cumorah Mission.

As the Church grew, the boundaries of the Eastern States Mission shrank. Before the **Southern States Mission** was formed in 1876, all states east of the **Mississippi** were part of the Eastern States Mission. At the turn of the century, the mission covered 200,000 square miles in 12 states, part of another, and **Ontario, Canada**. Many new missions were formed from the Eastern States Mission: **Virginia** (1902); Ontario (1919); **Maine** (1927); **Vermont** (1927); **New Hampshire** (1928); **West Virginia** (1928); **Maryland** (1928, 1960); **Rhode Island** (1937); **Massachusetts** (1937); **Connecticut** (1937); **Pennsylvania** (1960, 1964); **New Jersey** (1960); New York (1964). By 1973, the Eastern States Mission served an area of 15,000 square miles across New York, New Jersey, Massachusetts, Connecticut, and Pennsylvania.

Church membership in the Eastern States Mission fluctuated. About 900 members attended a regional conference in **Philadelphia** in 1840. Membership decreased when the Saints gathered to **Utah** and increased when gathering was deemphasized in the 1890s. At the end of the nineteenth century, the mission had 165 missionaries and 1,100 members in eight **conferences**. By 1973, just before it became the New York New York Mission, it comprised five **stakes** and 15,000 members. Membership had become ethnically diverse and located primarily in urban communities.

SOURCES

"Manuscript History of the Eastern States Mission." LDS Church Archives, Salt Lake City.

Smith, Joseph. *History of The Church of Jesus Christ of Latter-day Saints.* Edited by B. H. Roberts. 2d ed. rev. 7 vols. Salt Lake City: The Church of Jesus Christ of Latter-day Saints, 1932–51.

Whitman, Charles Walker. "A History of the Hill Cumorah Pageant (1937–1964) and an Examination of the Dramatic Development of the Text of *America's Witness for Christ.*" Ph.D. diss., University of Minnesota, 1967.

JED L. WOODWORTH

ECCLES, DAVID. Destined to become **Utah**'s richest industrialist, David Eccles was born 12 May 1849 in Paisley, **Scotland**, to Latter-day

Saint parents and raised in poverty. With little formal schooling, eight-year-old David peddled kitchen utensils and homemade resin sticks throughout the countryside to raise money for his blind father's **family**. In 1863 the family emigrated to **America**, under the sponsorship of the Church's **Perpetual Emigrating Fund**, and crossed the plains by wagon before settling in Huntsville, near **Ogden**. Independent, uninhibited, and unafraid, the enterprising young David set out on his own, working as a mill hand and freighter in **Oregon**, **Wyoming**, and Utah. The family returned to Ogden in 1869, where David purchased a lumber yard in the newly energized railroad boom town. Eventually called David Eccles & Company, this enterprise became the springboard to his vast fortune.

A lumberman at heart, Eccles expanded his business ventures into the Northwest, developing the mammoth Oregon Lumber Company and the narrow-gauge Sumpter Valley Railroad. Eventually his interests spread into the sugar beet, ranching, and financial industries. Mayor of Ogden in 1887, Eccles was also president of the Ogden First National Bank, parent charter bank of the First Security Bank System, which his son, Marriner, established in 1928. At the time of his death on 12 March 1912 in Ogden, Utah, Eccles was a multimillionaire.

A faithful tithe-paying member of the Church, Eccles married Bertha Marie Jensen in 1875 and married Ellen Stoddard as a plural wife in 1885. He had 21 children.

SOURCES

Arrington, Leonard J. *David Eccles: Pioneer Western Industrialist.* Logan, Utah: Utah State University, 1975.

Eccles, Marriner S. *Beckoning Frontiers—Public and Personal Recollections.* Edited by Sidney Hyman. New York: Alfred A. Knopf, 1951.

Hyman, Sidney. *Marriner S. Eccles: Private Entrepreneur and Public Servant.* Stanford: Graduate School of Business, Stanford University, 1976.

RICHARD E. BENNETT

ECCLES, MARRINER S. Remembered as **Utah**'s pragmatic conservative banker, Marriner Stoddard Eccles was born 9 September 1890 in **Logan**, Utah. He followed in the enterprising footsteps of his father, lumber magnate **David Eccles**. Upon his return from missionary duty to **Scotland**, his ancestral home, he spearheaded the amalgamation of several intermountain banks into the famed First Security Bank system in 1928. During the early days of the **great depression**, he masterminded strategies that kept his banks open while many others were closing their doors.

The Depression spurred Eccles, a thoughtful if not formally educated observer of economics, to move from accepting his father's beliefs in self-reliance, thrift, and prudent spending as antidotes to economic suffering to advocating positive government involvement in the economy. His highly debatable views caught the eye of President Franklin D. Roosevelt, who invited him in 1934 to become governor of the Federal Reserve Board in **Washington**. A **Republican** in a Democratic administration, Eccles predated the economic views of John Maynard Keynes by opposing efforts to balance the federal budget and by advocating massive deficit spending to spur consumption, reduce unemployment, and encourage business investment. A prime mover in establishing nationwide banking deposit insurance, Eccles was also the inspiration behind the Banking Act of 1935, which greatly strengthened the Federal Reserve Board and centralized the banking system of **America**.

After returning home, Eccles lost a 1952 nomination bid for Republican senator for the state of Utah to the incumbent, Arthur Watkins. Chairman of the Board of First Security Corporation for much of the rest of his life, Eccles continued to speak out on such debatable issues as supporting worldwide population control, strongly opposing America's involvement in the **Vietnam** War, and urging the reopening of full economic relations with mainland **China**. Eccles died 18 December 1977 in **Salt Lake City**.

SOURCES

Eccles, Marriner S. *Beckoning Frontiers—Public and Personal Recollections.* Edited by Sidney Hyman. New York: Alfred A. Knopf, 1951.

Hyman, Sidney. *Marriner S. Eccles: Private Entrepreneur and Public Servant.* Stanford: Graduate School of Business, Stanford University, 1976.

May, Dean L. "Success of Marriner S. Eccles's Economic Thought." *Journal of Mormon History* 3 (1976): 85–100.

RICHARD E. BENNETT

ECONOMIC HISTORY. The economic history of most churches, like that of other institutions, includes such matters as sources of income, disbursement into projects such as building chapels, and the impact of the rise and fall of the market and cycles of unemployment. All of these have influenced The Church of Jesus Christ of Latter-day Saints, of course, but in addition, **revelations** and leadership decisions have immersed the Church in an unusual variety of economic programs. To any who complain about such "nonspiritual" activity, the answer from the beginning has been: "Verily I say unto you that all things unto me are spiritual, and not at any time have I given unto you a law which was temporal" (D&C 29:34).

Much of the economic activity of the Church resulted from simple necessity, but it was also shaped by idealistic goals of oneness and equality: "If ye are not equal in earthly things ye cannot be equal in obtaining heavenly things" (D&C 78:6).

When converts joined the Church, they often wished to "gather"—to join the body of the **Saints**. This required planning and cooperation in selling previous property, pooling resources, and traveling by sea and land to **Ohio, Missouri, Illinois**, or, in the second half of the nineteenth century, **Utah**. The Saints constructed wagons, purchased teams, stockpiled provisions, chartered ships, and formed companies. Between 1852 and 1887, the **Perpetual Emigrating Fund** assisted in bringing about 26,000 people to the West.

Once they arrived at their destination, the immigrating Latter-day Saints often required further assistance. Public works programs helped sustain life while filling community needs, but as soon as possible the immigrants were encouraged to support themselves. Lands and houses were purchased, or people were formed into companies and sent to colonize new settlements. Partial early examples of this sequence can be found in Ohio, Missouri, and Illinois, but it was carried out most completely in the **Great Basin** in the second half of the nineteenth century. Each of many settlements—historians have enumerated well more than 300—had its own separate but similar history of settlers being called, moving to the new location, and attempting to establish a viable economic base. Church-appointed leaders played a prominent role throughout.

Individualistic capitalism was not the ideal. Some form of cooperation or pooling of resources seemed essential to survival. Prompted by revelations, **Joseph Smith** established a system of "consecration and stewardship," according to which Church members deeded over their property to the Church and then received back as a "stewardship" that portion considered suitable for their own needs (D&C 51:3). In Ohio and Missouri, the Saints repeatedly made efforts to establish this system, but it failed in part because of the selfishness of the Saints.

During the Utah period, especially during the 1870s and 1880s, efforts were made to renew some form of cooperation under such labels as the **law of consecration**, united order, or cooperatives, each with a different shade of meaning but all referring to Church-sponsored economic policy. The degree of implementation ranged from cooperative wholesale buying, production, and retail sales (through **ZCMI** and its affiliate local stores) all the way to some communities, most notably **Orderville**, where work assignments, clothing, and even meals were centrally organized. Abandonment of these efforts was forced by such realities as human nature, powerful competition from the surrounding capitalist economy, and relentless undercutting of Church economic activity by the federal government.

Church participation in the economy took another form during the 1890s, when funds were invested in the manufacture of sugar, hydro-electric power, the production of salt, and a lakeside resort, as well as other enterprises. But such sponsorship required heavy indebtedness. Soon after the turn of the century, under continued pressure from the government, the Church sold most of its business interests.

The voluntary payment of **tithing** and fast offerings became the Church's primary source of revenue as early as 1838, although much of this was payment in kind and not ready cash. Hampered by the **Edmunds-Tucker Act of 1887**, Church members became reluctant to contribute because the federal government escheated Church property. This happened again in the 1890s because of a long economic slump, but the paying of tithing enjoyed a resurgence under President **Lorenzo Snow**, and—along with fast offerings—has remained the primary basis of the Church's financial support.

During the 1930s, under conditions of the **great depression**, the welfare plan was organized. To assist in providing for basic human needs while avoiding "the evils of the dole," the program includes agricultural and production programs, to which Church members donate labor. Church-owned farms have been established in various states and in some foreign countries. **Deseret Industries** thrift stores provide employment and job training.

To assist others in times of need, the Church utilizes the resources of its ecclesiastical structure, the **Welfare Program**, and fast offerings, as well as humanitarian donations. A 1997 report showed that since 1985 the Church had supported 2,340 humanitarian projects in 137 countries at a cost of 162.5 million dollars. These projects included disaster relief efforts in **Mexico**, **Bangladesh**, **China**, the **Philippines**, Bosnia, **Croatia**, Rwanda, **Japan**, and North **Korea**.

The annual revenue from tithes and offerings as well as stock dividends is no longer reported publicly, but professional auditors assure proper accounting procedures. Church leaders state that tithing supplies most of the revenue, and most of the expenditure is for educational programs, **missionary work**, and the construction of chapels and **temples**.

In ways somewhat different from the past, then, the Church is involved in economic activities and programs. The original ideals are still acknowledged: "If ye are not one ye are not mine" (D&C 38:27). Looking forward to the second coming of Christ, the Church continues to assist its members to achieve greater self-sufficiency, reduce the extremes of poverty and suffering, and work toward greater equality.

SOURCES

Arrington, Leonard J. *Great Basin Kingdom: An Economic History of the Latter-day Saints.* Cambridge, Mass.: Harvard University Press, 1958.

Mangum, Garth L., and Bruce Blumell. *The Mormons' War on Poverty: A History of LDS Welfare, 1830–1990.* Salt Lake City: University of Utah Press, 1993.

Rudd, Glen L. *Pure Religion: The Story of Church Welfare Since 1930.* Salt Lake City: The Church of Jesus Christ of Latter-day Saints, 1995.

LEONARD J. ARRINGTON

ECUADOR. The Republic of Ecuador, located on the Pacific Coast of South America, has a Spanish and Quechua-speaking population that is 95% Roman Catholic. The Church was first introduced to the country in 1965 when **Elder Spencer W. Kimball** of the **Quorum** of Twelve **Apostles** sent a letter to J. Averil Jesperson, president of the Andes **Mission** in Lima, **Peru**, suggesting that missionary work be taken to Ecuador. Two weeks later four elders from Peru were sent to labor in Quito, Ecuador.

At the time the Ecuador Mission was created on 1 August 1970, membership was 1,000, and by the end of 1975 it had risen to 3,226. Hundreds of members attended newly organized **seminary** and **institute** programs. The first **stake** was organized in Guayaquil on 11 June 1978 with Lorenzo A. Garaycoa as president. Less than a month later, a second mission was opened in Guayaquil, and at the end of 1979 membership had accelerated to 19,000.

Some of the earliest proselyting in Ecuador took place among the Otavalo Indians near Quito. Among the first baptized was Rafael Tabango, who later became the first **branch** president, **district** president, and stake **patriarch** in Ecuador. In 1981 the first all-**Lamanite** stake in South America was created from among the Otavalo Indians.

In 1989 the headquarters for the South America North **Area** moved to Quito from Lima, Peru. Although President **Gordon B. Hinckley** had announced the coming of a **temple** in 1982, because of pending government approvals it was not until 1996 that ground was broken by Elder **Richard G. Scott**. In August 1997 President Hinckley traveled to Ecuador, speaking to some 15,000 members; he was the first Church president to visit the land. On 1 August 1999 the Guayaquil Ecuador Temple was dedicated. At the beginning of the year 2000 there were 146,420 members in the country living in 32 stakes and 373 **wards** and branches.

SOURCES

"Ecuador's 1st Stake Formed in Guayaquil." *Church News,* 8 July 1978, 12.

1999–2000 Church Almanac. Salt Lake City: Deseret News, 1998. 313–14.

Wells, Elayne. "In the Andes, Lehi's Children Grow Strong in the Gospel." *Church News,* 17 February 1990, 10.

REBECCA JACKSON

EDMUNDS ACT OF 1882. See **ANTIPOLYGAMY MOVEMENT.**

EDMUNDS-TUCKER ACT OF 1887. See **ANTIPOLYGAMY MOVEMENT.**

EDUCATION. From its beginning the Church has emphasized the importance of spiritual and secular education for its members (D&C 88:76–80, 118; 90:15; 93:36, 53). For early leaders, true education was learning those principles that would be valuable in this life and the next. **Joseph Smith** stated, "Knowledge saves a man, and in the world of spirits, a man cannot be exalted but by knowledge" (Smith, 357). **Brigham Young** added, "I shall not cease learning while I live, nor when I arrive in the spirit-world; but shall there learn with greater facility; and when I again receive my body, I shall learn a thousand times more in a thousand times less time" (*JD,* 8:10). The ideology espoused by Joseph Smith, Brigham Young, and their successors maintained it was a person's religious duty to gain knowledge.

The Church not only stressed the importance of education but also put its educational ideals into practice. The **School of the Prophets**, established in 1833, was one of the earliest programs for adult education in the **United States**. Many Latter-day **Saints** embraced American educational ideals, including the concept that schools were a place for the moral, intellectual, and social development of children. As the Saints moved from **Ohio** to **Missouri**, and then to **Illinois**, they founded schools for their children. In addition, when the **Nauvoo Charter** was written in 1840, it included the establishment of a university.

When the **pioneers** arrived in **Utah**, they immediately began to build community schools. In 1850 the territorial legislature established the **University of Deseret**, one of the first universities west of the **Mississippi**. During the last quarter of the nineteenth century, the Church also founded dozens of stake **academies**, which taught traditional subjects along with **Mormon** values. In 1888 a general Church board of education was instituted under the supervision of President **Wilford Woodruff** to direct the growing Church school system. From 1890 to 1930 the Church also sponsored children's religion classes, held in **ward meetinghouses**.

During the first decades of the twentieth century, as more Latter-day Saints had the opportunity to attend public schools, it became evident that the Church could not financially support the more than 30 **stake** academies that stretched from settlements in **Canada** to **Mexico**. Therefore, in 1920 the Church's board of education recommended that most academies be closed. At this time the Church began to head in a different educational direction. The few academies that were retained became junior colleges, such as Ricks College (later BYU–Idaho) in Rexburg, Idaho, and the **Brigham Young Academy** in **Provo, Utah**; the latter eventually became a full-fledged university. For secondary students, the Church would now supply religious education while the public school system would provide the secular.

In 1912 the first seminary was established, adjacent to Granite High School in **Salt Lake City**. Other **seminaries** were subsequently instituted to provide religious instruction for Latter-day Saint youth. Some school districts were willing to release students for one hour during the school day to participate in religious instruction. Other students attended classes in the early morning hours before school, and still others received instruction on a home-study basis. Beginning in 1926 at the University of **Idaho, institutes of religion** were built next to campuses where students attend non-Latter-day-Saint colleges and universities. These programs are designed to help Latter-day Saint youth develop a greater understanding and testimony of the gospel of **Jesus Christ** while they pursue their secular education.

In 1998 the **Church Educational System** was composed of seminaries and institutes in more than 90 countries. The Church also operated **Brigham Young University** in Provo, Utah; Brigham Young University–Hawaii Campus, in **Laie, Hawaii**; Ricks College (later BYU–Idaho) in

Rexburg, Idaho; and **LDS Business College** in Salt Lake City, Utah. Additionally, the Church offered adult and continuing education programs, as well as a few elementary and secondary schools in countries where public education was not provided for Latter-day Saint youth.

Latter-day Saints are taught at an early age the importance of reading the **standard works** and that "the glory of God is intelligence" (D&C 93:36). Leaders of the Church encourage members to acquire the highest possible level of education, and consequently the Saints often have more schooling than their peers. As the Church spreads throughout the world, its educational emphasis and activities continue to enrich the lives of its members.

SOURCES

Bennion, Milton Lynn. *Mormonism and Education.* Salt Lake City: Deseret Book, 1939.

Buchanan, Frederick S. "Education among the Mormons: Brigham Young and the Schools of Utah." *History of Education Quarterly* 22 (Winter 1982): 435–59.

Journal of Discourses [JD]. 26 vols. London: Latter-day Saints' Book Depot, 1854–86. Vol. 8.

Monnett, John Daniel. "The Mormon Church and Its Private School System in Utah: The Emergence of the Academies, 1880–1892." Ph.D. diss., University of Utah, 1984.

Smith, Joseph. *Teachings of the Prophet Joseph Smith.* Selected by Joseph Fielding Smith. Salt Lake City: Deseret Book, 1970. 357.

MARY JANE WOODGER

EDWARDS, LAVELL. LaVell Edwards, an active member of the LDS Church who served as a **bishop**, became one of the most successful college football coaches in history. Born 11 October 1930 in **Provo, Utah,** to Philo Taylor and Addie May Gurr Edwards, LaVell was an all-state football player in high school (1946 and 1947). He then played for Utah State Agricultural College, where he was team captain and earned all-conference honors (1950 and 1951). He married Patti Covey in the summer of 1951 and they became the parents of three children. LaVell played football in the army for three years (1952–54) and then began his high school coaching career. He was head football coach at Granite High School for eight years (1954–61) and then assistant coach at **Brigham Young University** for 10 years (1962–71). During LaVell's first year at BYU he was also called to be the bishop of a student ward.

Edwards became head coach at BYU in 1972 and over the next 28 years compiled a record of 251 wins and 95 losses. During that time his teams won 19 conference titles and played in 22 bowl games. He won the

National Championship in 1984, the same year he was named national coach of the year. At the end of 1999 only six coaches in the history of major college football had had more career victories. In August 2000 Edwards announced that he would retire at the end of the season.

SOURCE

Edwards, LaVell, with Lee Benson. *LaVell: Airing It Out.* Salt Lake City: Shadow Mountain, 1995.

ARNOLD K. GARR

EGYPT. Egypt has had a long and prominent role in the recorded history of God's dealings with his children, being especially noted in the Old Testament as a refuge in times of famine for **Abraham** and the **family** and offspring of Jacob, as well as for those escaping the Babylonians in the time of Lehi. In the New Testament, Egypt was also a place of refuge for Joseph, Mary, and **Jesus** to escape the murder of children in Bethlehem during Herod's reign. Egypt became a predominantly Christian land in succeeding centuries, but Christianity in that country has declined during the past millennium with the advent and growth of Islam. In the late twentieth century, Christians in Egypt composed about 10% of the total population.

Since the restoration of the Church through **Joseph Smith**, numerous **general authorities** and other Church members have visited Egypt, beginning with **Elder Orson Hyde** in 1841. In 1873 President **George A. Smith**, first **counselor** to **Brigham Young**, and other Church leaders visited Egypt, and similar visits have continued to the present time. During the last third of the twentieth century, members of the Church moved to Egypt to pursue diplomatic, business, or educational assignments and opportunities.

The formal organization of a **branch** and holding of regular services in Cairo date from 1974. Three members first met that summer in a Cairo hotel, and later in the fall the number of members increased to between 25 and 30. For some years thereafter, **meetings** were held in a large home (villa) of one of the branch members. Since 1982 the branch has met in a villa leased for holding religious meetings. Because Church members are foreigners living in Egypt for a limited time specified by contracts or assignments, branch membership numbers vary considerably from year to year, from 30 to as many as 150. Since 1980, couples have been assigned to Egypt to assist in fellowshipping and related branch activities.

The Cairo Branch was part of the Church **International Mission** from 1974 until 1987, when the **mission** was discontinued. The branch then became part of the **Austria** Vienna East Mission, and in 1990 became a part of the newly created Athens **Greece** Mission. At the beginning of the year 2000 there were about 100 members living in Egypt.

SOURCE

Church History of Cairo, Egypt. Cairo: Cairo Branch, 1992.

C. WILFRED GRIGGS

EGYPTIAN LANGUAGE. The **Book of Mormon** plates and the **book of Abraham**, both ancient documents that **Joseph Smith** translated, were written in Egyptian. The **Prophet** said that the **gold plates** from which he translated the Book of Mormon were written in "Egyptian characters" (Smith, 4:537). In fact, there seem to be two separate forms of Egyptian used on these plates. The language of most of the Book of Mormon, which was abridged by **Mormon** and his son **Moroni**, was called "reformed Egyptian," so designated, Moroni tells us, because it was "handed down and altered by us, according to our manner of speech" (Morm. 9:32). Thus, the "language of the Egyptians" used by Nephi (1 Ne. 1:2) had been modified during the 1,000-year period between Nephi and Moroni.

Why the Nephite prophets used Egyptian rather than Hebrew to record their sacred scripture was explained by Moroni, who said: "If our plates had been sufficiently large we should have written in Hebrew." Since the brass plates that Nephi and his brothers obtained from Laban were also written in Egyptian (Mosiah 1:4), this would have been a further incentive to use Egyptian. But why were the sacred scriptures of the **Jews**, including even some of the prophecies of Jeremiah (1 Ne. 5:13), written in Egyptian? The answer can be found by considering the lineage of Lehi and Laban, who were both of the tribe of Joseph (1 Ne. 5:14, 16). Joseph spent most of his adult life in **Egypt**. He was a distinguished member of the pharaoh's court and even married an Egyptian wife (Gen. 41:45). That the records of his posterity should be kept in Egyptian is not surprising.

The book of Abraham consists of "writings of Abraham while he was in Egypt" (Smith, 2:524). The Church now has in its possession ten fragments of some of the papyri that Joseph Smith obtained from **Michael Chandler**. In particular, the original of Facsimile No. 1 of the book of

Abraham survives. The writing on all these fragments is Egyptian, for the most part in the writing system called hieratic, an abbreviated form of hieroglyphic used in writing on papyri. These fragments include the original of Facsimile No. 1 but no other part of the text of the book of Abraham.

In July 1835 Joseph Smith recorded in his diary: "The remainder of this month, I was continually engaged in translating an alphabet to the book of Abraham, and arranging a grammar of the Egyptian language as practiced by the ancients" (Smith, 2:238). In 1935 some documents dating to the **Kirtland** period were discovered in the **Church Historian's office**. They seemed to be related to this alphabet and grammar mentioned by the Prophet. As **Hugh Nibley** has pointed out, none of these papers is written by the hand of Joseph Smith (except one brief page), but most are in the handwriting of **W. W. Phelps**, with some short appendages written by **Warren Parrish** (Nibley, 359). Nibley suggests that these papers are the result of Phelps and Parrish following the Lord's admonition to "study it out in your mind" (D&C 9:8) in an effort to understand the papyri (Nibley, 398). Unlike the book of Abraham, they were never published, were never represented as being the work of Joseph Smith, and were never put forward as divine **revelation**.

SOURCES

Nibley, Hugh. "The Meaning of the Kirtland Egyptian Papers." *BYU Studies* 11 (Summer 1971): 350–99.

Smith, Joseph. *History of The Church of Jesus Christ of Latter-day Saints.* Edited by B. H. Roberts. 2d ed. rev. 7 vols. Salt Lake City. The Church of Jesus Christ of Latter-day Saints, 1932–51.

MICHAEL D. RHODES

EIGHT WITNESSES OF THE BOOK OF MORMON. See WITNESSES OF THE BOOK OF MORMON.

EKA, DAVID W. David William Eka, one of the pioneering leaders of the Church in **Nigeria**, was born at a Protestant **mission** in Etinan, Nigeria, on 20 May 1945. Because of early religious training, he turned to **God** during the Biafran civil war and promised that if his life were spared, he would devote it to serving others. He subsequently raised orphaned children and provided love and support to many.

In 1974 David married Ekaete David, and they soon left for **England**

to further their education. Prior to leaving Nigeria, David had been introduced to the gospel by an uncle who had joined the Church in **America**.
In England, David was contacted by many missionaries but could not see
the need to be baptized again. Upon returning to Nigeria, he found the
Church had recently been established there. Though not yet baptized, he
helped translate the **Book of Mormon** into the Efik dialect. By the time
he finished, he knew it was true, so he and Ekaete were baptized. He
soon served as **branch** president, **counselor** to the **mission president**, and
as **district** president. On 15 May 1988, he became the president of the
new Aba Nigeria **Stake**—the first stake in this dispensation in which all
leaders were black. In November 1990 Brother Eka became a **regional
representative** and in October 1997 was sustained as an **area authority
seventy** to serve in **Africa**.

SOURCES

LeBaron, E. Dale, ed. *All Are Alike unto God.* Orem, Utah: Granite Publishing, 1990.
    55–64.
"Nigeria Marks Twin Milestones." *Church News,* 21 May 1988, 6.
Oral histories of early Church converts collected by E. Dale LeBaron. Copies at BYU
    Library, Provo, Utah; LDS Church Historical Library, Salt Lake City, Utah.

E. DALE LEBARON

ELDER. The calling of elder, an ordained office within the **Melchizedek
Priesthood**, existed in ancient Israel, among the Nephites, and in the
meridian of time. This office was **restored** in the latter days.

When **John the Baptist** restored the **Aaronic Priesthood** on
15 May 1829, he promised **Joseph Smith** and **Oliver Cowdery** that they
would subsequently receive the higher or **Melchizedek Priesthood** and
become the first and second elders of the Church (JS–H, 1:72). The exact
date of the conferral of the Melchizedek Priesthood is not known, but
after Joseph and Oliver arrived at the Whitmers' home in **Fayette, New
York**, in June 1829, they prayed for greater understanding. Joseph
records: "We had not long been engaged in solemn and fervent prayer,
when the word of the Lord came unto us in the chamber, commanding
us that I should ordain Oliver Cowdery to be an Elder in the Church of
Jesus Christ; and that he also should ordain me to the same office"
(Smith, 1:60–61). The Prophet also learned that he and Oliver were "to
defer [their] ordination" until a time when baptized members could meet
and sustain this action (Smith, 1:61). Although the Melchizedek

Priesthood may have been conferred by this point, the ordination to the office of elder required the consent of the brethren.

These instructions were carried out at the **organization of the Church** on **6 April** 1830. Joseph and Oliver ordained each other to the office of elder and officially became known as the First and Second Elders of the Church.

The duties of an elder as spelled out in modern **revelation** are to administer in spiritual things (D&C 107:12), such as blessing the sick (D&C 42:44), teaching and exhorting Church members, giving the gift of the Holy Ghost (D&C 20:42–45), and conducting the **meetings** of the Church (D&C 46:2). An elder may also perform any duty done by those who hold the Aaronic Priesthood.

In addition to being an ordained office of the Melchizedek Priesthood, the term *elder* may be used to designate any holder of that priesthood. Commonly, Church members refer to the **general authorities** and missionaries of the Church as elders even though these men might be ordained **high priests, seventies,** or **apostles.**

Sources

McConkie, Bruce R. *Doctrinal New Testament Commentary.* 3 vols. Salt Lake City: Bookcraft, 1965–73. 2:114–15.

———. *Mormon Doctrine.* 2d ed. Salt Lake City: Bookcraft, 1966. 214–15.

Smith, Joseph. *History of The Church of Jesus Christ of Latter-day Saints.* Edited by B. H. Roberts. 2d ed. rev. 7 vols. Salt Lake City: The Church of Jesus Christ of Latter-day Saints, 1932–51. 1:60–61.

Guy L. Dorius

ELDERS' JOURNAL (1837–38). The final issues of the *Messenger and Advocate* in August and September 1837 carried a prospectus signed by **Sidney Rigdon** announcing a new **periodical,** the *Elders' Journal.* "This paper is intended to be a vehicle of communication for all **elders** of the church . . . through which they can communicate to others, all things pertaining to their mission, and calling." The *Journal* was under the general editorship of **Joseph Smith** and was printed once a month. The subscription price was $1 per year.

Beginning in October 1837, two issues of the *Journal* were printed and published by **Thomas B. Marsh** in **Kirtland**. Apparently, the bulk of the editorial duties for these two numbers was discharged to **Don Carlos Smith**. The *Journal* ceased publication in Kirtland when Joseph Smith and Sidney Rigdon moved to **Far West, Missouri**, in January 1838. On 30 April 1838, a prospectus was issued announcing that the *Elders' Journal* would be revived in Far West on the same terms as before, with Joseph Smith as editor and Thomas B. Marsh as publisher. Two additional issues were published in Far West in July and August 1838 before the expulsion of the Saints from **Missouri** marked the end of the *Journal*. Each issue of the paper contained 16 pages in double columns, the four numbers continuously paged. The *Journal* consisted almost entirely of letters from the elders abroad and minutes of **conferences** and **council** meetings.

SOURCE

Jenson, Andrew. *Encyclopedic History of The Church of Jesus Christ of Latter-day Saints.* Salt Lake City: Deseret News, 1941. 218.

LYNDON W. COOK

ELDERS' JOURNAL (1903–07). See LIAHONA THE ELDERS' JOURNAL.

ELDREDGE, W. JAY. W. Jay Eldredge served as general superintendent of the **Young Men's Mutual Improvement Association** from 17 September 1969 to 25 June 1972 and was sustained as president of that organization on 9 November 1972. He had previously served as a **mission president** and as the first president of the Parleys **Stake**. He was born 27 April 1913 in **Salt Lake City** and married Marjory Hyde. They became the parents of five children.

GUY L. DORIUS

ELIAS. Elias is the **New Testament** (Greek) form of the name **Elijah** (as in Luke 4:25–26; James 5:17), signifying a forerunner, one who prepares the way "for a greater revelation of God" (Smith, 335–37). **John the Baptist** (JST Matt. 11:13–15; JST John 1:19–28), John the Beloved (D&C 77:14), Gabriel or Noah (Luke 1:19; D&C 27:7; Smith, 157), and even **Joseph Smith**, "that prophet" called and foreordained to prepare the way for the **Second Coming** (JST Matt. 17:14; JST John 1:22; Ehat and Cook, 370), have ministered in the "spirit of Elias."

On 3 April 1836 a heavenly messenger designated as Elias appeared in the **Kirtland Temple** to Joseph Smith and **Oliver Cowdery**. This Elias, whose specific identity is not given in the revelation, "committed the dispensation of the gospel of Abraham, saying that in us and our seed all generations after us should be blessed" (D&C 110:12). Elias restored the keys associated with eternal marriage, with what we know as the patriarchal order or the new and everlasting covenant of marriage, the marriage discipline that had been revealed to the ancient patriarchs. Thus all **Saints** who participate in this order of matrimony (temple marriage), and keep their covenants, receive all of the blessings promised to **Abraham**, Isaac, and Jacob.

SOURCES

Ehat, Andrew F., and Lyndon W. Cook, comps. and eds. *The Words of Joseph Smith.* Provo, Utah: Religious Studies Center, Brigham Young University, 1980.

Smith, Joseph. *Teachings of the Prophet Joseph Smith.* Selected by Joseph Fielding Smith. Salt Lake City: Deseret Book, 1970.

ROBERT L. MILLET

ELIJAH. A prophet to the northern kingdom of **Israel in the ninth century before Christ**, Elijah occupies a central position in Latter-day Saint doctrine regarding the sealing power of the **Melchizedek Priesthood**, **temple work**, and **family history**. Elijah's biblical ministry to Israel was characterized by powerful miracles and a forceful opposition to idol worship (1 Kgs. 17–2 Kgs. 2; 2 Chron. 21:12–15). This mission ended when he was translated and taken to heaven (2 Kgs. 2:11–12).

As prophesied in Malachi 4:5–6, Elijah's ministry to the inhabitants of the earth continued after his miraculous departure. His condition as a translated being allowed him, the "last Prophet that held the keys of the Priesthood" (*TPJS*, 172), to physically bestow those same "keys of the kingdom" (Matthew 16:9) on the apostles **Peter, James**, and **John** at the Mount of Transfiguration (Matthew 17:1–4). The priesthood keys spoken of refer to "the binding, or sealing power" that "make valid *all* the ordinances of the gospel" (*DS*, 2:119).

In 1823 the prophet **Moroni** quoted an alternative rendering of Malachi 4:5–6 to **Joseph Smith**, foreshadowing another visitation of Elijah in this latter dispensation (JS–H 1:36–39). On 3 April 1836, one week after the dedication of the **Kirtland Temple**, Elijah appeared as a resurrected being (D&C 133:55) to commit the keys of this dispensation to Joseph Smith and **Oliver Cowdery** (D&C 110:13–16). This bestowal of the sacred sealing power gave eternal validity to the performance of all gospel ordinances for both the living and the dead.

Elijah's latter-day appearance also awakened throughout the earth an interest in family history. Called "the spirit of Elijah," this emphasis on family ties reflects Malachi's observation that Elijah's coming would "turn the heart of the fathers to the children, and the heart of the children to their fathers" (Mal. 4:6). Manifestations of this spirit include the completion of one's family history and the performance of all gospel ordinances on behalf of one's ancestors.

SOURCES

Merrill, Byron R. *Elijah: Yesterday, Today, and Tomorrow.* Salt Lake City: Bookcraft, 1997.

Packer, Boyd K. *The Holy Temple.* Salt Lake City: Bookcraft, 1980.

Smith, Joseph. *Teachings of the Prophet Joseph Smith [TPJS].* Selected by Joseph Fielding Smith. Salt Lake City: Deseret Book, 1970.

Smith, Joseph Fielding. *Doctrines of Salvation [DS].* 3 vols. Compiled by Bruce R. McConkie. Salt Lake City: Bookcraft, 1954–56.

BYRON R. MERRILL

EL SALVADOR. The Church has grown rapidly in El Salvador, despite a prolonged civil **war** that severely hampered **missionary work** in the Central American country for more than a decade. On 2 March 1951, Ana Villasenor became the first person baptized in El Salvador. In 1965 the Guatemala–El Salvador **Mission** was organized.

In 1980, with Church membership standing at 14,000, civil war broke out in the country, forcing the closure of the mission. In 1984 the mission was reopened but relied solely on native missionaries. An earthquake on 10 December 1986 devastated the country. Among the **Saints** were two dead and five injured, and 700 were left homeless. The Church sent three planeloads of food, medical supplies, and tents. On 7 April 1990, **Elders Russell M. Nelson** and **Richard G. Scott** formally dedicated the land for the preaching of the gospel. Soon thereafter, the mission was divided, and baptisms increased dramatically. In 1992 the civil war ended, and North American missionaries returned. By the beginning of the year 2000 Church membership had reached 84,683 in 16 **stakes** and 152 **wards** and branches.

SOURCE

1999–2000 Church Almanac. Salt Lake City: Deseret News, 1998. 315–16.

LORENA CANNON

EMERGENCY PREPAREDNESS. The **scriptures** and the **prophets** have given repeated warnings that destructive events will occur. The Lord has urged his people to prepare for difficult times by putting away a year's supply or more of bare necessities so that they can be sustained when floods, earthquakes, famines, hurricanes, and other trials come. Only preparation—both spiritual and temporal—can dispel fear of these disasters.

The primary responsibility to prepare for and respond to emergencies rests with individual members and families. Nevertheless, when the Saints are doing all they can to provide for themselves and their families and still cannot meet their basic needs, the Church stands ready to help them; the Lord has declared that he will hear their cries and will not forsake them.

In managing the affairs of the Church, leaders have tried to set an example. They have, as a matter of policy, stringently set aside a percentage of the income of the Church each year against a possible day of need.

Sources

Church Welfare Resources. Salt Lake City: The Church of Jesus Christ of Latter-day Saints, 1991. 14.

Hinckley, Gordon B. "To the Boys and to the Men." *Ensign* 28 (November 1998): 51–54.

Kimball, Spencer W. *The Teachings of Spencer W. Kimball.* Edited by Edward L. Kimball. Salt Lake City: Bookcraft, 1982.

Providing in the Lord's Way. Salt Lake City: The Church of Jesus Christ of Latter-day Saints, 1990. 11.

GLEN L. RUDD

EMERITUS GENERAL AUTHORITIES. On 30 September 1978, the **First Presidency** announced the creation of a new "emeritus" status for **general authorities**, based on conditions of health or age. Announcing the change during **general conference**, as directed by President **Spencer W. Kimball**, President N. **Eldon Tanner** said the status was created "out of consideration for the personal well-being of the individuals, and with deep appreciation for their devoted service;" the brethren were "not being released but will be excused from active service" ("Revelation," 16). Seven members of the First **Quorum** of **Seventy** were the first to be given that status; they continued as members of the quorum and participated as much as possible in **meetings** and activities, while being relieved of many of the responsibilities.

Brethren given emeritus status have been members of the First Quorum of the Seventy. The **patriarch** to the Church, **Eldred G. Smith**, was also designated emeritus in 1979.

SOURCES

"News of the Church." *Ensign* 8 (November 1978): 99.
"Revelation on Priesthood Accepted, Church Officers Sustained." *Ensign* 8 (November 1978): 16.

DAVID KENISON

EMIGRATION. See GATHERING.

EMIGRATION CANYON, UTAH. See PIONEERS

EMMETT, JAMES. James Emmett, a **Latter-day Saint** frontiersman, was born in Boone County, **Kentucky**, 22 February 1803. He married Phoebe Jane Simpson, and in 1831 he was baptized by **Lyman Wight**. As a missionary in Kentucky, he taught the Butler, Hendricks, and Lewis families, who became stalwart **Saints**. In **Missouri** he was president of the Mirabile **Branch**. He fought in the **Battle of Crooked River**, and **Joseph Smith** sent him and John Butler on two dangerous proselyting **missions** among **Indian** tribes north and west of **Nauvoo** in 1840 to 1841. He later became a member of the **Council of Fifty**, a **Nauvoo** policeman, and one of Joseph Smith's 12 official bodyguards. Leaders asked him to participate in the **Oregon** and **California** exploring expedition, which trip he postponed to campaign for Joseph Smith for president.

After the **Martyrdom**, Emmett determined to fill the expedition mission. By September 1844 he and 150 recruits assembled near **Iowa** City. **Brigham Young** sent John Butler to help Emmett. In January 1845 the company moved up the Iowa River, lost members due to conflicts about consecration, crossed through wilderness to the southeastern tip of present **South Dakota**, and wintered (1845–46) at Camp Vermillion. The Twelve, disapproving of the expedition, monitored it but did not call it to return. Most in it were loyal Saints who ended up in **Utah**. An ineffective, authoritarian leader, Emmett antagonized his followers and **family**. Emmett's group joined Nauvoo **exodus** companies at **Council Bluffs**, where the Twelve assigned them to Bishop **George Miller's** advance company, which wintered (1846–47) at Ponca Camp. Emmett, disaffected from the Twelve, left the Church and died in Cottonwood, California, on 28 December 1852.

SOURCES

Bennett, Richard E. "Mormon Renegade: James Emmett at the Vermillion, 1846." *South Dakota History* 15 (Fall 1985): 217–33.

Hartley, William G. *My Best for the Kingdom: History and Autobiography of John Lowe Butler, a Mormon Frontiersman.* Salt Lake City: Aspen Books, 1993.

WILLIAM G. HARTLEY

EMMETT EXPEDITION. See EMMETT, JAMES.

ENCYCLOPEDIAS AND REFERENCE WORKS. There is a wide range of useful reference material concerning LDS Church history. Because the Church has emphasized record keeping ever since its inception, the body of historical information is vast; related reference works range from a broadly scoped *Church Almanac* to the geographically focused *Historical Atlas of Mormonism.* For many years, the most important works were written by Church **Historians** and assistant historians, but the second half of the twentieth century saw a trend toward many definitive works being written and compiled by scholars working at **Brigham Young University** or independent of the Church altogether. Consistent with this shift, many works began to be issued by large, commercial publishers, rather than the Church or **Deseret Book.**

Reference works on the LDS Church may be divided into four general categories: Encyclopedias, Biographical Reference Works, Bibliographies, and Electronic Reference Tools. (For further information related to encyclopedias and reference works, see also **Historians and Historical Writings**, **Historical Publications**, and **Periodicals**.)

ENCYCLOPEDIAS

Andrew Jenson's *Encyclopedic History of The Church of Jesus Christ of Latter-day Saints* stands as a foundation work for most Latter-day Saint historians since his time. The first to organize Latter-day Saint historical data into an encyclopedic form, Jenson characteristically covered both breadth and depth of subject. *The Encyclopedia of Mormonism* (1992), edited by Daniel H. Ludlow, is currently the best source for general information because of its accuracy, its four-volume breadth of information, and its relatively recent date of publication. **Joseph Fielding Smith's** *Essentials in Church History* includes an appendix that became a predecessor for the *Church Almanac,* which was published by the **Deseret News** annually, then biennially (beginning with the 1985 issue). This publication has gained a reputation as the best source for the most current biographies of general authorities, statistics, lists, and other such information on the Church.

Other useful encyclopedic works include Melvin R. Brooks, *Latter-day Saint Reference Encyclopedia* (2 vols., 1960 and 1965), mostly pertaining to important individuals in Church history and doctrinal issues; Hoyt W. Brewster Jr., *Doctrine and Covenants Encyclopedia* (1988); and Davis Bitton, *Historical Dictionary of Mormonism* (1994).

Similar reference works include Andrew Jenson's *Church Chronology: A Record of Important Events* (1899, 2d ed. rev. and enl., 1914), a day-by-day list of events important to the Church during its early decades; a three-volume pictorial guide book of Mormon sites titled *Historic Photographs and Guide* (1990–91) by Richard Neitzel Holzapfel and T. Jeffrey Cottle; the *Historical Atlas of Mormonism,* a unique collection of maps and related essays compiled by S. Kent Brown, Donald Q. Cannon, and Richard H. Jackson in 1994; Wayne L. Walquist, *Atlas of Utah* (1981); and Allan Kent Powell, *Utah History Encyclopedia* (1994), focusing on places and events important to the state of **Utah**; and *Sacred Places* (edited by LaMar C. Berrett), a multivolume, comprehensive guide to Latter-day Saint historical sites, the first volume of which was published in 1999.

BIOGRAPHICAL REFERENCE WORKS

Foremost among biographical works is Andrew Jenson's four-volume *Latter-day Saint Biographical Encyclopedia* (1901–36). Another important biographical reference, *Pioneers and Prominent Men of Utah* (1913), was written by Frank Esshom, featuring high-quality photographs and including many non-Mormons. The fourth volume of Orson F. Whitney's *History of Utah* consists of biographies of prominent Utahns.

In 1974 Lawrence R. Flake published *Mighty Men of Zion,* which contains biographies (averaging about two pages each) of all the general authorities up to that time. Twenty-six years later, Flake updated, corrected, and reconfigured the book, reducing its scope to **apostles** and members of the **First Presidency**; the new version was published in 2001 as *Prophets and Apostles of the Last Dispensation.* In 1984 BYU published

Marvin Wiggins, *Mormons and Their Neighbors,* an index to more than 75,000 biographical sketches from 1820 to the 1980s.

Richard S. Van Wagoner and Steven C. Walker wrote *A Book of Mormons,* which covers many of the legendary, notorious, and folk Mormons and **anti-Mormons** that are generally ignored in other places— focusing on the quirks or events that made them legendary. Susan Easton Black's mammoth *Membership of The Church of Jesus Christ of Latter-day Saints 1830–1848* (1989), containing nearly every member who joined during the first nineteen years of the Church, is useful because of its wide scope. For accuracy, the "Biographical Register" found on pages 521 to 607 of Dean C. Jesse, *Papers of Joseph Smith,* Vol. II, is one of the best biographical appendices on the Joseph Smith era.

Several books give biographical information on individuals named in the **Doctrine and Covenants**. In 1981 Lyndon W. Cook, *The Revelations of the Prophet Joseph Smith,* contained reliable biographical commentary on every section of the Doctrine and Covenants. This was followed in 1991 by George M. McCune, *Personalities of the Doctrine and Covenants,* and in 1997 by both Lynn F. Price, *Every Person in the Doctrine and Covenants,* and Susan Easton Black, *Who's Who in the Doctrine and Covenants.*

BIBLIOGRAPHIES

Published in 1976 and revised in 1992, *The Story of the Latter-day Saints* by James B. Allen and Glen M. Leonard included a definitive Latter-day Saint bibliography. In 1995 David J. Whittaker edited and contributed to *Mormon Americana*—exceptionally useful in its coverage not only of sources but of collections; the volume also includes 10 specialized bibliographic essays on such topics as photoarchives, folklore, and the visual and performing arts. Another useful tool is *A Descriptive Bibliography of the Mormon Church* by Peter Crawley, giving historical information for various Church publications; the first volume, covering 1830 to 1847, appeared in 1997.

Some more narrowly focused and helpful bibliographies also exist: *A Catalogue of Theses and Dissertations concerning The Church of Jesus Christ of Latter-day Saints, Mormonism and Utah* (1970), compiled by the College of Religious Instruction (now Religious Education) at Brigham Young University; and Davis Bitton, *Guide to Mormon Diaries and Autobiographies* (1977). Also the **Foundation for Ancient Research and Mormon Studies** biannually publishes the *FARMS Review of Books,* dedicated to discussing and reviewing literature on the **Book of Mormon**.

The *Review* regularly rebuts anti-Mormon attacks and in 1999 published a bibliography of all literature on the Book of Mormon. Publications from the **Mormon History Association** and the **Utah Historical Society** have also contained valuable bibliographical information.

In the year 2000 James B. Allen, David J. Whittaker, and Ronald Walker produced the most exhaustive bibliography yet, entitled *Studies in Mormon History,* consisting of an indexed bibliography (arranged both topically and by authors' last names) of all the scholarly work on Mormon history from 1830 to 1998. Many other individuals have made significant contributions to Latter-day Saint bibliography, including Chad Flake, Dale Morgan, Donald Perry, David L. Laughlin, and Ronald D. Dennis.

ELECTRONIC REFERENCE TOOLS

As computers and the Internet became more available and inclusive, electronic reference tools played an increasingly important role for historians, scholars, and students of Latter-day Saint history. Infobases (by Bookcraft) and GospeLink (by **Deseret Book**) each offered a searchable CD-ROM library of thousands of Latter-day Saint books and reference tools. In 1999 the two companies merged, the software along with them, so that all titles became available for both systems. Another important electronic tool, the Latter-day Saint Church's **FamilySearch**™, facilitates genealogy and family history work. FamilySearch™ can be found at www.familysearch.com.

RICHARD D. MCCLELLAN

ENDOWMENT. See TEMPLES AND TEMPLE WORK.

ENDOWMENT HOUSE. The Endowment House, formerly located in the northwest corner of the Temple Block (known today as **Temple Square**) in **Salt Lake City**, served as a "temporary temple" from 1855 until 1889. Designed by **Truman O. Angell**, it was dedicated on 5 May 1855 by **Heber C. Kimball**. The building was a two-story structure measuring 34 feet by 44 feet, with a 20-foot square entrance. An addition was erected later to accommodate **baptisms for the dead**. The first floor of the main building consisted of the entrance room and four **ordinance** rooms, with each room's floor placed at a different level to provide a sense of ascent as one moved through the rooms during the **endowment**

ceremony. The second floor consisted of the large celestial room and a much smaller **sealing** room. Ordinances, except endowments for the dead and sealing of children, were performed there from 5 May 1855 until 22 September 1889. The building was also used for prayer **meetings** and to **set apart** and instruct missionaries. By 1889, **temples** at St. George, **Logan**, and **Manti** were in full operation, and construction of the **Salt Lake Temple** was moving forward. In a symbolic effort to eliminate non-**Mormon** opposition to **plural marriage** and **statehood**, Church leaders razed the Endowment House, where many **plural marriages** had been performed previously.

SOURCES

Berrett, LaMar C. "Endowment Houses." *Encyclopedia of Mormonism*. Edited by Daniel H. Ludlow. 4 vols. New York: Macmillan, 1992. 2:456.

Tingen, James D. "The Endowment House: 1855–1889." Senior History Paper, December 1974, Brigham Young University.

RICHARD NEITZEL HOLZAPFEL

ENGLAND. Elders **Heber C. Kimball** and **Orson Hyde** of the Quorum of the Twelve **Apostles**—along with **Willard Richards**, **Joseph Fielding**, John Goodson, Isaac Russell, and John Snider—arrived in England on 19 July 1837. Eleven days later, on Sunday, 23 July, **Elder** Kimball baptized nine converts in the River Ribble in Preston, an event that was viewed by some 8,000 inquisitive bystanders. A week later a total of 50 had joined the Church. Despite opposition from ministers and the press, within nine months the number of converts had reached 1,500.

Nine members of the **Quorum** of the Twelve, including **Brigham Young**, labored in England at some time from 1840 to 1841. During this time they baptized more than 5,000 people. They also arranged for about 800 of these converts to emigrate to **America**. The flow of British converts helped vitalize the struggling Church in America, both then and for years later.

In 1850 the membership of the Church in Britain reached 30,747, while the general Church membership was 51,839. During the 1850s Latter-day Saint emigration was at its highest, with 16,342 British **Saints** sailing from **Liverpool**. Almost 15,000 more followed in the 1860s.

The Church faced severe opposition over the next few decades, and the work was slow. After the turn of the century **missionary work** increased. During **World War I**, local sisters took over proselyting activities. After the war missionary work increased, and **anti-Mormon** activity waned. This resulted in a membership increase, and in the mid-1930s a large building program began. During **World War II**, local members began "home missionary work." This increased the number of branches from 68 to 75, although these were later consolidated into 29 branches.

A **temple** was announced in 1953 for London. This, along with visits from Church leaders and the **Tabernacle Choir** over the following few years, lifted the spirits of the members. The **London Temple** was dedicated by President **David O. McKay** on 7 to 9 September 1958.

On 27 March 1960, the **Manchester** Stake was created and the **British Mission** was divided. The **seminary** program was introduced in the country in 1968. The Church continued to grow, and another large building program was inaugurated. There were 70,000 members by 1971, which increased to 91,000 by 1980.

The celebration of the Church's 150th anniversary in **Great Britain** in 1987 underscored the maturity of the Church. President Ezra Taft Benson and President Gordon B. Hinckley of the **First Presidency** joined former prime minister Edward Heath at a banquet, where they viewed a videotaped message from former U.S. president Ronald Reagan. Eight public markers were dedicated to honor important Church sites in the **British Isles**.

The London Temple was remodeled and then rededicated on 18 October 1992, and another temple in Preston was announced by President Hinckley. The ground for this new temple was broken on 12 June 1994, and it was dedicated on 7 June 1998 by President Hinckley.

By the beginning of the year 2000, there were 36 **stakes**, 289 wards and branches, and 6 **missions** in England, with a Church membership of 135,748.

SOURCES

Bloxham, V. Ben, James R. Moss, and Larry C. Porter, eds. *Truth Will Prevail: The Rise of The Church of Jesus Christ of Latter-day Saints in the British Isles, 1837–1997*. Cambridge: Cambridge University Press, 1987.

1999–2000 Church Almanac. Salt Lake City: Deseret News, 1998. 398–401.

DAVID COOK

ENSIGN, THE. Officially called *The Ensign of The Church of Jesus Christ of Latter-day Saints*, the *Ensign* (pronounced *N'sign*, not *N'sun*) is a monthly magazine for English-speaking adult members living primarily in the **United States**, **Canada**, the **United Kingdom** and **Ireland**,

Australia, and **New Zealand**. Sized 8.46 by 10.59 inches, it carries no advertising. It prints in its May and November issues proceedings of April and October **general conferences**. Ten additional issues further its purpose to strengthen members' faith, promulgate truths of the restored gospel, and keep members abreast of current vital policies, programs, and happenings. Its **First Presidency** messages are used in **home teaching**; its **visiting teaching** messages are used similarly. It also prints articles on **scripture**, doctrine, member experiences, support for families, single members, Church programs, auxiliaries, and Church news. Circulation in 1999 was near 800,000, making it one of the world's most widely circulated denominational magazines. Many articles are translated into some 37 languages for the Church's **International Magazines**. Staff-produced, the *Ensign* is overseen by appointed **general authorities** and enjoys the benefits of the Church's **correlation** process. The *Ensign* (a term rich in scriptural meaning) was formed in 1971 when the **Brethren** amalgamated the *Improvement Era, Relief Society Magazine,* and *Instructor* into one publication.

SOURCES

Green, Doyle L. "The Church and Its Magazines." *Ensign* 1 (January 1971): 12.

Todd, Jay M. "Ensign." *Encyclopedia of Mormonism.* Edited by Daniel H. Ludlow. 4 vols. New York: Macmillan, 1992. 2:460.

JAY M. TODD

ENSIGN PEAK. Anticipating the latter-day restoration, the ancient prophet Isaiah declared that the Lord would "lift up an ensign [or banner] to the nations" (Isa. 5:26; compare 11:12). On 26 July 1847, just two days after **Brigham Young** arrived in the **Salt Lake Valley**, he and seven others ascended a dome-shaped hill north of the present **Utah** State Capitol building. He had seen this prominent peak in a vision. As President Young raised a flag, he also symbolically lifted the "ensign to all nations," inviting them to gather to **Zion**. From Ensign Peak the group had an excellent panoramic view of the Salt Lake Valley and surrounding areas, the "resting place" God had designated for his people (Joseph F. Smith, 24:155–56).

Ensign Peak was the place where **Addison Pratt** received the **endowment** from Brigham Young before departing on his mission in 1849. A tribute to Ensign Peak was portrayed in the famous 1853 **Mormon** gathering hymn, "High on the Mountain Top," with text by Joel H. Johnson and music by Ebenezer Beesley.

SOURCES

Richards, Franklin D. *Journal.* Family collection. 5.
Smith, George Albert. *Journal of Discourses.* 26 vols. London: Latter-day Saints' Book Depot, 1854–86. 13:85–86.
Smith, Joseph F. *Journal of Discourses.* 26 vols. London: Latter-day Saints' Book Depot, 1854–86. 155–56.

JOHN M. BECK

EQUAL RIGHTS AMENDMENT. The Equal Rights Amendment, initiated during the early 1970s as a proposed amendment to the **United States Constitution**, was openly opposed by the Church. The proposed amendment stated: "Equality of rights under the law shall not be denied or abridged by the United States or by any State on account of sex." Proponents of the bill asserted that the amendment would extend social and economic equality to women.

In 1976 the First Presidency explained why the Church opposed the ERA: "While the motives of its supporters may be praiseworthy, ERA as a blanket attempt to help women could indeed bring them far more restraints and repressions. We fear it will even stifle many God-given feminine instincts. It would strike at the family, humankind's basic institution. ERA would bring ambiguity and possibly invite extensive litigation. Passage of ERA, some legal authorities contend, could nullify many accumulated benefits to women in present statutes" ("First Presidency," 2). Opposition by the Church was based on the belief that the proposal was misguided and would foster misunderstandings of gender roles and would have other unintended consequences. The amendment, first proposed in 1972, was vigorously debated in both the state and federal legislatures throughout the United States.

While some members of the Church favored passage, the vast majority of Latter-day **Saints** opposed the ERA. Throughout the United States, Saints effectively organized to prevent the bill from becoming law. In 1981 the proposal was defeated as proponents were unable to secure approval by two-thirds of the states within the 10-year time limit set forth in the Constitution.

SOURCES

Allen, James B., and Glen Leonard. *The Story of the Latter-day Saints.* 2d ed. Salt Lake City: Deseret Book, 1992. 659.

Church History in the Fulness of Times. Salt Lake City: The Church of Jesus Christ of Latter-day Saints, 1993. 586.

"First Presidency Opposes ERA." *Church News*, 30 October 1976.

Quinn, D. Michael. "The LDS Church's Campaign against the Equal Rights Amendment." *Journal of Mormon History* (Fall 1994): 85–155.

ROBERT C. FREEMAN

ERIE CANAL. Measuring 40 feet wide at the top and 4 feet in depth, the Erie Canal, or "Clinton's Ditch," was under construction for a period of eight years, 1817 to 1825. This exceptional engineering feat traversed 363 miles from Albany, **New York**, to Lake Erie at Buffalo, New York. From the Hudson River at Albany there was a rise in elevation of 565 feet to Lake Erie, which required 83 locks and 18 aqueducts to navigate.

From the beginning of the **Restoration** under the **Prophet Joseph Smith**, the Erie Canal became a principal thoroughfare for individuals and parties associated with the rise of Mormonism. For instance, **Palmyra, New York**, was a canal town, and the waterway provided ease of transit for **Oliver Cowdery** in the spring of 1830. **Abner Cole**, editor of the *Reflector,* observed: "The **apostle** to the Nephites (Cowdery) has started for the EAST, on board a boat, with a load of 'gold bibles,' under a command . . . to declare the truth (according to Jo[seph] Smith,) 'in all the principal cities in the Union'" ("Apostle," 28). The **Colesville, Fayette**, and **Manchester** branches of the Church used the Erie Canal as an important link in their emigration from New York to **Ohio** in April and May 1831.

SOURCES

"The Apostle to the Nephites." *Reflector* [Palmyra, New York], 1 June 1830, 28.

Porter, Larry C. "A Study of the Origins of The Church of Jesus Christ of Latter-day Saints in the States of New York and Pennsylvania, 1816–1831." Ph.D. diss., Brigham Young University, 1971. 296–308, 311–22.

Shaw, Ronald E. *Erie Water West: A History of the Erie Canal, 1792–1854*. Lexington: University of Kentucky Press, 1966.

LARRY C. PORTER

ESSENTIALS IN CHURCH HISTORY. For more than 50 years, *Essentials in Church History* stood as the most-often-read single volume of Church history. Written by **Joseph Fielding Smith**, it became a **priesthood** manual from 1922 to 1923, shortly after its initial publication. It contains the chronological history of the Church from the birth of **Joseph Smith**, along with an appendix of biographical information on each **general authority**, and is beneficial for both the casual reader and the serious scholar. Written to meet the specifications of a Church textbook and to build faith, it has been unfairly criticized by modern historians for bias and unscholarly methods. President Smith, who served for 49 years as Church Historian, interpreted history through the eyes of faith, seeing in it the fulfillment of **scripture** and prophecy. His study of the development of the Church is intertwined with commentary on the revelations of the **Restoration**, giving an increased historical context and spiritual perspective.

JOSEPH FIELDING MCCONKIE

ESTONIA. Estonia was dedicated for the preaching of the gospel on 25 April 1990 by **Elder Russell M. Nelson** of the Quorum of the Twelve **Apostles**. It was the first country in the former Soviet Union to be opened for **missionary work**. The first four missionaries arrived from the Finland Helsinki Mission in 1989. Shortly thereafter Estonia became part of the **Russia** St. Petersburg Mission. The first **branch** was established in Tallinn on 28 January 1990, with a missionary, Edler Hari Aho, as president.

Missionaries worked in Tallinn, the country's capital, and Tartu, the home of the largest and oldest university in the Baltic countries. A **district** was created in Estonia on 27 August 1997 under the direction of the **Europe** East **area** presidency. In the year 2000 there were 339 members living in three **branches** of the Church in Estonia: Tallinn had separate Estonian-and Russian-speaking branches, and Tartu had a single branch.

SOURCE

Browning, Gary. *Russia and the Restored Gospel.* Salt Lake City: Deseret Book, 1997. xvi-xxi.

MICHAEL MANOOKIN

ETERNAL MARRIAGE. See MARRIAGE.

ETHIOPIA. The east central African country of Ethiopia has been viewed as a seedbed for Christianity since apostolic times, and today half the population belongs to the Ethiopian Orthodox religion. About one-third follows the **Muslim** faith.

The Church was first introduced in Ethiopia by Latter-day Saint expatriates associated with embassies in the capital city of Addis Ababa. These members worshiped together in their homes. In March 1985 they received supplies from **Elders M. Russell Ballard** and Glenn L. Pace, who joined them for a sacrament meeting in the home of Harry Hadlock. Over the years the Church has donated millions of dollars for famine relief and irrigation development in Ethiopia and neighboring countries.

Ethiopia became part of the newly created **Kenya** Nairobi Mission in 1991. Brother Robert DeWitt, an official in the American embassy, held Ethiopia's first official Church meeting in his home in August 1992. Eugene and Ruth Hilton arrived 28 February 1993 as the country's first missionaries, and the first convert was Koyam Negash. The Church attained legal registration 16 September 1993, and on 5 January 1994 the first official **branch** in Addis Ababa was formed.

Girma Denisa, who joined the Church in 1973 while attending **Ricks College**, became the first Ethiopian branch president, as well as the first Ethiopian missionary. The **seminary** program was instituted in Ethiopia in 1995. In the year 2000 there were 257 members in one branch.

SOURCES

1999–2000 Church Almanac. Salt Lake City: Deseret News, 1998. 316–17.

Oral histories of early Church converts collected by E. Dale LeBaron. Copies at BYU Library, Provo, Utah; LDS Church Historical Library, Salt Lake City, Utah.

E. DALE LEBARON

ETOILE DE DESERET. See L'ETOILE.

EUROPE. In 1837, during some difficult days in **Kirtland**, the **Prophet Joseph Smith** called **Heber C. Kimball** to open a **mission** in **Great Britain**. In just over a month, **Elder** Kimball, **Orson Hyde**, and five other missionaries arrived in **England**; 11 days later they had their first baptisms. On the morning of that day (30 July 1837), the missionaries had a terrible experience with evil spirits and were almost overcome. Joseph Smith later remarked, "When I heard of it, it gave me great joy, for then I knew that the work of God had taken root in that land" (quoted in Whitney, 132).

Within nine months of the beginning of this first **mission** across the

Atlantic, more than 1,500 souls had been baptized into the Church. The mission to England, 1837 to 1838, provided a foundation for an even greater missionary effort in England, and from there radiating to the other nations of Europe. Joseph Smith soon after received a revelation instructing the Twelve to organize and prepare to depart on a mission overseas (D&C 118). Nine **apostles** served together in this second mission to England during 1840 and 1841. At the end of this mission, membership in the **British Isles** stood at more than 5,000, with about 1,000 others who had emigrated to the United States.

Early missionary labors on the continent met with limited success. This was largely due to the lack of religious freedoms, as well as the intense persecution, economic conditions, and political situation in many of the countries of Europe. During the late 1840s, some revolutions and other significant efforts helped to bring about freedom of religion to **Denmark**, the **Netherlands**, and **Switzerland**. Beginning in 1850 Denmark became a land of considerable success for the early missionaries. The gospel was also taken to the other Scandinavian countries, as well as to **Iceland**, **France**, **Germany**, and **Italy**. **Belgium** and the Netherlands followed in the early 1860s. Other countries with more limited freedoms did not receive the missionary message until later: **Hungary** in 1885 and **Romania** in 1899. Although missionaries were appointed in 1843 to **Russia**, they were unable to serve. It was not until 1903 that the land was dedicated for the preaching of the gospel, but even then missionary work was not yet possible.

From the beginning, missionaries taught their converts the importance of gathering to the headquarters of the Church in **America**. By 1900 more than 91,000 members from Europe had heeded the call to gather to **Zion**. The gathering of these members provided great strength to the Church in America, but congregations of **Saints** remained small throughout Europe, where religious persecution increased during the late nineteenth and early twentieth centuries.

In the early 1900s, a number of Church leaders encouraged Saints to stay in their countries rather than emigrate. In 1906 **Joseph F. Smith**, the first to visit Europe while serving as president of the Church, said that the day would come when temples of the Lord would dot the whole of Europe (Richards, 70). It took some time, however, for members to feel comfortable in staying and building the Church in their homelands.

Those Saints who did remain in Europe had to survive great challenges and difficulties, especially those in lands racked with **war** or political strife. Many are the stories of faithful Latter-day Saints sacrificing even their lives when necessary in defending their faith and also in sustaining the governments under which they lived during the two great wars of the twentieth century.

With the resurgence of missionary work in Europe following **World War II**, there was a renewal of emigration; but under President **David O. McKay**, efforts were made to provide members in other lands with the same blessings and opportunities found in the United States, including chapels, local leadership, and especially **temples**. In 1955 Elder **Spencer W. Kimball** told the Saints in Europe: "Stay where you are, you have received the gospel, the blessings will be brought to you, it will not be long until you have **stakes** and the brethren will come across the ocean to visit you. Eventually, temples will come and you will have all the blessings of Zion" (quoted in Kimball, 439). Elder Kimball later stated: "The First Presidency and the Twelve see great wisdom in multiple Zions, many gathering places where the Saints within their own culture and nation can act as a leaven in the building of the kingdom—a kingdom which seeks no earthly rewards or treasures" (quoted in Kimball, 440).

Taking the Church to the people was profoundly represented by the dedicating of temples in Europe, beginning with the **Swiss Temple** in 1955. A temple behind the Iron Curtain was dedicated in Freiberg, East Germany, in 1985. At the end of the twentieth century, additional temples throughout Europe followed, to the rejoicing of the Saints, confirming the pattern of establishing places of gathering in the lands where members live.

Following the fall of **communism** during the last two decades of the twentieth century, missions have been opened in **Yugoslavia**, **Poland**, Hungary, Russia, and other countries of the former eastern bloc. Plans to erect a temple in Kiev, **Ukraine**, were announced in 1998. At the beginning of the year 2000, there were 404,109 members in Europe (including Scandinavia, the United Kingdom, and Ireland), living in 100 stakes and about 57 missions.

SOURCES

Clark, James R., comp. *Messages of the First Presidency of The Church of Jesus Christ of Latter-day Saints.* 6 vols. Salt Lake City: Bookcraft, 1965–75. Vol. 2.

Kimball, Spencer W. *The Teachings of Spencer W. Kimball.* Edited by Edward L. Kimball. Salt Lake City: Bookcraft, 1982.

Richards, LeGrand. "'God Moves in a Mysterious Way.'" *Improvement Era* 73 (December 1970): 69–71.

Van Orden, Bruce A. *Building Zion: The Latter-day Saints in Europe.* Salt Lake City: Deseret Book, 1996.

Whitney, Orson F. *The Life of Heber C. Kimball, an Apostle: The Father and Founder of the British Mission.* Salt Lake City: Bookcraft, 1974.

A. BRYAN WESTON

EUROPEAN MISSION. From 1850 to 1929, the president of the British Mission, often an **apostle**, also supervised and assisted all other **missions** on the continent as president of the European Mission. Headquarters were first in **Liverpool** and then in London. After 1929 the presidencies of the British and European Missions were separated.

In 1946 **Elder Ezra Taft Benson** of the **Quorum** of the Twelve administered relief to the **Saints** during a nine-month term as European Mission president (he returned to the mission in 1964). When his successor, Alma Sonne, was released in 1949, the office was not filled until 1960, when **Alvin R. Dyer** set up a new headquarters in Frankfurt, **Germany.** His office trained **mission presidents** and administered the temporal affairs of the Church, including building, translation and publication, genealogical microfilming, and relations with governments, military, and the media. In 1961 a second supervisory office, the West European Mission, was created with headquarters in London. In 1965 the **First Presidency** announced that members of the Quorum of the Twelve would supervise 12 world **areas**, a move that foreshadowed the creation of area presidencies and ended the need for administrative arrangements like the European Mission.

SOURCES

Jenson, Andrew. *Encyclopedic History of The Church of Jesus Christ of Latter-day Saints.* Salt Lake City: Deseret News, 1941.

Scharffs, Gilbert W. *Mormonism in Germany.* Salt Lake City: Deseret Book, 1970.

Smith, Henry A. "Church Enlarges World Assignments of General Authorities." *Church News,* 19 June 1965, 3–5.

JOHN THOMAS

EVANS, RICHARD L. Elder Richard L. Evans, a member of the **Quorum** of the Twelve **Apostles** (1953–71) and previously a member of the First Council of **Seventy** (1938–53), served as the announcer and writer of the spoken text of the **Tabernacle Choir's** weekly broadcast, *Music and the Spoken Word,* from 1930 to 1971.

Richard Louis Evans was born the youngest of nine children on 23 March 1906 in **Salt Lake City**. His father died in an accident only ten weeks after he was born. His loving mother reared him on principles of sacrifice, courage, and faith.

He served a **mission** in **Europe**, during which he edited the *Millennial Star* and wrote a history of the **British Mission**. Afterwards, he earned his bachelor's and master's degrees from the University of Utah, and on 9 August 1933 he married Alice Ruth Thornley in the Salt Lake Temple. They had four sons. Brother Evans was the managing editor of the *Improvement Era* for 14 years and the senior editor for 21 years. He also directed the **Temple Square** Mission.

Elder Evans was on the Board of Regents of the **University of Utah** and Board of Trustees of **Brigham Young University**. He wrote a regular column for a national newspaper syndicate and published 17 books. As president of Rotary International (1966–67), he visited and spoke in more than 60 countries.

Remembered as the narrating voice for the Tabernacle Choir, Elder Evans began announcing the Choir's radio program when he was 24 years old. He continued this weekly assignment as writer, producer, and announcer until his death 41 years later, 1 November 1971, in **Salt Lake City**.

SOURCES

Evans, Richard L., Jr. *Richard L. Evans—The Man and the Message.* Salt Lake City: Bookcraft, 1973. 221.

Hanks, Marion D. "Elder Richard L. Evans, Apostle of the Lord." *Ensign* 1 (December 1971): 2–11.

LLOYD D. NEWELL

EVENING AND THE MORNING STAR, THE. Publication of the first Church newspaper, *The Evening and the Morning Star,* began in June 1832 at **Independence, Missouri**, and the last number was published in September 1834 at **Kirtland, Ohio**. After 14 numbers had been published, **Jackson County** citizens wrecked the **W. W. Phelps** printing office on 20 July 1833. Five months later, **Oliver Cowdery** resumed publication of the **periodical** in Kirtland, where he published an additional ten numbers.

The *Star* included 18 sections of the **Book of Commandments**, as well as extracts from the **Book of Mormon** and the **book of Moses**. It also addressed subjects such as the **organization of the Church**, the **law of consecration**, and the **vision of the three degrees of glory**. Its editors also presented commentaries on the Old and New Testaments.

From time to time the paper provided special instructions to the **Saints** concerning their **gathering** to **Zion** and their application of gospel principles. Special serials on "the Millennium," "the gospel," "the rise and progress of the Church," and the "second coming of the Savior" also appeared in the paper's pages. **Hymns** and **poetry** added additional flavor to the *Star.*

Commentaries on world governments, politics, and natural catastrophes kept the **Saints** abreast of world situations, and letters from missionaries kept them aware of the growth of the Church in **Zion** and throughout the **United States.**

Following the expulsion from Jackson County, Missouri, in 1833, the last 10 numbers of the *Star* detailed Mormon **persecution** and suffering at the hands of **Missouri** residents, as well as efforts for **redress** from the Missouri legislature and courts. Between January 1835 and October 1836 24 numbers were reprinted under the abbreviated title *Evening and Morning Star.*

SOURCE

Crawley, Peter. *A Descriptive Bibliography of the Mormon Church.* Vol. 1 (1830–1847). Provo, Utah: Religious Studies Center, Brigham Young University, 1997. 32–34, 50–51.

CLARK V. JOHNSON

EXODUS. See PIONEERS.

EXPLORER PROGRAM. See BOY SCOUTS.

EXPLORATION, MORMON.

Following the **Saints'** arrival in the **Salt Lake Valley**, **Brigham Young** straightway put forth an exploration program for the **Great Basin** to ascertain its lands and resources for large-scale colonization and economic development. For three decades thereafter the Church appointed, outfitted, and sustained several exploration and colonization parties. This system was an anomaly in western settlement, its social planning and organization a striking contrast to the spontaneity and individualism that propelled most other settlers.

The earliest **Mormon** explorations were of the Wasatch Front valleys to find settlement sites that together formed what is labeled the "inner cordon." But explorations and **colonization** extended outward, too, far beyond these valleys. With the 1855 **general conference**, efforts were stepped up to explore and colonize outlying areas such as **Las Vegas** and **Carson Valley, Nevada**; Elk Mountain (Moab), **Utah**; **Forts Bridger** and Supply, **Wyoming**; and Limhi Valley, Idaho—forming a supposed "outer cordon" of settlements.

Exploration and colonization also linked the Salt Lake Valley with southern **California**, creating an economic artery by a string of settlements—the "**Mormon Corridor**." By edict of the **Council of Fifty**, **Parley P. Pratt** directed many of the early explorations, and his reports led to most of the colonization sites (about 100 in the first decade) and points of resource production (like the **Iron Mission** near present Cedar City, Utah).

Mormon explorations decreased significantly after the **Utah War** (1857) with increased non-Mormon governmental control and the Saints' own waning zeal. The year 1860 brought a cursory survey of the **Uinta Basin**, and in 1876 Brigham Young sent a party to reconnoiter and colonize along **Arizona**'s Little Colorado River. By then much of the forbidding region was known, with the Saints' efforts in exploring and colonizing it a remarkable and unique endeavor.

SOURCES

Arrington, Leonard J. *Great Basin Kingdom*. Cambridge, Mass.: Harvard University Press, 1958.

Campbell, Eugene E. "Brigham Young's Outer Cordon: A Reappraisal." *Utah Historical Quarterly* 31 (Summer 1973): 220–53.

Hunter, Milton R. *Brigham Young, the Colonizer.* Salt Lake City: Deseret News Press, 1940.

Peterson, Charles S. *Take Up Your Mission: Mormon Colonizing along the Little Colorado, 1870–1900*. Provo, Utah: Brigham Young University Press, 1973.

FRED R. GOWANS AND S. MATTHEW DESPAIN

EXPLORATION, U.S. GOVERNMENT. U.S. military personnel carried out extensive **Great Basin** explorations during the mid-nineteenth century. Their maps, the roads they established, and the data they gathered helped local Latter-day Saints who could not have afforded such studies themselves. These surveyors became a link between exploration by **Indians** and fur trappers and later civilian scientists. Howard Stansbury and John W. Gunnison, members of the Army Corps of Topographical Engineers, came to the **Salt Lake Valley** in 1849. They surveyed the valley, studied the resident Indian tribes and the **Saints**, located a supply route north to the emigrant trail, and examined local natural resources. Their party completed surveys of the Jordan River and Utah Lake and was the first known to circumnavigate the Great Salt Lake by land. Returning to the East in 1850, they established a route later used by the Overland Stage, the **Pony Express**, and the Union Pacific **Railroad**. Gunnison wrote a book presenting an objective view of the Saints based on his year's stay in **Salt Lake City**. Commissioned in 1853 to lead the survey of a possible railroad route along the 38th parallel, Gunnison and seven of his men were attacked and killed by the Pahvant Indians along the Sevier River.

Between 1853 and 1869, further explorations took place: Edward G. Beckwith completed Gunnison's work and additional Great Basin railroad surveys; Lt. Colonel Edward J. Steptoe supervised some of the improvements along the **Mormon Corridor** road; Corpsman James Simpson located wagon roads east toward **Fort Bridger** and Denver and west to **California**; Joseph Ives and geologist John Newberry studied the plateaus of northern **Arizona** and southern **Utah**, including the floor of the Grand Canyon; and George Wheeler explored the area south of the 40th parallel through southeastern **Nevada** and western Utah, being the first since the mountain men to make this north-south crossing of the Great Basin.

In 1869 former military man John Wesley Powell and his party floated the Green and Colorado Rivers to the mouth of the Virgin River. Two years later he repeated this voyage with a sizable appropriation from Congress to map and study the Colorado Plateau region. He employed several Utahns in this second exploration, including Indian missionary **Jacob Hamblin**, who helped provision Powell's party. This extensive study was headquartered in Kanab, Utah, and was completed in 1879. In the process of their survey, the group named many prominent geographical sites in southeastern Utah.

Sources

Bartlett, Richard A. *Great Surveys of the American West.* Norman, Okla.: University of Oklahoma Press, 1962.

Goetzman, William H. *Army Exploration in the American West, 1803–1863.* New Haven, Conn.: Yale University Press, 1959.

Schubert, Frank N. *Vanguard of Expansion, Army Engineers in the Trans-Mississippi West, 1819–1879.* Washington, D.C.: Historical Division, Office of Administrative Services, Office of the Chief of Engineers, 1980.

Vivian Linford Talbot and Fred R. Gowans

EXPOSITOR. See NAUVOO EXPOSITOR.

EXTERMINATION ORDER. Following nearly three months of civil conflict in northern **Missouri**, on 27 October 1838 word reached Missouri Governor **Lilburn W. Boggs** in Jefferson City that the **Mormons** had attacked and annihilated a contingent of Ray County militia under the command of Captain **Samuel Bogart** on **Crooked River** in Ray County. Although the reports were spurious and greatly exaggerated, Boggs believed that the Mormons had perpetrated the conflict and that they were coming out in open rebellion against the state of Missouri by deliberately attacking state militia. This fact emerges clearly in the governor's letter, dated 27 June 1838 and known in Mormon historical circles as the "extermination order," which called for General John B. Clark of the state militia to march against the Mormons at **Far West**. "The Mormons [are] in the attitude of open and avowed defiance of the laws, and of having made open war upon the people of this state," he wrote. Hence, his order stated that they "must be treated as enemies, and must be exterminated or driven from the State . . . for the public peace." The militia moved quickly. Within three days 2,500 troops were positioned on the outskirts of Far West, calling for the surrender of the Mormons and demanding that they comply with the governor's mandate. Faced with no other alternative, on 31 October the Mormons capitulated and agreed to leave. During the winter and spring of 1839, nearly the entire Latter-day Saint community made their way east, where they obtained refuge and sanctuary with **Illinois**'s more hospitable citizens.

Interestingly, the first definition of the word *exterminate*, as defined in Webster's *American Dictionary of the English Language*, published in 1828, reads, "to drive from within the limits or borders." Therefore, contrary to popular opinion, the governor may not necessarily have been ordering the state militia or the citizens of Missouri to murder the Latter-day Saints. Given this definition, the order may have been interpreted to mean that the Mormons "must be exterminated or [*in other words*] driven from the State . . . for the public peace."

In the spirit of reconciliation, on 25 June 1976 while addressing an **RLDS** reunion of the members of the Far West **Stake** at Stewartsville, Missouri, Governor Christopher Bond formally rescinded Boggs's mandate and expressed personal regret "for the injustice and undue suffering which was caused by [the] 1838 order."

SOURCES

Baugh, Alexander L. "A Call to Arms: The 1838 Mormon Defense of Northern Missouri." Ph.D. diss., Brigham Young University, 1996.

————. "Missouri Governor Lilburn W. Boggs and the Mormons." *John Whitmer Historical Association Journal* 18 (1998): 111–32.

Le Sueur, Stephen C. *The 1838 Mormon War in Missouri.* Columbia, Mo.: University of Missouri Press, 1987.

ALEXANDER L. BAUGH

EXTRACTION PROGRAM. See FAMILY HISTORY.

EYRING, HENRY. Selected by *Chemical and Engineering News* as one of "the top 75 distinguished contributors to the chemical enterprise" during the magazine's 75-year lifetime, Henry Eyring also exhibited a profound commitment to the Church. He was born 20 February 1901 in **Colonia Juárez**, one of the Mormon **Mexican colonies**. The **family** moved to **Arizona** in 1912 to avoid the Mexican revolution. Henry earned a scholarship to the University of Arizona, where he received his bachelor's and master's degrees in mining engineering and metallurgy, respectively. In 1925 he went to Berkeley and obtained his Ph.D. in chemistry in 1927. After a brief period as an instructor of chemistry at the University of **Wisconsin**, he taught for 15 years at Princeton until 1946, when he became dean of the graduate school and professor of chemistry at the **University of Utah**.

His publications number more than 600. He was awarded 15 U.S. and international honorary degrees and received 18 prizes that include the National Medal of Science, the Priestly and Gibbs Medals, the Berzelius Medal of the Swedish Academy (awarded only once every 50 years), and **Israel's** Wolf Prize. He was a member of the National Academy of Sciences and served as president of the American Chemical Society and the American Association for the Advancement of Science.

Henry married Mildred Bennion and raised three sons, Edward M., Henry B., and Harden R. Following the death of Mildred, he married Winifred Brennan. His Church work included service as a **branch** president, **district** president, **stake** high councilor, and member of the general board of the **Sunday School**. He wrote two books, *The Faith of a Scientist* and *Reflections of a Scientist,* which record his views concerning the integration of twentieth-century science with Latter-day Saint theology. Henry Eyring died 26 December 1981.

SOURCES

"C&EN's Top 75—Contributors to the Chemical Enterprise." *Chemical and Engineering News* (12 January 1998): 171–75.

Eyring, Henry. *Reflections of a Scientist.* Edited by Harden Romney Eyring. Salt Lake City: Deseret Book, 1983.

HARDEN R. EYRING

EYRING, HENRY B. Henry Bennion Eyring, **apostle** and educator, was born 31 May 1933 in Princeton, **New Jersey**, the second of three sons. His parents, Dr. **Henry Eyring** and Mildred Bennion, moved from Princeton to **Salt Lake City** in 1946, where Dr. Eyring became one of the **University of Utah**'s most distinguished teachers and researchers. Henry attended East High School and then the University of Utah, where he graduated in 1955 with a B.S. in physics.

After college, Brother Eyring served as an officer in the U.S. Air Force and, during that time, as a **district** missionary in Albuquerque, **New Mexico**. Upon his release from the military, he entered the Harvard Business School, from which he earned M.B.A. and D.B.A. degrees. In June 1962, he married Kathleen Johnson of Palo Alto, **California**. They moved to that area, and from 1962 to 1971 Dr. Eyring taught at the Stanford Graduate School of Business. In 1964 and 1965, he was a visiting faculty fellow at the Sloan School of Management at the Massachusetts Institute of Technology. During their years at Stanford and MIT, the Eyrings were blessed with three sons, Henry Johnson, Stuart, and Matthew.

In 1971 while Brother Eyring was serving as **bishop** of the Stanford **Ward**, he was appointed president of **Ricks College** in **Rexburg, Idaho**. During their time in Rexburg, the Eyrings had another son, John. In 1977, Brother Eyring became deputy commissioner of the **Church Educational System** and the **family** moved to Bountiful, **Utah**, where two daughters, Elizabeth and Mary, were born. Brother Eyring served as deputy commissioner and then commissioner in the Church Educational System until April 1985, when he was called into the **presiding bishopric**. He served for seven years as first counselor to Bishop **Robert D. Hales**. In 1992, Bishop Eyring was called to the First Quorum of the **Seventy** and, for the second time, he became the Church's commissioner of education—a responsibility he continued to carry as an apostle.

On 1 April 1995, **Elder** Eyring was sustained to the Quorum of the Twelve Apostles, filling a vacancy created by the passing of President **Howard W. Hunter**. He was ordained an apostle five days later under the hands of President **Gordon B. Hinckley**.

SOURCE

"Elder Henry B. Eyring." *Ensign* 25 (May 1995): 105–6.

HENRY J. EYRING

TIMES AND SEASONS.

"Truth will prevail."

VOL. III. No. 9.]   CITY OF NAUVOO, ILL. MARCH, 1, 1842.   [Whole No. 45.

A FAC-SIMILE FROM THE BOOK OF ABRAHAM.
NO. 1.

EXPLANATION OF THE ABOVE CUT.

FIG. 1,—The Angel of the Lord.

2. Abraham, fastened upon an Altar.

3. The Idolatrous Priest of Elkenah attempting to offer up Abraham as a sacrifice.

4. The Altar for sacrifice, by the Idolatrous Priests, standing before the Gods of Elkenah, Libnah, Mahmachrah, Korash, and Pharaoh.

5. The Idolatrous God of Elkenah.

6. The   "   "   " Libnah.

7. The   "   "   " Mahmachrah.

8. The   "   "   " Korash.

9. The   "   "   " Pharaoh.

10. Abraham in Egypt.

11. Designed to represent the pillars of Heaven, as understood by the Egyptians.

12. Raukeeyang, signifying expanse, or the firmament, over our heads; but in this case, in relation to this sub̲ject, the Egyptians meant it to signify Shamau, to be high, or the heavens: answering to the Hebrew word, Shaumahyeem.

FACSIMILES. Joseph Smith published facsimiles from the book of Abraham in the *Times and Seasons* in March 1842. The facsimiles are now included in the Pearl of Great Price.

FACSIMILES. See **BOOK OF ABRAHAM.**

FAIRBANKS, AVARD. Latter-day Saint sculptor Avard Fairbanks (1897–1987) studied at the Art Student League in **New York** at the age of 13, and then at the Ecole Nationale des Beaux Artes in Paris. At the age of 17, he became the youngest artist ever admitted to the French Salon. He would later earn degrees from the **University of Utah,** Yale, and the University of **Michigan.** Fairbanks taught at several universities, including the University of Utah, where he organized the College of Fine Arts.

His Latter-day Saint sculptural works include the **Winter Quarters monument,** the *Restoration of the Aaronic Priesthood,* friezes on the **Hawaii Temple** and the **Brigham Young University** library, and the angel **Moroni** statue on the **temples** in **Washington, D.C.;** Denver, Colo.; West Jordan, Utah; and Mexico City, Mexico.

Among his non-Church monuments are Lycurgus, the ancient law-giver in Sparta (for which he was knighted by King Paul of **Greece**); the **Pony Express; Pioneer Family** (at the state capitol in Bismark); Daniel Jackling (at the **Utah** State Capitol); Prime Minister of **Canada** McKenzie King (at the Parliament Buildings in Ottawa); **George Washington** (at the **Washington** State Capitol Building), **Abraham Lincoln** (at Ford Theater and the U.S. Supreme Court), and John Burke, Abraham Lincoln, Esther Morris, and Marcus Whitman in the National Capitol Building.

SOURCE

Fairbanks, Eugene F. *A Sculptor's Testimony in Bronze and Stone, Sacred Sculpture of Avard T. Fairbanks.* Salt Lake City: Publishers Press, 1994.

RICHARD G. OMAN

FALKLAND ISLANDS. Located in the South Atlantic, the Falkland Islands are claimed both by **Great Britain** and by **Argentina**, which names them las Islas Malvinas. At the beginning of the year 2000, there were 11 Latter-day **Saints** in one **branch**.

RICHARD O. COWAN

FAMILY. Latter-day scriptures affirm that family relationships can endure beyond the grave and, in fact, are a basic requirement for exaltation in the highest degree of the celestial kingdom (D&C 131:1–4; 132:7–21). When grounded in Christian virtues, the family is the vehicle by which individuals are brought to **Christ**. **Marriage** and family are matters of covenant. When parents honor their covenants, protecting and nurturing each other and their children as Christ has commanded, family relationships will continue after mortality.

In some dispensations, **plural marriage**, under certain circumstances, has been permitted. In the nineteenth century it was authorized by revelation (D&C 132:34–66) but was later suspended as announced in the **Manifesto** of 1890.

The family, from the time of **Adam**, has been patriarchal, which means the husband and father is called to bear an obligation to bless his wife and children, and is to do so "only by persuasion, by long-suffering, by gentleness and meekness, and by love unfeigned; by kindness, and pure knowledge . . . and without guile" (D&C 121:41–42). **Brigham Young** noted, "It is the right of the head of a family to get revelations to guide and govern his family" (*HC*, 7:286). The wife and mother is to stand as a partner to a righteous husband; her prime calling is to nurture the children. Together, parents are united to protect and nourish the family as a shepherd guards the sheep (John 10:11, 14; D&C 50:44), or as a "hen gathereth her chickens under her wings" (Matt. 23:37).

It is possible for a father to dishonor his obligations and responsibilities. When he neglects family members, or actually mistreats them, he is guilty of what the **scriptures** call "unrighteous dominion" (D&C 121:39). In such cases "the heavens withdraw themselves; the Spirit of the Lord is grieved; and when it is withdrawn, Amen to the **priesthood** or the authority of that man" (D&C 121:37). President **Joseph F. Smith** counseled men regarding family conduct: "Fathers, if you wish your children to be taught in the principles of the gospel, if you wish them to love the truth and understand it, if you wish them to be obedient to and united with you, love them! And prove to them that you do love them by your every word or act to them. For your own sake . . . when you speak or talk to them, do it not in anger, do it not harshly, in a condemning spirit. Speak to them kindly; . . . use no lash and no violence, but . . . approach them with reason, with persuasion and love unfeigned. . . . You can't do it any other way" (Smith, 316). Consistent with this advice and in light of an 1831 revelation directing parents to teach their children (D&C 68:25, 28), President Smith and his counselors in 1915 encouraged the inauguration of regular **family home evenings**. This activity received further emphasis in the 1960s under President **David O. McKay** as part of **priesthood correlation**.

The 1995 **Proclamation on the Family** reflects the Church's commitment to these principles: "The family is ordained of God. Marriage between man and woman is essential to His eternal plan. Children are entitled to birth within the bonds of matrimony, and to be reared by a father and a mother who honor marital vows with complete fidelity. Happiness in family life is most likely to be achieved when founded upon the teachings of the Lord Jesus Christ" (*Ensign*, 102).

SOURCES

"The Family: A Proclamation to the World." *Ensign* 25 (November 1995): 102.

Roberts, B. H. *A Comprehensive History of The Church of Jesus Christ of Latter-day Saints, Century One.* 6 vols. Salt Lake City: The Church of Jesus Christ of Latter-day Saints, 1930. 7:286.

Smith, Joseph. *History of The Church of Jesus Christ of Latter-day Saints [HC].* Edited by B. H. Roberts. 2d ed. rev. 7 vols. Salt Lake City: The Church of Jesus Christ of Latter-day Saints, 1932–51. 1:60–61.

Smith, Joseph. F. *Gospel Doctrine.* Salt Lake City: Deseret Book, 1977. 316.

TERRANCE D. OLSON

FAMILY, A PROCLAMATION TO THE WORLD. See **PROCLAMATION ON THE FAMILY.**

FAMILY HISTORY. The **Prophet Joseph Smith** taught that for Latter-day **Saints** "the greatest responsibility in this world that God has laid upon us is to seek after our dead" (Smith, 356). In the **general conference** of 14 April 1894, President **Wilford Woodruff** taught: "We want the Latter-day Saints from this time to trace their genealogies as far back as they can, and be sealed to their fathers and mothers. Have children sealed to their parents, and run this chain through as far as you can get it" (Durham, 157). On 14 November 1894, the Church founded the **Genealogical Society of Utah**, which was dedicated to gathering records of forebears into a central library and teaching Church members and others how to discover ancestors. The Society was the forerunner of today's Family History Department and the **Family History Library** of the Church.

In 1938 the Genealogical Society began microfilming original records and making the films available to researchers in the Genealogical Society Library. In 1998 nearly two million rolls of microfilm were accessible at the Family History Library and at more than 3,000 Church-sponsored **Family History Centers** worldwide.

Church leaders used several means to promote genealogy and to help members find their ancestors. The Genealogical Society of Utah published The *Utah Genealogical and Historical Magazine* from 1910 to 1940, and the **Sunday Schools** of the Church past and present have taught **family** history courses. Teachers used manuals like **Archibald F. Bennett's** *Adventures in Research: Genealogical Training Class Sunday School Lessons.* Until 1967, **stakes** were encouraged to sponsor genealogical conferences. From 1966 to 1977 **Brigham Young University** and the Church sponsored annual **priesthood** genealogical seminars. Since 1978 BYU has sponsored annual genealogy and family history conferences in **Provo.** At least by 1912, genealogy classes were offered to Brigham Young University students and today are available at **Ricks College** (later BYU–Idaho), and many **institutes of religion.** BYU is the only university in the **United States** offering a B.A. degree in genealogy and family history.

In The Church of Jesus Christ of Latter-day Saints, the term *genealogy* was replaced by the term *family history* in 1987. **Elder Boyd K. Packer** explained these changes: "The word 'genealogy' often suggests a need for professional training. We hope the change in name to Family History, coupled with simplified materials and procedures, will make the work less technical and more appealing to members of the Church" (Packer).

Since 1970 the Church has used computers to help its members locate kindred dead. At the end of the twentieth century the Church's **FamilySearch**™ program, as well as Internet and CD resources, provided access to facts about millions of deceased persons in just seconds. **Personal Ancestral File 3.0®** and PAF Companion 2.0® allowed Latter-day Saints to create family records on home computers and share genealogical information with relatives using printed or electronic reports.

SOURCES

Allen, James B., Jessie L. Embry, and Kaulile Mehr. *Hearts turned to Fathers: A History of the Genealogical Society of Utah, 1894–1994.* Provo, Utah: BYU Studies. 1995. 77.

Bennett, Archibald F. *Adventures in Research: Genealogical Training Class Sunday School Lessons*. Salt Lake City: Deseret Sunday School Union Board, 1943.

Packer, Boyd K. "Name Change, Simplification for LDS Ancestral Research Program." News Release. 10 August 1987. Salt Lake City: The Church of Jesus Christ of Latter-day Saints Public Communications Department.

Smith, Joseph. *Teachings of the Prophet Joseph Smith*. Selected by Joseph Fielding Smith. Salt Lake City: Deseret Book, 1970.

Woodruff, Wilford. *The Discourses of Wilford Woodruff*. Complied by G. Homer Durham. Salt Lake City: Bookcraft, 1946.

RAYMOND S. WRIGHT

FAMILY HISTORY CENTERS. Family History Centers, which are branch libraries of the **Family History Library** in **Salt Lake City**, had been established in more than 3,000 locations worldwide by 1998. The **Genealogical Society of Utah** Library—known as the Family History Library as of 1987—was founded in 1894, and in 1938 it began to microfilm original Church records, vital records, censuses, probates, military and court records, as well as many other types of documents. These microfilmed records were originally available to researchers only at the library of the Utah Genealogical Society in Salt Lake City. In 1964 leaders of the Genealogical Society decided to circulate microfilms to branch libraries housed in Latter-day Saint **stake centers**. The first such library was a test site established at **Brigham Young University** in May 1964. **Logan, Utah**, became home to the second branch library in October of the same year. At the end of the twentieth century branch libraries were known as Family History Centers and served some two and a half million visitors each year. Family History Centers are staffed with volunteers, and most users are not Latter-day **Saints**. Each center has a collection of reference materials, microfilm readers, and, in most cases, computers with access to **FamilySearch®**, **Personal Ancestral File®**, and genealogical resources on CD.

SOURCES

Allen, James B., Jessie L. Embry, and Kaulile Mehr. *Hearts turned to Fathers: A History of the Genealogical Society of Utah, 1894–1994*. Provo, Utah: BYU Studies. 1995. 187–90, 260–84.

RAYMOND S. WRIGHT

FAMILY HISTORY LIBRARY. The Family History Library of The Church of **Jesus Christ** of Latter-day **Saints** was founded under sponsorship of the Church in 1894 as the **Genealogical Society of Utah** Library. Its **mission** remains focused upon collecting resources to aid Latter-day Saints in locating ancestors. About 800,000 visitors enter its doors every year to search for **family** members in original records copied upon some two million rolls of microfilm and in about 300,000 volumes of books. The Family History Department's international microfilming program, begun in 1938, provides a growing number of microfilmed records to library users. It is the largest genealogical library in the world in terms of its number of resources.

The first genealogical library was in a room of the **Church Historian's Office** at 58 East South Temple in **Salt Lake City**. The library's need to accommodate more resources and patrons led to several moves, each time into a facility larger than the old one: the entire third floor of the new Church Administration Building, opened at 47 East South **Temple** in 1917; the **Joseph F. Smith** Memorial Building at 80 North Main Street in 1934; the former Montgomery Ward department store at 107 South Main in 1962; and in November of 1973, the four-story west wing of the new **Church Office Building** at 50 East North Temple became the library's home. Twelve years later, in 1985, the library moved into its own building at 35 North West Temple. The library's name has changed since its founding. In 1944 it became simply The Genealogical Society Library; in 1976, the Genealogical Library; and in 1987, the Family History Library.

SOURCE

Allen, James B., Jessie L. Embry, and Kaulile Mehr. *Hearts turned to Fathers: A History of the Genealogical Society of Utah, 1894–1994.* Provo, Utah: BYU Studies. 1995. 46, 84, 123–24, 195–96.

RAYMOND S. WRIGHT

FAMILY HOME EVENING. Family home evening is a weekly gathering of family members for spiritual devotionals and family recreation. It began in the Granite **Stake** in **Salt Lake City**, and was known as the home evening gathering. After the program was reviewed by the **First Presidency** in 1915, President **Joseph F. Smith** announced the inauguration of a home evening program churchwide. This program was described as a time when parents would gather their children and teach them the word of the Lord. The program suggested that families participate in praying, singing hymns, reading scriptures, discussing family topics, and reviewing family duties; it even suggested serving refreshments. Church leaders were urged to set aside at least one evening a month for home evening, and no other activities were to conflict with the new program. With this announcement, President Smith promised: "If the **Saints** obey this counsel, we promise that great blessings will result. Love at home and obedience to parents will increase. Faith will be developed in the hearts of the youth of Israel, and they will gain power to combat the evil influence and temptations which beset them" (*Messages,* 339). Two years later, home evening was introduced to the **missions** throughout the Church.

The emphasis on home evening gradually declined until 1964, when the First Presidency announced that all parents would be provided a home evening manual and shown a filmstrip outlining the program's format. Rather than a monthly gathering, the emphasis was now to gather families weekly. During this period of renewed emphasis, the current title, "family home evening," was coined. In 1970, Monday was announced as the designated night for family home evening, and Church leaders were instructed not to schedule competing activities. The First Presidency authorized **ward** leaders to organize **single adults** not living at home into family home evening groups in 1973, with an individual designated as the leader.

Additional changes to family home evening were made in 1985, when manuals were replaced with a family home evening resource book. Video vignettes to supplement family home evening lessons were produced in 1987. family home evening has ample supplementary material, continued Church endorsement, and many prophetic promises.

SOURCES

Clark, James R., comp. *Messages of the First Presidency of The Church of Jesus Christ of Latter-day Saints.* 6 vols. Salt Lake City: Bookcraft, 1965–75. 4:339; 5:88–89, 191–92.

Lee, Harold B. "The Home Evening." *Improvement Era* 70 (January 1967): 22–23.

MATTHEW O. RICHARDSON

FAMILYSEARCH™. FamilySearch™ is a computer system and set of files and programs developed by the LDS Church to help simplify family history research internationally. It is available on compact discs and on the Internet at the Church's FamilySearch™ Internet **Genealogy** Service (www.familysearch.org). The following resource files are on compact disc:

- **Ancestral File**, containing more than 35 million names lineage-linked into families and pedigrees. Both living and deceased individuals are included.

- **International Genealogical Index**, an index more than 600 million names of deceased individuals submitted to the Family History Department. It also includes names that have been copied from vital records and other sources from around the world.

- U.S. Social Security Death Index identifies deceased persons from about 1962 to 1998.

- U.S. Military Index identifies servicemen and women who died in the Korean and **Vietnam wars**.

- Scottish Church Records, an index to Scottish church records dating from the late 1500s through about 1854.

- **Family History Library** Catalog (FHLC) identifies more than two million rolls of microfilm and thousands of books and other sources available at the Family History Library in **Salt Lake City**. FHLC serves as a guide to materials housed in the main library that can identify and link families.

- LDS Options (Ordinance Index and **TempleReady**), an index and a program that assist Latter-day **Saints** in providing **temple ordinances**.

FamilySearch™ on the Internet includes the following files and databases:

- Ancestral File, genealogies of deceased individuals only

- International Genealogical Index

- Pedigree Resource File

- Family History Library Catalog (FHLC)

- Research Guidance, a tool and a genealogical reference library of information containing 150 Family History Department research outlines that describe records in countries, states, and provinces, letter-writing guides, a glossary of word meanings, and other useful reference aids.

- **Family History Centers**, a list of more than 3,400 family history centers located throughout the world.

- Collaboration Lists for registering users of the new Internet service. Here users are able to preserve their genealogical records, contact other researchers, or add a Website to FamilySearch™ Internet. They can also e-mail others through family history mailing lists.

- "Search for Ancestors" allows those using the program to enter their ancestors' names or search by just a surname. Two other ways to search the linked Internet sites are "Keyword Search" and "Custom Search." These searches also check Research Guidance for pertinent references.

Internet Websites are categorized by topics, such as Census, Family Histories and Genealogies, Libraries, Migration, Military, Places, Vital Records, and others. This will lead the user to many different Internet sites for that particular subject. Researchers are able to give the developers feedback and offer suggestions about the site, learn more about the LDS Church, and learn about other family history products available on compact disc from the Family History Department. Some programs may be downloaded over the Internet, such as **Personal Ancestral File** 4.0.

KIP SPERRY

FARMS. See FOUNDATION FOR ANCIENT RESEARCH AND MORMON STUDIES.

FARMS REVIEW OF BOOKS. In 1989 the **Foundation for Ancient Research and Mormon Studies (FARMS)** began the annual publication of the *Review of Books on the Book of Mormon.* In order to accommodate the need to review an increasing number of books on the **Book of Mormon** and related subjects, the *Review* changed to a biannual publication in 1994 and then in 1996 changed its name to the *FARMS Review of Books.* The new name reflects the wider range of books and material that are increasingly being dealt with in the periodical, although the primary focus continues to be on the Book of Mormon.

M. GERALD BRADFORD

FARNSWORTH, PHILO T. Philo Taylor Farnsworth, world-renowned Latter-day Saint inventor and "the father of television," was born 19 August 1906 near Beaver, **Utah**. By age 12 he had moved to **Idaho**, and when he was 19 he married Elma "Pem" Gardner. They were the parents of four children.

At an early age Philo was familiar with the principles governing electronics, enabling him to visualize concepts based on scientific principles.

Many of his early dreams later became inventions. At age 14 he envisioned an early television set, and within months he had working designs completed to show its feasibility. By 1927 he developed vacuum tubes and was able to transmit and receive recognizable images on an early television prototype; before his 25th year, he lectured on research principles that are still in use within the television industry.

His accomplishments while working on television research included over 150 patents. His inventions included the first electronic microscope, infrared scopes for nighttime surveillance, electronic tubes for sonar underwater travel, radar screens, and air traffic control scopes.

Farnsworth died near **Salt Lake City** on 11 March 1971 at age 64.

SOURCE

Farnsworth, Elma G. "Pem." *Distant Vision: Romance and Discovery on an Invisible Frontier.* Salt Lake City: Pemberly Kent, 1990.

DAVID F. BOONE

FARR, LORIN. Lorin Farr, mayor, pioneer, Church leader, businessman, and personal friend of the **Prophet Joseph Smith**, was born 27 July 1820 in Waterford, **Vermont**, to Winslow Farr and Olive Hovey Freeman. When Lorin was eight years old he moved with his parents to Charleston, Vermont. While living there in 1832, his family was taught the gospel by two future **apostles—Lyman F. Johnson** and **Orson Pratt**. Lorin joined the Church that year along with other members of his **family.**

In 1837 his father sold their farm and the Farrs gathered with the Saints in **Kirtland, Ohio**. The following year, when Lorin was only 17, he walked to **Far West, Missouri**, where he lived with Joseph Smith for several months until the remainder of his family arrived. While he was staying in the Prophet's home, the Church experienced some of its worst **persecution**. During that time Lorin often slept on the floor by Joseph with a gun and sword at his side to help protect the Prophet from mob violence.

Lorin moved with his family to **Quincy, Illinois**, for a short time, and in the spring of 1840 the family settled in **Nauvoo**. In 1842 he served a mission in **Wisconsin** and **Illinois**, and the following year in the middle and eastern states. In 1845 Lorin married Nancy B. Chase. Like many Church leaders he practiced plural marriage; eventually he had five wives and 36 children.

In 1847 he went with the Church to the **Salt Lake Valley**. In 1850

Brigham Young called him to move to Ogden and preside over the Saints there. He was the first mayor of that city and stake president of the Weber Stake, and served in both of these positions for the next two decades. He was also a member of the first territorial legislature and one of the main contractors for the Central Pacific Railroad. Lorin Farr died 12 January 1909 in Hot Springs, Weber County, Utah.

SOURCES

Jenson, Andrew. *Latter-day Saint Biographical Encyclopedia.* 4 vols. 1901–36. Reprint, Salt Lake City: Western Epics, 1971. 1:749.

Pardoe, Thomas Earl. *Lorin Farr, Pioneer.* Provo, Utah: Brigham Young University, 1953.

ARNOLD K. GARR

FAR WEST, MISSOURI. Far West was established in Caldwell County approximately 60 miles northeast of Independence, Missouri. In 1833 and 1834, when the Saints had to leave Jackson County, some settled temporarily in Clay and Ray Counties. But with growing unrest, the local citizens were concerned that the Saints would stay permanently in their areas. On 29 June 1836, a mass meeting was held at the Liberty courthouse, where the local citizens passed a series of resolutions calling upon the Saints to withdraw from the county. The northern part of Missouri was sparsely settled and believed by most to be worthless (*CHC* 1:418), so Alexander W. Doniphan, a representative for Clay County to the Missouri legislature, proposed that a "Mormon" county be created out of the northern part of Ray County. Fearing that the organization of a county, especially for the "Mormons," might meet with opposition, the legislature created a bill that formed two counties out of the northern part of what was Ray County, one to be named Caldwell, and the other Daviess. This passed without much opposition (*CHC* 1:419).

William W. Phelps and John Whitmer selected the 640-acre site for Far West, which served as the county seat for Caldwell County. The agreement with the few people in the area was that the Mormons would also purchase the land owned by local residents. By the fall of 1838, the Saints had bought about 250,000 acres and had built nearly 200 homes, several dry goods stores, three family groceries, half a dozen blacksmith shops, and two hotels. On 26 April 1838, the Prophet Joseph Smith received section 115 of the Doctrine and Covenants, instructing that the city of Far West was to "be a holy and consecrated land unto [the Lord]; and it shall be called most holy, for the ground upon which thou standest is holy" (v. 7). In this same section of the Doctrine and Covenants, the Lord also commanded his people to build a **temple**. It was also here in Far West that the official name of the Church was designated: The Church of **Jesus Christ** of Latter-day Saints (v. 4).

Far West became the model for the general plan of laying out the cities of **Zion**. The town site was made one mile square, divided by streets running at right angles into regular blocks. A large public square was laid off in the center of the town, designed for a temple site and other public buildings (*CHC* 1:424). Though in 1836 Far West was a wilderness that few wanted, by 1838 the population numbered more than 5,000, and most were Latter-day Saints. During the winter of 1838 to 1839, members of the Church were forced to flee the city in consequence of the **extermination order** issued by Governor **Lilburn W. Boggs** on 27 October 1838.

SOURCE

Roberts, B. H. *A Comprehensive History of The Church of Jesus Christ of Latter-day Saints, Century One.* 6 vols. Salt Lake City: The Church of Jesus Christ of Latter-day Saints, 1930.

RALPH M. MCAFFEE

FAR WEST RECORD. The **Far West** Record, a compilation of minutes taken at various meetings of the Church from 1830 to 1844, provides rare insight into early Latter-day Saint history. Included in the record are such historical topics as the background of several **revelations** of **Joseph Smith**, the nature of revelation, early development of Church doctrine and policy, the **law of consecration**, Church disciplinary procedures, **priesthood** organization and duties, **missionary work**, and gifts of the Spirit. This record also provides useful genealogical information, including membership and ordination records for about 350 members.

The Far West Record is a record book into which loose copies of minutes were inserted. There are minutes of **meetings** held in **New York, Ohio, Indiana, Missouri,** and **Illinois.** The book was given to the **high council** at Far West, Missouri, in 1838 to be used for its minutes. The compilation was first named the "Far West Record" after the **Saints** settled in **Utah.**

The earliest meeting for which minutes are included in the Far West Record is the first **conference** of the Church, held 9 June 1830 at the **Whitmer farm** in **Fayette, New York.** The latest minutes found in the record were from the **Nauvoo** high council meeting held 15 June 1844, just 12 days before the **martyrdom** of the **Prophet** Joseph Smith.

The original manuscript is found in the archives of the LDS Church, and the record has been edited and published (1983) and is therefore accessible to the general public.

SOURCE

Cannon, Donald Q., and Lyndon W. Cook, eds. *Far West Record: Minutes of The Church of Jesus Christ of Latter-day Saints, 1830–1844.* Salt Lake City: Deseret Book, 1983.

DONALD Q. CANNON

FAST DAY. The ancient custom of fasting, the practice of abstaining from food and drink for religious purposes, was restored to the latter-day Church (D&C 88:76). Fast **meetings** were held sporadically until the **pioneers** came to **Utah. Brigham Young** then instigated a regular fast day on the first Thursday of each month. As the Church grew, the Thursday meetings presented problems for businesses that closed so that employees could attend the meeting. On 6 December 1896, the **First Presidency** changed fast day to the first Sunday of the month.

The Church as a whole observes fast day by foregoing food and beverages for 24 hours and contributing fast offerings—equivalent to the missed two meals—to the needy. On an individual basis, a person may choose to fast and pray for someone else needing spiritual support or to pray for personal guidance and blessings. If a person fasts with a purpose and a sincere intent, other benefits can also be realized, such as increased spirituality, self-discipline, and charity. The law of the fast is found in Isaiah 58:3–12.

An occasional fast is beneficial to the body, but members are cautioned to use common sense, because some health conditions do not tolerate fasting.

SOURCES

Leonard, Glen M. "Why Do We Hold Fast and Testimony Meeting on the First Sunday of the Month?" *Ensign* 28 (March 1998): 60–61.

Smith, Joseph F. "Observance of Fast Day." *Improvement Era* 6 (December 1902): 146–49.

Wengreen, A. Dean. "The Origin and History of the Fast Day in The Church of Jesus Christ of Latter-day Saints, 1830–1896." Master's thesis, Brigham Young University, 1955.

VENEESE C. NELSON

FATHER IN HEAVEN. See **GOD THE FATHER.**

FAUST, JAMES E. James Esdras Faust, **counselor** in the **First Presidency**, state legislator, and attorney, was born 31 July 1920 in Delta, Utah, to George A. and Amy Finlinson Faust. **Elder** Faust served a **mission** in **Brazil** from 1939 to 1942. Upon his return from missionary service, he entered the Army Air Corps, where he was commissioned as a second lieutenant. He served as an intelligence officer during **World War II**.

Brother Faust married Ruth Wright on 21 April 1943 in the **Salt Lake Temple**. They became the parents of five children. Upon his release from military service, Brother Faust attended the **University of Utah**, where he ran track and received a B.A. and then a juris doctorate in 1948. He established a law practice in **Salt Lake City**. Elected to the Utah House of Representatives at the age of 28, he also served as president of the Utah Bar Association and advisor of the American Bar Journal, and was appointed by President John F. Kennedy to the Lawyers Committee for Civil Rights and Racial Unrest. In 1970, Brother Faust was appointed to the board of directors of the **Deseret News** Publishing Company. In 1995, he received the Minuteman Award by the Utah National Guard and was awarded the Distinguished Lawyer Emeritus Award by the Utah Bar Association in 1996.

Elder Faust served as a stake president and **regional representative**, and was sustained as an **assistant to the Twelve** on 6 October 1972. On 1 October 1976, he was sustained to the presidency of the First Quorum of the **Seventy**. While serving as a **general authority**, Elder Faust has been an **area** supervisor (Brazil), president of the **International Mission**, managing director of the **Melchizedek Priesthood—MIA**, and director the Curriculum Department. He was sustained as a member of the Quorum of the Twelve **Apostles** on 30 September 1978 and ordained an apostle 1 October 1978, at age 58. Elder Faust was set apart as second counselor to President **Gordon B. Hinckley** on 12 March 1995.

SOURCES

Bell, James P. *In the Strength of the Lord: The Life and Teachings of James E. Faust.* Salt Lake City: Deseret Book, 1999.

Maxwell, Neal A. "President James E. Faust: Pure Gold." *Ensign* 25 (August 1995): 12–17.

1999–2000 Church Almanac. Salt Lake City: Deseret News, 1998. 17.

MATTHEW O. RICHARDSON

FAYETTE, NEW YORK. Peter Whitmer Sr. moved his family from Hamburg, **Pennsylvania**, to the township of **Fayette**, Seneca County, **New York**, in about 1809. There they eventually acquired ownership of a 100-acre farm three miles south and one mile west of Waterloo. The Whitmers' personal introduction to the **Joseph Smith Sr. family** came through **Oliver Cowdery**, a friend of **David Whitmer**. Oliver Cowdery and **Samuel Smith**, brother of the **Prophet**, stayed overnight with the Whitmers in the forepart of April 1829. Oliver then went down to **Harmony, Pennsylvania**, to meet **Joseph Smith Jr.** for the first time. Soon, because of mob hostility in Harmony, the Prophet and Oliver Cowdery had to suspend their **translation of the Book of Mormon** in May 1829. The two men were granted refuge at the **Whitmer farm**. David Whitmer picked the men up in his wagon during the latter part of May and delivered them to Fayette by 1 June. Soon afterwards **Emma Smith** joined her husband at the Whitmer home.

In that same month of June the work of translation of the Book of Mormon was completed at Fayette. Here the Three **Witnesses of the Book of Mormon**, Oliver Cowdery, David Whitmer, and **Martin Harris**, accompanied by the Prophet, were shown the **gold plates** and other Nephite artifacts by the **angel Moroni** in a secluded area of the farm. On that occasion the voice of **God** was heard bearing witness to the validity of the translation.

Also in June, in the chamber of the Whitmer log house, Joseph and Oliver received the word of the Lord, including an outline of the procedures to be followed on the day of the **organization of the Church**. Such organization was to be deferred until an unspecified date. Meanwhile, a number of believers were baptized for the remission of their sins by the Prophet and Oliver Cowdery under the authority of the **Aaronic Priesthood**.

Following the publication of the Book of Mormon in nearby **Palmyra, New York**, during March 1830, some 56 interested persons assembled with the Prophet at the Whitmer log house on **6 April 1830** to participate in the organization of the Church of Jesus Christ. Six persons, including the Prophet, were officially named to meet the legal requirements associated with the organization of a religious society in the state of New York (three to nine persons are required by law). Through the consent of the congregation, Joseph Smith and Oliver were accepted as spiritual leaders. They then exercised the keys they had received from **Peter, James, and John** to ordain one another first and second **elder**, respectively. **Confirmation** of membership and the gift of the Holy Ghost were bestowed by the laying on of hands to persons who had been baptized previous to the organizational meeting. Some additional **priesthood** ordinations were also carried out. The sacrament was administered for the first time in this dispensation and **revelation** was received. Between June 1829 and January 1831 in Fayette, the Prophet received 20 revelations, which are now recorded in the **Doctrine and Covenants**.

The first three **conferences** of the Church were conducted at the **Whitmer farm** in June and September 1830, and January 1831. The visit of **Sidney Rigdon** and **Edward Partridge** to Fayette from **Ohio** in December to January 1830 to 1831 precipitated inquiries that resulted in significant changes for the New York **Saints**. It was at the 2 January 1831 conference that the body of the Church received revelation from the Lord directing them to gather in Ohio (D&C 38; see also 37). The Prophet preceded them in January 1831, and the Fayette **Branch** as a whole moved to **Kirtland, Ohio**, in May 1831.

A later frame home built on the Whitmer farm between 1845 and 1851 has often erroneously been identified as the place where the Church was organized in 1830. By 1980 the Whitmer log home was reconstructed at the correct site, and a portion of the Church's sesquicentennial **general conference** was televised from there.

SOURCES

Anderson, Richard Lloyd. "Who Were the Six Who Organized the Church on 6 April 1830?" *Ensign* 10 (June 1980): 44–45.

Carmack, John K. "Fayette: The Place the Church Was Organized." *Ensign* 19 (February 1989): 14–19.

Faulring, Scott H. "The Articles and Covenants of the Church: D&C 20 and Its Antecedents." Provo: Foundation for Ancient Research and Mormon Studies, 1997. 1–24.

Porter, Larry C. "A Study of the Origins of The Church of Jesus Christ of Latter-day Saints in the States of New York and Pennsylvania, 1816–1831." Ph.D. diss., Brigham Young University, 1971. 243–68, 374–86.

LARRY C. PORTER

FELT, LOUIE B. Louie Bouton Felt, general **Primary** president for 45 years, served longer than any **auxiliary** president in the history of the Church. Sarah Louise Bouton was born 5 May 1850, in Norwalk, **Connecticut**, and met her future husband, Joseph H. Felt, while journeying to **Utah**. Though not blessed with children of her own, Louie had a profound influence on generations of Latter-day Saint children. She was called as the first general president of the Primary in 1880 and guided the organization through its formative years. Recognizing the need for better children's medical care, she established the **Primary Children's Hospital** in 1911, first as a convalescent home and later as a full-service hospital. Another of her long-lasting contributions was the *Children's Friend,* published first in 1902 as a guide to Primary workers. Eventually it became a magazine for children. Louie incorporated progressive educational concepts into the Primary curriculum, focusing on learning through active involvement. Released as president in 1925, Louie died 13 February 1928 in **Salt Lake City.**

SOURCES

Madsen, Carol Cornwall, and Susan Staker Oman. *Sisters and Little Saints: One Hundred Years of Primary.* Salt Lake City: Deseret Book, 1978.

Peterson, Janet, and LaRene Gaunt. *The Children's Friends: Presidents of the Primary and Their Lives of Service.* Salt Lake City: Deseret Book, 1996.

Harward, Conrad A. "A History of the Growth and Development of the Primary Association of the LDS Church from 1878 to 1928." Master's thesis, Brigham Young University, 1976.

JANET PETERSON

FEMINISM. See WOMEN, ROLE OF.

FICTION, MORMONS IN.

The generally lurid and sensational image of Mormons as portrayed in non-Mormon fiction throughout the nineteenth and much of the twentieth centuries mirrors, in both comic and serious ways, prevailing attitudes towards the Latter-day **Saints** and has occasioned longstanding and continuing negative consequences in Latter-day Saint public relations.

The comic image of the Latter-day Saints in nineteenth-century fiction centered principally in the Saints' practice of **plural marriage** and was widely exploited by numerous literary comedians in newspapers and from the lectern. Artemus Ward (Charles Farrer Browne), in his popular lecture "Artemus Ward among the Mormons" and his condensed novel "Reginald Gloverson" (*Travels,* 1865), was among the first to profit from mock confusions of multiple mothers-in-law, bunches of wives, and legions of children. In *Roughing It* (1872), Mark Twain followed Ward's lead in describing a fictitious visit of a **gentile** with **Brigham Young,** who, lamenting the complexities and expenses of multiple-marriages, advises his visitor to limit his own marrying to "ten or eleven wives; never go over it" (145). Twain also had fun with the **Book of Mormon**, calling it "chloroform in print"("Gentle Blasphemer," 146). Max Adeler (Charles Heber Clark) mocked polygamy in his popular comic novel *The Tragedy of Thompson Dunbar, A Tale of Salt Lake City* (1879), which details the perilous life of a polygamous husband who woos and weds an entire corps of Mormon widows. Marietta Holley, "the female Mark Twain," spoke her antipolygamy opinions on Mormon polygamy through acerbic Samantha Allen, who takes on Elder Judas Wart and the Mormon Church in *My Wayward Pardner; or, My Trials with Josiah, America, the Widow Bump, and Etcetery, by Josiah Allen's Wife* (1881).

Fiction writers capitalized on the rampant anti-Mormon sentiment of the nineteenth century to demonize Mormons in the kind of lurid and grossly sensational propaganda that typified anti-Catholic and anti-Masonic literature. In **England**, Sherlock Holmes, in Sir Arthur Conan Doyle's *A Study in Scarlet* (1888), solves a murder case in which Mormon Avenging Angels track a woman who has fled polygamy in **Utah** Territory; Robert Louis Stevenson's heroine in *The Dynamiter* (1925) likewise flees, only to be tracked down by the sinister Danites. German literature also has a venerable tradition of anti-Mormonism, exemplified in Balduin Möllhausen's *Das Mormonenmädchen* (1864) and in several of Karl May's popular Westerns (Cracroft, "Karl May"). The first full-length anti-Mormon American novel was John Russell's *The Mormoness; or, the Trials of Mary Maverick* (1853), which depicts the fate of those who fall into the "fatal snare of Joe Smith" (42). More than 50 anti-Mormon tales followed before the end of the century (Terryl L. Givens, 109–110); typical are *Bessie Baine: the Mormon's Victim* (1876) by M. Quad (Charles Bertrand Lewis); Mrs. A.G. Paddock, *The Fate of Madame La Tour: A Tale of Great Salt Lake* (1881); Jennie Switzer [Bartlett], *Elder Northfield's Home: Or, Sacrificed on the Mormon Altar* (1882); and Burt L. Standish, "Frank Merriwell among the Mormons: or, The Lost Tribes of Israel" (1897). These works feature such titillating mainstays of anti-Mormon fiction as abduction, torture in subterranean chambers, white slavery, enforced polygamy, secret and terrible temple rites, infant and human sacrifice, and other grisly crimes and atrocities. The women are always captives, never converts; even Jane Withersteen, the Mormon heroine of Zane Grey's popular *Riders of the Purple Sage* (1912), has to free herself from the tentacles of the Mormon serpent to flee to the arms of her Mormon-killer lover.

At the end of the twentieth century, Mormons and the LDS Church continued to be strangely caricatured in some literary works (Givens,

153–67). Since mid-century, however, in such works as Allen Drury's *Advise and Consent* (1960) and Tom Clancy's *Hunt for Red October* (1984) and *Clear and Present Danger* (1989), the Mormon in fiction has become a clean-cut paragon of moral rectitude: "successful, white, Anglo-Saxon, middle-class, suburban, one working parent in a traditional family with a stay-at-home mother and five children" (Givens, 163). Since society has now reached a point where "the politics of the periphery are working to devalue the center" (Givens, 164), Mormons again find themselves distinctively different because they are puritanical. Thus, the narrator in John Le Carré's *The Russia House* (1990) describes two stereotypical American CIA agents as radiating a "Mormon cleanliness" which he "found slightly revolting"(211). Turn-of-the-century Latter-day Saints, relieved at the change in the popular Mormon image, can endure more comfortably this current, albeit still distorted, stereotype of quintessential wholesomeness.

SOURCES

Cracroft, Richard H. "The American West of Karl May." Master's thesis, University of Utah, 1963. 114–20.

———. "Distorting Polygamy for Fun and Profit: Artemus Ward and Mark Twain among the Mormons." *BYU Studies* 14 (Winter 1974): 272–88.

———. "The Gentle Blasphemer: Mark Twain, Holy Scripture, and the Book of Mormon." *BYU Studies* 11 (Winter 1971): 119–40.

———. "'Ten Wives Is All You Need': Artemus Twain and the Mormons—Again." *Western Humanities Review* 38 (Autumn 1984): 197–211.

Givens, Terry L. *The Viper on the Hearth: Mormons, Myths, and the Construction of Heresy.* New York: Oxford University Press, 1997.

Twain, Mark. *Roughing It.* Edited by Hamlin Hill. New York: Penguin, 1981.

RICHARD H. CRACROFT

FIELDING, JAMES. Reverend James Fielding, a Protestant minister in Preston, **England**, learned about the restored gospel in letters from his brother Joseph and his sisters Mary and Mercy, who had been baptized in **Canada**. James was born 7 April 1793 in Halifax, England, one of ten children born to John Fielding and Rachel Ibbotson. After hearing about Mormonism, he invited the missionaries (including his brother **Elder Joseph Fielding**) to preach their first sermon on British soil in his Vauxhall Chapel on Sunday, 23 July 1837. Nine members of his congregation were baptized the following Sunday, leading him to close his chapel doors to the missionaries and eventually become a bitter enemy of the Church. Reverend Fielding died 7 December 1877.

SOURCES

Bloxham, V. Ben, James R. Moss, and Larry C. Porter, eds. *Truth Will Prevail: The Rise of The Church of Jesus Christ of Latter-day Saints in the British Isles, 1837–1997.* Cambridge: Cambridge University Press, 1987.

Garrard, LaMar. "Satan's Opposition to the Introduction of the Gospel to England." In *British Isles.* Edited by Donald Q. Cannon. Regional Studies in Latter-day Saint Church History series. Provo, Utah: Brigham Young University, 1990. 83–101.

DAVID COOK

FIELDING, JOSEPH. Along with six others, Joseph Fielding was the first to take the restored gospel to **England** in 1837. His brother, **James Fielding**, was pastor of the Church in Preston where the missionaries were given their first opportunity to preach. He labored in England for four years, serving for half that time as president of the British Mission.

Joseph was born 26 March 1797 in Honeydon, Bedfordshire, England. He emigrated to Toronto, **Canada**, in 1832, where four years later he met **Parley P. Pratt** and was baptized there.

He served in a bishopric as well as on the high council at **Winter Quarters**. In September 1848 he arrived in the **Salt Lake Valley**, where he lived until his death at **Mill Creek** 19 December 1863. His sister Mary was the wife of **Hyrum Smith**.

SOURCES

Diary of Joseph Fielding. Salt Lake City: Genealogical Society of The Church of Jesus Christ of Latter-day Saints, 1963. 1–165.

Jenson, Andrew. *Latter-day Saint Biographical Encyclopedia.* 4 vols. 1901–36. Reprint, Salt Lake City: Western Epics, 1971. 2:762–763.

CALVIN R. STEPHENS

FIELDING, MARY. See **SMITH, MARY FIELDING.**

FIFTY, COUNCIL OF. See **COUNCIL OF FIFTY.**

FIJI. The Church first went to Fiji in 1924 when member Mele Ashley emigrated from **Tonga** to Fiji with her children. In the 1950s other families from Tonga and **Samoa** moved to Fiji and began holding Church meetings in Suva. The first missionaries assigned to Fiji were Elders Boyd I.

Harris and Sheldon I. Abbott, from the Tonga Mission. These missionaries, with 14 Fijian members, organized the Suva **Branch** on 5 September 1954. In 1955 President **David O. McKay** visited Fiji; he met with the missionaries and attended Church services in a home. The Fiji **Mission** was created on 23 July 1971 and the Fiji Suva **Stake** was organized on 12 July 1983.

Over the years missionary work has moved slowly because of a government quota placed on missionary visas—at times as few as two were allowed. After a bloodless military coup in 1987, the quota was lifted. Since then Church **growth** has more than doubled.

In 1997 President **Gordon B. Hinckley** met with more than 10,000 members in a national stadium. In May 1999 the Church began construction on a temple in Suva, Fiji. By the beginning of the year 2000, there were 11,998 members, four stakes, and 41 **wards** and branches in a country with a population of 802,000 scattered over numerous islands.

SOURCES

Meek, Shirleen. "First Islands of Faith." *Ensign* 20 (December 1990): 32–37.
1999–2000 Church Almanac. Salt Lake City: Deseret News, 1998. 317–18.

CRAIG K. MANSCILL

FILLMORE, UTAH. Fillmore was the first capital of the territory of **Utah**, and was named after U.S. president Millard Fillmore, who had appointed **Brigham Young** as territorial governor. In 1851 the territorial legislature called for the area located near Chalk Creek on the east side of the Pauvant Valley to be colonized and established as the territorial capitol. The area was selected because of its central location within the territory. Shortly thereafter, a company of Latter-day **Saint** colonists moved there and began constructing homes. In 1852 construction of the territorial statehouse began under a design by **Truman Angell**. The south wing was completed in December 1855, and the fifth meeting of the legislature was held there the same month. By December 1856, the legislature chose to move the capital to Salt Lake City, where most of the state's population was located.

A **stake** was established in Fillmore on 9 March 1869. **Ira Nathaniel Hinckley**, grandfather of President **Gordon B. Hinckley**, served as president of the stake from 1877 to 1902.

SOURCES

Jenson, Andrew. *Encyclopedic History of The Church of Jesus Christ of Latter-day Saints.* Salt Lake City: Deseret News, 1941. 249–51.

Payne, Richard W. *The Legacy of the Lone South Wing.* Provo, Utah: Brigham Young University Press, 1970.

JEFFREY L. ANDERSON

FILMS. See MOTION PICTURES.

FINANCES. See ECONOMIC HISTORY.

FINLAND. Located in northern **Europe** between **Sweden** and **Russia**, Finland has a population of more than five million people, of which about 90% belong to the Lutheran Church. The first Latter-day Saint missionaries to serve in Finland were Carl and John Sundstrom, who came from Sweden in 1875. They served in the town of Vaasa, where they baptized Johanna Berg and Johanna Sundstrom the following year. Soon others converted, and by 1877 temporary **branches** were established in Vaasa, Sipoo, and Pietasaari. During these early years the elders labored among Swedish-speaking Finns. There was a law that prohibited anyone from "rising to speak," so missionaries learned to preach the gospel while sitting in their seats. The Church established its first long-lasting branch in the country at Larsmo in 1880, soon after Anders and Lovisa Stromberg were baptized. **Elder Francis M. Lyman** of the **Quorum** of the **Twelve** Apostles visited Finland in 1903 and on 4 August formally dedicated the land for preaching the gospel. Missionary activity in the country was sporadic for the next several decades.

On 16 July 1946 Elder **Ezra Taft Benson** rededicated the land, and in November of that year Elder Mark E. Anderson became the first missionary to preach the gospel in the Finnish language. In 1947 the Finnish mission was organized with Henry A. Matis as president. At the time there were only about 120 Latter-day Saints in the country. On 1 July 1948 the government officially recognized the Church and in 1954 the **Book of Mormon** was translated into Finnish. The country's first **stake** was organized in Helsinki on 16 October 1977 with Kari Haikkola as president. In that year there were approximately 3,600 members in the nation.

Starting in 1989 Finland became a gateway to missionary work in the Soviet Union, specifically in **Estonia** and Russia. On 1 July 1990 the Finland Helsinki East Mission was organized to serve members in the USSR. It was discontinued in 1992 when missions were established in both Moscow and St. Petersburg, Russia.

At the beginning of the year 2000, Finland had more than 4,403 members living in two stakes and 30 **wards** and branches. In the April 2000 **general conference** President **Gordon B. Hinckley** announced that the Church would build a **temple** in Helsinki.

SOURCES

Muistamme: We Remember, 1947–1997. Salt Lake City: Henry A. Matis Family Society. 1997.
1999–2000 Church Almanac. Salt Lake City: Deseret News, 1998. 318–19.

ARNOLD K. GARR

FIRESIDE. Since the 1930s Church members have used the term "fireside" to describe several different sizes and kinds of gatherings. Firesides provide an opportunity to gather people together in a warm, friendly atmosphere for gospel study and enrichment, inspiration, and social interaction. They are usually held Sunday evenings in homes, meetinghouses, or other locations with a featured speaker or theme.

Audiences range from a small group to thousands. Firesides have been held on a class, multiclass, **quorum**, **auxiliary**, **ward**, **stake**, regional, student-body, organization, and Church-wide level. Church-wide fireside broadcasts have targeted a variety of groups and topics: Christmas, families, finances, **missionary work**, morality, **priesthood**, **restoration**, **Primary**, **scouting**, **scriptures**, **single adults**, young adults, **Young Women**, and youth.

During 1960 two fireside series were presented over radio and by tape recording to Mutual-age audiences around the world. Since September 1992 the **Church Educational System** has sponsored young adult firesides almost monthly, transmitted by **satellite communications** to many North American locations.

SOURCES

Irvine, Arnold J. "Coast to Coast Firesides Prepared for Youth." *Church News*, 2 January 1960, 1, 8–9.
Pinnock, Florence B., ed. "'Come Join Us at Fireside.'" *Improvement Era* 64 (September 1961): 682–87.
Sheffield, Sheridan R., Scott Lloyd, and Mike Cannon. "Some Things Uniquely LDS." *Church News*, 25 January 1992, 8.

LARRY R. SKIDMORE

FIRST COUNCIL OF THE SEVENTY. See **SEVENTY.**

FIRST PRESIDENCY. The First Presidency is a **quorum** consisting of the president of the Church and his **counselors**. It is ordinarily made up of three individuals, although more members may be added as circumstances require. The First Presidency developed gradually by **revelation** as the Church grew from just six official members to a much larger body. At the organizational meeting of the Church on **6 April** 1830, the assembled group accepted **Joseph Smith** and **Oliver Cowdery** "as their teachers in the things of the **Kingdom of God**," and the two men then ordained each other to the office of **elder** in compliance with earlier revelation (Smith, 1:77–78). At the Church's first **conference**, held 9 June 1830, Joseph and Oliver, as first and second elder of the Church, issued licenses to **priesthood** holders.

At a conference held in **Amherst, Ohio**, 25 January 1832, Joseph Smith was ordained as president of the High Priesthood. He later chose **Sidney Rigdon** and **Jesse Gause** as his counselors. In March of that year, a revelation confirmed Brother Gause as a counselor to Joseph Smith, "Unto whom I have given the keys of the kingdom, which belong always unto the Presidency of the High Priesthood" (D&C 81:2). At a conference in **Independence, Missouri**, on 26 April 1832, Joseph was "acknowledged by the **High Priests** in the land of **Zion** to be president of the High Priesthood, according to commandment and ordination in Ohio, at the Conference held in Amherst January 25 1832" (Cannon and Cook, 44). Jesse Gause was excommunicated in December 1832, and **Frederick G. Williams** replaced him the following March (D&C 81; 90).

In February 1835, Joseph Smith organized the Quorum of the Twelve **Apostles** and the First Quorum of **Seventy**. Subsequently, the Lord gave a revelation explaining the relationship among the quorums. It declared: "Of the **Melchizedek Priesthood**, three Presiding High Priests, chosen by the body, appointed and ordained to that office, and upheld by the confidence, faith, and prayer of the church, form a quorum of the Presidency of the Church" (D&C 107:22).

Beginning with Joseph Smith, several presidents of the Church have named counselors in addition to the first and second counselor in the First Presidency. Several men who later served as president, first counselor, or second counselor in the First Presidency served for a time as additional counselors, among them **Lorenzo Snow, Joseph F. Smith, Joseph Fielding Smith,** and **Gordon B. Hinckley**.

While serving as first counselor in the First Presidency, President Hinckley declared, "When the President is ill or not able to function fully in all of the duties of his office, his two Counselors together comprise a

Quorum of the First Presidency. They carry on with the day-to-day work of the Presidency. In exceptional circumstances, when only one may be able to function, he may act in the authority of the office of the Presidency as set forth in the **Doctrine and Covenants**, section 102, verses 10–11" (Hinckley, 54).

SOURCES

Cannon, Donald Q., and Lyndon W. Cook, eds. *Far West Record: Minutes of The Church of Jesus Christ of Latter-day Saints, 1830–1844.* Salt Lake City: Deseret Book, 1983.

Hinckley, Gordon B. "God Is at the Helm." *Ensign* 24 (May 1994): 53–60.

1997–1998 Church Almanac. Salt Lake City: Deseret News, 1996.

Smith, Joseph. *History of The Church of Jesus Christ of Latter-day Saints.* Edited by B. H. Roberts. 2d ed. rev. 7 vols. Salt Lake City: The Church of Jesus Christ of Latter-day Saints, 1932–51.

Woodford, Robert J. "The Historical Development of the Doctrine and Covenants." Ph.D. diss., Brigham Young University, 1974.

RICHARD E. TURLEY JR.

FIRST QUORUM OF THE SEVENTY. See SEVENTY.

FIRST VISION. In the spring of 1820, **God** the Eternal Father and his Son **Jesus Christ** appeared and spoke to Joseph Smith, a 14-year-old farm boy, in a grove near his family's log home. This sacred experience initiated the marvelous work of the **Restoration** and became a cornerstone of Latter-day Saint faith.

Two years prior to this vision, Joseph's family had moved to a farm located in Manchester, New York. The family's temporary log home and the **Sacred Grove**, site of the First Vision, were located near the border of Manchester and Palmyra townships in western New York, about two miles southwest of Palmyra Village.

During the 10-year period following Joseph's experience (from 1832 to 1842), on at least four different occasions, Joseph Smith wrote or dictated to scribes accounts of his First Vision. They were prepared at different times, under different circumstances, for different audiences, and for different purposes. Therefore, these accounts emphasize different aspects of Joseph's experience. The **Prophet** never prepared a complete account describing everything he learned during this vision. In his most descriptive version, an account written in 1838 and included in the **Pearl of Great Price**, he declared, "Many other things did he say unto me, which I cannot write at this time" (JS–H 1:20). By examining all these accounts, one can gain a more complete understanding of who appeared to Joseph Smith, as well as the message that unfolded in 1820 (Backman, Appendix A-D).

Joseph Smith also related his experience to early converts and to nonmembers of the Church, who wrote accounts of the First Vision based on what they had learned from him. Although these contemporary accounts substantiate Joseph Smith's testimony, they do not include any major concepts not found in versions prepared by the Prophet (Backman, Appendix E-J).

As Joseph Smith described the background of his First Vision, he recalled that for about four years he was involved in a quest for religious truth. He realized that he needed a forgiveness of his sins and was seeking salvation. His quest for truth occurred during an age of intense **revivalism**. The Prophet observed that in the whole region, great multitudes were uniting themselves with different religious communities. Meanwhile, some denominations were "endeavoring to establish their own tenets and disprove all others. In the midst of this war of words and tumult of opinions," Joseph Smith asked, "Who of all these parties are right?" (JS–H 1:9–10). He also reasoned "that all could not be right, and that God could not be the author of so much confusion" (Backman, 169). Believing in the apostle James's declaration that prayers are answered (James 1:5), he retired to a secret place in a grove and engaged in supplication.

The first principle Joseph learned after beginning his prayer was that the power of evil is real and strong—suddenly he was almost overcome by the power of **Satan**. But the destructive force was replaced by a brilliant light, and he learned that God's power is stronger than Satan's and that God hears and answers prayer.

As Joseph looked into the light, he saw two personages who exactly resembled each other in features and likeness. The one personage addressed him by saying, "This is My Beloved Son. Hear Him" (JS–H 1:17).

As the Savior addressed him, Joseph Smith learned many other truths. He learned that his sins were forgiven and that Jesus atoned for the sins of mankind. He learned about the reality of the Second Coming and of an apostasy from the ancient Christian church. "They told me," he explained, "that all religious denominations were believing in incorrect doctrines, and that none of them was acknowledged of God as his church and kingdom. I was expressly commanded," he added, "to go not after them" and was promised "that the fulness of the gospel should at some future time be made known unto me" (Backman, 169).

In an account published in his 1835 diary, Joseph not only

emphasized that he saw two personages but said that he saw many **angels** during this vision (Backman, 159).

When Joseph Smith described the aftermath of this remarkable vision, he wrote in 1832: "my Soul was filled with love and for many days I could rejoice with great joy . . . the Lord was with me" (Backman, 159).

In other accounts Joseph Smith wrote that after informing some professors of religion of his experience, persecution erupted. He felt, he said, like Paul when he made his defense before King Agrippa. Responding to this verbal oppression, Joseph testified, "I had seen a vision; I knew it, and I knew that God knew it, and I could not deny it" (JS–H 1:25).

SOURCES

Backman, Milton V. Jr. *Joseph Smith's First Vision: Confirming Evidences and Contemporary Accounts.* 2d ed. rev. Salt Lake City: Bookcraft, 1980.

Jessee, Dean C., ed. *The Papers of Joseph Smith.* Vol. 1. Salt Lake City: Deseret Book, 1989.

MILTON V. BACKMAN Jr.

FISHING RIVER. The expedition known as **Zion's Camp** entered western Missouri in the summer of 1834, bringing wagons loaded with supplies to assist the **Saints** who had been exiled from **Jackson County** the previous November. They camped between the forks of Little and Big Fishing River on 19 June. During the night, a severe thunder storm with heavy rain caused the rivers to rise 30 to 40 feet, protecting the men from the mob army that had gathered to annihilate them.

While the members of Zion's camp were stopped at Fishing River, the Lord chastened them for disobedience, as foretold by the **Prophet Joseph Smith**. Cholera raged through the camp and nearby countryside, killing 13 men and one woman (Smith, 115–16, 120). On 22 June 1834, four days after their arrival, the Lord outlined in revelation the conditions by which **Zion** must be redeemed (D&C 105).

SOURCE

Smith, Joseph. *History of The Church of Jesus Christ of Latter-day Saints.* Edited by B. H. Roberts. 2d ed. rev. 7 vols. Salt Lake City: The Church of Jesus Christ of Latter-day Saints, 1932–51. 115–16, 120.

CLARK V. JOHNSON

FLAKE, GREEN. Green Flake, an 1847 **pioneer**, was an early African-American in **Utah**. Born a slave in January 1828 at Anson County, **North**

Carolina, he took his master's last name. After joining the Church with James Madison Flake's **family** in 1843 or 1844, he traveled with them to **Nauvoo**. His master sent him with **Brigham Young**, and Flake reportedly drove the first wagon into the Salt Lake Valley. Flake married Martha Crosby in 1848 and settled in Union, Utah, along with other African-Americans. Sources differ on when he was freed. Despite **priesthood** restriction, Flake and some descendants remained active **Latter-day Saints** and were important members of a small Utah African-American community. Green Flake died on 20 October 1903 in Idaho Falls, **Idaho**.

SOURCE

Carter, Kate B. "The Negro Pioneer." *Our Pioneer Heritage* 8 (1965): 500–4.

JESSIE L. EMBRY

FLETCHER, HARVEY. Harvey Fletcher, one of Mormonism's premier scientists of the twentieth century, was born 11 September 1884 in **Provo, Utah**. His accomplishments include foundational research in speech and hearing, the invention of the hearing aid, major improvements in the telephone to accurately reproduce the human voice, the development of amplifiers and loudspeakers, the invention of stereophonic sound (one of the earliest applications of stereophonic sound was the huge speakers for the **Hill Cumorah Pageant**), assembling and supervising the team that developed the transistor, and working with Warner Brothers to perfect the first sound film, *The Jazz Singer.* Two Nobel Prizes were awarded to men whose work derived from Harvey Fletcher's.

A graduate of **Brigham Young University** and the University of Chicago, Fletcher was appointed director of Bell Laboratories, the premier laboratory for electronic sound research in **America**. He served as the first president of the Acoustical Society of America, vice president of the American Association for the Advancement of Science, and professor of electrical engineering at Columbia University. Later he became the first dean of the College of Engineering at BYU.

Fletcher's Church service included the **Sunday School** general board, where he wrote many lesson manuals. He died 23 July 1981 in Orem, Utah.

SOURCE

Jackson, Kenneth T., ed. *Scribner Encyclopedia of American Lives.* New York: Charles Scribner's Sons, 1998. 280–82.

RICHARD G. OMAN

FLORENCE, NEBRASKA. See WINTER QUARTERS.

FLORIDA. In 1843 **Elders** William Brown and Daniel Cathcart were called to preach in Florida. Two years later **Phineas Young** distributed copies of the **Book of Mormon** in the area, but only nominal success was experienced at first. In 1895 the Florida **conference** was organized as part of the **Southern States Mission.**

The **Saints** did not escape all of the persecution of the South. In 1898 Elder George Canova, a **branch** president, was ambushed and killed, largely because of his membership in the Church. His assailant was never found. Elder Canova's grandson Alvin Chace became the first **stake president** in Florida.

In 1947 a stake was organized in Jacksonville, the first **stake** in the southeastern **United States. Elders Charles A. Callis** and **Harold B. Lee** directed the organization. The stake was unique in the Church as the first outside of the Intermountain West to be completely organized with local leadership.

Beginning in 1950 the Church purchased 316,000 acres of investment property near Orlando; this became the Deseret Ranch, one of the largest of its kind in the country. The relative lateness of the Church's development, the state's diverse demographic population, and the attraction of temperate climate all lessened the impact of emigration and contributed to substantial growth in Florida. With this rapid growth, stakes were soon organized in Orlando (1958), Tampa (1959), and Miami (1960), with numerous others added later.

In 1994 a **temple** was dedicated in Orlando. By the beginning of the year 2000 there were 24 stakes with 108,955 members living in 201 **wards** and **branches.**

SOURCES

Berrett, LaMar C. "History of the Southern States Mission, 1831–1861." Master's thesis, Brigham Young University, 1960.

Jenson, Andrew. *Encyclopedic History of The Church of Jesus Christ of Latter-day Saints.* Salt Lake City: Deseret News, 1941.

1999–2000 Church Almanac. Salt Lake City: Deseret News, 1998. 189–91.

Skousen, Mark. *Sunshine in the Soul: One Hundred Years of the Mormon Church in Florida.* Winter Park, Florida: Skousen Publishing, 1996.

DAVID F. BOONE

FOLKLORE. **Mormon** folklore is the "unofficial" history of the Latter-day **Saint** Church, consisting of that part of Latter-day Saint cultural life which Church members keep alive and pass on to succeeding generations through oral transmission or customary example rather than through book learning or formal instruction. Mormon folklore captures major events in the Mormon saga, from the **restoration** of the gospel to the contemporary worldwide expansion into all parts of the globe. It binds Church members together in a common cause and strengthens their sense of cultural identity.

Mormon lore falls into three broad categories. The first consists of things we make with words. These are stories—of hardships faithfully endured by **pioneer** ancestors, of present-day persecutions, of **missions**, of conversions, of God's interventions in individual lives, of admiration for Church authorities, of acts of sacrifice and kindness performed by charitable Church members, and of the day-to-day delights and sorrows of Church membership. Such stories are passed on orally; for example, a member hears in a family or church setting a faith-promoting story about a miraculous appearance of the Three Nephites, or listens in on a humorous tale about missionaries struggling to learn a new language, and then repeats the story to others.

In the second category are things we make with our hands—friendship quilts, cross-stitch renditions of the **temple** in which a couple was married, special family or holiday foods, "quiet books" designed to keep children constructively engaged during Church meetings, creative photograph albums, and **family histories**. A young girl who watches and assists her grandmother stitch a genealogy quilt learns to make her own quilts, and thus perpetuates a specific type of Mormon folklore that has existed for generations.

The third category consists of things we make with our actions—family holiday celebrations, "creative dating" practices, **scripture**-learning games, **family home evening** traditions, morning and evening prayer customs, and special ways of celebrating births and baptisms. Children participate in family Christmas rituals, for example, and later continue the traditions with their own children.

Because all these stories, objects, and practices spring from what is centrally important to Mormons and cease to exist once they no longer engage the core values and concerns of Church members, they provide the scholar excellent means of taking the pulse of Mormon cultural life. The study of Mormon folklore began in the 1930s and continues unabated today. As the Church grows and adapts to an ever-changing technological world, folklore will continue to provide insights into the heart of Latter-day Saint life that can be gained in no other way.

SOURCES

Fife, Austin, and Alta Fife. *Saints of Sage and Saddle: Folklore among the Mormons.* Bloomington: Indiana University Press, 1956.

Wilson, William A. "The Study of Mormon Folklore." *Utah Historical Quarterly* 44 (1976): 317–28.

———. "The Study of Mormon Folklore: An Uncertain Mirror for Truth." *Dialogue* 22 (Winter 1989): 95–110.

———. "Mormon Folklore: Cut from the Marrow of Everyday Experience." *BYU Studies* 33, 3 (1993): 521–40.

WILLIAM A. WILSON

FOLLETT, KING. See KING FOLLETT DISCOURSE.

FOLSOM, WILLIAM HARRISON.

William Harrison Folsom, one of the most creative and skilled architects of the first generation in **Utah**, had a long and prolific career that included, along with service as a Church and civic leader, the design and construction of a large portion of early Utah's most significant structures.

Born 25 March 1815, in Portsmouth, **New Hampshire**, the third child of a carpenter, he spent much of his youth in Buffalo, **New York**, where he learned his father's trade. When he married Zerviah Eliza Clark at the age of 22, he was already a skilled craftsman. While living in Buffalo, the couple embraced the restored gospel and accepted baptism in 1842. The next year they moved to **Nauvoo**, where William worked as a carpenter on the **Nauvoo Temple**. He served a **mission in Ohio** in 1844, returning to Nauvoo to continue working on the **temple** following the deaths of Joseph and **Hyrum Smith**. When most Church leaders and members left the city in early 1846, Folsom remained behind to help complete the interiors of the temple. In September he fought in the **Battle of Nauvoo** and was forced from the city with his **family**.

Folsom lived and worked for more than a decade in **Iowa** as a successful builder. Soon after arriving in **Salt Lake City** in 1860, he opened a shop on Main Street as an architect and builder. His first major project was the **Salt Lake Theater**, the largest and most opulent structure in the territory. He succeeded **Truman O. Angell** as Church architect in 1861, supervising construction of the **Salt Lake Temple**, making early designs for the **Salt Lake Tabernacle**, and designing the new city hall. Angell returned as Church architect in 1867, and Folsom served as an assistant Church architect for the next two decades. He served two missions to the eastern states in 1869 and 1870, and built a number of important commercial buildings and houses in the 1870s, including the elaborate **Gardo House** for **Brigham Young**, the **ZCMI** department store with its cast-iron facade, and extensive additions to the Devereaux Mansion.

In 1875 Folsom began work on the temple in **Manti, Utah**. He probably worked out the general plan of the building in Salt Lake City under the supervision of Brigham Young and Truman Angell before moving to Manti, where he remained for ten years, designing and supervising the exquisite details of the temple, perhaps his greatest artistic achievement. During those years he also designed a series of outstanding buildings, including the **Provo** Tabernacle, the Moroni Tabernacle, the Manti **Tabernacle**, and a new tower for the **St. George Temple**.

Following the dedication of the Manti Temple in 1888, Folsom returned to Salt Lake City. Over the next 12 years he served as a city building inspector, **home missionary**, and **patriarch**. He died in Salt Lake City on 19 March 1901, just six days short of his 86th birthday.

SOURCES

Anderson, Paul L. "William Harrison Folsom: Pioneer Architect." *Utah Historical Quarterly* (Summer 1976): 240–59.

Andrew, Laurel B. *The Early Temples of the Mormons.* Albany, N.Y.: State University of New York Press, 1978.

PAUL L. ANDERSON

FORD, THOMAS.

FORD, THOMAS. Thomas Ford was governor of **Illinois** when **Joseph** and **Hyrum Smith** were killed. Born 5 December 1800 in Fayette County, **Pennsylvania**, he was a lawyer and judge in Illinois before serving as that state's **Democrat** governor from 1842 to 1846. Fearing armed conflict in **Hancock County** following the destruction of the *Expositor* press, Ford promised Joseph the protection of the state if he would stand trial at Carthage. In his *History of Illinois,* Ford characterized Joseph as "the most successful imposter in modern times" (Smith, 35). He encouraged a trial for Joseph's alleged assassins and urged the **Saints** to leave Illinois. Ford died of tuberculosis 3 November 1850 in Peoria, Illinois.

SOURCES

Johnson, Allen, and Dumas Malone, eds. *Dictionary of American Biography.* New York: Charles Scribner's Sons, 1958. 3:520–21.

Smith, Joseph. *History of The Church of Jesus Christ of Latter-day Saints.* Edited by
    B. H. Roberts. 2d ed. rev. 7 vols. Salt Lake City: The Church of Jesus Christ of
    Latter-day Saints, 1932–51. 7:35.

ANDREW H. HEDGES

FORDHAM, ELIJAH. Elijah Fordham, best known for his miraculous
recovery from illness following a blessing by **Joseph Smith** in Montrose,
Iowa, in July 1839, also served in **Zion's Camp**, the **Nauvoo Legion**, and
various leadership positions. Born 12 April 1798 in **New York City**,
Fordham worked on both the **Kirtland** and **Nauvoo Temples**. He also
helped **Parley P. Pratt** establish the first **branch** of the Church at New
York City in 1837. Fordham served a mission to clear Joseph's name following the Prophet's 1843 arrest in Dixon, **Illinois**, and followed **Brigham
Young** to **Utah**. A father of 12 children, Fordham died 9 September 1879
in Wellsville, Utah.

SOURCES

Black, Susan Easton, comp. *Membership of The Church of Jesus Christ of Latter-day
    Saints, 1830–1848.* 50 vols. Provo, Utah: Religious Studies Center, Brigham Young
    University, 1984–88. 16:741–47.
Pratt, Parley P. *Autobiography of Parley P. Pratt.* Edited by Parley P. Pratt Jr. Salt Lake
    City: Deseret Book, 1985. 145, 254.
Smith, Joseph. *History of The Church of Jesus Christ of Latter-day Saints.* Edited by
    B. H. Roberts 2d ed. rev. 7 vols. rev. Salt Lake City: The Church of Jesus Christ of
    Latter-day Saints, 1932–51. 4:3nn.

ANDREW H. HEDGES

FORGERIES OF HISTORICAL DOCUMENTS. Throughout the
Church's history, perpetrators of forged historical documents have sought
to deceive Latter-day **Saints** and others in efforts to undermine the
Church and its leaders, distort history, or generate profits. Among the
earliest such attempts was the alteration of the 116 manuscript pages of
the Book of Lehi, lost by **Martin Harris**. Of the conspirators in this
instance, the Lord warned **Joseph Smith**, "**Satan** hath put it into their
hearts to alter the words . . . which you have translated . . . that . . . they
read contrary from that which you translated and caused to be written"
(D&C 10:10–11).

    Three of the best-known and most persistently cited forgeries are a
purported letter from Joseph Smith to **James J. Strang** that Strang used
to draw away followers after Joseph's death; a **pamphlet** attributed to

Oliver Cowdery titled *Defence in a Rehearsal of My Grounds for Separating Myself from the Latter Day Saints;* and a confession supposedly made by Oliver Overstreet claiming that he impersonated Oliver Cowdery and that the latter did not really return to the Church in 1848.

In more recent years, document dealer Mark W. Hofmann forged scores of documents, many of them related to Latter-day Saint history. Among the most notorious are the Anthon transcript, the **Joseph Smith III** blessing, and the Salamander Letter. Hofmann's greed finally proved his undoing as he promised to several persons a collection purportedly originating with early **apostle William E. McLellin**. Unable to produce the collection, Hofmann murdered two Church members before nearly dying himself when a bomb of his own making detonated in his car.

SOURCES

"James E. Talmage and the Fraudulent 'Michigan Relics.'" *Journal of Book of Mormon Studies* 7 (Spring 1998): 78.

Turley, Richard E., Jr. *Victims: The LDS Church and the Mark Hofmann Case.* Urbana: University of Illinois Press, 1992.

RICHARD E. TURLEY JR.

FORT BRIDGER, WYOMING. Fort Bridger was built in 1843 on Black's Fork of the Green River (in present southwestern **Wyoming**) by mountain men **Jim Bridger** and Louis Vasquez. It served as a trading, supply, and army post for nearly 50 years. Emigrants on the **Oregon-California** and **Mormon trails** stopped there to replenish supplies, refresh stock, and gather information. The LDS Church purchased the fort in 1855 after building another rival post, Fort Supply, 12 miles south in 1853. The **Mormons** used the two forts to control eastern access to **Utah** Territory, assist emigrants, and maintain friendly relations with **Indians**.

In 1857, as **Johnston's Army** approached during the Utah Expedition, the Mormons deserted and destroyed both forts and a new community called Supply City.

Rebuilt by the army in 1858, Fort Bridger served the **Pony Express**, Overland Stage, and Union Pacific **Railroad**. It was also used as the **Shoshone Indian** Agency, where Eastern Shoshones and Bannocks signed several treaties in 1863 and 1868. Fort Bridger was abandoned in 1890 and became a historic site in 1933. The **Saints** resettled the Bridger Valley in the 1890s, organizing the Fort Bridger **Branch** in 1896 and the Lyman **Stake** in 1926.

SOURCES

Fort Bridger Collection. LDS Church Historical Department, Salt Lake City.

Gowans, Fred R. "Fort Bridger and the Mormons." *Utah Historical Quarterly* 42 (Winter 1974): 49–67.

Gowans, Fred R., and Eugene E. Campbell. *Fort Bridger: Island in the Wilderness.* Provo, Utah: Brigham Young University Press, 1975.

———. *Fort Supply: Brigham Young's Green River Experiment.* Provo, Utah: Brigham Young University Press, 1976.

FRED R. GOWANS AND JAY H. BUCKLEY

FORT DOUGLAS, UTAH. Fort Douglas (originally Camp Douglas), located four miles east of **Temple Square** in **Salt Lake City** on the foothills of the Wasatch Mountain Range, was established to prevent **Indian** attacks along the overland mail route. It was founded by Colonel **Patrick E. Conner**, who arrived in Salt Lake City with a battalion of 750 **California Volunteers** on 20 October 1862. Conner and his volunteers, who published in 1864 an **anti-Mormon** newspaper, the *Union Vidette,* were regarded with great suspicion by the Saints. In 1863 the Bear River massacre between soldiers from the fort and hostile Indians brought greater security to the settlers in northern **Utah** and southern **Idaho**. Fort Douglas became an active Army and Navy reserve center in 1986.

SOURCES

Jenson, Andrew. *Encyclopedic History of The Church of Jesus Christ of Latter-day Saints.* Salt Lake City: Deseret News, 1941.

W. SIDNEY YOUNG

FORT HALL. Fort Hall was built in 1834 on the Snake River near the mouth of the Portneuf (at present-day Pocatello) as a supply station and place of refuge for **Latter-day Saints** and others. At first the fort served **Idaho** as a supply post for the fur trade and later it became a major supply depot and a rest stop along the **Oregon Trail**. In 1837 the fort was sold to the **Hudson's Bay Company**, who continued to supply emigrants until the post's abandonment in 1856. From 1856 to 1870, the fort was sometimes used as a trading, military, and overland stage post between **Salt Lake City** and Virginia City, **Montana**. In 1870 a "new" Fort Hall was built 40 miles northeast to protect the growing Mormon and non-Mormon settlements in the Snake River Valley.

SOURCES

Brown, Jennie Broughton. *Fort Hall on the Oregon Trail*. Caldwell, Idaho: Caxton Printers, 1934.

Robertson, Frank C. *Fort Hall: Gateway to the Oregon Country*. New York: Hastings House, 1963.

FRED R. GOWANS AND ANDREA G. RADKE

FORT LARAMIE, WYOMING. Fort Laramie, a famous trading post on the **Oregon Trail**, was founded by William Sublette and Robert Campbell in 1834 and later became part of the American fur company. Located at the confluence of the Laramie and North Platte rivers near the Black Hills, Fort Laramie overlooked the tall grass and nearby wetlands that had long attracted buffalo, deer, and antelope. From its beginning the fort's location was a favored rendezvous spot for fur trade with the Sioux and Cree Indian tribes.

With the swelling tide of overland emigration starting in 1843, the post also became a supply station and a way station. The **Mormon pioneers** of 1847 saw Fort Laramie as the halfway point to their Rocky Mountain destination and took full advantage of its blacksmithing, wagon repair, and provision-stocking facilities. At the time it measured 108 by 116 feet, with 15-inch walls and 16 rooms. Over the main entrance stood a square tower. James Bordeaux, a student of the Intermountain West who was then in charge of the fort, was especially kind to the Latter-day Saints and encouraged them to pursue the valley of Salt Lake as their final destination. Hundreds of other later companies, Mormon and otherwise, including the famous **handcart** companies, found safety, provisions, and supplies at Fort Laramie.

Because of the increasing **Indian** unrest, in 1849 the **United States** government purchased Fort Laramie and transformed it into a military post, maintaining it as such for the next 40 years. **Johnston's Army** made use of the fort en route to **Utah** in 1857. Today Fort Laramie is preserved as a famous tourist spot on the overland trail, some 60 miles north of Laramie, **Wyoming**.

SOURCES

Boyack, Hazel Noble. "Historic Fort Laramie: The Hub of Early Western History, 1834–1849." *Annals of Wyoming* 21 (July–October 1949): 170–80.

Hafen, LeRoy R., and Francis M. Young. *Fort Laramie and the Pageant of the West, 1834–1890*. Glendale, Calif.: Arthur H. Clark, 1938.

Nadeau, Remi. *Fort Laramie and the Sioux Indians.* Englewood Cliffs, N.J.: Prentice-Hall, 1967.

RICHARD E. BENNETT

FORT LEAVENWORTH. Fort Leavenworth, **Kansas,** a United States Army post and reservation, was the outfitting point for the Mormon Battalion as they reported for duty on 1 August 1846. Fort Leavenworth occupied 6,000 acres on the west bluff of the Missouri River in Leavenworth County—approximately three miles north of the city of Leavenworth and 25 miles northwest of Kansas City. The fort was established in 1827 by Colonel Henry Leavenworth to protect the old Santa Fe Trail, along which the Mormon Battalion would begin its 2,000-mile march. The Battalion encamped at the fort for 12 days, each member receiving a $42 uniform allowance, provisions, and equipment while there.

At the end of the twentieth century, Fort Leavenworth was still an active military installation, containing the Army's Command and General Staff College, the Army and Air Force military prison, a federal penitentiary, and the U.S. Disciplinary Barracks.

SOURCE

Walton, George H. *Sentinel of the Plains: Fort Leavenworth and the American West.* Englewood Cliffs, N.J.: Prentice-Hall, 1973.

W. SIDNEY YOUNG

FORT LIMHI, IDAHO. At the April **conference** of 1855, **Brigham Young** called 27 elders led by Thomas S. Smith to establish a farming settlement among the **Native Americans,** wherever they might be received. The group selected a post in east-central **Idaho,** which they called Fort Limhi after a king in the **Book of Mormon.**

For nearly three years, they found both temporal and spiritual success. In the winter of 1858, however, a band of Bannock warriors attacked the fort because they believed a local Nez Perce band was receiving preferential treatment by the Mormon missionaries. The **Saints** therefore abandoned their **mission** site and returned to **Utah.**

SOURCE

Arrington, Leonard. *History of Idaho.* 2 vols. Moscow, Idaho: University of Idaho Press, 1994. 1:165–81.

FRED E. WOODS

FORT SUPPLY, WYOMING. Mormons constructed Fort Supply on Smith's Fork of the Green River in present southwestern **Wyoming**. Built in 1853, 12 miles south of **Fort Bridger**, the Fort's purposes were to secure the eastern entrance to **Utah** Territory, aid emigrants, assist ferry operators, extend Mormon influence, and form an alliance with the Eastern **Shoshones**. The post existed until 1857, when the Mormons abandoned and destroyed the fort to prevent its use by **Johnston's Army** during the Utah Expedition. Prominent record-keepers included **John Brown**, Isaac Bullock, Jesse Crosby, Lewis Robison, and John Pulsipher.

───────

SOURCES

Camp Journal of Fort Supply. Manuscript History of Brigham Young. LDS Church Archives, Salt Lake City.

Gowans, Fred R., and Eugene E. Campbell. *Fort Bridger: Island in the Wilderness.* Provo, Utah: Brigham Young University Press, 1975.

───. *Fort Supply: Brigham Young's Green River Experiment.* Provo, Utah: Brigham Young University Press, 1976.

Twitchell, Jerry F. "History of Latter-day Saints in Bridger Valley, Wyoming." Master's thesis, Brigham Young University, 1959.

FRED R. GOWANS AND JAY H. BUCKLEY

FOSTER, CHARLES G. AND ROBERT D. See. *NAUVOO EXPOSITOR.*

FOUNDATION FOR ANCIENT RESEARCH AND MORMON STUDIES. Commonly know as FARMS, the Foundation for Ancient Research and Mormon Studies is a nonprofit research organization. Incorporated in 1979, FARMS is now formally affiliated with **Brigham Young University** in **Provo, Utah**. The Foundation sponsors research on the **Book of Mormon**, the **Bible**, other ancient scripture, and related subjects. It supports the preservation of ancient religious documents and publishes its research results for both scholars and the general public.

FARMS supports and coordinates work done by faithful scholars who are trained in various relevant academic disciplines such as history, linguistics, literary studies, art history, law, geography, archaeology, political science, and the comparative study of cultures. These scholars apply such disciplines to their study of the scriptures, according to established demands of scholarship.

The Foundation directs a subsidiary known as the Center for the Preservation of Ancient Religious Texts. The Center supports projects that preserve and make available to scholars ancient religious documents. Such projects include *The Dead Sea Scrolls on CD,* the *Journal of Book of Mormon Studies,* the *FARMS Review of Books,* newsletters, and hundreds of original or reprinted papers.

The results of FARMS-supported research are also shared through public presentations, including conferences, lectures, seminars, **radio** and **television** broadcasts, and, when invited, firesides. The work of the Foundation is supported by proceeds from the sale of publications and from donations.

M. GERALD BRADFORD

FOX, RUTH MAY. Ruth May Fox served the **Young Women** of the Church for 39 years as a general board member, counselor, and president. Born 16 November 1853 in Wiltshire, **England**, she married Jessie W. Fox Jr. in 1872, five years after emigrating to **Utah**. They became the parents of 12 children. Involved in the **woman suffrage** movement and community affairs, Ruth was also a writer. She was called to the general board of the Young Ladies Mutual Improvement Association in 1898 and as a counselor in the general presidency in 1905. In 1929 she became the third general president at age 75. Highlights of her administration include the organization's new name—the **Young Women's Mutual Improvement Association**, the girls' camp program, the **Lion House** as a social and learning center for young women, and traveling libraries to promote education. For the Church's centennial in 1930, Ruth penned the hymn "Carry On." Released in 1937 and promised that her "last days would be [her] best days," she lived to the age of 104 and died 12 April 1958 in Salt Lake City.

SOURCES

Brandley, Elsie T. "Ruth May Fox." *Young Woman's Journal* 40 (May 1929): 313.

Fox, Ruth May. "My Story." Privately published, December 1973. LDS Church Archives, Salt Lake City.

Peterson, Janet, and LaRene Gaunt. *Keepers of the Flame: General Presidents of the Young Women.* Salt Lake City: Deseret Book, 1993.

JANET PETERSON

FOX ISLANDS. **Wilford Woodruff**, one of the greatest Mormon missionaries, completed a successful mission to the Fox Islands. These islands are located 12 miles off the coast of Maine near Rockland. There are two islands, North Haven (North Fox Island) and Vinalhaven (South Fox Island).

Elder Woodruff probably became aware of the Fox Islands through his wife, Phoebe Carter Woodruff, whose family lived in Scarborough, **Maine**. His missionary companion, **Jonathan Hale**, was familiar with the Fox Islands, having previously traveled there to get a load of sheep.

The two elders landed on North Fox Island at 2 A.M. on a Sunday in August 1837. Their first preaching occurred in a Baptist church, which they visited that morning. Justin and Betsey Ames, a sea captain and his wife, were baptized in spite of opposition from their Baptist minister. Elder Woodruff and Elder Hale preached on the South Fox Island and incurred the opposition of the Methodist minister located there. Indeed, much of their missionary labors were performed in an atmosphere of hostility. Their zeal yielded dividends—enough people joined the Church to necessitate the organization of a **branch** on each of the islands.

In the fall of 1838, Wilford Woodruff helped 53 Saints from the Fox Islands gather to **Zion**. While their initial destination was **Missouri**, they stopped near Springfield, Illinois, because of hostilities in Missouri. They later joined the Saints in **Nauvoo**. The conversion of many souls, the establishment of two branches, and the gathering to Zion are evidence of Wilford Woodruff's successful mission to the Fox Islands.

SOURCES

Cannon, Donald Q. "Wilford Woodruff's Mission to the Fox Islands." In *New England.* Edited by Donald Q. Cannon. Regional Studies in Latter-day Saint Church History series. Provo, Utah: Brigham Young University, 1988. 85–89.

"Wilford Woodruff's Mission to Maine." *Improvement Era* 73 (September 1970): 82–86.

DONALD Q. CANNON

FRANCE. In July 1849, William Howell of Aberdare, **Wales**, was sent by the presidency of the **British Mission** to open **missionary work** in France. His first convert, Augustus Saint d'Anna, a young multilinguist, was baptized on 30 July 1849 in Le Havre, France. On 5 April 1850, the first French **branch** of the Church was organized with six members in Boulougne-sur-Mer.

The French Mission officially opened 18 June 1850 when **Elder John Taylor** of the Quorum of the Twelve **Apostles** and Curtis E. Bolton arrived in France. They organized the first Paris branch of the Church with eight members on 8 December 1850.

French translations of Church **literature** and **scripture** were among the first materials published by the Church in a language other than English. The *Etoile du Deseret* (Star of Deseret), the first **Mormon periodical** on continental **Europe**, was published monthly for one year beginning May 1851. Largely due to the efforts of **Louis A. Bertrand,** one of the original members of the Paris Branch, the **Book of Mormon** was translated into French and published in January 1852 under Elder Taylor's supervision.

By 24 July 1853, nine branches had been organized, serving 337 members, 289 of whom resided on the Channel Islands. The French mission closed in 1864 because of a general lack of success compared to other European **missions**, compounded by the government's edict that forbade gatherings of more than 20 people at a time. Louis A. Bertrand presided over the mission from 1859 until its closure.

Shortly after the turn of the century, Elder **Francis M. Lyman** of the Quorum of the Twelve dedicated France for missionary work, commencing a new era of the Church in that nation. The mission opened a second time in 1912, geographically covering all of French-speaking Europe. Presiding over it was one of the mission's 28 full-time elders, 23-year-old Edgar B. Brossard. During the first year, 62 people were baptized. Official missionary service, however, was discontinued again with the outbreak of **World War I**.

In 1924, the year the French mission reopened, there were 200 convert baptisms. Octave F. Orsenbach and Joseph E. Evans were among those who presided over the mission before it was closed again in 1939 when France entered **World War II**. Leon Fargier, a member in Valence, in nonoccupied France, almost single-handedly conducted the spiritual affairs of the Church in France until 1946 when the mission reopened after peace was established. The **Mormon Tabernacle Choir** performed in France in 1955, 1991, and 1998.

Membership consistently increased from 1,909 in 1959 to 16,500 in 1985. The first French **stake** was created in 1975 in Paris. At the beginning of the year 2000 there were 3 missions, 7 **stakes**, 132 **wards** and branches, and 30,541 members in France.

SOURCES

Marie, Alain. "Leon Fargier: His Faith Wouldn't Go Underground." *Ensign* 21 (September 1991): 29–31.

McClellan, Richard D. "Louis A. Bertrand: One of the Most Singular and Romantic Figures of the Age." Honor's thesis, Brigham Young University, 2000.

"Moments in History." *Church News,* 31 July 1971, 2.

1997–98 Church Almanac. Salt Lake City: Deseret News, 1996. 324–25.

Stocks, Hugh G. "Book of Mormon Translations." *Encyclopedia of Mormonism.* Edited by Daniel H. Ludlow. 4 vols. New York: Macmillan, 1992. 1:213–14.

CAMILLE FRONK

FREEMASONRY. See MASONRY.

"FREE PEOPLE OF COLOR." In the July 1833 edition of *The Evening and Morning Star,* the Church published an article "to prevent any misunderstanding . . . respecting Free people of color, who may think of coming to the western boundaries of **Missouri**, as members of the church" (*Star,* 109). The article indicated the Church's willingness to abide by the Missouri laws forbidding free blacks from living in the state unless they had obtained U.S. citizenship. Non-Mormon residents of **Jackson County**, however, misinterpreted the article and used it as evidence that the Saints were "tampering with [their] slaves" by "inviting free negroes and mulattoes . . . to become '**Mormons**,' and remove and settle among [them]" (Smith, 375). Initially written to counter the charge of the mob, the article actually became a cause of the Saints' persecution in Jackson County.

SOURCES

The Evening and the Morning Star 2 (July 1833): 109.

Smith, Joseph. *History of The Church of Jesus Christ of Latter-day Saints.* Edited by B. H. Roberts. 2d ed. rev. 7 vols. Salt Lake City: The Church of Jesus Christ of Latter-day Saints, 1932–51. 1:372–79.

ANDREW H. HEDGES

FREIBERG TEMPLE. At the end of **World War II**, approximately 10,000 members of the Church lived in eastern **Germany**, which became the Soviet zone of occupation and then the communist German Democratic Republic (GDR). Regular Church activities were permitted under certain restrictions, but for the most part members had no access to a **temple.** Certain persons, primarily older members, were permitted to travel to the temple in **Switzerland.** Many simply emigrated out of the country, but in 1961 the Berlin Wall prevented even that. Some persons were permitted to visit relatives in the Federal Republic of Germany (West Germany), but their visas did not normally permit travel to Switzerland. After many discussions between Church and government authorities, the government of the GDR offered property on the outskirts of the city of Freiberg and suggested that the Church build a temple inside the German Democratic Republic. In 1985 the Freiberg Germany Temple was dedicated; approximately 70,000 people toured the temple during the open house prior to dedication. The first **temple president** was **Henry Burkhardt.** At the end of the twentieth century, the temple served members from the countries of eastern **Europe.**

SOURCES

Burckhardt, Henry. Interview by Matthew K. Heiss. James Moyle Oral History Program, LDS Church Historical Department, Salt Lake City. 24 October 1991.

Davis, Garold N., and Norma S. Davis, comp. and trans. *Behind the Iron Curtain: Recollections of Latter-day Saints in East Germany, 1945–1989.* Provo, Utah: BYU Studies, 1996.

Monson, Thomas S. *Faith Rewarded.* Salt Lake City: Deseret Book, 1996.

GAROLD N. DAVIS

FRÉMONT, JOHN C. John Charles Frémont, **explorer,** cartographer, naturalist, and general, best remembered as the "pathfinder" of the American West, eventually became a friend of the **Mormons.** Born in Savannah, **Georgia,** on 21 January 1813, Frémont was a **railroad** surveyor at age 26. As a charter member of the U.S. Army's Corps of Topographical Engineers, he worked under Joseph Nicollet, **America's** first systematic cartographer, in mapping the Upper **Mississippi** regions in 1838 and 1839. Son-in-law of **Missouri's** first senator, Thomas Hart Benton, Frémont received the political and financial support to conduct several landmark expeditions into the American West at a time of budding interest in westward expansionism.

On his first expedition in 1842, he mapped the **Platte River** road as far west as the South Pass and the Wind River Mountains. During his second expedition, 1843 to 1844, Frémont discovered and named the **Great Basin** as a geologic and geographic entity. His internationally popular *Report of the Exploring Expeditions to the Rocky Mountains,* including his maps of the Platte River country and of the Great Salt Lake regions, were carefully studied by **Brigham Young** and other Mormon leaders in **Nauvoo** on the eve of the exodus. Frémont's works were frequently consulted throughout the Mormon march west and helped confirm the decision to settle in the **Salt Lake Valley**.

During his ill-fated third expedition, Frémont engaged in military action against Mexican authority in Monterey and became a prominent figure in America's claim to **California**. His independence, impetuosity, and sometimes imperious behavior, however, led him into conflict with such senior army officers as General Stephen W. Kearny, resulting in Frémont's court martial in 1848. Quickly pardoned by President **James Polk**, the undeterred, ever-adventurous Frémont conducted two other less-successful railroad surveying expeditions in the West in 1848 and 1853. During the latter, he and his snowbound, winter-starved exploring party were saved by Mormons in Parowan, **Utah**—a favor that led him to befriend Utah and the Mormon cause ever after.

Frémont's careful writings, numberless plant specimens, and detailed maps made him an almost legendary figure. He was nominated as the first presidential candidate of the newly formed **Republican Party** in 1856. During the **Civil War**, he briefly served as a general in the Union Army. Later he gained—and lost—vast fortunes in California land and mining interests. After serving for a short time as territorial governor of **Arizona**, he died on 13 July 1890 while on a visit to **New York City**.

SOURCES

Frémont, John Charles. *Report of the Exploring Expedition to the Rocky Mountains*. Ann Arbor, Mich.: University Microfilms, 1966.

Miller, David E. "John C. Frémont in the Great Salt Lake Region." *Historian* 11 (Autumn 1948) 14–28.

Nevins, Allen. *Frémont: The West's Greatest Adventurer.* 2 vols. New York: Harper Brothers, 1928.

Rolle, Andrew. *John Charles Frémont—Character as Destiny*. Norman, Okla.: University of Oklahoma Press, 1991.

Spence, Mary Lee. "The Frémonts and Utah." *Utah Historical Quarterly* 44 (Summer 1976): 286–302.

RICHARD E. BENNETT

FRENCH FARM. As **Saints** began to gather to the **Kirtland** area, a need arose to purchase lands for their settlement. In April 1833 the Church purchased Peter French's 103-acre farm for $5,000. The **Prophet Joseph Smith** sought inspiration concerning how to divide the newly purchased farm, and he received instructions that the **bishop** in Kirtland was to oversee the dividing of the land for inheritances (D&C 96). The most important determination was that the **Kirtland Temple** be built on a portion of the French farm.

Because much of the French farm was later deeded to **John Johnson**, including an inn that sat on the property, many believe that Johnson had donated a large portion of the funds used to purchase the farm after he sold his property in **Hiram, Ohio.**

SOURCE

Keith W. Perkins. "Land Ownership in Kirtland." *Historical Atlas of Mormonism.* Edited by S. Kent Brown, Donald Q. Cannon, and Richard H. Jackson. New York: Simon & Schuster, 1994. 22–24.

CRAIG J. OSTLER

FRENCH GUIANA. With a population of 163,000, French Guiana is an overseas department of **France** located on the northern coast of **South America.** In the early 1980s, Charles Fortin and Rosiette Fauvette became members of the Church and subsequently moved to French Guiana. **Elder Charles Didier** visited the area 4 March 1988 and organized a group in Kourou. Serge and Christie Bonnoit became the first converts in French Guiana in November of the same year. The first native Guyanaise convert was Michaela Papo, baptized 1 July 1989. By the beginning of the year 2000, the country had about 209 members and two branches.

SOURCE

1999–2000 Church Almanac. Salt Lake City: Deseret News, 1998. 320.

TODD KRUEGER

FRENCH POLYNESIA. French Polynesia, a French overseas territory, consists of five island groups (118 islands) and in 1999 had a total population of 220,000. Seventy-nine percent of the populace is Polynesian.

On 30 April 1844, three **elders—Addison Pratt**, Benjamin F. Grouard, and Noah Rogers—arrived at Tubuai Island, 350 miles south of Tahiti. They had been sent from **Nauvoo, Illinois**, in May 1843 by the **Prophet Joseph Smith**. They established the first foreign language **mission** of the Church. Pratt created **branches** on Tubuai, while Rogers went to islands in the northwest and Grouard went to Anaa in the Tuamotu Archipelago. Rogers returned to **America** in 1845. Pratt and Grouard baptized at least 2,000 Polynesians. From 1847 to 1848, Pratt went to Utah and returned in 1850 with reinforcements. Unfortunately, the French forced closure of the mission in 1852.

In 1892 French Polynesia was reopened by Elders Joseph W. Damron and William A. Seegmiller, sent from Samoa. Through the decades, international political and economic events have taken their toll on membership growth. Since 1950, however, the Church has experienced steady growth and progress. For example, the number and quality of buildings increased during the Building Missionary era of the 1950s and 1960s; temple excursions to New Zealand began in 1963; the Latter-day Saint Primary School was established from 1964 to 1982; the Tahiti Stake was created on 14 May 1972; and the Papeete Tahiti Temple was dedicated on 27 October 1983. In 1994 the French Polynesian Saints celebrated the sesquicentennial of the founding of the mission. At that time Elder Russell M. Nelson of the Quorum of the Twelve Apostles dedicated French Polynesia for the preaching of the gospel. At the beginning of the year 2000, membership stood at 16,230. In that same year, French Polynesia had 1 mission (Tahiti Papeete Mission), 6 stakes, and 3 districts with 45 wards and 28 branches. The Book of Mormon was first published in Tahitian in 1904.

SOURCES

Britsch, R. Lanier. *Unto the Islands of the Sea: A History of the Latter-day Saints in the Pacific.* Salt Lake City: Deseret Book, 1986. 1–90.

Ellsworth, S. George, and Kathleen C. Perrin. *Seasons of Faith and Courage: The Church of Jesus Christ of Latter-day Saints in French Polynesia, a Sesquicentennial History.* Sandy, Utah: Yves R. Perrin, 1994.

1999–2000 Church Almanac. Salt Lake City: Deseret News, 1998. 320–22.

R. LANIER BRITSCH

FRIBERG, ARNOLD. Arnold Friberg, a prominent Mormon artist, was born 21 December 1913 in Winnetka, Illinois, to Swedish immigrants. Friberg worked as a commercial artist and a master artist and became a member of the Royal Society of Arts. Raised in Phoenix, Arizona (where his family joined the Church), his schooling and career in art took him to New York, Chicago, and eventually to Salt Lake City, where he taught art and illustration at the University of Utah. In 1953, Arnold worked with Cecil B. Demille on the artistic design for the movie *The Ten Commandments.* He was nominated for an Academy Award for his work. He is best known in the Church for his Book of Mormon series, commissioned by the **Sunday School** and **Primary** organizations. This series contains eight paintings of Book of Mormon scenes. A man considered both spiritual and patriotic, Friberg has painted portraits of British royalty, American heroes (such as General **George Washington** kneeling in prayer at Valley Forge), and Canadian Mounties.

SOURCES

Anderson, Velan Max. "Arnold Friberg, Artist: His Life, His Philosophy, and His Works." Master's thesis, Brigham Young University, 1970.

Schwarz, Ted. *Arnold Friberg: The Passion of a Modern Master.* Flagstaff, Ariz.: Northland Press, 1985.

MATTHEW O. RICHARDSON

FRIEND, THE. First published in January 1971, the *Friend* **magazine** is the monthly Church publication for children under the age of 12. This magazine continues a tradition of publishing for children of the Church. **Elder George Q. Cannon** published the *Juvenile Instructor,* a "first-class child's paper," in January 1866. When this publication later became sponsored by the **Sunday School** organization, the **Primary** association commenced publishing the *Children's Friend* in January 1902, with the general Primary presidents serving as editors.

In June 1970 the **First Presidency** announced that Church magazines would "be unified into three publications," including one for children, which would be published "under the direct supervision of the First Presidency and the Council of the Twelve" and would "thereby become official organs of communication from the Church to its members throughout the world" (Letter).

Regarding the change in the name of the children's magazine, Elder **Gordon B. Hinckley** explained: "The name of the magazine will . . . simply be the *Friend,* dropping the word *Children's,* because when some youngsters get to be ten and eleven years of age, they think they are no longer children. But they still need a *Friend*" (98).

SOURCES

Cannon, George Q. *Juvenile Instructor* (1 January 1866): 3.

"Church Magazines to Be Combined into Three Publications." *Church News,* 6 June 1970. 3.

First Presidency letter to Stake Presidents, Bishops, Mission Presidents, District and Branch Presidents, 3 June 1970.

Gibson, Stephen W. "Magazines Make History." *Church News,* 6 June 1970, 8–9.

Hinckley, Gordon B. "A Friend for Every Child." *Improvement Era* 73 (December 1970): 97–98.

GARY GILLESPIE

FRONTIER GUARDIAN. The *Frontier Guardian,* western Iowa's first newspaper and a product of the **Mormon exodus,** served the citizens of Kanesville (**Council Bluffs**) from February 1849 to early 1852. Under the editorship of **Orson Hyde** (1805–78), a Mormon **apostle,** the semimonthly *Frontier Guardian* defended the Mormon faith while promoting local law and order at a time when thousands of restless gold seekers were passing through the area en route to **California.** In addition, taking a pro-Whig political stance, it sought to insure the political rights of the residents of Pottawattamie County in the new **Iowa** state legislature. The paper's primary purpose, however, was to encourage the emigration of Latter-day **Saints** everywhere to the Great **Salt Lake Valley.**

Stoutly religious, the *Frontier Guardian* ran front-page articles on the **Prophet Joseph Smith,** the **Book of Mormon,** baptism for the dead, and other Mormon doctrines. It likewise included minutes of **conferences, high council meetings,** instructions to **bishops,** and notices of excommunications. **Elder** Hyde, a former editor of the *Millennial Star* in **England,** was assisted by Daniel Mackintosh and by John Gooch, typesetter and printer.

Anxious to head west in 1852, Brother Hyde sold his enterprise to Jacob Dawson, a fellow Whig, for $2,000. Soon after, the paper was reissued under the name *Frontier Guardian and Iowa Sentinel,* a name later changed to the *Iowa Sentinel* and still later to the *Council Bluffs Nonpareil.*

SOURCES

Hill, Marvin S. "An Historical Study of the Life of Orson Hyde, Early Mormon Missionary and Apostle from 1805 to 1852." Master's thesis, Brigham Young University, 1955. Chapter 8.

Trumbo, Jean. "Orson Hyde's Frontier Guardian: a Mormon Editor Chronicles the Westward Movement Through Kanesville, Iowa." *Iowa Heritage Illustrated* 77 (Summer 1996): 74–85.

RICHARD E. BENNETT

FUNDAMENTALISTS. In the context of Mormonism, the term "fundamentalists" connotes the group of men and women who continue in the practice of **plural marriage** during the twentieth century. This group of schismatic Mormons attests to belief in the nineteenth-century doctrines of the Church, particularly the emphasis on plural marriage and the **law of consecration** and stewardship. Confused by what they perceived as ambiguous language in the **1890 Manifesto**, which signaled the end of Church-sanctioned plural marriage, many continued in the practice, either migrating to **Mexico** and **Canada** or moving increasingly apart from mainstream **Mormon** society. After the first decade of the twentieth century, so-called fundamentalists were excommunicated by the Church for their beliefs, and the line between these groups and Latter-day **Saints** became increasingly significant over time. By the 1920s many polygamists gathered in informally organized groups around various leaders who claimed continued priesthood authority to perform plural marriages. Men like Joseph W. Musser, John Y. Barlow, and Lorin C. Woolley each inspired different groups of fundamentalists to separate from The Church of Jesus Christ of Latter-day Saints and continue in their lifestyle, independent of Church approval. Later in the twentieth century, principle enclaves included the groups that settled in Short Creek, **Arizona**, led by LeRoy Johnson, and the United Apostolic Brethren located in Bluffdale, **Utah**, headed by Owen Allred.

SOURCE

Bradley, Martha Sonntag. *Kidnapped from That Land: The Government Raids on the Short Creek Polygamists.* Salt Lake City: University of Utah Press, 1993.

MARTHA SONNTAG BRADLEY

FUNK, RUTH HARDY. Ruth Hardy Funk, seventh general president of the **Young Women**, was born 11 February 1917 in Chicago, **Illinois**. An accomplished pianist, she declined a concert career to better serve her **family** and the Church. She grew up in **Salt Lake City, Utah**, where she met and married Marcus C. Funk. Ruth taught piano, led high school chorales, and served on the General **Music** Committee of the Church. Called as the general president of the Young Women's Association in 1972, she served until 1978. The organization was restructured as the **Aaronic Priesthood** MIA (Young Women) in 1972, then in 1974 as the Young Women. Sister Funk's presidency introduced the Young Womanhood Recognition program, which emphasized inner growth, goal setting, service, and accountability.

SOURCES

Ruth Hardy Funk Oral History. James Moyle Oral History Program, LDS Church Historical Department, Salt Lake City. 1979.

Peterson, Janet, and LaRene Gaunt. *Keepers of the Flame: General Presidents of the Young Women.* Salt Lake City: Deseret Book, 1993.

JANET PETERSON

FUR TRADE RENDEZVOUS. Four of the 16 fur trade rendezvous held between 1825 and 1840 took place in **Utah**. These sites, where trappers met caravans from the East to trade their furs for supplies, helped to open the mountain West for permanent settlers such as the **Mormons**.

Manual Lisa, **William H. Ashley**, Andrew Henry, and others lost the battle with the Blackfoot and Arikara Indians on the upper **Missouri River** in the early 1800s. Because of the abundance of beaver, the Henry-Ashley Company in the early 1820s moved trapping operations to the Green River of **Wyoming** and northern Utah in 1824.

With Henry-Ashley men in the mountains year-round after 1824, the fur trade caravan and the rendezvous system replaced the river system and the forts of the upper Missouri River. Pack mules and wagons replaced the boats previously used to haul supplies to traders and trappers on the river. Bringing supplies to preselected locations in the mountains replaced the forts formerly used to resupply trappers who became the "**mountain men**." Willow Valley (Cache) was the site of the 1826 and 1831 rendezvous. Sweet Lake (Bear Lake) was the site of the 1827 and 1828 rendezvous.

SOURCES

Billington, Ray Allen. *Westward Expansion: A History of the American Frontier.* 4th ed. New York: Macmillan, 1974. 384–85.

Gowans, Fred R. *Rocky Mountain Rendezvous: A History of the Fur Trade Rendezvous, 1825–1840.* Layton, Utah: Peregrine Smith Books, 1985.

FRED R. GOWANS AND JAMES WIRSHBORN

GENERAL CONFERENCE. Crowds at Temple Square during the 6 April 1906 general conference.

GABON. In 1992 the west central African nation of Gabon gave permission for the Church to be established there. This approval followed a visit to Salt Lake City by a diplomat of the Embassy of Gabon, with **Elder Neal A. Maxwell** of the Quorum of the Twelve **Apostles** and Elder Richard P. Lindsay of the **Seventy**. The diplomat was accompanied to **Salt Lake City** by Jerome Mickouma, a citizen of Gabon who had joined the Church several years earlier while working in **Washington, D.C.** On 1 February 1992, Gabon became part of the **Cameroon** Yaounde Mission, presided over by President Robert L. Mercer. Mission headquarters were later moved, and the **mission** became the **Ivory Coast** Abidjan Mission. At the end of 1997, there were fewer than 100 members living in the country.

SOURCE

1999–2000 Church Almanac. Salt Lake City: Deseret News, 1998. 323.

E. DALE LEBARON

GADSDEN PURCHASE. In 1853 the **United States** acquired the Gadsden Purchase from **Mexico** for $10 million. It was about 30,000 square miles and was located in Southern **Arizona** and **New Mexico**. When the **Mormon Battalion** left Santa Fe under the command of Colonel **Philip St. George Cooke**, its assignment was to open a wagon road through the relatively unknown territory between the Rio Grande and the Gila River. Skirting a mountain range, they pioneered and mapped a route via the Guadalupe Pass and San Pedro River in southeastern Arizona. Following the close of the **Mexican War**, interest in a southern transcontinental **railroad** increased. "Cooke's wagon road" was incorporated into the proposed route. The 1848 Treaty of Guadalupe Hidalgo, however, placed the international boundary along the Gila River, leaving the Battalion's route in Mexican territory. The purchase, negotiated by James Gadsden, U.S. ambassador to Mexico, was intended to remedy this problem.

The irregular frontier gave the United States control of the land through which Cooke and the Battalion had pioneered their wagon road. The boundary proceeded west from El Paso one hundred miles and then abruptly dropped south—just far enough to include the area where the Mormon Battalion had headed south in order to get through the mountains. The line continued west at that latitude far enough to include the Battalion's route from Guadalupe Pass to where it turned north along the San Pedro River to reach the Gila. The boundary then began angling northwest to a point to provide Mexico a land bridge to Baja California.

SOURCES

Garber, Paul Neff. *The Gadsden Treaty.* Gloucester, Mass.: Peter Smith, 1959.

Goetzmann, William H. *Army Exploration in the American West, 1803–1863.* New Haven: Yale University Press, 1959.

RICHARD O. COWAN

GALLAND, ISAAC. Isaac Galland, best remembered for selling land to **Mormons** who had been exiled from **Missouri**, was born 15 May 1791 in Somerset County, **Pennsylvania**. He spent his early years in **Ohio** and **Indiana**, where he married, speculated in land, and studied and eventually practiced some form of botanical medicine. As a frontier medical practitioner, Galland earned himself the title "doctor," which remained with him until his death. He relocated to **Illinois** in the early 1820s and about 1827 built the first cabin and established a trading post at Oquawka. By 1829 he had moved to **Lee County, Iowa**, where he founded the town of Nashville and continued to practice medicine and speculate in land. He became acquainted with the Mormons in November 1838 when he met Israel Barlow who, with other Mormons, was fleeing Missouri and seeking refuge in Illinois. Negotiations between Galland and Church authorities immediately ensued and continued until the following spring, when he sold nearly 18,000 acres of land (mostly in Lee County, Iowa) to the Mormons for about $50,000.00.

Galland converted to Mormonism in July 1839. An 1841 **revelation** (D&C 124) counseled the doctor to invest in the **Nauvoo House**, and soon thereafter Galland was sent to the east to solicit donations for its construction. While in Pennsylvania Doctor Galland wrote a seven-page defense of Mormonism (July 1841), but by 1842 he had withdrawn his fellowship. Except for a three-year stay in northern **California**, Galland lived the remainder of his life in Lee County, Iowa, where he died 27 September 1858. Despite Isaac Galland's only superficial interest in Mormonism, **Joseph Smith** and other authorities of the Church considered him a Mormon benefactor.

SOURCE

Cook, Lyndon W. "Isaac Galland: Mormon Benefactor," *BYU Studies* (Spring 1979): 261–84.

LYNDON W. COOK

GALLATIN ELECTION DAY. At the election held in Gallatin 6 August 1838, an incident took place which ignited the flames of antagonism between **Mormons** and **Missouri** mobocrats. This hostility culminated with Governor **Lilburn W. Boggs's extermination order**, enforced by the Missouri State Militia, which drove the Mormons from the state.

A few Mormons, as citizens of **Daviess County**, went to Gallatin to vote. Entering the town square, they found William P. Penniston haranguing the old settlers and warning them that the Mormons were "rascals" and would soon control the county if allowed to vote (Roberts, 1:447). Two men, Samuel Brown and Richard Weldon (also spelled Weldin or Welding) began to argue when Brown called Penniston's accusations untrue. Weldon struck Brown, and a general riot broke out as each side sought its rights. Following the affray, the Mormons retired without voting. Rumors quickly reached **Far West** and **Adam-ondi-Ahman** that two Mormons had been killed, several wounded, and others held prisoner by Missourians. **Sampson Avard** raised an armed force and rode to Gallatin to verify the rumors. **Joseph Smith**, **Hyrum Smith**, and **Elias Higbee** accompanied the group. As they neared Gallatin, they met some Mormons who, although badly bruised and hurt from their fight, assured their rescuers that no one had been killed. A temporary peace agreement was reached on both sides. Within a few weeks, however, events occurred at **Crooked River**, **DeWitt**, **Haun's Mill**, and Far West that forced the Mormons to leave Missouri (Smith, 3:58–61).

SOURCES

"Letter to General John B. Clark from B. M. Lisle, Adj.-General, 26 October 1838." *Document Containing the Correspondence, Order &c. In Relation to the Disturbances with the Mormons; and the Evidence Given before the Hon. Austin A. King, Judge of the fifth Judicial Circuit of the State of Missouri, at the Court-House in Richmond, in a*

Criminal Court of Inquiry, Begun November 12, 1838, on the Trial of Joseph Smith, Jr., and Others, for High Treason and Other Crimes Against the State. Published by Order of the General Assembly. Fayette, Mo.: Boon's Lick Democrat, 1841. 62–63.

Mormon Redress Petitions, Documents of the 1833–1838 Missouri Conflict. Edited by Clark V. Johnson. Provo, Utah: Religious Studies Center, Brigham Young University, 1992.

Roberts, B. H. *A Comprehensive History of The Church of Jesus Christ of Latter-day Saints, Century One.* 6 vols. Salt Lake City: The Church of Jesus Christ of Latter-day Saints, 1930. 1:447–48.

Smith, Joseph, *History of The Church of Jesus Christ of Latter-day Saints.* Edited by B. H. Roberts. 2d ed. rev. 7 vols. Salt Lake City: The Church of Jesus Christ of Latter-day Saints, 1932–51. Introduction, xxviii–xxix, 58–61, 176 fn.

CLARK V. JOHNSON

GAMBLING. Gambling most commonly takes the form of games of chance and involves the hope of receiving something of value with little or no effort. The Church opposes gambling in its various forms because of the moral, spiritual, and financial destruction of individuals, families, and communities that engage in it.

In 1925 the **First Presidency** took a stand against betting on horse races and similar practices that "encourage the spirit of reckless speculation" (quoted in Cowan). In the closing decades of the twentieth century, the Church likewise opposed the establishment of, and participation in, state-operated lotteries.

SOURCES

"Church's Stand on Gambling." *Ensign* 22 (March 1992): 74.

Cowan, Richard O. *The Latter-day Saint Century.* Salt Lake City: Bookcraft, 1985. 127.

McConkie, Bruce R. *Mormon Doctrine.* 2d ed. Salt Lake City: Bookcraft, 1966. 302–3.

Oaks, Dallin H. "Gambling—Morally Wrong and Politically Unwise." *Ensign* 17 (June 1987): 69–75.

BRIAN M. HAUGLID

GARDEN GROVE, IOWA. Mt. **Pisgah** and Garden Grove were the two temporary **Mormon** settlements in midsouthern **Iowa** from 1846 to 1851. On 24 April 1846, **Brigham Young's** company reached the site by Weldon Fork (creek), 144 miles from **Nauvoo.** Within two weeks they built log cabins, dug wells, plowed, planted gardens and farms, and fenced hundreds of acres, creating a stopover settlement where **Saints** from Nauvoo lacking outfits, resources, or health could stop, rest, and recruit. On 24 May President Young's company moved on, leaving hundreds there with Samuel Bent as president. Garden Grove residents traded with people in eastern Iowa towns and with **Missouri** farmers 50 miles south. In the spring of 1846, thousands more from Nauvoo reached Garden Grove by a new, more direct route, and many stayed. That fall, Garden Grove wagons helped rescue the last Saints forced from Nauvoo.

During Garden Grove's first year, some 70 died, including President Bent. As of February 1847, 120 families lived there. David Kington presided from late 1847 until 1851, when the Saints vacated Garden Grove in a wagon train of some 100 people. A modern monument and park mark the Saints' cemetery site. Today's town of Garden Grove is one mile east of where the Mormon settlement was located.

SOURCES

Bennett, Richard E. *Mormons at the Missouri, 1846–1852: "And Should We Die. . . ."* Norman, Okla.: University of Oklahoma, 1987.

Gunzenhauser, Karla. "The Settlement at Garden Grove, Iowa." *Nauvoo Journal* 6 (Fall 1994): 14–44.

Webb, Lynn Robert. "The Contributions of the Temporary Settlements Garden Grove, Mount Pisgah, and Kanesville, Iowa, to Mormon Emigration, 1846–1852." Master's thesis, Brigham Young University, 1954.

WILLIAM G. HARTLEY

GARDO HOUSE. In 1873 **Brigham Young** began construction on the Gardo House, the official **Salt Lake City** residence for the president of the Church. The building stood directly across South Temple Street from the **Beehive House**. Detractors called it Amelia's Palace after Brigham Young's wife Amelia Folsom Young, for whom it was rumored to have been built.

The Church acquired the house from the Brigham Young estate, and in 1881 **John Taylor** became the first president of the Church to occupy it. Mining magnate Edwin F. Holmes and his wife, Susannah, purchased the house in 1901 and made it a showplace for Salt Lake City society. The house was demolished in 1921 to make way for business buildings.

SOURCE

Bardsley, Ann Jardine. "Tracing the Lore of the Gardo House." *Deseret News,* 25 July 1985, C1.

W. RANDALL DIXON

GARMENTS. The latter-day restoration of temple **ordinances** included instructions concerning the wearing of the garment of the **priesthood**. Members of the Church who receive their endowments in the house of the Lord covenant to wear sacred priestly undergarments throughout their lives. The undergarments have symbolic marks of spiritual significance to the wearer. These garments are manufactured and distributed by an agency of the Church.

Historically, **Adam** and Eve received sacred clothing prior to being cast out of the Garden of Eden: "Unto Adam also and to his wife did the Lord God make coats of skins, and clothed them" (Gen. 3:21). Further, Aaron and his sons, as officiators in the tabernacle, wore special ceremonial clothing (Lev. 8:6–9). The Savior also wore the "garment," referred to by modern **Jews** as the tallith, that was prescribed in the Mosaic law (Matt. 14:36; Luke 8:44).

The garment serves as a reminder of covenants made in holy **temples**. Similarly, the Lord explained to **Moses** that the purpose of the garment worn by ancient Israelites was "that ye may look upon it, and remember all the commandments of the Lord, and do them" (Num. 15:39). In 1988 the **First Presidency** wrote that the garment "is an outward expression of an inward commitment to follow the Savior" (Letter). Additionally, the garment encourages modesty in clothing styles. The garment "strengthens the wearer to resist temptation, fend off evil influences, and stand firmly for the right" (Asay, 21).

Sources

Asay, Carlos E. "The Temple Garment: 'An Outward Expression of an Inward Commitment.'" *Ensign* 27 (August 1997): 19–23.

First Presidency Letter. 10 October 1988.

Packer, Boyd K. *The Holy Temple.* Salt Lake City: Bookcraft, 1980. 75–79.

CRAIG J. OSTLER

GATES, CRAWFORD. Crawford Gates, a composer, conductor, and educator, is best known for two major Mormon works: the successful musical play *Promised Valley,* and his music for the **Hill Cumorah Pageant**. Born 29 December 1921, Gates enrolled at **Brigham Young University** in 1946 to study composition. That same year the State of Utah commissioned him to write what became *Promised Valley* for the **pioneer** centennial (1947). Six years later he was commissioned to write the first original score for the Hill Cumorah Pageant (completed in

1957). From 1950 to 1966, he served at BYU as a composer, conductor, and eventually chair of the Department of **Music**, after which he took a position at Beloit College (**Wisconsin**) from 1966 to 1989. He conducted several regional symphony orchestras in the midwest and composed nearly 800 solo, chamber, and large ensemble works, including a new Hill Cumorah score (1988) and the oratorio *Vision of Eternity* (1993).

SOURCE

Gates, Crawford. "A Sacred Choral Pageant." *Music Journal* 19 (February 1961): 68–70.

MICHAEL HICKS

GATES, SUSA YOUNG. Respected as a writer, publisher, educator, missionary, **women's** rights advocate, and mother, Susa Young Gates was born in **Salt Lake City** on 18 March 1856 to **Brigham Young** and Lucy Bigelow Young, Brigham's 22d wife. Susa married at age 16 and had two children before divorcing. She then enrolled in **Brigham Young Academy** and founded the Department of **Music** while a student there. She later met Jacob F. Gates and was married to him in 1880; they had 11 children together, only four of whom survived to adulthood.

In addition to being a busy mother, Susa Gates served a **mission** with her husband and her young **family** to the **Sandwich Islands** from 1885 to 1889. She served as the official stenographer for the dedication of the **Salt Lake Temple** in 1893.

She was involved throughout her life in writing and **education**. Her literary and editorial work included the founding of both the *Young Woman's Journal* and the *Relief Society Magazine*; she contributed scores of articles to these **periodicals** and other publications. She wrote several novels and nonfiction books, including a biography of her father completed shortly before her own death. She also served on Church boards for the **Relief Society** and **Young Ladies' Mutual Improvement Association**.

As a member of the National Council of Women and the founder of the Utah Woman's Press Club, Susa was active in supporting women's issues. In her later years, she devoted most of her time to **genealogy** and **temple work**, completing several thousand **endowments**. She died in Salt Lake City on 27 May 1933.

SOURCES

Cracroft, R. Paul. "Susa Young Gates: Her Life and Literary Work." Master's thesis, University of Utah. 1951.

Person, Carolyn W. D. "Susa Young Gates." *Mormon Sisters: Women in Early Utah.* Edited by Claudia L. Bushman. Cambridge, Mass.: Emmeline Press, 1976. 198–223.

Plummer, Louise. "Gates, Susa Young." *Encyclopedia of Mormonism.* Edited by Daniel H. Ludlow. 4 vols. New York: Macmillan, 1992. 2:535–36.

DAVID KENISON

GATHERING. A biblical doctrine clarified by **Book of Mormon** and modern **revelations**, the "gathering" refers to a promise that in the last days scattered Israel will be gathered to **Jerusalem** and to a **New Jerusalem**. Much of that gathering will take place when believers seek safety during the destruction initiating the Millennium. These gatherings have a spiritual as well as a geographical component (D&C 133:14). Two preliminary gathering efforts have already taken place—Jewish people to the **Holy Land**, and early Latter-day Saint converts from among scattered Israel "leaving sinful Babylon" and gathering to centers in **Ohio**, **Missouri**, **Nauvoo**, and then the Rocky Mountains.

In Jerusalem on 24 October 1841, **Elder Orson Hyde** of the Twelve dedicated **Palestine** for the gathering of the **Jews**. In 1873 Elder **George A. Smith** of the **First Presidency** rededicated the land. Jewish migration to Palestine began in the late nineteenth century. British forces took Palestine from the Turks during **World War I**. By the Balfour Declaration of 1917, Britain committed itself to fostering a national home for Jewish people, despite Palestinian Arabs' opposition. During the 1930s and 1940s, Jewish refugees fled there in large numbers. In 1947 the United Nations partitioned Palestine into separate Jewish and Arab states. The Republic of **Israel** came into being on 14 May 1948. By the mid-1990s, Israel's population was 5.4 million out of 14 million Jewish people worldwide.

The "gathering" has been a practice, operational in the LDS Church from 1830 to the 1890s, wherein converts were commanded to relocate to where the Church was gathering. It was initiated by a September 1830 revelation stating that "the decree hath gone forth from the Father that they shall be gathered into one place upon the face of the land, to prepare their hearts and be prepared in all things against the day when tribulation and desolation are sent forth upon the wicked" (D&C 29:8). **Saints** gathered to **Jackson County, Missouri**, a place designated in revelations as **Zion**, where a New Jerusalem would be built. Persecution thwarted their efforts and drove them out, forcing them to gather elsewhere.

In 1836 at **Kirtland**, **Joseph Smith** received from **Moses** "the keys of the gathering of Israel" (D&C 110:11). Nauvoo replaced Kirtland and Missouri as the gathering center until persecutions pushed the Saints to the Intermountain West. There the gathering fulfilled prophecy that the house of the Lord would be established in the "top of the mountains" (Isa. 2:2).

During the nineteenth century, gathering was the next step after baptism. Converts first gathered from the **United States** and **Canada**. From 1840 to 1846 Church-sponsored immigrant companies moved some 4,000 British converts to Nauvoo. In 1844 Joseph Smith pronounced that "the whole of America is Zion" and that "henceforth wherever the Elders of Israel shall build up churches and **branches** unto the Lord throughout the States, there shall be a **stake** of Zion" (Smith, 6:318–19).

After relocating in the West, the Church sponsored large-scale emigration, giving assistance that included **Perpetual Emigrating Fund** Company loans (after 1849). In 1848 Saints in **Europe** were told to "emigrate as speedily as possible" (*Millennial Star,* 81–88). In 1852 the First Presidency said of Saints abroad: "It is time for them to gather, without delay, to Zion" (Clark, 2:98). The gathering had two primary purposes: to give the Church a strong, permanent base and to provide a place of refuge from persecution and sin. They sang with joy, "Oh Babylon, oh Babylon, we bid thee farewell" and "Israel, Israel, God is calling thee from lands of woe." The trek across sea, plains, and mountains required faith and sacrifice—leaving homes, jobs, and unconverted family members behind.

Between 1840 and 1890, some 85,000 converts emigrated from Europe during 333 emigrant voyages on Latter-day Saint-chartered sail and steam ships—perhaps 50,000 from the **British Isles**, 20,000 from **Scandinavia**, and 6,000 from continental Europe. From 1847 to 1868, at least 329 wagon and **handcart** companies moved more than 60,000 believers to **Utah**; afterward those gathering to Zion came by train.

By the 1890s the Church had ceased promoting the gathering to Utah. Latter-day Saint settlements could no longer absorb and support large numbers of newcomers. Further, emigration sapped mission-field branches of strength, hampering proselyting efforts. Saints were asked to "stay and build up the work abroad," and that policy is still in effect.

SOURCES

Clark, James R. comp. *Messages of the First Presidency of The Church of Jesus Christ of Latter-day Saints.* 6 vols. Salt Lake City: Bookcraft, 1965–75.

Hafen, LeRoy R., and Ann W. Hafen. *Handcarts to Zion: 1856–60.* Glendale, Calif.: Arthur H. Clark, 1960.

Hartley, William G. "Coming to Zion: Saga of the Gathering." *Ensign* 5 (July 1975): 14–18.

Larson, Gustive O. *Prelude to the Kingdom*. Francestown, N.H.: Marshall Jones, 1947.

Millennial Star 10 (15 March 1848): 81–88.

Mulder, William. *Homeward to Zion: The Mormon Migration from Scandinavia.* Minneapolis: University of Minnesota Press, 1957.

"Religious Information." *World Almanac and Book of Facts 1997*. Mahwah, N.J.: World Almanac Books, 1996. 644–46.

Smith, Joseph. *History of The Church of Jesus Christ of Latter-day Saints*. Edited by B. H. Roberts. 2d ed. rev. 7 vols. Salt Lake City: The Church of Jesus Christ of Latter-day Saints, 1932–51.

Sonne, Conway B. *Saints on the Seas: A Maritime History of Mormon Migration, 1830–1890*. Salt Lake City: University of Utah Press, 1983.

Stegner, Wallace. *The Gathering of Zion*. New York: McGraw-Hill, 1971.

Taylor, P. A. M. *Expectations Westward: The Mormons and the Migration of Their British Converts in the Nineteenth Century*. Ithaca, New York: Cornell University Press, 1966.

WILLIAM G. HARTLEY

GAUSE, JESSE. Jesse Gause, a counselor to **Joseph Smith** in "the ministry of the presidency of the **high Priesthood**" (quoted in Woodford, 363), was born about 1785 at East Marlborough, Chester, **Pennsylvania**. He left his Quaker affiliation to join with the United Society of Believers in Christ's Second Appearing (**Shakers**) in 1829. The year he joined the LDS Church is not known. On 8 March 1832 the Prophet penned, "Chose this day and ordained brother Jesse Gause and Brother **Sidney [Rigdon]** to be my councellors" (quoted in Woodford, 363; see also D&C 81, Introduction). Gause served for only six months as a counselor. His whereabouts after 1832 is unknown.

SOURCES

Quinn, D. Michael. "Jesse Gause: Joseph Smith's Little Known Counselor." *BYU Studies* 23 (Fall 1983): 487–93.

Woodford, Robert J. "Jesse Gause: Counselor to the Prophet." *BYU Studies* 15 (Spring 1975): 362–64.

SUSAN EASTON BLACK

GENEALOGICAL SOCIETY OF UTAH. Founded in 1894, the Genealogical Society of **Utah** (GSU) is today the microfilming arm of the **Family History** Department. With the advent of microfilming by the LDS Church in 1938, the GSU became a world leader in filming original records, mostly dating from the 1500s to the 1920s. Although it began with just a handful of books, the GSU, now known as the **Family History Library**, has become the largest genealogical research library in the world.

The Family History Library is located in a 142,000-square-foot building in downtown **Salt Lake City** and is open to the public at no charge. The library is arranged by geographical region, including North **America**, **Great Britain**, **Europe** and **Scandinavia**, Latin America, and other areas. About 2,700 patrons visit the library daily.

The library's microfilm collection preserves about 2 billion names found in a variety of sources—church registers, census records, wills, military records, land records, and many more. At the close of the twentieth century, more than 2 million rolls of microfilmed records were available, as well as 711,000 microfiche and more than 280,000 genealogy and local history books. Microfilming projects were continuing in nearly 50 countries. The collection grows at about 5,000 rolls of film and 1,000 books a month.

Family histories and genealogies for America and all foreign countries are located in the **Joseph Smith Memorial Building** (JSMB) in Salt Lake City. A copy of the 1920 U.S. census with related indexes on film, and original copies of some eight million family group records, are also located here.

Copies of most microfilms may be loaned to over 3,400 branch libraries of the main library, known as **Family History Centers**. Found in 65 countries and territories, they have many sources on compact disc, microfilm, microfiche, and book collections of varying sizes.

A list of Family History Centers may be found on the Internet at www.familysearch.org, under Libraries at www.lds.org and also at www.deseretbook.com/famhis. Information may also be obtained by telephone at (800) 346–6044.

―――――
SOURCE

Allen, James B., et al. *Hearts Turned to the Fathers: A History of the Genealogical Society of Utah, 1894–1994*. Provo, Utah: Brigham Young University, 1995.

KIP SPERRY

GENEALOGY. See **FAMILY HISTORY**.

GENERAL AUTHORITIES. A designation of the general leaders of the **Church**, the phrase "general authorities" was first used in scripture

as part of an 1834 revelation (D&C 102:32). This group has included the
First Presidency (1833–), Quorum of the Twelve Apostles (1835–),
patriarch to the Church (1834–1979), assistants to the Twelve
(1941–1976), the First Council of the Seventy (1835–1976), First
Quorum of the Seventy (1975–), Second Quorum of the Seventy (1989–),
and the presiding bishopric (1831–).

RICHARD O. COWAN

GENERAL CONFERENCE. Even before the Church was organized,
the Lord commanded the Saints "to meet in conference" from "time to
time" (D&C 20:61). Following the establishment of the Church, general
conferences, with few exceptions, have been held at least twice each year.
At these assemblies leaders conduct Church business and deliver significant discourses. The proceedings of these gatherings have been published
in the *History of the Church,* the *Journal of Discourses,* the *Millennial
Star,* the *Deseret News,* Conference Reports, and official Church magazines. Conference sessions are also broadcast around the world by television, radio, and the Internet. Church members and others can learn
much about Latter-day Saint history and doctrines from listening to and
reading the sermons that are delivered at these meetings.

At the Church's first conference in June 1830, the Articles and
Covenants were sustained. Brigham Young used general conference to
publicly call missionaries and colonizers. The practice of plural marriage
was first publicly announced at conference in 1852, and the Manifesto
ending the practice was sustained at another conference in 1890. The
Pearl of Great Price, including the Articles of Faith, was canonized as
scripture at the October 1880 conference. In the April 1976 conference,
two revelations were added to the standard works (now D&C 137; 138).

Since Brigham Young led the Saints to the Great Basin, most general
conference sessions have been held in Salt Lake City; a few, however,
were convened in Logan (1885), Provo (1886, 1887), and Coalville
(1886). Conference speakers have included Church presidents, apostles,
other general authorities, stake presidents, mission presidents, auxiliary
officers, representatives of the president of the United States and the Boy
Scouts of America, and the chief of staff of the United States Army.

When Latter-day Saints think of general conference, they think of
testimony, faith, and stories of sacrifice and devotion. They recall prayers
of faith and sacred hymns sung by choirs. They remember prophets,

seers, and revelators declaring the mind and will of God to the world and to his Saints.

SOURCES

Godfrey, Kenneth W. "150 Years of General Conference." *Ensign* 11 (February 1981): 66–71.

Lowe, Jay R. "A Study of the General Conferences of The Church of Jesus Christ of Latter-day Saints." Ph.D. diss., Brigham Young University, 1972.

Smith, Joseph. *History of The Church of Jesus Christ of Latter-day Saints.* Edited by B. H. Roberts. 2d ed. rev. 7 vols. Salt Lake City: The Church of Jesus Christ of Latter-day Saints, 1932–51.

KENNETH W. GODFREY

GENERAL COUNCIL. See COUNCIL OF FIFTY.

GENERAL HANDBOOK OF INSTRUCTIONS. See HAND-BOOKS.

GENERAL SMITH'S VIEWS OF THE POWERS AND POLICY OF THE GOVERNMENT OF THE UNITED STATES.

General Smith's Views, the platform for the **presidential campaign of Joseph Smith**, was published as a **pamphlet** in 1844. On 29 January, the same day the **Prophet** decided to run for president of the **United States**, he met with **William W. Phelps** and dictated to him the headings for the pamphlet. They completed work on the text 7 February, and the following night Phelps read it publicly for the first time. Strictly a political document, the pamphlet makes no mention of Joseph Smith's religious teachings. *General Smith's Views* was, essentially, an attempt to give pragmatic solutions to many of the nation's most pressing problems.

The most important plank in Joseph's platform concerned the powers of the president. Joseph wanted to give the chief magistrate "full power to send an army to suppress mobs . . . without the governor of a state to make the demand" (quoted in Garr, 156). He even advocated capital punishment for public officials who declined to protect the lives and property of citizens.

Slavery was another important issue in the platform. The Prophet recommended that slavery be abolished by the year 1850 at the latest. He would have congress "pay every man a reasonable price for his slaves out of the surplus revenue arising from the sale of public lands, and from the *deduction* of pay from members of congress" (quoted in Garr, 156). Joseph wanted to reduce congressional pay from $8 to $2 a day. He wanted to have only two members of the House of Representatives for every one million people. This would have reduced the number of representatives in the House from 223 to only 40 members. *General Smith's Views* also recommended prison reforms: "Let penitentiaries be turned into seminaries of learning," the Prophet declared (quoted in Garr, 157). He also wanted to do away with imprisonment for debt, which was still a lingering problem in some states. In addition, Joseph favored forming a national bank, eliminating military court martials for desertion, and annexing **Oregon** and **Texas**.

On 24 February, the Prophet had 1,500 copies of the pamphlet printed, and two days later he had the document mailed to the president of the United States and his cabinet, the justices of the Supreme Court, senators, representatives, editors of principal newspapers, postmasters, and other prominent citizens.

General Smith's Views is an intriguing document. With the luxury of hindsight, we can see that many of Joseph Smith's proposals came to pass, although not necessarily in the way he hoped: the power of the presidency was increased by **Abraham Lincoln** during the **Civil War**; the same bloody conflict also emancipated the slaves; the penal system improved, although not to the extent that Joseph prescribed; and, of course, Oregon and Texas soon became part of the Union. **Elder John A. Widtsoe** evaluated *General Smith's Views* as "an intelligent, comprehensive, forward-looking statement of policies, worthy of a trained statesman" (quoted in Garr, 159).

SOURCES

Garr, Arnold K. "Joseph Smith: Candidate for President of the United States." In *Illinois*. Edited by H. Dean Garrett. Regional Studies in Latter-day Saint Church History series. Provo, Utah: Brigham Young University, 1995. 151–68.

Smith, Joseph. *History of The Church of Jesus Christ of Latter-day Saints*. Edited by B. H. Roberts. 2d ed. rev. 7 vols. Salt Lake City: The Church of Jesus Christ of Latter-day Saints, 1932–51. 6:197–209.

ARNOLD K. GARR

GENTILE. Traditionally, a Gentile is one who is not of the Jewish faith or is of a non-Jewish nation, but the term technically has a variety of uses depending on historical context. Latter-days **Saints** use the term both in the traditional way and to refer to those who are not members of the Church.

SOURCE

"Gentile." Bible Dictionary. Appended to The Holy Bible, King James Version. Salt Lake City: The Church of Jesus Christ of Latter-day Saints, 1979. 679–80.

RICHARD NEITZEL HOLZAPFEL

GEORGIA. Missionaries coming from other southern states introduced the gospel in Georgia in 1843. Early growth was encouraging and, except for during times of emigration and **war**, has increased steadily. Georgia was included in the original **Southern States Mission** upon its organization in 1876. Most of the early converts emigrated. Some joined the body of the Church in **Nauvoo**; others traveled west and colonized in **Colorado, New Mexico, Arizona**, and **Utah**.

Partially because of missionary success, Georgia became a hotbed of **anti-Mormon** feelings, culminating in the persecution of missionaries and members. **Elder Joseph Standing** was killed (1879) by a mob in Varnell Station; others were mobbed, and some chapels were burned. Newspapers boasted, "There is no law in Georgia to protect the Mormons," but proselyting efforts continued, and in about 1900 the Church's public image began to improve.

In 1919 the Southern States Mission headquarters was transferred from **Tennessee** to Atlanta. In April 1980 a major dream was realized with the announcement of a **temple** in Atlanta. Elder **LeGrand Richards**, age 97, attended the dedication (1983) in the area where he had served as **mission president** from 1934 to 1937. In the year 2000 Georgia's Latter-day Saint population was 57,857, with 14 **stakes** and 116 **wards** and **branches**. Two **missions** were headquartered in Atlanta and Macon.

SOURCES

Berrett, LaMar C. "History of the Southern States Mission, 1831–1961." Master's thesis, Brigham Young University, 1960.

Jenson, Andrew. *Encyclopedic History of The Church of Jesus Christ of Latter-day Saints*. Salt Lake City: Deseret News, 1941.

1999–2000 Church Almanac. Salt Lake City: Deseret News, 1998. 191–93.

DAVID F. BOONE

GERMANY. The first Latter-day Saint missionary to Germany was James Howard, assigned by **British Mission** President **Brigham Young** in

1840. Discouraged by a lack of success, he returned to **England**. At the same time in **America**, **Joseph Smith** called apostle **Orson Hyde** to dedicate **Palestine** for the return of the **Jews**. On his way to and from this assignment to the **Holy Land**, **Elder** Hyde spent at least nine months of his 20,000-mile journey in Germany. During this time he wrote *Ein Ruf Aus Der Wueste (A Cry from the Wilderness)*, telling the story of Mormonism.

Latter-day Saint **apostles** and missionaries opened **missions** in **Scandinavia**, **France**, and **Italy** from 1849 to 1850 with encouragement to go to other areas "as instructed by the Spirit." These three missions probed into Germany, laying the groundwork for opening the first German mission in Hamburg in 1852, with Daniel Carn as president. During the same year, apostle **John Taylor**, heading the French Mission, directed the publishing of the first German **Book of Mormon**.

Carn met with great success at first, baptizing 12 persons and participating in a miraculous **healing**. Within a few weeks of his arrival, however, he was arrested and imprisoned. The U.S. consul obtained Carn's release, provided he leave Germany within eight days. Other missionaries arrived, and membership reached about 120, but after two years and more arrests, these elders were also expelled by German officials. The first German mission ended in 1854, with most of the converts migrating to **Utah**.

In the same year, 225 miles southeast of Hamburg in Dresden, where no **Latter-day Saint** missionary had yet set foot, a German educator, **Karl G. Maeser**, read an anti-Mormon **pamphlet** and became curious about the Church. Eventually he was able to join the Church and move to Utah. In 1868 Brigham Young called him to return to Germany and preside over the faltering Swiss-German Mission. During his two and a half years of leadership, about 600 new converts joined the Church. After Maeser returned to Utah, Brigham Young called him in 1876 as president of the recently formed **Brigham Young Academy** in **Provo**.

During the following decades, **missionary work** in Germany proceeded slowly and faced much opposition. When **World War I** began, missionaries were evacuated, leaving about 60 branches in Germany and **Switzerland**. Most of these branches survived the **war**. In 1919, following World War I, the Church purchased a large supply of food from the U.S. Army in France to distribute to needy **Saints** in Germany. In Hamburg the Church purchased the first building for Latter-day Saint worship in Germany. By 1924 the Swiss-German Mission had more total members than any LDS mission in the world with 1,795 new converts during the year. In the 1920s missionary work started in **Argentina** and **Brazil**, and the first converts were mostly German emigrants. In 1929 the Church built its first chapel in Selbongen (now part of **Poland**). By 1930 Germany had more non-English-speaking Latter-day Saints than any other nation—nearly 12,000. In that same year, Germany also had more Church members than any other country outside the United States.

In 1937 President **Heber J. Grant** visited Germany, combining portions of the Swiss-German Mission and the German-Austrian Mission into the new Swiss-Austrian Mission. He simultaneously created the first two all-German missions: the West German Mission with headquarters in Frankfurt and the East German Mission in Berlin.

In 1939, one week prior to Germany's invasion of Poland, 150 missionaries were evacuated from Germany. As happened during World War I, local German Saints were required to fill administrative and spiritual positions instead of relying on the missionaries from America. This furthered the development of leadership skills among the German Saints.

The only churches recognized by the German government during the war were the Lutheran, Catholic, and Latter-day Saint churches. Although German officials did not generally harass the Saints, leaders were often interrogated by the *Gestapo* (secret police). Nazi officials were usually satisfied when Mormon leaders quoted the Church's twelfth **Article of Faith**, which affirmed obedience to civil law and officers. One incident, however, caused great anxiety. In 1942 the German police arrested **Helmuth Hübener**, a 17-year-old Latter-day Saint boy. He and two younger members printed and distributed stories about the war that they heard on short-wave broadcasts from England. Although capital punishment for juveniles was illegal in Germany, the highest court of the land in Berlin ruled that these boys be tried as adults. They were judged guilty, and Hüebner was beheaded; the other two were sentenced to prison. After the war, this incident was often cited as an example of how perverted German jurisprudence had become. The two younger boys served prison terms until freed by Allied soldiers.

In devastated Germany, Latter-day Saint losses were also staggering. Bombs destroyed the mission home in Berlin and many LDS meeting halls. Some 600 Saints (5% of the members) lost their lives during the war. Most were soldiers. In Germany there were about 12,000 members at the end of the war (the same as at the beginning); some 600 baptisms had offset the fatalities. Two local German mission presidents lost their lives on the Russian Front. The aftermath of **World War II** was a greater ordeal for most Germans than the war itself; transportation and utility breakdowns, food and fuel shortages, and rampant disease created chaos.

After Germany's 1945 surrender, Latter-day Saint servicemen who were part of the United States occupation forces were the first to help the distressed German Saints. They shared their rations and gave hope and encouragement. Some soldiers formed a great love for the German Saints and after their discharge from the military were able to return as missionaries. On 14 January 1946, Elder **Ezra Taft Benson** of the Twelve became the European Mission president. He was the first American civilian permitted by the U.S. government to travel in war-ravaged Germany. He brought spiritual hope to the Saints and directed massive welfare shipments from Church headquarters. Although the Dutch suffered severely during the German occupation, in 1947 the Saints in **Holland** sent most of their 60-ton potato harvest to the German members in distress. Many Germans, members and nonmembers, reported that they could not have lived without this help. Baptisms in Germany also increased substantially in the years after the war.

By 1947 American missionaries began arriving, but dozens of local Germans were already at work. Russians refused entry of Americans into East Germany; however, some 30 to 40 native LDS missionaries continued working behind the Iron Curtain during the 28-year Communist occupation. The faithfulness and loyalty of Latter-day Saints during these most trying times is one of the great chapters of devotion in the history of the Church. Elder **Thomas S. Monson** occasionally visited the East German Saints and gave them strength to carry on.

In 1961 the Church created Germany's first **stakes** in Berlin, Stuttgart, and Hamburg. In 1965 the first German missionary called to serve outside Europe received his appointment to **California**. Hundreds of other German Latter-day Saints since then have served in missions around the world.

In 1955 the Church had completed its first European **temple** in Bern, Switzerland, which allowed the German Saints to fulfill their hopes and prayers for temple blessings. A miracle occurred in 1985 when the Church built the **Freiberg Temple**, Germany's first temple behind the Iron Curtain. This was several years before the fall of the Berlin Wall in 1989 and prior to German reunification in 1990. When the Frankfurt Germany Temple was completed in 1987, Germany became the first country outside the United States to have two temples.

German converts over the years have served in significant Church positions. In 1952 Carl W. Buehner became second counselor in the

presiding bishopric. In 1977 F. Enzio Bushe was called to the First Quorum of the **Seventy**. In 1994 Dieter Uchtdorf became a member of the Second Quorum of the Seventy, and then in 1996 he was sustained as a member of the First Quorum of the Seventy.

In 1996 President **Gordon B. Hinckley** held a regional conference in Berlin as part of a five-nation European tour. At the beginning of the year 2000 Germany had 36,303 members living in 14 stakes and 188 **wards** and **branches**.

SOURCES

1999–2000 Church Almanac. Salt Lake City: Deseret News, 1998. 323–26.

Scharffs, Gilbert. *Mormonism in Germany: A History of The Church of Jesus Christ of Latter-day Saints in Germany between 1840 and 1970.* Salt Lake City: Deseret Book, 1970.

GILBERT W. SCHARFFS

GERMANY DRESDEN MISSION. The Germany Dresden Mission was established in 1989 and operated behind the iron curtain for a short time. At the end of **World War II** in 1945, the eastern part of **Germany** became the Soviet Zone of Occupation and, in 1949, the communist German Democratic Republic. Foreign missionaries were not permitted to serve in the country, although local members were permitted to serve **missions** inside the GDR until the mid 1960s. At the April 1989 **conference** of the Church, President **Thomas S. Monson** reported on a meeting held the previous October in East Berlin with the head of the German Democratic Republic, Erik Honecker. At that meeting the Church was granted permission to open a mission inside the GDR with native and foreign missionaries.

The Germany Democratic Republic Dresden Mission began operating in the spring of 1989. At first missionaries were called from the other German-speaking missions of **Europe**. By June of 1989 there were 20 missionaries in the country and an office staff consisting of Wolfgang Paul, the **mission president**; Sister Norma Davis, secretary to the president; and **Elder** Garold Davis, finance secretary. A mission office was opened in the basement rooms of the Dresden chapel. All missionaries were called to attend a briefing in East Berlin at the headquarters of Hans Loeffler, the Minister for Ecclesiastical Affairs in the GDR, where ground rules for proselyting were given: no street meetings; no door-to-door contacting; missionaries were to be housed in members' apartments or in buildings occupied by the Church; and investigators were to be taught for the most part in chapels or in members' homes.

In November 1989 the Berlin Wall came down, and during the first four months of 1990, 80 new missionaries were brought in from the MTC in **Provo, Utah.** By the end of the first year of operation the mission had reported 669 baptisms.

SOURCES

Davis, Garold N., and Norma S. Davis., coll. and trans. *Behind the Iron Curtain: Recollections of Latter-day Saints in East Germany, 1945–1989.* Provo, Utah: Brigham Young University, 1996.

Monson, Thomas S. *Faith Rewarded.* Salt Lake City: Deseret Book, 1996.

GAROLD N. DAVIS

GHANA. The Republic of Ghana is located on the western coast of **Africa.** More than half of its population is Christian, and about one-third is **Muslim.**

Ghanaians, along with neighboring Nigerians, were among the earliest people of black Africa to embrace the Church and its teachings. In the early 1950s, many Ghanaians obtained missionary **pamphlets** and copies of the **Book of Mormon** from members or missionaries while traveling abroad, or from expatriate Latter-day **Saints** living in their country. As this **literature** was studied and shared, many letters were written to Church headquarters requesting more information, some even requesting membership. Literature was sent upon request, but inquirers were advised to be patient until missionaries could be sent. During the 1960s more letters of this nature came from Ghana and **Nigeria** than from the rest of the world combined. The desire for Church affiliation was so great that many congregations were organized and named "The Church of Jesus Christ of Latter-day Saints," though none of the participants were baptized members.

One of the earliest Ghanaians to pursue this course was Dr. Raphael A. F. Mensah of Accra, who obtained a copy of the Book of Mormon in the early 1960s. Determining that the book was true, he shared it with **Joseph W. B. Johnson.** After studying the book prayerfully for a month, Brother Johnson said he had heard the voice of God telling him that if he did the Lord's work, he and his land would be blessed. Together Dr. Mensah and Brother Johnson began publicly teaching and testifying of the Book of Mormon and the restored Church, and a congregation was established in Accra. Soon Brother Johnson moved to Cape Coast, where he gave his full time to this ministry. Over a period of 14 years (1964–78), Brother Johnson helped to build and organize at least 10 congregations bearing the Church's name and involving more than 1,000 unbaptized followers. Some of these followers, like **Priscilla Sampson-Davis,** who obtained a copy of the Book of Mormon while in the **Netherlands** in 1963, were already converted before finding Brother Johnson's congregations. The faith, courage, and patience of these converts is a unique and inspiring chapter in Church history. The leaders of this work officially registered the Church with the Ghanaian government in 1969, more than nine years before missionaries came to them. This was done without the knowledge of the **general authorities**, but it proved beneficial when the Church did send missionaries.

On 9 December 1978, just six months after the revelation allowing all worthy males to receive the **priesthood** (**Official Declaration 2**), Rendell N. and Rachel Mabey and Edwin Q. "Ted" and Janath Cannon arrived in Ghana after spending a month in Nigeria. They baptized 89 converts who had been waiting and praying for many years. Within a year, more than 400 people had been baptized, and a building program was commenced. Brother Johnson became the first Ghanaian **branch** president, and later he served as a **district** president, missionary, and **patriarch**.

The Africa West **Mission**, which included Nigeria and Ghana, was organized 1 July 1980. Five years later another Ghana Mission was created, but the rapid growth of the Church in Ghana contributed to severe government action against it. On 14 June 1989, the Ghana government expelled the missionaries and banned the Church from functioning, though members could hold services in their homes. On 1 December 1990, the government reversed its decision, and the Church was again able to resume activities.

In 1991 the first two **stakes** were created at Accra and Cape Coast. On 16 February 1998, President **Gordon B. Hinckley** became the first Church president to visit Ghana. On this occasion, he announced plans for the Accra **Temple**, the first in West Africa. In the year 2000, Ghana had 17,278 members living in 5 stakes and 60 **wards** and **branches**.

SOURCES

Brigham, Janet. "Nigeria and Ghana." *Ensign* 10 (February 1980): 73–76.

1999–2000 Church Almanac. Salt Lake City: Deseret News, 1998. 326–27.

Oral histories of early Church converts collected by E. Dale LeBaron. Copies at BYU Library, Provo, Utah; LDS Church Historical Library, Salt Lake City, Utah.

E. DALE LEBARON

GIBRALTAR. In 1852 missionaries were called to Gibraltar, a **British** Island fortress at the mouth of the Mediterranean Sea. One of these missionaries was Edward Stevenson, who had been born there 1 May 1820 and was called to the First Council of Seventies October 1894. A Latter-day **Saint group** was organized there in 1991, and it became part of the new Cadiz **Spain Stake** four years later. At the beginning of 2000, there were 24 members in one **branch.**

SOURCE

1999–2000 Church Almanac. Salt Lake City: Deseret News, 1998. 403.

RICHARD O. COWAN

GIBSON, WALTER MURRAY. Walter Murray Gibson, an unscrupulous adventurer, was born aboard ship in the Bay of Biscay on 16 January 1822 and raised in **South Carolina.** In **Utah** Gibson professed belief in "Mormonism" and was baptized 15 January 1860. In November of the same year, President **Brigham Young** called him on a **mission** to the **Pacific.**

Gibson arrived in **Hawaii** in June 1861. He showed his credentials, greatly impressing the superstitious native **Saints,** and declared himself the leader of the Church on the Islands. He sold the **priesthood** and offices in the Church and brought about wicked practices and immorality.

In 1864 President Young sent Elders **Lorenzo Snow** and **Ezra T. Benson,** along with **Joseph F. Smith** and others, to resolve the problem. After an investigation, Gibson was excommunicated from the Church in April 1864.

Gibson later became prime minister to Hawaiian King Kalakaua. He died 21 April 1888 in **San Francisco, California.**

SOURCES

Barrett, Gwynn. "Walter Murray Gibson: The Shepherd Saint of Lanai Revisited." *Utah Historical Quarterly* 40 (Spring 1972): 142–62.

Britsch, Lanier R. "The Founding of the Samoan Mission." *BYU Studies* 18 (Fall 1977): 12–26.

Smith, Joseph Fielding. *Life of Joseph F. Smith, Sixth President of The Church of Jesus Christ of Latter-day Saints.* Salt Lake City: Deseret Book, 1969.

JAN FELIX

GILBERT, A. SIDNEY. Algernon Sidney Gilbert was an influential member in **Ohio** and **Missouri,** designated in the **Doctrine and**

Covenants as an "agent unto the church" (D&C 53:4; 57:6). He was born 28 December 1789 in New Haven, **Connecticut**. By 1827 Gilbert and **Newel K. Whitney** had entered a mercantile partnership. While engaged in this business enterprise, Gilbert was baptized (1830).

He lived only four years after his baptism. During these years he established a mercantile store for the blessing of "the affairs of the poor" in **Independence, Missouri** (D&C 82:12). He was persecuted when mob action erupted in Independence. On 23 July 1833 he was one of six men who offered to give their lives as a ransom for the rest of the **Saints** in **Jackson County**. Although he abandoned his store and fled from mobs, he was instructed not to sell his store in Independence (D&C 101:96). Gilbert was obedient to the instruction. He built a new store in **Liberty**, Missouri, to care for the needs of the poor. Gilbert died of cholera in Clay County, Missouri, on 29 June 1834.

SOURCES

Bangerter, Geraldine Hamblin, and Susan Easton Black. *My Servant Algernon Sidney Gilbert: Provide for My Saints (D&C 57:10)*. Salt Lake City: Rollins, Hamblin, and Bangerter Families, 1989.

Smith, Joseph. *History of The Church of Jesus Christ of Latter-day Saints*. Edited by B. H. Roberts. 2d ed. rev. 7 vols. Salt Lake City: The Church of Jesus Christ of Latter-day Saints, 1932–51. 1:319; 2:118–19.

SUSAN EASTON BLACK

GILBERT, JOHN H. John Hulburd Gilbert, printer of the **Book of Mormon**, was born 13 April 1802 in the town of Richmond, Ontario County, **New York**, the only child of Russell and Phebe Hulburd Gilbert. Orphaned at an early age, John secured an apprenticeship in Canandaigua to learn the printer's trade. He then worked in Albany and Lewiston, New York.

In 1824 Gilbert moved to **Palmyra, New York**, formed a partnership with Pomeroy Tucker, and published the *Wayne Sentinel* from 1824 to 1827. **Egbert B. Grandin** then purchased the *Wayne Sentinel* from them in April 1827 and became editor and publisher. He subsequently hired John Gilbert to assist him in his print shop. John had married Chloe P. Thayer on 4 September 1827 in Palmyra. Coincidentally, Chloe's father, Joel Thayer, was among those who constructed the "Thayer & Grandin's Row," where John was employed by E. B. Grandin.

Following a second request by **Martin Harris**, in June 1829 Mr. Grandin asked Gilbert to help him estimate the cost of publishing the

"Mormon Bible." They agreed to printing and binding in leather 5,000 copies for $3,000. Around the middle of August, **Hyrum Smith** took the first foolscap pages of the manuscript to the printer. It required extensive punctuating by Gilbert, who even took some home to work on at night. As the primary compositor he set the type, made up the pages and forms, and did much of the press work.

The first edition of the Book of Mormon was released to the public from the E. B. Grandin Bookstore on 26 March 1830. According to **Pomeroy Tucker**—a local historian as well as Gilbert's partner—in 1847, this project was "the largest printing job ever done" in Wayne County. For the rest of his life, John Gilbert answered many questions about publishing the "Gold Bible." He died at Palmyra on Saturday, 26 January 1895 at the age of 92.

SOURCES

Skousen, Royal. "The Book of Mormon Critical Text Project." *Joseph Smith: The Prophet, the Man.* Edited by Susan Easton Black and Charles D. Tate. Provo, Utah: Religious Studies Center, Brigham Young University, 1993. 65–75.

Tate, Charles D. "John H. Gilbert's Work on the Book of Mormon." In *New York*. Edited by Larry C. Porter, Milton V. Backman Jr., and Susan Easton Black. Regional Studies in Latter-day Saint Church History series. Provo, Utah: Brigham Young University, 1992. 112–28.

LARRY C. PORTER

GLEANER. The Gleaner class was established in 1924 as part of the **Young Women** program of the Church. Golden Gleaner awards were instigated in 1940. In 1950 the class was divided into Jr. Gleaners, ages 16 to 18, and Gleaners, ages 19 to 29. In 1972, the Gleaners were integrated into Young Adults.

SOURCES

Josephson, Marba C. *History of the YWMIA.* Salt Lake City: The Church of Jesus Christ of Latter-day Saints, 1955. 72–89.

"2 Priesthood-Oriented MIAs." *Church News,* 11 November 1972. 3, 8.

VENEESE C. NELSON

GODBEITES. The "New Movement," led by William S. Godbe, was a short-lived attempt to bring Utah away from the philosophy of isolationism to that of integration into the national economy. This position was supported by Elias L. T. Harrison, who with Godbe edited the *Utah*

Magazine. This journal began in 1868 with the endorsement of Brigham Young but soon turned to criticizing his neglect of a mining industry that could bring much wealth and the finer things of the world to Utah.

As the eastern press increasingly publicized the conflict between Brigham Young and the Godbeites, Vice President Schuyler Colfax delivered a noted **anti-Mormon** speech in Utah. **Elder John Taylor** defended the Church from these attacks, but this only resulted in intensifying the anti-Mormon hysteria, both in the East and the West.

The Godbeites established a weekly newspaper, *The Mormon Tribune* (later the daily *Salt Lake Tribune*), which became a bitter weapon against the **Saints**. The *Salt Lake Herald*, on the other hand, defended Brigham Young's position. In essence, the Godbeite affair created an opportunity for federal officials and other citizens to attack the Church. This led to the formation of the gentile **Liberal Party**.

The Godbeites formed the "Church of **Zion**" in 1870, and several of their leaders were excommunicated from the LDS Church. A number of them, including **Edward Tullidge** (well-known **historian** and author), returned to full faith and fellowship in the LDS Church.

SOURCES

Bancroft, Hubert Howe. *History of Utah*. Salt Lake City: Bookcraft, 1964.

Neff, Andrew Love. *History of Utah, 1847 to 1869*. Salt Lake City: Deseret News Press, 1940.

Walker, Ronald W. *Wayward Saints: The Godbeites and Brigham Young*. Urbana: University of Illinois Press, 1998.

JAMES A. CARVER

GOD THE FATHER. Known by the name-title Elohim, God the Father is "the only supreme governor and independent being in whom all fullness and perfection dwell . . . [who is] omnipotent, omnipresent, and omniscient, without beginning of days or end of life" (*Lectures on Faith*, 2:2). One of his important attributes is that he knows all things (D&C 88:41). We know that we were created in the image and likeness of our Heavenly Father (Gen. 1:26–27), therefore he has a physical body of flesh and bones, which houses his spirit (D&C 130:22).

We currently know more about Elohim than did any other people, because he has appeared in this dispensation. Speaking of God the Father and his Son **Jesus Christ**, President **Harold B. Lee** gratefully acknowledged: "They are not an absentee Father and Lord" (Lee, 124). Indeed, Latter-day Saints believe that the Father and the Son have been seen more often than many realize. In 1820, they appeared to Joseph Smith in the First Vision at the Sacred Grove in New York (JS–H 1:11–20). In addition, there are at least four accounts of God the Father being seen by vision. First, at the Isaac Morley farm in Kirtland, when Joseph Smith had ordained the first high priests in June 1831, he testified: "I now see God, and Jesus Christ at his right hand" (quoted in Perkins, 96). Second, as part of the vision of the three degrees of glory received in 1831 at Hiram, Ohio, Joseph Smith and Sidney Rigdon saw the Savior, "even on the right hand of God" (D&C 76:22–24). Third, in 1833 when keys were bestowed upon two future counselors in the First Presidency—Sidney Rigdon and Frederick G. Williams—as part of the School of the Prophets on the second floor of the Whitney Store building, the group beheld a vision of the Father and the Son in the room. Fourth, on 21 January 1836 at the first meeting in the nearly completed Kirtland Temple, Joseph Smith and others saw a vision of the celestial kingdom and the "blazing throne of God, whereon was seated the Father and the Son" (D&C 137:3).

SOURCES

Dahl, Larry E., and Charles D. Tate Jr. *The Lectures on Faith in Historical Perspective.* Provo, Utah: Religious Studies Center, Brigham Young University, 1990.

"House of Revelation." *Ensign* 23 (January 1993): 31–37.

Lee, Harold B. "Stand Ye in Holy Places." *Ensign* 3 (July 1973): 124.

Perkins, Keith W. "The Prophet Joseph Smith in 'the Ohio': The Schoolmaster." *The Prophet Joseph, Essays on the Life and Mission of Joseph Smith.* Edited by Larry C. Porter and Susan Easton Black. Salt Lake City: Deseret Book, 1988. 90–114.

KEITH W. PERKINS

GOLD IN CALIFORNIA, DISCOVERY OF.

GOLD IN CALIFORNIA, DISCOVERY OF. The discovery of gold in California is significant to Church history for several reasons. First, Latter-day Saints were intimately involved. Second, in some ways gold sustained "modern Israel" just as manna had ancient Israel. Third, the gold rush made it difficult for the Church to sustain an organization in California.

Latter-day Saint pioneers were the first on the scene of the gold discovery and among the first to reap its benefits. The diary of Henry Bigler, a member of the Mormon Battalion, pinpoints the discovery's exact date—24 January 1848.

Although Captain Sutter paid his Mormon workmen only $1 per day, they stayed on the job. They sometimes made $25 per day panning gold after work. When **Brigham Young** said they would be better off in **Utah**, many left, bringing enough gold to Utah to give it a viable gold currency for several years. Also, gold rushers paid Church members along the trail for guides, supplies, and services, sometimes abandoning valuables to lighten their loads. It has been said that California gold was Utah's "most important crop" (Cowan and Homer, 125) until after 1851.

As rumors of rich sites spread, Church members remaining in California flocked to first one, then another, making it difficult to maintain any kind of Church order or structure. The allure of gold gradually diminished as Utah's economy became better established and gold became harder to find.

Sources

Arrington, Leonard J. *Great Basin Kingdom: An Economic History of the Latter-day Saints, 1830–1900.* Cambridge, Mass.: Harvard University Press, 1958.

Cowan, Richard O., and William E. Homer. *California Saints.* Provo: Religious Studies Center, Brigham Young University, 1996.

Davies, J. Kenneth. *Mormon Gold: The Story of California's Mormon Argonauts.* Salt Lake City: Olympus, 1984.

WILLIAM E. HOMER

GOLD PLATES. The golden plates, a set of thin metal sheets upon which ancient **prophets** wrote a religious history of the former inhabitants of **America**, were translated by **Joseph Smith** and published as the **Book of Mormon** in 1830. Following directions from the angel **Moroni**, Joseph Smith found the plates 22 September 1823, buried in the **Hill Cumorah** in a stone box with the **Urim and Thummim** and the breastplate. Four years later Joseph received the plates, and he completed the translation of the record sometime in the summer of 1829. Before the plates were returned to Moroni, 11 men were allowed to see them. These men became **witnesses of the Book of Mormon,** and their recorded testimonies concerning the reality of the plates appear in every edition of the book.

Joseph described the plates as having "the appearance of gold," each plate "not quite so thick as common tin" and measuring six inches by eight inches. The plates were "bound together in a volume as the leaves of a book, with three rings running through the whole." The volume measured "something near six inches in thickness, a part of which was sealed." The unsealed plates were "filled with engravings, in **Egyptian** characters, . . . small, and beautifully engraved" (Smith, 537).

SOURCE

Smith, Joseph. *History of The Church of Jesus Christ of Latter-day Saints.* Edited by B. H. Roberts. 2d ed. rev. 7 vols. Salt Lake City: The Church of Jesus Christ of Latter-day Saints, 1932–51.

ANDREW H. HEDGES

GOODYEAR, MILES. Miles Morris Goodyear, often deemed "**Utah's** first citizen," was born 24 February 1817 in Hamden, **Connecticut**. He ventured west with the Whitman-Spaulding missionary party (1836); took up fur trapping and trading in the Central Rockies (1836–45); and founded Utah's first settlement, Fort Bueneventura (1846), on the Weber River (antedating **Mormon** settlement by one year) to profit from overland emigrants.

In 1847 Goodyear met the Mormon **pioneer** company, praised the Wasatch Front to its leaders, and directed the company into the **Salt Lake Valley**. That same year **Brigham Young**, fearful that Fort Bueneventura might become a refuge for dissatisfied and apostate **Saints**, had the Church purchase it for $1,950. Modern-day **Ogden** developed from this settlement. Goodyear died 12 November 1849 in the Sierra **Nevada**.

SOURCES

Campbell, Eugene E. "Miles Morris Goodyear." *The Mountain Men and the Fur Trade of the Far West.* Edited by LeRoy Hafen. 10 vols. Glendale, Calif.: Arthur H. Clark, 1966–72. 2:179–88.

Morgan, Dale L. "Miles Goodyear and the Founding of Ogden." 2 parts. *Utah Historical Quarterly* 21 (July 1953): 195–218; (October 1953): 301–29.

FRED R. GOWANS AND S. MATTHEW DESPAIN

GOSPEL DOCTRINE. Gospel Doctrine, a compilation of the sermons and writings of **Joseph F. Smith**, sixth president of the Church, ranks among the classics of **Latter-day Saint literature**. Though one of the finest theologians in the history of the Church, President Smith never wrote a book. A committee under the direction of **Elder John A. Widtsoe** took the initiative to select and compile extracts from 50 years of President Smith's teachings to form the book. Arranged by topic, the book's 26 chapters cover virtually every facet of the gospel. They reflect President Smith's ministry, giving particular emphasis to his testimony of **Joseph Smith** and loyalty to the **revelations** of the **Restoration**. Perhaps no other book in the literature of the Church has been quoted more often by those in positions of leadership. After President Smith's death, *Gospel Doctrine* was used as a **priesthood** manual.

SOURCE

Smith, Joseph F. *Gospel Doctrine*. Salt Lake City: Deseret Book, 1939.

JOSEPH FIELDING MCCONKIE

GRANDIN PRINTING SHOP. "Thayer and Grandin's Brick Row," **Palmyra, New York**, is where Egbert B. Grandin printed, bound, and offered for sale the first edition of the **Book of Mormon**. Built by Joel and Levi Thayer and Philip Grandin (Egbert's brother), the federal-style structure was typical of **Erie Canal**–era commercial buildings.

The four-bay wide, three-story row housed various businesses. Egbert Grandin rented the west bay, establishing his bookstore and office on the ground level, bindery on the second, and printing shop on the third.

Grandin, editor of a weekly newspaper (*Wayne Sentinel*), contracted with **Joseph Smith** and **Martin Harris** to print the 5,000-copy edition of the Book of Mormon for $3,000. Printing was completed in March 1830, the binding months later.

The first public meeting in Palmyra of the Church of Christ (Latter-day Saints) was held in the row. The building was remodeled considerably in the following 150 years. The Church purchased the west half of the row in 1978 and opened it as an historic site in 1982. On 26 March 1998, following extensive restoration, the west bay with adjoining exhibits was dedicated by President **Gordon B. Hinckley** as the "Book of Mormon Historic Publication Site."

SOURCES

Enders, Donald L. "Two Significant Sites of the Restoration." *Ensign* 28 (September 1998): 30–37.
"Historic Discoveries at the Grandin Building." *Ensign* 10 (July 1980): 48–50.

DONALD L. ENDERS

GRANGER, OLIVER. Oliver Granger, an early **agent** for the Church, was born 7 February 1794 in Phelps, Ontario County, **New York**, to

Pierce and Clarissa Granger. A few months after the publication of the **Book of Mormon**, Oliver obtained a copy and was converted following a heavenly visitation from **Moroni**. This **angel** commanded Oliver to bear testimony that the Book of Mormon is true, and prophesied that he would "hereafter be ordained to preach the everlasting **Gospel** to the children of men" (Peterson).

Granger was baptized and ordained an elder in Wayne County, New York, in the early 1830s and moved to **Kirtland** in 1833 to be with the **Saints**. There he was appointed a member of the **high council**, served **missions** to the East, and helped with the building of the **temple**.

Oliver fled from religious persecutions to Missouri in 1838 but only one month after arriving there was called by revelation to return to Kirtland and settle the Church debts. In that same revelation, Oliver received a beautiful promise that his name would be held in "sacred remembrance from generation to generation, forever and ever" (D&C 117:12).

As an agent for the Church, Granger obtained property in Lee County, **Iowa**, for the Saints during the summer of 1839 and when he returned to Kirtland in 1840. There he served as an "attorney-in-fact" to eliminate all the Prophet's "outstanding debts" and to take care of other Church matters (Black, 108). On one occasion the First Presidency acclaimed him as being "a man of the most strict integrity and moral virtue; and in fine, to be a man of God" (Smith, 3: 350). Oliver died 25 August 1841 in Kirtland, Ohio.

SOURCES

Black, Susan Easton. *Who's Who in the Doctrine and Covenants*. Salt Lake City: Bookcraft, 1997. 107–8.

Cook, Lyndon W. *The Revelations of the Prophet Joseph Smith*. Provo, Utah: Seventy's Mission Bookstore, 1981. 230.

Peterson, H. Donl. *Moroni: Ancient Prophet, Modern Messenger.* Horizon Publishers & Distributors. 1983. 151–52.

Smith, Joseph. *History of The Church of Jesus Christ of Latter-day Saints*. Edited by B. H. Roberts. 2d ed. rev. 7 vols. Salt Lake City: The Church of Jesus Christ of Latter-day Saints, 1932–51. 3:350.

RACHEL WILKINS

GRANITE MOUNTAIN RECORDS VAULT. The Granite Mountain Records Vault is a storage facility located under 700 feet of granite in the side of a mountain in Little Cottonwood Canyon, 20 miles southeast of **Salt Lake City**. It houses microfilms of historical and genealogical records. The **Genealogical Society of Utah** began microfilming records in 1938, and as the collection of microfilms from various countries grew, the Church made plans for this permanent storage area.

The construction of the vault was completed by 1963 and cost $2 million. The vault consists of four tunnels, each measuring 190 feet long, 25 feet wide, and 15 feet high, all connected by three corridors on the ends and through the middle. The front tunnel contains office and laboratory space, and the other three tunnels are the storage vaults. An underground spring provides fresh water for the laboratory and offices. The spring and the depth of the tunnels provide optimal humidity and temperature control for microfilm storage.

The storage facility is designed to hold about 26 million 300-page volumes on microfilm and to withstand nuclear blasts and natural disasters. The collection increases by several thousand films each month. The Church creates microfilms from records of churches, government agencies, and libraries around the world to preserve the vital records and other documents and provide easier access for genealogists to identify their ancestors. These microfilms are available for use through the **Family History Library** and Family History Centers throughout the world.

SOURCES

Allen, James B., Jessie L. Embry, and Kahlile B. Mehr. "Hearts Turned to the Fathers: A History of the Genealogical Society of Utah, 1894–1994." *BYU Studies* 34 (1994–95).

Baldridge, Steven W. "Granite Mountain Record Vault." *Encyclopedia of Mormonism.* Edited by Daniel H. Ludlow. 4 vols. New York: Macmillan, 1992.

In a Granite Mountain. Pamphlet. Salt Lake City: The Church of Jesus Christ of Latter-day Saints, 1988.

CYNTHIA DOXEY

GRANT, HEBER J. Heber Jeddy Grant, the seventh president of the Church, was born in **Salt Lake City, Utah**, 22 November 1856. His father, **Jedediah M. Grant**, second **counselor** to President **Brigham Young**, died nine days later. His mother, Rachel Ridgeway Ivins Grant, carried the baby in her arms to her husband's funeral.

Heber C. Kimball, President Young's first counselor, after whom the infant was named, prophesied the child would become an **apostle**. Later, at a **Relief Society** meeting where little Heber was crawling on the floor, **Eliza R. Snow**, speaking in **tongues**, with an interpretation by **Zina D.**

Young, predicted the child would become one of the high leaders of the Church. Rachel Grant carried these predictions in her heart. As he grew, his mother admonished Heber to guard his thoughts and actions as he had important work to do. The son was inclined to dismiss these urgings as being the wishful thinking of a lonely mother for her only child.

Heber soon showed qualities of determination and tenacity that would typify his conduct throughout his life. For instance, when he was seven, financial problems made it necessary to sell the **family** home on main street, located on the site of the **ZCMI** Center. The boy was seen crying at the front gate and declaring, as he shook his fist at the house, "When I'm a man, I'll buy you back." Years later, during a time of financial turmoil in Salt Lake City, Heber J. Grant headed a syndicate that acquired this property, thus redeeming his boyhood boast.

When classmates ridiculed his handwriting, Heber declared defiantly that he would learn to write as well as the penmanship teacher. Through arduous practice over many months he became a classical penman, earning extra money by writing greeting cards and invitations. Embarrassed when playmates taunted his clumsiness, he announced with some stubbornness his intention to qualify for the championship baseball team of the territory. He accomplished this goal by strengthening his arm and perfecting his control through endless hours of throwing a baseball at the barn of his neighbor, **Bishop** Edwin D. Woolley. The bishop, annoyed by the seeming attempt of this loafer to destroy his barn, declared Heber Grant to be the laziest boy in the Thirteenth **Ward**. When he learned what prompted Heber's habit, his derision changed to admiration. Learning that bookkeepers at the Wells Fargo bank earned the princely sum of $150.00 a month, Heber determined to become one. After improving his penmanship he succeeded.

Although he was tone deaf, Heber was determined to learn to sing. For years he practiced singing at odd moments, whether in the bathroom, on the porch of his home on the Avenues overlooking **Salt Lake Valley**, or on long trips with Church or business associates. He ultimately was able to carry a tune tolerably well and occasionally would regale an audience with an impromptu solo during a talk. These and other similar incidents caused Heber J. Grant to adopt as a slogan one of the sayings of Ralph Waldo Emerson, edited to his own liking: "That which we persist in doing becomes easy, not that the nature of the thing has changed but that our power to do has increased." He had this saying printed on little cards, which he inserted in the envelopes containing calls to missionaries.

Heber's skill as a bookkeeper led to employment by an insurance agent, H. R. Mann, who later formed a brokerage partnership with Henry Wadsworth. When the partners moved from Salt Lake City, dissolving their business, Heber, who had been tutored by Mann and Wadsworth for five years, organized his own insurance and brokerage business. His business experience and contacts in the community were broadened when he served temporarily as an assistant cashier of Zions Savings Bank.

Fulfilling a vow to be married before he reached age 21, Heber married Lucy Stringham on 1 November 1877 in the **St. George Temple**, three weeks before his 21st birthday. Less than three years later, he was called as the president of the Tooele **Stake**. Shortly after he was installed, the Tooele stake **patriarch**, John Rowberry, gave Heber a patriarchal blessing. When he finished, the patriarch said he had seen something he dared not mention. At that moment it was revealed to Heber he would one day be the president of the Church. He never divulged this to anyone until it had become a fact.

He was called and **ordained** an apostle and set apart as a member of the Twelve in October 1882, several weeks before his 26th birthday. Concerned that one so young should be called to the apostleship, Elder Grant began to pray fervently for some divine witness of the reason for his early call. The answer came during an assignment to visit the **Navajo Indian** reservation in **Arizona**. It was then revealed to him that his call originated from a heavenly council, participated in by his natural father and by Joseph Smith, to whom his mother had been sealed. Thus, Heber J. Grant considered himself to stand in the patriarchal line of the Prophet Joseph Smith.

In 1884, Elder Grant was sealed to Augusta Winters and Emily Wells as plural wives. His three wives gave birth to a total of 12 children—ten girls and two boys. The boys died before reaching maturity. As the living allowance he received from the Church was minimal, Elder Grant continued his business activities to maintain his large family.

In 1901, he was called to open and preside over a **mission** in **Japan**. He labored there for two years. Language and cultural barriers limited his effectiveness. Only two known converts came out of this service, both of whom later fell away. Nonetheless, he predicted that the Church would realize a great harvest of converts in Japan, a prediction that was fulfilled following **World War II**. Elder Grant later presided over the **European Mission**. He took Emily and six of his daughters with him.

When Elder **Francis M. Lyman** died in November 1916, Elder Grant became the president of the **Quorum** of the Twelve Apostles. When

President **Joseph F. Smith** died in November 1918, Elder Grant became the president of the Church. His administration was marked by an increased rapport with the non-Mormon community through his business activities. During the 1930s he directed the establishment of the Church **welfare program**, assisted ably by his counselors and by **Harold B. Lee**, then a stake president in Salt Lake City.

In the early 1940s President Grant suffered a stroke, which limited his activities. He passed away quietly on 14 May 1945 in Salt Lake City. As his funeral cortege passed the Catholic cathedral on South Temple and Third East, the bells of the cathedral sounded as several priests stood in front to pay their respects to their friend. He was buried in the city cemetery overlooking the valley he loved.

SOURCE

Gibbons, Francis M. *Heber J. Grant: Man of Steel, Prophet of God.* Salt Lake City: Deseret Book, 1979.

FRANCIS M. GIBBONS

GRANT, JEDEDIAH M. Jedediah Morgan Grant, **counselor** in the **First Presidency** and mayor of **Salt Lake City**, was born 21 February 1816 in Windsor, **New York**. He was 17 at the time of his baptism, and the next year, after traveling to the Church's headquarters at **Kirtland**, he joined the historic **Zion's Camp** march. In 1839 he was called on a **mission** to the southern states. While he was serving in **Virginia**, a group of skeptical southerners did not believe the eloquent **Latter-day Saint** missionary when he told them that he had never "studied up" a sermon in his life, but delivered them spontaneously after filling his mind with **scriptures** and truths of the gospel. They mockingly challenged him to preach to them at an appointed date from a text they would furnish upon the spur of the moment. Thinking to make a fool of the naive young man in front of his audience, they handed him a blank piece of paper. Not to be thwarted by their cruel sense of humor, **Elder** Jedediah M. Grant without hesitation uttered a marvelous sermon on the theme of the blankness of Protestant doctrine, winning the good will of almost all there and convincing some of them that the true gospel had been restored.

In 1842 he was called by the **Prophet** to preside over the Church in Philadelphia. He returned to **Nauvoo** at the time of the **Martyrdom** and carried news of the tragedy to **Brigham Young** and the other **apostles**, who were on missions in the East. The next year, Brother Grant was ordained to the First Council of the **Seventy**. As captain of a company of one hundred, he trekked to the **Salt Lake Valley** in 1847, suffering the desolating loss of his beloved wife and tiny daughter as a result of the hardships. He later married Rachel Ivins; they were the parents of one child, **Heber J. Grant**.

In 1851 Jedediah Grant was elected the first mayor of Salt Lake City and retained that position until his death. He was chosen as second counselor to Brigham Young in 1854, and with this call came an ordination to the office of apostle. On 1 December 1856, just one week after the birth of his son, Heber, Elder Jedediah M. Grant died in Salt Lake City at the young age of 40.

SOURCES

Flake, Lawrence R. *Prophets and Apostles of the Last Dispensation*. Provo, Utah: Religious Studies Center, Brigham Young University, 2001. 251–53.

Walker, Ronald W. "Jedediah and Heber Grant." *Ensign* 9 (July 1979): 47–52.

LAWRENCE R. FLAKE

GRANT, ULYSSES S. Ulysses Simpson Grant, West Point graduate, Union commander, and president of the **United States** (1869–77), was the first U.S. president to visit **Utah**. Born 27 April 1822 in Point Pleasant, **Ohio**, Grant fought in the **Mexican War**, soldiered on the West Coast, and worked as a farmer, realtor, and store clerk. He distinguished himself in **Kentucky**, **Tennessee**, and **Mississippi Civil War** battles before **Abraham Lincoln** appointed him commander-in-chief.

Grant's positive contributions as president—a benevolent **Indian** policy, the protection of **African Americans**, and a settlement of claims against **Great Britain**—balance the regrettable fraud by his subordinates and his attempt to annex Santo Domingo.

Grant stood against **Mormon polygamy** and "theocracy" (Church influence in politics). He sent stern governors John Wilson Shaffer and George L. Woods, as well as Chief Justice James B. McKean, to Utah. During Grant's October 1875 visit to Utah, he met with **Brigham Young** and Governor George W. Emery. White-clad Latter-day Saint children lined South Temple to greet him. Grant died 23 July 1885 near Saratoga, **New York**.

SOURCES

Alexander, Thomas G. "A Conflict of Perceptions: Ulysses S. Grant and the Mormons." *Newsletter of the Ulysses S. Grant Association* 8 (July 1971): 29–42.

Grant, Ulysses S. *The Papers of Ulysses S. Grant.* Edited by John Y. Simon. 21 vols. Carbondale: Southern Illinois University Press, 1967–98.

————. *Personal Memoirs.* New York: C. L. Webster, 1894.

McFeely, William S. *Grant: A Biography.* New York: Norton, 1981.

THOMAS G. ALEXANDER

GRASSLI, MICHAELENE P.

GRASSLI, MICHAELENE P. Michaelene Packer Grassli, eighth general president of the **Primary**, was born 19 June 1940 in **Salt Lake City**. She married Leonard Grassli in the Idaho Falls **Temple** in 1961. They became the parents of three daughters.

Sister Grassli served for nearly 20 years at the general level of the Primary organization. In 1974 she was called to the general board, where she was a member of the Blazer scout committee. Six years later she became second **counselor** to President **Dwan J. Young**. In this position, she served on the National Cub Scout Committee and later received the Silver Beaver and Silver Antelope Awards.

Sister Grassli was sustained as Primary president at **general conference** on 2 April 1988. The following year the Church published the *Children's Songbook*. During a satellite broadcast on 23 January 1994 the **First Presidency** inaugurated "Focus on the Children," an ongoing program created to revitalize spiritual instruction for children in the home and in the Church. Sister Grassli also served on the Primary Children's Medical Center board of directors.

SOURCES

Grassli, Michaelene P. Interview by author. 15 September 1998.

Peterson, Janet, and LaRene Gaunt. *The Children's Friends: Primary Presidents and Their Lives of Service.* Salt Lake City: Deseret Book, 1996. 141–64.

JOANN M. BRITSCH

GRAU, GEORG.

GRAU, GEORG. Georg Grau, the first convert to the LDS Church in Ottoman **Palestine** during the nineteenth century, was born 4 March 1840 in Obermuehle Welzheim, Wuerttemberg, Germany. He emigrated from **Europe** to a German colony in Haifa (a coastal city in modern **Israel**) and was working there as a blacksmith when **Jacob Spori** came from Constantinople in 1886 to continue his missionary labors. **Elder** Spori had seen Grau and his blacksmith shop in a dream before he arrived in Haifa, and immediately upon landing he made his way to the shop. He was greeted enthusiastically by Grau, who told him that he in turn had seen Spori in a dream the previous night and wanted to hear his message. Grau was baptized 29 August 1886 in Acre (Haifa) Bay by Elder Spori and was ordained an elder on 3 September. Grau taught the gospel to his wife (Magdalena) and baptized her, as well as others, on 19 September 1886.

The conversions of Grau and his wife marked the beginnings of a **branch** of the Church in Haifa that grew to 25 converts over the next several years. In 1888 Elder **Ferdinand F. Hintze**, presiding elder of the Church in the Near East, visited the branch and found it in good order, ably led by Elder Grau. After his wife's death, Grau immigrated to **Utah** for a few years, but he returned to Palestine in the late 1890s as a missionary. He died 9 June 1901 and was buried with his wife in Haifa at a cemetery with other Latter-day **Saints**.

SOURCES

Baldridge, Steven W. *Grafting In: A History of the Latter-day Saints in the Holy Land.* Murray, Utah: Roylance Publishing, 1989. 5–6.

Galbraith, David B., D. Kelly Ogden, and Andrew C. Skinner. *Jerusalem, the Eternal City.* Salt Lake City: Deseret Book, 1996. 345–46.

ANDREW C. SKINNER

GREAT AWAKENING. A great awakening is a time when large numbers of people become concerned with their standing before **God**. It involves various reform efforts and increased church attendance. Historians recognize two great awakenings in American history—the first took place primarily in New England between 1739 and 1743, and the second embraced the first 50 years of the nineteenth century and provided the background for the "unusual excitement on the subject of religion" noted by **Joseph Smith** (JS–H 1:5). This second great awakening was strongest in the southern and western portions of the country and was characterized by highly emotional camp meetings and revivals, the fragmentation of established denominations, the establishment of several new sects, increased church activity among Americans, and a concern with reestablishing New Testament Christianity. So many revivals swept upstate **New York** during this period that the region became known as the "**Burned-Over District**."

SOURCE

Ahlstrom, Sydney E. *A Religious History of the American People.* New Haven: Yale University Press, 1972.

ANDREW H. HEDGES

GREAT BASIN. In 1847 **Brigham Young** chose the Great Basin as a refuge and **gathering** site for the **Saints**, following their expulsion from **Nauvoo, Illinois.** An area of some 220,000 square miles, the Great Basin stretches between **Utah's** Wasatch Mountains on the east and the Sierra Nevada range on the west and includes parts of southeastern **Idaho**, southeastern **Oregon**, southern **California**, and the Baja Peninsula. **John C. Frémont** gave the region its name in 1844 in recognition of the fact that none of the rivers in this area drained to the sea, but rather drained into extensive salt water lakes or simply disappeared into the ground in various sinks. Subsequent explorations and studies revealed that this basin was carved out by advancing ice sheets during the Pleistocene period, after which much of it filled with water in several large lakes. The largest of these lakes, Lake Bonneville, was more than 1,000 feet deep and covered some 19,750 square miles at its greatest extent.

Archeological evidence suggests that humans have lived in the Great Basin for some 9,000 years. The three largest **Indian** tribes using the area when the **Latter-day Saints** arrived were the Paiutes, Utes, and **Shoshoni**. Spaniards from **Mexico** began traveling through the area during the latter half of the eighteenth century, followed by French, English, and American fur trappers in the 1820s, 1830s, and early 1840s. Backed by the U.S. government, Frémont explored the region extensively in 1843 and 1844, publishing the results of his trip in 1845. Seeking a place of safety for the beleaguered **Saints**, Brigham Young and other Church leaders studied these trappers' and explorers' descriptions of the Great Basin extensively and found in the region's isolation, forbidding climate and geography, and potential for irrigation the characteristics they were looking for in a refuge.

SOURCES

Bennett, Richard E. *We'll Find the Place: The Mormon Exodus, 1846–1848.* Salt Lake City: Deseret Book, 1997.

Cline, Gloria Griffen. *Exploring the Great Basin.* Norman: University of Oklahoma Press, 1963.

Durham, Michael S. *Desert between the Mountains: Mormons, Miners, Padres, Mountain Men, and the Opening of the Great Basin, 1772–1869.* New York: Henry Holt, 1997.

ANDREW H. HEDGES

GREAT BRITAIN. See ENGLAND, IRELAND, SCOTLAND, and WALES.

GREAT DEPRESSION. See DEPRESSION, GREAT.

GREECE. On 19 September 1972, **Elder Gordon B. Hinckley** dedicated Greece for the preaching of the gospel in modern times. Before its organization as a **mission** 1 July 1990, Greece was part of the Austria Vienna East Mission, and before that it was part of the **International Mission**.

Missionaries first entered Greece near the turn of the century, after the Church received a letter from Rigas Profantis of Athens requesting more information about the restored gospel. Turkish **mission president** Ferdinand F. Hintze visited Greece in April 1899 and taught Profantis and his friend, Nicholas Malavetis, who had been searching for truth. Both were baptized 22 October 1905 by **J. Wilford Booth** of the Near East Mission.

In 1909 or 1910 the Church withdrew missionaries from Greece, and a **branch** was not organized until 1965. President **Ezra Taft Benson** visited the country in 1979.

Before the official organization of a mission in Greece, the Church in that nation consisted mainly of **United States** military and diplomatic personnel and their families. With the close of the American air bases in Greece, the Church created a large international branch of various nationalities and organized a small Greek branch in Athens. A small branch was also organized in the northern city of Thessalonica. The frequent denial of resident permits to United States missionaries was partially overcome by the recommendation that half of the missionaries called be European members, who did not need visas or resident permits.

By the beginning of the year 2000 there were 479 members of the Church in Greece living in 5 branches.

─────

Source

1999–2000 Church Almanac. Salt Lake City: Deseret News, 1998. 327.

R. Douglas Phillips

GREENE, JOHN P. John Portineus Greene, an early, prominent Latter-day Saint, was born 3 September 1793 in Herkimer, **New York**. Although he made many contributions to the early Church, including 11 missions in 10 years, he is perhaps best remembered for his role in two events: (1) the conversion of himself, his wife, his wife's brother (**Brigham Young**), and the entire Young **family** by one copy of the **Book of Mormon**

left at Greene's home; and (2) under his direction as Nauvoo city marshal the destruction of the *Nauvoo Expositor* press. The aftermath of the latter event, including the **martyrdom** of **Joseph Smith** in June 1844, caused Greene to become distraught and bedridden. He died in Nauvoo on 10 September of that year.

SOURCES

Manscill, Craig K. "A Period of Trial, Testing and Tutoring: New York, Pennsylvania Era Was Formative for Prophet." *Deseret News,* 21 May 1994.
Smith, Calvin N. "Noble Legacy Left by Early Convert." *Church News,* 28 September 1986. 8–10.

WILLIAM E. HOMER

GREENLAND. Although Greenland is the largest island in the world, it is sparsely populated, with only about 57,000 inhabitants. Greenland was administered by the Danish government until home-rule was granted in 1979. Between 1776 and 1950 the Danish government closed Greenland to outsiders. The earliest known LDS presence in Greenland began in 1944, when Latter-day **Saints** serving in the **United States** military came to the island. A branch was organized in 1953 but was discontinued in 1989. Thule Air Force Base remains the center for Church activity, where a small servicemen's group meets. At the beginning of the year 2000 Church membership numbered 14 living in one **branch**.

SOURCE

1999–2000 Church Almanac. Salt Lake City: Deseret News, 1998. 311.

JEFFREY L. ANDERSON

GRENADA. With an estimated population of 92,200, Grenada is composed of three mountainous islands in the eastern Caribbean. A majority of this parliamentary democracy's people are members of the Roman Catholic Church. **Elders** Robert W. Hoffmaster and Leonard G. Gill were the first missionaries in the country, arriving in May of 1985. The first **branch** of the Church was organized in the capital city of St. George on 3 September 1985. At the beginning of the year 2000, there were about 109 members living in one branch.

SOURCE

1999–2000 Church Almanac. Salt Lake City: Deseret News, 1998. 328.

TODD KRUEGER

GROUP. Any small gathering of Latter-day **Saints** may be known informally as a group. Specifically, men and women in military service away from regular Church units have been organized into groups. Also, when a **high priests quorum** or **elders quorum** comprises more than one **ward** or **branch**, the high priests in each ward or branch are organized as a group, and so are the elders. The presiding officer of such a group is known as a group leader.

RICHARD O. COWAN

GROVES, WILLIAM H. Latter-day **Saint** philanthropist William H. Groves endowed the LDS **Hospital**, the first of the Church's hospital systems. Born in **England** in 1834, Groves was a long-time dentist in **Salt Lake City**. He retired a widower with a small fortune but without any children. Shortly before his death in Salt Lake City on 26 April 1895, he willed all his real property, valued at $50,000, to the **presiding bishopric** of the Church. He asked Church authorities to found and manage a hospital in his name. Ten years later, the Dr. W. H. Groves LDS Hospital was opened in Salt Lake City.

SOURCES

"The Late Dr. Grove's Will." *Deseret Evening News,* 2 May 1895, 2.
Probate Record, Third District Court, Salt Lake County, Utah. Book K-1. 385–86.

JED L. WOODWORTH

GROW, HENRY. Architect and builder Henry Grow was born 1 October 1817 in Philadelphia, **Pennsylvania**. He converted to Mormonism in 1842 and soon gathered to **Nauvoo, Illinois**. In **Utah** he built mills, homes, bridges, and businesses—including the **ZCMI** store in **Salt Lake City** (1868). His work on the **Tabernacle** (1867), the Assembly Hall (1879), and the **Salt Lake Temple** (1893) are part of his enduring legacy. Of these, the arched roof of the Tabernacle without center supports is his most celebrated achievement. Married to three wives, he was the father of 27 children. Grow died on 4 November 1891 in Salt Lake City.

SOURCE

Jenson, Andrew. *Latter-day Saint Biographical Encyclopedia.* 4 vols. 1901–36. Reprint, Salt Lake City: Western Epics, 1971. 3:94–96.

RICHARD NEITZEL HOLZAPFEL

GROWTH. Since its founding the Church has grown tremendously, becoming established in more than 162 countries around the world.

SIZE AND GROWTH

Beginning in obscurity with six members on 6 April 1830, the LDS Church had grown to more than 11 million members by 2000. During the first two decades, Church membership grew mostly from new converts being baptized, but thereafter it grew primarily through natural increase. By the end of its first century, the Church counted 700,000 members. From 1930 on, the number of Church members increased exponentially—to 1.1 million in 1950, 2.9 million in 1970, 7.8 million in 1990, and 10.4 million at the end of 1998. Overall growth rates during the 1990s averaged about 3.6% per year.

After 1960, converts became the largest source of new members. To illustrate, the 23,000 convert baptisms in 1950 made up 39% of all new members. By 1970 the 55,000 convert baptisms made up 59% of all new members. In 1998 the 299,000 converts made up 80% of all new members.

Projections of Church membership forecast continued high growth. Projections are only estimates, but they can indicate future possibilities. Using an exponential growth model, sociologist Rodney Stark predicted in 1980 that if future growth continued at the same rate as in the past, membership would reach 23 million by the year 2020, and between 265 and 267 million by the year 2080. These projections were based on estimates of 50% growth per decade (4.14% per year). Revisiting his initial estimates in 1994, Stark found that growth between 1980 and 1994 had actually surpassed his projections, and prospects for continued growth looked good.

GEOGRAPHIC DISTRIBUTION

From the Church's beginnings in New York state, **missionary work** was an essential part of spreading the gospel to other eastern states, as well as into **Europe** and other countries outside the **United States**. Wars and economic depression slowed missionary work during the first half of the 1900s. Growth during these decades came mainly from U.S. converts and the children of members. In 1950 nine out of ten members lived in the United States; 40% lived in **Utah**. Since then, conversion outside the United States has changed the distribution dramatically. Beginning in 1997, half of all Latter-day **Saints** lived outside the United States and **Canada**.

Latin American members contributed significantly to the expansion outside the United States since 1950. Members in **Mexico** and Central and **South America** accounted for 2% of total members in 1960 but 36% in 1998. The number of members in **Asia**, the **Philippines**, and the South **Pacific** has increased steadily since 1960—from 3% of all members to 10% in 1998.

While the Church as a whole was growing at a rate of about 3.6% per year in the 1990s, this growth was not uniform throughout the world. In **Africa** it was growing about 10% per year (although the membership base was still small). South America had a rate of increase of almost 7% per year, while Mexico, **Central America**, Asia, and the Philippines were growing at almost 5% per year. Europe and the South Pacific had lower rates of about 3% per year, and the United States increased about 2% per year. Should these regional growth rates continue, a majority of all members will soon live in Latin America and Utah members will make up only a small portion of the worldwide Church.

The distribution of the million members baptized between 1996 and 1998 demonstrated the increasingly international makeup of Church members. New members in South America, Mexico, and Central America accounted for more than half of the total. Converts in the United States and Canada accounted for another third, while 10% of new members joined the Church in Asia, the Philippines, and South Pacific areas. New members in Europe added 3%, and new members in Africa added 2% of the million new members.

Additional members require additional **wards** and **branches**. The number of wards and branches increased from 1,541 in 1950 to 25,791 in 2000, when about 15,000 were outside the United States.

SOURCES

Heaton, Tim. "Vital Statistics." *Encyclopedia of Mormonism*. Edited by Daniel H. Ludlow. 4 vols. New York: Macmillan, 1992.

1999–2000 Church Almanac. Salt Lake City: Deseret News, 1998.

Stark, Rodney. "The Rise of a New World Faith." *LDS Social Life: Social Research on the LDS Church and Its Members*. Edited by James T. Duke. Provo, Utah: Religious Studies Center, Brigham Young University, 1998. 9–27.

KRISTEN L. GOODMAN AND DOUGLAS A. HOOPER

GUADELOUPE. See MARTINIQUE AND GUADELOUPE.

GUAM. After being ruled by Spain for more than 200 years, Guam became a territory of the **United States** following the **Spanish-American War** in 1898. The first known Latter-day **Saints** to visit this territory arrived when the United States retook the island from **Japan** in August 1944. Lewis W. Gale was among the first wave of U.S. Marines to land on the island. Six or seven Latter-day Saint soldiers, including Gale, held a Church **meeting** in a foxhole in 1944. From that time on, regular meetings were held by American military personnel. A chapel, made up of two quonset huts, was dedicated in 1953 at Agana, and Guam became a dependent **branch** of the Oahu-**Hawaii** Stake.

On 25 August 1955, President **Joseph Fielding Smith** visited Guam and dedicated it for the preaching of the gospel. The first full-time missionaries were **Elders** Danny Gallego and Paul Ray. Elder **Ezra Taft Benson** dedicated the first permanent chapel at Barrigada on 10 March 1970. In 1972 Guam became a **ward** in the Kaneohe **Stake**, which split into another ward in 1976. The two wards were reorganized into four branches on 1 April 1980, and the Guam **District** was organized. The **Micronesia**-Guam **Mission** was created the same day.

The first Chamorro **family** to join the Church, Don and Maria Calvo, were baptized in May 1977. Serving from 1979 to 1981, Herbert J. Leddy was the first missionary of Chamorro lineage; he labored in the **Tennessee** Nashville Mission. In November 1989 Brother Leddy became the first Chamorro member to be called as district president. Elder L. **Tom Perry** dedicated the Talisay chapel in 1985. Later that year the mission office and the missionary house located near the Talisay chapel were dedicated.

At the beginning of the year 2000, Guam had 1,476 members living in 4 branches.

Sources

"A Brief History of the Micronesia-Guam Mission, 1980–1990." Micronesia-Guam Mission, 1990.

Muller, Alan Edward. "A Historical Account of The Church of Jesus Christ of Latter-day Saints on Guam." Guam, 1 April 1955.

1999–2000 Church Almanac. Salt Lake City: Deseret News, 1998. 328.

W. James Jacob

GUATEMALA. Located in **Central America**, Guatemala is the northernmost country of the isthmus. It is about the size of **Tennessee**, with a population of approximately 12 million. The people are largely of Mayan descent. They live in rural settings and the principal language is Spanish.

The first resident member of The Church of Jesus Christ of Latter-day Saints was **John O'Donnal**. He arrived in Guatemala in 1942 as a U.S. government employee and set about to develop a commercial rubber industry. In 1946 he petitioned President **George Albert Smith** to send missionaries. The following year four missionaries arrived, and their first baptism was John O'Donnal's Guatemalan wife, Carmen Gálvez. A few years later a **branch** of the Church was organized in Guatemala City, and in 1955 the first chapel was constructed. The growth of the Church virtually exploded during the 1960s. From 1956 to 1966 the membership increased from 256 to more than 10,000 members. A year later the first **stake** was organized in Guatemala City.

The phenomenal growth of the Church since the first two decades has continued in subsequent years. The first mission based in Guatemala was established in 1976. This was followed by a second mission for the highland area in 1977. By 1993 the third and fourth **missions** had been added.

During the late twentieth century, Guatemala became a regional hub for Church administration and activity. The nexus of this activity was the Guatemala City **Temple**, completed in 1984. The Church also established in Guatemala City an Office of Temporal Affairs (1979), a **Missionary Training Center** (1985), and the Central America **Area** Office (1990). In 1989 **Elder Carlos H. Amado** was called to the **Seventy** and became the first Guatemalan **general authority**.

Approximately half of all Guatemalans are of Mayan descent. Many of these native **Indians** do not speak Spanish. This has prompted the Church to provide instruction and services in four of the indigenous languages. In 1975 missionaries began teaching the Cakchiquel Indians in their native language. This was followed by **missionary work** with the Quiché, Kekchí, and Mam Indian languages. Ten years later the first Indian stake was organized in the Cakchiquel area and named the Chimaltenango Stake. A unique development for the Church in Guatemala was implementing the concept of smaller rural chapels. Another innovation of the Indian program came during 1993 when the Church added the four native languages to the temple services in Guatemala City.

Even though the land of Guatemala has known years of political instability mixed with economic poverty, almost overnight it has become a fruitful field for The Church of Jesus Christ of Latter-day Saints.

Guatemala is a testament to Nephi's prophecy that "they [the **Lamanites**] shall be restored unto the knowledge of their fathers, and . . . of **Jesus Christ**" (2 Ne. 30:5).

At the beginning of the year 2000 the membership of the Church in Guatemala totaled 174,784 and included 40 stakes and 449 **wards** and branches.

SOURCES

1999–2000 Church Almanac. Salt Lake City: Deseret News, 1998.

O'Donnal, John Forres. *Pioneer in Guatemala.* Yorba Linda, Calif.: Shumway Family History Services, 1997.

KEITH J. WILSON

GURLEY, ZENOS H. See **REORGANIZED CHURCH OF JESUS CHRIST OF LATTER DAY SAINTS.**

GUYANA. Guyana, a republic on the northern coast of South America, has an estimated population of 708,000. It is part of the United Kingdom's Commonwealth of Nations, and the population speaks **American Indian** dialects and English. Approximately 37% of the people are Hindu, and the remainder are Christians. The first Latter-day Saint missionaries in the country were Benjamin and Ruth Hudson, who arrived 19 August 1988. The first convert in Guyana was Indra Sukhdeo, baptized 23 October 1988. The Church gained recognition in February of 1989, and a small **branch** was organized in Georgetown, the capital, the following month. At the beginning of the year 2000, the country had about 1,026 members and three branches.

SOURCE

1999–2000 Church Almanac. Salt Lake City: Deseret News, 1998. 331.

TODD KRUEGER

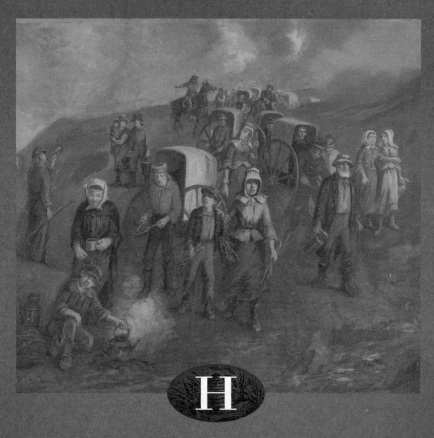

HANDCARTS. Many emigrant Saints formed handcart companies between 1856 and 1860, pulling and pushing their belongings to Utah, as depicted in Danquart A. Weggeland's oil painting *Handcart Pioneers*.

HAIGHT, DAVID B. David Bruce Haight, **apostle**, mayor, missionary, and businessman, was born 2 September 1906 in Oakley, **Idaho**, to Hector Caleb Haight and Clara Tuttle Haight. He received a teaching certificate from Albion State Normal School in Idaho and a B.A. in business administration from Utah State University in 1928. He married Ruby Olson on 4 September 1930 in the **Salt Lake Temple**. They became the parents of three children.

Brother Haight worked at **ZCMI** as a district and regional manager of a large retail store chain and owned a hardware business. He also served as a personal secretary to Secretary of Agriculture **Ezra Taft Benson** during the Eisenhower administration.

In 1943, Brother Haight was commissioned in the **United States** Navy and rose to the rank of commander. He served as mayor of Palo Alto, **California**, for two terms until he was called as president of the Scottish Mission in 1963. He was then assistant to President **Ernest L. Wilkinson** at **Brigham Young University**. Elder Haight served as a **regional representative** and was sustained as an **assistant to the Twelve** 6 April 1970. He was **ordained** an **apostle** on 8 January 1976 and sustained a member of the **Quorum** of the Twelve Apostles 3 April 1976 at age 69.

SOURCES

1999–2000 Church Almanac. Salt Lake City: Deseret News, 1998. 19.

Tate, Lucile C. *David B. Haight: The Life Story of a Disciple.* Salt Lake City: Bookcraft, 1987.

MATTHEW O. RICHARDSON

HAITI. The first member of the Church in Haiti was Alexandre Mourra, a prominent Haitian businessman who was baptized in 1977 in Fort Lauderdale, **Florida**. Missionaries from the **France** Paris Mission were sent to Haiti in June 1980. In October a **branch** was officially organized in Port-au-Prince, the capital.

On 17 April 1983, Haiti was dedicated for the preaching of the gospel by **Elder Thomas S. Monson** of the **Quorum** of the Twelve **Apostles.** On 4 August 1984, the Haiti Port-au-Prince Mission was officially opened, with James S. Arrigona as president.

The mission was evacuated in 1991 following the ouster of the country's president, Jean-Bertrand Aristide, by an army coup. Haiti was closed to foreign missionaries until July 1996, when President Aristide was reinstated by the **United States.** On 21 September 1997 the first **stake** in Haiti was organized, with Reynolds Antoine Saint-Louis as president. In the year 2000 there were 8,157 members and 19 **wards** and branches.

SOURCE

VanDenBerghe, Elizabeth, and Jed VanDenBerghe. "Haitian Saints See Hope in the Gospel." *Ensign* 21 (March 1991): 32–37.

PATRICK CANNON

HALE, EMMA. See SMITH, EMMA HALE.

HALE, ISAAC. Isaac Hale, **Emma Smith's** father, offered Joseph Smith protection while he was translating the plates. Born 21 March 1763 at Waterbury, **Connecticut,** Isaac met Joseph when the **Prophet** boarded at his home while working for **Josiah Stowell** in 1825. A devout Methodist, Isaac was suspicious of Joseph's prophetic calling and opposed his **marriage** to Emma, but he allowed Joseph and Emma to live near him between December 1827 and August 1830. Finally, in the face of mounting persecution, he asked the couple to leave. Author of an 1834 affidavit defaming Joseph's character, Isaac died 16 February 1842 in **Harmony, Pennsylvania.**

SOURCE

Black, Susan Easton. "Isaac Hale: Antagonist of Joseph Smith." In *New York.* Edited by Larry C. Porter, Milton V. Backman Jr., and Susan Easton Black. Regional Studies in Latter-day Saint Church History series. Provo, Utah: Brigham Young University, 1992. 93–111.

ANDREW H. HEDGES

HALES, ROBERT D. When he was called to be a member of the Quorum of the Twelve **Apostles** in April 1994, Robert Dean Hales had already served 19 years as a **general authority**. He was an **assistant to the Twelve**, a member of the First Quorum of the **Seventy**, and a **mission president** of the **England** London Mission. From 1985 to 1994 he was the **presiding bishop**.

Elder Hales was born 24 August 1932 in **New York City** to John Rulon and Marie Holbrook Hales. He and his wife, Mary Crandall, had two sons. Elder Hales received a bachelor's degree from the **University of Utah** and a master's degree from Harvard Business School. He served in the U.S. Air Force as a jet fighter pilot. Elder Hales had a distinguished business career, including executive positions with both national and international corporations. The Hales family lived in many cities in the **United States**, England, **Germany**, and **Spain** (Avant, 6).

Sources

Avant, Gerry. "New Apostle Aware of Heightened Role." *Church News,* 16 April 1994. 6.
Gaunt, LaRene. "Elder Robert D. Hales: Return with Honor." *Ensign* 24 (July 1994): 48–53.

Cynthia Doxey

HAMBLIN, JACOB. Noted for his peaceful missionary efforts among various tribes of **Indians** in the West, Jacob Hamblin also helped colonize parts of **Utah, Arizona**, and **New Mexico**. Born **6 April** 1819 in Salem, **Ohio**, Jacob was baptized 3 March 1842 in **Wisconsin** and moved to Nauvoo the same year. He moved to Tooele, Utah, in 1850. While defending the **Saints** in Tooele against Indians the following year, Jacob had it "forcibly impressed" upon his mind that it was "not [his] calling to shed the blood of the scattered remnant of Israel, but to be a messenger of peace to them" and that if he "would not thirst for their blood, [he] should never fall by their hands" (Hamblin, 24). He acted on these impressions and began learning the Indians' language in 1854 while serving as a missionary in southern Utah's Santa Clara Indian **Mission**. Called to preside over the mission in 1854, Jacob worked closely with the **Paiutes, Navajos**, and Hopi in the area over the next several years, earning their respect with his honesty and fairness. In December 1876, **Brigham Young ordained** him an "apostle to the **Lamanites**" (Jenson, 100) in St.

George. Jacob moved to Amity, Arizona, in 1878 and to Pleasanton, **New Mexico**, in 1882, where he died 31 August 1886.

Sources

Hamblin, Jacob. *Jacob Hamblin: His Life in His Own Words.* New York: Paramount Books, 1995.

Jenson, Andrew. *Latter-day Saint Biographical Encyclopedia.* 4 vols. 1901–36. Reprint, Salt Lake City: Western Epics, 1971. 3:100–1.

Peterson, Charles S. "Jacob Hamblin, Apostle to the Lamanites, and the Indian Mission." *Journal of Mormon History* 2 (1975): 21–34.

ANDREW H. HEDGES

HANCOCK, LEVI. Levi Ward Hancock, a member of the original Seven Presidents of **Seventy** (D&C 124:138), was born 7 April 1803 at Springfield, Hampdon, **Massachusetts**. He moved with his **family** to Chagrin (Willoughby), **Ohio**, and then to Rome, Ohio. He was converted to the Church after listening to the missionaries who had been called to teach the **Lamanites**. He was baptized by **Parley P. Pratt** 16 November 1830 and **ordained** an **elder** by **Oliver Cowdery**. He completed a successful **mission** to **Missouri** in 1831 (D&C 52:29) and was a member of the first **School of the Prophets** in **Kirtland** in 1833. He marched with **Zion's Camp** in 1834 and was a trusted friend of **Joseph Smith**, moving with him from Kirtland to Missouri and **Nauvoo**. He was the only **general authority** in the **Mormon Battalion**, serving as **chaplain**. He died in Washington, **Utah**, 10 June 1882, where in addition to his role as a general authority he had served as a **patriarch**.

Sources

Baird, Amy E., Victoria H. Jackson, and Laura L. Wassell, comp. "Autobiography of Levi Ward Hancock." Typescript in Keith Perkins's possession.

Jenson, Andrew. *Latter-day Saint Biographical Encyclopedia.* 4 vols. 1901–36. Reprint, Salt Lake City: Western Epics, 1971. 1:188.

KEITH W. PERKINS

HANCOCK, MOSIAH. Mosiah Hancock, **pioneer, missionary,** and colonizer, was born 9 April 1834 in **Kirtland, Ohio**, to **Levi Hancock** and Clarrissa Reed. Mosiah then moved with the Church and his family to **Missouri** and **Illinois**. His parents instilled in him a love for the **Prophet Joseph Smith**. His most poignant memory was that of viewing the dead bodies of Joseph and **Hyrum Smith**. Mosiah's father had him place one hand on the Prophet's breast, raise his other arm and swear he would never compromise the principles of Joseph Smith with those who fought against the gospel of **Jesus Christ**. Mosiah stated he was determined to fill this vow to the very letter. After the **Martyrdom**, the Hancock family made the trek across the plains and arrived in the **Salt Lake Valley** on 3 August 1848. As an adult, Mosiah lived in several places in northern **Utah** and for a time assisted in the construction of the Brigham Young Academy. He served **missions** for the Church in southern Utah and in the late 1870s helped colonize Taylor, **Arizona**. He died in Hubard, Graham County, Arizona, 14 January 1907.

SOURCE

Baird, Amy E., Victoria H. Jackson, and Laura L. Wassell, comp. "Autobiography of Mosiah Hancock." Typescript in Keith Perkins's possession.

KEITH W. PERKINS

HANCOCK COUNTY, ILLINOIS. Located in western **Illinois**, Hancock County was created in 1825 from unorganized territory and named for John Hancock, the first signer of the **Declaration of Independence**. The county has an area of 797 square miles. The Latter-day **Saints** established several settlements in Hancock County besides Nauvoo. Those 17 additional communities may be divided into categories. Major colonies included **Ramus** (later known as Macedonia and Webster) and Lima. Minor colonies included Plymouth, Green Plains, Yelrome (Tioga), and Camp Creek. Missionary towns, where Mormons lived among many non-Mormons, included **Carthage**, Bear Creek, LaHarpe, and Fountain Green. The **Nauvoo** suburbs included Stringtown, Mormon Springs, Rocky Run, Sonora, and Davis Mound. Warren was planned but never established.

The largest and most important of the settlements after Nauvoo was Ramus, which was subsequently called Macedonia and is now known as Webster. A stake was created in Ramus on 15 July 1840. The Saints in Ramus built their own meetinghouse, an unusual practice in the early Church. **Joseph Smith** visited Ramus frequently and received two revelations there (D&C 130; 131).

SOURCES

Cannon, Donald. "Spokes on the Wheel: Early Latter-day Saint Settlements in Hancock County, Illinois." *Ensign* 16 (February 1986): 62–68.

Rugh, Susan Sessions. "Conflict in the Countryside: The Mormon Settlement at
    Macedonia, Illinois." *BYU Studies* 32 (Winter-Spring 1991): 149–74.

DONALD Q. CANNON

HANDBOOKS. Since its beginning, the Church has set forth its organization in a number of publications that have served as handbooks to
help Latter-day **Saints** understand how the Church functions.

The earliest handbook in the Church was the "**Articles and Cove-
nants**," published as sections 20 and 22 of the **Doctrine and Covenants**.
At the first **conference** of the Church, held 9 June 1830, the Articles and
Covenants were read to the congregation and adopted. These sections
spelled out many of the basic procedures of the Church (Woodford,
292–93). The **revelation** that became section 136 of the Doctrine and
Covenants outlined the organization of the Church's migration from
Winter Quarters to the Salt Lake Valley.

Early Church leaders in **Utah** were heavily involved with the administration of **tithing**. In 1852 a printed circular was issued, giving **bishops**
instructions on how to settle tithing accounts at the end of the year. A
more detailed set of instructions was printed in 1859 (Hartley, 99–101).
By the 1880s these tithing instructions were sent out to **priesthood**
leaders on a yearly basis.

The First Presidency issued a particularly significant circular letter
11 July 1877, describing the organization of **stakes**, **wards**, and **quorums**
(Clark). These instructions provided the foundation for later handbooks.
Beginning in 1899 the annual tithing instructions were issued as a booklet.
In 1909 the instructions were expanded to include information on other
matters of organization. After 1910 the instructions were no longer issued
annually, but approximately every five years (May, 541). Starting in 1928
the word "handbook" was added to the title of the instructions. In 1960
the *Handbook of Instructions* became the *General Handbook of Instructions*.

In addition to these general handbooks, the organizations of the
Church such as the **Sunday School**, **Relief Society**, and **MIA** have issued
handbooks. While these organizations were created in the nineteenth
century, the publication of their handbooks began in the early twentieth
century.

In 1998 a new *Church Handbook of Instructions* was published.
Volume one is the successor of the general handbooks that began publication in 1899. Volume two is an effort to publish the organizational
handbooks for Church leadership in a single source. A number of

specialized handbooks, including full-time missionary handbooks, continue to be published separately.

SOURCES

Clark, James R., comp. *Messages of the First Presidency of The Church of Jesus Christ of Latter-day Saints.* 6 vols. Salt Lake City: Bookcraft, 1965–75. 2:283–95.

Hartley, William G. "Ward Bishops and the Localizing of LDS Tithing, 1847–1856." *New Views of Mormon History: A Collection of Essays in Honor of Leonard J. Arrington.* Edited by Davis Bitton and Maureen Ursenbach Beecher. Salt Lake City: University of Utah Press, 1987. 96–114.

May, Frank O. Jr. "General Handbook of Instructions." *Encyclopedia of Mormonism.* Edited by Daniel H. Ludlow. 4 vols. New York: Macmillan, 1992. 2:541.

Woodford, Robert J. "The Historical Development of the Doctrine and Covenants." Ph.D. diss. 2 vols. Brigham Young University, 1974.

GRANT ALLEN ANDERSON

HANDCART PIONEER MONUMENT. The Handcart Pioneer Monument on Temple Square celebrates the most distinctive means of transportation for the early Latter-day Saint pioneers as they crossed the plains to Zion. This monument commemorates the more than 4,000 pioneers who came by handcart between 1856 and 1860. Commissioned in 1925 by the Daughters of the Handcart Pioneers, the much smaller original sculpture was done for the Bureau of Information on Temple Square. In 1947 the monument was unveiled on Temple Square as part of the Pioneer Centennial.

The artist, Norwegian-born Torleif Severin Knaphus (1881–1965), studied art at the Kings Art School in Oslo. He joined the LDS Church in 1902 and immigrated to Utah in 1906. He later studied art in Paris and New York City. Among Knaphus's other works are sculptures in and on the Hawaii and Cardston Temples, as well as the Hill Cumorah Monument.

SOURCES

Hafen, Leroy R., and Ann W. Hafen. *Handcarts to Zion: The Story of a Unique Western Migration, 1856–1860.* Lincoln: University of Nebraska Press, 1992.

Porter, Elizabeth Cannon. "A Monument to the Handcart Pioneers." *Improvement Era* 28 (July 1925): 833–37.

RICHARD G. OMAN

HANDCARTS. As a means of overland transportation, handcarts were unique to the Latter-day Saint migration to Zion. A handcart consisted of a shallow wooden box mounted on an axle supported by two carriage-type wheels. The pioneers propelled the cart forward by pushing against a crossbar attached to shafts in front. Others pushed from the rear when needed. Usually one family or five people were assigned to a cart. Because loads had to be kept light, each emigrant was allowed on average only 17 pounds of baggage. A few wagons accompanied each handcart train to carry the heavy provisions and tents. Children age four and under, and occasionally the sick or elderly, rode; all others walked.

The handcart's primary advantage was its affordability, but there were some disadvantages. To maintain a strict budget, agents and handcart captains carefully rationed food, giving each adult only a pint of flour a day, sometimes with a little bacon and dried apples. With the small food allowance and arduous work of pulling carts and walking, the handcart **pioneers** were often hungry, tired, and footsore.

Brigham Young, as president of the **Perpetual Emigrating Fund** (PEF) Company, instituted the handcart plan that was used by a portion of the **pioneers** from 1856 through 1860. As early as 1852 he had suggested the use of handcarts, but Church emigration agents found other means and did not implement the plan that year. Then from 1854 to 1856, severe economic conditions in Utah, including grasshopper infestations and drought, greatly reduced donations and repayments to the Perpetual Emigrating Fund. An extremely large emigration from **Europe** funded by the PEF in 1855 drastically depleted funds available for emigration loans. Yet the urgent desire to gather Church membership to Zion, particularly the long-faithful poor **Saints**, was paramount. These three factors combined to necessitate the use of low-cost transportation in 1856.

President Young directed Church agents to set the handcart experiment in motion. The system proved financially successful, allowing the gathering of many Saints at minimal expense. Tragedy came, however, when two handcart companies started too late in 1856 to avoid being caught by **Wyoming** snow. In these companies, led by James G. Willie and Edward Martin, more than 200 people died, and many others endured starvation, exposure, frostbite, and frozen limbs. The system continued with modifications in 1857, 1859, and 1860, with strict instructions to begin the journey early.

Five handcart companies in 1856 and two in 1857 departed from Iowa City, **Iowa**, for a trek of approximately 1,300 miles. In 1859 and 1860, three companies began their journey at Florence, **Nebraska**, and walked 1,000 miles. Besides the 10 handcart companies that came to

Utah, one handcart train of missionaries left **Salt Lake City** for their **mission** assignments in the spring of 1857 to further prove the plan's feasibility.

A relatively small number of Saints journeyed to Zion by handcart compared to the vast majority, who came by wagon. Of the 70,000 immigrants to Utah from 1847 to 1869, only 3,000 (4.3%) traveled by handcart. The Church organized handcart companies during only 4 of those 22 years. Only in 1856, when some 2,000 Saints pushed and pulled their way to Zion, did the number of handcarts exceed the number of wagons crossing the plains with pioneers bound for Utah. In 1856, much of the expense of handcart emigration was financed by PEF loans. Because of this heavy debt, PEF assistance was limited in subsequent years, and most of the handcart travelers paid their own way. Church-sponsored wagon trains replaced the handcart system after 1860.

Though the number of handcart pioneers was small, the handcart experience has come to symbolize the faith, determination, and sacrifice of all the pioneers. The disaster that befell the thousand members of the Willie and Martin handcart companies has captured the hearts of Latter-day Saints worldwide and has brought attention to the Mormon migration experience. The dramatic and compassionate rescue of these suffering people by the Saints in Utah serves as an example of service and a source of pride for Church members today.

SOURCE

Hafen, LeRoy R., and Ann W. Hafen. *Handcarts to Zion: The Story of a Unique Western Migration, 1856–1860*. Lincoln: University of Nebraska Press, 1992.

LYNDIA CARTER

HAN IN SANG. While Han In Sang is distinguished as the first Korean to serve as a **mission president** and as the person who singularly translated the **Book of Mormon** into the Korean language, he is best known as the first Korean to be called as a **general authority** of the Church. He served in the Second Quorum of the **Seventy** between 1991 and 1996.

Brother Han was born in Ich'on, Kyonggi Province, about 30 miles south of Seoul, 10 December 1938. He was in elementary school when the **Korean War** broke out in 1950. His family was Buddhist, and as a youngster In Sang lived in a mountain setting near a Buddhist temple. When the Korean War ended, he was a junior high school student.

Brother Han was in high school in 1956 when a friend invited him to attend meetings of The Church of Jesus Christ of Latter-day Saints. He was baptized into the Church by missionary Claude W. Newman on 20 April 1957. He was **ordained** an **elder** by Elder **Gordon B. Hinckley** in 1961 and was ordained a **high priest** in 1973 by Elder **Spencer W. Kimball**.

Between 1961 and 1964, Brother Han served in the Marine Corps. After his release, he was called to serve a full-time proselyting **mission**; he was **set apart** 10 February 1964. Under the direction of mission president Gail E. Carr, Elder Han was assigned to work full time on the translation of the Book of Mormon into the Korean language. With much faith, prayer, and study, and after many trials and hardships, this historic work was completed in 1967.

Han In Sang was married to Lee Kyu In on 26 March 1966 by mission president Spencer J. Palmer at the mission headquarters in Seoul. Their marriage was sealed in the **Hawaii Temple** 23 August 1973.

Brother Han has served in many important Church positions, including manager of Translation Services and manager for temporal affairs in **Korea**. He served as a **branch** president (1964 and 1966); as president of the Seoul West **District** (1971); as president of the Korea Pusan Mission (1975–78); and as a **regional representative** (1978 and 1985).

After his release as a general authority in 1996, Han In Sang was called to serve as president of the Seoul Korea **Temple**.

SOURCES

Palmer, Spencer J. *The Church Encounters Asia.* Salt Lake City: Deseret Book, 1970. 178, 184–88.

Palmer, Spencer J., and Shirley H. Palmer. *The Korean Saints: Personal Stories of Trial and Triumph, 1950–1980.* Salt Lake City: Deseret Book, 1995. 89–100.

SPENCER J. PALMER

HANKS, EPHRAIM K. Ephraim Knowlton Hanks, courageous frontiersman and **pioneer**, has become a folk hero in Church history. Born 21 March 1826 in Madison, Ohio, Hanks served three years in the **United States** Navy and was also a **Mormon Battalion** soldier, a mail carrier across the plains (50 times), an Indian agent, a rescuer of the **handcart** pioneers in 1856, a Mormon Militia member, a settler at Mountain Dell, and a leader of settlements in Wayne County, **Utah**.

A skilled outdoorsman, Hanks knew no fear. Whether the difficulty involved a mountain storm, raging rivers, treacherous **Indians**, or the

United States Army, Hanks was equal to the task. He was a confidant of **Brigham Young**, who was his brother-in-law.

Throughout his life, Hanks felt he was on the Lord's errand. He saw his part in the daring rescue in 1856 of the handcart pioneers as commonplace, yet it was filled with privations and hardship on his part. His diplomacy among the Indians unquestionably aided in the safe travel of countless **Mormon** immigrants. He represented the best in moral and physical courage and played an integral part in the settlement of the **Great Basin**. His life was a pattern of strict obedience to Church leadership. He later served as a **stake patriarch** in Wayne County, Utah. Ephraim Hanks died 9 June 1896 in Pleasant Creek, Utah.

SOURCE

Hanks, Sidney Alvarus, and Ephraim K. Hanks. *Scouting for the Mormons on the Great Frontier.* Salt Lake City: Deseret News Press, 1948.

JOHN M. BECK

HARDY, RUFUS K. Rufus Kay Hardy, **mission president** and member of the First Council of the **Seventy**, was born 28 May 1878 in **Salt Lake City**. He was sent at age 22 to teach the gospel to the **Maoris** of **New Zealand**. He grew to love the people, absorbing their culture and learning to speak their language so fluently that he was often called to sit in council with their leaders. Accompanied by his wife, he returned again to the islands in 1907 as president of the New Zealand **Mission**.

Brother Hardy was ordained a seventy before his first mission, and he held that office in the **priesthood** throughout his life. He was made one of the presidents of the eighth **quorum** of seventies in 1906 and was called as a member of the First Council of the Seventy in October 1934. He died 7 March 1945 in Salt Lake City.

SOURCES

Flake, Lawrence R. *Mighty Men of Zion.* Salt Lake City: Karl D. Butler, 1974. 449.

"Rufus K. Hardy of the First Council of the Seventy." *Improvement Era* 35 (October 1932): 712–15, 735.

LAWRENCE R. FLAKE

HARMONY, PENNSYLVANIA. The township of Harmony was created in 1809 while still a part of Luzerne County, Pennsylvania. The village of Harmony was situated just two miles south of the

Pennsylvania–New York state line, on the east bank of the Susquehanna River. Harmony became part of Susquehanna County when it was divided from Luzerne in 1810. That portion of the township where Joseph Smith Jr. and the Isaac Hale family once lived became the township of Oakland when it divided from Harmony in 1853, and it remains such to this day.

Joseph Smith first visited the Isaac Hale home in the rural area of the "Great Bend" of the Susquehanna in the forepart of November 1825. He was in company with Josiah Stowell Sr. of the town of Bainbridge in Chenango County, New York. Stowell had employed Joseph and others to assist him in digging for a purported Spanish treasure. The men lodged at the Isaac Hale home until about 17 November 1825, when they discontinued their efforts and left the area. While living with the Hales, Joseph Smith had been attracted to Isaac's daughter Emma. He continued his courtship of Emma after moving to Stowell's place in Chenango County. Isaac Hale did not approve of Joseph's advances and refused to give his daughter's hand in marriage. The couple chose to elope, and they were married in South Bainbridge, Chenango County, 18 January 1827. They then went to Manchester, New York, to live with Joseph's parents.

Emma and Joseph visited the Isaac Hale family in August 1827 to obtain her dowry. Isaac invited Joseph to come and live with them, which offer Joseph deferred at the time. On 22 September 1827, Joseph went to the Hill Cumorah in Manchester and received the gold plates from Moroni, and by December 1827 the couple was eager to accept the Hale invitation to come to Harmony. Members of a mob in the Palmyra/Manchester area had made it almost impossible for Joseph to keep the plates safe or to engage in their translation.

In Harmony the Smiths procured a 13-acre lot from Isaac Hale and moved a small two-story frame house onto the site. It was in that home that Joseph undertook the translation of the Book of Mormon. Martin Harris was dispatched from Harmony by Joseph Smith in February 1828 to visit learned men in eastern New York with a transcript of characters and an interpretation of those characters. Martin next served as scribe for Joseph between 12 April and 14 June 1828, at which time he begged permission to take the manuscript, then numbering 116 pages, to show to select members of his family in the township of Palmyra. On 15 June, the day following Martin's departure, Emma gave birth to her first son, who did not survive. A Smith family Bible identifies his name as Alvin (see Youngreen).

Martin lost the manuscript that he had covenanted to keep safe and was no longer allowed to act as scribe. In the emergency, Emma, her brother Reuben Hale, and Joseph's brother **Samuel H. Smith** each gave minimal assistance in writing for Joseph until the arrival of **Oliver Cowdery**, a Manchester schoolteacher, who became Joseph's permanent scribe. By 7 April 1829, Oliver was occupied as the principal scribe for the translation. On 15 May 1829, Joseph and Oliver were visited by **John the Baptist** in answer to a prayer for guidance relative to their question of baptism and the authority to perform that ordinance. The heavenly messenger ordained the two men to the **Aaronic Priesthood** and com- missioned them to baptize each other and ordain one another to that priesthood. Soon afterward Joseph and Oliver were ordained to the **Melchizedek Priesthood** by the ancient **apostles Peter, James, and John**, who likewise appeared to them on the banks of the Susquehanna River.

It was in Harmony that the Lord revealed to Joseph the content of 15 sections now recorded in the **Doctrine and Covenants**. The Lord also gave to Joseph a "precious morsel" now comprising the first chapter of the book of **Moses** in the **Pearl of Great Price**.

Nathaniel Lewis, Emma's uncle and an ordained Methodist preacher, helped stir up the mob element in Harmony that forced Joseph and Oliver to flee for their safety during the latter part of May 1829. At the request of the **Prophet**, Oliver Cowdery had contacted his friend **David Whitmer**, who, in turn, obtained sanctuary for them at the home of his father, **Peter Whitmer Sr.**, in the township of **Fayette, New York**. They arrived at the **Whitmer farm** by 1 June 1829, and Emma soon followed. Most of the translation of the Book of Mormon was done in Harmony, but of necessity the final pages were completed at Fayette between 1 June and 1 July.

Joseph and Emma were back in their Harmony home by 3 October 1829. Their final departure from the Susquehanna area occurred in the latter part of August 1830, when they again went to live at the Whitmer farm in Fayette.

SOURCES

Jessee, Dean C., ed. *The Papers of Joseph Smith*. Vol. 1. Salt Lake City: Deseret Book, 1989. 8–10.

Porter, Larry C. "The Restoration of the Aaronic and Melchizedek Priesthoods." *Ensign* 26 (December 1996): 30–47.

———. "A Study of the Origins of The Church of Jesus Christ of Latter-day Saints in the States of New York and Pennsylvania, 1816–1831." Ph.D. diss., Brigham Young University, 1971. 111–14, 118–71.

Smith, Joseph. Letter to Oliver Cowdery. Harmony, Penn., 22 October 1829. LDS Church Archives, Salt Lake City.

Youngreen, Buddy. Personal interview by Larry C. Porter. Provo, Utah, 6 June 1988. Youngreen has the Joseph Smith family Bible, in which Emma records in her own hand under "Births" that of "Alvin Smith June 15th 1828."

LARRY C. PORTER

HARRIS, MARTIN. Martin Harris, one of the **Three Witnesses** to the divine origin of the **Book of Mormon**, financed the first publication of the book in 1830. Born 18 May 1783 in Easton, Washington County, **New York**, Harris died 10 July 1875 in Clarkston, Cache County, **Utah**. He was extolled by non-Mormon contemporaries for honesty, sincerity, memory, neighborliness, generosity, and civic spirit. His wife characterized him as industrious, attentive to domestic concerns, and an excellent provider and father.

Before Harris met **Joseph Smith** he had been looking for the restoration of biblical Christianity. He said in 1870, "I was inspired of the Lord and taught of the Spirit that I should not join any church" (interview by Edward Stevenson). By 1824, Harris had learned about the angel **Moroni's** appearances to Joseph Smith and about the **gold plates**. In the fall of 1827, he helped Joseph Smith protect the plates from thieves and financed the Prophet's move from **Manchester, New York**, to **Harmony, Pennsylvania**.

In February 1828, Harris visited Joseph Smith in Harmony and obtained a transcription and translation of characters from the plates. He took the documents to "learned men" in Utica, Albany, and **New York City**, where **Samuel L. Mitchill, Charles Anthon,** and **Luther Brodish** examined the texts. These visits fulfilled a prophecy in Isaiah 29:11–14.

From 12 April to 14 June 1828, Martin Harris served as Joseph Smith's scribe, producing 116 manuscript pages. Joseph let Martin take the pages to Palmyra, New York, to gain family support. During a three-week period when Harris visited relatives, attended to business, and served jury duty, the 116 pages were stolen. Martin's wife, Lucy, reportedly said that she burned them. The couple later divorced.

In June 1829, Joseph Smith, **Oliver Cowdery,** and **David Whitmer** were shown the golden plates by the angel Moroni. The angel then appeared to Martin Harris and Joseph Smith. Harris heard the voice of **God** declare that Joseph's translation was correct, and **Jesus Christ** commanded Harris to testify of what he had seen and heard. Palmyra's Egbert B. Grandin printed the Book of Mormon after Harris agreed to mortgage his home and some of his farm for $3,000 as security, which he sold on 7 April 1831 to pay the printing bill.

Martin Harris was present at the **organization of the Church** on 6 April 1830. In May 1831 he led 50 converts from Palmyra to **Kirtland, Ohio**. The same year, Harris accompanied Joseph Smith and others to **Missouri** to purchase property and designate the site for **Zion**. There he was asked to live the **law of consecration**.

In 1832, Harris and his brother Emer served a mission together, baptizing 100 people at Chenango Point (now Binghamton), New York. In January 1833, Martin Harris was imprisoned briefly in Springville, **Pennsylvania**, to stop his preaching.

Returning to Kirtland in January 1834, Harris became a member of the first Church **high council**. The same year, he went to **Jackson County, Missouri**, with **Zion's Camp** to assist persecuted **Saints**. On 14 February 1835, the Three Witnesses selected the first **Quorum** of the Twelve **Apostles**. In 1836, Harris attended the dedication of the **Kirtland Temple**. Later that summer, Martin's estranged wife, Lucy Harris, died. Martin married Caroline Young, **Brigham Young**'s niece, in November 1836.

Harris refused to join the **Kirtland Safety Society**. He was released from the high council on 3 September 1837 and was excommunicated during the last week of December 1837. He was baptized again on 7 November 1842.

Brigham Young invited Martin and Caroline Harris to join the **Saints** in the West. In 1856, Caroline and the children journeyed to Utah. The aging Harris remained in Kirtland with other relatives until 1870, supporting himself by his 90 acres. Harris prospered and acted as a self-appointed guide/caretaker of the deserted Kirtland Temple, listing himself in the 1860 census as "Mormon preacher."

In 1869 Brigham Young, William H. Homer, and other Latter-day Saints renewed their offers of assistance in bringing Harris to Utah. At age 87, Martin Harris, accompanied by **Edward Stevenson**, arrived by train in **Salt Lake City** on 30 August 1870. He accepted **rebaptism** as evidence of his reaffirmation of faith on 17 September 1870 and, at Brigham Young's invitation, publicly testified of the **Book of Mormon**. He traveled to Smithfield, Utah, where he lived with his son Martin Harris Jr. He moved to Clarkston in 1874.

Hundreds journeyed to Smithfield and Clarkston to hear Harris's testimony. He died at age 92 in July 1875 after bearing testimony of the Book of Mormon: "Yes, I did see the plates on which the Book of

Mormon was written. I did see the angel, I did hear the voice of God, and I do know that Joseph Smith is a true Prophet of God, holding the keys of the Holy Priesthood" ("Last Testimony").

SOURCES

Anderson, Richard Lloyd. *Investigating the Book of Mormon Witnesses.* Salt Lake City: Deseret Book, 1981.

Harris, Martin. Interview by Edward Stevenson, 4 September 1870. Stevenson Microfilm Collection. Vol. 32. LDS Church Archives, Salt Lake City.

———. "The Last Testimony of Martin Harris." Recorded by William H. Homer in a statement sworn before J. W. Robinson. 9 April 1927. LDS Church Archives, Salt Lake City.

James, Rhett Stephens. "Lucy Harris: Wife of the Witness," "The Legacy of Martin Harris: The Printing of the Book of Mormon," "The Martin Harris Festival, 1870–1995," "Martin Harris: The Witness," *Mormon Heritage Magazine* 2 (July–August 1995).

RHETT STEPHENS JAMES

HARRIS FARM. To pay for the printing of the first edition of the **Book of Mormon**, **Martin Harris** sold 151 acres (including his farmstead) to Thomas Lakey on 7 April 1831 for $3,000. From 1813 to 1830, Harris acquired approximately 260 acres in **Palmyra** Township and developed a quality farm one and one-half miles north of Palmyra Village on ground formerly owned by his parents.

On his farmstead Martin constructed a one-and-a-half-story New England–style frame house, a barn and outbuildings, and considerable fencing. Together with cultivated fields and an orchard, extensive meadows, pastures, woodlands, and a year-round creek, the farm was one of the best in Wayne County.

Eighty acres were purportedly deeded by Martin to Lucy Harris when they separated due to unresolved differences regarding **Joseph Smith's** work. Her 1820s home still stands. Martin's original home burned down in 1849, and William Chapman replaced it in 1849 and 1850 with the cobblestone structure that now stands on the site.

SOURCES

Anderson, Richard L. "Gold Plates and Printer's Ink." *Ensign* 6 (September 1976): 71–79.

Gunnell, Wayne Cutler. "Martin Harris, Witness and Benefactor to the Book of Mormon." Master's thesis, Brigham Young University, 1955.

Porter, Larry C. "The Book of Mormon: Historical Setting for Its Translation and Publication." *Joseph Smith: The Prophet, The Man.* Edited by Susan Easton Black and Charles D. Tate Jr. Provo, Utah: Brigham Young University, 1993. 49–64.

Donald L. Enders

HARRISON, BENJAMIN. Benjamin Harrison, 23rd president of the **United States**, granted amnesty to some **Mormon** polygamists in the late nineteenth century. He was born 20 August 1833 in North Bend, **Ohio**, at the home of his grandfather, William Henry Harrison, who was ninth president of the United States. Benjamin graduated from Miami University (Ohio) in 1852 and married Caroline Lavina Scott the following year. He studied law in Cincinnati and was admitted to the bar in 1854. Later that year he established a law practice in Indianapolis, **Indiana.** Before he became president in 1889, he served as a Union officer in the **Civil War** and as a U.S. senator from 1881 to 1887.

Harrison ran for president on a **Republican** platform that pledged to "stamp out the . . . wickedness of polygamy" among the Mormons (Roberts, 283). After he was elected, he appointed several officials for the territory of Utah, including Judge Charles Zane, who were openly antagonistic to the practice of **plural marriage**. When President **Wilford Woodruff** issued the **Manifesto** in 1890, however, Harrison gradually assumed a more moderate attitude toward the Saints. On 19 December 1891 Church leaders formally petitioned Harrison to grant general amnesty to all members who had practiced plural marriage. Harrison waited until 4 January 1893 to respond to the petition and then only gave amnesty to those who had complied with the antipolygamy laws since 1890. President **Grover Cleveland** issued a more general amnesty on 25 September 1894.

After Harrison lost his bid for reelection to Cleveland, he resumed a law practice in Indianapolis, where he died on 13 March 1901.

Sources

Roberts, B. H. *A Comprehensive History of The Church of Jesus Christ of Latter-day Saints, Century One.* 6 vols. Salt Lake City: The Church of Jesus Christ of Latter-day Saints, 1930. 6:283–89.

Sievers, Harry J. *Benjamin Harrison.* 3 vols. Chicago: H. Regnery Co., 1952–69.

Arnold K. Garr

HASLEM, JAMES H. James Holt Haslem, remembered for his role as messenger, carried dispatches to **Brigham Young** detailing problems emigrants from Missouri and Arkansas had caused the Indians in Iron County. He left Cedar City Monday afternoon, 7 September 1857, and arrived in **Salt Lake City** Thursday morning, having covered a distance of about 300 miles. After James had rested for a few hours, President Young had him return with word that the Indians must be restrained from harming the emigrants. James arrived home on Sunday, two days after the **Mountain Meadows Massacre**.

Born 16 September 1825 in Bolton, Lancashire, **England**, James was converted and baptized in November 1840. In 1851 he arrived in **Utah**, where he would have three wives and 20 children. James died 13 March 1913 at Wellsville, Utah.

SOURCE

Journal History. LDS Church Historical Department, Salt Lake City. 13 March 1913. 2.

CALVIN R. STEPHENS

HASTINGS, LANSFORD. Lansford Warren Hastings, an emigrant, author, and aspiring politician, wrote *The Emigrants' Guide to Oregon and California*, which was consulted by Church leaders prior to the trek west. Born about 1818 and raised in Mt. Vernon, **Ohio**, Hastings traveled on the **Oregon Trail** in 1842. In 1845 he published the *The Emigrants' Guide*. Hastings influenced the emigrant groups of 1846, including the **Donner-Reed party**, to travel the ill-advised route south of the Great Salt Lake.

While promoting his *Guide* in **New York City** in 1845, Hastings met Samuel Brannan, who published excerpts from the book in the *New York Messenger*. Selections were printed in the *Nauvoo Neighbor*. Church councils in **Nauvoo** consulted the *Guide,* though it focused mainly on the West Coast and included only a brief description of the **Salt Lake Valley**.

SOURCES

Andrew, Thomas. "Lansford W. Hastings and the Promotion of the Salt Lake Desert Cutoff: A Reappraisal." *Western Historical Quarterly* 4 (April 1973): 133–50.

Hastings, Lansford W. *The Emigrants' Guide to Oregon and California.* Cincinnati: George Conclin, 1845.

Kelly, Charles. *Salt Desert Trails.* Salt Lake City: Western Printing Company, 1930.

SCOTT ELDREDGE AND FRED R. GOWANS

HATCH, ORRIN G. Orrin G. Hatch (R-Utah), **United States** senator beginning in 1976, has distinguished himself as a public servant and devout Church member. He was born 22 March 1934 in Pittsburgh, **Pennsylvania**. He graduated from **Brigham Young University** in 1959 and from the University of Pittsburgh Law School in 1962. He married Elaine Hansen of Newton, **Utah**, in the **Salt Lake Temple** in 1957, and they became the parents of six children.

Hatch practiced law in Pennsylvania and then in Utah until his election to the Senate (his first elective office). He served as chairman of the Senate Judiciary Committee and championed numerous legislative causes, including the welfare reform bill and the Religious Freedom Restoration Act. In 1999 he became a candidate for the Republican nomination for president of the United States and then focused on reelection to the Senate in 2000. The recipient of many awards and honorary doctorates, Senator Hatch is a respected statesman as well as an author and a songwriter.

In the Church he has served as a missionary in the Great Lakes **Mission**, a **bishop**, **stake** high councilor, and gospel doctrine teacher.

SOURCE

Vetterli, Richard, and Brad E. Hainsworth. *In the Lions' Den: The Story of Senator Orrin Hatch*. Springville, Utah: Cedar Fort, 1994.

LLOYD D. NEWELL

HAUN'S MILL MASSACRE. Haun's Mill, named after the community's founder, Jacob Haun, was one of the first Latter-day **Saint** settlements founded in **Caldwell County**. Following his conversion to Mormonism, Haun emigrated from his home in Green Bay, **Wisconsin**, to western **Missouri**. Around 1834 he established a mill at a remote site on **Shoal Creek** in the northeastern part of what was then **Ray County**. The settlement included only a few families and less than a dozen cabins; however, approximately 75 Latter-day Saint families lived in the immediate area, mostly along Shoal Creek. A **branch** of the Church was established with David Evans as president.

On the afternoon of 30 October 1838, an extralegal force composed of more than 200 men primarily from Livingston and Daviess Counties attacked the settlement. Fifteen Latter-day Saints were killed during the attack or died shortly afterwards. Two others died within a few weeks. Another fourteen were wounded. There were no fatalities on the side of the Missourians. After securing the settlement, the vigilantes ransacked the homes and temporary shelters, taking household items and food and confiscating animals.

The dead were buried the following day. Fourteen of the victims were buried in a dry well: Elias Benner, John Byers, Alexander Campbell, Simon Cox, Josiah Fuller, Austin Hammer, John Lee, Thomas McBride, Levi N. Merrick, William Napier, George S. Richards (age 15), Sardius Smith (age 10), Warren Smith, and John York. The locations of the other three victims' remains are not known. Hiram Abbot lived for five weeks following the attack. Charles Merrick (age nine) was wounded while fleeing from the blacksmith shop and died four weeks later. The final fatality, Benjamin Lewis, was buried in an individual grave by his brother David Lewis.

Historians have often concluded that the attack made by the Livingston militia on the Haun's Mill community was associated with the 27 October **extermination order** of Governor **Lilburn W. Boggs**. Historical sources indicate that there was no connection with the governor's directive whatsoever, because the Livingston marauders did not learn about the order until 31 October, the day following the attack.

Sources

Baugh, Alexander L. "A Call to Arms: The 1838 Mormon Defense of Northern Missouri." Ph.D. diss., Brigham Young University, 1996.

———. "The Haun's Mill Massacre and the Extermination Order of Missouri Governor Lilburn W. Boggs." *Religious Studies Center Newsletter* 12 (September 1997): 1–5.

———. "Joseph Young's Affidavit of the Massacre at Haun's Mill." *BYU Studies* 38 (1999): 188–202.

Blair, Alma R. "The Haun's Mill Massacre." *BYU Studies* 13 (Autumn 1972): 62–67.

———. "The Haun's Mill Massacre." *Courage: A Journal of History, Thought, and Action* 2 (Summer 1972): 503–7.

ALEXANDER L. BAUGH

HAWAII. Church leaders sent **Addison Pratt** and three companions to the Sandwich Islands (Hawaii) in 1843. Pratt and company never reached Hawaii; however, they stopped at **French Polynesia**. In June 1846 the ship *Brooklyn* rested its 238 Latter-day Saint passengers at Honolulu for 10 days, but the Church was not established there at that time. On 12 December 1850, 10 **elders**, who had been sent from the gold fields of **California** by **apostle Charles C. Rich**, arrived at Honolulu to begin LDS **missionary work**.

Five of the first elders soon left the mission field, but the others—

Henry William Bigler, George Quayle Cannon, William Farrer, James Hawkins, and James Keeler—remained to establish a strong **mission**. Initial success came on the island of Maui, where the Kula **Branch** was formed 6 August 1851. By the time **Joseph F. Smith** came to Hawaii as a missionary in 1854, there were more than 4,000 Hawaiian **Saints** in 53 branches on all the principal islands. By that time Cannon, Farrer, and Hawaiian member **Jonatana H. Napela** had completed a Hawaiian translation of the **Book of Mormon**, which was published the next year.

In August 1854 the mission leased acreage on the island of Lanai and established a gathering place for the Hawaiian converts. The settlement taxed the energies and faith of members and missionaries. Following the departure of the **Utah** elders in 1858 (to defend **Zion** from the threat of **war**), the Hawaiian Saints floundered. Into their midst in 1861 came the adventurer **Walter Murray Gibson**, who usurped Church authority and began selling **priesthood** offices. The mistakes of that era were corrected with Gibson's excommunication in 1864 and the Church's purchase of 6,000 acres of land at **Laie**, Oahu, in January 1865. Laie then became the home of the Saints.

From 1865 to 1919, Laie was the center of the mission and of the Church-owned Laie sugar plantation. The central figure was Samuel E. Woolley, **mission president** and plantation manager from 1895 to 1921. The plantation era ended on 27 November 1919 when President **Heber J. Grant** dedicated the **Hawaii Temple**. Two years later the mission headquarters was moved to Honolulu, where it has remained since. In 1935 President Grant organized the Oahu **Stake**, the first stake outside of North America. Two years later, in 1937, President Grant sent Hilton A. Robertson to Hawaii to organize the Japanese Mission (later called the **Central Pacific Mission**). That mission was combined with the Hawaiian Mission in 1950.

In addition to its ecclesiastical, economic, and social concerns, the Church has devoted considerable resources to the **education** of the Hawaii members. Elementary schools were organized by missionaries in the early 1850s. For many years, until 1921, the Church operated Laie Elementary School. Religious education classes and later **seminary** and **institute** classes have been available. In 1955 President **David O. McKay** guided the organization of a junior college, the Church College of Hawaii. In 1959 it became a four-year college. It was renamed **Brigham Young University–Hawaii Campus** in 1974. The Church created the **Polynesian Cultural Center** in 1963 primarily to provide jobs and financial support for the CCH/BYU–Hawaii students. It has been one of Hawaii's major tourist attractions.

Since **World War II**, the Church has grown steadily. In the year 2000, 55,361 members (approximately 5% of the state's population) comprised 14 stakes and 111 **wards** and branches. On 23 and 24 January 2000 a small **temple** was dedicated at Kona, on the island of Hawaii.

SOURCES

Britsch, R. Lanier. *Moramona: The Mormons in Hawaii*. Laie, Hawaii: Institute for Polynesian Studies, 1989.

———. *Unto the Islands of the Sea: A History of the Latter-day Saints in the Pacific*. Salt Lake City: Deseret Book, 1986. 92–191.

1999–2000 Church Almanac. Salt Lake City: Deseret News, 1998. 193–95.

R. LANIER BRITSCH

HAWAII TEMPLE. When the Laie Hawaii Temple was dedicated on 27 November 1919 by President **Heber J. Grant**, it was the only **temple** in a **mission** of the Church. In 1864, when William W. Cluff was living in Hawaii, **Brigham Young** appeared to him in a **vision** and said, "Upon this land we will build a temple unto our God" (quoted in Woolley, 80).

In June 1915, President **Joseph F. Smith** dedicated a temple site at **Laie**, atop a gentle rise covered with luxurious semitropical vegetation.

The lack of building materials on the islands posed great challenges. Steel-reinforced concrete was made with crushed rock and coral. Construction came to a standstill because of the lack of lumber. Prayers were offered, and two days later a freighter was seen stranded on a coral reef. The captain offered to give his entire cargo of lumber to the **Saints** if they would unload it.

The temple's exterior walls have a creamy white surface adorned with 123 nearly life-size figures created by J. Leo and **Avard Fairbanks**, depicting four dispensations, from the time of **Adam** to the present. In the chapel are reproductions of these friezes. The temple's main rooms seat about 50 persons.

Cement-lined pools surrounded by tropical flowers and vegetation lead to the temple's entrance.

The total cost of the temple and grounds was $215,000.

SOURCES

Cowan, Richard O. *Temples to Dot the Earth*. Salt Lake City: Bookcraft, 1989.

Lundwall, N. B. *Temples of the Most High*. Salt Lake City: Bookcraft, 1949.

Woolley, Samuel E. Conference Report (October 1917): 76–82.

JAN FELIX

HAWKES, SHARLENE WELLS. See WELLS, SHARLENE.

HEALINGS. With the **restoration** of the gospel in this **dispensation** came the renewed understanding of gifts of the spirit. Healings were one of the gifts restored and taught to the early **Saints**. In 1830 the Lord declared: "And whoso shall ask it in my name in faith, they shall cast out devils; they shall heal the sick; they shall cause the blind to receive their sight, and the deaf to hear, and the dumb to speak, and the lame to walk" (D&C 35:9). Specifically concerning the sick, the Lord instructed, "The **elders** of the church, two or more, shall be called, and shall pray for and lay their hands upon them in my name," and those who are "not appointed unto death, shall be healed" (D&C 42:44, 48). Another revelation reiterated, "And again, to some it is given to have faith to be healed; and to others it is given to have faith to heal" (D&C 46:19–20).

Instances of miraculous healings began to appear early in Church history. On one occasion in 1831 **John Johnson**, his wife Alice (some have referred to her as Elsa), and a Methodist minister named **Ezra Booth** came to visit **Joseph Smith**. While there, one of them said to Joseph: "Here is Mrs. Johnson with a lame arm; has God given any power to man now on the earth to cure her?" Moments later Joseph rose and took Mrs. Johnson by the hand saying: "Woman, in the name of the Lord **Jesus Christ** I command thee to be whole." Mrs. Johnson returned home able to use her arm (Smith, 1:215–16).

There are many other examples of healings by faith. During the massacre at **Haun's Mill**, **Alma Smith**, son of Amanda Smith, was shot in the hip at point-blank range. The entire hip bone had been shot away. Already dead were Amanda's husband and her son Sardius. Not knowing what to do for her little boy, she prayed and was guided in the treatment of the wound. After treating it as directed by the Spirit, she asked her little boy if he had faith to be healed. He questioned her as to whether she had such faith. She testified that she had been shown in vision his treatment and recovery. He remained immobile for five weeks, after which time a flexible gristle had grown in the place of the missing hip and he was soon up and playing with the other children. Forty years later he showed no sign of being crippled (Jenson, 84–88). This is one of numerous examples of healings by faith without the advantage of priesthood presence.

Mass healings are exemplified by what **Wilford Woodruff** referred to as "a day of God's power" (Woodruff, 22 July 1839). During the summer of 1839 in **Nauvoo** the Saints were afflicted by a fever (malaria). Multitudes fell ill on both sides of the **Mississippi River**. On 22 July the Prophet Joseph Smith felt prompted to arise from his own sickbed and went forth healing many of the stricken. One notable example was **Elijah Fordham**. He was so ill he was unable to speak, yet he rose and was revived. Joseph sent Wilford Woodruff with a red silk handkerchief and told him the sick would be healed if he administered to them and wiped their faces with the cloth. Wilford kept the handkerchief and treasured it for the rest of his life.

Healings occur today with great regularity. By the power of the priesthood and the faith of the Saints, these miracles will continue to be highlights of faith in the lives of many.

SOURCES

Jenson, Andrew, ed. *The Historical Record*. Salt Lake City, 1888. 5:84–88.

Smith, Joseph. *History of The Church of Jesus Christ of Latter-day Saints*. Edited by B. H. Roberts. 2d ed. rev. 7 vols. Salt Lake City: The Church of Jesus Christ of Latter-day Saints, 1932–51. 1:215–16.

Woodruff, Wilford. *Leaves from My Journal*. 2d ed. Salt Lake City: Juvenile Instructor Office, 1882. 63.

GUY L. DORIUS

HEALTH MISSIONARIES. See **WELFARE PROGRAM.**

HEREFORDSHIRE, ENGLAND. See **ENGLAND.**

HIGBEE, CHAUNCEY. See *NAUVOO EXPOSITOR.*

HIGBEE, ELIAS. Church recorder, **temple** builder, and **missionary**, Elias Higbee remained faithful to the Church throughout his life. He was born 23 October 1795 in Galloway, **New Jersey**. In 1817 he married Sarah Ward and moved to Cincinnati, where he was first taught the gospel. After his baptism in 1832, Higbee moved to **Jackson County, Missouri**, but was soon driven by mobs to **Clay County**. **Orson Pratt** ordained him a high priest 7 August 1834. In the spring of 1835, Higbee began a one-year mission that led him through **Missouri, Illinois, Indiana, Ohio**, and finally to **Kirtland**, where he worked on the temple until its completion. After returning to his family in Missouri, Higbee moved to **Caldwell County**, where he served as the county's first judge. **Joseph Smith** called both **John Corrill** and Elias Higbee as Church historians in 1838. Mobs again forced Higbee to move in 1839, this time to **Nauvoo**, Illinois. During that same year, Higbee accompanied Joseph Smith to **Washington, D.C.**, to seek redress for losses the **Saints** had suffered in Missouri. In 1839, Higbee was placed on the building committee for the **Nauvoo Temple**. He labored in this capacity until he died of cholera on 8 June 1843 in Nauvoo, Illinois.

SOURCES

Jenson, Andrew. *Latter-day Saint Biographical Encyclopedia.* 4 vols. 1901–36. Reprint, Salt Lake City: Western Epics, 1971. 1:253.

Jessee, Dean C., ed. *The Papers of Joseph Smith.* Vol. 1. Salt Lake City: Deseret Book. 1989. 490.

JASON WAYNE HUGHES

HIGBEE, FRANCIS. See *NAUVOO EXPOSITOR*.

HIGH COUNCIL. On 17 February 1834, a general council was held at the **Prophet Joseph Smith**'s home. From this council of 24 **high priests**, 12 brethren were selected to become the first high council in the first **stake** of the Church. It was known as the **Kirtland** Stake, over which the **First Presidency** of the Church became the **stake presidency**. The purpose of the high council was to settle difficulties that arose in the stake and to assist the presidency in organizing and regulating Church affairs.

Through the years, the First Presidency has addressed the duties and responsibilities of the high council and, among other things, has encouraged the high council and the stake presidency to become one. The high council is to advise and counsel the stake presidency in matters related to Church and **disciplinary councils** (D&C 102), **Aaronic** and **Melchizedek Priesthood** matters, the **Relief Society** and **Young Women** organizations, **welfare** issues, **temple** programs, **emergency preparedness**,

public communications, and other administrative concerns. It also approves names of individuals who are presented to serve in the stake, and council members are often assigned to speak in **ward sacrament meetings**.

SOURCES

Clark, James R., comp. *Messages of the First Presidency of The Church of Jesus Christ of Latter-day Saints*. 6 vols. Salt Lake City: Bookcraft, 1965–75. 1:346; 2:348; 3:244; 4; 5:342–43; 6:273.

Fleming, Donovan E. "High Council." *Encyclopedia of Mormonism*. Edited by Daniel H. Ludlow. 4 vols. New York: Macmillan, 1992. 2:586–87.

STANLEY A. JOHNSON

HIGH PRIEST. The office of high priest is a division of the **Melchizedek Priesthood** with the primary purpose to "preside" and "administer in spiritual things" within the Church. While other priesthood offices had been identified previously, the office of high priest was not added until more than a year after the **organization of the Church**. Worthy brethren were first ordained to "the high priesthood," later referred to as the office of high priest, at the 3 June 1831 conference in **Kirtland, Ohio**.

Organized into a **quorum** with a president and **counselors**, high priests provided direction in the initial effort to build the **Kirtland Temple**, among other duties. In **Nauvoo** the high priests quorum planned a meeting hall as the seventies had done, but **Brigham Young** directed them to concentrate instead on finishing the **temple**, which they did. To expand their ministries and augment the work of the **bishops**, early **Utah** high priests served as "acting **teachers**" (now called **home teachers**). In 1877 the **First Presidency** specified that there should be one high priest quorum in every **stake**, and since 1956 the **stake president** has served as president of that quorum. Today, general and local authorities, all being high priests, continue in their responsibility for the spiritual welfare of the Church.

SOURCES

Hartley, William G. "Ordained and Acting Teachers in the Lesser Priesthood, 1851–1883." *BYU Studies* 16 (Spring 1976): 375–98.

Smith, Joseph. *History of The Church of Jesus Christ of Latter-day Saints*. Edited by B. H. Roberts. 2d ed. rev. 7 vols. Salt Lake City: The Church of Jesus Christ of Latter-day Saints, 1932–51. 1:175–76; 7:364.

RONALD O. BARNEY

HILL, GEORGE R. George Richard Hill, general superintendent of the **Sunday School** (1949–66), earlier served as a member of the general board of the **Young Men's** Mutual Improvement Association from 1926 to 1935. Prior to being Sunday School superintendent, he labored as second assistant (1934–43) and as first assistant (1943–49), serving a total of 32 years in that organization. He was born 10 April 1884 to George Richard Hill and Elizabeth Burch in **Ogden, Utah**. His wife, Elizabeth Odette McKay, was the sister of President **David O. McKay**. Hill received a B.S. from **Brigham Young University** in 1907 and a Ph.D. from Cornell in 1912. He subsequently became the director of the School of Agriculture at **Utah State University**. George Hill died 13 August 1971 in **Salt Lake City**.

SOURCE

Hill, George Richard. "Brigham Young University Oral History Interview." Brigham Young University Western Americana Special Collections, 1968.

MARY JANE WOODGER

HILL CUMORAH. The **gold plates**, from which the **Book of Mormon** was translated, were buried in a hill located in the township of **Manchester, New York**, about three miles southeast of the **Joseph Smith Sr.** farm. Just when this hill was first called Cumorah is difficult to determine, but by 1835 the name Cumorah seemed to be well known, at least among Church members. The U.S. Geological Survey of 1898 called the hill "Mormon Hill," and in 1952 the name appeared in the survey as "Hill Cumorah."

Mormon and **Moroni** are the only Book of Mormon writers to use the name Cumorah, and all references to it are associated with the hiding of the Nephite records and the destruction of the Nephite and Jaredite nations. We know of only one time when **Joseph Smith** used "Cumorah" in his personal writings (D&C 128:20). Some scholars suggest that the name *Cumorah* means "Arise-O-Light" or "Arise-**Revelation**" (Palmer, 21).

Those who assume that the final Book of Mormon events took place in what is now the northeastern **United States** believe that the hill in upstate New York is the only hill called Cumorah. Others conclude there must be two hills called Cumorah: one in **Central America**, where they believe the final battles of the Book of Mormon took place; and the other in New York, where Moroni ultimately buried the gold plates he later delivered to Joseph Smith.

Between 1914 and 1928, in a series of purchases, the Church

acquired the Hill Cumorah and several surrounding farms. In 1935, on the highest point of the hill, the Church erected a granite monument topped by a nine-foot statue of Moroni. Its base features four bronze-sculptured panels depicting Joseph Smith, the **Three Witnesses**, the **Eight Witnesses**, and Moroni's challenge to Book of Mormon readers as recorded in Moroni 10:4. The following year the Church opened a "bureau of information," or **visitors' center**, at the base of the hill.

In July 1936 the **Eastern States Mission** conducted a **pageant** in connection with its annual Pioneer Day conference; the audience sat on the lower slopes of the hill while the drama was staged on the level land below. The following year the arrangement was reversed; the audience sat at the foot of the hill while the drama unfolded on stages erected on the slopes above. At that time a newly arrived missionary, Harold I. Hansen, was named the pageant's dramatic director, a role he would play for the next four decades. In later years special effects, employing state-of-the-art technology, were added to the pageant.

SOURCES

Palmer, David A. *In Search of Cumorah: New Evidences for the Book of Mormon from Ancient Mexico*. Bountiful, Utah: Horizon, 1981.

Reeve, Rex C., Jr., and Richard O. Cowan. "The Hill Called Cumorah." In *New York*. Edited by Larry C. Porter, Milton V. Backman Jr., and Susan Easton Black. Regional Studies in Latter-day Saint Church History series. Provo, Utah: Brigham Young University, 1992. 71–79.

REX C. REEVE JR.

HILL CUMORAH MONUMENT. The Hill Cumorah Monument, created by Torlief S. Knapus (1881–1965) in 1935 by Church commission, commemorates the angel **Moroni** and special testimonies of the coming forth of the **Book of Mormon**. On the top of a tall shaft stands the heroic-sized, bearded, gold-leafed figure of the angel Moroni holding the ancient record and raising his arm to call upon the world to give heed to the message of the Book of Mormon. On the shaft are sculptures witnessing to the truthfulness of the Book of Mormon; on the base are three bronze bas reliefs that recount historic testimonies of Moroni and the **gold plates**, as well as one that gives Moroni's own spiritual promise to all who will read and pray about the book. On the west side, Moroni delivers the plates to **Joseph Smith**. On the south, Moroni and Joseph show the plates to the **Three Witnesses**. On the east panel, Joseph shows the plates to the **Eight Witnesses**. And on the north panel is written Moroni's promise (Moro. 10:4).

SOURCE

Giles, John D. "The Symbolism of the Angel Moroni Monument—Hill Cumorah." *Instructor* 86 (April 1951): 98–99.

RICHARD G. OMAN

HILL CUMORAH PAGEANT. See PAGEANTS.

HINCKLE, GEORGE M. George M. Hinckle, a missionary and Church official in **Missouri**, was condemned for treachery after surrendering **Joseph Smith** and other leaders at **Far West**. He was born 13 November 1801 in Jefferson County, **Kentucky**, and was baptized either there or in Missouri by 1832, after which he preached with Elisha Groves in the surrounding states. He was recommended for a second **mission** in 1834.

As a member of the Missouri high council from 1836 to 1838, he served on the Far West temple committee and played a significant role in disciplinary councils that excommunicated the Missouri presidency in the early months of 1838. Meanwhile, he operated a store and served in the militia.

He and **John Murdock** headed the settlement of **DeWitt** in June 1838, and that fall Hinckle defended **Mormon** towns. On 31 October, however, he surrendered the **Prophet** and others to General **Samuel Lucas** at Far West, turned over property and weapons the next day, and testified for the state at a hearing several days later in **Richmond**. The Prophet condemned him, and a council excommunicated him in **Quincy** on 17 March 1839. As late as August 1844 Hinckle wrote **William Phelps** asking that his name be cleared. He died outside the Church at Iowa in 1861.

SOURCES

Cannon, Donald Q., and Lyndon W. Cook, eds. *Far West Record: Minutes of The Church of Jesus Christ of Latter-day Saints, 1830–1844*. Salt Lake City: Deseret Book, 1983.

LeSuer, Stephen C. *The 1838 Mormon War in Missouri*. Columbia: University of Missouri Press, 1986.

JOHN THOMAS

HINCKLEY, ALONZO A. Alonzo Arza Hinckley, apostle, stake president, and missionary, was born 23 April 1870 at **Cove Fort** in south-central **Utah**, where his parents, Angeline and **Ira Hinckley**, were living in response to a call from **Brigham Young**. He lived most of his life in that area of Millard County. He married Rose May Robison, and they became the parents of 14 children.

When Alonzo's father was released in 1902 after 25 years of service as president of the Millard **Stake**, Alonzo succeeded him and served until the stake was divided in 1912; he then served as the first stake president of the new Deseret Stake until 1929. He was called as mission president of the California Mission in 1932. Two years later, while still a mission president, he was called by **Heber J. Grant** to serve as an apostle and was ordained 11 October 1934 at age 64; he continued to serve as mission president until 1935. **Elder** Hinckley became seriously ill and died 22 December 1936 in **Salt Lake City** at age 66, after only two years of service as an apostle.

Marion G. Romney reported that when doctors told Elder Hinckley his illness would be fatal, he wrote to the **First Presidency**: "I assure you I am not deeply disturbed over the final results. I am reconciled and I reach my hands to take what my Father has for me, be it life or death. . . . As to the future, I have no misgivings. It is inviting and glorious, and I sense rather clearly what it means to be saved by the redeeming blood of **Jesus Christ** and to be exalted by his power and be with him ever more" (quoted in Romney, 20).

Alonzo A. Hinckley was the uncle of **Gordon B. Hinckley**.

SOURCES

Jenson, Andrew. *Encyclopedic History of The Church of Jesus Christ of Latter-day Saints.* Salt Lake City: Deseret News, 1941. 505.

1999–2000 Church Almanac. Salt Lake City: Deseret News, 1998. 60.

Romney, Marion G. Conference Report (October 1965): 20.

DAVID KENISON

HINCKLEY, GORDON B. Gordon Bitner Hinckley, 15th president of The Church of **Jesus Christ** of Latter-day **Saints**, was born 23 June 1910 in **Salt Lake City, Utah**. He was the eldest of five children born to Bryant S. and Ada Bitner Hinckley, although at birth he joined a household of six children. Bryant's first wife had died two years earlier, leaving him with eight children, two of whom were reared by their mother's parents. The

family lived in the Salt Lake Liberty **Stake**, the largest stake in the Church at that time, where Gordon's father served as **stake president**.

After graduation from LDS High School (and despite the economic difficulties of the **great depression**), Gordon pursued his studies at the **University of Utah**, graduating in English with a minor in Latin and Greek. In 1933 he was called to the European Mission, with headquarters in London, where he served as assistant to **apostle Joseph F. Merrill**, the **mission president**. Although he had always been full of faith, his mission solidly placed him on the path of complete devotion to the gospel. Upon his release in 1935, Gordon planned to return to graduate school in journalism. These plans were circumvented when Elder Merrill asked him to report to the **First Presidency** concerning the need among **missions** for written and visual materials. After Elder Hinckley completed his presentation, President **Heber J. Grant** requested that the young elder become the executive secretary to the newly formed **Radio, Publicity, and Mission Literature Committee**.

In 1937, Gordon married Marjorie Pay, a bright and beautiful young woman who had grown up across the street. Her belief in the gospel, devotion to her husband, love for their children, cheerfulness, and independent manner created a happy and faith-filled home. Theirs was a partnership rooted in mutual respect and love. Together they reared five children in East Mill Creek, a rural community about 10 miles southeast of the center of Salt Lake City.

From 1935 on, with one brief interruption during **World War II**, Gordon worked full time for the Church. For 40 years he served directly with the Missionary Committee, much of that time as executive secretary. Under the direction of President **David O. McKay**, he worked to develop a process by which the **temple endowment** could be given in multiple languages. Other assignments included overseeing **world's fair** exhibits and writing and producing numerous films, radio programs, **pamphlets**, and tracts for missionary work and **visitors' centers**. He also wrote a biography of **James H. Moyle** and the book *What of the Mormons?*, which was later renamed *Truth Restored* and became a widely used brief history of the Church.

His ecclesiastical callings included stake **Sunday School** superintendent (1935–37); general Sunday School board member (1937–46); second **counselor**, first counselor, and president of the Salt Lake East Mill Creek Stake (1946–58).

In 1958 he was called as an **assistant to the Twelve**. When the Church was first divided into geographic **areas** he was assigned to supervise the work in **Asia** (1960–68). Continuing his heavy involvement with the Missionary Department and other assignments in Salt Lake City, he traveled extensively during these years, initiating the work in the **Philippines**, helping to establish the Church in postwar **Korea**, and encouraging the fledgling work in other countries.

On 30 September 1961, Elder Hinckley was called to the **Quorum** of the Twelve **Apostles**, where he would serve for the next 20 years. He continued to gain experience that would prepare him for coming challenges, such as supervising the missions in Asia, **South America**, and **Europe**; serving on the Missionary Executive Committee; working with Church business entities (Deseret Management Corporation, **Bonneville Corporation**, **Deseret News** Publishing Company); dedicating **Vietnam** and **Greece** for the preaching of the gospel; participating in campaigns to oppose **liquor-by-the-drink** legislation in **Utah** and the **Equal Rights Amendment**; serving on various community boards; chairing the Children's **Correlation Committee**; participating in the dedication of restored buildings in **Nauvoo**; chairing the **Melchizedek Priesthood** Executive Committee; and participating in several **temple** dedications.

Elder Hinckley was called 15 July 1981 to serve as an additional counselor in the First Presidency when President **Spencer W. Kimball** developed health problems. Although he felt overwhelmed by the calling, President Hinckley expressed his desire to do whatever he could to lighten the burdens of the **prophet** he loved. Less than two years later President **N. Eldon Tanner**, first counselor, died. The First Presidency was reorganized, naming President **Marion G. Romney** as first counselor and President Hinckley as second counselor. Within a month after President Tanner's death, President Romney's health was such that he could no longer participate in the administrative duties of the First Presidency. Because President Kimball became less able to carry on the daily workload of the presidency, by mid-1982 the day-to-day responsibilities of the First Presidency had shifted almost entirely to President Hinckley. The Quorum of the Twelve, led by President **Ezra Taft Benson**, shared the load, and President Hinckley never failed to express gratitude for their great unity and support. In turn, he was "faithful to the scope and limits of his stewardship . . . unwilling to move ahead on decisions of any magnitude without the full support of his **Brethren**." He never intruded on matters that "belonged solely to the President. . . . Short of assuming that prophetic mantle, he moved as far as he could" (Dew, 401). The Church continued to build and dedicate temples and hold regional **conferences**; local congregations became fully supported by the tithes and offerings from the general membership with the elimination of **ward** budget funds; and the First Quorum of the **Seventy** began to administer to the worldwide membership through the establishment of area presidencies. With the calling of two new apostles in 1984, President Hinckley reassured members that "we are on occasion able to converse with [President Kimball] and he has given his authorization to that which has been done. We would not have proceeded without him" (quoted in Dew, 403).

With the death of President Kimball in November 1985, the First Presidency was again reorganized. President Ezra Taft Benson called Elder Hinckley to serve as first counselor and **Thomas S. Monson** as second counselor. The Church continued to move forward, and President Hinckley once again did all he could to sustain and support the prophet. His assignments included participating in several temple dedications; taking part in the dedication of historical sites in Nauvoo, **Carthage, Wyoming,** and **Cove Fort**; and dedicating the **Joseph Smith Memorial Building**. As President Benson aged, Presidents Hinckley and Monson shouldered more of the daily business of the Church. Once again, the unity of the Brethren and a clear understanding of the limits of their stewardship prevailed.

Following the death of President Benson in 1994, **Howard W. Hunter** was ordained and set apart as president. He once again called President Hinckley as first counselor and President Monson as second counselor. President Hunter's death in March 1995 resulted in another reorganization of the First Presidency. Gordon B. Hinckley became the fifteenth president of The Church of Jesus Christ of Latter-day Saints 12 March 1995, with President Thomas S. Monson as first counselor and President **James E. Faust** as second counselor.

President Hinckley's administration became noted for its energetic and unprecedented forward movement in many areas. Buildings and improvements in downtown Salt Lake City included the **Conference Center**, which enlarged the possible audience of general conference from about 6,000 in the Tabernacle to more than 20,000 in the new structure; and the closing of Main Street between North Temple and South Temple, creating a pedestrian mall between **Temple Square** and the Church office block.

Often expressing gratitude for an increase in the positive visibility of the Church in the media, President Hinckley supported this view with interviews on national television, notably with Mike Wallace on

60 Minutes and Larry King on *Larry King Live,* as well as with press conferences in many countries throughout the world.

Retention of new converts with continuing attention to the individual was a matter President Hinckley emphasized. "Every convert needs a friend, a responsibility, and to be nourished by the good word of God." His messages often stressed tolerance and respect for those not of the LDS faith.

Perfectly suited to the age of technology, President Hinckley was eager to use it to move the work forward. Disseminating information about the Church, broadcasting **general conference** and other **meetings**, and facilitating **family history** work are just a few of the initial uses of this powerful tool.

In September 1995 President Hinckley introduced "**The Family: A Proclamation to the World**," a declaration outlining doctrines on the family and exhortations about its preservation. "Why do we have this proclamation on the family now? Because the family is under attack. All across the world families are falling apart. The place to begin to improve society is in the home" (Hinckley, 209).

During the late 1990s more than half the Church membership was living outside the **United States**, and the total passed 10 million.

Continuing the work of accelerated temple building begun under President David O. McKay and emphasized during subsequent administrations, President Hinckley announced in 1997 a plan for smaller temples that was revolutionary in increasing the number of these sacred structures. The first of these was dedicated less than one year later. With a goal of more than 100 temples in operation by the close of the year 2000, Church members enthusiastically greeted the announcements of temples in historic places such as **Palmyra**, **Winter Quarters**, and **Nauvoo**. Temples were an enduring theme of President Hinckley's administration.

In keeping with President Hinckley's reverence for the past and eye to the future, the 1997 sesquicentennial anniversary of the arrival of the **pioneers** in the **Salt Lake Valley** was celebrated worldwide. Activities on every continent reminded members of the roots of the Restoration.

A biography of President Hinckley, *Go Forward with Faith,* and a compilation entitled *Teachings of Gordon B. Hinckley,* both appeared in the 1990s. For a national audience, he wrote *Standing for Something: Ten Virtues That Will Heal the Hearts and Homes of America,* published by Random House in 2000.

President Hinckley's energetic travels excited Church members worldwide. He held many large meetings, such as the one in Santiago, Chile, which 57,500 attended in April 1999. Traveling to every continent, he expressed an urgency to see the Saints, "to feel of their hearts, to see that they're trying to do the right thing" (*Church News*). He possessed an extraordinary ability to use both the spoken and written word effectively, making it possible for him to teach straightforwardly without offense, to inspire and motivate without discouraging, and to convey gospel truth heart to heart. He came to be loved for his quick wit, optimism, and compassion for individuals. Members resonated with his powerful testimony of the Savior and optimistic vision of the future of the restored gospel of Jesus Christ. His sound financial sense, integrity, breadth of knowledge, problem-solving and decision-making capabilities, coupled with his humility and commitment to the Lord, made him a leader of giant stature.

President Hinckley expressed his excitement and optimism concerning the future of the latter-day work on the eve of the new millennium: "Our job is to just keep moving forward. As I have said again and again, to go forward with faith in the ultimate destiny of this work. What we've seen in the past just indicates something remarkable and glorious and wonderful for the future. . . . I believe we don't actually realize the magnitude of what's happening. It's really tremendous" (*Church News*).

SOURCES

Church News, 11 December 1999. 5.

Dew, Sheri L. *Go Forward with Faith: The Biography of Gordon B. Hinckley.* Salt Lake City: Deseret Book, 1996.

Hinckley, Gordon B. *Teachings of Gordon B. Hinckley.* Salt Lake City: Deseret Book, 1997.

1999–2000 Church Almanac. Salt Lake City: Deseret News, 1998.

VIRGINIA H. PEARCE

HINCKLEY, IRA N. Ira Nathaniel Hinckley, known as a pioneer, fort builder, mayor, **stake president**, and patron of education and community development, was born 30 October 1828 in Leeds County, **Ontario, Canada**. His father and mother both died by the time he was 14, his mother having joined the LDS Church and moved to Springfield, **Illinois**, before her death in 1841. Ira helped build wagons in **Nauvoo** for the trek to **Utah** and lost both his wife of two years and half-brother to cholera en route, arriving in October 1850. For the next six years he worked as a blacksmith, farmer, stockman, policeman, and an excavator at the **Salt Lake Temple** stone quarry.

In 1856 Ira superintended the building of Horseshoe Fort, 30 miles west of **Fort Laramie**, for the **Y.X. Company**. He labored for several years with groups under the direction of **Brigham Young** and the U.S. Army to protect vulnerable mail and telegraph lines; he served these groups as a blacksmith, veterinary surgeon, superintendent, and builder. In 1867 Ira built **Cove Fort** in a strategic location between **Fillmore** and Beaver. Throughout the next few years many inhabitants of Cove Fort froze to death due to the harsh winter conditions. In 1992 Ira's grandson, Elder **Gordon B. Hinckley**, dedicated the newly restored Cove Fort as a Church historic site.

Ira Hinckley was the fifth mayor of Fillmore, where he invested much of his small fortune in projects for community and educational development, including helping found and finance an **academy**. He was president of the Millard Stake for 25 years and stake **patriarch** from 1896 until his death on 10 April 1904 in **Provo, Utah**. He married four times and fathered 21 children. Ira's grandson, Gordon B. Hinckley, was set apart as the 15th president of the Church on 12 March 1995.

SOURCES

Cannon, Donald Q., and Richard D. McClellan. "Building Utah: Contributions of Eastern Canadians." Manuscript in authors' possession.

Hinckley, Lorin A. *Arza Erastus Hinckley and Ira Nathaniel Hinckley: Descendants and Ancestors*. Salt Lake City: Hinckley Family, 1979. Introduction.

Hinckley, Parnell. *Ira Nathaniel Hinckley, 1828–1904 and Angeline Wilcox Noble, 1831–1912*. Ojai, Calif.: L.B. Hunter, 1994.

Porter, Larry C. "Cove Fort." *Utah History Encyclopedia*. Edited by Allan Kent Powell. Salt Lake City: University of Utah, 1994. 119–20.

RICHARD D. MCCLELLAN

HINCKLEY, MAY G. May Green Hinckley, third general president of the **Primary**, was born 1 May 1881 in Brampton, **England**. The promise in her **patriarchal blessing** that she would be a mother to many children was fulfilled in an unusual way. May did not marry until she was 50 years old. She thus "mothered" Bryant S. Hinckley's 13 children (including **Gordon B. Hinckley**), missionaries in the Northern States Mission over which her husband presided, and thousands of **Primary** children as she served as general Primary president. When President **Heber J. Grant** issued the call, he told her, "May, we're going to give you 102,000 children" ("Leader," 20). During her three years of service (1940–43), the Primary introduced its seal and colors—red, yellow, and blue; simplified the program to meet wartime needs; stressed more spiritual instruction; and continued the *Children's Friend* and **Primary Children's Hospital**. May died at age 62 on 2 May 1943 in **Salt Lake City**.

SOURCES

"English-Born Leader Guides Destiny of 102,000 Children." *Church News,* 4 April 1964. 20.

Harward, Conrad A. "A History of the Growth and Development of the Primary Association of the LDS Church from 1878 to 1928." Master's thesis, Brigham Young University, 1976.

Madsen, Carol Cornwall, and Susan Staker Oman. *Sisters and Little Saints: One Hundred Years of Primary.* Salt Lake City: Deseret Book, 1978.

Peterson, Janet, and LaRene Gaunt. *The Children's Friends: Presidents of the Primary and Their Lives of Service.* Salt Lake City: Deseret Book, 1996.

JANET PETERSON

HINTZE, FERDINAND F. Ferdinand Friis Hintze, known as the father of the Armenian **Mission**, was born 13 May 1854 in Roskilde, **Denmark**. He was baptized on his eighth birthday and immigrated to **Utah** with his parents in 1864. He served five **missions**. Prior to his labors in the Near East, Ferdinand served twice in the Central States Mission and once in **Scandinavia**. Early in 1887 **Elder** Hintze arrived in **Turkey**, where he joined **Joseph Tanner** and **Jacob Spori** as one of the first missionaries in the Near East. In September of that year, he was called as president of the Turkish Mission, and his work among the Armenian people began to flourish. Later, with the help of a Turkish convert named Haig Jevahirdjian, Ferdinand translated the **Book of Mormon** and the **Doctrine and Covenants** into Turkish.

During his second mission to Turkey (1897–1900), Ferdinand traveled to **Palestine** with **apostle Anthon H. Lund**. On 8 May 1898, they ascended the Mount of Olives and dedicated the land for the gathering of Judah and Israel.

At home in **Salt Lake City**, Ferdinand was involved in farming and mining interests. He had four wives and 32 children. He died 9 March 1928 in Salt Lake City.

SOURCES

Hansen, A. J. "Ferdinand Friis Hintze." Manuscript. Rexburg, Idaho. 1928.

Scandinavian Jubilee Album. Salt Lake City: n.p., 1900. 120.

LaMar C. Berrett and Blair G. Van Dyke

HIRAM, OHIO. Hiram, Ohio, was the home of the **Prophet Joseph Smith** from 12 September 1831 to 1 April 1832 and is acknowledged as the "birthplace" of the **Doctrine and Covenants**. The township of Hiram lies approximately 30 miles south of **Kirtland**. Hiram residents John and Alice Johnson, newly converted to the gospel, had a comfortable farm and invited Joseph and Emma to live with them.

While the Prophet lived in Hiram, he received 15 **revelations**. A conference of the Church was held in Hiram in November 1831, at which it was determined to publish a selection of revelations that had been received through Joseph Smith. Several revelations were received in connection with this conference. Prominent was the "preface" to the **Book of Commandments**, now section one of the Doctrine and Covenants.

A primary work of the Prophet at Hiram was the revision of the **Bible**. **Sidney Rigdon**, scribe for the **Joseph Smith Translation of the Bible**, moved to Hiram to continue assisting in this work. It was while engaged in this translation during February 1832 that Joseph and Sidney beheld a series of **visions**, including the one recorded in Doctrine and Covenants 76.

At Hiram, on the night of 24 March 1832, Joseph and Sidney were dragged from their beds, beaten, tarred, and feathered. Joseph and Sidney escaped with their lives, though they bore the marks of this abuse until their deaths. Ten-month-old Joseph Smith Murdock, whom Joseph and Emma had adopted with his twin sister, Julia, and who was just recovering from the measles, died as a consequence of exposure to the cold night air during the attack.

Soon after this horrible experience, the Johnsons sold their farm and moved to Kirtland. The money received for the farm was given to the Church. The funds were used to help purchase the **French farm**, upon which the **Kirtland Temple** was built. Today the Church owns the Johnson home and farm, which are open as a **visitors' center**.

Sources

Backman, Milton V. *Heavens Resound: A History of the Latter-day Saints in Ohio 1830–1838.* Salt Lake City: Deseret Book, 1983.

Perkins, Keith W. "Land Ownership in Kirtland." *Historical Atlas of Mormonism.* Edited by S. Kent Brown, Donald Q. Cannon, and Richard H. Jackson. New York: Simon & Schuster, 1994. 22–24.

Smith, Joseph. *History of The Church of Jesus Christ of Latter-day Saints.* Edited by
   B. H. Roberts. 2d ed. rev. 7 vols. Salt Lake City: The Church of Jesus Christ of
   Latter-day Saints, 1932–51. 1:215–65.

CRAIG J. OSTLER

HISTORIAN, CHURCH. When the Church was formally organized,
the Lord commanded through the **Prophet Joseph Smith**: "Behold, there
shall be a record kept among you" (D&C 21:1). The **Articles and
Covenants** of the Church, the basis for Church administration,
specifically provided that "a regular list of all the names of the whole
church . . . be kept in a book by one of the elders, whomsoever the other
elders shall appoint from time to time" (D&C 20:82).

   At a **conference** of the Church held 9 June 1830, **Oliver Cowdery**,
second elder of the Church, was "appointed to keep the Church record
and Conference minutes until the next conference." He did so, and
during the following conference, held 26 September 1830, "**David
Whitmer** [was] appointed to keep the Church records until the next
Conference." Despite Brother Whitmer's appointment, he kept no minutes of the 2 January 1831 conference (Cannon and Cook, 2–5).

   Oliver Cowdery, however, continued keeping a record that, according
to his successor, **John Whitmer**, covered the history of the Church up to
12 June 1831. The manuscript of this history was apparently lost and,
despite periodic efforts over the years to locate it, has never been found.
Still, Oliver's extant writings, including a series of letters published in the
Messenger and Advocate in 1834 and 1835, have provided important
source materials for writing the history of the Church's earliest days.

   In a **revelation** given 3 March 1831, the Lord directed that John
Whitmer "should write and keep a regular history" and "keep the church
record and history continually; for Oliver Cowdery I have appointed to
another office" (D&C 47:1, 3). In compliance with this commandment,
on 9 April 1831 Brother Whitmer received his appointment "to keep the
Church record & History" (Cannon and Cook, 5).

   After a series of intervening clerks, historians, and recorders, **Willard
Richards** became Church historian in 1842. He was called as Church
recorder in 1843 and became a major force behind the compilation of
Joseph Smith's history. When Elder Richards died in 1854, **George A.
Smith** succeeded him, continuing as Church historian and general
Church recorder until 1870. Under his direction, the writing and publi-
cation of Joseph's history was completed, and the history of **Brigham**

Young became a major emphasis. After **Albert Carrington** served as Church historian and recorder for four years, **Orson Pratt** received the assignment, which he filled from 1874 until his death in 1881.

Wilford Woodruff, whose diary remains one of the principal sources for nineteenth-century Church history, became Church historian and recorder in 1883. He continued in that position until he became president of the Church in 1889. **Franklin D. Richards** succeeded him as Church historian and recorder, serving until his death in 1899. **Anthon H. Lund** served from 1900 to his death in 1921.

Joseph Fielding Smith had labored for nearly two decades in the Church historian's office, 15 of those years as assistant Church historian, when he was called as Church historian and recorder in 1921. He served until becoming Church president in 1970 and was succeeded by **Howard W. Hunter**, who served from 11 February 1970 to 14 January 1972.

From 1842 until 1972, the Church historian and recorder was a member of the **First Presidency** or **Quorum** of Twelve **Apostles** and had supervised the operations of the Church Historian's Office. On 14 January 1972, the Church Historian's Office was renamed the Historical Department, and the responsibilities of the Church historian and general recorder were assigned to a managing director. Under this reorganization, a **general authority** with the title of managing director remained in charge of the department.

The new Historical Department had three divisions: the Archives Division, the Library Division, and the History Division. Each division head received a title reflecting that division's purpose. Thus Earl E. Olson became Church archivist, Donald T. Schmidt Church librarian, and **Leonard J. Arrington** Church historian. Later, a new Arts and Sites Division was created, headed by Church curator **Florence Jacobsen** (Allen and Leonard, 608). The Arts and Sites Division became the Museum Division after the opening of the Museum of Church History and Art.

In 1978 **G. Homer Durham** became the Church historian as the general authority department head. He passed away on 10 January 1985 and was succeeded by Dean L. Larsen, who was sustained as Church historian and recorder at the April 1985 general conference. He was formally released from that calling at the October 1997 general conference, when he was designated an emeritus member of the First Quorum of **Seventy**.

John K. Carmack of the Seventy succeeded Elder Larsen as executive director of the Historical Department in 1989 and served until 1991, when he was called to serve in the Asia area presidency. He was followed in the position by three other members of the Seventy: Loren C. Dunn, who served from 1991 to 1993; Stephen D. Nadauld, who served from 1993 to 1996; and Marlin K. Jensen, who served from 1996 to 1998. In 1998, Elder Carmack once again became executive director of the department, occupying the position until 1999, when Elder Dunn again succeeded him, serving for the next year.

The executive director of the department has been assisted by another Seventy designated as assistant executive director. Elders Carmack, Dunn, Nadauld, and Jensen each served as assistant executive directors prior to their appointments as executive director. Other members of the Seventy who have served as assistant executive directors in the Historical Department have been Richard P. Lindsay (1989–90), Alexander B. Morrison (1993–95), Ben B. Banks (1998–99), and Jay E. Jensen (1999–2000).

On 1 June 2000, the Historical Department and the Family History Department were combined to form the Family and Church History Department. Under the guidance of the Church leaders, the staff of the new department continues to fulfill the commandment that a record be kept.

SOURCES

Allen, James B., and Glen M. Leonard. *The Story of the Latter-day Saints.* 2d ed. Salt Lake City: Deseret Book, 1992.

Cannon, Donald Q., and Lyndon W. Cook, eds. *Far West Record: Minutes of The Church of Jesus Christ of Latter-day Saints, 1830–1844.* Salt Lake City: Deseret Book, 1983.

Historical Department Office Journal. Historical Department. The Church of Jesus Christ of Latter-day Saints, Salt Lake City.

Searle, Howard Clair. "Early Mormon Historiography: Writing the History of the Mormons, 1830–1858." Ph.D. diss., University of California at Los Angeles, 1979.

Smith, Joseph Fielding. *Essentials in Church History.* Salt Lake City: Deseret Book, 1974.

Smith, Joseph Fielding, Jr., and John J. Stewart. *The Life of Joseph Fielding Smith, Tenth President of The Church of Jesus Christ of Latter-day Saints.* Salt Lake City: Deseret Book, 1972.

RICHARD E. TURLEY JR.

HISTORIANS AND HISTORICAL WRITING. The LDS Church has always been concerned with keeping and writing its history. Although official **Church historians** have made a significant contribution, over the years LDS historical writing has not been limited to institutional personnel. Many others, including non-Mormons, have made distinctive contributions.

Like all historical writing, the recording of Latter-day Saint history has been affected by many factors. These include the faith or nonfaith assumptions of its writers, the insights provided by newly available sources, the application of new techniques for interpretation (for example, modern demographic techniques), important intellectual and historiographical trends (focuses on economic history, psychological history, and sociology of religion, for instance), and the need to respond to the changing interests of society and the Church (in recent times LDS historical writing has paid more attention to **women**'s history, ethnic histories, international concerns, and so forth).

Perhaps as many as 900 significant historical books and articles were written about the Saints in the nineteenth century. Many were bitterly **anti-Mormon**, including the first book on the origin of the Church, **Eber D. Howe**'s *Mormonism Unvailed* (the preferred spelling of the time), published in 1834, which set the tone for most anti-Mormon writing for many decades. As the century progressed, however, a few non-Mormons, such as John W. Gunnison and **Hubert Howe Bancroft**, produced significant histories with a remarkably balanced approach; several travelers' accounts, such as **Richard Burton**'s *City of the Saints* (1861) and Elizabeth Kane's *Twelve Mormon Homes Visited in Succession on a Journey through Utah and Arizona* (1874) provided important, often positive, insights into the Latter-day Saint community.

The Latter-day **Saints** recounted their own history in Church **periodicals**, early missionary **pamphlets**, published missionary journals, biographical studies, and several other important monographs and compilations. Of all these, one project stands out. Begun under the direction of **Joseph Smith** as a kind of Church annals, compiled by various scribes and historians, and completed 16 years after the Prophet's death, this history drew from a variety of sources, including the writings of Joseph Smith and his associates. Compiled in chronological order, the material read like a first-person account by Joseph Smith, which made it impossible for readers to distinguish between what was actually written or dictated by him and what came from other journals. Nevertheless, it is still the most significant published collection of early LDS historical material extant. First published serially in the *Deseret News* and the *Millennial Star,* it was later edited by **B. H. Roberts** and published from 1910 to 1912 as a six-volume work titled *History of The Church of Jesus Christ of Latter-day Saints: Period I: History of Joseph Smith, the Prophet, by Himself.* A companion volume 7, with the subtitle *Period II: From the Manuscript History of Brigham Young and Other Original Documents,* was added in 1932.

Another lasting contribution came from assistant Church historian **Andrew Jenson**, who, among other things, produced the monumental four-volume *LDS Biographical Encyclopedia* (1901–36). He also began the compilation of the Journal History, a chronological scrapbook of documentary and other historical material. Even though it eventually became little more than newspaper clippings, this collection, consisting of more than 800 legal-size volumes, remains an invaluable resource.

Significant LDS historical writers of the early twentieth century included **Susa Young Gates, Preston Nibley**, and **Joseph Fielding Smith**. The latter's highly popular one-volume *Essentials in Church History* went through numerous editions and revisions from 1922 to the mid-1970s. The best and most prolific LDS historian of this era was B. H. Roberts. His six-volume *A Comprehensive History of The Church of Jesus Christ of Latter-day Saints, Century I* (1930) provided an important new synthesis of the whole of LDS history as well as the first extensive treatment of many pivotal events.

Sometime before 1950 the writing of Latter-day Saint history began to take on a new professionalism as young scholars, both Mormon and non-Mormon, emerging from some of America's best graduate schools began to ask new questions and apply newly learned techniques from various disciplines. As part of this "new Mormon history," important new interpretations of Mormon frontier and group life, for example, came from the pens of Lowry Nelson, Nels Anderson, and Hamilton Gardner, while **Milton R. Hunter** published a ground-breaking study of **Brigham Young**'s colonization efforts. The most controversial new studies, however, were psychological biographies, the best known of which was *No Man Knows My History*, a biography of Joseph Smith published in 1945 by **Fawn McKay Brodie**, a disaffected Mormon. Brodie explained Joseph Smith and the **Book of Mormon** in completely naturalistic terms and was hailed by scholars for her brilliant writing and seemingly thorough research. Several "replies" soon appeared, but since no other biography comparable in style of scholarship was forthcoming, Brodie's book became a standard reference for non-Mormon writers for decades to come. Meanwhile, in 1950, **Juanita Brooks** published her *Mountain Meadows Massacre*, still the most important work on that tragic episode. In her endeavor to get at the heart of issues that were both important and controversial, and in her remarkably balanced presentation, Brooks was an appropriate forerunner to the tremendous scholarly advances in LDS history that were coming.

Leonard J. Arrington, an economist turned historian, led and

exemplified the careful scholarship and new approaches that character-
ized Mormon historical writing over the next half century. In his *Great
Basin Kingdom: An Economic History of the Latter-day Saints* (1958),
Arrington asked perceptive questions and opened new vistas for historical exploration. The most prolific LDS historian of his time (some 250
Mormon-related books and articles), he played a pivotal role in helping
Latter-day Saint history gain new respect in academic circles and in 1965
was instrumental in organizing the **Mormon History Association**. In
1972 he was asked to head the history division of the newly organized
Historical Department of the Church. Two important books from this era
were *The Story of the Latter-day Saints,* by James B. Allen and Glen M.
Leonard, and *The Mormon Experience,* by Arrington and Davis Bitton. The
first, intended primarily for Church members, told the traditional
Mormon story with a new synthesis, took into account recent scholarship, placed the Church more fully in its broader context, confronted
many thorny historical issues not dealt with in most earlier Mormon-
written texts, and dealt with the twentieth century in more detail than
any previous one-volume work. *The Mormon Experience* was intended for
the wider, non-Latter-day Saint audience and, accordingly, was published
by a national press. Responding in part to current scholarly trends and
interests, it was topical and more analytical in nature, treating such
themes as women's history and the Church's adjustment to the twentieth
century.

At the same time, scholars in the history division pioneered new
approaches to the study of Latter-day Saint women, studied institutional
administrative history, examined economic history in more detail, edited
and published significant diaries and other primary sources, dealt with
changes in Church policies and practices, and helped open up studies of
the international Church. In 1982 members of the history division were
moved to Brigham Young University as the **Joseph Fielding Smith
Institute** for Church History. In the next 16 years the Smith Institute produced more than 40 books and monographs and more than 300 historical
notes, reviews, book chapters, and articles. Perhaps the most important
was Arrington's biography, *Brigham Young: American Moses* (1985).

Members of the Department of Church History and Doctrine at BYU
also published significant books and hundreds of articles on Latter-day
Saint history, including the Regional Studies in Latter-day Saint Church
History, a series of volumes of collected essays on specific geographic
areas. BYU faculty members were highly productive, as were faculty

members at other colleges and universities, especially in **Utah**. Several nonacademics produced equally significant works.

The years from 1950 to 1997 yielded nearly 1,500 theses and dissertations, more than 2,000 books, and more than 7,100 articles on Mormon-related issues. While seemingly every subject imaginable was covered, the era also saw the growth of special interest in women's history, biography, and the publication of professionally edited historical documents, including autobiographies, journals, and letters.

In women's studies, an important monograph to appear was Jill Mulvay Derr, Janath Russell Cannon, and Maureen Ursenbach Beecher, *Women of Covenant: The Story of Relief Society* (1992). Incorporating the best modern scholarship and dealing with numerous sensitive issues in a straightforward yet faithful manner, this work was the culmination of years of study of this remarkable women's organization.

Representative of the numerous well-reviewed, full-length biographies to appear were Edward L. Kimball and Andrew E. Kimball Jr., **Spencer W. Kimball**: *Twelfth President of The Church of Jesus Christ of Latter-day Saints* (1977); Richard L. Bushman, *Joseph Smith and the Beginnings of Mormonism* (1984); James B. Allen, *Trials of Discipleship: The Story of **William Clayton**, a Mormon* (1987); Levi S. Peterson, *Juanita Brooks: Mormon Woman Historian* (1988); Thomas G. Alexander, *Things in Heaven and Earth: The Life and Times of **Wilford Woodruff**, a Mormon Prophet* (1991); Ronald W. Walker, *Wayward Saints: The **Godbeites** and Brigham Young* (1998, a collective biography); and Davis Bitton's excellent and long-awaited *George Q. **Cannon**: A Biography* (1999). In addition, other biographies of several Latter-day Saint Church presidents have provided significant insights, such as those by Sheri L. Dew: *Ezra Taft Benson: A Biography* (1987) and *Go Forward with Faith: The Biography of **Gordon B. Hinckley** (1996).

In the last half of the twentieth century, the rich variety of important works covering thousands of topics demonstrated not only an amazing growth of historical scholarship among the Saints but also a continued and growing interest on the part of respected non-Mormon scholars. One significant work was by non-Mormon Jan Shipps: *Mormonism: The Story of a New Religious Tradition* (1985). This work was an important new interpretation of the place of Mormonism in its broader religious and intellectual environment.

The student of Latter-day Saint history may be helped in navigating the overwhelming maze of Mormon historical writing by the explosion of another important genre: the publication of various **encyclopedias and**

reference works, particularly bibliographical guides to Latter-day Saint sources and literature. Especially important was Davis Bitton's *Guide to Mormon Diaries and Autobiographies* (1977). The only general guide to Mormon collections in various depositories around the United States was David J. Whittaker's edited volume *Mormon Americana: A Guide to Sources and Collections in the United States* (1995). The most comprehensive of these guides to Mormon historical writings, produced by James B. Allen, Ronald W. Walker, and David J. Whittaker, is *Studies in Mormon History, 1830–1997: An Indexed Bibliography.*

SOURCES

Alexander, Thomas G. "Historiography and the New Mormon History: A Historian's Perspective." *Dialogue* 19 (Fall 1986): 25–49.

Allen, James B. "Since 1950: Creators and Creations of Mormon History." *New Views of Mormon History.* Edited by Davis Bitton and Maureen Ursenbach Beecher. Salt Lake City: University of Utah Press, 1987. 407–38.

Arrington, Leonard J. "In Praise of Amateurs." *Journal of Mormon History* 17 (1991): 35–42.

———. "The Writing of Latter-day Saint History: Problems, Accomplishments, and Admonitions." *Dialogue* 14 (Autumn 1981): 119–29.

Bitton, Davis, and Leonard J. Arrington. *Mormons and Their Historians.* Salt Lake City: University of Utah Press, 1988.

Jessee, Dean C. "The Reliability of Joseph Smith's History." *Journal of Mormon History* 3 (1976): 23–46.

Perkins, Keith W. "Andrew Jenson: Zealous Chronologist." *Supporting Saints.* Edited by Donald Q. Cannon and David J. Whittaker. Provo, Utah: Religious Studies Center, Brigham Young University, 1985. 83–89.

Shipps, Jan. "Background Books: The Mormons' Progress." *Wilson Quarterly* 15 (Spring 1991): 48–50.

Walker, Ronald W. "Toward a Reconstruction of Mormon and Indian Relations, 1847–1877." *BYU Studies* 29 (Fall 1989): 23–42.

Whittaker, David J. "Mormon Studies: Progress and Prospects." *Mormon Identities in Transition.* Edited by Douglas J. Davies. London and New York: Cassell, 1996. 213–24.

JAMES B. ALLEN

HISTORICAL DEPARTMENT. See HISTORIAN, CHURCH.

HISTORICAL PUBLICATIONS.

HISTORICAL PUBLICATIONS. From the organization of the Church in the 1830s, both **Mormons** and non-Mormons have evidenced an interest in the history and culture of the Latter-day **Saints**. Particularly significant are efforts by twentieth-century Mormon **historians** to chronicle and interpret their past.

Among secondary works the most extensive overview of Church history available is **B. H. Roberts**'s aptly titled work *A Comprehensive History of The Church of Jesus Christ of Latter-day Saints* (6 vols., 1930). Though more than a half century old, Roberts's opus remains a useful source of information. Standard one-volume treatments of LDS history include the influential but now outdated **Joseph Fielding Smith**, *Essentials in Church History* (1922); James B. Allen and Glen M. Leonard, *The Story of the Latter-day Saints* (2d ed., 1992), which is a balanced summary with a superb bibliography; and *Church History in the Fulness of Times: The History of the Church of Jesus Christ* (1989; 2d. ed. expected in 2000), an attractively illustrated textbook intended both for **Church Educational System** religion classes and general use. Perhaps the most valuable interpretive synthesis remains **Leonard J. Arrington** and Davis Bitton, *The Mormon Experience* (1979). Other volumes of value include Arrington, *Great Basin Kingdom: An Economic History of the Latter-day Saints, 1830–1900* (1958), a seminal study of nineteenth-century Church **economic** programs; and Richard O. Cowan, *The Latter-day Saint Century* (revised ed., 1999), which emphasizes the rapid growth and expanding frontiers of the worldwide Church. A readable study intended for young Latter-day Saints, primarily focusing on the nineteenth-century Church, is Dean Hughes, *The Mormon Church: A Basic History* (1986).

Among collections of primary documents relating to Church history, the best is *History of The Church of Jesus Christ of Latter-day Saints* (7 vols., 1901–32). Edited by B. H. Roberts, this collection remains an important source for early Church history through 1846. Other valuable collections include the authoritative edition of **Joseph Smith**'s documents, edited by Dean C. Jessee, *The Papers of Joseph Smith* (2 vols., 1989, 1992; additional vols. anticipated). *Early Mormon Documents* (2 vols., 1996, 1998; 3d vol. anticipated), edited by Dan Vogel, is a helpful collection of documents that deals with the origins of Mormonism.

Since around 1960 there has been a remarkable increase in books, monographs, and professional journal articles dealing with the history of the Latter-day Saints. Several **periodicals**, most of them independent, have surfaced as vehicles of expression for this deluge of interest in Mormon history (as well as Mormon culture and **literature**). Journals that range from devoting at least some space to historical matters to being full-fledged Mormon history periodicals include *BYU Studies* (1959–); *Dialogue* (1966–); *Journal of Mormon History* (1974–); *Sunstone*

(1975–); *John Whitmer Historical Association Journal* (1980–); and *Mormon Historical Studies* (2000). In recent years and months, other journals dealing with LDS history have surfaced, especially on the Internet.

Currently a number of presses or publishing firms produce Mormon historical writing, some of them a good deal of it. These include **Deseret Book**, Bookcraft (acquired in 1999 by Deseret Management Corporation, the parent company of Deseret Book), Horizon, and Signature Books. The University of **Illinois** Press continues to issue books of merit on Mormon history, and in 1998 **Brigham Young University** Press was revived and promises to become an important source of Mormon history titles. Another organization of note, the Religious Studies Center, an arm of Religious Education at Brigham Young University, has issued several LDS historical works.

As the Church continues to grow and flourish, becoming an even more influential and visible organization, it is expected that there will be a correspondingly greater interest in its history. In short, it appears that the recent upsurge in interest in LDS Church history is but a harbinger of things to come.

SOURCES

Allen, James B., and Glen M. Leonard. *The Story of the Latter-day Saints*. Salt Lake City: Deseret Book, 2d ed. 1992. 673–762.

———, Ronald W. Walker, and David J. Whittaker. *Studies in Mormon History, 1830–1997*. Urbana and Chicago: University of Illinois Press, 1999, 2000.

Draper, Larry W. "Publications." *Encyclopedia of Mormonism*. Edited by Daniel H. Ludlow. 4 vols. New York: Macmillan, 1992. 3:1173–77.

Flake, Chad J., ed. *A Mormon Bibliography, 1830–1930*. Salt Lake City: University of Utah Press, 1978.

PAUL H. PETERSON

HISTORICAL RECORD. See HISTORICAL PUBLICATIONS.

HISTORICAL SETTING OF THE RESTORATION. See RESTORATION, HISTORICAL SETTING.

HISTORICAL SITES.

In 1903 President **Joseph F. Smith** authorized the first purchase of a Church historical site—**Carthage Jail**, the place of **Joseph** and **Hyrum Smith**'s **martyrdom** in 1844. Soon other sites, including portions of the original temple lot in **Independence, Missouri** (1904), the birthplace of the Prophet Joseph Smith in **Vermont** (1905), and the **Joseph** and **Lucy Mack Smith** farm in upstate **New York** (1907), were purchased by the Church as the efforts to capture the past through historic sites began in earnest.

During the ensuing decades of the twentieth century, the Church identified, purchased, marked, and restored numerous historic sites, including the **Hill Cumorah (Manchester, New York)**, **Grandin Printing Shop (Palmyra, New York)**, **Martin Harris Farm** (Palmyra, New York), **Whitmer Farm (Fayette, New York)**, **Johnson Farm (Hiram, Ohio)**, Newel K. **Whitney Store** and Home (**Kirtland, Ohio**), **Liberty Jail** (Liberty, **Missouri**), **Winter Quarters** (Omaha, **Nebraska**), Beehive House (**Salt Lake City, Utah**), Jacob Hamblin Home (Santa Clara, Utah), and **Brigham Young**'s winter Home (**St. George, Utah**).

Additionally, a number of other organizations, including **Daughters of Utah Pioneers**, Missouri Mormon Frontier Foundation, the **RLDS** church, **Nauvoo Restoration Inc.**, and **Mormon** Historic Sites Foundation have marked historic sites. Likewise, local, state, and federal governmental agencies, working either alone or with other groups (including the LDS Church), have identified and marked Mormon historic sites that are part of not only the story of the LDS Church but also the regional, state, or national story.

Several important efforts beyond the confines of the United States have added to the number of sites identified, sometimes in cooperation with the LDS Church (such as the 1987 sesquicentennial celebration of the arrival of Mormonism in the **British Isles**). In 1995, the government of **Canada** named the **Cardston Alberta Temple** a Canadian Historical Site, honoring the national, historic, and architectural significance of the first LDS temple built in that country.

The Church's main focus in work with historic sites has been to mark the Mormon Trail from Vermont to Utah. These efforts attempt to help visitors understand the important people and events of the Church's story—particularly the historical beginnings of the **Restoration** during the nineteenth century.

Additionally, unlike movies and books, which may allow intellectual and emotional connections with events or persons, historical sites provide visitors with a three-dimensional experience that offers a sense of reality other mediums are unable to reproduce as effectively. Standing in Carthage Jail or the **Sacred Grove**, people are often moved by the sense of the actual events associated with the site.

Two of the most visited sites in the last decades of the twentieth century were **Temple Square** in Salt Lake City, Utah, and the restored properties of **Nauvoo, Illinois**. The Church hosted an average of about five million visitors each year at Temple Square in the late 1990s. Nauvoo became the second most visited site by the early 1980s, and the reconstruction of the **Nauvoo Temple**, announced in 1999, only increased interest in this community.

Unlike many other religious bodies, Latter-day Saints have not tried to create shrines or pilgrimage sites per se. In fact, the phenomenal interest in Church historic sites manifested by North American Saints should be understood in the context of American culture. U.S. citizens enjoy visiting museums and historical sites. American Latter-day Saints, sharing similar interests, often combine a visit to Church historical sites with a visit to significant non-LDS sites. Many Latter-day Saints experience deep religious attachments to sacred places where events that are part of their doctrinal belief system occurred.

───────

SOURCES

Hudman, Lloyd, and Richard H. Jackson. "Mormon Pilgrimage and Tourism." *Annals of Tourism Research* 19, 1 (1992): 107–21.

Jackson, Richard H. "Historical Sites." *Encyclopedia of Mormonism*. Edited by Daniel H. Ludlow. 4 vols. New York: Macmillan, 1992. 2:592–95.

Olson, Steven L. "Museums and Historic Sites of Mormonism." *Mormon Americana: A Guide to Sources and Collections in the United States*. Edited by David J. Whittaker. Provo, Utah: BYU Studies, 1995. 523–37.

T. JEFFERY COTTLE AND RICHARD NEITZEL HOLZAPFEL

HISTORY OF THE CHURCH. A manuscript written by **Joseph Smith** and his secretaries known as "History of the Church" is located in the Church Historian's Office; however, the work most commonly known as the *History of the Church* is a seven-volume account compiled from this history. The first six volumes record the unfolding of the Restoration between 1820 and the death of the Prophet Joseph Smith in 1844. Volume 7 records Governor **Thomas Ford**'s history of **Illinois, John Taylor**'s memoirs of the **Martyrdom**, and **Brigham Young**'s account of the historical events from the death of the **Prophet** to the **Saints'** arrival in **Salt Lake City**, focusing on events from 1844 to 1848.

An extensive collection of copies of materials written by the **Prophet** Joseph Smith and his clerks was gathered by **Elder B. H. Roberts**, a member of the First Council of the **Seventy**. Elder **Francis M. Lyman**, a member of the **Quorum** of the Twelve **Apostles**, suggested that Elder Roberts compile his notes into a suitable form to give better clarity to the early documents of Church history. President **George Q. Cannon** felt that the cost to have B. H. Roberts compile such a record was too high and offered to produce the same document at his own expense. With the endorsement of **President Lorenzo Snow**, George Q. Cannon began the exhaustive work. Shortly after the project began, however, President Cannon died, and Elder Roberts was asked to complete the project. With the approval of the **First Presidency**, Elder Roberts was asked to complete the work as he saw fit.

History of the Church concentrates primarily on the words of the Prophet Joseph Smith. In fact, it is written as if the words were his own, even though often they are not. B. H. Roberts provided extensive footnotes throughout the work that render historical illumination and contextual understanding. Prior to its publication, the text was reviewed and approved by Elder **Anthon H. Lund**, a member of the Quorum of the Twelve and Church historian, and by President **Joseph F. Smith**. *History of the Church* has become the accepted historical source of the early Church and is a treasured resource among historians and members of the Church alike.

SOURCES

Church History in the Fulness of Times. Salt Lake City: The Church of Jesus Christ of Latter-day Saints, 1993. 477.

Smith, Joseph. *History of The Church of Jesus Christ of Latter-day Saints.* Edited by B. H. Roberts. 2d ed. rev. 7 vols. Salt Lake City: The Church of Jesus Christ of Latter-day Saints, 1932–51. 1:iii-viii.

MATTHEW O. RICHARDSON

HOFMANN, MARK W. See FORGERIES OF HISTORICAL DOCUMENTS.

HOLLAND. See NETHERLANDS.

HOLLAND, JEFFREY R. Jeffrey Roy Holland, educator and **apostle**, was born 3 December 1940, in **St. George, Utah**. He was the second son of Frank and Alice Holland. As a youth he earned money working as a newspaper carrier, a grocery bagger, and a service station attendant.

During his high school years he was a student leader and excelled in sports. While serving a **mission** in **Great Britain**, his president, **Marion D. Hanks**, gave him special responsibility to train missionaries.

After Jeffrey returned home, his life moved quickly. He co-captained **Dixie College's** basketball team, married Patricia Terry, and transferred to **Brigham Young University**, where he majored in English. Excelling in his studies, he was awarded a teaching fellowship in the College of Religious Instruction and received a master's degree in Religious **Education**. One of only two people selected to teach **institute** fulltime without prior **seminary** experience, he was sent to Hayward, **California**. After a short time there, he was appointed director of the institute adjacent to the University of **Washington** in Seattle and became the **bishop** of a singles' **ward**.

In 1970 the Hollands moved to New Haven, **Connecticut**, where Jeffrey earned a Ph.D. in American studies at Yale. He was next appointed an instructor at the Salt Lake Institute, where he taught for a few months before being called as director of the **Melchizedek Priesthood MIA**. In 1974 he was appointed dean of Religious Instruction at BYU and two years later he was called as commissioner of Church Education. In 1980 he became president of Brigham Young University. In **general conference** of April 1989 he was sustained as a member of the First **Quorum** of the **Seventy**; his call to the Quorum of the Twelve **Apostles** came on 23 June 1994, and he was sustained 1 October 1994.

As he began his service in the Quorum of the Twelve, he told Church members, "I pledge everything I have and everything I know how to give to witnessing and reaffirming the divinity of the Savior's life and the restoration of his gospel. My greatest joy and my solemn obligation is to testify of Jesus Christ wherever I may go and with whomever I may be for as long as I shall live" (quoted in Searle, 15).

SOURCE

Searle, Don L. "Elder Jeffrey R. Holland." *Ensign* 24 (December 1994): 10–15.

KENNETH W. GODFREY

HOLY LAND.

HOLY LAND. The small geographical region known as the Holy Land to **Jews**, **Muslims**, and Christians is also regarded as a homeland to Israelis and Palestinians. Although it has been the scene of wars, bloodshed, idolatry, and evil practices of every hue, it is revered for its associations with sacred events of the past, present, and future. Great men and women, righteous pillars of virtue and spiritual wisdom, have endowed the land with the "spirit of place." Above all, it was the land of the Savior's birth, life, ministry, and great atonement for all mankind.

The Latter-day **Saints**' love of sacred accounts in the **scriptures**, particularly those related to the Savior, is somehow transferred to a love for this land. Visits are largely motivated by Church members' desires to more deeply appreciate the events and teachings that transpired there. Therefore, as Latter-day Saints journey, physically or mentally, to the Holy Land, they come away spiritually rejuvenated.

The Holy Land was under Roman and Byzantine rule until the Arabs conquered Jerusalem in 638. Between 1099 and 1199, crusaders from Western **Europe** took control. In 1517 the Ottoman Turks began centuries of rule, during which visits from the outside became almost impossible. Following a brief Arab uprising (1831–40), the Turks regained control but were forced to implement reforms, which once again opened the Holy Land to visitors.

Elder **Orson Hyde** was the first Latter-day Saint to visit this area. On 24 October 1841, he ascended the Mount of Olives and offered a prayer of dedication, blessing the land for the return of Abraham's descendants. Other dedicatory prayers followed. In 1884 **Jacob Spori** opened missionary work at Haifa and made a few converts among German Christians living there.

In 1896 Theodore Herzl published *The Jewish State,* which led to an increased influx of Jews. **World War I** brought Turkish rule to a close in 1917, when Palestine became part of the British Mandate. For three decades British officials attempted to maintain peace between Arabs and Jews. In 1947 the United Nations devised a plan to partition Palestine, leading to the establishment of a separate state of Israel the following year.

In 1968 **Brigham Young University** conducted its first semester abroad in the Holy Land. Then in 1972 President **Harold B. Lee** became the first **prophet** to visit the area in nearly 2,000 years. While there, he organized the first Jerusalem **branch** of the Church. Seven years later the five-acre Orson Hyde Memorial Garden was dedicated on the slopes of the Mount of Olives. The multimillion-dollar Brigham Young University **Jerusalem Center for Near Eastern Studies** was dedicated by **Elder Howard W. Hunter** in 1989. The **Mormon Tabernacle Choir** made its first tour of the Holy Land three years later. Out of respect for local sensitivities and under an agreement with the Israeli government, the Church refrained from proselyting in Israel during the final decades of the twentieth century. At the beginning of the year 2000, there were 165 Latter-day Saints residing in 2 branches.

SOURCES

Galbraith, David B., D. Kelly Ogden, and Andrew C. Skinner. *Jerusalem, The Eternal City.* Salt Lake City: Deseret Book, 1996.

Ogden, D. Kelly, and Jeffrey R. Chadwick. *The Holy Land.* Jerusalem: HaMakor, 1990.

DAVID B. GALBRAITH

HOME MISSIONARIES. Beginning in the 1850s, **Brigham Young** appointed home missionaries to travel among the **Saints** to call Church members to repentance. Like full-time missionaries, they traveled in pairs and depended on those whom they visited for support. Typically they preached to Church members in regularly scheduled **meetings.** During the latter part of the nineteenth century, similar groups of missionaries were called to promote involvement in such auxiliary organizations as **Relief Society, Primary, Young Men's Mutual Improvement Association,** and **Sunday School.**

During the twentieth century, the role of home missionaries was substantially changed. Recently returned full-time missionaries were appointed to accompany **high councilors** in their **ward** preaching assignments. By 1912 home missionaries, frequently members of local seventies **quorums,** were called to carry the gospel to nonmembers living in the area. Thus, they were forerunners of **stake missionaries.**

SOURCE

Humpfrey, A. Glen. "Missionaries to the Saints." *BYU Studies* 17 (Autumn 1976): 74–100.

PAUL EDWARDS DAMRON

HOME TEACHING. Since 1830 leaders have assigned **priesthood** bearers to visit members in their homes. During the nineteenth century, such visitors were called teachers, acting teachers, or block teachers. After 1908 they were called ward teachers, and since the 1960s, home teachers. Initially, **teachers** and **priests** or **Melchizedek Priesthood** bearers who were called as acting teachers or acting priests, with help from **deacons,** did the visiting, fulfilling scriptural assignments for teachers and priests to "visit the house of each member," to watch over and strengthen the **Saints**, to help them do their duties, and to pray (D&C 20). At that time deacons, teachers, and priests were adults.

A teachers **quorum** directed visiting in the **Missouri** period. In **Nauvoo** the priests quorum did the visiting, assisted by teachers and deacons. In **Utah**, **Brigham Young** wanted "the best men" to be the teachers. In 1870 **wards** had between 18 and 24 block teachers, each pair of whom visited 8 to 20 families. Most **bishops** met monthly with their ward's acting teachers. In 1877 the **First Presidency** instructed that some boys should receive **Aaronic Priesthood** ordination and be taken along as trainees by the block teachers. Brigham Young's deathbed wish was that priests and teachers do more thorough visiting.

Between 1908 and 1912, the Church introduced the ward teaching system. Because **elders**, scripturally, are to "watch over the church" (D&C 20), ward teaching was defined as Melchizedek Priesthood work as well as Aaronic. To be a ward teacher was a ward calling, not a quorum responsibility, and bishops directed the ward teaching. Route sizes were reduced to eight families and then to five in 1938.

In January 1964, as part of priesthood **correlation** changes, home teaching replaced ward teaching, with Melchizedek Priesthood quorums supervising it instead of bishops. Youthful priests, teachers, and sometimes deacons have continued to serve as junior companions.

Since 1911 instructions regarding what to teach during visits have varied, from using lessons prepared by stakes or by the Church, to letting the Spirit direct, to using a First Presidency's message from the *Ensign* magazine.

Sources

Anderson, Rex A. "A Documentary History of the Lord's Way of Watching over the Church by the Priesthood through the Ages." Master's thesis, Brigham Young University, 1974.

Phelps, Gary L. "Home Teaching—Attempts by the Latter-day Saints to Establish an Effective Program during the Nineteenth Century." Master's thesis, Brigham Young University, 1975.

WILLIAM G. HARTLEY

HONDURAS. **Missionary work** in Honduras began shortly after the **Central America Mission** was created in the bordering country of **Guatemala** in 1952. **Elders** James T. Thorup and George W. Allen, who had been serving in Guatemala, arrived in Tegucigalpa, Honduras, 10 December 1952. On 21 March 1953 they baptized the country's first five converts, and the following day they organized a **branch**. The San Pedro Sula Honduras **Stake** was formed 10 April 1977. Organized in 1980, the Honduras Mission experienced notable success, its Church membership increasing by 10 times in the first 15 years. In 1990 the mission was reorganized as the Honduras San Pedro Sula Mission (including the country of **Belize**) in the north and the Tegucigalpa Mission in the south. Most of those serving in these missions were Hondurans, many being new converts. By the beginning of the year 2000, Honduras had 95,750 members with 20 stakes and 216 **wards** and branches.

SOURCES

"Growth Leads to Four New Missions." *Church News,* 3 February 1990. 7.
"Honduras Mission Formed." *Church News,* 10 November 1979. 4.
1999–2000 Church Almanac. Salt Lake City: Deseret News, 1998. 332–33.
"Twenty-three New Stakes: Honduras, Norway, and Venezuela Get First Stake." *Ensign* 7 (August 1977): 77–78.

LISA KURKI

HONG KONG. The first Latter-day **Saint** missionaries arrived in Hong Kong in the spring of 1853; however, they met with little success and left four months later. As a result of **wars** and uncertainties in **China**, missionaries did not return to Hong Kong for nearly 100 years. **Elder Matthew Cowley** of the Quorum of the Twelve **Apostles** officially established the Hong Kong **Mission** in 1949. The first missionaries, Elders Grant Heaton and William Paalani, arrived in early 1950. The first recorded baptisms occurred 31 December 1950. **Missionary work** in Hong Kong was suspended during the **Korean War** and was not reestablished until 1955 when 26-year-old Grant Heaton was called as **mission president.**

By 1960 Church membership had grown to 1,700 members in eight branches. The Hong Kong **District** was established in 1965, coinciding with the publication of the **Book of Mormon** in Chinese. The first **stake** in Hong Kong was organized 25 April 1976, with a membership of nearly 3,500. Church membership grew fivefold over the next 20 years, resulting in a membership of 20,256 by the year 2000. In that year Hong Kong had 5 stakes and 39 **wards** and **branches.**

On 26 May 1996, President **Gordon B. Hinckley** dedicated the **Hong Kong Temple.** The unique structure serves as **temple, meetinghouse,** and mission office. Despite some initial concerns, the reversion of Hong Kong to the **People's Republic of China** on 1 July 1997 has not affected the status of the Church nor its operation in Hong Kong.

SOURCES

Britsch, R. Lanier. *From the East: The History of the Latter-day Saints in Asia, 1851–1996.* Salt Lake City: Deseret Book, 1998. 231–50.
1997–1998 Church Almanac. Salt Lake City: Deseret News, 1996.

JEFFREY RINGER

HONG KONG TEMPLE. Church leaders felt the need to have a **temple** functioning in Hong Kong before the British colony reverted to the jurisdiction of mainland **China** in 1997. President **Gordon B. Hinckley**, a counselor in the **First Presidency**, visited the area several times to find a suitable site. During his 1992 visit, he felt prompted to use the site where **mission** headquarters and a small chapel were then located. He sketched the general plan for this unusual building. Temple facilities, accessible from a special entrance, would occupy only the top three floors and the basement of the seven-story building. A separate public entrance led to facilities on the other floors, including the new chapel and mission offices. The temple was dedicated by President Hinckley on 26 May 1996.

SOURCES

Cowan, Richard O. *Temples to Dot the Earth.* Springville, Utah: Cedar Fort, 1997. 196, 198.
Dew, Sheri L. *Go Forward with Faith: The Biography of Gordon B. Hinckley.* Salt Lake City: Deseret Book, 1996. 481–82.

RICHARD O. COWAN

HORNE, MARY ISABELLA HALES. Mary Isabella Hales, a leading figure in the **Relief Society**, was born 20 November 1818 in Rainham, Kent, **England**, the oldest of seven children. In April 1832 her family left England and settled in Toronto, **Ontario**, Canada.

She met her husband, Joseph Horne, in the spring of 1834 at a Methodist camp meeting and was married 9 May 1836: Three weeks later they heard **Orson Pratt** preach. The following week, **Parley P. Pratt** preached, and soon Mary and all her **family** were baptized.

Mary met the **Prophet Joseph Smith** in the summer of 1837 while he served a mission to Toronto. In March 1838 her family left with a small company of **Saints**, arriving in **Far West, Missouri**, in August. They suffered the violent expulsion of the Saints from **Missouri** and later left their home in **Nauvoo** to cross the plains into the **Salt Lake Valley** with the second company of **pioneers** in 1847.

Mary was an original member of the Relief Society organized in 1842. In 1870 the Senior Cooperative **Retrenchment** Association was formally organized with Mary as president (1870–1904). Additionally, she served as Salt Lake Stake Relief Society president (1877–1903); member of the central board of the Relief Society (1880–1905), which later became the general board; member of the **Deseret Hospital** committee (1882–94); counselor to **Zina D. H. Young** in the Deseret Silk Association; and president of the Women's Cooperative Mercantile and Manufacturing Institution (1890–1905).

Mary Horne was the mother of 15 children, including three sets of twins. She died 25 August 1905 in Salt Lake City at the age of 86.

––––––––

SOURCES

Church History in the Fulness of Times. Salt Lake City: The Church of Jesus Christ of Latter-day Saints, 1989. 409.

Horne, Mrs. Joseph. "Migration and Settlement of the Latter-day Saints." Typescript, 1884. Bancroft Library, University of California–Berkeley.

Kramer, Lyneve Wilson, and Eve Durrant Wilson. "Mary Isabella Hales Horne: Faithful Sister and Leader." *Ensign* 12 (August 1982): 63–66.

Madsen, Susan Arrington. "Mary Isabella Horne." *Encyclopedia of Mormonism.* Edited by Daniel H. Ludlow. 4 vols. New York: Macmillan, 1992. 2:657–59.

W. JEFFREY MARSH

HOSPITALS. Financial resources, availability of health care, and the needs of the **Saints** helped guide Church policy on hospitals in the nineteenth and twentieth centuries. Members of the Church who lived in the 19th century were generally not opposed to hospitals but did not often use them, in part because few existed in **Utah** and the surrounding territories, where most of the Saints lived. Local itinerant physicians drew upon folk training and reading from eastern medical journals to perform minor surgeries and mete out prescriptions. Nearly all babies were delivered in homes, most without trained nurses or midwives. **Brigham Young** sought to improve conditions when he sent **Ellis Shipp** and other Latter-day Saint **women** to the East for medical training beginning in the 1870s. They later helped organize the Deseret Hospital, which opened in **Salt Lake City** in 1882 but closed in 1894 after the **antipolygamy** movement of the 1880s and a nationwide financial panic in 1893 caused the Church to go deeply into debt.

After the Church recovered financially, thousands of Saints increasingly looked to Church-sponsored hospitals for modern scientific health care. The Dr. **W. H. Groves** LDS Hospital opened in Salt Lake City in 1905, the first of 16 hospitals the Church either owned or managed in **Utah, Idaho,** and **Wyoming.** Saints were asked to patronize these institutions and were reminded that charity cases were taken upon recommendation by the local **bishop** and an attending physician. **Priesthood** leaders encouraged young women, especially in the first half of the century, to attend nursing schools conducted at three of the largest Church hospitals. By 1970 about half of all Church members lived near enough to access one or more Church hospitals, which cared for upwards of 500,000 patients yearly.

Church hospitals were jettisoned in the late twentieth century. The U.S. government had become the largest financier of health care, and the poor and elderly were increasingly assisted. These factors, combined with escalating medical costs and the growing financial demands of a global Church, made hospitals no longer integral to the Church's mission. The **First Presidency** gave the Church hospitals to the public in September 1974, when the net worth of the entire network was about $60 million. A nonprofit organization, Intermountain Health Care (IHC), took control of the hospitals and in 2000 still managed them.

After divestiture, the Church worked to spread the benefits of hospitals to members and nonmembers across the world. Funds were directed toward indigent countries and localities lacking in modern health care facilities, medicines, and trained personnel. Fast offerings continued to assist with hospitalization costs for needy Saints, and subsidies were increasingly directed toward mental health care headed by **LDS Family Services.**

SOURCES

Bush, Lester E. Jr. *Health and Medicine among the Latter-day Saints: Science, Sense, and Scripture.* New York: Crossroad, 1993.

Vitelli, Tom. *The Story of Intermountain Health Care.* Salt Lake City: Intermountain Health Care, 1995.

JED L. WOODWORTH

HOTEL UTAH. Heralded as one of the grandest hotels in the world, the Hotel Utah opened in 1911. The 10-story building had a classic revival style and was topped with a white dome in the shape of a beehive. The exterior was a smooth, white terra-cotta with white glazed brick. The structure was a riveted steel frame encased in concrete, with concrete floor slabs. The public spaces were elaborately detailed with the finest finishes.

The Hotel Utah became a symbol of stability and community cooperation as the stockholders represented a cross section of the community. "The Hotel" was a meeting place for kings, presidents, celebrities, and LDS **conference** visitors.

The building acquired a significant addition in 1975 and was placed on the National Register of Historic Places in 1979. It was closed in 1987 in preparation for its conversion to the **Joseph Smith Memorial Building**, which was completed in 1993.

SOURCES

Arrington, Leonard J., and Heidi S. Swinton. *The Hotel: Salt Lake's Classy Lady: The Hotel Utah, 1911–1986.* Salt Lake City: Publisher's Press, 1986.

Jackson, Roger P. "The Joseph Smith Memorial Building: The Renovation of a Utah Landmark." *Heritage: The Utah Heritage Foundation Newsletter* 27 (November-December 1993): 5–10.

ROGER P. JACKSON

HOUSE OF THE LORD. Written in 1912 by **James E. Talmage**, a member of the **Quorum** of the Twelve **Apostles**, *House of the Lord* is one of the most clear and thorough discussions of the history and purpose of **temples** and temple **ordinances** ever written. In light of threats and attempted blackmail by enemies of the Church to publish unauthorized pictures of the temple's interior, **Elder** Talmage was assigned by the Church to publish this volume explaining the significance of LDS temples. Originally the volume contained high quality photographs of both the exteriors and interiors of temples, in particular the **Salt Lake Temple**, taken by Ralph Savage. Through the years it was published with various revisions and appendices added to the text and with modern photographs to replace those taken by Savage. The original text and photographs have recently been reprinted.

SOURCES

Talmage, James E. *The House of the Lord: A Study of Holy Sanctuaries Ancient and Modern.* Salt Lake City: Signature, 1998.

DAVID ROLPH SEELY

HOWE, EBER D. Eber D. Howe, printer and the founding editor of the *Painesville Telegraph,* contributed to negative views of the **Saints** in **Ohio**. He was born 9 June 1798 in Clifton Park, **New York**. During the early to mid-1830s, Howe, whose wife and sister had joined the Church, frequently wrote or published articles in his newspaper that were critical of **Joseph Smith** and the Latter-day Saints. In 1834, Howe published the infamous exposé *Mormonism Unvailed.* His antagonistic writings helped fuel the fires of religious and social intolerance in and around **Kirtland**. In his autobiography, Howe described the nonbelievers' negative feelings toward the Kirtland Saints. He wrote, "All [the Saints'] vain babblings and pretensions were pretty strongly set forth and noticed in the columns of the *Telegraph* . . . and many of our citizens thought it advisable to take all the legal means within their reach to counteract the progress of so dangerous an enemy in their midst, and many law suits ensued" (*Autobiography,* 44–45). These outside pressures, combined with internal dissent, eventually forced the Latter-day Saints to leave northeast Ohio in 1838. Howe sold his newspaper business in 1839 and 1840 and remained in Painesville, where he died 11 November 1885.

SOURCES

Backman, Milton V., Jr. *The Heavens Resound: A History of the Latter-day Saints in Ohio, 1830–1838.* Salt Lake City: Deseret Book, 1983.

Howe, E. D. *Autobiography and Recollections of a Pioneer Printer.* Painesville, Ohio: Telegraph Steam Printing House, 1878.

———. *Mormonism Unvailed; or, A Faithful Account of That Singular Imposition and Delusion, from Its Rise to the Present Time.* Painesville, Ohio: E. D. Howe, 1834.

Obituary Index to the *Painesville Telegraph.* Morley Library, Painesville, Ohio.

SCOTT H. FAULRING

HOWELLS, ADELE C. Adele Morris Cannon Howells, the fourth general **Primary** president, was born 11 January 1886 in **Salt Lake City, Utah**. She and her husband, David Parrish Howells, a wealthy businessman, traveled the world and lived in **Los Angeles, California**. After his death, she accepted a call as **counselor** to Primary president **May Green Hinckley** and returned to Utah. Adele succeeded May as president in July 1943 and served until her death on 14 April 1951 in Salt Lake City. As editor of the *Children's Friend,* Adele commissioned a series of **Book of Mormon** paintings by **Arnold Friberg**. As administrator of **Primary Children's Hospital**, she oversaw the building of the large new **hospital**.

During her tenure The Primary sponsored **radio** and TV programs for children and published *The Children Sing.*

SOURCES

Madsen, Carol Cornwall, and Susan Staker Oman. *Sisters and Little Saints: One Hundred Years of Primary.* Salt Lake City: Deseret Book, 1978. 99, 106, 117–33.

Peterson, Janet, and LaRene Gaunt. "Adele Cannon Howells." *The Children's Friends: Presidents of the Primary and Their Lives of Service.* Salt Lake City: Deseret Book, 1996. 59–76.

Shumway, Naomi M. "Primary." *Encyclopedia of Mormonism.* Edited by Daniel H. Ludlow. 4 vols. New York: Macmillan, 1992. 3:1146–50.

JANET PETERSON

HUBBLE, MS. In February 1831 Ms. Hubble, a convert in **Kirtland**, claimed to have revelations in behalf of the Church. She proclaimed that she should be appointed as a teacher to the Church of Christ, but **Joseph Smith** discerned her misrepresentation. After this one appearance, she slipped into historic obscurity; however, this incident brought forth **Doctrine and Covenants** 43, which clarified the order of **revelation** for the Church.

SOURCE

Smith, Joseph. *History of The Church of Jesus Christ of Latter-day Saints.* Edited by B. H. Roberts. 2d ed. 7 vols. rev. Salt Lake City: The Church of Jesus Christ of Latter-day Saints, 1932–51. 1:56–69.

MARY JANE WOODGER

HÜBENER, HELMUTH G. Helmuth Günther Hübener was born in 1925 and beheaded 29 October 1942, having been convicted of high treason by the infamous Nazi "blood tribunal." He and two other Latter-day Saint teenagers from Hamburg, Karl-Heinz Schnibbe and Rudolf Wobbe, were arrested in February 1942 for illegally listening to the British Broadcasting Company and distributing dozens of leaflets written by Helmuth denouncing national socialism. His friends were sentenced to hard labor, surviving the war despite incredible hardships. The Hübener group is one of the noteworthy resistance groups in the Third Reich. Though Hübener was only a youth, his moral courage and keen intellect—viewed by the Nazis as a danger greater than armed resistance drove him to point out that Hitler's policies were leading to disaster.

SOURCES

Holmes, Blair R., and Alan F. Keele. *When Truth Was Treason: German Youth against Hitler. The Story of the Helmuth Hübener Group, Based on the Narrative of Karl-Heinz Schnibbe.* Urbana and Chicago: University of Illinois Press, 1995.

Schnibbe, Karl-Heinz, with Alan F. Keele and Douglas F. Tobler. *The Price: The True Story of a Mormon Who Defied Hitler.* Salt Lake City: Bookcraft, 1984.

Wobbe, Rudi, and Jerry Borrowman. *Before the Blood Tribunal.* American Fork, Utah: Covenant Communications, 1992.

ALAN KEELE

HUDSON'S BAY COMPANY. "The Company of Adventurers of England Trading into Hudson's Bay," the oldest continuously operating company in the world, received a royal charter from King Charles II in 1670. The Hudson's Bay Company was granted a fur-trading monopoly over Rupert's Land, a vast uncharted territory of more than 1.5 million square miles. After amalgamating with its Montreal-based rival, the North-West Company, in 1821, the "Company," under the capable leadership of Sir George Simpson, established networks of inland trading posts and conducted explorations throughout the vast reaches of the West and into the frozen tundras of the Arctic. In an attempt to delay the inevitable American migrations into Oregon country, Simpson appointed capable chief factors or post commanders, such as Dr. John McLoughlin at Fort Vancouver on the Columbia. He also encouraged **Peter Skene Ogden's** discovery of the Great Salt Lake in 1825 and acquired American fur-trading posts, such as Fort Hall, Idaho (1842), on the **Oregon Trail.**

Simpson knew of **Brigham Young's** plans for exodus and ordered a "policy of conciliation" with the Latter-day **Saints.** Captain Johnnie Grant, chief Company trader at Fort Hall, developed a short but important commercial trade with the early **Latter-day Saint** settlers in the **Salt Lake Valley.** With the signing of the Oregon Treaty in 1846, the Company gradually evacuated the American Northwest for safer hunting grounds in British territories to the north but was ever wary of the long-rumored Mormon interest in Vancouver Island as a possible alternative settlement—a rumor the Company took seriously, especially during the **Utah War** of 1857.

Eventually the Hudson's Bay Company ceded all of Rupert's Land to **Canada** in 1869 and for decades afterward operated a large number of trading posts in northern Canada. In the late twentieth century the "Bay" was one of Canada's most successful department stores, employing thousands of Canadians, including several Latter-day Saints.

SOURCES

McCue, Robert J. "British Columbia and the Mormons in the Nineteenth Century." *The Mormon Presence in Canada.* Edited by Brigham Young Card et al. Edmonton: University of Alberta Press, 1990. 35–52.

Newman, Peter. *Company of Adventurers.* Markham, Ontario: Viking Penguin, 1985.

Rich, E. E. *Hudson's Bay Company, 1670–1870.* 3 vols. New York: Macmillan, 1960.

RICHARD E. BENNETT

HUMANITARIAN AID. Since its beginnings, the Church has been involved in helping not only its own poor and needy but also those of other faiths. For example, during **World War I** the **United States** government needed wheat for the war effort and asked to purchase wheat that had been stored by the **Relief Society**. The Church offered it free, but the government insisted on buying it. When the war was over, the money was used to replenish the wheat storage.

In the mid-1980s, a severe drought caused great suffering to millions of people in **Africa**. The Church held two special fasts to raise money, particularly for the people of **Ethiopia**. After those fasts, the Church formally organized the Humanitarian Service Division of Welfare Services, which is funded entirely by freewill donations.

The guiding purpose of Humanitarian Service is to strengthen families through relief and development activities among the world's poor and needy populations. From 1985 to 1997, the Church assisted in more than 2,785 relief and self-reliance projects in more than 146 countries. In 1997 alone, the humanitarian effort sponsored 568 relief and development projects. In 1997 approximately 400 **Welfare Services missionaries**, including full-time couples, were serving humanitarian missions in more than 45 countries.

SOURCES

Ferguson, Isaac C. "Freely Given." *Ensign* 18 (August 1988): 10–15.

Monson, Thomas S. "Our Brothers' Keepers." *Ensign* 28 (June 1998): 33–39.

Van Orden, Del. "Am I My Brother's Keeper?" *Church News,* 29 November 1997. 3.

GLEN L. RUDD

HUNGARY. The first missionary arrived in Hungary from the German-Swiss Mission in 1885, but he spent only three months there before returning to Vienna. The first Hungarian to join the Church appears to have been Brother Markow, who was baptized in 1887. In 1888 Ferdinand Hinthze, president of the Turkish Mission, visited Hungary to meet Mischa Markow so they could preach the gospel together. Because they were unsuccessful in their efforts to find investigators, they soon left Hungary, but Markow returned 12 years later. He baptized several people in Timsora and established the first Hungarian branch of the Church.

In 1909 John Ensign Hill from the Swiss-German Mission was assigned to study Hungarian and be the first official missionary to preach the gospel in Hungary. **Elder** Hill was able to build a good relationship with the local civil authorities, which led to the recognition of the Church in November 1911. Altogether, 106 people had been baptized by 1914, when all the missionaries were taken out of **Europe** because of **World War I.** By the time of the evacuation, only 40 members were left. Half of the entire membership emigrated, many of them to **Salt Lake City.**

A new era for the restored gospel in Hungary began in October 1984, when the **Mormon Tabernacle Choir** participated in a European tour. A highly favorable reaction to a telecast led to a Hungarian television crew being sent to **Utah** to make a short documentary about the Latter-day Saints. Soon the Church received requests from Hungarians for more information.

The desire to learn more about the Church on the part of many Hungarians, along with the improving relationship between the **United States** and Eastern European countries, led to Elder **Russell M. Nelson's** visit to Hungary in April 1987. He visited government officials, and in June 1988 the Hungarian government officially recognized the Church. Just a month later, Hungary was attached to the Austria Vienna East Mission, and missionaries again contacted the people of Hungary.

In October 1989 President **Thomas S. Monson** of the **First Presidency** dedicated a meetinghouse in Budapest. In 1990, a separate Hungary Budapest Mission was established, and by the year 2000 there were approximately 3,191 members in the country living in 19 branches.

SOURCE

Cowan, Richard O. "Mischa Markow: Mormon Missionary to the Balkans." *BYU Studies* 11 (Winter 1970): 92.

JOZSEF KUCSKAR

HUNT, JEFFERSON. Jefferson Hunt, colonizer and officer in the **Mormon Battalion,** was born in Bracken County, **Kentucky,** 20 (or 22) January 1804. He and his wife joined the Church while living in Edwards County, **Illinois.** They moved to **Clay County** and then to **Caldwell County, Missouri.** Later in **Nauvoo,** Jefferson Hunt served as a major in the **Nauvoo Legion.** When the call came for the Latter-day Saints to enlist for service against **Mexico,** he joined the Mormon Battalion and was chosen captain of the first company. When commanding officer **Captain James Allen** died at **Fort Leavenworth,** Jefferson became the interim commander until a new leader was appointed. He marched with the battalion all the way to **California.**

Hunt then migrated to **Salt Lake Valley,** arriving in October of 1847. Shortly thereafter, he served a mission to California to obtain provisions. In the spring of 1849, he helped to settle **Provo, Utah,** remaining there until 1851, when he was called back to California to help establish the settlement of **San Bernardino.** As a representative to the state legislature from that area, he became known as the "Father of the San Bernardino Valley." He lived there until 1857. After his return to Utah, he lived in **Ogden** Valley, where the town of Huntsville was named in his honor. He later moved to Oxford, **Idaho,** where he died 11 May 1879.

Sources

Jenson, Andrew. *Latter-day Saint Biographical Encyclopedia.* 4 vols. 1901–36. Reprint, Salt Lake City: Western Epics, 1971. 4:747

Merrill, Byron R., and Patrick J. Thurston. "Jefferson Hunt: Senior Captain of the Mormon Battalion." In *California.* Edited by Regional Studies in Latter-day Saint Church History series. Provo, Utah: Brigham Young University. 1998. 57–79.

Roberts, B. H. "Jefferson Hunt." *A Comprehensive History of The Church of Jesus Christ of Latter-day Saints, Century One.* 6 vols. Salt Lake City: The Church of Jesus Christ of Latter-day Saints, 1930.

Lawrence R. Flake

HUNTER, EDWARD. Edward Hunter, **presiding bishop** of the Church (1851–83), was born 22 June 1793 at Newton, **Pennsylvania.** Baptized 8 October 1840, he moved to **Nauvoo** in mid-1842. A wealthy man, he generously consecrated his resources to the Church. Hunter served as a **bishop** in Nauvoo, **Winter Quarters,** and **Salt Lake City,** and he became presiding bishop 7 April 1851, succeeding **Newel K. Whitney.** In 1856 Leonard W. Hardy and **Jesse C. Little** became his **counselors.** During his term, the number of **wards** in the Church increased from

40 to 300, and the number of members in the West increased from 11,000 to 120,000. Bishop Hunter oversaw **tithing** operations at the general tithing office and in the wards (primarily tithes in kind and labor tithing), directed work of ward bishops, promoted **Aaronic Priesthood quorums,** helped the needy, and welcomed and assisted emigrant company arrivals. He died in Salt Lake City 16 October 1883 at age 90.

SOURCES

Hartley, William G. "Edward Hunter: Pioneer Presiding Bishop." *Supporting Saints: Life Stories of Nineteenth-Century Mormons.* Edited by Donald Q. Cannon and David J. Whittaker. Provo, Utah: Religious Studies Center, Brigham Young University, 1985.

Hunter, William E. *Edward Hunter, Faithful Steward.* N.p.: Mrs. William E. Hunter, 1975.

WILLIAM G. HARTLEY

HUNTER, HOWARD W. Howard William Hunter, 14th president of the Church, served as **prophet** just nine months, the shortest term of any Church president in this dispensation. Yet in that short time, his life and teachings made a profound impact on the **Saints.**

Howard W. Hunter was born 14 November 1907 in Boise, **Idaho,** a son of John William and Nellie Marie Rasmussen Hunter. His father, who worked as a railroader, was not a member of the Church. His mother, who descended from Scandinavian **pioneers,** was active in the small Latter-day Saint congregation in Boise and saw to it that Howard and his sister, Dorothy, were active also. Howard was not baptized until he was 12 because his father wanted to be sure he understood the importance of the baptismal covenant. He became active in **scouting** and earned his Eagle. In his teens Howard learned to play several musical instruments and organized a dance band; after high school graduation, the band provided music on a cruise ship to the Far East. When he returned home two months later, Howard learned that his father had been baptized in his absence.

In 1928 Howard moved to **Los Angeles,** where he decided to make his home. On 10 June 1931, Howard was married to Clara May (Claire) Jeffs in the **Salt Lake Temple.** They had three sons, the eldest of whom died in infancy. For several years Howard worked fulltime while attending evening classes at Southwestern University School of Law, graduating cum laude in 1939. Within a few years, he had a thriving practice in business law and was on the boards of more than 20 corporations. He was also a highly respected Church leader, serving as a **bishop**, high councilor, and **stake president**. He also became a member of the **Los Angeles Temple** and regional welfare committees.

On 10 October 1959, Howard W. Hunter was sustained in **general conference** as a member of the **Quorum of the Twelve Apostles**. He was ordained an **apostle** five days later. Over the next 18 months, he traveled each week between **California**, where he was turning over his legal practice to a partner, and **Salt Lake City**, where he carried out his responsibilities as a **general authority**. His study and practice of law and his Church leadership experiences greatly influenced his service as a general authority. An early assignment was to review applications for divorce clearances and for cancellations of **sealings**, which involved both legal and ecclesiastical considerations.

As an apostle for nearly 35 years, **Elder** Hunter met with Saints throughout the world and was involved with many programs that would have far-reaching effects on the Church for generations to come. For example, as president of the **Genealogical Society** (later renamed the **Family History** Department), he oversaw the implementation of computer technology to make the voluminous records needed for family research and **temple work** more readily available and manageable. As Church historian and recorder, he directed a reorganization of the **Church Historian's Office** with a professional staff. As president and chairman of the board of the **Polynesian Cultural Center** in Laie, **Hawaii**, he oversaw a huge expansion of the center's physical facilities and programs. Today it provides employment opportunities for many Polynesian students attending **Brigham Young University–Hawaii** and is one of the most popular tourist attractions on the island.

For more than 10 years, as an emissary of the **First Presidency**, Elder Hunter represented the Church in very difficult and often tense negotiations with Israeli officials to secure a site for the **Brigham Young University Jerusalem Center for Near Eastern Studies**. Elder **Jeffrey R. Holland** of the Quorum of the Twelve, then president of BYU, said that "without President Howard W. Hunter . . . there would have been no BYU Jerusalem Center" (*Church News*, 9).

President Hunter had many personal challenges during his apostolic service. In October 1983 his wife, Claire, died after suffering with deteriorating physical and mental health for more than 10 years. Beginning in 1980, he too began experiencing numerous physical problems, including cancer surgery, a heart attack, quadruple bypass surgery for blockages in his coronary arteries, back surgery and the loss of the use of his legs, gastrointestinal bleeding, and near-fatal complications from gall-bladder surgery. These must have been lonely times for President Hunter. His life was considerably brightened when on 12 June 1990, he married Inis Egan Stanton in the Salt Lake Temple.

On 10 November 1985, Howard W. Hunter was set apart as acting president of the Quorum of the Twelve, serving in the stead of President **Marion G. Romney**, who had ill health. Following the death of President Romney, President Hunter became president of the Twelve on 2 June 1988. Six years later, on 5 June 1994, he was set apart as 14th president of the Church, after the death of **Ezra Taft Benson**. He set the theme for his administration at a press conference the next morning: "First of all, I would invite all members of the Church to live with ever more attention to the life and example of the Lord **Jesus Christ**, especially the love and hope and compassion He displayed," and second, "I also invite the members of the Church to establish the temple of the Lord as the great symbol of their membership and the supernal setting for their most sacred covenants" (*Church News*, 6).

President Hunter kept up a busy pace. During his presidency, he dedicated the Orlando **Florida** and Bountiful **Utah** Temples and announced plans for new **temples** to be built in **Tennessee**, **Bolivia**, and **Brazil**. He participated in services in **Nauvoo** and Carthage, **Illinois**, commemorating the sesquicentennial of the **martyrdom** of the Prophet **Joseph Smith**; traveled to meetings with the Saints in the **United States**, **Canada**, **Mexico**, and **Switzerland**; and installed a new president of BYU–Hawaii.

On 18 January 1995, the Church issued a statement that President Hunter had prostate cancer that had spread to the bone. He died two months later on 3 March in Salt Lake City at the age of 87. Though his term as prophet was short, his message of love and compassion, based on the example of the Savior, resonated with the Saints. In his last general conference address on 2 October 1994, he reiterated what had become the focus of his life and ministry: "I bear witness that Jesus is the Christ, the Savior of the world. Certainly he is the center of our worship and the key to our happiness. Let us follow the Son of God in all ways and all walks of life. Let us make him our exemplar and guide" (Hunter, 87).

Sources

Church News, 11 March 1995.

Hunter, Howard W. "Follow the Son of God." *Ensign* 24 (November 1994): 87.

Knowles, Eleanor. *Howard W. Hunter.* Salt Lake City: Deseret Book, 1994.

Eleanor Knowles

HUNTER, MILTON R. Milton Reed Hunter, member of the First
Council of the **Seventy** and **historian**, was born 25 October 1902 in
Holden, **Utah**, to John Edward and Margaret Teeples Hunter. His grandparents, converts to the Church in **Scotland**, were among Utah's early
pioneers. Reared in rural Utah, he participated in the typical activities of
farm life.

A history major and English minor, Hunter graduated in 1929 from
Brigham Young University, where he was the student body president and
a champion wrestler. He also attended the **University of Utah** (1925–26).
He later received distinguished service awards from both schools. He
obtained his M.A. from BYU in 1931 and his Ph.D. in 1935 from the
University of **California** at Berkeley in western history, with a minor
emphasis in anthropology and archaeology.

These interests remained with him throughout his life. Many of his
22 books and more than 250 articles focused on either Utah history or
Book of Mormon archaeology. Two of his Utah history books were
adopted by the state for textbooks in the public schools, and two others
were used as college textbooks. Three of his books were used as study
courses in the **Melchizedek Priesthood** quorums, **MIA**, and the institute
of religion program. He led many archaeology tours to **Mexico, Central
America**, and **South America**. Milton married Ferne Gardner in the
Logan Temple on 30 July 1931, and they became the parents of seven
children.

Milton turned down a position at Berkeley so that he could work for
the Church. An institute teacher at the Utah State Agricultural College,
Milton R. Hunter was called to the First Council of the Seventy on
6 April 1945 at age 42 and served in that capacity until his death on
27 June 1975 in **Salt Lake City**.

SOURCES

Durham, G. Homer. "Milton R. Hunter of the First Council of the Seventy."
Improvement Era 48 (May 1945): 241, 287.
Flake, Lawrence R. *Mighty Men of Zion*. Salt Lake City: Deseret Press, 1974. 455–56.

LINDA HUNTER ADAMS

HUNTSMAN, JON M. Jon M. Huntsman, a prominent and influential Latter-day Saint businessmen, is chairman and chief executive officer
of Huntsman Corporation and Huntsman Chemical Corporation, which
operate more than 80 sites in 23 countries. He was born 21 June 1937 in

Blackfoot, **Idaho**. He and his wife, Karen Haight Huntsman, are the parents of nine children.

As a member of the Church, Jon Huntsman has served in many capacities, including president of the **Washington D.C.** Mission, **stake president**, **regional representative**, and **area authority seventy**.

Jon Huntsman is well known for his philanthropic work. The scope of his humanitarian service has included international funding for institutions benefiting the homeless, abused women, the ill, and the under-privileged. His service also includes membership on the National Board of Governors of the American Red Cross, as well as cochairmanship of the National Prostate Cancer Coalition.

Huntsman donated more than $100 million to establish the Huntsman Cancer Institute at the **University of Utah**. Under his direc-tion, a concrete manufacturing facility was developed in **Armenia** to pro-vide materials to rebuild homes destroyed in the 1988 earthquake. Other beneficiaries of the Huntsman family's generosity include institutions of higher education and environmental and religious organizations.

Jon Huntsman has received numerous humanitarian awards from such organizations as the Horatio Alger Association and the National Conference of Christians and Jews and from Pope John Paul II for his contributions in behalf of those who suffer.

SOURCES

Anders, George. "The Benefactors: Brushes with Death Turn the Very Wealthy into Medical Medicis." *Wall Street Journal,* 6 January 1998. A1.

Cannon, Mike. "The Huntsmans: A Family of Faith and Philosophy." *Deseret News,* 8 February 1998, A1.

CYNTHIA DOXEY

HURLBUT, DOCTOR PHILASTUS.

Doctor Philastus Hurlbut (spelled "Hurlburt" in some earlier LDS publications), collector of the 16 affidavits hostile to **Joseph Smith** that formed the basis of **E. D. Howe's** *Mormonism Unvailed,* threatened Joseph's life in **Kirtland**. Named "Doctor" by his parents, Hurlbut was **ordained** an **elder** 18 March 1833 and excommunicated three months later for "un-Christian conduct with women" (Smith, 1:352) while on a **mission**. Hurlbut gathered the affi-davits in the vicinity of **Palmyra** shortly after his excommunication, after which he was arrested for his threats against Joseph's life and ordered by the court in Chardon, **Ohio**, to "be of good behavior . . . to the said Joseph Smith" (Smith, 2:49).

SOURCES

Roberts, B. H. *A Comprehensive History of The Church of Jesus Christ of Latter-day Saints, Century One.* 6 vols. Salt Lake City: The Church of Jesus Christ of Latter-day Saints, 1930. 1:41–46.

Smith, Joseph. *History of The Church of Jesus Christ of Latter-day Saints.* Edited by B. H. Roberts. 2d ed. rev. 7 vols. Salt Lake City: The Church of Jesus Christ of Latter-day Saints, 1932–51. 1:334, 352–55; 2:49.

ANDREW H. HEDGES

HUTCHINS, COLLEEN. As Miss **America** of 1952, Colleen Kay Hutchins, a resident of Southern **California** born 23 May 1926 in **Salt Lake City**, was perhaps the first Latter-day Saint media "superstar." She was described by the Miss America Pageant director as "the busiest and most popular of all Miss Americas" (quoted in Green, 396). She was crowned at a time when **television** was sweeping North America and Miss America was idealized. Hundreds of front-page stories about her appeared in newspapers throughout the country, and she was featured in national **magazine**s and **radio**, as well as on TV. Outspoken about her beliefs, she was for many people, particularly those living outside the Western United States, their first acquaintance with a Latter-day Saint. Colleen married Ernest Vandeweghe, and in the year 2000 they were living in Indian Wells, California.

SOURCE

Green, Doyle L. "Colleen Hutchins—Miss America—1952." *Improvement Era* 55 (June 1952): 396–97, 464–66.

WILLIAM E. HOMER

HYDE, ORSON. Orson Hyde, an **apostle**, missionary, and government leader during the **Utah** territorial period, is perhaps best remembered for offering the dedicatory prayer of the **Holy Land**. Born 8 January 1805 in Oxford, **Connecticut**, he joined the Church in 1831. He participated in the march of **Zion's Camp** in 1834, and in 1835 he was ordained an original member of the **Quorum** of the Twelve Apostles organized in this dispensation. In May 1839, in connection with a disciplinary proceeding, he was removed from the Quorum. Later in the same year he was reinstated.

In the April 1840 general conference in Nauvoo, Orson Hyde was called on a missionary journey, which culminated in his offering a dedicatory prayer in the Holy Land. The prayer, given 24 October 1841, was a highlight of his ministry. Soon after his return, Hyde was called upon to help supervise the completion of the **Nauvoo Temple** and the **exodus** of the Latter-day **Saints** to the **Great Basin**.

After his arrival in the **Salt Lake Valley**, Hyde became active in government. He possessed a keen intellect and served in several governmental positions, including associate judge of the Supreme Court of Utah and member of the territorial legislature, where he served as president of the Senate. His contributions to government were in addition to his responsibilities as the senior apostle in the Quorum of the Twelve. **Elder** Hyde eventually served as president of the Twelve for 27 years from December 1847 until April 1875, when a change in the determination of seniority in the Quorum elevated **John Taylor** to the position of president. Orson Hyde died in Spring City, Utah, 28 November 1878 and was eulogized as an "apostle of the Lord Jesus Christ, Defender of truth, [and] preacher of righteousness" (quoted in Black, 144).

SOURCES

Hyde, Myrtle Stevens. *Orson Hyde: The Olive Branch of Israel.* Sandy, Utah: Agreka, 2000.

Black, Susan Easton. *Who's Who in the Doctrine and Covenants.* Salt Lake City: Bookcraft, 1997. 141–44.

Flake, Lawrence R. *Prophets and Apostles of the Last Dispensation.* Provo, Utah: Religious Studies Center, Brigham Young University, 2001. 329–32.

ROBERT C. FREEMAN

HYMNS AND HYMNBOOKS. In July 1830 **Joseph Smith** received a revelation calling his wife, Emma, "to make a selection of sacred hymns . . . to be had in my church" (D&C 25:11). Initially, this "selection" meant gathering hymn texts from Protestant sources and deciding which of them should be sung in Latter-day Saint **meetings**. In time the selected hymn texts, along with some newly written ones, were published in the Church newspaper *The Evening and the Morning Star* (1832–34), whose editor, **William Wines Phelps** followed a charge from Church leaders to correct the texts Emma had selected by changing doctrinal statements, tone, point of view, and so forth. In 1835 the selected, corrected, and newly written hymn texts were published in the hymnbook bearing Emma's name.

For the rest of the century, that book provided the pattern for a succession of official and unofficial LDS hymnbooks that were pocket-sized and contained texts (without music notation) divided into such sections as "Missionary Hymns," "Sacrament Hymns," "Farewell Hymns," and so forth. The most notable of these successors to Emma's book was the one produced by the British Mission in 1840, which featured many new hymn texts (such as those by **apostle Parley P. Pratt**) and many borrowed ones. This hymnbook eventually went through dozens of editions and revisions and became the model for the various hymnbooks in other languages that sprang up in the late nineteenth century.

In the second half of the nineteenth century, as Church auxiliaries such as the **Sunday School, Mutual Improvement Association,** and **Primary** Association were formed, they produced their own songbooks. These songbooks relied heavily on new texts and, for the first time, new tunes written by British immigrant musicians and published (complete with **music** notation) in the *Juvenile Instructor*. These musicians also presided over the making of the *Latter-day Saints' Psalmody* (1889), the first Church-authorized collection of music-notated settings for all the hymn texts in the British-derived hymnal.

By the early twentieth century, essentially three sacred songbooks with printed music were in use by adults in the English-speaking Church: the *Psalmody, Deseret Sunday School Songs* (1909), and *Songs of Zion,* an eclectic, widely used collection produced by a coalition of **mission presidents** in 1908. In 1927 the *Psalmody* was superseded by the single-volume *Latter-day Saint Hymns,* which featured dozens of new hymn texts and tunes and also incorporated the more popular gospel songs that characterized the Sunday School book and *Songs of Zion.* In 1948, following the **First Presidency's** decision to have only a single hymnbook for all adult meetings, the Church Music Committee created *Hymns: The Church of Jesus Christ of Latter-day Saints,* which contained many new Latter-day Saint hymns and well-known non-Latter-day Saint hymns absent from earlier hymnbooks. After undergoing a radical revision in 1950, this hymnbook (and its variants in other languages) stood until a new hymnbook appeared in 1985. This last edition, intended as much for **family** as for congregational use, continued the pattern of the previous one, broadening its scope to include more Protestant-based hymns, new Latter-day Saint hymns, and, for the first time, children's songs.

SOURCES

Davidson, Karen Lynn. *Our Latter-day Hymns: The Stories and the Messages.* Salt Lake City: Deseret Book, 1988.

Hicks, Michael. *Mormonism and Music: A History.* Urbana: University of Illinois Press, 1989.

MICHAEL HICKS

INDIA. Elder Horace Hayes, R. Lanier Britsch, and Randy Booth introduce Brigham Young University's Young Ambassadors to India's prime minister Indira Gandhi in January 1982.

ICARIANS. The Icarians were a group of French communal idealists, a small branch of whom established themselves in **Nauvoo, Illinois**, after the exodus of the Latter-day Saints from the area. Headed by Etienne Cabet, the Icarian movement became extremely influential in **France** during the political turmoil leading up to the Revolution of 1848. With a sour turn of political affairs in France and the failure of the first "Icaria" in **Texas**, Cabet himself (with a remnant of about 300 men, women, and children from the Texas group) established a new society at Nauvoo in 1849. The group purchased, at minimal cost, the abandoned homes of the Saints and the largely destroyed **Nauvoo Temple**, which they intended to reroof—until some of the walls were blown over the following year.

Though the Nauvoo Icarians had found moderate economic success and peaked at about 500 members by the mid-1850s, Cabet was forcefully expelled in 1856 and died 8 November of that year. In 1857 the group moved to Corning, **Iowa**, and from there split into several factions, finally dying out by 1895.

Meanwhile, **John Taylor** and Curtis Bolton had come into contact with the Icarians in Paris, where in December 1850 they baptized **Louis Bertrand**, the political editor of the group's **periodical**. Church leaders made use of the Icarian failures to illustrate the need for the gospel to establish a utopian society. For example, John Taylor regularly cited a discussion he had had with Louis Krolikowski, another Icarian leader in Paris, in which Taylor chided the group for their inability to succeed where all things were already prepared for them and contrasted their failures to the success of the Latter-day Saints in **Utah** (*JD*, 5:237–38; 11:54; 13:228–9).

SOURCES

Johnson, Christopher. *Utopian Communism in France: Cabet and the Icarians, 1839–1851*. Ithaca and London: Cornell University, 1974.

Journal of Discourses [JD]. 26 vols. London: Latter-day Saints' Book Depot, 1854–86. 1:134.

McClellan, Richard D. "Louis A. Bertrand: One of the Most Singular and Romantic Figures of the Age." Honor's Thesis, Brigham Young University, 2000.

Wells, Junius F. "The Icarians." *Improvement Era* 16, 12 (October 1913): 1170–75.

RICHARD D. MCCLELLAN

ICELAND. The first Icelandic converts, Thorarinn Haflidasson Thorason and Gudmund Gudmundson, were baptized in **Denmark** in 1851 under the direction of **Erastus Snow**, an **apostle** and the president of the Scandinavian Mission. They were then set apart as missionaries to Iceland. Benedikt Hanson, his wife, and several others were soon baptized. The first branch was organized 19 June 1853 by Johan P. Lorentzen, an elder sent from Denmark. Gudmund Gudmundson was the branch president.

The first Icelandic **pioneers** to **Utah** were Samuel Bjarnson, his wife, Margaret, and Helga Jonsdottir. They arrived September 1855 and were sent by **Brigham Young** to Spanish Fork, where most Icelandic converts settled.

In 1873 **Elders** Magnus Bjarnasson and Loftur Jonsson reorganized a branch in Iceland. Many of the converts were from the Westmann Islands. Eventually, most of the members emigrated to **America**.

An Icelandic mission existed from 1894 to 1900. **Missionary work** there was discontinued in 1914. In 1975, Byron and Melba Geslison and their twin sons, David and Daniel, reopened the work under the Danish Mission. A branch with more than 40 members was established 8 August 1976 in Reykjavik. Elder **Joseph B. Wirthlin** dedicated the land for **missionary work** 18 September 1977. The **Book of Mormon** was translated into Icelandic and published in 1980. Branches of the Church were subsequently established in Keflavik and Akureryi. At the beginning of the year 2000 there were 248 members of the Church living in one **district** with two branches.

Spanish Fork is the oldest settlement of Icelanders in America, and Utah has the second largest population of Icelandic descendants outside of Iceland. The first visit to Utah by an Icelandic president was in 1997 when Olafur Ragnar Grimsson participated in the annual Iceland Day celebration sponsored by the Icelandic Association of Utah.

SOURCES

Geslison, Byron T. "The Icelandic Settlement in Utah." Submitted to the Utah State Historical Society, 16 August 1992.

Harris, Tod. "Gospel Touches Remote Iceland." *Church News,* 6 August 1994, 6, 12. *1999–2000 Church Almanac.* Salt Lake City: Deseret News, 1998. 334–35.

CLARK T. THORSTENSON

IDAHO. The emergence of the Latter-day Saints in Idaho occurred in six progressive stages. The first commenced in 1855 when the **Fort Limhi** Mission was established among **Native Americans** in east-central Idaho.

The second movement began in 1860 in the fertile areas of Cache Valley. The town of Franklin was then established as the first white settlement in Idaho. Under the leadership of Preston Thomas, the Franklin **Saints** were very successful in farming and in getting along with the local Indians.

In 1863 Idaho became a territory. That year commenced the third stage of Latter-day Saint migration into Idaho. This migration was led by **Charles C. Rich**, who directed a group of 40 Latter-day Saint families to settle in a town they called Paris, located in the Bear Lake Valley. Soon more than a dozen villages sprang up in the area, and several buildings were constructed.

The fourth stage of Latter-day Saint migration in Idaho occurred in 1873 when two families migrated from Willard, **Utah**, to the upper Cassia Creek area. Soon other Latter-day Saint families followed, and Cassia County became widely populated with Latter-day Saints in such towns as Oakley, Elba, Almo, Heyburn, and Burley.

The extension of the Utah Northern **Railroad** from Franklin to the Upper Snake River Valley (1874–78) provided another stimulus for the Saints to move into Idaho. The settlements grew nearly as quickly as the tracks, which continued north to **Montana**. The railroad brought commerce and provided a better means for farmers to sell their produce. Under the direction of such Church leaders as **William B. Preston**, Thomas E. Ricks, and William F. Rigby, the Saints harnessed the Snake River and found great success in irrigation practices. By the time Idaho became a state in 1890, the Upper Snake River Valley was already widely settled by Latter-day Saints. More than 25,000 Saints had settled in Idaho, which meant that about one-fourth of the population of Idaho was Latter-day Saint.

The final stage of LDS movement into Idaho involved individuals rather than communities. For example, in 1905 when the Milner Dam was completed, people from the Teton area moved into the areas of Magic Valley, Boise, and Payette. Twentieth-century reclamation projects also brought an increase of the Latter-day Saint population into such cities as Rupert, Emmet, and American Falls.

These progressive stages, combined with the posterity of the Saints who previously settled there, account for the fact that by the year 2000, about 28% of Idaho's population was Latter-day Saint. Of those 343,489 Latter-day Saints living in the state of Idaho, about one-third currently live in the Upper Snake River Valley. Approximately 60,000 are located in the Boise region.

Idaho has produced three presidents of the Church: **Harold B. Lee**, **Ezra Taft Benson**, and **Howard W. Hunter**. As of the year 2000 there were two **temples** in Idaho: the Idaho Falls Idaho Temple (dedicated in 1945) and the Boise Idaho Temple (completed in 1984). Idaho is home to **Ricks College** (later BYU–Idaho), one of the Church's four institutions of higher learning.

SOURCES

Arrington, Leonard J. "The Mormon Experience in Idaho." Address to faculty, administration, spouses, and students at Ricks College, 6 April 1994.

1999–2000 Church Almanac. Salt Lake City: Deseret News, 1998. 195–96.

FRED E. WOODS

IDAHO TEST OATH OF 1885. See REXBURG, IDAHO.

ILLINOIS. Headquarters of the Church from 1839 to 1846, Illinois has witnessed a resurgence of Latter-day Saint membership within its boundaries. Before 1839 only a handful of **Saints** lived in Illinois. Then, in that year, thousands of Latter-day **Saints** crossed the **Mississippi River**, having been forcibly expelled from **Missouri**. The citizens of **Quincy** nobly provided refuge for most of the exiles. Eventually the Saints converged on eastern **Iowa** and western Illinois.

Many of the Saints settled in Commerce, later called **Nauvoo, Illinois**. As **Joseph Smith** noted, Nauvoo was the hub of the wheel with smaller settlements in Iowa and Illinois being the spokes. Before the Saints' exodus to the West, several thousand Latter-day Saints lived in Illinois. They built a **temple** on the crest of the hill overlooking the **Mississippi River**. Many of the Saints received their endowments in the **Nauvoo Temple**.

When serious trouble emerged in 1845 and 1846, most of the Saints abandoned Nauvoo, crossed the Mississippi, and took up temporary refuge in the Iowa Territory before continuing on to the **Rocky Mountains**. The temple they left behind was soon destroyed by fire and later a tornado.

Latter-day Saint missionaries from **Utah** reentered Illinois in the late nineteenth century as part of the Northwestern Mission, later the Northern States Mission, with headquarters in Chicago. Considerable growth took place in the early twentieth century, and by 1930 the state had nearly 3,000 members. The first **stake** organized in Illinois since the 1840s was in Chicago in 1936.

Interest in LDS history led to a resurgence of the Church in western Illinois. Dr. **J. LeRoy Kimball** purchased the **Heber C. Kimball** home at Nauvoo in 1954 and subsequently restored it. Interest in this restoration led to the creation of **Nauvoo Restoration, Inc.**, in 1962. Later, dozens of Latter-day Saints' homes from the 1840s were restored. Nauvoo soon became the destination of thousands of tourists each year, both Latter-day Saints and members of other faiths.

Meanwhile, the Church population in Illinois has grown dramatically, especially in the Chicago area. Several stakes have been organized, and a temple was dedicated in the Chicago suburb of Glenview in 1985. In October 1999 the Church began to rebuild the Nauvoo Temple on its original site.

By the beginning of the year 2000, Illinois had 46,135 members, 12 stakes, and 115 **wards** and **branches**.

Sources

Godfrey, Kenneth W. "Illinois." *Historical Atlas of Mormonism*. Edited by S. K. Brown, D. Q. Cannon, and R. G. Jackson. New York: Simon & Schuster, 1994. 60–61.
1999–2000 Church Almanac. Salt Lake City: Deseret News, 1998. 200–202.

Donald Q. Cannon

IMMIGRATION AND EMIGRATION. See GATHERING.

IMPROVEMENT ERA, THE. The *Improvement Era* began as the official organ of the **Young Men's** Mutual Improvement Association, but later expanded and addressed itself more to the adults of the Church. Executives in the MIA, concerned with lack of communication between Church leadership in **Salt Lake City** and young men worldwide, introduced the *Improvement Era* in November 1897. According to editor and Church president **Joseph F. Smith**, the *Era* was "devoted to the uplifting of the youth of **Zion**" (Green, 13).

As the *Improvement Era* received sponsorship from other Church agencies, its objectives broadened. It was now to be "the voice of the Church," a gospel-centered "interpreter" of world events, and a source of "increasing knowledge" and entertainment (Widtsoe, 2).

To further these objectives, historical articles, stories, poetry, instructions for priesthood leaders, ward teaching messages, and **general conference** addresses were printed. Special features included the "Spoken Word" essays of **Richard L. Evans**; a question/answer column, "Evidences and Reconciliations," by **John A. Widtsoe**; and the "Era of Youth," a precursor to the *New Era*. In 1971 the *Improvement Era* was replaced by the ***Ensign***.

SOURCES

Bitton, Davis. "*Improvement Era.*" *Historical Dictionary of Mormonism.* Metuchen, N.J.: Scarecrow Press, 1994. 115–16.

Green, Doyle L. "The *Improvement Era*—The Voice of the Church (1897–1970)." *Improvement Era* 73 (November 1970): 12–20.

Widtsoe, John A. "Looking Forward with the *Improvement Era.*" Address delivered at the 1935 MIA June Conference.

KRISTIN B. GERDY

INDEPENDENCE, MISSOURI. See JACKSON COUNTY, MISSOURI.

INDEPENDENCE, MISSOURI, PRINTING OFFICE.

Published materials produced by the early Church's printing office at Independence, **Missouri**, 1832 to 1833, are touchstones of the history of the **Restoration** and continue to testify of the vision of early members. Established to provide a communication link between Church centers in **Ohio** and **Missouri** and to generate needed sources of employment and income, the press was intended to favorably influence the public mind.

W. W. Phelps was designated printer to the Church. On 8 August 1831, **Bishop Edward Partridge** purchased lot 76 in the original "Town Plat of Independence" (on Liberty Street between Lexington and Kansas Streets) for the printing establishment. The completed office was dedicated 29 May 1832. The first paper published in Independence, *The Evening and the Morning Star,* appeared within a few days. Desirous to make the Church's modern-day scripture available, Phelps also began work on the **Book of Commandments**.

Unfortunately, the content of the **Latter-day Saint** newspaper proved a growing sore spot among nonmember residents of **Jackson County**. Amid escalating local hostility, nonmembers meeting at the courthouse on Saturday morning, 20 July 1833, decided to destroy the printing office and Phelps's residence. The demolition took about one hour, effectively interrupting all publication.

Following the destruction, Church leaders and members were pursued, ending with the tarring and feathering of Edward Partridge and Charles Allen on the public square. Some printed material for the Book of Commandments survived, and though the work was incomplete, Church members treasured the few volumes of scripture assembled from salvaged pages.

In 1907 the Church established a new printing office in Independence called **Zion's Printing and Publishing Company**, which served the missions of the Church for nearly half a century.

SOURCES

Parkin, Max. *A History of the Latter-day Saints in Clay County, Missouri, from 1833 to 1837.* Ph.D. diss., Brigham Young University, 1976.

RONALD E. ROMIG

INDIA. India first received the gospel through Joseph Richards, who arrived in Calcutta in mid-1851 as a short-term missionary. He baptized four people—James Patric Meik and Mary Ann Meik, Matthew McCune, and Maurice White—and organized the first **branch** of the Church in **Asia**. William Willes and Hugh Findlay arrived late that year and early the next, having been called by **Elder Lorenzo Snow**. Before the early **mission** was closed in 1856, 17 missionaries served in India, Burma, Siam (**Thailand**), and Ceylon (Sri Lanka). They preached the restored gospel in most of India's important cities, organized a number of branches, translated and published **pamphlets** in five Indian languages, and bore witness to thousands of British military men and their families. Although baptisms were relatively few, some families of converts immigrated to **Zion**.

In the late twentieth century, India was approximately two-thirds the size of the contiguous 48 states of the United States but had a population roughly four times as large—about 1 billion. The Church has never lost interest in India as a mission field, but local restrictions and international events have made advancement into that nation difficult. Beginning in 1964, baptisms were performed as requested by Indian citizens. From then until 1969, when the administration of missionary work in India was transferred to **Singapore**, the nation was under the Southern Far East Mission president in **Hong Kong**. Beginning in 1978 Church-representative couples temporarily stayed in various Indian cities. At the request of citizens, they also taught the gospel and baptized. The Church gained legal recognition in 1982, although that status did not permit proselyting of the gospel by foreigners.

In 1985 young Indian elders and sisters began active missionary work in their own country, and convert baptisms became steady. In January 1993 the India Bangalore Mission was created with Gureharan Singh Gill as president. Between 1993 and 1995 a number of foreign elders were sent into India on tourist visas. The government stopped that procedure in late 1995, leaving missionary work to be accomplished almost entirely by Indian members.

At the beginning of the year 2000, there were 2,435 members living in 4 **districts** and 18 branches.

SOURCE

Britsch, R. Lanier. *From the East: The History of the Latter-day Saints in Asia, 1851–1996.* Salt Lake City: Deseret Book, 1998. 8–33, 506–55.

R. LANIER BRITSCH

INDIANA. A rich history of early **missionary work** is part of Indiana's legacy of continual Church growth. In 1831 **Samuel H. Smith** and **Reynolds Cahoon** first preached the gospel in Indiana. In that same year, the Church established branches in the state and on 29 November held a conference that was attended by **Oliver Cowdery**, **John Whitmer**, **Thomas B. Marsh**, and others. In the spring of 1832, **Joseph Smith** and **Newel K. Whitney** visited Greenville, Indiana, and in 1834 **Zion's Camp** peacefully passed through the state en route to **Missouri**.

The state was included in the Northwestern States Mission as early as 1882. During the first decade of the twentieth century, a small group of **Saints** met regularly in Indianapolis at the home of Edward and Anna Faulting. In 1913 a **branch** was officially organized in the city, and in 1927 the Church built a **meetinghouse** that was dedicated by President **Heber J. Grant**. The first **stake** was created in Indianapolis on 17 May 1959.

The Church's **seminary** and **institute** programs were introduced in the state during the 1960s, blessing the lives of hundreds of high school students and young adults.

At the beginning of the year 2000 Indiana had 33,058 members living in 10 stakes with 88 wards and branches.

SOURCES

Jenson, Andrew. *Encyclopedic History of The Church of Jesus Christ of Latter-day Saints.* Salt Lake City: Deseret News, 1941. 361.
1999–2000 Church Almanac. Salt Lake City: Deseret News, 1998. 218–19.

GARY L. ALLEN

INDIAN PLACEMENT PROGRAM. The Church formally organized the Indian Student Placement Program in July 1954. Previous to this time (1947–54), a small number of students had been placed in foster homes in four western states. During the 1970s an average of 2,500 students per year left what they considered inadequate educational opportunities on reservations to live with LDS foster families. While living with these families, students would attend the local public school during the academic year and then return to their homes each summer. This gave many Indian youth a better opportunity to develop leadership, academic, and intercultural skills.

Native American parents were expected to initiate the request for their children to be placed in the program. Each student had to be at least eight years old and a baptized member of the Church. The foster **family** welcomed the student into their home as a regular family member, providing a home, financial support, and clothing.

The Church began limiting the placement of students once the reservations began to improve their educational institutions. During the 1980s only high school students could participate in the program. In 1990 about 500 high school students took part in the program. In 1998 only five students remained, and they continued until graduation. From 1954 to 1998 about 35,000 Native Americans participated in the program.

LDS **Social Services** continues to serve Native Americans in their own areas. They provide local support and counseling in parenting, **marriage** enrichment, and overcoming substance abuse. The program has helped in the partial fulfillment of the prophecy that "the **Lamanites** shall blossom as the rose" (D&C 49:24).

SOURCES

De Hoyos, Genevieve. "Indian Student Placement Services." *Encyclopedia of*

Mormonism. Edited by Daniel H. Ludlow. 4 vols. New York: Macmillan, 1992. 2:679–80.

Kimball, Spencer W. *Faith Precedes the Miracle.* Salt Lake City: Deseret Book, 1972. 339–58.

LDS Social Services–Native American Services. *"Go amongst Thy Brethren."* Pamphlet. Salt Lake City: The Church of Jesus Christ of Latter-day Saints, 1999.

BRIAN L. SMITH

INDIANS. See NATIVE AMERICANS.

INDIAN SEMINARY. The Church established the Indian Seminary program in the 1950s and 60s to extend religious education opportunities to Indian youth. At this time, most Native Americans attended federally funded schools, set up both on and off of their reservations. When the Intermountain Indian School opened at **Brigham City, Utah,** in 1949, of its 600 **Navajo** students 6 were Latter-day Saints. In 1954 **Boyd K. Packer** was called to develop a program that would strengthen these youth, and by 1956 the first Indian chapel and **seminary** building were dedicated at the school. After meeting with government officials at Washington, D.C., in 1958, Boyd K. Packer and **A. Theodore Tuttle** visited federal Indian schools throughout the West, establishing seminary programs wherever there were enough LDS students. Missionaries assigned to Indian reservations encouraged parents to enroll their children in religion classes, and even many non-Latter-day Saint parents signed their children up for seminary. This led to many conversions. The **Indian Placement Program** also contributed to the number of youth able to participate in Indian Seminary. In 1959 J. Edwin Baird was called as the first full-time coordinator of the Indian Seminary program, and by 1961 enrollment was 3,528 students at 85 schools. In the 1970s programs such as Indian Seminary declined as more Indian students attended public schools and participated in the Church's traditional seminary program.

SOURCE

Berrett, William E. *A Miracle in Weekday Religious Education.* Salt Lake City: Salt Lake Printing Center, 1988. 103–21.

LISA KURKI AND JOHN P. LIVINGSTONE

INDONESIA. Indonesia, the world's most populous Islamic country, was dedicated for **missionary work** 26 October 1969 by **Elder Ezra Taft**

Benson. The first six missionaries arrived in January 1970. In 1975 the Indonesia Jakarta Mission was created out of the Southeast **Asia** Mission, with Hendrik Gout as president. During the first decade of missionary work, branches were established in eight of the largest cities on Java, the main island of Indonesia. Obtaining visas was a constant problem, and door-to-door contacting was prohibited. In 1978 the Indonesian government severely restricted foreign missionary work, and the last foreign elders left the country in August 1981. Local missionaries continued the work, and in 1995 the Indonesia Jakarta Mission was reopened under the leadership of Vern M. Tueller. At the beginning of the year 2000 there were 5,339 members, 3 districts, and 21 branches (mostly on Java, but also on Medan and Menado). There were 29 local missionaries serving, as well as 3 foreign couples representing LDS Charities.

SOURCE

Britsch, R. Lanier. *From the East: A History of the Latter-day Saints in Asia, 1851–1996.* Salt Lake City: Deseret Book, 1998.

CHAD EMMETT

INSPIRED VERSION OF THE BIBLE. See JOSEPH SMITH TRANSLATION OF THE BIBLE.

INSTITUTES OF RELIGION. In the 1920s the Church inaugurated institutes of religion, a program of religious instruction for the growing number of Latter-day **Saints** attending public colleges and universities. Church leaders had in place a strong **seminary** program that provided religious instruction for high school students, but nothing had been done for Church members enrolled in higher **education**. Three LDS professors at the University of **Idaho** asked the **First Presidency** to construct a building in Moscow, Idaho, that would serve as a chapel where students could worship, meet in **Sunday School** and MIA, and support each other in their faith. Responding to this call for help, in 1926 President **Heber J. Grant** sent **J. Wyley Sessions** to Moscow, where he was to take care of Latter-day Saint students and make recommendations as to "what the Church should do for its members registered at all state universities" (quoted in Arrington, 140). Soon Sessions recommended that a building be erected wherein students could not only worship but also be instructed and helped to "attain a deeper understanding of their faith and the church, and to help them with intellectual and other problems which arise at the University" (Arrington, 141). Church leaders responded affirmatively to Sessions's recommendations, and he taught the first institute class during the fall of 1927. The first institute building, erected in Moscow, Idaho, was dedicated 28 September 1928 by President **Charles W. Nibley**. Other institutes were soon constructed adjacent to Utah State Agriculture College (Utah State University) in **Logan, Utah**; Idaho Southern Branch College (Idaho State University) in Pocatello, Idaho; and the **University of Utah** in **Salt Lake City**.

In 1938 Church leaders sent **Elder John A. Widtsoe** to **Los Angeles**, where he founded an institute adjacent to the University of Southern **California**. This was the first institute outside the Intermountain West. The institute program slowly grew, and by 1950 there were at least a dozen institutes, located mostly in Utah, **Wyoming**, Idaho, and California.

As the Church grew and more of its members enrolled in universities all over the world, the institute program expanded. Highly educated instructors taught classes on the **Book of Mormon**, the Old and New Testaments, **Doctrine and Covenants**, **Pearl of Great Price**, Church history, courtship and marriage, world religions, and Christian history as well as several seminars for graduate students.

The first student **stake** was organized in 1956. Student stakes were often headquartered in institute buildings. A decade later, the **Latter-day Saint Student Association** was organized to promote and coordinate activities for students. Both the student stakes and the student association contributed to the effectiveness of the institute program.

J. Wyley Sessions taught 57 students in the first institute class. From that rather small beginning, the program grew until in 1999 hundreds of thousands of students were enrolled in classes in more than a hundred countries. Those university students who registered for and attended classes often graduated from universities with their faith intact, even strengthened, and with their knowledge of the **scriptures** deepened and enlarged.

SOURCES

Arrington, Leonard J. "The Founding of the LDS Institute of Religion." *Dialogue* 2 (Summer 1967): 138–47.

Berrett, William E. *A Miracle in Weekday Religious Education.* Salt Lake City: Salt Lake Printing Center, 1988.

KENNETH W. GODFREY

INSTRUCTOR, THE. See *JUVENILE INSTRUCTOR.*

INTELLECTUAL HISTORY. Mormonism's intellectual history encompasses the formation and development of ideas relative to the doctrines, ritual practices, principles, economics, and social structures of the Church. These ideas may be either initiated by **revelation** from God or by thoughtful individuals. The claim to revelation makes the Church distinct from the world.

Revelations in this dispensation began with those received through the **Prophet Joseph Smith,** such as the communications recorded in the **Doctrine and Covenants,** the translation of the **Book of Mormon,** the **Joseph Smith Translation of the Bible,** and the **Pearl of Great Price.** Some of the Prophet's contemporaries elaborated on the revelatory flow of ideas given through him. While others, including later prophets, aided in the crystallization of doctrinal thought, within the Church it is a fundamental principle that God continues to reveal ideas, doctrines, and principles through **prophets, seers, and revelators.** As such, the religious beliefs of the Church are anchored in revelation, and the teachings of the living prophets are preeminent in determining the direction of Latter-day Saint religious thought and practice.

Historians such as **Leonard J. Arrington,** Richard F. Haglund, and David J. Whittaker have suggested various models describing the stages of Latter-day Saint intellectual history. Their models may be combined to include five main periods.

RESTORATION AND FORMATION (1830–44)

From the **organization of the Church** to the **martyrdom** of Joseph Smith, most of the key concepts relating to a variety of doctrines and practices were revealed to the Prophet. Nineteenth-century religious thought embraced many ideas, practices, and beliefs that were at odds with the revelations received by Joseph Smith. For instance, *creation ex nihilo* (creation of existence out of nonexistence), trinitarianism, baptism of infants, and *sola scriptura* (the belief that doctrine can only come from the **Bible**) were all countered by latter-day revelations, and Joseph Smith often elaborated on these newly revealed truths. Foundational revelations and teachings of the Prophet that became part of the Church's beliefs during the **New York** period deal with such subjects as continuing revelation, faith, repentance, baptism by immersion, reception of the Holy Ghost by the laying on of hands, the necessity of **priesthood** authority, the importance of **missionary work**, the fall of **Adam** and the atonement of Christ, agency and accountability, gifts of the Spirit, and **America** as a promised land and site of the future **New Jerusalem**, or **Zion** (Allen and Arrington). During the **Ohio**, **Missouri**, and **Illinois** periods, revelations and teachings of the Prophet included **tithing**, premortal existence, the **three degrees of glory**, eternal **marriage** (including **plural marriage**), eternal progression, **salvation for the dead**, and significant developments in Church organization.

ELABORATION (1844–67)

Beginning with the death of Joseph Smith, this period continued through the organization of the **School of the Prophets** in **Utah**. Secretaries to **Brigham Young**, editors and writers for various publications, and educators and independent writers such as **Willard Richards, Orson Pratt, Orson Hyde, Franklin D. Richards,** and **John Taylor** all contributed to the elaboration of intellectual materials. Through publications such as the *Journal of Discourses,* various matters were addressed and elaborated upon. For instance, **Elder** Orson Pratt expands our understanding of the future state in the spirit world in his address entitled "The Increased Powers and Faculties of the Mind in a Future State" (*JD,* 2:235–48).

PURIFICATION (1867–1914)

Church leaders saw this as a time for the **Saints** to band together as increased commercial interaction and denominational academies encroached into LDS communities. At this time the **Young Men** and **Young Women** organizations were formed. In addition, more than two dozen LDS **academies** were established. During this period it was necessary to refine what could and should be taught in these organizations. Journals such as the **Woman's Exponent** and *Juvenile Instructor* show that numerous issues of a religious and secular nature were editorialized and discussed. **James E. Talmage** also published his seminal *Articles of Faith,* which served to refine Latter-day Saint thought on many doctrinal subjects.

ADAPTATION AND CONFRONTATION (1914–45)

A rise in industrial technology, two world **wars**, and an increase in secularism contributed to a higher level of Church involvement in world affairs. During this period, some Latter-day Saints studied and received higher degrees from notable universities. Such prominent **general author-ities** as **B. H. Roberts** and **John A. Widtsoe** made significant contributions to ancient studies, philosophy, and **science**. In *The Doctrine of Deity,* Elder Roberts demonstrates a Latter-day Saint view of God while confronting theological issues with Reverend Van der Donckt of the Catholic Church in Pocatello, **Idaho**. Elder Widtsoe formulates an organized theological discussion in his *Rational Theology.*

GLOBALIZATION (1945–PRESENT)

Because of computer technology and satellite transmission, Church information and teachings have been made much more accessible world-wide. Due to significant international growth during the latter half of the twentieth century, curriculum writers and others who communicated Latter-day Saint thought had to consider how best to relate gospel prin-ciples to many cultures. During this period the Church curriculum was modified to feature a study of the standard works and teachings of latter-day prophets; this gave the many new members around the world a better understanding of the fundamental sources of Latter-day Saint thought. The Church also simplified programs and lesson manuals to present the doctrines and practices of the restored gospel for small units among ethnic minorities in urban areas and in developing regions worldwide.

SOURCES

Allen, James B., and Leonard J. Arrington. "Mormon Origins in New York: An Introductory Analysis." *BYU Studies* 9 (Spring 1969): 241–74.

Arrington, Leonard J. "The Intellectual Tradition of the Latter-day Saints." *Dialogue* 4 (Spring 1969): 13–26.

Haglund, Richard F., Jr., and David J. Whittaker. "Intellectual History." *Encyclopedia of Mormonism.* Edited by Daniel H. Ludlow. 4 vols. New York: Macmillan, 1992. 2:685–91.

Journal of Discourses [JD]. 26 vols. London: Latter-day Saints' Book Depot, 1854–86.

BRIAN M. HAUGLID

INTERESTING ACCOUNT OF SEVERAL REMARKABLE VISIONS. While serving a mission in Edinburgh, **Scotland**, in 1840, **Orson Pratt** of the Quorum of the Twelve **Apostles** published a 31-page booklet entitled *Interesting Account of Several Remarkable Visions, and of the Late Discovery of Ancient American Records.* This tract tells of the **First Vision** and the coming forth of the **Book of Mormon**. It ends with "a sketch of the faith and doctrine of this Church" (Pratt, 24) that bears obvious similarity to, and appears to have been a model for, the **Articles of Faith**, which were refined and published by **Joseph Smith** in 1842. Perhaps the most important aspect of **Elder** Pratt's booklet is that it presents the earliest published account of Joseph Smith's First Vision. The tract was later republished with minor changes in the **United States** and in **Europe**.

Sources

Crawley, Peter. *A Descriptive Bibliography of the Mormon Church: Volume One, 1830–1847*. Provo, Utah: Religious Studies Center, Brigham Young University, 1997. 127–29, 160–61, 191–92.

England, Breck. *The Life and Thought of Orson Pratt*. Salt Lake City: University of Utah, 1985. 67–71.

Pratt, Orson. *Interesting Account of Several Remarkable Visions*. Edinburgh, 1840.

Kent P. Jackson

INTERMOUNTAIN HEALTH CARE, INC. See HOSPITALS.

INTERNATIONAL GENEALOGICAL INDEX. The International Genealogical Index (IGI) is a computerized index to millions of names of deceased individuals from around the world that have been submitted to the **Family History** Department. It also includes names that have been copied from vital records and other sources internationally. An emphasis is placed on North American and British records. The compact disc and Internet versions do not contain names of living individuals, nor do they show LDS **temple ordinance** dates. The IGI serves as an index to parish registers and other vital records, such as New England town records. Numerous birth, christening, and **marriage** records are indexed. Most records date from the 1500s to the late nineteenth century. The IGI is part of the **FamilySearch**™ computer system available on compact discs and also on the Internet at FamilySearch™ Internet **Genealogy** Service (www.familysearch.org). An older version is available on microfiche at **Family History Centers**.

Kip Sperry

INTERNATIONAL MAGAZINES. See *LIAHONA* MAGAZINE.

INTERNATIONAL MISSION. Organized on 9 November 1972, the International Mission was created to serve all members of the Church living outside of **stakes** and **missions**. At that time, for example, the **Switzerland** Zurich Mission served all Latter-day Saints in the **Middle East** and **Africa** except those in the South African Mission, but responsibility for those two areas was transferred to the International Mission in June 1974.

Headquartered in **Salt Lake City**, the International Mission did not proselyte but organized members into **branches** and groups, provided study and lesson materials, **family home evening** manuals, Church **magazines**, and sacrament cups. The mission arranged for baptisms, **priesthood** ordinations, and **temple** recommends; it also kept membership records and received tithes and offerings.

Members planning to move into International Mission **areas** were encouraged to contact headquarters before moving. They would receive helpful materials and instructions to make their residence abroad more beneficial from the start. They also received names and addresses of any members residing in their area. Regular letters of instruction and encouragement were sent so they could feel part of the Church and realize their responsibility to be good examples.

The International Mission was discontinued on 15 August 1987 after enough area authorities were called to serve members worldwide. Remaining needed services were assigned to the International Services Division of the Missionary Department.

SOURCES

Cannon, Edwin Q., Jr. "I Have a Question." *Ensign* 13 (February 1983): 20–21.
"International Mission in Its Tenth Year." *Church News*, 6 February 1982, 3.
"Mission Organized to Aid Unattached." *Church News*, 16 December 1972, 4.

EDWIN Q. CANNON JR.

IOSEPA, UTAH. To provide a **gathering** place, or colony, for faithful Hawaiian Latter-day **Saints** eager to come to **Zion**, in 1889 the **First Presidency** purchased a ranch in Skull Valley, Tooele County, 75 miles southwest of **Salt Lake City**. Named *Iosepa* (the Hawaiian word for "Joseph" in honor of **Joseph Smith** and **Joseph F. Smith**), the community lasted 28 years and, at its peak, numbered more than 275 souls.

The settlement, however, was never a thriving success. The aridity of the desert soil, the grinding isolation, and the extremes in temperature were all in stark and disappointing contrast to the temperate, balmy climate of the Hawaiian Saints' island home. Furthermore, Iosepa was victimized by smallpox, leprosy, and other contagious diseases. Nevertheless, the community persevered in faith and hope and likely would have persisted had the Church not announced in 1915 plans for the building of a **temple** in **Hawaii**, now officially part of the **United States**. With transportation funded by the Church, most settlers decided to return and relocate on the Church plantation at **Laie**, Oahu. Soon afterwards, in 1917, the Church sold the Iosepa ranch.

SOURCES

Arrington, Leonard J. "The L.D.S. Hawaiian Colony at Skull Valley." *Improvement Era* 57 (May 1954): 314–15, 366–67.

Atkin, Dennis H. "A History of Iosepa, the Utah Polynesian Colony." Master's thesis, Brigham Young University, 1958.

RICHARD E. BENNETT

IOWA. Iowa is important to early Latter-day Saint history because of 12 major developments, 10 of them prior to 1860. (1) After the "**Mormon War**" in **Missouri**, some LDS militiamen fled north into the **Iowa** Territory in late 1838, pioneering a road called the Mormon Trace. (2) Early in 1839, Latter-day Saint exiles from Missouri settled across the river from **Nauvoo** in what became the **Zarahemla Stake**, which included several congregations and was centered in **Montrose**. (3) In 1844–45, the James **Emmett Expedition** of more than 150 Saints from the Nauvoo area moved up the west shore of the **Mississippi River**, then followed the Iowa River into central Iowa and on to present **South Dakota**. (4) **Saints** involved in the 1846 three-stage mass **exodus** from **Illinois** crossed Iowa heading west. This movement included the initial group of some 2,000 **pioneers**—the "Camp of Israel"—led by **Brigham Young**, which left Nauvoo in February (the winter exodus); the larger wave of some 11,000 departures in April, May, and June (the spring exodus); and the final group of poor Saints, whom mobs drove from Nauvoo in September (the fall exodus). (5) More than 500 members of the Church enlisted in the **Mormon Battalion** and departed from the **Council Bluffs** area in July 1846. (6) **Garden Grove** and **Mount Pisgah** were operated as temporary **Latter-day Saint** settlements near the center of southern Iowa between 1846 and 1852. Both have cemetery **monuments** honoring those who died there. (7) On 5 December 1847 the **Quorum** of the Twelve **Apostles** met in **Orson Hyde's** home at Kanesville to reorganize the **First**

Presidency. They sustained Brigham Young as president, with **Heber C. Kimball** as first counselor and **Willard Richards** as second counselor. On 27 December the Saints gathered in the log **tabernacle** in Kanesville and sustained the new First Presidency. (8) Kanesville (Council Bluffs) developed as a Latter-day Saint city between 1848 and 1852 and had more than 90 satellite settlements and clusters of Latter-day Saints within 40 miles of its center. At its peak, Kanesville had more than 3,000 inhabitants. Between 1848 and 1852, an estimated 46 separate Latter-day Saint wagon trains started west from Kanesville. (9) Keokuk served for a year (1853) as the Saints' outfitting camp for nine covered wagon companies. (10) Seven handcart companies (1856–57) and nine wagon trains (1856–58) outfitted at Iowa City, the western **railroad** terminus, and traveled to Council Bluffs. (11) **The Reorganized Church of Jesus Christ of Latter Day Saints (RLDS)**, formed in 1860, made Lamoni, Iowa, its headquarters in the 1880s. The organization's president, **Joseph Smith III**, lived there. The RLDS Church established its Graceland College in Lamoni in 1895. (12) The LDS Church began to establish branches in the later nineteenth century and **wards** and **stakes** in the twentieth century.

A branch at Keokuk existed in 1875, and one in Council Bluffs by 1878. By 1878 Iowa was a missionary **conference** in the Northern States **Mission**, and in 1889 it became part of the Northern States Mission. By 1930 the Eastern and Western Conferences in Iowa included branches in Ames, Boone, Davenport, and Sioux City. The Cedar Rapids Stake (1966) was the first stake organized in Iowa since the 1840s, and it was followed by stakes at Des Moines (1970), Davenport (1978), Ames (1995), Sioux City (1996), and Council Bluffs (1999). The Iowa Des Moines Mission was created in 1976. At the beginning of the year 2000, Iowa had 17,465 Latter-day Saints in 6 stakes and 49 wards and branches.

SOURCES

Hartley, William G. "Mormons and Early Iowa Hisotry (1838–1858): Eight Distinct Connections." *Annals of Iowa* 59 (Summer 2000): 217–60.

Jenson, Andrew. *Encyclopedic History of The Church of Jesus Christ of Latter-day Saints.* Salt Lake City: Deseret News, 1941. 366–67.

1999–2000 Church Almanac. Salt Lake City: Deseret News, 1998. 203–4.

WILLIAM G. HARTLEY

IRAN. Organized in July 1975, the short-lived Iran Tehran Mission was the only Latter-day Saint mission headquartered in the **Middle East** since 1950. Dean B. Farnsworth served as mission president until July 1978;

he was then replaced by William J. Attwooll, who remained in Iran until his evacuation with the other missionaries the following December. The Iranian government granted the Church official legal recognition in 1977, the first Middle Eastern country to do so.

The opportunity to establish the mission resulted from the Shah's efforts to promote national development through a policy of openness to Western economic and political values, including tolerance of non-**Muslim** religions. The missionaries, a total of 18 (all elders), learned to speak Farsi but were not allowed to discuss their religious views openly or to initiate gospel discussions. Much of their time, therefore, was spent in nonproselyting activities, such as teaching English in schools, assisting with local **Boy Scout** programs, and contacting referrals from Latter-day Saint **visitors' centers** around the world. **Missionary work** was further hampered because none of the LDS **scriptures** except the **Bible** had been translated into Farsi; however, the mission managed to have some tracts, as well as a 2,000-word English-Farsi glossary of the **Book of Mormon**, translated and published. Few Iranians embraced Mormonism (about 15 altogether) due in part to the daunting problems that Muslim converts to Christianity often faced in Islamic societies: ostracism, unemployment, disinheritance, and even threat of death. For this reason, Iranians who joined the Church abroad and returned to Iran usually did not acknowledge their conversion or participate fully in Latter-day Saint activities. After the revolution of the late 1970s, however, some Iranians who fled the country but had had contact with the missionaries or other Latter-day Saints in Iran joined the Church in **Europe** and North **America**.

Despite these difficulties in proselyting, the missionaries strengthened the Church in other ways: providing leadership in the main branches and groups (located in Tehran, Shiraz, Isfahan, Ahwaz, and Charchesmeh), visiting Church members in outlying areas, and teaching and baptizing non-Iranian expatriates (mostly Filipinos, Koreans, and Americans). Two **apostles, Elders Thomas S. Monson** and **Howard W. Hunter**, visited Iran on separate occasions. Unlike **Palestine** in the Turkish-Armenian Mission, which was dedicated on numerous occasions, an apostolic prayer dedicating the land for missionary work was never offered in Iran. Because of increased fighting between Islamic revolutionary forces and the Shah's army, President Attwooll and the missionaries were evacuated from Iran in December 1978 and reassigned to other mission fields. A final sacrament meeting was held in May 1979; after that, all Church activities ceased. In December of that year an apartment building owned by the Church and used for meetings, offices, and living quarters was confiscated by the Iranian government and reconverted into public housing. In the year 2000 the Church had no official presence or organized units in Iran.

SOURCES

Farnsworth, Dean Burton. "Oral History." Interview by Matthew K. Heiss. Orem, Utah, 1990. Typescript. James Moyle Oral History Program, LDS Church Historical Department, Salt Lake City.

Interviews with Dean B. Farnsworth and William J. Attwooll, former presidents of the Iran Tehran Mission; Kent Bowman, Chris Soelberg, and Nels Draper, returned missionaries; and David Farnsworth, former Church legal counsel for the Middle East.

"President's Correspondence, 1974–1977." Tehran District, Iran Tehran Mission. LDS Church Archives, Salt Lake City.

JAMES A. TORONTO

IRAQ. See MIDDLE EAST and MUSLIMS.

IRELAND. Reuben Hedlock was the first missionary to visit Belfast, Ireland, arriving in May 1840; however, he stayed only three days. Two months later, 28 July 1840, **Elder John Taylor** arrived in the Emerald Isle and introduced the gospel. He was accompanied by two native Irishmen, William Black and James McGuffie, who had joined the Church in **England**. The three went to Newry in Northern Ireland, likely the hometown of James McGuffie. Elder Taylor arranged for the use of the town hall the evening of 28 July, and more than 600 gathered to hear him preach the first message of the restored gospel in Ireland.

Three days later, 31 July 1840, Elder Taylor baptized Thomas Tait in nearby Loughbrickland, making the Irish farmer and friend of James McGuffie the first convert to the Church in Ireland. James McGuffie baptized a few more converts in Newry before the three missionaries sailed for **Scotland** in August 1840.

Other missionaries followed, but progress was slow. Between 1840 and 1850, fewer than 200 converts joined the Church in Ireland. Many who did join emigrated to gather with other Latter-day **Saints**. Little proselyting was accomplished during the height of the Irish famine of 1845–47. Between 1840 and 1850, the population in Ireland decreased by half—from eight million to four million. Upwards of one million died of starvation, and another three million emigrated. An unknown but apparently large number of Irish famine emigrants did, however, join the

Church in Scotland, England, **Wales**, **Canada**, the **United States**, and other countries to which they fled. This trend of Irish conversions outside of Ireland fulfilled, in part, the latter-day **revelation** that many would be warned and called "by the voice of famines" (D&C 43:25).

Missionary work in Ireland had all but ceased by 1850 when missionaries returned once again. Elder Edward Sutherland, a native of Dublin, went to that region during the summer of 1850 to open it for the gospel. By 1 September 1850, he and his companion, Elder H. E. Bowering, had baptized six converts, most of whom were Sutherland's relatives.

Several missionary campaigns in both north and south Ireland were hampered by religious opposition, famine, and internal political strife. Church growth in Ireland was also affected by the **emigration** of many of those who joined. By the turn of the century, less than 800 converts had been gained in Ireland during the 60-year period.

Shortly after 1900, several German Latter-day Saint families immigrated to Dublin, where they formed the nucleus of the Church for many years. Many of these members were pork butchers by trade. By 1920 branches of the Church were established in the Belfast Conference with approximately 225 members, and another 60 members were in and around Dublin. Missionaries were again withdrawn from Ireland during **World War II**, with limited growth occurring during that time.

LDS missionaries returned to Ireland in 1946 after World War II ended. Growth continued, and the Irish **Mission** was organized on 8 July 1962. Twelve years later the Belfast **Stake** was organized on 9 June 1974. A stake was created in Dublin on 12 March 1995, and in the year 2000 there were 2,341 members in the Republic of Ireland and approximately 5,516 members in Northern Ireland. In that same year the mission headquarters of the Church was in Dublin.

SOURCES

Barlow, Brent A. "History of The Church of Jesus Christ of Latter-day Saints in Ireland Since 1840." Master's thesis, Brigham Young University, 1968.

Bloxham, V. Ben, James R. Moss, and Larry C. Porter, eds. *Truth Will Prevail: The Rise of The Church of Jesus Christ of Latter-day Saints in the British Isles, 1837–1997.* Cambridge: Cambridge University Press, 1987. 299–331.

1999–2000 Church Almanac. Salt Lake City: Deseret News, 1998. 336–37, 401.

BRENT A. BARLOW

IRON MISSION. The Iron Mission was originally organized to satisfy increasing needs for ore within the provisional **state of Deseret**, but it led to the colonization of two important communities in southern Utah. After **Parley P. Pratt** returned from an expedition in the spring of 1850, reporting large quantities of readily accessible iron ore in southern Utah, the general assembly of the provisional state of Deseret organized Iron County and elected **George A. Smith** as chief justice. The area to be settled was most of southern **Utah**, including what are now Piute, Washington, Iron, Kane, Garfield, and Beaver Counties, as well as some of **Nevada** (Dalton, 6). Located more than 200 miles south of **Provo** and in the heart of some of the most active **Indian** areas in the territory, the mission's first settlement, Parowan, reached far beyond the Church's colonization efforts up to that time.

On 15 December 1850, a meeting was held in Provo, and for the first time members of the Iron Mission met together. The group voted unanimously to sustain George A. Smith as president and leader of the expedition. With 120 men, 31 women, 101 wagons, and 50,000 plus pounds of seed, the group marched toward Iron County. On 13 January 1851, after traveling for 28 days in the cold winter weather, the **pioneers** arrived in the Little Salt Lake Valley (Parowan Valley) and made their camp next to a fresh spring in present-day Parowan. The company had made roads through snow and ice, fording the rivers and streams with little forage available to their livestock.

The pioneers found that there was a good supply of land, quality timber available in the mountains, and plenty of water. Soon they had established iron works 20 miles to the south at Coal Creek (present-day Cedar City). Iron production reached its peak in 1855, when about 6,100 pounds of ore were processed in one run. By late 1856, however, iron production had come to a near standstill due to a lack of expertise, hostile Indians, inclement weather, personnel problems, and the incipient **Utah War.** These problems contributed to Brigham Young's decision to close down the works in 1857, but the communities of Cedar City and Parowan continued.

Source

Dalton, Luella Adams, comp. *History of the Iron County Mission.* Parowan, Utah, 1973.

Ralph M. McAffee

IRRIGATION. Latter-day **Saints** have figured prominently in the development of irrigation in North **America**. They were among the first Euro-Americans to irrigate lands in **Utah**, **Nevada**, **Wyoming**, and

Alberta, Canada. Moreover, in **Arizona**, **Colorado**, **New Mexico**, **Idaho**, and northern **Mexico**, the Saints opened large, new areas to irrigated farming. The Saints' earliest attempts at irrigation probably occurred in **California**, as emigrants who had traveled there aboard the *Brooklyn* in 1846 established the town of New Hope. Church members' initial irrigation of planted fields in Utah occurred 23 July 1847 and provided a model for subsequent irrigation efforts in the **Great Basin**.

Prior to their arrival in the West, the Saints were aware of general irrigation processes, and some had observed irrigation. Settling near creeks and rivers flowing out of the mountains, they generally established small irrigation systems suitable for sustaining individual settlements. By 1865 the Saints had built more than 1,000 miles of canals in Utah, largely by using rudimentary surveying techniques and excavating equipment, including plows and other simple implements. Five years later, Church members tilled at least half of all the irrigated land in the western United States. The Saints helped to develop western water laws based upon the legal doctrine of prior appropriation. They also devised a system of watermasters to supervise and manage water use locally.

Although few non-Mormons adopted the Saints' cooperative, village-based approach to irrigation, the Saints' success with irrigation attracted the attention and admiration of numerous visitors. In 1891, William Smythe, one of the nation's foremost irrigation enthusiasts, termed Utah "the arid region as we hope it will soon appear to the eye of the world" (Arrington and May, 14). Church members played important roles in lobbying for federal aid for irrigation at the National Irrigation Congress's founding meeting, held in **Salt Lake City** in 1891. Some of the nation's foremost early irrigation scientists and water lawyers were Latter-day Saints. In the twentieth century, as the federal government became heavily involved in constructing and administering irrigation systems through the Bureau of Reclamation, Church members held significant administrative posts in the Bureau's local, regional, and national offices. In 1923 and 1924, **Elder John A. Widtsoe** served on a landmark commission that significantly altered the bureau's policies.

Sources

Arrington, Leonard J., and Dean May. "'A Different Mode of Life': Irrigation and Society in Nineteenth-Century Utah." *Agriculture in the Development of the Far West.* Edited by James H. Shideler. Washington: Agricultural History Society, 1975. 3–20.

Harper, Kelly C. "The Mormon Role in Irrigation Beginnings and Diffusions in the Western States: An Historical Geography." Master's thesis, Brigham Young University, 1974.

Jackson, Richard H. "Righteousness and Environmental Change: The Mormons and the Environment." *Essays on the American West, 1973–74.* Edited by Thomas G. Alexander. Provo, Utah: Brigham Young University Press, 1974. 21–42.

BRIAN Q. CANNON

ISAACSON, THORPE B. **Counselor** to President **David O. McKay**, Henry Thorpe Beal Isaacson was born 6 September 1898 in Ephraim, **Utah**. Brother Isaacson was well educated, attending four institutions of higher learning. Eventually he served as a member of the board of regents for the **University of Utah**, vice president of the board of trustees at **Brigham Young University**, and president of the board of trustees at Utah State University. On 12 December 1946, he began his **general authority** service as second counselor to **presiding bishop LeGrand Richards** and continued from 1952 as first counselor to **Joseph L. Wirthlin**. In September 1962 he became an **assistant to the Twelve**, and four years later he was set apart as an additional counselor in the **First Presidency** under President David O. McKay. One of his great contributions as a general authority was made at his request—he wanted to work with adult **Aaronic Priesthood** holders. He encouraged and inspired countless of these brethren and innovated successful programs for their benefit. When the First Presidency was dissolved at the death of President McKay, Elder Isaacson returned to his position as an assistant to the Twelve. He died less than a year later on 9 November 1970 in **Salt Lake City**.

SOURCES

Flake, Lawrence R. *Prophets and Apostles of the Last Dispensation.* Provo, Utah: Religious Studies Center, Brigham Young University, 2001. 297–99.
"Thorpe B. Isaacson of the First Presidency." *Improvement Era* 69 (November 1966): 1078.
Zobell, Albert L., Jr. "Thorpe B. Isaacson." *Improvement Era* 68 (December 1965): 1078–81.

LAWRENCE R. FLAKE

ISLE OF MAN. The Isle of Man is a tiny island in the Irish Sea off the coasts of **England, Scotland**, and **Ireland**. It was a part of the **British Mission**, which was organized in 1837. **John Taylor**, Hiram Clark, and William Mitchell were the first missionaries called to this island. They arrived at the city of Douglas on 17 September 1840 and were later joined by Joseph Cain, **Joseph Fielding**, and James Blakeslee. The initial labors of these missionaries resulted in the conversion of approximately 100 people. Many of these converts would immigrate to the **United States**.

The first convert on the Isle of Man was most likely Samuel Pitchforth, followed by his mother, Ann Pitchforth, and his sisters Mercy, Sarah, and Annie. After immigrating to **Nauvoo**, Ann Pitchforth became the plural wife of John Taylor.

Samuel Pitchforth settled in Nephi, **Utah**. He named the small community of Mona, Utah (seven miles north of Nephi), for the Isle of Man, which had been named Mona by Julius Caesar.

SOURCES

Cannon, Mike. "Early Church Leaders Visited Isle of Man." *Church News*, 23 September 1995, 10.

Smith, Paul Thomas. "Among Family and Friends: John Taylor's Mission to the British Isles." *Ensign* 17 (March 1987): 36–41.

JAMES A. CARVER

ISRAEL. See HOLY LAND.

ITALY. Italy was one of the first non-English-speaking countries opened to missionary work (1850), and despite political, economic, and sectarian challenges during the past 150 years, the Church has gradually established a solid presence there.

Italy attracted the attention of early Church leaders because of its prominent role in religious and cultural history and its strategic geographical location in the Mediterranean world. During the October 1849 general conference, President Brigham Young called the first missionaries to begin preaching the gospel on the continent of Europe. Among these were **Lorenzo Snow**, an apostle, and Joseph Toronto, an Italian convert, who were assigned to open missionary work in Italy. While in England, en route to Italy, Elder Snow called Elder Thomas (T. B. H.) Stenhouse and Elder Jabez Woodard to serve in the new mission. Having arrived in Genoa on 25 June and assessed conditions and prospects, Elder Snow decided to begin proselyting among the **Waldensians**, a small Protestant community in the Piedmont region of northwest Italy. On 19 September 1850, Elders Snow, Stenhouse, and Woodard (Toronto had left to teach his family in Sicily) ascended a prominent mountain peak near the city of La Tour (Torre Pellice). Elder Snow offered a prayer dedicating Italy to the preaching of the gospel and organized the Italian

Mission. The missionaries immediately began to teach the gospel openly, and a few weeks later, on 27 October Elder Snow baptized the first convert, Jean Bose. The first Italian edition of the Book of Mormon was published in London in 1852 under the supervision of Lorenzo Snow.

During the next 15 years, missionary work was hindered by opposition from ministers, anti-Mormon literature, deeply rooted religious and political traditions, and the poverty of the people. By the time the mission closed in 1867, about 180 persons had been baptized: approximately 70 of these immigrated to Utah, and the remainder either apostatized or were excommunicated. Many prominent Latter-day Saint families—Beus, Cardon, Malan, Bertoch, Pons, and Chatelain—are descendants of these original Waldensian converts.

Intermittent efforts to preach the gospel in Italy were carried out over the next century. In the late nineteenth century, a few missionaries, including some of Waldensian descent (for example, Jacob Rivoir, James Bertoch, and Paul Cardon), renewed proselyting efforts in northern Italy. In 1933 Elder Riccardo Robezzoli of the Swiss-German Mission worked briefly among relatives in the Trento region of Italy, but Italian officials stopped him. Some Italians were converted before World War II by reading Latter-day Saint publications. The most prominent example is that of Vincenzo di Francesca, whose conversion story was told in a 1988 Church film, *How Rare a Possession.* During World War II, Latter-day Saint servicemen's branches were established in several locations in Italy, but no formal proselyting efforts were undertaken. During the 1950s and early 1960s a number of Italians (including Pietro and Felicità Snaidero, Santo Beltrame, Luigi Pittini, Giovanni Morandini, and Adelia Lucchi) were baptized through informal Latter-day Saint contacts in Italy. In April 1963 the first member conferences were held in Vicenza, and in March 1964 a new Italian translation of the Book of Mormon was published. Elder Ezra Taft Benson went to Rome in November 1964 to discuss with Italian government officials the prospects for reopening missionary work in Italy, and later that month he organized the Italian District of the Swiss Mission. By February 1965, 22 elders from the Swiss Mission were assigned to preach the gospel in seven cities in Italy.

On 2 August 1966 Elder Benson reestablished the Italian Mission in Florence with John Duns Jr. as president, and in November 1966 he rededicated Italy for the preaching of the gospel at Torre Pellice, near the site of Elder Snow's 1850 dedicatory prayer. The Italian Church **periodical** *La Stella* (*The Star*) commenced circulation in June 1967 and was thus published until its title, along with those of all other Church international magazines, was changed to *Liahona* in January 2000. By June 1971 Church growth necessitated the formation of two missions, and by 1977 four missions had been organized: Italy Rome, Italy Catania, Italy Milan, and Italy Padova. A major historical event was the first visit of a Church president to Italy—President Spencer W. Kimball arrived in August 1977. After years of groundwork, a milestone was achieved on 22 February 1993 when Italian president Oscar Luigi Scalfaro signed papers granting formal legal status to the Church. A total of three stakes exist in Italy: the first was established in Milan (June 1981), the second in Venice (September 1985), and the third in Puglia (March 1997). The **Church Educational System**, which has operated in Italy since 1975, includes five full-time supervisors, 220 teachers, and about 1,500 students enrolled in seminary and institute classes.

Despite continuing challenges of secularism and materialism and the ongoing problems of economic stagnation and out-migration in southern Italy, the Church continued to grow and consolidate its presence in Italy. At the beginning of the year 2000, total membership reached 18,599, organized into 3 stakes and 15 districts with 133 wards and branches.

SOURCES

Bennett, Archibald F. "The Vaudois of the Alpine Valleys and Their Contribution to Utah and Latter-day Saint History." Manuscript. LDS Church Historical Library, Salt Lake City. 1960.

Homer, Michael W. "The Church's Image in Italy from the 1840s to 1946: A Bibliographic Essay." *BYU Studies* 31 (1991): 2.

———. "'For the Strength of the Hills We Bless Thee': Italian Mormons Come to Utah." Manuscript. LDS Church Historical Library, Salt Lake City.

———. "The Italian Mission: 1850–1867." *Sunstone* 7 (May-June 1982): 16–21.

Jacobs, L. R. "Mormon Non-English Scriptures, Hymnals, & Periodicals, 1830–1986: A Descriptive Bibliography." Ithaca, N.Y.: L. R. Jacobs, 1986.

"Manuscript History of the Italian Mission." Church Historical Department Archives, Salt Lake City.

Snow, Lorenzo. *The Italian Mission.* London: W. Aubrey, 1851.

Toronto, James A. "Giuseppe Efisio Taranto: Odyssey from Sicily to Salt Lake City." *Pioneers in Every Land: Inspirational Stories of International Pioneers Past and Present.* Salt Lake City: Bookcraft, 1997.

JAMES A. TORONTO

IVINS, ANTHONY W. Anthony Woodward Ivins is noted for his missionary efforts among the **Lamanites** and for establishing the **Mexican colonies**. Rancher, businessman, and counselor to President **Heber J.**

Grant, he was born 16 September 1852 at Toms River, **New Jersey**. He married Elizabeth Ashby Snow in **Salt Lake City**, and they had nine children.

Ivins was with the first missionaries sent to **Mexico** (October 1875). They recorded no baptisms, but they located sites for future **Mormon** colonies. In 1878 Ivins served a **mission** with **Erastus Snow** to the **Navajo** and Pueblo Indians in **Arizona** and **New Mexico**. He was president of the Mexican Mission (1883–84) and called as president of the Colonia Juárez Stake on 9 December 1895.

Subsequent callings include membership in the Quorum of the Twelve **Apostles** (1907–21); **Young Men** general superintendent (1918–21); second counselor in the **First Presidency** (1921–25); and first counselor in the First Presidency (1925–34).

As a member of the First Presidency, President Ivins was involved with numerous significant events, including the first radio broadcast on the KZN radio station with President Heber J. Grant (6 May 1922); the dedication of the Mesa **Arizona Temple** site (28 November 1921); and the launching of the Church **Welfare Program** (1933). He died 23 September 1934 in Salt Lake City.

SOURCES

Church History in the Fulness of Times. Salt Lake City: The Church of Jesus Christ of Latter-day Saints, 1989. 496, 506, 621.

Roberts, B. H. *A Comprehensive History of The Church of Jesus Christ of Latter-day Saints, Century One.* 6 vols. Salt Lake City: The Church of Jesus Christ of Latter-day Saints, 1930. 5:475, 578, 586; 6: 262, 493.

Rubalcava, Boanerges. "The Church in Mexico and Central America." *Encyclopedia of Mormonism.* Edited by Daniel H. Ludlow. 4 vols. New York: Macmillan, 1992. 2:897–902.

W. JEFFREY MARSH

IVORY COAST (COTE D'IVOIRE). Ivory Coast is situated just west of **Ghana** on the Gulf of Guinea. Its people speak French and tribal languages, and its dominant faiths include Islam, Christianity, and tribal religions. Expatriate Latter-day Saint families, including those of Barnard and Cherry Silver and Terry and Bobby Broadhead, lived in Ivory Coast as early as the 1970s.

Two families from Ivory Coast might be considered **pioneers** in joining the Church. Lucien and Agathe Affoue were baptized in 1980 in Lyon, **France**, while Lucien was attending the university. Brother Affoue served in the Bordeaux **Branch** presidency, and the **family** was sealed in the **Swiss Temple** before returning to Abidjan, Ivory Coast, in March 1984. They began holding Church **meetings** in their home and prayed for the fellowship of other Latter-day **Saints**.

Phillipe Assard was baptized in Germany in 1980. His wife, Annelies, had joined the Church in 1976. Because of his strong desire to help establish the gospel in his homeland, Brother Assard moved his family back to Ivory Coast in 1986. He and his wife received their **patriarchal blessings** and were sealed in the Swiss Temple. Before leaving **Germany** he obtained a list of all known members of the Church in Ivory Coast.

Upon arriving home, Brother Assard wrote letters to these Church members, and the Lucien Affoue family was the first to respond. The two families rejoiced in meeting together and sharing the gospel with others, although Brother Assard, a qualified engineer, was without a job for a year.

In 1987 **Elder Marvin J. Ashton** of the Quorum of the Twelve **Apostles** created the first branch in Ivory Coast, with Terry Broadhead, an expatriate Latter-day Saint, as president and Brother Assard as counselor. Brother Assard later became the first native branch president and then **district** president. In 1988 the Affoue family moved to Bouake, Ivory Coast, where Brother Affoue served as a branch president and **counselor** to the **mission president**. In that same year the Church called Barnard and Cherry Silver to be the first official missionaries to serve in the country.

On 11 March 1990, Ivory Coast had its first district conference, held in Abidjan. About 200 of the 350 members attended. The Church received legal recognition 19 April 1991. Ivory Coast was part of the Ghana Accra Mission until 1992, when it was placed under the newly created **Cameroon** Yaounde Mission. A year later it became the Ivory Coast Abidjan Mission. On 17 August 1997, the Abidjan Ivory Coast **Stake** was created with Phillipe Assard as president. By the beginning of the year 2000, there were 5,402 members living in 1 **stake** and 14 **wards** and branches.

Sources

Mercer, Robert L. "Pioneers in Ivory Coast." *Ensign* 27 (September 1997): 25–30.

1999–2000 Church Almanac. Salt Lake City: Deseret News, 1998. 339–40.

Oral histories of early Church converts collected by E. Dale LeBaron. Copies at BYU Library, Provo, Utah; LDS Church Historical Library, Salt Lake City, Utah.

Silver, Cherry. "When a Woman Is Alone." *Ensign* 18 (June 1978): 40–43.

E. DALE LEBARON

JAPAN. Officers of the Mutual Improvement Association in a small branch in Japan around 1916.

JACK, ELAINE L. For more than 20 years, Elaine Low Jack served as a member of the **Relief Society** general board, as **counselor** in the **Young Women** general presidency, and as the 12th general president of the Relief Society. Born 22 March 1928 in **Cardston, Alberta**, Canada, she settled in **Utah** after her marriage to Joseph E. Jack. During her administration (1990–97), the Relief Society celebrated its sesquicentennial in 1992 with an innovative worldwide **satellite** broadcast. Other highlights of her administration included the initiation of the gospel **literacy** effort and cosponsorship of the **BYU** Women's Conference. Sister Jack returned to Cardston in 1997, when her husband was called as president of the **Cardston Alberta Temple**, which her stonemason grandfather had helped build.

SOURCES

Derr, Jill Mulvay, Janath Russell Cannon, and Maureen Ursenbach Beecher. *Women of Covenant: The Story of the Relief Society.* Salt Lake City: Deseret Book, 1992. 401–20.
"New Relief Society General Presidency Called." *Ensign* 10 (May 1990): 110–11.
Peterson, Janet, and LaRene Gaunt. *Elect Ladies: Presidents of the Relief Society.* Salt Lake City: Deseret Book, 1990. 201–10.

JANET PETERSON

JACK-MORMONS. The term *Jack-Mormon* was originally used by residents of **Jackson County, Missouri**, to describe nonmembers of the Church in **Clay County**, Missouri, who sympathized with the plight of the **Saints**. Today, the term describes members of the Church who are lukewarm in their commitment to living gospel principles, honoring their covenants, and sharing the gospel.

SOURCES

Church History in the Fulness of Times. Salt Lake City: The Church of Jesus Christ of Latter-day Saints, 1993. 137.

McConkie, Bruce R. *Mormon Doctrine.* 2d ed. Salt Lake City: Bookcraft, 1966. 390–91.

MATTHEW O. RICHARDSON

JACKSON COUNTY, MISSOURI. Six months after **Joseph Smith** organized the Church in **Fayette, New York**, he received a **revelation** stating that the City of **Zion**, a contemporary **New Jerusalem**, was to be built by the Latter-day **Saints** "on the borders by the **Lamanites**" (D&C 28:9). This revelation fostered an interest among the Saints to commence building the millennial Zion on the American frontier.

In the summer of 1831, Joseph Smith and others arrived at **Independence**, Jackson County. The **Prophet** identified **Missouri** as "the land of promise" and Independence as "the center place" of Zion, with a site for a **temple** just west of town (D&C 57:2–3). Before returning east, Joseph appointed officers to purchase land in Jackson County, establish a store and a Church press in Independence, and promote a systematic gathering of Church members to the county. During the next two years, the Latter-day **Saints** established five settlements west of Independence, where they practiced economic principles of **consecration**. Their press published *The Evening and Morning Star,* a religious newspaper, and was printing the **Book of Commandments**, a collection of revelations received by Joseph Smith.

Despite the Saints' enthusiasm for Jackson County, it proved to be a troublesome place for them. Rough-hewn Independence was a backward American outpost and a raw outfitting station for the **Santa Fe Trail**. The speech, manners, and customs typical of Latter-day Saints, most of whom were from the northeastern United States, were in striking contrast with the individualism and frequent lawlessness of the resident southern settlers. Moreover, some perceived the **Mormons** as possessing unconventional religious teachings and practices, which intensified feelings against the Latter-day Saints.

Violence erupted in the summer of 1833, after a citizens' manifesto was circulated, containing grievances against the Latter-day Saints over political, religious, economic, and social concerns, including a marked objection to their immigration to the county. In July, a strident body of more than 400 citizens met at the courthouse in Independence and savagely demonstrated against the Saints. They tarred and feathered **Bishop Edward Partridge** (the leading Church officer) and Charles Allen, tore down the Church printing house, and attacked the Mormon-owned store. The citizens believed that the only acceptable solution was for the

Latter-day Saints to leave the county, which, under duress, they agreed to do. The Saints hesitated in withdrawing, however, because state authorities recommended that they seek redress in the courts; consequently, the citizens undertook ruthless measures to drive them away.

Violence raged that fall as a mob attacked a Latter-day Saint settlement eight miles west of Independence. The mob destroyed several houses, whipped the men, and terrorized the women and children. In November, attacks on their settlements continued and disorder increased. Expecting protection in return, an armed company of Latter-day Saints turned over its weapons to the military authority at Independence. Thereafter, mobs fearlessly attacked unprotected villages and drove 1,200 suffering and unprepared Latter-day Saints from the county. Most Latter-day Saints fled northward and crossed the **Missouri River** into **Clay County**, where they spent the harsh winter in exile in makeshift shelters, awaiting deliverance.

SOURCES

Allen, James B., and Glen M. Leonard. *The Story of the Latter-day Saints.* 2d ed. Salt Lake City: Deseret Book, 1992. 69, 92–98.

Parkin, Max H. "Missouri's Impact on the Church." *Ensign* 9 (April 1979): 57–63.

Smith, Joseph. *History of The Church of Jesus Christ of Latter-day Saints.* Edited by B. H. Roberts. 2d ed. rev. 7 vols. Salt Lake City: The Church of Jesus Christ of Latter-day Saints, 1932–51. 1:372–440.

MAX H. PARKIN

JACOBSEN, FLORENCE S.

JACOBSEN, FLORENCE S. Florence Smith Jacobsen, the sixth general president of the **Young Women's Mutual Improvement Association,** was born in **Salt Lake City, Utah,** 7 April 1913. Her passion for Church history developed early in her life and shaped much of her service. Following a **mission** to **New York City** with her husband, Ted C. Jacobsen, Florence served on the YWMIA general board. Two years later, in 1961, she was called as the auxiliary's president. The YWMIA supervised the **Beehive, Mia Maid, Laurel,** and **Gleaner** classes as well as the Young Marrieds and Special Interests program. Working with the YMMIA leaders, Florence planned June **conferences** (Churchwide **auxiliary** leadership conferences held in **Salt Lake City**), served as associate general manager of the *Improvement Era,* and helped organize the **Mormon Youth Symphony.** When she learned that the **Lion House,** then under the jurisdiction of the YWMIA, was slated for destruction, she worked to save and restore the building. The 1969 YWMIA centennial was celebrated in the

Lion House, where **Brigham Young** had created the organization. Florence also restored or refurbished the homes of **Joseph Smith Sr.** (**Manchester, New York**), **Wilford Woodruff** (**Nauvoo, Illinois**), Brigham Young (Nauvoo, Illinois), and **Peter Whitmer Sr.** (**Fayette, New York**). A year after her release as president in 1972, Florence became Church curator (later director of the Arts and Sites Division of the Historical Department). She suggested building the **Museum of Church History and Art** and supervised the restoration of numerous historic sites. She retired from the position in 1985.

SOURCES

A Century of Sisterhood: Chronological Collage, 1869–1969. Salt Lake City: YWMIA, 1969.

Peterson, Janet, and LaRene Gaunt. *Keepers of the Flame: Presidents of the Young Women.* Salt Lake City: Deseret Book, 1993. 81–97.

JANET PETERSON

JAMAICA. Jamaica is the third largest island in the Caribbean and has a population that is 90% black. In 1853, missionaries were sent to the **West Indies** and labored in Jamaica. They experienced some success but were eventually driven from the island by mobs.

By 1970 several American Latter-day Saint families working on the island began worshipping together. In 1973 Brother Paul Schmeil introduced the gospel to Victor E. Nugent. On 20 January 1974, Victor and Verna Nugent, along with their son Peter, were the first Jamaicans baptized into the Church.

On 5 December 1978, **Elder M. Russell Ballard** dedicated Jamaica for the preaching of the gospel. In the year 2000, there were 4,240 members living in 2 districts and 16 **branches**.

SOURCES

Crockett, David R., and Victor E. Nugent. "LDS Church History in Jamaica." Manuscript.

Farr, Aaron F. Diary. LDS Church Archives, Salt Lake City.

Millett, Richard L. "Jamaica: A Tropical Paradise and the Beginning of the Work." Manuscript.

1999–2000 Church Almanac. Salt Lake City: Deseret News, 1998. 340.

DAVID R. CROCKETT

JAMES. See PETER, JAMES, AND JOHN.

JAPAN. On 4 February 1901, President **Lorenzo Snow** announced the call of **Elder Heber J. Grant** of the Quorum of the Twelve **Apostles** and three companions—Horace S. Ensign, Louis B. Kelsch, and 18-year-old Alma O. Taylor—to open the Japanese Mission. They arrived at Yokohama on 12 August 1901. On 1 September Elder Grant dedicated Japan for the preaching of the restored gospel.

Progress was slow, and in 1924 Heber J. Grant, as president of the Church, closed the mission. The most notable accomplishment of the mission was the publication of Alma O. Taylor's Japanese translation of the **Book of Mormon** in 1909. From 1924 to 1945, minimal Church activities were carried on in Japan, but some baptisms were performed in the late 1930s by Hilton A. Robertson, president of the **Japanese Mission in Hawaii**. The Church had little presence in Japan until **World War II** ended in August 1945.

Latter-day Saint servicemen recommenced missionary work in Japan after the war. The first baptisms were Tatsui and Chiyo Sato on 7 July 1946. They had been taught the gospel by Ray Hanks and C. Elliott Richards and were baptized by Richards and **Boyd K. Packer**, respectively. Brother Sato later retranslated the Book of Mormon and also translated the **Doctrine and Covenants** and the **Pearl of Great Price** into Japanese.

Members from the early mission commenced holding Sunday services shortly following the war. By the time Edward L. Clissold arrived in Japan as **mission president** in March 1948, 43 members and investigators were already holding **Sunday School meetings**. Five elders arrived on 26 June—Paul C. Andrus, Wayne McDaniel, Koji Okauchi, and brothers Harrison "Ted" and Raymond C. Price—to begin proselyting activities. Initial efforts brought considerable success.

While missionaries were working to establish a solid membership base among the Japanese in the early 1950s, the **Korean War** brought hundreds of Latter-day Saint servicemen to Japan and **Korea**. Mission president Vinal Mauss organized servicemen's groups in both countries. With the influence and teaching of **Latter-day Saint** military personnel, Koreans began to join the Church. This led to the opening of formal **missionary work** in Korea in April 1956. South Korea became a separate mission in 1962.

In 1965 mission president Dwayne N. Andersen led 164 Japanese **Saints** to the **Hawaii Temple**, the first of a number of such excursions.

That same year, **Adney Y. Komatsu**, the first person of Japanese ancestry to so serve, began his years as mission president. At the end of Komatsu's mission term, Japan was divided into two missions, the first of many such divisions. In 1975 Komatsu was called as an **assistant to the Twelve** and in 1976 to the First Quorum of the **Seventy**. He was the first person of Asian ancestry to become a general authority.

In March 1970 the Church opened an exhibition at Expo '70, the Osaka **World's Fair**. In that same month, two new missions were organized, and the Tokyo **Stake**, Japan's first, was created, with Kenji Tanaka as president. Five years later, from 8 to 10 August 1975, President **Spencer W. Kimball** presided over the first **area conference** in Japan. During that conference he announced the forthcoming **Tokyo Japan Temple**. It was dedicated 27 October 1980 by President Kimball.

On 1 October 1977, **Yoshihiko Kikuchi**, a native of Japan, was sustained to the First Quorum of the Seventy. He was the first native Asian general authority. In 1991 Tokyo became home to the Asia North Area presidency, an area that included Japan, Korea, and eastern Siberia. A major event after that time was a devastating earthquake in Kobe in January 1995, in which one member was killed and a number of members were left homeless. This crisis provided opportunity for the Church to provide much Christian service. In May 1996, President **Gordon B. Hinckley**, who had been influential in the history of the Church in Japan, visited the country, the first president of the Church to do so since President Kimball had visited in 1980. Two years later, on 7 May 1998, President Hinckley announced plans to build a **temple** at Fukuoka, on the western island of Kyushu. Construction began in the spring of 1999.

By the year 2000, Japan had eight missions and 110,987 members living in 30 stakes, 20 **districts**, and 317 **wards** and **branches**.

SOURCES

Britsch, R. Lanier. "The Blossoming of the Church in Japan." *Ensign* 22 (October 1992): 32–38.

———. *From the East: The History of the Latter-day Saints in Asia, 1851–1996*. Salt Lake City: Deseret Book, 1998. 43–169.

1999–2000 Church Almanac. Salt Lake City: Deseret News, 1998. 341–43.

R. LANIER BRITSCH

JAPANESE/CENTRAL PACIFIC MISSION IN HAWAII. In

November 1936, Church president **Heber J. Grant** announced the opening of the Japanese Mission in Hawaii and the call of Hilton A. and Hazel

Robertson to lead the **mission**. In 1924 President Grant had closed the Church's mission in **Japan** while Robertson was serving as president. The new mission, an extension of the Church's efforts in Japan, focused only on Japanese and Americans of Japanese ancestry. The missionaries did most of their teaching among teenagers and young adults who spoke English; nevertheless, they learned Japanese to communicate more effectively with the parental generation.

Although missionaries from this mission were not sent to open work in Japan after **World War II** (as many had hoped), they did teach the restored gospel to many young men and women who, after baptism, served in Japan. When the mission was combined with the Hawaiian mission in 1950, there were 671 members. This group, hardly more than a large ward, provided numerous Church leaders in **Hawaii** and Japan. Among them were Adney Y. Komatsu and Sam K. Shimabukuro, both of whom afterward served as general authorities of the Church, and Chieko Okazaki, who served as first **counselor** of the general **Relief Society** presidency. Many others served as missionaries in Japan, as **mission president** couples, and as **temple presidents and matrons**.

Source

Britsch, R. Lanier. *From the East: The History of the Latter-day Saints in Asia, 1851–1996.* Salt Lake City: Deseret Book, 1998. 71–79.

R. Lanier Britsch

JENSON, ANDREW. Assistant **Church historian** Andrew Jenson was born 11 December 1850 in Torslev, **Denmark**, to Christian Jenson and Kirsten Andersen. His parents joined the Church in 1854 and were among the first converts in their part of Denmark. Baptized 2 February 1859, Andrew emigrated with his **family** from Denmark in 1866. His **pioneer** journal provides rich details of the journey to **Utah**. In 1875 he married Kirsten Marie Pedersen and later Emma Howell and Bertha Howell. In 1879 he published *Joseph Smith's Levnetslob,* the first Church book published in Utah in a foreign language. He served many **missions** for the Church—both proselyting and historical gathering missions. His mission in 1888 to early Church history sites in **Missouri, Illinois, Ohio,** and **New York** with **Elders Edward Stevenson** and Joseph S. Black, laid a foundation for his future historical works. He was set apart by Elder **Franklin D. Richards** on 16 April 1891 as a historian in the Church. Andrew Jenson became the most traveled Church historian ever. His journals contain details about early Church history that would have otherwise been lost. His many historical works, including *Historical Record, Biographical Encyclopedia, Church Chronology, Encyclopedic History of the Church,* and others, laid a foundation upon which many subsequent historians have built. He died 18 November 1941 in **Salt Lake City.**

SOURCES

Jenson, Andrew. *Autobiography of Andrew Jenson.* Salt Lake City: Deseret News, 1938.
———. *Latter-day Saint Biographical Encyclopedia.* 4 vols. 1901–36. Reprint, Salt Lake City: Western Epics, 1971. 1:261–63.
Perkins, Keith W. *Andrew Jenson, Zealous Chronologist.* Provo, Utah: Brigham Young University, 1974.

KEITH W. PERKINS

JERUSALEM CENTER FOR NEAR EASTERN STUDIES. In October 1979, during a trip to Jerusalem to dedicate the newly created **Orson Hyde** Memorial Garden on the Mount of Olives, President **Spencer W. Kimball** announced that under direction of the **First Presidency, Brigham Young University** would build a center in Jerusalem with facilities to accommodate local LDS **branches,** BYU's travel study programs, and visitors. The center would be known as the Jerusalem Center for Near Eastern Studies.

Negotiations for the site and appropriate zoning and building permits extended from 1980 to 1984, as did the design and architectural work. Construction began in August 1984. So, too, did opposition to both the Center's construction and the formal presence of Latter-day **Saints** in the **Holy Land.** By December 1985, opposition had increased to the point that the Labor government faced a vote of no confidence in the Knesset. The immediate threat to the government was defused by the appointment of a committee of cabinet members, evenly divided between those for and those against the completion of the Center, who were to hold hearings and recommend a course of action for the government. At the same time, a Knesset subcommittee requested that the Center, Church, and university give an official promise not to proselyte **Jews** in **Israel.** BYU president **Jeffrey R. Holland** provided an official undertaking on behalf of the university to this effect in August 1985. The commitments in this undertaking were later incorporated in the land-lease document, which President Holland signed for the university and President **Howard W. Hunter** signed for the Church.

In spite of this assurance, virulent opposition continued, and in response, in May 1986, 154 members of the U.S. Congress sent a letter to Israel's prime minister and all members of the Knesset in support of the completion of the Center and BYU's continued activities in the Holy Land. Shortly afterward, Israel's attorney general issued a report concluding that there was no merit in charges that the Church and university had obtained a land-lease commitment in illegal or unethical ways, and the ministerial committee issued a recommendation that construction be allowed to continue. In response, the Israeli cabinet gave final authorization for a lease on the property to extend for 49 years, with the recommendation that there be formed a public activities review committee, consisting of members appointed by the city and national governments, which would oversee the Center's public activities for the first 10 years of the lease. Students moved into the Center in March 1987 while it was still under construction. The lease was signed in May 1988. Twelve months later, President Hunter returned to Jerusalem and dedicated the building.

The Center's site, on Mt. Scopus looking southwest down the Kidron Valley to the walled Old City and beyond, is stunning. Virtually every window in the building, whose eight stories step down the mountainside, frame a view of the Old City with the hills of Bethlehem on the far horizon. Particularly in the soft light of early evenings and mornings, the Old City is a glowing presence in the building. The Center, in turn, is a landmark of considerable distinction in Jerusalem with its modern arches, cream limestone, glass, and teak exterior, and masterful landscaping. Tens of thousands of individuals visit the building each year to enjoy tours, concerts, symposia, lectures, and the beauty, tranquillity, and peace the building exudes.

But for all of its beauty and its physical and cultural presence in Jerusalem, the Center's most important contribution is to the lives of some 800 BYU students who worship, study, reflect, and live within its walls each year. The Center's integrated curriculum—Old and New Testament and ancient and modern Near Eastern history and culture—is embedded in an intensive and rich field trip and cocurricular program that focuses on scriptural, historical, and cultural experiences. As students seek knowledge, understanding, and spirituality, they find themselves, they find the Lord, and they fall in love with the land, cultures, and peoples of the Near East.

SOURCE

Galbraith, David B., D. Kelly Ogden, and Andrew C. Skinner. *Jerusalem, the Eternal City.* Salt Lake City: Deseret Book, 1996. 450–73.

JAMES R. KEARL

JESUS CHRIST. Jesus Christ is the central figure in the doctrine and practices of The Church of Jesus Christ of Latter-day Saints. He is God the Second, the Redeemer (*TPJS*, 190). Through the scriptures of the **Restoration**, we come to know Jesus Christ as

1. *The Firstborn.* Modern **revelation** attests that Jesus was the firstborn spirit child of **God the Father** and thus the heir to all that God the Father possesses (D&C 93:21–22).

2. *Jehovah—the Great I AM.* Jesus was and is Jehovah, the Lord Omnipotent (Mosiah 3:5). In the premortal life, he volunteered to put into full effect all the terms and conditions of the Father's plan (Moses 4:1–4). It was Jehovah who manifested himself to the ancient prophets in both the old and new world (1 Ne. 19:8–10). Under the direction of the Father, he oversaw the creation of worlds without number (3 Ne. 9:15; D&C 76:24; Moses 1:33; 7:30).

3. *The Only Begotten in the Flesh.* Jesus is the Son of Man, meaning the Son of Man of Holiness (Moses 6:57). From Mary, a mortal woman, he inherited mortality, the capacity to die. From Elohim, his exalted Sire, he inherited the powers of immortality, the power to atone for the sins of mankind, to rise from the dead, and to initiate the rise from the grave of all mortals (John 10:17–18; 2 Ne. 2:8; Hel. 5:10; D&C 93:11).

4. *The Father and the Son.* Though it is true that the word *Father* is used in regard to Elohim as the Father of our spirits (Heb. 12:9), Jesus is also known as the Father—Father as Creator of the heavens and the earth (Alma 11:39), Father through spiritual rebirth (Mosiah 5:7; 15; D&C 25:1), and Father by divine investiture of authority.

5. *Gracious Savior.* The first words spoken by the Lord to **Joseph Smith** in this dispensation attest to the atoning mission of the Savior: "Joseph, my son, thy sins are forgiven thee. . . . Behold, I am the Lord of glory. I was crucified for the world that all those who believe on my name may have eternal life" (Backman, 157; spelling and punctuation standardized). Christ our Advocate pleads our cause before the Father (D&C 38:4; 45:3–5). The Atonement, truly infinite and eternal in scope (2 Ne. 25:16; Alma 34:9–14), reaches beyond this earth to all his creations (D&C 76:22–24, 40–42; Moses 1:32–35).

6. *The Deliverer among the disembodied.* Latter-day revelation certifies to the immortality of the soul and of the continuation of the work of salvation beyond the veil of death. It was revealed to President **Joseph F. Smith** that Jesus, between the time of His death and resurrection,

ministered in the postmortal spirit world. There the Master taught the gospel and organized his servants so that the word of truth could be carried to all who would repent and receive the gospel (D&C 138).

7. *The King of kings and Lord of lords.* The call of Joseph Smith signaled the reestablishment of the **kingdom of God** on earth, this time to remain forever. The work of restoration will continue into the Millennium. Jesus the Christ will then, in that day of peace and glory, reign as the Second David, the King of Israel and of all the earth, the King of kings (D&C 65:5–6).

Jesus Christ revealed himself, in company with his Eternal Father, to Joseph Smith in the **Sacred Grove** in the spring of 1820 (JS–H 1:17–18). He appeared to and conversed with the Prophet in the **vision of the three degrees of glory** (D&C 76:14) and in the **Kirtland Temple** (D&C 110:1–10). Further, he spoke again and again to and through the Prophet Joseph in the revelations we have in the **Doctrine and Covenants**. The divine word is delivered, repeatedly: "Listen to the voice of Jesus Christ, your Redeemer, the Great I AM" (D&C 29:1). And as the Lord was with Joseph Smith, so will he be with all of those called to shoulder the responsibility of leading his latter-day work. For example, in 1898 the Lord appeared to **Lorenzo Snow** in the **Salt Lake Temple**, directing him to proceed immediately with the organization of the **First Presidency**. President **Joseph Fielding Smith** testified: "I desire to say that no man of himself can lead this church. It is the Church of the Lord Jesus Christ; he is at the head. . . . If this were the work of man, it would fail, but it is the work of the Lord, and he does not fail. And we have the assurance that if we keep the commandments and are valiant in the testimony of Jesus and are true to every trust, the Lord will guide and direct us and his church in the paths of righteousness, for the accomplishment of all his purposes" (in CR, 113).

Latter-day Saints worship Christ the Son as he is acknowledged as the source of truth and redemption, as the light and life of the world, as the Perfect Example (2 Ne. 25:29; 3 Ne. 11:11; 27:27; D&C 93:12–20). Thus "we talk of Christ, we rejoice in Christ, we preach of Christ, . . . that our children may know to what source they may look for a remission of their sins" (2 Ne. 25:26). Joseph Smith stands as the preeminent prophetic witness and revealer of Christ to this dispensation. Through what the Prophet Joseph has made known, we are invited to come unto Christ—to learn of him, to listen to his words, to walk in the meekness of his Spirit (D&C 19:23)—and thereby grow into a meaningful spiritual union with that Lord who has purchased us with his blood (D&C 38:4).

SOURCES

Backman, Milton V., Jr. *Joseph Smith's First Vision*. Salt Lake City: Bookcraft, 1971.

Smith, Joseph. *Teachings of the Prophet Joseph Smith [TPJS]*. Selected by Joseph Fielding Smith. Salt Lake City: Deseret Book, 1938.

Smith, Joseph Fielding. Conference Report [CR] (April 1970): 113–14.

ROBERT L. MILLET

JESUS THE CHRIST. One of the great works on Latter-day Saint theology, *Jesus the Christ* was written by **Elder James E. Talmage**. The content of the book originated as a series of lectures, which Talmage began in 1904, on the life and mission of the Savior. The **First Presidency** asked Elder Talmage to write the lectures in book format. On 14 September 1914, Elder Talmage began preparing the manuscript but was constantly interrupted. Consequently, he was provided a room in the **Salt Lake Temple** to work on the manuscript. Working long hours every day, Elder Talmage finished the manuscript on 19 April 1915 in only seven months and five days. After a review by a committee of the First Presidency, and the **Quorum of the Twelve Apostles**, the book was published by the Church in 1916. *Jesus the Christ* details the Savior's mission and life from premortal life to his second coming.

SOURCE

Talmage, John R. *The Talmage Story: Life of James E. Talmage*. Salt Lake City: Bookcraft, 1972. 181–87.

MATTHEW O. RICHARDSON

JEWS. Latter-day Saint scriptures discuss the "return of the Jews" as part of the gathering of Israel and envision the partnership of "Ephraim" with "Judah" (Jews) in promulgating scriptures (2 Ne. 29) and building millennial capitals (Ether 13).

Contacts between Latter-day Saints and Jews began early. In 1836 **Joseph Smith** hired Cincinnati-based **Joshua Seixas** to teach Hebrew in **Kirtland, Ohio**. In 1841 **Elder Orson Hyde** traveled to the **Holy Land** and offered a dedicatory prayer on the Mount of Olives. More than a century later (1979), the Orson Hyde Memorial Garden was created to commemorate that event. In 1900 the Church donated land for **Salt Lake**

City's first synagogue, contributing to the Saints' positive relationship with Jews in **Utah**. Zionist migration to Palestine and the creation of modern Israel triggered conversionist expectations among Latter-day Saints. Early missionary efforts included proselyting among the Jews in **New York** from 1922 to 1932. Later the Church operated Jewish missions (1954–59) in seven U.S. cities. In 1959 Church officials directed that Jews not be targeted in proselyting. When signing the lease for **Brigham Young University's Jerusalem Center** (built 1984–87), Latter-day Saint leaders pledged not to proselyte in Israel.

SOURCES

Green, Arnold H. "Gathering and Election: Israelite Descent and Universalism in Mormon Discourse." *Journal of Mormon History* 25 (Spring 1999): 195–228.

———. "Jews in LDS Thought." *BYU Studies* 34, 4 (1994–95): 137–64.

———. "A Survey of LDS Proselyting Efforts to the Jewish People." *BYU Studies* 8 (Summer 1968): 427–43.

Madsen, Truman, ed. *Reflections on Mormonism: Judeo-Christian Parallels.* Provo, Utah: Religious Studies Center, Brigham Young University, 1978.

ARNOLD H. GREEN

JOHN. See PETER, JAMES, AND JOHN.

JOHN JOHNSON FARM. See JOHNSON FARM.

JOHNSON, BENJAMIN F.

Benjamin Franklin Johnson was a trusted friend and confidant of the Prophet **Joseph Smith** in **Nauvoo** and one of the youngest members of the **Council of Fifty**. Born 28 July 1818, in Pomfret, **New York**, he was the 10th of 16 children born to Ezekiel and Julia Hills Johnson. He was 13 years old in 1831, when most of his **family** joined the Church and moved to **Ohio**. There Benjamin met the Prophet Joseph Smith and became a careful observer of the events in **Kirtland**, **Missouri**, and **Illinois**. He became a defender of **plural marriage**, a principle he learned from the Prophet, and eventually married seven wives, who bore him 45 children.

In a meeting of the Quorum of the Twelve **Apostles** and the Council of Fifty prior to the **Martyrdom**, Benjamin heard the Prophet's final charge to the Twelve, when Joseph declared with great power that they now held the keys necessary to bear off the **kingdom of God** to all the world and that they would be accountable before God for doing so. After the Prophet's death, Benjamin witnessed the process of **succession** as he saw the mantle of the Prophet Joseph Smith fall upon **Brigham Young**.

During the next 60 years, under the leadership of President Young and his successors, Benjamin became a prominent colonizer in four **Utah** counties and in **Arizona** and **Mexico**. He served **missions** in the eastern **United States** and **Hawaii**. For the last 20 years of his life, Benjamin served as a **patriarch** in Arizona. Just before his death on 18 November 1905 in **Mesa, Arizona**, Benjamin F. Johnson testified that Joseph Smith and his successors were prophets of God.

SOURCES

Johnson, Benjamin F. *My Life's Review: The Autobiography of Benjamin F. Johnson.* Edited by Lyndon W. Cook and Kevin V. Harken. Provo: Grandin Book, 1997.

LeBaron, E. Dale. *Benjamin F. Johnson, Friend to the Prophets.* Provo: Grandin Book, 1997.

E. DALE LEBARON

JOHNSON, JOHN. John Johnson was the father of latter-day **apostles** **Luke** and **Lyman Johnson** and was affectionately known as Father Johnson among the **Saints**. He was born 11 April 1778, in Chesterfield, Cheshire, **New Hampshire**. His conversion to Mormonism was inspired by the miraculous **healing** of his wife, Elsa (or Alice). She was instantly healed of chronic rheumatism when **Joseph Smith** said, "Woman, in the name of the Lord **Jesus Christ** I command thee to be whole" (Smith, 1:216). From 12 September 1831 to 28 March 1832, Joseph Smith resided with Johnson in his farmhouse in **Hiram, Ohio**. Soon after the tarring and feathering of the Prophet near the house, Father Johnson sold his 304-acre farm, moved to **Kirtland, Ohio**, and opened an inn near Newel K. **Whitney's store**. He is remembered for displaying in his inn the mummies and papyri obtained from **Michael Chandler**, for his work on the **Kirtland Temple**, and for his appointment by **revelation** to the Kirtland **high council** (D&C 102:3). In September 1837 he was rejected as a high councilor and later became disaffected from the Church. This sequence of events gave rise to the false conclusion that he had been excommunicated. He died 30 July 1843 in Kirtland at age 64.

SOURCES

Johnson, Luke. "History of Luke Johnson by Himself." *Millennial Star* 26 (1864): 834–35.

Porter, Larry C., and Susan Easton Black, eds. *The Prophet Joseph Smith: Essays on the Life and Mission of Joseph Smith*. Salt Lake City: Deseret Book, 1988. 173.

SUSAN EASTON BLACK

JOHNSON, JOSEPH W. B. Joseph William Billy Johnson was born 17 December 1934, in Lagos, Nigeria, and became one of the earliest converts to the Church in **Ghana**. He is regarded as one of the Church's foremost **pioneers** there. He became converted to the gospel many years before he could be baptized, but over those years his great desire was to share this "good news" with his fellow Ghanaians.

Johnson was raised as a Catholic and believed that church's teachings to be true, but he felt that no religion could provide answers to the many troubling questions about life and its purpose. In 1964 Dr. A. Frank Mensah from Accra, Ghana, shared with him a copy of the **Book of Mormon**, the *Joseph Smith Testimony* **pamphlet**, and other Church literature. As Johnson prayerfully read this material, he felt the Spirit and became convinced that it was really the word of God. One morning while praying he saw the heavens open and angels singing praises to God; a voice said: "Johnson, Johnson, Johnson. If you will take up my work as I will command you, I will bless you and bless your land." With deep emotion he replied, "Lord, with thy help I will do whatsoever you will command me" ("Gospel," 41).

Brother Johnson felt that he was called by God to preach the restored gospel to the people of Ghana, and he immediately began teaching and testifying in public squares, on the streets, and in homes. Nevertheless, he was surprised that this message of truth brought such opposition and persecution. He received support and encouragement from President **David O. McKay** as well as from expatriate Latter-day Saints living in Ghana.

Through 14 years of preaching, Brother Johnson established ten congregations with more than a thousand followers, none of whom were yet baptized members of the Church. He testified that he had received divine guidance in his work and also sometimes manifestations through dreams or visions. He claimed to have seen **visions** of a deceased brother, as well as ancestors desiring **baptism for the dead** and teaching him the doctrine. Brother Johnson received spiritual strength from his dreams of the Prophet Joseph Smith and President Brigham Young, who also assured him that missionaries would soon come. Brother Johnson and many of his followers also saw the long-awaited arrival of the missionaries in dreams and described the coming event clearly for others.

At midnight on 9 June 1978, Brother Johnson heard a shortwave news broadcast from **England** that announced President **Spencer W. Kimball's** revelation that all worthy males could receive the priesthood. He burst into tears of joy, knowing that the Church would soon come to his land.

On 9 December 1978, six months after the announcement of the revelation that would open the floodgates for the Church to go to Africa, Brother Johnson was baptized and became Ghana's first **branch** president. In 1980 **Elders Boyd K. Packer** and **James E. Faust** organized the first two Ghanaian **stakes** in Accra and Cape Coast, the centers where Brother Johnson had earlier established his congregations. Johnson was later ordained Ghana's first stake **patriarch**.

SOURCES

"Gospel Pioneers in Africa." *Ensign* 20 (August 1990): 40–43.

LeBaron, E. Dale, ed. *"All Are Alike unto God."* Orem, Utah: Granite Publishing, 1998. 15–28.

Oral histories of early Church converts collected by E. Dale LeBaron. Copies at BYU Library, Provo, Utah; LDS Church Historical Library, Salt Lake City, Utah.

E. DALE LEBARON

JOHNSON, LUKE S. Luke Samuel Johnson, one of the original members of the **Quorum** of the Twelve **Apostles**, was born 3 November 1807, in Pomfret, Vermont. In the fall of 1831, Luke became acquainted with **Joseph Smith** while the Prophet was living in Luke's parents' home in **Hiram, Ohio**. Luke was baptized by the Prophet Joseph Smith and soon afterward filled a **mission** to southern **Ohio**.

On at least two occasions, Luke protected Joseph Smith from the designs of his enemies and once helped **Joseph Smith Sr.** avoid an illegal trial by telling the court jokes while Father Smith escaped through a window. On a mission through **Virginia** and **Kentucky** in 1832, Elder Johnson and two companions baptized more than one hundred persons. When the Quorum of the Twelve was first organized on 14 February 1835, Brother Johnson was chosen to be an **apostle**. He was disfellowshipped during the widespread **apostasy** resulting from the failure of the **Kirtland Safety Society** in 1837 and was excommunicated in 1838.

Brother Johnson was rebaptized in 1846 and traveled with **Brigham Young** the next year to **Utah**. He died 9 December 1861 in Salt Lake City.

SOURCES

Flake, Lawrence R. *Prophets and Apostles of the Last Dispensation.* Provo, Utah: Religious Studies Center, Brigham Young University, 2001. 363.

Smith, Calvin N. "Among First Apostles, 3 'Forgotten.'" *Church News,* 25 February 1989. 7.

LAWRENCE R. FLAKE

JOHNSON, LYMAN E. When the **Quorum** of the Twelve **Apostles** was organized in February 1835, Lyman Eugene Johnson was the first to be sustained a member of that body. Born 24 October 1811, in Pomfret, **Vermont**, he was only 23 years old at the time of his calling to the Twelve. He served several **missions** in the eastern states and one to **Nova Scotia**. He also participated in the march of **Zion's Camp**. In September 1837 he was disfellowshipped by his quorum, but upon his repentance and confession a few days later, he was reinstated. Not long thereafter he joined with those seeking to overthrow the Church in **Kirtland** and was excommunicated 13 April 1838. He died 20 December 1856, in a drowning accident near Prairie du Chien, **Wisconsin**.

SOURCES

Flake, Lawrence R. *Prophets and Apostles of the Last Dispensation.* Provo, Utah: Religious Studies Center, Brigham Young University, 2001. 363–64.

Smith, Calvin N. "Among First Apostles, 3 'Forgotten.'" *Church News,* 25 February 1989. 7.

LAWRENCE R. FLAKE

JOHNSON FARM. The John Johnson farm figured predominantly, if only briefly, in the early establishment of the Church. Sixteen sections of the **Doctrine and Covenants** and a significant portion of the revision of the **Bible** were received in this **Hiram, Ohio**, home, where several **conferences** of the Church were also held. Hiram was settled between 1815 and 1818 by a group of families from **Vermont**, including the **John Johnson** family (1818). When he built his frame house in 1828–29, it was the largest in the area. After **Joseph Smith Jr.** healed the rheumatic arm of Johnson's wife, Elsa (or Alice), in **Kirtland, Ohio**, the Johnson family were converted to the gospel, along with a friend and minister **Ezra Booth.**

On 12 September 1831, Joseph, Emma, and the Murdock twins (Joseph and Julia, infant children of **John Murdock** adopted by the Smiths) moved into the Johnson home. **Sidney Rigdon** moved into the log cabin across the street. They had come for a peaceful setting in which to work on the translation of the **Bible.** In November a group of priesthood brethren gathered in the Johnson home and voted to print the **Book of Commandments.**

Unfortunately, the Johnson farm did not long remain a peaceful setting. By September Ezra Booth and **Symonds Ryder,** another influential leader in Hiram, had apostatized. They organized serious **persecutions** against the Prophet following their separation from the Church, and on 1 December 1831 the Lord commanded Joseph to stop translating and meet his enemies in public and in private to confound them (D&C 71). A series of debates followed.

On 16 February 1832, Joseph Smith and Sidney Rigdon received the **vision of the three degrees of glory** in an upper room of the Johnson home (D&C 76). On 24 March a mob led by Ryder tarred and feathered Joseph and Sidney, dragging them from their homes in the middle of the night. Five days later, 10-month-old Joseph Murdock died, in part due to exposure he endured that night.

In the beginning of April, Joseph and Sidney traveled to **Missouri** while Emma and Julia Murdock relocated to Kirtland. During the winter of 1832–33, the Johnsons sold their farm of 304 acres in Hiram for $3,000, which was donated to the Church, and moved to Kirtland. John Johnson's sons **Luke** and **Lyman** later became members of the **Quorum** of the Twelve **Apostles,** and his daughter Marinda married **Orson Hyde.**

In 1956 the Church bought the Johnson home and 160 acres of land. The house was restored as a **historical site,** and the land became one of the Church's **welfare program** farms, producing strawberries (86,000 pounds in 1999) and several varieties of apples.

───────

SOURCE

Documents in the collection of Richard L. McClellan, resident of Chesterland, Ohio.

RICHARD L. MCCLELLAN

JOHNSTON'S ARMY. In 1857 President **James Buchanan** sent 2,500 soldiers to **Utah** Territory under the command of General William S.

Harney to put down a supposed rebellion of Latter-day Saints. Recruited from many enlistment centers in the East, the large army consisted of Americans, Germans, Irish, and others. Harney was replaced by General Albert Sidney Johnston, from whom the army got its name.

The first companies left **Fort Leavenworth** over a period of weeks in May 1857. They included companies of infantry, artillery, and dragoons. Supply wagons and vehicles carrying officers' wives were part of the entourage, which was several miles long.

When the **Latter-day Saints** in Utah received word that the army was coming, they feared for their lives. On 15 September 1857, territorial governor **Brigham Young** declared martial law and mobilized the local militia, known as the Nauvoo Legion. Major **Lot Smith** led a band of Latter-day Saints to eastern Utah, now **Wyoming**, with orders to harass the approaching army. He was told to destroy the trains and stampede the animals but to take no lives. He succeeded in burning more than 50 wagons and capturing more than one thousand head of cattle. These tactics delayed the army and caused them to winter in Wyoming before entering the **Salt Lake Valley**. In the meantime mediators from **Washington, D.C.**, met with Latter-day Saint officials and negotiated a peaceful solution to the crisis.

After wintering at Camp Scott near **Fort Bridger**, Johnston's army marched into **Salt Lake City**, halting just long enough for army bands to play several patriotic and army tunes. It took all day for the whole force to march through the city and across the Jordan River, where they camped at about present-day Twenty-first South and Redwood Road. Following a few days of rest, the men were ordered on to Cedar Valley, where they set up **Camp Floyd**. By 1861 all troops had been reassigned to other areas, and the camp was shut down. Many of the soldiers and officers went on to serve in the **Civil War**.

SOURCES

Furniss, Norman F. *The Mormon Conflict, 1850–1859*. New Haven: Yale University Press, 1960.

Godfrey, Audrey M. "A Social History of Camp Floyd, Utah Territory, 1858–1861." Master's thesis, Utah State University, 1989.

Langley, Harold D., ed. *To Utah with the Dragoons*. Salt Lake City: University of Utah Press, 1974.

Moorman, Donald R., and Gene R. Sessions. *Camp Floyd and the Mormons: The Utah War*. Salt Lake City: University of Utah Press, 1992.

AUDREY M. GODFREY

JOHNSTON'S ATOLL. An island in the North Pacific about a third of the way from Hawaii to the Marshall Islands, Johnston's Atoll has an area of 2.8 square kilometers. No indigenous people live on the island, but some 1,200 U.S. military personnel and civilians are stationed there. There were 17 Latter-day Saints organized into 1 branch during the year 2000.

EMILY C. ZEIGLER

JOHN THE BAPTIST. Because John the Baptist was a descendant of Aaron through his priestly father, Zacharias, and his mother, Elisabeth (Luke 1:5), he was a natural heir to the keys and powers of the Aaronic Priesthood. He was the epitome of the law of Moses, which existed to bring people to Christ (Gal. 3:24). His lineage, premortal foreordination, and earthly ordination (D&C 84:28) made him the Elias to prepare the way for the Messiah, proclaim his divinity, and baptize him. John performed no miracles (John 10:41); his mission was to identify the Messiah to the Jews and prepare them to receive salvation through Jesus Christ. Most, if not all, of the Twelve Apostles were first tutored by John. Jesus praised him as a shining light (John 5:33–35) and as more than a prophet (Luke 7:24–28). At age 32 John was beheaded by Herod's order (Mark 6:17–29); he was resurrected after Jesus' resurrection (D&C 133:55). Under the direction of Peter, James, and John, the resurrected John the Baptist ordained Joseph Smith and Oliver Cowdery to the Aaronic Priesthood 15 May 1829, near Harmony, Pennsylvania. The powers and keys of the ancient Aaronic Priesthood were thus established on earth in the dispensation of the fulness of times and are operative in the Church (D&C 13; 27:7–8; 84:26–28; 107:1; JS–H 1:68–72).

SOURCE

Matthews, Robert J. *A Burning Light: The Life and Ministry of John the Baptist.* Provo, Utah: Brigham Young University Press, 1972.

ROBERT J. MATTHEWS

JOHN THE REVELATOR, See PETER, JAMES, AND JOHN.

JOHN WHITMER HISTORICAL ASSOCIATION. Organized in 1973, the John Whitmer Historical Association promotes the study of the history of the Reorganized Church of Jesus Christ of Latter Day Saints, as well as some early **Mormon** history. Meetings are open to all and are held annually on the last full weekend in September in various locations and historic sites important to the **Restoration**. The *John Whitmer Historical Association Journal* is published yearly and includes scholarly papers, book reviews, and other features. A newsletter is published several times a year, and a web page is also sponsored on the Internet. Scholarship grants are offered to students of Restoration history.

BARBARA J. BERNAUER

JONES, DAN. One of the great missionaries of the Church, Dan Jones was born 4 August 1810, in Halkyn, Flintshire, North **Wales**, to Thomas Jones, a lead miner, and Ruth Roberts. He began a life of sailing at about age 17. He married Jane Melling on 3 January 1837, and by 1840 they had moved to **St. Louis, Missouri**. Skeptical of the many negative reports about the Latter-day Saints, Jones sought out the missionaries. He was baptized in the icy waters of the **Mississippi River** on 19 January 1843; three months later he met the Prophet **Joseph Smith** while landing *The Maid of Iowa* (a steamboat in which he owned half interest) at **Nauvoo**.

Jones was with the Prophet Joseph in the **Carthage Jail** the night before the **Martyrdom**. He was the recipient of the Prophet's last recorded prophecy—that he (Jones) would not be killed by the enemy and that he would return to Wales and fulfill the mission to which he had been called earlier. He survived three attempts on his life during the next 36 hours and eventually served two **missions** to Wales. He is credited with baptizing about 2,000 people there. He died 3 January 1862 in **Provo, Utah**.

His first wife, Jane, preceded him in death. His second wife, Elizabeth Jones Lewis, and his third wife, Mary Matilda LaTrielle, both survived him, as did six children, two by each of the three wives.

SOURCES

Dennis, Ronald D. *The Call of Zion: The Story of the First Welsh Mormon Emigration.* Provo, Utah: Religious Studies Center, Brigham Young University, 1987.

——, ed. and trans. *Prophet of the Jubilee.* Provo, Utah: Religious Studies Center, Brigham Young University, 1997.

——. *Welsh Mormon Writings from 1844 to 1862: A Historical Bibliography.* Provo, Utah: Religious Studies Center, Brigham Young University, 1988.

Jenson, Andrew. *Latter-day Saint Biographical Encyclopedia.* 4 vols. 1901–36. Reprint, Salt Lake City: Western Epics, 1971. 3:659.

RONALD D. DENNIS

JONES, DANIEL W. Daniel Webster Jones, a heroic rescuer of the 1856 Martin Handcart Company, ranks high in the annals of Latter-day Saint stalwarts. Born 26 August 1830, in Booneslick, Missouri, Jones joined the Missouri Volunteers with Colonel Alexander Doniphan in the Mexican War. After the war in 1850, he came into contact with the Latter-day Saints when he accidentally shot himself while herding sheep near present-day Green River, Utah, and was taken by his friends to the closest Mormon settlement, Spanish Fork in Utah Valley. His life was saved by the efforts of Bishop and Sister Isaac Higbee. Later Daniel found work in Manti, Utah, and under the tutelage of Isaac Morley, joined the Church, being baptized in icy water in the middle of the winter.

In 1856, when the call was sounded for volunteers to rescue handcart pioneers, Daniel was among the first to respond. He had been shown extraordinary kindness, and now it was his turn to repay. With three brethren he found the Martin Company 16 miles above the Platte River Bridge near present-day Casper, Wyoming. Brigham Young asked Daniel and his companions to remain and guard supplies that were left behind.

Jones later became a tireless settler and missionary in the Church. He settled Jonesville (near Mesa, Arizona), was the first missionary and later the first president of the Mexican Mission (1876–77), and was the first to translate portions of the Book of Mormon into Spanish. Jones died 20 (or 29) April 1915, in Lehi/Mesa, Arizona.

SOURCES

Stegner, Wallace. *The Gathering of Zion.* Lincoln: University of Nebraska Press, 1992. 260–75.

Tullis, F. Lamond. "Early Mormon Exploration and Missionary Activities in Mexico." *BYU Studies* 23 (Summer 1982): 289–310.

JOHN M. BECK

JORDAN. In 1989 Jordan became the first Arab country to conclude a formal agreement with the Church, granting permission to lease property, engage in humanitarian projects, sponsor educational programs, and promote cultural exchanges. This agreement was the result of positive relations between the Jordanian ambassador to the United States, Muhammad Kamal, and Latter-day Saint officials at Brigham Young University and Church headquarters.

At the suggestion of Kamal (who was later appointed to the Jordanian senate by King Hussein) and with his personal intervention, the Church signed an agreement with the Jordanian government to establish the Center for Cultural and Educational Affairs in the capital city, Amman, where the Church leased and renovated a villa (the former Swiss embassy) in the diplomatic district of Jebel Amman to serve as the site for the Center. The **First Presidency** appointed Vernon Tipton, a retired BYU professor, to be the first director of the Center. Tipton and his wife, Norma, served from January 1989 until their evacuation from Jordan when the Gulf War began in August 1990. The Center was closed upon their departure and remained inoperative until February 1992. Subsequent directors were Paul and Daphne Sharp (February 1992–July 1993), William and Michele Wilson (August 1993–July 1995), James and Diane Toronto (August 1995–June 1998), and Thomas and Diane Kay (beginning June 1998). At the time the Center was established, it was the only Latter-day Saint building in the **Middle East** publicly displaying the name of the Church.

The presence of the Center has opened the way for increased cooperation and interaction between the Church and Jordanian institutions. The Center has coordinated academic agreements and cultural exchanges between BYU and the University of Jordan and Yarmouk University; given ongoing humanitarian assistance to the Soldier's Family Welfare Society (a charitable organization that provides economic, medical, and educational assistance to poor families in Zarqa); started community health programs in Bakaa, a Palestinian refugee camp north of Amman; overseen admissions procedures and scholarship opportunities for Jordanian students applying to BYU; and arranged for performances of BYU musical groups in the national Jordanian Jarash Festival and in the Royal Cultural Center. As in other Middle Eastern Islamic countries, the Church strictly observes a nonproselyting policy but is allowed to provide religious services as part of the Christian community. In 1998 services were held in three cities—Amman, Irbid, and Husn—for approximately 100 members, most of whom were European, Asian, and American expatriates and Arab (Jordanian, Egyptian, and Iraqi) Christians.

SOURCES

Interviews by the author with Muhammad Kamal, Vernon and Norma Tipton, and William and Michele Wilson.

Correspondence and files in the Center for Cultural and Educational Affairs, Amman, Jordan.

JAMES A. TORONTO

JOSEPH, CITY OF. See NAUVOO, ILLINOIS.

JOSEPH FIELDING SMITH INSTITUTE FOR LATTER-DAY SAINT HISTORY. The primary responsibility of **Brigham Young University's** Joseph Fielding Smith Institute for Latter-day Saint History is to research, write, and publish Latter-day Saint history from the perspective of faith and according to the highest scholarly standards. In 1972 the **Church Historian's Office** was reorganized into the Historical Department of the Church, and **Leonard J. Arrington**, a historian from Utah State University, was called to head the new history division. He gathered a staff and over the next eight years launched an ambitious program of scholarly publication, producing numerous books and articles, contributing frequently to Church publications, and launching an extensive oral history program.

It was decided in 1980 that a university would provide a better setting for research and publication, so the history division became the Smith Institute and was moved to BYU. Arrington continued to serve as director until 1986, when Ronald K. Esplin succeeded him. In 1999 the Institute's organization was broadened. Esplin created an executive committee of BYU faculty members chaired by Richard L. Bushman, to direct the Institute's scholarly program. The Institute became a center with expanded resources that helped support a network of Latter-day Saint scholars. To promote the publication and marketing of quality history and biography, the Institute added a publishing division under John W. Welch of *BYU Studies* and formalized an alliance with **Deseret Book Company**. A revitalized collaboration with the Historical Department of the Church increased resources available for documentary editing, one of the Institute's major emphases.

Although the Smith Institute faculty members taught history and Church history, their principal assignment remained the scholarly research and writing about the Latter-day Saint past. From time to time other faculty members also served with the Institute.

SOURCES

Arrington, Leonard J. *Adventures of a Church Historian.* Urbana: University of Illinois Press. 1998.

Esplin, Ronald K., comp. *Celebrating the LDS Past: Essays Commemorating the 20th Anniversary of the 1972 Founding of the LDS Church Historical Department's "History Division."* Provo, Utah: Joseph Fielding Smith Institute for Church History, Brigham Young University. 1992.

RONALD K. ESPLIN

JOSEPH SMITH, PRESIDENTIAL CAMPAIGN OF. See **PRESIDENTIAL CAMPAIGN OF JOSEPH SMITH.**

JOSEPH SMITH–HISTORY. Joseph Smith–History (JS–H) is a section of the **Pearl of Great Price** that records excerpts from the **Prophet Joseph Smith's** official testimony and history. He began to prepare these excerpts in 1838, and they were published serially under the title "**History of the Church**" in the *Times and Seasons* in **Nauvoo, Illinois**, beginning 15 March 1842. This autobiographical account begins by introducing briefly the Prophet's ancestry, birth, and **family** and religious circumstances. It then describes some of the Prophet's most significant experiences associated with the early period of the **restoration** of the gospel, from the spring of 1820 through May 1829. These include the **First Vision**, in which he saw **God the Father** and **Jesus Christ**; the persecution he endured as certain professors of religion learned of his experiences; visitations to the Prophet by the angel **Moroni**; his receiving the **gold plates**; his early associations with **Martin Harris** and **Oliver Cowdery**; and the restoration of the **Aaronic Priesthood** as well as the **ordinance** of baptism.

In 1851 **Elder Franklin D. Richards**, then an apostle and president of the **British Mission**, collected and published materials that he called the "Pearl of Great Price." As he indicated in the preface to the first edition, he did this so that Church members might have greater access to the priceless truths and early documents of the Restoration and thereby be better able to defend their faith. In this "choice selection" Elder Richards included excerpts from Joseph Smith's official history.

Joseph Smith–History became officially accepted **scripture** when Church members voted to canonize the Pearl of Great Price at the October 1880 **general conference**. For several years, Joseph Smith–History was published separately as a pamphlet entitled *Joseph Smith's Own Story* and was used as a missionary tract. The same text is still used as a missionary brochure under the title of *The Testimony of the Prophet Joseph Smith*.

SOURCES

Clark, James R. *The Story of the Pearl of Great Price.* Salt Lake City: Bookcraft, 1965. 186–98, 201–5.

Hunter, Milton R. *Pearl of Great Price Commentary.* Salt Lake City: Bookcraft, 1963. 225–26.

Jessee, Dean C. "The Writing of Joseph Smith's History." *BYU Studies* 11 (Summer 1971): 439–73.

ANDREW C. SKINNER

JOSEPH SMITH HOMES, NEW YORK. Two homes built by the Joseph Smith Sr. family—a log house near their farm in **Manchester, New York**, and a frame house on the farm—were settings for significant events in the **restoration** of the gospel.

Constructed from 1818 to 1819, the one-and-one-half-story log home had a kitchen, "best room," and a bedroom, as well as sleeping rooms above. The Smiths were residing there when the **First Vision** occurred (1820), when the angel **Moroni** appeared to Joseph Jr. in an upstairs bedroom (1823), and when the printer's copy of the **Book of Mormon** manuscript was recorded by **Oliver Cowdery** (1829–30).

The Smiths moved into their one-and-a-half-story, New England-style, central-chimney frame house in October and November of 1825. They never completed it. They lost title to the farm in December 1825 but remained for four years as renters. For safekeeping the Book of Mormon plates were placed under the brick hearth in the "west room," parlor (1827). In this home Oliver Cowdery obtained his testimony of Joseph Smith's divine call. During the spring of 1829, the Smiths moved back into the log home, where Hyrum and his family were living.

The log and frame homes and their adjoining outbuildings, orchard, fencing, gardens, and woodlands were restored by the Church to their 1820s character. The project was completed in the year 2000.

SOURCES

Berge, Dale L. "Archaeological Work at the Smith Log Home." *Ensign* 15 (August 1985): 24–26.

Enders, Donald L. "A Snug Log House." *Ensign* 15 (August 1985): 14–23.

———."Two Significant Sites of the Restoration." *Ensign* 28 (September 1998): 30–37.

DONALD L. ENDERS

JOSEPH SMITH–MATTHEW. See JOSEPH SMITH TRANS-LATION OF THE BIBLE.

JOSEPH SMITH MEMORIAL BUILDING. The Joseph Smith Memorial Building, built in 1911 as the **Hotel Utah**, opened in 1993 after extensive remodeling. The building's classic revival architecture is richly ornamented on both the interior and exterior. Original features of the structure were carefully preserved to maintain the look and feel of the original building. The ornate columns, plaster moldings, and finishes of the original spaces were retained in the lobby and meeting rooms on the street and mezzanine levels. All of the guest rooms were removed to build modern offices for Church departments. The Lafayette Ballroom was made into a chapel for worship services of downtown congregations, and the Grand Ballroom was remodeled to accommodate a 500-seat theater for showing Church films (the first was *Legacy*). The tenth floor was entirely removed and rebuilt with two public restaurants and reception accommodations. The ninth floor has additional reception rooms with a view toward **Temple Square**. This mixed-use facility also houses a computer center for family history research and an outlet store for the Distribution Center.

SOURCE

Jackson, Roger P. "The Joseph Smith Memorial Building: The Renovation of a Utah Landmark." *Heritage: The Utah Heritage Foundation Newsletter* 27 (November–December 1993): 5–10.

ROGER P. JACKSON

JOSEPH SMITH TRANSLATION OF THE BIBLE. The Joseph Smith Translation of the Bible is a revelatory translation of the King James Version. The **Prophet Joseph Smith** began the work in June 1830, being divinely commissioned (D&C 35:20; 76:15–18). He spoke of the translation as a "branch of [his] calling" as a prophet (Smith, 1:238). He said the translation came "by the power of God" (Manuscript, 1). Most of the translation had been accomplished by 2 July 1833; nevertheless, the Prophet continued to edit and improve the text, working to prepare a manuscript for the press up until the time of his death in 1844. It is probable that further refinements would have been made if he had lived to publish the entire work. A few extracts were published during the Prophet's lifetime in *The Evening and the Morning Star*, the *Times and Seasons*, the **Lectures on Faith**, and on a single-page tract.

The Prophet's translation of the **Bible** had a direct and substantial effect on Church history, doctrine, and official **literature**. Joseph Smith and his scribes, consisting at various times of **Oliver Cowdery**, **John Whitmer**, **Sidney Rigdon**, **Emma Smith**, and **Frederick G. Williams**, devoted much time and energy to making the translation while living at **Harmony, Pennsylvania**; **Fayette, New York**; **Kirtland, Ohio**; **Hiram, Ohio**; and **Nauvoo, Illinois**. Because it was a day-to-day activity, the translation is mentioned frequently in the seven-volume *History of the Church* (for example, *HC*, 1:131–33, 170, 211, 215, 219, 238, 242,

245, 253, 255, 273, 295, 322, 324, 331, 341, 365, 368–69; 4:137, 164, 187, 493, 517–18; 6:164–65; 7:260), in the **Doctrine and Covenants**, and in early Church **magazines**.

Translating the Bible was evidently a learning experience for the Prophet, for many **revelations** containing clarification of doctrine were received in connection with various biblical passages encountered during the translation. Entire sections of the Doctrine and Covenants, such as 76, 77, and 91, as well as parts of many other sections, were received in the process.

The 467-page manuscript prepared by the Prophet and his scribes is helpful in determining the proper historical role of the Joseph Smith Translation. Several parts of the manuscript contain dates and geographical locations showing when and where particular parts of the Bible were being translated, thus making it possible for us to see the chronological relationship to the Doctrine and Covenants. Occasionally a doctrinal concept is expressed in the manuscript at an earlier date than the same concept appears in in the Doctrine and Covenants. For example, the manuscript for the Prophet's translation of Genesis 17:11, written in early 1831, contains information about children becoming accountable at eight years of age. This is similar to the teaching of Doctrine and Covenants 68:25–28, dated November 1831. It is easily discerned that the age of accountability was known to the Prophet through the translation of Genesis more than six months before it appeared in the Doctrine and Covenants. That the translation often came first suggests primacy and originality and gives it a dignity that would have been overlooked if we did not know of the dates in the manuscript.

Specific instructions concerning the JST were given to Joseph by revelation and cited in the Doctrine and Covenants. Certain passages speak of relevant and practical issues, such as which parts of the Bible to translate next (45:60–62; 90:13), which parts not to translate (91:1–6), where the Prophet should live so as to be able to translate (41:7), when to stop temporarily (37:1), and who should serve as scribe (35:20; 47:1). The Lord gave encouragement to persist and continue until the translation was finished (73:3–4), commandments to hasten in the work (93:53), and finally, instruction to print the translation (94:10; 104:58; 124:89). As the early revelations in the Doctrine and Covenants dealt with the translation and publication of the **Book of Mormon**, so the later revelations dealt with the translation and publication of the Joseph Smith Translation.

The **Pearl of Great Price** is also enriched by the Joseph Smith

Translation and contains two substantial excerpts from it: the **Book of Moses** (27 pages) and Joseph Smith–Matthew (more than 3 pages). These two documents are rich in doctrinal and theological information.

In addition to having an impact on the history, doctrine, and **scripture** of the Church, the printed Joseph Smith Translation (a publication of the Reorganized Church of Jesus Christ of Latter Day Saints) is an effective source of spiritual knowledge, enabling readers to better understand the Bible. The Joseph Smith Translation contains at least 3,410 verses rendered differently from their counterparts in the King James Version. These are additional verses or enlargements of existing verses. The account of Enoch in Joseph Smith Translation Genesis 6 and 7 (Moses 6–7) contains 5,200 more words about Enoch than the King James Version does. One Old Testament book is omitted in the Joseph Smith Translation because, the manuscript states, The Songs of Solomon are "not inspired." The biblical messages are often clarified, made more consistent, and focused doctrinally.

More than 700 passages from the Joseph Smith Translation are provided in the footnotes and the appendix of the Latter-day Saint edition of the King James Version, first issued in 1979. A comparison of the texts of these passages with the King James Version soon demonstrates the valuable doctrinal contribution of the Joseph Smith Translation. The Joseph Smith Translation restores a great deal of scripture and doctrine lost from the Bible through the centuries, as specified in 1 Nephi 13 and Moses 1:40–41.

The manuscript of the Joseph Smith Translation and the King James Version used by the Prophet Joseph Smith were retained by the Prophet's **family** after his death and are now the property of the **Reorganized Church of Jesus Christ of Latter Day Saints** in **Independence, Missouri**. It is by their generosity that scholars have been permitted to use the materials in recent years.

Although not the official Bible of The Church of Jesus Christ of Latter-day Saints, the Joseph Smith Translation is a valuable source of biblical understanding. It is the most effective Bible in the world in bearing witness of the Lord **Jesus Christ**. That the Prophet Joseph Smith could produce such a work is tangible evidence that he was inspired by the same Lord Jesus Christ.

SOURCES

Joseph Smith Translation Manuscript. Reorganized Church of Jesus Christ of Latter Day Saints Archives, Independence, Missouri.

Matthews, Robert J. "A Plainer Translation," *Joseph Smith's Translation of the Bible: A History and Commentary.* Provo, Utah: Brigham Young University Press, 1975.

Millet, Robert L., and Robert J. Matthews. *Plain and Precious Truths Restored.* Salt Lake City: Bookcraft, 1995.

Smith, Joseph. *History of The Church of Jesus Christ of Latter-day Saints.* Edited by B. H. Roberts. 2d ed. rev. 7 vols. Salt Lake City: The Church of Jesus Christ of Latter-day Saints, 1932–51. 1:60–61.

ROBERT J. MATTHEWS

JOURNAL OF BOOK OF MORMON STUDIES. The *Journal of Book of Mormon Studies* is a biannual scholarly periodical published by the **Foundation for Ancient Research and Mormon Studies (FARMS)**. While the *Journal* is intended to communicate with the average nonacademic reader, it is still designed to serve the academic community and to shed fresh light on the **Book of Mormon** by encouraging and publishing scholarly studies. Each issue includes several regular features: "Reports and Commentary on the News," "Names in the Book of Mormon," "Answers to Book of Mormon Inquiries," and reports on related research.

M. GERALD BRADFORD

JOURNAL OF DISCOURSES. The 26-volume *Journal of Discourses* contains stenographic reports of sermons of Church leaders and others, given between 1851 and 1886. It was published in England and originally issued twice monthly in individual numbers. Each volume consists of a 16-page signature (the first dated 1 November 1853), with the intent that the 24 numbers would be bound together at the end of the year, producing a single volume.

Topics of the reports cover a multitude of subjects, including practical counsel. Nevertheless, most of the discourses contain historical and doctrinal themes. A **First Presidency** letter, dated 1 June 1853, appeared in the first volume and provided the historical background for the appearance of the *Journal.* The letter indicated that English convert **George D. Watt**, at the behest of **Brigham Young**, learned shorthand so he could report "the public Sermons, Discourse, Lectures, &c., delivered by the Presidency, the Twelve, and others" in **Salt Lake City**. Watt proposed "to publish a *Journal* of these Reports, in England, for the benefit of the **Saints** at large." The First Presidency requested the Latter-day Saints' cooperation in the "purchase and sale" of the *Journal* to help sustain Watt in his services.

During the *Journal's* history of more than 30 years, several reporters and publishers continued the tradition of providing published copies of the talks of Church leaders for an increasing membership. Since the discourses are not canonized, they contain less-than-official statements on policies and doctrines of the Church. Nevertheless, the *Journal* constitutes an important source on what LDS leaders considered timely and important during this critical period of Church history. Because copies of the *Journal* had become quite rare in the first half of the twentieth century, a photo lithographic reprint was released in 1956, bringing the reports back into circulation for another generation of interested readers.

SOURCE

Watt, Ronald G. "Journal of Discourses." *Encyclopedia of Mormonism.* Edited by Daniel H. Ludlow. 4 vols. New York: Macmillan, 1992. 2: 769–70.

RICHARD NEITZEL HOLZAPFEL

JOURNAL OF MORMON HISTORY. The *Journal of Mormon History* is a scholarly **periodical** devoted to **Mormon** history. It publishes articles that bring to light important information regarding the Mormon experience. Not many years after the founding of the **Mormon History Association** in 1965, its officers began discussing the feasibility of publishing a **journal** that would reflect the work of only the best Mormon **historians**. Such discussions continued until 1974, when **Weber State University** history professor Richard W. Sadler was appointed editor of an annual journal that would be funded by subscription and sponsored by the MHA. With the help of **Brigham Young University** history professors Thomas G. Alexander and James B. Allen, as well as historians Maureen Ursenbach and Glen M. Leonard, the 72-page *Journal* appeared that year, containing four articles.

Since 1980 the *Journal* has published the O. C. Tanner lecture, which has been delivered at the annual meetings of the Mormon History Assocation by some of the nation's most illustrious scholars of religion and history. The *Journal* also encourages and publishes review articles and bibliographical essays comparing and evaluating work on a given topic. In 1992 the MHA decided to publish the *Journal* biannually. It more than doubled in size with the addition of letters to the editor, book reviews, and advertising.

SOURCE

Bitton, Davis. "Taking Stock: The Mormon History Association after Twenty-Five Years." *Journal of Mormon History* 17 (1991): 1–27.

KENNETH W. GODFREY

JOURNALS. The terms *journal, diary,* and *daybook* refer to a personal record of one's activities kept day by day, or at least recorded soon after the events described. By contrast, *memoirs, reminiscences,* and *autobiographies,* with their different shades of meaning, are retrospective accounts looking back over one's life. From the beginning of the Church in 1830, journals were kept, with a strong conviction that the events they recorded were of great significance. "We urge every person in the Church to keep a diary or a journal from youth up, all through life," said President **Spencer W. Kimball** at **general conference** in October 1977.

One of the most common types of journal kept within **Latter-day Saint** culture is the missionary journal, as hundreds of thousands of missionaries, following instructions, have dutifully recorded their experiences while serving full-time **missions**. But daily records are not limited to missions. Numerous journals recount exploration, ocean and overland journeys, the establishment of settlements, ecclesiastical and political events, and the details of daily life. Whether or not the journal includes any emotions, reflection, or introspection depends entirely on the diarist. Presidents and **apostles**, from **Joseph Smith** to the present, have kept journals. Of great value is the journal of **Wilford Woodruff**, kept from his conversion in 1834 to his death in 1898. Ordinary Latter-day Saints have also kept journals that tell the reader much about what life was like in their particular settings. Journals kept by Latter-day Saint women are often especially poignant in recounting the countless challenges of everyday life and the ups and downs of emotion they experienced.

The value of keeping personal journals is evident on at least three levels. First, the journal keeper becomes more conscious of activities, is sometimes able to answer questions or resolve disputes by bringing forth specific entries, and can, if desired, relive experiences that otherwise would be forgotten. Second, a journal helps families appreciate the challenges and achievements in the lives of their parents or grandparents and facilitates the perpetuation of both life experiences and testimony. Finally, even while recognizing the inevitable bias of any one person's version of events, historians and biographers find journals immensely valuable as primary sources. Details that otherwise would be lost—as well as the texture of life as it is lived—are captured in such personal writings.

Hundreds of Mormon journals have been published, and many more remain unpublished. A standard finding aid is Bitton's *Guide,* still useful for its nearly 3,000 synopses and valuable index. Since the publication of the *Guide* in 1977, many additional journals have been acquired by libraries and research repositories. Continuing technological advances have allowed access to many journals, both published and unpublished, on compact disks or the Internet.

SOURCES

Bitton, Davis. *Guide to Mormon Diaries and Autobiographies.* Provo, Utah: Brigham Young University Press, 1977.

Godfrey, Kenneth W., Audrey M. Godfrey, and Jill Mulvay Derr. *Women's Voices: An Untold History of the Latter-day Saints, 1830–1900.* Salt Lake City: Deseret Book, 1982.

DAVIS BITTON

JST. See JOSEPH SMITH TRANSLATION OF THE BIBLE.

JUAN FERNÁNDEZ ISLAND. See BROOKLYN.

JUÁREZ STAKE. See MEXICAN COLONIES.

JUBILEE. In 1880, the Latter-day Saints celebrated the 50th anniversary of the **organization of the Church** with a jubilee, based on the biblical jubilee observed by the Israelites every 50 years. At the April **conference** of that year, President **John Taylor** forgave half of the debt, which was $802,000 owed to the **Perpetual Emigrating Fund** by the "worthy poor." In addition, the Church distributed 1,000 cows and 500 sheep to the poor and asked the **Relief Society** to join in helping by lending wheat to struggling farmers, to be repaid without interest the following year. Individual members were asked to follow the example set by the Church so that poverty might be abolished among the Saints.

RICHARD NEITZEL HOLZAPFEL

JUNE CONFERENCE. See CONFERENCES.

JUVENILE INSTRUCTOR. When **George Q. Cannon**, a **counselor** to President **Brigham Young**, launched the *Juvenile Instructor* in January 1866, it was the first children's magazine to be published west of the **Mississippi River**. **Elder** Cannon was the editor and publisher as well as the founder and owner. Conceived as an alternative to what he considered the "degrading fiction" of the time, the attractive, four-page semimonthly magazine contained not only a wealth of religious material but also articles relating to history, **literature**, **science**, and geography. Over the years, poetry, biographical sketches, games, and beautiful engravings graced its growing number of pages. The *Juvenile Instructor* served as the official voice of the Church's **Sunday School**, over which President Cannon presided as general superintendent for more than three decades (1867–1901). Just four months before Cannon's death on 12 April 1901, the **Deseret Sunday School Union** purchased the magazine from the Cannon **family**. In 1929 it was renamed the *Instructor* and became more and more a resource for teachers. When the Church consolidated its magazines in 1971, the *Instructor* ceased publication after a remarkable life span of 104 years.

SOURCES

Flake, Lawrence R. "The *Juvenile Instructor* and Its Functions in Religious Education." Master's thesis, Brigham Young University, 1969.

Green, Doyle L. "The Church and Its Magazines." *Ensign* 1 (January 1971): 12–15.

LAWRENCE R. FLAKE

KIRTLAND TEMPLE. The west pulpits of the lower assembly room of the first temple erected by the Church, dedicated in 1836.

KANE, THOMAS L. Thomas L. Kane was born 27 January 1822, the son of prominent Democrat and **Pennsylvania** judge John K. Kane. He forsook a promising career in law and a clerkship in the U.S. District Court to support a host of humanitarian causes, such as abolitionism, education for women, and prison reform. Because of his concern for the downtrodden, the displaced, and the misunderstood, Kane developed an abiding interest in the Latter-day Saints.

Colonel Kane's involvement with the **Mormons** began in 1846 when, hearing of their persecutions and being anxious that they retain their allegiance to **America**, he traveled overland to **Council Bluffs**. In flight to a new **Zion** in the West, the Saints were skeptical of President James K. Polk's invitation to enlist in the **Mexican War**. Kane greatly assisted **Brigham Young** by defraying suspicions and helping enlist the 500-man **Mormon Battalion**. At the same time, he persuaded the U.S. government to allow the Latter-day Saints to establish their **Winter quarters** temporarily on **Indian** lands across the **Missouri** River from Council Bluffs. Taken seriously ill, Kane was nursed back to health by the Latter-day Saints, a kindness he never forgot. Returning to the East, "the fragile idealist" published his well-known address, "The Mormons," in which he pleaded fairness and understanding of their cause. In return, the Saints renamed their frontier settlements at Council Bluffs "Kanesville."

From 1849 to 1850, Kane gave generous assistance to the Mormon petition for **statehood**. Though Congress rejected the notion of the State of **Deseret**, opting for territorial status instead, Kane was instrumental in negotiating key governmental concessions to the Latter-day Saints, including the appointment of Brigham Young as governor of **Utah** Territory.

Another significant contribution to Latter-day Saint history came later during the crisis of the so-called **Utah War**. Acting impetuously and under bad advice, President **James Buchanan** had dispatched an army of 2,500 troops to put down an alleged Mormon insurrection and to install

Alfred Cumming of **Georgia** as the new territorial governor. Sensing the risk of bloodshed, Kane promptly set sail for **California**, again at his own expense yet with presidential blessing. From there he traveled by overland wagon to **Salt Lake City** in the winter of 1858–59. After counseling with Brigham Young, Kane traveled east to **Fort Bridger**, where he met the army and brokered yet another compromise. In return for guaranteeing Cumming's appointment, the Saints received assurance of noninterference by the army and a safe return to their evacuated homes.

After serving with distinction as a Union officer during the **Civil War**, Kane lived out the rest of his life on a Pennsylvania farm. In 1872 he returned to Utah and assisted Brigham Young in writing his will by preparing documents that later established **Brigham Young Academy**, **Brigham Young College**, and other schools. Six years after President Young's death, Kane himself died of pneumonia on 26 December 1883, in Philadelphia.

A "Friend of the Mormons," Kane is well remembered in Utah with both a city and a county named after him. In 1959 the state erected a heroic-sized statue in his memory in the Utah State Capitol Building.

SOURCES

Arrington, Leonard J. "'In Honorable Remembrance': Thomas L. Kane's Services to the Mormons." *BYU Studies* 21 (Fall 1981): 389–402.

Poll, Richard D. "Thomas L. Kane and the Utah War." *Utah Historical Quarterly* 61 (Spring 1993): 112–35.

Zobell, Albert L. *Sentinel in the East: A Biography of Thomas L. Kane.* Salt Lake City: Printing Company, 1965.

RICHARD E. BENNETT

KANESVILLE, IOWA. See COUNCIL BLUFFS IOWA.

KANOSH. Kanosh was head chief of the Pahvant band of **Ute Indians**, claiming the area around the present location of Fillmore, **Utah**. Already an important Ute leader when the **Mormons** arrived in Utah in 1847, Kanosh was one of the first Indians to receive the **endowment**, making attempts to adopt Latter-day **Saint** religion and culture much earlier and more enthusiastically than other **Native Americans**. Like his Latter-day Saint mentors, Kanosh was a **polygamist**. Among others, he married Sally, an adopted Paiute daughter of **Brigham Young**, essentially making him the son-in-law of the Church president. Kanosh's marriage to Sally and his relationship with Brigham Young cemented a Pahvant-Mormon alliance that made Kanosh's band the most favorable to Mormon settlement of all the Indians associated with the Northern Ute Tribe. Occasionally this alliance drew the Church into serious conflicts with non-Mormon whites who had little to do with the Latter-day Saints. This was the case with both the Gunnison Massacre and the Pahvant-Gentile conflict, which led to the **Mountain Meadows Massacre**. Both incidents involved Kanosh's tribe, eventually drew in Latter-day Saints, and played major roles in sharpening the **anti-Mormon** policy of the U.S. government. During the **Black Hawk War** of the 1860s and early 1870s, however, Kanosh and his Pahvants were advocates of peace during a time when most Utes were covertly or overtly belligerent toward the Latter-day Saints. During this significant Mormon-Indian conflict, Brigham Young repeatedly used his good relations with Kanosh to attempt to broker peace with other **Native Americans**.

SOURCE

Pailla, Paul. "Kanosh." *Utah History Encyclopedia.* Edited by Allan Kent Powell. Salt Lake City: University of Utah Press, 1994. 297–98.

JOHN A. PETERSON

KANSAS. The restored gospel was first carried to the area later known as Kansas when **Oliver Cowdery** and **Parley P. Pratt** fulfilled a **mission** to the **Lamanites,** as instructed by the Lord (**Doctrine and Covenants** 28 and 32). The mission ended prematurely because of pressure from government-appointed Indian agents. They threatened military intervention if the missionaries did not leave peacefully because the elders had not met government conditions to be in Indian territory.

Ironically, members of the Church next entered Kansas as soldiers of the U.S. military. The **Mormon Battalion** left **Fort Leavenworth**, Kansas, in 1846 on the longest infantry march in U.S. history.

Although some immigrants passed through Kansas in the 1850s, the Church did not establish a permanent presence in the state until 1882, when Joseph F. Doxford, James Mellor, and Marcus L. Shepherd preached and organized a branch near Salina. On 24 June 1962, President **Joseph Fielding Smith** organized the Wichita **Stake**, the first in Kansas. In the year 2000, six stakes, 45 **wards**, and 24 branches served the 27,232 Church members scattered across the state.

SOURCE

1999–2000 Church Almanac. Salt Lake City: Deseret News, 1998. 220–21.

STERLING KNAPP

KAPP, ARDETH G. Ardeth Greene Kapp, the ninth **Young Women** general president, was born 19 March 1931 in southern **Alberta, Canada.** She married Heber Kapp in the **Cardston Alberta Temple** on 28 June 1950. Graduating with a bachelor's degree from the **University of Utah** and a master's degree from **Brigham Young University**, she taught elementary school and supervised student teachers. She served on the Youth Correlation Committee of the Church and as second counselor to Young Women general president **Ruth Hardy Funk.** Ardeth also served with her husband as he presided over the Canada Vancouver Mission. She was Young Women general president from 1984 to 1992.

Under her visionary leadership, the Young Women values were developed, as well as the Young Women theme, age group recognitions, and Young Women motto—"Stand for Truth and Righteousness." In addition to her Church service, Sister Kapp is widely known as a speaker and author. She has also served on the boards of directors for numerous Church and community organizations.

SOURCES

Arnesen, Karen T. "Ardeth Greene Kapp: A Prairie Girl, a Young Woman Still." *Ensign* 15 (November 1985): 35–39.

Kapp, Ardeth G. *Lead, Guide, and Walk Beside.* Salt Lake City: Deseret Book, 1998.

Peterson, Janet, and LaRene Gaunt. *Keepers of the Flame: Presidents of the Young Women.* Salt Lake City: Deseret Book, 1993. 137–57.

CAROLYN J. RASMUS

KEARNS, THOMAS. Thomas Kearns was a **Utah mining** entrepreneur, newspaperman, U.S. Senator, and noteworthy critic of **Mormon** leaders. He was born 11 April 1862, in Oxford County, **Ontario, Canada.** Raised on a farm in O'Neill, **Nebraska,** Kearns migrated west, arriving in Park City, **Utah,** in 1883. Here he worked and prospected, ultimately discovering and developing the Silver King Mine, which made him a multimillionaire.

Meanwhile, Kearns married Jennie Judge, with whom he had three children. He entered politics as a **Republican** and was elected alderman in Park City. In 1901 he was elected U.S. Senator by the Utah legislature with the active support of LDS Church president **Lorenzo Snow,** though Kearns was a Catholic. As senator, Kearns supported **Theodore Roosevelt's** conservation/irrigation programs, secured regimental post status for **Fort Douglas**, and opened the Uintah **Indian** Reservation to white settlement.

Kearns turned against the LDS Church when he ran for reelection in 1905 and failed to receive the support of President **Joseph F. Smith**. By this time he and David Keith had purchased the *Salt Lake Tribune*, using this newspaper to attack the Church and its influence on politics. He utilized the columns of the *Salt Lake Tribune* to support the **anti-Mormon American Party**. Later his attitude toward the Church mellowed. Kearns died on 18 October 1918, of a stroke at age 56. His impressive home on South Temple Street in **Salt Lake City** was donated by his **family** to the state in 1937 and for most of the time since has served as the official residence for Utah's governors.

SOURCES

Bringhurst, Newell G. "Thomas Kearns: Irish-American Builder of Utah." *Journal of the West* 31, 2 (April 1992): 24–32.

Malmquist, O. N. *The First 100 Years: A History of the Salt Lake Tribune, 1871–1971.* Salt Lake City: Utah State Historical Society, 1971.

NEWELL G. BRINGHURST

KENNEDY, DAVID M. David Matthew Kennedy was a special representative of the **First Presidency** from 1974 to 1990, as well as a distinguished national leader in banking and government. Born 21 July 1905, in Argyle, **Utah**, he was reared in Randolph, Utah. He married Lenora Bingham and then filled a two-year **mission** to **England**.

Kennedy earned a law degree from George Washington University and a graduate degree in banking from Rutgers University. After working for the Federal Reserve System (1930–46), he accepted a position with the Continental **Illinois** National Bank and Trust Company of Chicago. He was eventually elected president of the bank and later chairman and CEO. Early in the 1950s, Kennedy took leave from the bank to serve for a time as assistant to the secretary of the treasury in the U.S. government.

In 1968 Kennedy returned to government service when he was appointed secretary of the treasury by President Richard M. Nixon. He later served as U.S. ambassador-at-large and ambassador to NATO.

In 1974 President Spencer W. Kimball called Kennedy to be a special representative of the First Presidency. He was very successful in establishing good relations with national leaders and helping the Church gain recognition in several countries. In 1985 the international studies center at **Brigham Young University** was named the David M. Kennedy Center for International Studies. Kennedy died 1 May 1996, in **Salt Lake City**.

SOURCES

Hickman, Martin Berkeley. *David M. Kennedy: Banker, Statesman, Churchman.* Provo, Utah: Deseret Book and David M. Kennedy Center for International Studies, 1997.

Kennedy Oral History. David M. Kennedy Oral History. Interviews by Gordon Irving, 1981–85. 3 vols. Typescript. James Moyle Oral History Program, LDS Church Historical Department, Salt Lake City.

Kennedy Papers. David M. Kennedy Paper. Brigham Young University Library, Provo, Utah.

RAY C. HILLAM

KENTUCKY. The first Latter-day Saint missionary to serve in Kentucky was **Samuel Smith**, younger brother of the **Prophet** Joseph. Louisville was a common stop along the route from **Kirtland, Ohio**, to the Latter-day Saint **Missouri** settlements. An early branch of the Church was established south of Cincinnati. Some of the first missionaries included **Orson Pratt**, **Wilford Woodruff**, and **David Patten**.

Early converts emigrated from Kentucky in 1836 and periodically thereafter until emigration was discontinued around the turn of the century. Proselyting efforts ceased during the **Civil War** but were renewed before the organization of the **Southern States Mission**, to which Kentucky was assigned in 1876.

Significant persecution followed growth in Kentucky until the Church's image improved early in the twentieth century. By the beginning of the year 2000, Kentucky had 22,952 Church members, 6 **stakes**, and 64 **wards** and **branches**. The Louisville Kentucky Temple was dedicated 19 March 2000.

SOURCES

Berrett, LaMar C. "History of the Southern States Mission, 1831–1861." Master's thesis, Brigham Young University, 1960.

Jenson, Andrew. *Encyclopedic History of The Church of Jesus Christ of Latter-day Saints.* Salt Lake City: Deseret News, 1941.

1999–2000 Church Almanac. Salt Lake City: Deseret News, 1989. 205–6.

DAVID F. BOONE

KENYA. The Church began to take root in Kenya nearly 20 years before it was officially recognized by the Kenyan government. Since two-thirds of the people in Kenya were Christians, many became interested in the restored gospel when Latter-day Saint expatriates arrived in the 1970s. Church **meetings** were held in their homes, and many discussions occurred between Kenyans and Latter-day Saints. The first Kenyan converts were Elizaphan Osaka, his wife, Ebisiba, and their two oldest children. They were baptized 21 October 1979. Brother Osaka, a former minister, was ordained a priest at the time of his baptism. In September 1980 the first full-time missionaries arrived in Kenya: Farrell and Blanch McGhie of Palo Alto, **California**.

On 10 May 1981, a Kenya **District** was formed with branches in Nairobi and Kiboko. The first Kenyan missionaries were Benson and Nickson Kasue, brothers who were called in 1983 to serve in the California Los Angeles **Mission** and the **Washington, D.C.** North Mission, respectively. Joseph Sitati became the first Kenyan **branch** president in 1988, and he and his **family** were the first Kenyans to receive **temple** blessings.

After a prolonged and unsuccessful effort to have the Church registered in Kenya, the government required the Church to withdraw all full-time missionaries, which was done in July 1989. Brother Sitati was then called as the first Kenyan district president, serving from 1989 to 1991. During this time most Church meetings were held in small groups in homes. Following further struggle with government officials, along with much prayer and fasting by members and many converts who were not yet baptized, the Church received official recognition on 25 February 1991.

The Kenya Nairobi Mission was created in July 1991 with Larry Brown presiding and more than 30 missionaries serving during the first year. The mission included the countries of Kenya, **Uganda**, **Tanzania**, and **Ethiopia**. Kenya was dedicated for the preaching of the gospel by **Elder James E. Faust** on 24 October 1991. Since that time, the Church has provided relief efforts for the people of the area, who have been chronically affected by severe drought and other conditions. The Church has also organized humanitarian projects in Kenya, including an effort in 1994 to establish water taps in hundreds of families' homes.

By 1994 four districts had been created and the first **meetinghouse** was completed, for the Langata Branch in Nairobi. On 17 February 1998, the members throughout eastern **Africa** were strengthened by the visit of President **Gordon B. Hinckley**, the first Church president to visit that region. About 900 members in Nairobi attended, and the prophet promised that they would continue to see the Church grow in their area.

At the beginning of the year 2000, there were 4,039 Latter-day Saints living in Kenya, organized into 2 districts and 17 branches.

SOURCES

1999–2000 Church Almanac. Salt Lake City: Deseret News, 1998. 343–44.

Oral histories of early Church converts collected by E. Dale LeBaron. Copies at BYU Library, Provo, Utah; LDS Church Historical Library, Salt Lake City, Utah.

E. DALE LEBARON

KEYS OF THE PRIESTHOOD. See PRIESTHOOD.

KIKUCHI, YOSHIHIKO. Elder Yoshihiko Kikuchi was the first native-born Japanese **general authority**. He was sustained to the First Quorum of **Seventy** on 1 October 1977 at age 36. He was born 25 July 1941, in Horoizumi, Hokkaido, **Japan**, where he was raised as a Buddhist. He joined the Church at age 15 and later married Toshiko Koshiya. They became the parents of four children. He graduated from **Asia** University of Tokyo and was the president of a Japanese food storage company.

In addition to his call as a general authority, he served as both a proselyting and building missionary, a translator, a **counselor** in the Japan Tokyo **Mission**, a counselor and later president of the Tokyo Japan **Stake**, and president of the **Hawaii** Honolulu Mission and the Tokyo Japan Temple. As a general authority he served as an Area Supervisor, in several **Area** Presidencies, and in the management of several departments at Church headquarters.

SOURCES

Avant, Gerry. "Hard Work, Poor Health: War's Tragedies Lead to Gospel." *Church News,* 29 October 1977, 5.

Morris, Larry E. "Elder Yoshihiko Kikuchi: Steadfast amid Change." *Ensign* 14 (December 1984): 40–44.

Rodriguez, Derin Head. "Yoshihiko Kikuchi." *From Every Nation.* Salt Lake City: Deseret Book, 1990. 48–63.

GLENN N. ROWE

KIMBALL, HEBER C. Heber Chase Kimball (1801–1868), a counselor in the **First Presidency**, was one of the early Church's most colorful figures, and few Church leaders have exceeded his total devotion to the restored gospel. For more than 36 years, in 10 states and in **England**, he faithfully served his God and his people and strove to build both the spiritual and material **kingdom**. From his acceptance of the new faith in 1832 until his death in 1868, he was in the forefront of the excitement, drama, and turbulence of **Mormon** history.

Kimball was born 14 June 1801, in Sheldon, **Vermont**, to Solomon and Anna Kimball. In 1832 he was living with his wife and family in **Mendon, New York**, when they were baptized into the Church. Subsequently he served eight missions between 1832 and 1840, including two to England (1837 and 1840), where he headed the first Latter-day Saint mission outside the United States. He moved to **Kirtland, Ohio**, in 1832 and participated in the Zion's Camp march in 1834. One year later he became a member of the original **Quorum** of the Twelve **Apostles**.

In 1838 Elder Kimball followed **Joseph Smith** to **Far West, Missouri**, from which place the **Saints** were driven during the following winter. Thereafter he helped create new headquarters in **Nauvoo, Illinois**. Seven years later, in 1846 when the Church was driven from Nauvoo, he traveled with the Saints across Iowa. The next year he went in the vanguard company of pioneers to the Salt Lake Valley. Returning to Kanesville, he was called as first counselor to Brigham Young in December 1847.

Elder Kimball married 43 wives and had 65 children and at least 300 grandchildren. By hard work he amassed land, cattle, and property worth more than $100,000. From 1848 to his death 20 years later, he participated fully in the political, economic, social, and cultural development of **Utah**. He became chief justice of the provisional **State of Deseret** in 1849, served in the **Utah** territorial legislature from 1851 to 1858, generally presided over all **temple** work under the direction of Brigham Young, assisted in colonizing the **Great Basin**, and helped foster economic independence in the region.

President Kimball died 22 June 1868 in Salt Lake City from a subdural hematoma after being thrown from his wagon by a lunging horse. His funeral was the largest ever held in Utah Territory. On 25 June the *New York Times* commented, "The Mormons, by the death of Heber Kimball, have lost their most prominent man next to Brigham Young. He illustrated in himself all the more striking peculiarities of the Mormon leaders—their energy and astuteness, their self-sacrifice and selflessness, their devotion to the Church, and their power over its devotees" (quoted in Kimball, *Heber C. Kimball*, 229).

SOURCES

Kimball, Stanley B. *Heber C. Kimball: Mormon Patriarch and Pioneer.* Champaign: University of Illinois Press, 1988.

———, ed. *On the Potter's Wheel: The Diaries of Heber C. Kimball.* Salt Lake City: Signature Books, 1987.

Whitney, Orson F. *The Life of Heber C. Kimball.* 2d ed. Salt Lake City: Stevens & Wallace, 1945.

STANLEY B. KIMBALL

KIMBALL, J. GOLDEN. A **general authority** and folk figure, Jonathan Golden Kimball was a popular speaker known for his wit and colorful language. On one occasion **Elder** Kimball asked a congregation of **Saints,** "Brothers and sisters, how many of you would give your life for the Church?" Nearly every hand went up. He then asked, "How many of you pay a full **tithing?**" Only a few hands went up. A moment of silence passed. Elder Kimball then remarked, "**Bishop,** it looks like these people would rather die than pay their tithing."

That members of the Church today continue to tell "J. Golden Kimball stories" is strong evidence of the impression made by this unique leader. A rare combination of spontaneous wit, homespun philosophy, and a genuine testimony of the gospel enabled Elder Kimball to communicate effectively with nearly all his listeners.

The son of **Heber C. Kimball,** Golden was born 9 June 1853 in Salt Lake City. He served two years as a missionary in the southern states under President **B. H. Roberts,** and then in 1891 he returned to the South as **mission president** for three years. During this assignment he was called to the First Council of the **Seventy** on 5 April 1892. He served for nearly half a century until his death in an automobile accident near Reno, **Nevada,** on 2 September 1938.

SOURCES

Flake, Lawrence R. *Mighty Men of Zion.* Salt Lake City: Karl D. Butler, 1974. 429.

Richards, Claude. "J. Golden Kimball: Friend and Teacher." *Improvement Era* 41 (October 1938): 635–38.

Woller, Tony. "Elder J. Golden Kimball: A Great, Mormon Folk Hero." *(BYU) Daily Universe,* 30 March 1976, 7B.

LAWRENCE R. FLAKE

KIMBALL, J. LEROY. See **NAUVOO RESTORATION, INC.**

KIMBALL, SARAH GRANGER. Noted for her advocacy of women's issues, Sarah Granger was born 29 December 1818, in Phelps, **New York,**

to Oliver (see D&C 117:12–15) and Lydia Dibble Granger. She joined the Church in 1833 and moved with her family to Kirtland, Ohio.

In Nauvoo, Illinois, Sarah invited several women to her home on 4 March 1842 to discuss how to organize a sewing society to assist temple workers. This led to the formal organization, 13 days later, of the Female Relief Society of Nauvoo, antecedent of the modern Relief Society.

Sarah married Hiram Kimball, and they moved to Salt Lake City (1851). Widowed in 1863, she taught school to support her family. Her positions included president of the Fifteenth Ward Relief Society for more than 40 years, general secretary of the Relief Society under President Eliza R. Snow, vice president of the General Relief Society, and president of the Utah Woman Suffrage Association. She died 1 December 1898 in Salt Lake City.

SOURCES

Kimball, Sarah M. "Auto-Biography." *Woman's Exponent* 12 (1 September 1883): 51.

Richards, Mary Stovall. "Sarah Granger Kimball." *Encyclopedia of Mormonism.* Edited by Daniel H. Ludlow. 4 vols. New York: Macmillan, 1992. 2:784–85.

Winder, Barbara W. "Relief Society in Nauvoo." *Encyclopedia of Mormonism.* Edited by Daniel H. Ludlow. 4 vols. New York: Macmillan, 1992. 3:1207–8.

W. JEFFREY MARSH

KIMBALL, SPENCER W. Spencer Woolley Kimball, 12th president of the Church (1973–85), was born 28 March 1895 in Salt Lake City, the son of Andrew Kimball and Olive Woolley. In 1898 his family moved to Thatcher, Arizona, where his father had been called to serve as president of the St. Joseph Stake.

After graduating from high school in 1914, Spencer served a mission to the central states. Two years later he returned to Arizona and attended college, but after one semester he received notice to report for army service in World War I. He and Camilla Eyring, a high school teacher, married while he awaited induction; however, the war ended before Spencer was called to active duty. He began work as a bank teller and served in the Church as stake clerk under his father. When his father died, the new stake president chose Spencer as one of his counselors.

After several years Spencer and a partner began an insurance and real estate business. Although times were hard during the great depression, the business furnished income for Spencer's family, which now included four children.

When the stake was divided in 1938, Spencer became president of the new Mt. Graham Stake, which included wards stretching from Safford, Arizona, to El Paso, **Texas**. In 1943 Spencer was called to the Quorum of the Twelve, the first **apostle** in nearly a century to be called from outside of **Utah**.

Elder Kimball's major assignments as an apostle included visiting stake quarterly **conferences**, supervising **missions** in **South America** and **Great Britain**, counseling people with moral problems, assigning missionaries, and promoting Church programs for the benefit of the **Lamanites**.

Notable for his energy and commitment to hard work, Elder Kimball struggled through a plague of boils, heart attacks, recurrent cancer of the larynx, open heart surgery, and many lesser ills. Removal of most of his vocal cords resulted in his having only a distinctive, weak, hoarse voice, which caused people to listen attentively.

Just after Christmas of 1973, President **Harold B. Lee** died unexpectedly after serving as president of the Church for just 17 months. Spencer W. Kimball, the senior apostle, succeeded him as president of the Church. Despite years of serious physical problems, he began his service in reasonably good health for a man of 78. Though people expected that his might be a brief administration, President Kimball's 12 years as **prophet** saw major developments. These included expansion of Church membership and programs, as well as some clarification of Church doctrine.

Strong growth occurred throughout the Church as **missionary work** spread. More missionaries than ever were being sent to South America, **Asia**, **Africa**, and—though to a limited extent—behind the Iron Curtain. The missionary force increased from 17,000 to 29,000, and the number of converts grew from 80,000 in 1974 to 198,000 in 1985. During these years, total Church membership increased from 3.3 million to 5.7 million.

The **First Presidency** and other Church leaders conducted **area conferences** in an attempt to spread the gospel. These conferences took place in 60 population centers on six continents between 1974 and 1980. An even greater number of **solemn assemblies**, special meetings for instruction of local **priesthood** leaders, were held independent of the area conferences.

During these years, the Church acquired **satellite** technology that fostered its ability to communicate with widely scattered congregations. Genealogical research also benefited from computer technology, and an expanded name-**extraction program** increased performance of vicarious **ordinances** for the dead.

An effort to extend gospel blessings to more people resulted in the building of several **temples**, scattered across the world. The smaller size of many of these buildings allowed for greater numbers to be constructed. Operating temples increased from 15, when President Kimball was sustained as prophet, to 36, at his death, with 11 more under construction or authorized.

President Kimball reorganized the First Quorum of **Seventy** in 1975. This **quorum** expanded to absorb all of the **assistants to the Twelve** in 1976. The seven quorum presidents were called for an undetermined length of time, rather than receiving a lifetime calling. Beginning in 1984, some Seventies were called for limited terms of three to five years. **Emeritus** status for **general authorities** other than apostles was instituted in 1978, permitting a less demanding schedule for leaders in poor health or of advanced years (generally age 70).

As many Church programs expanded, some also diminished. Stake welfare farms with labor furnished by local members became less common, and programs specific to the Indians of the **United States** and **Canada** declined as the need diminished. Local fundraising for chapels also largely decreased as building construction costs were almost completely provided by the tithing funds of the Church.

The most dramatic event of President Kimball's years as prophet was the announcement in June 1978 of a revelation allowing worthy men of all races to hold priesthood office and all worthy members to participate in temple ordinances. Members of the Church had long hoped for such a change. It came after substantial consideration by the First Presidency and the Quorum of the Twelve, when intensive prayer by President Kimball gave him clarity of direction, followed by a spiritual confirmation experienced by these brethren while gathered in the temple. Missionary work in black Africa and such mixed-raced countries as **Brazil** soon began to flourish.

A new edition of the **standard works** appeared with important study aids. Two new sections, reporting visions experienced by **Joseph Smith** and **Joseph F. Smith**, were added to the **Doctrine and Covenants.** The announcement of the 1978 revelation on priesthood was also added to the book as an **official** "Declaration." The **Book of Mormon** was given the subtitle "Another Testament of Jesus Christ," emphasizing the book's Christian character.

The Church faced a difficult issue during the 1970s when the **Equal Rights Amendment** to the Constitution of the United States was proposed. In the public arena the Church actively opposed the amendment, urging that although its objectives of equal treatment for women and men were in most respects laudable, the broad language of the amendment posed the risk of its being used to weaken the family as the central institution of society. The Church's position produced a great deal of negative publicity.

The First Presidency again became directly involved politically when in 1981 it issued a statement opposing the government's proposal to base a huge system of MX missiles in the Utah-**Nevada** desert. Church leaders criticized both the arms race generally and the proposed location in particular.

The 12 years of President Kimball's administration involved Cold War tensions, detente, and the weakening of Soviet control over Eastern **Europe**. Growing secularism and sexual permissiveness threatened moral standards that the Church upheld. During this period of worldwide instability, the Church attracted favorable attention through its efforts to protect the family and encourage morality.

In doctrinal matters, President Kimball expressly rejected the Adam-God theory, and a First Presidency statement confirmed that divine inspiration has come to many philosophers, reformers, and religious figures.

In 1979 President Kimball suffered a brain hemorrhage that required surgery. This condition recurred two months later, and then again in 1981. After the third operation, President Kimball's health declined, leaving him largely inactive. In 1981 he called **Gordon B. Hinckley** as a third counselor, and because of the poor health of counselors **N. Eldon Tanner** and **Marion G. Romney**, President Hinckley took the lead during the last several years of President Kimball's administration, always being careful to consult with the aging president and the Quorum of the Twelve before taking action on an issue.

President Kimball died in Salt Lake City 5 November 1985 at age 90 from the cumulative effects of aging. Among his most prominent personal traits were his humility, ceaseless work, kindliness, and open expressions of affection. The people reciprocated his love. His wife, Camilla, intelligent and independent, had supported him faithfully in every endeavor. She survived him by two years.

SOURCES

Kimball, Edward L., and Andrew E. Kimball Jr. *Spencer W. Kimball.* Salt Lake City: Bookcraft, 1977.

Kimball, Spencer W. *The Teachings of Spencer W. Kimball.* Edited by Edward L. Kimball. Salt Lake City: Bookcraft, 1982.

Miner, Caroline E., and Edward L. Kimball. *Camilla.* Salt Lake City: Deseret Book, 1980.

Edward L. Kimball

KIM HO JIK. Dr. Kim Ho Jik, a famous and influential Korean member of The Church of Jesus Christ of Latter-day Saints, is credited as being the first Korean convert. He was born 16 April 1905, in Pyŏktong-gun, Korea.

Although already prominent as a teacher, educator, and college president in **Korea**, Kim fulfilled a long-standing aspiration to study in the United States by enrolling in a doctoral program in nutrition at Cornell University in 1949. During his studies he met a Latter-day Saint student named Oliver Weyman, who taught him concerning the restoration of the gospel of Jesus Christ. Brother Kim was baptized in the **Susquehanna River** by Don C. Wood on 31 July 1951. He finished his graduate program and returned to Korea in 1952, a time when the country had been devastated by the Korean War.

Kim had a deep conviction that the Lord had sent him to **America** so that he could gain a knowledge of the gospel. He was a fine scholar and a man of impeccable humility and integrity. He was also a deeply spiritual man who freely applied his distinguished academic and social credentials to the work of the Lord. Kim was directly instrumental in gaining legal recognition for the Church and giving it credibility in Korea. He repeatedly testified of the truthfulness of the gospel in both public and private, explaining that the Spirit of the Lord had commanded him to "feed my sheep." Thus, he worked tirelessly in missionary service among Korean students and with the initial foreign full-time missionaries.

After his return to Korea in 1952, Kim was appointed by President Rhee Syngman to serve as vice minister of education for the Republic of Korea. He later served as a professor at Hongik College in Seoul, as dean of animal husbandry at Konguk University in Seoul, and as a member of the Korean National Academy of Arts and Sciences. He also served as vice chairman of the Seoul City Board of Education.

On 2 August 1955, Dr. Kim Ho Jik was set apart as president of the Korean **District** of the Northern Far East Mission, headquartered in Tokyo. The blessing was given by Elder **Joseph Fielding Smith** of the Quorum of the Twelve **Apostles** when he visited Korea to dedicate the land for the preaching of the gospel. Kim retained that calling until his death. With his knowledge of both Korean culture and the gospel, his delightful sociability, and his impeccable command of the English language, he served as a unique magnet and powerful catalyst in bringing high-quality Korean converts into the Church and in laying foundations for growth and development during the first decade of Church history in Korea. Dr. Kim died 31 August 1959.

SOURCES

Kim Jung Sook, "Kim Ho Jik: A Tribute to My Father." *The Korean Saints: Personal Stories of Trial and Triumph, 1950–1980.* Edited by Spencer J. Palmer and Shirley H. Palmer. Salt Lake City: Deseret Book, 1995. 23–25.

Palmer, Spencer J. *The Church Encounters Asia.* Salt Lake City: Deseret Book, 1970. 94–100.

SPENCER J. PALMER

KINDERHOOK PLATES. In April 1843, some alleged New World antiquities were presented to **Joseph Smith** for his opinion. The six small, bell-shaped brass plates with strange engravings were reported to have been excavated in Kinderhook, Illinois, about 70 miles south of Nauvoo.

Although Joseph Smith and the Saints were intrigued by the plates, no effort was made to purchase them or translate them. Eventually all but one of the plates disappeared. The surviving plate is the property of the Chicago Historical Society.

From the plates' alleged discovery until 1981, many scholarly arguments were made for and against their genuineness. Finally, in 1980–81, the Chicago Historical Society granted permission to make "destructive" tests on the remaining plate. The tests, performed by D. Lynn Johnson of Northwestern University, proved that the plates were of nineteenth-century manufacture, and there appears no reason to accept the Kinderhook plates as anything but an unsuccessful frontier hoax designed to embarrass Joseph Smith.

SOURCES

Kimball, Stanley B. "Kinderhook Plates." *Encyclopedia of Mormonism.* Edited by Daniel H. Ludlow. 4 vols. New York: Macmillan, 1992. 2:789–90. There is an error on 790. It should read "etched, not engraved."

———. "Kinderhook Plates Brought to Joseph Smith Appear to Be a Nineteenth-Century Hoax." *Ensign* 11 (August 1981): 66–74.

Ricks, Wallaby W. "The Kinderhook Plates." *Improvement Era* 65 (September 1962): 636–37, 656, 658, 660.

Smith, Joseph. *History of The Church of Jesus Christ of Latter-day Saints.* Edited by B. H. Roberts. 2d ed. rev. 7 vols. Salt Lake City: The Church of Jesus Christ of Latter-day Saints, 1932–51. 5: 372–78.

STANLEY B. KIMBALL

KINGDOM OF GOD. The phrase "kingdom of God" as used in scripture has reference either to God's celestial kingdom in heaven or to his kingdom on earth. The kingdom of God on earth is The Church of Jesus Christ of Latter-day Saints, whose purpose is to prepare its members to live forever in the kingdom of God in heaven (Hinckley, 97). During the Millennium, when Christ will reign personally, the kingdom of God on earth will exercise political as well as ecclesiastical jurisdiction. **Joseph Smith** was prompted to pray that the Lord's kingdom on earth might go forth so that his millennial heavenly kingdom might come (D&C 65:6). In anticipation of this expanded kingdom, the **Prophet** organized, under the name Kingdom of God, a body commonly known as the **Council of Fifty** to function in political affairs. Some early Church leaders have made the distinction between this more narrow definition of the Kingdom of God and the Church as a whole. Elder **James E. Talmage**, however, clarified that the Kingdom of God "does not aspire to temporal domination among nations. It seeks not to overthrow any existing forms of government" (in Talmage, 129).

SOURCES

Brinley, Douglas. "I Have a Question." *Ensign* 26 (January 1996): 60–61.

Hinckley, Gordon B. "Rise to a Larger Vision of the Work." *Ensign* 2 (May 1996): 97.

McKay, David O. "Some Characteristics of 'the Kingdom.'" *Improvement Era*, August 1954. 557–58.

Smith, Joseph. *History of The Church of Jesus Christ of Latter-day Saints.* Edited by B. H. Roberts. 2d ed. rev. 7 vols. Salt Lake City: The Church of Jesus Christ of Latter-day Saints, 1932–51. 7:382, note.

Smith, Joseph Fielding. *Teachings of the Prophet Joseph Smith.* Salt Lake City, Utah, 1976:271–27.

Talmage, James E. Conference Report, April 1916. 129.

CRAIG K. MANSCILL

KING FOLLETT DISCOURSE. Joseph Smith's most famous sermon, the King Follett Discourse was given at **general conference** in **Nauvoo** on 7 April 1844. During the course of his sermon, Joseph Smith discussed 158 different doctrinal topics. In this address the **Prophet** paid tribute to King Follett, a member of the Church who had died in an accident a month earlier. Hence, the sermon has been called the King Follett Discourse.

During the Nauvoo period, Joseph Smith taught the **Saints** through a series of sermons, culminating in the King Follett Discourse, which brought together ideas that had been developing over a long period of teaching the Saints and receiving revelation. The sermon contains many of the unique doctrines of the **Restoration**, such as the existence of intelligence, the nature of creation as organization, **God** as an exalted man, and mankind's potential to become as God is.

April conference in 1844 was held in the East Grove, one of the outdoor amphitheater locations used for public **meetings**. The number in attendance was several thousand, perhaps 8,000. More inflated numbers have been given, but they are likely inaccurate.

As the Prophet spoke, four men recorded or made notes of his sermon: **Wilford Woodruff, Willard Richards, William Clayton**, and **Thomas Bullock**. Although Woodruff is the best known of the recorders, he was not officially assigned to take notes, having recorded various sermons of Joseph Smith out of a natural desire to make a historical record. Richards was the Prophet's personal secretary and was assigned to take notes. Clayton, another private secretary, had also been assigned to record the events of the conference. Bullock was the most skillful recorder and served in a number of clerical posts in Nauvoo. The original notes prepared by these men have been preserved. As a result, a fairly accurate version of the sermon is now available. The King Follett Discourse has been more frequently published than any other of Joseph Smith's sermons—by more than thirty times.

SOURCES

Cannon, Donald Q. and Larry E. Dahl. "The King Follett Discourse: Joseph Smith's Greatest Sermon in Historical Perspective." *BYU Studies* 18 (Winter 1978): 179–92.

———. *The Prophet Joseph Smith's King Follett Discourse: A Six-Column Comparison of Original Notes and Amalgamations.* Provo, Utah: Religious Studies Center, Brigham Young University, 1983.

DONALD Q. CANNON

KIRIBATI. The first members of the Church from Kiribati, an island country in Micronesia, joined while attending a secondary school in the country of **Tonga**. Under British rule, secondary school opportunities in Kiribati were limited to 5 or 6% of the population. In 1972 Waitea Abiuta, principal of a small elementary school on the capital island of Tarawa, wrote to secondary schools throughout the world, asking that some of his students be granted the opportunity to further their schooling abroad. One of those letters reached Liahona High School in Tonga. After careful consideration, 12 students were selected to attend Liahona starting in 1973.

All 12 students joined the Church at Liahona; six of them were then called to serve **missions** in 1975. After serving for six months in the Nuku'alofa-Tonga Mission, they were transferred to the **Fiji**-Suva Mission. President Kenneth Palmer of the Fiji-Suva Mission, accompanied by the six Kiribati missionaries, arrived at Tarawa 19 October 1975 to begin proselyting among the people of Kiribati.

Among the first converts was Waitea Abiuta. Not long after Waitea's baptism, President Palmer set him apart as the first **branch** president of Kiribati on 24 January 1976. The Church continued to grow, and Waitea's elementary school became the center of Church activity. Many expatriate service missionaries were called to serve education missions to teach at this school. Grant Howlett, his wife, Patricia, and their family were the first to come. Brother Howlett succeeded in securing official government recognition for the Church on 29 June 1977. The Church later purchased the school, renaming it Moroni Community School. When the school moved out of the elementary sector and became a secondary school, its name was changed to Moroni High School. In 1998 Moroni High School had more than 400 students.

The Church has steadily grown in Kiribati, spreading to several outer islands. The Tarawa-Kiribati **District** was organized 19 January 1988, with Iotua Tune called as the first district president. On 10 August 1996, **Elder L. Tom Perry** chose the site of the **World War II** Battle of Tarawa (fought in 1943) as the place to dedicate Kiribati and six additional island countries and provinces for the preaching of the gospel. The following day he organized the first **stake** in **Micronesia**—the Tarawa-Kiribati Stake. At the beginning of the year 2000, there were 7,964 members in the country, living in 1 stake, 1 district, and 23 **wards** and branches.

SOURCES

Britsch, R. Lanier. *Unto the Islands of the Sea: A History of the Latter-day Saints in the Pacific.* Salt Lake City: Deseret Book, 1986. 515–21.

Jacob, W. James. "A Beacon to the Isles of the Sea: The Development of the Church in Kiribati through Education." LDS Church Archives, Salt Lake City.

1999–2000 Church Almanac. Salt Lake City: Deseret News, 1998. 344.

W. JAMES JACOB

KIRTLAND, OHIO.

Early Church headquarters and site of the Church's first temple, Kirtland served as the Church's organizational, teaching, and spiritual center from 1831 to 1838. This small northeast Ohio town near Cleveland was named after **Judge Turhand Kirtland**, a landowner and surveyor. The first **converts** in Kirtland were **baptized** in November 1830, when four missionaries to the **Lamanites—Oliver Cowdery, Parley P. Pratt, Peter Whitmer Jr.**, and **Ziba Peterson—** stopped on their way to the **Missouri** frontier. They converted **Sidney Rigdon** and such members of his congregations as **Newel K. Whitney, Frederick G. Williams, Isaac Morley, Lyman Wight**, and **John Murdock**. These conversions ignited a blaze of new Church growth. Within a month, Church membership approximately doubled as more than 120 converts accepted baptism. **Joseph Smith** was commanded to move the Church from **New York** to Ohio in December 1830, thereby establishing Kirtland as Church headquarters for the next several years. Joseph and **Emma Smith** led the way, arriving about 1 February 1831.

Organizational Development

Most of the offices and organizational structure of the Church were put in place in Kirtland. This included the **First Presidency, Quorum of the Twelve, Quorums of the Seventy, patriarchs**, and **high priests**. In Kirtland, the first stake of the Church was organized, the first **high council** established, and the first **bishop** called. The Kirtland period marked a great expansion in organized **missionary work**. Missionaries were sent from Kirtland throughout the **United States**, Eastern **Canada**, and **England**. Kirtland became the Church's first gathering place. Saints from New York and from other areas gathered to Kirtland.

Teaching and Scriptures

Kirtland is often identified with the formal beginning of Church education. In 1833 the **School of the Prophets** convened in an upstairs room of the Newel K. Whitney store. Subsequent sessions were conducted in the schoolhouse-printing office, where the *Lectures on Faith* were given, as well as in the temple. The reception of scripture in the Kirtland period is astounding. Sixty-five sections of the current **Doctrine and Covenants** (almost half) were received in the Kirtland area. These many revelations included the **Word of Wisdom, priesthood** principles and instruction, and the doctrine of **three degrees of glory**.

The Church's welfare system is based on principles established by revelations received in Kirtland; not only was the **law of consecration** first implemented there, but out of it grew the United Firm, or as it is often called, the united order. The Newel K. Whitney store became the first **bishop's storehouse** of the Church.

Other Kirtland schooling encompassed Joseph's translation activities. The Church purchased four mummies and accompanying papyrus scrolls from **Michael Chandler** in Kirtland. The **book of Abraham** was translated from these documents. Joseph Smith also completed almost all of his inspired translation of the **Bible** while he resided in the Kirtland area. The first edition of the Doctrine and Covenants was printed there, as was the second edition of the **Book of Mormon** and the first collection of hymns. Joseph translated parts of both the **Book of Moses** and the book of Abraham in Kirtland, and they were later added to the **Pearl of Great Price**.

The Prophet also taught the Saints about future events from prophecies given in Kirtland, such as his prophecy of the **Civil War**, which came to pass almost three decades later. Although the Kirtland period preceded the Saints' going west by more than 10 years, two prophecies uttered in Kirtland foretold the Saints' journey to the Rocky Mountains. Joseph Smith further prophesied there that "this Church will fill North and **South America**—it will fill the world" (Woodruff, 57).

PENTECOSTAL PERIOD

Experiences similar to New Testament Pentecostal outpourings also took place in Kirtland—unparalleled spiritual manifestations were granted. As documented in many histories, the **Savior** appeared in vision to Joseph Smith at least 10 times in Kirtland, and four of those visions included God the Father. **Journals** and histories reflect the appearance of at least eight prophets from past dispensations, including **Adam, Abraham, Moses, Elias, Elijah, Peter, James, and John**. Great Pentecostal manifestations occurred. Although they primarily surrounded the Kirtland Temple dedication, other manifestations accompanied meetings in the Whitney store. Manifested in these Pentecostal experiences were angels, visions, prophesying, the gift of tongues, the sound of mighty wind, choirs of angels, and a pillar of fire (Anderson, 169–77). Of this period, Joseph Smith said, "The occurrences of this day shall be handed down upon the pages of sacred history, to all generations" (Smith, 2:432–33).

KIRTLAND'S DECLINE

The fortunes of the Church in Kirtland declined after the temple dedication in 1836. The Church incurred debt from building the temple, buying land, and assisting needy members in Missouri. To help with banking needs, Joseph Smith established the **Kirtland Safety Society** in January 1837. It struggled for about six months before Joseph's involvement ended and the institution subsequently failed. An economic panic was spreading throughout the country, resulting in the collapse of many banks in the nation. Nevertheless, the failure in Kirtland caused bitterness within and without the Church. Persecution became intense, forcing Saints to abandon their homes and property and migrate to Missouri. Joseph and Emma fled Kirtland in January 1838. The largest block of Saints left in July of the same year in "Kirtland Camp," a group of more than 500 emigrants organized by the Seventy. Although some Saints remained and new settlement even occurred in the 1840s, meaningful Church presence effectively ended in 1838.

Rebuilding Kirtland

Realizing that the Church would leave its temple and relocate, Joseph Smith, **Hyrum Smith**, and **Brigham Young** prophesied that the Lord would one day rebuild Kirtland. A revelation in 1841, after the Saints had left the area, declares, "I, the Lord, will build up Kirtland" (D&C 124:83). Speaking in the name of the Lord, Church Patriarch Hyrum Smith prophesied that the rebuilding of Kirtland would come for future generations. He said that, although the Saints must leave their land and property in Kirtland, "yet your children may possess them, but not until many years shall pass away . . . thus saith the Lord, . . . and then I will send forth and build up Kirtland, and it shall be polished and refined according to my word" (Smith, 4:443–44). In 1979, President **Ezra Taft Benson** declared these prophecies to be fulfilled as he broke ground for the Church's first building in Kirtland since 1836. Responding to the prophecy in the **Doctrine and Covenants**, President Benson declared, "That prophecy is being fulfilled today." Then, reflecting on Hyrum Smith's prophecy, President Benson said, "Those many years have, I feel, passed away and now is the time . . . to arise . . . and look forward to great progress in this part of the Lord's vineyard." Church membership increased and new wards and **branches** were established. Two years after President Benson's visit, the meetinghouse was completed just below the temple hill; four years after his visit, the Kirtland **Stake** was organized again, becoming the first stake there since the Prophet Joseph Smith left.

The Church purchased property and restored historical sites such as the Newel K. **Whitney store** (1984) and the Johnson home. In April 2000, the Church announced plans to build and restore a historic village around the Whitney Store, including the Newel K. Whitney home, the John Johnson (French) Inn, the Kirtland schoolhouse, a tannery, an ashery, and a new visitors' center.

SOURCES

Anderson, Karl Ricks. *Joseph Smith's Kirtland, Eye Witness Accounts.* Salt Lake City: Deseret Book, 1989.

Backman, Milton V., Jr. *The Heavens Resound: A History of the Latter-day Saints in Ohio 1830–1838.* Salt Lake City: Deseret Book, 1983.

Benson, Ezra Taft. Kirtland Ward Meetinghouse Groundbreaking Address. LDS Church Archives, Salt Lake City. 14 October 1979.

Smith, Joseph. *History of The Church of Jesus Christ of Latter-day Saints.* Edited by B. H. Roberts. 2d ed. rev. 7 vols. Salt Lake City: The Church of Jesus Christ of Latter-day Saints, 1932–51.

Woodruff, Wilford. Conference Report (April 1898): 57–58.

KARL RICKS ANDERSON

KIRTLAND CAMP.

KIRTLAND CAMP. Impoverished Kirtland **Saints** who could not afford to go to **Missouri** in the early months of 1838 were organized into the Kirtland Camp by the First Council of the **Seventy** under the direction of **Hyrum Smith**. Their journey took them from **Kirtland, Ohio**, to **Far West** and **Adam-ondi-Ahman**, Missouri. The camp originally consisted of 529 individuals and grew to 620. They departed Kirtland 6 July 1838 and arrived at Adam-ondi-Ahman on 4 October. **Oliver Granger**, the Church **agent**, stated that Kirtland Camp "would be the greatest thing ever accomplished since the organization of the Church or even since the exodus of Israel from **Egypt**" (Smith, 3:96).

SOURCES

Smith, Joseph. *History of The Church of Jesus Christ of Latter-day Saints.* Edited by B. H. Roberts. 2d ed. rev. 7 vols. Salt Lake City: The Church of Jesus Christ of Latter-day Saints, 1932–51. 3:87–148.

KEITH W. PERKINS

KIRTLAND SAFETY SOCIETY.

KIRTLAND SAFETY SOCIETY. To meet the critical banking needs of the Latter-day Saint community in northeastern Ohio, **Joseph Smith** and several associates organized the Kirtland Safety Society in 1837. During the previous six years, **Kirtland** had experienced rapid population growth and economic expansion. Joseph Smith and other Church leaders had participated in this expansion by purchasing land and merchandise and by extending credit to members who had migrated to Kirtland. In order to finance their purchases, Church leaders had, themselves, obtained credit from lenders and merchants in **New York**, Cleveland, and Buffalo. Because most of their assets were held as nonliquid land and most of their liabilities were in the form of short-term (90- to 180-day) notes, Church leaders had a cash-flow problem. Hence, they had trouble paying their debts. It was rightly believed that this problem would be alleviated by the establishment of a bank, which could convert long-term assets (land) into liquid assets (bank notes). A bank would also serve the important purpose of providing credit and a circulating medium of exchange to the growing community. The **Ohio** state legislature nevertheless, turned down the **Saints** and all others applying for bank charters in 1836 and 1837.

Determined to provide the advantages of a bank to their community, on 2 January 1837 Church leaders formed a joint-stock company called the "Kirtland Safety Society Anti-Banking Company," which began issuing its own "anti-banking" notes in payment of Church obligations. Between January and November 1837, about $100,000 in notes was issued by the Kirtland Safety Society. While the notes did circulate as a medium of exchange, heavy demand for redemption in specie (coined money) depleted the bank's small reserve and led to the suspension of specie payments within a month after the first issue.

Although the Kirtland Safety Society continued to operate with notes backed by land values, the notes circulated at a sharp discount. The spread of the national bank panic of 1837 in May and June placed further pressure on the Kirtland institution, and it finally ceased operations in November 1837.

SOURCES

Adams, Dale W. "Chartering the Kirtland Bank." *BYU Studies* 23 (Fall 1983): 467–82.

Arrington, Leonard J. *Great Basin Kingdom: An Economic History of the Latter-day Saints, 1830–1900.* Cambridge: Harvard University Press, 1958.

Hill, Marvin S., C. Keith Rooker, and Larry T. Wimmer. "The Kirtland Economy Revisited: A Market Critique of Sectarian Economics." *BYU Studies* 17 (Summer 1977): 391–475.

Sampson, D. Paul, and Larry T. Wimmer. "The Kirtland Safety Society: The Stock Ledger Book and the Bank Failure." *BYU Studies* 12 (Summer 1972): 427–36.

L. DWIGHT ISRAELSEN

KIRTLAND TEMPLE.

KIRTLAND TEMPLE. The Kirtland Temple was the first large-scale building enterprise undertaken by the **Saints** and served as the pattern for subsequent **temples** constructed by the Church. Revelations given in the spring of 1833 instructed the Saints to build three identically sized buildings in **Kirtland**: one "a house, in the which I [the Lord] design to endow those whom I have chosen with power from on high" (D&C 95:8, 13–17), one for "the work of the presidency" (D&C 94:3–9), and another "for the work of the printing" (D&C 94:10–12). Only the first of these buildings, the Kirtland Temple, was constructed according to these specifications.

The plans for the Kirtland Temple were developed at the same time as the drawings and specifications were prepared for the Independence Temple, and the two structures would have been similar if construction had gone forward in **Independence**. **Joseph Smith**, **Sidney Rigdon**, and **Frederick G. Williams** saw the temple in **vision** (Robinson, 8) and then communicated simple instructions dealing primarily with size and functional layout to craftsmen, who then used traditional methods and carpenters' pattern books to complete construction.

A feature distinguishing the temple from contemporary American **meetinghouses** was its two congregational meeting rooms, one above the other. Also unique to the temple are the dual sets of pulpits in each of these rooms, one for the **Aaronic Priesthood** on the east, and the other for the **Melchizedek Priesthood** on the west. Five small rooms used by the **First Presidency**, **quorum** presidencies, the **School of the Prophets (or Elders)**, and the Kirtland High School were located on the attic level.

Construction began 5 June 1833, with **Hyrum Smith** and **Reynolds Cahoon** digging the foundation and Harry Stanley and **George A. Smith** hauling the first load of stone. When asked if the temple should be built of logs or lumber, the **Prophet** declared that he had been shown a different plan—the temple should be built of substantial masonry. When brick-making efforts failed, the Saints took the advice of **Artemus Millet**, supervisor of the work, and used a rubble sandstone masonry covered with a unique plaster containing old glass and pottery. Construction proceeded slowly during most of 1834 because of the large number of brethren absent with **Zion's Camp**. With their return in the fall, the number of workers escalated. Other important contributions to the construction were made by Jacob Bump and **Truman O. Angell** on the interior woodwork; **John Corrill**, who superintended later phases of the work; and **Brigham Young**, who built the windows and superintended the painting of the lower rooms.

Incident to the dedication of the temple on 27 March 1836, the Saints experienced a season of spiritual manifestations, including the appearance of the Savior and other heavenly messengers to Joseph Smith and Oliver Cowdery (D&C 110). The ordinance of the washing of feet was conducted, and the promise to be "endowed with power from on high" (D&C 38:32) was fulfilled prior to brethren being sent on **missions** (Smith, 2:429–32). The temple was the center of Church administration, and a school met there during the week. The collapse of the **Kirtland Safety Society** Anti-Banking Company, however, coupled with the large debt owed on the temple and land purchased in Kirtland, led to a series of economic failures and defaults that intensified opposition to Joseph Smith and necessitated his departure from Kirtland on 12 January 1838. By July of that year, most of the Saints had followed the Prophet to **Missouri.**

A congregation of Saints continued to worship in the temple from 1839–41, at which time they were instructed to gather to **Nauvoo, Illinois.** The few who remained continued to meet there until 1845, when control of the temple passed on to various apostate groups. The **Reorganized Church of Jesus Christ of Latter Day Saints** successfully obtained clear title to the building in 1880. The RLDS Church repaired the temple, replacing missing or damaged woodwork, and upgraded it with lighting, heating, and protective systems. Used as a meetinghouse for many years, it became prominent in RLDS culture through the "temple reunion" camp meetings held on the grounds in the early decades of the twentieth century. At the end of the twentieth century the temple was maintained as a historic property with guided tours.

SOURCES

Backman, Milton V., Jr. *The Heavens Resound: A History of the Latter-day Saints in Ohio, 1830–1838.* Salt Lake City: Deseret Book, 1983.

Cowan, Richard O. "The House of the Lord in Kirtland: A 'Preliminary' Temple." In *Ohio.* Edited by Milton V. Backman Jr. Regional Studies in Latter-day Saint Church History series. Provo, Utah: Brigham Young University, 1990. 105–22.

Launius, Roger D. *The Kirtland Temple: A Historical Narrative.* Independence, Mo.: Herald House, 1986.

Robison, Elwin C. *The First Mormon Temple: Design, Construction, and Historic Context of the Kirtland Temple.* Provo, Utah: Brigham Young University Press, 1997.

Smith, Joseph. *History of The Church of Jesus Christ of Latter-day Saints.* Edited by B. H. Roberts. 2d ed. rev. 7 vols. Salt Lake City: The Church of Jesus Christ of Latter-day Saints, 1932–51.

ELWIN C . ROBISON

KISSI, EMMANUEL A. Dr. Emmanuel Abu Kissi, an early convert and Church leader from **Ghana**, was born 24 December 1938 in

Abomosu, Ghana. He joined the Church in 1979, less than a year after the **revelation** allowing all worthy males to receive the **priesthood**. He was completing his training as a surgeon in London, **England**, when missionaries called on him.

From his youth, Brother Kissi was driven by two goals: to become a medical doctor and to find greater doctrines than those offered by the Christian churches in Ghana. While completing his M.D. in Ghana, Brother Kissi married Elizabeth Bamfo, who became a qualified nurse and midwife. To achieve his spiritual goals, he earnestly studied Christian religions and the **Bible** but continued to feel a spiritual hunger.

When he and his wife were taught by the missionaries, Dr. Kissi was skeptical until reading the **Book of Mormon**, *Jesus the Christ,* and *A Marvelous Work and a Wonder.* He observed: "I realized that **Joseph Smith** had the same problem that I had. . . . It wasn't difficult for me to understand him" (quoted in LeBaron, "Gospel Pioneers," 43).

Soon after his baptism, Dr. Kissi was offered attractive professional opportunities in England, which he declined. He observed: "England wants me, but Ghana needs me. Before I joined the Church, I was anxious to return to Ghana because I knew my people would need my medical skills. But, after I joined, I knew they needed my testimony of the gospel even more" (Oral histories).

Dr. Kissi and his wife, Elizabeth, established a medical clinic in Accra, Ghana, which they named Deseret Hospital. His Church service, which began soon after the Church was established in Ghana, included callings of **branch** president, **district** president, counselor in the Ghana Accra Mission presidency, and **regional representative**. Dr. Kissi served as the presiding Church officer in Ghana from June 1989 through November 1990, at which time the Ghanaian government ordered a freeze on all Church activities and properties and expelled all foreign Church representatives, including the **mission president**.

In 1999 Dr. and Sister Kissi built a new and expanded medical clinic in Accra so that they could better help the people.

Sources

LeBaron, E. Dale, ed. *All Are Alike unto God.* Orem, Utah: Granite Publishing, 1998. 29–42.

———. "Gospel Pioneers in Africa." *Ensign* 20 (August 1990): 40–43.

Oral histories of early Church converts collected by E. Dale LeBaron. Copies at BYU Library, Provo, Utah; LDS Church Historical Library, Salt Lake City, Utah.

E. Dale LeBaron

KNIGHT, AMANDA INEZ. See ALLEN, AMANDA INEZ KNIGHT.

KNIGHT, JESSE. A self-made millionaire and dedicated member of the Church, Jesse Knight was born 6 September 1845 in **Nauvoo, Illinois**, to Newel and Lydia Knight. When he was a year old, Jesse's father died, but Jesse reached **Utah** with the rest of his **family** in 1850. He received no formal schooling, but worked from an early age at logging, freighting, dairying, and ranching. On 18 January 1869, he married Amanda McEwan, and they had five children. The family lived on a ranch near Payson, Utah. Jesse distanced himself from Mormonism until life events made him seek God and embrace the faith. He then received spiritual confirmations and prophetic dreams, including inspiration to claim and develop Humbug Mine near Eureka, Utah. This venture produced $10 million in silver, the basis for Jesse's subsequent wealth.

In 1906 Jesse formed the Knight Investment Corporation, which in time included some 80 corporations. In 1908 he erected a monument at Niobrara, Nebraska, memorializing his father, **Newel Knight**, who had died there (1847).

Throughout his life Jesse believed his wealth was a trusted stewardship given to him for the purpose of doing good and building up the Church. To benefit Church members, he invested in farmlands and a sugar factory in **Alberta, Canada**, and promoted rural electrification, canals, and industries in Utah. His large loans saved Church credit at two critical times. Later Jesse became a trustee and financial backer of **Brigham Young Academy** (BYU), where the Amanda Knight Hall, Knight-Mangum Building, and Jesse Knight Humanities Building were named for him and members of his family. He died 14 March 1921 in **Provo**, Utah.

SOURCES

Knight, Jesse William. *The Jesse Knight Family: Jesse Knight, His Forebears and Family.* Salt Lake City: Deseret News, 1940.

Petersen, Richard H. "Jesse Knight, Utah's Mormon Mining Mogul." *Utah Historical Quarterly* 57 (Summer 1989), 240–53.

Reese, Gary Fuller. "'Uncle Jesse,' the Story of Jesse Knight, Miner, Industrialist, Philanthropist." Master's thesis, Brigham Young University, 1961.

WILLIAM G. HARTLEY

KNIGHT, JOSEPH, SR. The father of a large **family** that displayed great devotion to the restored gospel, Joseph Knight Sr. (later known as Father Knight) was born 26 November 1772 in Oakham, **Massachusetts**. In about 1795, Joseph married **Polly Peck,** and in 1808 they moved to **Colesville, New York**. In late 1826, Joseph hired the **Prophet Joseph Smith** to help with farm and millwork. He lent Joseph Smith his sleigh so the latter could court **Emma Hale**. When Joseph Knight Sr. visited the Smith home in Palmyra in September 1827, Joseph and Emma used his wagon to pick up the **gold plates** at the **Hill Cumorah**. He also provided paper for the **Book of Mormon** translation, as well as food and supplies.

Father Knight was baptized 28 June 1830. Joseph, Polly, and their seven children and spouses joined the Church, as did three of Mother Polly's siblings (Pecks), their spouses, and Father Knight's sister. Together they became the **Colesville Branch** of nearly 60 members. The family moved to **Ohio** and were later among the first Latter-day **Saint** settlers in **Jackson County, Missouri**. Polly died there 6 August 1831. Father Knight later married Phoebe Crosby Peck, and they had two children. A dozen Knight-related families (named Knight, Slade, DeMille, Stringham, Peck, Culver, Johnson, Cleveland, and Rich) lived in and near **Nauvoo**. While living in Nauvoo, Joseph Smith paid tribute to Father Knight and his family for their help, friendship, and loyalty since the 1820s. More than a dozen **Doctrine and Covenants** sections contain directives for the Knight relatives.

During the Nauvoo exodus, Father Knight died at **Mt. Pisgah, Iowa**, 2 February 1847. After 1846 nearly all living Knight family adults—about two dozen—as well as their children went west to **Utah**. The Knight's lasting devotion provides a remarkable "family witness" of Joseph Smith's character and prophetic work.

SOURCES

Hartley, William G. *Stand by My Servant Joseph: A History of the Joseph Knight Family and the Restoration*. Salt Lake City: Deseret Book, 2001.

Jesse, Dean C. "Joseph Knight's Recollections of Early Mormon History." *BYU Studies* 17 (Autumn 1976): 29–39.

Porter, Larry C. "A Study of the Origins of The Church of Jesus Christ of Latter-day Saints in the States of New York and Pennsylvania, 1816–1831." Ph.D. diss., Brigham Young University, 1977.

WILLIAM G. HARTLEY

KNIGHT, LUCY JANE BRIMHALL. Lucy Jane Brimhall and Amanda Inez Knight, both called to labor in Great Britain, were set apart as the first official, single sister missionaries in the Church on 1 April 1898. Born 13 December 1875, in Spanish Fork, **Utah**, to George Henry and Alsina Elizabeth Wilkins Brimhall, Lucy graduated from **Brigham Young Academy** in 1895. After serving her mission she married J. William Knight in 1899. The couple moved to **Canada** for seven years and helped found Raymond, **Alberta**. The mother of two sons, Lucy served as first **counselor** in the general **Relief Society** presidency from 1921 to 1928. She was active in the Red Cross, National Conference of Social Workers, and National Council of Women. She died 31 March 1957, in **Provo**, Utah.

SOURCE

Fritzen, Mary Jane Groberg. *Lucy Jane (Jennie) Brimhall Knight: An Expression of Love and Gratitude for Her Exemplary Life.* Idaho Falls, Idaho: Delbert V. and Jennie H. Groberg, 1997.

JULIE HUNSAKER

KNIGHT, NEWEL. Newel Knight was born 13 September 1800, in Marlborough, **Vermont**, to **Joseph Knight** and **Polly Peck**. He married Sally Colburn 7 June 1825, and they had two children. Newel was baptized in May 1830, when **Joseph Smith** worked for the Knight **family** in **Colesville, New York**, and taught them the gospel. Joseph Smith cast an evil spirit from Newel at Colesville, thus performing the Church's first **miracle**. Newel was a close friend of Joseph and served as both president of the Colesville **Branch** and religious leader for the large Knight family network when they moved to **Ohio**, **Missouri**, and then **Illinois**. Called to the first **high council** in Missouri in July 1834, he served on four high councils during the next 12 years. Sally died 15 September 1834, and Newel married Lydia Goldthwaite Bailey in **Kirtland, Ohio**, on 24 November 1835—the first **marriage** ceremony Joseph Smith performed by **priesthood** authority. Newel built mills in Missouri and **Nauvoo**. He and Lydia had seven children, including **Jesse Knight** (later a **Utah** millionaire).

Newel Knight left Nauvoo in the spring 1846 phase of the exodus. In July **Brigham Young** sent Newel ahead, with family, as captain of a Young-selected wagon company. Accompanied by a wagon train assembled by **Heber C. Kimball**, they joined **Bishop George Miller's** advance company at Grand Island, **Nebraska**, and all wintered far north, creating the Ponca Encampment (September 1846–March 1847) of some 100 families. There Newel died 11 January 1847. Lydia and her family moved to **Winter Quarters** and **Kanesville**, then crossed the plains in 1850. She died 3 April 1884 in **St. George, Utah.** In 1908 their son Jesse erected a monument at present-day Niobrara, Nebraska, honoring Newel and the Ponca Encampment.

SOURCES

Gates, Susa Young. *Lydia Knight's History: The First Book of the Noble Women's Lives Series.* Salt Lake City: Juvenile Instructor Office, 1883.

Hartley, William G. *Stand by My Servant Joseph: A History of the Joseph Knight Family and the Restoration.* Salt Lake City: Deseret Book, 2001.

Knight, Newel. "Newel Knight's Journal." *Scraps of Biography.* Reprinted as part of *Classic Experiences and Adventures.* Salt Lake City: Bookcraft, 1969.

WILLIAM G. HARTLEY

KNIGHT, POLLY. Polly Knight, matriarch of a prominent early family in the Church, was born 16 April 1774, in Guilford, **Vermont,** to Joseph Peck and Elizabeth Read. She married **Joseph Knight Sr.** in about 1795. In 1808 they moved to **Colesville, New York,** where the Knights befriended **Joseph Smith** by 1826. Polly was baptized 28 June 1830 by **Oliver Cowdery.** She bore seven children, including **Newel Knight,** all of whom joined the Church. Polly was the first **Saint** to die in **Jackson County, Missouri** (6 August 1831); Joseph Smith preached at her funeral.

SOURCES

Hartley, William G. *Stand by My Servant Joseph: A History of the Joseph Knight Family and the Restoration.* Salt Lake City: Deseret Book, 2001.

Smith, Joseph. *History of The Church of Jesus Christ of Latter-day Saints.* Edited by B. H. Roberts. 2d ed. rev. 7 vols. Salt Lake City: The Church of Jesus Christ of Latter-day Saints, 1932–51. 88, 199.

WILLIAM G. HARTLEY

KOMATSU, ADNEY Y. Adney Yoshio Komatsu, the first **general authority** of Japanese and Asian descent, was sustained 4 April 1975 as **assistant to the Quorum of the Twelve Apostles** and on 1 October 1976 as a member of the First **Quorum** of the **Seventy.** He was born 2 August 1923, in Honolulu, **Hawaii.** Reared a Buddhist, he joined the Church at age 17. He married Judy Nobue Fujitani, and they became the parents of four children. During **World War II** he served in the Army's 441st counterintelligence corps, and his career was in banking.

He was president of the Northern Far East **Mission, regional representative, area** supervisor, and a member of several area presidencies. He also served in the general **Sunday School** presidency and as the **Tokyo Temple** president. On 2 October 1993, Elder Komatsu became an **emeritus general authority**.

SOURCES

Britsch, R. Lanier. *From the East: The History of the Latter-day Saints in Asia, 1851–1996.* Salt Lake City: Deseret Book, 1998. 124–27.
"His Mother Received a Promise." *Church News,* 3 May 1975, 7.
Rodriguez, Derin Head. *From Every Nation.* Salt Lake City: Deseret Book, 1990. 1–16.

GLENN N. ROWE

KOREA. With a population of about 47 million as of December 1998, the Republic of Korea has the largest Christian population by percentage (49%) on the Asian continent. The restored gospel was first introduced into the country during the **Korean War** period (1950–53) through Latter-day Saint servicemen.

Korea was greatly blessed with a number of remarkable pioneer members, including **Kim Ho Jik,** who was baptized 29 July 1951, in the **Susquehanna River** near **Harmony, Pennsylvania,** while earning his Ph.D. at Cornell University. He became the first native Korean to join the Church. Politically, Kim attained the office of vice-minister of education for South Korea, the highest-ranking position a member of the Church had ever held in Asia to that point. Until his untimely death at age 54, Kim laid a solid foundation for the Korean Church and its growth.

On the morning of 2 August 1955, President **Joseph Fielding Smith** dedicated the land of Korea for the preaching of the restored gospel. On the day of dedication, President Smith set Kim Ho Jik apart as president of the Korean **District** of the Northern Far East Mission, then headquartered at Tokyo, **Japan.**

The first Korean Mission was created 8 July 1962, with Gail E. Carr (then age 32) as president. He had just completed his B.A. at the University of Southern **California** in Asian studies and spoke both Korean and Japanese fluently. The Church membership in Korea was then approximately 1,600.

A watershed in Korean Church history occurred 8 March 1973, when the first continental Asian **stake** was organized in Seoul, with Rhee Ho Nam as president. It was the third stake in the Orient and the 604th stake in the world.

Another new era dawned in Korea on 14 December 1985, when the first LDS **temple** on the Asian mainland was dedicated. President **Gordon B. Hinckley**, first counselor in the **First Presidency**, dedicated the Seoul South Korea Temple, the 37th operating temple.

Korean **Saints** were greatly honored when **Han In Sang** was called to the Second Quorum of the **Seventy** on 1 June 1991, becoming the first Korean **general authority**. Blessed with unusual ability and talent, **Elder** Han well deserves the designation "first." He was the first Korean to serve a full-time mission, the first Korean to serve as a **mission president**, and the first Korean to be sustained as a **regional representative**. Also, at the age of 26, he translated the **Book of Mormon** into Korean.

At the beginning of the year 2000, the Church in Korea had a membership of 71,166, representing .14% of the population. It had four missions, 17 stakes, and 175 **wards** and **branches**.

SOURCES

Britsch, R. Lanier. *From the East: The History of the Latter-day Saints in Asia, 1851–1996.* Salt Lake City: Deseret Book, 1998.

Choi Dong Sull. "A History of The Church of Jesus Christ of Latter-day Saints in Korea, 1950–1985." Ph.D. diss., Brigham Young University, 1990.

1999–2000 Church Almanac. Salt Lake City: Deseret News, 1998. 344–45.

DONG SULL CHOI

KOREAN WAR. The agonies endured by many Korean people during the Korean War (1950–53) prepared the way for the acceptance of Mormonism in **Korea**. Some of the displaced, hungry, and fearful Koreans who fled as far south as Pusan were friendshipped by Latter-day **Saint servicemen**, taught the hopeful and happy message of the restored gospel, and baptized into the Church. Dr. **Kim Ho Jik**, who is credited with being the first Korean to join the Church, was baptized 29 July 1951, in the **United States**. Shortly thereafter, he returned to Korea and joined with new converts located mostly in Pusan and Seoul. A good number of the earliest converts to the Church who later became **bishops**, as well as members of **stake** presidencies and **temple** presidencies, were baptized by servicemen before the arrival of the first full-time proselyting missionaries in 1956.

The sorrows associated with the Korean War are almost indescribable. In 1968, however, **Elder Gordon B. Hinckley** called attention to the "silver thread, small but radiant with hope, shining through the dark tapestry of war" in Korea. He observed that the Korean War afforded an opportunity for "the establishment of a bridgehead, small and frail now; but which somehow, under the mysterious ways of **God**, will be strengthened." Elder Hinckley predicted that a great work would spring forth, affecting many of Heavenly Father's children: "This marvelous membership is the sweet fruit of seed once planted in dark years of war and in troubled days immediately following, when good men of the **priesthood**, both civilian and military, through the example of their lives and the inspiration of their precepts, laid a foundation on which a great work has been established" (Hinckley, 24).

SOURCES

Britsch, R. Lanier. *From the East: The History of the Latter-day Saints in Asia, 1851–1996.* Deseret Book, 1998. 170–81.

Hinckley, Gordon B. Conference Report, April 1968.

Palmer, Spencer J., and Shirley H. Palmer. *The Korean Saints: Personal Stories of Trial and Triumph, 1950–1980.* Salt Lake City: Deseret Book, 1995. 1–3.

SPENCER J. PALMER

KSL. The call letters KSL signify the respected **Salt Lake City**-based radio and television stations with which the Church has been affiliated since 1925.

KSL radio evolved from the independent station KZN that first aired in Salt Lake City in 1922. The call letters were changed to KSL when the Church bought controlling interest in the station on 21 April 1925. KSL radio is a clear-channel station with massive geographic coverage, transmitting at 50,000 watts (the maximum allowable power). KSL has been affiliated with the CBS Radio Network, KSL-AM (1160 on the dial), since 1932 and has been the home of *Music and the Spoken Word* since 1929. The Church's semi-annual **general conference** broadcasts have been aired on KSL since 1924. KSL-FM was created in 1946 and sold in 1978.

KSL-TV went on the air 1 June 1949. It became an NBC affiliate station in 1995, after 45 years of affiliating with CBS. It has a large survey area that includes seven western states. The first color broadcast was in 1964. KSL television has earned many honors and awards from every television industry organization and is recognized as a leader in the field.

Both KSL radio and KSL television are known for their audience loyalty, strong local news, technological excellence, and extensive community involvement. In 1964 Bonneville International Corporation was created as the parent company of KSL.

SOURCES

Christensen, Bruce L. "Broadcasting." *Encyclopedia of Mormonism.* Edited by Daniel H. Ludlow. 4 vols. New York: Macmillan, 1992. 1:232–34.

Madsen, Arch L. "KSL Radio." *Encyclopedia of Mormonism.* Edited by Daniel H. Ludlow. 4 vols. New York: Macmillan, 1992. 2:800.

LLOYD D. NEWELL

KUWAIT. See **MIDDLE EAST** and **MUSLIMS.**

LAMANITES. Little Soldier, a Shoshoni, was one of many Native American converts to the Church during the pioneer period in Utah.

LABAN, SWORD OF. Nephi described the sword of Laban in the **Book of Mormon** (1 Ne. 4:9): "I drew it forth from the sheath thereof; and the hilt thereof was of pure gold, and the workmanship thereof was exceedingly fine, and I saw that the blade thereof was of the most precious steel." Nephi brought the sword to the promised land, and it became a prototype for sword making in Book of Mormon warfare. It probably was a symbol of kingship, a national treasure, as were other artifacts mentioned in the Book of Mormon. **Brigham Young** said that **Oliver Cowdery** and **Joseph Smith** saw the sword of Laban in the **Hill Cumorah** (Young, 19:38). A revelation given through Joseph Smith told the **Three Witnesses** that they would see the plates, the sword of Laban, and other sacred objects (D&C 17:1). David Whitmer later testified that this promise was realized.

Sources

Cook, Lyndon W., ed. *David Whitmer Interviews: A Restoration Witness.* Orem, Utah: Grandin Book, 1991. 26.

Nibley, Hugh. *The Book of Mormon.* Vol. 5 of *Collected Works of Hugh Nibley.* Salt Lake City: Deseret Book and Provo, Utah: Foundation for Ancient Research and Mormon Studies, 1988. 107–8.

Young, Brigham. *Journal of Discourses.* 26 vols. London: Latter-day Saints' Book Depot, 1854–86. 19:38.

ROBERT L. MARROTT

LABOR MISSIONARY PROGRAM. See **BUILDING MISSIONARIES.**

LAIE, HAWAII. Laie is located near the northeastern corner of the island of Oahu, about 35 miles from Honolulu, and is the spiritual, educational, and cultural center of the Church in the **Pacific** Basin. It has been an almost completely **Mormon** town since 26 January 1865, when Francis Hammond purchased Thomas Dougherty's 6,000-acre Laie plantation with $14,000 that had been lent to him by the Church.

Laie has struggled both as a business enterprise and as a "gathering place" through most of its history. At first missionaries tried several different crops as they attempted to establish a place for Hawaiian **Saints** to develop western skills and work habits. By 1868 sugar was the mainstay. Laie had its own mule-powered mill, and until 1919 it was the headquarters of the Hawaiian **Mission**.

Although the "gathering place" concept never materialized, and Laie never did become the population center of the Church in the Pacific, its significance as the spiritual focus was assured with the dedication of the Laie **Hawaii Temple**, 27 November 1919. The educational emphasis was added in 1955 when President **David O. McKay** dedicated the Church College of **Hawaii** (CCH). To help provide employment for the students, the **Polynesian Cultural Center** (PCC) opened in October 1963 and came to be regarded as the top commercial tourist attraction in the state, as well as a financial boon for both the community and the college. In 1974 CCH was absorbed by **Brigham Young University** and became **BYU–Hawaii**. With 2,000 students from **Asia**, the Pacific Basin, and the mainland, this university forms perhaps the most "international" campus in the world.

Today, with the Laie Hawaii Temple, BYU–Hawaii, and the PCC, Laie is home to approximately 7,000 residents.

SOURCES

Britsch, R. Lanier. *Moramona: The Mormons in Hawaii*. Laie, Hawaii: Institute for Polynesian Studies, 1989.

Law, Reuben D. *The Founding and Early Development of The Church College of Hawaii*. St. George, Utah: Dixie College Press, 1972.

KENNETH W. BALDRIDGE

LAMANITE MISSION OF 1830–1831. The Lord commanded **Oliver Cowdery** to "go unto the **Lamanites** and preach my gospel unto them"(D&C 28:8). **Peter Whitmer Jr.**, **Parley P. Pratt**, and **Ziba Peterson** were also called to this mission (D&C 30:5, 32:1–3). The group left **Fayette, New York**, in late October 1830 for Buffalo, where they met with Lamanites and left copies of the **Book of Mormon** with them. Next, they traveled to the **western reserve**, stopping at **Kirtland, Ohio**. There Parley P. Pratt renewed his acquaintance with **Sidney Rigdon**, a Reformed Baptist minister whom he knew from their days as students at a Baptist seminary. Rigdon was impressed with the gospel message and was baptized. After three weeks of preaching, about 130 individuals had joined the Church in Kirtland. Missionary work continued in the area surrounding Kirtland. **Frederick G. Williams**, a new convert, joined the missionaries and they visited the Wyandot tribe near Sandusky, **Ohio**.

After preaching in the Kirtland area, the missionaries continued to the Lamanite lands. On 20 December they left Cincinnati by steamer, but after a few days the river froze. They walked 200 miles to **St. Louis, Missouri**, then walked more than 300 miles of snow-covered prairies to **Independence, Jackson County, Missouri**. They covered almost 1,500 miles, preaching the gospel to anyone who would listen. In Independence, Whitmer and Peterson set up a tailor shop, while the other three visited the **Delaware Indian** tribe in the **Kansas** Territory. They met with Chief William Anderson Kithtilhund, the Delaware nation leader, and taught him and other Delaware leaders about the **Book of Mormon** and the restored gospel. After several days, the Indian Agency removed the missionaries because they did not have permission to enter the reservation. It appears, however, that the forces behind this expulsion were the ministers of other religions, especially Reverend Issac McCoy, who objected to the Mormon missionaries' presence among the Indians.

The missionaries returned to Independence. Parley P. Pratt traveled to St. Louis to obtain the necessary permission to preach to the Native Americans. After failing to obtain this permission, he continued to Kirtland, Ohio, to report to Joseph Smith the problems faced by the missionaries. Meanwhile, the other missionaries preached the gospel around Jackson County, baptizing as many as 50 individuals.

Although it appears that they failed in the stated purpose of preaching the gospel to the Lamanites, the mission was important in the development of the early Church. The missionaries established a **branch** of the Church in Kirtland, which later became a center place of the Church and opened the door for Jackson County to become identified as the center place of **Zion** (see D&C 57).

SOURCES

Backman, Milton V., Jr. *The Heavens Resound: A History of the Latter-day Saints in Ohio.* Salt Lake City: Deseret Book, 1983.

Pratt, Parley P. *Autobiography of Parley P. Pratt.* Edited by Parley P. Pratt Jr. Salt Lake City: Deseret Book, 1985. 47–62.

H. DEAN GARRETT

LAMANITES. Descendants of ancient **Book of Mormon** peoples are often called *Lamanites*. This term was first used in the Book of Mormon when Jacob enumerated the various factions into which the people had split, about a half century after Lehi's colony left Jerusalem. At this time the Lamanites were typically described as an idle people cursed because of their unrighteousness. A mark of dark skin was placed upon the Lamanites in order to distinguish them from the Nephites and prevent mingling in **marriage** and the possible resultant mixing of beliefs, values, customs, and behaviors (2 Ne. 5:21–24).

In much of the remainder of the text of the Book of Mormon there are accounts of numerous wars and hostilities between the Nephites and Lamanites. By 29 B.C., the formerly righteous Nephites had dwindled in unbelief and the Lamanites had become a more righteous people (Hel. 6:1). For example, Samuel, a Lamanite **prophet**, came to call the Nephites to repentance and prepare them for the coming of the Lord (Hel. 13–15).

Following the Savior's ministry among the peoples of the Book of Mormon (3 Ne. 11–26), there was a 200-year period of peace, in which there was complete economic, social, and religious unity. "There were no robbers, nor murderers, neither were there Lamanites, nor any manner of -ites; but they were in one, the children of **Christ**, and heirs to the **kingdom of God**" (4 Ne. 1:17). Afterward, iniquities returned, and "there was a great division among the people," those who rejected the gospel calling themselves "Lamanites" (4 Ne. 1:35, 38).

In the great final battle at Cumorah, as recorded in the Book of Mormon, the Nephites, who had become even more wicked, were destroyed, and the Lamanites were spared. These surviving Lamanites were actually descendants of both the original Nephites and Lamanites. Today Latter-day Saints typically identify American **Indians**, the indigenous peoples of Latin America, and Polynesians of the **Pacific** as "Lamanites." The Book of Mormon speaks of the time when the "scales of darkness" would fall from the eyes of the Lamanites, and they would once again become a "pure and delightsome people" (2 Ne. 30:6). President **Spencer W. Kimball** frequently spoke of this glorious destiny.

SOURCES

Kimball, Spencer W. *The Teachings of Spencer W. Kimball.* Edited by Edward L. Kimball. Salt Lake City: Bookcraft, 1982. 594–620.

LEWIS R. CHURCH

LAMBDA DELTA SIGMA. Lambda Delta Sigma was originally a fraternity established in 1936 by **Lowell L. Bennion** at the **institute of religion** adjacent to the **University of Utah**. Shortly after its establishment, it expanded to include women. In 1967 it was reorganized under the Church's direction as the women's sorority, while Sigma Gamma Chi, signifying Service to God and Country, became the men's fraternity. The purpose of Lambda Delta Sigma is to provide college women with opportunities to "increase personal *spirituality,* experience bonds of *sisterhood,* value *scholarship,* extend *support* to **family**, Church, and community, and render Christlike *service*" (Leader Handbook, 1).

SOURCE

Church Educational System. *Lambda Delta Sigma Leader Handbook*. Salt Lake City: The Church of Jesus Christ of Latter-day Saints, 1996.

CYNTHIA DOXEY

LANE, GEORGE. Reverend George Lane was a participant in the revivalism that swept western New York in the early 1820s. Born near Kingston, Ulster County, **New York**, on 13 April 1784, he joined the Methodist Episcopal Church during the winter of 1802–03. In July 1819 he was serving an appointment as presiding **elder** of the Susquehanna **district** for that denomination. **Oliver Cowdery** identifies him as one of those who helped kindle the spiritual yearnings that led young Joseph Smith to the Sacred Grove, stating that it was through Lane's instruction that "our brother's mind became awakened" (Porter, 338). **William Smith**, the brother of the Prophet, said that Joseph was in attendance when Lane preached a sermon on "What church shall I join?" and used as his text James 1:5. William further observed, "When Joseph went home and was looking over the text he was impressed to do just what the preacher had said, and going out in the woods . . . kneeled down and prayed" (Porter, 338). Reverend Lane's sister, Irene Lane Foote, was baptized into the Church on 28 February 1846 in the Montebello **Illinois** Branch. Reverend George Lane died at Wilkes-Barre, **Pennsylvania**, on 6 May 1859.

SOURCE

Porter, Larry C. "Reverend George Lane—Good 'Gifts,' Much 'Grace,' and Marked 'Usefulness.'" *BYU Studies* 9 (Spring 1969): 321–40.

LARRY C. PORTER

LANGHEINRICH, PAUL. Paul Langheinrich was a Latter-day Saint German genealogist who from 1945 to 1953 was involved in rescuing records that became the foundation for the modern-day Deutsche Zentralstelle für Genealogie (German Central Office for **Genealogy**) in Leipzig and the German collection of the **Family History Library** in **Salt Lake City**. He was born 19 February 1895, in Oberplanitz, Saxony, **Germany**, and died 12 April 1979, in Salt Lake City.

In August 1945, Paul Langheinrich began to locate parish records stored in mines and castles in eastern Germany and gather them to then East Berlin. Among the rescued records were thousands of microfilms of parish registers and thousands of parish register originals. Langheinrich microfilmed the unpreserved church books and added these films to the others he had found. In 1967 the original books as well as the microfilms were turned over to the newly established Zentralstelle für Genealogie in Leipzig. Some of the records preserved on microfilm by Paul Langheinrich contained church records of christenings, marriages, and burials that no longer exist in their original form.

SOURCES

Babbel, Frederick W. *On Wings of Faith.* Salt Lake City: Bookcraft, 1972. 57–59.
Mehr, Kahlile. "The Langheinrich Legacy. Record Gathering in Post-War Germany." *Ensign* 11 (June 1981): 23–25.
———. "Preserving the Source: Early Microfilming Efforts of The Genealogical Society of Utah 1938–1950." Master's thesis, Brigham Young University, 1985.

RAYMOND S. WRIGHT

LANGUAGE TRAINING MISSION. See **MISSIONARY TRAIN-ING CENTERS.**

LAS VEGAS, NEVADA. In general conference of April 1855, President **Brigham Young** called 30 men to establish a **mission** at the **Las Vegas** Springs. These missionaries were to instruct the Paiutes in farming and the gospel and construct a fort, where travelers between **Salt Lake City** and **San Bernardino, California**, could find protection, water, and rest. The first of these missionaries arrived at Las Vegas on 14 June 1855.

While completing a 150 square-foot fort and the accompanying mud-walled corral, they cleared the land, planted crops, and diverted irrigation water from Las Vegas Creek. They also discovered the Potasi lead deposit, established a post office, and began formalized instruction in **Native American** languages.

In 1856 a group of 30 mining missionaries was sent to Las Vegas. They were called to mine lead in the Potasi Mountains and ship it back for use in Salt Lake City. Internal dissension between the idealistic **Indian** missionaries and the hard driving mining missionaries, along with the inability of the group to grow sufficient food, led to the official disbanding of the Las Vegas Mission in 1857. Some of the group stayed until September 1858.

The present Las Vegas town site was established in 1905 by a **railroad** land auction. Latter-day Saints from farming communities moved to the new town to find jobs or start businesses. Beginning with a **Sunday School** formed by Newell Leavitt, the Las Vegas **Branch** grew until 1 June 1923 when the Las Vegas **Ward** of the Moapa Stake was created. Slow but continuous **growth** resulted in the creation of the Las Vegas **Stake** in 1954.

Church growth was rapid after the first stake organization. At the end of the twentieth century there were more than 160 wards and 18 stakes in the Las Vegas Valley. As a testament to the growth, maturity, and dedication of the LDS community in Southern Nevada, the Las Vegas Nevada **Temple** was dedicated on 16 December 1989.

SOURCES

Arrington, Leonard J. *The Mormons in Nevada.* Las Vegas: Las Vegas Sun, 1979.
The Guide to LDS in Southern Nevada. Las Vegas: Kanet Communications, 1997.
Hunter, Milton R. *Brigham Young the Colonizer.* Santa Barbara, Calif.: Peregrine Smith, 1973.

DAVID R. ROWBERRY

LATTER-DAY SAINTS' EMIGRANTS' GUIDE. The *Latter-day Saints' Emigrants' Guide,* published in February 1848, served as an aid to future **pioneers** and travelers on the trail from **Council Bluffs, Iowa,** to the **Salt Lake Valley.** Written by **William Clayton** following his journey with the vanguard company of Latter-day Saints in 1847, it included very accurate mileage and detailed descriptions of springs, creeks, landmarks, and camp locations along the trail. Clayton employed the use of an **odometer,** which he had developed with **Orson Pratt.** Clayton proposed using a mechanical odometer, Orson Pratt designed it, and Appleton Harmon constructed it. With these mileages and careful observations,

Clayton's guide was well respected and used by thousands of others in their journey west.

SOURCES

Clayton, William W. *The Latter-day Saints Emigrants' Guide.* Edited by Stanley B. Kimball. Gerald, Mo.: Patrice Press, 1983.

GUY L. DORIUS

LATTER-DAY SAINT HOSPITAL. See HOSPITAL.

LATTER-DAY SAINTS' MILLENNIAL STAR. See MILLEN-NIAL STAR.

LATTER-DAY SAINT STUDENT ASSOCIATIONS.

Latter-day Saint college students have often organized themselves into various associations. The first of these groups began in 1869 at the **University of Deseret** in **Salt Lake City**, when young scholars formed a debating society called **Delta Phi**. The ideals of this society included scholarship, spirituality, service, and brotherhood and sisterhood in the gospel.

At the end of **World War I**, returned missionary students at the **University of Utah** noticed a drift away from gospel ideals. To reestablish those ideals, the Friars' Club was organized on 24 November 1920. Soon colleges in **Ogden** and **Logan** created Friars' Clubs, and **Brigham Young University** converted their Doctors of Divinity group into a Friars' Club. Friars' Clubs were exclusively for men.

In December 1931 the first **Deseret Club** was formed to meet the needs of LDS students at the University of **California–Los Angeles**. Its purpose was to provide LDS college students an opportunity for social and spiritual activities with other Church members. Deseret Clubs were formed in many other places with large populations of LDS college students. In 1936 the Deseret Clubs were brought under the charge of the Church Department of **Education**, with Franklin L. West as commissioner.

In 1966 the Church General Board of Education asked Church Education to unify all Latter-day Saint college students and correlate their Church and social activities. In 1971 the Latter-day Saint Student Association (LDSSA) was established. It functioned as an arm of the **priesthood** to help the **family** and priesthood leaders of college students make the teachings of the gospel a major force in the lives of LDS college students.

In 1995 the **Church Educational System** invited all **single adults**, enrolled in college or not, to participate in the Latter-day Saint Student Association. At the end of the twentieth century there were more than 200,000 students active in the Association.

SOURCE

Berrett, William E. *A Miracle in Weekday Religious Education.* Salt Lake City: Salt Lake Printing Center, 1988. 133–37.

CRAIG K. MANSCILL

LATTER-DAY SAINTS' UNIVERSITY. Latter-day Saints' University was a forerunner to the **LDS Business College**. When it was established in 1886 it was called Salt Lake Stake Academy (1886–90). Its other names were Latter-day Saints' College (1890–1901, 1927–31), Latter-day Saints' University (1901–27), and LDS Business College (1931–present). At the end of the nineteenth century, the institution was "designed as the summit of the Church's educational system" (Alexander 163). Located in the center of **Salt Lake City**, it was replaced by **Brigham Young University** as the Church's primary educational institution in 1907.

As with other Church-sponsored educational institutions, the university suffered from a lack of finances. Eventually this lack of funding caused all but the business department of the university to close. In 1931 the business department changed its name to LDS Business College.

SOURCES

Alexander, Thomas G. *Mormonism in Transition: A History of the Latter-day Saints, 1890–1930.* Urbana: University of Illinois Press, 1986. 163–70.

Hilton, Lynn M. *The History of LDS Business College and Its Parent Institutions, 1886–1993.* Salt Lake City: LDS Business College, 1995.

CRAIG L. FOSTER

LATVIA. Latvia (population approximately 2.5 million) declared its independence from the **Soviet Union** on 20 August 1991, but the light of the gospel had previously penetrated this precinct behind the Iron Curtain. Missionary **Mischa Markow** had preached the gospel there on 9 October 1903. Three families had asked to be baptized, but Mischa had to leave the country.

By October 1991, a Latvian convert, baptized in **Holland**, had returned to his homeland—becoming the first Church member there in modern times. Missionary work in Latvia officially began in June of the following year, with the arrival of four elders and a missionary couple serving under the **Russia** St. Petersburg **Mission**. The first convert within Latvia (Gunars Kavals) was baptized soon thereafter on 25 July. Elder James E. Faust dedicated Latvia for the preaching of the gospel on 17 March 1993. On 1 July of that same year the Latvia Riga Mission (which also included **Lithuania** and **Estonia**) was organized. When headquarters moved three years later, the name was changed to the Lithuania Vilnius Mission. At the beginning of the year 2000, Latvia had 178 Church members, 4 **branches**, and 1 **district**.

SOURCES

Browning, Gary. *Russia and the Restored Gospel.* Salt Lake City: Deseret Book, 1997.
"Four European Lands Dedicated." *Church News,* 12 June 1993, 3.
1999–2000 Church Almanac. Salt Lake City: Deseret News, 1998. 346.

EMILY C. ZEIGLER

LAUREL CLASS. See YOUNG WOMEN.

LAW, WILLIAM. William Law was a counselor in the **First Presidency** who later became an enemy of the **Prophet Joseph Smith**. The son of Richard Law and Mary Wilson, he was born 8 September 1809, at Tyrone County, Northern **Ireland**. The family immigrated to Mercer County, **Pennsylvania**, about 1818. Law attended schools in Pittsburgh and Philadelphia and later relocated to Churchville, Peel County, Ontario (**Upper Canada**), where land was offered free. He married Jane Silverthorn about 1833, and they became the parents of eight children.

In 1836 the Laws were converted to the Church in Upper Canada by **John Taylor** and **Almon W. Babbitt**. In 1839, touched by the spirit of gathering, Law led a seven-wagon caravan of Latter-day Saints to **Nauvoo**, arriving in early November. In the spirit of unity and common purpose, he immediately invested in Nauvoo's future and was soon called to serve as second counselor to Joseph Smith in January 1841 (D&C 124:91). Also that year, Law became a captain in the **Nauvoo Legion**. He and his brother Wilson established and operated a steam-powered grain and sawmill, speculated in real estate, and owned a dry-goods store.

Although William Law and Joseph Smith shared much the same vision concerning proselyting, economic development, and political solidarity, they were divided by social background, interests, temperament, and methodology. The Prophet preferred a full-blown theocracy; William's vision was for a coherent, democratic society. Despite his initial enthusiasm, by 1843 Law felt threatened by Joseph Smith's leadership.

By early 1844, William broke with the Prophet and was excommunicated 18 April 1844. Amid a highly charged atmosphere, Law used the *Nauvoo Expositor* to publicize his growing opposition to the Prophet. The destruction of the *Expositor* press led to Joseph's arrest and eventual **martyrdom**. Labeled an apostate, William left Nauvoo with his family in June 1844.

Law continued for a decade as a merchant in northern **Illinois** but eventually turned his attention to medicine. Regionally acknowledged as a competent physician and surgeon, Dr. Law practiced for nearly 40 years near Apple River, Illinois, and at Shullsburg, **Wisconsin**. He died there of pneumonia at the age of 82 on 19 January 1892.

SOURCES

Cook, Lyndon W. *William Law.* Orem, Utah: Grandin Book, 1994.

LYNDON W. COOK

LAW, WILSON. See *NAUVOO EXPOSITOR.*

LAW OF ADOPTION. See **ADOPTION, LAW OF.**

LAW OF CONSECRATION. See **CONSECRATION, LAW OF.**

LAYTON, CHRISTOPHER. Mormon colonizer Christopher Layton was born in Thorncut, Bedfordshire, **England**, on 8 March 1821. In 1843, one year after his conversion, he migrated to **America**. In 1846 Layton participated in the march of the **Mormon Battalion** through **Arizona** to **California**. By 1852 he settled with his family in Kaysville, **Utah**. In the spring of 1883, Layton was called to Arizona, where he became the first president of the St. Joseph **Stake**. In addition to his Church responsibilities, Layton was involved in several business interests, including the operation of a number of stage lines. In 1898 poor health necessitated his release as **stake president**. His successor was Andrew Kimball, father of future Church president **Spencer W. Kimball**. Christopher Layton died 7 August 1898, in Kaysville, Utah.

SOURCES

Layton, Christopher. *Autobiography of Christopher Layton with an Account of His Funeral, a Personal Sketch, etc., and Genealogical Appendix.* Edited by John Q. Cannon. Salt Lake City: Deseret News, 1911.

McIntyre, Myron W., and Noel R. Barton, eds. *Christopher Layton.* Salt Lake City: Publishers Press, 1966.

ROBERT C. FREEMAN

LDS BUSINESS COLLEGE.

LDS BUSINESS COLLEGE. Located in central **Salt Lake City**, the LDS Business College is a fully accredited two-year school owned and operated by the LDS Church. The institution opened as the **Salt Lake Stake** Academy on 15 November 1886, after **Karl G. Maeser** was asked to establish in Salt Lake City an institution similar to the **Brigham Young Academy** in **Provo**. Originally housed in the **Social Hall**, the academy was designed to educate students in grades 7 and 8; however, the school quickly expanded to include instruction for the upper grades. In 1890 the school's name changed to Latter-day Saints' College. In 1901 it became **Latter-day Saints' University**; in 1927 it returned to Latter-day Saints' College. The location of the campus also changed often, but each site has been within a half mile of **Temple Square**. The business department was added in 1896, eventually accommodating a junior college curriculum. In 1931 financial crises brought on by the **great depression** required the closure of all curriculum departments, with the exception of business. Since that time the school has continued as the LDS Business College, with a curriculum emphasis on fundamental business skills, career preparation, and ethics in the business profession.

SOURCE

Hilton, Lynn M. *The History of LDS Business College and Its Parent Institutions, 1886–1993.* Salt Lake City: LDS Business College, 1995.

CAMILLE FRONK

LDS MESSENGER AND ADVOCATE.

LDS MESSENGER AND ADVOCATE. See *MESSENGER AND ADVOCATE, LATTER-DAY SAINTS'.*

LDSSA. See LATTER-DAY SAINT STUDENT ASSOCIATIONS.

LDS STUDENT ASSOCIATION. See LATTER-DAY SAINT STUDENT ASSOCIATIONS.

LEAGUE OF NATIONS. President Woodrow Wilson's plan for a League of Nations created a stir in **Utah** in 1919, as it did elsewhere. Church members were found on both sides of the debate. For example, **Reed Smoot**, Republican senator and **apostle** opposed ratification of the treaty, believing it would compromise American sovereignty. **B. H. Roberts** of the Seventy, on the other hand, favored the League. Both sides cited scriptures to bolster their positions. President **Heber J. Grant** declared his personal support of the League but stated that his endorsement was made "on the basis of his own opinion, rather than scripture," lamenting that the standard works had been dragged into this matter (Allen, 95). The Church did not declare an official stand on this issue and directed the Saints not to allow themselves to be divided over it. On 23 September, President Wilson's pro-League speech in the Salt Lake **Tabernacle** was enthusiastically received, but the treaty was rejected by the Senate in November, and Democrats helped defeat an amended version of the treaty in March 1920.

SOURCES

Alexander, Thomas G. *Mormonism in Transition.* Urbana: University of Illinois Press, 1986.

Allen, James B. "Personal Faith and Public Policy: Some Timely Observations on the League of Nations Controversy in Utah." *BYU Studies* 14 (Fall 1973): 77–95.

JOHN THOMAS

LEBANON. Lebanon is the ancient and modern name of the region immediately north of what is called today the state of Israel. Anciently Lebanon was known for its impressive cedar forests (1 Kgs. 4:33; 5:6; 2 Ne. 12:13; 24:8). Isaiah prophesied that the land would again become a fruitful field, a sign associated with the coming forth of the **Book of Mormon** and the restoration of the gospel (Isa. 29:17–18). Modern **prophets** indicate that this is being fulfilled (Smith, 98).

In the early nineteenth century, Lebanon (specifically Beirut) became for a time the headquarters of Protestant efforts to proselyte **Jews** and

Muslims of the Near East. During **Orson Hyde's** famous journey to Jerusalem in 1841 to dedicate the **Holy Land** for the gathering of Abraham's posterity, he docked in Beirut, where he regained his health before continuing his **mission**. In the last decades of the nineteenth century the country became part of the LDS Church's Turkish Mission, opened by **Elder Jacob Spori** in 1884. In 1921 Lebanon became part of the Armenian Mission; in 1933 part of the **Palestine**-Syrian Mission; and in 1950 part of the Near East Mission that was discontinued in January 1951. Between 1965 and 1975, when missionaries from the Swiss Mission served in Beirut, a **branch** of the Church operated there, but civil war forced Church activities to cease. A Church branch was reestablished in 1990, and by the beginning of the year 2000 this branch held 139 members. The Church's presence in Lebanon has generally been tenuous, tied to the fortunes of the country itself, which has suffered variously from war, political instability, and material privations.

SOURCES

Lindsay, Rao. "A History of the Missionary Activities of The Church of Jesus Christ of Latter-day Saints in the Near East, 1884–1929." Master's thesis, Brigham Young University, 1958.

1997–1998 Church Almanac. Salt Lake City: Deseret News, 1996. 412.

Smith, Joseph Fielding. *The Restoration of All Things.* Salt Lake City: Deseret Book, 1973. 53.

ANDREW C. SKINNER

LEBOLO, ANTONIO. Giovanni Pietro Antonio Lebolo was born 22 January 1781, in Castellamonte, a small city near Turin in northwestern **Italy**. He was an artifacts dealer and explorer. Current research has documented that Lebolo was in Egypt between 1817 and 1821. While there, he worked for Bernardino Drovetti in upper Egypt near Thebes. In one of his excavations, he discovered 11 Egyptian mummies and papyri; a portion of these writings led to the **book of Abraham**, now found in the **Pearl of Great Price**. The artifacts were shipped to Italy and eventually sent to **America**.

Oliver Cowdery reported that some of Lebolo's artifacts were secured by **Michael Chandler** in 1833 (Smith, 2:348). Chandler displayed the mummies for the next two years and sold all but four of them before arriving in **Kirtland**. He sold the last four mummies and some papyri to the **Prophet Joseph Smith**. Lebolo was 49 years old when he died at his home in Castellamonte, 19 February 1830.

SOURCES

Church News, 19 May 1985. 6.

Peterson, H. Donl. "Antonio Lebolo: Excavator of the Book of Abraham." *BYU Studies* 31 (Summer 1991): 5–29.

———. *The Story of the Book of Abraham.* Salt Lake City: Deseret Book, 1995. 36–85.

Smith, Joseph. *History of The Church of Jesus Christ of Latter-day Saints.* Edited by B. H. Roberts. 2d ed. rev. 7 vols. Salt Lake City: The Church of Jesus Christ of Latter-day Saints, 1932–51.

BRIAN L. SMITH

LECTURES ON FAITH. The Lectures on Faith are seven "lectures on theology" (Smith, 2:176) delivered by the presiding officers of the Church and some of the **elders** to the **School of the Elders**, in the printing office in **Kirtland, Ohio**, during the latter part of November and the first three weeks of December 1834. Authorship studies point to **Sidney Rigdon** as a major contributor to the writing of the lectures, and acknowledge that others, including **Joseph Smith**, **Oliver Cowdery**, **Parley P. Pratt**, and **William W. Phelps**, may also have had a hand in their composition.

Joseph Smith was well acquainted with the content of the lectures, inasmuch as he attended the School of the Elders and spent the month of January 1835 "preparing the lectures on theology for publication in the book of **Doctrine and Covenants**" (Smith, 2:180). According to President **John Taylor**, the lectures were "published with the sanction and approval of the **Prophet** Joseph Smith" (quoted in Woodford, 1:87).

In the original printing the lectures filled 74 pages. The lengths of the lectures differ, the longest being lecture 2 and the shortest being lecture 5. The format consists of numbered paragraphs in which principles are stated and scriptures quoted. Lectures 1 through 5 each end with a question-and-answer section—a catechism pertaining to the principles stated in the lecture. These sections are often about as long as the lectures themselves. There are no questions and answers at the end of lecture 6; rather, the following note appears: "This lecture is so plain and the facts set forth so self-evident that it is deemed unnecessary to form a catechism upon it. The student is, therefore, instructed to commit the whole to memory." Lecture 7 ends with a simple "Amen."

The lectures focus on different topics related to faith. Lecture 1 explains what faith is, and lecture 2 describes how mankind comes to know about God. Lectures 3 and 4 make clear the necessary and unchanging attributes of God, while lecture 5 deals with the nature of God the Father, his Son Jesus Christ, and the Holy Ghost. Lecture 6 proclaims that the willingness to sacrifice all earthly things is prerequisite to gaining faith unto salvation, and lecture 7 treats the fruits of faith—perspective, power, and eventually perfection.

From 1835 to 1921, the Lectures on Faith were published as part of the Doctrine and Covenants. The "Explanatory Introduction" of the 1921 edition states: "Certain lessons, entitled 'Lectures on Faith,' which were bound in with the Doctrine and Covenants in some of its former issues, are not included in this edition. Those lessons were prepared for use in the School of the Elders, conducted in Kirtland, Ohio, during the winter of 1834–1835; but they were never presented to nor accepted by the Church as being otherwise than theological lectures or lessons."

In addition to having been published as part of the Doctrine and Covenants, the lectures have been issued individually as a series in periodicals as well as together in single volumes. Between 1840 and 1843, Parley P. Pratt printed all seven lectures serially in the Millennial Star in England. After he was excommunicated, Sidney Rigdon also published the lectures serially from October 1845 to March 1846 without Church approval. About 1940, N. B. Lundwall included the Lectures on Faith, along with a number of other items, in one volume. In 1952, the Reorganized Church of Jesus Christ of Latter Day Saints published the lectures, and in 1985 Deseret Book Company of Salt Lake City released a hardbound edition. In 1990 the BYU Religious Studies Center published a volume entitled The Lectures on Faith in Historical Perspective. This volume contains a newly edited version of the lectures themselves, charts comparing the texts of various editions of the lectures from 1835 to 1990, a brief summary concerning authorship and history of the lectures, a discussion of each lecture, and a selected bibliography pertaining to the lectures.

SOURCES

Dahl, Larry E., and Charles D. Tate, eds. The Lectures on Faith in Historical Perspective. Provo, Utah: Religious Studies Center, Brigham Young University. 1990.

Smith, Joseph. History of The Church of Jesus Christ of Latter-day Saints. Edited by B. H. Roberts. 2d ed. rev. 7 vols. Salt Lake City: The Church of Jesus Christ of Latter-day Saints, 1932–51.

Woodford, Robert J. "The Historical Development of the Doctrine and Covenants." 3 vols. Ph.D. diss., Brigham Young University, 1974.

LARRY E. DAHL

LEE, ANN. Ann Lee was considered by the "United Society of Believers in Christ's Second Appearing"—commonly called **Shakers**—to be Christ at his Second Coming. She was born in **Manchester, England**, on 29 February 1736. She joined Jane and James Wardley's "Shaking Quaker" sect in 1758. After the deaths of her four children, Ann rose to prominence in the society by advocating celibacy. Following a series of visions she had while in prison for disturbing the Sabbath, Ann assumed leadership of the sect as the female Christ. Emigrating to **America** in 1774, she helped establish a Shaker community at Watervliet, **New York**, where she died 8 September 1784. In the spring of 1831, **Joseph Smith** received a revelation in **Kirtland, Ohio**, refuting several doctrines advocated by Ann Lee and the Shakers, such as a female Christ, celibacy, and abstinence from meat (D&C 49).

Sources

Ahlstrom, Sydney E. *A Religious History of the American People.* New Haven, Connecticut: Yale University Press, 1972. 492–94.

Andrews, Edward Deming. *The People Called Shakers.* New York: Dover, 1963. 3–50.

Andrew H. Hedges

LEE, HAROLD B. A monumental plaque near President Harold B. Lee's birthplace reads: "Harold B. Lee, eleventh president of The Church of Jesus Christ of Latter-day Saints, touched and changed countless lives." Harold Bingham Lee was born 28 March 1899, on a farm near Clifton, **Idaho**, the second son of Samuel Marion and Louisa Emeline Bingham Lee. On the farm Harold learned the value of hard work, thrift, sharing, determination, and independence. The chores started shortly after daybreak and continued until evening, when they were done with the aid of a lantern.

As a small boy, Harold saw some broken-down buildings in his neighbor's yard and imagined they were castles to be explored. As he started toward the buildings, he heard a voice say, "Harold, don't go over there." President Lee stated: "I looked in every direction to see where the speaker was. I wondered if it was my father, but he couldn't see me. There was no one in sight. I realized that someone was warning me of an unseen danger. . . . From that time on, I accepted without question the fact that there were processes not known to man by which we can hear voices from the unseen world, by which we can have brought to us the **visions** of eternity" (Lee, 17).

Harold was able to start school a year early at age five, because he could write his name and the alphabet. This set a pattern of high achievement for the rest of his life. While in high school, he participated in such extracurricular activities as debate and basketball, and he played in several bands and orchestras. He learned to play the trombone, mandolin, organ, and piano. Later as an **apostle** he often played piano accompaniment for the **general authorities** in their meetings.

Harold earned a teaching certificate at Albion State Normal School in Idaho. In 1916, at the age of 17, he began his first teaching job at the Silver Star School near Weston, Idaho. He certified by examination to teach 15 subjects. He was hired as principal, teacher, custodian, and groundskeeper for the one-room school. The wide age span of his 20–25 students from first to eighth grade challenged him and prepared him to teach widely and effectively. In 1917, at age 18, he became principal of the district school in Oxford, Idaho, where he served for three winters.

At age 21 (1920), he was called by President **Heber J. Grant** to serve in the Western States **Mission**, headquartered in Denver, **Colorado**. Elder Lee's missionary experience developed his ability to organize and motivate the Saints. After serving only nine months, he became a well-respected conference president. He returned home in early December of 1922. President Knight, his **mission president**, saw in this young missionary an undeniable capacity for leadership.

While on his mission Elder Lee met a sister missionary from **Utah** named Fern Lucinda Tanner. They later renewed their friendship while attending the **University of Utah** and were married in the **Salt Lake Temple** on 14 November 1923. Fern's wedding ring was purchased with the money Harold received from the sale of his trombone. During the early years of their marriage, money was scarce. Harold worked in a grocery store and a gasoline station while completing school during the evenings. He later became principal of Whittier School and then of the Woodrow Wilson School in the Granite School District of **Salt Lake City** from 1923 to 1928. Together he and Fern raised two daughters, Maurine and Helen.

Harold was appointed to the city commission by the mayor of Salt Lake City in 1932. One year later he was elected to that same position. Many felt that he should run for the office of governor or for the U.S. Senate. In 1936 he resigned his position on the city commission to devote his time to a call to help develop the Church's **welfare program**.

Previous to this time, the **great depression** had hit the **United States**. In 1930, when unemployment climbed drastically, more than half of the membership of the Pioneer **Stake** (where he was serving as president) was out of work. President Lee labored tirelessly as he prayed for solutions to help the suffering members. About 4,800 of the 7,500 members in his stake needed employment assistance. A welfare program was developed, and employment was found for many of the members. In 1936, under assignment from President Heber J. Grant, he traveled with Elder **Melvin J. Ballard** throughout the Church to help develop a Churchwide welfare plan. The following announcement was given: "Stake President Harold B. Lee is brought into the welfare organization with a wealth of experience gained from operation of a program in his own stake similar to that being projected for the church. President Lee had proved that it can be done and that it is a program worthy of the support of the entire church and to him is falling the task of completing much of the detail of organization." (Smith, 338).

In 1941, at the age of 42, Harold B. Lee was ordained an apostle by President Heber J. Grant, filling the vacancy left by the passing of Elder **Reed Smoot**. As the newest apostle, he was at least 20 years younger than all the other members of the **Quorum**. President **David O. McKay** appointed Elder Lee as chairman of the Church **Correlation** Committee in 1961. With faith and courage, Elder Lee accepted the calling and petitioned the Lord for his will concerning the correlation of all the organizations of the Church.

Elder Lee's wife of 39 years passed away on 21 September 1962. It was a time of great sorrow for him. He was married in the Salt Lake Temple to Freda Joan Jensen on 17 June 1963. At the time of their marriage, she was a member of the **Primary** general board and director of elementary education in the Jordan School District in the Salt Lake area.

On 23 January 1970, when **Joseph Fielding Smith** became president of the Church, Harold B. Lee was sustained as first **counselor** in the **First Presidency** and president of the Quorum of Twelve Apostles. Two years later, on 7 July 1972, he became president of the Church. President Lee enjoyed mingling with the people, attending **area conferences** in **England**, **Mexico**, and **Germany**; he was the first Church president to visit **Israel**. Concerning his new calling, he said, "Never think of me as the head of the Church, Jesus Christ is the head of this Church, I am only a man, his servant" (Tanner, 90).

President Lee served as president for just over 17 months. His death in Salt Lake City on 26 December 1973 came as a surprise to most members of the Church. For so many years he had been one of the youngest members of the Quorum of the Twelve. He had served as an apostle for 31 years.

SOURCES

Fielding, Lavina. "In Memoriam: President Harold B. Lee, 1899–1973." *Ensign* 4 (February 1974): 7–23.

Gibbons, Francis M. *Harold B. Lee, Man of Vision, Prophet of God.* Salt Lake City: Deseret Book, 1993.

Goates, L. Brent. *Harold B. Lee, Prophet and Seer.* Salt Lake City: Bookcraft, 1985.

Lee, Harold B. "The Way to Eternal Life." *Ensign* 1 (November 1971): 9–17.

Nibley, Preston. *The Presidents of the Church.* Salt Lake City: Deseret Book, 1974. 427–57.

Smith, Henry A. "Church-Wide Security Program Organized." *Improvement Era* 39 (June 1936): 333–38.

Tanner, N. Eldon. "A True Servant of God." *Ensign* 4 (February 1974): 91–94.

BRIAN L. SMITH

LEE, JOHN D. John Doyle Lee, born 12 September 1812, at Kaskaskia, **Illinois**, was a man whose name will always be associated with the **Mountain Meadows Massacre**. After his baptism on 17 June 1838, he immediately began throwing his energies into building the kingdom. He moved with his family to southern **Utah** during 1850–51, where he was industrious, ambitious, and devoted to the Church and his growing family.

In 1857, Lee got involved in the massacre at Mountain Meadows, and although he was not a major leader or decision maker, he carried out his part. He was tried by civil authorities for his participation and found guilty. He was also stripped of his Church membership and **priesthood blessings**. Lee was executed by government authorities at the site of the massacre on 23 March 1877. He is buried in Panguitch, Utah.

On 20 April 1961, the **First Presidency** and **Quorum of the Twelve** met together, and "it was the action of the Council after considering all the facts available that authorization be given for the re-instatement to membership and former blessings to John D. Lee" (Brooks, 376). On 8 and 9 May the required ordinances were performed in Lee's behalf in the **Salt Lake Temple**.

SOURCES

Brooks, Juanita. *John Doyle Lee: Zealot, Pioneer Builder, Scapegoat.* Glendale, Calif.: Arthur H. Clark, 1972.

KARL F. BROOKS

LEE, REX E. From July 1989 until 31 December 1995, Rex E. Lee served as president of **Brigham Young University**. He had previously been U.S. solicitor general—the chief appellate advocate for the federal government during the first four years of the Reagan administration (1981–85). During his tenure as solicitor general and in his private legal practice, he argued a total of 59 cases before the U.S. Supreme Court.

Rex was born 27 February 1935, in Los Angeles, California, and grew up in St. Johns, **Arizona**. After serving a **mission** for the Church in **Mexico**, he graduated from Brigham Young University in 1960, serving as student body president his final year. He married Janet Griffin in 1959, and they became the parents of seven children.

In 1963 Rex graduated first in his class from the University of Chicago Law School. He then served as a law clerk to Justice Byron R. White at the U.S. Supreme Court. In 1971, at the age of 37, Rex was asked to be the founding dean of the **J. Reuben Clark** Law School at BYU. He later served as assistant U.S. attorney general (1975–77) during the Ford administration.

In 1987 Rex was diagnosed with cancer. He battled the illness and the effects of its treatments for nine years. He died in **Provo, Utah**, in March 1996.

SOURCES

Lee, Rex E., and Janet Lee with Jim Bell. *Marathon of Faith.* Salt Lake City: Deseret Book, 1996.

JANET LEE

LEE COUNTY, IOWA. Lee County, located across the **Mississippi River** from **Nauvoo**, was the scene of many Latter-day Saint developments between 1839 and 1853. Iowa's most southeastern county, its main cities are Ft. Madison (north), **Montrose** (middle), and Keokuk (south).

While fleeing **Missouri** in 1839, some 40 LDS families, including those of **Brigham Young, John Taylor,** and **Wilford Woodruff**, occupied Old Fort Des Moines's deserted army barracks at Montrose. On 22 July 1839, a great day of **healing, Joseph Smith** and five **apostles** came to the barracks, where they healed Brigham Young and **Elijah Fordham**.

In late 1839 the Church purchased a townsite named Zarahemla at Montrose's west side and created the Iowa **Stake**. When this became Zarahemla Stake in 1841 (with **John Smith** as president), it included eight **branches** and nearly 700 members. For a brief time Zarahemla

Stake was the second largest community of **Saints** in **America**. Ambrosia Branch (Hawley's Settlement), three miles west of Montrose, once had 109 members. In 1839 the Church bought some 20,000 acres three miles south of Montrose and established Nashville. In 1839 some Saints settled in Keokuk, 10 miles south of Montrose. The Church bought land there and established a **branch**.

In Montrose on 6 August 1842, according to Anson Call, Joseph Smith pronounced his **Rocky Mountain prophecy**. On 23 June 1844, the **Prophet** fled from Nauvoo by boat to Montrose, planning an escape to the West, but he returned to Nauvoo at the urging of others and was ultimately killed at **Carthage Jail**.

During the exodus from Nauvoo, February through October 1846, Saints crossed to Montrose, Nashville, and Ft. Madison to begin their trek west. The **pioneers'** first camp, at **Sugar Creek**, was seven miles west of Montrose, and their next two campsites (Sugar Creek #2 and Lick Creek) were in Lee County. Poor Saints forced from Nauvoo in September 1846 camped at Potter's Slough, 1.5 miles north of Montrose's riverfront. On 9 October the **Poor Camp** Saints experienced the **miracle of the quail** when exhausted quail fell to the ground, easy to catch and cook for food.

In 1853 at Keokuk's north edge, some 2,000 Saints from **Europe** and the United States outfitted and assembled into nine wagon trains. Many of the men performed vital street grading work for Keokuk before heading across Iowa for **Utah**.

SOURCES

Black, Susan Easton, and William G. Hartley, eds. *The Iowa Mormon Trail: Legacy of Faith and Courage.* Orem, Utah: Helix Publishing, 1997.

Brown, S. Kent, Donald Q. Cannon, and Richard H. Jackson, eds. *Historical Atlas of Mormonism.* New York: Simon & Schuster, 1994. 58–59.

Kimball, Stanley B. "Nauvoo West: The Mormons of the Iowa Shore." *BYU Studies* 18 (Winter 1978): 132–42.

Smith, Joseph. *History of The Church of Jesus Christ of Latter-day Saints.* Edited by B. H. Roberts. 2d ed. rev. 7 vols. Salt Lake City: The Church of Jesus Christ of Latter-day Saints, 1932–51.

Deseret News, 1964. 3:345, 4:4, 6:548–49.

WILLIAM G. HARTLEY

LESOTHO. Lesotho, a mountainous enclave in **South Africa** with a population of two million, gained its independence from the **United Kingdom** in 1966. The Church was slowly established there with scattered LDS **families**, mainly from the **United States**, living in the country.

In July 1988, the first **branch** of the Church was formed at Maseru as part of the South African **Mission**. The Church registered with the government on 6 July 1989, and the first missionaries entered the country in September 1989. After the first local baptisms on 17 December, 1989, the Church grew to such an extent that a house was purchased on 2 January 1994 for meetings. The **seminary** program was introduced in 1991. A second branch of the Church was organized at Mazenod on 4 July 1993 but was disbanded due to lack of facilities for meetings. In the year 2000 there were 411 members living in Lesotho.

SOURCE

1999–2000 Church Almanac. Salt Lake City: Deseret News, 1998. 346–47.

H. DEAN GARRETT

L'ETOILE. The first **Mormon periodical** published on the European continent, *L'Etoile*—originally entitled *Etoile du Deseret* (Star of Deseret) —was established in May 1851 by **Louis A. Bertrand,** one of eight original members of the Paris **Branch**. Its purpose was to extend **missionary work,** since the French government forbade **meetings** of 20 people or more. The magazine was edited by **Elder John Taylor** of the Quorum of the Twelve and published monthly for only a year. The first ten issues were printed in Paris; the last two in **Liverpool, England.** In 1928 the periodical was resumed under the shortened name *L'Etoile.* Initially published in Geneva, its production moved to Frankfurt when the *Unified Magazine* was introduced in 1967. *L'Etoile* retained its original name both as a part of the *Unified Magazines* and as a part of the "**International Magazines,**" introduced in 1974. By the year 2000, the titles of all international Church periodicals, including *L'Etoile,* had been changed to *Liahona.*

SOURCES

"Church Publications." *Liahona* 1 (May 1907): 85.
1974 Church Almanac. Salt Lake City: Deseret News, 1974. 202.

CAMILLE FRONK

LIAHONA THE ELDERS' JOURNAL. *Liahona the Elders' Journal* (1907–45) was the longest running and most widely circulated **mission periodical** that the Church ever issued in North **America.** It was created on 6 April 1907, when the *Elders' Journal,* published by the **Southern States Mission** from 1903 to 1907, merged with *The Liahona,* a multi-mission publication issued by the Central States Mission. The magazine was published in **Independence, Missouri,** and in its prime had a circulation of close to 20,000 readers.

The official publication for all the **Mormon** missions of North America, *Liahona the Elders' Journal* printed editorials, sermons, articles, and poetry that were of interest to missionaries, the general membership, and those of other faiths who were investigating the Church. The periodical helped build a feeling of community among **Saints** who lived away from the Mormon settlements in the Intermountain West. This was especially so in the early part of the century before the automobile, airplane, radio, and telephone came of age. The *Liahona* went to thousands of investigators as a tract and assisted in the conversion process on numerous occasions. In some cases it was even the primary instrument of conversion. Duplication with other periodicals and continued financial problems eventually led to the magazine's demise in 1945. The *Liahona* remains a storehouse of information for historians interested in the activities of the Saints living in the North American missions during the first half of the twentieth century.

SOURCES

Garr, Arnold K. "A History of *Liahona the Elders' Journal,* A Magazine Published for the Mormon Missions of America, 1903–1945." Ph.D. diss., Brigham Young University, 1986.

———. "Liahona the Elders' Journal." In *Missouri.* Edited by Arnold K. Garr and Clark V. Johnson. Regional Studies in Latter-day Saint Church History series. Provo, Utah: Brigham Young University, 1994. 173–88.

ARNOLD K. GARR

LIAHONA (DIRECTOR OR COMPASS). The Liahona was the instrument presented to Lehi by the Lord to help guide his **family** through the wilderness (1 Ne. 16:10; Alma 37:38–40). The Lord promised the Three **Witnesses of the Book of Mormon** that they would have "a view of the plates, and also of the breastplate, the sword of Laban, the **Urim and Thummim** . . . and the miraculous directors" (D&C 17:1). That they indeed saw the Liahona is attested by **David Whitmer,** who stated that the **angel** "showed to [them] the plates, the sword of

Laban, the Directors, the Urim and Thummim, and other records"
(Anderson, 80).

SOURCE

Anderson, Richard Lloyd. *Investigating the Book of Mormon Witnesses.* Salt Lake City:
Deseret Book, 1981.

ALEXANDER L. BAUGH

LIAHONA MAGAZINE. The *Liahona* magazine is the official international magazine of The Church of Jesus Christ of Latter-day Saints.
Published in English and more than 40 other languages, it includes
articles and art on gospel topics for Latter-day Saints worldwide. The title
Liahona is a **Book of Mormon** term meaning "compass" or "director."

The first non-English Latter-day Saint magazine was published in
Wales in 1846. In 1967 and 1968 all official non-English LDS magazines
were combined into one publication produced in **Salt Lake City** under
the general designation "Unified Magazines." In 1974, this collective title
was changed to "International Magazines." Originally most language
editions carried different titles, such as *Der Stern* (German), *L'Étoile*
(French), *La Stella* (Italian), and *Tambuli* (English). Beginning in January
2000, all were titled *Liahona.*

Except for 16-page customized news inserts, the content of all
language editions is identical. Because the magazine includes articles for
adults, youth, and children, some pieces are selected from the *Ensign,
New Era,* and *Friend.* Other articles by and about Saints around the world
are published first in the *Liahona.* The *Liahona* includes articles from the
First Presidency of the Church, **general conference** addresses, and messages to be shared by **home teachers** and **visiting teachers**. Also included
are articles on Church history and doctrine, helps for leaders and teachers, features on topics such as marriage and parenthood, articles and
activities for youth and children, and faith-promoting narratives.

During the decade of the 1990s, the number of language editions of
the magazine grew substantially—from 19 (in January 1990) to 42 (in
January 2000). The magazine was published in Albanian, Armenian,
Bulgarian, Cebuano, Chinese, Czech, Danish, Dutch, English, Estonian,
Fijian, Finnish, French, German, Haitian, Hiligaynon, Hungarian,
Icelandic, Ilokano, Indonesian, Italian, Japanese, Kiribati, Korean,
Latvian, Lithuanian, Malagasy, Mongolian, Norwegian, Polish,
Portuguese, Romanian, Russian, Samoan, Spanish, Swedish, Tagalog,

Tahitian, Thai, Tongan, Ukrainian, and Vietnamese. Frequency of publication—monthly, bimonthly, quarterly, semiannually, or annually—varies by language edition, based primarily upon the number of Church members speaking the language. Subscribers may receive any language edition anywhere in the world.

SOURCES

Gardner, Marvin K. "A Magazine for All the World." *Liahona* (October 1998): 32–35.
Kelly, Brian K. "International Magazines." *Encyclopedia of Mormonism.* Edited by Daniel H. Ludlow. 4 vols. New York: Macmillan, 1992. 2:697. See also Appendix 3, "Church Periodicals," 4:1659–64.

MARVIN K. GARDNER

LIAHONA PERIODICALS, HISTORICAL OVERVIEW OF. Over the years, the **Book of Mormon** term *Liahona* has been used as the title for several Latter-day **Saint** publications. In 2000 it was the title of the Church's official international magazine, *Liahona.*

On 6 April 1907 the Central States Mission printed a multimission publication entitled *The Liahona.* Soon it merged with the *Elder's Journal* to become *Liahona the Elders' Journal,* which was published until 1945. In that year the title *Liahona* was given to the Mexican Mission's Spanish-language periodical, formerly known as *In Yaotlapiyoui* and *El Atalaya.* In 1951 the Brazilian Mission changed its Portuguese publication from *A Gaivota* to *A Liahona.* From 1963 to 1971, the **Indian** Committee of the Church published a periodical known as *The Liahona* for American Indians.

In 1967 and 1968, all official non-English LDS magazines were consolidated into one magazine produced in **Salt Lake City.** Although they were known collectively as the Unified Magazines and, beginning in 1974, as the International Magazines, they continued using their individual titles. Thus, the Spanish and Portuguese magazines continued using the title *Liahona,* while other non-English LDS magazines had different titles.

When the Samoan magazine began in 1968, it was titled *O Le Liahona.* In January 1995 the title of the Thai magazine, *Khao San Sitichon,* was changed to *Liahona.* In April 1995 the English international magazine, *Tambuli,* and the Indonesian magazine, *Teran Osza,* were also changed to *Liahona.*

Since June 1993, all new language editions of the Church's international magazine have been titled *Liahona,* beginning with Russian, Czech, and Hungarian. In January 1999 and January 2000, the titles of all remaining non-English language editions were changed to *Liahona*. In January 2000, there were 42 language editions of the *Liahona*.

SOURCES

Encyclopedia of Mormonism. Edited by Daniel H. Ludlow. 4 vols. New York: Macmillan, 1992. Appendix 3, "Church Periodicals," 4:1659–64.

Garr, Arnold K. "A History of *Liahona the Elders' Journal:* A Magazine Published for the Mormon Missions of America, 1903–1945." Ph.D. diss., Brigham Young University, 1986.

Historical files, *Liahona* magazine, Salt Lake City, Utah.

MARVIN K. GARDNER AND BRIAN M. HAUGLID

LIBERAL PARTY. The Liberal Party was organized at Corinne, Utah, in July 1870 under the chairmanship of **Patrick Edward Connor**. Opposed to **Mormon** "theocracy" (Church influence in politics) and **polygamy**, Protestants, Catholics, **Jews**, and **Godbeites** organized the Liberal Party after running William McGroarty for Congress in 1867. Its only pre-1888 success came in 1874 when its candidates captured the Tooele County government.

After 1887 some Latter-day Saints and **Gentiles** promoted cooperation. The founding of chambers of commerce in 1887 preceded the 1888 victory in **Salt Lake City** of a "Citizen's" ticket of both People's (Mormon) and Liberal Party candidates. After 1887 a few Liberals won election to the legislature. In 1889 Fred J. Kiesel won election as mayor of **Ogden**, and in 1890 George M. Scott won in Salt Lake City. In 1890 the fusionist Workingman's Party won in Salt Lake County.

Following the division of the Latter-day Saint people into the two national political parties in 1891, cooperation increased, and the Liberal Party lost membership, until a convention dissolved the party in December 1893.

SOURCES

Alexander, Thomas G. *Mormonism in Transition: A History of the Latter-day Saints, 1890–1930.* Urbana: University of Illinois Press, 1986.

Baskin, Robert N. *Reminiscences of Early Utah.* N.p.: R.N. Baskin, 1914.

Madsen, Brigham D. *Glory Hunter: A Biography of Patrick Edward Connor.* Salt Lake City: University of Utah Press, 1990.

THOMAS G. ALEXANDER

LIBERIA. The Republic of Liberia is located on the west coast of **Africa**. The official language is English, and the population is 20% **Muslim**, 20% Christian, and 60% followers of tribal beliefs.

The founders of Liberia were wealthy white Americans who in 1816 used private funds to free and resettle slaves back in Africa. The name Liberia refers to the liberty that the settlers were seeking, and the name of the capital, Monrovia, refers to James Monroe, the American president at the time of the colonization. Liberia gained independence in 1847, and it is the oldest black republic in Africa. During the 1990s the country was wracked by civil war, bloody factional fighting, and the collapse of the central state.

Among the early Church members in Liberia was Thomas Peihopa of **New Zealand**, who began teaching a **Sunday School** class in 1985 and had some 80 people participating. Expatriates Steven P. and Barbara Wolf, who were in Liberia on a military assignment, held Church meetings in their home in 1986.

J. Duffy and Jacelyn Palmer, along with Philander and Juanita Smartt, began formal **missionary work** in Liberia in 1987. The first convert was John Tarsnoh, who was baptized 22 August 1987. Five days later 47 converts were baptized in a lagoon, and the New Kru Town and Congo Town **Branches** were organized. Liberia was dedicated for the preaching of the gospel on 2 September 1987 by **Elder Marvin J. Ashton**, and on 1 March 1988 the Liberia Monrovia Mission was created. Two years later the mission had one **district** and eight branches, with several newly converted young men serving full-time missions. Due to a civil **war**, the missionaries were transferred to Freetown, **Sierra Leone**, on 8 May 1990, and the mission was closed in April 1991. During the war, only about 400 Church members remained in Liberia, the rest fleeing to neighboring countries.

Some of the members returned at the war's conclusion, but the missionaries were not reassigned until conditions were more settled. Church leaders discouraged large gatherings, advising members to meet in homes instead. In 1992, after other violence erupted and abated, members started regrouping. By the spring of 1993, seven of the eight branches had been reorganized. Even though missionary work was halted in Liberia, 43 young men and **women** from the country served missions elsewhere. Church members returned to their homes in the late 1990s and by the beginning of the year 2000 there were 2,694 members in 12 branches.

SOURCES

Middleton, John, ed. *Encyclopedia of Africa South of the Sahara.* 4 vols. New York: Macmillan Library Reference USA, 1997. 2:568–76.

1999–2000 Church Almanac. Salt Lake City: Deseret News, 1998. 347.
Oral histories of early Church converts collected by E. Dale LeBaron. Copies at BYU Library, Provo, Utah; LDS Church Historical Library, Salt Lake City, Utah.

E. DALE LEBARON

LIBERTY JAIL. Joseph Smith, Hyrum Smith, and four others entered Liberty Jail in **Clay County, Missouri,** on 1 December 1838 and remained there until **6 April** 1839, awaiting trial on charges stemming from the Missouri conflict in the fall of 1838.

Liberty Jail was a sturdy structure about 14 feet square, with only one small, heavily barred window measuring one foot by two feet. The interior consisted of two rooms, one upper and one lower. The lower room, or "dungeon," was lighted by two narrow window grates with heavy iron bars and was accessed by a trap door. The outside wall was made of rough-hewn limestone, two feet thick, and the inside wall consisted of 12-inch hewn oak logs. A 12-inch space filled with loose rock separated the two walls. Combined, the walls made a formidable barrier four feet thick.

While incarcerated, Joseph Smith wrote a poignant letter, extracts of which are found in **Doctrine and Covenants** 121–23. Because this long epistle contains some of the **Prophet's** most heart-rending pleas for help and understanding, coupled with an awe-inspiring and profound response from the Lord, **B. H. Roberts** called Liberty Jail a "prison-temple" (Roberts, 1:521). Today the Church operates a visitors' center at the site where tourists may see the partially reconstructed jail.

SOURCES

Holzapfel, Richard Neitzel, and T. Jeffery Cottle. *Old Mormon Kirtland and Missouri.* Santa Ana, Calif.: Fieldbrook, 1991. 218–25.
Roberts, B. H. *A Comprehensive History of The Church of Jesus Christ of Latter-day Saints, Century One.* 6 vols. Salt Lake City: The Church of Jesus Christ of Latter-day Saints, 1930. 1:521ff.

T. JEFFERY COTTLE AND RICHARD NEITZEL HOLZAPFEL

LIBRARIES. The archive maintained by the Historical Department of the Church is the most important of all Latter-day Saint library collections. It contains personal papers of Church leaders and invaluable manuscripts that document many early developments in Latter-day **Saint** history. Next in importance is the Harold B. Lee Library's Special Collections at **Brigham Young University.** This collection contains the manuscript materials, diaries, **journals,** and private papers of many prominent Church officials and members. BYU's collection of printed LDS works is probably the most complete in existence. The **RLDS** Church collections at **Independence, Missouri,** contain many of the earliest materials important to the development of the Church during **Joseph Smith's** life. The original manuscripts of many of Joseph's translation works are particularly valuable.

Herbert Howe Bancroft gathered many valuable manuscripts in preparing his landmark series of volumes on Western American history. Added to these, collections of Hugh E. O'Niel and Dale L. Morgan complete the core of the outstanding collection at the University of **California's** Bancroft Library in Berkeley. The Henry E. Huntington Library in San Marino, California, has acquired many rare manuscripts and publications.

The **University of Utah** began its collection in 1850 as the University of Deseret with a $5,000 congressional appropriation to establish a territorial library. Located in **Salt Lake City,** it is the alma mater of many loyal Church officials who gave their papers to the "U," which has acquired an impressive collection of manuscript and printed materials. The **Utah State Historical Society** began accumulating materials in 1897 and has developed a large archive, which includes important **family** collections. Utah State University Special Collections in **Logan** began slowly in 1916, but has been aggressive in recent decades in collecting important manuscripts and rare published materials. **Weber State University** in **Ogden, Utah**—a much later arrival—has acquired a few important materials.

Harvard has collected many important and rare specimens of **Mormon** Americana under the immediate supervision of famed historian Frederick Jackson Turner. Its most unique acquisition was the Eli H. Pierce collection, with the most complete known set of **pamphlets** for and against the Church. The **New York** Public Library has the Schroeder Collection of mostly **anti-Mormon** materials. Yale, Princeton, Cornell, **Michigan,** and **Wisconsin** hold the best of the other university collections. The National Archives and the Library of Congress have good collections of printed materials and copies of valuable manuscripts. Important libraries in the states where the Church had an early presence also have useful holdings, including the Chicago Historical Society, the University of Chicago, and Southern **Illinois** University.

SOURCE

Whittaker, David J., ed. *Mormon Americana: A Guide to Sources and Collections in the United States.* Provo, Utah: BYU Studies, 1995.

ALAN K. PARRISH

LIBYA. See **MIDDLE EAST.**

LICENSES. Even in its early stages, the Church instituted procedures to organize members effectively. One such procedure was licensing—Church leaders issued licenses to all men holding **priesthood** offices and to all missionaries called to preach the gospel. This regulated the conduct of Church members, since only those with a bona fide license could serve in the Church. This custom also served another important purpose. The license of an **elder** provided him with credentials that allowed **Mormons** and non-Mormons to rest assured that he represented the Church.

The first licenses were handwritten statements signed by the appropriate Church authority. Later, the Church began to use a printed form that included a space for the elder's name, the date, the place, and the clerk's name. Today ordination certificates and the documents given to full-time missionaries when they are set apart are types of licenses.

SOURCE

Cannon, Donald Q. "Licensing in the Early Church." *BYU Studies* 22 (Winter 1982): 96–105.

DONALD Q. CANNON

LIGHTNER, MARY ELIZABETH ROLLINS. See **ROLLINS, MARY ELIZABETH.**

LINCOLN, ABRAHAM. Abraham Lincoln, the 16th president of the United States, was born 12 February 1809 in Harden County, **Kentucky**. The Church first came in contact with Lincoln when the **Saints** migrated to **Nauvoo, Illinois**. He was then a member of the Illinois General Assembly, having served four consecutive two-year terms (1834–42). Lincoln was one of **Illinois'** state legislators who advocated a policy of fairness and tolerance toward the Saints. His vote helped secure passage of the **Nauvoo Charter** in the State House of Representatives in December 1840. No evidence has been found that Lincoln ever met the **Prophet Joseph Smith** while the two lived in Illinois, even though both were men of some notoriety. Some historians have proposed that the two could not have escaped such a meeting in 1843 while Joseph was on trial in Springfield (Lincoln's home), having been accused of complicity in the attempted assassination of **Missouri** former governor **Lilburn Boggs**.

After the death of Joseph Smith in 1844, Lincoln seemed to remain impartial and open-minded toward the Church, though he did so in the face of tremendous opposition. The fledgling **Republican Party** called for the extinction of those "**twin relics of barbarism**"—**slavery** and **polygamy** (Hubbard, 95). Lincoln responded to the speeches of **Stephan A. Douglas** (delivered between 1857 and 1860) by pointing out the inconsistency between Douglas's idea of popular sovereignty and his denunciation of the **Mormons** as "alien enemies and outlaws." Lincoln also saw Douglas's advocating the repeal of **Utah's** territorial status as a way of trying to destroy Mormonism (Hubbard, 96–97).

When Lincoln was elected president of the **United States** on 6 November 1860, the Saints had already been settled in their mountain home for several years while the rest of the nation careened toward the brink of destruction. By the time of his inauguration on 4 March 1861, several states had seceded from the Union and **civil war** was only weeks away. The rest of Lincoln's life was consumed by all aspects of America's most wrenching and deadly conflict and, consequently, he did not spend a great deal of time on other issues, the Latter-day Saints included. There are a few noteworthy events, however, that illuminate shifting Latter-day Saint views on President Lincoln.

Despite Lincoln's impartiality toward the Saints, many critical opinions about him were voiced publicly by Church leaders before and after his inauguration. When word reached **Utah** in 1860 that Lincoln had been elected, **John D. Lee** referred to him as "the Black Republican" (Hubbard, 97). In a **Tabernacle** address on 10 February 1861, President **Brigham Young** spoke of the weakness of Lincoln's political position and mockingly called him "King Abraham" (*JD*, 8:323–324). Again, during April 1861 **general conference**, President Young explicitly stated that the president was "like a rope of sand, or like a rope made of water. He is as weak as water" (Young, 9:4). These very negative attitudes seem to have been motivated by fear of stated Republican aims to eradicate the linked practices of slavery and polygamy, fear of the unleashed fury which would inexorably lead to the dissolution of the divinely inspired union, fear of Lincoln's assumed total agreement with Republican goals as well as his powerlessness to control the monumental carnage of the civil war prophesied by the Prophet Joseph Smith, and sympathy for the notion of states' rights.

President Lincoln's first official communication with the Church after becoming president was a letter to Brigham Young on 28 April 1862, asking him to raise a company of cavalry for 90 days' service to protect the newly completed transcontinental **telegraph** (1861) and overland mail against **Indian** attacks. Despite President Young's prompt reply and stated allegiance to **Washington**, Congress still passed **anti-Mormon** legislation that year. Known as the **Morrill Anti-Bigamy Act**, it called for penalties against anyone practicing polygamy and limited the amount of property the Church could own to a value of $50,000. President Lincoln signed the bill on 8 July 1862 but did not press for its enforcement.

President Young became anxious to know explicitly what future course Lincoln intended to pursue regarding "the Mormons," and sent **Thomas Stenhouse**, a Church member then in good standing who was in **Washington, D.C.**, transacting business, to visit Lincoln. When Brother Stenhouse presented his issue for Lincoln's consideration, the president was reportedly silent for some moments. He then said that when he was a boy on the farm in Illinois and had to clear the land of timber, occasionally he would come to a log that was too hard to split, too wet to burn, and too heavy to move, so he ploughed around it. He told Stenhouse, "You go back and tell Brigham Young that if he will let me alone, I will let him alone" (Hubbard, 103).

Historian George U. Hubbard has rightly regarded this episode as the real turning point in the LDS attitude toward Abraham Lincoln. It reflected "the kind of governmental policy which the Mormons had sought in vain for the past thirty-three years"—no special privileges, but freedom to worship God without unjust interference (Hubbard, 103). President Lincoln's second inauguration on 4 March 1865 was a time of great jubilation in Utah. Celebrations were held throughout the state, but the happiness was short-lived as word of the president's assassination spread across the country. President Lincoln died 15 April 1865 in Washington, D.C. Church members greatly mourned Lincoln's passing, and a memorial service was held in his honor on Sunday, 16 April in the **Salt Lake Tabernacle**. Since that time Church leaders have highly praised Lincoln, teaching that he was foreordained and reserved for his unique time and circumstance in mortality (Hubbard, 108).

SOURCES

Hubbard, George U. "Abraham Lincoln As Seen by the Mormons." *Utah Historical Quarterly* 31 (Spring 1963): 91–108.

Skinner, Andrew C. "Lincoln's Presidency." *Encyclopedia of North American History.* Edited by John C. Super. Tarrytown, N.Y: Marshall Cavendish Corp., 1999. 697–701.

Young, Brigham. *Journal of Discourses [JD]*. 26 vols. London: Latter-day Saints' Book Depot, 1854–86.

Andrew C. Skinner

LION HOUSE. The Lion House was built from 1854 to 1856 in Salt Lake City to house the families of **Brigham Young**. It is distinguished by the statue of a lion above the front porch and by its many gothic-style gables. Brigham Young died there in 1877. Members of the Young family continued to occupy the house until 1900, when the Church acquired it. Over succeeding years it served many uses, including that of a **Church Office Building**, classrooms and dormitory for **Latter-day Saints' University**, and a social center for young women. Since 1968 it has housed a reception center and cafeteria.

Sources

Gates, Susa Young. *The Life Story of Brigham Young*. New York: Macmillan, 1930. 322–63.

Spencer, Clarissa Young. *Brigham Young at Home*. Salt Lake City: Deseret Book, 1974. 23–31.

W. Randall Dixon

LIQUOR BY THE DRINK. During the late 1960s, the phrase "liquor by the drink" described a legislative bill that was proposed to remove restrictions on the sale of alcohol by the drink within **Utah**. The proposal pitted groups who advocated increased access to liquor against those who opposed loosening restrictions on alcohol. The LDS Church was the most notable opponent to the bill, basing its opposition on issues of safety, health, crime, and associated government costs. **Apostles Marion G. Romney, Howard W. Hunter**, and **Gordon B. Hinckley** were designated spokesmen for the Church in expressing opposition. In the end, the measure was defeated by a nearly two-to-one margin.

Sources

Allen, James B., and Glen M. Leonard. *The Story of the Latter-day Saints*. 2d ed. Salt Lake City: Deseret Book, 1992. 620.

Dew, Sheri L. *Go Forward with Faith*. Salt Lake City: Deseret Book, 1997. 291–94.

Robert C. Freeman

LITERACY. In 1972 the Church determined that an ongoing literacy effort was needed to help all members read and understand the gospel for themselves. From their experiences in Central and **South America**, Church leaders had learned that many members lacked essential literacy skills. To address this reality, they initiated a pilot literacy project in **Bolivia** and then appointed a task group to determine the best way for the Church to proceed in providing literacy education where needed.

In 1979 the **Church Educational System** accepted the responsibility to develop basic Spanish literacy materials that would enable the **Saints** to read the scriptures and other publications in order to more fully participate in Church programs. The success of the Spanish literacy materials written by M. Nelson Dibble and a team of Church educators led to the development of English literacy materials in 1990. As a result, the English literacy program *Ye Shall Have My Words* was published to complement the existing Spanish materials.

The literacy effort received further attention in 1992 when the **Relief Society** organization, under the leadership of **Elaine L. Jack**, selected literacy as a service priority. Working with the Church Educational System, the Relief Society promoted literacy using the existing Spanish and English materials. With the encouragement of the **First Presidency**, materials were distributed to the **wards** and **stakes**, and training was provided to Relief Society volunteers. The objectives were to teach literacy skills to those who could not read or write and to encourage family and individual gospel study. The Church's commitment to literacy development remains a priority of the Relief Society organization and Church Educational System.

SOURCES

Derr, Jill M., Janath R. Cannon, and Maureen U. Beecher. *Women of Covenant: The Story of the Relief Society.* Salt Lake City: Deseret Book, 1992.

Dockstader, Julie A. "Literacy: Not Just Reading and Writing." *Church News*, 7 September 1996, 8–10.

Gospel Literacy Guidelines for Priesthood and Relief Society Leaders. Pamphlet. Salt Lake City: The Church of Jesus Christ of Latter-day Saints, 1993.

Hinckley, Gordon B. "Ambitious to Do Good." *Ensign* 22 (March 1992): 2–6.

DENNIS A. WRIGHT

LITERARY FIRM. The Literary Firm was a business partnership organized by Church leaders in November 1831 for the purpose of printing the official literature of the Church. The members of the firm included

Joseph Smith, Oliver Cowdery, Martin Harris, Sidney Rigdon, John Whitmer, W. W. Phelps, Frederick G. Williams, and Jesse Gause. The partners of the firm had dedicated themselves in their respective responsibilities so that the profits from the sale of Church publications would not only benefit them personally but also the Church at large.

Agenda items for the Literary Firm initially included the printing and distribution of (1) the **revelations**, (2) the **New Translation of the Bible**, (3) a Church hymnal, (4) a Church **almanac**, (5) Church newspapers (*The Evening and the Morning Star, Messenger and Advocate, Northern Times*, the **Kirtland** reprint of *The Evening and the Morning Star*, and the *Elders' Journal*), and (6) children's **literature**. In 1837, the company printed a second edition of the **Book of Mormon**. The firm was undercapitalized at organization and subsequently suffered from poor cash flow and frequent turnover in management. By 1838, after nearly five years of operation, it began to dissolve.

LYNDON W. COOK

LITERATURE.

LITERATURE. Mormon literature includes, in a variety of genres, the literary expression of the distinctive history, theology, and culture of the Latter-day Saints. It can be traced through four distinct historical periods: The Foundation (1830–80), Home Literature (1880–1930), The "Lost Generation" (1930–60), and New Impulses (1960–present).

THE FOUNDATION (1830–80)

Mormon literature begins with the **Book of Mormon** (1830), which includes the genres of sacred narrative history, divine **revelation**, and spiritual biography interspersed with doctrinal sermons, letters, devotional poetry, and elements of epic poetry (see Rust; Jorgensen). Recent literary studies identify the ancient linguistic, literary, and anthropological roots of the Book of Mormon (Nibley; Welch; Sorenson). Two additional, distinctive foundational works of Mormon literature are the **Doctrine and Covenants** (Walker) and the **Pearl of Great Price**, which, with the Holy **Bible**, make up the sacred writings of the Church.

The letters, **journals**, and discourses of **Joseph Smith Jr.**, together with his doctrinal, historical, and autobiographical writings, are foundational literary documents, many of which are contained in *History of The Church of Jesus Christ of Latter-day Saints* (1902). The literary power of the Prophet's several autobiographical accounts of the **First Vision** and of subsequent events of the **Restoration** have received increased scholarly attention in recent years (Allen; Lambert and Cracroft; Jessee; King), as has his landmark "**King Follett Discourse**" (Larson).

Latter-day Saint discourses or sermons, regularly recorded and published in the *Journal of Discourses* and **Conference Reports** (1850–present), provide a major literary archive, establish doctrine, and set the literary standard for the Church. The Latter-day Saint **hymn**, the principal poetic form of the nineteenth-century Church, reflects LDS theology, history, and faith across different periods, as in the hymns of **W. W. Phelps**, **Parley P. Pratt**, and **Eliza R. Snow**. Pratt's classic *Autobiography of Parley P. Pratt* (published posthumously, 1874) is a gem of early **Mormon** autobiography. The diaries, journals, and letters of the **Saints** tell in spare, unadorned, and almost modern prose of trials and triumphs on their literal and spiritual journeys to **Zion**. The early Saints, however, saw fiction as a waste of time. **Brigham Young** decried novel reading (Young, 9:173), and **George Q. Cannon** wrote in the *Juvenile Instructor,* "This habit of novel-reading is very common in these days, and is the cause of many of the evils which prevail in the world" (4).

HOME LITERATURE (1880–1930)

Under mounting pressure from both increasing Gentile influence in **Utah** Territory and **Latter-day Saint** youth eager to be more open to eastern cultural influences, Church leaders turned growing literary interests to LDS advantage by promoting a "Home Literature," written by Latter-day Saints for Latter-day Saint audiences, teaching and portraying Mormon ideals and doctrines. Nephi Anderson asserted that "a good story is artistic preaching" (Anderson, 271). In *Added Upon* (1898), the first LDS novel, Anderson follows his characters on their salvation journeys from premortal life through exaltation. The novel, never out of print, has spawned such spinoffs as *Saturday's Warrior* (1974) and *My Turn on Earth* (1977).

Other important literary works of the Home Literature period include an ambitious epic poem about the Restoration, *Elias, an Epic of the Ages* (1904), by **Orson F. Whitney**. LDS classics of the period are *Joseph Smith the Prophet-Teacher* (1905) and *A Comprehensive History of The Church of Jesus Christ of Latter-day Saints* (1930), by **B. H. Roberts** and *The Articles of Faith* (1899) and *Jesus the Christ* (1915), by **James E. Talmage**.

THE "LOST GENERATION" (1930–1960)

The counter-reaction by young Mormon writers in the 1930s and 40s to perceived provinciality and the overt moralism of Home Literature gave rise to a generation of expatriate, alienated writers called Mormondom's "Lost Generation" (Geary). Several of them reached large national audiences and shaped national perceptions of the Saints: Vardis Fisher's *Children of God: An American Epic* (1939); Maurine Whipple, *The Giant Joshua* (1941); Virginia Sorensen's *A Little Lower Than the Angels* (1942), *The Evening and the Morning* (1949), and short story collection, *Where Nothing Is Long Ago: Memoirs of a Mormon Childhood* (1963); Samuel W. Taylor's *Family Kingdom* (1951) and his comic Mormon novel, *Heaven Knows Why* (1948). Fawn McKay Brodie's psychobiography *No Man Knows My History* (1945) initiated a new era of Mormon studies as LDS scholars responded to her interpretation of the life of Joseph Smith, and Juanita Brooks aired long-closed closets in her ground-breaking history, *The Mountain Meadows Massacre* (1950).

New Impulses (1960–present)

Contemporary Mormon literature, in responding to a postwar generation accustomed to literary realism and desiring to express themselves as human beings and Latter-day Saints in the modern world, has tended to divide into two divergent but not always disparate literary streams: New Home Literature, which self-consciously teaches, cautions, models, and posits LDS solutions to the problems of modern life, and New Realism, which examines life from the perspective of generally faithful but uncomfortable Latter-day Saints who, not content with facile answers, reexamine traditional and orthodox Latter-day Saint solutions and answers to life's problems and questions.

New Home Literature ranges from an outpouring of didactic popular novels aimed at **Latter-day Saint** teenagers and young adults to the well-crafted historical fiction of Gerald N. Lund, the reception of whose multivolume series *The Work and The Glory* (1990–98), has been a literary phenomenon in Mormon letters. There is an increasing trickle of fiction that undertakes to examine the Mormon/human condition faithfully but artistically, as in Dean Hughes's series, *Children of the Promise* (1997–2000), about a Mormon family swept up in **World War II. Latter-day Saint** authors have found large national audiences for their values-based children's, teenager, young adult, and comic fiction. Nonfiction Home Literature, consisting principally of the collected discourses and biographies of **general authorities** and the devotional commentaries and personal essays of prominent Latter-day Saints, has also found a large LDS readership.

New Realists, such as Orson Scott Card, Douglas H. Thayer, Phyllis

Barber, Donald R. Marshall, Levi S. Peterson, and, in nonfiction, Edward A. Geary and Terry Tempest Williams, differ primarily from New Home Literature authors in their artistic purposes. New Realists escaped the limitations of didacticism to refract Mormon light onto different surfaces to achieve different artistic effects. Mormon poetry, thanks to Clinton F. Larson's influence and the recent advent of trained poets who are faithful Latter-day Saints, is establishing a growing body of contemporary poetry that is innately but not distinctively LDS. A number of poets have published collections of their verse: Edward L. Hart, Marden J. Clark, John Sterling Harris, Carol Lynn Pearson (who achieved national prominence with *Beginnings,*[1974]), Emma Lou Thayne, Lewis Horne, Kathy Evans, Linda Sillitoe, Susan Elizabeth Howe, and Lance Larsen. Mormon playwrights have been increasingly successful in narrowing the canvas from sweeping epics to the **drama** of individual Mormon lives. The future of Mormon letters appears rich, varied, and promising.

SOURCES

Allen, James B. "The Significance of Joseph Smith's 'First Vision' in Mormon Thought." *Dialogue* 1 (Fall 1966): 29–45.

Anderson, Nephi. *Improvement Era* 1 (February 1898): 271

Cannon, George Q. *Juvenile Instructor* 5 (8 January 1870): 4.

Cracroft, Richard H., and Neal E. Lambert. *A Believing People: The Literature of the Latter-day Saints.* Provo, Utah: BYU Press, 1974; Salt Lake City: Bookcraft, 1979.

England, Eugene. "Mormon Literature: Progress and Prospects." *Mormon Americana: Guide to Sources and Collections in the United States.* Edited by David J. Whittaker. Provo, Utah: BYU Studies, 1995: 455–505.

Geary, Edward A. "Mormondom's Lost Generation: The Novelists of the 1940s." *BYU Studies* 18 (Fall 1977): 89–98.

Jessee, Dean. *The Personal Writings of Joseph Smith.* Salt Lake City: Deseret Book, 1984.

Jorgensen, Bruce W. "The Dark Way to the Tree: Typological Unity in the Book of Mormon." *Literature of Belief: Sacred Scripture and Religious Experience.* Edited by Neal E. Lambert. Religious Studies Monograph series. Provo, Utah: Religious Studies Center, Brigham Young University, 1981. 5:217–31.

Journal of Discourses. 26 vols. London: Latter-day Saints' Book Depot 1854–86.

King, Arthur Henry. "Joseph Smith As a Writer." *The Abundance of the Heart.* Salt Lake City: Bookcraft, 1986. 197–205.

Lambert, Neal E., and Richard H. Cracroft. "Literary Form and Historical Understanding: Joseph Smith's First Vision." *Journal of Mormon History* 7 (1980): 31–42.

Larson, Stan. "The King Follett Discourse: A Newly Amalgamated Text." *BYU Studies* 18 (Winter 1978): 193–208.

Nibley, Hugh. *Lehi in the Desert & The World of the Jaredites.* Salt Lake City: Bookcraft, 1952; 1980.

Rust, Richard D. *Feasting on the Word: The Literary Testimony of The Book of Mormon.* Salt Lake City: Deseret Book and FARMS, 1997.

Sorenson, John L. *An Ancient American Setting for the Book of Mormon.* Salt Lake City: Deseret Book; Provo, Utah: FARMS, 1985.

Walker, Steven C. "Doctrine and Covenants as Literature." *Encyclopedia of Mormonism.* Edited by Daniel H. Ludlow. 4 vols. New York: Macmillan, 1992. 1:427.

Welch, John W. "Chiasm in the Book of Mormon." *BYU Studies* 10 (February 1969): 69–84.

RICHARD H. CRACROFT

LITHUANIA. Lithuania is a republic on the east coast of the Baltic Sea and was formerly part of the Soviet Union. Missionaries preached in this land as early as 1937.

One of the first members of the Church from Lithuania was Irute Meskiene. She was baptized in **Hungary** in 1988. The first permanent missionaries were called to the republic in 1992.

On 20 May 1993, **Elder M. Russell Ballard** dedicated Lithuania for the preaching of the gospel. The service was attended by 27 people. Earlier he had said to the missionaries: "From this small beginning, you will see the Church grow and prosper here. There will be many **branches** and then a **district** and, in the Lord's due time, there will be **stakes**. Who knows, if we could look out 50 years, perhaps a small **temple**" ("Four European Lands," 7).

In 1996 the **mission** headquarters was moved from **Latvia** to Lithuania, and the mission was renamed the Lithuania Vilnius Mission. By the beginning of the year 2000 there were 499 members in 3 branches.

SOURCES

"Four European Lands Dedicated." *Church News,* 12 June 1993.

1999–2000 Church Almanac. Salt Lake City: Deseret News, 1998. 347–48.

DAVID R. CROCKETT

LITTLE, FERAMORZ. Feramorz Little was a mayor, world traveler, and business partner of **Brigham Young**. Born 14 June 1820 in Aurelius, New York, to James and Susan Little, Feramorz was also the nephew of Brigham Young. Since James Little died when Feramorz was four, Brigham played a significant role in Feramorz's life. There must have been high regard between the two, because they consistently entered into business ventures together and President Young eventually named a son Feramorz Little Young (Cook, 280).

From 1872 to 1873 Feramorz joined President **George A. Smith**, along with **apostles Lorenzo Snow** and **Albert Carrington**, on a dedicatory **mission** to **Palestine**. He is known for his civic, business, and philanthropic efforts rendered throughout his life. He served three consecutive terms as mayor of **Salt Lake City**. A prominent banker and industrialist, he built the first dam across the Jordan River, allowing for greater irrigation of the **Salt Lake Valley**. He had extensive lumber holdings and built the **Utah** state prison at its present locale. His many business enterprises left Feramorz very comfortable financially. He consistently drew from these resources to assist the poor and needy. Feramorz granted these gifts and endowments in general anonymity, so only his closest associates were aware of his extensive generosity. Feramorz Little died 14 August 1887 in Salt Lake City.

SOURCES

Cook, Lyndon W. *The Revelations of the Prophet Joseph Smith.* Provo, Utah: Seventy's Mission Bookstore, 1981. 280.

Jenson, Andrew. *Latter-day Saint Biographical Encyclopedia.* 4 vols. 1901–36. Reprint, Salt Lake City: Western Epics, 1971. 2:485–87.

BLAIR G. VAN DYKE

LITTLE, JESSE C. Jesse Carter Little is best remembered as president of the Eastern and Middle States **Mission** (1846–52). He was born 26 September 1815 in Belmont, Waldo County, **Maine**. He later served as a **counselor** to Edward Hunter in the presiding bishopric.

As president of the **Eastern States Mission**, Brother Little was the voice of the Church and chief negotiator for government services in **Washington, D.C.**, during the critical **exodus** era in Church history. With the aid of **Thomas L. Kane**, he persuaded President **James K. Polk** to ask **Brigham Young** and the Latter-day Saints, who were then encamped near **Council Bluffs** on the **Missouri River** in July 1846, to form a **Mormon Battalion** that would march west to **California** in **America's war** with **Mexico**.

Little interrupted his eastern mission to go to the **Great Basin** in 1847, but he soon returned to his duties as **mission president** in the East. In 1852 he returned to **Utah**, where he settled permanently. After his service in the presiding bishopric (1856–1874), he moved to Littleton, Morgan County, Utah. He died 26 December 1893 in **Salt Lake City**.

SOURCES

Bennett, Richard E. *Mormons at the Missouri, 1846–1852: "And Should We Die."* Norman, Okla.: University of Oklahoma Press, 1987.

Jenson, Andrew. *Latter-day Saint Biographical Encyclopedia.* 4 vols. 1901–36. Reprint, Salt Lake City: Western Epics, 1971. 1:242–43.

RICHARD E. BENNETT AND JONATHAN T. BOWNS

LITTLE SOLDIER, CHIEF. Chief Little Soldier was a **Native American** leader of the "Weber-Utes" (a **Shoshone**-speaking Gosiute band in the Weber and Morgan County, **Utah,** area in the nineteenth century) and a noted friend and ally of the early **Mormon** settlers of northern Utah.

Born at Red Butte Canyon east of **Salt Lake City** in about 1821, Little Soldier became acquainted with **Brigham Young** and the Latter-day Saints soon after their July 1847 entry into his homeland. He retained a generally amicable relationship with them until his death 37 years later.

In 1874, Little Soldier and his people traveled to a small Church-sponsored farm near Franklin, **Idaho.** While there, they were converted to the gospel and were baptized on 6 June. After his baptism, Little Soldier was **ordained** an **elder.** On 15 June 1875, he and his wife, Wango-bit-y, were sealed at the **Endowment House** at Salt Lake City. In 1876, Little Soldier and his people joined other Native Americans in establishing farms at Lemuel's Garden in Box Elder County, Utah. He became one of the first Native Americans in the **United States** to apply for homestead lands. Toward the end of his life, Little Soldier returned to the **Ogden** area, where he died 22 April 1884.

SOURCES

"An Exemplary Indian." *Deseret Evening News,* 24 April 1884.

Christensen, Scott R. "Chief Little Soldier: Shoshone Chieftain, Mormon Elder." *Pioneer* 42 (Winter 1995): 16–19.

Hill, George Washington. "A Brief acct of the Labors of G W Hill while engaged on a mission to the House of Israel, October 1, 1876." Manuscript. LDS Church Archives, Salt Lake City.

SCOTT R. CHRISTENSEN

LIVERPOOL, ENGLAND. The chief port of **England** in the nineteenth century, Liverpool became a center for Latter-day Saint emigration and publication. During the heaviest period of emigration between 1850 and 1869, more than 30,000 British **Saints** left from Liverpool. The harbor was a busy one, receiving 20 ships on 19 July 1837, the day the *Garrick* docked, carrying the first seven missionaries to England.

Though every missionary arrived in or left from Liverpool, it was not until January 1840 that **Elder John Taylor** began to do **missionary work** there. On Sunday, 2 February, he gave the first Latter-day Saint public discourse in Liverpool to a crowd of 300 in a hall he hired. After his speech, ten people came forward to be baptized. When **Brigham Young** landed in Liverpool with four other **apostles** on 6 April 1840, they found John Taylor mightily engaged in his labors with almost 30 members in Liverpool. Among the first to be baptized was George Cannon, brother to Elder Taylor's wife, Leonora. His 12-year-old son, George Q., later served as first counselor to Presidents Taylor, Woodruff, and Snow. On 27 July 1840, Elder Taylor hired the Music Hall on Bold Street for 12 months for the purpose of giving public lectures on the doctrines and history of the Church. This building is one of a very few still standing from that era. In the period from 1840 to 1855, the Liverpool Branch had 2,000 converts.

Because printing was cheaper there than in **America**, Liverpool became the book and **pamphlet** supply depot for the Church throughout the world. The *Millennial Star* was published there for a time. In 1851 the first editions of the **Pearl of Great Price** were also printed in Liverpool. The *Journal of Discourses* began there on 1 November 1853 as a 16-page semimonthly **periodical**.

———

SOURCES

Allen, James B., Ronald K. Esplin, and David J. Whittaker. *Men with a Mission: The Quorum of the Twelve Apostles in the British Isles, 1837–1841.* Salt Lake City: Deseret Book, 1992.

Bloxham, V. Ben, James R. Moss, and Larry C. Porter, eds. *Truth Will Prevail: The Rise of The Church of Jesus Christ of Latter-day Saints in the British Isles, 1837–1997.* Cambridge: Cambridge University Press, 1987.

Evans, Richard L. *A Century of "Mormonism" in Great Britain.* Salt Lake City: Publishers Press, 1984.

DAVID COOK

LOGAN, UTAH. See CACHE VALLEY.

LOGAN TEMPLE. Brigham Young presided at the groundbreaking ceremonies for the Logan Utah **Temple** on 17 May 1877. **Truman O. Angell** was the architect and **Charles O. Card** the superintendent of construction. Temple construction took exactly seven years; the dedicatory services, presided over by President **John Taylor**, were held 17 May 1884, making it the second temple completed in **Utah**. Built from siliceous limestone quarried in Green Canyon north of Logan, the temple proper measures 171 feet long, 95 feet wide, and 86 feet high, with the east and west towers rising 170 and 165 feet respectively. Approximately 25,000 persons participated in the building's construction, estimated to have cost $607,000. Since its dedication the temple has undergone a number of renovations, the most extensive taking place from 1976 to 1979 when the interior portion of the building was demolished and redesigned and a new annex constructed. President **Spencer W. Kimball** presided at the rededication of the Logan Temple beginning 13 March 1979.

<hr />

SOURCES

Arrington, Leonard J., and Melvin T. Larkin. "The Logan Temple and Tabernacle." *Utah Historical Quarterly* 41 (Summer 1973): 301–14.

Carmack, Noel A. "Labor and Construction of the Logan Temple, 1877–1884." *Journal of Mormon History* 22 (Spring 1998): 52–79.

Olsen, Nolan Porter. *Logan Temple: The First 100 Years*. Providence, Utah: Keith W. Watkins and Sons, 1978.

ALEXANDER L. BAUGH

LONDON TEMPLE. The London England Temple was the second **temple** built by the Church in **Europe** and one of five dedicated by President **David O. McKay**, who took a personal interest in every phase of its development. The site was selected by June 1952 and was purchased the following year. The groundbreaking ceremony took place Saturday, 27 August 1955, under the direction of President McKay. More than 1,000 people attended, and **music** was provided by the **Mormon Tabernacle Choir**.

Faced with cut white Portland limestone, the temple measures 84 by 159 feet with a tower rising 156 feet 9 inches from ground level. The final 33-foot spire is sheathed in lead-coated copper. The temple was toured by 76,324 people, after which it was dedicated in six sessions, 7–9 September 1958, by President McKay.

During extensive remodeling in the early 1990s, the floor space was increased from 34,000 to 42,652 square feet, and three more endowment rooms were added. President **Gordon B. Hinckley** then rededicated the temple 18–20 October 1992 in ten sessions.

In both dedicatory prayers, Presidents McKay and Hinckley expressed appreciation for the Magna Carta, which guaranteed fundamental freedoms and was signed centuries earlier in the same county of Surrey, where the temple is located.

―――――

SOURCES

Bloxham, V. Ben, James R. Moss, and Larry C. Porter, eds. *Truth Will Prevail: The Rise of The Church of Jesus Christ of Latter-day Saints in the British Isles, 1837–1997.* Cambridge: Cambridge University Press, 1987.

Cowan, Richard O. "The Church Comes of Age in Britain." In *British Isles.* Edited by Donald Q. Cannon. Regional Studies in Latter-day Saint Church History series. Provo, Utah: Brigham Young University, 1990. 194–214.

1999–2000 Church Almanac. Salt Lake City: Deseret News, 1998. 458–59.

DAVID COOK

LOS ANGELES, CALIFORNIA. Los Angeles has been the site of Latter-day Saint activity for more than a century and a half. In 1847 most of the **Mormon Battalion** was ordered to Los Angeles, where its members helped erect Fort Moore and raised the American flag as part of the community's first 4th of July celebration. Other **Saints** came when the nearby **San Bernardino** colony was established in 1851. Even after most Latter-day Saints returned to **Utah** in 1858 following the coming of **Johnston's Army**, many stayed behind; however, for three decades there was no official Church organization in southern **California**.

By 1890 Latter-day Saints were meeting in the home of Eliza Wollacott near the present civic center. A branch was officially organized in 1895, and soon Church membership in the south exceeded that in the northern part of the state. Following the 1906 **San Francisco** earthquake, headquarters of the California **Mission** were moved to Los Angeles.

The first LDS chapel in the area (1913) was located on Adams Blvd. The first urban **stake** outside of the Intermountain West was organized here (1923). A new stake center, the Wilshire **Ward** chapel (1929), became a recognized landmark.

Church membership continued to expand, especially following **World War II**, and the number of stakes and wards multiplied. Church members made significant contributions to civic and cultural life, some becoming well known in the entertainment industry.

For decades Los Angeles Saints had participated in excursions to do temple work in **Arizona** and **St. George** until the **Los Angeles Temple** was completed in 1956. It was the largest **temple** in the Church at the time.

During the later twentieth century, Church growth was especially rapid among Hispanics and Asians. In 1984 the Spanish-speaking Huntington Park West Stake became the Church's first stake organized for an ethnic minority.

By the 1990s there were more than 40 stakes in the Los Angeles metro area, with Church membership exceeding 400,000.

SOURCES

Cowan, Richard O., and William E. Homer. *California Saints: A 150-Year Legacy in the Golden State.* Salt Lake City: Bookcraft, 1996.

Orton, Chad M. *More Faith Than Fear: The Los Angeles Stake Story.* Salt Lake City: Bookcraft, 1987.

RICHARD O. COWAN

LOS ANGELES TEMPLE. At the time of its dedication in 1956, the Los Angeles California Temple was the Church's largest temple. The site had been selected by President Heber J. Grant in 1937, but construction was postponed because of World War II. In 1949 President George Albert Smith expressed his desire that the temple make an architectural and cultural contribution to Los Angeles.

Because of rapid postwar growth in California, architect Edward O. Anderson designed the temple to accommodate three hundred persons per session and added a large priesthood assembly room on the upper floor. The temple was constructed of reinforced concrete, specifically engineered to withstand California earthquakes. Faced with perfectly matched crushed-stone panels, the temple reflected Mayan architecture. Measuring 364 feet long by 241 feet wide, it contained 190,000 square feet. Surmounted by a tower more than 257 feet high, the temple was the second tallest structure in Los Angeles at the time it was completed and was visible from ships 25 miles out to sea. A 15½-foot gold-leafed statue of Moroni was sculpted by Millard F. Malin. The temple's large ordinance rooms featured beautiful murals.

Under the direction of the local temple building committee headed by the Pasadena Stake president, Howard W. Hunter, California Saints contributed generously to the building fund, raising more than one-and-a-half times the amount requested. Nearly 700,000 people visited the temple during a 51-day open house. The temple was dedicated in eight sessions, 11–14 March 1956, by President David O. McKay. Apartments for temple workers and visitors were opened in 1966.

SOURCES

Anderson, Edward O. "The Los Angeles Temple." *Improvement Era* 56 (April 1953): 225–27; 58 (November 1955): 802–7 and color insert.

Cowan, Richard O. *Temples to Dot the Earth.* Springville, Utah: Cedar Fort, 1997. 152–6, 179, 262.

Cowan, Richard O., and William E. Homer. *California Saints: A 150-Year Legacy in the Golden State.* Provo: Religious Studies Center, Brigham Young University, 1996. 347–50.

Orton, Chad M. *More Faith Than Fear: The Los Angeles Stake Story.* Salt Lake City: Bookcraft, 1987.

RICHARD O. COWAN

LOST MANUSCRIPT. From 12 April to 14 June 1828, **Martin Harris** served as **Joseph Smith's** scribe, producing 116 manuscript pages. To gain family support, he persuaded Joseph to let him take the pages to **Palmyra, New York,** to show his family. During a three-week period when he visited relatives, attended to business, and served jury duty, the 116 pages were stolen, altered, and reportedly destroyed by his wife, Lucy.

In the preface of the 1830 edition of the **Book of Mormon,** Joseph Smith wrote: "I would inform you that I translated . . . one hundred and sixteen pages, the which I took from the Book of Lehi . . . which said account, some person or persons have stolen [and altered the words], and being commanded of the Lord that I should not translate the same over again . . . if I should translate the same over again, they would publish that which they had stolen [and altered to discredit] this work." The book of Lehi contained largely secular history; another portion of the Book of Mormon taken from the small plates of Nephi contained a religious account of the same time period.

SOURCES

James, Rhett Stephens. *The Man Who Knew: The Early Years, 1824–1830.* Cache Valley, Utah: Martin Harris Pageant Committee, 1983.

———, and Beverly Scott. "Lucy Harris: Wife of the Witness." *Mormon Heritage Magazine* 2, 2 (July/August 1995): 7–13.

RHETT STEPHENS JAMES

LOTTERIES. Government-sponsored lotteries are considered a form of gambling by the Church. These are games of chance that take "without giving value in return" and "where the winner has been enriched at the expense of a multitude of losers." Some attempt to justify lotteries by presenting them as an innocent way of generating revenue for government needs and programs. Regardless of noble ideals, public lotteries violate the moral standards of the **Church,** which has long opposed gambling in its various forms; the Church encourages its members to oppose the legalization and government sponsorship of lotteries. The **First Presidency** has stated that "experience has clearly shown gambling to be harmful to the human spirit, financially destructive of individuals and families, and detrimental to the moral climate of communities" ("Stand," 74). Not only can lotteries become an addictive obsession, but they also foster the ruinous belief that one can get something for nothing.

SOURCES

"Church's Stand against Gambling." *Ensign* 22 (March 1992): 74.
"First Presidency Issues Statement against Gambling." *Church News,* 5 October 1986, 4.
"Gambling Is 'Morally Wrong, Politically Unwise,' Says Elder Oaks." *Ensign* 17 (March 1987): 76–77.

MATTHEW O. RICHARDSON

LOUISIANA. Missionary work began in Louisiana as a result of individuals writing to the **Prophet Joseph Smith** in **Nauvoo** requesting **elders** to preach, even providing money to help defray expenses. **Elder** Harrison Sagers was sent in 1841, and he baptized several converts.

Between 1841 and 1855, New Orleans was the principal port for Latter-day Saint immigrants arriving from **Europe**. During most of this time, a **branch** of the Church functioned in the city.

Louisiana was originally a part of the **Southern States Mission** but was later assigned to the Central States Mission. The Church experienced some persecution, but in most cases local residents defended the missionaries.

The first **stake** was organized in New Orleans in 1955, and by the year 2000 six additional stakes had been added to serve 24,143 **Saints** living in 63 **wards** and **branches**. A **mission** was headquartered in Baton Rouge, which was also the site of a **temple** that was dedicated in the year 2000.

SOURCE

1999–2000 Church Almanac. Salt Lake City: Deseret News, 1998.

DAVID F. BOONE

LOZANO, AGRICOL. An attorney and prominent Church leader in **Mexico**, Agricol Lozano was born to Latter-day Saint parents Josefina

Herrera and Agricol Lozano in Tula, Hidalgo. The eldest of 13 children, he excelled in track during his youth. After serving a **mission**, Agricol enrolled at the University of Mexico and eventually reached his goal of becoming an attorney. Lozano served as a **high councilor**, president of three **stakes**, **regional representative**, and president of the Mexico City **Temple**. In 1993, when Mexico's new constitution allowed official recognition of churches, Agricol, the Church's legal counsel, was chosen to officially receive the "certificate of registration" from Mexico's government officials. He wrote several articles and books, including *Historia del Mormonismo en Mexico*.

SOURCES

Hart, John L. "Mexico Formally Registers Church." *Church News,* 17 July 1993, 3.
Moreno, Erin K. "Mexico City Temple Leader Devoted Lifetime to Church." *Church News,* 23 October 1993, 10.

CLARK V. JOHNSON

LUCAS, SAMUEL D. Samuel D. Lucas was a prominent merchant, official, and militia member in **Independence** who played a leading role in the expulsion of the **Saints** from **Jackson County** and later from the state of **Missouri**. Born in **Kentucky** on 17 July 1799, he settled in Independence before 1827. He was elected a county judge there in 1831 and served as court clerk from 1842 to 1865.

Lucas and other leading citizens signed a "Secret Constitution" in 1833 that resulted in the forced departure of Latter-day Saints from Jackson County later that year. In 1838 he led the 4th Division of the Missouri militia against the **Saints** in **Caldwell County**. Lucas laid siege to **Far West**, dictated the surrender of **Joseph Smith** and other Church leaders, and sentenced the prisoners to death, and then confiscated their property. When **Alexander Doniphan** refused to carry out the death sentence, Lucas took the prisoners to Independence. Ironically, once in Jackson County, Lucas treated the prisoners quite mildly, placing them in a house, feeding them at a hotel, and allowing them to walk about the area freely during the few days before they were returned to **Richmond** for a court hearing.

Lucas remained in Independence during the **Civil War**; he died there on 23 February 1868.

SOURCES

Jesse, Dean C. "'Walls, Grates, and Screeking Iron Doors': The Prison Experience of Mormon Leaders in Missouri, 1838–1839." *New Views of Mormon History.* Edited by Davis Bitton and Maureen U. Beecher. Salt Lake City: University of Utah Press, 1987. 19–42.

LeSuer, Stephen C. *The 1838 Mormon War in Missouri.* Columbia: University of Missouri Press, 1986.

Wilcox, Pearl G. *Jackson County Pioneers.* Independence, Mo.: Pearl G. Wilcox, 1975.

John Thomas

LUCIFER. See SATAN.

LUND, ANTHON H. Anthon Hendrik Lund was born in Aalborg, Denmark, 15 May 1844. When he was three years old his mother died and his father was drafted into the military. Anthon was raised by his grandmother, who joined the Church when Anthon was nine years old. He was baptized on his twelfth birthday. A brilliant young man, he was first in his class in Aalborg Public School and learned English by taking private lessons. At age 13 Anthon was called on a **mission** to teach English to the Scandinavian **Saints** who were emigrating to **America**. When he was 18 years old he moved to the United States, settling in **Utah**. In 1870 he married Sarah Ann Preston, and they moved to Ephraim. The couple had nine children.

Brother Lund held many prominent Church positions, making two missionary journeys to **Scandinavia**, the second time as president of the mission. In 1889 he became a member of the **Quorum** of the Twelve **Apostles**, and in 1893 he was called as president of the **European Mission**. Brother Lund was appointed to succeed **Franklin D. Richards** as Church historian in 1900 and was called as second counselor in the **First Presidency** under **Joseph F. Smith** in 1901. During Joseph F. Smith's presidency, he was called to be first counselor and retained this position under **Heber J. Grant**. Elder Lund died 2 March 1921 in Salt Lake City.

SOURCES

Flake, Lawrence R. *Prophets and Apostles of the Last Dispensation.* Provo, Utah: Religious Studies Center, Brigham Young University, 2001. 191–94.

Jenson, Andrew. *Latter-day Saint Biographical Encyclopedia.* 4 vols. 1901–36. Reprint, Salt Lake City: Western Epics, 1971. 3:753.

Lives of Our Leaders. Salt Lake City: Deseret News, 1901. 206.

Lawrence R. Flake

LUXEMBOURG. Only one branch of the Church exists in Luxembourg, a small nation located between **Germany**, **France**, and **Belgium**. The first formal proselyting began in 1963 when missionaries from the Franco-Belgian **mission** entered the country. A branch was formed in the mid-1960s, but it was discontinued in 1971. Luxembourg became part of the Belgium Brussels Mission in 1974. A branch was again organized in 1988. In 1994 Luxembourg was placed under the Metz France **District**. At the beginning of the year 2000 the country had 155 members living in 1 branch.

SOURCES

Luxembourg Branch Historical Report. LDS Church Archives, Salt Lake City.
1999–2000 Church Almanac. Salt Lake City: Deseret News, 1996. 348.

JEFFREY L. ANDERSON

LYMAN, AMASA M. Missionary, colonizer, cabinet-maker, and **apostle**, Amasa Mason Lyman was born 30 March 1813 in Lyman, **New Hampshire**. Bereft of his parents at a young age, Lyman passed an unhappy childhood being raised by his uncle, a strict disciplinarian and zealous religionist, who instilled in him a love of reading, philosophy, and universal truth. In 1832 he converted to Mormonism and shortly afterwards filled the first of 16 **missions** for the Church. Lyman was a faithful member of **Zion's Camp** who suffered in the subsequent **Missouri** persecutions. Also a close friend and confidant of **Joseph Smith**, he became a member of the **Quorum** of the Twelve in August 1844. Nine years earlier he had married Louise Maria Tanner, the first of his eight wives.

Lyman played a key role in the **exodus** west in 1847, encouraging the sick detachment of the **Mormon Battalion** in **Pueblo** to come to the **Salt Lake Valley**. In 1849 he and **Charles C. Rich** supervised the short-lived, conflict-torn **Latter-day Saint** settlement in **San Bernardino** with Lyman elected first mayor of that southern **California** town in 1853.

While serving yet another mission, this time to **England** (1860–63), **Elder** Lyman gave a sermon at Dundee, Scotland, in which he denied the necessity of Christ's atoning sacrifice. Upon his return he became involved in spiritualism, headed up the short-lived New Movement or "Church of **Zion**" in the so-called **Godbeite anti-Mormon** movement, and was ultimately excommunicated from the Church in 1870. He died on 4 February 1877 in Fillmore, Utah. His baptism was reconfirmed and his **priesthood** blessings restored in 1909. His son **Francis M. Lyman** was called to the apostleship in 1881, as was his grandson **Richard R. Lyman** in 1918.

SOURCES

Arrington, Leonard J. *Charles C. Rich—Mormon General and Western Frontiersman.* Provo, Utah: Brigham Young University Press, 1974.

Hefner, Loretta. "From Apostle to Apostate." *Dialogue* 16 (Spring 1983): 90–104.

Lyman, Albert R. *Amasa Mason Lyman: Trailblazer and Pioneer from the Atlantic to the Pacific.* Delta, Utah: Melvin A. Lyman, 1957.

Walker, Ron W. *Wayward Saints—The Godbeites and Brigham Young.* Urbana: University of Illinois Press, 1998.

RICHARD E. BENNETT

LYMAN, AMY BROWN. Amy Brown Lyman, the eighth general president of the **Relief Society**, served during the period of **World War II**. She incorporated new technology, such as the use of office machines and uniform record keeping, into the Relief Society and was responsible for documenting the history of its organization. Born 7 February 1872 in Pleasant Grove, **Utah**, she later attended **Brigham Young Academy** and taught at her alma mater for four years. She married **Richard R. Lyman** on 9 September 1896, and they had two children. When Richard was studying at the University of Chicago, Amy took classes in social welfare at the same university and worked at Hull House, a social settlement organization that provided community services and recreational facilities for the poor. Her experiences in Chicago greatly influenced her 30 years of service in the Relief Society, which included being the founder, teacher, and director of the Church's **Social Services** Department, general board member, assistant secretary-treasurer, and first counselor. She died 5 December 1959 in **Salt Lake City**.

SOURCES

Derr, Jill Mulvay, Janath Russell Cannon, and Maureen Ursenbach Beecher. *Women of the Covenant: The Story of the Relief Society.* Salt Lake City: Deseret Book, 1992.

Hefner, Loretta L. "The Decade Was Different: Relief Society's Social Services Department, 1919–1929." *Dialogue* 15 (1982): 65–72.

Lyman, Amy B. *In Retrospect: Autobiography of Amy Brown Lyman.* Salt Lake City: Deseret Book, 1945.

Peterson, Janet, and LaRene Porter Gaunt. *Elect Ladies: Presidents of the Relief Society.* Salt Lake City: Deseret Book, 1990.

MARY JANE WOODGER

LYMAN, FRANCIS M. Francis Marion Lyman was born 12 January 1840 in Good Hope, **Illinois**, to **Amasa M. Lyman** and Maria Louisa Tanner. When only eight years old, Francis crossed the plains, driving an ox team in the absence of his father, who had gone ahead to the Salt Lake Valley with **Brigham Young** and the first company. In 1860 he filled a two-and-a-half-year **mission** to **England**, leaving his wife, Rhoda Ann Taylor, and their first child in a one-room cabin he had built. On his return trip from England he was in charge of a company of 800 emigrants.

Called in 1877 to move to Tooele and preside over the **stake** there, Francis Lyman became active in politics and was elected county recorder and also a representative to the territorial legislature. In 1880 he was called to make a tour of the **branches** of the Church in southern **Utah**, **Arizona**, and **New Mexico**. While on this trip, 27 October 1880, he was chosen as a member of the Quorum of the Twelve Apostles. On 6 October 1903 he became president of that Quorum. He died 18 November 1916 in **Salt Lake City**.

SOURCES

Flake, Lawrence R. *Prophets and Apostles of the Last Dispensation.* Provo, Utah: Religious Studies Center, Brigham Young University, 2001. 337–39.
"In Honor of President Francis M. Lyman." *Improvement Era* 21 (January 1917): 193.
Lives of Our Leaders. Salt Lake City: Deseret News, 1901. 110.

LAWRENCE R. FLAKE

LYMAN, RICHARD R. On 6 April 1918, Richard Roswell Lyman was sustained as a member of the **Quorum** of the Twelve **Apostles**, where he served for 25 years before his excommunication in 1943. He was born in Fillmore, **Utah**, on 23 November 1870. His father, **Francis M. Lyman**, was an apostle, as was his grandfather, **Amasa M. Lyman**, who also served for a short time as a **counselor** to **Joseph Smith**.

A fine student, Richard was educated in the Tooele, Utah, public schools, the **Brigham Young College** in **Logan**, **Utah**, and the **Brigham Young Academy** in **Provo**, where he served as student body president. After his graduation he went east and earned a bachelor's degree in engineering from the University of **Michigan** and a Ph.D. in engineering from Cornell University. He then returned to Utah and was appointed head of the department of engineering at the **University of Utah**. He also served as chairman of the Utah Road Commission and vice chairman of the Utah

Water Storage Commission. He devised a numerical system for naming city streets. Dr. Lyman was a consulting engineer for the Grand Coulee Dam in Washington, the Columbia Basin water project, and the Metropolitan Water District of Los Angeles. In 1915 his essay on the flow of streams won the James R. Coe gold medal, the highest award given to civil engineers in the **United States**.

He married **Amy Brown**, who became a noted sociologist and served as general president of the **Relief Society** during the war years (1940–45). They had two children. While **Elder** Lyman was an apostle, he also served as second assistant in the general **Young Men's Mutual Improvement Association** (1918–21) and presided over the **European Mission** (1936–38).

On 12 November 1943, Church members learned of his excommunication for violation of the law of chastity. On 27 October 1954, he was rebaptized into the Church. He died 31 December 1963 in **Salt Lake City**.

SOURCE

Flake, Lawrence R. *Prophets and Apostles of the Last Dispensation*. Provo, Utah: Religious Studies Center, Brigham Young University, 2001. 443–45.

KENNETH W. GODFREY

MORONI. For Latter-day Saints, the angel Moroni symbolizes the restoration of the gospel and representations of him cap many temples. This one, atop the Salt Lake Temple, was placed 6 April 1892.

MACAU. Macau (also spelled Macao) is a small, densely populated territory of Portugal located 60 kilometers from **Hong Kong** on the southeastern coast of **China**. At the beginning of the year 2000, there were 871 Latter-day Saints (organized into two branches) among the nearly half million inhabitants.

EMILY C. ZEIGLER

MACK, LUCY. See **SMITH, LUCY MACK**.

MACK, SOLOMON. Solomon Mack, **Lucy Mack Smith's** father, was known for his adventurous, accident-prone life. Born 15 September 1732 in Lyme, **Connecticut**, Solomon spent most of his childhood as an indentured servant. After obtaining his freedom, he married Lydia Gates in 1759. He fought in the French and **Indian** War and later in the Revolutionary War. Solomon's efforts to support his eight children were hampered by unscrupulous business partners, shipwrecks, and injuries sustained while felling trees and by falling on a water wheel. Broken and discouraged, in 1811 he turned to religion. He died 23 August 1820 in Gilsum, **New Hampshire**.

SOURCES

Anderson, Richard Lloyd. *Joseph Smith's New England Heritage.* Salt Lake City: Deseret Book, 1971. 5–26.

Bushman, Richard L. *Joseph Smith and the Beginnings of Mormonism.* Urbana and Chicago: University of Illinois Press, 1984. 11–19.

Smith, Lucy Mack. *History of Joseph Smith by His Mother.* Rev. ed. Edited by Scot Facer Proctor and Maurine Jensen Proctor. Salt Lake City: Bookcraft, 1996.

ANDREW H. HEDGES

MADAGASCAR. Madagascar is the fourth largest island in the world. Located off the southeastern shore of **Africa** in the Indian Ocean, its population speaks French, and the official language is Malagasy. The country's religious distribution is 41% Christians, 7% Muslims, and 52% followers of traditional faiths.

One of the first converts from Madagascar was Razanapanala Ramianadrisoa, who was baptized 1 November 1986 in Talence, **France**, while attending school. A year later he was ordained an **elder**. He then returned to Madagascar in 1988 and began teaching the gospel to a small group of people in his father's home. He contacted President Girard Giraud-Carrier of the Mascarene Islands **Mission**, who visited him on 9 November 1988. In 1990 Jean-Claude Rafenonirina was the first person to be baptized in Madagascar. The first **branch** of the Church was organized 23 September 1990 with some 50 people in attendance, and Razanapanala Ramiandrisoa was sustained as the branch president. Fred L. and Eileen Forsgren arrived 3 March 1991 as the first missionaries to Madagascar. The following year **seminary** and **institute** programs were established.

On 13 July 1993, Madagascar granted the Church legal status. The Madagascar Antananarivo Mission was created 1 July 1998. On 9 May 1999, more than 600 people attended the dedication of the first Church building in Madagascar, which served as mission headquarters and a **meetinghouse** for two branches. In 1999 the translation of the **Book of Mormon** into Malagasy was nearing completion. By the beginning of the year 2000, there were 1,349 members in 1 **district** with 6 branches.

SOURCES

Hogensen, Marvyn, and LaVeeta Hogensen. "Rich Harvest of Souls on Island of Madagascar." *Church News*, 4 February 1995, 8ff.

Middleton, John, ed. *Encyclopedia of Africa South of the Sahara.* 4 vols. New York: Macmillan Library Reference USA, 1997. 3:72–89.

1999–2000 Church Almanac. Salt Lake City: Deseret News, 1998. 348–49.

Oral histories of early Church converts collected by E. Dale LeBaron. Copies at BYU Library, Provo, Utah; LDS Church Historical Library, Salt Lake City, Utah.

E. DALE LEBARON

MAESER, KARL G. Karl Gottfried Maeser was principal of Brigham Young Academy and general superintendent of the LDS Church school system. Born 16 January 1828 in Saxony, **Germany**, he worked as a teacher in Dresden and married the schoolmaster's daughter, Anna Meith, in 1854.

Maeser heard about the LDS Church through an **anti-Mormon** pamphlet and was baptized a member in October 1855. He and his **family** left Germany for the **Utah** territory in 1856. En route to Utah, Maeser served two **missions**, the first in the British Isles and the second in the southern states.

After his arrival in Utah, Maeser worked as a teacher and school administrator. He served a mission to Germany and **Switzerland** from 1867 to 1870. He married Emilie Damke as a plural wife in 1875.

In 1875 **Brigham Young** asked Maeser to go to **Provo** and be the principal of Brigham Young Academy. During the next 16 years, Maeser advanced the school from a student body of only 29 students to an enrollment of more than 400 students in several departments. Maeser believed in educating the whole person and combined academic learning, religious teachings, and character development as part of the curriculum.

In 1888 he was named general superintendent of LDS Church schools, and in 1898 he wrote *School and Fireside*. Maeser died 15 February 1901 in **Salt Lake City**.

SOURCES

Burton, Alma P. *Karl G. Maeser: Mormon Educator.* Salt Lake City: Deseret Book, 1953.

Tobler, Douglas F. "Karl G. Maeser's German Background, 1828–1856: The Making of Zion's Teacher." *BYU Studies* 17 (Winter 1977): 155–75.

CATHERINE BRITSCH FRANTZ

MAGAZINES. See PERIODICALS.

MAGIC. See TREASURE HUNTING AND MAGIC.

MAHLANGU, MOSES. Moses Mahlangu was a **pioneer** of the Church in **South Africa**. He found the gospel through his personal search for true religion and became converted, but waited many years to be baptized. While he waited he tirelessly shared the gospel and gained many followers, who joined him in studying, living, and sharing the gospel as they waited and prayed to receive all of its blessings.

Moses was born in 1925 in Boshoek, South Africa, to a **family** of 15 children. From his early childhood, he sought to learn about God. His love of the Lord and of people motivated him to learn nine languages so he could teach others. In 1964, while serving as a Christian preacher to many Africans in various townships, Moses found a copy of the **Book of Mormon**. The bottom of the title page was torn off, however, so he did not know what church had published it. He studied it diligently and began to incorporate its teachings in his sermons and in his discussions with fellow preachers.

A few years later, he discovered the name of the Church and made contact with the **mission president** in Johannesburg, requesting to be baptized. Because of apartheid laws in South Africa, which prevented him from meeting with a white congregation, he was told that he would have to wait. Nevertheless, he went frequently to the mission offices to replenish his supply of missionary **pamphlets** and copies of the Book of Mormon. Moses regularly held **meetings** in his home and traveled to many African townships to teach people about Christ's restored Church. After waiting 16 years to join the Church, Moses was baptized in June 1980 along with his family and many others who were prepared through his teaching.

SOURCES

LeBaron, E. Dale, ed. *"All Are Alike unto God."* Orem, Utah: Granite Publishing, 1998. 185–95.

Oral histories of early Church converts collected by E. Dale LeBaron. Copies at BYU Library, Provo, Utah; LDS Church Historical Library, Salt Lake City, Utah.

E. DALE LEBARON

MAID OF IOWA. The *Maid of Iowa* was a small sidewheel steamboat that was first launched on the **Mississippi River** in the fall of 1842. It was built and owned by Levi Moffit and **Dan Jones**, but within two years **Joseph Smith** had bought the shares owned by each. During the **Nauvoo** period, the *Maid of Iowa* brought hundreds of LDS British converts from **New Orleans** to Nauvoo. This steamboat was small, as was her captain, **Dan Jones**, an energetic Welshman who later brought thousands of converts into the Church in **Wales**.

LDS immigrant accounts provide a vivid picture of the opposition encountered aboard the *Maid of Iowa*, which was well known along the Mississippi. One derogatory term used by **Gentiles** for passengers aboard the *Maid* was "Joe's rats." On one occasion, a river rogue tried to light the vessel on fire with a "half-consumed cigar." On another voyage, a larger steamboat tried to run her off the river and would have succeeded had not Captain Jones threatened to shoot their pilot. In contrast, passenger accounts reveal that Brother Joseph and other **Saints** were at the Nauvoo shores to welcome the incoming converts on the boat.

The *Maid of Iowa* was also used for Nauvoo pleasure cruises and hauling food for workers on the **Nauvoo Temple**. In 1845, after the **martyrdom** of Joseph and **Hyrum Smith**, Church leaders directed that the vessel be sold. A year later, the *Maid* was reported lost.

SOURCES

Enders, Donald L. "The Steamboat *Maid of Iowa:* Mormon Mistress of the Mississippi." *BYU Studies* 19 (Winter 1979): 321–35.

Sonne, Conway B. *Ships, Saints and Mariners: A Maritime Encyclopedia of Mormon Migration, 1830–1890.* Salt Lake City: University of Utah Press, 1987. 134–35.

FRED E. WOODS

MAINE. The history of the Church in Maine began on 19 September 1832 when **Orson Hyde** and **Samuel Smith** preached the gospel there for the first time. They baptized Timothy Smith on 31 October 1832 and organized a branch in Saco, York County. Other missionaries would follow, including **Wilford Woodruff** and Jonathan Hale, who served successful missions in 1837 on the **Fox Islands**. These two elders converted approximately 100 people and organized two branches. Many of these converts migrated to **Illinois** in 1838.

Through the years, those who accepted the gospel in Maine experienced some of the same challenges the entire Church faced in the early days of the **Restoration**. Yet persecution in the state was relatively mild. That may be why Governor Hugh J. Anderson of Maine was one of those to whom **Brigham Young** wrote, requesting asylum for the **Saints** at the time they were facing expulsion from **Illinois**.

Nearly 500 converts were "gathered" out of the state between 1832 and 1847. Then in 1850, Brigham Young admonished all the Saints in Maine to migrate to the Intermountain West. For the next half century, activities in the state were minimal.

In 1904 missionaries began preaching the gospel in Portland, where a branch was soon established. In 1909 the Maine **Conference** was organized, and in 1925 the state was placed under the jurisdiction of the Canadian Mission. The first meetinghouses were built in 1957 in Portland and Bangor. The Maine **Stake** was established at Augusta in

1968, and as of the year 2000 there were 8,569 members living in 2 stakes and 26 **wards** and **branches**.

SOURCES

Cannon, Donald Q. "Wilford Woodruff's Mission to the Fox Islands." In *New England*. Edited by Donald Q. Cannon. Regional Studies in Latter-day Saint Church History series. Provo, Utah: Brigham Young University, 1988. 85–99.

Damron, Paul Edwards. "The Narrative of the Saints in Maine from 1831 to the 1900s." Manuscript. LDS Church Archives, Salt Lake City.

1999–2000 Church Almanac. Salt Lake City: Deseret News, 1998. 208.

PAUL EDWARDS DAMRON

MALAWI. Malawi is a relatively small nation of 74,000 square miles, located in southeastern **Africa**. One third of its 10 million inhabitants are Christian, and more than half follow traditional religions. Their official languages are English and the African dialect Chickewa.

One of the first Malawians to join the Church was Folias Paul Mwale, who was baptized in **Canada** while there as an exchange student in 1987. McFarlane Njolomole Phiri, baptized in July 1992, was the first to accept the gospel in Malawi itself. He had actually been converted in 1979 and spent the next twelve years corresponding with the Church, seeking additional **literature** and membership, while sharing his faith with others. These early **pioneers** in Malawi received support and encouragement from Jerry R. Mills, a former **bishop** assigned to the U.S. Embassy in Malawi, and other Latter-day Saint expatriates and Peace Corps workers living in the country.

In July 1992 Elder and Sister Brian J. Peedle from the Zimbabwe Harare Mission were sent to Malawi to teach and baptize those who had been patiently waiting for Church membership. Within four days they baptized 33 persons and 13 brethren were **ordained priests**. Soon, the new members constructed a small **meetinghouse** in Sitima Village near Liwonde with materials provided by the Church. On 25 April 1995 the LDS Church was officially registered by the Malawi government. In September 1998, the Church sent funds to assist many who were facing starvation. In May 1999 the first **branch** was officially organized in Sitima Village with McFarlane Phiri as the branch president and his brother

Kennedy as first counselor—both having been ordained elders previously. In the year 2000 there were 181 members living in 2 branches.

SOURCE

Oral histories of early Church converts collected by E. Dale LeBaron. Copies at BYU Library, Provo, Utah; LDS Church Historical Library, Salt Lake City, Utah.

E. DALE LEBARON

MALAYSIA. Part of the **Singapore** Mission since 1980, Malaysia has experienced steady Church growth since expatriate members began living there in the 1960s. Latter-day Saint missionaries who served in **India** and Burma in the 1850s were the first to preach the gospel along the Malay Peninsula. Today, the dominantly Muslim government does not allow **missionary work** by outside churches, but local citizens may teach the restored gospel to non-Muslims. The first Malaysian **elders** called to teach there (1980) were David Soon Ewe Seang and Chong Sun Fu, ethnic Chinese Saints who had joined the Church in **England** and **Australia**. A succession of local elders and sisters has served over the years since. Even before 1980 couples had served in Kuala Lumpur as Church representatives and strengthened the growing **branches**. By the beginning of the year 2000, membership had grown to 1,141 members living in 12 branches and 2 **districts**.

SOURCE

Britsch, R. Lanier. *From the East: The History of the Latter-day Saints in Asia, 1851–1996.* Salt Lake City: Deseret Book, 1998. 470–75.

R. LANIER BRITSCH

MALTA. The Republic of Malta is located in the Mediterranean Sea south of **Italy** and north of Libya. It consists of the main island of Malta, the adjacent Gozo, and the very small island of Camino. Malta's population is about 365,000. Maltese, a Semitic language closely related to Arabic, is spoken by most Maltese people at home and is taught in the schools. At the same time, as a result of a long period of British rule, English is widely understood and used.

In 1852 **Lorenzo Snow** visited Malta, baptized three people, and called Thomas Obray to lead the **mission** there. Despite opposition, converts were made among both the Maltese people and the British military personnel. A floating **branch** was organized on a ship headed for the conflict in Crimea. The branch and mission were closed in 1856.

In July 1979 Maltese-born Elder Victor Bonnici and Elder Paul M. Anderson of the Italy Catania Mission were sent to resume work on Malta. Then after another hiatus of nearly a decade, a couple was called to serve an 18-month mission there, and elders from the Italy Catania Mission were assigned there to proselyte. Since then, except for a brief period of withdrawal during the Gulf War, scores of elders and sister missionaries have proselyted there, with the invaluable help of couple missionaries. Missionaries are tutored in the Maltese language. Both the English and Maltese languages are used in the Malta branch.

Faithful Maltese Latter-day Saints have filled positions ranging from branch president, **Relief Society** president, and priesthood leadership positions, to instructor and historian assignments. The first full-time missionary called from the Malta membership, Sister Suzanne Portelli, served in the **Temple Square** Mission and in **Alabama**.

A private newsletter, *Il Moghdija* (The Path), is published twice a year in **Salt Lake City**, with the purpose of encouraging the work on Malta and maintaining connections between Maltese members and returned missionaries worldwide. By the beginning of the year 2000 Malta had 1 branch and 120 members.

———

Source

1999–2000 Church Almanac. Salt Lake City: Deseret News, 1998. 350.

JoAn Bitton

MANCHESTER, ENGLAND. **William Clayton** is credited with the first preaching of the gospel in Manchester, England, shortly after he gave up his business pursuits and devoted himself wholly to Church activities in October 1838. Many believed and were baptized, and he soon organized a thriving branch that grew to 240 members by 1840—the largest branch of the Church in Britain at that time.

Manchester served as the headquarters of the Church in **England** during the time **Brigham Young** and his fellow **apostles** were serving their **missions** in the country (1840–41). It was also the city from which President Young directed the **British Mission**. During the same period, Elder **Parley P. Pratt** served there as the first editor of the *Millennial Star.*

His **hymn** "The Morning Breaks" appeared in the newspaper's premier issue in May 1840.

Brigham Young served much of the 376 days he spent in Britain in Manchester, where he hired Carpenter's Hall for regular meetings. He was the first apostle to preach there. He organized the local priesthood to occupy about 40 street-preaching stations throughout the city each Sabbath. At these the congregation was notified of the **meetings** at Carpenter's Hall. At the last **general conference** held in Manchester before the apostles returned to **America** on 16 April 1841, nine of the apostles were present.

The Manchester **Stake**, the first in Britain, was created on 17 March 1960 by Elder **Harold B. Lee** of the Quorum of the Twelve Apostles and was divided in March 1961. Manchester hosted the first **area conference** of the Church on Sunday, 29 August 1971, which was presided over by President Joseph Fielding Smith and attended by more than 10,000 people.

SOURCES

Allen, James B., and Thomas G. Alexander. *Manchester Mormons—The Journal of William Clayton*. Salt Lake City: Peregrine Smith, 1974.

Bloxham, V. Ben, James R. Moss, and Larry C. Porter, eds. *Truth Will Prevail: The Rise of The Church of Jesus Christ of Latter-day Saints in the British Isles, 1837–1997*. Cambridge: Cambridge University Press, 1987.

Evans, Richard L. *A Century of "Mormonism" in Great Britain*. Salt Lake City: Publishers Press, 1984.

DAVID COOK

MANCHESTER, NEW YORK. See PALMYRA/MANCHESTER, NEW YORK

MANIFESTO (1890). The publication of the Manifesto in September 1890 began the end of **plural marriage** among faithful Latter-day Saints.

Plural marriage generated more opposition to the Church than any other doctrine or practice, except possibly the ecclesiastical control of government. Since Congress exercised plenary power over territories, it could legislate for **Utah** (1850–96) on matters reserved to the states under the federal system. Acts passed in 1862, 1874, 1882, and 1887 (see **Antipolygamy Movement**) restricted the authority of local government, disfranchised polygamous men and all women, imprisoned polygamists, and escheated the Church's secular property to support the territorial schools.

In a series of rulings beginning in 1879, the U.S. Supreme Court upheld these laws. Enforcement led to the jailing of more than 1,000 polygamous men and some women who refused to cooperate with the law. In May 1890 the Supreme Court opened the door to the possible confiscation of the Church's **temples** and chapels.

Latter-day Saints attempted to mitigate the effect of these laws. The Church distributed property to **stakes** and **wards**, men hid out, women refused to testify, and members moved to **Mexico** and **Canada**.

In addition, the **general authorities** began to restrict plural marriages. In 1888 the Quorum of the Twelve **Apostles** instructed Church leaders to stop preaching plural marriage. The **First Presidency** issued a directive on 30 June 1890 prohibiting new plural marriages in the United States. President **Wilford Woodruff** had demolished the **Endowment House**, where such sealings had occurred, in the spring of 1889.

In the meantime, in an attempt to gain statehood for Utah, Church leaders had begun to build bridges with national political leaders. They achieved greater success at first with the Democrats, who tended to hold more liberal views than Republicans on local self-government and, to a lesser extent, on matters of personal lifestyles. Nevertheless, the Church leadership courted the Republicans through a group of **California** business associates.

In early September 1890 the receiver, Henry W. Lawrence, entered a suit for the confiscation of the Church's religious properties, including the **temples**. President Woodruff went to California to confer with **Isaac Trumbo**, a Republican businessman, and other leaders who had advised the Church on this matter.

Returning to Utah and giving these problems prayerful consideration, he consulted with his counselors and with members of the Quorum of the Twelve. Inspired to act for the temporal salvation of the Church, he issued the Manifesto on 24 September 1890. The declaration said that the Church was not then preaching plural marriage, that he had earlier ordered the demolition of the Endowment House, and that he intended "to submit to [the] laws" of the land and to use his influence with the members of the Church "to have them do likewise." The membership sustained the Manifesto on 6 October. Beginning in 1908 it was placed in the **Doctrine and Covenants** as an official declaration; in the 1981 edition it became known as Official Declaration 1.

SOURCES

Alexander, Thomas G. *Things in Heaven and Earth: The Life and Times of Wilford Woodruff, a Mormon Prophet.* Salt Lake City: Signature Books, 1991.

Larson, Gustive O. *The "Americanization" of Utah for Statehood.* San Marino, Calif.: Huntington Library, 1971.

Lyman, Edward Leo. *Political Deliverance: The Mormon Quest for Utah Statehood.* Urbana: University of Illinois Press, 1986.

THOMAS G. ALEXANDER

MANIFESTO, POLITICAL. Church leadership approved the Political Manifesto in October 1895 as a means of securing approval to release **general authorities** from some of their duties so they could engage in political activities. Several general authorities and a number of local leaders served in the 1895 **Utah** state constitutional convention without formal approval, and on 2 October 1895 **Elder Moses Thatcher** of the Twelve told the **First Presidency** that since the Church had formally withdrawn from politics, individuals ought to continue to make their own political decisions. **Joseph F. Smith**, second counselor in the First Presidency, disagreed, and at a general **priesthood** meeting on 7 October 1895, he said that all Church members should secure the approval of their presiding officers before running for political office.

Presidents **Wilford Woodruff** and **George Q. Cannon** felt that the scope of this statement was too broad. Therefore, Cannon drafted a document which said that general authorities who had committed their full time to Church service must secure approval from the First Presidency before accepting a nomination for office. The First Presidency, **Quorum of the Twelve** (except Thatcher), **patriarch to the Church**, First Council of the **Seventy**, and **presiding bishopric** approved the document. Thatcher was dropped from the **Quorum**, and both the Political Manifesto and the disciplining of Thatcher created a political furor over ecclesiastical influence in Utah politics.

SOURCES

Alexander, Thomas G. *Things in Heaven and Earth: The Life and Times of Wilford Woodruff, a Mormon Prophet.* Salt Lake City: Signature Books, 1991.

Lyman, Edward Leo. "The Alienation of an Apostle from His Quorum: The Moses Thatcher Case." *Dialogue* 18 (Summer 1985): 67–91.

Reasoner, Calvin. *Church and State: The Issue of Civil and Religious Liberty in Utah.*
Salt Lake City: Juvenile Instructor Press, 1896.

THOMAS G. ALEXANDER

MANIFESTO, SECOND. The Church announced the Second
Manifesto in April 1904 to end the practice of members entering into new
plural marriages. After the approval of the original Manifesto in October
1890, a number of Church members entered into plural marriages with
the approval of general and local authorities. The election of **Reed Smoot**
as U.S. Senator from **Utah** in January 1903, and the investigation that
followed, led to a public clamor throughout the United States over plural
marriage.

Unwilling to order the dissolution of marriages contracted between
1890 and 1904, the **First Presidency** and **Quorum of the Twelve Apostles**
agreed to prohibit new plural marriages. On 6 April 1904, President
Joseph F. Smith announced the Second Manifesto, which prescribed
excommunication for anyone who performed or entered into a new
plural marriage. The members approved the Second Manifesto in **general
conference** on a motion of **Francis M. Lyman**, president of the Quorum
of the Twelve. Two members of the Twelve, **John W. Taylor** and **Matthias
F. Cowley**, who could not support this action, resigned in 1905.

Hearing of new plural marriages, in 1909 the First Presidency called
President Lyman to chair an investigating committee. The investigation
led to the excommunication of a number of members and leaders for performing and entering into plural marriages. Elders **Taylor** and **Cowley** were
among those disciplined in 1911.

SOURCES

Alexander, Thomas G. *Mormonism in Transition: A History of the Latter-day Saints,
1890–1930.* Urbana: University of Illinois Press, 1986.
Hardy, B. Carmon. *The Mormon Polygamous Passage.* Urbana: University of Illinois
Press, 1992.
Jorgensen, Victor W., and B. Carmon Hardy. "The Taylor-Cowley Affair and the
Watershed of Mormon History." *Utah Historical Quarterly* 48 (Winter 1980): 4–36.

THOMAS G. ALEXANDER

MANITOBA, CANADA. Gateway to the Canadian Northwest,
Manitoba ("Land of the Great Spirit") became a province of **Canada** in
1870. **Mormon** missionaries began serving in the province during the last

two decades of the nineteenth century. Thomas Brandley labored among his Mennonite relatives in 1884, while Jacob Johnson worked with his Icelandic kin in 1893. **Charles Ora Card** was sending missionaries east from **Cardston** to Winnipeg and Brandon throughout the 1890s. While a "Sister Williams" was the first known convert in Manitoba (1897), the first **family** to join the Church was the Cornelius de Winter family, baptized in the Red River in Winnipeg in 1901. The Winnipeg **Branch**, formed in 1910, was the first in western Canada outside of **Alberta**. Since the beginning of the twentieth century, the Church has been actively proselyting continuously with modest but steady success. In 1978 a **stake** was organized in Winnipeg.

While membership is concentrated in this city, **wards** and branches are scattered over a vast territorial expanse stretching from the nickel-mining town of Thompson in the far north to Dauphin, Brandon, Selkirk, and other more southerly communities. Willing to share a harsh and sometimes unforgiving continental climate with their neighbors, members played an active role in assisting Winnipeg and surrounding communities during the devastating 1997 Red River Flood that inundated thousands of square miles in southern portions of the province. At the beginning of the year 2000, the province had 12 wards and branches with 3,866 **Saints**.

SOURCE

Pruden, Hal. *Mormons in Manitoba.* Winnipeg: Winnipeg Manitoba Stake, 1988.

RICHARD E. BENNETT

MANSION HOUSE. The Mansion House was a two-story frame house and the second home of the **Joseph Smith family** in **Nauvoo**. Construction began in 1842, and by August 1843 the Smiths were occupying three of the 22 rooms. "The Mansion, being large and convenient," said the **Prophet**, "renders travelers more comfortable than any other place on the Upper **Mississippi**" (Smith, 6:33). Joseph welcomed paid guests to the Mansion House until January 1844, when the hotel portion was leased to Ebenezer Robinson.

After the deaths of Joseph and **Hyrum Smith**, thousands of sorrowful **Saints** viewed the brothers' remains in the Mansion House. Joseph's widow, **Emma Smith** Bidamon, resided in the house until the 1870s. Then Alexander and **David H. Smith** and their families became occupants. In 1890 the hotel wing of the Mansion House was removed.

Restoration work has preserved the remainder of the structure. The Mansion House is currently owned by the **Reorganized Church of Jesus Christ of Latter Day Saints**.

SOURCES

Holzapfel, Richard Neitzel, and T. Jeffery Cottle. *Old Mormon Nauvoo and Southeastern Iowa: Historic Photographs and Guide.* Santa Ana, Calif.: Fieldbrook Productions, 1990.

Shields, Steven L. *An Illustrated History of Nauvoo.* Independence, Mo.: Herald Publishing House, 1992.

Smith, Joseph. *History of The Church of Jesus Christ of Latter-day Saints.* Edited by B. H. Roberts. 2d ed. rev. 7 vols. Salt Lake City: The Church of Jesus Christ of Latter-day Saints, 1932–51. 1:60–61.

SUSAN EASTON BLACK

MANTI, UTAH. Manti is located 123 miles south of **Salt Lake City** in the Sanpete Valley. It was the fourth town founded by the **Saints** in **Utah** (after Salt Lake City, **Ogden**, and **Provo**). Chief Walker (**Walkara**) sent a delegation of **Ute Indians** to Salt Lake City in June 1849 to request **Mormon** colonists for Sanpitch Valley to teach the Indians how to build homes and till the soil. **Brigham Young** responded by sending an exploring party to the area with Chief Walker acting as guide. They reached the present site of Manti on 20 August 1849, where the Indians entertained them. The group reported favorable conditions for founding a colony, and Brigham Young responded by sending 50 families from Salt Lake City and Centerville in the fall of 1849. The colonists settled on the site of Manti on 22 November 1849 under **Isaac Morley's** secular and ecclesiastical leadership.

Morley suggested the name from the location mentioned in the **Book of Mormon**. The first settlers settled on City Creek, but three feet of snow fell on the camp the first night. The settlers then moved their camp south of Temple Hill. Their first homes were dugouts, which did little to protect the **pioneers** from heavy snows, loss of animals, famine, and serious Indian troubles. In time, however, the agricultural community became known as the "granary of Utah."

As immigrants from **Scandinavia** poured into Utah, they settled in the Sanpete Valley, which was very close to their native climate. The Manti settlement may have failed had it not been for the hardy Scandinavians whose heritage is still evident today among the names, architecture, and customs of the people, including the annual Scandinavian Days celebration.

Manti was incorporated in 1851 with **Dan Jones** as mayor. The city suffered during the **Walker War** from 1853 to 1854 and the **Black Hawk War** from 1865 to 1867. **Wilford Woodruff** dedicated the **Manti Temple** on 21 May 1888. Manti is perhaps best known today for the Church-sponsored Mormon Miracle **Pageant**, presented annually for two weeks on Temple Hill with a cast of roughly 800 and an estimated audience of 128,000.

SOURCES

Antrei, Albert C., ed. *The Other Forty-Niners: A Topical History of Sanpete County, Utah, 1849–1983.* Salt Lake City: Western Epics, 1982.

History of Sanpete and Emery Counties, Utah. Ogden, Utah: W. H. Lever, 1898.

Jenson, Andrew. *Encyclopedic History of The Church of Jesus Christ of Latter-day Saints.* Salt Lake City: Deseret News, 1941.. 471–72.

J. MICHAEL HUNTER

MANTI TEMPLE. The Manti Utah Temple was the third **temple** completed in **Utah. Brigham Young** designated its location in 1875. The ground for the temple was surveyed and laid out in 1877 by Jesse Fox, surveyor general of Utah Territory. He was assisted by **Truman O. Angell** and **William Folsom,** Church architects. Brigham Young dedicated the site 25 April 1877. William Folsom was appointed general superintendent, and Canute Peterson became the assistant superintendent. A buff-colored stone and oolite limestone obtained from nearby quarries were used in the temple's foundation and walls. The completed temple measured 168 feet long by 95 feet wide. The east tower was 179 feet high and the west tower 169 feet. President **Wilford Woodruff** offered the dedicatory prayer at private services 17 May 1888. Approximately 5,400 people attended the public services 21 through 23 May 1888 with **Elder Lorenzo Snow** offering the dedicatory prayer.

After renovations, the temple was rededicated 14 through 16 June 1985, with President **Gordon B. Hinckley** presiding. The Manti Temple is a marvel to many for its beauty, its architectural design, and its unique history.

SOURCES

Anderson, Lewis R. "The Manti Temple." *Improvement Era* (March 1908): 414–18.

Stubbs, Glen R. *Temple on a Hill.* Rexburg, Idaho: Ricks College Press, 1988.

Talmage, James E. *The House of the Lord*. Salt Lake City, Utah: Deseret News, 1912.

GLEN R. STUBBS

MANUSCRIPT FOUND. See SPAULDING THEORY.

MAORI PROPHETS. In ancient times, priests or *tohunga* supervised worship among the Maori—the Polynesians of **New Zealand**. After the introduction of Christianity in the late eighteenth century, some tohunga continued in their former roles as oracles, healers, and admonishers of the people, but they did so in the name of the new religion. Among these tohunga were five who prophesied signs, beliefs, practices, and events that were later identified with the Latter-day Saint Church.

For example, in 1830 Arama Toiroa counseled his descendants to leave the Protestant church they had joined and wait for the church that manifested specific signs and practices. Fifty-four years passed before **Mormon elders** visited his village, Korongata. The prophesied signs were recognized, and the entire village joined the Church. Three other tohunga—Toaroa Pakahia, Apiata Kuikainga, and King Tawhiao—made similar prophecies.

Best known among the prophecies were those of Paora Potangaroa of the Ngatikahungunu tribe. In 1881 Paora, following a period of fasting and prayer, told the leaders of his tribe: "The church for the Maori people has not yet come among us. You will recognize it when it comes. Its missionaries will travel in pairs . . . come from the rising sun . . . visit us in our homes . . . learn our language and teach us the gospel in our own tongue. When they pray they will raise their right hands" (quoted in "Maori Traditions," 42). He then gave what has been called a covenant: a forecast of sacred events soon to come. Within months Latter-day Saint elders came among his people and fulfilled Paora's prophetic words.

Knowledge of these prophesies among the Maori was partially responsible for the rapid expansion of the Church among them during the 1880s and 1890s.

SOURCES

Britsch, R. Lanier. "Maori Traditions and the Mormon Church." *New Era* 11 (June 1981): 38–46.

———. *Unto the Islands of the Sea: A History of the Latter-day Saints in the Pacific*. Salt Lake City: Deseret Book, 1986. 272–78.

R. LANIER BRITSCH

MAORIS. The original Polynesian inhabitants of **New Zealand**, the Maoris first joined the Church in significant numbers in the 1880s. Some who converted did so, in part, because the characteristics and messages of **Mormon** elders fulfilled earlier prophecies of Maori tohungas or **priests**, who had talked about the coming of a church for the Maori people. Other Maoris were impressed with the devotion of missionaries who were willing to endure privation to live with them and who took great pains to learn their language. Missionaries found the Maori people easy to love because of their genuineness, hospitality, and great faith.

From the 1880s until the 1950s, **missionary work** in New Zealand was concentrated among the Maori people. Most of the more than 70,000 Church members in New Zealand are Maoris. Perhaps the most famous missionary to the Maoris was the beloved **Elder Matthew Cowley**, later called the "**apostle** to the Polynesians," who spent ten years among them as a proselyting elder and later as a **mission president**.

SOURCE

Britsch, R. Lanier. *Unto the Islands of the Sea: A History of the Latter-day Saints in the Pacific.* Salt Lake City: Deseret Book, 1986. 253–345.

PAUL H. PETERSON

MARKHAM, STEPHEN. Stephen Markham was an early **pioneer** who repeatedly sacrificed his earthly possessions for the Church. He was born 9 February 1800 in Avon, Ontario, **New York**, and at age two moved with his mother to **Ohio** after his father was shot during soldier training. Several years later Markham heard the gospel and was baptized in July 1837. Though he had been a successful farmer, he obeyed **Joseph Smith**'s request to sell all of his possessions and assist 60 people in moving from **Kirtland, Ohio**, to **Far West, Missouri**. In **Missouri** Markham raised funds to help other **Saints** who had suffered from mob attacks. Later he helped to move the **Prophet**'s **family** from Missouri to **Illinois** and served as a bodyguard to Joseph Smith. Brother Markham again demonstrated loyalty to the Prophet when he sold his only home and used the funds to pay expenses from Joseph Smith's lawsuits.

After the **Martyrdom, Brigham Young** appointed Markham as one of the leaders in the original pioneer company. After leading several groups of pioneers to the **Great Basin**, he settled in **Utah** County. In 1853 he was ordained a **bishop**, and in 1856 he was assigned to a colonizing mission at **Fort Supply** near the Green River. He died 10 March 1878 in Spanish Fork, Utah.

SOURCE

Jenson, Andrew. *Latter-day Saint Biographical Encyclopedia.* 4 vols. 1901–36. Reprint, Salt Lake City: Western Epics, 1971. 3:676–77.

LISA KURKI

MARKOW, MISCHA. Mischa Markow was one of the first Latter-day Saint missionaries to southeastern **Europe**. He was born 21 October 1854 to a Serbian family living in Czernyn, Torontal Megye, **Hungary**. Following a pilgrimage to the **Holy Land** he went to Alexandria, Egypt. President **Jacob Spori** of the Turkish mission, then visiting Palestine, saw in a vision a man in Alexandria to whom he could teach the gospel, so he immediately went there. Both boarded the same ship bound for Constantinople. Aboard ship Spori recognized Markow as the man he had seen in his dream, taught him the gospel, and baptized him in Constantinople on 1 February 1887. A year later Markow was ordained an **elder** and sent as a missionary to **Belgium**, where he labored until emigrating to **Utah** in 1892. On 24 May 1893 he married Nettie Hansen in the newly dedicated **Salt Lake Temple**, and the couple became the parents of two children.

On 21 April 1899 Markow was set apart as a missionary to the Balkans. After being banished from **Serbia** and Hungary, he went to **Romania**, where he baptized seven converts before once again being expelled. In **Bulgaria** he was hindered by the forces of **anti-Mormonism**. After being banished from Hungary he finished his mission in **Germany** before returning to Utah in 1901.

In 1903 Markow was called on yet another mission, this time to **Russia**, but met the same opposition. After only a month in Russia he reported to the Turkish mission, where he served until 1905. Afterwards, he worked as a barber in **Salt Lake City** until his death on 19 January 1934.

SOURCES

Cowan, Richard O. "Mischa Markow: Mormon Missionary to the Balkans," *BYU Studies* 11 (Fall 1970): 92–99.

Kehr, William Hale. "Missionary to the Balkans Mischa Markow," *Ensign* 10 (June 1980): 29–32.

Van Orden, Bruce A. *Building Zion: The Latter-day Saints in Europe.* Salt Lake City: Deseret Book, 1996. 110–12.

RICHARD O. COWAN

MARKS, WILLIAM. An early **stake president** who eventually left the Church, William Marks was born 15 November 1792 in Rutland, Rutland County, **Vermont.** He married Rosannah R. Robinson on 2 May 1813, and they became the parents of 11 children. Marks joined the Church in about 1835 in upstate **New York;** he was ordained a **priest** prior to 3 April 1835 and an **elder** before 3 June 1836. In May 1837 Marks took over the Church-operated newspaper, the *Latter-Day Saints' Messenger and Advocate* and moved to **Kirtland, Ohio,** that same year, where he became a member of the Kirtland **high council** and an **agent** to Bishop **Newel K. Whitney** in September.

In 1838 he was made president of the Kirtland Stake. He was also called to be a leader in **Far West, Missouri** (D&C 117:1, 10), but due to the expulsion of the Mormons from the state, Marks did not assume this responsibility. He left Kirtland and settled temporarily in **Quincy, Illinois,** in 1839. On 6 May 1839, he was appointed to preside over the Saints residing in Commerce, Illinois. On 5 October 1839, Marks was named president of the Nauvoo Stake. In Nauvoo he served in prominent civic positions, was among the first to receive his endowment (4 May 1842), and became a member of the **Council of Fifty** (19 March 1844). Although he initially sympathized with Sidney Rigdon's succession claims, he ultimately acknowledged the right of the Twelve to lead the Church. Still, on 7 October 1844, the Saints at Nauvoo rejected Marks as stake president, and soon thereafter he left Nauvoo and left the Church.

Settling in Fulton City, Illinois, he maintained a distant and brief relationship with Sidney Rigdon's movement. In 1846, Marks was appointed counselor to **James Jesse Strang** and assumed this position the following year at Voree, **Wisconsin.** By 1850 he broke with Strang and relocated at Shabbona, Illinois, where he became postmaster. In 1852, he joined Charles B. Thompson's Jehovah's Presbytery of Zion and became first chief of its quorum of traveling teachers. The following year he left Thompson, and in 1855 he helped form a church organization with John C. Gaylord and **John E. Page.** Marks also assisted in founding the **Reorganized Church of Jesus Christ of Latter Day Saints** in 1860 and was a participant in the ordination of **Joseph Smith III** as its president. In April 1863 he was appointed as counselor to Joseph Smith III and served in this capacity until his death. Following the death of his first wife in 1862, Marks married Julia A. Durfee Muir in 1866. He died in Plano, Kendall County, Illinois, 22 May 1872.

SOURCE

Cook, Lyndon B. *The Revelations of the Prophet Joseph Smith.* Provo, Utah: Seventy's Mission Bookstore, 1981. 230–231.

LYNDON W. COOK

MARRIAGE. With the **restoration** of the gospel came a fuller understanding of the sacred nature of marriage. The 1995 **Proclamation on the Family** declared that "marriage between a man and a woman is ordained of God." The complete meaning of this phrase has come over time. In the "law of the Church," received through the **Prophet Joseph Smith** in February 1831, the Lord instructed, "Thou shalt love thy wife with all thy heart, and shalt cleave unto her and none else" (D&C 42:22). Countering the **Shakers'** doctrine of celibacy, the Lord also stated: "And again, verily I say unto you, that whoso forbiddeth to marry is not ordained of God, for marriage is ordained of God unto man" (D&C 49:15–16). Following the restoration of the sealing keys by **Elijah** (D&C 110:13–16), Joseph Smith gave greater emphasis to the "new and everlasting covenant of marriage." He taught that this covenant was a requirement to attain the highest degree in the celestial kingdom (D&C 131:1–2), and the means of becoming like God (D&C 132:19–24). About this time the Prophet Joseph Smith began teaching selected Saints the principle of **plural marriage**. In 1890, following enactment of oppressive **antipolygamy** laws, President **Wilford Woodruff's Manifesto** announced that the Church would no longer sanction this practice.

Divine revelations and repeated teachings of living prophets provide a more exalted understanding of the relationship between husband and wife. Therefore the Church has continued to give emphasis to the sanctity of marriage and the family.

SOURCE

Dorius, Guy L. "Marriage and Family: 'Ordained of God.'" *The Doctrine and Covenants: A Book of Answers.* Edited by Leon R. Hartshorn, Dennis A. Wright, and Craig J. Ostler. Salt Lake City: Deseret Book, 1996. 155–68.

GUY L. DORIUS

MARRIAGE, PLURAL. See PLURAL MARRIAGE.

MARRIOTT, J. WILLARD, SR. John Willard Marriott Sr. was born 17 September 1900 in a two-room farmhouse in Marriott, Utah, and later became a well-known Latter-day Saint philanthropist and founder of a billion-dollar international business conglomerate. The son of Hyrum Willard and Ellen Morris Marriott, he received his education from Weber College (1922) and the **University of Utah** (1926). He married Alice Sheets on 9 June 1927 and was the father of two sons—John Willard (1932) and Richard Edwin (1939). Starting in 1927 with an A & W root beer stand in **Washington, D.C.**, Marriott eventually operated 125 hotels, 2,500 fast food restaurants, cruise ships, amusement parks, and the largest airline catering service in the world by the time he died 13 August 1985.

Marriott served a **mission** for the Church in the **Eastern States Mission** from 1919 to 1921 and was later the president of the Washington D.C. **Stake**. In 1976, he helped bring the **Tabernacle Choir** to Washington, D.C., for the country's bicentennial celebration. His many philanthropical contributions include the Marriott Center and the Marriott School of Management at **Brigham Young University**, the Marriott Library at the University of Utah, and the Marriott Allied Health Sciences Building at **Weber State University**.

SOURCES

O'Brien, Robert. *Marriott: The J. Willard Marriott Story.* Salt Lake City: Deseret Book, 1977.

"Philanthropist J. Willard Marriott dies at 84." *Church News,* 18 August 1985. 7.

J. MICHAEL HUNTER

MARSH, THOMAS B. Thomas Baldwin Marsh was the first president of the **Quorum** of the Twelve **Apostles** in this dispensation. Born 1 November 1799 (or 1800) at Acton, **Massachusetts**, and left motherless at age 7, Thomas ran away at 14 and found his way to **New York City**. After marrying Elizabeth Godkin in 1820, he worked in a Boston type foundry. An unsatisfied religious seeker, he was led westward in 1829, where he learned of the **Book of Mormon** being printed in **Palmyra**. He returned home with some unbound pages and joined the Church with Elizabeth shortly after its organization.

Thomas helped lead migrating **Saints** to **Ohio** and was **ordained** an **elder** and then a **high priest**. He also served **missions** and was on a **high council**. Chosen as an apostle in 1835, he presided over the quorum as its oldest member. Having served faithfully and defended **Joseph Smith** against dissidents, in 1838 Thomas became estranged over leaders' decisions regarding his wife's dishonest domestic dealings. In October 1838 Thomas left the Church and swore an affidavit against Joseph Smith, asserting treason. The cruel **extermination order** followed. Thomas later blamed his apostasy on his tendency to magnify Joseph Smith's shortcomings while minimizing his own.

Thomas remained in **Missouri** and outside the Church nearly two decades before begging for reconciliation, expressing his realization: "[The Church had] lost nothing by my falling out of the ranks; but O what have I lost?" (quoted in Cook, 398). He died in full fellowship at **Ogden, Utah**, in January 1866.

Sources

Anderson, A. Gary. "Thomas B. Marsh: The Preparation and Conversion of the Emerging Apostle." In *New York*. Edited by Larry C. Porter, Milton V. Backman Jr., and Susan Easton Black. Regional Studies in Latter-day Saint Church History series. Provo, Utah: Brigham Young University, 1992. 129–48.

———. "Thomas B. Marsh: Reluctant Apostate." In *Missouri*. Edited by Arnold K. Garr and Clark V. Johnson. Regional Studies in Latter-day Saint Church History series. Provo, Utah: Brigham Young University, 1994. 13–26.

Cook, Lyndon W. "'I Have Sinned Against Heaven and Am Unworthy of Your Confidence, but I Cannot Live without a Reconciliation': Thomas B. Marsh Returns to the Church." *BYU Studies* 20 (Summer 1980): 389–400.

Esplin, Ronald K. "'Exalt Not Yourselves': The Revelations and Thomas B. Marsh, an Object Lesson for Our Day." *The Heavens Are Open*. Salt Lake City: Deseret Book, 1993. 112–29.

———. "Thomas B. Marsh as President of the First Quorum of the Twelve 1835–1838." *Hearken O Ye People: Discourses on the Doctrine and Covenants*. Sandy, Utah: Randall, 1984. 167–90.

STEVEN C. HARPER

MARSHALL ISLANDS.

Called by Robert Louis Stevenson the "Pearl of the **Pacific**," Majuro is the capital island of the 31 Marshall Islands. Most Latter-day Saints living in the Marshall Islands reside at Majuro. On 3 February 1977, Elders William Wardel and Steven Cooper were the first missionaries to arrive in Majuro. They taught and baptized Misao Lokeijak, who first learned about the Church in **Hawaii**. Lokeijak became the first **branch** president in the Marshall Islands when the Laura Branch was formed on 11 May 1978.

By 1979 membership had grown to 177 members. Two **meeting-houses** were dedicated for the Laura and Rita branches on 13 and 14 January 1986. In 1990 the membership in Majuro reached 1,100. At the beginning of the year 2000 the country had 3,369 members living in 10 branches.

SOURCES

"A Brief History of the Micronesia-Guam Mission, 1980–1990." Micronesia-Guam Mission, 1990.

Micronesia-Guam Mission Historical Report. Archives, Historical Department, The Church of Jesus Christ of Latter-day Saints, Salt Lake City.

1999–2000 Church Almanac. Salt Lake City: Deseret News, 1998. 350–51.

W. JAMES JACOB

MARTIN HARRIS FARM. See HARRIS FARM.

MARTINIQUE AND GUADELOUPE. Islands located in the eastern Caribbean, Martinique and Guadeloupe are departments of **France.** A combined estimated population of 723,000 residents is nearly equally divided between the two islands. The first Latter-day Saint **missionaries** to serve in the area were Elders Mark Richards, Stan Jones, and David Simons. They arrived 4 May 1984. Some of the earliest converts to the Church in Guadeloupe were members of the Claire Dinane family. By the year 2000, there was one **branch** in Martinique with 143 members and two branches in Guadeloupe with 195 members.

SOURCE

1999–2000 Church Almanac. Salt Lake City: Deseret News, 1998. 322.

TODD KRUEGER

MARTINS, HELVÉCIO. Helvécio Martins, the first **general authority** of African descent, was born 27 July 1930 in Rio de Janeiro, **Brazil.** A descendant of African slaves, he was raised in a **family** of limited means. He left school at age 12 to help support his family but several years later at the urging of his wife-to-be, Rudá Tourinho Assis, he returned to school. He completed a degree in economics in 1962 and began working in Brazil's largest corporation, a public oil company called Petrobras. Eventually, he became head of one of the divisions and was involved in government decisions regarding oil distribution and price setting. He also taught economics at the State University of Rio de Janeiro School of Finances and Administration. He and his family joined the LDS Church in 1972. He served in several Church positions, including public relations director of the Brazil North Region and member of the public relations committee for the dedication of the **São Paulo Temple**. After the **revelation** that extended priesthood authority to all worthy males in 1978, Elder Martins served in the Rio de Janeiro **Stake** presidency and as a **bishop**, before serving as president of the Brazil Fortaleza **Mission** between 1987 and 1990. In 1990 he was called as a member of the Second **Quorum** of the **Seventy**. Released in 1995, Helvécio Martins was a leader in the development of the Church in Brazil and an example of faith for members of the Church throughout the world.

SOURCES

Grover, Mark L. "Mormonism in Brazil: Religion and Dependency in Latin America." Ph.D. diss., Indiana University, 1985.

————."The Mormon Priesthood Revelation and the São Paulo Temple." *Dialogue* 23 (Spring 1990): 39–54.

Martins, Helvécio. *The Autobiography of Elder Helvécio Martins.* Salt Lake City: Aspen Books, 1994.

MARK L. GROVER

MARTYRDOM, THE.

MARTYRDOM, THE. On a hot, humid afternoon in June 1844, **Joseph Smith** and his older brother Hyrum were murdered while incarcerated in the **Carthage Jail** in **Illinois**. For the first time since the Church was organized 14 years earlier, it was left without its founding **Prophet**. "Many marveled because of [Joseph's] death," but **Brigham Young**, in a revelation received at **Winter Quarters**, declared that "it was needful that [Joseph] should seal his testimony with his blood, that he might be honored and the wicked might be condemned" (D&C 136:39). The Martyrdom was a tragic and pivotal moment in Latter-day Saint history.

Early in the spring of 1844, a group of men (as many as 200, mostly apostate **Mormons**) met in secret in **Nauvoo** and united in a conspiracy to destroy Joseph Smith. Their anger was directed not only at him but also toward some of the doctrines he taught, such as **plural marriage**, sealing people up to eternal life, the establishment of the political kingdom of God, and temple rituals. While the conspirators met, the anti-Mormon political party of Hancock County formulated plans to kill the Prophet and expel his followers from the state. Their anger focused on the political power of the Latter-day Saints, the Nauvoo Legion, the size of Nauvoo, and the Latter-day Saints' growing economic power.

After the Nauvoo city council declared the anti-Mormon *Nauvoo Expositor* a nuisance and destroyed the press, unrest in Hancock County reached a boiling point. Joseph Smith, Nauvoo's mayor, declared martial law, and the Nauvoo Legion was mustered to defend the city. The conspirators, who also owned the *Expositor,* swore out warrants for the Prophet's arrest, charging him with riot. Governor Thomas Ford assured Joseph Smith that he would be protected if he came to Carthage and stood trial.

Joseph went to Carthage with other members of the city council, posted bail for the riot charge, and was rearrested on a charge of treason based on his having declared martial law (treason was a nonbailable offense). He was then taken to Carthage Jail.

On 27 June 1844, Thomas Ford left Carthage and traveled to Nauvoo, where he spoke to a large gathering of Saints. While he was away, a mob of 200 men, faces blackened, assaulted the jail late in the afternoon. Both Joseph and Hyrum were shot four times and killed. John Taylor was hit five times, but he lived. Willard Richards, also in the jail, survived with only a bullet grazing his ear.

Joseph and Hyrum were buried in Nauvoo, and no one was ever convicted for their murder. Public sentiment stood in the way of justice. John Taylor wrote that the prophet left "a fame and name that cannot be slain" (D&C 135:3).

After a few weeks, Brigham Young and the Quorum of the Twelve Apostles were sustained by Church members to lead the organization Joseph had founded. By the fall of 1846, most Latter-day Saints were headed west in quest of a new Zion.

SOURCES

Blake, Reed. *24 Hours to Martyrdom.* Salt Lake City: Bookcraft, 1973.

Oaks, Dallin H., and Marvin S. Hill. *Carthage Conspiracy.* Urbana: University of Illinois Press, 1975.

KENNETH W. GODFREY

MARTYRS, LATTER-DAY. Elder Bruce R. McConkie taught that the "laying down of one's life, standing alone is not . . . martyrdom"; rather, a

martyr's death must result from a refusal to deny the gospel (470). During this dispensation there are far more who fit into this category than can be listed here.

Best known, perhaps, are the **Prophet Joseph** and Church **Patriarch Hyrum Smith**, who died in the **Carthage Jail** on 27 June 1844, as well as their brother Samuel, who later died from the effects of this same tragedy. Those who died from the attack at **Haun's Mill**; from other mobbings in **Missouri, Ohio**, and **Illinois**; and from hardships along the **pioneer** trail to the **Great Basin** and beyond are also considered martyrs.

Missionaries have been particularly vulnerable. Around the world they put their lives on the line every day, and some have paid the ultimate sacrifice. In the **Southern States Mission**, a place which historian **Andrew Jenson** described as "the scene of more persecution than any other LDS Mission" (821), half a dozen missionaries lost their lives as a direct result of persecution; other dozens lost their lives due to exposure, improper diets, illness, disease, and other factors.

Many other members likewise died for their testimonies as a result of persecution. In the **Middle East** at least five individuals were buried far from home due to infectious diseases and lack of medical assistance. Today in **Turkey, Israel**, and **Syria** the presence of missionary graves are a reminder of these **Saints'** sacrifice for the truth.

SOURCES

Jenson, Andrew. *Encyclopedic History of The Church of Jesus Christ of Latter-day Saints.* Salt Lake City: Deseret News, 1941. 821.

McConkie, Bruce R. *Mormon Doctrine.* 2d ed. Salt Lake City: Bookcraft, 1966. 469–70.

Smith, Joseph. *History of The Church of Jesus Christ of Latter-day Saints.* Edited by B. H. Roberts. 2d ed. rev. 7 vols. Salt Lake City: The Church of Jesus Christ of Latter-day Saints, 1932–51.

DAVID F. BOONE

MARVELOUS WORK AND A WONDER, A. Considered a classic for latter-day missionaries, *A Marvelous Work and a Wonder* (first published in 1950) has been translated into 18 languages and has sold more than two million copies—more than any other Latter-day Saint book except the **Book of Mormon**. In 1937, **LeGrand Richards**, then president of the **Southern States Mission**, prepared an outline for a series of discussions his missionaries could use for the systematic and logical presentation of the gospel: "The Message of Mormonism." While serving as **presiding bishop**, he received so many requests for the outline that he prepared a manuscript for a book based on how he would teach these discussions if he were to meet with a **family** once a week for six months. *A Marvelous Work and a Wonder,* with its straightforward and persuasive manner, has been the means of introducing thousands to the basic doctrines of the restored gospel.

SOURCES

Richards, LeGrand. *A Marvelous Work and a Wonder.* Salt Lake City: Deseret Book, 1950. xi-xiv.

Tate, Lucile C. *LeGrand Richards—Beloved Apostle.* Salt Lake City: Bookcraft, 1982.

A. LeGrand Richards

MARYLAND. By 1837 Latter-day Saint missionaries began proselyting in present-day Maryland. Early missionaries, including **Erastus Snow**, William Bosley, **Jedediah M. Grant**, and John F. Wakefield, were assigned to labor in the state and experienced some success.

Often associated with the north, Maryland was temporarily included in the **Southern States Mission**, then transferred to the Northern States Mission, and in 1893, to the **Eastern States Mission**. Little **missionary work** was performed in Maryland during the nineteenth century.

After 1900 success increased. In 1940 the Washington **Stake** (including parts of Maryland) was organized, with **Ezra Taft Benson** as its first president. The **Washington, D.C. Temple**, actually located in Kensington, Maryland, was dedicated in November 1974. In the year 2000 Church membership in Maryland included 34,113 members in 8 stakes and 78 **wards** and **branches**.

SOURCES

Berrett, LaMar C. "History of the Southern States Mission." Master's thesis, Brigham Young University, 1960.

Jenson, Andrew. *Encyclopedic History of The Church of Jesus Christ of Latter-day Saints.* Salt Lake City: Deseret News, 1941.

1999–2000 Church Almanac. Salt Lake City: Deseret News, 1998. 208–9.

David F. Boone

MASONRY. As were **Mormons** and Catholics, the Masons were the object of persecution in early American history. A fraternal order established to provide protection for its members and service to others, the

Masons engaged in secret rituals which often led to wild speculations as to what transpired inside their temples. Masons believe their roots extend back as far as King Solomon and the building of his temple, and perhaps even to **Adam**.

A few early Latter-day Saint converts, including **Hyrum Smith, Heber C. Kimball, Newel K. Whitney, John C. Bennett**, Lucius N. Scovil, Noah Rodgers, and James Adams, were Masons before they were Latter-day Saints.

In the early summer of 1841, the Masonic order in **Illinois** granted a recess dispensation for the **Saints** to establish a lodge in **Nauvoo, Illinois**. Within a few months, more than 1,500 Latter-day Saint men, including **Joseph Smith**, had been initiated into lodges in Nauvoo and **Iowa**. There were more Latter-day Saint Masons than non-LDS Masons in all the other Illinois lodges combined. Though Joseph Smith attended few Masonic meetings, he seems to have supported Church members' involvement in this organization. Some believe he encouraged the growth of Masonry among Latter-day Saints so that Church members would be better protected than they had been in **Missouri**. Also, many of the state's leading politicians were Masons, and the **Prophet** might have hoped to improve the Church's political standing through involvement with Masonry. Others believe that Joseph Smith saw Masonry as another avenue for the Saints to influence and serve those outside the Church.

Not many months passed before Masons accused the Mormon lodge of initiating women into the order in violation of Masonic rules. Other Masons charged the Latter-day Saints with stealing their temple ceremony from the Masons. Latter-day Saints, including Joseph Smith, believed that the Masonic ceremony and the temple endowment had a common origin—ancient temple ceremonies—and this accounted for any similarities between the two rituals. Women did receive their endowments in Nauvoo in a private ritual, but they were never initiated as Masons.

By 1843, the dispensation of the Mormon Masonic lodges was suspended, even though some non-LDS Masons argued that Mormon Masonry was suspect simply because of its LDS members. After the martyrdom of Joseph Smith, the Illinois Grand Lodge withdrew all fellowship with LDS lodges, and all LDS Masons were suspended. This suspension included the Rising Sun Lodge at **Montrose, Iowa**, whose procedures had never been suspect.

Latter-day Saint enthusiasm for Masonry may have contributed to the conflict in **Hancock County**, Illinois, between Mormons and non-Mormons. Since the expulsion of the Latter-day Saints from Illinois,

Masonry has not played a significant role in Latter-day Saint history. Masons have joined the Church and served both organizations well, but their numbers are few.

SOURCES

Godfrey, Kenneth W. "Joseph Smith and the Masons." *Journal of the Illinois State Historical Society* 64 (1971): 79–90.

Hogan, Mervin B. *Mormonism and Freemasonry: The Illinois Episode.* Salt Lake City: Campus Graphics, 1980.

KENNETH W. GODFREY

MASSACHUSETTS. Massachusetts was the home of five generations of **Joseph Smith's** ancestors, as well as many prominent leaders in the early days of the Church, including **Thomas B. Marsh, John Boynton, Ezra T. Benson, Orson Spencer, Isaac Morley, Franklin D. Richards,** and **Edward Partridge.** Missionaries first proselyted in Massachusetts in 1832. Because of the doctrine of the **gathering,** the Church remained quite small there during much of the nineteenth century. Most of the growth in Church membership occurred after **World War II** and centered around Harvard and other universities in the Bay State. The Boston **Stake,** the first in New England, was created in 1962. Ground was broken for a **temple** in the Boston area in 1997. By the year 2000, Massachusetts had 21,106 members of the Church, 4 stakes, 49 **wards** and **branches,** and one **mission**—the Massachusetts Boston Mission.

SOURCES

Berrett, LaMar C., ed. *New England and Eastern Canada.* Vol. 1 of *Sacred Places.* Salt Lake City: Bookcraft, 1999. 1–57.

1999–2000 Church Almanac. Salt Lake City: Deseret News, 1998. 210–11.

DONALD Q. CANNON

MAUGHAN, PETER. Peter Maughan, who became a colonizer, **pioneer, stake president** and **bishop,** was born 7 May 1811 in Cumberland, **England,** the fifth child of William and Martha Wilson Maughan. He married Ruth Harrison 1 October 1831, and they became the parents of six children. Peter and Ruth joined the Church in 1838 and were active in the Alston branch. Ruth died 26 March 1841 after giving birth to their sixth child. **Brigham Young** counseled Peter to immigrate to **Nauvoo.** He and five of his children arrived in **America** 19 May 1841; his baby daughter, Ruth, was buried at sea.

While traveling in a wagon train from Kirtland to Nauvoo, Peter met a young widow, Mary Ann Weston Davis, whom he married on 2 November 1841. They had eight children. After being driven out of Nauvoo, Peter and his sons went to New Diggens, **Wisconsin**, and earned $800 by working in the lead mines. Using this money to equip the family for the trip to the **Salt Lake Valley**, they arrived 17 September 1850 and settled in Tooele, west of **Salt Lake City**, where he became the county clerk and assessor.

In 1856, under the direction of Brigham Young, Peter Maughan led a group of settlers from Tooele to **Cache Valley**, settling in the south end of the valley. Here they established Maughan's Fort, later to be known as Wellsville. Other communities soon followed, and Peter Maughan was called by Brigham Young as a regional presiding bishop, overseeing the **wards** and **branches** of Cache Valley. In 1860, Maughan was directed by the **prophet** to move his family to **Logan**. He served as the president of the Cache Stake as well as probate judge of Cache County and a member of the territorial legislature. He was also a colonel in the **Nauvoo Legion of Utah**.

Peter entered **plural marriage** 8 December 1866, marrying Elizabeth Francis Preator in the **Endowment House** in Salt Lake City. They had three children. He died of pneumonia in Logan, Utah, 24 April 1871 and was buried in the Logan cemetery.

SOURCES

Jenson, Andrew. *Latter-day Saint Biographical Encyclopedia.* 4 vols. 1901–36. Reprint, Salt Lake City: Western Epics, 1971. 1:758–9.

Powell, Allen Kent, ed. *Utah History Encyclopedia.* Salt Lake City: University of Utah Press, 1994. 360–61.

Wellsville History Committee. *Windows of Wellsville, 1856–1984.* Wellsville, Utah: Wellsville History Committee, 1985.

H. DEAN GARRETT

MAURITANIA. See MIDDLE EAST and MUSLIMS.

MAURITIUS. The island of Mauritius, located east of **Madagascar**, has an ethnically mixed population of more than one million persons of European, Indian, African, and Chinese origin. Colonized by **France** and then a member of the British empire, Mauritius became an independent nation in 1968.

In 1980 missionary couples began serving in Mauritius, where they found several individuals who had already been baptized members of the Church. The first Mauritius **branch** of the Church was organized in 1982 under the direction of the **International Mission**. In 1985 the first pros-elyting young adult missionaries arrived, establishing the Church more firmly. Mauritius was officially dedicated by **Elder Marvin J. Ashton** on 22 November 1988. By the year 2000 the country had 277 members living in 1 branch.

SOURCES

"Mauritius, Reunion Dedicated for Missionary Work." *Ensign* 19 (March 1989): 76.
Wheelwright, Max. "Tiny Branches Bear Fruit in Mascarene Islands." *Ensign* 16 (February 1986): 79–80.

CYNTHIA DOXEY

MAVIMBELA, JULIA N. At the **Brigham Young University** com-mencement of August 1995, Julia N. Mavimbela, a black South African, was presented a Presidential Citation and Medallion for "commitment to community, faithfulness to God," and "service to others." Born 20 Dec-ember 1917 in Standerton, South Africa, Julia faced and overcome many hardships and challenges throughout her life. She was raised in a poor farming area and her father died when she was four, leaving the **family** in dire circumstances. Through hard work and persistence, she graduated from a teacher's college—a rare accomplishment for an African woman at that time. She taught elementary school and later became one of the first black female principals in the nation.

Julia gave up her career when she married. In 1955 her husband, John, was killed in a tragic accident. She was left destitute with six chil-dren and struggled intensely.

Fluent in seven languages, Julia established literacy programs. She served as president and vice president of the National Women of South Africa. To help promote a peaceful transition to democracy for all races in South Africa, she organized Women for Peace, a multiracial organiza-tion that brought her in contact with the major political leaders of South Africa. To help Africans overcome racial hatred, she involved hundreds of children in beautifying some weed-covered, rodent-infested areas of land in Soweto by planting gardens. Her message was: "Love will not come without forgiving others. Where there has been a blood stain, a beautiful flower must grow" (quoted in LeBaron, 176).

In 1981 Julia met the missionaries and joined the Church after two months of earnest study and prayer. She has served as a **Relief Society** president, Church public affairs director, and **temple** worker.

──────

SOURCES

LeBaron, E. Dale, ed. *"All Are Alike unto God."* Orem, Utah: Granite Publishing, 1998. 171–84.

Oral histories of early Church converts collected by E. Dale LeBaron. Copies at BYU Library, Provo, Utah; LDS Church Historical Library, Salt Lake City, Utah.

E. DALE LEBARON

MAXWELL, NEAL A. A member of the **Quorum** of the Twelve **Apostles**, Neal Ash Maxwell became known as an articulate defender of the faith. Born 6 July 1926 in **Salt Lake City, Utah**, he raised award-winning pigs in his youth. During **World War II** he enlisted in the Army and saw action on Okinawa. He filled a **mission** to eastern **Canada** from 1947 to 1949 and married Colleen Fern Hinckley in 1950. Maxwell received bachelor's and master's degrees in political science from the **University of Utah**. From 1952 through 1956 he worked for U.S. senator Wallace F. Bennett. He served as dean of students and executive vice president at the University of Utah. In 1970, he was appointed commissioner of education for the Church, initiating an era of reorganization and tremendous growth.

Elder Maxwell was among the first group of **regional representatives** called in 1967. In 1974, he was called as an **assistant to the Twelve**; in 1976, to the presidency of the **Quorum** of the **Seventy**; then, in 1981, to the Quorum of the Twelve.

Among the memorable events in Elder Maxwell's travels were the creation of the first **stake** in black **Africa** in 1988 and the dedication of **Mongolia** for the preaching of the gospel in 1993.

Shortly after his seventieth birthday, Elder Maxwell was diagnosed with leukemia. His ministry thereafter was characterized by attentiveness to those struggling with illness or tragedy.

Known for his ability to compress meaning and feeling into compact verbal images, Elder Maxwell became a powerful teacher and defender of the faith. His organizational abilities and keen intellect made him an effective and admired leader in the Church. He was known for his love of the scriptures and his ability to show their relevance to daily life.

SOURCES

Durham, Lowell M., Jr. "The New Brethren." *New Era* 4 (June 1974): 7–8.

Eyring, Henry B. "Elder Neal A. Maxwell: Pursuing 'A More Excellent Way.'" *Ensign* 17 (January 1987): 6–11.

Hafen, Bruce C. "Elder Neal A. Maxwell: An Understanding Heart." *Ensign* 12 (February 1982): 6–13.

CORY H. MAXWELL

MCCONKIE, BRUCE R.

Bruce Redd McConkie, a member of the **Quorum** of the Twelve **Apostles**, was a powerful doctrinal teacher and one of the Church's most prolific gospel writers. Towering in stature and mighty in testimony, he was born 29 July 1915 in Ann Arbor, **Michigan**. In 1937 he married Amelia Smith. After graduating with a juris doctorate from the **University of Utah**, he served as a city prosecutor, an intelligence officer in **World War II**, and an editorial writer for the *Deseret News*. At age 31 he was called to the First Quorum of the **Seventy**. His service included presiding over the Southern Australian **Mission** from 1961 to 1964. In 1972 Elder McConkie was called to fill the vacancy in the Quorum of the Twelve caused by the death of his father-in-law, President **Joseph Fielding Smith**.

A major accomplishment in Elder McConkie's life was his contribution to the 1981 edition of the LDS scriptures, a contribution which included writing chapter headings and section summaries. His published writings include *Mormon Doctrine*, a three-volume New Testament commentary, a six-volume series on the life of Christ, and a commentary on the **Articles of Faith**. He also penned the words for the well-loved hymn "I Believe in Christ."

On 19 April 1985, only days before his death, Elder McConkie gave one of the most memorable talks ever heard in **general conference**. He testified of Christ, saying: "I am one of his witnesses, and in a coming day I shall feel the nail marks in his hands and in his feet and shall wet his feet with my tears. But I shall not know any better then than I know now, that he is God's Almighty Son" (McConkie, 12).

SOURCES

Flake, Lawrence R. *Prophets and Apostles of the Last Dispensation.* Provo, Utah: Religious Studies Center, Brigham Young University, 2001. 513–16.

McConkie, Bruce R. Conference Report (April 1985): 9–12.

Young, S. Dilworth. "Elder Bruce R. McConkie of the Council of the Twelve." *Ensign* 3 (January 1973): 5–11.

Joseph Fielding McConkie

MCKAY, DAVID LAWRENCE. David Lawrence McKay served as general superintendent of the Deseret **Sunday School** from 1966 to 1971. He had served previously as second assistant from 1949 to 1952 and as first assistant from 1952 to 1966. He was born 30 September 1901 in **Ogden, Utah**, the oldest son of **David O. McKay**, ninth president of the Church. He later married Mildred Dean Calderwood. When President McKay became ill, David Lawrence read several of his father's sermons in **general conference**. He also served as a mission president. He died 27 October 1993 in **Salt Lake City**.

―――――

Source

McKay, David Lawrence. *My Father, David O. McKay*. Edited by Lavina Fielding Anderson. Salt Lake City: Deseret Book, 1989.

Mary Jane Woodger

MCKAY, DAVID O. When David Oman McKay became the ninth president of The Church of Jesus Christ of Latter-day Saints on 9 April 1951, he had served 45 years as a **general authority**. At age 77, he still had a tall, impressive physique and a head of thick, white, wavy hair. After meeting President McKay, many would comment that he not only acted like a prophet, he also looked like one.

Born 8 September 1873 in the small **Utah** town of Huntsville, David was the third child of David and Jeanette Evans McKay. His father came from **Scotland**, and his mother was from **Wales**. Both had immigrated to **Ogden, Utah**, in 1859. Though David's father lacked formal **education**, he taught himself the necessary skills to be elected to the Utah state legislature. David's parents were married in 1867 and made their home in Huntsville, Utah. President McKay credited his parental home as the chief component in molding his character. He often spoke of his parents, family, upbringing, and beginnings in a small rural town.

When David was seven, his two older sisters died within days of one another, and his father was called on a mission to Scotland. During his father's two-year absence, David assumed responsibilities that surpassed his years and experience. As a youth he was also involved in **ward** activities, serving as **deacons** president at 12, **Sunday School** secretary at 15, and Sunday School teacher at 20.

David's parents made sure that education played a key role in the lives of their children. Because of this emphasis in their home, President McKay was the first prophet with a college degree. He was educated in the Huntsville community school and then Weber Stake Academy, where he developed a love for learning and a keen interest in literature. He spent many hours memorizing passages from such authors as Robert Burns, William Shakespeare, and Ralph Waldo Emerson. Later, as a general authority, he often used their words in his sermons.

In 1893, at the age of 20, David became principal of the school in Huntsville. A year later he enrolled at the **University of Utah**, where he played on the school's first official football team, became class president, and graduated in 1897 as the valedictorian of his class.

After completing his education at the University of Utah, David was called to serve a mission to Great Britain from 1897 to 1899, where he presided over the Scottish conference. During his mission, two experiences made indelible impressions on him. When he was in Stirling, Scotland, he saw the phrase "Whate'er thou art, act well thy part" carved above a front door. He internalized the meaning of the inscription, and it became his personal motto, which he incorporated into many of his speeches. The other experience took place during a priesthood meeting when James McMurrin, a counselor in the mission presidency, said: "Brother David, **Satan** has desired you that he may sift you as wheat, but God is mindful of you, and if you keep the faith, you will yet sit in the leading councils of the Church" (Morrell, 731).

As a young returned missionary, he became the second assistant in the Weber Stake Sunday School superintendency and developed new programs. His innovations were noticed by the general leadership of the Church, who would soon draw him into their ranks.

During his mission David had corresponded with Emma Ray Riggs, whom he had met while boarding at her mother's house during his college years. Their courtship began to blossom through the mail. Emma Ray, who was born 23 June 1877, graduated from the University of Utah in 1898, and was teaching at Madison School in Ogden when she married David O. McKay on 2 January 1901. They were the first couple to be sealed in the **Salt Lake Temple** in the twentieth century. They became the parents of seven children.

David began his teaching career in 1899 at Weber Stake Academy. In

1902 he was made principal, and in 1908 he became the president of the board, a position he held until 1922.

David O. McKay's greatest opportunity to influence the Church's educational ideas, policy, and practices came on 9 April 1906 when he was ordained an **apostle**. The very nature of his unique assignments within the Quorum of the Twelve suggests the scope of his influence on Church education policy.

When Elder McKay was sustained as an apostle, he also became the second assistant to the general superintendent of the Deseret **Sunday School** Union. He was called as first assistant in 1909. The same innovations he used in the Weber Stake Sunday School were quickly put into practice by the entire Church. Seeing a need for uniform lessons, he wrote *Ancient Apostles,* which was prepared as one of the first Sunday School lesson manuals. Elder McKay's name became synonymous with the Sunday School.

He became the first general authority directly in charge of the Church's entire education program, being called as the general superintendent of the Deseret Sunday School Union in 1918 and as the Church commissioner of education the following year. Commissioner McKay made a proposal that changed Church education forever. In 1920 he advised that most Church-owned **academies** be closed and be superseded by **seminaries** and **institutes of religion** adjacent to schools.

Other experiences prepared David O. McKay to lead a worldwide Church. At the request of President **Heber J. Grant** in 1920, he toured all the Church **missions** and schools throughout the world. During this trip, he had powerful revelatory experiences concerning the future of the Church worldwide. In 1922 he was called as president of the **European Mission**, where he showed a remarkable ability to improve the Church's image through positive public relations. It was while he had this calling that he coined the motto "Every member a missionary."

After he became president of the Church in 1951, David O. McKay continued to be supportive of Church education. He directed the expansion of **Brigham Young University** and **Ricks College** (later BYU–Idaho). He founded the Church College of **Hawaii** (later **Brigham Young University–Hawaii Campus**); he also supported the continuation and development of seminaries and institutes, along with Church schools in the Pacific and in Latin America, where public schooling was not available.

President McKay's administration was marked by incredible growth. Church membership tripled, the missionary force grew sixfold, and for the first time **temples** were erected in **Europe** (**Switzerland**, 1955) and the South Pacific (**New Zealand**, 1958). Under his direction, films were used to present the temple ceremony in various languages. President McKay traveled more miles than all of his predecessors combined. In 1952 he visited nine European countries, and in 1954 he was the first prophet to tour **South Africa**.

During his administration the number of **stakes** grew from 184 to 500 as new stakes were formed in **Australia**, **Argentina**, **Brazil**, **England**, **Germany**, **Guatemala**, **Japan**, **Mexico**, the **Netherlands**, **Peru**, Switzerland, **Samoa**, Scotland, **Tonga**, and **Uruguay**. To accommodate this tremendous growth, members of the First Quorum of the **Seventy** were made **high priests** in 1961, and the new office of **regional representative** of the Twelve was established in 1967. As his health began to decline in 1965, he also called additional counselors into the **First Presidency**.

President McKay's sermons often discussed the sanctity of marriage and the home. The maxim "No other success can compensate for failure in the home" became his byword as he called on parents to spend more time with their children and to teach them about character and integrity. His marriage of more than 60 years became the model union for Latter-day Saints. His powerful sermons on the subjects of the Savior, the Atonement, the **restoration** of the gospel and spirituality were well received. He was also seen by members of other faiths as an important leader, meeting often with government officials from the **United States** and abroad. Surprisingly active in his elderly years, he continued to conduct the business of the Church into his tenth decade. In the late 1960s President McKay's health began to fail, and he was confined to a wheelchair. He passed away 18 January 1970 in **Salt Lake City, Utah**, at the age of 96. He had served 64 years as a general authority, longer than anyone else during the present dispensation.

SOURCES

Allen, James B. "David O. McKay." *The Presidents of the Church.* Edited by Leonard J. Arrington. Salt Lake City: Deseret Book, 1986. 274–313.

Ashton, Emma Rae McKay. "Emma Ray Riggs McKay." *Instructor* 102 (June 1967): 402.

McKay, David Lawrence. *My Father, David O. McKay.* Edited by Lavina Fielding Anderson. Salt Lake City: Deseret Book, 1989.

Morrell, Jeanette McKay. *Highlights in the Life of President David O. McKay.* Salt Lake City: Deseret Book, 1967.

———. "Life of President David O. McKay." *The Relief Society Magazine* (November 1953): 730–36.

Woodger, Mary Jane. "Educational Ideas and Practices of David O. McKay, 1880–1940." Ed.D. diss., Brigham Young University, 1997.

MARY JANE WOODGER

MCKAY, THOMAS E. Thomas Evans McKay was born 29 October 1875 in Huntsville, Utah. In 1899 he graduated from the **University of Utah** and took a job as principal of Pingree Elementary School. He served a **mission** in **Germany** from 1900 to 1903, and then he taught for six years at the schools that later became **Weber State University** and **Utah State University**. In 1909 he was called as president of the Swiss-German Mission, and in 1912 he married Fawn Brimhall. They became the parents of five children.

Thomas served for 20 years as a **stake president**. As a public official, he was elected to the Utah state house of representatives and also the state senate, where he served as president for two terms. **Elder** McKay was sustained as **assistant to the Quorum of the Twelve Apostles** (one of the original five assistants) on 6 April 1941. He served in this calling for 17 years until his death in Salt Lake City on 15 January 1958.

SOURCE

Flake, Lawrence R. *Mighty Men of Zion*. Salt Lake City: Karl D. Butler, 1974. 323–24.

BARBARA MCKAY SMITH

MCLELLIN, WILLIAM E. William E. McLellin was an early missionary, **apostle**, and **Book of Mormon** champion. He was born 18 January 1806 in Smith County, Tennessee. He was converted to the restored gospel when he was 25 years old, and almost immediately he was baptized and ordained an **elder**. He served a **mission** in the Midwest, worked at building up **Zion** in **Missouri**, and in 1835 was called as one of the original members of the **Quorum** of the Twelve Apostles, in which capacity he visited the eastern states and **Ontario, Canada**. He also taught school in **Kirtland, Ohio,** and served a mission in the southern states.

In spite of his dedicated service, his relationship with Church leadership was troubled from time to time, sometimes exceedingly, and in 1838 he was branded as an apostate and excommunicated. Like some other early Church leaders who were cut off, McLellin afterwards united with several other **Mormon schismatic groups**. He never tarried with any of them for long, and continued to maintain not only that the Book of

Mormon was true, but also that it was precisely what it claimed to be. He died 24 April 1883 in **Independence, Missouri**.

McLellin's missionary journals, which were published in 1994, recount his struggles to be faithful. They also provide invaluable details about the Church's beginnings and information about early Latter-day Saint preaching.

SOURCES

Grandstaff, Mark R. "Having More Learning Than Sense: William E. McLellin and the Book of Commandments Revisited." *Dialogue* 26 (Winter 1993): 23–50.

Porter, Larry C. "The Odyssey of William Earl McLellin: Man of Diversity, 1806–83." *The Journals of William E. McLellin, 1831–1836.* Edited by Jan Shipps and John W. Welch. Provo, Utah: BYU Studies, 1994.

JAN SHIPPS

MEDICINE. Throughout the history of the Church, faithful Latter-day Saints have turned to both sacred and secular resources when faced with personal and family illness. Anchored doctrinally by an early revelation that directed "whosoever among you are sick, and have not faith to be healed, but believe, shall be nourished with all tenderness, with herbs and mild food" (D&C 42:43–44), the afflicted turned early both to the ministrations of **elders** and to the healing herbs of botanic practitioners.

Given the limited medical knowledge of mid-nineteenth century **Saints**, distinctions between **priesthood** and medical ministrations soon blurred, with consecrated oil assuming the role of a divine therapeutic (applied directly and repeatedly to the afflicted area) and occasionally **rebaptism** for the direct relief of symptoms.

In the 1870s, at a time when modern scientific medicine was beginning to unfold, **Brigham Young** sent young Latter-day Saints to medical programs in the East so they could bring back to the larger LDS community the benefits of the latest thinking. The return of these physicians brought transition to the germ theory of disease, preventive medicine, and modern hospital care.

Church members were encouraged early to protect their health through the tenets of the **Word of Wisdom**. In the early twentieth century, however, the promotion of LDS health achieved a new level of attention through a renewed emphasis on the Word of Wisdom, special health sections in Church periodicals, and Church-supported community action programs. Concurrent with this emphasis, the role and form of priesthood healings were clarified, rebaptisms for health discontinued, and any directly therapeutic overtones from anointing eliminated.

Emerging from these developments was a symbiotic relationship combining the unique contributions of priesthood administration and medical practice. Church members were strongly encouraged to seek the blessings of the **priesthood** and to turn early to the best in modern medicine. This perspective remains that of the present-day Church, now including the embrace of such late twentieth-century medical developments as psychopharmacology, organ transplantation, and revolutionary procedures in reproductive medicine.

SOURCES

Bush, Lester E., Jr. *Health and Medicine among the Latter-day Saints: Science, Sense, and Scripture.* New York: Crossroad, 1993.

———. "The Mormon Tradition." *Caring and Curing: Health and Medicine in the Western Religious Traditions.* Edited by Ronald L. Numbers and Darrel W. Amundsen. Baltimore: Johns Hopkins University, 1998. 397–420.

LESTER BUSH

MEETINGHOUSES. Early Latter-day Saint meetings were held in houses, groves of trees, or available buildings. The first specifically **Mormon** structure was the log hall built in July 1831 in Kaw Township, **Jackson County, Missouri.** Next was the 1836 temple in **Kirtland, Ohio,** abandoned two years later when the evicted **Saints** left for Missouri. While in **Nauvoo,** the Church built another temple for special meeting purposes. Regular Sabbath-day meetings continued in groves and houses.

Forced out of Nauvoo in 1846, the Saints headed west and stopped for the winter near present Omaha, **Nebraska.** In this area they built two meetinghouses. Continuing west, the first Saints entered the Great **Salt Lake Valley** in 1847. Housing was the first priority, and meetings were again held outdoors and in members' homes. Buildings were of log, stone, or adobe, and schools doubled as meetinghouses. By 1859 about 90 of these modest combined school-meetinghouses were constructed. An adobe meetinghouse, sometimes called the "Old Tabernacle," was completed in 1852 on the southwest corner of the temple block. It was large enough to seat 2,500 people.

Between 1860 and 1877, a second generation of 200 meetinghouses was built with a distinctive pioneer vernacular style plus elements of the Greek Revival. Brick was made and used from 1863. The famous **Salt Lake Tabernacle** was constructed in 1867.

From 1878 to 1899 a continued momentum in building was necessitated by the influx of converts. They spread throughout the state and built their meetinghouses where they settled. The larger communities built impressive **tabernacles**, some still standing.

The first two decades of the twentieth century introduced more stylish buildings, influenced by the Gothic and Romanesque Revival and even the new Prairie architecture. These meetinghouses included a limited number of classrooms and a small "amusement hall," sometimes located in the basement.

The next period, 1920 through 1933, brought 350 meetinghouses in the ever-popular Colonial Revival style, many of which are still in use.

Between 1934 and 1950 the Church ceased to provide complete sets of plans, but maintained control as to size and cost of buildings. Local architects were used, and the latest styles of Art Deco, Moderne, and International appeared in about 12% of the buildings. The remaining 88% continued with the popular simplified Colonial Revival and other architectural styles.

The pace of building construction quickened to such a point that in 1945 the office of the Building Committee was established. During the 1950s the Building Committee designed meetinghouses with the addition of enlarged recreation halls, which accommodated activities such as basketball. These halls were positioned to serve as overflow spaces for the chapels. A group of Salt Lake architects once again provided plans for hundreds of buildings.

Beginning in 1958, "phase buildings" were designed to expand in stages to provide for the growing congregation. All of these meetinghouses accommodated the priesthood and auxiliary programs for various age groups. These buildings are still designed and constructed for the benefit of the Saints worldwide.

RICHARD W. JACKSON

MEETINGS. **Revelations** instruct Church members to "meet together often" in order to edify and instruct each other and to partake of the **sacrament** (D&C 20:55, 75; 43:8). On the Lord's day (Sunday) members are to keep themselves unspotted from the world by going to "the house of prayer" and partaking of the sacrament (D&C 59:9). Those who conduct meetings are to be "directed and guided by the Holy Spirit" (D&C 46:2; 20:45). **Priesthood** officers "are to meet in **conference** once in three months" or whenever business requires it (D&C 20:61–62). Children should be brought "unto the **elders** before the church" to be blessed (D&C 20:70). Officers are instructed not to exclude nonmembers from public meetings, members from sacrament meetings, or investigators from **confirmation** meetings (D&C 46:3–6).

The first record of a Church Sabbath meeting, a 9 June 1830 conference, opened with singing followed by a prayer, the sacrament, confirmations, ordinations, and "much exhortation and instruction." By 1831 the Sunday meeting schedule was a morning meeting and an afternoon meeting, with the sacrament being administered at one of them. **Saints** often had a mid-week evening prayer meeting, with testimony sharing, from the 1830s to the 1870s.

Until the 1860s the "house of prayer" was a private home, a small schoolhouse, or, for large gatherings, an outdoor meeting. At **Nauvoo**, community-wide meetings took place (if weather allowed) in outdoor groves and at the **temple** site. In the Great **Salt Lake Valley**, the Sunday community-wide morning and afternoon meetings were in the outdoor bowery, the Old **Tabernacle**, and then the new Tabernacle. During winter, Sunday meetings took place in private homes until wards built **meetinghouses**, after which sacrament meetings became ward meetings. During the **Utah War**, no sacrament meetings were held for ten months. Until the mid 1860s the pioneers had few formal meetings to attend, and the first ward meetinghouses were too small for most members to attend sacrament meeting. With bigger chapels, attendance increased.

Ward meetings came to include Sunday School (by 1860s), Relief Society (after 1867), **YLMIA** and **YMMIA** and Primary (by 1870s), **quorum** gatherings, ward priesthood meetings (after 1908) on Monday nights and then on Sundays, and weekday **religion classes** (1905–29).

In 1896, fast day was changed from the first Thursday of each month to the first Sunday so that working people and students could attend the ward fast meetings. Starting in 1909 LDS **hymnbooks** were tailored for congregational singing, rather than mainly for choirs. **Stake conferences** have been held since the 1830s, quarterly at first, but semiannually since 1979. General conferences have been held semiannually since the 1830s, usually in April and October. They have been broadcast by **radio** (1924), **television** (1953), and **satellite** television systems (1980).

SOURCES

Hartley, William G. "Common People: Church Activity during the Brigham Young Era." *Nearly Everything Imaginable: The Everyday Life of Utah's Mormon Pioneers.* Edited by Ronald W. Walker and Doris R. Dant. Provo, Utah: Brigham Young University Press, 1999. 249–95.

"Mormon Sundays." *Ensign* 8 (January 1978): 19–25.

Walker, Ronald W. "'Going to Meeting' in Salt Lake City's Thirteenth Ward, 1849–1881: A Microanalysis." *New Views of Mormon History: A Collection of Essays in Honor of Leonard J. Arrington.* Edited by Davis Bitton and Maureen Ursenbach Beecher. Salt Lake City: University of Utah Press, 1987.

WILLIAM G. HARTLEY

MELCHIZEDEK PRIESTHOOD. As revealed to the **Prophet Joseph Smith**, this higher **priesthood**, which comprehends or encompasses the **Aaronic** and Levitical priesthoods (Smith, 166), holds "the keys of all the spiritual blessings of the Church" and "the mysteries of the kingdom of heaven" (D&C 107:18–19); it "holds the right of presidency, and has power and authority over all offices in the church in all ages of the world" (D&C 107:8). Like God himself, the Melchizedek Priesthood is eternal. The Prophet Joseph Smith said, "The priesthood is an everlasting principle, and existed with God from eternity, and will to eternity" (Smith, 157).

The Melchizedek Priesthood was instituted "prior to the foundation of this earth" and "is the channel through which the Almighty commenced revealing his glory at the beginning of the creation of this earth, and through which he has continued to reveal himself . . . and through which he will make known his purposes to the end of time" (Smith, 166–67). Hence, it was referred to in New Testament times as "without descent, having neither beginning of days, nor end of life" (JST Heb. 7:3). The **Book of Mormon** prophet Alma taught that all those who are ordained to the Melchizedek Priesthood in mortality were foreordained in our premortal existence to hold that priesthood (Alma 13:3–7).

Before the time of the **patriarch** Melchizedek, this higher priesthood was called "the Holy Priesthood after the Order of the Son of God." But out of respect or reverence for the name of Deity, its name was changed to the Melchizedek Priesthood in honor of the great patriarch (D&C 107:2–4). When worthy men are **ordained** to this priesthood, they both imitate the Lord **Jesus Christ** and possess the power to become as he is: "And all those who are ordained unto this priesthood are made like unto the Son of God, abiding a priest continually" (JST Heb. 7:3). In fact, the Melchizedek Priesthood is the power by which men and women also become like our Father in Heaven, heirs of his kingdom and joint heirs with Jesus Christ, possessing every power and every blessing the Father and the Son possess (Smith, 308–9, 322).

The Melchizedek Priesthood and its keys were held anciently by the chief **apostles, Peter, James, and John** (Smith, 158). After centuries of apostasy, the Melchizedek Priesthood and the keys to direct its use were restored to the Prophet Joseph Smith under the hands of these three apostles. Though the exact date is unknown, this event evidently occurred sometime shortly after the **restoration** of the Aaronic Priesthood (15 May 1829) by **John the Baptist**, who said that he acted under the direction of the chief apostles and that the restoration of the Melchizedek Priesthood was to follow "in due time" (JS–H 1:72). Joseph Smith later indicated that he had met Peter, James, and John "in the wilderness between **Harmony**, Susquehanna county, and **Colesville**, Broome county, on the **Susquehanna river**" (D&C 128:20). That the promised restoration had occurred was clearly attested by the Lord in August of 1830 when he spoke to the Prophet about "Peter, and James, and John, whom I have sent unto you, by whom I have ordained you and confirmed you to be apostles" (D&C 27:12).

SOURCES

McConkie, Bruce R. *Mormon Doctrine.* 2d ed. Salt Lake City: Bookcraft, 1966. 475–83.

Porter, Larry C. "The Restoration of the Priesthood." *Religious Studies Center Newsletter* 9, 3 (May 1995): 1–12.

———. "The Restoration of the Aaronic and Melchizedek Priesthoods." *Ensign* 26 (December 1996): 30–47.

Smith, Joseph. *Teachings of the Prophet Joseph Smith.* Joseph Fielding Smith, comp. Salt Lake City: Deseret Book, 1970.

ANDREW C. SKINNER

MELCHIZEDEK PRIESTHOOD, RESTORATION OF.

The **Aaronic Priesthood**, with the authority to baptize, was bestowed on **Joseph Smith** and **Oliver Cowdery** by **John the Baptist** on 15 May 1829 on the banks of the **Susquehanna River** in **Harmony, Pennsylvania**. The **Melchizedek Priesthood** was conferred shortly thereafter, apparently during that very month, on the heads of those same men by the ancient **apostles Peter, James, and John**. These heavenly ministers appeared to Joseph and Oliver while "in the wilderness between Harmony, Susquehanna county [Pennsylvania] and **Colesville**, Broome county [**New York**], on the Susquehanna river, declaring themselves as possessing the keys of the kingdom, and of the dispensation of the fulness of times" (D&C 128:20).

Joseph Smith and Oliver Cowdery received all the power and authority necessary to organize and direct the Church of **Jesus Christ** and to perform additional saving priesthood **ordinances**. Not only did Peter, James, and John ordain them to the holy Melchizedek Priesthood, but they also conferred the keys and authority pertaining to the apostolic office. The **scriptures** and historical evidence, as well as the testimony of contemporaries closely associated with the **Prophet**, attest that these brethren had received the Melchizedek Priesthood and exercised its keys when they organized the Church on **6 April** 1830. Ordinations of other brethren to various offices in the Aaronic and Melchizedek Priesthoods were performed by Joseph Smith and Oliver Cowdery both on the day of the **organization of the Church** and at the first **conference**, held 9 June 1830.

SOURCES

Anderson, Richard Lloyd. "Melchizedek Priesthood Restoration in the Combined Comments of Joseph Smith and Oliver Cowdery." Manuscript in author's possession.

Cannon, Brian Q., and BYU Studies staff, eds. "Priesthood Restoration Documents." *BYU Studies* 35 (1995–96): 162–207.

Porter, Larry C. "The Priesthood Restored." *The Pearl of Great Price.* Edited by Robert L. Millet and Kent P. Jackson. Vol. 2 of Studies in Scripture series. Salt Lake City: Randall Book, 1985.

———. "The Restoration of the Aaronic and Melchizedek Priesthoods." *Ensign* 26 (December 1996): 30–47.

LARRY C. PORTER

MENDON, NEW YORK. Mendon Township, Monroe County, **New York**, is situated 12 miles south of Rochester, New York. John Young, the father of **Brigham Young**, moved to the town of Mendon in 1827 and located 1.6 miles south of the village of Mendon. Brigham and Miriam Works Young moved to John Young's farm in the spring of 1829 and built a home and mill site. **Phineas H. Young**, Brigham's brother, was living in nearby Victor, Ontario County, New York, in the spring of 1830.

In April 1830, **Samuel H. Smith**, brother of the **Prophet**, visited with Phineas H. Young at the Tomlinson Inn in Mendon. Samuel sold a **Book of Mormon** to Phineas, and that copy began to circulate among the Youngs. During June 1830, Samuel again returned to the Mendon area, placing a copy of the Book of Mormon in the home of **John P. Greene** and his wife Rhoda Young, a sister of Brigham. Samuel Smith's placement of these copies, along with the follow-up missionary efforts of elders from Bradford and Tioga counties, resulted in many baptisms in Mendon. Brigham Young was baptized in his own mill stream by Eleazer Miller on

15 April 1832 (*JD*, 9:219). **Heber C. Kimball** was baptized by Alpheus Gifford, 16 April 1832. The Mendon Branch met in the Tomlinson Inn, which was owned by convert Nathan Tomlinson.

SOURCES

Esplin, Ronald K. "Conversion and Transformation: Brigham Young's New York Roots and the Search for Bible Religion." *Lion of the Lord: Essays on the Life & Service of Brigham Young.* Edited by Susan Easton Black and Larry C. Porter. Salt Lake City: Deseret Book, 1995. 20–53.

Journal of Discourses [JD]. 26 vols. London: Latter-day Saints' Book Depot, 1854–86.

Palmer, Richard F., and Karl D. Butler. *Brigham Young: The New York Years.* Provo, Utah: Charles Redd Center for Western Studies, Brigham Young University, 1982. 17–72.

LARRY C. PORTER

MENLOVE, COLEEN K. Coleen K. Menlove was sustained in **general conference** on 2 October 1999 as general president of the **Primary**. She was born 1 July 1943 in **Salt Lake City** to Robert D. and Marjory Moon Kent. Coleen was afflicted with polio in her youth, and her parents demonstrated unfailing care in facilitating therapy and recovery.

In 1964 she married Dean W. Menlove, and the next year she graduated from the **University of Utah** with a bachelor's degree in elementary education. In 1973 she received a master's degree in education curriculum from **Brigham Young University** and taught professionally part-time from 1985 to 1999. In addition to actively participating in education-related organizations, she published a text on early childhood education. Prior to her call as general Primary president, Sister Menlove served as **stake** Primary president, a member of Church writing committees, and a member of the **Young Women's** general board.

SOURCES

"Colleen K. Menlove: Primary General President." *Ensign* 29 (November 1999): 107.

"This Teacher Will Share Her Spiritual Talents." *Church News,* 30 October, 1999.

ROBERT C. FREEMAN

MERRILL, JOSEPH F. Joseph Francis Merrill was born of humble means to Marriner W. Merrill and Mariah Loenza Kingsbury on 24 August 1868 in Richmond, **Utah.** Educated as a **scientist,** Joseph earned degrees at the **University of Utah,** the **University of Michigan,** and Johns Hopkins University. He taught at the University of Utah, where he became dean of the School of Mines and Engineering. While serving as a member of the Granite **Stake** presidency, he originated the idea of a released-time **seminary** at Granite High School. When Brother Merrill became the Church commissioner of education in 1928, he expanded the idea and is now considered the father of the Church's seminary program. Brother Merrill was ordained a member of the **Quorum** of the Twelve Apostles on 8 October 1931 and served in that capacity until his death in **Salt Lake City** on 3 February 1952.

SOURCES

Benson, Ezra Taft. "Elder Joseph F. Merrill." *Relief Society Magazine* 39 (April 1952): 217–18.

Flake, Lawrence R. *Prophets and Apostles of the Last Dispensation.* Provo, Utah: Religious Studies Center, Brigham Young University, 2001. 457–59.

Hinckley, Gordon B. "Elder Joseph F. Merrill." *Improvement Era* 55 (March 1952): 144–47, 203–5.

LAWRENCE R. FLAKE

MERRILL, MARRINER W. Marriner Wood Merrill was born in Sackville, **New Brunswick**, **Canada**, on 25 September 1832. He joined the Church in 1852 and immigrated to Utah the following year. In November 1853 he married Sarah Atkinson. In 1860 they were called to settle **Cache Valley** in northern Utah. Merrill's record of community building there is impressive. He helped explore the valley, built a grist mill, served as **bishop** in Richmond, acted as director of the Utah Northern Railroad, helped establish the Cache Valley Dairy Association, was counselor in the **stake** presidency, served as president of the **Logan Temple**, and was on the board of trustees for **Brigham Young College.**

In 1889 Church leaders called Marriner W. Merrill as an **apostle.** For a time he served concurrently in the **Quorum** of the Twelve and as president of the Logan Temple; he also helped with the dedication of the **Salt Lake Temple** in 1893. He died 6 February 1906 in Richmond, Utah.

SOURCES

Cannon, Donald Q., and Richard D. McClellan. "Building Utah: Contributions of Eastern Canadians." Manuscript.

Esshom, Frank Elwood, *Pioneers and Prominent Men of Utah.* Salt Lake City: Utah Pioneers Book Publishing Company, 1913. 379.

Pollock, Gordon Douglas. *Northern Voices: A Folk History of Mormonism among British Americans.* Halifax, Nova Scotia: Kelso Associates, 1995.

DONALD Q. CANNON

MESA, ARIZONA. Mesa is located in the Salt River Valley of Central Arizona and is the home of the **Arizona Temple**. Founded in 1877 by **Mormon pioneers**, Mesa is the largest of the surviving LDS Arizona colonies. Today the city has an estimated population of 375,000, making it the second largest city in the state.

The first party to settle Mesa was composed of approximately 80 pioneers led by Charles Crismon, Francis M. Pomeroy, Charles I. Robson, and George W. Sirrine. The first years in Mesa were filled with obstacles as the pioneers combated heat, drought, floods, and rattlesnakes. Early discouragements, however, soon gave way to growth and progress. For example, success in irrigation was greatly assisted through the use of an ancient canal.

These Arizona pioneers organized the community of Mesa with wide streets, building lots according to the pattern established in **Salt Lake City**. As news of the success in Mesa reached Church headquarters, other families were dispatched to the area. In 1880 "The Mesa Union" was instituted to implement principles of the united order, but this experiment was short-lived.

By 1894 Mesa's population reached 648, and in 1920 the census recorded that 3,036 lived in the city. In 1927 the seventh temple of the Church, located at the center of Mesa, was dedicated. In the years since that time, the community has grown from a modest agricultural town composed of miles of citrus groves and cotton fields to its position today as a thriving suburb of Phoenix, the nearby capital of Arizona. At the end of 1998, Church members in Mesa were organized into approximately 15 stakes. Among the many distinguished Church leaders from Mesa was **Delbert L. Stapley** (1896–1978), who was a member of the **Quorum** of the Twelve **Apostles** from 1950 to 1978.

SOURCES

McClintock, James H. *Mormon Settlement in Arizona.* Tuscon, Ariz: The University of Arizona Press, 1985.

1997–98 Church Almanac. Salt Lake City: Deseret News, 1996. 190–92.

ROBERT C. FREEMAN

MESSENGER AND ADVOCATE, LATTER-DAY SAINTS'. The *Latter-day Saints' Messenger and Advocate* was published in Kirtland as the Church's official monthly newspaper between October 1834 and September 1837. Each issue was 16 pages of double columns, and each year's last issue contained an index for the year. Succeeding *The Evening and the Morning Star,* the *Messenger and Advocate* was dedicated to promulgating and defending the beliefs and doctrines of the Church. Articles on a variety of topics—including the **Word of Wisdom**, the early history of the Church, and the millennium—appeared in its pages, as did itineraries of missionaries, obituaries, marriages, and news from various branches of the Church. **Oliver Cowdery**, **John Whitmer**, and Warren A. Cowdery served as editors at various times, and **Frederick G. Williams**, **Joseph Smith**, **Sidney Rigdon**, and **William Marks** were identified as publishers. Contributors to the paper included Joseph Smith, Oliver Cowdery, and several members of the **Quorum** of the Twelve **Apostles**.

SOURCE

Caldwell, J. Leroy. "Messenger and Advocate." *Encyclopedia of Mormonism.* Edited by Daniel H. Ludlow. 4 vols. New York: Macmillan, 1992. 2:892.

ANDREW H. HEDGES

MEXICAN COLONIES. Harassed, hunted, and persecuted because of their practice of **plural marriage**, a band of faithful **Saints** left the **United States** with mixed emotions on 5 March 1885 and crossed the border into **Mexico**, seeking refuge and the right to live their religion in peace. With the passage of the Edmunds Bill in 1882 and subsequent measures, stalwart citizens of good repute were regarded as felons by federal authorities.

Having heard of the great abuse heaped upon the Saints by the government in **Arizona**, President **John Taylor** paid them a visit and recommended that they seek refuge in Mexico. Soon Saints from Arizona, **New Mexico**, and Utah were heading south.

The Church leaders had long been looking to Mexico with the idea of establishing colonies for the purpose of spreading the gospel. Various exploration parties had been sent. The first (1875) included **Daniel W. Jones** and **Meliton Trijo**. Mexico was dedicated in 1879; however, it was not until they faced the persecutions stemming from polygamy that the Saints began establishing colonies in that country.

Between 1885 and 1909 there were ten colonies established. In Chihuahua these included Colonia Díaz (1885), Colonia Juárez (1885), Colonia Pacheco (1887), Cave Valley (1887), Colonia Dublán (1888), Colonia García (1894), and Colonia Chuichupa (1894). In Sonora settlements were established in Colonia Oaxaca (1892), Colonia Morelos

(1899), and Colonia San José (1909). The Mexican Revolution of 1910 caused an abrupt upheaval in the lives of the colonists and brought about the 1912 exodus from the colonies. Of the approximately 4,000 Saints that fled to the United States, only about a fourth ever returned to Mexico.

By the late twentieth century, Colonia Juárez and Colonia Dublán remained home to fewer than 500 descendants of the original colonizers. Nonetheless, the colonies continued to fulfill such important **missions** as educating the youth of **Zion** in the Church school, Academia Juárez; spreading the gospel to the nation; and providing leadership for Church missions throughout Latin America. On 6 and 7 March 1999 the Church dedicated a **temple** in Colonia Juárez—a monument to the faith and courage of those who went before.

SOURCES

Hatch, Nelle Spilsbury. *Colonia Juárez*. Salt Lake City: Deseret Book, 1954.

Johnson, Annie R. *Heartbeats of Colonia Diaz*. Salt Lake City: Publishers Press, 1972.

The Mormon Colonies in Mexico. Korea: Creative Graphics International, 1985.

RELVA L. WHETTEN

MEXICAN WAR. Following the annexation of **Texas**, a dispute remained between the United States and **Mexico** over the southern boundary of the **United States**. Mexico claimed lands and territories as far north as the Nueces River, while the United States claimed that the boundary was the Rio Grande River, 100 miles further south. To enforce the U.S. claim, President **James K. Polk** ordered a military force, under the command of General Zachary Taylor, south to the Rio Grande River.

Concurrently, Polk secretly received word that the Mexican government would favor a proposal to sell **California** and **New Mexico** to the United States. Consequently, President Polk sent John Slidell to Mexico City, authorizing him to pay $40,000,000 for the desired territories (Polk, 68–69). Much to the president's surprise, the Mexican government refused to receive the U.S. envoy.

When Mexican forces fired on a small U.S. Army unit consisting of 60 men, killing 16 and capturing the rest, Congress approved Polk's message declaring war on Mexico. The Mexican government claimed that it was only when the U.S. Army infringed on their territorial rights and fired at them that the fighting occurred (Polk, 72–73).

Polk ordered General Taylor to invade Mexico from the North. He also ordered Colonel Stephen W. Kearny to march with a small force, open a wagon road to California, and claim California for the Union. As part of Kearny's force, Polk authorized the formation of the **Mormon Battalion**, commanded by **Colonel James Allen**. Without waiting for Allen's Battalion, Kearny left Fort Leavenworth, Kansas, giving instructions for Allen to follow him.

Advancing overland, Taylor won battles at Contreras, Churubusco, and Matamoras (Jackman, 865). When the Mexican government refused to entertain peace proposals offered by the U.S. government, Admiral Winfield Scott landed his marines at Vera Cruz and advanced over land to Mexico City. During the following weeks, the Marines won decisive battles at Molino del Rey, Chapultepec, and ultimately captured Mexico City (*Dictionary*, 610).

Nicholas P. Trist, envoy of the United States, successfully negotiated the Treaty of Guadalupe Hidalgo, which was signed 2 February 1848 and ratified by the U.S. Congress on 30 May 1848, ending the war with Mexico (*Jackman*, 931).

SOURCES

Concise Dictionary of American History. Edited by Wayne Andrews. New York: Charles Scribner's Sons, 1967.

Jackman, William J. *History of the American Nation.* Chicago: Western Press Association, 1911.

Polk, James K. "Reasons for the War with Mexico." *America* 7 (1846): 68–73.

CLARK V. JOHNSON

MEXICO. By the year 2000, Mexico had 846,931 Latter-day Saints—more than any other country outside the **United States**. They were grouped into 179 **stakes** and 18 **missions**. The country's first Latter-day Saint **temple**, located in Mexico City, opened in 1983. By the beginning of the year 2000, eleven additional temples for Mexico had been dedicated or were under construction. Native Mexicans now preside over almost all the stakes, **wards**, missions, districts, and **branches**. From a difficult beginning, the Church in Mexico is now well established and widely valued.

The Church's initial move into Mexico was motivated principally by two goals: to find Native Americans (**Lamanites**) interested in the **Book of Mormon** and to explore for colonization sites for persecuted **Utah Saints**. Thus in 1875, with 1,500 copies of newly translated sections of the Book of Mormon in hand (*Trozos Selectos del Libro de Mormon*), seven missionaries left **Salt Lake City** on horseback for Mexico. They were **Daniel W. Jones**, Helaman Pratt, James Z. Stewart, **Anthony W. Ivins**, Robert H. Smith, Ammon M. Tenney, and Wiley Jones (Daniel W. Jones's son). Only Daniel W. Jones and Ammon Tenney spoke Spanish. They preached as they traveled, distributed the *Trozos Selectos,* and explored for places of possible refuge during their nearly year-long journey. They reported to **Brigham Young** that the Casas Grandes area of the state of Chihuahua was a promising site for colonization. After 1885 the Church established colonies there—Juárez, Dublán, Díaz, Cave Valley, Pacheco, García, and Chuichupa—for members who had been practicing **polygamy**.

In 1879 missionaries went directly to Mexico City. Dr. Plotino C. Rhodakanaty had read a copy of the *Trozos Selectos* and forcefully requested that missionaries be sent to Mexico. The Church sent newly ordained **apostle Moses Thatcher**, James Z. Stewart, and **Melitón Gonzales Trejo**. They preached, visited government dignitaries, baptized, and started several branches of the Church. Silviano Arteaga, Fernando A. Lara, Ventura Páez, and Lino Zárate were among Mexican members of the time noted for their dedication and sacrifice.

With periodic changes in personnel, **missionary work** in central Mexico continued through 1889, with particular emphasis on the rural valleys surrounding Mexico's famous natural landmark, the volcano Popocatépetl. Except for their **Mexican colonies** in the north, Latter-day Saints then abandoned the country for more than a decade. The struggle over polygamy until 1890 with the U.S. government was debilitating, so during the following decade the Church focused inwardly for a time to recoup its strength. In 1901 the Church reopened its Mexican mission, sending Ammon M. Tenney to Mexico City to preside. He visited all the old branches and found that many members had remained faithful during the missionaries' 12-year absence.

From 1901 to mid-1912, normal Church activities resumed, and a modest but consistent growth unfolded; however, the Mexican Revolution (1910–17) frustrated the Church's efforts both in central Mexico and in its northern Chihuahua colonies. In 1912 missionaries were again withdrawn from central Mexico, and the northern colonies were abandoned. During the **war**, neither individuals nor their property were safe.

From 1912 until 1917, when the civil war finally ended, Mexican members had to perform Church activities much on their own. They were remarkably dedicated, even in the face of severe deprivation and some loss of life, such as the death of branch president **Rafael Monroy**.

In keeping their faith alive during these and subsequent trying times, many Mexican members were aided by **Rey L. Pratt**, who presided over them in absentia (from the U.S. border) but found every way possible to make his spiritual presence felt. Thus, through the revolution and until his death in 1931, Pratt established an enduring legacy for the Church in Mexico.

The years of functional independence from Salt Lake City contributed to some Mexican members' desire to have a **mission president** from among their own people. When the Church replaced the deceased Rey Pratt with his brother Harold, about a third of the Mexican members refused to accept him. On this crucible the Third Convention was born. Mainline Latter-day Saints and Third Convention Latter-day Saints existed side-by-side for more than a decade. They agreed on almost everything except who their mission president should be.

In 1946, when the mission president issue ceased to be so troubling, President **George Albert Smith** visited Mexico to preside over the reunification of the Church there. Most of the Third Convention members returned to the main body, and thereafter the Church began to flourish as never before. It constructed buildings, founded schools, established its first stake outside the colonies in 1961, and began a prodigious building and leadership development effort that today involves the lives of hundreds of thousands of Mexicans. Though the faith's rapid expansion in Mexico was not achieved without severe, even uncommon challenges, the Church has developed a membership and institutional base there that augurs well for its future.

SOURCES

Johnson, Clark V. "Mormon Education in Mexico: The Rise of the Sociedad Educativa y Cultural." Ph.D. diss., Brigham Young University, 1977.

Tullis, LaMond. *Mormons in Mexico: The Dynamics of Faith and Culture.* Logan: Utah State University Press, 1987.

———. "Reflections on a Mexican Legacy." Martin B. Hickman Outstanding Scholar Lecture. Brigham Young University, 6 March 1997.

———. "A Shepherd to Mexico's Saints: Arwell L. Pierce and the Third Convention." *BYU Studies* 37, 1 (1997–98): 127–57.

F. LaMond Tullis

MEXICO CITY TEMPLE. The Mexico City D. F. Temple, the largest outside of the **United States** and fifth largest in the world, was dedicated 2 December 1983 by President **Gordon B. Hinckley**, a **counselor** in the

First Presidency. Plans to build the **temple** were announced 21 March 1976 to Church leaders from **Mexico** and **Central America**. Because of legal requirements concerning the ownership of religious buildings in Mexico, sensitive negotiations with government officials continued for more than three years before construction could begin. Ground was broken 25 November 1979 under the direction of **Elder Boyd K. Packer** of the Quorum of the Twelve **Apostles**, who offered the dedicatory prayer in Spanish.

The temple measures 178 by 214 feet and is surmounted by a 140-foot tower. Designed by Emil B. Fetzer, the building features modern adaptations of traditional Mayan **architecture**. The upper portion of the white cast-stone exterior is highly ornamented, and the temple was one of three buildings to receive an international award for the effective use of precast concrete. Its foundation was especially designed to enable the building to withstand earthquakes. Its 128,000-square-foot interior includes four ordinance rooms, each seating 120 persons.

SOURCE

Cowan, Richard O. *Temples to Dot the Earth.* Springville, Utah: Cedar Fort, 1997. 184–87.

RICHARD O. COWAN

MIA. The abbreviation MIA was commonly used for the **Mutual Improvement Associations** and their programs. Activities sponsored jointly by the **Young Men's** and **Young Women's** organizations were also commonly called "Mutual."

RICHARD O. COWAN

MIA MAID CLASS. See YOUNG WOMEN.

MICHIGAN. Lucy Mack Smith accompanied the first missionaries to preach the gospel in Michigan (D&C 52:7–8). While visiting her brother's family in Pontiac in 1831, she warned a hostile minister that members of his congregation would soon be converted—a prophecy that was fulfilled in 1833 when one-third of the group, including a deacon, accepted the message of Latter-day Saint missionary Jared Carter. Missionary work flourished from 1831 to 1834. Early missionaries included **David Patten** (1832), **Joseph Smith, Joseph Smith Sr.**, **Hyrum Smith**, the **Three Witnesses** (1834), and **Parley** and **Orson Pratt** (1839). After the death of Joseph Smith in 1844, the faithful **Saints** gathered to **Nauvoo**. The apostate **James J. Strang** and his followers settled on Beaver Island in Lake Michigan from 1849 to 1856.

Missionary work resumed in 1876, proceeding under direction of the Northwestern States Mission (organized 1878), and the Northern States Mission (organized 1889). Many of the converts in this period migrated to **Utah**. In 1915 German E. Ellsworth, president of the Northern States Mission, organized a branch in Detroit that built the first LDS **meetinghouse** in Michigan in 1928. The first **stake** was organized in Detroit in 1952 with **George W. Romney** as president. Membership grew from 7,183 in 1945 to 36,888 at the beginning of the year 2000. In October 1999 President **Gordon B. Hinckley** dedicated the Detroit Michigan **Temple**.

SOURCES

Brown, Hilda Faulkner. *The Michigan Mormons, 1985.*
1999–2000 Church Almanac. Salt Lake City: Deseret News, 1998. 211–12.

DAVID ROLPH SEELY

MICROFILMING. See FAMILY HISTORY.

MICRONESIA. Micronesia is made up of hundreds of islands scattered across more than half the width of the Pacific Ocean. In addition to the four states listed below, **Kiribati**, the **Marshall Islands**, the **Northern Marianas**, Belau, and **Guam** all make up what Western colonizers have labeled Micronesia. Under the direction of **Elder** John H. Grogberg, President William W. Cannon of the **Hawaii** Honolulu Mission expanded his **mission** into many areas of Micronesia in the 1970s. The Micronesia-Guam Mission was created 1 April 1980 with Ferron C. Losee as president. At the beginning of the year 2000 there were 3,008 members living in all of Micronesia. At that time, the following four states were under the Federated States of Micronesia:

CHUUK (TRUK)

Elders Dan Baldwin and Torlik Tima were sent by President Cannon to open the islands of Chuuk for missionary work on 7 July 1977. Three months later, on 22 October, T. M. Conrad Mailo and his wife, Nisor Cerly David, became the first Trukese converts. The next convert was a friend of Mailo and Nisor called Happiness Ichin. Happiness became the first Micronesian Elder to serve in his own islands. Mailo became the first **branch** president of the Moen Branch. Membership reached 170 in 1980. President Ferron Losee dedicated the first chapel in Truk on 24 April 1983, and the Chuuk **District** was created 8 January 1985. In 1990 membership grew to 350, and two chapels were operating.

Primary general president **Michaeline P. Grassli** and Primary board member Virginia H. Pearce visited Chuuk, Pohnpei, Kosrae, and Kawajalein in June 1991.

KOSRAE

The initial attempt to establish missionaries on Kosrae was hindered by a state resolution that was adopted to keep future religions from entering the island. The first missionaries had little success because of opposing churches who continued to warn their members not to listen to the elders' message. Finally, on 26 April 1986 Isidro Abraham became the first Kosraean to be baptized. Kosrae became a district on 14 March 1990 with only 64 members. The Malem **meetinghouse** was dedicated 3 December 1992, and an additional meetinghouse in Lelu was dedicated in January 1993.

POHNPEI

The capital and largest island of the Federated States of Micronesia is Pohnpei. The first missionaries to arrive on the island were Elders George L. Mortensen and Aldric Porter on 23 October 1976. It was some time before the first baptism occurred on 7 February 1981. A new chapel was completed in January 1982, and the Pohnpei District was organized on 22 November 1985. By 1990 membership was 464; in 1999 it was approximately 1,100.

YAP

In the early part of 1977, Charles Keliikipi was chosen to organize an efficient police department on Yap under a two-year contract. President William W. Cannon assigned him to organize the Church on Yap while he worked there. Later that year Elders David S. Ige and Douglas Andrews served as the first missionaries in the island. The first convert came in March 1978, and soon several families joined the Church.

The first meeting place was a Yapese hut. Later a chapel was completed on 13 January 1981, and the first service was held on 18 January 1981. By 1990 there were approximately 150 members living on the island.

SOURCES

"A Brief History of the Micronesia-Guam Mission, 1980–1990." Micronesia-Guam Mission, 1990.
Micronesia-Guam Mission Historical Report. LDS Church Archives, Salt Lake City.
1999–2000 Church Almanac. Salt Lake City: Deseret News, 1998. 358.

W. JAMES JACOB

MIDDLE EAST. Having played a prominent role in Christian history and doctrine, the Middle East has been of interest to Latter-day Saints from the earliest days of their history. Yet political turmoil in the Ottoman Empire, two world wars, and restrictions imposed by local governments have challenged the Church's efforts to establish official presence in the Middle East. Despite these many difficulties, the Church has grown in various Middle Eastern countries, due mostly to the influx of expatriate Church members who work there. Before 1950 Church activities were limited to **Turkey, Syria, Lebanon, Palestine,** and **Egypt,** but since then they have also occurred in **Iran, Jordan, Israel,** the West Bank, and the Arab countries of North Africa and the Gulf.

The history of the Church in the Middle East dates from 1841, when **Elder Orson Hyde,** an **apostle,** prayed on the Mount of Olives near Jerusalem for the gathering of Abraham's children (especially the **Jews**) to Palestine, for the building up of Jerusalem, and for the rearing of a temple. Latter-day Saint **missionary work** in the Middle East began in 1884 when **Jacob Spori** opened the Turkish Mission in Istanbul. The largest branches of the Church, consisting mostly of Armenian converts, were established in the cities of Aintab, Turkey, and Aleppo, Syria. The mission closed in 1909 because of the increasing political turmoil in the Ottoman Empire.

In 1921, after **World War I,** the mission was reopened in Aleppo and named the Armenian Mission. In 1928 its headquarters were moved to Haifa in Palestine, but the mission was closed that December with the sudden death of Joseph Booth, the mission president (the fifth Latter-day

Saint missionary to die while serving in the Middle East). The mission was established again in 1933 as the Palestine-Syrian Mission but was closed in 1939 with the outbreak of **World War II**. In 1947 the mission reopened, and in 1950 it was renamed the Near East Mission. It was discontinued for the last time in January 1951.

For the next 20 years, Church activity in the Middle East consisted mostly of individual members and small groups scattered in various countries and a few missionaries from the Swiss Mission assigned to work in Lebanon. In 1969 a Church group was organized in Jerusalem to accommodate **Brigham Young University** faculty and students involved in a Near Eastern Studies program. Other events there included the organization of the first **district** (1977), the dedication of the Orson Hyde Memorial Garden on the Mount of Olives (1979), and the dedication of the BYU **Jerusalem Center for Near Eastern Studies** (1989).

The advent of the Cold War in the 1950s, the dramatic increase in oil revenues which occurred in the early 1970s, and the signing of the Camp David peace accord in 1979 brought an influx of expatriate businessmen, consultants, engineers, educators, and military advisers to the Middle East. Among these workers were many LDS professionals and their families who desired to organize themselves for purposes of worship and fellowship. Governments began gradually and discreetly to allow more non-Muslim groups to hold religious services.

Beginning in the late 1950s, small branches with mostly expatriate members were established in Turkey at Istanbul, Ankara, Adana, Izmir, and Sinop. A branch of the Church has been operating in Cairo, Egypt, since 1974. The Iran Tehran Mission was organized in July 1975, the first LDS mission headquartered in the Middle East since 1950, but the missionaries were evacuated in December 1978 when fighting between government and revolutionary forces began to intensify. In 1989 Jordan became the first Arab country to sign a formal agreement with the Church, allowing it to lease property and establish the Center for Cultural and Educational Affairs in Amman. A branch of the Church operated in Beirut, Lebanon, between 1965, when the first missionaries were assigned there from the Swiss Mission, and 1975, when Church activities ceased with the outbreak of civil war. A branch was reestablished in Beirut in May 1990 at the end of the civil war. An expatriate branch was organized in Damascus, **Syria**, in December 1997. Small groups and branches of expatriate members have also been organized intermittently since 1950 in Morocco, Libya, Tunisia, Algeria, Sudan, and Iraq.

The presence of Church members in the Gulf is a result of the relocation of Latter-day Saint expatriates for temporary residence and work. Government officials in Bahrain, Kuwait, the United Arab Emirates, Qatar, Saudi Arabia, Oman, and Yemen have allowed foreign residents to hold religious services on condition that these activities remain low-key and that Islamic laws and traditions, including the restriction against proselyting, be respected. Dubai granted legal status to the Church in 1993, and Bahrain officially recognized the Church in 1997.

Despite its reputation for vigorous missionary activity in other areas of the world, the Church has observed religious restrictions in the Middle East by making nonproselyting commitments to government leaders and by issuing strict instructions for members to honor these commitments. In the 1990s the Church adopted a formal policy of not proselyting, teaching, or baptizing **Muslims** who either live in or plan to return to the Middle East. This step was taken to accommodate Islamic laws that stipulate legal and social sanctions for Muslims who convert to other faiths.

The Church has refrained from taking sides on the Arab-Israeli question; rather, the position of Church leaders is best revealed by the manner in which they have quietly sought to cultivate good relations and a reputation for impartiality with both Israelis and Palestinians. The following statement by Elder **Howard W. Hunter**, then a member of the Twelve, is characteristic of this attitude: "Both the Jews and the Arabs are children of our Father. They are both children of promise, and as a church we do not take sides. We have love for and an interest in each" (Hunter, 35–36).

LDS **scriptures** and publications have been translated into several Middle Eastern languages: the **Book of Mormon** in Arabic, Hebrew, Farsi, Turkish, Urdu, and Armenian; the **Doctrine and Covenants** and the **Pearl of Great Price** in Arabic and Armenian; and *Gospel Principles* and several **pamphlets** in Arabic, Armenian, Urdu, Farsi, and Turkish.

SOURCES

Baldridge, Steven. *Grafting In: A History of the Latter-day Saints in the Holy Land.* Murray, Utah: Roylance Publishing, 1989.

"Correspondence, 1932–1955." Near East Mission. LDS Church Archives, Salt Lake City.

"History." Palestine-Syrian Mission. LDS Church Archives, Salt Lake City.

Hunter, Howard W. "All Are Alike unto God." *1979 BYU Devotional Speeches of the Year.* Provo, Utah: Brigham Young University Press, 1980. 32–36.

Lindsay, Rao H. "A History of the Missionary Activities of The Church of Jesus Christ of Latter-day Saints in the Near East, 1884–1929." Master's thesis, Brigham Young University, 1958.

"Papers of Joseph Wilford Booth." Special Collections and Manuscripts, Brigham Young University Library, Provo, Utah.

Peterson, Daniel C. *Abraham Divided: An LDS Perspective on the Middle East.* Salt Lake City: Aspen Books, 1995.

"Turkish Mission." Manuscript History. LDS Church Archives, Salt Lake City.

JAMES A. TORONTO

MILITARY. As early as 1832, in the "**prophecy on war**," the Lord spoke of **wars** being poured out in the latter days (D&C 87) and admonished members of the Church to develop insights into the background and causes of "wars and the perplexities of nations" (D&C 88:78–79). Not being immune to the consequences of the vices of the world, Church members have occasionally had to assume a military posture as a people and to participate in military activities as law-abiding citizens at the call of their countries.

The **scriptures** instruct: "renounce war and proclaim peace" (D&C 98:16) and "seek peace and pursue it" (Ps. 34:14). While peace is the Lord's lofty standard, some wars are commanded by him and are for righteous and just causes. President **David O. McKay** explained that there are at least two reasons why a person's going to war can be justifiable—defense against aggression and loyalty to one's country (McKay, 70–74). The Lord has directed that his people "be subject to the powers that be, until he reigns whose right it is to reign" (D&C 58:22), and to "uphold the respective governments in which they reside" (D&C 134:5). "Obedient to these principles," the First Presidency explained, "the members of the Church have always felt under obligation to come to the defense of their country when a call to arms was made" (First Presidency, 93).

The first half-century of the Church's existence witnessed numerous military-related activities, including **Zion's Camp**, the **Nauvoo Legion**, the march of the **Mormon Battalion**, defenses against **Indian** disturbances during the **pioneer** era in the **Great Basin**, and the conflict known as the **Utah War**.

In the **Spanish-American War**, Church members formed the core of two artillery units, and 13 LDS soldiers gave their lives. More than 20,000 Church members served in uniform in **World War I**, of whom about 600 died. In **World War II** approximately 100,000 members served in the military, representing about 12 to 15% of the Church's total membership. Nearly 6,000 of these died. These numbers indicate the tremendous contribution in manpower and sacrifice of lives Church members have made. The Church was comparatively small during these war years, and it demonstrated patriotism in numbers disproportionate to its membership. Perhaps because of the many contributions the Church made to war efforts, the American liberty ships *S.S. Joseph Smith* and *S.S. Brigham Young* were named in honor of its first two presidents.

Approximately 20,000 Latter-day Saints served during the Korean War of the early 1950s. Then, during the 12-year Vietnam conflict of the 1960s and 70s, a total of about 100,000 Church members served, with as many as 30,000 on active duty at one time.

In the early 1950s, the Church approved the establishment of the Reserve Officer Training Corps at **Brigham Young University**. Air Force and Army Detachments there maintained distinguished records of accomplishment and trained thousands for future service. At one time, 1.5% of all officers in the U.S. military were Church members.

During early military participation in Southeast Asia, **Elder Gordon B. Hinckley** spoke of a positive aspect of war, saying that through the dark and bloody tapestry of conflict shines a silver thread—that of missionary opportunities. During all major wars the number of full-time missionaries permitted to serve was greatly reduced, but Latter-day Saint servicemen and their families have been responsible for tremendous success in sharing the gospel with others who were also serving their country. Latter-day Saints in uniform were particularly successful missionaries among the local populations during periods immediately following wars in **Japan**, **Germany**, **Korea**, and other areas.

From 1941 to 1969, military activities were coordinated at Church headquarters through the General Servicemen Committee, originally headed by **Harold B. Lee**. During World War II **Hugh B. Brown**, who had served as a colonel in the Canadian Army in World War I, was named Servicemen Coordinator. Under his direction, **chaplains** served in all branches of the service, as they had in the Spanish-American War and World War I. Special servicemen groups were formed and selected people were set apart to preside over these groups, wherever they might be needed—whether on a military base, a warship at sea, or in a combat zone. In 1969 the name of the Servicemen Committee was changed to Military Relations Committee, and since 1997 it has been known as the Military Relations Department.

SOURCES

Boone, Joseph F. *The Roles of The Church of Jesus Christ of Latter-day Saints in Relation to the United States Military 1900–1975.* Ph.D. diss., Brigham Young University, 1975.

McKay, David O. Conference Report (April 1942): 70–74.
"Message of the First Presidency." Conference Report (April 1942): 93.

Joseph F. Boone

MILLENNIAL STAR, THE. The *Millennial Star* was established in 1840 by the **Quorum** of the Twelve **Apostles** while they were on their **mission** in **Great Britain**. It was a major source of information on Church doctrines and events for more than a century. The Quorum of the Twelve named it *The Latter-day Saints' Millennial Star* and elected **Parley P. Pratt** as editor. For nearly 100 years the president of the **British** or **European Mission**, who was generally a member of the Quorum of the Twelve, served as its editor. These editors form an impressive "Who's Who" of early Church leaders, including six future presidents of the Church.

Just ten years into the *Star's* history, more than half of the total Church membership resided in Great Britain, but members from all over the world subscribed to the *Star* and corresponded with its editors. Hence, many extremely important developments were reported in its pages, especially in the first 25 volumes. As the proportion of Church membership in Great Britain diminished, so did the significance of the *Millennial Star.* When it was discontinued at the end of 1970 (when the *Ensign, New Era,* and *Friend* replaced several existing Church magazines), it had been published monthly, biweekly, or weekly for 130 years. At the time the *Millennial Star* ceased publication, it held the distinction of being the longest running Church **periodical**.

Sources

Jenson, Andrew. *Encyclopedic History of The Church of Jesus Christ of Latter-day Saints.* Salt Lake City: Deseret News, 1941. 506–8.
Peterson, Stanley A. *Encyclopedia of Mormonism.* Edited by Daniel H. Ludlow. 4 vols. New York: Macmillan, 1992. 906.

Alan K. Parrish

MILLER, GEORGE. George Miller was an early prominent member of the Church who later apostatized. He was born 25 November 1794 near Standardville, **Virginia**. Miller was baptized into the Church on 12 August 1839 by **John Taylor**. He was a carpenter, lumberman, and farmer. He was among the first to be taught and participate in **washings and anointings**, and the **endowment** of the **temple**.

Miller served in several prominent organizations in **Nauvoo**: the

Board of Trustees of the **University of Nauvoo**, the Nauvoo Agricultural and Manufacturing Association, and **Nauvoo House** Association, for which he procured lumber. He achieved the rank of brigadier-general in the **Nauvoo Legion**.

Miller was appointed by revelation 19 January 1841 to take the place of **Bishop Edward Partridge**, who had died. In October of the same year, after **Don Carlos Smith** died, Miller was also sustained as a president of the **high priests quorum** in Nauvoo.

On the trek west, Miller (one of the captains) became disaffected with **Brigham Young**'s leadership. He lost fellowship 3 December 1848 and moved to **Texas** to be with his old friend, **Lyman Wight**. Miller became alienated with Wight in 1849, and in 1851 he moved to be with **James J. Strang** on Beaver Island, where he was deputy sheriff. He left Beaver Island after Strang was shot in 1856. Miller died in Illinois that same year.

SOURCES

Cook, Lyndon W. *The Revelations of the Prophet Joseph Smith.* Salt Lake City: Deseret Book, 1985. 249, 268.

Smith, Joseph. *History of The Church of Jesus Christ of Latter-day Saints.* Edited by B. H. Roberts. 2d ed. rev. 7 vols. Salt Lake City: The Church of Jesus Christ of Latter-day Saints, 1932–51. 3:336; 4:276ff; 5:1–2, 74, 105, 120 (note); 7:247.

ROBERT L. MARROTT

MILLET, ARTEMUS. Artemus Millet was superintendent and head mason during the building of the **Kirtland Temple**. He was born 11 September 1790, in Westmoreland, Cheshire County, **New Hampshire**. At a young age he took up the trade of a mason, working to support his widowed mother. He gained valuable experience as he applied his trade during the **War** of 1812 and at various large stone building sites. Artemus had married and acquired some status of wealth while building bridges in upper Eastern **Canada** when he came in contact with the restored gospel.

While walking around the Kirtland temple grounds, the **Prophet Joseph Smith** asked, "Who can we get to superintend this work?" **Lorenzo Young** replied that he knew a man who could take charge of the work—Artemus Millet. The Prophet then turned to **Brigham Young** and said, "I give you a **mission** to go to Canada and baptise Brother Artemus Millet, and bring him here. Tell him to bring a thousand dollars with him" (Anderson, 16).

Artemus and his wife were baptized on 18 February 1832 by Brigham Young and confirmed by **Joseph Young** in Longborough, Canada. In April, Artemus closed his business, moved to Kirtland, and worked on the temple until it was completed. He oversaw the construction of the building and also gave support to it financially.

In **Nauvoo** he again applied his trade and helped construct the **Nauvoo Temple**. Artemus immigrated to **Utah** in 1850 and continued to construct buildings in various settlements. He died 19 November 1874 in Scipio, Utah, at age 84.

SOURCES

Anderson, Karl Ricks. *Joseph Smith's Kirtland Eyewitness Accounts*. Salt Lake City: Deseret Book, 1989. 15–16.

Millet Family History, "A Brief History of Artemus Millet," Manuscript. 70–71. LDS Church Archives, Salt Lake City.

Robinson, Elwin C. *The First Mormon Temple*. Provo, Utah: Brigham Young University Press, 1997. 33–34, 168.

CRAIG K. MANSCILL

MINING. When **Brigham Young** reentered the Great **Salt Lake Valley** in the fall of 1848, he faced an unanticipated challenge—the lure of gold, reportedly "mountains" of it, discovered in **California** earlier that year. A dilemma arose concerning how to take advantage of the gold and yet retain the manpower essential to the **pioneer** economy. Brigham Young's resultant policy was publicly to discourage the **Saints** from going off to California to mine, while at the same time sending men on confidential gold-mining missions for the benefit of the kingdom.

Between 1848 and 1851, more than $71,000 in gold was deposited to Brigham Young's "Daily Transactions in Gold Dust" account, serving for a time as the backing for the Mormon money system and for several years as the primary source of currency for the purchase of imports needed by the isolated, fledgling **Utah** economy.

Coal was discovered near present-day Coalville in the mid-1850s. Initially used for heating, coal became increasingly important with the coming of the **railroad** in 1869. The smelting industry, associated with the discovery of silver- and gold-bearing ores in Bingham Canyon that same year, also made mining a dominant, but troublesome, industry in Utah.

The social result of these mines was the inundation of an essentially agrarian community with an endless supply of often antagonistic non-**Mormon** miners. While the mines were economically beneficial, the cultural, religious, and political contrasts with the Saints' conservative faith produced a persistent tension between the Latter-day Saints and the non-Mormon-dominated mining communities.

SOURCES

Arrington, Leonard J. *Great Basin Kingdom.* Cambridge: University Press, 1958.

Campbell, Eugene E. "Mormon Gold Mining Mission of 1849." *BYU Studies* 2 (Winter 1960): 19–31. August 1959.

Davies, J. Kenneth. *Mormon Gold: The Story of California's Mormon Argonauts.* Salt Lake City: Olympus Publishing, 1984.

J. KENNETH DAVIES

MINISTERING OF ANGELS. See ANGELS.

MINNESOTA. After less-successful attempts to establish the Church in Minnesota in 1854, 1857, and 1868, Bengt Wulffenstein, who had been converted in **Sweden,** found several relatives there and started to hold meetings with them in 1875. He eventually organized Minnesota's first branch, in Freeborn County. This was the first time the restored gospel was preached to Scandinavians in **America.** Following a migration of 27 **Saints** from Minnesota to **Utah** in 1885, missionaries were sent to Minnesota as part of the Northwestern States Mission. In 1925 the state of Minnesota became part of the North Central States Mission, and the Minnesota Stake was organized on 29 November 1960. The Church has continued to grow steadily in Minnesota. On 9 January 2000 the St. Paul Minnesota Temple was dedicated, at which time there were 6 **stakes,** 63 **wards** and **branches,** one **mission,** and 22,941 members.

SOURCES

Jenson, Andrew. *Encyclopedic History of The Church of Jesus Christ of Latter-day Saints.* Salt Lake City: Deseret News, 1941. 514.

1997–1998 Church Almanac. Salt Lake City: Deseret News, 1996. 228.

MARY JANE WOODGER

MIRACLE OF FORGIVENESS, THE. The *Miracle of Forgiveness* was written by **Elder Spencer W. Kimball** and published in 1969. It is still recognized among Church members as the outstanding treatise on repentance. Elder Kimball was prompted to write the book after years of counseling troubled individuals, missionaries, and other members of the Church seeking forgiveness. He decided in 1959 to convert notes and scriptures he had made for repenting individuals into an "extensive treatise on repentance." After eight years of exhaustive work, the manuscript was submitted as a two-volume work. After two more years of reduction, the book was published and has gone through more than 26 printings.

SOURCES

Gibbons, Francis M. *Spencer W. Kimball: Resolute Disciple, Prophet of God.* Salt Lake City: Deseret Book, 1995. 253–55.
Kimball, Edward L. *Spencer W. Kimball.* Salt Lake City: Bookcraft, 1977. 378–403.

MATTHEW O. RICHARDSON

MIRACLE OF THE QUAIL. See QUAIL, MIRACLE OF.

MIRACLE OF THE SEAGULLS. See SEAGULLS, MIRACLE OF.

MIRACLES. Miraculous happenings hold much the same place in Church history as they did during the time of **Christ** and the early **apostles.** Latter-day miracles have not been widely publicized, nor have they been used to advertise the authenticity of the restored gospel; they have simply come to pass when they were needed.

There are many different kinds of miracles. **Joseph Smith's visions** and **revelations,** for example, must be regarded as miraculous. Others have experienced similar phenomena. **Sidney Rigdon** was present when Joseph Smith received the vision (D&C 76), and **Oliver Cowdery,** along with the Prophet, received keys from heavenly messengers and saw Jesus himself (D&C 110). At the dedication of the **Kirtland Temple,** a number of people saw and heard **angels.**

The best-known miracles are often **healings.** For example, when an epidemic of malaria infected many residents of **Nauvoo,** including Joseph Smith, the **Prophet** exercised his faith to be healed himself and then went through the town and surrounding areas on both banks of the Mississippi River healing scores of people. Many others have also healed people, from Lorenzo Snow's raising Ella Jensen from the dead in 1891 to **Matthew**

Cowley's restoring numerous sick and afflicted persons to good health in the 1930s and 40s.

Instances of divine intercession have come in different forms. Joseph Smith cast an evil spirit out of **Newel Knight**. Later Newel Knight instantly healed **Philo Dibble** of a lethal gunshot wound. The "poor camp" of Nauvoo refugees were saved from starvation by the arrival of huge flocks of quail. **Joseph F. Smith** and **George Q. Cannon** received the gift of **tongues**, each becoming fluent in the Hawaiian language almost instantaneously.

Miracles have been the subject of much discourse and many questions over the years. What is their nature? Where do they come from? What is their purpose? Can we call upon them? In the introduction to Joseph Smith's *History of the Church,* the **Prophet** explains that miracles come from spiritual gifts, such as those listed in I Corinthians 12 or **Doctrine and Covenants** 46 and 84, and are administered by the Holy Ghost. Church officials, priesthood holders, and other people of great faith have asked for and received miracles. The origin of these miracles is divine, not of man. **Brigham Young** spoke on miracles several times, making clear his view of the scriptural explanations: miracles come about through the Lord's use of natural laws that we do not yet understand. They come nearly always in response to prayer. They can work only through the faith of both petitioner and recipient. Miracles cannot prove the truthfulness of anything and can only enhance faith, not create it. He stated: "Miracles, or these extraordinary manifestations of the power of God, are not for the unbeliever; they are to console the **Saints**, and to strengthen and confirm the faith of those who love, fear, and serve God, and not for outsiders" (*JD*, 12:97).

SOURCES

Journal of Discourses [JD]. 26 vols. London: Latter-day Saints' Book Depot, 1854–86. 1:91; 3:45–46, 205; 4:338; 7:148; 8:42; 12:97; 13:91.

Smith, Joseph. *History of The Church of Jesus Christ of Latter-day Saints.* Edited by B. H. Roberts. 2d ed. rev. 7 vols. Salt Lake City: The Church of Jesus Christ of Latter-day Saints, 1932–51. 1:lxxvi–lxxvii; 4:6.

DALE BEECHER

MISSIONARY HOME. During the early 1920s, Church leaders became concerned for the welfare of missionaries coming to **Salt Lake City** to be endowed and **set apart**. They purchased and remodeled a home just north of the **Beehive House**. It was dedicated 3 February 1925 as a mission home. Groups of up to 100 missionaries stayed there free of charge for one week, learning gospel principles, missionary methods, and procedures, as well as how to work with auxiliary organizations, how to conduct family history research, and how to care for themselves. LeRoi C. Snow, son of **Lorenzo Snow**, served many years as director.

An adjoining home was purchased in 1926. With rapid Church expansion following the 1950s, the program was moved to a former hotel on North Main Street and then to a remodeled elementary school across from Church headquarters on North Temple Street. The Missionary Home in Salt Lake City continued to function until 1978, when it was superseded by the **Missionary Training Center** in **Provo**.

SOURCE

Snow, LeRoi C. "The Missionary Home." *Improvement Era* 31 (May 1928): 552–54.

RICHARD O. COWAN

MISSIONARY TRAINING CENTERS. In an 1832 **revelation**, the Lord directed the **elders** of the Church to conduct a "**solemn assembly**" to be known as the "**School of the Prophets**," in which they were to study "the doctrine of the kingdom" together with a variety of secular subjects so that they might "be prepared in all things" for their **mission** to warn the world (D&C 88:70–81, 137).

Early Church schools, such as **Brigham Young Academy** in 1883 and **Ricks College** in the early 1900s, included programs for training missionaries. Elder **B. H. Roberts** taught missionary classes at the LDS University in **Salt Lake City** beginning in 1902.

In 1925 the Church opened the **Missionary Home** in Salt Lake City. For the next several decades, it provided a week-long training experience for outgoing missionaries.

In December 1961 the Missionary Language Institute was opened at Brigham Young University for 29 missionaries experiencing lengthy delays in receiving visas to enter **Mexico** and **Argentina**. These missionaries lived in a hotel in **Provo, Utah**, and attended classes and meetings in various buildings on BYU campus. In addition to studying Spanish, they also gained self-discipline and the missionary spirit.

To enhance the stature of this program, Church leaders made its director a **mission president** and changed the name to Language Training Mission (LTM). Soon Portuguese and German were added to the curriculum. In 1968 the decision was made to offer training in all 16 languages then being used by missionaries. Separate LTMs were created at Ricks College to teach Dutch and the Scandinavian languages and at the **Church College of Hawaii** to teach the languages of the **Pacific** and **Asia**.

As the number of missionaries expanded during the 1970s, facilities at BYU became increasingly inadequate. The **general authorities** decided to construct a multimillion-dollar complex in Provo and to consolidate all language training. When the first phase of this complex was opened in 1976, the LTMs in **Idaho** and **Hawaii** were closed.

In 1978 the Missionary Home in Salt Lake City was closed, and all missionaries reported directly to Provo, whether or not they needed language training. To reflect its broadened scope, the name of the facility was changed to Missionary Training Center (MTC). Rigorous instruction in foreign languages and missionary methods was given by experienced returned missionaries attending nearby BYU. Missionaries were grouped into **branches** with leaders drawn from the surrounding community. Regular **temple** attendance and weekly devotional assemblies addressed by general authorities also enhanced spiritual growth. A regular exercise program promoted physical fitness.

Missionaries called from outside of the **United States** and **Canada** typically reported directly to their assigned fields without an MTC experience. In 1977, however, the first **area** MTC was established in **Sao Paulo, Brazil**. By 1999 international MTCs had been established at 14 other locations in Latin America, **Europe**, the Pacific, and Asia. The objective was to give all missionaries the benefit of quality training, enabling them to better proclaim the gospel of **Jesus Christ** to the world.

SOURCE

Cowan, Richard O. "Missionary Training Centers." *Encyclopedia of Mormonism.* Edited by Daniel H. Ludlow. 4 vols. New York: Macmillan, 1992. 2:913–14.

RICHARD O. COWAN

MISSION OF THE TWELVE TO BRITAIN. See BRITISH MISSION.

MISSION PRESIDENT.
Even before the Church was organized, the Lord emphasized the importance of sharing the gospel. To provide structure to this effort, the Church organized missions and placed mission

presidents at the head. The first mission president was **Heber C. Kimball,** who began serving in the **British Mission** in 1837.

The duties and terms of mission presidents have evolved over the years. By the end of the twentieth century a man and his wife were called by the **First Presidency** to serve full time for three years. They were not paid, although they were given a modest living allowance. Many presidents leave full-time employment, to which they return when their service is complete.

The mission president is given the priesthood keys to administer the programs of the mission under the direction of the **area** presidency. He and his two counselors constitute the mission presidency. The mission president's primary responsibility is to supervise proselyting efforts and assure the well-being of his missionaries, typically numbering between 120 and 200. He orients, interviews, motivates, counsels, teaches, supervises, and disciplines them. In developing areas where **stakes** have not yet been organized, mission presidents also supervise all Church programs, **districts,** and **branches.**

SOURCES

Day, Gerald. "Mission President." *Encyclopedia of Mormonism.* Edited by Daniel H. Ludlow. 4 vols. New York: Macmillan, 1992. 3:914–15.

McConkie, Bruce R. *Mormon Doctrine.* 2d ed. Salt Lake City: Bookcraft, 1966. 509–10.

1999–2000 Church Almanac. Salt Lake City: Deseret News, 1998. 414–37, 552–53.

RANDY BOTT

MISSION REPRESENTATIVES.

MISSION REPRESENTATIVES. The mission representatives were 29 experienced leaders, appointed in 1972, who worked under the First Council of the **Seventy** to strengthen proselyting in both **stake** and full-time **missions.** Some served simultaneously as **regional representatives** to train leaders and members in mission **districts** and **branches.** In 1974 the responsibility of the mission representatives was given to regional representatives, and this distinct calling was discontinued.

SOURCE

Church News, 1 July 1972, 3–16; 17 March 1973, 6; 2 November 1974, 13.

RICHARD O. COWAN

MISSIONS AND MISSIONARY WORK.

MISSIONS AND MISSIONARY WORK. From the earliest moments in Latter-day Saint history, taking the restored gospel to the world was central to the meanings and purposes of the Church. The **Prophet Joseph Smith** accepted the Savior's charge to "go ye therefore, and teach all nations" (Matt. 28:19), as found in the New Testament. Modern **revelations** in the **Book of Mormon** and the **Doctrine and Covenants** reinforced the necessity of gleaning chosen Israel from the nations of the earth (for examples, see D&C 4:4; 11:3; 12:3; 31:4.) Shortly after the **organization of the Church** on 6 April 1830, the Prophet sent his brother Samuel, armed with copies of the newly published Book of Mormon, as the first called missionary of the Church. Four other missionaries—**Oliver Cowdery, Peter Whitmer Jr., Parley P. Pratt,** and **Ziba Peterson**—were soon called to the **Lamanite Mission.** By the end of 1830, 280 converts had been baptized into the newly organized Church.

Early missionary work was centered in eastern **United States** and **Canada.** The first mission outside of North **America** was to **Great Britain** in 1837. This also appears to be the earliest use of the term *mission* as a designated ecclesiastical unit of the Church. In 1843 Joseph Smith sent **elders** to the Society Islands (**French Polynesia**). This was the first non-English-speaking mission of the Church. From June 1844, when Joseph Smith was martyred, until the Church was established in **Utah,** the expansion of missions proceeded haltingly—only the Welsh mission in 1845 and the **California** mission in 1846 were founded. But in the early 1850s, President **Brigham Young** and his associates determined that the Church was again strong enough to continue its mission of taking the restored gospel to the nations.

The Scandinavian, French, Italian, Swiss, and Sandwich Islands (**Hawaii**) missions were opened in 1850. During the next five years, missionary work opened in **Australia, Chile, India,** Burma, **Malta, Germany,** Gibraltar, **Hong Kong, New Zealand, South Africa,** Siam, (**Thailand**) and American **Indian** Territory. Success and longevity varied from mission to mission, but the gospel was going forth. From 1864, when a mission opened in the **Netherlands,** until the beginning of the twentieth century, only **Mexico, Turkey, Samoa,** and **Tonga** were added as new mission areas outside of North America. Inside the United States, however, various regional missions were developed.

In 1901, **Japan**—the twenty-first mission worldwide—was the first mission outside of North America founded in the twentieth century. Even while the Church endured two world wars and the **great depression,** the number of missions more than doubled to 43 by 1950. Since then the number of missions has exploded to 333 (1999), with approximately

60,000 missionaries serving in more than 160 countries and territories worldwide. The greatest growth in numbers of missions and numbers of converts has come in Mexico, Central and **South America**, **Africa**, and **Asia**. During the 1990s a number of missions were organized in Eastern **Europe** and the former **Soviet Union**.

THE NATURE AND METHODS OF LDS MISSIONARY WORK.

Latter-day Saint missions differ from Protestant and Roman Catholic missions, which are generally staffed by professionals who devote their lives to proselyting, creating mission theology, teaching and administering schools, translating or retranslating the **Bible** into new languages, carrying out medical and social services, and studying mission work anthropologically, historically, or sociologically (missiology). Latter-day Saints do not separate missionary work from the principal purposes and undertakings of the Church. Indeed, missionary work for the living and the dead (as done in LDS **temples**) is the heart and focus of the Church. To a considerable degree, the history of the Church is the history of missionary work, and vice versa.

Missionary work has been the life blood or ever-revitalizing force within the Church. The essence of this work has been to bear witness of the truth that Joseph Smith is a **prophet, seer, and revelator** called by God, that the Book of Mormon was translated by Joseph Smith from ancient records and is another testament that Jesus is the Christ, that **Jesus Christ** and **God the Father** live and guide the Church, and that the Church is led by a series of prophets of God. Many other doctrines and explanations regarding organization, **priesthood**, revelation, social order (beliefs regarding the **family**), **scriptures**, **education**, and intelligence, are available and may be shared by **Mormon** elders and sisters. But the essence of the message and witness has been the teachings mentioned here in combination with the basic gospel message that every person must have faith in the Lord Jesus Christ, repent of his or her sins, be baptized by one holding priesthood authority, be confirmed by the laying on of hands for the gift of the Holy Ghost, and endure—that is, remain faithful in keeping the Lord's commandments and serving in His Church until one's work in mortality is done. The plan of salvation and the purpose of mortality are taught to all investigators who study with the missionaries. During the nineteenth century, missionaries frequently warned their hearers of the impending second coming of the Lord and told them that the day of judgment was at hand. New members were strongly encouraged to gather to **Zion** in the Mountain West. Since the beginning of the twentieth century, Saints around the world have been encouraged to remain in their home countries to build up the Church there. Considering the current growth and demographics of the Church, such counsel makes obvious sense.

During the first 40 or 50 years after the Church was organized, most missionaries were married men who left their families for various lengths of time—from a few days or weeks up to a few years—to serve without any financial support from their families or the Church. They were usually assigned to work in pairs. They traveled without "purse or scrip" and depended on the good will and generosity of the people they met. The belief existed among them that the willingness of individuals and families to sustain them as the Lord's servants was one of the major tests of worthiness to receive the restored gospel. During the twentieth century, particularly since **World War II**, most missionaries or their families have provided a major share of their support. The Church has paid the cost of transportation to and from the mission field.

Latter-day Saint missionary work has always been well structured and organized. Strict rules of behavior and protocol have been important. Even though during the early decades individual missionaries frequently had greater personal discretion than today, a strict rule of celibacy and separation of the sexes among single missionaries has always prevailed. All missions and missionaries have been organized under an **apostle**, a **seventy**, a **mission president**, or some order of priesthood supervision. Within missions a variety of organizational patterns have been used, but reporting lines have been important and carefully adhered to. Leaders of the Church have stressed from the beginning that order was to abound within the Church, and members were to be provided with evidence of their fellowship with the Saints, that is, with membership certificates.

During the twentieth century, missionary work has become increasingly structured. Young elders (men ages 19 to 26) served for two years; young sisters (women ages 21 and older) served for 18 months. Older couples served a period of 12 to 24 months. Prior to being called to service, missionaries were carefully screened regarding worthiness, testimony of the gospel, **and** physical and mental health. Once in the mission field, uniform rules of study, work hours, service time, and preparation time are followed by all young missionaries. Most LDS missionaries proselyte full time, usually 60 to 70 hours a week. Several methods are used in finding potential investigators: house-to-house tracting (knocking on doors and leaving printed information) is most common, but referrals by members who introduce the potential convert to the missionaries in the member's own home are the most successful. Street meetings and mall presentations have occasionally been used in some areas. The Church operates a number of **visitors' centers** at historic sites and at temples, where missionaries provide printed materials, media presentations, historical summaries or lectures, and warm hospitality. Missionaries use various other approaches in different parts of the world.

Before World War II, LDS missionaries did not use a uniform plan for teaching the gospel. The doctrines taught were the same everywhere, of course, but the manner and order of presentation and emphasis varied. In the late 1940s, Elders Richard L. Anderson in the Northwestern States Mission and Willard A. Aston in the Great Lakes Mission created systematic missionary plans. In addition to making the message clearer and simpler, the plans made it possible to transfer missionaries from place to place and still maintain continuity among missionary teachers. The success of such plans became obvious to the Church Missionary Committee, which created a uniform system for teaching investigators that was announced to mission presidents in June 1961. From that time, missionary teaching has been similar worldwide.

Because LDS missionaries are lay members, outside observers have at times suggested that they are not "trained for the ministry." Although formal divinity training is not part of the LDS system, missionaries, especially those who are reared in the Church and who participate fully in its programs, have ample opportunity to study the gospel in formal settings. In addition to three hours of Sunday services in which all aspects of the gospel are taught, young Latter-day Saints also have the opportunity to study the gospel in their homes, as well as in weekday religion classes at the high school (seminary) and university (institute) levels. Prospective missionaries who attend the Church's institutions of higher learning also receive religious instruction.

After a missionary receives his or her call to serve, materials for study are supplied for further preparation. This is true also for mission presidents and their wives. Upon entering missionary service, missionaries report to one of many **Missionary Training Centers** throughout the world for instruction in basic methods of teaching the gospel and, if assigned to a foreign language mission, eight weeks of intensive language instruction. This has not always been the pattern of language instruction. Prior to the early 1960s, missionaries were required to learn foreign languages while in the mission field.

Translation work has been an obvious requirement for successful planting of the gospel. As a rule, the first materials translated have been tracts, **pamphlets**, the Joseph Smith testimony of his **First Vision**, and the Book of Mormon. Until the mid-1960s, the responsibility to translate these materials and others like them first rested upon the local leadership. Then in the mid-1960s, the Translation Department was created to coordinate these activities throughout the world. Local offices were established in Asia, Europe, and Latin America. Through the **Salt Lake City** offices and the various centers, all translation work and printing are coordinated from beginning to distribution in the **stakes** and missions. The work of the Translation Department has greatly enhanced the ability of missionaries—foreign and local—to communicate with potential and new members of the Church.

In the late 1990s, each mission was organized with a president, usually a middle-aged or older married man, who, along with his wife, had many years of experience in Church administration and gospel teaching. Mission presidents and their wives, who generally served for three years, were usually given a support stipend from the Church, but sacrifice was always involved.

A second type of mission is the stake mission. Stake missions are organized to include missionaries who live at home and serve on a part-time basis, but who coordinate closely with full-time missionaries. **Stake missionaries** are organized under a stake mission presidency that is directed by the **stake president**.

In addition to full-time proselyting missionaries, in the late 1990s more than 137,600 additional missionaries were also serving the Church in varied assignments. Church Service Missionary assignments include helping with temple work, the Church Educational System, family history, health, agriculture, welfare services, LDS charities, leadership, and hosting. Many Church Service Missionaries serve in the central offices of the Church in a variety of assignments.

PROPHETIC LEADERSHIP OF THE MISSIONARY EFFORT AND EXPANSION OF THE FAITH.

After the **Quorum** of the Twelve Apostles was selected and organized in 1835, the primacy of the role of the Twelve in spreading the gospel to the nations was soon evident. Not only did some of the Twelve accept missionary calls to **England** in 1837, but they also took charge, as directed by the First Presidency, of the Church as it grew in America and Canada, in the British Isles, in Europe, and in the **Pacific** and Asian regions. Since that time the **First Presidency** and the Quorum of the

Twelve have directly administered the expansion of the Church throughout the nations.

Every Church president has contributed to missionary work and the worldwide **growth** of the Church, in recent years the work has moved forward more rapidly. The 1950s and 1960s provided conditions that allowed President **David O. McKay** to travel throughout the world. His statement, "Every member a missionary" (a rephrasing of the Lord's commandment that every member should "warn his neighbor" [D&C 88:81]), was an inspired missionary slogan during his time and has been reiterated frequently since. Between 1951 and 1970, Church membership grew from 1.14 million to 2.9 million members.

In 1974 President **Spencer W. Kimball** further awakened the Church to its missionary responsibility with an address titled "When the World Will Be Converted." While liberal and mainline Protestant and Catholic mission theorists were calling for the end of using words such as *convert*, *conversion*, and *missions*, President Kimball and other LDS leaders were marshaling the forces of the Church to begin one of the greatest periods of missionary activity the world has known. President Kimball emphasized the responsibility of "every able worthy" young priesthood holder to "shoulder the cross" and serve a mission (Kimball, 8). During his presidency (1973–85), missionary numbers expanded from 17,258 to 29,265. The young men and women of the Church "lengthened their stride and quickened their pace" to carry the gospel to the world. Total numbers of members grew from 3.3 million to 5.9 million, and the number of missions climbed to 188.

President **Ezra Taft Benson** emphasized studying the Book of Mormon and using it as a proselyting tool. During his presidency (1985–94), missionary numbers grew to 47,311. Membership also expanded dramatically to 9.02 million at the time of his passing. The number of missions grew to 303.

President **Gordon B. Hinckley** vigorously continued the Church's emphasis on taking the gospel to all the world's peoples. By 1998 the number of full-time proselyting missionaries expanded to almost 60,000 and the number of missions to 331 (only 110 of which were in North America). Of collateral significance was his leadership in using all legitimate forms of media (print, **radio**, **television**, Internet, etc.) to bring the Church "out of obscurity" (D&C 1:30) and his continual traveling to all parts of the earth to strengthen members and encourage missionary work.

For many decades after the large emigration of 19th-century Saints from the British Isles and **Scandinavia** to Zion (1850–90), most Church members lived in the United States. Then in February 1996 membership outside the United States for the first time exceeded that within. The Church had become a truly international organization. In 1999 Church membership reached 10,354,241.

SOURCES

Britsch, R. Lanier. "Mormon Missions: An Introduction to the Latter-day Saints Missionary System." *Occasional Bulletin of Missionary Research* 3 (January 1979): 22–27.

Cleverly, Dean B. "Missions." *Encyclopedia of Mormonism.* Edited by Daniel H. Ludlow. 4 vols. New York: Macmillan, 1992. 915–20.

Condie, Spencer J. "Missionary, Missionary Life." *Encyclopedia of Mormonism.* Edited by Daniel H. Ludlow. 4 vols. New York: Macmillan, 1992. 2:910–13.

Day, Gerald J. "Mission President." *Encyclopedia of Mormonism.* Edited by Daniel H. Ludlow. 4 vols. New York: Macmillan, 1992. 2:914–15.

Kimball, Spencer W. "When the World Will Be Converted." *Ensign* 4 (October 1974): 3–14.

1999–2000 Church Almanac. Salt Lake City: Deseret News, 1998.

Whittaker, David J. "Mormon Missiology: An Introduction and Guide to the Sources." *The Disciple as Witness.* Edited by Stephen D. Ricks, et al. Provo, Utah: Foundation for Ancient Research and Mormon Studies, 2000. 435–514.

R. LANIER BRITSCH

MISSISSIPPI. Early missionaries to Mississippi included John Hunter and Benjamin Clapp in 1839. By April 1842 nearly 100 Latter-day Saints from Mississippi, mainly from Monroe County, arrived in **Nauvoo**. Despite this emigration, sufficient members remained or were baptized to form a branch in Monroe County the following year. In 1846 the **Mississippi Saints**, including members from Mississippi and neighboring states, started west. They arrived in the **Great Basin** in July 1847.

Missionary work continued in Mississippi until disrupted by the **Civil War,** and it resumed with significant success in the early 1870s. Persecution also increased, but efforts to expel missionaries from the state failed. In 1888 missionary Alma Richards was murdered, and his assailants and their motives were never ascertained.

In 1891 a Latter-day Saint community called Republican Square was established in southern Mississippi, by and for African-American converts, but it gradually dissolved as members immigrated west or died.

In 1996 descendants of early Mississippi **pioneers** dedicated a monument at Mormon Springs, a place celebrated for decades as the site for early convert baptisms. In 1999 plans were announced to erect a temple at Jackson, and by the beginning of the next year there were 4 **stakes** in Mississippi and 17,578 members.

SOURCES

Berrett, LaMar C. "History of the Southern States Mission, 1831–1861." Master's thesis, Brigham Young University, 1960.

Jenson, Andrew. *Encyclopedic History of The Church of Jesus Christ of Latter-day Saints.* Salt Lake City: Deseret News, 1941.

1999–2000 Church Almanac. Salt Lake City: Deseret News, 1998. 214–15.

DAVID F. BOONE

MISSISSIPPI RIVER. The Mississippi River was an important artery for Latter-day Saint **immigration** from December of 1840 until March of 1855. During this period more than 90 voyages, carrying about 18,000 **Saints**, entered **America** through the port of **New Orleans**, which was the best choice economically and also offered accessible water travel inland.

The gathering place for the Saints from the spring of 1839 until February of 1846 was **Nauvoo**. During this period, about 5,000 British converts crossed the Atlantic and came up the **Mississippi** on steamboats to the city. After the Nauvoo exile, the Mississippi River was still used for Latter-day Saint immigration, but beginning in early 1847, most immigrating Saints docked at **St. Louis** and headed west on the **Missouri River** to trailheads before beginning their westward trek to **Salt Lake City**.

This choice to no longer use New Orleans—and thus the Mississippi —for immigration resulted from a letter written by **Brigham Young** to emigration agent **Elder Franklin D. Richards**, stationed in **Liverpool**. "You are aware of the sickness liable to assail our unacclimated brethren on the Mississippi river, hence I wish you to ship no more to New Orleans, but ship to Philadelphia, Boston, and **New York**" (Young, 684). Yet before the Saints left the Mississippi they had planted their unique story on "Old Man" River, and their influence stretched from the shores of Nauvoo and St. Louis into the many settlements of the LDS immigrants in the West.

SOURCE

Young, Brigham. "Foreign Correspondence." *Millennial Star* 16 (28 October 1854): 684.

FRED E. WOODS

MISSISSIPPI SAINTS. As the Latter-day Saint exodus from **Nauvoo** (1846) progressed, similar preparations were being made elsewhere. Converts from **Mississippi** living in Nauvoo were sent home to prepare other **Saints** for the trek west.

About 45 individuals from several southern states made up the nucleus of the group that left from Monroe County, Mississippi, and traveled 800 miles to **Independence, Missouri**, where they were joined by others. They continued as far west as **Fort Laramie, Wyoming**, but were unable to find the Vanguard Pioneer Company. The Mississippi contingent began looking for a place to winter. They ultimately located 250 miles south in **Pueblo, Colorado**.

This settlement, which they called **Mormon** Town, consisted of cabins built from cottonwood logs. They planted crops, and the emigrants spent a comfortable and fairly prosperous winter. They learned that the pioneers had stopped at **Council Bluffs** and **Winter Quarters**. They also learned that about 500 men had formed the **Mormon Battalion** to assist the **United States** in the **Mexican War**. Three groups from the Battalion joined them in Pueblo during the winter of 1846–47.

When news arrived that the **pioneers** were preparing to resume their westward travel, Mississippi Latter-day Saints returned to the **Platte River** and followed the Vanguard Company until they arrived in the **Great Basin** 29 July 1847.

The Mississippi Saints remained as a group in Holladay and Cottonwood, **Utah**, and many later moved to colonize **San Bernardino, California** (1850). They were called back, due to the **Utah War**. Many settled in southern Utah settlements, and others joined Latter-day Saint colonization efforts in **Arizona**, **New Mexico**, and **Colorado**.

SOURCES

Carter, Kate B., comp. *Our Pioneer Heritage.* Vol. 2. Salt Lake City: Daughters of Utah Pioneers, 1958–77. 421–76.

DAVID F. BOONE

MISSOURI. The Missouri period has often been considered the darkest era in the history of the Church. During the years 1831 through 1839, the **Saints'** hope of establishing a Mormon utopia or the latter-day **Zion** in **Jackson County, Missouri**, brought with it misunderstandings, jealousies, mob action, confiscation and destruction of property, killings, and civil conflict. The resulting animosity and hatred led to the eventual expulsion of more than 10,000 Latter-day Saints by order of the state's chief executive. To Missouri historians, Mormonism in Missouri in the 1830s merits only a few pages and footnotes in their histories. But to the Latter-day Saints, the scenes that transpired on Missouri soil—principally in Jackson, Clay, Ray, Carroll, Caldwell, Daviess, and Livingston Counties—constitute a dramatic epoch in Latter-day Saint history, in addition to being an integral part of the Church's spiritual heritage.

Significantly, the story of the Latter-day Saints in Missouri did not end with Governor Lilburn W. Boggs's 1838 executive order calling for the removal of the Latter-day Saints. Some, mostly former Mormons, remained, making Missouri their permanent home. Beginning in the mid-1840s and through the late 1850s, St. Louis became a place of temporary settlement for Latter-day Saints before they immigrated to the West. During the mid-nineteenth century, thousands of Latter-day Saint emigrants found passage from St. Louis up the Missouri River through Kansas City, St. Joseph, and other points of departure further north before crossing the plains by wagon and later by rail.

In the late 1860s, Missouri, but particularly the Independence area, once again became a gathering place for restoration groups. In 1867, under the direction of Granville Hedrick, members of the Church of Christ (Temple Lot) moved from Illinois to Jackson County and subsequently purchased the main temple site property. The Church of Christ (and a few offshoots) has retained a presence in the area, but its numbers are small. An even smaller Mormon faction known as the Church of Christ (Cutlerite) relocated from Minnesota to Independence in the late 1920s, although today the organization consists of only one congregation.

In the late 1860s, members of the Reorganized Church of Jesus Christ of Latter Day Saints also began relocating in the Independence area. By 1873 a branch of the church was organized, and in 1892 the first chapel, known as the Stone Church, was completed. In 1906 Church president Joseph Smith III moved from Lamoni, Iowa, to Independence and took up permanent residence, but it was not until 1920 that Independence became the official RLDS church headquarters. Throughout the remainder of the twentieth century, the RLDS church presence in the greater Kansas City area has been substantial, although in recent times a number of RLDS congregations have broken off to form the Restoration Branches. Construction of the RLDS auditorium (1926–62) and temple (dedicated 1994) has helped to establish the RLDS Church as the dominant restoration religion in the west central regions of the state.

The Church of Jesus Christ of Latter-day Saints, headquartered in Utah, has made significant inroads toward reestablishing an official presence in Missouri. Beginning in 1904, Church president **Joseph F. Smith** authorized the purchase of 25 acres of Independence property, including 11 acres of the original temple lot. That same year the Central States Mission was created with headquarters in Independence, and a Church publishing house began operations, publishing *Liahona the Elders' Journal*, as well as other missionary-related **periodicals**. Additional buildings have been constructed over the years on the LDS Independence property, including the first chapel (1914), a mission home (1920), a new mission office (1955), a **visitors' center** (1971), and a **stake** center (1980). Church **growth**, particularly during the last 50 years, has been remarkable. At the end of the twentieth century there were 51,187 members and 13 stakes in Missouri. Perhaps the most visible presence of the Church is the St. Louis Temple, completed in 1997.

Mormonism in Missouri from the 1830s to the 1860s was troubled and temporary, but times have changed. Members of The Church of Jesus Christ of Latter-day Saints look forward to the day when Zion, or the **New Jerusalem**, will be established in Missouri in anticipation of the millennial reign of **Jesus Christ** (10th Article of Faith).

SOURCES

Baugh, Alexander L. "A Call to Arms: 1838 Mormon Defense of Northern Missouri." Ph.D. diss., Brigham Young University, 1996.

Garr, Arnold K., and Clark V. Johnson, eds. *Missouri*. Regional Studies in Latter-day Saint Church History series. Provo, Utah: Brigham Young University, 1994.

Gentry, Leland H. "A History of the Latter-day Saints in Northern Missouri from 1836 to 1839." Ph.D. diss., Brigham Young University, 1965.

ALEXANDER L. BAUGH

MISSOURI COMPROMISE. The **Missouri** Compromise, drawn up in 1820, was the agreement reached between northern and southern factions in Congress that allowed Missouri to enter the Union as a slave state. When the **Saints** began moving to Missouri in 1831, they found themselves in the midst of slave holders who quickly grew jealous of the nonslaveholding Saints' increasing influence in the state. The Compromise called for admitting **Maine** to the Union as a free state at the same time Missouri was admitted as a slave state, and forbade the introduction of slavery into the rest of the **Louisiana** Purchase north of Missouri's southern boundary. When "popular sovereignty" of the

Kansas-Nebraska Act replaced the Missouri Compromise in 1854, the Saints were propelled into the national political arena when **Republicans**, who were antagonistic toward **Mormons**, pointed to **plural marriage** in **Utah** as an example of what could go wrong if the people of a territory were allowed to govern themselves.

SOURCE

Roberts, B. H. *A Comprehensive History of The Church of Jesus Christ of Latter-day Saints, Century One.* 6 vols. Salt Lake City: The Church of Jesus Christ of Latter-day Saints, 1930. 529.

ANDREW H. HEDGES

MISSOURI RIVER. The **Missouri** River, one of the most prominent waterways in North **America**, is also mentioned in Latter-day Saint **scripture**. On 20 March 1839, **Joseph Smith** recorded this passage: "As well might man stretch forth his puny arm to stop the Missouri river in its decreed course, or to turn it up stream, as to hinder the Almighty from pouring down knowledge from heaven upon the heads of the Latter-day Saints" (D&C 121:33).

Once called the "Pekitanoni" or "muddy water" by the Osage **Indians**, the Missouri is America's longest river and most favored natural highway to the West. Discovered by Marquette and Joliet in 1643, the Missouri was later conquered in 1806 by Lewis and Clark, who charted its 2,564 miles of twisting and ever shifting channels from its source in the Rocky Mountains to its confluence with the **Mississippi River** at **St. Louis.** With the siren call of "manifest destiny," Americans began their mighty westward caravans to the valleys of **Oregon** and the coasts and gold fields of **California** in earnest, beginning in 1842. By 1869 an estimated 270,000 had found a new life west of the Missouri (Unruh, 85).

The **Saints** set out "across the wide Missouri" as early as 1831, when **Oliver Cowdery** and the missionaries to the Lamanites preached the gospel to the **Delaware Indians**, then located just west of **Independence, Missouri.** Driven out of Missouri by their persecutors in 1838 and 1839 and later out of **Nauvoo, Illinois,** the Saints established their **Winter Quarters** on the west bank of the Missouri (or "misery bottoms") on the present site of **Florence, Nebraska,** in the fall of 1846. They also established other settlements in the Missouri River valley including Kanesville (now Council Bluffs), Iowa. For years afterwards, thousands of Latter-day Saint emigrants sailed up the river from **New Orleans** to disembark at Florence to continue their overland journey to the Great Salt Lake.

Unfortunately, the worst steamboat catastrophe on the Missouri River, the 1852 explosion of the *Saluda* near Lexington, Missouri, claimed many Latter-day Saint lives.

SOURCES

Chappell, Phillip Edward. *A History of the Missouri River.* 1911.

Nasatir, A. P., ed. *Before Lewis and Clark—Documents Illustrating the History of the Missouri 1785–1804.* 2 vols. Lincoln: University of Nebraska Press, 1990.

Unruh, John D. Jr. *The Plains Across—The Overland Emigrants and the Trans-Mississippi West, 1840–60.* Urbana: University of Illinois Press, 1982.

RICHARD E. BENNETT

MITCHILL, SAMUEL L. Along with **Charles Anthon**, Samuel Latham Mitchill was one of the scholars whom **Martin Harris** consulted regarding a small sample of **Book of Mormon** writing and translation in 1828. Mitchill was born in 1764 at North Hempstead, Long Island, New York. He became an M.D., a "living **encyclopedia**," a "chaos of knowledge," and an accomplished linguist living in **New York City**. His erudition is emphasized not because he knew much about **Egyptian** languages but because Martin Harris sought out the best scholars in the **United States** at that time. According to Harris, Mitchill "sanctioned what Professor Anthon had said" about the Egyptian characters being authentic. Samuel L. Mitchill died in 1831 in New York City.

SOURCES

Kimball, Stanley B. "I Cannot Read a Sealed Book." *Improvement Era* 60 (February 1957): 80–82, 104, 106.

———. "Charles Anthon and the Egyptian Language." *Improvement Era* 63 (Oct. 1960): 708–10, 765.

———. "The Anthon Transcript: People, Primary Sources, and Problems." *BYU Studies* 10 (Spring 1970): 325–52.

Roberts, B. H. *A Comprehensive History of The Church of Jesus Christ of Latter-day Saints, Century One.* 6 vols. Salt Lake City: The Church of Jesus Christ of Latter-day Saints, 1930. 102.

STANLEY B. KIMBALL

M-MEN. Mutual-Men (M-Men) was for many years the counterpart to Gleaners in the Mutual Improvement Association of the Church. Created in 1920 for young men ages 17 to 21, the organization regularly participated in Churchwide athletic, dramatic, and musical competitions. In 1971, M-Men became known as Young Adults.

SOURCES

Strong, Leon M. "A History of the Young Men's Mutual Improvement Association, 1875–1938." Master's thesis, Brigham Young University, 1939.

Williams, John Kent. "A History of the Young Men's Mutual Improvement Association, 1839 to 1974." Master's thesis, Brigham Young University, 1976.

JED L. WOODWORTH

MONEY, MORMON. Mormon notes first appeared at **Kirtland** and **Nauvoo** as currency and to raise funds. They were issued by the **Kirtland Safety Society**, **Nauvoo House** Association, **Nauvoo Legion**, Nauvoo City, Nauvoo **Music** Association, and the **Seventies Hall**. In 1849 in **Utah** the Church issued Valley Notes in various denominations and then minted **California** gold dust into coins with face values of $2.50, $5, $10, and $20. Most of the coins were dated 1849 and 1850. The Church mint closed in 1860. About 1857 the Deseret Currency Association's paper money circulated, bearing **Brigham Young's** signature. In the 1850s, the General **Tithing** Office and local tithing offices issued a tithing scrip, at first handwritten, then printed, bearing various denominations, and redeemable in meat, produce, and commodities at tithing offices. Until the early 1900s, the Church used tithing scrip to pay its employees and to help **welfare** recipients. Collectors today pay high prices for the old "Mormon money."

SOURCES

Arrington, Leonard J. *Great Basin Kingdom: An Economic History of The Latter-day Saints, 1830–1900.* Lincoln: University of Nebraska Press, 1966. 55–56, 71–72, 144.

1980 Church Almanac. Salt Lake City: Deseret News, 1980. 327–32.

Wilde, Elaine Pugmire. "The Mint: Making Money in Pioneer Utah." *Pioneer* (Summer 1995): 14–19.

WILLIAM G. HARTLEY

MONGOLIA. Through 1990 and 1991, **Elders** Merlin Libbert and Monte J. Brough of the **Asia Area** presidency visited Mongolia and contacted government and educational leaders. The Church was invited to send mature couples with experience in education to advise, consult, and teach in the schools and higher education institutions in the capital city of Ulaanbaatar. In September of 1992, the first couple was called as missionaries, followed by five other couples. Six young elders were sent in August 1993.

The couples and elders were assigned to work with the Ministry of Science and Education, and began working in the schools. They were free to teach the gospel and engage in Church activity outside of their classroom activities. The first investigators came from the missionaries' students. They held their first meetings in the missionaries' apartments, and their first converts came in February 1993. Elder **Neal A. Maxwell** and Elder Kwok Yuen Tai dedicated Mongolia for the preaching of the gospel in April of 1993, and baptisms came regularly after that time.

By the year 2000 Mongolia had 1,850 members, making up nine **branches**. Many of the local members were serving in branch and **district** positions. More than 80 members from Mongolia had served full-time missions in various parts of the world. There were also about 80 young missionaries and couples serving in Mongolia.

SOURCE

1999–2000 Church Almanac. Salt Lake City: Deseret News, 1998. 358–59.

KENNETH H. BEESLEY

MONROY, RAFAEL. Rafael Monroy was a Mexican **martyr** born 21 October 1878 in Octopam, Hidalgo (about 50 miles northwest of Mexico City). He lived in San Marcos, Hidalgo, with his wife and daughter. In May 1913 Rafael's sisters Jovita and Guadalupe persuaded him to attend a Latter-day Saint Church **conference**. Afterwards Rafael had a dream in which he saw himself preaching what he had learned at the conference. On 10 June 1913, he was baptized (Young, 98–99). After the **family** joined the Church, friends ignored them, and business at the family store decreased (de Montoya, 28). During the Mexican revolution (1910–17), as various factions fought to gain control, missionaries were withdrawn from the country. Before leaving **Mexico, Mission president Rey L. Pratt** ordained Rafael an **elder** and set him apart as president of the small San Marcos **Branch**. Under Rafael's direction, the small branch grew until 22 attended Sunday **meetings**.

During this time, the Zapatistas defeated the Carancistas and occupied San Marcos. The Zapatistas accused Rafael of concealing weapons and of being a Carancista Colonel. Even though these charges were denied, Zapatista commanders arrested Rafael and Vicente Morales, another Church member. Rafael's three sisters, Natalia, Jovita, and Guadalupe, importuned the commanding general, assuring him of the prisoners' innocence. As a result, they, too, were arrested and jailed.

Hoping to force them to confess and to renounce their new faith, soldiers put ropes around the prisoners' necks and threatened to hang them but to no avail; the prisoners maintained their innocence and refused to renounce their religion (Monroy, 33). About 8:30 P.M. on 17 July 1915, Rafael Monroy and Vicente Morales were shot by a firing squad, becoming martyrs for The Church of Jesus Christ of Latter-day Saints (Monroy, 34; Young, 150).

SOURCES

de Montoya, Rosa Jimenez Uda. "Historia de la Iglesia de Jesucristo de los Santos de los Ultimos Días de la Rama de San Marcos." Edited by Guadalupe Monroy. Tula Hidalgo. Manuscript. Photocopy in possession of the author. 1934.

Tullis, LaMond F. *Mormons in Mexico: The Dynamics of Faith and Culture.* Logan: Utah State University Press, 1987. 103.

Young, Walter Ernest. "The Diary of W. Ernest Young." Manuscript. Brigham Young University Library, Provo, Utah. 1973.

CLARK V. JOHNSON

MONSON, THOMAS S. Thomas Spencer Monson, counselor to three presidents of the Church and president of the Quorum of the Twelve Apostles, was born 21 August 1927 in Salt Lake City to G. Spencer and Gladys Condie Monson. A naval veteran of World War II, Brother Monson attended the University of Utah, where he graduated with honors in business management in 1948. He received a master of business administration degree from Brigham Young University in 1974, and in 1981 BYU conferred upon him an honorary doctor of laws degree. He married Frances Beverly Johnson on 7 October 1948 in the Salt Lake Temple. They became the parents of three children. Brother Monson began his professional career with Deseret News Publishing Company in 1948, where he was a sales manager and assistant general manager. In 1962 he was named the general manager of Deseret Press.

Thomas S. Monson's service in the Church has been exceptional. On 7 May 1950, at age 22, he was called to be a bishop in a Salt Lake City ward with over 1,000 members and 86 widows. There he gained experience in welfare service and gospel instruction and fine-tuned his personal spiritual attentiveness. In June 1955, Thomas Monson was sustained as second counselor in the Salt Lake Temple View Stake, and in 1959 he was called as president of the Canadian **Mission**, headquartered in **Toronto**. On 4 October 1963, at age 36, Thomas S. Monson was sustained as a member of the Quorum of the Twelve and **ordained** an apostle 10 October of that year. **Elder** Monson was set apart as second counselor to President **Ezra Taft Benson** on 10 November 1985 at age 58. He was set apart as second counselor to President **Howard W. Hunter** on 5 June 1994, and on 12 March 1995, President Monson was set apart as the president of the Quorum of the Twelve and the first counselor in the **First Presidency** to President **Gordon B. Hinckley**.

SOURCES

Church News. 26 April, 1975. 5–13.

Gibbons, Francis M. "President Thomas S. Monson." *Ensign* 25 (July 1995): 7–11.

Holland, Jeffrey, R. "President Thomas S. Monson: Man of Action, Man of Faith, always 'on the Lord's Errand.'" *Ensign*, February 1986. 10–17.

MATTHEW O. RICHARDSON

MONTANA. The first two Latter-day Saints in what would become the state of Montana were E. W. Van Etten, who traded with the Flathead **Indians** in the 1850s, and Mrs. Henry G. Miller (Minnie), the first white woman to live in western Montana. The gold rush in the 1860s brought other members of the Church to the territory of Montana, both as gold seekers and freighters for the miners. A company formed by Latter-day Saint leaders built a **railroad** from **Ogden, Utah**, to Butte, Montana, in 1884.

Latter-day Saint settlers of **Alberta, Canada**, passed through the state during the 1880s and 1890s, but no unit of the Church was established until 1897, when Phineus Tempest, who had been called as **mission president** in Montana the year before, established a **branch** in Lima. The following year the new **mission** became part of the Northwestern States Mission.

The **growth** of the Church has been slow but steady in the last one hundred years. A **temple** was dedicated in Billings on 20–21 November 1999. As of 2000, Montana had 11 stakes with 39,842 members.

SOURCE

1999–2000 Church Almanac. Salt Lake City: Deseret News, 1998. 217–18.

ELAINE MCMEEN FLAKE

MONTROSE, IOWA. Montrose, Iowa, located across the **Mississippi River** from **Nauvoo, Illinois,** had been a trading site for the Sac and Fox Indians since the famed explorers Marquette and Joliet visited them in 1674. In 1799 Louis Tesson, the first white man to settle in the area, set up a trading post with the nearby tribes and planted extensive orchards. After 1824 the Indians began selling off most of their 119,000-acre half-breed tract to newcomers and land speculators, including James White, David W. Kilbourne, and **Isaac Galland.** Kilbourne named the site "Mount of Roses" because of the many wild roses blooming on nearby bluffs—a name soon shortened to Montrose. In 1834 the U.S. Army established Fort Des Moines at Montrose to protect the rights of the Indians from unlawful encroachments by dishonest land speculators.

With the rising tide of Latter-day Saint refugees streaming into the area from **Missouri** in 1839, Galland, later a Mormon convert, sold the Church large plots of land on both sides of the river, including several thousand acres in and near Montrose. **John Taylor, Wilford Woodruff,** and **Brigham Young** set up temporary residences in the abandoned Fort before moving across the river into Nauvoo. It was here that **Joseph Smith** performed several miraculous **healings** among the sick in 1839. Eventually enough Latter-day Saints settled in and around Montrose (about 600) that the short-lived **Iowa** or Zarahemla **Stake** was organized in 1841 (D&C 125:3–4). Gradually most of the Saints crossed over the river into Nauvoo. Montrose was later remembered as the sad gathering place of many in the "poor camps" in the wake of the Battle of Nauvoo in September 1846. The "**miracle of the quails**" occurred in October 1846 not far from Montrose.

The present city of Montrose was incorporated in 1857, and for several years it was a thriving sawmill and ship repair center on the upper Mississippi. The construction of the Keokuk Dam in 1912 flooded part of the original townsite. Today Montrose is a quiet river town of barely 1,000 inhabitants.

Sources

Cook, Lyndon W. "Isaac Galland—Mormon Benefactor." *BYU Studies* 19 (Spring 1979): 261–84.

Hancock, Russell (Mrs.). *Montrose in Retrospect.* Montrose: Telcon, 1969.

Kimball, Stanley B. "Nauvoo West: The Mormons of the Iowa Shore." *BYU Studies* 18 (Winter 1978): 132–42.

RICHARD E. BENNETT

MONUMENTS AND MARKERS. Government agencies, private organizations, historical societies, and the Church continue to erect monuments and markers honoring people, places, and events significant to the Latter-day Saints. Monuments are usually defined as structures, such as buildings or sculptures, erected as memorials. Markers, on the other hand, are usually defined as any object used to mark or identify some historical event or person, including tombstones. Both monuments and markers provide visitors to **historic sites** with significant information about the site, event or person for whom the monument or marker was created.

The earliest LDS monument erected was Cyrus Dallin's **Brigham Young** Monument, completed in 1900, honoring the **pioneers** and Brigham Young. A few years later, in 1905, the Church commissioned **Junius F. Wells** to erect the **Joseph Smith** Monument in **Sharon, Vermont**, to honor the one-hundredth anniversary of the **Prophet**'s birth, December 23, 1905.

One of the most dramatic monuments, *A Tragedy of Winter Quarters*, was created by **Avard Fairbanks** in 1937. This impressive monument depicts a couple huddled together over the open grave of a young child, and honors the nearly 400 Latter-day Saints who died at Winter Quarters (1846–48).

The largest monument in **Utah** was dedicated in 1947, celebrating the 100th anniversary of the pioneers' arrival in the Great Basin. The Utah State Commission, representing various faiths, selected **Mahonri M. Young**, a grandson of Brigham Young, to design the monument, which stands at the mouth of **Emigration Canyon** in **Salt Lake City**.

Another massive monument project was announced in 1975 at the annual **Relief Society** conference in Salt Lake City. Two and half years later, the Monument to Women, located in the sculpture garden of the Nauvoo Restoration's Visitors Center in **Nauvoo, Illinois**, was dedicated.

Another monument of particular note was the completely renovated **Hotel Utah** in Salt Lake City, which, when completed in 1993, was renamed the "**Joseph Smith Memorial Building**."

Besides erecting and dedicating numerous monuments, Church and civic leaders have also made a concerted effort to place markers in an effort to remind, identify, and celebrate historical events such as the rise of Mormonism, the **Mormon Trail** from Nauvoo to Salt Lake City, the founding of pioneer businesses, Church organizations, and pioneer communities. Beginning in the late 1930s, one organization—the International **Daughters of Utah Pioneers** (DUP)—became the prime mover in erecting markers to honor events and historic sites. As of March 2000, the DUP has erected 526 historical markers throughout North America, the **British Isles**, and Continental **Europe**. Additionally, the **Sons of the Utah Pioneers** (SUP) have also been involved in marking sites.

During the last two decades of the twentieth century, many private organizations and local government agencies increased the number of monuments and markers erected throughout North America and the world, honoring the Latter-day Saint past (e.g., the Mormon Historic Sites Foundation, established in 1992). All in all, monuments and markers remind visitors of important people, places and events that shaped the present.

RICHARD NEITZEL HOLZAPFEL

MOORE, REVEREND GEORGE. During the 1840s Reverend George Moore had extensive contact with **Joseph Smith** and other **Saints** in **Nauvoo**. He recorded his experiences in a diary, which provides useful insights into the history of the Church. Born 4 May 1811 in Sudbury, **Massachusetts**, George Moore was educated at Harvard and enjoyed close friendships with Ralph Waldo Emerson and Henry David Thoreau. In 1841 he took a position as a Unitarian minister in **Quincy, Illinois**, thus coming in contact with the Latter-day Saints at Nauvoo. Many of his journal entries indicate his awareness of and interest in the Latter-day Saint people: "Visited the Mormon **Temple**. The situation is beautiful, commanding an extensive view—overlooking a large bend of the river" (105). Reverend Moore died 11 March 1847.

SOURCES

Cannon, Donald Q. "Reverend George Moore Comments on Nauvoo, the Mormons, and Joseph Smith." *Western Illinois Regional Studies* 5 (Spring 1982): 5–16.
George Moore Diary. American Antiquarian Society, Worcester, Massachusetts.

DONALD Q. CANNON

MORGAN, JOHN. John Morgan, a **general authority** and president of the **Southern States Mission**, was born in Greensburg, **Indiana**, 8 August 1842. After formal schooling he enlisted with the Union Army during the **Civil War**, where he was wounded and decorated twice for bravery. Following his military career and additional schooling, he went on a cattle drive to the west and decided to remain in **Salt Lake City** because he was intrigued with the **Mormons**.

In Salt Lake he established the Morgan Commercial College, which taught business skills and attracted the children of many prominent Church leaders. Strongly convinced of the value of public education, he closed his own school in deference to the **University of Deseret**. While in Salt Lake, Morgan had a dream that foreshadowed his future, including his conversion to Mormonism and missionary service in the South.

Within ten years, Morgan was proselyting in the Southern States Mission, over which he was eventually called to preside (1878–84). Legendary for his zeal, he traveled widely and wrote *The Plan of Salvation,* a **pamphlet** that has been used by missionaries since.

Morgan was called to the First Council of the **Seventy** in 1884, and as a general authority he returned to preside over the Southern States **Mission** a second time (1886–88). During his presidency he frequently led groups of southern emigrants to Latter-day Saint settlements in **Arizona**, **Utah**, **New Mexico**, and especially in the San Luis Valley, **Colorado**, where he lived for a time.

His contributions included pioneering bureaus of information (or visitors' centers), the use of **Articles of Faith** missionary cards, and the practice of sustaining Church authorities in local **conferences**. For years he was involved in politics and was active in petitioning for Utah's **statehood**. He died in Preston, **Idaho**, in 1894.

Sources

Jenson, Andrew. *Latter-day Saint Biographical Encyclopedia.* 4 vols. 1901–36. Reprint, Salt Lake City: Western Epics, 1971. 1:204–5.

Richardson, Arthur. *The Life and Ministry of John Morgan.* Salt Lake City: n.p., 1965.

David F. Boone

MORLEY, ISAAC. Isaac Morley, a **general authority** and colonizer, was born 11 March 1786 in Montague, **Massachusetts**. A veteran of the **War** of 1812, he and his wife, Lucy Gunn, were among the first converts to the Church in northern **Ohio**, joining in 1830. Less than a year later, Brother Morley was called as first **counselor** to **Edward Partridge** (the Church's first **bishop**), a position he filled until Bishop Partridge's death in 1840. When a mob tarred and feathered Bishop Partridge and destroyed the Church printing office in **Independence**, Bishop Morley and five other brethren offered themselves to the mob as a ransom for the **Saints**, agreeing to be scourged or even killed.

Other trials he suffered for the kingdom included three weeks of imprisonment in Richmond, **Missouri**; the burning of his home, cooper's shop, and barn in **Nauvoo**; and the loss of his wife at **Winter Quarters**. In **Utah Brigham Young** put Brother Morley in charge of the settling of the Sanpete Valley, a region that became known as the granary of the Church. He baptized the famous **Indian** Chief **"Joseph" Walker** and served in the territorial government. He died 24 June 1865 in Fairview, Utah.

Of Bishops Morley and Partridge the Lord said, "Behold I am well pleased with my servant Isaac Morley and my servant Edward Partridge, because of the integrity of their hearts in laboring in my vineyard" (Smith, 2:302).

SOURCES

Flake, Lawrence R. *Mighty Men of Zion.* Salt Lake City: Karl D. Butler, 1974. 491.

Green, Forace. *Testimonies of Our Leaders.* Salt Lake City: Bookcraft, 1958. 317.

Morley, Richard Henry. "The Life and Contributions of Isaac Morley." Master's thesis, Brigham Young University, 1965.

Smith, Joseph. *History of The Church of Jesus Christ of Latter-day Saints.* Edited by B. H. Roberts. 2d ed. rev. 7 vols. Salt Lake City: The Church of Jesus Christ of Latter-day Saints, 1932–51.

LAWRENCE R. FLAKE

MORLEY'S SETTLEMENT. Morley's Settlement was a Latter-day Saint community from 1839 to 1845, founded 25 miles south of **Nauvoo, Illinois,** by **Isaac Morley.** The settlement was sometimes termed "Yelrome"—Morley spelled backward—and was part of the Lima **Stake,** which included 400 to 500 members at Morley's Settlement and nearby Lima. Morley's Settlement was a farm settlement that spread out for a mile. Its center, Morley Town, had four stores and a chair and cooper shop. Morley Town's site, at the south end of present Tioga, Illinois, has a historical marker. **Anti-Mormon** parties attacked Morley's Settlement 9 through 13 September 1845 and burned some 125 **Mormon** buildings there and in Lima. Members fled to Nauvoo for safety. When a group returned to harvest crops on 15 November, attackers killed Edmund Durfee. Local officials refused to try the accused murderers. The **Saints** abandoned the town a year later when they fled to the West.

SOURCES

Hartley, William G. *The 1845 Burning of Morley's Settlement and Murder of Edmund Durfee.* Salt Lake City: Primer Publications, 1997.

Jenson, Andrew. *Encyclopedic History of The Church of Jesus Christ of Latter-day Saints.* Salt Lake City: Deseret News, 1941. 434.

WILLIAM G. HARTLEY

MORMON. Almost from its beginning, The Church of Jesus Christ of Latter-day Saints and its members have been identified with the name *Mormon*. The **Book of Mormon** is named after Mormon, who was responsible for abridging a thousand years of history contained on Nephite records, from which the Prophet **Joseph Smith** made his translation.

Mormon introduces himself as "a disciple of **Jesus Christ**, the Son of God" (3 Ne. 5:13). He was commissioned to make a record that would help his latter-day readers to know their Redeemer (3 Ne. 5:13–26). When Mormon was 10 years old, a prophet told him where the Nephite records were deposited. When he was 15, he saw the resurrected Lord. At the age of 16, he was appointed leader of the Nephite armies. Mormon was engaged in continual conflict until he was 40 years old, at which time a ten-year truce was declared. During this period Mormon cried repentance to his people, but to no avail. Finally, at the age of 74, he led his people in their last struggle against the Lamanites, which ended at the **Hill Cumorah**. Mormon was wounded in battle and was later killed.

Sources

Smith, Joseph Fielding. *Doctrines of Salvation: Sermons and Writings of Joseph Fielding Smith*. 3 vols. Edited by Bruce R. McConkie. Salt Lake City: Bookcraft, 1954–56.

CALVIN R. STEPHENS

MORMON BATTALION. On 26 January 1846 **Brigham Young** authorized **Jesse C. Little** to meet with national leaders in **Washington, D.C.**, to seek aid for migrating Latter-day Saints. On 3 June 1846, Little met with President **James K. Polk**. The president offered aid to the **Mormon pioneers** by permitting them to raise a battalion of five hundred men. Little's assurance to Polk that his proposal would be looked upon with favor, and the subsequent ratification by Brigham Young and his council, committed a battalion of Latter-day Saints to join the Commander of the West, Colonel Stephen Watts Kearny, to fight for the **United States** in the **Mexican War**.

Kearny appointed **Captain James Allen** to enlist soldiers from the encamped Latter-day Saints in **Iowa** Territory. Allen's recruitment efforts were personally endorsed by Brigham Young, who exclaimed, "Let the 'Mormons' be the first to set their feet on the soil of **California**" (Roberts, 3:79). He wrote, further, that "hundreds would eternally regret that they did not go, when they had the chance" (Black and Poreter, 155). On 16 July 1846 and for several succeeding days, an estimated 520 men were mustered into the Mormon Battalion at **Council Bluffs, Iowa** Territory. Captain Allen automatically became a Lieutenant Colonel following the enlistment of the first four and one-half companies recruited on the 16th.

The Mormon Battalion left Council Bluffs 21 July 1846, accompanied by 35 women and 42 children. Shortly after trekking to **Fort Leavenworth**, Colonel Allen died. Prior to his death, Allen had sent respective companies of the battalion ahead under the command of Captain **Jefferson Hunt**. His command was soon overtaken by First Lieutenant A. J. Smith, a regular army officer who marched the men toward Santa Fe.

While on the Arkansas River, Smith sent a sick detachment of disabled men, along with some women and children, to Fort **Pueblo (Colorado)** under the command of Captain Nelson Higgins. The first men of the battalion approached Santa Fe on 9 October 1846 and were heralded by a hundred-gun salute. In Santa Fe, Smith was relieved of his command by Lieutenant Colonel **Philip St. George Cooke**.

Cooke ordered women and children to accompany the sick of a second detachment to Fort Pueblo under **Captain James Brown**, instead of continuing the march toward California. The remaining soldiers, with four officers' wives and a wife of a private, left Santa Fe for California on 19 October 1846. The soldiers journeyed down the Rio Grande del Norte before a third sick detachment was sent to Pueblo under the command of Second Lieutenant William W. Willis.

Near what today is Hatch, **New Mexico**, the remaining battalion members headed west—away from the Rio Grande. Cutting across the southeast corner of present-day **Arizona**, the column moved into Old **Mexico**, reaching the ruins of the abandoned Rancho San Bernardino on 2 December 1846. They reentered Arizona and marched along the San Pedro River. While moving up the San Pedro, the battalion was attacked by wild cattle. Despite a few injuries, the battalion continued their march towards Tucson, where they anticipated a fight with the garrisoned Mexican soldiers, but no conflict ensued.

On 21 December 1846 the battalion encamped on the Gila River. Two weeks later they crossed the Colorado River into California. By 29 January 1847, they were camped at the **San Diego** Mission. Their military march of nearly 2,000 miles from Council Bluffs to California had ended.

To complete their enlistment, battalion soldiers were assigned to garrison duty at San Diego, San Luis Rey, and Los Angeles, while others were designated to accompany General Kearny back to Fort Leavenworth. The battalion soldiers were mustered out of the military on 16 July 1847 at Los Angeles. Eighty-one men reenlisted and served eight additional months (20 July 1847–14 March 1848) in California in Company A of the Mormon Volunteers, commanded by Captain Daniel C. Davis.

The men of the Mormon Battalion are remembered for their loyalty to the United States during the Mexican War and the unprecedented distance of their march from Council Bluffs to California. They are also acknowledged for their participation in the early development of the West, and the building of the first wagon road over the southern route from California to Utah in 1848.

SOURCES

Black, Susan Easton, and Larry C. Porter. *Lion of the Lord: Essays on the Life and Service of Brigham Young.* Salt Lake CIty: Deseret Book, 1995.

Cooke, Philip St. George. *The Conquest of New Mexico and California in 1846–1848.* Chicago: Rio Grande Press, 1964.

———. "Cooke's Journal of the March of the Mormon Battalion, 1846–1847." *Exploring Southwestern Trails, 1846–1854.* Vol. 7 of Southwest Historical series. Edited by Ralph P. Bieber and Averam B. Bender. Glendale, Calif.: Arthur H. Clark, 1938.

Golder, Frank Alfred. *The March of the Mormon Battalion from Council Bluffs to California: Taken from the Journal of Henry Standage.* New York: Century, 1928.

Larson, Carl V., comp. *A Data Base of the Mormon Battalion: An Identification of the Original Members of the Mormon Battalion.* Providence, Utah: K. W. Watkins, 1987.

Ricketts, Norma B. *The Mormon Battalion: U.S. Army of the West, 1846–1848.* Logan, Utah: Utah State University Press, 1996.

Roberts, B. H. *A Comprehensive History of The Church of Jesus Christ of Latter-day Saints, Century One.* 6 vols. Salt Lake City: The Church of Jesus Christ of Latter-day Saints, 1930.

Tyler, Daniel. *A Concise History of the Mormon Battalion in the Mexican War, 1846–1847.* Glorieta, New Mexico: Rio Grande Press, 1969.

Yurtinus, John F. "A Ram in the Thicket: The Mormon Battalion in the Mexican War." 2 vols. Ph.D. diss., Brigham Young University, 1975.

LARRY C. PORTER, CLARK V. JOHNSON, AND SUSAN EASTON BLACK

MORMON BATTALION MONUMENT. The Mormon Battalion Monument, which stands on the grounds of the Utah State Capitol, was sculpted by Gilbert Riswold in 1927. Shaped like the mountains and buttes of the Battalion's desert journey, this monument supports a heroic-sized bronze battalion soldier. Carved into the pink granite are the upper torsos of an Anglo woman and an Indian woman. There are also four bas-relief scenes outlining the history of the battalion: "The Enlistment," including their families and **Brigham Young** at **Council Bluffs**; "The March," as they built the first wagon road through the southwest to the Pacific; "The Arrival of the Pueblo Detachment in the **Salt Lake Valley**," five days after the arrival of Brigham Young; and finally, "Discovery of Gold—**California**, January 24, 1848," showing four of the returning Battalion digging the millrace for John Sutter and panning for gold.

Another Mormon Battalion Monument, with just a single bronze figure, commissioned by the Church and sculpted in 1969 by Edward Fraughton, stands in a park above "Old Town," north of San Diego.

SOURCES

Bitton, Davis. "The Ritualization of Mormon History." *Utah State Historical Society Quarterly* 43 (Winter 1975): 67–85.

Ricketts, Norma Baldwin. *The Mormon Battalion U.S. Army in the West, 1846–1848.* Logan: Utah State University Press, 1996.

Tyler, Daniel. *A Concise History of the Mormon Battalion in the Mexican War, 1846–1847.* Salt Lake City: Infobases Collector's Library, 1981. Infobases.

RICHARD G. OMAN

MORMON CORRIDOR. The Mormon Corridor was a line of Church-established settlements stretching from the **Salt Lake Valley** to southern **California**. It was created to facilitate an alternate route for immigration and to provide a Pacific port for commercial purposes. The possibility of using the Colorado River as a shipping route also contributed to the establishment of the Mormon Corridor.

Most of the corridor settlements were founded during the 1850s along a line through central and southern **Utah**, approximating present-day Interstate 15. **Salt Lake City** and **San Bernardino, California**, marked the extreme ends of the corridor, San Bernardino being served by the seaport of San Pedro. For a time the only Mormon Corridor colony that existed between San Bernardino and the Utah settlements was **Las Vegas**, located on the Spanish Trail.

Rationale for the corridor's existence was eventually undercut by congressional rejection of the state of Deseret, the subsequent establishment of the Utah Territory, and the ability to transport immigrants from the east coast by rail. The abandonment of Las Vegas and San Bernardino during the **Utah War** also made the Mormon Corridor less viable.

Although the purpose for the Mormon Corridor eventually ended, the settlements became permanent, most continuing to the present day.

SOURCES

Arrington, Leonard J. *Great Basin Kingdom: An Economic History of the Latter-day Saints, 1830–1900.* Cambridge: Harvard University Press, 1958.

Campbell, Eugene E. *Establishing Zion: The Mormon Church in the American West, 1847–1869.* Salt Lake City: Signature Books, 1988.

Peterson, Charles S. *Utah: A History.* Nashville: American Association for State and Local History, 1977.

MICHAEL N. LANDON

MORMON CREED. The phrase "mind your own business" and its variants was adopted by nineteenth-century **Saints** as "the Mormon Creed," and was known among American frontiersman as "the eleventh commandment." In 1843 **William Smith** was the first to publish the idea that the Saints' creed was "to mind their own business, and let everybody else do likewise." Other Church leaders soon adopted the phrase, though usually dropping its second half. By the mid-1850s, the Mormon Creed was best known as simply "mind your own business." In that form it was quoted in countless sermons, songs, and newspaper editorials—even appearing on a fixture in the **Logan Temple**. For decades a Latter-day Saint was said to be living his religion if he was "minding his own business," especially during the **antipolygamy** campaigns, which heightened the Saints' need for circumspection. In the closing years of the century, the phrase began to wane, and nowadays it is virtually unknown.

SOURCES

Hicks, Michael. "Minding Business: A Note on the 'Mormon Creed.'" *BYU Studies* 26 (Fall 1986): 125–32.

MICHAEL HICKS

MORMON HISTORICAL STUDIES. Inaugurated in 2000, this independent periodical, published biannually by the **Mormon Historic Sites Foundation**, includes essays, biographies, documents, book reviews, historical site descriptions, and archival listings associated with the **Mormon** experience. Previously, from 1989 through 1999, the periodical was published independently under the title *Nauvoo Journal.*

ALEXANDER L. BAUGH

MORMON HISTORY, JOURNAL OF. See JOURNAL OF MORMON HISTORY.

MORMON HISTORY ASSOCIATION. The Mormon History Association (MHA), founded in 1965, has become the premier organization for the scholarly presentation, publication, and discussion of Latter-day Saint history. In the aftermath of World War II, Latter-day Saints began attending graduate schools in larger numbers. Historians, scholars from other disciplines, and well-informed amateurs interested in Church history published and met together to confer. On 9 September 1965, a group of professors and institute teachers met in the Merrill Library at Utah State University during the annual meeting of the Utah Conference on Higher Education. They agreed to organize MHA at the American Historical Association convention in San Francisco, 28 December 1965.

The 52 persons at the organizational meeting included professors, institute teachers, representatives of the Church Historian's Office, Latter-day Saints, Reorganized Latter Day Saints, and members of other faiths. The group elected Leonard J. Arrington as its first president. Until 1972, when membership reached more than 300, MHA held its meetings at the conferences of other historical associations. Thereafter, MHA has held an annual conference at sites alternating between the Mountain West and other areas. The annual meetings follow a traditional format including scholarly papers, tours to historic sites, an invited lecture (funded by Obert C. Tanner), and a presidential address. Unlike most historical associations, MHA also sponsors a Sunday morning devotional service.

At first MHA relied on *BYU Studies* and *Dialogue: A Journal of Mormon Thought,* professional journals, Church magazines, and a newsletter for publication and information. In 1974, when membership reached nearly 1,000, MHA inaugurated the *Journal of Mormon History.* Increased membership and interest led to its conversion to a semiannual publication in 1992.

SOURCES

Arrington, Leonard J. *Adventures of a Church Historian.* Urbana: University of Illinois Press, 1998.

Beecher, Maureen Ursenbach. "*Entre Nous:* An Intimate History of MHA." *Journal of Mormon History* 12 (1985): 43–52.

"Recollections on the Founding and Purpose of the Mormon History Association, 1965–1983." *Journal of Mormon History* 10 (1983): 91–103.

THOMAS G. ALEXANDER

MORMONISM UNVAILED. *Mormonism Unvailed* was the first book-length anti-Mormon attack on Joseph Smith and the Book of Mormon. It was published in 1834 by E. D. Howe. This nearly 300-page book is a disjointed collection of distorted or falsified information. Although the title page lists Howe as author, disgruntled ex-Mormon Doctor Philastus Hurlbut gathered most of the book's contents, including a series of contrived affidavits from the Smith family's western New York acquaintances. In Hurlbut's standardized style, these derogatory statements described Joseph Smith and his family as nefarious and shiftless people. *Mormonism Unvailed's* most absurd claim is that the historical foundation of the Book of Mormon story had originated in an unpublished romance written by Solomon Spaulding in 1812 (see Spaulding Theory). When Howe sold his newspaper firm in 1839 or 1840, he unwittingly left behind the suppressed Spaulding manuscript. Forty-four years later, the person who purchased Howe's business rediscovered Spaulding's novel, compared it with the Book of Mormon, and discredited one of *Mormonism Unvailed's* principal assertions.

SOURCES

Backman, Milton V., Jr. *The Heavens Resound: A History of the Latter-day Saints in Ohio, 1830–1838.* Salt Lake City: Deseret Book, 1983.

E. D. Howe. *Autobiography and Recollections of a Pioneer Printer.* Painesville, Ohio: Telegraph Steam Printing House, 1878.

———. *Mormonism Unvailed; or, A Faithful Account of That Singular Imposition and Delusion, from Its Rise to the Present Time.* Painesville, Ohio: E. D. Howe, Published by the Author, 1834.

Spaulding, Solomon. *Manuscript Found: The Complete Original "Spaulding Manuscript."* Edited by Kent P. Jackson. Provo, Utah: Religious Studies Center, Brigham Young University, 1996.

SCOTT H. FAULRING

MORMON MIRACLE PAGEANT, THE. See PAGEANTS.

MORMON TABERNACLE CHOIR. See TABERNACLE CHOIR.

MORMON TRAIL. Since its formative days in upstate New York, the Church set a trail westward, first to Ohio and later to Missouri. The "Mormon Trail," however, is popularly identified with the forced exodus of thousands of Latter-day Saints beginning in February 1846 from their beloved city of **Nauvoo, Illinois**, on the banks of the **Mississippi River**, to the **Salt Lake Valley** in July 1847. Although many thousands of individuals were beginning to move west in the 1840s along the **California** and **Oregon** trails in search of new opportunities and economic fortune, nothing in American history compares with this forced expulsion of an entire religion.

Brigham Young set the Saints westward on a march of approximately 1,300 miles along a trail of hope and faith that eventually stretched across **Iowa, Nebraska**, and **Wyoming** to the **Great Basin**. Their muddy march across Iowa in what was one of the wettest springs on record began at the **Sugar Creek** encampment across the Mississippi from Nauvoo and continued up the "agency road" on the north side of the Des Moines River (through Farmington, North Bentonsport, and Keosauqua) before heading west to Richardson Point, Locust Creek, and Pleasant Grove. Farther west at their encampments at **Garden Grove** and at **Mt. Pisgah**, near the headwaters of the Grand River, they established way stations or temporary farm acreages for those who would follow later. From Mt. Pisgah they continued to rely on the maps of J. N. Nicollet and followed **Indian** trails to **Council Bluffs**, where they arrived well behind their time and too late that year to reach the mountains.

After establishing a **"Winter Quarters"** across the **Missouri River** in what is today Florence, Nebraska (a suburb of Omaha), Brigham Young and a handpicked band of **pioneers** continued their march westward in the spring of 1847, relying heavily on the maps of the pathfinder **John C. Frémont**. In contrast with the **Oregon Trail**, which hugged the southern banks of the **Platte River** west, the **Mormons** set their own course and deliberately followed along the north side of the Platte to avoid contact with potential **Missouri** enemies heading west and to set a clear course for the many thousands to follow. Later both the Union Pacific mainline and Interstate 80 followed this course from Omaha west to North Platte. From the Elkhorn, the vanguard company traveled west through the heart of Pawnee country up the North Fork of the Platte River to Ash Hollow, Chimney Rock, Scottsbluff, and eventually to **Fort Laramie** in the shadows of the Black Hills.

After fording the North Fork of the Platte River near present-day Casper, Wyoming, the **pioneer** company struck west for the Sweetwater River, passing by Independence Rock, Devil's Gate, and then over **South Pass**. They continued on to Sandy Creek and Green River before heading down to **Fort Bridger** (near present-day Evanston, Wyoming). Anxious to strike a settlement in either the Salt Lake or **Cache Valley** and to plant crops, Brigham Young chose to follow the so-called "Hastings

Cutoff." Soon after leaving Fort Bridger, they came down Red Fork (Echo Canyon), and rather than follow treacherous Weber Canyon, they took the arduous overland trail that the ill-fated **Donner-Reed Party** had blazed the year before over Big and Little Mountains. They entered the Salt Lake Valley from the mouth of **Emigration Canyon** in July 1847.

One of their number, **William Clayton**, kept meticulous records of their journey, which were later published as *The Latter-day Saints' Emigrants' Guide*—one of the most respected popular trail guides of its time. The Mormon Trail is today a national historic site as proclaimed by the U.S. National Park Service, and it was well remembered in the highly publicized 1997 commemorative Mormon Trail Wagon Train reenactment.

SOURCES

Bennett, Richard E. *We'll Find the Place—The Mormon Exodus 1846–1848.* Salt Lake City: Deseret Book, 1997.

Black, Susan Easton, and William G. Hartley, eds. *The Iowa Mormon Trail: Legacy of Faith and Courage.* Orem, Utah: Helix Publishing, 1997.

Clayton, William. *The Latter-day Saints' Emigrants' Guide.* Edited by Stanley B. Kimball. Gerald, Mo.: Patrice Press, 1983.

Stegner, Wallace. *The Gathering of Zion: The Story of the Mormon Trail.* Salt Lake City: Westwater Press, 1964.

RICHARD E. BENNETT

MORMON VILLAGE. See CITY PLANNING.

MORMON WAR. From August through November 1838 a number of civil disturbances broke out between the **Saints** and other residents of northern **Missouri**. Known as the "1838 Mormon War," this conflict included the following incidents: (1) the confrontation between Latter-day Saints and Missouri vigilantes in **Daviess County**, leading to the intercession by regional state militia (August through mid-September); (2) the Latter-day Saint defense against "county regulators" at **De Witt**, Carroll County, and the regional state militia's response to this disturbance (August through October 10); (3) the expulsion of non-Mormon residents of Daviess County by Mormon militia (mid-October); (4) the encounter between Latter-day Saints and Missouri militia at **Crooked River** in **Ray County** (October 25); (5) governor **Lilburn W. Bogg's** "**extermination order**" (October 27); (6) the attack on the Mormon settlement at **Haun's Mill** by Missouri vigilantes primarily from

Livingston and Daviess Counties (October 30); (7) the Latter-day Saint defense of **Far West** against vigilante and state militia forces (October 28–31); and (8) the surrender of the **Saints** at Far West and the military occupation conducted by the state militia (November 1–29). The Mormon War ended in the winter of 1838–39 with the expulsion of more than 10,000 Saints from the state of Missouri.

SOURCES

Baugh, Alexander L. "A Call to Arms: The 1838 Mormon Defense of Northern Missouri." Ph.D. diss., Brigham Young University, 1996.

Gentry, Leland H. "A History of the Latter-day Saints in Northern Missouri from 1836–1839." Ph.D. diss., Brigham Young University, 1965.

LeSueur, Stephen C. *The 1838 Mormon War in Missouri*. Columbia: University of Missouri Press, 1987.

ALEXANDER L. BAUGH

MORMON YOUTH CHORUS AND SYMPHONY. The **Mormon** Youth Chorus and Symphony (MYCS) was first organized and sponsored by the Church in 1969 to provide **music** for weekly **radio** broadcasts distributed throughout the **United States** and other countries. After a time the radio broadcasts ceased, but the group continued to perform, increasing musical appreciation and understanding between peoples and cultures. The MYCS included 400 young vocalists and instrumentalists who volunteered their time and talents during weekly rehearsals as well as approximately 30 concerts per year.

The group rehearsed and performed regularly at the **Tabernacle** on **Temple Square** and in concert halls throughout the United States, including the Hollywood Bowl, the Kennedy Center, and Madison Square Garden. The MYCS performed and recorded for both television and radio and was featured with many prominent performers including Bing Crosby, Gene Kelly, Nat "King" Cole, Johnny Mathis, and Burl Ives. One of their television specials, "Christmas World," received two Emmy Awards in 1980 for Best Entertainment Program in the western regional division. Other award-winning television specials included "Carnival of the Animals" and "America, America, America." They also had over two dozen commercial sound recordings to their credit. The group was dissolved in 1999, at the time its conductor, Robert C. Bowden, retired.

SOURCES

Mormon Youth Chorus and Symphony. Pamphlet. Salt Lake City: The Church of Jesus Christ of Latter-day Saints, 1996.

Mormon Youth Chorus and Symphony: Twenty-Fifth Anniversary Commemorative Program. Salt Lake City: The Church of Jesus Christ of Latter-day Saints, 1994.

CYNTHIA DOXEY

MOROCCO. See MIDDLE EAST and MUSLIMS.

MORONI. Moroni is the name of two great Nephite **prophets** in the **Book of Mormon**—the first was a general who liberated his people, and the second was the son of Mormon (the abridger of the Book of Mormon) who lived during the closing years of Nephite history. The second may have been given his name because of his father's admiration for General Moroni (Alma 48:17–18). As the last of the Nephite prophet-historians, Moroni finished the record of his father's life, abridged twenty-four gold plates containing Jaredite history (the Book of Ether), and concluded the Book of Mormon with ten chapters of his own instruction on doctrinal matters, including some epistles and teachings of his father, Mormon. In approximately A.D. 421 Moroni sealed the sacred record and hid it in the earth (the **Hill Cumorah**), to come forth in the latter days as prophesied.

Nothing more is known of Moroni until modern times when, as a resurrected personage, he began visiting **Joseph Smith** on 21 September 1823 to instruct him about the engraved plates, the coming forth of the Book of Mormon, and Joseph's role in the fulfilment of prophecy (JS–H 1:29–42). It was later revealed to the Prophet that Moroni acted under the direction of the Lord, who committed to him "the keys of the record of the stick of Ephraim," that is, the Book of Mormon record (D&C 27:5; compare Ezek. 37:15–37). During the evening of Moroni's first appearance, he came to Joseph Smith three times, and returned a fourth time the next morning, always repeating the same instructions (JS–H 1:43–49). Joseph went to the hill that he had been shown in vision the night before and again met Moroni, who showed him the plates. Joseph was told not to take the plates, but to return to that exact spot the same time every year until the time was right for him to receive the plates four years later (JS–H 1:50–54). Joseph obeyed these instructions and was given charge of the plates on 22 September 1827 (JS–H 1:59).

Between 1823 and 1829, Moroni appeared more than 20 times to the Prophet, instructing him on such matters as the plates, the **gathering** of Israel, the coming of **Elijah**, and the Second Coming of the Savior. Moroni's appearances to Joseph Smith partially fulfilled the apostle John's vision of another angel, flying "in the midst of heaven, having the ever-lasting gospel to preach unto them that dwell on the earth" in the last days (Rev. 14:6–7; McConkie, 514). Moroni was the angel who showed the gold plates to the Three Witnesses of the Book of Mormon and took them back after the translation had been accomplished (JS–H 1:60). Additionally, sources indicate that Moroni appeared to several others, including **W.W. Phelps** and **Heber C. Kimball**. He may also have been the angel who appeared to Mary Whitmer and Oliver Granger (Peterson, 114–16, 151–52).

Elder **Orson Hyde** of the **Quorum** of the Twelve **Apostles** taught that Moroni's grand ministry involves watching over **America**. He referred to Moroni as the "Prince of America" and said that he "presides over the destinies of America, and feels a lively interest in all our doings" (JD, 6:368). Elder Hyde further stated that Moroni helped guide **Christopher Columbus** through dreams and visions, was in the camp of **George Washington** directing affairs by an invisible hand, and led our founding fathers on to victory, "and all this to open and prepare the way for the Church and **kingdom of God** to be established on the western hemi-sphere, for the redemption of Israel and the salvation of the world" (JD, 6:368). In speaking directly "unto all the ends of the earth" at the end of his mortal life, Moroni left a testimony of the Savior's redemptive power and an invitation to "come unto Christ" that are among the most moving and powerful statements in all of scripture (Moro. 10:24–34).

SOURCE

Journal of Discourses [JD]. 26 vols. London: Latter-day Saints' Book Depot, 1854–86.

Peterson, H. Donl. *Moroni: Ancient Prophet, Modern Messenger.* Bountiful, Utah: Horizon Publishers, 1983.

ANDREW C. SKINNER

MORRILL ANTI-BIGAMY ACT OF 1862. See ANTI-POLYGAMY MOVEMENT.

MORRIS, GEORGE Q.

MORRIS, GEORGE Q. George Quayle Morris, named after his grand-father **George Q. Cannon**, served as a member of the **Quorum** of the Twelve **Apostles**. Born 20 February 1874 in Salt Lake City, he grew up working at his father's tile and monument company. After attending

Brigham Young Academy and the University of Utah, he fulfilled a mission in the British Isles. Resuming work in his father's company, he headed the committee responsible for erecting the "This Is the Place" Monument at the mouth of Emigration Canyon. He served for 24 years on the general board of the YMMIA, becoming general superintendent. He also served as chairman of the *Improvement Era* committee and was instrumental in combining that magazine with the *Young Woman's Journal* in 1929.

In 1948 he was called to preside over the Eastern States Mission, a position he held in 1951 when he was made an assistant to the Twelve. In April 1954, at the age of 80, he became an apostle—the oldest man to be called to the Quorum. He served faithfully in the Twelve until his death on 23 April 1962 in Salt Lake City.

SOURCES

Christensen, M. Elmer. "George Q. Morris." *Improvement Era* 65 (June 1962): 392.

Flake, Lawrence R. *Prophets and Apostles of the Last Dispensation.* Provo, Utah: Religious Studies Center, Brigham Young University, 2001. 501–3.

Stevens, Stringham A. "George Quayle Morris: The New Superintendent of the Young Men's Mutual Improvement Association." *Improvement Era* 40 (May 1937): 282–83, 294, 364.

LAWRENCE R. FLAKE

MORRISITES. In the 1860s a group of over 400 former Latter-day Saints followed Joseph Morris, an English convert who claimed to have received revelations affirming that he had been reincarnated with the spirit of Moses and was the seventh angel of the book of Revelation. He claimed that he was not to form a new church but to preside over and set straight the LDS Church, whose leaders had gone astray.

The Morrisites established a colony at Kington Fort in Weber County, Utah. Morris claimed that the Lord would take care of them, so they did not have to plant crops nor pay debts. Some members defected. Three defecting Morrisite men were kidnapped and returned to Kington Fort. The government issued writs that were destroyed by Morris. Finally, Frank Fuller, the acting governor of Utah Territory, sent a posse of 250 men with deputy marshall Robert T. Burton, a faithful Latter-day Saint, to make arrests. A three-day seige followed, in which Morris was killed. Burton later faced indictments but was cleared. The convicted members of the Morrisites were all pardoned by the **anti-Mormon** Governor Stephen S. Harding. The Morrisite movement ended soon thereafter.

SOURCES

Cannon, M. Hamlin. "The Morrisite War." *The American West* 7 (November 1970): 5.

Roberts, B. H. *A Comprehensive History of The Church of Jesus Christ of Latter-day Saints, Century One.* 6 vols. Salt Lake City: The Church of Jesus Christ of Latter-day Saints, 1930.

ROBERT L. MARROTT

MOSES. The great Old Testament prophet Moses led the ancient Israelites out of Egyptian bondage and revealed God's law to them.

Moses plays an important role in Latter-day Saint history. The **Restoration** sheds much light on his work and clarifies important points about his ministry. The **Book of Mormon** explains more clearly than does the **Bible** the destiny of the house of Israel and the meaning of the Law of Moses, especially its relationship to the Atonement. The **Joseph Smith Translation of the Bible** reveals important new information about Moses not found in other Bibles, including his magnificent vision in Moses 1 and other important doctrinal additions (see JST Ex. 33:20; 34:1–2; JST Deut. 10:2).

Moses came to the **Prophet Joseph Smith** as part of the restoration of the gospel. On 3 April 1836, Moses appeared in the **Kirtland Temple** to restore "the keys of the gathering of Israel from the four parts of the earth, and the leading of the ten tribes from the land of the north" (D&C 110:11). With these keys, **missionary work** is fully empowered, and "the literal gathering of Israel and . . . the restoration of the Ten Tribes" is taking place (A of F 10).

KENT P. JACKSON

MOSES, BOOK OF. See **BOOK OF MOSES**.

MOTHER IN HEAVEN. The role of a Mother in Heaven was expressed by the **First Presidency** (1909) when they stated that "all men and women are in the similitude of the universal Father and Mother" ("Origin," 1667). "**The Family: A Proclamation to the World**" (1995) declares that all human beings are spirit sons or daughters of "heavenly parents" and that gender is an essential, permanent "characteristic of individual premortal, mortal and eternal identity and purpose."

The term "Mother in Heaven" does not appear in the **scriptures**, but since full salvation means to become like God, includes begetting children in eternity (D&C 132:19–32), and is attained only by a man and a woman in celestial **marriage**, it follows that there is a Heavenly Father and also a Heavenly Mother. This concept appears in the LDS **hymn** "O My Father" (*Hymns* #292). The implication of **Doctrine and Covenants** 20:19 is that Heavenly Mother should not be worshiped, hence not prayed to, by mortal man.

SOURCES

The First Presidency of the Church. "The Origin of Man." 1909. *Encyclopedia of Mormonism.* Edited by Daniel H. Ludlow. 4 vols. New York: Macmillan, 1992. 4:1665–69.

The First Presidency and Quorum of the Twelve Apostles of The Church of Jesus Christ of Latter-day Saints. "The Family: A Proclamation to the World." Salt Lake City: The Church of Jesus Christ of Latter-day Saints, 1995.

Hinckley, Gordon B. "Daughters of God." *Ensign* 21 (November 1991): 97–100.

Hymns of The Church of Jesus Christ of Latter-day Saints. Salt Lake City: The Church of Jesus Christ of Latter-day Saints, 1985.

McConkie, Bruce R. *Mormon Doctrine.* 2d ed. Salt Lake City: Bookcraft, 1966. 516–17.

ROBERT J. MATTHEWS

MOTION PICTURES. Latter-day Saints have been portrayed in numerous movies from the early 1900s to the present. The earliest, *A Trip to Salt Lake City* (1905), involved a polygamous husband trying to give his wives and children a drink of water aboard a train to **Utah**. A Danish film, *A Victim of the Mormons* (1911), depicted the familiar stereotype of a young woman kidnapped and married against her will in the **Salt Lake Temple**. **Danites**, secret oaths, and the perilous plight of a young gentile girl trapped into a **marriage** with a Mormon **apostle** summed up *A Mormon Maid* (1917). *Trapped by the Mormons* (1922) showed a predatory, vampirelike Mormon missionary victimizing **England**'s female population. **Utah** Senator (and Church **apostle**) **Reed Smoot** successfully prohibited the film's distribution in the **United States**. Reminiscent of nineteenth-century pulp novels, these films, and others that followed, deeply concerned President **Heber J. Grant**. During the 1920s more than 30 films depicted aspects of Mormonism. The usual approach dealt with **plural marriage**, the clannish and conspiratorial Mormon culture, and Danite raids.

In 1940 a major biographical movie on **Brigham Young** released by 20th Century Fox forever changed the negative film stereotypes of Latter-day Saints. *Brigham Young* was distinguished by the Church's cooperation with the studio on the development of the script and the film's unprecedented sympathetic portrayal of **Saints** as victims rather than perpetrators of violence. President Grant called it a "friend maker" and urged Saints to not criticize its partly fictional account of Young, played by Dean Jagger (who joined the Church in 1972), and **Joseph Smith**, played by Vincent Price.

Director John Ford's affectionate tribute to the Saints in *Wagonmaster* (1950) dramatized the courageous journey of Hole-in-the-Rock Saints to southern Utah. By this time Latter-day Saints, largely accepted into the American mainstream, had established careers in front of and behind the camera, including **Ogden** native Moroni Olsen, a veteran character actor of more than 300 films, and actress Laraine Day. From the 1960s through the 80s films—including *Paint Your Wagon* (1969), *The Getaway* (1972), *The Duchess and the Dirtwater Fox* (1976), and *Fletch* (1985)—touched briefly but humorously on Mormonism. In 1977, a Utah-based company's feature film *Brigham* was released largely to audiences in the Intermountain West. This positive but bland drama of the Church's origins and trek west failed to create believable characters.

The Avenging Angel (1995), a TV movie broadcast worldwide, dealt with a plot against Young by a former wife and the maneuverings of his power-hungry associates. Charlton Heston's brief but impressive Brigham Young graced this otherwise forgettable film. *The Avenging Angel* was as false to Utah events as the earlier films that so disturbed President Grant. In 1997 the futuristic science fiction action thriller *Starship Troopers* identified a Fort Joseph Smith that was wiped out by alien creatures.

Mormonism in the movies largely followed contemporary cultural perceptions, from malicious and polygamous through the early 1930s to, by 1940, an unfairly persecuted law-abiding minority. Subsequently, Latter-day Saints have been treated more fairly in film, but not without some humor about their distinctive beliefs and colorful history.

SOURCES

D'Arc, James V. "Darryl F. Zanuck's *Brigham Young:* A Film in Context." *BYU Studies* 29:1 (Fall 1989): 5–33.

Nelson, Richard Alan. "From Antagonism to Acceptance: Mormons and the Silver Screen." *Dialogue: A Journal of Mormon Thought* 10 (Spring 1977): 58–69.

JAMES V. D'ARC

MOUNTAIN MEADOWS MASSACRE. On 11 September 1857, more than 100 emigrants, principally from **Arkansas**, were massacred at Mountain Meadows in Southern **Utah**. At first Native Americans were blamed for the massacre, but later Latter-day Saints and **Brigham Young** were accused of participating in and ordering the extermination of the Fancher Train. The massacre at Mountain Meadows is one of the most tragic events in Utah history.

There is no universal agreement among historians as to the causes of this tragedy, who was to blame, or the exact sequence of events. Still, scholars have reached a consensus relative to some fundamental facts. As early as the summer of 1857, Latter-day Saint leaders learned that a federal army of more than 2,000 men was coming to Utah to put down a supposed rebellion and install a new territorial governor. Brigham Young declared martial law, forbade the Saints to sell produce to wagon trains traveling through the territory, sought to win the support of Native Americans in case of war, called home missionaries and **Mormon** settlers in outlying areas, and sent members of the **Quorum** of the Twelve **Apostles** throughout Utah to preach. **George A. Smith** traveled in Southern Utah, extolling the Saints to be ever ready to defend **Zion**.

During the summer of 1857, a wagon train led by Charles Fancher made its way through the territory and then camped at Mountain Meadows near Enterprise, Utah, to allow their animals to rest and graze before continuing on to **California**. It appears that some of these emigrants told a few Latter-day Saints that when they had transported their families to the Golden State they were going to return, join the army, and subdue the Saints.

While resting their animals, the emigrants were attacked by Native Americans. Church leaders sent **James H. Haslem** on horseback to **Salt Lake City** for instructions from Brigham Young. President Young told Haslem to make certain that the emigrants safely left Utah. While Haslem made his ride, meetings were held in Cedar City, and Latter-day Saints were sent to confer with Native American leaders. Before Haslem had returned, Saints joined the attacking **Indians**. After the emigrants surrendered their weapons, they were all killed, except for 18 very young children. The dead were quickly buried in shallow graves, and **John D. Lee**, the "Indian farmer" for that region, rode to Salt Lake City and told Brigham Young and other leaders that Indians were solely responsible for the massacre. Brigham Young used this information in his report to federal officials.

Only a few days after the massacre, rumors began circulating throughout the country that Native Americans were not the only guilty people at Mountain Meadows that September. Almost 20 years after the massacre, John D. Lee was arrested, tried, convicted, and shot for the role he played at Mountain Meadows. Though other Latter-day Saints were as culpable as Lee, he was the only one executed.

Evidence shows that Brigham Young did not order the massacre nor know beforehand that it was going to take place. It remains difficult to understand how Latter-day Saints could have participated in such a horrible, tragic affair.

SOURCES

Brooks, Juanita. *John Doyle Lee*. Logan, Utah: Utah State University Press, 1992.

———. *The Mountain Meadows Massacre*. Palo Alto, Calif.: Stanford University, 1951.

Godfrey, Kenneth W. "The Mountain Meadows Massacre and Its Historians: Separating Myth from Reality." Paper presented at the Mormon History Association Meetings, St. George, Utah, May 1992.

KENNETH W. GODFREY

MOUNT PISGAH. Mount Pisgah was established by the **Mormon pioneers** in Union County, **Iowa**, as a settlement on the trail from **Garden Grove, Iowa**, to **Winter Quarters, Nebraska**. Shortly after the first pioneers arrived in Garden Grove, **Parley P. Pratt** led a party to explore the area. As he rode his horse, he "came suddenly to some round and sloping hills, grassy and crowned with beautiful groves of timber," which he called Mount Pisgah. In a few days, the traveling **Saints** arrived and "established a settlement, and surveyed and enclosed another farm of several thousand acres. This became a town and a resting place for the Saints for years" (Pratt, 342–43). It was from Mount Pisgah that 65 men were recruited into the **Mormon Battalion** during the **Mexican War**.

The settlement was maintained from 1848 to 1852. The living conditions were poor, and during the town's first six months, between 160 and 300 individuals died. The Church bought two acres in 1888 and built a monument to these pioneers.

SOURCES

Black, Susan Easton, and William G. Hartley, eds. *The Iowa Mormon Trail: Legacy of Faith and Courage*. Orem, Utah: Helix Publishing, 1997.

Pratt, Parley P. *Autobiography of Parley P. Pratt*. Edited by Parley P. Pratt Jr. Salt Lake City: Deseret Book, 1976. 242–43.

H. DEAN GARRETT

MOYLE, HENRY D. Henry Dinwoodey Moyle, counselor in the First Presidency, was born in Salt Lake City, 22 April 1889, to James H. Moyle and Alice E. Dinwoodey. He studied at the University of Utah, the University of Chicago, Harvard Law School, and a world-famous school of mines in Freiburg, Gemany, where he had previously served a full-time mission for the Church. In addition to his law practice, he taught part time for a quarter of a century at the University of Utah. He also headed successful business ventures involving trucking, railroads, oil, ranching, banking, finance, and insurance. He was a soldier in World War I and director of the Petroleum Industries Council in World War II.

While accomplishing much in the world, Brother Moyle still found time to serve in the Church. From 1927 to 1937 he was president of the Cottonwood Stake. He was later appointed chairman of the General Church Welfare Committee, where he used his tremendous knowledge of business, finance, ranching, and science to help extend this program all over the world.

On 10 April 1947, President George Albert Smith ordained him a member of the Quorum of the Twelve Apostles. In June 1959 he became second counselor to President David O. McKay and was appointed chairman of the Missionary Committee. Under the direction of President McKay, he greatly increased the amount of proselyting activity in the Church, virtually doubling the number of missionaries in the field. On 12 October 1961, Elder Moyle became President McKay's first counselor. He served in that position until he died 18 September 1963 in Deer Park, Florida.

Blessed with an abundance of this world's goods, President Moyle was an extremely generous man; however, he realized he could share more important blessings than temporal wealth with his fellow men. He said: "We may sometimes find satisfaction in sharing our material wealth with others. But far greater satisfaction comes from sharing ourselves, our time, our energy, our affection, and particularly in imparting to others our testimony of God, the power of God unto salvation, the knowledge we possess of God and His purposes" (Green, 202).

SOURCES

Flake, Lawrence R. *Prophets and Apostles of the Last Dispensation.* Provo, Utah: Religious Studies Center, Brigham Young University, 2001. 213–16.

Green, Forace. *Testimonies of Our Leaders.* Salt Lake City, Bookcraft, 1958. 202.

Lee, Harold B. "President Henry Dinwoodey Moyle, Second Counselor in the First Presidency." *Relief Society Magazine* 46 (August 1959): 499–500.

LAWRENCE R. FLAKE

MOYLE, JAMES H. James Henry Moyle was known for his contributions as an attorney and politician as well as his service as a missionary and **mission president**. He was born 17 September 1858 in **Salt Lake City**. In his youth, he learned stone-cutting and masonry from his father, but his ambition was always to become a lawyer. He graduated from the **University of Deseret** in 1879. After serving as a missionary in the **Southern States Mission** for two years, he returned to school in **Utah** and then earned a law degree at the University of **Michigan** from 1882 to 1885. After returning to practice law in Salt Lake City, he was elected county attorney and a member of the Utah legislature. He was a recognized leader in the **Democratic party**, and ran unsuccessfully for Utah governor in 1900.

Moyle served as assistant secretary of the U.S. Treasury from 1917 to 1921 and as U.S. commissioner of customs for many years. He served as the president of the **Eastern States Mission** from 1928 to 1933. He is also remembered for an interview he conducted with **David Whitmer** in 1885 in **Richmond, Missouri**, shortly before Whitmer's death, in which the elderly witness reaffirmed his testimony of **Joseph Smith** and the **gold plates**.

Moyle married Alice Evelyn Dinwoodey in 1887, and they were the parents of eight children. Their oldest son, **Henry D. Moyle**, was ordained an **apostle** in April 1947 and served as a **counselor** to President **David O. McKay**. James H. Moyle died in Salt Lake City on 19 February 1946 at the age of 87.

SOURCES

Evans, John Henry. *James Henry Moyle.* Edited by Gordon B. Hinckley. Salt Lake City: Deseret Book, 1951.

Sessions, Gene A., ed. *Mormon Democrat: The Religious and Political Memoirs of James Henry Moyle.* Salt Lake City: The James Moyle Genealogical and Historical Association, 1975.

Whitney, Orson F. *History of Utah.* 4 vols. Salt Lake City: George Q. Cannon & Sons, 1901–04. 4:564–5.

DAVID KENISON

MOZAMBIQUE. Mozambique is located on the southeast coast of **Africa** and covers 309,496 square miles. In 1999 its population was about 17 million, and the nation's official language was Portugese. Most also spoke one of six Bantu languages. About 30% of the people were Christian, 55% followed tribal religions, and the remainder were **Muslim**.

Mozambique is one of the poorest countries in the world, and the Church has provided its people with much **humanitarian aid**. Following a drought in 1992 (the worst in 100 years) and a flood in 2000, the Church shipped a million pounds of food and relief items to Mozambique.

One of the country's first citizens to join the Church was Chico Tomo Antonio Mapenda, who was baptized in 1990 in East **Germany** while attending school there. He was converted by teachings and **literature** provided by Church members behind the Iron Curtain, and he was ordained a **priest** before returning to Africa. Upon his return to Mozambique, Chico taught and converted scores of others, including **family** members. By 1998 they had organized three unofficial **branches** of the Church, as only Chico was a baptized member. The Church was legally recognized in Mozambique in 1996. When the first missionaries arrived three years later they found hundreds waiting to be baptized in Beira, Maputo, and Marromeu. The latter city alone had more than 500 people waiting for the missionaries. They were under the leadership of Francisco Dique Sousa, a former Protestant minister who had become converted through reading a copy of the **Book of Mormon**. He had unofficially organized these unbaptized followers into nine branches and had built six **meetinghouses**.

On 29 October 1999 **Elder Richard G. Scott** of the Quorum of the Twelve dedicated the country for the preaching of the gospel. At the beginning of the year 2000, there were 311 baptized members in Mozambique, residing in 3 official branches, with many more waiting to be baptized.

SOURCES

Hollsinger, Don. Interview by E. Dale LeBaron. Brigham Young University, 21 April 1998.

Middleton, John, ed. *Encyclopedia of Africa South of the Sahara.* 4 vols. New York: Macmillan Library Reference USA, 1997. 92–98.

1999–2000 Church Almanac. Salt Lake City: Deseret News, 1998. 359.

Oral histories of early Church converts collected by E. Dale LeBaron. Copies at BYU Library, Provo, Utah; LDS Church Historical Library, Salt Lake City, Utah.

E. DALE LEBARON

MUDDY MISSION. During a **general conference** in the fall of 1864, **Anson Call** of Davis County, **Utah**, was directed by the **First Presidency** to find a place for a warehouse and landing on the **Colorado** River in

Nevada, establish a road, and build up a colony of **Saints** nearby. On 8 January 1865, the first missionaries arrived at what would be called the Muddy Mission.

Villages were built at St. Thomas, St. Joseph, Simonsville, and other sites in the Muddy Valley. Those called to serve there struggled with the heat, primitive conditions, and isolation. Poor relations with local **Native Americans** resulted in a call to centralize their efforts, but the settlements did not thrive.

Early in 1870 **Brigham Young** went to the Muddy and observed the desolate situation of the Saints. As a result, he released them from their responsibilities, allowing them to return to their former homes or move to more successful areas.

SOURCES

Fleming, L. A. "The Settlements on the Muddy: 1865 to 1871—'A God-forsaken place.'" *Utah Historical Quarterly* (Spring 1967): 147–72.

Godfrey, Audrey M. "Colonizing the Muddy River Valley: A New Perspective." *Journal of Mormon History* (Fall 1996): 120–42.

AUDREY M. GODFREY

MURDOCK, JOHN. John Murdock, a valiant missionary and Church leader, was the first **mission president** in **Australia**. He was born 15 July 1792 in Kortwright, **New York**, to John and Eleanor Murdock. **Parley P. Pratt** baptized him 5 November 1830 in **Kirtland, Ohio**, while Pratt was traveling to **Missouri** on a **mission** to the **Lamanites**. John's wife, Julia, died six hours after giving birth to twins, leaving him to raise five children. The twin babies were given to Joseph and **Emma Smith** to raise.

According to the **Prophet's** promise, John Murdock beheld the face of the Savior in vision while attending the **School of the Prophets** in the spring of 1833. He traveled to Missouri as a member of **Zion's Camp** in 1834. John served in the Church on **high councils** in **Far West** and **Salt Lake City** and presided as **bishop** both in **Nauvoo** and in the Salt Lake Fourteenth **Ward**. He also presided over a mission in Australia in 1851. Upon returning home to Lehi, **Utah**, he was ordained a **patriarch**. He died 23 December 1871 in Beaver, Utah, having been a faithful member of the Church since his baptism.

SOURCES

Black, Susan Easton. *Who's Who in the Doctrine and Covenants*. Salt Lake City: Bookcraft, 1997. 201–4.

Jenson, Andrew. *Latter-day Saint Biographical Encyclopedia.* 4 vols. 1901–36. Reprint, Salt Lake City: Western Epics, 1971. 2:362–64.

John Murdock Journal. Typescript. Special Collections, Brigham Young University Library, Provo, Utah.

CRAIG J. OSTLER

MURPHY, DALE. As a baseball all-star, **bishop**, and **mission president**, Dale Murphy was one of the best-known and most respected Latter-day Saints in the later twentieth century. He was born 12 March 1956 in Portland, **Oregon**, to Charles Milton and Betty Louise Bryan Murphy. An exceptional high school baseball player, Dale became the first draft pick of the Atlanta Braves in 1974. He spent the next four years playing in the minor leagues. He became interested in Mormonism in 1975 when he saw one of his teammates, Barry Bonnell, reading the **Book of Mormon** on the bus at night with the help of a flashlight. Dale was baptized later that year at the end of the baseball season. On 29 October 1979 he married Nancy Thomas in the **Salt Lake Temple**. They became the parents of eight children.

Dale played major league baseball from 1977 to 1993, all but two and one half years for Atlanta. During his career he won two Most Valuable Player awards, five Gold Gloves, played in seven All-Star Games and hit 398 home runs. The Braves retired his number in 1994.

After Dale retired from baseball he moved to Alpine, **Utah**, where he served as a **high councilor**, bishop, and stake president's counselor. He presided over the Massachusetts Boston **Mission** from 1997 to 2000.

SOURCES

Church News, 1 March 1997. 5.

Murphy, Dale. *Murph.* Salt Lake City: Bookcraft, 1986.

1998 Braves Media Guide. Atlanta: Tucker/Castleberry, 1998. 309.

ARNOLD K. GARR

MUSEUM OF CHURCH HISTORY AND ART. Since its opening in April 1984, the Museum of Church History and Art has expanded a long-standing Church commitment to collect, care for, and interpret important objects related to Latter-day Saint history. The museum presents historical exhibitions on major themes from Church history and highlights other historical and religious topics. Exhibits feature historical artifacts, **art**, architectural elements, photographs, books, manuscripts, films, maps, and models.

The Church museum builds on an interest launched by **Lucy Mack Smith** in **Kirtland**, promoted by **Philo Dibble** and others in **Nauvoo** and **Winter Quarters**, and first realized when **John W. Young** and Guglielmo G. R. Sangiovanni launched the Salt Lake Museum and Menagerie in 1869. Known for most of the next half-century as the **Deseret** Museum, Young's education-oriented institution reached its professional pinnacle in the 1890s under Dr. **James E. Talmage**. The museum closed in 1918 and dispersed its natural history specimens to area universities. Historical and prehistorical materials joined a small collection on **Temple Square**. The Temple Square **Mission** shepherded and expanded this assemblage in the LDS Church Museum, an annex to the Bureau of Information. When the Bureau closed in 1976, the collection moved first to storage and then to a new 60,500-square-foot facility west of the **Salt Lake Tabernacle**. As the heir of a century-old collection, the Museum of Church History and Art adopted new professional standards for storing, cataloging, and displaying the artifacts and accepted a stewardship over headquarters art.

The museum presents major Church history themes in two long-term exhibitions, *A Covenant Restored* and *Presidents of the Church*. Supplementing these mainstays are *Portraits of Church Leaders, Foundations of Latter-day Saint Art,* and numerous short-term displays. Temporary exhibits have included images of **Joseph Smith**, the Paris art missionaries, the **Salt Lake Temple** centennial, the **Relief Society** sesquicentennial, New Testament themes for children, triennial international art competitions, **Native American** art, and the history of the Church **welfare program** and **humanitarian aid**.

Besides exhibits, the museum offers group tours, school outreach, children's interactive activities, lectures, films, a museum store, and other educational programs. The museum restores and furnishes Church historical sites, marks other sites, and helps prepare interpretive materials for site missionaries.

Annual attendance of a mostly regional audience averages three hundred thousand. Admission is free, and the museum is open daily, including most holidays.

SOURCES

Eubanks, Lila Carpenter. "The Deseret Museum." *Utah Historical Quarterly* 50 (Fall 1982): 361–76.

Jacobsen, Florence Smith. "LDS Museums." *Encyclopedia of Mormonism.* Edited by Daniel H. Ludlow. 4 vols. New York: Macmillan, 1992. 2:971–73.

Leonard, Glen M. "Antiquities, Curiosities, and Latter-day Saint Museums." *The Disciple as Witness: Essays in Honor of Richard Lloyd Anderson.* Edited by Stephen D. Ricks, Donald W. Parry, and Andrew H. Hedges. Provo: Foundation for Ancient Research & Mormon Studies, 2000.

GLEN M. LEONARD

MUSIC. Music has always played a vital role in the spiritual and cultural life of Latter-day Saints. In the early days of the Church, **hymns** were an important part of members' daily lives, as were folk songs and other forms of traditional music. Music was an expression of faith and testimony. It gave the Saints hope and courage. It was used to comfort and console, to entertain, and to bring enrichment to life. It was a source of strength to the early **Saints** as they sought to live the gospel through times of trial and testing. It sustained them as they crossed the plains.

Music and other arts were fostered under **Brigham Young's** leadership as soon as the Saints were settled in the **Salt Lake Valley**. The **Tabernacle Organ** and the Mormon **Tabernacle Choir** are reminders of this legacy. Music also thrived in **Mormon** settlements established throughout the West, providing a source of recreation as well as spiritual uplift. Bands and other musical organizations flourished, and the weekly choir practice was often the social centerpiece of a community.

The hymns of the Church were established from the beginning as the basic musical form of worship. One of the first **revelations** given to the **Prophet Joseph Smith** after the **organization of the Church** instructed **Emma Smith** to "make a selection of sacred hymns" (D&C 25:11). In 1835 she published *"A Collection of Sacred Hymns, for the Church of the Latter Day Saints."* This first hymnbook stands as a foundation of the Church's musical tradition, with almost a third of its texts still found in the current hymnbook.

Many hymnbook editions have been published through the ensuing decades. In 1985 an edition was issued as a sesquicentennial commemoration of Emma Smith's original hymnbook. This new hymnbook serves as a resource for the Church **meetings**, including congregational singing, choirs, prelude music, and special musical selections. It is also used by Latter-day Saint families and individual members.

Hymns in this publication were "selected to meet the varied needs of today's worldwide Church membership" (*Hymns,* ix). This hymnbook has been translated into over 20 languages, with more to come. Smaller

selections of hymns and children's songs, often included as part of the
Gospel Principles manual, have also been published in almost 100 languages to serve the developing areas of the Church.

Today the Church continues to foster music as an important tool to
bless Latter-day Saints, to fill homes with the sound of worthy music, to
inspire love and unity among **family** members, to bring a spirit of beauty
and peace into homes, and to serve as a source of strength and blessing in
the personal lives of members (See *Hymns*, x). Music also remains an
important element in Church meetings. Improving congregational
singing, establishing ward choirs, fostering effective and appropriate
music, and meeting music training needs continue to be important
focuses as the Church establishes its global presence.

SOURCE

Hymns of The Church of Jesus Christ of Latter-day Saints. Salt Lake City: The Church of
    Jesus Christ of Latter-day Saints, 1985.

MICHAEL F. MOODY

"MUSIC AND THE SPOKEN WORD." "Music and the Spoken
Word," the traditional Sunday program of the **Mormon Tabernacle
Choir**, first aired in 1929, making it the longest continuous network
broadcast (CBS Radio) in the world. The weekly program made its **television** debut in 1962 and is now broadcast by more than 600 **radio**
stations, television stations, and cable systems throughout the **United
States** and in several other countries. The Choir broadcast originates
from the **Tabernacle** on **Temple Square** each Sunday at 9:30 A.M. (MT)
and is open to the public. "Music and the Spoken Word" is produced and
distributed by Bonneville Communications and began on station **KSL** in
Salt Lake City.

The program is 30 minutes long and consists of sacred **hymns** and
choral works accompanied by the **Tabernacle organ**, as well as a two-
and-a-half minute inspirational message, the "Spoken Word," delivered
by the choir announcer. For seven decades and thousands of broadcasts,
the opening hymn has remained "Gently Raise the Sacred Strain," and
the signature signoff is "May peace be with you, this day and always."

For 41 years **Richard L. Evans** inspired millions of listeners as the
voice, producer, and writer of the program (1930–71). He was followed

by J. Spencer Kinard (1972–90) and then Lloyd D. Newell (beginning in 1990) as announcer and "voice of the Tabernacle Choir."

SOURCES

Evans, Paul H. "Mormon Tabernacle Choir Broadcast." *Encyclopedia of Mormonism.* Edited by Daniel H. Ludlow. 4 vols. New York: Macmillan, 1992. 2:952.
"Tabernacle Choir Broadcasts 3,500th Program." *Ensign* 26 (November 1996): 109–10.

LLOYD D. NEWELL

MUSLIMS. The historical and doctrinal association between Muslims and **Mormons** dates from the earliest period of Latter-day **Saint** Church history and has often been explored by both LDS and non-LDS commentators. The first Church members to experience prolonged exposure to Muslim languages, cultures, and religious beliefs were the missionaries who served (beginning in 1884) in **Turkey, Syria, Lebanon,** and **Palestine**, countries which all have predominant or significant Muslim populations. Although the early missionaries focused their labors among the Christian Armenian and expatriate European communities, their daily interaction with Muslims heightened awareness of the Church's relationship to Islam and produced a growing body of personal correspondence and published materials dealing with this theme.

Since the final closure of the Near East Mission in 1951, Church members continued to have a significant presence in Muslim areas such as the Levant, North **Africa**, the Gulf, and the **Indonesian** archipelago. By adopting a policy of nonproselyting in Islamic countries of the **Middle East**, the Church has sought to respect Islamic laws and traditions that prohibit conversion of Muslims to other faiths. Greater contact between Muslims and Latter-day Saints worldwide has led to increased interfaith dialogue and cooperation in recent years: visits of Muslim dignitaries and delegations at Church headquarters in **Salt Lake City**; Muslim use of Church canning facilities to produce *halal* (ritually clean) food products; Church humanitarian aid and disaster relief sent to numerous Muslim countries; academic agreements and cultural exchanges between **Brigham Young University** and various educational and governmental institutions in the Islamic world; and the existence of the Muslim Student Association at BYU.

Treatment of Mormon-Muslim parallels by non-LDS Christian authors has been, for the most part, polemical in nature, intended to disparage **Joseph Smith** and the Church by making superficial comparisons to the arch-rival of Western civilization, Muhammad, the prophet of Islam. These writings typically dwell on **plural marriage**; the humble origins and charismatic leadership of two false prophets, both dangerous enemies of Christianity; persecution and exodus; the sensuous, "unspiritual" nature of Mormon and Muslim theology; and the ideas of covenant and community.

Generally speaking, Latter-day Saint writings have portrayed Mormonism's relationship to Islam in a positive light. Some early editorials in the *Times and Seasons* reflect traditional Christian antipathy toward Islam. But Latter-day Saint leaders **George A. Smith** and **Parley P. Pratt**, speaking in **general conference** in 1855, treated extensively and in complimentary terms the role of Islam in religious history. More contemporary Latter-day Saint authors have noted that the Church teaches many principles and values that Muslims share: faith in God, belief in **prophets**, emphasis on strong families, giving to the poor, fasting, prayer, honesty, hard work, and loyal citizenship. While there are many commonalities between Islam and Mormonism, some fundamental tenets of LDS thought contradict Muslim belief: the divinity of **Jesus Christ**, eternal progression, an anthropomorphic **God**, modern **scriptures**, and continuing **revelation** through living prophets.

SOURCES

Green, Arnold H. "World Religions (Non-Christian) and Mormonism: Islam." *Encyclopedia of Mormonism*. Edited by Daniel H. Ludlow. 4 vols. New York: Macmillan, 1992. 4:1592–93.

Palmer, Spencer J., ed. *Mormons and Muslims*. Provo, Utah: Religious Studies Center, Brigham Young University, 1983.

Peterson, Daniel C. *Abraham Divided: An LDS Perspective on the Middle East*. Rev. ed. Salt Lake City: Aspen Books, 1995.

Pratt, Parley P. *Journal of Discourses*. 26 vols. London: Latter-day Saints' Book Depot, 1854–86. 3:38, 41.

Smith, George A. *Journal of Discourses*. 26 vols. London: Latter-day Saints' Book Depot, 1854–86. 3:31–32.

Toronto, James A. "Islam." *Religions of the World: A Latter-day Saint View*. Edited by Spencer J. Palmer, et al. Provo, Utah: Brigham Young University, 1997. 213–41.

JAMES A. TORONTO

MUSSER, AMOS MILTON. Amos Milton Musser was a prominent and vocal defender of the faith in territorial **Utah**. Born 20 May 1830 in Donegal Township, Lancaster County, **Pennsylvania**, Musser joined the

Church in 1851 and traveled to Utah that same year. He spent the rest of his life building up the kingdom, spiritually and physically.

Musser was one of the first missionaries to **India** in 1853. After his return he served 18 years as a traveling **bishop** for the Church. He was also assistant **Church historian**, superintendent of the **Deseret Telegraph**, and territorial fish and game commissioner. Musser introduced both the telephone and telegraph into Utah. He died in Salt Lake City on 24 September 1909.

SOURCES

Britsch, R. Lanier. *Nothing More Heroic: The Compelling Story of The First Latter-day Saint Missionaries in India.* Salt Lake City: Deseret Book, 1999.

Brooks, Karl. "The Life of Amos Milton Musser." Master's thesis, Brigham Young University, 1961.

CRAIG L. FOSTER

MUTUAL IMPROVEMENT ASSOCIATION. The Mutual Improvement Association, also known as MIA, was part of the title of both the **Young Men's** and **Young Women's** organizations of the Church until the 1970s. When the transcontinental railroad came to Utah in 1869, Brigham Young was concerned that it would subject Church members to worldly influences, and that the young women might become discontent with their unassuming and virtuous lifestyle. This concern resulted in the 1875 organization of the Young Ladies Mutual Improvement Association, with Ella V. Empey as president. Initially called the Young Ladies Department of the Cooperative **Retrenchment** Association, President Young's plea was for young women to "retrench" in their diet, dress, and speech. The title Young Women's Mutual Improvement Association (YWMIA) was adopted in 1934.

In June of 1875, President Young appointed **Junius F. Wells** to organize the Young Men's Mutual Improvement Association (YMMIA), beginning with the **Salt Lake** Thirteenth **Ward**. H. A. Woolley was called as its first president, and 19-year-old **Heber J. Grant** as a **counselor**. By 1876 there were 57 associations formed with 1,200 members. From 1879 to 1899, the *Contributor,* a monthly periodical edited by **Elder** Wells, was the official organ of the Young Men's association. It was soon followed with the YMMIA general board's publication of the *Improvement Era.* During the 1970s the title Mutual Improvement Association (and its acronym MIA) was dropped from the name of both organizations. In

1974 the girls auxiliary was named simply Young Women, and in 1977 the boys organization became known as "Young Men."

SOURCES

Encyclopedia of Mormonism. Edited by Daniel H. Ludlow. 4 vols. New York: Macmillan, 1992. 2:565, 621; 3:1223, 1617.

Improvement Era 1 (December 1897): 85–93.

Jenson, Andrew. *Encyclopedic History of The Church of Jesus Christ of Latter-day Saints.* Salt Lake City: Deseret News, 1941. 968–70.

KIM C AVERETT

NAUVOO. Bishop Edward Hunter's two-story brick home in Nauvoo, the city that was the gathering place for the Saints between 1839 and 1846.

NADAULD, MARGARET D.

NADAULD, MARGARET D. In October 1997 Margaret Dyreng Nadauld was called as the general president of the **Young Women**. Born 21 November 1944 in **Manti, Utah**, to R. Morgan and Helen Bailey Dyreng, Margaret married Stephen D. Nadauld on 19 July 1968. They became the parents of seven sons. Margaret received a B.S. in secondary **education** from **Brigham Young University** in 1967. Before her appointment as Young Women president, she served on the **Relief Society** general board. She also supported her husband in his responsibilities as president of **Weber State** College, as a **regional representative**, and as a member of the Second Quorum of the **Seventy** from 1991 to 1996.

SOURCE

Dockstader, Julie A. "Prayer Sustained Her in Childhood, Now As Youth Leader." *Church News,* 18 October 1997, 11.

MARY JANE WOODGER

NAMES OF THE CHURCH. See CHURCH, NAMES OF.

NAMIBIA. The Republic of Namibia was known as South West Africa until 1990, when it became an independent nation. Its citizens speak Afrikaans, English, German, and indigenous languages. In 1999, 90% were Christian, predominantly Lutheran.

The LDS Church was not formally organized in Namibia until 1973. Otto Krauss became the presiding **elder**, and the first missionaries, Elders Daniel Gustafson and Douglas Stone of the **South Africa** Johannesburg **Mission**, arrived in 1978. In October of that year, Church members made a 2,000-mile round trip to join 5,000 other **Saints** at the South Africa **area conference** with Presidents **Spencer W. Kimball** and N. **Eldon Tanner** and Elders **Gordon B. Hinckley**, **Neal A. Maxwell**, and James A. Cullimore.

In 1983 Namibia's first **branch** was organized in Windhoek with Dieter Greiner as president. On 22 August 1992, Elder **Russell M. Nelson** dedicated Namibia for the preaching of the gospel. Andre Van der Merwe was the first missionary called from Namibia, serving in the South Africa Johannesburg Mission in 1992. By the beginning of the year 2000 there were 261 members living in 1 branch.

SOURCES

Middleton, John, ed. *Encyclopedia of Africa South of the Sahara.* 4 vols. New York: Macmillan Library Reference USA, 1997. 3:262–69.

Newman, Mark, and Greg Hagen. "Gospel Springs Forth in Harsh Desert Land of New African Nation." *Church News,* 5 October 1991, 8.

1999–2000 Church Almanac. Salt Lake City: Deseret News, 1998. 359–60.

Oral histories of early Church converts collected by E. Dale LeBaron. Copies at BYU Library, Provo, Utah; LDS Church Historical Library, Salt Lake City, Utah.

E. DALE LEBARON

NAPELA, JONATANA. Napelakapuonamahanaonaleleonalani (Jonatana Napela), a great Church leader in Hawaii, was born 11 September 1813 of royal parentage. During a **mission** to **Hawaii**, Elder George Q. Cannon was led to Napela, and he and his wife, Kiti, were baptized 5 January 1852.

After his baptism, Napela preached the gospel almost every Sunday and became a steward of **tithing** funds. In 1853 he began teaching new elders the Hawaiian language. When the mission in Hawaii was closed (1858–64), Napela gave civility and courtesy, but not support, to the apostate **Walter Gibson**, self-appointed Church leader for the islands.

In 1873 Kiti contracted leprosy, requiring her to live in the leper colony at Kalaupapa. Napela joined her, and they became leaders in the colony. Napela finally contracted leprosy and died 6 August 1879 in Kalaupapa, Molokai. Kiti died two years later.

During the dedicatory prayer of the **Hawaii Temple**, President **Heber J. Grant** said, "We thank Thee for raising up Thy servant Elder J. H. Napela, that devoted Hawaiian, who assisted Thy servant President **George Q. Cannon** in the translation of the **Book of Mormon**" (Lundwall, 153).

SOURCES

Lundwall, N. B., comp. *Temples of the Most High.* Salt Lake City: Bookcraft, 1947.

McKay, David O. *Cherished Experiences from the Writings of David O. McKay.* Compiled by Clare Middlemiss. Salt Lake City: Deseret Book, 1976.

Spurrier, Joseph H. *Sandwich Island Saints.* Oahu, Hawaii: J. H. Spurrier, 1989.

JAN FELIX

NATIVE AMERICANS. The indigenous peoples of North America have always occupied a special position in Latter-day Saint theology. Among them are descendants of the **Book of Mormon** peoples who were of the house of Israel through Joseph.

Joseph Smith understood the role Native Americans were to play in the **Restoration.** Just six months after the founding of the Church, he sent four men, including two **witnesses of the Book of Mormon,** "into the wilderness among the **Lamanites.**" This "**Lamanite Mission**" was generally well received by the Catteraugus, Wyandot, Shawnee, and **Delaware Indians.**

In the West, with motives both religious and practical, **Brigham Young** encouraged the **pioneers** to "feed rather than fight" the Indians. President Young authorized **missions** in 1855 to the Eastern **Shoshone** of **Wyoming** and to the Lemhi Shoshone in **Idaho's** Salmon River country. Other missionary activity was carried out among the **Utes,** Paiutes, Gosiutes, **Navajo,** Hopi, and Zuni in the West, and among the Catawba in **South Carolina.**

In the nineteenth century, the Church established a handful of farms, mostly in **Utah,** where Native Americans could be taught both Mormonism and agrarianism. Most of these farms did not survive long, but the **Washakie** community in Box Elder County, Utah, home to the Northwestern Shoshone, thrived for 80 years.

Early in the twentieth century, the Church established a presence at Fort Peck, **Montana,** among the Sioux and Assiniboin tribes. Many joined the Church. Similar efforts were undertaken at a few other reservations. With the encouragement of **Elder George Albert Smith,** the Navajo-Zuni Mission was formed in 1943 (later expanded into the Southwest Indian Mission). In 1964 the Northern Indian Mission, with headquarters in **South Dakota,** was formed.

The **Indian Placement Program,** adopted by the Church in 1954, attempted to improve educational opportunities for Indian children by placing them during the school year with Latter-day Saint families. At its high point in the early 1970s, the program involved 7,000 children yearly. The Church also began the Indian **Seminary Program** in the 1950s.

Eventually it spread to nearly 200 federal and public schools. The program was merged with the seminary system between 1980 and 1982.

SOURCES

Dibble, Charles E. "The Mormon Mission to the Shoshoni Indians." *Utah Humanities Review* 1 (January, April, July 1947): 53–73, 166–77, 279–93.

Whittaker, David J. "Mormons and Native Americans: A Historical and Bibliographical Introduction." *Dialogue* 18 (Winter 1985): 33–64.

SCOTT R. CHRISTENSEN

NAURU. Nauru is a small, one-island nation in the middle of the Pacific and is one of the wealthiest countries on earth because of its rich phosphate deposits. The earliest members of the Church from Nauru actually joined while residing in the nearby country of **Kiribati**. Following their stay, they returned to Nauru with the gospel. In 1995 the first **branch** was organized, with Taoki Buautua of Kiribati called as president. On 10 August 1996, at a former **World War II** battle spot on the beach at Betio, Tarawa, Kiribati, **Elder L. Tom Perry** dedicated a total of four countries, one being Nauru, and three provinces of **France** for the preaching of the gospel.

In 1999 Jean Tefan, president of the **Fiji**-Suva Mission, traveled to Nauru regularly to do **missionary work**. As of 1999 no full-time missionaries had been assigned to this country, but by the end of the year Nauru had a **branch** with 96 members.

SOURCES

"Elder Perry Creates First Kiribati Stake, Dedicates Islands." *Church News*, 21 September 1996, 3.

Fiji-Suva Mission Historical Report. Archives, Historical Department, The Church of Jesus Christ of Latter-day Saints, Salt Lake City.

1999–2000 Church Almanac. Salt Lake City: Deseret News, 1998. 360.

W. JAMES JACOB

NAUVOO, BATTLE OF. Only a few Latter-day Saints still lived in **Hancock County, Illinois**, the summer of 1846. Though most of the **Saints** were emigrating west, about 600 of the poor and sick still resided in Nauvoo. They became worried when accounts reached **Nauvoo** of Mormons being whipped in outlying areas. Many so-called new citizens had purchased Mormon homes and property, and remaining Saints were concerned that non-Mormons were making plans to drive all the Latter-day Saints from Nauvoo. Their fears were realized when the **anti-Mormons** again united in what detractors called "a renegade Army," captained by James W. Singleton and Thomas S. Brockman. In late August they decided to launch an attack against the City of Joseph (Nauvoo).

Learning of their plans, Jack Carlin organized the new citizens and the few able-bodied Latter-day Saints and prepared to defend the city. This makeshift army manned two cannons crafted from a steamboat shaft and a barricade on the north side of Mullholland Street facing Carthage. The anti-Mormon forces camped one mile east of the city on property owned by **William Law** near **Joseph Smith's** farm. War, everyone knew, was imminent.

The Latter-day Saints had a prayer meeting each morning at the **temple** and asked **God** to protect them. On 10 September there was some firing, and Nauvoo's army hid in a cornfield hoping to ambush the enemy. There were brief skirmishes on 11 and 12 September, which included some gunfire, but it was early on the morning of 13 September when the anti-Mormon forces began their march on the city. Cannons roared, banners waved, and the smoke of muskets filled the Nauvoo air. Latter-day Saints retreated, firing from buildings and through windows, but they were no match for the superior forces. The battle lasted one hour and 45 minutes, and the city's defenders were forced to the river, but not before several were killed. At the water's edge they signaled their surrender. The citizens gave up their arms, and the Latter-day Saints said they would depart. The army agreed to protect the sick and the helpless. **Daniel H. Wells**, not a Latter-day Saint at this time, helped negotiate the peace accord, which was signed 16 September 1846.

After the agreement was signed, a mob in violation of its provisions overran the city, threw many Saints into the river, and desecrated the temple. As in February, long lines of Saints, together with their wagons and cattle, were seen crossing the river, and a tent city arose on the **Iowa** side. **Emma Smith** escaped the battle with her family and friends by going north to Fulton City, Iowa. Mormon Nauvoo was no more.

SOURCES

Miller, David E., and Della S. Miller, *Nauvoo: City of Joseph.* Santa Barbara: Peregrine Smith, 1974. 199–202.

Roberts, B. H. *A Comprehensive History of The Church of Jesus Christ of Latter-day Saints, Century One.* 6 vols. Salt Lake City: The Church of Jesus Christ of Latter-day Saints, 1930. 2–23.

KENNETH W. GODFREY

NAUVOO, ILLINOIS. Beginning in 1839, Nauvoo served as the gathering place and headquarters of The Church of Jesus Christ of Latter-day Saints. The city grew so rapidly that it rivaled Chicago in population. Latter-day Saint refugees from **Missouri** lived first in **Quincy** and then in Commerce, **Illinois**. They made their first land purchases at Commerce in May 1839, and additional property was purchased later.

In July 1839 the **Saints** began to feel the effects of their suffering in Missouri. Their weakened condition, coupled with the malaria-infested swampland along the **Mississippi**, caused many to fall ill with ague, fever, malaria, and typhoid. Although ill himself, **Joseph Smith** arose from his bed and went about healing the sick. One of the most remarkable examples of faith-healing in LDS history, which **Wilford Woodruff** called "a day of God's power," occurred at this time as Joseph Smith visited **Elijah Fordham**. The **Prophet** commanded him in the name of **Jesus Christ** to be made well. Elijah got up from his bed, ate a bowl of bread and milk, and then assisted Joseph Smith in healing others. In the midst of poverty, sickness, and the task of building a new city, the Twelve started on their mission to **England**. Their valiant efforts paid rich dividends because the **mission of the Twelve** reaped a bountiful harvest of souls.

In August 1839 Joseph Smith named the new settlement Nauvoo, declaring that the name was Hebrew for beautiful situation (the name of the post office was not changed from Commerce to Nauvoo until April 1840).

In the summer of 1840 the first converts from England arrived in Nauvoo. In August 1840 the Prophet first taught the doctrine of **baptism for the dead** in a funeral sermon for Seymour Brunson. In December 1840 the **Nauvoo Charter** was granted by the state of Illinois. This charter proved to be a great blessing for the citizens of Nauvoo because it afforded them a measure of self-government. The **First Presidency** described the Charter as one of the most liberal ever granted. It went into effect with the municipal election in February 1841. It also provided for the creation of the **University of Nauvoo** and the **Nauvoo Legion**. The City Council created these two institutions soon after the first election.

In March 1841 work began on the **Nauvoo Temple**, in accordance with a revelation received in January of that year (D&C 124). During construction the Saints discovered they could not find the pine lumber they needed in Illinois, so they opened the **Wisconsin** Pineries in the Black River Falls area. Those involved in this project cut timber and formed it into rafts, which they floated downstream to Nauvoo. As construction on the temple progressed, baptisms for the dead were moved, in November 1841, from the Mississippi River to the font of the unfinished building.

In December Joseph Smith opened his **Red Brick Store**. This two-story building on Water Street became the hub of community activity as well as a general store. It ranks as one of the most important buildings in Nauvoo. On 15 March 1842 the Nauvoo Masonic Lodge was formed there, and two days later the Nauvoo Female **Relief Society** was organized in the large assembly room on the second floor. In May the first endowments were initiated on the upper floor of the store. That same month Joseph became the mayor of Nauvoo, and **Stephen A. Douglas** visited the city. During the summer, while across the river in Montrose, Joseph Smith prophesied that the Saints would eventually move to the Rocky Mountains.

In 1843 someone attempted to kill former Governor **Lilburn Boggs** of Missouri and suspicion focused on Joseph Smith and **Orrin Porter Rockwell**. To clear himself of all charges, the Prophet agreed to appear before Judge Nathaniel Pope in Springfield, Illinois. After listening to all arguments, Judge Pope cleared Joseph Smith of any involvement in the Boggs case. While he was in the Illinois capital Joseph Smith had the opportunity to meet with several prominent people, including Stephen A. Douglas, Justin Butterfield, and Governor Thomas Ford, to explain some of the tenets of Mormonism.

The year 1843 was significant in relation to **plural marriage**. In May, for example, Eliza and Emily Partridge were sealed to Joseph Smith. **Emma Smith** had chosen the Partridge sisters as wives for her husband.

In 1843 there was more trouble with Missouri. Governor Ford of Illinois, acting upon the request of Governor Reynolds of Missouri, issued an arrest warrant for Joseph Smith. In the meantime Joseph Smith was arrested while he was visiting relatives near Dixon, Illinois. Eventually, Joseph and others appeared in court in Nauvoo, where Joseph was released on a writ of habeas corpus. Thus, Nauvoo officials overturned an order of the governor of Illinois.

In August 1843 Joseph Smith and his family moved into the **Mansion House**, the first home they ever built for themselves. Part of the home was used as a hotel. Missionaries continued to leave for **missions** from Nauvoo, and emigrants continued to arrive there, primarily from England. Those arriving were mostly from the working classes, which had been adversely affected by deteriorating economic conditions in England.

In early 1844 Joseph Smith announced that he would run for the presidency of the **United States**. The **Council of Fifty** supported this **presidential campaign**, and political missionaries were sent out in April and May.

In the meantime a conspiracy had formed against Joseph Smith, with the Laws, Fosters, and Higbees as leaders. They succeeded in publishing only one issue of the *Nauvoo Expositor* on 7 June 1844. Given the inflammatory nature of the articles in the paper, the city council ordered the destruction of the press. This and other actions led to charges of treason against Joseph Smith. On 22 June Joseph and a few others crossed the Mississippi and planned to seek refuge somewhere in the West. After being accused by some friends of abandoning them, Joseph returned and went to Carthage to answer charges against him. On 25 June the Prophet and others were incarcerated in the **Carthage Jail**. Two days later, Joseph Smith and his brother Hyrum were martyred there. The next day their bodies were taken to Nauvoo. After a viewing and public funeral, they were buried secretly in the basement of the **Nauvoo House**.

On 8 August the Saints met to resolve the issue of **succession in the presidency**. **Brigham Young** was chosen to lead the Church in his role as president of the **Quorum** of the Twelve Apostles. Most of the Saints supported him, but a few chose to follow others. Work continued on the temple with the capstone being place on 23 September. In December the new **Seventies Hall** was dedicated.

In 1845 the Saints began to call Nauvoo "The City of Joseph," honoring the Prophet, because the city had lost its charter. Those accused of murdering him and his brother were acquitted in a jury trial. In the wake of this decision, hostilities escalated between Mormons and non-Mormons in **Hancock County**. Mobs burned the homes of several Latter-day Saints in outlying settlements. As a consequence of these events the Saints began preparations for their eventual journey across the plains. In the midst of such preparations, work continued on the temple. In late 1845 and early 1846 more than 5,000 Saints received their temple **endowments**. Nevertheless, the **exodus** from Nauvoo began when the first residents left the city on 4 February 1846. Even though most had departed, the Nauvoo Temple was dedicated in May. In September the **Battle of Nauvoo** took place, and within a month all had evacuated except for a few who were left behind to dispose of the Saints' property.

Much of the property that had belonged to the Latter-day Saints, including the temple, was acquired by a French communal group led by Etienne Cabet in 1849. He and some 500 followers, known as the

"**Icarians**," sought to establish a Utopian society in the midst of the deserted town site until Cabet and others were expelled after a power struggle in 1856. For the next hundred years, Nauvoo averaged a population of just over a thousand.

In 1962 the Latter-day Saints returned to Nauvoo with the founding of **Nauvoo Restoration, Incorporated** (NRI). NRI was the creation of **Dr. J. LeRoy Kimball**, who pioneered the effort to restore many Nauvoo homes from the 1840s. This effort continues, and each year Latter-day Saint missionaries host visitors in the restored buildings of old Nauvoo. In 1999 the Church began to build a new Nauvoo Temple on the site of the first one, which had been destroyed by fire and a tornado 150 years earlier.

SOURCES

Cannon, Janath R. *Nauvoo Panorama.* N.p.: Nauvoo Restoration, 1991.

Miller, David E. and Della S. *Nauvoo; City of Joseph.* Salt Lake City: Peregrine Smith, 1974.

DONALD Q. CANNON

NAUVOO CHARTER. Only a few months after the first Latter-day Saints settled on a horseshoe bend of the **Mississippi River**, the Church in December 1839 petitioned the **Illinois** state legislature "to define new boundaries of **Nauvoo** and Commerce" (Wall, 491). Nothing was done by the legislature at this time, so in the October 1840 semiannual **conference** of the Church, a committee composed of **Joseph Smith**, **John C. Bennett**, and Robert B. Thompson was appointed to draft a bill for the incorporation of the city of Nauvoo. After a one hour recess the committee reported to the conference the outlines of a charter (likely the document had been composed before the conference convened).

John C. Bennett was then authorized "to superintend the bill through the Legislature" (Wall, 492). The General Assembly met on 23 November and the second bill of the session, "an act to incorporate the city of Nauvoo," (Wall, 493) was introduced. Twenty-one days later the bill passed and Nauvoo became a city. Joseph Smith said that he had "concocted [the Nauvoo Charter] for the salvation of the Church" (Roberts). One of the reasons the charter passed legislative scrutiny so quickly was because it was similar to others that had already been granted to Chicago, Galena, Quincy, Springfield, and Alton.

The Nauvoo City Council "was granted authority to pass any laws not repugnant to the constitution of the **United States** or the constitution of Illinois" (Reinterpretation, 67). Thus, city officials could enact legislation without adhering to state laws, which made Nauvoo "truly a state within a state" (Reinterpretation, 67). The Charter contained 28 sections and authorized a council composed of four aldermen, nine councilors, and a mayor. It granted the formation of a municipal court, only the third such created in Illinois, and the mayor served as its chief justice with the aldermen doubling as associate justices. The city court possessed the power to issue writs of habeas corpus.

The Charter authorized the creation of the **University of Nauvoo**. The city council "possessed the authority to initiate and perpetuate appointments," whereas the boards of trustees of other Illinois universities were "named in the legislative act" (Reinterpretation, 75). Members of the board of trustees also served on the city council.

Section 25 of the Charter gave authority to establish a military organization known as the **Nauvoo Legion**. Officers of this legion received their commissions from the governor of the state. The Charter also created a "Court-Marshal to be composed of the commissioned officers of said legion" (Reinterpretation, 76).

The Latter-day Saints relied on the Nauvoo Charter "to be an unbreachable wall defending the rights of **Zion**" (Wall, 496). In contrast, "many of their non-Mormon neighbors came to view it as an offensive barrier" (Wall, 496) and argued that it "exacerbated the Mormon problem by isolating and thereby alienating the officers of the city from the rest of the county and state" (Wall, 496–97). Still the Latter-day Saints rejoiced when their charter was granted, providing them a government within a government.

SOURCES

Kimball, James L. Jr. "A Wall to Defend Zion: The Nauvoo Charter," *BYU Studies* 15 (Summer 1975): 491–97.

———. "The Nauvoo Charter: A Reinterpretation," *Journal of the Illinois State Historical Society* 64 (Spring 1971): 66–78.

Roberts, B. H. *A Comprehensive History of The Church of Jesus Christ of Latter-day Saints, Century One.* 6 vols. Salt Lake City: The Church of Jesus Christ of Latter-day Saints, 1930. 2:55.

KENNETH W. GODFREY

NAUVOO EXPOSITOR. The *Nauvoo Expositor* was a short-lived, dissenting newspaper published in **Nauvoo, Illinois**. Its purpose was to denounce the **Prophet Joseph Smith** and promote the "unconditional repeal of the Nauvoo city charter" (Smith, 6:443).

On 7 June 1844 the first and only issue of the **anti-Mormon** newspaper appeared, with Sylvester Emmons as editor. Angry local residents decried the false printed assertions and the negative depiction of religious life and politics in Nauvoo.

Joseph Smith, acting as mayor of Nauvoo, summoned the city council to discuss the explosive tensions between the newspaper proprietors and **Mormon** citizens that threatened peace in the community. The council reviewed the **United States** Constitution, the **Illinois** Constitution, and the **Nauvoo Charter** provisions during their 14 hours of deliberations. On Monday, 10 June 1844, the council resolved that the *Nauvoo Expositor* and its printing office were "disturbers of the peace" and that the paper was "a public nuisance" and should be removed "without delay" (Smith, 6:434, 448).

John P. Greene (city marshal and faithful Latter-day Saint) and members of the **Nauvoo Legion** destroyed the "press, type, printed paper, and fixtures" of the *Expositor* in two hours (Smith, 6:432). Although the swift action was heralded by many Nauvoo residents, it served to heighten anti-Mormon sentiment in nearby communities. The *Quincy Whig* denounced the destruction as "high-handed outrage." Legal charges, arrest warrants, incarceration, and the **martyrdom** of Joseph Smith and his brother Hyrum on 27 June 1844 stemmed from the destruction of the *Nauvoo Expositor.*

SOURCES

Oaks, Dallin H. "The Suppression of the *Nauvoo Expositor.*" *Utah Law Review* 9 (Winter 1965): 862–903.

Oaks, Dallin H., and Marvin S. Hill. *Carthage Conspiracy: The Trial of the Accused Assassins of Joseph Smith.* Urbana: University of Illinois Press, 1979.

Smith, Joseph. *History of The Church of Jesus Christ of Latter-day Saints.* Edited by B. H. Roberts. 2d ed. rev. 7 vols. Salt Lake City: The Church of Jesus Christ of Latter-day Saints, 1932–51. 1:60–61.

SUSAN EASTON BLACK

NAUVOO HOUSE. On 19 January 1841, the Lord commanded **Joseph Smith** to build a boarding house "unto his name," where traveler and Saint could "contemplate the glory of **Zion**" (D&C 124:60; D&C 124:22–24, 56–83, 111–22). Joseph Smith donated the land, and architects **William Weeks** and Lucien Woodworth drew plans for an L-shaped hotel. Construction began in 1841 and halted in 1844. "It [is] best to let the Nauvoo House remain as it is until the **temple** is completed," said Joseph Smith on 4 March 1844 (Smith, 6:230).

On 18 August 1845 work began anew, but construction stopped again because of persecution. It was not until the 1870s that the smaller Riverside Mansion or Bidamon House was erected from portions of the unfinished structure. Lewis Bidamon and his wife, **Emma Smith** Bidamon, resided in the house until their deaths.

Bishop E. L. Kelly, trustee in trust for the **Reorganized Church of Jesus Christ of Latter Day Saints**, purchased the house and surrounding acreage on 13 October 1909. The property remains in RLDS possession.

SOURCES

Holzapfel, Richard Neitzel, and T. Jeffery Cottle. *Old Mormon Nauvoo and Southeastern Iowa: Historic Photographs and Guide.* Santa Ana, Calif.: Fieldbrook Productions, 1990.

Shields, Steven L. *An Illustrated History of Nauvoo.* Independence, Mo.: Herald Publishing House, 1992.

Smith, Joseph. *History of The Church of Jesus Christ of Latter-day Saints.* Edited by B. H. Roberts. 2d ed. rev. 7 vols. Salt Lake City: The Church of Jesus Christ of Latter-day Saints, 1932–51. 1:60–61.

SUSAN EASTON BLACK

NAUVOO JOURNAL. See MORMON HISTORICAL STUDIES.

NAUVOO LEGION. The Nauvoo Legion was a unit of the **Illinois** state militia, created as part of the charter granted to the city of **Nauvoo** by the state legislature. Service in the Legion satisfied the military obligations required of adult males in the state. Entitled to a portion of public arms, the Legion was at the disposal of the mayor and governor to enforce laws and provide defense. The legislature provided that anyone in **Hancock County** could join the Legion, and **Joseph Smith** clearly stated that it was not to be an exclusively **Mormon** organization. The Legion was an important part of the parade on the occasion when the cornerstones were placed for the **Nauvoo Temple**. It was also called out at the time of the **Prophet's martyrdom** in June 1844, to guard Nauvoo from attack.

On 10 June 1843, the Legion authorized the building of an arsenal to house its arms. The site was located just west of the temple on Knight

Street. The arsenal was later used by the **Icarians**, then became part of St. Mary's Academy, and in 1967 was torn down.

In 1845 the state of Illinois revoked the **Nauvoo Charter**, ending the authority of the Legion. Some of its members felt they still had the right to defend their homes, and a few of its members were involved in the **Battle of Nauvoo** in September of 1846. Militias were organized during the forced **exodus** from Nauvoo and after the Saints' arrival in **Utah**. Although they had no connection to the state of Illinois, they were still called the Nauvoo Legion, to honor the Nauvoo organization.

SOURCE

Flammer, Philip M. "Nauvoo Legion." *Encyclopedia of Mormonism.* Edited by Daniel H. Ludlow. 4 vols. New York: Macmillan, 1992. 3:997–99.

MIKE TRAPP

NAUVOO NEIGHBOR. The *Nauvoo Neighbor,* which replaced the *Wasp,* was a secular paper published in **Nauvoo, Illinois,** nearly every Wednesday from May 1843 to November 1845. **John Taylor,** who was also editor of the *Times and Seasons,* enlarged and renamed the paper. The two publications were printed in the same building.

Although some articles initially appearing in the *Nauvoo Neighbor* were reprinted in the *Times and Seasons,* the two papers were different. The *Times and Seasons* was subsidized by the Church and maintained a religious orientation. The *Neighbor* included foreign, domestic, and local news, poetry, **literature**, advertisements, ordinances passed by the city council, and articles on religion, agriculture, homemaking, manufacturing, and commerce. The advertisements provide helpful insights into the multiple businesses established in that community.

SOURCE

Nauvoo Neighbor, 1843–45. Brigham Young University Library, Provo, Utah.

MILTON V. BACKMAN JR.

NAUVOO RESTORATION, INC. Nauvoo Restoration, Inc. (NRI), officially incorporated in July 1962, is the agency responsible for most of the historical restoration accomplished in the city of **Nauvoo, Illinois.** Organized by Dr. J. LeRoy Kimball under the "General Not for Profit Corporation Act" of the state of Illinois, NRI is now sponsored by The

Church of Jesus Christ of Latter-day Saints. NRI's stated objectives are "to acquire, restore, protect and preserve, for the education and benefit of its members and the public, all or a part of the old city of Nauvoo, Illinois, and the surrounding area, in order to provide an historically authentic physical environment for awakening a public interest in, and an understanding and appreciation of, the Story of Nauvoo." In order to achieve these goals, NRI works in cooperation with the Illinois State Historical Society and The National Park Service. By the year 2000 NRI had restored or developed more than 30 sites and properties in the historic village for tourists and visitors.

SOURCES

Baugh, Alexander. "Returning to Nauvoo." *Nauvoo Journal* 11:2 (Fall 1999): 1–3.

Holzapfel, Richard N., and Jeffrey Cottle. *Old Mormon Nauvoo*. Provo, Utah: Grandin, 1990. 67–68.

Nauvoo Restoration, Inc. *What Is Nauvoo Restoration, Incorporated?* Pamphlet. Nauvoo Restoration, Inc., 1970.

DONALD Q. CANNON

NAUVOO TEMPLE. The Nauvoo Temple, dedicated in 1846, was the second **temple** built by the Latter-day Saints. Because temple **ordinances** and **salvation for the dead** were revealed during the early 1840s, the Nauvoo Temple included accommodations for these sacred rites—a baptismal font in the basement and specialized rooms on the top floor. Like the earlier **Kirtland Temple**, the body of the building consisted of two large auditoriums, one above the other.

In 1839, following their expulsion from **Missouri**, the **Saints** began building what would become the city of **Nauvoo**. On 15 August 1840, **Joseph Smith** first taught that the **Saints** could be baptized in behalf of their deceased loved ones. A **revelation** received on 19 January 1841 affirmed that a font for these baptisms "belongeth to my house" and gave instructions for building the temple (D&C 124:25–44). On 6 April cornerstones were laid, and by November of that year the basement was enclosed and a baptismal font dedicated.

The first **endowments** were given 4 May 1842 in the large upper room of Joseph Smith's **Red Brick Store**. Following instructions (D&C 131:1–4) and a revelation on eternal marriage, recorded in 1843 (D&C 132), a number were performed.

Meanwhile, the Saints devoted their energies to building the temple. Joseph Smith, who testified he had seen the temple in **vision**, gave instructions to architect **William Weeks**. Light gray limestone was quarried nearby, while timber was brought from "pineries" in southern **Wisconsin**. Many donated every tenth working day to temple construction, while others contributed funds, notably Joseph Toronto's gift of $2,500 in gold coins. **Women** created a "penny fund" and, under the direction of Joseph Smith, were organized as the **Relief Society** to aid temple workmen.

Work on the temple was pushed forward even after the **martyrdom** of Joseph Smith on 27 June 1844, the capstone being placed 24 May 1845. The temple measured 128 by 88 feet, and its tower rose to a height of 165 feet. The temple's main floor "grand hall" seated 3,500; as at **Kirtland**, there were pulpits at each end, and the seating was reversible so the congregation could sit facing either direction. The temple's exterior featured ornamental moon, sun, and star stones, perhaps reminders of the three degrees of glory.

By December 1845, the temple's attic was completed to the point that ordinances could be inaugurated. The attic's central council hall was temporarily partitioned and furnished to represent stages in man's eternal progression back into the presence of God; here some 5,500 received their endowment. Small rooms along each side served as offices; some contained altars where sealings were performed. These ordinances went forward amid the hectic preparation for the **exodus** west, which got underway on 4 February 1846. Instructions that only those receiving the sacred ordinances should enter the temple may be the origin of the issuing of temple **recommends**.

Most of the Saints had left the area before the temple's formal dedication. The temple was dedicated in a private service on 30 April 1846 and also in a public ceremony the following day, when Elder **Orson Hyde** gave the dedicatory prayer. Following a devastating fire on 9 October 1848, believed to be arson, only the exterior walls remained standing. A portion of these were leveled by a tornado in 1850, and within a few years nothing was left standing.

The Church reacquired the site of the Nauvoo Temple in 1937. It was planted in grass, and a line of stones outlined the place where the temple had stood. In 1999 President **Gordon B. Hinckley** announced plans to rebuild the Nauvoo Temple, and on 24 October of that year, ground was broken and construction started.

SOURCES

Brown, Lisle G. "The Sacred Departments for Temple Work in Nauvoo: The Assembly Room and the Council Chamber." *BYU Studies* 19 (Spring 1979): 361–74.

Cowan, Richard O. *Temples to Dot the Earth*. Springville, Utah: Cedar Fort, 1997.

Kimball, Stanley Buchholz. "The Nauvoo Temple." *Improvement Era* 66 (November 1963): 974–82.

McGavin, E. Cecil. *The Nauvoo Temple*. Salt Lake City: Deseret Book, 1962.

RICHARD O. COWAN

NAVAJO INDIANS. The Navajo Indians, the largest tribe in the **United States**, numbered about 225,000 by the end of the twentieth century. Most lived in the Four Corners region of **Arizona**, **New Mexico**, and **Utah**. In 1855 **Mormon** missionaries from the Elk Mountain **Mission** in southeastern Utah were sent to trade and investigate the possibilities of engaging in missionary work among the Navajo. **Jacob Hamblin** was appointed president of the Southern Indian Mission in 1857. His efforts as missionary and diplomat helped to establish friendly relations between the Navajos and Latter-day Saints. After preaching to a large number of Navajos at Fort Defiance, Arizona, in 1870, Hamblin signed a treaty with the Navajo Headmen that allowed the Navajos to visit Utah to trade.

The first record of Navajos being baptized was in 1875 at Kanab. Latter-day Saint settlements were established among the Navajos on the San Juan River of southern Utah, west of the Hopi Mesas, and on the Little **Colorado** River in northeastern Arizona in the 1870s. Intense missionary activities took place among the Navajos between 1875 and 1887. Organized relations among the Navajos and Latter-day Saints did not resume until 1936, when the Snowflake Stake Mission actively began proselyting the Navajo with considerable success. The Snowflake Stake Mission later became the Southwest Indian Mission, and finally the Albuquerque Mission.

SOURCES

Flake, David Kay. *History of Southwest Indian Mission*. N.p., 1965.

Locke, Raymond Friday. *The Book of the Navajo*. Los Angeles: Mankind, 1976.

McPherson, Robert S. *The Northern Navajo Frontier, 1860–1900: Expansion through Adversity*. Albuquerque: University of New Mexico, [1988].

FRED R. GOWANS AND V. ROBERT WESTOVER

NEBRASKA. The area now known as Nebraska played an important role in Church history for a few critical years before being largely abandoned by the **Saints**. In recent decades the influence of the Church in Nebraska has again grown. In 1846 when Church members were forced to leave **Nauvoo**, they traveled for some 300 miles across **Iowa** into "**Indian** country." The exiled Saints arranged with the federal Indian agent to settle on the west banks of the **Missouri River** in the area they called **Winter Quarters**, where the city of Omaha, Nebraska, now lies.

The winter of 1846–47 was harsh, with many perishing on the banks of the Missouri River. The Saints were eager to move on to the West. The route used by the **pioneers** followed the **Platte river** southwest through Nebraska, then the North Platte northwest towards an important landmark known as Chimney Rock, then on to **Ft. Laramie**, in an area now part of **Wyoming**.

Converts to the Church continued to come to Winter Quarters to prepare for the journey west. But in the spring of 1848 they evacuated the settlement on request from Indian agents and moved back across the river to **Kanesville, Iowa**. Starting in 1854, the town of **Florence** was established at the site of Winter Quarters and soon became a thriving city. Tens of thousands of pioneer emigrants came there to be outfitted with wagons or **handcarts** for the thousand-mile journey to the **Salt Lake Valley**. Many of them worked in exchange for supplies, and so Church members were instrumental in helping to establish many of the towns in the area. Other Saints were called to build up settlements along the trail, such as Genoa (100 miles west of Florence), to assist future pioneers. The completion of the transcontinental railroad in 1869 changed the nature of emigration, and most of the Latter-day Saints left Nebraska.

After this time, **missionaries** did some work in Nebraska, often as part of journeys to other missions farther east. There were about a thousand members in the state by 1930. The first stake created in Nebraska was called the Winter Quarters Stake, organized in 1960 and including parts of Iowa. It was later renamed the Omaha Nebraska Stake. Additional stakes were created in 1974 (Bellevue Nebraska Stake, later renamed Lincoln Nebraska), 1986 (Papillion Nebraska, later renamed Omaha Nebraska Papillion), and 1991 (Kearney Nebraska). The Nebraska Omaha Mission was created in 1993. At the time, there were 1.9 million people living in the mission boundaries and a total of 12,532 members in four **stakes** and one **district**. By the beginning of the year 2000 there were 18,613 LDS members in Nebraska living in 54 **wards** and **branches**.

A new **Mormon Trails** Center was dedicated in Omaha in 1997 by President **Gordon B. Hinckley** at the original site of Winter Quarters. In 1999, the Church acquired rights to the "Mormon Pioneer Cemetery" (adjacent to the Center) from the city of Omaha, where several Saints were buried during the winter of 1846–47. Then, in 1999, construction began on the Omaha Nebraska Temple on 1.9 acres adjacent to the cemetery. The temple's name was soon changed to the Winter Quarters Nebraska Temple.

SOURCES

Bennett, Richard E. *Mormons at the Missouri, 1846–1852.* Oklahoma: University of Oklahoma Press, 1987.

1999–2000 Church Almanac. Salt Lake City: Deseret News, 1998.

DAVID KENISON

NELSON, RUSSELL M. Renowned heart surgeon Russell Marion Nelson was sustained as a member of the **Quorum** of the Twelve **Apostles** 7 April 1984. He was born 9 September 1924 in **Salt Lake City** to Marion C. and Edna Anderson Nelson. He married Dantzel White in 1945 in the **Salt Lake Temple**, and they became the parents of nine daughters and one son.

He graduated from college with highest honors, receiving both his B.A. and M.D. degrees from the **University of Utah**. He furthered his training at the University of **Minnesota**, where he received a Ph.D. While in Minnesota, he was involved in innovative research on a mechanical heart device. He then served two years as a physician in the U.S. Army. Upon his discharge, and after a brief term at **Massachusetts** General Hospital in Boston, he and his family returned to Salt Lake City. There he offered distinguished service at both the University of Utah and in private practice until his call to the apostleship. His accomplishments included the first open heart surgery in **Utah**. Additionally, he provided leadership in several medical organizations and wrote and lectured widely in his field. He also operated on **Spencer W. Kimball** before the latter became president of the Church. **Elder** Nelson's extensive experience in the Church before becoming a member of the Twelve included service as **stake president**, **regional representative**, and general **Sunday School** president.

SOURCES

"Elder Russell M. Nelson of the Quorum of the Twelve Apostles." *Ensign* 14 (April 1984): 87–88.

Nelson, Russell M. *From Heart to Heart: An Autobiography.* Salt Lake City: Nelson, 1979.

"New Apostle Has a Flair with the Heart." *Church News,* 22 April 1984, 4.

1997–1998 Church Almanac. Salt Lake City: Deseret News, 1996. 17.

ROBERT C. FREEMAN

NETHERLANDS. The Netherlands, also known as Holland, comprises 12 provinces, including those of North and South Holland. Dutch is the official language of this constitutional monarchy, located on the north-western boundaries of **Europe**, although Frisian is also spoken in the northern provinces. In 1998 the population was approximately 16 million. Although many thousands have joined the Church in the Netherlands over the years, significant numbers immigrated to America.

Elder Orson Hyde of the Quorum of the Twelve **Apostles** visited Jewish rabbis in Rotterdam and Amsterdam in 1841 en route to his **mission** in the **Holy Land**. His brochure "A Message to the Hebrews" was translated into Dutch.

Full-time **missionary work** began on 5 August 1861 with the arrival of two missionaries, Paul August Schettler and Anne Wiegers van der Woude. The first baptisms took place in Friesland on 1 October 1861. In 1936 a monument commemorating this event was erected near the site in Broeksterwoude. The first branch was organized in Amsterdam in 1862. The **Book of Mormon** was translated in 1890, and six years later the Dutch magazine, *De Ster,* began publication.

Missionary work began under the Swiss-Italian-German Mission, but on 1 November 1864 the Netherlands Mission was organized. To reflect the mission's labors with the Flemish-speaking people of northern **Belgium**, the name was changed on 31 January 1891 to the Netherlands-Belgium Mission. The name reverted to the Netherlands Mission on 15 May 1914, although missionary work continued in Flanders. On 10 June 1974 the **First Presidency** designated the name Netherlands Amsterdam Mission.

One of the most noteworthy events of the Church in the Netherlands was the magnanimous outpouring of love by Dutch **Saints** following **World War II**. In 1947 they grew and shipped 75 tons of potatoes to suffering German Saints, and the following year they sent another 90 tons of potatoes and 9 tons of herring. In 1953 President **David O. McKay** visited Queen Juliana in her palace, and two years later, August 1955, the Church was given official recognition in the land.

On 12 March 1961, the first non-English-speaking stake of the entire Church was organized in The Hague, South Holland, with J. Paul

Jongkees as president. Initially called the Holland **Stake**, it was later changed to The Hague Netherlands Stake. The Apeldoorn and Rotterdam Stakes now encompass the rest of the country, with the exception of several Church units in southern Netherlands, which are part of the Antwerpen Belgium Stake.

In August 1999 the Church announced the construction of The Hague Netherlands Temple. By the beginning of the year 2000, there were 7,627 Church members living in three stakes and 43 **wards** and **branches**.

Among prominent Church leaders with connections to the Netherlands are native-born Elder Jacob de Jager, emeritus member of the First Quorum of the **Seventy**, and **Alonzo A. Hinckley, Sylvester Q. Cannon**, and **LeGrand Richards**, who served as missionaries in the Netherlands and were later called to the Quorum of the Twelve Apostles.

SOURCES

Lyon, T. Edgar. "Landmarks in the Netherlands Mission." *Improvement Era* 39 (September 1936): 546–47, 573.

1995–1996 Church Almanac. Salt Lake City: Deseret News, 1994. 263–65.

Tobler, Douglas F., Barton W. Marcois, and J. L. W. van Langendijk. "Geschiedenis van de Mormoonse Kerk in Nederland en Vlaanderen." *Horizon* (March 1982): 46–55; (July 1982): 48–55; (September 1982): 51–56; (March 1983): 47–53; (May 1983): 50–57; (September 1983): 53–60.

Warner, Keith C. *History of the Netherlands Mission.* Master's thesis, Brigham Young University, 1967.

HOYT W. BREWSTER Jr.

NEVADA. In June 1850 Hampton Beatie and six other Latter-day Saints from **Salt Lake City** built a trading post in the **Carson Valley**. Their one-story log cabin with no roof or floor was the first permanent structure built by settlers in Nevada. This outpost was a critical resupply station for travelers to **California**. Beatie sold the post to Stephen Moore and returned with his companions to Salt Lake City. John Reese, Beatie's subsequent employer, was intrigued by his stories and, along with Stephen Kinney and 18 other men, left for Carson Valley in the spring of 1851.

Reese purchased the original Beatie site plus additional land and constructed a two-story log cabin that housed a store and hotel. Reese's station, later renamed **Mormon** Station, developed into a multiservice outpost, boasting a blacksmith shop and livery stable with flour and sawmills nearby. Mormon and non-Mormon settlers soon followed.

The **Utah** territorial legislature formally organized this area as Carson County in 1854. This was the first true county government in what is now Nevada. **Brigham Young** appointed **Elder Orson Hyde** to carry out this mandate and serve as probate judge and ecclesiastical leader of the community. Orson Hyde and 35 other men arrived in the Carson Valley in June of 1855 and, shortly thereafter, changed the name of this area to Genoa and designated it the county seat. By the spring of 1856, an official Latter-day Saint colonizing **mission** of 65 families had settled in Carson Valley. Mormon presence in this promising colony ended in 1857 when Brigham Young called all Latter-day Saints back to defend Salt Lake City against the advancing **Johnston's Army**.

During the same period that the Hyde party was sent to Carson Valley, Brigham Young called thirty men to establish a mission at the **Las Vegas** Springs. These missionaries instructed the Paiutes in farming and the gospel, constructed a fort to accommodate travelers between Salt Lake City and **San Bernardino**, and discovered a lead deposit in the Potasi Mountains. A group of 30 mining missionaries was sent to the Las Vegas Mission in 1855 to mine the lead in the Potasi Mountains and ship it back for use in Salt Lake City. Internal dissension between the idealistic **Indian** missionaries and the hard-driving mining missionaries, and the inability of the group to grow sufficient food, led to the official disbanding of the Las Vegas Mission in 1857. The Old Fort eventually became a ranch headquarters and the foundation for the city of Las Vegas.

Panaca, the oldest continuous Latter-day Saint settlement in the state, was founded in May 1864 by colonists from **St. George**. In December of that same year, **Anson Call** established Call's Landing, which served as an important inland dock for navigation on the Colorado River.

In 1864 President Young called on Church members to establish communities in Meadow Valley (in what is now Lincoln County) and along the Colorado, Muddy, and Virgin rivers in present-day Clark county. The Latter-day Saints settled the towns of St. Thomas, St. Joseph, Overton, West Point, Junction City, and Bunkerville. They were assigned to raise food for people traveling the trail between California and Utah Territory, to provide **cotton** for a factory near St. George, and to teach the Indians. Bunkerville retains historical significance as one of the settlements that practiced the united order for a time, and in 1912 Overton became the headquarters for the **Moapa Stake**—the first permanent stake in Nevada.

The completion of the **railroad** from Salt Lake City to **Los Angeles** in

1905 facilitated the establishment of Las Vegas as a town site. Latter-day Saints from Utah and neighboring settlements moved to the new town to find jobs or start businesses. Beginning with a **Sunday School** formed by Newell Leavitt, the Las Vegas **Branch** grew until it was formed into a ward on 1 June 1923. Slow but continuous **growth** resulted in the creation of the Las Vegas Stake in 1954. Growth has been rapid ever since.

Members of the Church also gathered in Western, Northern, and Eastern Nevada. The first stake in Northern Nevada was organized at Ely in 1926. This was followed by the Reno Stake in 1941. Although not as rapidly as in the Las Vegas area, growth has continued, especially in the Reno, Sparks, and Carson Valley areas.

As a testament to the growth, maturity, and commitment of the Latter-day Saints, the Church dedicated the Las Vegas Nevada Temple on 16 through 18 December 1989. Eleven years later the Church dedicated the Reno Nevada Temple on 23 April 2000. At the beginning of the year 2000, Nevada reported 30 stakes, 279 wards and branches, two missions, and a membership of 143,372.

SOURCES

Arrington, Leonard J., and Davis Bitton. *The Mormon Experience.* New York: Knopt, 1979.

Arrington, Leonard J., Feramorz Y. Fox, and Dean L. May. *Building the City of God.* Salt Lake City: Deseret Book, 1976.

Hall, Ashley J. "The Las Vegas Mormon Mission." Las Vegas, Nevada, 1999.

———. "Regional Welfare Center with Multiple Facilities Dedicated in Las Vegas." *Church News,* 20 November 1993. 11.

Hulse, James W. "Panaca: Mormon Outpost among Mining Camps, The Afterlife of St. Mary's County, or Utah's Penumbra in Eastern Nevada." *Utah Historical Quarterly* 55 (1987).

Kanet Communications. *The Guide to LDS in Southern Nevada.* Las Vegas, Nev.: Kanet Communications, 1997.

Southern Nevada Public Affairs Council. "A Legacy of Service, Latter-day Saints in Southern Nevada." Las Vegas, Nev.: Southern Nevada Public Affairs Council, 1997.

State of Nevada, Parks Division. "The Old Fort." Las Vegas, Nev.: State of Nevada, Parks Division, 1994.

———. "Mormon Station State Historic Park." Carson City, Nev.: State of Nevada, Parks Division, 1996.

DAVID R. ROWBERRY

NEW BRUNSWICK, CANADA. **Lyman E. Johnson** arrived in New Brunswick in the summer of 1836, preaching first in St. John. Finding no

success there, the young **apostle** moved northeast to Sackville, where he converted 19 people, some of whom gathered to **Kirtland** in 1838. In 1844 Jesse W. Crosby and Benjamin Brown worked along the upper St. John River Valley, converting some 40 members. **Wilford Woodruff** visited his friend, Captain Joseph Russell, a wealthy shipbuilder on the Miramichi River, in 1849. Crosby returned to the province in 1852, and in 1853 he led 24 members from New Brunswick and **Nova Scotia** to **Utah**. In this company was 21-year-old **Marriner Wood Merrill**. In the following year, most of the remaining New Brunswick **Saints** gathered to Utah.

Although Merrill, William Atkinson, Matthew Phillips, and Charles Shelton returned to the province, there was no sustained missionary activity in New Brunswick until Nephi Jensen reestablished a **mission** there in December 1919. The **great depression** of the 1930s and **World War II** inhibited missionary activity, and only with the conclusion of that war did missionaries return to New Brunswick. The first **stake** was organized at St. John in 1988, and by the end of the twentieth century there were 2,060 Church members in 7 wards and branches in the province.

SOURCE

1999–2000 Church Almanac. Salt Lake City: Deseret News, 1998.

GORDON POLLOCK

NEW CALEDONIA. Latter-day Saints from **French Polynesia** were the first to establish the Church in New Caledonia, a French Overseas Territory in the South **Pacific** that is part of Melanesia. President Kendall Young of the French Polynesia **Mission** obtained official recognition for the Church in New Caledonia and in 1961 organized the Noumea **Branch**. Government permission to proselyte came six years later. On 2 May 1968, **Elder Thomas S. Monson** dedicated the islands for the preaching of the gospel. The first missionaries were French speakers Harold and Jeannine Richards, who arrived in July 1968. In 1975 New Caledonia was transferred to the **Fiji** Suva Mission. The Noumea Branch was first divided a year later. By 1978, 382 members were in the **area**, and a third branch was organized. In the year 2000, 1,449 Latter-day Saints made up nine branches and one **district**.

SOURCES

Britsch, R. Lanier. *Unto the Islands of the Sea: A History of the Latter-day Saints in the Pacific.* Salt Lake City: Deseret Book, 1986. 511–14.

Johnson, R. Val. "Islands of Light." *Ensign* 30 (March 2000): 31–35.

1999–2000 Church Almanac. Salt Lake City: Deseret News, 1998. 322–23.

R. LANIER BRITSCH

NEW DEAL. In October 1929 the United States began to slide into the great depression, which was more severe than any other depression in the nation's history. As the crisis deepened, general and local Church leaders and local governments tried to find jobs for the unemployed and offer relief for the unemployable. By the winter of 1932–33, more than 25% of the nation's workforce and 36% of those in Utah could not find jobs. Since 80% of the Church membership lived in Utah, and Latter-day Saints made up approximately 70% of Utah's population, both Church and government leaders faced a daunting task.

In 1932 Utah and the nation turned to the Democratic Party. Electing New York Governor Franklin D. Roosevelt as president of the United States and Davis County businessman and stake president Henry H. Blood as governor of Utah, the people chose substantial Democratic majorities for the legislature and Congress. Promising "a New Deal for the American people," Roosevelt proposed programs that Congress enacted to promote relief, recovery, and reform. States cooperated by appropriating matching funds to hire people to construct public buildings, sewer systems, roads, dams, water systems, and other projects. By 1936, as a result of employment on government projects, Utah's unemployment rate had declined to 6%. Even with reduced unemployment, the Church could not provide enough work and relief for needy members through its newly inaugurated Welfare Plan.

The opinions of some Church leaders concerning the New Deal changed over time. In 1933 a number of general authorities, including Anthony W. Ivins of the First Presidency, Stephen L Richards and Joseph F. Merrill of the Quorum of the Twelve Apostles, and B. H. Roberts of the Seventy, praised the New Deal and its programs. By 1936, however, the views of Richards and Merrill had changed, and Ivins and Roberts had died. At the same time, Church president Heber J. Grant and first counselor J. Reuben Clark vigorously opposed the New Deal.

Nevertheless, many members felt quite differently. Despite an unsigned front-page editorial in the *Deseret News* in October 1936 that praised Republican candidate Governor Alfred M. Landon of Kansas and attacked President Roosevelt without naming either, more than 69% of Utahns voted Democratic. A number of prominent Latter-day Saints, including **Marriner S. Eccles**, Robert H. Hinckley, and Elbert D. Thomas, were leaders in the New Deal.

SOURCES

Arrington, Leonard J. *Utah, the New Deal, and the Depression of the 1930s.* Dello G. Dayton Memorial Lecture, 25 March 1982. Ogden, Utah: Weber State University Press, 1983.

Derr, Jill Mulvay, Janath Russell Cannon, and Maureen Ursenbach Beecher. *Women of Covenant: The Story of Relief Society.* Salt Lake City: Deseret Book, 1992.

Hinton, Wayne Kendall. "The New Deal Years in Utah: A Political History of Utah, 1932–1940." Master's thesis, Utah State University, 1963.

Mangum, Garth L., and Bruce D. Blumell. *The Mormons' War on Poverty.* Salt Lake City: University of Utah Press, 1993.

THOMAS G. ALEXANDER

NEWEL K. WHITNEY STORE. See WHITNEY STORE.

NEW ERA, THE. The *New Era* is the Church's official magazine for youth ages 12 through 18. It began publication in January 1971 and has been published monthly ever since, except during the years 1979 through 1985, when January and February issues were combined in response to rising printing, paper, and mailing costs. Jay M. Todd was the first managing editor, followed by Brian K. Kelly (1972–89), Richard M. Romney (1989–98), and Larry A. Hiller (1998–).

Originally, the target readership included Latter-day Saints up to age 26. There was a strong emphasis on material of interest to—and written on the level of—a college-age audience. Later readership was refocused on just those in the **Young Men** and **Young Women** programs, and the reading level and content gradually changed to reflect the needs and interests of a younger audience.

During the early years, the *New Era* featured numerous general interest articles. Since the mid-1980s, however, the *New Era* has focused exclusively on increasing faith, testimony, gospel knowledge, and righteous living among Latter-day Saint youth. Special issues have featured such topics as leadership (1979), courtship and marriage (1987), service (1988), **family** (1991), and the **Savior** (1994).

LARRY A. HILLER

NEWFOUNDLAND, CANADA. Newfoundland began as an English fishing station in 1610 and is **Canada's** North Atlantic Island Sentinel. Under naval governorship for decades, this colony was not given its own assembly until 1832. Known for its rugged terrain, rocky coastlines, and a fiercely independent populace, Newfoundland finally became part of the Canadian Confederation 1 April 1949 under the spirited leadership of Premier Joey Smallwood. Today Newfoundland owns Labrador on the Canadian mainland, northeast of **Quebec**, and continues to forge a hard economy of cod-fishing, mining, lumbering, oil drilling, and hydro-electric power.

Though Latter-day Saints had previously lived in Newfoundland (at Argentia and other **United States** and Canadian air force bases built during **World War II**), serious **missionary work** began on the island when **Elders** H. Curtis Page and John M. Scowcroft of the New England Mission landed at St. John's, the capital city, in 1948. From there the work spread to Cornerbrook, Grand Falls, Concepcion Bay, Gander, and elsewhere. The first convert, Lavenia W. Mercer, was not baptized until August 1950. The first **branch** to be organized was St. John's in 1957, with Wilbur Q. Moses as president. By the beginning of the year 2000, out of a population of 563,000, there were but 3 branches and 585 faithful members.

SOURCE

1999–2000 Church Almanac. Salt Lake City: Deseret News, 1998. 292.

RICHARD E. BENNETT

NEW GUINEA. See PAPUA NEW GUINEA.

NEW HAMPSHIRE. In search of work and land to farm, the **Smith family** moved to West Lebanon, New Hampshire, in approximately 1811. In 1813 typhoid fever swept through the area, and seven-year-old Joseph became ill, leading to a severe infection in his leg that would eventually require four surgeries. Although conventional medical practices of the day recommended the amputation of **Joseph Smith's** leg, the Smith family's fortunate residence in New Hampshire put them in contact with Dr. Nathan Smith, a pioneering surgeon from Dartmouth Medical College who oversaw Joseph's surgery and, at the urging of Joseph's mother, was able to save his leg. Shortly after the surgery, the family moved to **Vermont**.

The Church's first official contact with New Hampshire took place in 1832, when **Elders Orson Pratt** and **Lyman E. Johnson** spent 26 days preaching in the town of Bath, leading to 20 baptisms. Missionaries began to pass through New Hampshire, and within a year the first **branch**, consisting of 15 members, was organized in Dalton, Coos County. Membership grew slowly over the next 12 years, but with the **martyrdom** of Joseph Smith in 1844, most of the **Saints** in New Hampshire migrated to the West.

Following this **exodus** to the **Salt Lake Valley**, the Church in New Hampshire did not grow significantly, and in 1869 **missionary work** was discontinued. In 1893 New Hampshire was organized as part of the New England **Conference**, and missionary efforts resumed. By 1945 a branch was organized in Concord, and in 1970 the Merrimack (Nashua) Stake was created with **wards** in Keene, Laconia, Manchester, and Concord. By the year 2000, the state had 7,296 members living in 3 stakes and 20 wards and branches.

SOURCES

Church History in the Fulness of Times. Salt Lake City: The Church of Jesus Christ of Latter-day Saints, 1993. 22–23.
1999–2000 Church Almanac. Salt Lake City: Deseret News, 1998. 222–23.

JONATHAN HART

NEW JERSEY. In 1832 **Lyman Johnson** and **Orson Pratt** brought the gospel to New Jersey. By 1848 the state had 21 branches of the Church, and many New Jersey **Saints** made the **pioneer trek** west.

Industry and education brought many Latter-day Saints to New Jersey. Among them was **Ernest L. Wilkinson**, later a president of **Brigham Young University**, who served as **branch** president in Newark in 1920. A professor at Princeton University, **Henry Eyring** was another well-known member of the Church.

In the year 2000 New Jersey had 5 stakes and 25,945 members. Its two missions have had considerable success, especially in the inner cities. The state has attracted immigrants from many countries and boasted as many as 16 foreign-speaking wards and branches in 1998.

SOURCES

Jenson, Andrew. *Encyclopedic History of The Church of Jesus Christ of Latter-day Saints.* Salt Lake City: Deseret News, 1941.
1999–2000 Church Almanac. Salt Lake City: Deseret News, 1998. 223–24.

R. WILLIAM BURNETT

NEW JERUSALEM. For millennia the Lord's people have anticipated the building of a holy city, known as **Zion** or the New Jerusalem, to which **Jesus Christ** will come in glory (Moses 7:62; Ezek. 48:30–35; Rev. 21:1–4). The **Book of Mormon**, published in 1830, declared that this city would be on the American continent (Ether 13:2–3). The following year the Lord revealed that it would be a place of gathering and refuge in preparation for the time that he would come to his **temple** (D&C 42:35–36; 45:66–67) and that the center place would be at **Independence, Jackson County, Missouri** (D&C 57:1–3). On 3 August 1831 **Joseph Smith** placed a cornerstone to mark the site of the future **temple**. In June 1833 the **Prophet** released his "plat" for the City of Zion, showing that there would be 24 temples at its center serving a variety of **priesthood** functions. Unfortunately, attacks against the **Saints** in Jackson County became more violent the following month, and by November they were forced to flee.

Even after **Brigham Young** led the Mormon **pioneers** to **Utah** in 1847, their hope to build the New Jerusalem and its future glorious temple remained bright. Church leaders spoke of how the kings of the earth would look to Zion for knowledge and how the Savior would eventually come to his temple in the New Jerusalem. Brigham Young envisioned the beauty of the temple with its towers and gardens and stressed that the Saints must prepare before they could build it. When the American **Civil War** failed to open the way for an immediate return to Jackson County, the Saints increasingly looked to a more distant time when they would build the great temple of the New Jerusalem. **Orson Pratt**, for example, often spoke of the different and glorious nature of the future temple (*JD*, 19:19; 21:330–31; 24:24).

As Church activity in Missouri expanded during the twentieth century, the Saints continued their interest in the future New Jerusalem. **Elder Alvin R. Dyer**, who had served as a **mission president** in Missouri, spoke of "a temple complex such as has never been known." The main thrust of modern Church leaders' counsel has been the necessity of the Saints to develop Zion-like attributes, rather than emphasizing the time for the establishment of Zion.

SOURCES

Cowan, Richard O. "The Great Temple of the New Jerusalem." In *Missouri*. Edited by Arnold K. Garr and Clark V. Johnson. Regional Studies in Latter-day Saint Church History series. Provo, Utah: Brigham Young University, 1994. 137–54.

Dyer, Alvin R. "Center Place of Zion." BYU Devotional Address, 7 February 1967.

Journal of Discourses [JD]. 26 vols. London: Latter-day Saints' Book Depot, 1854–86.

McConkie, Bruce R. *The Millennial Messiah: The Second Coming of the Son of Man.* Salt Lake City: Deseret Book, 1982. 301–7.

RICHARD O. COWAN

NEW MEXICO. As early as 1831, the Latter-day Saints knew about the "Navashoe" (**Navajo**), a civilized nation west of Santa Fe, but their first contact with New Mexico did not come until 1846 when the **Mormon Battalion** passed through on its historic march to the Pacific. The Battalion's map became the basis of a proposed **railroad**, leading to the 1853 **Gadsden Purchase**, which brought southwestern New Mexico and southern **Arizona** into the **United States**.

Beginning in the 1860s, missionaries to the Navajo and other tribes of northern Arizona probably crossed into New Mexico. In 1875, missionaries en route to **Mexico** baptized more than 100 among the Zuni.

In the 1870s, Latter-day Saints established settlements in northwestern New Mexico and southwestern **Colorado**, organizing the Young **Stake** in 1912. That year's exodus from the **Mexican Colonies** during the revolution brought many Saints into southwestern New Mexico, Virden being one of their early settlements.

New Mexico blends three cultures. During parts of the twentieth century, overlapping **missions** served **Native Americans**, Hispanics, and Anglos. The Albuquerque Stake (1957) was the first stake entirely within New Mexico. In 1997, plans were announced for a **temple** at Albuquerque. By the beginning of the year 2000 New Mexico had 57,807 members living in 12 stakes and 121 **wards** and **branches**.

SOURCE

1999–2000 Church Almanac. Salt Lake City: Deseret News, 1998. 224–25.

RICHARD O. COWAN

NEW ORLEANS, LOUISIANA. In the winter of 1840–41, two **elders** were sent to New Orleans to proselyte. They soon sent word to **Joseph Smith** that help was needed to save this wayward cosmopolitan city. Harrison Sagers was thereafter sent, and by the spring of 1841, the elders had rented a house and were preaching the gospel. They experienced persecution and limited success in this Roman Catholic area of Louisiana, which remains the only state that designates parishes instead of counties.

From December 1840 to March 1855, New Orleans was the main port for European Latter-day Saints immigrating to **Nauvoo** and later the Rocky Mountains. This port received more than 90 voyages with a total of over 18,000 Saints embarking from **Liverpool, England**. New Orleans provided a first glimpse of **America**, and for some the despicable slave markets left an abhorrent impression as they commenced their inland journey to **Zion**.

As the twentieth century dawned, **missionary work** swelled Church growth in New Orleans and throughout the state of **Louisiana**. These converts heeded a call to build Zion locally, and by 1997 the New Orleans Louisiana **Stake** was one of seven stakes in the state.

SOURCES

Buice, David. "When the Saints Came Marching In: The Mormon Experience in Antebellum New Orleans, 1840–1855." *Louisiana History* 23, 2 (1982): 221–37.

1999–2000 Church Almanac. Salt Lake City: Deseret News, 1998. 206–8.

FRED E. WOODS

NEW TRANSLATIONS. See JOSEPH SMITH TRANSLATION OF THE BIBLE.

NEW YORK. The state of New York, often referred to as the cradle of Mormonism, provided the setting for many of the most important events in Church history. In 1820 the **Restoration** began in the region of **Palmyra/Manchester, New York**. Here, in the **Sacred Grove**, **Joseph Smith** experienced his **First Vision**, in which **God the Father** and **Jesus Christ** appeared to him. Three years later the angel **Moroni** visited the boy **prophet** and told him of the **gold plates**, which contained "an account of the former inhabitants of this continent, and the source from which they sprang" (JS–H 1:34) and had been deposited in the **Hill Cumorah**. Joseph translated much of the plates in **Harmony, Pennsylvania**, but the work was completed at the **Whitmer farm** in **Fayette, New York**. In 1830 the Book of Mormon was published at the **Grandin Printing Shop** in Palmyra, and on **6 April** of that year the **organization of the Church** took place in Fayette. **Samuel H. Smith**, one of the first missionaries of the Church, preached in western New York, eventually leading to the conversion of **Brigham Young** and **Heber C. Kimball**.

In December 1830 and January 1831 Joseph Smith received

revelations commanding the **Saints** to gather in **Ohio** (D&C 37:3; 38:32). In early 1831 most of the faithful members (about 200) left New York. By the time they departed, Joseph Smith had received revelations in the state of New York that later amounted to 24 sections of the **Doctrine and Covenants**.

In 1837 **Parley P. Pratt** served a mission in **New York City**, where he organized a **branch**. While living there he published the **pamphlet**, *Voice of Warning*. The **Eastern States Mission** was organized in 1839 with headquarters in New York City. **John P. Greene** was called to be its first president. Between 1840 and 1890 approximately 50,000 Latter-day Saint immigrants from **Europe** came through the port of New York. In 1844 and 1845 the Church published a periodical in New York City entitled *The Prophet;* **Samuel Brannan**, **William B. Smith**, and Parley P. Pratt served as its editors. On 4 February 1846 Brannan led a group of over 230 saints from New York to **California** by way of Cape Horn on the ship *Brooklyn.* In 1855 **John Taylor** published a newspaper called *The Mormon* in New York City that counteracted negative articles written about the Church in the Eastern press. This periodical was discontinued in 1857 when, as a result of the **Utah War**, missionaries and colonists returned to **Utah**. From then until the 1890s there was relatively little missionary activity in the state.

In 1893 the Eastern States Mission was reorganized (after being discontinued three different times during the previous half century) and headquarters were established in Brooklyn. In 1907 leaders of the Church began buying sites in western New York that were significant to Church history, such as the Joseph Smith farm, the Peter Whitmer farm, and the Hill Cumorah; eventually the Church established **visitors centers** in all of these places. The first twentieth-century **stake** east of the Rocky Mountains was established in 1934 in New York City. Three years later in western New York the Church began producing the Hill Cumorah **Pageant**, "America's Witness for Christ," which annually attracts approximately 100,000 people during its seven nights of performance. In 1964 the Church built a pavilion at the New York **World's Fair** where the film "Man's Search for Happiness" was shown.

In 1980, the 150th anniversary of the Church was commemorated in both Fayette and **Salt Lake City**. During the April **general conference** of that year, President **Spencer W. Kimball** addressed the Church via **satellite** broadcast, originating from the newly rebuilt Peter Whitmer log home, on the site where the Church was first organized.

In the later 1990s President **Gordon B. Hinckley** was involved in several important events associated with the state. In September 1995 he announced in General Conference that the Church would build a **temple** in White Plains, New York (later designated the Harrison New York Temple). That same year he spoke to a gathering of business executives and media representatives in New York City. This led to his appearance on the national telecast "60 Minutes" the following April. President Hinckley dedicated the restored Grandin Print Shop in Palmyra on 26 March 1998. The building was renamed the "Book of Mormon Historical Publication Site." The next day President Hinckley dedicated a replica of the **Joseph Smith Sr.** Log Home, which had been constructed earlier in the year on the site where the Angel Moroni first appeared.

On 26 April 1998 President Hinckley spoke at a **conference** in Madison Square Garden to an audience of about 20,000. In February 1999 the Church announced it would build a temple in Palmyra, New York. The temple was dedicated 6 April 2000.

The number of members living in the state increased significantly during the twentieth century. In 1900 there were only a few hundred members. By the beginning of the year 2000, there were 60,516 Church members living in 14 stakes and 161 **wards** and branches.

SOURCES

Bushman, Richard L. *Joseph Smith and the Beginnings of Mormonism.* Urbana and Chicago: University of Illinois Press, 1984.

1999–2000 Church Almanac. Salt Lake City: Deseret News, 1998. 225–27.

Porter, Larry C. "A Study of the Origins of The Church of Jesus Christ of Latter-day Saints of New York and Pennsylvania, 1816–1831." Ph.D. diss., Brigham Young University, 1971.

Porter, Larry C., Milton V. Backman, and Susan Easton Black, eds. *New York.* Regional Studies in Latter-day Saint Church History series. Provo, Utah: Brigham Young University, 1992.

Woolf, William. "The Church in New York City." *Improvement Era* (December 1938). 728–30, 754–56.

ARNOLD K. GARR

NEW YORK CITY. New York City first received the gospel when Elder **Parley P. Pratt** arrived as a missionary in July 1837. Two years later the **Prophet Joseph Smith** sent **John P. Greene** to preside over the **Saints** there, and soon afterwards the **Eastern States Mission** was organized with headquarters in New York City. Several Church publications were printed there—Parley P. Pratt's *Voice of Warning,* as well as the *New York Messenger* and *The Mormon.* Between 1840 and 1890, New York City also served as the port of entry for approximately 50,000 Saints traveling from **Europe.**

In 1934, New York City became the first place east of the intermountain area to have a **stake** organized. This city hosted the 1964–65 **World's Fair** and became the site of the Church's popular exhibit featuring the film *Man's Search for Happiness.* The success of this presentation led to further technological developments in Latter-day Saint **missionary work.**

On 25 May 1975, President **Spencer W. Kimball** dedicated a large new **visitors' center**, along with a stake center, a genealogical library, and headquarters for the New York New York City Mission, at Lincoln Square. Serving a diverse group of Saints, the Church in New York City has offered meetings in English and several foreign languages, including Spanish, Korean, and American Sign Language. Though at the end of the twentieth century many in this city faced problems of inner city life, such as crime, poverty, and abuse, the Church continues to grow, and the retention rate of new members has been reported as better than 70% (Gaunt, 43).

SOURCES

Cannon, Mike. "Diversity of Saints Find Unity in Gospel in New York City." *Church News,* 27 August 1994, 9.

Cowan, Richard O. *The Latter-day Saint Century.* Salt Lake City: Bookcraft, 1999.

Gaunt, LaRene. "Testimonies from the Inner City." *Ensign* 22 (April 1992): 36–43.

Jenson, Andrew. *Encyclopedic History of The Church of Jesus Christ of Latter-day Saints.* Salt Lake City: Deseret News, 1941. 578–79.

"New York Visitors' Center Dedicated." *Ensign* 5 (June 1975): 77.

LISA KURKI

NEW ZEALAND. In August 1853 Augustus Farnham, president of the Australian Mission, received permission from the **First Presidency** to visit New Zealand. In October 1854 he and N. William Cooke arrived, and missionary work began among the Pakeha (Pa-key-ha), or English-speaking people. Six months later, in April 1855, the first branch of the Church in New Zealand was organized with 20 members.

In December 1871, the first company of 11 Saints emigrated from New Zealand to **Utah.** In 1875, five elders from **Zion** arrived to labor in the country. In 1879, the headquarters of the Australian Mission was transferred to New Zealand. William Bromley arrived as **mission president** in January 1881, and he had a strong impression to present the gospel to the **Maori** people. In October of that same year, the first Maori joined the Church.

In January 1886, a native school was opened in Nuhaka by Sondra Sanders. After two years of work, the **Book of Mormon** was translated into the Maori language by Ezra F. Richards and Sondra Sanders and was published early in 1889. Years later, from 1918 to 1919, **Matthew Cowley** retranslated the Book of Mormon and also translated the **Doctrine and Covenants** and the **Pearl of Great Price** into the Maori language.

Construction began on the Maori Agricultural College in 1911, and it was completed and dedicated in April 1913. In 1931, the college was destroyed by an earthquake. In September 1948, **Elder** Matthew Cowley announced that a new school would be built. Property was purchased the following year, and the George R. Beisinger family arrived from **America** in 1950 to supervise the construction of the school, as well as a chapel. **President David O. McKay**, who in 1921 was the first **general authority** to visit New Zealand, visited the country again in January 1955. Later that year, he announced that a **temple** was to be built in New Zealand for the South Pacific. The temple was dedicated by President McKay on 20 April 1958. The Church College of New Zealand was dedicated 24 April 1958. The first **stake** was organized by Elder **Marion G. Romney** on 18 May 1958. By early in the year 2000 there were 89,952 members of the Church living in 25 stakes and 211 **wards** and **branches**.

——— ——

SOURCES

Rudd, Glen L. "New Zealand: a Short Collection of History." Manuscript. 1993. 1–9, 16.

Smith, Henry A. *Matthew Cowley: Man of Faith*. Salt Lake City: Bookcraft, 1954. viii.

GLEN L. RUDD

NEW ZEALAND TEMPLE.

NEW ZEALAND TEMPLE. Dedicated by President **David O. McKay** in 1958, the Hamilton **New Zealand** Temple was the first built in the southern hemisphere. As early as 1928, **mission president**, John E. Magleby, had prophesied that a temple would be built in the Waikato Valley. In 1954 President McKay assigned Wendell B. Mendenhall, supervisor of the Church's building program in the **Pacific**, to confidentially investigate potential **temple** sites. Mendenhall was impressed with the hill overlooking the Church College, which also commanded a spectacular view of the entire Waikato River Valley. Ground was broken on 21 December 1955 by the mission president, Ariel S. Ballif, no **general authority** being present. Although construction was carried out by volunteer "labor missionaries," government inspectors found the quality of work to be excellent. Women assisted with landscaping and by weaving carpets. The cornerstone was laid 22 December 1956 by **Elder Hugh B. Brown**, an **assistant to the Twelve**. The temple and adjacent college were dedicated by President McKay on 20 April 1958. The temple measures 159 by 84 feet and contains 38,000 square feet of floor space. Its tower rises 157 feet above ground level.

SOURCES

Allred, Gordon T. "The Great Labor of Love." *Improvement Era* 61 (April 1958): 226–29, ff.

Cowan, Richard O. *Temples to Dot the Earth.* Springville Utah: Cedar Fort, 1997. 163–67.

Howe, Allie. "A Temple in the South Pacific." *Improvement Era* 58 (November 1955): 811–13.

RICHARD O. COWAN

NIBLEY, CHARLES W. Charles Wilson Nibley, a prominent Church, business, and political leader in the Intermountain West, has left an inspiring legacy of faith and perseverance. In 1860 the Nibleys settled in **Cache Valley** of northern **Utah**, and Charles (born 5 February 1849 in Hunterfield, Scotland) began a life of caring for animals, including some of **Brigham Young's** cattle. Later he sold salt to miners in **Montana**. He found the acquisition of wealth comparatively easy and soon was involved in the lumber business in **Oregon** and the sugar beet industry in Utah and **Idaho**. He also served on the board of directors of roughly a dozen companies and became one of Utah's wealthiest citizens. The love of money was never a prime motivator in his life, and he gave away much of his wealth before his death.

Nibley's Church activities were as impressive as his business achievements. He served in the **British Mission** in 1877, where he formed a deep and rare friendship with his mission president, **Joseph F. Smith**. In December 1907 President Smith called him as the Church's **presiding bishop**. In this capacity he revamped the **tithing** system, replacing tithing in kind with an all-cash system. He traveled extensively with President Smith, touring **Europe** and assisting in selecting the **Hawaii Temple** site.

He loved to play golf, and **Heber J. Grant** was frequently his partner. In 1925 President Grant called him to become his **counselor** in the Church's **First Presidency**. Charles had three wives and fathered 24 children. He died 10 December 1931 and was buried in the **Logan**, Utah, cemetery.

SOURCES

Flake, Lawrence R. *Prophets and Apostles of the Last Dispensation.* Provo, Utah: Religious Studies Center, Brigham Young University, 2001. 269–71.

Reminiscences of Charles W. Nibley. Salt Lake City: Stevens & Walis, 1933.

KENNETH W. GODFREY

NIBLEY, HUGH W. As historian, linguist, and scriptorian, Hugh Winder Nibley stands as one of the most influential Latter-day Saint scholars of religious studies in the twentieth century.

Born 27 March 1910 in Portland, **Oregon**, his childhood awakened in him an enduring sensitivity to mankind's stewardship over the earth and an inexhaustible curiosity. After serving in the Swiss-German **Mission**, he completed his bachelor's degree in history at UCLA in 1934. A university fellow, he earned his doctorate at the University of **California** at Berkeley in 1938.

After teaching social philosophy at the Claremont Colleges in California and serving in army intelligence during **World War II**, he dedicated his academic career to The Church of Jesus Christ of Latter-day Saints. At the behest of **Elder John A. Widtsoe**, he joined the faculty of **Brigham Young University** in 1946, where he taught and worked for over 50 years.

His publications cover ancient history, classics, **education**, Egyptology, early **Israel**, Christian origins, **Book of Mormon**, **temple** worship, Church history, society, and the gospel. His works are characterized by an urgent sense of placing immediate priority on eternal values and patterns. LDS historical topics in the *Collected Works of Hugh Nibley* include works on **Joseph Smith** and **Brigham Young**.

SOURCES

Midgley, Louis. "Hugh Winder Nibley: Bibliography and Register." *By Study and also by Faith.* 2 vols. Edited by John M. Lundquist and Stephen D. Ricks. Salt Lake City: Deseret Book and FARMS, 1990. 2:xv-lxxxvii.

JOHN W. WELCH

NIBLEY, PRESTON. A prominent author, compiler, and assistant Church historian, Preston Nibley was born 26 May 1884 in **Logan, Utah**. A son of Charles W. and Ellen Ricks Nibley, he attended the Agricultural College in Logan, where he edited the student newspaper. He served a full-time mission to **Germany** (1903–06), then majored in journalism at the University of Chicago (1906–09). He married Anna Doney Parkinson in 1908. In 1911 the family moved to **Salt Lake City**, where he served in **stake** and **ward YMMIA** organizations. In 1919 he was called to the general board of the YMMIA.

Preston's business interests were in real estate and manufacturing, but his real passions were history and writing. He wrote four books and compiled/edited 11 others, most of which are now out of print. He presided over the Northwestern States Mission from 1937 to 1941. Following this assignment, he worked in the **Church Historian's Office**. Beginning in 1948, and for a decade thereafter, he toured the stakes of the Church to assist in compiling and updating stake histories.

He was appointed assistant Church historian in 1957. He retired in 1963 when his health began to fail. Preston Nibley died in 2 January 1966 in Salt Lake City.

SOURCES

"Funeral Service for Preston Nibley." Manuscript. Used by permission.
Jenson, Andrew. *Latter-day Saint Biographical Encyclopedia.* 4 vols. 1901–36. Reprint, Salt Lake City: Western Epics, 1971. 3:686.
Nibley, Preston P. "Some Recollections of My Father." Manuscript. Used by permission.

GERALD L. HOMER

NICARAGUA. Nicaragua first received the gospel in 1953 when **Elders** Manual Arias and Archie R. Mortensen arrived from the recently created Central America **Mission**. Their first convert was Jose D. Guzman, baptized 11 April 1954. The country's civil war forced foreign missionaries to withdraw in 1978; however, local **Saints** continued to build up the Church. In 1987 the government allowed some of the members to travel to the **Guatemala** City **Temple** to receive their **ordinances**. By 1989 missionaries had returned, and the Nicaragua Managua Mission was created 15 October 1989. The following years brought steady **growth**, and the Church extended **literacy** and **welfare service** programs to improve the lives of many Nicaraguans. In 1997 President **Gordon B. Hinckley** became the first Church president to visit Nicaragua in more than 40 years. By the beginning of the year 2000, the country had 31,747 members in 77 **wards** and **branches** comprising 1 **stake** and 11 **districts**.

SOURCES

Avant, Gerry. "Nicaraguans Eager to Learn, Improve Lives through Gospel." *Church News,* 22 November 1980, 6.

1999–2000 Church Almanac. Salt Lake City: Deseret News, 1998. 363–64.

LISA KURKI

NIGERIA. Nigeria is located on the west coast of Africa and has an estimated population of 110 million—the largest of any country on that continent. In 1999 it had a military government, and the official language
was English. Of the population, 50% were **Muslim**, 40% were Christian,
and 10% followed traditional religions.

Years before the arrival of missionaries, a number of Nigerian
Christians obtained Latter-day Saint **literature** while traveling abroad or
from Latter-day Saint expatriates living in their country. By 1964 Church
headquarters in **Salt Lake City** received letters that requested information; the Church sent this information, which led to the conversion of
hundreds. Though unofficial, several groups identifying themselves as
"The Church of Jesus Christ of Latter-day Saints" legally registered with
the Nigerian government. Glen G. Fisher visited Nigeria in 1960, following his service as president of the **South Africa Mission**. He then reported
to Church president **David O. McKay** in Salt Lake City that the groups
were sincere and recommended that missionaries be sent. The following
year the **First Presidency** sent LaMar Williams on a month-long fact-
finding assignment to Nigeria, following which Brother and Sister
Williams were called, along with other couples, to serve as missionaries
there. It was reported that more than 15,000 Nigerians were participating in many congregations that were pleading and praying for baptism.
Visa problems prevented missionaries from being sent, however, and
plans were terminated in 1965 with the outbreak of civil **war in Nigeria**.

When the **revelation** extending the **priesthood** to all races (**Official
Declaration 2**) was announced 9 June 1978, the way was opened for the
gospel to go to Nigeria, as well as to all of Africa. In August that year,
Merrill Bateman and Edwin Q. Cannon were sent to assess the situation
in Nigeria.

Elder Cannon and his wife, Janath, together with Rendell and Rachel
Mabey, arrived in Nigeria in November 1978 as special representatives of
the Church's **International Mission**. They taught the gospel to many who
had been meeting as Latter-day Saints and praying that Church representatives would come. On 21 November 1978, **Anthony Ozodimma
Obinna** became the first baptized member in Nigeria. He had previously
organized a congregation with the Church's name and had been waiting
for the missionaries. That same day several others were also baptized, and

the Aboh **Branch** was created with Brother Obinna as president. His brothers Francis and Raymond were called as his **counselors**, and his wife, Fidelia, was set apart as the branch **Relief Society** president.

On 1 July 1980, the Africa West Mission was organized, and five years later it became the Nigeria Lagos Mission. By 1987 membership in Nigeria approached 10,000. On 15 May 1988, **Elder Neal A. Maxwell** organized the Aba Nigeria **Stake**, with **David W. Ekka** as president—the first stake in which all the priesthood leadership was black.

Despite challenges of poverty and political turmoil, Church growth in Nigeria has been exceptional, with Nigerians serving in leadership positions on every level, including three **area authority seventies**: Christopher N. Chukwurah, David W. Ekka, and Emmanuel O. Opare Sr. Elder Opare was also called as a counselor in the Africa West **Area** presidency in 1998.

On 14 February 1998, President **Gordon B. Hinckley** visited Port Harcourt, Nigeria, addressing 1,150 priesthood leaders and more than 12,000 members in a regional **conference**. By the beginning of the year 2000, there were 42,746 Church members living in 11 stakes and 185 **wards** and **branches**. At the April 2000 general conference President Hinckley announced that the Church would construct a temple in Aba, Nigeria.

SOURCES

Brigham, Janet. "Nigeria and Ghana." *Ensign* 10 (February 1980): 73–76.

"Church Spreads in Nigeria, Ghana." *Church News,* 22 December 1979, 5.

LeBaron, E. Dale, ed. *All Are Alike unto God.* Orem, Utah: Granite Publishing, 1998. 116–38. 53–102.

Mabey, Rendell N., and Gordon T. Allred. *Brother to Brother.* Salt Lake City: Bookcraft, 1984.

Middleton, John, ed. *Encyclopedia of Africa South of the Sahara.* 4 vols. New York: Macmillan Library Reference USA, 1997. 3:307–23.

"Nigeria Marks Twin Milestones." *Church News,* 21 May 1988, 6.

1999–2000 Church Almanac. Salt Lake City: Deseret News, 1998. 364–66.

Oral histories of early Church converts collected by E. Dale LeBaron. Copies at BYU Library, Provo, Utah; LDS Church Historical Library, Salt Lake City, Utah.

E. DALE LEBARON

NIUE. Niue is a small island 300 miles southeast of **Samoa**. The first Latter-day Saint missionaries arrived there in 1952, baptizing 65 converts by the end of that year. The first **meetinghouse** built by labor missionaries was dedicated in 1958. The Church in Niue is administered by the

New Zealand Auckland mission. By the year 2000 Niue had 230 Latter-day Saints living in four **branches**.

SOURCES

Britsch, R. Lanier. *Unto the Islands of the Sea: A History of the Latter-day Saints in the Pacific.* Salt Lake City: Deseret Book. 1986.
1999–2000 Church Almanac. Salt Lake City: Deseret News. 1998. 366.

ERIC B. SHUMWAY

NORTH CAROLINA. The restored gospel was introduced in North Carolina by **Elder Jedediah M. Grant** in 1838. He had unusual success and was in time joined by other missionaries. Even with assistance, the missionaries were unable to fill all of the appointments to preach. Early **branches** were organized in Surry and Stokes Counties. Groups of converts emigrated, gathering to Latter-day Saint communities in the West. Little additional proselyting was performed in North Carolina until after the **Civil War**, when a native southerner, Henry G. Boyle (1869), had unusual success. Acts of violence, particularly mobbings, threats, and whippings, were common, but opposition reached a new level when a Latter-day Saint **meetinghouse** was burned at Harker's Island.

With the gradual improvement of the Church's **public image** after the turn of the century, mob action virtually ceased, and membership grew substantially when, during the 1890s, Church leaders encouraged converts to remain in their local areas. This change in policy also helped to provide seasoned and experienced leaders. The Kingston **Stake** was created in 1961, followed by stakes in Greensboro and Raleigh in the next few months. On 18 December 1999 the Raleigh North Carolina Temple was dedicated. By the year 2000 there were 56,261 **Saints** in North Carolina in 12 stakes and 2 **missions** located in Charlotte and Raleigh.

SOURCES

Berrett, LaMar C. "History of the Southern States Mission, 1831–1861." Master's thesis, Brigham Young University, 1960.
Jenson, Andrew. *Encyclopedic History of The Church of Jesus Christ of Latter-day Saints.* Salt Lake City: Deseret News, 1941.
1999–2000 Church Almanac. Salt Lake City: Deseret News, 1998. 227–29.

DAVID F. BOONE

NORTH DAKOTA. Proselyting in North Dakota commenced in 1883, but with little success until about 1914 when missionaries began teaching

Native Americans. Soon the state's first **branch** was created at Sully Lake with 40 members from the Fort Berthold Reservation under their own leadership. By 1930, there were **meetinghouses** at Sully Lake and Grand Forks, with a statewide membership of 145. In 1977, the Fargo Stake was created, making North Dakota the last state to have its first stake established. A second stake was created at Bismark in 1996. The Church dedicated a **temple** at Bismark on 19 September 1999. At the end of that year, North Dakota had 5,070 members living in two stakes and 15 **wards** and branches.

SOURCES

Jenson, Andrew. *Encyclopedic History of The Church of Jesus Christ of Latter-day Saints.* Salt Lake City: Deseret News, 1941. 587–58.

1999–2000 Church Almanac. Salt Lake City: Deseret News, 1998 229.

VAUGHN R. PICKELL

NORTHERN IRELAND. See IRELAND.

NORTHERN MARIANA ISLANDS. The islands of Saipan, Tinian, and Rota make up the Mariana Islands and are part of the **Guam District** in the **Micronesia**-Guam **Mission**. The first members to Saipan were American servicemen in 1944. **Elder L. Tom Perry** was among this group. These LDS servicemen built a chapel on Saipan during their stay. Initial missionary efforts in the early 1970s were halted by local threats on the missionaries.

Under the **Hawaii**-Honolulu Mission, Elders Callis Carleton and Jeff Frame were sent to Saipan in January 1975. They, too, experienced opposition but soon found some success with the help of the Gonzalez **family**. Alfred "Mustang" Gonzalez arrived at Saipan on 16 July 1975. A member from Hawaii, Gonzalez became the construction manager of the Saipan International Airport. He brought his family later that year. Early converts were Brad T. and Jean Nago, who joined the Church on 24 January 1976. Later Nago replaced Gonzalez as **branch** president of Saipan's Chalan Laulau Branch when the Gonzalez family returned to Hawaii.

Elders Stephen Jones and Kamealoha Kaniho were assigned to open Rota to missionary work on 5 September 1986, and on 14 August 1992, Elders James Adamson, and Ryan C. McCune opened Tinian for proselyting.

President **Gordon B. Hinckley** and Elder **Joseph B. Wirthlin**, along with their wives, stopped to visit 10 missionaries and about 60 of Saipan's 300 members on 1 June 1996 while their plane refueled en route home from **Asia**. By the dawn of the year 2000 there were 870 members on the islands residing in 1 branch.

SOURCES

"A Brief History of the Micronesia-Guam Mission, 1980–1990." Micronesia-Guam Mission, 1990.

Micronesia-Guam Mission Historical Report. Archives, Historical Department, The Church of Jesus Christ of Latter-day Saints, Salt Lake City.

Muller, Alan Edward. "A Historical Account of The Church of Jesus Christ of Latter-day Saints on Guam." Guam, 1 April 1955.

1997–1998 Church Almanac. Salt Lake City: Deseret News, 1996. 368–69.

W. JAMES JACOB

NORTHWEST TERRITORIES. A sparsely populated region of **Canada**, the Northwest Territories had 188 members in one **branch** at the beginning of the year 2000. The Yellowknife branch may be the largest in the Church in terms of the area it covers—half a million square miles.

SOURCE

1999–2000 Church Almanac. Salt Lake City: Deseret News, 1998. 297.

EMILY C. ZEIGLER

NORWAY. Norwegian boat captain Svend Larsen and Danish missionary Hans Frederik Petersen took the gospel to Norway on 11 September 1851. Larsen, who had heard the gospel in **Denmark**, returned and was baptized in Aalborg on 23 September. By 7 October Peterson and Larsen were back in Norway with a third missionary. The first baptisms in Norway soon followed on 26 November 1851 with John Olsen, a master blacksmith, and his assistant, Peter Adamsen.

The first branch in Norway was organized in Risør on 16 July 1852 with 18 members. Eighteen additional branches were organized by 1905.

Norway was organized as a **district** of the Scandinavian Mission and named the Brevik Conference. Its first Church **conference** was held 14 August 1852 in Brevik. **Missionary work** progressed slowly. By 1857 there were 310 members. In the early 1860s, the Church established a foothold in the capital city, and the Brevik Conference was renamed the Christiana (Oslo) Conference.

On 1 April 1920, Norway became a separate **mission,** with August S. Schow as its first president. The first Church-owned **meetinghouse/** mission office was built by the members in 1871 at Oslo. It was torn down and rebuilt in 1903 and used by the Church until 1964. In 1961 the first traditional Latter-day Saint chapel was built in Trondheim.

When **World War II** started, missionaries from the United States and the **mission president** left Norway, and a local member, Olaf Sønsteby, functioned as acting mission president. Norway suffered under Nazi occupation, but the members remained faithful and held regular Church meetings.

The Danish **Book of Mormon** was used in Norway until 1950, when it was replaced by a Norwegian translation. It was followed by the **Doctrine and Covenants** in 1954 and the **Pearl of Great Price** in 1955. The first Norwegian **hymn** book was printed in 1938. In 1937 the Norwegian Mission began publishing *Lys over Norge* (Light over Norway), a Church **magazine.**

The first **regional representative/mission representative** to Norway was Dean A. Peterson (1972). The **seminary** program began in 1973, and the **institute** program began in 1975. Ole Podhorny was the first full-time **Church Educational System** coordinator/director. The first **stake** was organized in Oslo on 22 May 1977 under the direction of President **Thomas S. Monson,** and the first **stake president** was Oswald Bjareng. On 4 November 1979, **Elder Bruce R. McConkie** dedicated Norway. In 1988 the Church was registered for the first time with the Norwegian government. As of the year 2000 there were 4,120 members living in one stake and three **districts.**

Church members knighted by the kings of Norway include John Langeland (1983) and Erlend D. Peterson (1997). Prominent LDS Norwegians in the **United States** include **John A. Widtsoe** (educator and **apostle**); Grant Johannessen (concert pianist); and Thorleif Knaphus (sculptor).

Sources

Encyclopedia of Mormonism. Edited by Daniel H. Ludlow. 4 vols. New York: Macmillan, 1992.

Freidel, H. *Under Nordlysets Himmell: Jesu Kristi Kirke i Norge: Den norske misjons historie, 1851–1966.* Oslo: Jesu Kristi Kirke av Siste Dagers Hellige Misjonskontoret, 1966.

1999–2000 Church Almanac. Salt Lake City: Deseret News, 1998. 367.

Zobel, Albert L. Jr. *Under the Midnight Sun: Centennial History of Scandinavian Missions.* Salt Lake City: Deseret Book, 1950.

Erlend D. Peterson

NOVA SCOTIA, CANADA. In the autumn of 1843, Robert Dixon, a native of Onslow, Nova Scotia, returned to the province and began **missionary work** for the Church. In Halifax he gathered followers who persisted in their new beliefs, despite derision by the city's press and the Strangites, a **Mormon schismatic group**. Between 1853 and 1855, virtually all believers left the province to gather to **Zion**.

In 1920 Nephi Jensen of **Utah** reestablished a Latter-day Saint mission in Nova Scotia. Records indicate a membership of more than 100 during these years, with the most success found in Halifax and Windsor. Prior to **World War II**, missionaries were withdrawn. Latter-day Saint missionary activity recommenced after the **war**, laying the foundation of the contemporary Church. The first **stake** was organized in 1985 at Dartmouth. On 14 November 1999 a **temple** was dedicated near Halifax, and by the year 2000 there were 4,268 Church members living in 18 wards and branches in Nova Scotia.

SOURCE

1999–2000 Church Almanac. Salt Lake City: Deseret News, 1998.

GORDON POLLOCK

NOVELS. See FICTION, MORMONS IN.

THE CHURCH OF JESUS CHRIST OF LATTER-DAY SAINTS
OFFICE OF THE FIRST PRESIDENCY
SALT LAKE CITY, UTAH 84150

June 8, 1978

To All General and Local Priesthood Officers of The Church of Jesus Christ
of Latter-day Saints Throughout the World

Dear Brethren:

As we have witnessed the expansion of the work of the Lord over the
earth, we have been grateful that people of many nations have responded to
the message of the restored gospel, and have joined the Church in ever-
increasing numbers. This, in turn, has inspired us with a desire to extend
to every worthy member of the Church all of the privileges and blessings
which the gospel affords.

Aware of the promises made by the prophets and presidents of the Church
who have preceded us that at some time, in God's eternal plan, all of our
brethren who are worthy may receive the priesthood, and witnessing the
faithfulness of those from whom the priesthood has been withheld, we have
pleaded long and earnestly in behalf of these, our faithful brethren,
spending many hours in the Upper Room of the Temple supplicating the Lord
for divine guidance.

He has heard our prayers, and by revelation has confirmed that the long-
promised day has come when every faithful, worthy man in the Church may
receive the holy priesthood, with power to exercise its divine authority,
and enjoy with his loved ones every blessing that flows therefrom, including
the blessings of the temple. Accordingly, all worthy male members of the
Church may be ordained to the priesthood without regard for race or color.
Priesthood leaders are instructed to follow the policy of carefully interviewing all candidates for ordination to either the Aaronic or the Melchizedek Priesthood to insure that they meet the established standards for
worthiness.

We declare with soberness that the Lord has now made known His will for
the blessing of all His children throughout the earth who will hearken to
the voice of His authorized servants, and prepare themselves to receive
every blessing of the gospel.

Sincerely yours,

The First Presidency

OFFICIAL DECLARATION 2. The First Presidency issued a letter dated 8
June 1978, announcing that "all worthy males" could be ordained to the priesthood. This
letter is known today as Official Declaration 2.

OAKLAND TEMPLE. Since **Brigham Young's** 1847 prophecy that "in process of time the shores of the Pacific may be overlooked from the temple of the Lord" (quoted in Cowan and Homer, 98) there was talk of a Latter-day Saint temple at **San Francisco** Bay. In 1924 **Elder George Albert Smith** gazed across the Bay from atop the Fairmont Hotel in San Francisco and saw in **vision** a "white temple of the Lord upon those [Oakland] hills" (quoted in Cowan and Homer, 269). Soon after this vision, the search for a site began. Several were offered, but only one, which was not for sale, seemed right. During **World War II** this site was purchased piece by piece. The final plot was purchased in 1947 and construction began in 1962. On 17 November 1964, the gleaming white temple with its oriental motif and panoramic view was dedicated by President **David O. McKay**, who had recently suffered a stroke.

At 82,000-plus square feet, the Oakland California Temple is one of the Church's largest, and its location on a freeway exit makes it one of the more accessible. Also constructed on the 18-acre site were a 77,000-square-foot interstake center with a 2,200-seat auditorium and a 22,000-square-foot **visitors' center** and **family history library**, making "Temple Hill" in Oakland somewhat analogous in size, configuration, and usage to **Temple Square** in **Salt Lake City**.

SOURCE

Cowan, Richard O., and William E. Homer. *California Saints.* Provo, Utah: Religious Studies Center, Brigham Young University, 1996.

WILLIAM E. HOMER

OAKS, DALLIN H. Best known for his service as an **apostle**, educator, and scholar, Dallin Harris Oaks was born 12 August 1932 in **Provo, Utah**, to Dr. Lloyd E. and Stella Harris Oaks. As a young man he earned degrees from **Brigham Young University** and the University of **Chicago**

Law School, later serving as a law clerk to Chief Justice Earl Warren of the U.S. Supreme Court. After this experience in **Washington, D.C.**, he practiced law with a large Chicago firm for three years and then returned to the University of Chicago as a law professor, where he distinguished himself in legal scholarship and served for a time as acting dean. He also served as the executive director of the American Bar Foundation.

From 1971 to 1980 he was president of Brigham Young University. Under his leadership the university made significant improvements in teaching effectiveness and scholarly achievement. He directed the founding of the **J. Reuben Clark** Law School, where he also taught. During his time at BYU, he became a national spokesman for the independence of private higher educational institutions, serving for a time as president of the American Association of Presidents of Independent Colleges and Universities.

In January 1981, Dallin H. Oaks became a justice on the **Utah** Supreme Court, where he was later honored by the Utah State Bar as Judge of the Year. In 1984, at the age of 51, he was called to serve in the Quorum of the Twelve Apostles. While this calling necessitated that he promptly conclude his duties with the court, he was able to finish his five-year term as chairman of the board of the Public **Broadcasting** Service.

As an apostle, **Elder** Oaks has spoken and written much about inward matters of the heart and the necessity of proper motives and desires. He has also illuminated particular doctrines and suggested principles that should guide personal decision making, contrasting the Lord's way with the way of the world. As a legal scholar and later as an apostle, he has published a number of books, including *Carthage Conspiracy* (with Marvin J. Hill), *Pure in Heart, The Lord's Way,* and *His Holy Name.* Elder Oaks and his wife June Dixon, who died in 1998, were the parents of six children. In August 2000 he married Kristen M. McMain.

SOURCE

Searle, Don L. "Elder Dallin H. Oaks: It Begins by Following the Other Apostles." *Ensign* 14 (June 1984): 14–19.

DALLIN D. OAKS

OBINNA, ANTHONY U. Anthony Uzodimma Obinna was a **pioneer** of the Church in Nigeria, born 15 April 1928 in Aboh Mbaisi. He was the first African to be baptized by missionaries sent to west **Africa** following the 1978 revelation allowing all worthy males to receive the **priesthood**.

Anthony's father was a highly respected village leader and judge. He had three wives and 24 children, few of whom were educated. In their African religion, the **family** worshiped idols, but Anthony embraced Christianity. He also became a schoolteacher.

In 1965 Anthony had a remarkable dream of the Savior, who showed him the rooms of a most beautiful building. He did not recognize the building until 1971 when he saw a picture of the **Salt Lake Temple** in a *Reader's Digest* article entitled "The March of the Mormons." He soon obtained literature from the Church, which he prayerfully studied, and gained a testimony of the gospel. He then became a prolific letter writer, seeking baptism for himself and for a congregation that he established, which included his extended family. After years of pleading for membership, in 1978 he learned of the revelation that would allow him to receive the priesthood. He immediately wrote to President Spencer W. Kimball: "We are happy for the many hours in the upper room of the temple you spent supplicating the Lord to bring us into the fold" (LeBaron 41).

At the time of his baptism, he was ordained a **priest** and set apart as Africa's first black **branch** president. He then baptized his wife, Fidelia, who became the first black **Relief Society** president there. His little congregation was the first **branch** of the Church in which all members were black. On 28 January 1989, Brother and Sister Obinna were sealed in the **Logan Temple**. He passed away at his home in Aboh Mbaisi on 25 August 1995.

SOURCES

LeBaron, E. Dale. "Gospel Pioneers in Africa." *Ensign* 20 (August 1990): 40–43.

Oral histories of early Church converts collected by E. Dale LeBaron. Copies at BYU Library, Provo, Utah; LDS Church Historical Library, Salt Lake City, Utah.

E. DALE LEBARON

ODOMETER. Two wooden odometers were designed, built, and used by **Brigham Young's pioneer** company of 1847. The first, made by Appleton M. Harmon near North Platte, **Nebraska**, measured the distance from that point to the **Salt Lake Valley** (12 May to 24 July 1847). The second, made by William A. King during the company's three-week stop in the valley, measured the total distance (1,032 miles) of the return journey to the **Missouri River** (17 August to 21 October 1847).

The first machine was designed to count the rotations of a wagon wheel that was 4'8" in diameter. Three hundred and sixty rotations of that wheel equaled one mile exactly. The initial design specifications for the machine were developed by **Orson Pratt**, but these were significantly modified for reasons of practicality and operational elegance. The specifications of the model are fully documented in **William Clayton's journal**.

The design features of the second odometer are unknown, though evidence suggests that they were an extension of the first odometer's operational characteristics.

William Clayton, a member of the pioneer company, was the driving force that brought the odometer project to fruition and meticulously monitored the operation of both instruments. Prompted by Clayton's talents as a record keeper and his desire for precision, Brigham Young directed him to compile the odometer-measured distances into a useful and accurate trail guide. The result was the publication of *The Latter-Day Saints' Emigrants' Guide* in March 1848.

SOURCES

Clayton, William. *William Clayton's Journal.* Salt Lake City: Deseret News, 1921. 152–53.

Pratt, Orson. *The Orson Pratt Journals.* Edited by Elden Jay Watson. Salt Lake City: Elden Jay Watson, 1975. 391–92.

Wright, Norman E. "The Mormon Pioneer Odometers." *BYU Studies* 30 (Fall 1997): 82–115.

NORMAN E. WRIGHT

O'DONNAL, JOHN F. John Forres O'Donnal was the first member and prominent leader of the Church in **Guatemala**. He was born 1 April 1917 in La Madera, **New Mexico**. He arrived in Guatemala in 1942 as a young college graduate. His assignment from the U.S. government was to initiate and develop rubber production. Shortly thereafter he petitioned the Church to send missionaries to Guatemala, and the first native convert was his wife, Carmen Gálvez.

He truly became a **pioneer** of the **Restoration** in this land. He became the first **district** president, the first **mission president** of the Guatemalan highlands (Quetzaltenango), and the first **temple president**. President **Gordon B. Hinckley** summarized his contribution by calling him "the father, the grandfather and the great-grandfather of the Church in Guatemala" (quoted in O'Donnal, 353).

SOURCE

O'Donnal, John Forres. *Pioneer in Guatemala.* Yorba Linda, Calif.: Shumway Family History Services, 1997.

KEITH J. WILSON

OFFICIAL DECLARATION 1. See MANIFESTO (1890).

OFFICIAL DECLARATION 2.

In 1969 the First Presidency stated: "From the beginning of this dispensation, the Prophet Joseph Smith and all succeeding presidents of the Church taught that blacks were not yet to receive the priesthood, for reasons which are known to God, but which He has not made fully known to man" (Letter). Church presidents had also stated that at some future time all priesthood blessings would be available to all worthy members.

President Spencer W. Kimball, whose clarion call during his ministry was to take the gospel to every nation, kindred, tongue, and people, was particularly aware of many throughout the world who could not receive the priesthood, and he pleaded long and earnestly in their behalf. In the Salt Lake Temple, President Kimball met on several occasions with his counselors and members of the Quorum of the Twelve Apostles to discuss this issue. In such a meeting on 1 June 1978, President Kimball asked his brethren to express their feelings regarding this matter. Only ten of the Twelve were present, since Elder Mark E. Petersen was in South America and Elder Delbert L. Stapley was in the hospital. Elder David B. Haight recalled that as each person spoke, there was "an outpouring of the Spirit which bonded our souls together in perfect unity" (quoted in Tate, 279). Then President Kimball suggested that they have prayer at the altar. President Gordon B. Hinckley recalled: "There was a hallowed and sanctified atmosphere in the room. For me, it felt as if a conduit opened between the heavenly throne and the kneeling, pleading prophet of God who was joined by his Brethren. . . . Every man in that circle, by the power of the Holy Ghost, knew the same thing. . . . Tremendous eternal consequences for millions over the earth are flowing from that manifestation" (Hinckley, 70).

An official announcement of this revelation, dated 8 June 1978, was released to the world the following day. This **revelation**, which was accepted as an official declaration by a sustaining vote of the Church membership in **general conference** on 30 September, made it possible for every nation, kindred, tongue, and people to receive all the blessings of the gospel of **Jesus Christ**. This revelation opened the way for the gospel to go to **Africa** and to billions of people on the other side of the veil.

In November 1978 Elder and Sister Rendell N. Mabey and Elder and Sister Edwin Q. Cannon Jr. were the first missionaries called to establish the Church in black Africa. They were sent to **Nigeria** and **Ghana** in West Africa, where thousands had been waiting and pleading for Church membership over a period of 20 years, and many congregations had been organized using the name of the Church, even though the participants were not baptized members. In less than ten years, Elder **Neal A. Maxwell** of the Quorum of the Twelve organized a **stake** in Aba, Nigeria—the first stake in which all members were black.

By 1998—20 years after the revelation—there were an estimated one half million members with African roots, with about 100,000 each in Africa and the **Caribbean**, and another 300,000 in **Brazil**.

SOURCES

First Presidency letter to all priesthood leaders, 15 December 1969.

Grover, Mark L. "The Mormon Priesthood Revelation and the Sao Paulo, Brazil Temple." *Dialogue* (1990): 39–53.

———. "Religious Accommodation in the Land of Racial Democracy: Mormon Priesthood and Black Brazilians." *Dialogue* (1984): 22–34.

Hinckley, Gordon B. *Ensign* 18 (October 1988): 69–72.

Kimball, Spencer W. *The Teachings of Spencer W. Kimball.* Edited by Edward L. Kimball. Salt Lake City: Bookcraft, 1982.

"Nigeria Marks Twin Milestones." *Church News,* 21 May 1988, 6.

Tate, Lucile C. *David B. Haight: The Life Story of a Disciple.* Salt Lake City: Bookcraft, 1987.

E. DALE LEBARON

OGDEN, PETER SKENE. Peter Skene Ogden was a fur trapper who worked in the **Utah** area before the coming of the **Mormons**. Born in 1794 to a colonial lawyer in **Quebec**, Ogden abandoned the legal career his father desired and became a fur trapper, **Indian** fighter, outlaw, explorer, and businessman. At 17 he joined the Montreal-based fur cartel, North West Company, and was one of the most partisan employees during the years of fierce competition and war with the **Hudson's Bay**

Company. After the merger of these two companies in 1821, he was appointed a clerk in the Columbia District.

Ogden explored and trapped beaver in what was to become Utah Territory. From 1828 through 1829 he traveled extensively in northwestern Utah, sighting the Great Salt Lake. In 1835 he was appointed the youngest chief factor (trader) in the Hudson's Bay Company. Beginning in 1847, as chief factor at Fort Vancouver, he was the immediate superior to the trader at **Fort Hall** (Pocatello, **Idaho**), who had many dealings with the Latter-day Saints. He died at **Oregon** City in 1854.

SOURCES

Cline, Gloria Griffen. *Peter Skene Ogden and the Hudson's Bay Company.* American Exploration and Travel series, no. 64. Norman, Okla.: University of Oklahoma Press, 1974.

Funk, Ann. "Peter Skene Ogden: Nevada's First Great Explorer." *Humbolt Historian* 11 (1988): 24–28.

LaLande, Jeffrey M. *First over the Siskiyous: Peter Skene Ogden's 1826–1827 Journey through the Oregon-California Borderlands.* Portland: Oregon Historical Society Press, 1987.

Miller, David E. "Peter Skene Ogden's Trek into Utah, 1828–1829." *Pacific Northwest Quarterly* 51 (1960): 16–25.

Socwell, Clarence P. "Peter Skene Ogden: Fur Trader Extraordinaire; Trapping, Exploration and Adventure on the Canadian and American Frontiers." *American West* 10 (1973): 42–47, 61.

"Through a 'strange country . . . covered with lakes' Peter Skene Ogden and the Hudson's Bay Company in the Klamath Basin." *Journal of the Shaw Historical Library* 8 (1994): 1–28.

FRED R. GOWANS AND LYN CLAYTON

OGDEN, UTAH. Ogden was the first permanent settlement in **Utah** originating with a fort and some cabins built by **Miles Goodyear** in 1845 and 1846. In November 1847, just four months after the arrival of the **pioneers**, Church leaders approved the purchase of Goodyear's claim (nearly all of present Weber County) at a cost of $1,950. Soon **Captain James Brown** and other settlers occupied the fort and established other forts and communities along the Weber and Ogden Rivers.

Early governments, secular and ecclesiastical, were combined under Church leadership. In 1849 James Brown was elected Weber River Precinct leader and bishop of the Weber River **Ward**. On 31 January 1850, Weber County was organized, and on 6 February 1851, Ogden City (named after **Peter Skene Ogden**) was incorporated. On 5 March 1850, the **Saints** in Weber County were organized as the Weber Branch, with

Lorin Farr appointed to govern in spiritual matters and Isaac Clark in temporal matters. On 25 January 1851, the Weber **Stake** of **Zion** was created with Lorin Farr as president. At that time Ogden was divided into two wards: Ogden North Ward (Farr's Fort) with Erastus Bingham as **bishop**, and Ogden South Ward (Brown's Fort) with Isaac Clark as bishop.

Church growth boomed. By 1856 Ogden was divided into four wards. In 1863 the ward areas were designated as *districts*, but in 1877 the term *ward* was used again. In 1908 the Ogden-Weber area was divided into three stakes: Weber, North Weber, and Ogden. By 1930 there were four stakes and 36 wards in the area. In 1998 there were 30 stakes (14 in Ogden City) and 227 wards in Weber County.

The Ogden-Weber area has made some overall contributions to the Church in leaders, service, and accomplishments. Several **general authorities** have come from this region: President **David O. McKay**; **Thomas E. McKay, assistant to the Twelve Apostles**; and members of the Quorums of **Seventy**: S. Dilworth Young, **Franklin D. Richards**, William J. Critchlow Jr., Marlin K. Jensen, Keith Wilcox, Stephen D. Nadauld, Joseph Murin, Gary J. Coleman, Dennis B. Neuenschwander, and Ronald T. Halverson.

Important Church activities and facilities throughout the years in the Ogden-Weber area include the Weber Stake Academy, the Ogden Tabernacle, the Ogden Tabernacle Choir, the Church Storehouse and Canning Plant, and the Ogden Utah Temple.

SOURCES

Jenson, Andrew. *Encyclopedic History of The Church of Jesus Christ of Latter-day Saints.* Salt Lake City: Deseret News, 1941. 605–14; 931–32.

Roberts, Richard C., and Richard W. Sadler. *A History of Weber County.* Salt Lake City: Utah State Historical Society, 1997. 51–101.

RICHARD C. ROBERTS

OHIO. During most of the 1830s, Latter-day Saints gathered in two regions in the United States—northeastern Ohio and western **Missouri**. Ohio was the first gathering place, and since **Joseph Smith** lived there during most of that decade, **Hiram** and **Kirtland** served as the principle headquarters of the Church. Ohio was a place of unusual **revelation**, of significant doctrinal and organizational development, and of powerful spiritual manifestations. Half of all the revelations in the **Doctrine and Covenants** were received while the Prophet lived in Ohio. Moreover, for seven years (1831–38) Kirtland was the center for missionary expansion. Latter-day **Saints** also built their first **temple** in Kirtland, and within two years of its completion, they were forced by increasing threats and mob activity to abandon the community where they had experienced some of the most significant developments in the history of the **Restoration**.

The first missionaries arrived in what was known as the **Western Reserve** (northeastern Ohio) at the end of October 1830, less than seven months after the organization of the Church. These traveling **elders**, known as the four **Lamanite** missionaries, were heading for the frontier west of Missouri to preach to the Indians. One of the elders, **Parley P. Pratt**, lived in northeastern Ohio but was converted in New York while preaching **restorationist** views. Elder Pratt introduced the gospel to **Sidney Rigdon**, one of the leading reformed Baptists in Ohio. Within a month Elder Rigdon and approximately 120 others were baptized into the new faith. That number represented a group larger than the membership of the Church in New York state. After learning of the conversions in the Western Reserve, Joseph Smith received revelations calling him and all early converts to gather to Ohio (D&C 37–38).

Between January and June 1831, approximately 200 members living in upstate and western New York migrated to Kirtland and the vicinity. Because Church members did not own sufficient land in Kirtland to provide for all these immigrants, many settled in Thompson on a farm owned by **Leman Copley**. After Copley left the Church, most of the New York Saints migrated to western Missouri.

During the summer of 1831, Joseph Smith and Sidney Rigdon traveled to the Missouri frontier and there dedicated the area of **Independence** as a gathering place for the Saints, identifying a temple site in that community. Soon many of the Saints in Ohio migrated to western Missouri.

Joseph Smith, however, did not remain in Missouri in 1831. Instead, he returned to Kirtland and then promptly moved to Hiram, which became a headquarters of the Church for about six months. In March 1832 Joseph Smith and Sidney Rigdon were severely beaten by a mob. Amid increased threats, they returned with their families to Kirtland, where Joseph lived until 1838.

The basic pattern of Church government that has continued to the present day was established in Ohio between 1831 and 1836. **Edward Partridge** was called to serve as the first **bishop** in 1831, with two counselors called that same year. The **First Presidency** was organized in 1832, with Joseph Smith as president and Sidney Rigdon and **Jesse Gause** (replaced by **Frederick G. Williams**) as counselors. **Joseph Smith Sr.** was called in 1833 as the first **patriarch**. Twelve men were called as **apostles** in February 1835, forming the Quorum of the Twelve Apostles, and in that same month the original Quorum of the **Seventy** was organized, with seven presidents called to preside. Meanwhile, in 1831 the first **high priests** were called to serve, and in 1835 **Aaronic Priesthood** quorums were constituted.

While Joseph Smith received many revelations relating to Church government, he received many **visions** and revelations that helped Latter-day Saints gain an enlarged understanding of the beliefs and principles of the restored gospel. While working on a new translation of the **Bible** in the **John Johnson** farmhouse in Hiram, Ohio, Joseph Smith and Sidney Rigdon saw in vision the Father and Son and learned about the **three degrees of glory** (D&C 76). Included among the revelations and visions he received in Kirtland was the prophecy on **war** (D&C 87), the revelation known as the **word of wisdom** (D&C 89), the revelation on **priesthood** (D&C 107), and the vision of the celestial kingdom in which members learned principles relating to the redemption of the dead (D&C 137). Joseph Smith and **Oliver Cowdery** also received keys of the priesthood by **Moses, Elias,** and **Elijah** during a visitation in 1836 in the **Kirtland Temple** (D&C 110).

Ohio was in some respects centrally located, and during the 1830s missionaries left Kirtland to serve throughout the **United States, Canada,** and **Great Britain**. During a turbulent period in the Church, Elder **Heber C. Kimball** and others traveled in 1837 to **England**, where they had unusual success.

One of the most significant accomplishments of Latter-day Saints in Kirtland was the building of their first temple. In December 1832 Joseph Smith received a revelation to build a house of the Lord in that community (D&C 88). At that time there were only about 200 members in the township. During the ensuing five years, however, LDS membership in Kirtland increased from 200 to 2,000. During three of these years, amid poverty and persecution, Latter-day Saints constructed their first temple, which was dedicated on 27 March 1836. In that building, Latter-day Saints experienced the greatest pentecostal season in the history of the restoration movement.

The magnificence and size of the Kirtland Temple in what was then a small rural farming community (a township of 162 families in 1830 with a population of 1,018) was just one indication of the strength of the new religious movement that had moved into Kirtland. Many non-Mormons viewed Latter-day Saints as a political, social, religious, and economic threat. In 1837 Latter-day Saint membership exceeded that of the combined population of all other settlers in that township. Prior to 1837 few Latter-day Saints had been elected to public office. In that year, however, this religious group gained political control of every office in the local government. Moreover, most Latter-day Saints supported the **Democratic Party**, and most settlers in that region were Whigs. Many teachings of Church members, especially their belief in a restoration by a prophet who instructed members by revelation, were offensive to some. The strength of an organized movement was offensive to others. Many thought that their traditional lifestyle was in jeopardy.

In late 1837 threats by mobs increased. In December Brigham Young fled from his home in order to preserve his life, and in January 1838 Joseph Smith followed. Amid increased threats and violence, nearly all Kirtland Saints migrated westward to Missouri before the end of July of that year.

Following the exodus of most Latter-day Saints, the temple underwent many changes. For several decades it was used for educational and religious purposes, then it was abandoned. In 1880 members of the **Reorganized Church of Jesus Christ of Latter Day Saints** gained possession of the vacant structure. Almost 80 years later, in 1959, members of this faith engaged in a successful restoration of the building that guaranteed its use for half a century. This sacred edifice is now designated as a National Historic Landmark.

The return of Latter-day Saints to northeastern Ohio began in the 1950s with the completion in 1954 of a **meetinghouse** in Cleveland. This was the first structure built by Latter-day Saints in that region since 1836. Twenty-three years later, the first **ward** was organized in Kirtland, and in 1983 a **stake** was organized there.

Members continue to reflect on the importance of their heritage, as is evident by the restoration in 1984 of one of the most important landmarks in early Kirtland, the **Newel K. Whitney Store**, a temporary home of Joseph Smith and site of many important revelations. On 4 and 5 September 1999 the Church dedicated a temple in Columbus, Ohio. At the beginning of the year 2000, Ohio had 47,437 members living in 10 stakes and 115 wards and **branches**.

SOURCES

Anderson, Karl Ricks. *Joseph Smith's Kirtland: Eyewitness Accounts.* Salt Lake City: Deseret Book, 1989.

Backman, Milton V. *The Heavens Resound: A History of Latter-day Saints in Ohio, 1830–1838.* Salt Lake City: Deseret Book, 1983.

MILTON V. BACKMAN JR.

OKLAHOMA. Although missionaries arrived unofficially in Oklahoma in 1840, the commencement of official **missionary work** there did not begin until 1855. On 26 June of that year, President **Brigham Young** created the Indian Territory Mission, with Henry W. Miller as the first president. Work in the area was hampered during the first several years due to disease, death, and **war**. Early success eventually came among **Indians**, however, and the work gradually spread to the non-Indian people living in the area. Nevertheless, on 23 May 1860 the mission was discontinued.

On 29 March 1883 the mission was permanently reopened, but membership did not increase significantly until the 1950s. In 1960 Oklahoma's first **stake** was organized in Tulsa, followed by a second in Oklahoma City later that same year. In March 1999 the Church began construction on a **temple** in Oklahoma City. At the beginning of the year 2000, continued growth had resulted in a total of seven stakes and two **missions** with 33,721 members living in 75 **wards** and **branches**.

SOURCES

Kimball, Spencer W. Conference Report (30 September 1950): 63–69.

1999–2000 Church Almanac. Salt Lake City: Deseret News, 1998. 231–32.

CONNIE R. LANKFORD

OMAN. See MIDDLE EAST.

ONTARIO, CANADA. Formerly known as Upper **Canada**, Ontario was the first place outside the **United States** to hear the restored gospel. **Mormon** missionaries, including **Brigham Young, John E. Page, Parley P. Pratt**, and a score of others, traveled throughout the province in the 1830s and 40s. **Joseph Smith** himself visited the province in 1833, baptizing several people in the Mt. Pleasant-Brantford areas. Perhaps the most famous early converts were **John Taylor** and **Joseph Fielding**, recent immigrants from **England** through whom Mormonism soon spread to

Great Britain. Some 2,500 people converted to Mormonism in these early years.

With the call to gather with the Church in the West, the Latter-day Saint presence in Ontario dwindled into near obscurity, despite the forays of such fine missionaries as William Segmiller and Abraham Losee in the 1870s and 80s.

The Church did not return to the province in earnest until after **World War I**, when the Canadian **Mission** was established in 1919 under President James Hart. Since that time, the Church has very gradually moved forward in what has become Canada's most populous province (10.5 million in 1999) under the direction of such **mission presidents** as J. Earl Lewis, **Thomas S. Monson**, and **M. Russell Ballard**. By the beginning of the year 2000, the province had 40,289 members, 9 **stakes**, and 92 **wards** and **branches** in all major communities from Thunder Bay in the far northwest to Cornwall near the Quebec border; from Timmins in the north to Windsor in the southwest. A fitting testimony to Church growth in Ontario and to the faithfulness of these Canadian **Saints** was the dedication of the Toronto Ontario **Temple** in 1990.

SOURCES

Bennett, Richard. "Canada: From Struggling Seed, the Church Has Risen to a Branching Maple." *Ensign* 18 (September 1988): 30–45.

———. "'Plucking Not Planting': Mormonism in Eastern Canada 1830–1850." *The Mormon Presence in Canada*. Edited by Brigham Y. Card, et al. Edmonton: University of Alberta Press, 1990. 19–34.

RICHARD E. BENNETT

ORCHESTRA AT TEMPLE SQUARE. The Orchestra at **Temple Square** is an all-volunteer orchestra, organized in 1999, that functions as a concert orchestra with scheduled performances and as a resource for other instrumental needs at Temple Square. Under the direction of Barlow Bradford, the orchestra performed with the **Tabernacle Choir** and the Temple Square Chorale, and at special events and recording sessions as needed.

The Mormon Tabernacle Choir, **Temple Square Chorale and Training School**, and the Orchestra at Temple Square were originally united under the direction of a Church-service president, Wendell Smoot, and a full-time professional music director, Craig Jessop.

LLOYD D. NEWELL

ORDAIN. Like some other ecclesiastical or theological terms, *ordain* has received a more specific meaning over the years. In the early days of the Church, this term referred to both ordaining to priesthood offices and to setting men and women apart for other callings (see, for example, D&C 25:7). Now *ordain* refers specifically to installing a brother in one of the priesthood offices—deacon, teacher, priest, bishop (in the **Aaronic Priesthood**), elder, high priest, patriarch, seventy, or apostle (in the **Melchizedek**).

These ordained offices are received permanently and can be lost only through excommunication. Other ecclesiastical offices are received by being **set apart**, from which an individual is regularly released following a period of service.

SOURCE

Cowan, Richard O. *Answers to Your Questions about the Doctrine and Covenants.* Salt Lake City: Deseret Book, 1996. 3.

RICHARD O. COWAN

ORDERVILLE, UTAH. Situated in Kane County, **Utah**, Orderville was founded by **Mormon pioneers** in 1875. As the name implies, Orderville was one of more than 150 united order communities instituted during the 1870s. It was founded on principles of cooperation, communal living, and hard work. Orderville was arguably the most successful of these "order" communities, remaining intact for more than a decade. Several factors accounted for this longevity, including isolation from outside influences. Orderville grew from a population of less than a hundred in 1876 to more than 600 by 1882. Over time, however, the call of fashion and material things threatened to dissolve the Order. By 1884 rules of remuneration were modified, allowing laborers to be paid according to individual skills. This change, along with fear of prosecution under the **Edmunds Act of 1882**, threatened the Order's existence. In 1886, following the counsel of **Elder Francis M. Lyman**, local leaders discontinued the Order. Although no longer an Order community, its pioneer legacy lives on. In 1999 Orderville was a quiet town with a population of approximately 500.

SOURCES

Israelsen, L. Dwight. "An Economic Analysis of the United Order." *BYU Studies* 30 (Summer 1978): 536–62.

Pendleton, Mark A. "The Orderville United Order of Zion." *Utah Historical Quarterly* 7 (October 1939): 141–59.

ROBERT C. FREEMAN

ORDINANCES. For Latter-day Saints, the word "ordinance" is most often used to identify or describe authoritative rituals, rites, or ceremonies. Some ordinances are essential to exaltation, and others, while a source of strength in mortality, are not absolutely required. Saving ordinances include baptism, **confirmation** (having the gift of the Holy Ghost bestowed), ordination to the **Melchizedek Priesthood** (for men), the **temple endowment**, and eternal **marriage**. Ordinances or rituals that are not considered essential to exaltation include the **sacrament** (communion or the Lord's supper), blessing and naming infants, anointing and blessing the sick, consecrating olive oil for blessings, dedicating graves, settings apart to Church positions, dedicating homes, blessings of comfort, and father's blessings. Such ordinances are performed in the name of **Jesus Christ** and by the authority of the **priesthood**. The saving ordinances, including baptism and sealing, are preformed in the name of all three members of the Godhead.

The word *ordinance* is also defined as "direction, decree, command, law, principle, order, or rule." **Elder Boyd K. Packer** pointed out that "the word 'ordinance' comes from the word 'order'" (145). Hence, ordinances help put our lives into the proper order from an eternal perspective.

SOURCE

Packer, Boyd K. *The Holy Temple.* Salt Lake City: Bookcraft, 1980. 145.

ROBERT L. MARROTT

OREGON. During the early 1840s, when **Mormon** persecution was intense, people both in and out of the **Church** wondered if the **Saints** would move to the Oregon Territory. **Henry Clay**, a presidential candidate, suggested that the Saints go there. **Orson Hyde** went to **Washington, D.C.**, to find out if the **United States** would annex Oregon and if the government would protect the Saints if they migrated to the territory. Before Oregon became a state in 1858, LDS settlers and missionaries found it generally an unwelcome place to preach and settle. The territorial legislature even proposed a bill to ban different races, **Mormons**, and skunks from settling in the territory.

Elder Charles C. Rich called Elder R. Boyd Stewart to serve a mission to Oregon on 25 September 1850. Four years later, others were called to go to the Oregon and **Washington** territories. During the **Utah War** of 1857, many Saints left Oregon to return to Utah. The Northwestern States Mission was organized for a second time on 26 July 1897. By the end of the nineteenth century, missionaries were beginning to have significant success, and Latter-day Saints became involved with timber companies, ranches, sugar beet farms, and the defense industry in Oregon. The Union **Stake** (now the LaGrande Oregon Stake) was organized 9 June 1901 in eastern Oregon. The Portland Oregon **Temple** was dedicated in 1989, and the Medford Oregon Temple was dedicated in the year 2000. The LDS population in 1980 was 94,000, and in the year 2000 it had grown to 134,438 members living in 35 stakes and 274 wards and branches. This made the LDS Church the second largest church in Oregon.

SOURCES

1999–2000 Church Almanac. Salt Lake City: Deseret News, 1998. 232–34.

Oregon Statesman. 26 December 1854.

Smith, Joseph. *History of The Church of Jesus Christ of Latter-day Saints.* Edited by B. H. Roberts. 2d ed. rev. 7 vols. Salt Lake City: The Church of Jesus Christ of Latter-day Saints, 1932–51.

BRIAN L. SMITH

OREGON TRAIL. In 1847 the **Mormon pioneers** followed part of the **Oregon** Trail on their trek to the **Salt Lake Valley.** The trail originated in the late 1820s, when fur traders followed already existing animal and **Indian** trails to outline what would become the "Great Platte River Road." By 1830 the Oregon Trail, named from **John Charles Frémont's** explorations in the early 1840s, consisted of two segments: American trappers and early emigrants expanded the eastern arm along the Platte and Sweetwater Rivers, while British trappers developed the western arm along the Columbia and Snake Rivers. In 1843 mass migrations began traveling to the Oregon country from **Independence, Missouri;** this movement continued steadily through the 1850s. In 1847 Latter-day Saints began using the Oregon Trail, commencing at **Fort Laramie** and leaving it at the parting of the trails, about 100 miles northeast of Fort Bridger. The Latter-day Saints reopened the north side of the **Platte River** from Grand Island, **Nebraska,** to Fort Laramie, following the old fur trade route along the north side of the Platte River. The Saints provided services along the trail until the transcontinental **railroad** caused over-land migration to decline in 1869.

SOURCES

Ghent, W. J. *The Road to Oregon: A Chronicle of the Great Emigrant Trail.* New York: Longmans, Green, and Company, 1929.

Lavendar, David. *Westward Vision: The Story of the Oregon Trail.* Lincoln: University of Nebraska Press, 1985.

Parkman, Francis. *The Oregon Trail.* Edited by E. N. Feltskog. Lincoln: University of Nebraska Press, 1994.

Unruh, John D. Jr. *The Plains Across.* Chicago: University of Illinois Press, 1979.

FRED R. GOWANS AND ANDREA G. RADKE

ORGAN, TABERNACLE. See **TABERNACLE ORGAN.**

ORGANIZATION OF THE CHURCH. During the month of June 1829 the Lord gave the **Prophet Joseph Smith** and **Oliver Cowdery** an explicit revelation describing the procedures to be followed on the actual day of Church organization the following year. Joseph explained that they retired to the chamber (or bedroom) of the **Peter Whitmer Sr. home**, and while praying for direction, received key instruction: "The word of the Lord came unto us in the chamber, commanding us that I should **ordain** Oliver Cowdery to be an **Elder** in the Church of **Jesus Christ**; and that he also should ordain me to the same office," but wait until "such times as it should be practicable to have our brethren, who had been and who should be baptized, assembled together, when we must have their sanc-tion to our thus proceeding to ordain each other, and have them decide by vote whether they were willing to accept us as spiritual teachers or not." They were also told to administer the sacrament, "ordain such men as the Spirit should dictate," and then bestow the gift of the Holy Ghost by the laying on of hands upon those who had been baptized previously (Smith, 1:60–61).

Doctrine and Covenants 20, "the most elaborate and detailed of any revelation given to the Prophet Joseph Smith prior to the organization of the Church" (Faulring, 1), has been referred to as the "Constitution of the Restored Church" and was accepted as the major part of the "Articles and Covenants of the Church." The Prophet testified that this revelation had been received from Jesus Christ "by the spirit of prophecy and revelation," and "pointed out to us the precise day upon which, according to his will and commandment, we should proceed to organize his Church" (D&C 20, headnote). The first verse of the revelation states: "The rise of the Church of Christ in these last days, being one thousand eight hundred and thirty years since the coming of our Lord and Savior Jesus Christ in the flesh, it being regularly organized and established agreeable to the laws of our country, by the will and commandments of God, in the fourth month, and on the sixth day of the month which is called April" (D&C 20:1).

It is evident that the organizers of this religious society not only sought to meet the commandments of God but also made a conscious effort to satisfy the legalities governing the incorporation of a religious society in the state of **New York** (Carmack, 15). **David Whitmer** affirmed that such an incorporation was their intent and that it had a practical side: "The world had been telling us that we were not a regularly organized church, and we had no right to officiate in the ordinance of marriage, hold church property, etc., and that we should organize according to the laws of the land. On this account we met at my father's house in Fayette, N.Y., on **April 6**, 1830, to attend to this matter of organizing according to the laws of the land" (Whitmer, 32–33). The original incorporation entry has never been found among the court records in Seneca County, despite an extensive search.

Section III of the 1813 New York "Act to provide for the Incorporation of Religious Societies," under which the Church would have been legally formed, specified: "It shall be lawful for the male persons of full age, belonging to any other church, congregation or religious society, now or hereafter to be established in this state, and not already incorporated, to assemble at the church **meetinghouse**, or to the place where they statedly attend for divine worship, and, by plurality of voices, to elect any number of discreet persons of their church, congregation or society, not less than three, nor exceeding nine in number as trustees, to . . . transact all affairs relative to the temporalities thereof. . . . That on the said day of election, two of the elders . . . to be nominated by a majority of the members present, shall preside at such election" (Van Ness, 214). While the act allowed for three to nine trustees, the Prophet arbitrarily selected six. According to an 1862 deposition by **Joseph Knight Jr.**, the six men who were responsible for organizing the Church were Oliver Cowdery, Joseph Smith Jr., **Hyrum Smith, Peter Whitmer Jr., Samuel H. Smith**, and David Whitmer. These names were given to Joseph Knight by Oliver Cowdery. Some of these men had been baptized previously, but all were baptized on the day of organization (Smith, 1:76).

An announcement of the organizational **meeting** was sent to the prospective membership. Joseph Smith stated, "We . . . made known to our brethren that we had received a commandment to organize the Church; and accordingly we met together for that purpose, at the house of Mr. **Peter Whitmer, Sen.**, (being six in number) on Tuesday, the sixth day of April, A.D., one thousand eight hundred and thirty" (Smith, 1:75–77).

Other individuals were there besides the six organizers named. On 2 January 1887 David Whitmer told **Edward Stevenson** about the organizational meeting. Edward recorded: "6 elders were at Peter Whitmer's. David's father's 2 rooms were filled with members—about 20 from Colesville, 15 from Manchester Church and about 20 from around about Father Whitmers. About 50 members & the 6 Elders were present. . . . And [David Whitmer] believes that Martin Harris was ordained at Conference" (Stevenson, 129).

That Joseph and Oliver had previously received the keys of the **Melchizedek Priesthood** under the hands of **Peter, James, and John** is further affirmed by the proceedings of the organizational meeting held on 6 April 1830. Without those keys, Joseph Smith and Oliver Cowdery would not have been authorized or would not have had the **priesthood** power to take the actions they took on that day. It was likewise imperative that they obtain the consent of the brethren over whom they would preside before they could function as officers within the Church. Joseph's exacting account of the sequence followed in that meeting closely parallels the outline which the Lord had given to him and Oliver in June of the previous year. The Prophet stated: "Having opened the meeting by solemn prayer to our heavenly Father, we proceeded, according to previous commandment, to call on our brethren to know whether they accepted us as their teachers in the things of the **Kingdom of God**, and whether they were satisfied that we should proceed and be organized as a Church according to said commandment which we had received. To these several propositions they consented by a unanimous vote" (Smith, 1:77).

The congregation accepted Joseph and Oliver as spiritual leaders. They then exercised the keys given them by Peter, James, and John to ordain one another first and second elder, respectively. The gift of the Holy Ghost and confirmation of membership were bestowed by the laying on of hands to persons who had been baptized previous to the organizational meeting. The Prophet affirmed that "the Holy Ghost was poured out upon us to a very great degree—some prophesied, whilst we all praised the Lord, and rejoiced exceedingly" (Smith, 1:77–78).

Revelation concerning the Prophet's calling as "a **seer**, a translator, a prophet, an **apostle** of Jesus Christ" was received and sustained by those present (D&C 21:1). Some additional ordinations to different priesthood offices were carried out. The sacrament was also administered during the course of the meeting and Joseph concluded, "We dismissed with the pleasing knowledge that we were now individually members of, and acknowledged of God, 'The Church of Jesus Christ,' organized in accordance with commandments and revelations given by Him to ourselves in these last days, as well as according to the order of the Church as recorded in the New Testament" (Smith, 1:78–79).

Responses to the newly organized Church of Christ can be measured in the numerous baptisms that resulted in the respective branches at Fayette, **Colesville**, and **Manchester**, New York, where individuals were moved upon by the Holy Ghost to be numbered with the Church and kingdom of God on earth.

SOURCES

Anderson, Richard Lloyd. "The House Where the Church Was Organized." *Improvement Era* 73 (April 1970).

———. "Who Were the Six Who Organized the Church on 6 April 1830." *Ensign* 10 (June 1980).

Carmack, John K. "Fayette: the Place the Church Was Organized." *Ensign* 19 (February 1989).

Faulring, Scott H. *The Articles and Covenants of the Church: D&C 20 and Its Antecedents.* Provo, Utah: Foundation for Ancient Research & Mormon Studies, 1997.

Porter, Larry C. "Organizational Origins of the Church of Jesus Christ, 6 April 1830." In *New York.* Edited by Larry C. Porter, Milton V. Backman Jr., and Susan Easton Black. Regional Studies in Latter-day Saint Church History series. Provo, Utah: Brigham Young University, 1992.

———. "The Restoration of the Aaronic and Melchizedek Priesthoods." *Ensign* 26 (December 1996).

———. "A Study of the Origins of The Church of Jesus Christ of Latter-day Saints in the States of New York and Pennsylvania, 1816–1831." Ph.D. diss., Brigham Young University, 1971. 96–103, 198–222, 252–68.

———. "Was the Church Legally Incorporated at the Time It Was Organized in the State of New York?" *Ensign* 8 (December 1978) 26–27.

Smith, Joseph. *History of The Church of Jesus Christ of Latter-day Saints.* Edited by B. H. Roberts. 2d ed. rev. 7 vols. Salt Lake City: The Church of Jesus Christ of Latter-day Saints, 1932–51. 1:60–61.

Stevenson, Edward. "Journal of Edward Stevenson." Manuscript. 2 January 1887. 129.

Van Ness, William P., and John Woodworth, revisors. *Laws of the State of New York, Revised and Passed at the Thirty-Sixth Session of the Legislature*. Albany, New York: H. C. Southwick & Co., 1813.

Whitmer, David. *An Address to All Believers in Christ*. Richmond, Mo.: David Whitmer, 1887.

LARRY C. PORTER

THE FAMILY

A PROCLAMATION TO THE WORLD

The First Presidency and Council of the Twelve Apostles
of The Church of Jesus Christ of Latter-day Saints

WE, THE FIRST PRESIDENCY and the Council of the Twelve Apostles of The Church of Jesus Christ of Latter-day Saints, solemnly proclaim that marriage between a man and a woman is ordained of God and that the family is central to the Creator's plan for the eternal destiny of His children.

ALL HUMAN BEINGS—male and female—are created in the image of God. Each is a beloved spirit son or daughter of heavenly parents, and, as such, each has a divine nature and destiny. Gender is an essential characteristic of individual premortal, mortal, and eternal identity and purpose.

IN THE PREMORTAL REALM, spirit sons and daughters knew and worshiped God as their Eternal Father and accepted His plan by which His children could obtain a physical body and gain earthly experience to progress toward perfection and ultimately realize his or her divine destiny as an heir of eternal life. The divine plan of happiness enables family relationships to be perpetuated beyond the grave. Sacred ordinances and covenants available in holy temples make it possible for individuals to return to the presence of God and for families to be united eternally.

THE FIRST COMMANDMENT that God gave to Adam and Eve pertained to their potential for parenthood as husband and wife. We declare that God's commandment for His children to multiply and replenish the earth remains in force. We further declare that God has commanded that the sacred powers of procreation are to be employed only between man and woman, lawfully wedded as husband and wife.

WE DECLARE the means by which mortal life is created to be divinely appointed. We affirm the sanctity of life and of its importance in God's eternal plan.

HUSBAND AND WIFE have a solemn responsibility to love and care for each other and for their children. "Children are an heritage of the Lord" (Psalms 127:3). Parents have a sacred duty to rear their children in love and righteousness, to provide for their physical and spiritual needs, to teach them to love and serve one another, to observe the commandments of God and to be law-abiding citizens wherever they live. Husbands and wives—mothers and fathers—will be held accountable before God for the discharge of these obligations.

THE FAMILY is ordained of God. Marriage between man and woman is essential to His eternal plan. Children are entitled to birth within the bonds of matrimony, and to be reared by a father and a mother who honor marital vows with complete fidelity. Happiness in family life is most likely to be achieved when founded upon the teachings of the Lord Jesus Christ. Successful marriages and families are established and maintained on principles of faith, prayer, repentance, forgiveness, respect, love, compassion, work, and wholesome recreational activities. By divine design, fathers are to preside over their families in love and righteousness and are responsible to provide the necessities of life and protection for their families. Mothers are primarily responsible for the nurture of their children. In these sacred responsibilities, fathers and mothers are obligated to help one another as equal partners. Disability, death, or other circumstances may necessitate individual adaptation. Extended families should lend support when needed.

WE WARN that individuals who violate covenants of chastity, who abuse spouse or offspring, or who fail to fulfill family responsibilities will one day stand accountable before God. Further, we warn that the disintegration of the family will bring upon individuals, communities, and nations the calamities foretold by ancient and modern prophets.

WE CALL UPON responsible citizens and officers of government everywhere to promote those measures designed to maintain and strengthen the family as the fundamental unit of society.

This proclamation was read by President Gordon B. Hinckley as part of his message at the General Relief Society Meeting held September 23, 1995, in Salt Lake City, Utah.

PROCLAMATION ON THE FAMILY. From time to time, LDS Church leaders have issued official proclamations. This one, the Proclamation on the Family, was read for the first time during a general Relief Society meeting, 23 September 1995.

PACIFIC. The Pacific Ocean, which occupies one-third of the earth's surface, is the largest physical feature on the globe. Its population, however, is relatively small: only 31.3 million, including **Australia**'s 18.4 million, in 1998. Geographers broadly classify the peoples of the Pacific as Polynesian, Melanesian, and Micronesian. Although the Pacific islands have a romantic legacy of balmy beaches and easy living, the reality for most islanders has been more difficult, including drought, hurricanes, earthquakes, isolation, and poverty. The high volcanic and continental islands (**New Zealand**, **Samoa**, and **Papua New Guinea**) have provided considerable food variety and consistent supply, but the low islands or atolls (Ha'apai in **Tonga** and the Tuamotus of **French Polynesia**) have provided only simple food and are vulnerable to hurricanes and drought.

Latter-day Saint presence in the Pacific began among the Polynesians of French Polynesia in 1844, among the Melanesians of **Fiji** and **New Caledonia** a century later, and in **Micronesia/Guam** during the 1970s. The most significant recent growth areas include **Kiribati**, Papua New Guinea, and **Vanuatu**. By the late 1990s the Church was established in Australia, French Polynesia, **Hawaii**, New Zealand, Samoa, Tonga, the **Cook Islands**, and **Niue** in Polynesia; in Fiji, New Caledonia, Papua New Guinea, and Vanuatu in Melanesia; in Guam, the **Marshall islands** of Arno and Mili, Kwajalein/Ebeye, and Majuro; the Micronesian islands of Chuuk [Truk], Kosrae, Pohnpei, and Yap; and the **Northern Mariana islands** of Saipan, Rota, and Tinian. Palau and Kiribati are also part of Micronesia. Most of the Pacific islanders had been Christianized before Latter-day Saint missionaries arrived.

Pacific Latter-day Saint population was 418,831 in 2000. The largest memberships were in Australia (99,000); New Zealand (89,952); Samoa (71,277); Hawaii (55,361); and Tonga (44,819—40% of the nation's population, the highest percentage of Latter-day Saints in the world).

For the first hundred years of LDS Pacific history, the focus was on Polynesia and Australia. The Church has had an enduring interest in

Polynesians. They have been considered descendants of Israel since George Q. Cannon's revelation to that effect during his missionary days in Hawaii (1850–54), and the presidents of the Church have identified the Polynesians as the posterity of father Lehi in the **Book of Mormon**. This conviction, and the attendant belief that these peoples deserve special attention, has been backed by considerable Church resources: gathering places in Lanai and **Laie, Hawaii**, and Mapusaga and Sauniatu, Samoa; schools (French Polynesia and Hawaii had the Church's first mission schools—New Zealand, Samoa, Tonga, Fiji, and Kiribati—the latter two being in Melanesia and Micronesia, respectively); translations of **scriptures**—first by missionaries and later by translation services; **temples**—Hawaii, New Zealand, **Tahiti**, Samoa, Tonga, and Sydney, and under construction Adelaide, Brisbane, and Melbourne, Australia; Suva, Fiji; and Kailua-Kona, Hawaii; and the **Polynesian Cultural Center** in Hawaii, which the Church opened in 1963 to preserve the cultures of the Pacific and to provide employment for students at Church College of Hawaii (now **BYU–Hawaii**). Nowhere else has the Church created flagship communities with housing, schools, and temples as it has done in Laie, Hawaii; Pesega, Samoa; Liahona, Tonga; and Temple View, New Zealand.

The Pacific provides several firsts in Church history: the first foreign language mission (French Polynesia); the first mission schools; the first temple dedicated outside continental North America (Hawaii 1919); the first stake outside North America (Oahu Stake in Hawaii, 1935); the **labor missionary program** in the 1950s and 1960s; the first countries to handle their own missionary work (Samoa and Tonga); and the first country to be entirely covered by **stakes** (Samoa).

At the end of the twentieth century, the Church was mature in most Pacific nations. French Polynesian Saints celebrated the Church's sesquicentennial in their islands in 1994. Hawaii reached its sesquicentennial anniversary in 2000, and Australia and New Zealand in 2001 and 2004. (The first missionary to Australia, 17-year-old William Barratt, arrived in 1841, but little was accomplished until missionaries were sent from **Utah** in 1851.) Samoa and Tonga celebrated their Church centennials in 1988 and 1991.

In 1999 the Church in the Pacific was administered by three **Area** Presidencies: Australia New Zealand Area with headquarters in Sydney, Australia; Pacific Islands Area with headquarters in Auckland, New

Zealand; and Hawaii as part of the North America West Area with head-quarters in **Salt Lake City**.

SOURCES

Britsch, R. Lanier. *Unto the Islands of the Sea: A History of the Latter-day Saints in the Pacific*. Salt Lake City: Deseret Book, 1986.
1999–2000 Church Almanac. Salt Lake City: Deseret News, 1998.

R. LANIER BRITSCH

PACKER, BOYD K. Boyd Kenneth Packer, an **apostle** and Church educator, was born 10 September 1924 in **Brigham City, Utah**, to Ira Wright and Emma Jensen Packer. He was the tenth of eleven children. As a child he was deeply observant of nature, especially birds, and he later became a skilled artist.

After graduating from Box Elder High School, he trained as a bomber pilot in the U.S. Air Force, serving in the **Pacific** Theater during **World War II**. While in the military, he determined that he would become a teacher.

After returning home he married Donna Edith Smith. During the years they were rearing their ten children, Brother Packer taught **seminary**, served as a city councilman, fulfilled calls in the Church, and continued his education. He earned his bachelor's and master's degrees from Utah State University and a doctor's degree in educational administration from **Brigham Young University**.

Brother Packer served as a supervisor of seminaries and **institutes of religion** until called as an **assistant to the Twelve** Apostles in 1961. Among his many assignments were president of the New England Mission and member of the administrative council and board of trustees of BYU.

On 6 April 1970, he was sustained to the Quorum of the Twelve Apostles; he was ordained an **apostle** on 9 April 1970. Elder Packer was set apart as acting president of the Quorum of the Twelve on 5 June 1994, and again on 12 March 1995.

His many published works include *Teach Ye Diligently, That All May be Edified*, and *The Holy Temple*. His biography, *A Watchman on the Tower*, details many events of his life.

Elder A. Theodore Tuttle, his close friend and fellow supervisor of seminaries and institutes of religion, wrote of his "ready wit and keen sense of humor," his deep spirituality, his "tremendous powers of concentration and capacity for work," and "his commitment to home and family" (Packer, vii-viii). The combination of these qualities, added to his spiritual powers, vision, wisdom, and penetrating expression, make him one of the most often quoted **general authorities** of our day.

***

SOURCES

Packer, Boyd K. *Teach Ye Diligently.* Salt Lake City: Deseret Book, 1975. viii.

Tate, Lucile C. *Boyd K. Packer, a Watchman on the Tower.* Salt Lake City: Bookcraft, 1995.

KENNETH W. PACKER

PAGE, HIRAM. Hiram Page was one of the **eight witnesses** of the **gold plates.** He was born in 1800 at Vermont. As a student of folk medicine, Page used his personal seer stone to receive insight regarding the newly organized Church. In an 1830 revelation (D&C 28), the **Prophet Joseph Smith** declared that Hiram had been deceived and that his ideas were false. After much deliberation, Church members sustained Joseph's leadership, and Hiram Page and his associates acknowledged their error.

Hiram Page faithfully followed the Prophet to **Ohio** and then on to **Independence** and **Far West, Missouri.** Here he lost faith in the leadership of Joseph Smith and was excommunicated. He left the Saints and lived the remainder of his days in Excelsior Springs, Missouri. While he never returned to the Church, his testimony of the reality of the gold plates remained constant throughout his life. Page died 12 August 1852, near Excelsior Springs, Missouri.

***

SOURCES

Black, Susan Easton. *Who's Who in the Doctrine and Covenants.* Salt Lake City: Bookcraft, 1997. 207–10.

McCune, George M. *Personalities in the Doctrine and Covenants.* Salt Lake City: Hawkes, 1991. 82.

Wright, Dennis A. "The Hiram Page Stone: A Lesson in Church Government." *The Doctrine and Covenants, a Book of Answers.* Edited by Leon R. Hartshorn, Dennis A. Wright, and Craig J. Ostler. Salt Lake City: Deseret Book, 1996. 85–94.

DENNIS A. WRIGHT

PAGE, JOHN E. John Edward Page, a member of the **Quorum** of the Twelve **Apostles**, was born 25 February 1799 in Trenton, Oneida, **New York**. He was a believing Methodist before joining the Church in 1833.

In May 1836 he was called on a mission to **Canada**. During his two years in that country, Page baptized nearly 600 people and traveled 5,000 miles preaching the gospel. After leaving Canada he settled in **Missouri**, where he suffered persecution for his religious beliefs. Page was ordained an apostle on 19 December 1838 in **Far West, Missouri**. His service in the Quorum of the Twelve did not match his earlier missionary zeal in Canada. He failed to fulfill a mission call to **England** and to accompany **Orson Hyde** to **Palestine**. Nevertheless, he retained his fellowship in the Twelve until advocating the apostate claims of **James J. Strang** as successor to Joseph Smith. On 9 February 1846, Page lost his apostolic authority and in June 1846 was excommunicated.

Thereafter he became affiliated with various schismatic groups. Although Page became president of the Strangite apostles and editor of the *Zion's Reveille* publication, by 1849 he had renounced Strangism. He then united with the James C. Brewster faction of Mormonism for a short period. By the 1860s he was an apostle and president of the high priesthood in the Church of the Temple Lot (Hedrickites). Page died 14 October 1867 in Sycamore, DeKalb, **Illinois**, at age 68.

Sources

Black, Susan Easton. *Who's Who in the Doctrine and Covenants*. Salt Lake City: Bookcraft, 1997. 210–13.

Quist, John. "John E. Page: An Apostle of Uncertainty." *Journal of Mormon History* 12 (1985): 53–68.

Susan Easton Black

PAGEANTS. The purpose of Church pageants is to celebrate, through **drama** and **music**, an event, place, or person in religious history. These pageants provide opportunities for local members to develop talents and for those of other faiths to learn more about the Church and be invited to meet with the missionaries. There are eight officially recognized pageants sponsored by the Church.

Calgary Pageant. "The Nativity Pageant," performed in Calgary, **Alberta**, is presented annually during the week before Christmas. Begun in 1963, this 20-minute pageant presents the story of the birth of the Savior as recorded in the second chapter of Luke.

Castle Valley Pageant. This production, begun in 1978, is held five miles from Castle Dale, **Utah**. It portrays the settlement of Emery County by Latter-day Saint **pioneers** sent from Sanpete County by President **Brigham Young**.

Clarkston Pageant. "**Martin Harris**, the Man Who Knew" tells how Martin Harris assisted in the publication of the **Book of Mormon**. Since 1983 it has been performed annually in Clarkston, Utah.

Hill Cumorah Pageant. "America's Witness for Christ" is held annually near **Palmyra, New York**. It tells the story of the coming forth of the Book of Mormon through the **Prophet Joseph Smith** and portrays Christ's resurrection and ministry to the Nephites. This pageant was first produced in 1937.

Manti Pageant. "The **Mormon** Miracle Pageant" has been performed in the small Utah community of Manti since 1967. This production tells the story of the restoration of the gospel, the westward movement of the pioneers, and the **Saints'** entry into Sanpete County.

Nauvoo Pageant. The musical drama "The City of Joseph" has been performed in **Nauvoo, Illinois**, since 1976. This pageant focuses on the establishment of Nauvoo and the building of the **Nauvoo Temple**.

Oakland Pageant. Begun in 1964, this pageant tells the story of the restoration of the gospel and of the movement of Latter-day Saints to **California**. All performances are held indoors in the large interstake center **meetinghouse** on Temple Hill in Oakland, California.

Mesa Pageant. Begun in 1938, "Jesus the Christ" portrays the Messiah and his mission according to holy **scripture**. It has grown to become one of the world's largest Easter pageants.

SOURCES

Woodbury, Lael J. "Pageants." *Encyclopedia of Mormonism.* Edited by Daniel H. Ludlow. 4 vols. New York: Macmillan, 1992. 3:1057.

ALBERT JAY BLAIR

PAINESVILLE TELEGRAPH. The *Painesville Telegraph* was a bitter **anti-Mormon** newspaper in its early days. It was published in Painesville, **Ohio**, about ten miles east of **Kirtland**. In 1822 **Eber D. Howe** started the paper, which he edited until 1835. Howe apparently became antagonistic toward the Church after his wife and sister were converted to Mormonism, and he printed more anti-Mormon articles in the *Telegraph* than were published in any other Ohio **periodical** during his time. The newspaper referred to Latter-day Saints as the "dregs of [their] community" and as "profound believers in witchcraft, ghosts, [and] goblins" (quoted in Backman, 53–54). Howe also printed derogatory statements, written by himself and others, about **Joseph Smith**, the **Book**

of Mormon, and the Three Witnesses. Many of the paper's articles were reprinted throughout the state. In addition to his work on the *Telegraph,* Howe cooperated with **Doctor Philastus Hurlbut**, who had twice been excommunicated for immoral conduct, in publishing the first anti-Mormon book, *Mormonism Unvailed* (1834). He also attacked the authenticity of the Book of Mormon, arguing that **Sidney Rigdon** pilfered and plagiarized the **Spaulding manuscript.**

SOURCES

Allen, James B., and Arrington, Leonard J. "Mormon Origins in New York: An Introductory Analysis." *BYU Studies* 9 (Spring 1969): 245–48.

Backman, Milton V., Jr. *The Heavens Resound.* Salt Lake City: Deseret Book, 1983. 53–54.

KEITH W. PERKINS

PALAU/BELAU. Palau is a former trust territory of the United States in the western **Pacific**. It gained its independence in 1994. Of the approximately 18,000 inhabitants, 370 of them (at the beginning of the year 2000) were Latter-day Saints organized into one **branch**.

EMILY C. ZEIGLER

PALESTINE. See HOLY LAND, MIDDLE EAST, and MUSLIMS.

PALMYRA-MANCHESTER, NEW YORK. In 1816 the **Joseph Smith Sr. family** moved from Norwich, **Vermont**, to the village of Palmyra, Palmyra Township, Ontario County (later Wayne Co., 1823), **New York**. Tradition has located their initial home on the southeast corner of what became Johnson and Vienna Streets, but substantiating evidence is lacking. Tax records indicate that the family was situated near the west end of Main Street from 1817 to 1819, and in 1820, two miles south of the village on Stafford Road, very near the Palmyra-Farmington (Manchester in 1822) township line. At some juncture between 1818 and 1820, the Smiths began building a log home on the west side of Stafford Road on the south end of the Palmyra township. Two archaeological digs in 1982 and 1997 verified the site and identified important features of the log home.

In the early spring of 1820, Joseph Smith Jr., then 14 years of age, went into the woods near this log house and with childlike faith knelt in prayer. His petition for guidance resulted in the **First Vision**, in which he witnessed the appearance of the Father and the Son and was instructed by the Savior. A daughter, Lucy, was born to Joseph Sr. and **Lucy Mack Smith** in the log home, 18 July 1821. The first appearances of the angel **Moroni** in and near this house, and at the **Hill Cumorah**, occurred 21–22 September 1823. Alvin, the eldest son, died here on 19 November 1823. After the Smiths moved into their new frame home just across the line, in the Manchester township, perhaps in the spring of 1825, the log house became the dwelling place of Hyrum and Jerusha Barden Smith following their marriage on 2 November 1826. Through an unfortunate set of circumstances, the Smiths lost their new home and farm within five years. Because they had not been able to make the requisite annual payment in 1825, the property passed into the hands of a new receiver, Lemuel Durfee Sr., on 20 December 1825. Durfee, however, was known to the Smiths and considered a friend. He allowed them to remain on the land and make their rental payments in property improvements and other labor.

As newlyweds, Joseph Jr. and **Emma Hale Smith** went to Manchester to live with his parents and to farm with them during the 1827 season. On 22 September Joseph and Emma went to the Hill Cumorah, and Joseph ascended its slopes to meet with the angel **Moroni**, from whom he received the **gold plates**, **Urim and Thummim**, and other sacred objects. The Prophet's attempts to familiarize himself with the record and begin the work of translation were thwarted by mobs seeking to take the plates from him. In December 1827 Joseph and Emma accepted an invitation from her parents to move about one hundred miles southeast to **Harmony, Pennsylvania**. Their friend, **Martin Harris**, paid for any local indebtedness of the couple.

Oliver Cowdery boarded with Joseph Smith Sr. during 1828 and 1829 while filling an appointment as a teacher in the small frame schoolhouse to the south of the Smith home on Stafford Road in Manchester. Gaining the Smiths' confidence, he learned of Joseph's work of translation being carried out in Harmony. Having received a witness of the work's truthfulness, Oliver accompanied Samuel Smith during the forepart of April 1829 to Harmony, where Cowdery acted as scribe to Joseph for the translation. In the spring of 1829, Joseph Sr. and Lucy Smith were forced to leave their Manchester frame home when Durfee foreclosed and required them to vacate. Having no other place to go, they returned to their original log house and lived with Hyrum and Jerusha. The Eight **Witnesses to the Book of Mormon** assembled at this home and then sought a secluded place in the woods to view the gold plates at the hands of the **Prophet**.

While the Book of Mormon was being printed, Joseph Smith, **Oliver Cowdery**, **Hyrum Smith**, and others operated out of the log house as they worked with Egbert B. Grandin to produce the first edition. These men continued to function from this location after Joseph's departure for Harmony in late September 1830. Following the publication of the Book of Mormon at the **Grandin Printing Shop** 26 March 1830, and the **organization of the Church** at **Fayette** on **6 April** of the same year, the log home became a nucleus for the emerging Manchester **Branch**. **Revelation** was received here, and some baptisms took place along nearby Hathaway Brook (Crooked Creek). Hyrum Smith left the log house in October 1830 to preside over the **Colesville** Branch. Joseph and Lucy Smith moved to Waterloo, New York, in October or November 1830, leaving the old home to others.

The LDS Church has completed a modern-day reconstruction of the Smith log home and of the Grandin Printing Shop. They were dedicated by President **Gordon B. Hinckley** on 27 March 1998. The following year plans were announced to construct a **temple** at Palmyra. On 6 April 2000 President Hinckley dedicated the Palmyra temple.

Sources

Berge, Dale L. "Archaeological Work at the Smith Log House." *Ensign* 15 (August 1985): 24–26.

———. "The Boyhood Home of Joseph Smith, Palmyra, New York: Historical and Archaeological Aspects of Life in a Frontier Log House." Manuscript in author's possession.

Bushman, Richard L. *Joseph Smith and the Beginnings of Mormonism*. Urbana: University of Illinois Press, 1984.

Enders, Donald L. "A Snug Log House." *Ensign* 15 (August 1985): 14–23.

———. "Two Significant Sites of the Restoration." *Ensign* 28 (September 1998): 30–37.

Gill, Greg. "President Hinckley Dedicates Historic Sites." *Church News*, 4 April 1998. 3, 6, 12.

Jessee, Dean C., ed. *The Papers of Joseph Smith*. Vol. 1. Salt Lake City: Deseret Book, 1989.

Porter, Larry C. "A Study of the Origins of The Church of Jesus Christ of Latter-day Saints in the States of New York and Pennsylvania, 1816–1831." Ph.D. diss., Brigham Young University, 1971. 35–110.

LARRY C. PORTER

PAMPHLETS. From the Church's earliest years, its missionaries have taken seriously the commandment to "publish glad tidings." At first they delivered their messages of the **Restoration** only orally, but soon members took up the pen to defend and explain the history and doctrines of the Church. These printed works ranged from one-page broadsides to books of several hundred pages. Historically, the most common form of their printed works were pamphlets, works generally ranging from 8 to 32 pages in length. These shorter works were well suited for inexpensive and fast production, they could be narrowly focused to address a specific issue, and they were also quick and easy to read. Pamphlets in Mormonism, as in the larger culture, were the ideal vehicle for debate and argument in an age of the democratic press.

Pamphlets published by Latter-day Saints first appeared in the 1830s, especially after 1835 when missionaries began to enter into the cities of the **United States** and **Canada**. Here they found the potentially larger audiences much harder to reach with just their oral presentations. Thus **Orson Hyde's** short work *Prophetic Warning to All the Churches*, published in Toronto in 1836, and **Parley P. Pratt's** *Voice of Warning*, issued in **New York City** in 1837, were significant works in the emergence of **Mormon** pamphleteering.

The 1840s saw the proliferation of pamphlets. Some were accounts of the **Missouri** persecutions, and others appeared as part of the founding of the **British Mission**. The Pratt brothers (Parley and Orson) were authors of important early Latter-day Saint pamphlets, as were other **apostles** like **John Taylor** and **Lorenzo Snow**. By the 1880s more than 70 individuals had published pamphlets, with almost every item growing out of a missionary context. For example, Latter-day Saint missionaries in **India** in the 1850s issued some 30 tracts, mostly addressed to an English audience there.

By the end of the nineteenth century, most of the missionary literature in use was being written by Church leaders or mission presidents. Works by **B. H. Roberts, John Morgan, Ben E. Rich, Joseph Fielding Smith,** and **James E. Talmage** were more commonly used in the missionary effort before the 1950s. In more recent times, literature issued by the Church for its **missionary work** has been the standardized product of the Missionary Committee and the **Priesthood Correlation** Committee of the Church.

Taken together, these written items provide students of Mormonism with insights into the faith, as well as the history and testimony of their authors and the Church they served. They offer another avenue for the study of Latter-day Saint history. Few, of course, could be considered literary masterpieces, and most are now forgotten, having only appeared in small editions of one printing. But together they testify to the value and significance of the printing press as a technological agent in the spread of the gospel message.

SOURCES

Crawley, Peter. *A Descriptive Bibliography of the Mormon Church, Volume One, 1830–1847.* Provo, Utah: Religious Studies Center, Brigham Young University, 1998.

———. "Parley P. Pratt, Father of Mormon Pamphleteering." *Dialogue* 15 (Autumn 1982): 13–26.

Flake, Chad J. *A Mormon Bibliography, 1830–1930: Books, Pamphlets, Periodicals, and Broadsides Relating to the First Century of Mormonism.* Salt Lake City: University of Utah Press, 1978. A ten-year supplement appeared in 1989, and a title index to both volumes was published in 1992, all by the same press.

Whittaker, David J. "Early Mormon Pamphleteering." Ph.D. diss., Brigham Young University, 1982.

———. "Mormon Imprints as Sources for Research: A History and Evaluation." Edited by James B. Allen, Ronald W. Walker, and David J. Whittaker. Urbana: University of Illinois Press.

———. "The Web of Print: Toward a History of the Book in Early Mormon Culture." *Journal of Mormon History* 23 (Spring 1997): 1–41.

DAVID J. WHITTAKER

PANAMA. The first Latter-day **Saint branch** in Panama was organized in 1941 for American servicemen working on the Panama Canal. Within a year, this branch had grown from 10 to 100 members. Some of these Saints shared their religion with the San Blas **Indians**, whose cultural beliefs had prepared them to receive the gospel. Proselyting was limited, however, because the Church did not gain official government recognition until several years later. In 1952 Panama became part of the newly created **Central America Mission**, and in 1961 **Elder Marion G. Romney** of the **Quorum** of the Twelve **Apostles** visited the country, offering a copy of the **Book of Mormon** to its president. When Panama granted the Church official recognition four years later, **mission president** Ted E. Brewerton began full-time **missionary work** there. Nelson L. Altamirano became president of the country's first **stake** in 1979, and ten years later the Panama Panama City Mission was organized. Although North American missionaries were required to leave Panama in 1988, the Saints in this country were strengthened by the additional leadership opportunities. In 1997 about 3,000 gathered in Panama City to hear President **Gordon B. Hinckley.** By the beginning of the year 2000 there were 35,257 members of the Church in Panama with seven stakes and 110 **wards** and branches.

SOURCES

Hart, John L. "New Missions Are Evidence of Church's Dynamic Growth." *Church News,* 25 February 1989. 3.

1999–2000 Church Almanac. Salt Lake City: Deseret News, 1998. 368–69.

"Panama Gains First Stake from Costa Rica Mission." *Church News,* 22 December 1979. 7.

"San Blas Indians." *Church News,* 2 June 1979. 16.

LISA KURKI

PAPUA NEW GUINEA. Papua New Guinea, a new frontier for the Church in the **Pacific**, is composed of hundreds of small islands where nearly 700 village languages are spoken. In July 1980 President Dennis D. Flake of the **Australia** Brisbane **Mission** was authorized to begin proselyting work among the native people. The following month a missionary couple, Douglas and Eva Johnson, arrived. They established a small **branch** and began teaching the gospel.

On 19 October in Port Moresby, four children were baptized, the first to accept the gospel. Government restrictions permitted only one or two missionary couples at a time in the country. In spite of this, during the first three years 716 people were baptized, nine branches and a mission **district** were organized, and three full-time missionaries were called. On 14 April 1983 **Elder L. Tom Perry** of the Quorum of the Twelve **Apostles** dedicated the nation for the preaching of the gospel. Since then the Church has grown steadily. Chapels have been built, a mission was organized in February 1992, and the first **stake** was established in October 1995. At the beginning of the year 2000, the country had about 8,954 members and 27 **wards** and branches.

SOURCES

Flake, Deanna C., comp. "Australia Brisbane Mission History, July 1980–June 1983."

Flake, Dennis D. Personal Journal and Records, 1980–1983.

1997–1978 Church Almanac. Salt Lake City: Deseret News, 1996. 371.

DENNIS D. FLAKE

PAPYRI. See BOOK OF ABRAHAM.

PARAGUAY. Paraguay is a landlocked country in the center of **South America** with a population of mixed Spanish and **Indian** descent, and its official languages are Spanish and Guarani. Its population is 87% Roman Catholic.

The Church was first brought to Paraguay when Samuel J. Skousen, who worked in the U.S. Embassy in Asuncion, introduced the gospel to Carlos Alberto Rodriguez and his wife, Mafalda, who were later baptized. On 26 July 1948, the first **branch** was organized in Asuncion with Skousen as president. In 1949 the **First Presidency** gave President Frederick S. Williams of the **Uruguay Mission** permission to open Paraguay for **missionary work**. The first missionaries did not enter the country until 9 January 1950, and their first baptism was not until 1951. Later that year two branches were organized.

At the time the Paraguay Mission was created in 1977, there were 2,063 members in the country. Two years later, on 25 February, the first **stake** was organized in Asuncion with Carlos Ramon Espinola as president. By 1980 there were only 2,232 members of the Church in Paraguay, but **growth** escalated during that year when almost an entire colony of Chulupi (Nivacle Indians) were baptized. In 1990 there were about 12,000 members in the country, but by 1995 the number doubled to 24,000 because of an increase in missionary work. On 1 July 1998 a second mission was created, and by the beginning of the year 2000 there were 44,632 members in 6 stakes and 123 **wards** and branches. In the April 2000 **general conference** President **Gordon B. Hinckley** announced the construction of the Asuncion Paraguay Temple.

───────

SOURCES

"The Church in Uruguay and Paraguay." *Ensign* 5 (February 1975): 30–32.

Curbelo, Nestor. "Acts of Faithfulness Write Story of Church Growing in Paraguay." *Church News,* 27 May 1995. 10.

───────. "'Heart' of South America Opening to Gospel." *Church News,* 27 May 1995. 8.

"Paraguayan Indians—Branch Thrives in Jungle." *Church News,* 27 November 1983. 4.

REBECCA JACKSON

PARMLEY, LAVERN W. Lavern Watts Parmley, leader in the **Primary** for 33 years as a general board member, counselor, and president, was born 1 January 1900, in Murray, **Utah**. She married Thomas J. Parmley, a **University of Utah** physics professor. Reared with eight brothers, she claimed that boys were her "speciality," and in her Primary service she administered the boys' programs—the Trail Builders, Cub Scouts, and **Boy Scouts**. LaVern was the first woman to serve on a national scout committee and to receive the Silver Buffalo. She became the fifth general Primary president in 1951, following nine years of service in the presidency. She reorganized age groups and classes, incorporated **scouting** into the Primary program, standardized responsibilities of Primary presidencies, streamlined **stake** boards, served as editor of the *Children's Friend*, and oversaw the completion and then expansion of the **Primary Children's Hospital**. She felt that administering the hospital and seeing "how many children it has helped" was "the most rewarding thing" she had ever done (Parmley Oral History, 100). A lasting contribution of her administration was the introduction in 1957 of a new Primary song, "I Am a Child of God," written by Naomi W. Randall. Sister Parmley was released in 1974 and died on 27 January 1980 in **Salt Lake City**.

SOURCES

LaVern Watts Parmley Oral History. 1974. James Moyle Oral History Program, LDS Church Historical Department, Salt Lake City.

Madsen, Carol Cornwall, and Susan Staker Oman. *Sisters and Little Saints: One Hundred Years of Primary.* Salt Lake City: Deseret Book, 1978. 117, 135–78.

Peterson, Janet, and LaRene Gaunt. "LaVern Watts Parmley." *The Children's Friends: Presidents of the Primary and Their Lives of Service.* Salt Lake City: Deseret Book, 1996. 79–101.

JANET PETERSON

PARRISH, WARREN. Warren Parrish was a clerk and scribe for **Joseph Smith** in the 1830s. He was born in New York in 1803 and was baptized by **Brigham Young** in 1833. He participated in the **Zion's Camp** expedition in 1834. He also recorded one of the accounts of Joseph Smith's **First Vision**.

At the time of the Panic of 1837, Parrish was the cashier in the **Kirtland Safety Society** Anti-Banking Company. He was accused of embezzling between $20,000 and $25,000 of the society's funds when it was failing. He led a party of some nine men, three of whom were in the **Quorum** of the Twelve **Apostles**, which tried to overthrow Joseph Smith as president of the Church and replace him with **David Whitmer**. As a result, Parrish was excommunicated from the Church. He organized the Church of Christ in 1837, wrote against Joseph Smith, and renounced the

Book of Mormon. By 1844 he was a Baptist minister. Parrish died in 1887 at Emporia, Kansas.

SOURCES

Roberts, B. H. *A Comprehensive History of The Church of Jesus Christ of Latter-day Saints, Century One*. 6 vols. Salt Lake City: The Church of Jesus Christ of Latter-day Saints, 1930. 1:404–8.

Smith, Joseph. *History of The Church of Jesus Christ of Latter-day Saints*. Edited by B. H. Roberts. 2d ed. rev. 7 vols. rev. Salt Lake City: The Church of Jesus Christ of Latter-day Saints, 1932–51. 2:484–88, 528.

ROBERT L. MARROTT

PARTRIDGE, EDWARD. Edward Partridge, the first **bishop** of the Church, was described as a man whose "heart is pure," even "like unto Nathaniel of old, in whom there is no guile" (D&C 41:11). A quiet, humble man, he gave everything he had for the building up of the **kingdom of God**.

Edward Partridge was born 27 August 1793 in Pittsfield, **Massachusetts**. In 1891 he married Lydia Clisbee, and they became the parents of seven children. He was a hatter by trade and eventually moved to Painesville, **Ohio**, where he opened a store. In 1828 Edward and Lydia joined **Sydney Rigdon's** Campbellite congregation.

The Partridges were still **Campbellites** when Lydia was converted by **Oliver Cowdery** and his companions. Edward Partridge was unsure, but after a visit to **Joseph Smith** in **New York**, he was baptized by the Prophet on 11 December 1830. Within two months of his baptism, he was called as bishop to the Church.

Four months after his appointment as bishop, Edward Partridge accompanied Joseph Smith to **Independence, Missouri**, where he remained as bishop of **Zion**. Joined shortly thereafter by his **family**, he worked under difficult conditions to build up the Church in Missouri. Conflict between members of the Church and the native Missourians increased during this troublesome time.

On 20 July 1833, an armed mob tarred and feathered Edward Partridge. By November of that same year, the Partridges and other members of the Church were forced to flee their homes in **Jackson County**. Shortly after the **Saints'** flight into **Clay County**, Partridge was called on a **mission** that lasted more than a year. During that time, he attended the dedication of the **Kirtland Temple**.

When he returned to Missouri, Edward Partridge experienced the persecution of the Saints, including imprisonment in Richmond Jail and forced removal from the state. His family left most of their possessions behind and eventually joined him in **Illinois**.

After moving to Commerce (**Nauvoo**), Illinois, Edward Partridge continued to serve the Church as bishop. The effects of the suffering in Missouri and the chills and fevers prevalent in Commerce led to his death in Nauvoo on 27 May 1840.

SOURCES

Jennings, Warren A., ed. "'What Crime Have I Been Guilty of?': Edward Partridge's Letter to an Estranged Sister." *BYU Studies* 18 (Summer 1978): 520–28.

Jesse, Dean. "'Steadfastness and Patient Endurance': The Legacy of Edward Partridge." *Ensign* 9 (June 1979): 40–47.

CRAIG L. FOSTER

PATRIARCH AND PATRIARCHAL BLESSINGS.

A patriarch, also known as an evangelist, holds an ordained office in the **Melchizedek Priesthood**. Patriarchs are selected by the Twelve **Apostles** (D&C 107:39–40) and may be **ordained** by one of the Twelve or by a **stake president**. Every stake in the Church usually has one or two ordained patriarchs.

A patriarchal blessing is given to build faith in **Jesus Christ** and to encourage the recipient to face the problems of life and strive for spiritual excellence. Patriarchs also declare by revelation the individual's lineage, that is, the tribe of Israel through which blessings can come. Realization of the promises depends on personal faithfulness.

The individual (usually more than 12 years of age) seeking a blessing is interviewed by his or her **bishop** before contacting the patriarch. A copy of the blessing is given to the recipient, and a copy is sent to the Church **Historical Department** in **Salt Lake City**.

Generally one patriarchal blessing is adequate for each person. Blessings are sacred and personal, and they should not be shared beyond the **family**. Every father, as a natural patriarch, can bless his family, but only blessings by ordained patriarchs are placed on file at Church headquarters.

SOURCE

McConkie, Bruce R. *Mormon Doctrine.* 2d ed. Salt Lake City: Bookcraft, 1966. 241–42, 558, 559–60.

ROBERT J. MATTHEWS

PATRIARCH TO THE CHURCH. On 18 December 1833, **Joseph Smith ordained** his father, **Joseph Smith Sr.**, to hold "the keys of the patriarchal **priesthood** over the **kingdom of God** on earth" (Bates, 34). Thus arose an office known as "**Patriarch** over the whole Church," "Patriarch of the Church" or "Presiding Patriarch." In 1942 the title "patriarch to the Church" was officially adopted. In addition to Joseph Smith Sr., seven other members of the **Smith family** have held this office: **Hyrum Smith, William Smith**, Joseph Smith Sr.'s brother John, Hyrum's son John, **Hyrum G. Smith, Joseph F. Smith II**, and **Eldred G. Smith**. Although the office generally passed from father to eldest son, any member of the Smith family was eligible to serve. Typically, months and even years elapsed between the death of one patriarch and the ordination of another. In 1979, Eldred Smith was designated patriarch emeritus, and no successor was named because of "the availability of patriarchal service throughout the world"(Bates, 216). Although Hyrum, the second patriarch, was ordained by his father, all subsequent patriarchs to the Church were ordained by the presiding authority in the Church. In 1919, the **First Presidency** and **Quorum** of the Twelve **Apostles** decided that the patriarch to the Church ranked between the Twelve and the First Council of **Seventy** in the Church hierarchy.

The patriarch to the Church possessed authority to pronounce **patriarchal blessings** and to seal those blessings. He was particularly responsible for the fatherless and members living in regions without local patriarchs. Beyond these duties, the patriarch's responsibilities fluctuated depending upon the attitudes of the Church authorities and depending upon the patriarch's own views and disposition. At times the patriarch was sustained as a **prophet, seer and revelator**. In addition to pronouncing blessings, the patriarch to the Church sometimes spoke in **general conference**, set apart missionaries, and accompanied other **general authorities** to **stake conferences**. Until 1942 the patriarch to the Church supervised, presided over, and sometimes ordained local patriarchs.

SOURCE

Bates, Irene E., and E. Gary Smith. *Lost Legacy: The Mormon Office of Presiding Patriarch*. Urbana: University of Illinois Press, 1996.

Stephens, Calvin R. "Patriarch to the Church." *Encyclopedia of Mormonism*. Edited by Daniel H. Ludlow. 4 vols. New York: Macmillan, 1992. 3:1065–66.

BRIAN Q. CANNON

PATTEN, DAVID W. David Wyman Patten was the first **apostle** to be martyred in this dispensation. He was born 14 November 1799 in Theresa, **New York**. He was introduced to the Church by his brother, John, who baptized him 15 June 1832 in **Indiana**. On 14 February 1835, he was chosen as one of the first members of the **Quorum** of the Twelve Apostles. On 2 May 1835, when seniority in the quorum was based on age, **Thomas B. Marsh** was thought to be the oldest and was appointed quorum president. Historical records, however, indicate that Patten was actually older than Marsh. Had that been known, Patten would likely have been the quorum president. He died 25 October 1838 in Caldwell County, Missouri, from a wound received in the Battle of **Crooked River**. He and his wife, Phoebe Ann Babcock, left no children. References to Patten in the **Doctrine and Covenants** include section 114 and verses 19 and 130 of section 124.

SOURCES

Baugh, Alexander L. "The Battle between Mormon and Missouri Militia at Crooked River." In *Missouri*. Edited by Arnold K. Garr and Clark V. Johnson. Regional Studies in Latter-day Saint Church History series. Provo, Utah: Brigham Young University, 1994. 85–103.

Jenson, Andrew. *Latter-day Saint Biographical Encyclopedia*. 4 vols. 1901–36. Reprint, Salt Lake City: Western Epics, 1971. 1:76–80.

Wilson, Lycurgus A. *Life of David W. Patten, the First Apostolic Martyr.* Salt Lake City: Deseret News, 1904.

ALEXANDER L. BAUGH

PEARL OF GREAT PRICE. In 1850 **Elder Franklin D. Richards**, president of the **British Mission**, found that the **Saints** in his area had very little access to Church literature (even the scriptures). He compiled some of his favorite documents of the **Restoration** into a tract that was published in 1851 in **Liverpool** as the Pearl of Great Price. Elder **Orson Pratt** was assigned to prepare the first American edition of the Pearl of Great Price in 1878, and the Saints voted in the October 1880 conference to accept the Pearl of Great Price as one of the books within their **standard works**.

Over the years a number of items were deleted from the Pearl of Great Price (including several revelations which were already in the **Doctrine and Covenants** and the poem "O, Say What Is Truth"), until by 1921 it contained what exists in the present volume. Two revelations that were added to the Pearl of Great Price in April 1976 were moved to the

Doctrine and Covenants in June 1979, becoming sections 137 and 138. The Pearl of Great Price now includes the following:

1. *Selections from the book of Moses*. The book of Moses is **Joseph Smith**'s inspired translation of Genesis 1:1–8, 18 (Moses 2–8), along with the record of an experience that **Moses** had with God and **Satan** on an unnamed mountain (Moses 1), which record serves as a divine prologue to the book of Genesis and the **Bible**. Prominent doctrines include the work and glory of God, the premortal existence, the creation and fall of **Adam** and Eve, and the proclamation of the gospel to and by such ancients as Adam, Enoch, and Noah. Hence, this book is the beginning of the **Joseph Smith Translation** of the Bible.

2. *The book of Abraham*. The book of Abraham is an excerpt from the Prophet Joseph's translation of some Egyptian papyri that came into the possession of the Church in the summer of 1835. The translation was published in the *Times and Seasons* in 1842. Prominent doctrines include **Abraham**'s quest for the high **priesthood**, the origin of the pharaohs, Abraham's lesson in astronomy and priesthood government, and the creation.

3. *Joseph Smith–Matthew*. Joseph Smith–Matthew is Joseph Smith's translation of Matthew 24, the Olivet Discourse. The Joseph Smith Translation distinguishes between the events leading up to the destruction of Jerusalem in 70 A.D. and the events leading up to the Lord's second coming in glory.

4. *Joseph Smith–History*. The excerpt from Joseph Smith's **History of the Church** recorded in Joseph Smith–History discusses such matters as the **First Vision**, the coming of **Moroni**, the translation of the golden plates, and the restoration of the **Aaronic and Melchizedek Priesthoods**.

5. *The Articles of Faith*. In a letter to John Wentworth, editor of the *Chicago Democrat*, Joseph Smith recited a brief history of the Church. This history has come to be known as the **Wentworth Letter**. The last part of this letter contains 13 statements of belief known as the Articles of Faith. Though not comprehensive in scope, the list sets forth such fundamental doctrines as the Godhead, the Fall and the Atonement, the gospel, priesthood and Church government, revelation and scripture, and the virtuous life.

When Elder **Franklin D. Richards** compiled the Pearl of Great Price, he probably did not realize how meeting the Saints' pressing need in one specific location could over time prove to be such a blessing to the entire Church. The Pearl of Great Price stands as a powerful evidence of the divine calling of the **Prophet** Joseph Smith. It demonstrates how the Almighty has dispensed his everlasting gospel to his chosen servants from the beginning and how he does now reveal and "will yet reveal many great and important things pertaining to the **kingdom of God**" (A of F 1:9).

SOURCE

Peterson, H. Donl. *The Pearl of Great Price: A History and Commentary.* Salt Lake City: Deseret Book, 1987.

ROBERT L. MILLET

PECK, POLLY. See KNIGHT, POLLY.

PENNSYLVANIA. Several important events in Latter-day Saint history occurred in Pennsylvania during the early nineteenth century. The **Prophet Joseph Smith** met his future wife, **Emma Hale** (1825), completed much of the **Book of Mormon** translation (1828–29), and received several **revelations** (1828–29; D&C 3–13; 24–27). The restoration of the priesthood to the earth (1829; D&C 13) occurred in Pennsylvania, and there the revelation of Moses chapter 1 (1830) launched the **Joseph Smith Translation** of the Bible.

After Joseph Smith obtained the **gold plates** in September 1827, he found refuge in Pennsylvania from the storm of opposition against his effort to translate them in **New York**. It was at Harmony, Pennsylvania, in May 1829, that Joseph Smith and **Oliver Cowdery** reached a passage in the Book of Mormon translation that discussed the necessity of baptism. As they prayed for guidance on the subject, **John the Baptist** appeared and gave them authority to baptize (JS–H 1:68–75). In June 1829 Joseph Smith moved to **Fayette, New York**, where they completed the translation and accomplished the **organization of the Church** (1830). Soon thereafter, **missionaries** traveled to Pennsylvania, mainly concentrating their efforts in the northern counties of the state, and by the end of the year there were about 125 members living there. Erie County, in the northwestern corner of the state, was another early field of missionary labor because of its geographic proximity to **Kirtland, Ohio,** (40 miles away), and its location on the main route of travel between New York and Ohio.

In the latter half of the 1830s, missionary efforts shifted from the northern Pennsylvania counties to the western and southern counties. In 1839 branches were established in southeastern Chester and Philadelphia counties. Three Pennsylvania converts—**Jedediah M. Grant**, Joshua

Grant Jr., and Benjamin Winchester—may have been the first missionaries to visit Philadelphia. By 1839 there were approximately 40 members within 60 miles of that city, where Joseph Smith organized a **branch** on 23 December of that year.

During the 1830s as many as 14 branches were organized in the state, mostly in sparsely settled counties. During this period most areas followed a similar pattern: first, missionary activity; second, branch organization; third, a growth period; fourth, loss of membership due primarily to the gathering to Ohio; and finally, either the stabilization of a branch or its disorganization. As a result only three units—Brandywine, Philadelphia, and Leechburg—continued to function until the early 1840s.

Branches were again established in 1886, and in 1897 the East and West Pennsylvania districts were created as part of the **Eastern States Mission**. By 1930, there were almost 800 members with branches in Philadelphia, Pittsburgh, and Wilson.

Membership increased during **World War II**, necessitating the establishment of additional branches. The Church organized the first Pennsylvania stake in Philadelphia on 16 October 1960 with some 2,000 members.

With the expansion of missionary work, a separate Pennsylvania mission was organized in 1970. By the beginning of the year 2000, there were 3 missions headquartered in Pennsylvania, and the 37,749 Church members in the state were organized into 10 **stakes** and 102 **wards** and branches.

Sources

Holzapfel, Richard Neitzel. "Pennsylvania." *Historic Atlas of Mormonism.* Edited by S. Kent Brown, et al. New York: Simon & Schuster, 1994. 16–17.
1999–2000 Church Almanac. Salt Lake City: Deseret News, 1998. 235–36.

Richard Neitzel Holzapfel

PENROSE, CHARLES W. Charles William Penrose was called to the **Quorum** of the Twelve **Apostles** in 1904 after serving in the Church for many years as a missionary, newspaper editor, assistant **Church historian**, and author of numerous **pamphlets** and books. He was sustained as second **counselor** to **Joseph F. Smith** in the **First Presidency** in 1911, and ten years later he became first counselor. He served in that position until his death in 1925.

Charles was born in London, **England** on 4 February 1832 to Richard and Matilda Penrose. A precocious child who taught himself how to read when he was only four, Penrose was introduced to the Church while still a teenager. He was the only member of his **family** to join the Church, yet he remained on good terms with his mother and sisters (his father had died) for the remainder of their lives.

After serving a ten-year mission in England, he returned to **Utah** in 1862 and began a career in business. In 1865 he received a call and went back to England for another three-year **mission**. When he returned to Utah, he became the editor of Ogden's newspaper, the *Junction*, and then moved to **Salt Lake City** to edit the *Deseret News*. He also served as editor of the *Salt Lake Herald* and was inducted into Utah's newspaper hall of fame.

Active in politics, Penrose was elected to the territorial legislature and helped secure statehood for Utah. He was a masterful writer and wrote a widely read series of tracts titled *Rays of Living Light*, which was used in all the Church's missions. He also wrote several books and composed well-known **hymns** such as "Oh Ye Mountains High." He was a fine public speaker and could discourse for hours at a time without using notes.

After his call as an apostle in 1904, he served as the **European Mission** president, returning to England for the last time. By the end of this mission he had served in **Great Britain** as a missionary for a total of 17 years. President Penrose died 15 May 1925 in Salt Lake City.

SOURCES

Godfrey, Kenneth W. "Charles W. Penrose: The English Mission Years." *BYU Studies* 27 (Winter 1987): 113–25.

———. "Charles W. Penrose and His Contributions to Utah Statehood." *Utah Historical Quarterly* 64 (Fall 1996): 356.

KENNETH W. GODFREY

PEOPLE'S PARTY. The People's Party, founded in 1870, was the political arm of the Church for two decades. The Latter-day Saints established the organization in response to the **Liberal Party**, which had been founded earlier in the year by a group of Protestants, Catholics, **Jews**, and **Godbeites**. The *Deseret News* became the voice of the People's Party, which also received support from the *Salt Lake Herald*.

The People's Party was a dominant force in **Utah** territorial **politics** throughout its existence. The party's candidates for delegate to the U.S.

Congress won elections every two years from 1870 to 1890; William H. Hooper won in 1870, **George Q. Cannon** was victorious from 1872 to 1882, and John T. Caine was elected from 1882 to 1890. Other prominent leaders in the party were **Franklin S. Richards** and **Charles W. Penrose**.

As a prerequisite for Utah becoming a state, its citizens were admonished to dissolve their territorial parties and actively affiliate with the two national parties—**Republican** and **Democrat**. Thus the People's Party was officially discontinued 10 June 1891.

SOURCES

Jenson, Andrew. *Encyclopedic History of The Church of Jesus Christ of Latter-day Saints.* Salt Lake City: Deseret News, 1941. 650.

Larson, Gustive O. *The "Americanization" of Utah for Statehood.* San Marino, Calif.: Huntington Library, 1971.

Lyman, Edward Leo. *Political Deliverance: The Mormon Quest for Utah Statehood.* Urbana and Chicago: University of Illinois Press. 1986.

ARNOLD K. GARR

PEOPLE'S REPUBLIC OF CHINA. See CHINA, PEOPLE'S REPUBLIC OF.

PERIODICALS. Since the beginning of the Church, desires to spread the gospel, answer **anti-Mormon** attacks, inform members of the Church community, and discuss doctrinal and historical ideas have promulgated a great variety of Church-related periodicals. More than a hundred in number, these have ranged from one-issue journals that never got off the ground to a 150-year-old newspaper, *Deseret News*, possibly the most influential in the Intermountain West.

EARLY CHURCH PERIODICALS

Beginning in the early 1830s, the Church published several periodicals for the sake of informing the members and defending Church doctrines. The first of these was *The Evening and the Morning Star* (June 1832–June 1833; December 1833–September 1834). Originally published in **Independence, Missouri**, this paper lasted 14 numbers (or issues) before an angry mob ordered its editor, **W. W. Phelps**, to discontinue publication. When he refused they destroyed the press. The periodical's headquarters were then moved to **Kirtland, Ohio**, where an additional

10 numbers were produced, edited by **Oliver Cowdery.** Between January 1835 and October 1836, all 24 numbers were edited and reprinted under the abbreviated name *Evening and Morning Star.* In October 1834 *The Latter Day Saints' Messenger and Advocate* began as a continuation of the *Star.* It was edited by Oliver Cowdery (two different times), **John Whitmer,** and Warren A. Cowdery before it was suspended in September 1837.

The Elders' Journal succeeded the *Messenger and Advocate* in 1837. Edited by **Joseph Smith Jr.** and published by **Thomas B. Marsh,** two numbers (October and November) appeared in Kirtland before the press was destroyed by fire. Numbers 3 and 4 appeared in July and August 1838 at **Far West, Missouri.** Forced to flee Far West, the **Saints** buried the type in a Church member's backyard until the following spring, when it was taken to **Illinois** and used for publishing *The Times and Seasons* (November 1839–February 1846). Published regularly (for the first year, monthly, and then semi-monthly) until 1846, *The Times and Seasons* parallels the history of the Church at Nauvoo. **Ebenezer Robinson,** who had, along with **Don Carlos Smith,** first published the paper, reluctantly sold it to the **Quorum** of the Twelve **Apostles** after they expressed an interest in it during November and December 1841. After this, *The Times* was edited by Joseph Smith and **John Taylor.**

SECULAR PERIODICALS

Aside from many of the early doctrine-oriented periodicals, the communities of the Church produced several papers that were, more or less, secular journals. Important among these were the *Upper Missouri Advertiser,* edited by W. W. Phelps in Independence from 1832 until 1833; the *Northern Times,* edited by **Frederick G. Williams** in Kirtland during 1835; the *Wasp,* published weekly in Nauvoo from April 1842 until April 1843; and the *Nauvoo Neighbor,* a continuation of the *Wasp,* edited by **William Smith** and John Taylor from 1843 until 1846.

The longest running of any Church-related publications and by far the largest of the Church's secular periodicals, the *Deseret News* was established in 1850 and is one of the most important newspapers in the Intermountain West. Among its editors have been three apostles: **Willard Richards, George Q. Cannon,** and **Charles W. Penrose.** Beginning in 1931 the *Deseret News* contained a supplement titled the **Church News,** with the purpose of updating Church members on the activities of the growing Church. This supplement was also sent out separately to members worldwide.

POLEMIC PERIODICALS

Soon after the Church formally announced the practice of **plural marriage**, **Brigham Young** appointed several men to go to various cities to establish periodicals to respond to antipolygamy polemic. These periodicals all affirmed the notion that "it is better to represent ourselves than to be represented by others" (quoted in Garr, 32). *The Seer* was edited by **Orson Pratt** and published from 1853 to 1854 in both **Washington, D.C.**, and **Liverpool, England**. It was followed by the *St. Louis Luminary* (November 1854–December 1855), established by **Erastus Snow**; the *Mormon,* founded by John Taylor in **New York City** in February 1855; and the *Western Standard* of **San Francisco**, edited by George Q. Cannon, beginning in February 1856.

MISSION PERIODICALS

During the last half of the nineteenth century, the Church allowed or caused its leaders to establish several periodicals to serve the needs of members in various missions. The purpose of these periodicals was to share with the Saints living in peripheral areas information, doctrine, and sermons readily available to those residing nearer the center of the Church. The first of the mission periodicals, and the only international one published during Joseph Smith's life, was the *Millennial Star.* Established by the Quorum of the Twelve on their mission to Great Britain in 1840, this periodical contributed to the conversion of more than 5,000 people in a year's time. It was edited first by **Parley P. Pratt**; after him each British **Mission president** acted as editor until the periodical was discontinued in 1970. Also based in Great Britain, the *Journal of Discourses* (1854–86) was published as a periodical in Liverpool to share general authorities' sermons given in **Utah** with British and European members.

A few early periodicals also served specific missions in the **United States**. In New York City during 1844 and 1845, the *Prophet* was edited by Parley P. Pratt, **Samuel Brannan**, and William Smith. The *Elders' Journal* (not to be confused with the 1837 periodical of the same name) was established in 1903 to serve the **Southern States Mission.** In 1907 it merged with the recently established *Liahona* as *Liahona the Elders' Journal* and, modeled after its Great Britain counterpart, the *Millennial Star,* this new periodical served all North American missions from 1907 to 1945.

One of the largest groups of Church-related periodicals includes those for speakers of languages other than English. Three of the earliest and most prominent among these were the *Skandinaviens Stherne* (Danish), beginning in 1851; *L'Etoile* (French), also first produced in 1851; and *Der Stern* (German), beginning in 1869. By the mid-twentieth century, Church periodicals had been published in Welsh, Tahitian, Swedish, Spanish, Maori, Hawaiian, Czech, Portuguese, Tongan, Norwegian, and Finnish.

Auxiliary Periodicals

During the last quarter of the nineteenth century, the various **auxiliaries** of the Church began printing their own materials. Generally the periodicals were first edited and published by private individuals in behalf of the auxiliaries, then taken over by the auxiliaries themselves. The first of these, the **Woman's Exponent** (1872–1914), was replaced by the *Relief Society Magazine* (1914–70). Titled the *Relief Society Bulletin* for its first year of publication, by the time it was discontinued in 1970 the *Relief Society Magazine* had the largest circulation of any auxiliary Church periodical.

The Contributor (1879–96) was originally edited by **Junius F. Wells** and published for the **Young Men's** Mutual Improvement Association. It was replaced by the *Improvement Era* (1897–1970) under the direction of the YMMIA. Slowly, after merging with the *Young Woman's Journal* (1889–1929, originally published by **Susa Young Gates** for the **Young Women's** auxiliary), the *Improvement Era* became the "voice of the Church," addressing itself more and more to adults.

The *Juvenile Instructor,* established by George Q. Cannon in 1866, was bought by the **Sunday School** in 1901 and became their official organ. As the Sunday School added more adult classes, the scope of this periodical also changed, and in 1930 its name was changed to, simply, the *Instructor.* From 1902 until 1970, the **Children's Friend** served as the official Primary organ.

Consolidated Periodicals

In 1971, under the direct supervision of the **First Presidency** and the Quorum of the Twelve, all auxiliary periodicals were consolidated into three periodicals published by the Church. The **Ensign** was established for adults (18 and older), the **New Era** for youth (12 to17), and the **Friend** for children (11 and under).

The various foreign magazines had also been systemized, containing translations selected from the Church's basic English magazines, and an additional section devoted to the specific cultures or countries to which each magazine was sent. Beginning in 1967, all international periodicals were consolidated into a Unified Magazine (redesignated International Magazine in 1974). Under both the Unified and International Magazine programs, these magazines retained their original titles and the cultural sections were produced by local editors. By the year 2000, however, all international periodicals had been renamed *Liahona*.

SCHOLARLY PERIODICALS

During the last half of the twentieth century, several scholarly non-Church-sponsored periodicals and journals dealing with LDS topics emerged. Among these, several were published by **Brigham Young University** and its dependents, such as *BYU Studies* (since 1959); the **Foundation for Ancient Research and Mormon Studies'** *Journal of Book of Mormon Studies* (since 1992); and the Religious Studies Center's *Religious Educator* (since 2000).

Other periodicals concerned with Latter-day Saint history and ideas, but published by independent organizations, have included *Dialogue: A Journal of Mormon Thought* (since 1966), seeking an unbiased viewpoint; the Mormon History Association's *Journal of Mormon History* (since 1974), presenting scholarly treatments of historical topics; *Sunstone* (since 1975), dedicated to an intellectual representation of differing viewpoints; the *John Whitmer Historical Association Journal* (since 1981), with a core interest in Reorganized Latter Day Saint history; and the Mormon Historic Sites Foundation's *Mormon Historical Studies* (known as the *Nauvoo Journal* from 1989 until 1999), with a primary interest in the nineteenth-century Latter-day Saint experience.

Periodicals have played an important role in the history of the LDS faith—a faith strengthened by discourse and the exchange of ideas and information. Church-related periodicals have provided a forum for ongoing doctrinal, secular, historical, and cultural discussion.

SOURCES

Crawley, Peter. *A Descriptive Bibliography of the Mormon Church.* Vol. 1. Provo, Utah: Religious Studies Center, Brigham Young University, 1997.

Encyclopedia of Mormonism. Edited by Daniel H. Ludlow. 4 vols. New York: Macmillan, 1992. 4:1659–64.

Garr, Arnold K. "A History of *Liahona the Elders' Journal*." Ph.D. diss., Brigham Young University, 1986. 21–53.

Jenson, Andrew. *Encyclopedic History of The Church of Jesus Christ of Latter-day Saints.* Salt Lake City: Deseret News, 1941.

1989–1990 Church Almanac. Salt Lake City: Deseret News, 1988. 187–91.

RICHARD D. MCCLELLAN

PERPETUAL EMIGRATING FUND. The Perpetual Emigrating Fund (PEF) was officially launched in the fall of 1849, but the concept behind it emerged a decade earlier, when **Brigham Young** proposed a covenant that the **Saints** assist the poor who were trying to escape the **Missouri** persecutions. A few years later, the Saints followed this same pattern once again when they faced exile and covenanted in the **Nauvoo Temple** to assist the poor in gathering west. A few months later, at **Winter Quarters**, Brigham Young received "The Word and Will of the Lord," which firmly ratified the covenant and declared, "Let every man use all his influence and property to remove this people to the place where the Lord shall locate a stake of **Zion**" (D&C 136:10).

The PEF derived its name from the fact that after the immigrants settled in the **Great Basin**, they were expected to pay back the fund, thus making it perpetual. By 1887, however, when the **Edmunds Tucker Act** disincorporated the Church and dissolved the PEF, only about one-third had fully repaid their debt; one-third had paid a portion and one-third had paid nothing at all. The program was successful in providing some financial assistance for nearly half of the 100,000 Saints who emigrated during its existence, while those who did not need monetary assistance certainly benefited from the procedures of the organization.

The core of the Perpetual Emigrating Fund's success is found in the commitment of faithful covenant Saints to gather their brothers and sisters from afar. Not only were many willing to contribute funding, but they were also willing to respond to a call to leave their homes and serve as immigration agents at ocean ports and frontier posts under the direction of the **priesthood**. Thus, they helped fulfill an earlier revelation "to bring to pass the gathering of my elect . . . unto one place" (D&C 29:7).

SOURCES

Hartley, William G. "How Shall I Gather?" *Ensign* 27 (October 1997): 5–17.

Larsen, Gustive O. "Story of the Perpetual Emigrating Fund." *Mississippi Valley Historical Review* 18 (September 1931): 184–94.

FRED E. WOODS

PERRY, L. TOM. Lowell Tom Perry, an **apostle, stake president**, and businessman, was born 5 August 1922 in **Logan, Utah**, the son of Elsie Nora Sonne and Leslie Thomas Perry. He attended Utah State Agricultural College in 1940–41 before serving a Northern States Mission. Six weeks after he returned home from his mission, he was drafted into the armed services, and he volunteered for duty in the Marine Corps. Following his release from the Marine Corps in the fall of 1946, he returned to Utah State Agricultural College, where he graduated with a degree in business in 1949. He remained at Utah State an additional year to do graduate work in finance.

On 18 July 1947, Brother Perry married Virginia Lee of Hyde Park, Utah. They became the parents of three children: Barbara, Lee, and Linda Gay. Virginia Lee Perry died 14 December 1974, and Elder Perry married Barbara Taylor Dayton on 28 April 1976.

Brother Perry began his business career in 1951 as an internal auditor with the C. C. Anderson Company. He later worked as a controller, secretary-treasurer, and vice president for firms in Sacramento, **California** (1954–62); **New York, New York** (1962–66) and Boston, **Massachusetts** (1966–72).

In October 1972, while serving as president of the Boston Massachusetts **Stake**, L. Tom Perry was called to be an **assistant to the Council of the Twelve**. Eighteen months later, 16 April 1974, he was sustained a member of the **Quorum** of the Twelve Apostles and ordained as an apostle on 11 April 1974. His major Church assignments as a member of the Quorum of the Twelve have included chair of the Church Bicentennial Committee (1973–76), chair of the Missionary Executive Committee (1986–93), chair of the Priesthood Executive Council (1993–94), and chair of the Church Board of Education and the BYU Board of Trustees executive committee (1995–present).

SOURCE

Perry, Lee. "Elder L. Tom Perry of the Council of the Twelve." *Ensign* 5 (February 1975): 8–17.

LEE PERRY

PERSECUTION. The first generation of Latter-day Saints faced the constant possibility of vocal opposition and physical violence. To help them understand these challenges to their faith, Church leaders and members drew from **scriptures**, new **revelation**, and their personal and group experiences to formulate an explanation for religious persecution.

The misunderstandings, fears, and encounters that prompted the search for meaning ranged widely. Ministers warned their flocks against "the Mormonites" and published critical tracts. **Missouri** settlers waged legal and militant battle against Latter-day Saint newcomers and expelled them under threat of extermination. Lawsuits followed **Joseph Smith** constantly. Vigilantes in **Illinois** burned homes and killed the **Prophet** and **patriarch**. Apostates in each gathering place challenged Church leaders. Zealous members sometimes provoked reactions with their own intemperate declarations of rights or militant actions. Opposition followed the Saints west. It took the familiar form of challenges to theocratic influence in government and business. The expanding practice of **plural marriage** raised new criticisms. In time, the new medium of film spawned **anti-Mormon** movies about these topics in the **United States** and abroad. Hecklers in some areas targeted missionaries with rotten eggs, dung, and rocks. Later controversial issues included the roles of **blacks** and **women** in the Church.

To explain harassment, Latter-day Saints defined a philosophy of persecution containing the following points: (1) God's work in all ages faces hostility. Consider the parallel reactions to the visions of Paul and Joseph Smith and the mistreatment of apostle-missionaries. (2) Ever-present contenders include the advocates of false religions, but truth ultimately will prevail. (3) Resistance impacts the Saints positively, creating greater unity and determination to accomplish God's work. (4) For individuals, opposition is a necessary part of the gospel plan. Challenges refine and test the faith of believers and give them spiritually valuable experience.

Outside commentators have noted that it was the closed, controlling nature of Latter-day Saint society and the actions of a few militant Latter-day Saints that prompted mistrust. Their neighbors saw attempts by Latter-day Saints to create a closely knit religious society as an unacceptable mingling of theocratic influence in local affairs. All this came in a time of Jacksonian democracy when individualism, grass-roots republican values, and religious pluralism were thriving. When the Saints refused to abandon their ideal of a gathered **Zion** society, religious and political foes created negative images of the Church and its leaders through public discourse and they sometimes resorted to physical violence.

Twentieth-century Church leaders have expressed concern that acceptance by the world and times of peace and prosperity without persecution might cause indifference that weakens members in their faith. Citing the lessons of past persecutions, authorities have encouraged tolerance and love toward others and an increased dedication to the Lord's work. They have warned against riches, pride, and the praise of secular society and have invited members to steel themselves against future trials by developing a deep personal testimony.

SOURCES

Arrington, Leonard J. "Why Did the Latter-day Saints Experience Persecution?" *Improvement Era* 73 (August 1970): 49–53.

Cannon, George Q. *The History of the Mormons: Their Persecutions and Travels.* Salt Lake City: Juvenile Instructor Office, 1890.

Hallwas, John E. "Mormon Nauvoo from a Non-Mormon Perspective." *Journal of Mormon History* 16 (1990): 53–70.

Paul, Rodman W. "The Mormons, from Poverty and Persecution to Prosperity and Power." *American Heritage* 28 (June 1977): 74–83.

GLEN M. LEONARD

PERSONAL ANCESTRAL FILE. Personal Ancestral File (PAF) is a popular computer genealogy program for recording, organizing, managing, and sharing genealogical information. It is available for personal computers (PCs) in Windows and MS-DOS formats, and for Macintosh computers. This program allows users to share genealogical information through GEDCOM (Genealogical Data Communications). **Genealogy** files may be added to PAF from **FamilySearch**™ (such as **Ancestral File** on compact discs) by using GEDCOM, or from another genealogy program.

The most recent version of PAF, available in a Windows-based format, may be downloaded at no cost from FamilySearch™ Internet Genealogy Service (www.familysearch.org). Beginning with version 5.0, one can add digitized pictures, video clips, and sound files. Users can create multimedia interactive scrapbooks and slide shows.

Users may print "Modified Register" **family history** books in descendancy order and create an index. They may also print Ahnentafel charts in ancestor order. This program allows users to print scrapbooks that show pictures, calendars, and print quality pedigree charts and family group records. Users are able to share genealogy information with others in an attractive format.

With the Match/Merge feature, one can find and merge duplicate names. Another important features is that users can export genealogical data for other researchers, contribute to Ancestral File and FamilySearch™ Internet, or copy files to other electronic databases. Users may also publish genealogy on the Internet with the Create Web Page feature.

KIP SPERRY

PERU. Official **missionary work** in Peru began in 1956, when former **mission president** Frederick S. Williams of the **Uruguay** Mission moved there with his **family.** Brother Williams requested permission from the **First Presidency** to establish a **branch** and begin proselyting, and six months later **Elder Henry D. Moyle** of the **Quorum** of the Twelve **Apostles** organized the first branch in Peru. In August of that year, four full-time missionaries entered the country, and by the end of 1959 Elder **Harold B. Lee** had established the Andes Mission, including Peru, **Chile,** and later **Bolivia,** with headquarters in Lima. James Vernon Sharp became the first mission president.

On 22 February 1970, Elders **Gordon B. Hinckley** and **Theodore Tuttle** created Peru's first **stake** in Lima, with Roberto Vidal as president. Missionary success continued, and by 1977 Church membership in Peru reached 17,000. That year President **Spencer W. Kimball** visited the country, speaking to about 7,900 **Saints.** In addition to the Church's proselyting efforts, **welfare service missionaries** extended programs to promote **literacy,** cancer prevention and other health care, as well as self-reliance and preparedness.

In January 1986 President Gordon B. Hinckley dedicated the country's first **temple** in Lima, and two years later Elder **M. Russell Ballard** created seven new Peruvian stakes in a single weekend, bringing the country's total to eighteen. President Gordon B. Hinckley visited Lima in 1996 as part of a six-nation South American tour. He addressed 35,000 people, many of whom had traveled long distances by bus to attend. On 15 August 1998, the Church created the South America West Area, which included Peru and Bolivia, with headquarters in Lima. At the beginning of the year 2000, Peru had seven missions, and its Church membership was 333,828 with 81 stakes and 838 **wards** and branches.

SOURCES

1999–2000 Church Almanac. Salt Lake City: Deseret News, 1998. 371–73.
"Peru." *Ensign* 7 (February 1977): 37–40.

"Prophet Visits South America." *Church News,* 16 November 1996. 3.

Warnick, Lee. "Eighteen Stakes Created from Eleven." *Church News,* 6 February 1988. 3.

Lisa Kurki

PETER, JAMES, AND JOHN. Peter, James, and John, three **apostles** of **Jesus Christ** in New Testament times, were called and **ordained** to the priesthood by Jesus himself (John 15:16). As apostles, they are special witnesses, particularly of Christ's resurrection from the dead (Acts 1:22; 4:33). Although not specifically designated as a **First Presidency** in current New Testament records, they exercised that level of administration and were given experiences not afforded other members of the Twelve, including being with Jesus when he raised a 12-year-old girl from the dead (Mark 5:35–42), being ministered to by **Moses** and **Elias** on the Mount (Matt. 17:1–9), and witnessing Jesus' sufferings in Gethsemane (Mark 14:32–42; 1 Pet. 5:1).

Peter, the chief apostle, possessing the keys of the kingdom (Matt. 16:16–18), took the lead in the Church after the departure of Jesus (Acts 1–10), and every listing of the Twelve in the New Testament places Peter first (Matt. 10:2; Mark 3:16; Acts 1:13).

Peter and James (as resurrected beings) and John (as a translated being), still holding the keys of their ministry, personally ordained **Joseph Smith** and **Oliver Cowdery** to the **Melchizedek Priesthood** by the laying on of hands. This occurred between **Harmony, Pennsylvania**, and **Colesville, New York**, during the latter part of May 1829 (D&C 128:20). By this event, the keys and powers of the ancient Melchizedek Priesthood were established on earth in the **dispensation of the fulness of times**, and are now operative in the Church (D&C 27:12–13; 107:1; 112:30–32).

SOURCE

Porter, Larry C. "The Restoration of the Aaronic and Melchizedek Priesthoods." *Ensign* 26 (1996): 30–47.

Robert J. Matthews

PETER FRENCH FARM. See FRENCH FARM.

PETERSEN, MARK E. Mark Edward Petersen, a twentieth-century **apostle** and newspaper executive, was born with his twin sister on

7 November 1900 in **Salt Lake City.** As a youth he delivered papers for the *Deseret News.* Following a **mission** to **Nova Scotia,** he became a reporter for that same paper, covering the "Church beat." He pursued his career in the newspaper business with such excellence that he rose to general manager in 1941 and became president of the Deseret News Publishing Company in 1952. He was a prolific writer, authoring more than 40 books, many missionary **pamphlets,** and literally thousands of editorials in the *Church News* for more than half a century. An ardent Church worker throughout his life, **Elder** Petersen served in two **stake** presidencies, on the board of directors of the **Genealogical Society,** and on the general board of the **Deseret Sunday School Union.** When he was sustained a member of the **Quorum** of the Twelve **Apostles** in April 1944, he bore powerful testimony: "I know that Jesus is the **Christ** and the son of God. . . . I shall take great pleasure in declaring His word for the remainder of my life" (quoted in Monson, 13).

When Elder Petersen died of cancer on 11 January 1984 in Salt Lake City, Elder **Thomas S. Monson** wrote: "He personified righteousness, he exemplified industry, he demonstrated love. How he will be missed in mortality!" (Monson, 6).

SOURCES

Evans, Richard L. "Mark E. Petersen." *Improvement Era* 62 (February 1959): 117.

Flake, Lawrence R. *Prophets and Apostles of the Last Dispensation.* Provo, Utah: Religious Studies Center, Brigham Young University, 2001. 477–79

Monson, Thomas S. "Mark E. Petersen: A Giant among Men." *Ensign* 14 (March 1984): 6–13.

LAWRENCE R. FLAKE

PETERSON, ZIBA. Ziba Peterson is best known as one of the four missionaries called to serve on the **Lamanite Mission of 1830–31.** He was born in 1818 at Burke County, **North Carolina.** He was baptized on 18 April 1830 by **Oliver Cowdery** and later that year was **ordained** an **elder** in the **Melchizedek Priesthood.** In October of 1830, Ziba was called with Oliver Cowdery, **Peter Whitmer Jr.,** and **Parley P. Pratt** to serve a mission to the **Lamanites** (D&C 32:3). They traveled to **Jackson County, Missouri,** where Peterson and Whitmer opened a tailor shop. The others went to preach to the **Delaware Indians** but were ejected from the Indian Territory. Cowdery and Peterson then preached the gospel in the Jackson County area. In Lafayette county they baptized as many as 40 to 50 individuals, including the Hopper family.

When **Joseph Smith** arrived in Jackson County, he received a **revelation** in which Peterson was reprimanded for unspecified conduct (D&C 58:60). Four days later on 4 August 1831, Ziba was publicly reprimanded in a conference, where he confessed his sins. On 11 August 1831 Peterson married Rebecca Hopper, and the couple had eight children. When the missionaries returned to **Kirtland**, he stayed in **Missouri**. In 1833, when the **Saints** were driven out of Jackson County, Peterson remained and ended his affiliation with the Church. In 1848 he and his family moved to **California**. He was elected sheriff of Dry Diggins, later known as Hangtown because of the hanging of two thieves that Peterson supervised. He died at "Hangtown" (Placerville, El Dorado), California, in 1849.

SOURCES

Cook, Lyndon B. *The Revelations of the Prophet Joseph Smith.* Salt Lake City: Deseret Book, 1995. 128, n. 5.

Garrett, H. Dean. "Ziba Peterson: From Missionary to Hanging Sheriff." *Nauvoo Journal* 19 (Spring 1997): 24–32.

H. DEAN GARRETT

PETER WHITMER FARM. See **WHITMER FARM**.

PETITIONS FOR REDRESS. See **REDRESS PETITIONS**.

PHELPS, WILLIAM W. William Wines Phelps, a **counselor** in the first **stake** in **Missouri** and both clerk and scribe to **Joseph Smith**, was born 17 February 1792 in Hanover, **New Jersey**, to Enon Phelps and Mehitabel Goldsmith. After purchasing a copy of the **Book of Mormon** from **Parley P. Pratt** and meeting Joseph Smith, William was baptized 10 June 1831 in **Kirtland, Ohio**. He assisted **Oliver Cowdery** with the selection and printing of books for the Church's schools, edited *The Evening and the Morning Star,* prepared and printed **revelations** for the *Book of Commandments,* helped with the compilation of the *Doctrine and Covenants,* acted as scribe for Joseph Smith in translating the **book of Abraham**, and assisted **Emma Smith** in compiling and printing the Church's first hymnbook. William also wrote several **hymns**, including "The Spirit of God," "Now Let Us Rejoice," "Redeemer of Israel," and "Praise to the Man." He assisted in the construction of the **Kirtland**

Temple, served in the Utah state legislature, and was a regent for the University of Deseret.

William Phelps was excommunicated from the Church on 10 March 1838 as a result of misusing Church funds and selling lands contrary to counsel. He was reinstated in July 1840 after repenting and seeking Joseph Smith's pardon. He died a faithful member of the Church on 7 March 1872 at Salt Lake City.

SOURCE

Cook, Lyndon W. *The Revelations of the Prophet Joseph Smith.* Provo, Utah: Seventy's Mission Bookstore, 1981.

SYDNEY MARIE HUGHES

PHILIPPINES. During the Spanish-American War in 1898, servicemen Willard Call and George Seaman served as Latter-day Saint missionaries in the Philippines, but they performed no baptisms. Until World War II, no further LDS activity occurred in this Southeast Asian nation. From 1944 to 1946, however, American LDS servicemen were again in the Philippines—this time in large numbers—and were organized into servicemen's groups. With the military buildup of the Korean War beginning in 1950, Latter-day Saint groups were again organized, this time under leadership of the Japanese (Far East) Mission. In 1953 President Vinal G. Mauss organized the Luzon Servicemen's District. At a servicemen's conference on 21 August 1955, Elder Joseph Fielding Smith, president of the Quorum of the Twelve Apostles, transferred the Philippines to the new Southern Far East Mission in Hong Kong and offered a prayer dedicating the Philippines for the preaching of the restored gospel.

In May 1960 Elder Gordon B. Hinckley encouraged Robert S. Taylor, president of the Southern Far East Mission, to make the necessary preparations to open proselyting in the Philippines. A year later they completed visa arrangements. On 28 April 1961, Elder Hinckley met with about 100 members at the American War Memorial Cemetery in Manila and rededicated the country. A few weeks later, 5 June 1961, President Taylor transferred four elders—Raymond L. Goodson, Nester O. Ledesma, Kent C. Lowe, and Harry J. Murray—to Manila.

Conversions were initially steady but later grew into a great flood of baptisms. The Philippines Mission was created on 28 June 1967 with Paul S. Rose as president. The first division of the mission occurred in 1974, leading ultimately to the 13 missions that existed in 1999.

On 20 May 1973, Augusto A. Lim was sustained as president of the Manila **Stake**, the first stake organized in the Philippines. In June 1992 Lim was called as the first Filipino to serve as a **general authority** of the Church.

The presence of the Church in the Philippines is substantial. By early in the year 2000 there were 441,359 members in 68 stakes; **wards** and **branches** totaled 1,051. The Church has grown rapidly in the Philippines, partly because of the 92% Christian population and the widespread use of English. A **Missionary Training Center** (1983), numerous **institutes** and **seminaries** (beginning 1972; in 1995 there were 11,848 institute students and 11,282 daily and home-study seminary students), hundreds of chapels, a large Church administration center, and a well-used **temple** manifest the strength of the Church. The Manila Philippines Temple was dedicated 25–27 September 1984 by President Gordon B. Hinckley. In 1987 Manila became the headquarters for the Philippines-Micronesia **Area** of the Church.

In contrast to the Church's substantial growth, members have suffered from natural disasters—volcanoes, earthquakes, typhoons, and floods—and ongoing economic difficulties. The Church has done much to alleviate suffering and to help members improve their employment.

The most important historic event since the temple dedication was President Gordon B. Hinckley's visit to Manila and Cebu in May–June 1996. He spoke to 35,000 at Amoranto Sports complex and to 9,200 in Cebu. He was warmly welcomed and shared his delight with what he called the "miracle of Manila."

SOURCES

Britsch, R. Lanier. *From the East: The History of the Latter-day Saints in Asia, 1851–1996.* Salt Lake City: Deseret Book, 1998. 318–73.

1999–2000 Church Almanac. Salt Lake City: Deseret News, 1998. 373–76.

R. LANIER BRITSCH

PHOTOGRAPHS AND PHOTOGRAPHERS. For more than 150 years, the camera has been an untiring eyewitness to the growth of the LDS Church throughout North **America** and the world. Photographers recorded important images of the **City of Joseph** as the **Saints** began the exodus to the Rocky Mountains. They also captured the beauty of the **Great Basin** and recorded the ingenuity of the Saints who transformed the **Mormon Corridor** into a productive agricultural region. Additionally, they have preserved the everyday events that lie at the heart of Latter-day Saint culture and society.

Through these images, photographers captured the indomitable spirit of the early **pioneer** Saints. That spirit enabled the LDS Church to thrive despite almost constant **persecution**, internal division following **Joseph Smith's** death, a long and difficult migration west, a fragile pioneer economy, and a federal campaign against the corporate Church in the 1880s.

Photographs are unique documents. Whereas libraries collect multiple copies of books and other published materials in relatively uniform sizes, photographs differ greatly in size and format. Therefore, they are usually housed in archival collections. Those collections of interest to historians and others vary widely in size and subject. Notwithstanding this variety, many repositories hold significant collections of great research value. These collections contain a wide range of material, such as one-of-a-kind daguerreotypes, ambrotypes, tintypes, multiproduced cartes de visite, stereographs, paper prints, and numerous fragile glass-plate negatives. Additionally, private collectors have preserved rare and important images.

The increased attention to LDS Church history and **family** history in the 1980s and 1990s brought to light some remarkable, previously unpublished photographs of people, places, and events that provide a fuller view of the past.

Prominent Latter-day Saint and **Utah** photographers include Lucian Foster (actively photographing between 1845–47), Marsena Cannon (1850–60), Charles R. Savage (1860–1906), James Shipler (1860s–1914), Charles W. Carter (1864–90s), Edward Martin (1865–70s), Charles W. Symons (1867–1913), James Fennemore (1870–80s), James H. Crockwell (1880–1900), Charles Ellis Johnson (1880s–1910s), George Edward Anderson (1880s–1928), Elfie Huntington (1892–1940), and Harold Allen (1940s–1980).

In addition to these, other photographers recorded people and places of interest to those who study the LDS culture and history. In this group are Thomas Easterly, William Henry Jackson, J. J. Reilly, Charles Wieftle, C. L. Pond, A. J. Russell, and various photographers employed by Underwood and Underwood and Company. These pioneer landscape and portrait photographers passed through **Palmyra, New York; Kirtland, Ohio; Independence, Missouri; Nauvoo, Illinois; Salt Lake City, Utah;** and other core Latter-day Saint regions during the nineteenth century, capturing important images that preserve the texture of Latter-day Saint life during that time.

Because of the Church's complex history, every photograph of the LDS experience is a historical record. As primary sources of historical information, photographs provide a window to the past and are of priceless historical value.

SOURCE

Holzapfel, Richard Neitzel, and T. Jeffery Cottle. "Mormon-Related Material in Photoarchives." *Mormon Americana: A Guide to Sources and Collections in the United States.* Edited by David J. Whittaker. Provo, Utah: BYU Studies, 1995. 506–21

T. JEFFERY COTTLE AND RICHARD NEITZEL HOLZAPFEL

PINEGAR, PATRICIA P. Patricia Peterson Pinegar, the ninth general president of the **Primary**, was born 3 February 1937, in Cedar City, **Utah**. As a child, Sister Pinegar lived in Utah, **Hawaii**, and **California**. She married Ed J. Pinegar, and they became the parents of eight children. Sister Pinegar's view of the worldwide Church broadened when she served with her husband in presiding over the **England** London South **Mission** and the **Missionary Training Center** in **Provo, Utah**.

Calls to serve on the Primary general board and in the **Young Women** general presidency preceded Sister Pinegar's October 1994 call as Primary general president. Her simple faith, firm commitment to following priesthood leaders, love of the **scriptures**, and desire to bless the lives of children guided her in this service. Sister Pinegar was released as president in the October 1999 **general conference**.

SOURCES

Dockstader, Julie A. "New Callings." *Church News*, 5 November 1998. 6–7.

Peterson, Janet, and LaRene Gaunt. *The Childrens' Friends.* Salt Lake City: Deseret Book, 1996. 167–84.

JAMIE L. GLENN

PIONEER COMMEMORATIONS. The date of 24 July has long been celebrated as "Pioneer Day" in **Utah** and in many congregations of Latter-day Saints around the world. It is a day to commemorate the arrival of the main group of **pioneers** in the **Salt Lake Valley** in 1847. Some have noted in the celebrations the symbolism of escape from oppression and delivery to the promised land, similar to what Jewish people celebrate during their annual Passover.

There is no record of any special commemoration of the pioneer arrival on the first anniversary in 1848, but on 24 July 1849, after two years of hard work, the Utah settlers rejoiced with a day of parades, patriotic speeches, pageantry, and feasting. Community celebrations were common through the nineteenth century, providing the hard-working pioneers with a time for relaxing and remembering. The tradition carried into the twentieth century, and the date was eventually reserved as an official state holiday in Utah.

Wilford Woodruff, one of the original pioneers from the 1847 company, presided over the 50-year commemoration in 1897—a "jubilee" celebration. Special programs were held throughout the Church. The **Brigham Young Monument** in downtown **Salt Lake City** was unveiled as part of the festivities.

The centennial celebration of 1947 included a cross-country tour with many Church leaders participating; they followed the **Mormon Trail** in cars decorated as covered wagons. The **This Is the Place Monument** was dedicated at the mouth of Emigration Canyon in Salt Lake.

The sesquicentennial celebration of 1997 included a more authentic wagon train that followed the entire Mormon Trail from **Nauvoo, Illinois**, to Salt Lake City. A new Mormon Trail Center was dedicated at **Winter Quarters**, in Omaha, **Nebraska**. Special **conferences** and festivities were held throughout the Church.

SOURCES

Olsen, Steven L., "Commemorations" and "Centennial Observances." *Encyclopedia of Mormonism*. Edited by Daniel H. Ludlow. 4 vols. New York: Macmillan, 1992. 1:258–59, 260–62.

Roberts, B. H. *A Comprehensive History of The Church of Jesus Christ of Latter-day Saints, Century One.* 6 vols. Salt Lake City: The Church of Jesus Christ of Latter-day Saints, 1930. 3:492ff; 5:615ff; 6:349ff.

DAVID KENISON

PIONEERS. Celebrated in song and sculpture, **pageant** and parade, the **Mormon** pioneer continues to claim a sacred legacy in Latter-day Saint history. Connoting far more than a mere immigrant, the term 'pioneer' has been reserved for those who are among the first to enter or settle a region. In Latter-day Saint history, such a definition extends far beyond **Brigham Young** and the vanguard companies that toiled their way from

Nauvoo, Illinois, to the **Salt Lake Valley** in 1847, to include those who came in later years and settled hundreds of Latter-day Saint communities throughout the Intermountain West. Though they have sometimes been overly glorified, "nothing," as one historian wrote, "can detract from the sheer fact of their achievement—the numbers involved, the organization required, and the dedicated effort it took" (Leonard, 6).

The precise number of Latter-day Saint converts and children who came to **Utah** is a subject of ongoing debate. During the overland trail period, from Brigham Young's initial company in 1847 until the coming of the transcontinental **railroad** in 1869, the best estimate is that over 60,000 came to Utah.

If the "pioneering generation" encompasses Latter-day Saint migration in all of the nineteenth century (including the "Pullman pioneers," who came by train), the corresponding figure is at least 105,000 adults with half again as many children. Of this later figure, approximately 50,000 originated in the British Isles, some 30,000 in **Scandinavia,** and the rest in towns and cities in the United States and **Canada.**

Most came by wagon along the **Mormon Trail** in 224 companies that were outfitted first at **Winter Quarters** and Florence, **Nebraska.** The famous **Perpetual Emigrating Fund,** established in 1849, served as one of **America's** most successful emigration agencies by lending funds to help pay passage costs, appointing agents at disembarkation points, and extending whatever assistance was required. From 1856 to 1860 thousands pulled and pushed their wooden **handcarts** across the plains and over the Rocky Mountains. Beginning in 1861, "Church trains" were composed of wagons sent east loaded with supplies which were dropped off at strategic points along the trail. The empty wagons then picked up the European immigrants and brought them to **Zion.** Their cost was reduced because the Saints donated most of the supplies and wagons and the young teamsters had been called to this service as missionaries. As the Union Pacific Railroad progressed towards the Rocky Mountains, the jumping-off point moved ever westward.

Unlike the comparatively free-wheeling, contemporaneous migrations to **Oregon** and the gold fields of **California** (quests for improved individual opportunities), the Latter-day Saint migration was a model of discipline, organization, and cooperation—an entire church on the move to a new **Zion.** Less motivated, perhaps, than others by economics, the Mormon pioneer was part of a Church-sponsored, systematic migration seeking a common good. Following patterns of organization laid down in the "Word and Will of the Lord" (D&C 136) received by Brigham

Young in Winter Quarters in 1847, they often came as entire families and were carefully organized into companies that crossed ocean and plain under the shepherding influence of the Church.

Faith was the prime motivation for these pioneers, many of whom had been persecuted for their beliefs and left family members never to see them again—all in the name of the restored gospel of **Jesus Christ**. For many, such a journey of more than 9,000 miles by sea and by land marked the greatest experience of their lives and the deepest expression of their faith. Approximately 6,000 died making the attempt, several hundred of whom perished in the remarkable handcart companies. Although there were inevitably some who fell away, most Mormon pioneers blazed their trail of hope and faith to their new home "far away in the West."

Throughout the Church today this pioneer heritage continues. There are more modern pioneers in far distant lands who, taking their cue from their nineteenth-century predecessors and with similar faith and determination, are establishing the Church in the face of great personal trial, misunderstanding, and difficulty.

SOURCES

Bayshore, Mel. "It is Impossible to Identify the Exact Number of Pioneers." *Church News*, 5 July 1997. 4.

Bennett, Richard E. *We'll Find the Place: The Mormon Exodus, 1846–1848*. Salt Lake City: Deseret Book, 1997.

Campbell, E. E. "The Mormon Migration to Utah." *Utah's History*. Edited by Richard D. Poll. Provo, Utah: Brigham Young University Press, 1970. 113–132.

Hafen, LeRoy R., and Ann W. Hafen. *Handcarts to Zion: The Story of a Unique Westward Migration, 1856–1860*. Glendale, California: A. H. Clark, 1960.

Leonard, Glen M. "Westward the Saints: The Nineteenth-Century Mormon Migration." *Ensign* (10 January 1980): 6–13.

Stegner, Wallace. *The Gathering of Zion: The Story of the Mormon Trail*. Lincoln: University of Nebraska Press, 1964.

Taylor, P. A. M. "The Mormon Crossing of the United States, 1840–1870." *Utah Historical Quarterly* 25 (1957): 318–337.

RICHARD E. BENNETT

PIONEER TREK OF 1847. From the moment the first Latter-day Saints left their homes in **Nauvoo, Illinois**, in early 1846 on their exodus to the West, their leader, **Brigham Young**, had hoped to send ahead an advance company of the Twelve **Apostles** to find a new home "over the mountains." Delayed by incessantly wet spring weather and stymied by his own people who feared being left behind, Brigham finally made it across **Iowa** well behind schedule. Weakened, lacking adequate provisions, and in no condition to move any further west, the Saints established their **Winter Quarters** refuge on **Indian** lands at the **Missouri River**, west of **Council Bluffs**, in October 1846.

During the ensuing winter, more careful plans were laid for an early spring departure, not of the entire people (then numbering some 11,000) but of a small, unfettered band of hand-picked **pioneers** to accompany the Twelve westward. Especially needed were skilled farmers, teamsters, blacksmiths, machinists, carpenters, millwrights, surveyors, and stonemasons—faithful men who could bridge a continent and build a colony.

The group left Winter Quarters 5 April 1847. This select company consisted of 143 men, three women, and two children, averaging 31 years of age; 76 of these individuals had come from New England and 11 from **Great Britain**. Constantly reminded by Brigham Young that they would find their place if they followed their God, the valiant little company escaped Indian depredation and fatal illness in the process of blazing the famous **Mormon Trail** along the north bank of the **Platte River** to Ash Hollow, along the **Oregon Trail** to **Fort Bridger**, and eventually over the **Hastings** Cut-Off to the Great Salt Lake. **Orson Pratt** and **Erastus Snow** first sighted the valley on 21 July 1847, and by the 24th Brigham Young and the entire group had arrived.

Once in their chosen valley, they went to work irrigating the land, planting crops, exploring surrounding territories, surveying a new city, and laying out a temple lot. While some remained to meet the incoming immigrant company of some 1,400 Saints, many returned to Winter Quarters that fall to promote the exodus to the West. The original 1847 pioneers laid a foundation on which a church, a state, and an entire people would later build.

SOURCES

Bennett, Richard E. *We'll Find the Place: The Mormon Exodus, 1846–1848.* Salt Lake City: Deseret Book, 1997.

Jenson, Andrew. *Day by Day with the Utah Pioneers, 1847: A Chronological Record of the Trek across the Plains.* Provo, Utah: Griffin Associates, 1934.

1997–1998 Church Almanac. Salt Lake City: Deseret News, 1996. 97–159.

Stegner, Wallace. *The Gathering of Zion: The Story of the Mormon Trail.* Lincoln: University of Nebraska Press, 1981.

RICHARD E. BENNETT

PITT, WILLIAM. William Pitt, a British convert, left-handed fiddler, flutist, and all-around musician, was born 16 August 1813 in Dymock, **England**. He later became the leader of the Nauvoo Brass Band. Pitt brought with him from England a large collection of music arranged for brass instruments. The band was organized in 1842 to accompany drills of the **Nauvoo Legion**, but its role soon expanded to include social and religious gatherings and other celebrations. It even raised funds and built the **Nauvoo** Concert Hall in 1843.

When the **pioneers** crossed **Iowa** in 1846, the band provided nightly entertainment for weary **Saints**, as well as money and provisions from concerts along the route. Pitt was one of three band members to travel west with the original pioneer company.

He was ordained a priest 14 June 1840 under the hands of **Willard Richards** and **Wilford Woodruff**. In 1852 Pitt returned to England on a full-time mission. Later his band was revived for a time in **Salt Lake City**, where he died 21 February 1873.

SOURCES

Church History in the Fulness of Times. Salt Lake City: The Church of Jesus Christ of Latter-day Saints, 1989. 310.

Purdy, William E. "They Marched Their Way West: The Nauvoo Brass Band." *Ensign* 10 (July 1980): 20–23.

Smith, Joseph. *History of The Church of Jesus Christ of Latter-day Saints.* Edited by B. H. Roberts. 2d ed. rev. 7 vols. Salt Lake City: The Church of Jesus Christ of Latter-day Saints, 1932–51. 4:135.

GERALD L. HOMER

PLATES, GOLD. See GOLD PLATES.

PLATTE RIVER. The Platte River provided a superb natural highway for **Mormon Pioneers** and other settlers of the West. It meanders from its origin in the high mountains of **Colorado** to its confluence with the **Missouri River**. Too shallow and sluggish for paddle wheelers and large fur boats, the "mile-wide and inch deep" river received its full share of scornful derision. Washington Irving considered it the most magnificent and useless river in **America**. Another called it "a complete burlesque in all the rivers of the world . . . a wide sheet of water only three or four feet deep, running over a vast level of sand . . . and which thus eternally creeps along" (Evans). To the **Mormons**, who chose to follow the much less traveled north bank of the Platte from the Elkhorn to Ash Hollow, the Platte gave direction, refreshment, and diversion from the unending dreariness of their westward march.

Since the discovery of South Pass in 1812 and John C. Frémont's exploratory expeditions in 1842, the Platte became the favored route of the overland immigrant. Between 1841 and 1866, an estimated 350,000 travelers chose to follow the Platte River Valley west.

Today a source of irrigation, environmental protection, and agricultural development, the Platte is as much a living symbol of the past as it is a vital portion of **Nebraska's** economy. Both the main line of the Union Pacific **Railroad** and Interstate 80 follow its course, busy testaments to the river's endless place in Nebraska's past and future.

SOURCES

Evans, James W. Journal. Bankcroft Library, Berkeley, California. 1 June 1850.

Frémont, John C. *Report of the Exploring Expedition to the Rocky Mountains in the Year 1842, and to Oregon and Northern California in the Years 1843–44.* Washington: Gales and Seaton, 1845. Executive Doc. (U.S. Congress House); 28th Congress, 2d Session, #174.

Mattes, Merrill J. *The Great Platte River Road: The Covered Wagon Mainline via Fort Kearny to Fort Laramie.* Lincoln: University of Nebraska, 1987.

RICHARD E. BENNETT

PLURAL MARRIAGE. Doctrine and Covenants 132 states that by God's command men are permitted to have more than one wife. The roots of this **revelation** extend back to the earliest days of the Church—perhaps to as early as when the **Prophet** was working on what came to be known as the **Joseph Smith Translation of the Bible.** He wondered why the Lord justified certain Old Testament prophets in "having many wives and concubines" (D&C 132:1). In answering the Prophet's questions, God declared that under certain conditions, when he wanted to "raise up seed unto [himself]," he authorized faithful disciples to practice plural marriage (Jacob 2:30).

The introduction of plural marriage is obscured because of the desire for confidentiality, but it appears that Joseph Smith entered the practice about 1835, Fanny Alger becoming his first plural wife. A careful study of available documents reveals that 29 women were sealed to the Prophet before his death in 1844 (Anderson and Faulring, 77–79).

Joseph Smith taught the principle of plural marriage to members of the **Quorum** of the Twelve **Apostles** and to some other worthy men and women whom he trusted, and a few of them entered the practice before the Latter-day Saints left **Nauvoo**. The men and **women** who were asked to practice plural marriage also received instructions to pray and receive divine confirmation before doing so. Those who received the affirmation and practiced plural marriage believed that living this principle helped ensure exaltation.

After the Saints arrived in the **Salt Lake Valley** and were safely established, **Brigham Young**, in a special August 1852 conference, asked **Orson Pratt** to publicly announce that **Mormons** were practicing plural marriage. In his discourse **Elder** Pratt gave the specific reasons for plural marriage: (1) to multiply and replenish the earth; (2) to take part in the promises made to Abraham; (3) because in ancient times, polygamy was more common than monogamy; (4) to reform the world morally and socially; and (5) to give good homes to the many spirit children of God who were waiting to come to earth and be trained properly (Whittaker, 303). Elder Pratt also argued that the **Constitution** granted religious freedom, including the Saints' right to practice polygamy.

Federal officials thought otherwise and in 1862 passed the Morrill Anti-Bigamy Act, which prohibited plural marriage in the territories of the **United States**. Church members claimed the law was unconstitutional, and following the **Civil War**, **George Reynolds**, a devout Latter-day Saint, agreed to stand trial and be convicted so that his case could be appealed to the Supreme Court. To the Saints' disappointment, in 1879 the Court declared the Morrill Act of 1862 constitutional. This sparked a vigorous **antipolygamy movement**. Other laws against plural marriage were subsequently passed—the Edmunds Act of 1882 and the Edmunds-Tucker Act of 1887. These stiffened the fines, lengthened jail time, and made it easier to gain convictions.

Only a minority of Church members practiced plural marriage, (approximately 20%, varying from community to community), but almost every Latter-day Saint was affected in some way by polygamy. As prosecutions intensified during the mid-1880s, many men went into hiding, leaving women and children to care for farms, gardens, and livestock. Federal officials often visited the territory's communities looking for the husbands of polygamous wives. Latter-day Saint men who were captured, tried, and convicted served time in prison, including **general authorities Lorenzo Snow** and **George Q. Cannon**. President **John Taylor** died while in hiding.

At the close of the 1880s, Congress considered passing a law that would deny every Latter-day Saint the right to vote, because they belonged to an organization that sanctioned polygamy. The government also took control of much of the property and funds of the Church. After mighty prayer, President **Wilford Woodruff** received a revelation from God telling him that the Saints were to stop the practice of plural marriage. On 24 September 1890 he issued an official declaration called the **Manifesto**, which said: "we are not teaching polygamy or plural marriage, nor permitting any person to enter into its practice" (Official Declaration 1).

Evidence shows that a few Latter-day Saints entered plural marriages after the Manifesto, so in 1904 President **Joseph F. Smith** issued another declaration, sometimes called the **Second Manifesto**, stating that those who took additional wives would be excommunicated from the Church. Those men who had plural families when the Manifesto was issued, for the most part, continued their support, and over time plural marriage in The Church of Jesus Christ of Latter-day Saints ended.

SOURCES

Anderson, Richard Lloyd, and Scott H. Faulring. "Review of Todd Compton, *In Sacred Loneliness: The Plural Wives of Joseph Smith.*" *FARMS Review of Books* 10, 2 (1998): 67–104.

Bachman, Danel W. "New Light on an Old Hypothesis: The Ohio Origins of the Revelation on Eternal Marriage." *Journal of Mormon History* 5 (1978): 19–32.

Bennion, Lowell. "The Incidence of Mormon Polygamy in 1880: 'Dixie' versus Davis Stake." *Journal of Mormon History* 11 (1984): 27–42.

Embry, Jessie L. *Mormon Polygamous Families.* Salt Lake City: University of Utah Press, 1987.

Foster, Lawrence. *Religion and Sexuality.* Urbana and Chicago: University of Illinois Press, 1984.

Hardy, V. Carmon. *The Mormon Polygamous Passage.* Urbana: University of Illinois Press, 1992.

VanWagoner, Richard S. *Mormon Polygamy: A History.* Salt Lake City: Signature Books, 1986.

Whittaker, David J. "The Bone in the Throat: Orson Pratt and the Public Announcement of Plural Marriage." *The Western Historical Quarterly* 18 (July 1987): 303.

KENNETH W. GODFREY

POCATELLO (SHOSHONI CHIEF). Pocatello was a prominent Indian leader who converted to Mormonism. Born about 1815 to Widzhebu ("Cunning Eye") and an unknown father in southern **Idaho**'s Grouse Creek area, he belonged to the Northwestern Shoshoni band. The exact origin of the name *Pocatello* is uncertain. Natives referred to him as

Tonaioza ("Buffalo Robe") during his lifetime. In the late 1850s an army officer nicknamed him "White Plume."

By about 1847 Pocatello had assumed leadership of his band. During the 1850s through 1870s, he and his men were widely feared and blamed, often erroneously, for raids on stage stations and massacres of travelers along the **Oregon**, **California**, and **Salt Lake City** to **Montana** trails. Many of his people were killed by emigrants passing through Shoshoni lands. In 1864 **Abraham Lincoln** issued a stay of execution on Pocatello's behalf; the chief had been arrested on charges of threatening the lives of stage station attendants and appropriating food from them.

In 1868 the Shoshoni and Bannock tribes were assigned to live on the newly-created **Fort Hall** Reservation near present-day Blackfoot, Idaho. Chief Pocatello didn't reside there permanently until about 1872, when he settled at Bannock Creek. Apparently he refused to play a prominent role in reservation affairs.

On 5 May 1875 the chief converted to Mormonism. He was baptized by Hyrum W. Mikesell in Salt Lake City, **Utah**, and ordained to the **priesthood** office of **elder**. Several of Pocatello's band were also baptized the same day. The chief predicted that many of his people would soon follow suit, and by the following August, 574 Shoshoni had been baptized by George W. Hill.

Reportedly, Chief Pocatello died in October 1884 and was buried in a spring in the Snake River bottoms now covered by American Falls Reservoir. Eighteen of his horses were killed and buried with him. The city of Pocatello, Idaho, adopted his name in the 1880s.

SOURCES

"Lamanite Baptisms in May, June and July 1875." LDS Church Historical Department, Salt Lake City, Utah.

Madsen, Brigham D. *Chief Pocatello, the "White Plume."* Salt Lake City: Bonneville Books, University of Utah Press, 1986.

Trenholm, Virginia Cole and Maurine Carley. *The Shoshonis: Sentinels of the Rockies.* Norman: University of Oklahoma Press, 1964.

JAY G. BURRUP

POETRY. See LITERATURE.

POLAND.
Much of the early missionary success in present-day Poland occurred in areas occupied by ethnic Germans. In 1928 a **meetinghouse**

was dedicated in Selbongen, then East Prussia. At the end of **World War II**, parts of **Germany** were ceded to Poland, and most ethnic Germans were forced to leave Poland. It was under these conditions that President **Ezra Taft Benson** visited the nation in 1947. Though a few members of the Church remained in Poland after the **war**, government restrictions severely limited the Church's activity. On 30 May 1977, the Church received official recognition from the government, and President **Spencer W. Kimball** visited the country on 24 August 1977. A few missionary couples began serving in Poland following official recognition, and young adult missionaries entered in 1988. On 1 July 1990, the Poland Warsaw Mission was created from the **Austria** Vienna East Mission. By the year 2000 there were 1,094 members living in 11 **branches** in the country.

Sources

1999–2000 Church Almanac. Salt Lake City: Deseret News, 1998. 377.
Poland Warsaw Mission Historical Reports. Church Historical Department, Salt Lake City.

Jeffrey L. Anderson

POLAND ACT. See ANTI-POLYGAMY MOVEMENT.

POLICIES, PRACTICES, AND PROCEDURES. See HANDBOOKS.

POLITICAL MANIFESTO. See MANIFESTO, POLITICAL.

POLITICS.

Religious freedom was a necessary condition for the **restoration** of the gospel of **Jesus Christ** and the founding of The Church of Jesus Christ of Latter-day Saints. A culture of religious pluralism and the absence of a state church permitted **Joseph Smith** and the early **Saints** to proselyte their message of continuing **revelation** and the **Book of Mormon** as a second witness of **Jesus Christ**. But politics in **Missouri** and **Illinois** also meant that the early Church experienced **persecution** and even an **extermination order** issued by Missouri Governor **Lilburn Boggs** (Roberts, 175). The fact that the Bill of Rights protections did not yet apply to state actions meant that U.S. president **Martin Van Buren** could say in response to Joseph Smith's plea for federal assistance, "Your cause is just but I can do nothing for you" (Allen and Leonard, 144).

The Twelfth **Article of Faith** of the Church states, "We believe in being subject to kings, presidents, rulers, and magistrates, in obeying, honoring, and sustaining the law." Accused of being opposed to obeying the law of the land, the Church adopted Section 134 of the **Doctrine and Covenants**. Important statements in that section, seen by members as **scripture**, include that "governments were instituted of God for the benefit of man" (verse 1); that God holds man accountable for their acts in making laws and administering them (verse 1); that political officials who "administer the law in equity and justice should be sought for and upheld" (verse 3); that members "sustain and uphold the respective governments in which they reside" (verse 5); and that church and state should be separated (verse 9). Members living in situations without religious freedom have been encouraged to "live as far as possible all the commandments of God and the teachings of the Church, under the existing laws of the country" (Tanner, 353). Where conditions of greater freedom exist, members are urged "to strengthen the community in which we live, from a civic and political as well as a religious standpoint" (Moyle, 62–63).

Joseph Smith, himself mayor of **Nauvoo, Illinois**, and a candidate for president of the **United States**, encouraged the early Saints to be involved in government and politics. For example, Joseph Smith openly praised Illinois Democratic gubernatorial candidate, **Stephen A. Douglas**, urging the Saints to vote for him (Poll, 105). **Brigham Young** followed in Joseph Smith's footsteps, serving as first **Deseret** and later **Utah** Territorial Governor (1849–57) and taking a keen interest in the political affairs of the day. Latter-day Saint apostle **Reed Smoot** served in the U.S. Senate for thirty years, until his defeat in 1932, and Elder **Ezra Taft Benson** served as Secretary of Agriculture during the Eisenhower presidency (1953–61). The era of LDS apostles and **prophets** holding political office ended with Ezra Taft Benson. During the 1990s, LDS members of Congress represented **Arizona, California, Idaho, Nevada, New Hampshire, Oklahoma, Oregon**, Utah, and **American Samoa**. Because of the concentration of LDS membership in the Intermountain West, the LDS Church has been important in the politics of this region.

Utah was repeatedly denied statehood because of **plural marriage** and perceptions that the Church dominated Utah politics and economics. Federal government policies against polygamy as well as the lack of governmental responsiveness to religious persecution in Missouri and

Illinois fostered among the Saints a distrust and hostility towards government. But the next hundred years saw this hostility change to fervent patriotism. Members are regularly encouraged to participate in politics and to vote in elections.

During the last third of the twentieth century, the Church took stands on questions of a moral nature. The most visible examples include opposition to **Liquor-by-the-Drink** in Utah in 1968, to the lottery in Idaho in 1988, to parimutuel **gambling** in Utah in 1992, and to same sex marriage in **Hawaii** and **Alaska** in 1998 and in California in 2000. On a national level, the Church opposed the **Equal Rights Amendment** in the 1970s and the deployment proposed for the MX missile in the early 1980s.

Examined collectively, Latter-day Saints are more conservative and more **Republican** than the general population. The tendency to be Republican is even stronger among younger members. In a national study done by Kenneth D. Wald, Latter-day Saints were the most Republican and conservative of all religious groups (Wald, 79). Yet Latter-day Saints scored much higher than most religious groups on racial liberalism and were more inclined to civil liberties than **black** Protestants and evangelical Protestants. Latter-day Saints were the least supportive of federalism (Wald, 80–89). That major studies of religion and politics now include Latter-day Saints as a separate category is evidence of the growing numbers and importance of Latter-day Saints in American politics.

SOURCES

Allen, James B., and Glen M. Leonard. *The Story of the Latter-day Saints.* 2d ed. Salt Lake City: Deseret Book, 1992.

Poll, Richard D. *Utah's History.* Logan, Utah: Utah State University, 1989.

Roberts, B. H. *A Comprehensive History of The Church of Jesus Christ of Latter-day Saints, Century One.* 6 vols. Salt Lake City: The Church of Jesus Christ of Latter-day Saints, 1930.

Tanner, N. Eldon. "Submission to Secular Authority." *Instructor* (October 1963).

Wald, Kenneth D. *Religion and Politics in the United States.* 2d ed. Washington, D.C.: C Q Press, 1992.

DAVID MAGLEBY

POLK, JAMES K. James Knox Polk was president of the **United States** (1845–49) at a time when the country experienced tremendous territorial growth. He was also a friend of the **Mormons** and assisted them in their migration to the West. Born 2 November 1795 near Pineville, **North**

Carolina, James moved with his family to central **Tennessee** when he was about 11 years old. He attended the University of North Carolina, where he graduated first in his class. Polk then returned to Tennessee where he practiced law. He married Sarah Childress in 1824 and served in the U.S. House of Representatives from 1825 to 1839, serving as Speaker of the House the last four years. He was governor of Tennessee from 1839 to 1841 and became president of the United States in 1845.

Polk was serving as chief executive when the Latter-day Saints were planning their **pioneer trek** from **Illinois** to the **Salt Lake Valley.** Church leaders heard that President Polk had advocated a series of forts or blockhouses to be built along the **Oregon Trail** to benefit American citizens as they moved west. **Brigham Young** sent **Jesse C. Little** to **Washington, D.C.,** to negotiate an agreement with President Polk, whereby the **Saints** would build the blockhouses in return for federal assistance to aid them in their western migration. By the time Little reached the nation's capital, however, the United States had already declared war on **Mexico**, and the country's priorities had changed. President Polk asked Little if 500 of the Latter-day Saints who were on their way west would be willing to enlist in the U.S. Army and assist with the war effort. The Church ultimately agreed, which led to the organization of the **Mormon Battalion.** As a result of the Saints' participation, they received soldiers' pay and clothing—allowance money that was greatly needed. It also gave the **pioneers** a justifiable reason to establish temporary settlements on **Indian** lands. Brigham Young stated that President Polk's request to organize the battalion was "the first offer we have ever had from the government to benefit us" (quoted in Allen and Leonard, 238). President Young later sent Polk a formal resolution of gratitude, which pledged to him the faith and prayers of the Saints. Polk served only one term as president and died of cholera just three months later on 15 June 1849. He was buried in Nashville, Tennessee.

SOURCES

Allen, James B. and Glen M. Leonard. *The Story of the Latter-day Saints.* 2d ed. Salt Lake City: Deseret Book, 1992.

Roberts, B. H. *A Comprehensive History of The Church of Jesus Christ of Latter-day Saints, Century One.* 6 vols. Salt Lake City: The Church of Jesus Christ of Latter-day Saints, 1930.

Sellers, Charles G., Jr. *James K. Polk: Jacksonian.* Princeton: Princeton, 1957.

ARNOLD K. GARR

POLYGAMY. See PLURAL MARRIAGE.

POLYNESIAN CULTURAL CENTER. The Church-sponsored
Polynesian Cultural Center (PCC), situated in **Laie, Hawaii**, on the north
end of the island of Oahu near the **BYU–Hawaii campus** and the **Hawaii
Temple**, first began operation in October 1963. The initial complex consisted of a 750-seat auditorium, a lagoon, food and concession areas, and
six Polynesian villages representing the islands and peoples of **Samoa,
Fiji, Tonga, Tahiti, Hawaii**, and the **Maoris** of **New Zealand**. In 1976 the
center underwent a major expansion when the lagoon was enlarged and
a Marqueasan village and 2,500-seat amphitheater were added. Additional
renovations took place again in 1984 and 1991. The premier attraction
of the PCC is the night show, where guests enjoy authentic Polynesian
songs and dances performed by islanders in native costumes and dress.
Since its establishment, the PCC has (1) helped to preserve many of the
Polynesian cultural traditions; (2) provided part-time employment and
work scholarships to support students from the South **Pacific** attending
BYU–Hawaii; (3) provided cultural entertainment for millions of visitors
to the Center (25 million as of September 1997); (4) provided full-time
employment for business and entertainment professionals, staff, and
maintenance personnel; and (5) helped to present a favorable image of
the Church.

SOURCES

Ferre, Craig. "A History of the Polynesian Cultural Center's 'Night Show':
    1963–1983." Ph. D. diss., Brigham Young University, 1988.

Forester, Rubina. "The Polynesian Cultural Center: The Realization Gone Far beyond
    the Dream." *Mormon Pacific Historical Society Proceedings: Seventh Annual
    Conference, Mormon History in the Pacific.* Laie, Hawaii: Brigham Young
    University–Hawaii, 1986. 60–72.

Webb, Terry Douglas. "Mormonism and Tourist Art in Hawaii." Ph.D. diss., Arizona
    State University, 1990.

Whitehurst, James. "Mormons and the Hula: The Polynesian Cultural Center in
    Hawaii." *Journal of American Culture* 12 (Spring 1989): 1–5.

ALEXANDER L. BAUGH

POLYSOPHICAL SOCIETY. The Polysophical Society, perhaps
organized as early as 1852, was meeting regularly by 1854 in the home
of its founder, **Lorenzo Snow**, in **Salt Lake City**. Its purpose was to promote intellectual advancement and appreciation for the arts. The society's

well-attended meetings were later moved to larger facilities. Their success inspired the creation of numerous similar societies. Despite the society's popularity, it was discontinued in 1856, and its activities were merged into those of the "Deseret Theological Class."

SOURCES

Coombs, Isaiah Moses. Diary. Vols. 1–2. Archives Division, Historical Department, The Church of Jesus Christ of Latter-day Saints, Salt Lake City.
Heinerman, Joseph. "Early Utah Pioneer Cultural Societies." *Utah Historical Quarterly* 47 (Winter 1979): 70–89.
Snow, Eliza R. *Biography and Family Record of Lorenzo Snow, One of the Twelve Apostles of The Church of Jesus Christ of Latter-day Saints.* Salt Lake City: Deseret News, 1884.

SCOTT BRADSHAW

PONY EXPRESS, THE.

Utah's communication isolation ended after 3 April 1860, when eastern express contractors established a transcontinental mail service—the legendary Pony Express. A relay of wiry riders and quick horses carried mail between St. Joseph, **Missouri**, and Sacramento, California, in 10 days. Operated by Russell, Majors, and Waddell, the Pony Express lasted only until October 1861—a brief year and a half. At the initial rate of $5 per half ounce, the Pony Express carried urgent business letters in specially designed leather packs called *mochilas*. These were easily transferred from one horse to another at stations spaced from 10 to 15 miles apart. Each rider would ride approximately 75 to 100 miles to a point where more substantial lodging and corrals were provided. The trail paralleled the **pioneer** route from **Wyoming** into the **Salt Lake Valley**. It then headed south almost to Lehi and turned west through the desert, toward the Sierra and California. Under the leadership of Howard Egan, **Mormons** rode the Utah portion of the route that operated day and night.

Although most mail carried on the Pony Express was bound for California, a few lightweight newspapers were delivered in Salt Lake City, enabling the *Deseret News* to reprint news that was only a few days old. When the transcontinental **telegraph** system was completed 24 October 1861, the Pony Express ended, leaving behind stories of heroic riders, colorful station keepers, and an organization still hoping for a profitable mail contract over the now-proven Central Route.

SOURCES

Bluth, John F. "Confrontation with an Arid Land: The Incursion of Gosiutes and Whites into Utah's Central West Desert, 1800–1978." Ph.D. diss., Brigham Young University. 1979.

Haymond, Jay M. "Pony Express in Utah." *Utah History Encyclopedia.* Edited by Allan Kent Powell. Salt Lake City: University of Utah Press, 1984.

Loving, Mabel. *The Pony Express Rides On.* St. Joseph, Mo.: Roibidoux Printing Co., 1961.

JOHN BLUTH

POOR CAMP. In the latter part of September of 1846, approximately 640 **Saints** who remained in **Nauvoo** crossed the frigid waters of the **Mississippi River** into **Lee County, Iowa**. These desperate ill-equipped Saints were known as the "poor camp." The main body of Saints left Nauvoo between February and May of 1846, yet **anti-Mormon** sentiment continued among enemies of the Church who feared that the **Mormons** would never completely leave Illinois. This fear culminated in the **Battle of Nauvoo** and final mediation that required the remaining Saints to leave immediately. Scattered along the **Iowa** banks of the **Mississippi River** with rampant sickness, meager accommodations, and little food, the Saints were nearly destitute. In the midst of this suffering, the Lord sent hundreds of quail, wearied from a long flight, into the poor camp like manna from heaven. The hungry Saints easily caught and killed the tired quail. The **miracle of the quail** coupled with a rescue mission sent by **Brigham Young** provided the physical and spiritual sustenance the Saints needed to rejoin the main body of Saints.

SOURCES

Allen, James B., and Glen M. Leonard. *The Story of the Latter-day Saints.* 2d ed. Salt Lake City: Deseret Book, 1992. 230–234.

Church History in the Fulness of Times. Salt Lake City: The Church of Jesus Christ of Latter-day Saints, 1993. 317–19.

Roberts, B. H. *A Comprehensive History of The Church of Jesus Christ of Latter-day Saints, Century One.* 6 vols. Salt Lake City: The Church of Jesus Christ of Latter-day Saints, 1930. 3:135–136.

RUSSELL C. RASMUSSEN

PORTUGAL. Members of the U.S. armed forces stationed in Portugal in the early 1970s were the first members of the Church in this southwest European nation. After a revolution in May 1974, which resulted in a statute granting religious freedom, the Church gained official recognition. In that same year, **David M. Kennedy**, representing the **First Presidency**, received permission from the government for the Church to officially enter the country.

In November 1974 the Portugal Lisbon **Mission** was created with William Grant Bangerter as its first president. The first four missionaries were transferred from a mission in **Brazil**, and the work progressed so rapidly that there were more than 1,000 members by July 1978.

By the year 2000, Portugal had the second largest membership of any European country, with 35,248 members living in 5 **stakes**. In July of 1998, the Mormon **Tabernacle Choir** visited and performed in Lisbon.

SOURCES

"A Half Century of Modern Church Expansion: 1947–97." *Church News,* 27 September 1997. 8.

"Musical Ministry Has Big Impact." *Church News,* July 18, 1998. 11.

1999–2000 Church Almanac. Salt Lake City: Deseret News, 1998. 405–6.

KYLE R. WALKER AND FRANCISCO XAVIER DIAS

POSTAGE STAMPS. See STAMPS.

PRATT, ADDISON. Addison Pratt is best known for the two **missions** he served to the Society Islands (**French Polynesia**) between 1843 and 1852. He also served as **branch** president in **San Francisco** in 1848. Born 21 February 1802 in Winchester, **New Hampshire**, Addison worked as a sailor on whaling and trading ships as a young man, visiting ports between the Mediterranean Sea and the Hawaiian Islands. He married Louisa Barnes 3 April 1831 and was baptized in **Kirtland** on 18 June 1838. Addison was called with three others in May 1843 to go on a mission to the South **Pacific**. He established the first branch of the Church in the Pacific Islands at Tubuai, in the Society Islands, shortly after his arrival there 30 April 1844. Overcoming opposition from Anglican missionaries in the area, he established several more branches on neighboring islands before leaving for **California** in May 1847. After meeting his **family** in **Utah** in 1848, he was called again to serve in the Society Islands. Accompanied by his wife and four daughters, he arrived in **Tahiti** in May 1850. Banished from the Society Islands by French authorities in 1852, Addison made his way back to California, where he left the Church and became a spiritualist. He died 14 October 1872 in Anaheim, California.

SOURCES

Ellsworth, S. George. *The Journals of Addison Pratt.* Salt Lake City: University of Utah Press, 1990.

Jenson, Andrew. *Latter-day Saint Biographical Encyclopedia.* 4 vols. 1901–36. Reprint, Salt Lake City: Western Epics, 1971. 3:698–99.

ANDREW H. HEDGES

PRATT, ORSON. Orson Pratt, one of the most influential leaders of the early Church, was born in Hartford, New York, on 19 September 1811. He was an **apostle**, missionary, editor, mathematician, scientist, and philosopher—a truly gifted individual.

Raised on a farm, he nevertheless found the time to develop his intellectual skills through a combination of personal study and formal schooling. A fervent student of the **scriptures**, Orson was anxious to find the truth in religious matters. Orson's brother **Parley P. Pratt** taught him about the Church and baptized him on his nineteenth birthday.

After being ordained an **elder** by **Joseph Smith** in October 1830, Orson undertook the first of many **missions**, preaching initially in **Colesville, New York.** In 1834 Orson marched with **Zion's Camp** to help redeem lost lands in **Jackson County, Missouri.** This was a formative experience in which young Orson had close daily contact with Joseph Smith.

In February 1835 **David Whitmer, Oliver Cowdery**, and **Martin Harris** ordained Orson Pratt as one of the original Twelve Apostles. In this capacity, Orson continued serving as a missionary, as well as carrying out administrative tasks.

Between 1839 and 1841 Elder Pratt served in the highly successful **mission of the Twelve to Britain.** In 1840 in Edinburgh he published his first missionary **pamphlet**, entitled *Interesting Account of Several Remarkable Visions*, which included one of the earliest published accounts of the **First Vision**.

From 1841 to 1844 Orson was in **Nauvoo**, where he filled various leadership roles and taught at the **University of Nauvoo**. In the meantime he became an avid student of mathematics, increasing his studies in algebra, trigonometry, and calculus.

Orson left Nauvoo on 14 February 1846 with his **family**—four wives and three children. One of his wives, Louisa Chandler Pratt, died of typhus fever on 12 June 1846. As a part of the vanguard company of **Mormon** pioneers, he helped with scientific observations and records. He and **Erastus Snow** were the first **pioneers** to enter the **Salt Lake Valley**. Upon arrival he began a survey of the valley.

More missionary work followed as Pratt was appointed president of the **European Mission** in April 1848. For three years he served as president, preacher, writer, and editor. In 1852 in **Washington, D.C.**, he began publication of *The Seer,* a periodical which defended and explained the tenets of Mormonism, including polygamy. Orson had been assigned to make the first public announcement and defense of **plural marriage** earlier that year. In 1864 he served a mission in **Austria**. Finding Austrian laws too restrictive, he did some Church work in **England** before returning home.

In August the famed Pratt-Newman Debates took place. Orson Pratt debated Mormonism with Dr. John Newman, Methodist Chaplain of the U.S. Senate. From the LDS perspective Elder Pratt emerged victorious.

In 1874 Pratt became **Church historian**, a position which he held until his death. He supervised the preparation of new editions of the **Book of Mormon** and **Doctrine and Covenants**. In company with **Joseph F. Smith** he visited various Latter-day Saint historical sites, and he had a successful interview with **David Whitmer**.

Orson Pratt died in **Salt Lake City** on 3 October 1881. He left 10 wives and 45 children. He was revered as one of the best minds in early Mormonism. The epitaph he had written for his gravestone sums up his life: "My body sleeps for a moment, but my testimony lives and shall endure forever."

SOURCES

England, Breck. *The Life and Thought of Orson Pratt.* Salt Lake City: University of Utah Press, 1985.

Pratt, Orson. *The Essential Orson Pratt.* Salt Lake City: Signature Books, 1991.

DONALD Q. CANNON

PRATT, PARLEY P. Parley Parker Pratt, missionary, pamphleteer, and poet, stands as one of the most influential early Latter-day Saints. The third of five sons of Jared and Charity Dickinson Pratt, Parley was born in Burlington, Otsego County, **New York**, 12 April 1807. He moved around New York during his early years as his father struggled to support his **family**. While Parley had little opportunity for **education**, his mother taught him to read the **scriptures**, and as a boy he learned to love books. At age 20 he married Thankful Halsey, took his bride to **Ohio**, and there, through the preaching of **Sidney Rigdon**, aligned himself with the followers of Alexander Campbell. In August 1830 Parley and Thankful sold their Ohio home and started for New York. En route he happened

upon a Baptist deacon who spoke of a "very strange book" in his possession, and the next day he eagerly read the deacon's copy of the **Book of
Mormon**, convinced that its message was true. In **Palmyra** he met **Hyrum
Smith**, and about 1 September 1830 he was baptized by **Oliver Cowdery**
in Seneca Lake.

Less than two months after his baptism, Parley left with Oliver
Cowdery, **Peter Whitmer Jr.**, and **Ziba Peterson** on the **Lamanite Mission
of 1830–1831**, which would take him to the western border of **Missouri**.
Pausing in Ohio, he introduced his new religion to his friend Sidney
Rigdon, helping to convert him and a number of the **Campbellite** con-
gregation. The following year he settled with the Saints in **Jackson
County, Missouri**, then fled with them into **Clay County** in November
1833, and returned to Jackson County with **Zion's Camp** in 1834. In
February 1835 he was chosen as a member of the original **Quorum** of the
Twelve **Apostles**.

Parley P. Pratt first wrote for the Church in December 1833 in a
Missouri handbill concerning the Jackson violence; he issued a pamphlet
16 months later that described his unsuccessful attempt to preach the
gospel in Mentor, Ohio; and he published a book of his poems in the
summer of 1835—the first book of Latter-day Saint poetry. So in **New
York City** in the summer of 1837, when his preaching fell on deaf ears,
he instinctively turned to the written word and in two months produced
one of the most important LDS books, *Voice of Warning*. Six months later,
when a Methodist cleric attacked the Latter-day Saints in print, Parley
wrote *Mormonism Unveiled: Zion's Watchman Unmasked*, the earliest
surviving reply to an **anti-Mormon** work, which, like *Voice of Warning*,
established a model to be used by **Mormon** pamphleteers for another
century.

Returning from his New York **mission** in the spring of 1838, Parley P.
Pratt settled again in Missouri, in time to be caught up in the violence
that fall. For eight months he languished in **Richmond** and Columbia
jails before escaping on 4 July 1839. As he waited to sail to England with
the Twelve, he wrote a number of **hymns** and two essays entitled *Late
Persecution,* and *Millennium and Other Poems*. These were published in
New York the following year. In England he served as the founding editor
of the *Millennial Star,* one of the Church's longest-running **periodicals**;
helped compile a hymnal, which included about 40 of his own songs;
reprinted his *Voice of Warning;* and published ten tracts.

Parley's stay in **Nauvoo** lasted three years, interrupted by missions to
the East Coast. In February 1846 he evacuated the city with his **family**

and headed into Iowa; 19 months later he entered the **Salt Lake Valley**. In March 1851 he left his Utah home for the Pacific coast, and in San Francisco that summer, he composed *Proclamation to the People of the Coasts and Islands of the Pacific,* which C. W. Wandell published in Sydney, **Australia**, that November. It was the first Latter-day Saint book published outside of North America or Western **Europe**, and the first book associated with the extraordinary effort that sent Latter-day Saint missionaries to **South America, Africa, India, China**, and Australia. Parley himself went to **Chile** in September, and upon his return to San Francisco the following spring, he published *Proclamacion Extraordinaria*— the first Latter-day Saint book in Spanish. In San Francisco he began another work, his great synthesis of Mormon doctrine, *Key to the Science of Theology,* published in **Liverpool, England**, in 1855. Parley P. Pratt's last mission began in September 1856, and during the winter of 1856–57 he toured the eastern states. Near Van Buren, **Arkansas**, on 13 May 1857, he was murdered by the former husband of one of his plural wives.

A century and a half after his death, few Latter-day Saints read Parley P. Pratt's doctrinal books and tracts. But their content, in one form or other, has survived—perpetuated in the books of later writers who used Parley's works as their points of departure. Latter-day Saints still sing his hymns, seven of which are in the current LDS hymnal. And they read his posthumously published *Autobiography*—one of Mormondom's treasures.

SOURCES

Crawley, Peter. *A Descriptive Bibliography of the Mormon Church.* Vol. 1. Provo, Utah: Religious Studies Center, Brigham Young University, 1997.

———. "Parley P. Pratt: Father of Mormon Pamphleteering." *Dialogue* 13 (Winter 1980): 26–37.

Pratt, Parley P. *Autobiography of Parley P. Pratt.* Edited by Parley P. Pratt Jr. Salt Lake City: Deseret Book, 1985.

Pratt, Steven. "Eleanor McLean and the Murder of Parley P. Pratt." *BYU Studies* 15 (1975): 225–56.

PETER CRAWLEY

PRATT, REY L. Rey Lucero Pratt was a member of the First Council of **Seventy** and "father" of the Mexican Mission. His name is forever linked to the history of the Church in Latin America. Born in **Salt Lake City, Utah**, to Helaman Pratt and Emmeline Billingsley 11 October 1878, Rey moved with his family to Colonia Dublan, Chihuahua, **Mexico** after marrying Mary Stark in 1900. Pratt was called on a mission to Mexico in 1906, then in 1909 he became president of the Mexican Mission. This mission later included all Spanish-speaking residents of the western **United States**.

On 29 January 1925 **Elder** Pratt was ordained a member of the First Council of the Seventy, and later that year he was called with **Elders Melvin J. Ballard** and **Rulon S. Wells** to open missionary work in **South America**—an endeavor that had been attempted previously by his grandfather, **Parley P. Pratt**. Rey L. Pratt returned to presiding over the Mexican Mission, but at the age of 52 he died from complications of a hernia operation on 14 April 1931 in Salt Lake City.

Rey L. Pratt translated scriptures and missionary tracts, and he compiled a Spanish **hymnal**. Elder Ballard said, "I see him in the spirit world teaching the Gospel to millions of the descendants of Lehi who have gone ahead of him" (Ballard, 282).

SOURCES

Beecher, Dale F. "Rey L. Pratt and the Mexican Mission." *BYU Studies* 15 (Spring 1975): 293–307.

Melvin J. Ballard . . . Crusader for Righteousness. Salt Lake City: Bookcraft, 1966.

KENNETH REY CALL

PRAYER CIRCLE. Prayer circles, which have their origin in ancient times (see, for example, 1 Tim. 2:8), have generally been associated with the **temple** endowment, which was first given 4 May 1842; however, two types of circles were organized apart from the temple. The first was composed of especially invited individuals. At **Nauvoo** in 1843, for example, a circle was organized with the **Prophet Joseph Smith** as its leader. Similar circles were created in the **Salt Lake Valley** beginning in 1851. These "special prayer circles" were discontinued by the **First Presidency** in 1929 because this privilege was not available to all worthy members.

The second type of prayer circle was composed of members of designated ecclesiastical bodies, such as the Nauvoo **high council**, beginning in 1845. Some early **meetinghouses** included "prayer circle rooms" with lockers where needed temple clothing could be kept. **Ward** bishoprics, priesthood **quorums**, and other local bodies secured First Presidency authorization to form prayer circle groups. In 1978, however, the First Presidency and Quorum of the Twelve **Apostles** decided that the rapidly multiplying number of **stakes** made it too difficult to supervise these circles, so they were discontinued. Since then authorized prayer circles have been limited to the temples.

SOURCES

Nibley, Hugh. "The Early Christian Prayer Circle." *BYU Studies* 19 (Fall 1978): 41–78.

Quinn, D. Michael. "Latter-day Saint Prayer Circles." *BYU Studies* 19 (Fall 1978): 79–105.

RICHARD O. COWAN

PRESIDENCY OF THE CHURCH. See FIRST PRESIDENCY.

PRESIDENTIAL CAMPAIGN OF JOSEPH SMITH. Joseph

Smith's presidential campaign, which was one of the most intriguing third-party movements in American history, took place in the year 1844. After President **Martin Van Buren** and the federal government refused to act on the **Mormon Petitions for Redress** concerning the **Missouri** persecutions, **Joseph Smith** lost confidence in the presidency of the **United States**. In 1843 he wrote **John C. Calhoun**, Lewis Cass, Richard M. Johnson, **Henry Clay**, and Martin Van Buren—the five leading candidates for the presidency—and asked each of them the same question: "What will be your rule of action relative to us as a people, should fortune favor your ascension to the chief magistracy?" (Smith, 65). Van Buren and Johnson never responded and the other three expressed an unwillingness to help the Church.

Soon thereafter the **Prophet** held an historic meeting in the **Nauvoo** mayor's office on 29 January 1844, where the **Quorum** of the Twelve **Apostles** and others present decided Joseph Smith, himself, would run for president. On that same day he met with **William W. Phelps**, who helped him write a platform that was published as a **pamphlet**, *General Smith's Views of the Powers and Policy of the Government of the United States*. The use of the title "General" (of the **Nauvoo Legion**) rather than "prophet" or "president" set the strictly political tone for the tract. Joseph advocated giving power to the president to suppress mobs. He also favored abolishing **slavery**, reducing both the number and pay of the House of Representatives, reforming the prison system, eliminating court martials for desertion, forming a national bank, and annexing **Oregon** and **Texas**.

On 9 April during a regular session of **general conference**, Brigham

Young called for volunteers to serve political/religious **missions**, and 244 stepped forward. During the next few days additional missionaries were called, bringing the total to at least 340. These electioneer missionaries, added to the number of those who had been called to serve traditional missions during that same year, brought the total number of missionaries to 586. This was, by far, the largest number of missionaries called to serve in a single year up to that time. On 15 April the electioneer missionaries were assigned to campaign and preach in all 26 states of the Union and in the **Wisconsin** territory.

Joseph Smith's original choice as a running mate for the office of vice-president was **James Arlington Bennett**; however, Bennett declined the offer. On 17 May a political convention was held in Nauvoo that formally nominated Joseph Smith as president and **Sidney Rigdon** as his vice-presidential running mate. The delegates planned to have a national convention in Baltimore, **Maryland**, on 13 July and appointed **Willard Richards**, **John Bernhisel**, William W. Phelps, and Lucian R. Foster to serve as a central committee. Whether or not Joseph believed that he could be elected cannot be known with certainty, but his *Views* were widely reported in the press. The campaign ended prematurely on 27 June when the Prophet was **martyred** at the **Carthage Jail**.

––––––

SOURCES

Garr, Arnold K. "Joseph Smith: Candidate for President of the United States." In *Illinois*. Edited by H. Dean Garrett. Regional Studies in Latter-day Saint Church History series. Provo, Utah: Brigham Young University, 1995. 151–68.

Smith, Joseph. *History of The Church of Jesus Christ of Latter-day Saints.* Edited by B. H. Roberts. 2d ed. rev. 7 vols. Salt Lake City: The Church of Jesus Christ of Latter-day Saints, 1932–51. 6:65.

ARNOLD K. GARR

PRESIDING BISHOP. The presiding bishop is a **general authority** who, together with his **counselors**, oversees the temporal affairs of the Church under the direction of the **First Presidency**. On 4 February 1831, the Lord directed that **Edward Partridge** "be appointed by the voice of the church, and ordained a **bishop**" (D&C 41:9). A later **revelation** declared that "other bishops [would] be set apart unto the church, to minister even according to the first" (D&C 68:14). In December 1831 **Newel K. Whitney** was also called to be a bishop (D&C 72:8). For a period of time, Bishop Partridge served as "the bishop in **Zion**" and

Bishop Whitney as "the bishop in **Ohio**" (D&C 84:104). As the Church grew, more bishops were called and given local jurisdictions.

To help maintain order in the Church, revelations clarified that **Joseph Smith** and his counselors were to oversee the work of the bishopric (D&C 78:9; 82:12; 107:64–68). Bishop Partridge died in 1840, and an 1841 revelation called **George Miller** to "the office of a bishopric, like unto my servant Edward Partridge, that he may receive the consecrations of mine house, that he may administer blessings upon the heads of the poor of my people" (D&C 124:21). The revelation also called "Vinson Knight, **Samuel H. Smith**, and Shadrach Roundy . . . to preside over the bishopric" (D&C 124:141).

At the time of this call to be presiding bishop, Vinson Knight was serving as a bishop in **Nauvoo**. Depending on how the historical evidence is interpreted, Bishop Knight either did not serve at all as presiding bishop, or he served as one of three presiding bishops, the other two being Bishops Whitney and Miller. In any case, he did not serve as the sole presiding bishop of the Church before his death on 31 July 1842. The first person to serve in a sole capacity with that title was Newel K. Whitney, who was sustained as such on **6 April 1847**.

Edward Partridge is considered the first presiding bishop of the Church because (1) when originally appointed in **Kirtland**, he was the only bishop and had general Church jurisdiction; (2) for a time Bishop Whitney reported stewardships to him (D&C 72:5–6; 13–18); and (3) he was the first called of the four early bishops (Partridge, Whitney, Miller, and Knight) who collectively were sometimes referred to as presiding bishops.

SOURCES

Brandt, Edward J. "The Office of Bishop in The Church of Jesus Christ of Latter-day Saints, 1830–1839." Religion 541 term paper, Brigham Young University, 1967.

Pace, Donald Gene. "The LDS Presiding Bishopric, 1851–1888: An Administrative Study." Master's thesis, Brigham Young University, 1978.

Taylor, John. *Items on Priesthood.* Salt Lake City: Deseret News, 1881. 18–40.

Watson, Elden Jay. "Early Development of the Presiding Bishopric." Manuscript. LDS Church Historical Department, Salt Lake City. 1973.

RICHARD E. TURLEY JR.

PRESIDING HIGH PRIEST. See FIRST PRESIDENCY.

PRESIDING PATRIARCH. See PATRIARCH TO THE CHURCH.

PRESTON, WILLIAM B. William Bowker Preston, a **presiding bishop** of the Church, was born in Halifax, **Virginia**, 24 November 1830, to Christopher Preston and Martha Mitchell Clayton. He was baptized in 1857 by **George Q. Cannon**. In 1858 he married Harriet A. Thatcher and served as a minuteman in the **Utah War**. He was called as the first bishop of **Logan** by **Orson Hyde** in 1859 and later as president of the Cache County **Stake**. From 1866 to 1869 he was a missionary in **Europe**, where he labored as the president of the Newcastle and Durham conference. In 1884 he was called as the presiding bishop, where he served until 1907, when he was released because of his failing health. Bishop Preston died 2 August 1908 in Salt Lake City.

SOURCE

Jenson, Andrew. *Latter-day Saint Biographical Encyclopedia.* 4 vols. 1901–36. Reprint, Salt Lake City: Western Epics, 1971. 1:232; 3:771.

MARY JANE WOODGER

PRIEST. Those who hold the office of priest in the **Aaronic Priesthood** are to preach, teach, expound, exhort, baptize, and administer the **sacrament**; visit members in their homes, exhorting them to pray vocally and secretly and to fulfill family duties; **ordain** other priests, **teachers**, and **deacons**; assist **elders**; and conduct **meetings** whenever higher officers are absent (D&C 20). A priests **quorum** can have up to 48 members and is presided over by a **bishop** (D&C 107:87–88).

During the nineteenth century almost all priests were adults. At the Church's first **conference**, held 9 June 1830, three priests were present: **Joseph Smith Sr.**, 59; **Hyrum Smith**, 30; and **Martin Harris**, 47. The average age of those in the **Nauvoo** priests quorum was 29. During the **Brigham Young** period, **Melchizedek Priesthood** bearers served as *acting* priests. In 1908 the Church set the ages for priests at 18–21. Currently the age range is 16–18.

During the 1830s and 1840s in **Missouri**, the **Kirtland** region, and **mission** areas, priests presided in small **branches** where no elders were present, served on proselyting missions, and visited members' homes, much like today's **home teachers**. After 1908 **wards** assigned the young priests, instead of older men, to bless the sacrament. In 1912, when ward teaching was formalized, instructions emphasized that there was no more important work in the Church than ward teaching and that every priest should be assigned to do it in partnership with an experienced adult ward teacher.

SOURCES

Hartley, William G. "From Men to Boys: LDS Aaronic Priesthood Offices, 1829–1996." *Journal of Mormon History* 22 (Spring 1996): 80–136.

Palmer, Lee A. *Aaronic Priesthood through the Centuries.* Salt Lake City: Deseret Book, 1964.

WILLIAM G. HARTLEY

PRIESTHOOD. see AARONIC PRIESTHOOD AND MELCHI-ZEDEK PRIESTHOOD.

PRIESTHOOD AND THE BLACKS. see OFFICIAL DECLA-RATION 2.

PRIESTHOOD BLESSINGS. See BLESSINGS.

PRIESTHOOD CORRELATION. See CORRELATION.

PRIESTHOOD MEETINGS. See MEETINGS.

PRIESTHOOD OFFICES.
After a man has had the Aaronic or Melchizedek Priesthood conferred upon him, he is ordained to an office of the priesthood. These offices are appointments to serve in specific ways within the priesthood. The priesthood is greater than any of its offices. Both the Aaronic and Melchizedek Priesthood were restored to Joseph Smith and Oliver Cowdery without ordination to any specific office. The first reference to priesthood offices came in June 1829 when Joseph and Oliver prayed at the Whitmer home for greater understanding. Joseph states: "we had not long been engaged in solemn and fervent prayer, when the word of the Lord came unto us in the chamber, commanding us that I should ordain Oliver Cowdery to be an Elder in the

Church of **Jesus Christ**; and that he also should ordain me to the same office; and then to ordain others." Joseph also notes that they were to defer their ordination until their brethren could be present to sustain them (Smith, 1:60–61). At the **organization of the Church** on **6** April 1830, Joseph and Oliver were ordained elders and sustained by the brethren present.

As the Church has grown, additional offices of the priesthood have been restored. At the organization of the Church, the priesthood offices mentioned were elder, **priest**, **teacher**, and **deacon** (D&C 20:38–60). In 1831 came the offices of **bishop** and **high priest** (D&C 41:9; Smith, 1:176), and in 1833 came the office of patriarch. In 1835 the offices of **apostle** and **seventy** were restored (Smith, 2:187, 201–2).

The offices of the **Aaronic Priesthood** in the Church today are deacon, teacher, priest, and bishop. The offices of the Melchizedek Priesthood are elder, high priest, **patriarch**, seventy, and apostle. Priesthood bearers belong to **quorums** according to their office. At a **ward** level there are quorums of deacons, teachers, priests, and elders with presidents over each (the bishop being president of the priests). At the **stake** level there is a quorum of high priests presided over by the **stake president**, and at the general Church level there are quorums of seventy and the Quorum of the Twelve Apostles.

SOURCES

Harper, Bruce T. "Priesthood Offices." *Encyclopedia of Mormonism.* Edited by Daniel H. Ludlow. 4 vols. New York: Macmillan, 1992. 3:1143–44.

McConkie, Bruce R. *Mormon Doctrine.* 2d ed. Salt Lake City: Bookcraft, 1966. 595–97.

Smith, Joseph. *History of The Church of Jesus Christ of Latter-day Saints.* Edited by B. H. Roberts. 2d ed. rev. 7 vols. Salt Lake City: The Church of Jesus Christ of Latter-day Saints, 1932–51.

GUY L. DORIUS

PRIESTHOOD QUORUMS. See QUORUM.

PRIMARY. On 25 August 1878, a chapel full of children met in Farmington, **Utah**, at the first meeting of the newly organized Primary Association. A century later more than a million and a half children were enrolled in this worldwide organization for Latter-day Saint youth ages 3 to 12. In the intervening years, the Primary Association sponsored a children's hospital, published a **magazine**, created radio and television programs, initiated a series of popular **Book of Mormon** paintings, implemented a teacher-training program, and provided instruction for thousands of children in the principles of the gospel through study of the **Articles of Faith**.

The Primary Association developed out of a concern for the social and spiritual well-being of **Zion's** youth. This concern, expressed by Latter-day Saint leaders and mothers, prompted **Aurelia Spencer Rogers** to put the question to **Eliza R. Snow** in 1878: "Could there not be an organization for little boys and have them trained to make better men?" (Rogers, 208). In her unofficial role as "presidentess of Mormon women," Eliza R. Snow was in a position to answer in the affirmative, and with the enthusiastic support of President John Taylor, the Primary Association, girls included, was launched.

In June 1880 **Louie B. Felt** was appointed the association's first general president, and she served for 45 years. By the mid-1880s, Primaries functioned in nearly every Latter-day Saint community. Eliza R. Snow furnished songs, biblical catechisms, and a series of books containing recitations and dialogues for the weekly **meetings**. Along with her counselor **May Anderson**, who succeeded her as president, Sister Felt studied and then adopted the child-centered principles of progressive education in developing a curriculum for the Primary. Dedicated teachers; activities such as dancing, singing, **drama**, arts and crafts; and close cooperation between home and school became central features of the week-day meetings.

In 1902 the Primary board established the *Children's Friend* to provide course material and instruction for Primary teachers and leaders. It soon included stories, projects, and **music** for children, and after 1961 it was exclusively a children's magazine. In 1971 responsibility for the magazine was transferred to the Church Publications Committee, which began producing the *Friend*.

President Felt also established a hospital fund and oversaw the construction of a children's convalescent hospital in **Salt Lake City** in 1922. Thirty years later a much larger **Primary Children's Hospital** was built, dedicated, and sustained in large measure from the birthday pennies and weekly contributions of Primary children. The Primary retained jurisdiction over the hospital until 1975, when the Church transferred ownership to a nonprofit organization.

In 1952, under the presidency of **LaVern W. Parmley**, Cub and Boy Scouting was added to the Primary program. Primary teachers became the first women scout leaders, and since then women have been regular scouters, serving on local and national boards, and receiving scouting awards.

In recent decades, under the Church correlation program of the 1960s and the consolidated meeting schedule of 1980, the Primary has adjusted its curriculum. Primary meetings were moved from weekdays to Sundays, replacing Junior **Sunday Schools**, and the Primary was given full responsibility for all formal religious instruction of Latter-day Saint children. Activities were minimized and spiritual training strengthened. Once each year the Primary has presented a sacrament service program, reflecting the scriptural foundation of the weekly lessons. The scriptural emphasis of the Primary in recent years has produced a generation of **scripture**-literate and spiritually oriented young people throughout the Church, well prepared for the responsibilities and opportunities of adult membership.

SOURCES

Madsen, Carol Cornwall, and Susan Staker Oman. *Sisters and Little Saints, One Hundred Years of Primary.* Salt Lake City: Deseret Book, 1978.

Rogers, Aurelia Spencer. *Life Sketches of Orson Spencer and Others, and History of Primary Work.* Salt Lake City: George Q. Cannon & Sons, 1898.

Shumway, Naomi M. "Primary." *Encyclopedia of Mormonism.* Edited by Daniel H. Ludlow. 4 vols. New York: Macmillan, 1992. 4:1146–50.

CAROL CORNWALL MADSEN

PRIMARY CHILDREN'S HOSPITAL. "The child first and always" is the creed of Primary Children's Hospital. The work began in 1911 when **Primary** leaders first sponsored a children's convalescent ward at LDS Hospital. In 1922 a 35-bed facility opened across from **Temple Square**. The facility quickly became inadequate to serve the numerous children needing care. To raise money for building and sustaining a full hospital, Primary children donated pennies—one for each year of their age. In 1952, a 70-bed hospital, complete with a large playroom and schoolroom, was dedicated. In 1975 the Church divested itself of operating 15 **hospitals** in three western states, including the Primary Children's Hospital and established a nonprofit, non-Church organization called Intermountain Health Care Inc. to assume ownership of the hospitals. A new hospital on the **University of Utah** campus was announced in 1985. Completed in 1991, the new Primary Children's Medical Center had more than 75 special treatment programs, including cancer treatment and organ transplant services, and has become a world-renowned leader in pediatric medicine. Community support continues through the "Pennies by the Inch" campaign, wherein donors contribute pennies for each inch of their height.

SOURCES

Divett, Robert T. "Medicine and the Mormons." *Bulletin of the Medical Library Association* 50 (January–October 1962): 1–15.

Josephson, Marba C. "Of Such Is the Kingdom of Heaven: The Primary Children's Hospital." *Improvement Era* 55 (October 1952): 714–45.

Rich, Catharine A, comp. *The Primary Children's Hospital.* Salt Lake City: Deseret Book, 1967.

KRISTIN B. GERDY

PRINCE EDWARD ISLAND, CANADA. The first Latter-day Saint missionary to Prince Edward Island was John Skerry, a cooper from Halifax who was converted there in 1843. Touring the island in 1845, Skerry had little success in Charlottetown, the colony's capital, but was more fortunate in the western section of the island. There he converted members of the Maxfield **family**, who were prosperous farmers and mill owners in Bedeque and Wilmot. The Saints on the island were then left to their own devices until the summer of 1849 when **Wilford Woodruff** visited and reorganized them, and only the members in the western portion of the island had remained active.

In the following year, the Maxfield family chartered a vessel and left for **Utah**. With the family's departure, Mormonism effectively ceased to exist on Prince Edward Island. Only following **World War II** was the Church reestablished on the island, and by the year 2000 there were about 391 members in 3 branches.

SOURCE

1999–2000 Church Almanac. Salt Lake City: Deseret News, 1998.

GORDON POLLOCK

PRINTING OFFICE, INDEPENDENCE, MISSOURI. See INDEPENDENCE, MISSOURI, PRINTING OFFICE.

PROCLAMATION ON THE FAMILY. During his address at the general Relief Society meeting on 23 September 1995, President Gordon B.

Hinckley read a statement entitled "The Family: A Proclamation to the World," issued by the **First Presidency** and the Quorum of the Twelve **Apostles**. Prior to his announcement and reading of the proclamation, the **prophet** cited many instances of the problems faced by families and individuals in society. He stated that this proclamation was "to the Church and to the world as a declaration and reaffirmation of standards, doctrines, and practices relative to the family which the prophets, seers, and revelators of this Church have repeatedly stated throughout its history" (Hinckley, 100).

The Church has issued only a few such documents. The rarity of these pronouncements underscores the importance of the subject of the proclamation on the family. This, along with its intended audience, which is the whole world, and its prophetic authorship, emphasizes the document's importance.

The proclamation declares the sacredness of marriage between a man and a woman and its centrality to the great plan of the Creator. The divine heritage of human beings as spirit sons and daughters of God is proclaimed with reference to gender as a premortal, mortal, and eternal characteristic of identity. The right of children to be born into families with a father and mother at the head is taught with the caution that the sacred powers of procreation should be exercised within the bonds of marriage. The proclamation reveals that families can be eternal when husbands and wives enter into sacred temple ordinances and covenants.

It further emphasizes the sacred nature of parenting, explaining that fathers and mothers should teach their children and provide for their physical and spiritual needs. The document suggests that the teachings of Jesus Christ are the most effective basis for teaching and nurturing families. The unique responsibilities of both fathers and mothers are enumerated, with warning given to those who violate covenants and in other ways contribute to the disintegration of the family. The proclamation calls upon individuals and governments to strengthen and support the family as the fundamental unit of society.

Sources

"'Best Season,' but also Time of Turmoil." *Church News,* 23 September 1995. 3.

Fyring, Henry B. "The Family." CES Satellite Fireside, 5 November 1995.

"The Family: A Proclamation to the World." *Ensign* 25 (November 1995): 102.

Hinckley, Gordon B. "Stand Strong against the Wiles of the World." *Ensign* 25 (November 1995): 98–101.

Guy L. Dorius

PROCLAMATIONS. Since the **organization of the Church** in 1830, Church leaders have written many letters, documents, declarations, proclamations, and public announcements. Some of these have been signed by the **First Presidency**, some by the First Presidency and the **Quorum** of the Twelve, and some by the Twelve **Apostles** alone. These have been sent to the members of the Church and, at times, they have been addressed to the world at large. The subject matter has included a variety of topics including instruction, warnings of judgments to come, statements regarding Church growth, and invitations to assist in the work. Some of them have been classified as "Official Declarations (e.g., **Official Declaration 1** and **Official Declaration 2**)," "Doctrinal Expositions," or "Epistles." Only five formal declarations have been given the title "Proclamation":

1. Proclamation of the First Presidency of the Church to the **Saints** Scattered Abroad (15 January 1841, **Nauvoo, Illinois**). At the time this proclamation was published the First Presidency was comprised of **Joseph Smith**, **Sidney Rigdon**, and **Hyrum Smith**. The proclamation speaks of the development of the Church in spite of all the persecution suffered in **Missouri** and discusses the settlement of Nauvoo and the opportunities available there.

2. Proclamation of the Twelve Apostles (**6 April** 1845, in **New York City**, and on 22 October 1845, in **Liverpool, England**). On 19 January 1841, Joseph Smith had received a significant revelation commanding him to "make a solemn proclamation" to the rulers of all nations (D&C 124:2–14, 16–17, 107). It was not until 1845, however, after the death of the **Prophet**, that the Quorum of the Twelve under the leadership of **Brigham Young** finally completed this assignment. The resulting 16-page **pamphlet** was printed in New York and reprinted in Liverpool. Some discrepancy exists with regard to the author of this document. James R. Clark (1:252) quoted William H. Reeder Jr.'s statement that **Wilford Woodruff** was the author. While it is certain that Wilford Woodruff published the proclamation, B. H. Roberts, in a footnote in the *History of the Church,* indicates that the author was **Parley P. Pratt** (7:558). The proclamation was signed by the Quorum of the Twelve Apostles because there was no First Presidency at the time it was published. In this proclamation, the Twelve announced to the rulers of the nations of the earth that **God** has spoken once again in our day and that the gospel of **Jesus Christ** has been fully restored to the earth. The solemn warning spoke not only of blessings, but of impending judgments that would come to a wicked

world. All were invited to come unto Christ and assist in preparing the world for the coming of the Savior.

3. Proclamation of the First Presidency and the Twelve Apostles (21 October 1865). This proclamation was written for the benefit of the members of the Church. A member of the Quorum of the Twelve had published his own ideas and theories about the nature of the Godhead in official Church publications without clearing them with his brethren. This proclamation clarified that "no member of the Church has the right to publish any doctrines, as the doctrines of The Church of Jesus Christ of Latter-day Saints, without first submitting them for examination and approval to the First Presidency and the Twelve" (Clark, 2:239).

4. Proclamation of the First Presidency and the Quorum of the Twelve Apostles of The Church of Jesus Christ of Latter-day Saints (6 April 1980). This proclamation was an important part of the general conference commemorating the 150th anniversary of the **organization of the Church**. Part of the Sunday morning session was broadcast from the restored **Peter Whitmer Sr.** home in **Fayette, New York**. President **Spencer W. Kimball** spoke about the Restoration of the Church on that location 150 years earlier. Elder **Gordon B. Hinckley** then read the proclamation which was broadcast via **satellite** to the **Tabernacle** in Salt Lake City, and was published as part of the conference proceedings. The proclamation bore testimony of the **Restoration**, summarized the extent of Church growth, and called upon all people to forsake evil and turn to God ("Proclamation").

5. The Family: A Proclamation to the World (30 September 1995, in **Salt Lake City**). This proclamation testified that gender is an eternal attribute of each individual, called upon men and women to fulfill their responsibility as parents, and warned that the disintegration of the family would undermine society. President Gordon B. Hinckley declared: "We commend to all a careful, thoughtful, and prayerful reading of this proclamation. The strength of any nation is rooted within the walls of its homes. We urge our people everywhere to strengthen their families in conformity with these time-honored values" ("Family" 101).

Sources

Clark, James R., comp. *Messages of the First Presidency of The Church of Jesus Christ of Latter-day Saints.* 6 vols. Salt Lake City: Bookcraft, 1965–75. 1:125–132, 252–266; 2:235–240.

"The Family: A Proclamation to the World." *Ensign* 25 (November 1995): 101–102.

Matthews, Robert J. "Proclamations." *Encyclopedia of Mormonism.* Edited by Daniel H. Ludlow. 4 vols. New York: Macmillan, 1992.

"Proclamation from the First Presidency and the Quorum of the Twelve Apostles of The Church of Jesus Christ of Latter-day Saints, April 6, 1980." *Ensign* 10 (May 1980): 52–53.

Reeder, William H., Jr. "Proclamation of the Twelve Apostles on the Death of Joseph Smith." *Improvement Era* 52 (March 1949): 149, 176–177.

Smith, Joseph. *History of The Church of Jesus Christ of Latter-day Saints*. Edited by B. H. Roberts. 2d ed. rev. 7 vols. Salt Lake City: The Church of Jesus Christ of Latter-day Saints, 1932–51.

JACK L. RUSHTON

PROHIBITION. Latter-day Saints first became associated with prohibition in 1833 when **Joseph Smith** received the **Word of Wisdom**. Among other things, this revelation advised against the consumption of strong drinks. Although many nineteenth-century Church members interpreted this counsel to imply moderate or limited consumption rather than total abstinence, Latter-day Saint communities were generally known for their temperateness and lack of drunkards.

Latter-day Saints became actively involved in the prohibition sentiment that engulfed the **United States** in the early twentieth century. In both April and October **general conferences** of 1908, **Joseph F. Smith** and numerous other **apostles**, all of abstinent bent, vigorously endorsed both complete Word of Wisdom compliance and prohibition legislation. But within months of this endorsement, President Smith moderated his prohibition advocacy, believing the claim of senator-apostle **Reed Smoot** that too vigorous and too early an embrace of prohibition would result in a loss of newly acquired **Gentile** friends, erode the **Republican party** power base, and furnish fodder for the **anti-Mormon American party**. Elder **Heber J. Grant**, although loyal to his file leader, continued to be a zealous supporter of prohibition.

By at least 1916, President Smith and Elders Grant and Smoot were on the same prohibitionary page. Sensing that the time was "now right," the **Brethren** unitedly pushed for legislation. In August 1917 **Utah** went "dry," an especially satisfying occasion for Heber J. Grant, who had labored mightily for ten years in prohibition causes.

But President Grant's satisfaction was short-lived. Eventually, many government officials, law enforcement officials, and citizens decided that the costs of enforcing prohibition were too great. In 1933, the hundredth anniversary of the Word of Wisdom, Utah, a predominantly Latter-day Saint state, had the dubious distinction of becoming the thirty-sixth and last state necessary to repeal prohibition. It was one of the great disappointments of President Grant's life.

Despite this failure, prohibitionary sentiment continued to characterize the LDS community. Largely because of LDS influence, since 1935 Utah has eschewed the unregulated sale of liquor, selling it through state-operated stores. In addition, in the twentieth century, abstinence from alcoholic drinks, tobacco, tea, and coffee has became not only a criterion for Church fellowship but, for outsiders, perhaps the single most distinguishing characteristic of Latter-day Saint people.

SOURCES

Alexander, Thomas G. *Mormonism in Transition.* Urbana: University of Illinois Press, 1986. 16–59, 258–271.

Powell, Allen Kent. "Prohibition." *Utah History Encyclopedia.* Edited by Allen Kent Powell. Salt Lake City: University of Utah Press, 1994. 444–446.

Thompson, Brent G. "Standing between Two Fires: Mormons and Prohibition, 1908–1917." *Journal of Mormon History* 10 (1983): 35–52.

PAUL H. PETERSON

PROMISED VALLEY. See PAGEANTS.

PROPHECIES. Latter-day Saints believe that prophecy is a form of **revelation** and is one of the gifts of the Spirit outlined by Paul (1 Cor. 12:10; D&C 11:25). This gift is given to men and women. The testimony of Jesus is the spirit of prophecy (Rev. 19:10), for by revelation, or by the power of the Holy Ghost, individuals gain a witness that **Jesus Christ** is the Redeemer and the Son of God.

Prophecies also refer to the inspired declarations of **prophets.** Latter-day Saints believe that the Lord revealed his will to others through prophets during the centuries covered in the Old and New Testament and the **Book of Mormon.** They further teach that the **Restoration** of the fulness of the gospel that commenced with **Joseph Smith** included a return of gifts of the Spirit and a return to prophets who instruct others through revelation. The **Articles of Faith** not only emphasize that the gift of prophecy is a basic belief but specify that men should be called by prophecy (meaning by revelation or divine inspiration) and the laying on of hands to preach the gospel and administer in its **ordinances.**

During the history of the restored Church, prophets have predicted many future events. Although some of these prophecies, such as events before and during the millennium, have not yet been fulfilled, portions of many prophecies, including those of Joseph Smith, have been fulfilled.

One of the frequently cited revelations of Joseph Smith is known as the **Prophecy on War**, or the **Civil War** prophecy. This revelation, now published in the **Doctrine and Covenants**, was initially recorded during the **South Carolina** nullification crises of 1832–33. In November 1832 a South Carolina convention declared that a federal law (Tariff of 1832) was null and void in that state, beginning 1 February 1833. Responding to this unprecedented action, President Andrew Jackson urged Congress to appropriate money for **war**. Although there was talk of war, no other southern state supported South Carolina in the nullification crisis of 1832. Early in 1833 Congress passed a new tariff bill, South Carolina rescinded her nullification ordinance, and peace was restored.

Meanwhile, on 25 December 1832, amid an apparent crisis, Joseph learned that a war would begin in South Carolina; that the southern states would be divided against the northern states; that the southern states would call on other nations for help, even the nation of **Great Britain**; and that the war would lead to the death and misery of many souls (D&C 87:1–3). He later added that the crisis might develop over the issue of slavery (D&C 130:12–13). All these events were fulfilled by the tragic war between the states (1861–65). Portions of this prophecy relate to future wars and include an admonition to stand in holy places during these periods of conflict.

Although the Civil War prophecy was not published by the Church until 1851, it was recorded in a Church minute book in the early 1830s and circulated by missionaries during that same decade.

Joseph Smith also uttered many prophetic statements concerning the LDS colonization of the Rocky Mountain region. He taught in the early 1840s that the Saints would continue to suffer affliction, but within five years would be out of the power of their enemies, that they would be driven to the Rocky Mountains, that many would die of exposure or disease, and that they would become a mighty people in the midst of the Rockies. He also identified **pioneers** who would establish settlements and build cities in the Rocky Mountain country. Moreover, he prepared maps identifying the basic route that the Saints would take on their westward journey.

In another prophetic declaration, the Prophet informed **Stephen A. Douglas**, who was then a local judge, that he would aspire to the presidency of the **United States**; that if he turned his hand against the Saints he would feel the weight of the hand of the Almighty, and that he would live to see and know that this prediction was true. The rise and demise of Stephen A. Douglas during the pre–Civil War years, and his denunciation of the Saints in **Utah** shortly before the Lincoln-Douglas debates, aptly verified Joseph Smith's prophetic remarks.

Many other prophecies of Joseph Smith related to his **martyrdom**. Shortly before his death, he predicted that the next time he was captured by a mob he would be killed. As he headed to Carthage, he declared that he was going like a lamb to the slaughter. Nevertheless he affirmed, "I have a conscience void of offense towards God, and toward all men. I shall die innocent, and it shall yet be said of me—he was murdered in cold blood" (D&C 135:4). Soon he was illegally imprisoned and murdered in the **Carthage Jail**.

SOURCES

Cannon, Donald Q. "Prophecy of War." *The Doctrine and Covenants.* Edited by Robert L. Millet and Kent P. Jackson. Vol. 1 of Studies in Scripture series. Salt Lake City: Deseret Book, 1989. 335–39.

Christian, Lewis Clark. "A Study of Mormon Knowledge of the American Far West Prior to the Exodus." Master's thesis, Brigham Young University, 1972.

McConkie, Bruce R. *A New Witness for the Articles of Faith.* Salt Lake City: Deseret Book, 1985.

MILTON V. BACKMAN JR.

PROPHECY ON WAR. See **WAR, PROPHECY ON.**

PROPHET, SEER, AND REVELATOR. The title *prophet, seer, and revelator* designates functions of each of the governing leaders of The Church of Jesus Christ of Latter-day Saints—the members of the **First Presidency** and **Quorum** of the Twelve **Apostles.** Nonetheless, only one man at a time, the president of the Church, is designated as *the* prophet, seer, and revelator. He holds complete authority and responsibility for the overall direction of the Lord's kingdom on earth, including presiding over the high **priesthood** of the Church, administering the **ordinances** of salvation, and declaring and interpreting doctrine (D&C 107:9, 65–66, 91–92; 28:2–3).

The responsibilities, operations, and powers associated with the calling of prophet, seer, and revelator are distinct yet overlapping. A preeminent responsibility of a prophet is to be God's mouthpiece and to stand as a witness of the divinity of Jesus Christ to all the world, for the "testimony of Jesus is the spirit of prophecy" (Rev. 19:10). The **Book of Mormon** repeatedly and unequivocally teaches that all the holy prophets testified of Christ (Jacob 4:4–5; Mosiah 13:33). In modern times, the members of the Quorum of the Twelve Apostles, who are sustained as prophets, are called to be "special witnesses of the name of Christ in all the world" (D&C 107:23). A revelator is one who comes to know the mind and will of God and is authorized to make it known to the people of the world. A seer "is a revelator and a prophet also" (Mosiah 8:16)— one called and empowered like Enoch of old to spiritually see "things which [are] not visible to the natural eye" (Moses 6:36), to see things "afar off" (D&C 101:54).

The practice of formally sustaining the leadership of the Church as prophets, seers, and revelators began early in this dispensation. At the dedication of the **Kirtland Temple**, 27 March 1836, Joseph Smith "called upon the quorums and congregation of Saints to acknowledge the Twelve Apostles, who were present, as Prophets, Seers, Revelators, and special witnesses to all the nations of the earth" (Smith, 109).

SOURCE

Smith, Joseph. *Teachings of the Prophet Joseph Smith.* Selected by Joseph Fielding Smith. Salt Lake City: Deseret Book, 1970. 109.

ANDREW C. SKINNER

PROSELYTING PLANS. See MISSIONARY WORK.

PROSPECTIVE ELDERS. A prospective **elder** is a male Church member, age 19 or older, who does not hold the **Melchizedek Priesthood.** Married brethren who are younger than 19 and do not hold the Melchizedek Priesthood are also prospective elders. Richard O. Cowan explains that "as early as 1911 the General Priesthood Committee considered what should be done for these men," and "in 1926 the Presiding Bishopric emphasized that these 'overgrown members' of **Aaronic Priesthood quorums** cannot be dropped, but should be invited to attend whatever priesthood class was closest to their age and interests" (160–61). At this time brethren so categorized were known as "Adult Aaronic Priesthood" and were under the supervision of their ward bishopric. In 1952 **presiding bishop Joseph L. Wirthlin** announced a plan approved by the **First Presidency** and Quorum of the Twelve **Apostles**

that called for a change in the title "Adult Aaronic Priesthood" to "Senior Aaronic Priesthood." The latter term, however, never completely replaced the former within the vernacular of the lay members of the Church. It was not until 1972 that the designation of "prospective elder" came into being. Thereafter, instead of having their own class, these men would meet with the elders quorum, which had been given responsibility for them.

SOURCES

Church Handbook of Instructions. Book 2. Salt Lake City: The Church of Jesus Christ of Latter-day Saints, 1998.

Conference Report (October 1952): 78–83.

Cowan, Richard O. *The Church in the Twentieth Century.* Salt Lake City: Bookcraft, 1985.

Goates, L. Brent. *Harold B. Lee: Prophet and Seer.* Salt Lake City: Bookcraft, 1985.

Widtsoe, John A. *Priesthood and Church Government.* Salt Lake City: Deseret Book, 1939. 306.

C. ROBERT LINE

PROVO, UTAH. The area encompassing the picturesque community of Provo, Utah, between the east shore of **Utah** Lake and the majestic Wasatch Mountains, has been home to **Native Americans**, fur trappers, and, for 150 years, a bustling, predominantly Latter-day Saint community.

The original inhabitants of the area were **Ute Indians**. Spanish fathers Dominguez and Escalante met these local Native Americans in 1776 when they visited the area. Provo takes its name from **Etienne Provost**, one of the fur trappers who frequented the area in the early nineteenth century.

Provo became one of the first Latter-day Saint colonies in Utah outside **Salt Lake Valley** when it was settled in 1849. When U.S. troops were sent to **Salt Lake City** to put down the "Mormon insurrection" in 1858, thousands of Latter-day Saints temporarily moved to Provo. "The Move" and the "**Utah War**" that precipitated the settlement came to a quick end, and Salt Lakers returned to their homes.

Provo was Utah's second largest city until **Ogden** surpassed it after being chosen as Utah's primary **railroad** terminus in 1869. Because Provo was removed from major rail routes, it retained its distinctly Latter-day Saint character and soon came to be known as the "Garden City" because of its extensive fruit orchards, trees, and gardens.

From humble beginnings in downtown Provo in 1875, Brigham

Young Academy (later **Brigham Young University**) grew into the nation's largest Church-sponsored university. BYU is now a major research institution known nationally for its excellent academic and sports programs. The city and the university have enjoyed a symbiotic relationship as Provo has grown from a quiet, small Latter-day Saint city to a substantial modern metropolitan area.

Provo has served as the focal point of Utah Valley industry, commerce, government, and religious life. Agriculture and woolen goods were eventually replaced by the Geneva Steel plant and high-technology companies. The massive **William Folsom**–designed **tabernacle** completed in 1896 served as the most prominent local Church symbol until the **Provo Temple** was constructed in 1972 at the mouth of Rock Canyon.

Provo has been home to a number of prominent Americans and Latter-day Saints. Among these are Church **apostles Reed Smoot** (also a U.S. senator) and **Dallin H. Oaks** (also a president of Brigham Young University and Utah Supreme Court justice); Supreme Court justice George Sutherland; Jack Dempsey, one-time heavyweight champion of the world; and numerous other Church, political, sports, and business figures.

SOURCES

Cannon, Kenneth L. II. *A Very Eligible Place: Provo and Orem, an Illustrated History.* Northridge, Calif.: Windsor Publications, 1987.

Jensen, J. Marinus. *History of Provo, Utah.* Provo, Utah: J. Marinus Jensen, 1924.

Moffitt, John Clifton. *The Story of Provo, Utah.* Provo, Utah: John Clifton Moffitt, 1975.

Moffitt, John Clifton, and Marilyn McMeen Miller. *Provo: A Story of People in Motion.* Provo, Utah: Brigham Young University Press, 1974.

W.P.A. Writers' Project. *Provo: Pioneer Mormon City.* Portland: Binford & Mort, 1942.

KENNETH L. CANNON

PROVOST, ETIENNE. Etienne Provost, one of the earliest and most persistent trappers of the Far West, was born 21 December 1785 in Chambly, **Canada**. He pushed over the Wasatch Mountains and into the **Great Basin** of Utah in 1824. There he was attacked by Snake **Indians** and viewed the Great Salt Lake prior to **Jim Bridger**'s discovery. He spent the winter on the Green River, and in the spring witnessed the famous confrontation between **Peter Skene Ogden** and Johnson Gardner, leader of a group of Ashley's men near the present city of **Ogden, Utah**. He later joined forces with **William H. Ashley** and was at the first rendezvous on

Henry's Fork of the Green in July 1825. In 1849 the Latter-day Saints founded a town along the Provo River and named it **Provo** in honor of Etienne Provost.

SOURCES

Hafen, LeRoy. "Etienne Provost." *The Mountain Men and the Fur Trade of the Far West.* Edited by LeRoy Hafen. 10 vols. Glendale, Calif.: Arthur H. Clark, 1966–72. 371–85.

Tykal, Jack B. *Etienne Provost, Man of the Mountains.* Liberty, Utah: Eagle's View Publishing, 1989.

FRED R. GOWANS AND KERRY OMAN

PUBLIC AFFAIRS. Due to an increasingly effective Public Affairs Department, the Church received more media coverage during the closing decade of the twentieth century than ever before in its history. From President **Gordon B. Hinckley**'s "Sixty Minutes" television appearance, to CNN's "Larry King Live," to numerous national and international interviews, Public Affairs personnel were behind the scenes, carefully cultivating media interest in the history, lifestyle, and beliefs of Latter-day Saints. Such innovations have always been part of LDS Public Affairs.

In 1935 Gordon B. Hinckley was called to the newly organized **Radio, Publicity, and Missionary Literature Committee** to utilize the communications media to further **missionary work**. During following decades the first **Tabernacle Choir** and Philadelphia Symphony recordings were made and press coverage for the **Hill Cumorah Pageant** in **New York** began. These breakthroughs were followed by the creation of the Church Information Service in 1957, which was then absorbed into the External Communications Department in 1972.

The following year, in a surprising break from traditional committee oversight, Managing Director Wendell J. Ashton was instructed to bring "external communications" under the direction of the **First Presidency**, as the Public Communications Department. His specific charge was to be proactive with the media, broadening the program worldwide.

When **Visitors' Center** exhibits and television media were added to the department's responsibilities, Ashton sought assistance from advertising executive and **Brigham Young University** Public Relations Director Heber Wolsey. The first "Homefront Series" of **radio** and **television** public service announcements were created under his direction. A quarter of a century later this series continued to receive innumerable awards for excellence, opening doors for missionaries and garnering positive publicity for the Church.

By 1978 Wolsey, who had then been appointed Managing Director, initiated the Church's first venture into paid advertising. For the first time Public Communications Councils were established outside of **Salt Lake City**, in **Los Angeles**, New York, and **Washington, D.C.** Priesthood leaders were requested to call individuals from those areas who had career experience in public relations, journalism, film, television, and community service to develop ways to "bring the Church out of obscurity" (D&C 1:30).

In 1983 the name of the department became Public Communications/Special Affairs under managing director Richard Lindsay. Community and government relations were added to its focus, and emphasis was placed on generating and distributing news through the Public Affairs network to media contacts. The Homefront campaigns and paid media ads were assigned to the Missionary Department.

In 1989 Bruce Olsen, a career public relations professional, was named to head the department, guiding it through rapid technological innovations to better meet the numerous challenges that come from ever-increasing media focus worldwide. In 1991 the First Presidency announced yet another name change—Public Affairs Department. For the 1997 Pioneer Sesquicentennial celebration, the department generated more worldwide print and electronic media coverage than at any other time.

The Public Affairs program has extended the Church's influence around the world, and in every **stake** Church members seek opportunities for reaching out to their communities more than ever before.

SOURCE

Haglund, Elizabeth M. "Public Relations." *Encyclopedia of Mormonism.* Edited by Daniel H. Ludlow. 4 vols. New York: Macmillan, 1992. 3:1177–79.

KEITH ATKINSON AND LEANNE HULL

PUBLIC IMAGE. The public's attitude about the Church, its programs, and its members has exerted a powerful influence on the course of Latter-day Saint history. Popular misunderstanding during the Church's early decades led to intense persecution and suffering. During the last half of the nineteenth century, the relative isolation of the Latter-day Saints in the Rocky Mountains made misunderstanding and misrepresentation more likely. For example, the press widely condemned the practice of **polygamy** and described the Church's hierarchy as a "menace."

Following President **Wilford Woodruff**'s 1890 **Manifesto** officially announcing the suspension of plural marriage, Mormonism cooled as a controversial issue. The periodical press began to recognize in the Latter-day Saint people some of the virtues then being advocated by the American populist movement—industry, thrift, temperance, self-reliance, and so forth. In 1893 the **Tabernacle Choir** created goodwill and favorable publicity during its first major concert tour.

Because of the reformist attitude during the "Progressive Era" at the beginning of the twentieth century, the election to Congress of two **general authorities**, **B. H. Roberts** and **Reed Smoot**, sparked a revival of earlier **anti-Mormon** agitation. After Reed Smoot was finally given his Senate seat in 1907, Mormonism again declined as a controversial issue. During **World War I**, the Mormon Church and people demonstrated their loyalty to the **United States**. In the following decade, as Latter-day Saints began moving into such areas as **California**, thereby becoming more integrated with American national life, the nation exhibited a more sympathetic understanding.

During the 1930s, new features appeared in the popular image of Latter-day Saints that have been characteristic ever since. The Church's image finally became predominantly positive. Writers in the press also became more interested in the programs of the Church rather than in its theology. Specifically, the **Welfare Program** attracted widespread admiration.

During the second half of the twentieth century, more and more Latter-day Saints were achieving prominence in government service, in professional circles, and in a variety of other fields. These individuals had a very positive influence on the public's attitude. While praising the Saints for their achievements, the press almost always explicitly identified them as Mormons. The virtues of their religion were often described as contributing to their personal success. For example, articles about golfer Johnny Miller, quarterback **Steve Young**, the Osmond **family**, or U.S. Senator **Orrin Hatch** often discuss the Latter-day Saint health code in the **Word of Wisdom**, family solidarity, or the gospel's emphasis on high moral standards.

Even though there have been a few negative themes in recent years, such as misunderstandings about the Church's position on **blacks** and on women's rights, the public attitude has continued to be largely positive.

The importance of this fact is seen in the large number of converts who first became interested in the restored gospel because of favorable publicity about the Tabernacle Choir, prominent Latter-day Saints, or Church programs. Along with the key roles being played by the Church public relations organization and proselyting missionaries, the wholesome examples set by individual Latter-day Saints everywhere must be acknowledged as one of the most important factors in bringing others to faith in the gospel of **Jesus Christ**.

SOURCES

Cowan, Richard O. "Mormonism in National Periodicals." Ph.D. diss., Stanford University, 1961.
Pelo, Dale P. "Mormonism in National Periodicals, 1961–70." Master's thesis, Brigham Young University, 1973.
Shipps, Jan. "'Is Mormonism Christian?' Reflections on a Complicated Question." *BYU Studies* 33, no. 3 (1993): 438–65.

RICHARD O. COWAN

PUBLIC WORKS. Between 1850 and 1870, the Church operated a Public Works Department to provide employment for new immigrants to Utah, develop several manufacturing industries in the area, and construct public and private buildings. Established 26 January 1850 with **Daniel H. Wells** as its superintendent, the department was headquartered on the northeast corner of the **temple** block in **Salt Lake City**. At its height, the department employed 2,000 carpenters, blacksmiths, painters, stone masons, and other skilled laborers, who used their expertise to develop Utah's first paper mill, pottery shop, machine shop, and foundry. In various "factories" in the territory, the department also produced bullets, buckets, nails, buttons, carding machines, and milling machinery. Public Works employees also helped build dams, roads, walls, bridges, and canals, and helped erect a number of buildings, including the Council House, Old **Tabernacle**, **Social Hall**, **Tithing** Store and Storehouse, **Salt Lake Theater**, **Salt Lake Tabernacle**, and **the Salt Lake Temple**. The functions carried out by the department were transferred to the **presiding bishop** in 1870.

A great benefit to the Church at large, the Public Works Department was also a boon for its employees. Employment in the department gave new immigrants time to adjust to conditions in Utah, opportunities for making new friends, a source of income, and means for paying off their debt to the **Perpetual Emigrating Fund** as well as for paying tithing.

SOURCE

Arrington, Leonard J. *Great Basin Kingdom: An Economic History of the Latter-day Saints*. Lincoln: University of Nebraska Press, 1958.

ANDREW H. HEDGES

PUBLISHERS AND BOOKSTORES. Mormonism began with a

book—the **Book of Mormon**. Since E. B. **Grandin**, a publisher and book-seller in **Palmyra, New York**, released the ancient record in March 1830, there has been a market for LDS material to supplement official Church publications.

With the establishment of **George Q. Cannon** and Sons in 1866, the modern LDS publishing and bookstore business really began. Over the years, this and other companies combined to form **Deseret Book Company** in 1919. Deseret Book dominated the Latter-day Saint market during most of the twentieth century as the largest LDS publisher and bookstore chain in North America.

Other groups and individuals attempted to carve a place for themselves in the market dominated by Deseret Book. John K. Orton established Bookcraft in 1942 and eventually became the second largest LDS publisher, with such popular works as *Mormon Doctrine* by **Bruce R. McConkie** (1958) and *The Work and the Glory* series (1991–1999) by Gerald N. Lund. Other publishers, such as Signature Books (1981) and Covenant Communication (1984), found niches in the LDS publishing market. Additionally, university presses, including **Brigham Young University** (with the Religious Studies Center and **BYU Studies**), the University of **Illinois, University of Utah**, and Utah State University, also published books of interest to the Latter-day Saints. Even national book publishers, such as Macmillan and Alfred A. Knopf of **New York**, have targeted the Latter-day Saint market from time to time.

Although many independent outlets, including some "garage businesses," provided consumers with options beyond Deseret Book's stores, the company virtually monopolized the market in the Intermountain West in the 1990s. As a result, publishers like Bookcraft and Covenant began placing their products in national bookstore chains such as B. Dalton, Media Play, and Barnes and Noble. As "e-commerce" began to take off in the late 1990s, online purchasing, through such international sellers as Amazon.com, greatly enhanced people's opportunities to purchase LDS-related material no matter where they lived. Several independent bookstores, including Zion's Bookstore (Sam Weller's), and Benchmark Books, specialized in rare and out-of-print materials.

The publishing and bookstore business took a dramatic shift in 1999, when the two largest publishers, Deseret Book and Bookcraft, merged, creating a megacompany with several imprint organizations under its umbrella.

SOURCE

Knowles, Eleanor. *Encyclopedia of Mormonism.* Edited by Daniel H. Ludlow. 4 vols. New York: Macmillan, 1992. 1:374.

RICHARD NEITZEL HOLZAPFEL

PUEBLO, COLORADO. As a frontier trading post founded in 1842, Pueblo provided protection and commerce for travelers along the **Arkansas** River. In 1846, 43 **Mississippi Saints** arrived at Pueblo while waiting for the Latter-day Saint westward migration to resume.

The Mississippi Saints established their settlement (**Mormon** Town) just west of the post. They built cabins from cottonwood logs, planted gardens, built a meeting/school house, and appeared more permanent than their intended temporary status.

By September, 45 individuals, including families, known as the first sick detachment from the **Mormon Battalion**, arrived in Pueblo, led by Nelson Higgins. Another detachment of 128 sick and trail-worn soldiers, including families, arrived in November under the leadership of **James Brown**. Finally in January 1847, a third group of 62 arrived under the leadership of Lieutenant W. W. Willis. By February the Latter-day Saint population of Pueblo expanded to almost 300 people.

Mormon children born in Pueblo are credited with being the first Anglo births in **Colorado**. By summer, groups of the **Saints** left, traveled north to rendezvous with the Vanguard **Pioneer** Company near **Fort Laramie, Wyoming**, and followed the **Mormon Trail** west. By late 1848 Mormon Town was deserted.

SOURCES

Carter, Kate B., ed. *Heart Throbs of the West.* 3 vols. Salt Lake City: Daughters of Utah Pioneers, 1947–48.

Lecompte, Janet. *Pueblo, Hardscrabble, Greenhorn.* Norman, Okla.: University of Oklahoma Press, 1978.

Porter, Larry. "The Mormon Battalion's Two-Thousand-Mile March from the Missouri River to the Pacific Ocean." In *California.* Edited by David F. Boone, et al. Regional Studies in Latter-day Saint Church History series. Provo, Utah: Brigham Young University, 1998. 31–56.

Scararcello, Mary Lindenmuth. *Mormon Pioneers in Pueblo, Colorado, 1846–1900.* N.p., 1993.

DAVID F. BOONE

PUERTO RICO. Between 1940–42, two LDS families held Church meetings in their homes in San Juan, Puerto Rico. In 1950, Melvin J. Rudd was called as a group leader, and meetings continued to be held near Ramey Air Force Base.

The first formal meetings of the Church in Puerto Rico were held in the military chapel at Fort Buchanan in 1953. In 1955, the San Juan and Ramey **Branches** were organized, and an island-wide **conference** was held. Puerto Rico was part of the **Southern States Mission** until 1960, when the Florida **Mission** was organized and took in the Caribbean Islands. In 1964, President Ned Winder of the Florida Mission organized the Caribbean District. Gardner H. Russell was called as **district** president.

The third Caribbean conference was held in 1968. James Dalton was called as president of the San Juan Branch. On 7 September 1968, a groundbreaking ceremony was held for the Jardines de Caparra meeting-house, which was the first chapel in the Caribbean. Dr. Carlos Lastra of the University of Puerto Rico assisted President Glen L. Rudd of the **Florida** Mission and Gardner Russell in the groundbreaking. The chapel was dedicated in March 1970 by Elder Stirling W. Sill.

In 1969, President Rudd assigned six Spanish-speaking missionaries to Puerto Rico. In 1979, the Puerto Rico San Juan Mission was created, and the first stake was organized in 1980 by **Elder Ezra Taft Benson.** **President Spencer W. Kimball** visited the Puerto Rico Saints in 1981. By the year 2000, there were 23,223 members with 4 stakes and 55 wards and branches.

SOURCE

1999–2000 Church Almanac. Salt Lake City: Deseret Book, 1998. 379–81.

GLEN L. RUDD

PYPER, GEORGE D. Elder George Dollinger Pyper was called as general **Sunday School** superintendent in 1934. He had labored 16 years previously as second assistant superintendent to Elder **David O. McKay**. His prior Church service included that of general secretary to **auxiliaries** and Church committees, associate editor of the *Juvenile Instructor* magazine, and tour manager for the **Tabernacle Choir**. He wrote the music to **Joseph Fielding Smith**'s poem "Does the Journey Seem Long?" (**Hymn** #127) and was a prolific opera and funeral soloist in the community. He also wrote *The Romance of an Old Playhouse* and *Stories of Latter-day Saint Hymns*.

Born 21 November 1860 in **Salt Lake City** to Alexander C. Pyper and Christiana Dollinger, he was employed early in the **silk industry** and at **ZCMI**. Other work experience included clerk of the police court (1875–82); justice of the peace (1884); alderman and police judge (1886–90); and secretary of the Deseret Agricultural and Manufacturing Society. In 1898 he became associated with the old **Salt Lake Theater**, which he managed from 1904 to 1929. Elder Pyper served on the first **education** and library boards in Salt Lake City. He died 16 January 1943.

SOURCES

Brooks, Melvin R. *LDS Reference Encyclopedia*. Salt Lake City: Bookcraft, 1960. 401.

Davidson, Karen Lynn. *Our Latter-day Hymns: The Stories and the Messages*. Salt Lake City: Deseret Book, 1988. 428.

Jenson, Andrew. *Latter-day Saint Biographical Encyclopedia*. 4 vols. 1901–36. Reprint, Salt Lake City: Western Epics, 1971. 1:669, 685; 4:220.

GERALD L. HOMER

QUAIL, MIRACLE OF. A group of poor Saints, forced from their homes in Nauvoo in 1846, gather up "manna sent from heaven" when an exhausted flock of quail land in their camp, as depicted in C. C. A. Christensen's painting from the 1880s.

QATAR. See **MIDDLE EAST** and **MUSLIMS.**

QUAIL, MIRACLE OF. An 1846 event known as the miracle of the quail reminded the **Saints** of how the Lord had provided food to the Israelites in the wilderness (Num. 11:13–33). On 10 September 1846 the **Battle of Nauvoo** commenced with about 160 remaining Saints defending the city against a mob of about 1,200. The battle ended on 16 September with the Saints surrendering and then being driven across the **Mississippi River** into **Iowa.** Some 640 Latter-day Saints, known as "the **poor camp**," were stretched along the Iowa side of the river, unable to move because they lacked wagons and teams. Here they suffered from hunger and inadequate shelter for several weeks. On Friday morning, 9 October, thousands of exhausted quail who had flown some distance began to drop into the camps of the starving Saints.

SOURCES

Bagley, Will, ed. *The Pioneer Camp of the Saints—The 1846 and 1847 Mormon Trail Journals of Thomas Bullock.* Spokane: Arthur H. Clark, 1997. 76.

Little, James A. *From Kirtland to Salt Lake City.* Salt Lake City: Juvenile Instructor Office, 1890. 74–75.

Roberts, B. H. *A Comprehensive History of The Church of Jesus Christ of Latter-day Saints, Century One.* 6 vols. Salt Lake City: The Church of Jesus Christ of Latter-day Saints, 1930. 3:134–36.

CALVIN R. STEPHENS

QUEBEC, CANADA. "La Belle Province de Quebec" remains North America's gritty reminder of the glorious history of New **France**, a French-Canadian, French-speaking Roman Catholic heritage as old as Jacques Cartier and his arrival at Hochelaga (**Montreal**) in 1534–35.

Although early Latter-day Saint missionaries realized significant success in nearby Upper **Canada** (**Ontario**) in the 1830s, Lower Canada (Quebec) remained virtually impregnable to Latter-day Saint and Protestant incursions of any kind. Though some 23 converts from the Hatley area in the "southern townships" did join and migrate west in 1837, the Church remained a virtual nonentity in the province for the next century.

With the organization of the Canadian **Mission** in 1919, however, missionary work in eastern Canada revitalized. Yet it was not until the late 1950s, with the waning of Catholic influence in the province and the rise of a new, more secular and liberalized "Quebecois" society, that the Church experienced significant modern **growth**. Concentrated initially in Montreal, Church membership at the end of the twentieth century included congregations in Quebec City, Chicoutimi, Rimouski, Val d'Or, and elsewhere. Less inclined to migrate west to larger English-speaking Latter-day Saint centers than their Ontario counterparts, the Quebec **Saints** have tended to stay home and build up the Church within their own communities—a positive sign for future growth. At the beginning of the year 2000, out of a population of 7.3 million, there were some 8,500 members residing in 27 wards and branches in 2 **stakes**—all anxiously anticipating the completion of the Montreal Quebec **Temple**.

Sources

Bennett, Richard. "Canada, from Struggling Seed, the Church Has Risen to Branching Maple." *Ensign* 18 (September 1988): 30–45.

———. "A Study of The Church of Jesus Christ of Latter-day Saints in Upper Canada 1830–1850." Master's thesis, Brigham Young University, 1975.

Louder, Dean. "Canadian Mormon Identity and the French Fact." *The Mormon Presence in Canada.* Edited by Brigham Y. Card, et al. Edmonton: University of Alberta Press, 1990. 302–28.

Richard E. Bennett

QUINCY, ILLINOIS. Quincy, **Illinois**, located 45 miles south of **Nauvoo** on the **Mississippi River**, became a refuge for members of the Church fleeing the persecution in **Missouri** during the winter of 1839. With a population of only 1,200, the people of Quincy provided food and shelter for as many of the **Saints** as they could. **Emma Smith**, wife of the **Prophet Joseph Smith**, found a place of peace on the outskirts of Quincy after walking across the ice of the frozen Mississippi River with her four children. She remained in Quincy until her husband was released from the **Liberty Jail**.

The Democratic Association of Quincy was active in helping the Saints find places to stay, food to eat, and even jobs for the exiled members of the Church. In the third week of February 1839, the association met three times to consider ways of helping the homeless. They heard reports from leaders of the Church and even passed resolutions condemning Missouri's treatment of the **Mormons**.

Thousands of Latter-day Saints arrived at the western bank of the Mississippi River across from Quincy during the winter and spring of 1839. Elizabeth Haven wrote that in late February "about 12 families crossed the river into Quincy every day and about 30 more are constantly at the other side waiting to cross, it is slow and grimy, there is only one ferry boat to cross in" (quoted in Barlow, 143). Between 8,000 and 10,000 members of the Church arrived on the banks of the Mississippi River in the winter and spring of 1839, searching for a place of safety. The village of Quincy could not accommodate all of the suffering Saints, so the surrounding farmlands and counties did whatever they could to help. Quincy became a lasting example of benevolent people extending help to those in need.

SOURCE

Barlow, Ora H. *The Israel Barlow Story and Mormon Mores.* Salt Lake City: Ora H. Barlow, 1968.

RALPH M. MCAFFEE

QUINCY, JOSIAH. Josiah Quincy, one of several notable visitors to **Nauvoo**, belonged to a prominent New England **family** whose ties included the famous presidential Adams clan of Quincy, **Massachusetts**. Josiah was born 26 January 1802 in Plymouth, Massachusetts, to a father by the same name.

On 15 May 1844 Josiah and his cousin Charles Francis Adams visited **Joseph Smith** at the **Mansion House** in Nauvoo. The **Mormon Prophet** autographed the **Book of Mormon** Josiah had purchased, which is now owned by the LDS Church. The two visitors paid 25 cents each to have **Lucy Mack Smith** show them the mummies of **Pearl of Great Price** fame. Soon after this visit, Quincy served as Mayor of Boston (1845–49). Before his death in 1882, he wrote a book, *Figures of the Past*, whose final chapter is entitled "Joseph Smith at Nauvoo." While Quincy's evaluation of Joseph Smith is generally skeptical, he did make some statements in praise of the Mormon prophet. He wrote: "It is by no means improbable that some future text-book, for the use of generations yet unborn, will contain a question something like this: What historical American of the nineteenth century has exerted the most powerful influence upon the destinies of his countrymen? And it is by no means improbable that the answer to that interrogatory may be thus written: *Joseph Smith, the Mormon Prophet*" (Quincy, 376). Quincy died in 1882.

SOURCES

Berrett, LaMar C., ed. *New England and Eastern Canada*. Vol. 1 of *Sacred Places*. Salt Lake City: Bookcraft, 1999.

Quincy, Josiah. *Figures of the Past: From the Leaves of Old Journals*. Boston: Roberts Brothers, 1896.

DONALD Q. CANNON

QUORUM. President **Boyd K. Packer** defined quorums of the **priesthood** as "selected assemblies of brethren given authority that [the Lord's] business might be transacted and His work proceed" (quoted in Christofferson, 41). **Elder Stephen L Richards** defined a quorum as "three things: first, a class; second, a fraternity; and third, a service unit" (quoted in Christofferson, 41).

Quorums exist at both the general and local level of Church government. The presiding quorums of the Church include the **First Presidency** (D&C 107:22), the Quorum of the Twelve **Apostles** (D&C 107:23–24), and the **Seventy** (D&C 107:25–26). The First Presidency, which consists of the president and generally two **counselors**, "constitute a quorum . . . to receive the oracles for the whole church" (D&C 124:126). The senior member of the Quorum of the Twelve Apostles becomes president of the Church upon the death of the previous president. The next senior member becomes President of the Quorum of the Twelve Apostles unless called to serve as a counselor in the First Presidency, in which case the next senior member after him becomes the Acting President of the Quorum of the Twelve. The President of the Quorum of the Twelve serves without counselors (D&C 124:127). Seven presidents preside over the Seventy (D&C 107:93–96; 124:138).

By **revelation**, "every decision made by . . . these quorums must be by the unanimous voice of the same; that is, every member in each quorum must be agreed to its decisions, in order to make their decisions of the same power or validity one with the other" (D&C 107:27). "A majority may form a quorum when circumstances render it impossible to be otherwise" (D&C 107:28).

Though quorums of seventy were once organized on the local level, since 1986 only two kinds of local Melchizedek Priesthood quorums have existed. The first was the high priests quorum, organized on a stake level and overseen by a presidency (D&C 124:133–136), which is now the stake presidency. The other is the elders quorum (D&C 107:89), organized at the ward level and overseen also by a president and two counselors (D&C 124:137).

Aaronic priesthood quorums, also organized on a ward level, include **priests** quorums (D&C 107:87), **teachers** quorums (D&C 107:86), and **deacons** quorums (D&C 107:85). The president of the priests quorum is the **bishop** (D&C 107:88).

SOURCES

Christofferson, D. Todd. "The Priesthood Quorum." *Ensign* 28 (November 1998): 40–42.

Church Handbook of Instructions. Salt Lake City: The Church of Jesus Christ of Latter-day Saints, 1998.

Widtsoe, John A. *Priesthood and Church Government in The Church of Jesus Christ of Latter-day Saints.* Salt Lake City: Deseret Book, 1965.

RICHARD E. TURLEY JR.

QUORUM OF THE TWELVE APOSTLES. See APOSTLES.

RELIEF SOCIETY. Made for the Jubilee celebration in 1880, this banner celebrates the mission of the Relief Society women's organization of the Church.

RADIO. See BROADCASTING.

RADIO, PUBLICITY, AND MISSION LITERATURE COMMIT-
TEE. In 1935 the Church officially organized the Radio, Publicity, and
Mission Literature Committee to oversee all public relations efforts. The
committee was composed of six members of the Quorum of the Twelve
Apostles, with Elder Stephen L Richards as chair and Elders Melvin J.
Ballard, John A. Widtsoe, Charles A. Callis, Alonzo A. Hinckley, and
Albert E. Bowen as members. A young returned missionary, Gordon B.
Hinckley, was appointed as executive secretary to manage the day-to-day
operations. The first materials developed by this committee were slide presentations, pamphlets, brochures, and audio presentations that were used
by missionaries throughout the world. In addition to creating missionary
materials, this committee worked with the media to project the image of
the Church more accurately. Radio programs dramatized Church history
and were broadcast by more than 400 stations around the United States.
The committee also oversaw the development of materials for exhibits and
pavilions at world's fairs and international expositions. This committee was
the precursor to several later Church departments and organizations, such
as the Church Information Service in 1957 and the Department of Public
Communications in 1972.

SOURCES

Cowan, Richard O. *The Latter-day Saint Century.* Salt Lake City: Bookcraft, 1999. 107,
275–77.

Dew, Sheri L. *Go Forward with Faith: The Biography of Gordon B. Hinckley.* Salt Lake
City: Deseret Book, 1996. 85–105.

BRENT L. TOP

RAILROADS. Within a month of the organization of the Church in
April 1830, railroad travel began in America with the opening of the

Baltimore and Ohio Railroad. **Oliver Cowdery** remembered taking "the rail road car for Schenectady, New York, the first passengers' car on the new road" (*Messenger*, 374). Soon missionaries and converts were availing themselves of this smoke-belching thunder of the British Industrial Revolution as it spread tracks throughout **Europe** and America.

With the subsequent decline of steamboat travel, railroads became the favored choice for Latter-day Saint emigrants. In 1855 **Brigham Young** encouraged valley-bound European immigrants to stop sailing to **New Orleans** and up the river system to **Nebraska** and to disembark on the East Coast and take the "cars" as far west as the latest railroad terminal point. Between 1847 and 1869, of the approximately 70,000 Mormon **pioneers** who crossed the plains, almost half traveled by railroad for at least one stage of their journey. Thereafter many more thousand "Pullman pioneers" made the journey to **Utah** by rail.

Hard on the heels of wagon-westering America, plans were laid for the building of the great transcontinental railroad. Some contended that the Latter-day Saints would oppose the coming of the railroad, and with it the arrival of "American civilization," ending Latter-day Saint autonomy in the West. Brigham Young welcomed it, however, and had petitioned as early as 1852 that the proposed railroad pass through Utah Territory. "We want to hear the iron horse puffing through this valley," he once said (*JD*, 12:54). Like Americans elsewhere, the Latter-day Saints celebrated the driving of the last spike on 10 May 1869 at Promontory Point, Utah. Although Brigham Young well understood that though the railroad would bring more Gentiles to the **Great Basin** and inevitably influence Latter-day Saint life, it was a new technology to be welcomed. The railroad would facilitate Latter-day Saint **immigration** to Utah, link Latter-day Saint settlements throughout the Intermountain West, improve communications, and spur on mining and other economic resource developments.

To counter the undesirable elements of railroad construction gangs and to ensure local financial benefit, Church leaders spearheaded a movement to have the Latter-day Saints lay as much of the track as possible. Local **ward priesthood** councils or "**schools of the prophets**" were established in most communities to lead out in construction and in retarding degrading influences. Consequently, not only did the Saints contract and build the Union Pacific and Central Pacific lines throughout much of Utah, they also constructed several feeder lines. These included the Utah Central, the Utah Northern, the Utah Southern, and other railroads in the 1870s, most of which eventually became part of the

Union Pacific Railroad system. Others later worked on the construction of the Denver and Rio Grande Western, the Northern Pacific, the Great Northern, the Santa Fe, and even the Canadian Pacific Railroad. It is estimated that Latter-day Saint construction crews built more than 1,000 miles of railroad throughout the Intermountain West. The Union Pacific Railroad's main line west followed parts of the **Mormon Trail** along the north banks of the **Platte River**. Likewise, the Southern Pacific incorporated parts of the **Mormon Battalion** trail through present-day **New Mexico** and **Arizona**.

The "ribbon-of-steel" has also ever been a path for missionary work. Though most modern missionaries reach their destinations by air, train travel is still used in many parts of the world. The Church invested in various railroad interests from time to time, with several Church leaders serving on boards of directors of the Union Pacific and other major western railroads.

SOURCES

Arrington, Leonard J. *Great Basin Kingdom: An Economic History of the Latter-day Saints, 1830–1900.* Cambridge, Mass.: Harvard University Press, 1958. 235–92.

Journal of Discourses [JD]. 26 vols. London: Latter-day Saints' Book Depot, 1854–86. Vol. 12.

Kimball, Stanley B. "Sail and Rail Pioneers Before 1869." *BYU Studies* 35, 2 (1995): 7–42.

Messenger and Advocate 2 (September 1836): 374.

RICHARD E. BENNETT

RAMUS, ILLINOIS. Ramus, **Illinois**, originally known as the Perkins Settlement, was settled in 1826 by Ute Perkins and his large **family** from **Tennessee**. The town is located about 20 miles southeast of **Nauvoo**. The first Latter-day Saint missionary in Ramus was Joel Hills Johnson. In April 1839 he converted Ute Perkins and some of his family and organized a small **branch**.

Johnson, his mother, and his seven siblings joined the Perkins family in Ramus in February 1840. The Perkins and Johnson families were the backbone of the community, accounting for 10% of the population. **Joseph Smith** considered it the "first spoke" of a wheel of settlements with Nauvoo as the hub. **Hyrum Smith** organized a **stake** at Ramus 9 July 1840 with Joel H. Johnson as president. Ebenezer Page was chosen as **bishop**, with Elijah B. Gaylord and William G. Perkins as **counselor**s. The **prophet**'s uncle **John Smith** became **stake president** in 1843, and on

18 February 1845 William G. Perkins was **ordained** bishop with Andrew H. Perkins as his counselor. The influence of the **Saints** from Ramus in **Hancock County** is evidenced by the election of Andrew H. Perkins as county commissioner from 1843 to 1845. At the Church's peak in Ramus there were between 500 and 600 members living there. Joseph Smith visited frequently, staying with the Perkins and Johnson families. There he gave some significant doctrinal addresses, a few excerpts now composing Doctrine and Covenants 131. The name Ramus was changed in 1843 to Macedonia and then to Webster.

SOURCES

Jenson, Andrew. *Encyclopedic History of The Church of Jesus Christ of Latter-day Saints.* Salt Lake City: Deseret News, 1941. 690–91.

Rugh, Susan Sessions. "Conflict in the Countryside: The Mormon Settlement at Macedonia, Illinois." *BYU Studies* 32 (Winter-Spring 1992): 149–74.

KEITH W. PERKINS

RAROTONGA. See COOK ISLANDS.

RAY COUNTY, MISSOURI. Following the expulsion of the **Mormons** from **Jackson County** in 1833, most Church members found refuge across the **Missouri River** in **Clay County**. An unknown number of **Saints** also settled in some of the sparsely inhabited regions of Ray County, east of Clay County. At the time, the boundaries of Ray ran from the Missouri River north to the **Missouri-Iowa** border, encompassing what are today **Caldwell**, **Daviess**, and Harrison counties. During the summer of 1836, Latter-day Saint leaders in Missouri began exploring the less-settled regions of Ray County for possible settlement. On 8 August **W. W. Phelps** and **John Whitmer** of the Missouri presidency negotiated the purchase of a one-mile square plot, situated a mile south of Shoal Creek and approximately 30 miles north and slightly west of **Richmond**, the county seat. After the purchase, Latter-day Saints began moving into the area for permanent settlement. On 29 December, the Missouri legislature divided Ray County and created two new counties—Caldwell and Daviess, with the former being established exclusively for Latter-day Saint occupation.

The following represent the most significant events associated with LDS history in Ray County: (1) **Zion's Camp** passed through Ray County en route to western Missouri in June 1834. (2) The **Battle of Crooked**

River took place in northwestern Ray County on 25 October 1838, resulting in the deaths of **apostle David W. Patten**, Gideon Carter, and Patrick O'Banion, and Moses Rowland—a Missourian. (3) From 12 to 29 November 1838, 64 Latter-day Saint prisoners, including **Joseph Smith**, were arraigned before circuit court judge Austin A. King in the Richmond courthouse. It was during this confinement that Joseph Smith rebuked the guards for their vile conduct and foul language. (4) Following their estrangement from the Church in 1838, Jacob Whitmer, John Whitmer, and **David Whitmer**, along with **Oliver Cowdery** (who married Elizabeth Ann Whitmer), took up residence in Richmond. Jacob and David Whitmer remained Richmond residents the rest of their lives. (5) Several members of the family of **Peter Whitmer Sr.** (also known as Peter Whitmer III) are buried in the Richmond Pioneer Cemetery, including Peter, his wife **Mary Whitmer**, and **Jacob Whitmer**. Oliver Cowdery died in Richmond on 3 March 1850, and he too is buried in the Pioneer Cemetery. (6) In November 1911, the Church erected and dedicated an 11-foot, 18-ton granite monument in honor of the **Three Witnesses** in the Richmond Pioneer Cemetery. The monument is in the approximate location of Cowdery's grave. (7) A statue of **Alexander Doniphan**, legal defender of Joseph Smith and the Latter-day Saints during the Missouri period, stands in the Richmond public square.

SOURCES

Anderson, Richard Lloyd. "Ray County in Mormon History." *Ray County, Missouri, History.* Marceline, Mo.: Walsworth, 1974. 223–29.

Black, Susan Easton. "The Evils of Rumor: Richmond, Missouri, 1836–1838." In *Missouri.* Edited by Arnold K. Garr and Clark V. Johnson. Regional Studies in Latter-day Saint Church History series. Provo, Utah: Brigham Young University, 1994. 119–35.

LeSueur, Stephen C. "'High Treason and Murder': The Examination of Mormon Prisoners at Richmond, Missouri, in November 1838." *BYU Studies* 26 (Spring 1986): 3–30.

Wells, Junius F. "Oliver Cowdery Monument at Richmond, Missouri." *Improvement Era* 15 (January 1912): 251–72.

ALEXANDER L. BAUGH

RAYS OF LIVING LIGHT. Before the Church provided official missionary discussions, **elders** used an accumulation of valuable tracts and **pamphlets** that discussed the fundamentals of the gospel and helped bring thousands to a knowledge of the faith. A widely circulated series of 13 tracts written by Elder **Charles W. Penrose** was entitled "Rays of

Living Light." Beginning in 1898, this series was translated into more foreign languages than any other Latter-day Saint **literature** originating during its time. The "Rays of Living Light" tracts can be read in their original text in volume 1 of the *Scrapbook of Mormon Literature*. They also appear in *Handbook of the Restoration*.

SOURCES

Godfrey, Kenneth W. "Charles W. Penrose: The English Mission Years." *BYU Studies* 27 (Winter 1987): 113–24.

Handbook of the Restoration: A Selection of Gospel Themes. Independence, Mo.: Zion's Printing and Publishing, 1944. 103–77.

Jenson, Andrew. *Latter-day Saint Biographical Encyclopedia.* 4 vols. 1901–36. Reprint, Salt Lake City: Western Epics, 1971. 1:256.

Rich, Ben E. *Scrapbook of Mormon Literature.* Chicago: Henry C. Etten, 1913. 1:202–76.

TIMOTHY W. BOTHELL

REBAPTISM. Rebaptism, a common gospel practice in the nineteenth century, often served as a symbol for rededication. For example, Church members were sometimes rebaptized when beginning any new phase of their religious life, such as marriage or entering into a united order, or when "commencing life anew" at a new gathering place (such as the **Salt Lake Valley**). There were also instances when members were rebaptized for a restoration of health.

Rebaptism was not uncommon in the **Joseph Smith** era, but became an even more accelerated practice during **Brigham Young**'s administration. Many **Saints** in **Nauvoo** were rebaptized during a general **reformation** in May 1842. Most Church members were rebaptized soon after entering the Salt Lake Valley for the first time. During the **Mormon** Reformation of 1856 to 1857, rebaptism was a requirement to maintain good standing in the Church. So frequent was rebaptism in **Utah** that **ward** membership forms first issued in 1877 contained columns for recording rebaptisms.

Elder George Q. Cannon's talk in **general conference** in October 1897 signaled an end to the practice of rebaptism. Elder Cannon explained that many people had come to think of rebaptism as an easy way to obtain forgiveness. "It is repentance from sin that will save you," Elder Cannon reminded the Saints, "not rebaptism." Rebaptism was officially discontinued in 1922.

Today, rebaptism is practiced only for excommunicated members who desire to return to the Church or in the unlikely event that one's membership records have been lost.

SOURCES

Allen, James B., and Glen M. Leonard. *The Story of the Latter-day Saints.* 2d ed. Salt Lake City: Deseret Book, 1992. 430–31.

Quinn, D. Michael. "The Practice of Rebaptism at Nauvoo." *BYU Studies* 18 (Winter 1978): 226–32.

Talmage, James E. *Articles of Faith.* Salt Lake City: The Church of Jesus Christ of Latter-day Saints, 1960.

PAUL H. PETERSON

RECOMMEND. See TEMPLE RECOMMEND.

RECORD KEEPING. At the time of the Church's organization on 6 April 1830, the Lord commanded, "Behold, there shall be a record kept among you" (D&C 21:1). This injunction has been followed throughout the history of the Church. While speaking with the newly appointed **Quorum** of the Twelve **Apostles** on 27 February 1835, **Joseph Smith** reminded them to appoint recorders to keep track of the proceedings of **meetings** and the decisions made. He told them they would "find it of infinite worth" to have such a record (Smith, 2:198–99).

Keeping records has been a commandment throughout the earth's history. **Adam** kept a book of remembrance, "for it was given unto as many as called upon God to write by the spirit of inspiration" (Moses 6:5–6). The importance of keeping records is also evident in the **Book of Mormon**. Lehi's sons were sent back to Jerusalem for the records contained on plates of brass and Nephi was commanded to write the history and ministry of his people. King Benjamin explained, "Remember that were it not for these plates, which contain these records and these commandments, we must have suffered in ignorance, even at the present time, not knowing the mysteries of God" (Mosiah 1:3). Christ emphasized record keeping when he chastised the Nephites for not keeping a complete record of important events.

Today the Church keeps records of **revelations**, including the **prophets'** words in the **general conference** reports and Church **magazines**. The Church also records the names of those who receive religious **ordinances**, and it keeps membership records, both of which help Church leaders to know the status and needs of individuals. Preserving histories of peoples, cultures, and places has been important in the

Church. The **Historical Department** has collected many documents related to the Church's history. Members have also been instructed to preserve their own **family** and personal histories, including **journals**, for their posterity.

SOURCES

Kimball, Spencer W. "President Kimball Speaks Out on Personal Journals." *Ensign* 10 (December 1980): 60–61.

Smith, Joseph. *History of The Church of Jesus Christ of Latter-day Saints.* Edited by B. H. Roberts. 2d ed. rev. 7 vols. Salt Lake City: The Church of Jesus Christ of Latter-day Saints, 1932–51. 2:198–99.

Thompson, Heber M. "What Is the Purpose and History of Church Membership Records?" *Ensign* 24 (June 1994): 59–60.

CYNTHIA DOXEY

RED BRICK STORE. Joseph Smith's Red Brick Store played an important role in the life of **Nauvoo** in the 1840s. Not only did the store provide **sugar**, molasses, salt, and other supplies, but the building also housed Joseph Smith's office. It was the scene of many important meetings that still affect men and women of the Church today.

The store was opened for the first time on 5 January 1842. At times, the second story assembly room was used as a school, where the youth of the area learned reading, writing, chemistry, and other subjects. The Nauvoo Masonic Lodge also met in the assembly room, where Joseph Smith became a first-degree **mason** on 15 March 1842. Two days later the Female **Relief Society** of Nauvoo was organized in this same room. The benevolent organization was led by **Emma Smith** as president. On 4 May 1842 Joseph Smith gave the **endowment** to seven brethren in the assembly room of the store, which had been divided by temporary partitions to represent different stages of our eternal progress back to the presence of **God**.

The building stood until 1890, when it was demolished and the brick used to build a meat market on Mulholland Street. The foundation then became a curiosity and a tourist site. The **Reorganized Church of Jesus Christ of Latter Day Saints** undertook the reconstruction of the Red Brick Store in the late 1970s, and it was opened for tours in 1980, with various goods typical of the 1840s available to the visitor for purchase.

SOURCES

Cowan, Richard O. *Temples to Dot the Earth.* Salt Lake City: Bookcraft, 1989. 53–55.

Derr, Jill Mulvay, Janath Russell Cannon, and Maureen Ursenbach Beecher. *Women of Covenant.* Salt Lake City: Deseret Book, 1992. 23–58.

Holzapfel, Richard Neitzel, and T. Jeffrey Cottle. *Old Mormon Nauvoo and Southeastern Iowa: Historic Photographs and Guide.* 2d ed. Santa Anna, Calif.: Fieldbrook Productions, 1991. 144–47.

MIKE TRAPP

REDEEMING THE DEAD. See DEAD, REDEEMING THE.

REDRESS PETITIONS. Because of the **Mormon War** in **Missouri**, **Joseph Smith** spent the winter of 1838 and 1839 confined in jail at **Liberty, Missouri**. While there he asked the **Saints** to prepare affidavits to secure redress from the federal government for the losses caused by their recent expulsion from Missouri. Beginning in December 1839, the **Mormons** commenced recording their Missouri experiences and swearing to their authenticity before civil authorities. These officials were justices of the peace, clerks of the circuit court, and notary publics, who possessed the seals of their respective offices. The Latter-day Saints presented these legal documents to the federal government on at least three different occasions in a concerted attempt to obtain reparation for their sufferings in Missouri.

The petitions give insights about the petitioners themselves. "Of the 678 petitioners who personally filed affidavits, 70 were women and 608 were men. At least 25 men and 10 women were illiterate; . . . twenty-five witnessed the **Haun's Mill massacre**; . . . 8 claimed personal knowledge of the events and sufferings at **DeWitt**; 5 were at the **Gallatin** election; 3 described the events at **Crooked River**; and 23 were at **Adam-ondi-Ahman**. An astounding 106 men and 3 women were taken prisoner by the Missouri militia or mobs" (Johnson, xxvii). The Saints lost personal property and 6,501 acres of land, for which they claimed $2,275,789.00 (Johnson, xxvii).

Presently, researchers have discovered 823 documents signed by 678 individuals, making this the largest collection of records pertaining to any one period in LDS Church history. Most of these records are in **Washington, D.C.**

SOURCES

Johnson, Clark V., ed. *Mormon Redress Petitions, Documents of the 1833–1838 Missouri Conflict.* Provo, Utah: Religious Studies Center, Brigham Young University, 1992.

CLARK V. JOHNSON

REEDER, BERTHA S. Bertha Stone Reeder served 13 years (1948–61) as the fifth general president of the **Young Women's Mutual Improvement Association**. Born 28 October 1892 in **Ogden, Utah**, Bertha married Christopher Aadnesen in 1912. After his death, she married William H. Reeder III. Sister Reeder served on the **Primary** general board prior to her husband's call to preside over the New **England Mission**. Under her direction as YWMIA president, the Individual Award program was adopted, the camping program expanded, and the "Era of Youth" section inaugurated in the *Improvement Era.* Bertha, again a widow, married I. L. (Lee) Richards in 1964. She died 26 December 1982 in Pocatello, **Idaho**.

SOURCES

Bertha Stone Reeder Oral History. 1974. James Moyle Oral History Program, LDS Church Historical Department, Salt Lake City.

A Century of Sisterhood: Chronological Collage, 1869–1969. Salt Lake City: YWMIA, 1969.

Peterson, Janet, and LaRene Gaunt. "Bertha Stone Reeder." *Keepers of the Flame: Presidents of the Young Women.* Salt Lake City: Deseret Book, 1993. 67–79.

JANET PETERSON

REFERENCE WORKS. See ENCYCLOPEDIAS AND REFERENCE WORKS.

REFORMATION. The **Mormon** reformation, a short but highly spirited reform movement, was initiated and conducted by Church leaders between September 1856 and April 1857. For some years Church leaders had urged the necessity of reform. The beginning of the reform crusade in 1856 was both an indication of **Brigham Young's** concern about the **Saints'** collective spiritual complacency and a reflection of the high level of compliance with gospel requirements that he and other leaders expected from Church members.

The immediate seeds of the reformation were possibly planted in a **prayer circle** meeting on 7 September 1856. On this occasion Brigham Young expressed a desire to go through the territory with the **First Presidency** and the Twelve and "make a great wake" by preaching the gospel. A week later, President Young sent counselor **Jedediah M. Grant** to preach reform in settlements north of **Salt Lake City**. In a stirring address to assembled Saints at Kaysville, **Utah**, Grant told Church members to repent of their sins, recommit to live gospel principles more fully, and to signify that commitment through **rebaptism**. About 500 Saints did so.

The early weeks of the reformation were characterized by rousing repentance sermons, anxious confessions, and mass rebaptisms. Much of the controversy about the bold and sometimes threatening rhetoric of the reformation, including many of the so-called "blood atonement" statements, can be traced to this brief period. Gradually, the revivalistic phase gave way to a more judicious, measured reform movement.

Home missionaries played a major role in the reformation, at least near the center of the Church. Missionaries were equipped with a 27-question catechism designed to measure the worthiness (and identify areas of needed improvement) of families in their assigned wards. Most of the families were rebaptized in large ward services in April 1857, signifying an end to the reformation.

Reformation fervor ultimately reached nearly all Latter-day Saint settlements and **missions** throughout the world. While reform procedures varied from place to place, recommitment to gospel principles and rebaptism were constants that characterized reform movements everywhere. Saints who refused to be rebaptized were dropped from Church membership rolls.

There were three obvious effects of the reformation. First, for many Latter-day Saints, the reform movement was a time of spiritual rejuvenation. Accepting the admonitions of their leaders at face value, they happily engaged in gospel "self-improvement programs." Throughout the Church, there was an increase in tithing and free-will offerings. Second, the reformation had the effect of separating "wheat from chaff." Hundreds of Saints, discomfited by alleged reform excesses and the emphasis on stricter compliance with gospel requirements, chose to sever their ties with the Church. Third, the reformation provided a fair amount of grist for anti-Mormon writers, who for decades characterized the reformation as an uncontrolled period of religious zealotry.

In truth, both critics and apologists have claimed too much. Clearly, the overall course of reform was more controlled and restrained than many have supposed. Conversely, it would seem that the overall community spiritual gains were of short duration, the thrust of reform being first interrupted and then eclipsed in the summer of 1857 by war fervor following the news that a government-sponsored army expedition was on its way to Utah territory. For most Saints, the reformation was over less than a year after it began.

SOURCES

Alexander, Thomas G. "Wilford Woodruff and the Mormon Reformation." *Dialogue* 25 (Summer 1992): 25–39.
Peterson, Paul H. "Brigham Young and the Mormon Reformation." *Lion of the Lord.* Edited by Susan E. Black and Larry C. Porter. Salt Lake City: Deseret Book, 1995.
———. "The Mormon Reformation of 1856–1857: The Rhetoric and the Reality." *Journal of Mormon History* (1989): 59–87.

PAUL H. PETERSON

REFORMED EGYPTIAN. See EGYPTIAN.

REGIONAL REPRESENTATIVE.

REGIONAL REPRESENTATIVE. The first 69 regional representatives of the Twelve were announced by a First Presidency letter in **general conference** on 29 September 1967. They were set apart 2 October 1967 and began their duties 1 January 1968. The name was shortened to regional representative in July 1977. To meet the "worldwide demands of the Church," their calling was "to carry counsel to and to conduct instructional meetings in groups of stakes or regions" (CR, 25–26).

Not considered **general authorities**, they accepted temporary assignments from the First Presidency, received direction from them and the Quorum of the Twelve **Apostles**, and reported to an area supervisor. Regional representatives offered leadership training to priesthood and auxiliary leaders and encouraged progress in specific geographical areas.

As announced in the general conference of April 1995, all 284 currently serving regional representatives were honorably released 15 August 1995. From 1967 to 1995 a cumulative total of 1,072 men served as regional representatives.

SOURCES

Conference Report [CR] (September-October 1967): 25–26.
"Regional Representative Program Starts 10th Year within Leadership Ranks." *Church News,* 6 November 1976. 4.
Walker, Joseph. "A Statistical Look at Regional Representatives." *Church News,* 16 January 1983. 8–10.

LARRY R. SKIDMORE

REID, ROSE MARIE. Rose Marie Reid, a world-renowned swimsuit designer during the 1950s and 60s, also distinguished herself as a speaker, writer, and businesswoman. She was born 12 September 1906 in **Cardston, Alberta, Canada**. She designed her first swimsuit for her husband, Jack Reid, from an old duck coat. He wore it at the Crystal Pool in Vancouver, **British Columbia**, as a lifeguard. Jack took her first design to the Hudson Bay Department Store. She was surprised when her first suits sold well, grossing $10,000 the first year.

Rose Marie later designed suits for the British Empire games in **Australia**. In one season sales went from $30,000 to $300,000, and the products were sold throughout **Canada** in more than 500 retail stores. By 1946, she had captured about 50% of the swimsuit market in Canada (Burr, 35).

That same year, Reid moved to **Los Angeles, California**, and began competing against such clothier giants as Jantzen, Catalina, and Cole, using her own label, "Rose Marie Reid." Her designs were featured in *Life* magazine. In 1951, Reid created the heralded "Hourglass" swimsuit, which catapulted her into the international markets (Burr, 91). By 1959, production was up to 10,000 suits a day, and worldwide distribution reached into 46 countries, making Reid the largest manufacturer of ladies' swimsuits in the world (Burr, 97). She was one of the *Los Angeles Times's* 10 Women of the Year in 1955 and in 1958 was awarded Designer of the Year, the most prestigious award in her field.

Reid's business left her little time to hold a regular Church position. Because she felt a great need to serve in the Church, she asked her **stake mission president** what she could do. He suggested to Church leaders that she be set apart as a missionary at large. This was done 26 April 1953 (Burr, 107). In her travels she accounted for hundreds of converts. Her work among the Jewish community was especially impressive. **Elder LeGrand Richards** asked her to draft a set of lessons especially for the Jewish people. These lessons were later used in Los Angeles with great effect.

Reid's prominence and her native wit made her a favorite speaker at **BYU** devotionals. She spent the last years of her life in **Provo, Utah**, living with her daughter Carole Reid Burr. She died 18 November 1978.

SOURCES

Burr, Carole Reid, and Roger K. Petersen. *Rose Marie Reid: An Extraordinary Life Story.* American Fork, Utah: Covenant Communications, 1995. 35, 91, 97, 107.

ROGER K. PETERSEN

RELIEF SOCIETY. The Latter-day Saint **women's** Relief Society is a counterpart and complement to adult men's **priesthood quorums.** It is "divinely made, divinely authorized, divinely instituted, divinely ordained of God to minister for the salvation of the souls of women and of men" (Smith, 184). The Relief Society was organized 17 March 1842 by the **Prophet Joseph Smith,** who taught its members that "the same organization existed in the church anciently" and that "the organization of the Church of Christ was never perfect until the women were organized" (quoted in Derr, 41). The Relief Society operates at general, **stake,** and **ward** levels under the direction of three-member presidencies, subject to presiding priesthood authorities. Its motto, "Charity Never Faileth," describes the charitable and **humanitarian** service central to its identity. Weekly Relief Society **meetings** serve as a forum for doctrinal teaching, spiritual sharing, and sisterly association.

1842–1844

In 1842 at **Nauvoo, Illinois, Sarah M. Granger Kimball** and her neighbors organized a women's sewing society to provide shirts for **temple** workmen. Following the pattern of other female benevolent societies, **Eliza R. Snow** drafted a constitution and bylaws for the group. The Prophet Joseph Smith praised her charter, but proposed the sisters be organized instead "under the priesthood after a pattern of the priesthood" (Derr, 27). At his request, 20 women gathered on 17 March 1842 in the room above his **Red Brick Store.** They elected **Emma Smith** their president (1842–44), she selected two **counselors,** and they were set apart for their callings by the laying on of hands by priesthood leaders. The presidency appointed a secretary and treasurer. The Prophet explained that the presidency's decisions, together with the minutes of society proceedings, were to be the group's constitution. In subsequent meetings, Joseph Smith commissioned the sisters to relieve the poor and save souls. He taught the sisters charity, mercy, harmony, unity, the exercise of spiritual gifts, and the blessings of forthcoming **temple ordinances.** "I now turn the key to you in the name of God," he declared, "and this Society shall rejoice and knowledge and intelligence shall flow down from this time" (minutes quoted in Derr, 47).

The Female Relief Society of Nauvoo, as they voted to call themselves, admitted new members individually by vote. They met weekly in the spring and summer to hear instructions from their presidency and priesthood leaders; share testimonies; receive donated money, goods, and services; and plan how to assist the needy with food, housing, and employment. In 1843, the expanding group was divided into wards. Committees were appointed to visit homes; these women were later known as visiting teachers. There were 1,341 members in March 1844, when President Emma Smith's conflicts with priesthood leaders over the practice of **plural marriage** resulted in the cessation of society meetings.

1844–1900

Relief Society did not function formally during the Saints' westward trek and early years in **Utah**, though women ministered to the needy and gathered informally to visit, spin and sew, and sustain one another spiritually through prayer, testimony, and the exercise of spiritual gifts. In 1854, a few women, eager to answer **Brigham Young**'s call to provide **clothing** for destitute **Native Americans**, initiated their own Indian relief societies. Endorsing the movement, President Young recommended that **bishops** organize in each ward a branch of the Relief Society. These ward societies assisted new immigrants and the poor and addressed other local needs. Most of them discontinued their meetings following the massive move south in 1858, incident to the **Utah War**.

During 1866 an 1867, Brigham Young reemphasized the importance of Relief Society to help relieve the poor and promote home industry. He called Eliza R. Snow (1867–87), one of his plural wives and former secretary of the Female Relief Society of Nauvoo, to help bishops reorganize societies in each ward. She visited virtually every ward, reading from the Nauvoo minutes she had preserved and giving sisters instructions regarding the responsibilities of officers, visiting teachers, and members. The women cared for the poor and heartily responded to President Young's counsel on economic cooperation and self-sufficiency, exercising much local initiative in forwarding the **silk industry**, grain storage, home manufacture, and cooperative stores. They built their own meeting halls, sponsored their own semimonthly newspaper, the *Woman's Exponent* (1872–1914), encouraged women's medical training, founded the **Deseret Hospital**, and worked under the direction of priesthood leaders to organize and nurture local units of **Retrenchment**, or **Young Ladies Mutual Improvement Association** (1869), and **Primary** Association (1878).

During the presidency of **Zina D. H. Young** (1888–1901), as Latter-day Saints endured nearly a decade of crushing federal prosecution for **plural marriage** (which culminated in the **Manifesto** of 1890), Relief Society women reached beyond **Utah** to increase good will. Focusing on common concerns, such as international peace and the advancement of women, the Relief Society became a member of the International (1888) and National Councils of Women (1891), sent exhibits and representatives to the Columbia Exposition in Chicago (1892–93), and joined suffrage advocates in successfully campaigning for inclusion of **woman suffrage** and equal rights in Utah's new state constitution (1895).

During widespread celebration of the Relief Society Jubilee in March 1892, sisters remembered their Nauvoo origins and Joseph Smith's prophetic promises. They celebrated local society history and international expansion. Some sisters feared that incorporation as the National Woman's Relief Society (1892–1945), with a general board composed of stake Relief Society presidents, would secularize the society, but relieving the poor and saving souls remained the essence of its work.

1901–1940

Between 1895 and 1905, Relief Society membership increased 50%, bringing the total to 33,000 members. When President **Bathsheba W. Smith** (1901–10), her counselors, and general board found it difficult and expensive to visit and communicate with local units, they conveyed general instructions through the society's first handbook (1902) and hoped ten-cent membership dues, initiated in 1898, would defray other expenses. They established the society's first official headquarters on the second floor of the newly completed Bishop's Building in **Salt Lake City** (1909). In 1902 the board invited stakes to prepare lesson outlines for their individual use. Covering many subjects, but known widely as "mothers' work," the lessons attracted a new generation of young mothers to the Relief Society.

During the presidency of **Emmeline B. Wells** (1910–21), younger board members successfully pushed the board to issue standardized lessons in the new *Relief Society Bulletin* (1914), quickly transformed into the *Relief Society Magazine* (1915–70). The lessons formalized the schedule and agenda of Relief Society meetings, which, in the nineteenth century, had been loosely structured around charity work, sewing, **scripture** study, and testimony bearing. The new lessons featured a different topic each week of the month—theology, culture, homemaking arts—and designated time for charity work and testimonies. Topics changed over time, but this plan largely characterized Relief Society meetings for most of the twentieth century. The society standardized its record-keeping and more closely coordinated its expanding charity work with public agencies by establishing the Relief Society **Social Services** Department (1919–69). After the U.S. government purchased 200,000 bushels of

Relief Society wheat in 1918 during the closing months of **World War I**, the grain storage program, advanced by local units for nearly 50 years, became a wheat trust fund (1918–76).

Under the direction of **Clarissa S. Williams** (1921–28), interest from the wheat trust fund enabled Relief Society women to address the health needs of mothers and children by establishing baby clinics, milk depots, and two stake maternity hospitals (Cottonwood, Utah, and **Snowflake, Arizona**). Particularly in Utah, the society's close cooperation with public and private charity agencies facilitated the distribution of aid to those in need. Bishops and Relief Society presidents were directed to meet regularly to coordinate ward charity work, and Relief Society rooms in ward **meetinghouses** officially replaced the sisters' own halls, both signaling the developing correlation of Church programs.

During the **great depression** the Church inaugurated its own **welfare plan**, directed by priesthood leaders at general, regional, and local levels. To **Louise Y. Robison** (1928–39) fell the responsibility of encouraging Relief Society women's active involvement in new welfare projects. Women sewed clothing and bedding and produced and preserved food to fill regional bishops' storehouses with necessities for the poor. Lending its full support to the new priesthood program, Relief Society gradually relinquished some of its own welfare initiatives, including the collection of Relief Society charity funds by visiting teachers (1944). Its weekly education program placed increasing emphasis on strengthening the home and **family**.

1940–1970

During **World War II**, under the direction of **Amy Brown Lyman** (1940–45), Relief Society encouraged simplification, thrift and conservation, nursing and first-aid training, and Red Cross work. As the war fragmented families and the number of women employed outside the home increased, Relief Society accentuated the importance of family life, particularly mothering and homemaking. During the war, European sisters pulled together to share supplies and soothe sorrow and anxiety. After the war, European Saints helped each other, and sisters in the **United States** and **Canada** worked in connection with the Church's welfare program to send clothing, food, and quilts to **Europe**. Hawaiian sisters sent provisions to **Japan**.

An increasing consciousness of the worldwide nature of Relief Society marked the long presidency of **Belle S. Spafford** (1945–74). Although membership, attendance, and **visiting teaching** had declined during the war, all three increased dramatically in the postwar years, particularly in the Far East, **Mexico**, and **South America**. The *Relief Society Magazine* was printed in Spanish (1966), and new cultural refinement lessons featured **literature**, **art**, and **music** from various nations. A new Relief Society building, announced in 1945, built by the donations of sisters worldwide and matching funds from the Church, was dedicated in 1956. It headquartered the society's officers and publications as well as the Relief Society Social Services Department, which offered services for adoption, Indian student placement, and youth guidance and foster care.

1971–2000

Foreseeing further international growth, the **general authorities** instituted a far-reaching program of **correlation** that consolidated under priesthood leadership the **magazines**, lessons, reporting, and finances of Relief Society and other **auxiliaries**. Relief Society's social services department was also placed under priesthood direction. Counterbalancing this abridgment of the society's duties was responsibility for a membership that expanded significantly after September 1971, when dues were eliminated and all adult Latter-day Saint women were automatically enrolled as Relief Society members. **Barbara B. Smith** (1974–84) guided Relief Society in restructuring its program to meet the needs of this larger and more diversified membership, which included young, single, and working women. The Relief Society building became a resource and training center, helping local officers keep current on the changing program.

Women's varied lives and contributions were celebrated in 13 bronze statues comprising the Relief Society Monument to Women at Nauvoo, Illinois, erected through contributions of sisters worldwide (1978). As the burgeoning feminist movement challenged women's traditional commitments, the general presidency affirmed women's essential role in family, Church, and community life and established a center for scholarly research on women at Brigham Young University (1978). President Barbara Smith joined Church leaders in opposing an **Equal Rights Amendment** to the U.S. **Constitution**.

A general meeting for all Relief Society sisters, initiated under the direction of President **Spencer W. Kimball** (1978), became an annual event and set the tone for the emphasis on personal righteousness that continued through the end of the century. **Barbara W. Winder** (1984–90) addressed this theme as she traveled to selected areas worldwide with the general presidents of Young Women and Primary. With the size of their general boards greatly reduced, the three women's presidencies worked closely together, and all three were housed in the Relief Society Building.

As the Church expanded in new areas like **Africa**, the emphasis was placed on strengthening local Relief Societies and reaching individual women. **Elaine L. Jack** (1990–97) and her counselors sought to make leadership training more equitable throughout the world. They contributed to a new correlated handbook and traveled as widely as possible, inviting local sisters to discuss their diverse achievements, challenges, and needs. In celebration of the society's sesquicentennial (1992), the presidency and board emphasized the importance of increasing literacy worldwide and encouraged local units to compile their histories and initiate community service projects. Women leaders together with priesthood leaders addressed contemporary problems such as single parenting and abuse, and praised the continuing strength and contributions of Latter-day Saint women.

During the presidency of **Mary Ellen Smoot** (1997–) Relief Society shifted to a new curriculum shared with priesthood quorums and based on the teachings of latter-day prophets (1998). By the year 2000 the society's membership numbered more than 4 million in 161 countries. A prelude to the new millennium, the "Relief Society Declaration" (1999) proclaimed Relief Society a "worldwide sisterhood . . . united in our devotion to Jesus Christ." The declaration recapitulated the principles that had guided Relief Society women for nearly 16 decades, including the importance of increasing testimonies and spiritual strength; fortifying **marriage**, family, and home; loving learning and delighting in service and good works; sustaining priesthood authority, delighting in the blessings of the temple, and striving for exaltation.

SOURCES

Derr, Jill Mulvay, et al. *Women of Covenant: The Story of Relief Society.* Salt Lake City: Deseret Book, 1992.

Smith, Joseph F. *Teachings of Presidents of the Church: Joseph F. Smith.* Salt Lake City: The Church of Jesus Christ of Latter-day Saints, 1998.

JILL MULVAY DERR

RELIEF SOCIETY MAGAZINE, THE. The *Relief Society Magazine* was first published in 1915 to bring **Relief Society** lessons to women of the Church. It superseded both the *Woman's Exponent* (the unofficial Relief Society publication that was begun in 1872) and the *Relief Society Bulletin,* which had been printed during 1914. The subscription rate for the **magazine** started at $1 per year and was later raised to $2. In the editorial of the first issue, the editor promised that the publication would be "filled with the Spirit of the Lord from cover to cover" (quoted in Sharp, 13–14).

Besides making available the monthly lessons, the magazine contained articles on child care, current events, **fiction**, **poetry**, recipes, and counsel from **priesthood** and Relief Society leaders. It reported activities of **ward** and **branch** Relief Societies and featured a photographic section on their events and on the handicraft of various individuals. The magazine also published advertisements that reflected women's interests, including the newest technological inventions to help the homemaker.

For 56 years, Relief Society **women** enjoyed a publication written solely for them and their interests in a format sanctioned by Church leaders. The last issue appeared in December 1970 when the Church switched to three consolidated magazines for members—the *Ensign*, the *Friend*, and the *New Era*.

SOURCES

Godfrey, Audrey M. "Selling the Good Life: A Look at Advertising in the Relief Society Magazine, 1914–1970." *Mormon Heritage Magazine* 2 (May–June 1995): 32–39.

Sharp, Marianne C. "*Relief Society Magazine's* Fiftieth Anniversary." *Relief Society Magazine* 50 (January 1963): 12–16.

AUDREY M. GODFREY

RELIGION CLASS. Religion Class was organized in 1890 when a **Utah** territorial law prohibited religious instruction in public schools. Like the Primary, the Religion Class in each **ward** conducted a class at the **meetinghouse** for children of elementary school age one afternoon each week. While Primary featured activities, Religion Class stressed instruction. The Religion Class Association was listed with the Church's other **auxiliaries** at times such as in **general conference**. In 1929, as part of an effort to simplify the Church's activities, the Religion Class program was discontinued, and its functions were absorbed by the Primary.

SOURCES

Cowan, Richard O. *The Latter-day Saint Century.* Salt Lake City: Bookcraft, 1999. 106–7.

Jenson, Andrew. *Encyclopedic History of The Church of Jesus Christ of Latter-day Saints.* Salt Lake City: Deseret News, 1941. 697.

RICHARD O. COWAN

RELIGIOUS EDUCATOR, THE. The *Religious Educator: Perspectives on the Restored Gospel* is a journal created in March 2000 and published twice a year (Fall and winter) under the auspices of the Religious Studies Center at **Brigham Young University**. It is intended to provide insights and ideas for those involved in teaching the restored gospel of **Jesus Christ** at every level—from paid professionals to those who are called to teach in the branches and wards of the Church. Articles address a variety of topics directly related to all facets of teaching the restored gospel, as well as the doctrine and history of the **Restoration**, and generally fall into regularly featured categories that include pedagogy, scripture and doctrine, church history, and devotion.

Andrew C. Skinner

RELIGIOUS LIBERTY. Religious liberty is an important principle of The Church of Jesus Christ of Latter-day Saints. It is closely linked to the doctrine of free agency and has been recognized from the earliest days of the Church as a key belief. It is affirmed both in the 11th **Article of Faith** and the declaration of belief regarding governments and laws recorded in Section 134 of the **Doctrine and Covenants**. The **Book of Mormon** also recognizes the importance of religious liberty (Alma 30:7–9). In a speech delivered on 9 July 1843, **Joseph Smith** declared, "I am bold to declare before Heaven that I am just as ready to die in defending the rights of a Presbyterian, a Baptist, or a good man of any denomination; for the same principle which would trample upon the rights of the Latter-day Saints would trample upon the rights of the Roman Catholics, or of any other denomination who may be unpopular and too weak to defend themselves. It is a love of liberty which inspires my soul—civil and religious liberty to the whole of the human race" (Smith, 5:498).

Church members protested violations of their religious freedom rights in **Missouri** and **Illinois**. Later in the nineteenth century, many laws that infringed upon beliefs of Church members were challenged. The most famous of these cases, *Reynolds v. United States*, 98 U.S. 145 (1878), was one of the earliest U.S. Supreme Court cases to interpret the Free Exercise Clause of the First Amendment. It rejected claims that a law prohibiting plural marriage violated the religious liberties of **Latter-day Saints**. The practice of **plural marriage** was left behind by revelation, beginning with the **Manifesto (1890)**, and the Church never sought to revisit this decision. In the twentieth century, the Church actively supported religious freedom. It played a major role in the broad-based coalition that supported enactment and defense of the Religious Freedom Restoration Act and the Religious Liberty Protection Act. It also supported the principle of religious liberty in a variety of contexts around the world.

SOURCES

Smith, Joseph. *History of The Church of Jesus Christ of Latter-day Saints.* Edited by B. H. Roberts. 2d ed. rev. 7 vols. Salt Lake City: The Church of Jesus Christ of Latter-day Saints, 1932–51. 5:498.

COLE DURHAM

REORGANIZED CHURCH OF JESUS CHRIST OF LATTER DAY SAINTS (RLDS).

The Reorganized Church of Jesus Christ of Latter Day Saints emerged following the death of **Joseph Smith Jr.** The RLDS Church believes that Joseph Jr. set apart his oldest son, Joseph III, to be his successor. At the time of the **Prophet's** death, however, his son was only 11 years old and could not accept the prophetic mantle.

A number of **Saints** who did not follow **Brigham Young** west awaited divine instruction regarding continuation of their faith. **Jason W. Briggs** was one of them. He joined the **Mormon** Church in **Wisconsin** in 1841, and after the **Martyrdom** associated with Brigham Young for approximately two years before joining with **James J. Strang.** In 1850 he united with a small group led by the Prophet's younger brother **William B. Smith** (who had been excommunicated by Brigham Young), which strongly advocated the principle of lineal succession in the presidency. In 1851 Briggs felt impressed to remain faithful in preaching the gospel and to accept the principle of lineal succession and God's laws, believing that if these conditions were met, the true church would arise and establish **Zion.**

Zenos Hovey Gurley Sr. in Yellowstone, Wisconsin, almost simultaneously reported a similar experience. Gurley, having a Methodist background, had been baptized by LDS missionary James Blakeslee in April 1838 in Ontario, **Canada.** Upon his move to **Far West,** Missouri, Gurley was ordained a **seventy** (at that time not a general authority office). From **Nauvoo,** Gurley went on **missions** through **Illinois,** actively raising funds for the **Nauvoo Temple.** After the Martyrdom, Gurley and those close to him joined James J. Strang but had the same misgivings Briggs did about Strang's emerging theology. Weeks later, Gurley and his followers heard about Briggs's experience and joined with them to await future divine direction.

A growing dissatisfaction arose among other splinter factions as they rejected their leaders. Many joined with Briggs and Gurley in espousing the lineal principle of presidential succession. This group provided the nucleus for a "New Organization" of the church. They first met in June 1852. In this conference several important principles became foundational to the emerging church: common consent; orderly transition of prophetic leadership; continuity of **priesthood** function with its origins through Joseph Smith Jr.; allegiance to the **Bible**, the **Doctrine and Covenants**, and the **Book of Mormon**; and an unabashed denunciation of **plural marriage** and any group that practiced it.

With renewed zeal, missionaries were sent out from the New Organization with a **pamphlet** describing their beliefs and calling for a "reorganization" of the Church. In 1856 the group approached **Joseph Smith III** at his home in Nauvoo, Illinois, encouraging him to join them. The young Smith, now approximately 24 years old, rebuffed their offer, telling them he needed to feel a personal call before fellowshipping with any of the movements. Three years later, and with the support of his mother, **Emma Hale Smith** Bidamon, Joseph III went to **William Marks**, former Nauvoo **Stake president** and close friend of the **family**, to discuss his decision to join the newly reorganized church. This contact was crucial, because Marks had already fellowshipped with the new movement. On **6 April** 1860, Joseph III and his mother, Emma, attended a **general conference** of the Reorganized Church of Jesus Christ of Latter Day Saints, in which Joseph received unanimous support to carry the prophetic mantle of the church.

Joseph Smith III headquartered the RLDS Church in Nauvoo from 1860 to 1866 and then moved the church east to Plano, Illinois, staying there until 1881. From Plano, Smith established the church in Lamoni, **Iowa**, where it remained officially until 1920. As early as the 1870s, however, RLDS Church members returned to **Independence, Missouri**, to live peacefully among the people of Jackson County, providing opportunity for RLDS stakes to be established.

After presiding over the church 54 years, Joseph III died in Independence. His oldest son, Frederick Madison Smith, accepted the prophetic mantle in May 1915, serving until his death in March 1946. During his administration, F. M. Smith stressed the importance of establishing Zionic conditions and the gathering to the center place. Upon his death, his younger brother, Israel A. Smith, became president and served in that capacity until his death in June 1958. Israel challenged the RLDS to develop spiritually and to embrace a unity of purpose in their faith. In October 1958 William Wallace Smith (half-brother to Israel Smith) was ordained to the presidency. Under his administration, the RLDS Church took great strides to become a "world church." In July 1976 he formally announced his son, Wallace B. Smith, as prophet and president-designate. Two years later, W. Wallace Smith was accorded the honor of president emeritus in his retirement from church leadership after ordaining his son as president of the church. Under Wallace B. Smith's leadership, priesthood ordination was extended to women, international ministries were expanded, and the **temple** in Independence was constructed. In 1996 Wallace B. Smith ordained W. Grant McMurray as prophet-president of the Church, departing for the first time from the principle of lineal descent. Under President McMurray's direction, the RLDS Church, with its quarter-million members, embraced peace, reconciliation, and healing of the spirit as it ministered in nearly 40 nations worldwide. At the April 2000 world conference the church decided that as of 1 January 2001 it would be known as the Community of Christ, although its legal name would remain unchanged.

SOURCES

Blair, Alma R. "The Reorganized Church of Jesus Christ of Latter Day Saints: Moderate Mormons." *The Restoration Movement: Essays in Mormon History.* rev. ed. Edited by F. Mark McKiernan, Alma R. Blair, and Paul M. Edwards. Independence, Mo.: Herald Publishing House, 1992.

Howard, Richard P. *The Church through the Years.* 2 vols. Independence, Mo: Herald Publishing House, 1992–93.

Newell, Linda King, and Valeen Tippetts Avery. *Mormon Enigma: Emma Hale Smith.* 2d ed. Urbana: University of Illinois Press, 1994.

MARK A. SCHERER

REPUBLICAN PARTY. Founded in 1854 by Whigs, Free-Soilers, and other anti-slavery forces, the Republican Party has played the role of both antagonist and advocate of Latter-day Saint causes. During its first national election in 1856, the party vigorously attacked the Latter-day Saint practice of **plural marriage**. It cleverly connected polygamy with slavery, calling them the "**twin relics of barbarism**." For the next third of a century the party continued its assault on the Church. All of the major antipolygamy legislation, including the Morrill Anti-Bigamy Act (1862), the Edmunds Act (1882), and the Edmunds-Tucker Act (1887), received strong Republican support.

In the late 1880s the relationship between the Church and Republicans began to improve. Before that time Latter-day Saints had been working for years with the **Democratic Party** to achieve **statehood** for Utah but to no avail. After Democratic president **Grover Cleveland** lost his bid for reelection in 1888, some Church leaders, such as **George Q. Cannon**, began working with prominent national Republicans to gain statehood. Republican support for the cause began to swell after President **Wilford Woodruff** issued the **Manifesto (1890)** on plural marriage. Some of the leading Republicans who worked for statehood were **Isaac Trumbo**, Leland Stanford, Morris M. Estee, James S. Clarkson, and James G. Blaine.

One of the prerequisites for Utah becoming a state was that the Church would have to discontinue its **People's Party** and the citizens of the territory would have to align themselves with the two national political parties—Republican and Democratic. The Republican Party in Utah was established on 20 May 1891, and three weeks later on 10 June the People's Party was dissolved. Because of members' previous clashes with the national Republican Party, many Church leaders feared that most of the **Saints** would flock to the Democratic Party and in so doing alienate Republican friends who were working diligently for statehood. Therefore, several **general authorities** used their influence both publicly and privately to encourage members to affiliate with the Republicans. This effort led to a strong and viable Republican Party in Utah by 1892. National Republicans, in turn, used their influence, along with Democrats, to pass the Utah Statehood Bill in Congress on 16 July 1894. Eighteen months later, on 4 January 1896, Utah became a state.

During the twentieth century the Republican Party enjoyed considerable success among Mormons, especially in Utah, and several prominent Latter-day Saint Republicans were elected or appointed to national office. **Elder Reed Smoot** represented Utah in the U.S. Senate from 1903 to 1933 while serving simultaneously as a member of the **Quorum** of the Twelve **Apostles**. **J. Reuben Clark** served as undersecretary of state (1928–30) and ambassador to **Mexico** (1930–33) before being called as a counselor in the **First Presidency** in 1933. Wallace F. Bennett served Utah in the U.S. Senate from 1951 to 1975. Elder **Ezra Taft Benson**, a member of the Quorum of the Twelve, served as U.S. secretary of agriculture during President Dwight D. Eisenhower's administration (1953–61). Two Latter-day Saints served in President Richard M. Nixon's cabinet: **David M. Kennedy** was secretary of treasury (1969–71) and **George Romney** was secretary of housing and urban development (1969–72). **Terrel H. Bell** served as U.S. secretary of education during President Reagan's administration (1981–85). Utah elected **Orrin Hatch** to the U.S. Senate in 1976, where he was still serving at the end of the century.

Latter-day Saints were especially inclined to vote Republican in the 1980s. During the 1984 presidential election a higher percentage of people in Utah voted for Ronald Reagan than in any other state, prompting sociologist Rodney Stark to call it the most Republican state in the nation. In the same election 85% of the Latter-day Saints throughout the country voted for Reagan. One study, completed in 1988, claimed that 46% of the Latter-day Saints in the United States were Republicans, compared with 27% of Protestants, 18% of Catholics, and 11% of Jews.

SOURCES

Alexander, Thomas G. *Mormonism in Transition: A History of the Latter-day Saints, 1890–1930*. Urbana and Chicago: University of Illinois Press, 1986. 1–59.

Bahr, Stephen J. "Social Characteristics." *Encyclopedia of Mormonism*. Edited by Daniel H. Ludlow. 4 vols. New York: Macmillan, 1992. 1375–76.

Larson, Gustave O. *The "Americanization" of Utah for Statehood*. San Marino, Calif.: Huntington Library, 1971.

Lyman, Edward Leo. *Political Deliverance: The Mormon Quest for Utah Statehood*. Urbana and Chicago: University of Illinois Press, 1986.

Sillito, John. "Republican Party." In *Utah History Encyclopedia*. Edited by Allan Kent Powell. Salt Lake City: University of Utah Press. 1994. 461–62.

ARNOLD K. GARR

REPUBLIC OF CONGO. See CONGO.

RESTORATION. The Restoration—the process of reestablishing on earth the fulness of the gospel of **Jesus Christ**, the authority to act in Jesus' name, and the true Church of Jesus Christ—began in 1820 through the **Prophet Joseph Smith**.

The Latter-day Saint concept of restoration includes a belief that in earlier times Christ's Church was on earth with its true teachings and authority. During Jesus' earthly ministry, he established his Church, and after his ascension it was administered by him through his **apostles**. In the days of the apostles, the Church was acknowledged by Christ, and his works were in it.

Latter-day Saints believe that during the first century A.D., Christians began to bring into the Church doctrinal and behavioral ideas that were alien to what Jesus and his apostles had taught. As the apostles died, the widespread acceptance of false teachings, coupled with rebellion against priesthood authority, led to the Christian church's no longer being acknowledged by Christ as his own. Without apostles during subsequent centuries, revealed doctrine was transformed under the influence of Greek philosophical ideas to create the incorrect beliefs and practices that now characterize traditional Christianity. Latter-day Saints call this cumulative process the Apostasy.

Joseph Smith was the Prophet of the Restoration, whose calling was to restore to the world what had been lost and transformed since Jesus' earthly ministry. The restoration of pure doctrine began with the **First Vision** in 1820, when **God the Father** and his Son Jesus Christ appeared to Joseph Smith. This event restored the important truths that the Father, the Son, and the Holy Ghost are separate and distinct beings, and that humans are, just as the Bible teaches, created in God's image.

The doctrinal restoration continued as the Prophet was tutored by the angel **Moroni** beginning in 1823. Moroni instructed Joseph Smith regarding the Prophet's own calling and mission, the **Book of Mormon**, keys of the **priesthood**, spiritual gifts, the gathering of Israel, the destruction of the wicked and the purification of the earth, Jesus' second coming, and the Millennium (JS–H 1:33–41).

The Book of Mormon, published early in 1830, restores pure doctrine regarding the Fall, the Atonement, **revelation**, **scripture**, the house of Israel, and the law of **Moses**. Revelations from 1828 until Joseph Smith's death in 1844 continued the restoration of lost truth. Collected in the **Doctrine and Covenants**, these revelations restore knowledge concerning the function and organization of Christ's Church, qualities of righteous living, the building of **Zion** on earth, life after death, the second coming of Jesus, and eternal rewards and punishments.

The **Joseph Smith Translation of the Bible**, undertaken from 1830 to 1833, restores lost truths regarding the nature of deity, the infinite scope of God's work, the mission of Jesus Christ, the plan of salvation, the character of **Satan**, the Fall, the antiquity of the gospel, the last days, and the establishment of Zion. The **book of Abraham**, a translation revealed to Joseph Smith from 1835 to 1842, restores truths regarding the premortal existence of humankind, the purpose of life on earth, and the Abrahamic covenant. Still more doctrinal light was restored in Joseph Smith's sermons and writings, in which he opened the heavens with revealed knowledge about the nature of God and eternal human possibilities.

In all, the doctrinal restoration was an explosion of light and knowledge, and the teachings cited above are illustrative of many more.

The restoration of authority to act in God's name began on 15 May

1829 when **John the Baptist** restored the lesser, or **Aaronic, Priesthood,** which includes the authority to baptize and administer the **sacrament** of the Lord's Supper. The higher authority, or **Melchizedek Priesthood,** was restored not long thereafter, giving the power to establish the Church and preside over its work. In subsequent years, the keys for specific callings were restored to the Church, including the keys of the gathering of Israel (D&C 110:11), the covenant of Abraham (D&C 110:12), and the **sealing** power (D&C 110:13–16). With these restored spiritual powers, Joseph Smith and those ordained by him have been authorized by God to act in his name, perform sacred **ordinances** acknowledged by him, build **temples,** conduct the affairs of the Church, and seal actions in heaven that are sealed on earth.

After being lost from the earth for many centuries, the Church of Jesus Christ was reestablished on **6 April** 1830. It is the same Church that existed in ancient times, and it is led by Jesus Christ today through his modern apostolic servants, just as it was in the days of **Peter, James, and John.** With its revealed doctrine and authority, it is Christ's restored Church, empowered by him to do his work.

SOURCES

Bushman, Richard L. *Joseph Smith and the Beginnings of Mormonism.* Urbana and Chicago: University of Illinois Press, 1984.

Jackson, Kent P. *From Apostasy to Restoration.* Salt Lake City: Deseret Book, 1996.

Smith, Joseph. *History of The Church of Jesus Christ of Latter-day Saints.* Edited by B. H. Roberts. 2d ed. rev. 7 vols. Salt Lake City: The Church of Jesus Christ of Latter-day Saints, 1932–52. xxiii–xciv, 1–80.

KENT P. JACKSON

RESTORATION, HISTORICAL SETTING.

The **restoration** of the gospel took place in a time of religious excitement when people throughout the **United States** were unusually concerned about salvation. For 30 years prior to the organization of the Church in 1830, the nation had been undergoing the **Second Great Awakening,** led by evangelical preachers who "awakened" hearers to concerns about their souls. Like so many others, **Joseph Smith** was moved by the revivalists to ask what he must do to be saved. Propelled by this wave of religious interest, the evangelical denominations mushroomed, none more dramatically than the Methodists. Between 1770 and 1830, the Methodists enlarged from a tiny sect of around a thousand members to nearly half a million. Joseph

Smith and **Brigham Young**, along with many other early Latter-day Saints, had been attracted to Methodism for a time.

Although Presbyterians, Congregationalists, Baptists, and Methodists took the lead in the revivals, the religious excitement did more than add numbers to the mainline churches. The search for salvation led people into new doctrines and church practices. Universalists, such as Joseph's grandfather **Asael Smith**, insisted that the atonement of Christ saved everyone—without the anguished conversions of the revivalists. Alexander Campbell, the founder of the Disciples of Christ, sought to recover the pure practices of early Christianity, teaching his own form of "restoration." New churches, new doctrines, and new leaders proliferated. **Visions** and religious dreams gave people premonitions of what was to come. Many believed they were visited by angels or were carried into heaven, where they saw God and Christ.

The burden of deciding which of the many churches was true rested on individual believers. Although Joseph Smith consulted with a Methodist minister about his religious problems, he knew he must find the truth for himself. In an earlier era, religious seekers would have turned automatically to the local pastor for guidance, but by 1830 the monopoly of the local churches had been broken. The rise of new religious sects, migration from old regions to new, and belief in freedom of conscience cut people loose from traditional denominations. Joseph's father and mother had no minister to turn to with their religious questions. Like most Americans, they were on their own. That independence, though perplexing for seekers, freed them from tradition and prepared them to accept new teachings. Self-reliant individuals, thirsting for religious knowledge, collected around emerging religious leaders like Joseph Smith.

Joseph's visions and **revelations** shocked people less then than they do today. Not only were visions and dreams common; many people believed the times called for extraordinary spiritual gifts. Most Christians looked forward to the return of **Jesus Christ** when the world would be redeemed. Some believed the millennium would come in gradually through natural human means; others expected God to rid the world of the wicked and set up a kingdom for the returning Savior. These millenarians were not surprised by reports of spiritual gifts. Intervention from heaven was to be expected as the Second Coming drew near. In that atmosphere of searching and expectation, the message of the Restoration fell on listening ears.

SOURCES

Cross, Whitney R. *The Burned-Over District: The Social and Intellectual History of*

Enthusiastic Religion in Western New York. Ithaca, N.Y.: Cornell University Press, 1950.

Hatch, Nathan O. *The Democratization of American Christianity.* New Haven, Conn.: Yale University Press, 1989.

Wood, Gordon S. "Evangelical America and Early Mormonism." *New York History* 61 (October 1980): 359–86.

RICHARD L. BUSHMAN

RESTORATIONISTS. Following the American Revolution, a number of preachers in the new nation rejected all major denominations and denounced the popular creeds of Christendom. Although leaders of this restorationist movement disagreed on a number of doctrinal issues, they were united in their quest to restore Christianity as defined in the New Testament. This movement was the first religious development in the United States that led to the creation of a number of enduring religious societies.

One of the unusual characteristics of the **restoration** movement of the late eighteenth and early nineteenth centuries was that independent congregations in pursuit of the apostolic church and teachings sprang forth almost simultaneously in different parts of **America**. In the 1790s, followers of James O'Kelly, a Methodist preacher, began organizing what were eventually called Christian churches in **North Carolina** and **Virginia**. In the early 1800s, followers of Abner Jones and Elias Smith, Baptist preachers, organized groups in New England that adopted the name Eastern Christians. Meanwhile, followers of Barton Stone, a Presbyterian preacher, organized Christian churches in **Kentucky**.

Another distinct restoration movement emerged in **Ohio** in the 1820s. Two of the most influential Baptist preachers of that movement were Alexander Campbell and **Sidney Rigdon**. Beginning about 1830, followers of Campbell began calling themselves **Disciples of Christ**. One reason for the selection of this name was to differentiate this new group from various independent congregations who called themselves Christians.

In the late 1990s, the largest religious community in the United States, known by the name "Church of Christ," had historical roots that dated back to an agreement of cooperation endorsed by Stone and Campbell in 1832.

SOURCE

Backman, Milton V. *Christian Churches of America: Origins and Beliefs.* New York: Charles Scribner's Sons, 1983.

MILTON V. BACKMAN JR.

RETRENCHMENT. In 1869, **Brigham Young** became concerned with the way Latter-day Saint **women** were being affected by outside influences. He directed the formation of a "retrenchment" movement to encourage women to devote more energy to spiritual and mental progress and less to concerns of fashion and vanity. He called **Mary Isabella Horne** to head the movement, which continued for some 35 years.

Retrenchment Associations were soon formed throughout the Church; they did not necessarily correspond to **ward** or **stake** boundaries, and women were encouraged to visit other groups. The **meetings** were held every few weeks, during which the sisters were invited to express their feelings about their faith or give extemporaneous speeches on topics assigned by the leaders. The sisters often shared information about "home industries," including food production and storage, making of **clothing**, etc. Later, when **polygamy** became controversial, the meetings provided a chance for the women to reaffirm their commitments and to receive reassurance and encouragement from each other.

Brigham Young also formed his own daughters into a "Young Ladies Retrenchment Association," with Emma Young Empey as president. This effort helped the young women learn about subjects similar to those studied by the adult women, and encouraged them to develop commitment to the Church's standards. The youth retrenchment programs evolved into the **Young Women's Mutual Improvement Association.**

SOURCES

Humphreys, A. Glen. "Missionaries to the Saints." *BYU Studies* 17 (Autumn 1976): 74–100.

Madsen, Carol Cornwall. "Retrenchment Association." *Encyclopedia of Mormonism.* Edited by Daniel H. Ludlow. 4 vols. New York: Macmillan, 1992. 3:1223–25.

DAVID KENISON

REUNION. Reunion, a small volcanic island in the Indian Ocean, was introduced to The Church of Jesus Christ of Latter-day Saints in 1979. The first members on Reunion were Alain and Danielle Chion-Hock, converts from **France.** Alain baptized his sister Rose Tahi Soui Tchong on 4 November 1979, making her the first convert on the island.

Under direction of the **International Mission, Elder** Joseph T. Edmunds and his wife, Ruth, opened a **mission** on the island in late 1979. They were joined by other couples within months. The islands were transferred to the **South Africa** Johannesburg Mission in 1986, and on 1 July 1988 the Mascarene Islands Mission was created, with 400 members of the Church on the islands. At that time there were three **branches** on Reunion. **Seminary** classes began in 1993, and on 1 July 1998 the island was placed in the **Madagascar** Antanarivo Mission. By the beginning of the year 2000, 695 members lived on the island, composing one district with four branches. Reunion is part of the **Africa** Southwest **Area** of the Church.

SOURCE

1999–2000 Church Almanac. Salt Lake City: Deseret News, 1998. 323.

GUY L. DORIUS

REVELATION. Revelation is the inspiration of the Holy Ghost given to man and the life blood of the gospel. **Joseph Smith** stated: "No man can receive the Holy Ghost without receiving revelations. The Holy Ghost is a Revelator" (Smith, 328). The restored Church is led by revelation, and it is only by the power of personal revelation that one can receive a knowledge and confirmation that the gospel is true.

Revelation is not limited to the **prophet** or the **apostles**. It is a blessing each individual can receive. Because God operates on eternal principles, any individual who abides the laws is entitled to receive revelation (McConkie, 152). Joseph Smith taught: "A person may profit by noticing the first intimation of the spirit of revelation; for instance, when you feel pure intelligence flowing into you, it may give you sudden strokes of ideas, so that by noticing it, you may find it fulfilled the same day or soon" (Smith, 151).

A correct knowledge of God can only come through personal revelation and through the ordinances God has set forth for that purpose. Intellectual efforts alone, even when sincerely made, cannot produce a testimony as firm as can a witness from the Holy Ghost. Joseph Smith taught, "Could you gaze into heaven five minutes, you would know more than you would by reading all that ever was written on the subject" (Smith, 324). The mind or intellect is not to be overlooked in our effort for answers, however. We are expected to mix reason and revelation as we prepare ourselves for inspiration. We must study the issue out in our *minds* and feel that the answer is right in our *hearts* (D&C 9:7–8).

The most common way the Lord communicates with individuals is through feelings and promptings. These promptings of the Spirit often include feelings of confidence, comfort, joy, and love. More dramatic forms of revelation are given from time to time. Some, such as **Moses** and

Joseph Smith, have talked with God face to face; others have entertained angels and had dreams or **visions**. Some have experienced an audible voice or inspired thoughts in their mind.

The Lord determines who receives revelation and when, how, and what is revealed. We become more receptive to revelation when we meet the personal conditions that the Lord has given us. These can include searching the scriptures, pondering, keeping the commandments, and asking in true faith. When revelation comes, it is often given in increments that allow us to spiritually mature.

Personal revelation is for our own benefit and edification. Revelation for the Church comes only through the properly constituted authorities.

SOURCES

McConkie, Mark L., ed. "How to Obtain Personal Revelation." *Doctrines of the Restoration: Sermons and Writings of Bruce R. McConkie.* Salt Lake City: Bookcraft, 1989. 151–58.

Oaks, Dallin H. "Teaching and Learning by the Spirit." *Ensign* 27 (March 1997): 6–14.

Packer, Boyd K. "Revelation in a Changing World." *Ensign* 19 (November 1989): 14–16.

Smith, Joseph. *Teachings of the Prophet Joseph Smith.* Selected by Joseph Fielding Smith. Salt Lake City: Deseret Book, 1969.

BRIAN L. SMITH

REVELATIONS, UNCANONIZED. Not all **revelations** have been canonized (officially accepted by vote as part of the **standard works**). For example, the **Doctrine and Covenants** contains only some of the revelations given through **Joseph Smith**. Because divine guidance, or inspiration, is a form of revelation, there is an infinite number of such communications. There are, however, dozens of recorded revelations that read like those in the Doctrine and Covenants, at least 45 of which have been published in *History of the Church*. Revelations selected for inclusion in the scriptural canon generally shed light on gospel doctrines and practices, while those not chosen tend to be more personal. Typical of the uncanonized revelations was a communication addressed to **Brigham Young** in 1838: "Verily thus saith the Lord, let my servant Brigham Young . . . there provide for his **family** . . . until I shall command him to go hence, and not to leave his family until they are amply provided for. Amen" (Smith, 3:23). Others during the Joseph Smith period include: **Reynolds Cahoon** to set his house in order (*HC*, 2:229), **Harvey Whitlock's** sins to be forgotten if he repents (*HC*, 2:315), **Orson Hyde's mission** to **Palestine**

revealed (*HC*, 4:113, 375–76), and the Twelve to edit *Times and Seasons* (*HC*, 4:503).

Revelation has continued to guide the Church since Joseph Smith's time. Some examples of uncanonized but accepted revelations include a **vision** of **Salt Lake** and future **temples** (*JD*, 1:133), instructions to perform temple work for the signers of the **Declaration of Independence** and others (*JD*, 19:229), inspiration regarding the calling of **general authorities** and the need for the Church to be guided through appointed channels (Clark, 2:348–54), admonition for **Saints** to trace **genealogy** and be sealed to ancestors (Clark, 3:251–60), Christ's personal instruction to **Lorenzo Snow** (Snow, 677), word of the Lord on **tithing** (Clark, 3:312), instruction to **Harold B. Lee** concerning the **welfare** plan (Lee, 124), and the **Proclamation on the Family** ("Family," 102).

SOURCES

Clark, James R., comp. *Messages of the First Presidency of The Church of Jesus Christ of Latter-day Saints.* 6 vols. Salt Lake City: Bookcraft, 1965–75.

Journal of Discourses [JD]. 26 vols. London: Latter-day Saints' Book Depot, 1854–86.

Lee, Harold B. Conference Report, (October 1972): 124.

Smith, Joseph. *History of The Church of Jesus Christ of Latter-day Saints.* Edited by B. H. Roberts. 2d ed. rev. 7 vols. Salt Lake City: Deseret Book, 1932.

"The Family: A Proclamation to the World." *Ensign* 25 (November 1995): 102.

Snow, LeRoi C. "An Experience of My Father's." *Improvement Era* 36 (September 1933): 677, 679.

RICHARD O. COWAN

REVENUE CUTTER. The *Revenue Cutter* was a medium-sized, leather-skinned boat used by the 1847 **Mormon pioneers** during the trek to the Great **Salt Lake Valley**. It was used to ferry men, materials, and freight across rivers and streams and was capable of carrying between 1,500 and 1,800 pounds. How the skiff got its name is not known. Prior to the American Revolution, however, a *Revenue Cutter* was a type of boat used to enforce the colonial navigation acts. An early definition of "revenue" was that of property belonging to everyone, implying that the boat was to be group-owned and used for the common good of the entire company. A "cutter" was a name for a small boat.

ALEXANDER L. BAUGH

REVIEW OF BOOKS ON THE BOOK OF MORMON. See FARMS REVIEW OF BOOKS, THE.

REVISION OF THE BIBLE. See JOSEPH SMITH TRANSLA-TION OF THE BIBLE.

REVIVALISM. One of the significant and unusual characteristics of religion in pre-**Civil War America** was revivalism. The first wide-spread revival in this land occurred between 1739 and the early 1740s. Another series of religious quickenings, sometimes referred to as the **Second Great Awakening**, began about 1800, reached its peak intensity in the 1830s and 1840s, and continued to the mid-1850s.

One of the ecclesiastical storm centers of early America was upstate and western **New York**. In 1819 and 1820, the period of the **First Vision**, there were more reports of revivals in that region than in any other section of America.

Three forces merged in the young republic, creating conditions favorable for perhaps the world's greatest revival. First, the United States was a land of religious pluralism. All major Christian faiths from western **Europe** were transplanted to this land. As early Protestant and Catholic settlers migrated westward, they carried with them multiple religious cultures. Second, a new birth of religious freedom followed the American Revolution, and this new liberty opened the door for increased diversity and a new evangelism. Third, many in this land had lost their identity with organized religion. This trend was accentuated by the westward expansion.

Responding to problems and challenges in the new nation, many religious leaders adopted various missionary techniques that proved successful during the Second Great Awakening. Using camp meetings, protracted meetings, and daily prayer meetings, itinerant ministers traveled throughout America awakening vast numbers to new religious responsibilities. Large numbers of people, including **Joseph Smith**, asked the question, "Which church should I join?" During this age of intense revivalism (between 1800 and 1860), Church membership in the United States increased from less than 10% to approximately 23%.

SOURCES

Backman, Milton V. *American Religions and the Rise of Mormonism.* 2d ed. Salt Lake City: Deseret Book, 1970.

———. "Awakenings in the Burned-Over District: New Light on the Historical Setting of the First Vision." *BYU Studies* 9 (1969): 301–20.

Hudson, Winthrop S. *Religion in America.* 3d ed. New York: Charles Scribner's Sons, 1965.

MILTON V. BACKMAN JR.

REXBURG, IDAHO. Rexburg was founded as a Latter-day Saint agricultural settlement in 1883 and named for prominent early settler Thomas Edwin Ricks. In 1888 Bannock **Stake** Academy was established, which later became **Ricks College** and later still, BYU–Idaho. A two-year institution, Ricks has served as a major educational and social center for thousands of Church members and an economic bulwark for the region. Rexburg's population in 1998 was 14,447. Ten stakes were centered in Rexburg, including five at Ricks College.

Latter-day Saint settlers colonized the Rexburg area during construction of the **Utah** and Northern Railroad from Utah to **Montana.** As Utah's prime agricultural land became less available to immigrants and subsequent generations of Latter-day Saint families, many Utahns looked to sparsely settled southeastern **Idaho** for economic opportunities.

Encouraging this migration, the **First Presidency** eventually appointed **William B. Preston,** president of the Cache Stake, to oversee the orderly colonization of the Rexburg area and advise the **Saints** to gather in villages, cooperate in building public works, and respect the **Indians'** water claims and rights on their reservations.

The Bannock **Ward,** centered in the Rexburg area, was organized on 18 December 1882. Rexburg's town site was selected on 11 March 1883. Construction began immediately on irrigation canals. The widely diffused water eventually transformed the region's arid plains into fertile fields yielding exceptional grain and hay crops and world-famous potatoes.

Vitriolic **anti-Mormonism,** aimed at eliminating polygamy and stifling Church members' political power in Idaho, intensified between 1884 and 1892. Idaho's antipolygamy test oath of 1885 deprived the Saints of the right to vote, serve as jurors, hold public office, and teach school. In 1888 hundreds of Saints in Rexburg and southeastern Idaho temporarily "resigned" their membership in the Church to circumvent the despised test oath and vote. Territorial marshals and deputies doggedly pursued and arrested polygamous Church leaders and members. To ensure convictions, an open venire system allowed the marshal to handpick jurists.

By 1900 Rexburg's population approached 1,400. A stake **tabernacle** designed in Italianate style was constructed in 1911. After spirited but failed attempts to move the Fremont County seat to Rexburg from St. Anthony, Rexburgites finally prevailed upon the legislature in 1913 to create Madison County and designate Rexburg as the new county's seat of government.

The collapse of the Teton Dam and subsequent disastrous flooding in June 1976 brought the Rexburg area to national attention. Thousands of volunteers from neighboring Idaho stakes and adjoining states flocked to help the stricken residents clean up and begin life anew.

SOURCES

Crowder, David L. *Rexburg, Idaho: The First 100 Years, 1883–1983*. Caldwell, Idaho: Caxton, 1983.

"Manuscript History of Fremont Stake." LDS Church Historical Department, Salt Lake City.

Wells, Merle W. *Anti-Mormonism in Idaho, 1872–1892*. Provo, Utah: Brigham Young University Press, 1978.

JAY G. BURRUP

REYNOLDS, ALICE LOUISE. Alice Louise Reynolds was the second female professor in the state of **Utah** and the first at **Brigham Young University**. She taught English **literature** for more than four decades. Born 1 April 1873 in **Salt Lake City** to George and Mary Ann Tuddenham Reynolds, she devoted her life to the pursuit and dissemination of knowledge. She started school when only four years old, graduating from Brigham Young Academy in 1890. She continued her education at various universities: Columbia, Cornell, and the Universities of **Michigan**, **California** at Berkeley, Chicago, London, and Paris. As a professor, she received high praise from students for her kindness and was renowned for her encyclopedic knowledge of world affairs. An advocate for **women's suffrage**, she was a delegate at many political conventions. Active in the **Relief Society**, she served on the general board and as editor of the *Relief Society Magazine* for seven years. Alice also wrote lessons for the Relief Society, **Sunday School**, and **MIA** organizations. She devoted 34 years to the Library Committee of BYU, overseeing the addition of more than seven thousand volumes to the library's holdings during that time. A loyal friend and intellectual, Alice died 6 December 1938.

SOURCES

Keele, Reba L. "Alice Louise Reynolds." *Sister Saints*. Edited by Vicky D. Burgess-Olson. Provo, Utah: Brigham Young University, 1978. 275–87.

Lyman, Amy Brown. *A Lighter of Lamps: The Life Story of Alice Louise Reynolds.* Provo, Utah: Alice Louise Reynolds Club, 1947.

Reynolds, Alice Louise. Autobiography, 1937. Archives Division, Historical Department of The Church of Jesus Christ of Latter-day Saints, Salt Lake City.

JULIE HUNSAKER

REYNOLDS, GEORGE. George Reynolds was a member of the First Council of **Seventy** and personal secretary to five presidents of the Church. He was born 1 January 1842 in **England** to George Reynolds and Julia Ann Tautz. As a boy, George became friends with a young servant maid, and upon learning she was a member of the Mormon Church, he asked to go with her to meetings. On his first visit he became convinced of the truthfulness of the gospel and requested that the **elders** of that **branch** baptize him; however, because he was only nine years old, he had to have his parents' approval, which they refused to give. For the next five years George attended Church as his parents would allow. When he learned of the Second Coming, he became fearful it would take place before he could be baptized. Therefore, at the age of 14, he went to a branch where he was unknown and was baptized the following Sunday.

From 1856 until 1865 George served in various positions in the Church, such as street preacher, **branch president**, and emigration clerk for the **British Mission**. Soon after immigrating to **Utah** in 1865, George became a secretary to **Brigham Young**. He eventually joined the **Nauvoo Legion**, became a regent of the **University of Deseret**, was an associate editor of the *Deseret News* and *Juvenile Instructor*, and became director of **ZCMI**, Zion's Savings Bank (see **Zion's Bank**), and **Deseret Telegraph** Line. After six years of service in the Church in Utah, George was called back to England to help edit the *Millennial Star.* He remained in England for only a short time, though, due to illness.

In 1874 Church leaders asked George to volunteer himself to be tried under the **Morrill Anti-Bigamy Act of 1862** to test the law's constitutionality, fully expecting that it would be thrown out as an infringement on the freedom of religion. Much to their surprise, he was convicted and served a year-and-a-half sentence (1879–81) in a Utah territorial penitentiary. While in prison, George did a great deal of writing, including work on his massive *Complete Concordance to the Book of Mormon,* which took him 21 years to complete.

In 1890 he was sustained a member of the First Council of the Seventy and served in that position until his death on 9 August 1909.

___

SOURCE

Van Orden, Bruce A. *George Reynolds: Prisoner for Conscience' Sake*. Salt Lake City: Deseret Book, 1992.

SYDNEY MARIE HUGHES

REYNOLDS V. UNITED STATES. See ANTI-POLYGAMY MOVEMENT.

RHEE HO NAM. Rhee Ho Nam, a vigorous and compassionate **pioneer** in the establishment and growth of The Church of Jesus Christ of Latter-day Saints in **Korea**, was born in Shimonoseki, **Japan**, on 28 February 1934. He and his family returned to Korea at the end of the **Korean War**. At age 20 he was taught the gospel by Calvin R. Beck, a U.S. military officer residing in Seoul, and was baptized by Alan Potts, another American LDS army officer, on 5 September 1954. He was confirmed a member of the Church by Elder **Harold B. Lee** of the Quorum of the Twelve **Apostles**.

In 1965, Brother Rhee was called to serve as first **counselor** in the Korean mission presidency. In 1967, he and his wife, Youn Soon, presented the first copies of the newly translated and published Korean language **Book of Mormon** to President **David O. McKay**. While in **Salt Lake City**, Brother and Sister Rhee were sealed by Elder **Gordon B. Hinckley** in the **Salt Lake Temple**, and they later received their **patriarchal blessings** from Church **Patriarch Eldred G. Smith**.

Rhee Ho Nam was selected in 1972 to serve as Korea area director of the **seminaries** and **institutes** of the Church. He organized more than 80 seminary classes throughout the country and established Institutes of Religion classes in Pusan, Taegu, Kwangju, and Seoul. On 8 March 1973, Brother Rhee was called by **Spencer W. Kimball**, president of the Council of the Twelve, to serve as president of the Seoul Korea **Stake**, the first stake of the Church to be organized on the Asian mainland.

Between 1978 and 1981, Brother Rhee served as president of the Korean Pusan **Mission**. After his release, he was called as **regional representative** of the Seoul region. He was active in preparations for the construction, groundbreaking (9 May 1983), and dedication of the Seoul

Korea **Temple** (14 December 1985). He conducted the first **endowment** session in that temple.

Rhee Ho Nam moved to the **United States** in 1986. He was later joined by his wife and four children. In 1987 he began teaching language classes as a faculty member of the Department of Asian and Near Eastern Languages at Brigham Young University; he has served as **bishop** of the Asian ward in **Provo, Utah**, and as a **branch** president in the **Missionary Training Center.**

SOURCES

Palmer, Spencer J. "Rhee Ho Nam: Hallmarks of a Korean Pioneer." *Pioneers in Every Land.* Salt Lake City: Deseret Book, 1997. 57–73.

Palmer, Spencer J., and Shirley H. Palmer. *The Korean Saints: Personal Stories of Trial and Triumph, 1950–1980.* Salt Lake City: Deseret Book, 1995. 184–90.

SPENCER J. PALMER

RHODE ISLAND. Important events in Rhode Island helped prepare the way for the **restoration** of the gospel in the latter days. Roger Williams, the founder of the Baptist movement in **America**, established Providence, Rhode Island, in 1636. He believed in freedom of thought and worship, separation of church and state, and equality for all men. These precepts eventually spread throughout America and helped provide an environment wherein the Church could one day be established.

In 1832 **Elder Orson Hyde** and **Samuel Smith** were the first Latter-day Saint missionaries to preach the gospel in Rhode Island. They did baptize some converts, but antagonists soon forced the elders to leave the state—throughout the rest of the nineteenth century small branches were sporadically organized and discontinued.

In 1905 a **branch** was established in Providence. By 1944 Elder **John A. Widtsoe** dedicated a remodeled private library as a branch **meetinghouse**. Rhode Island's first **stake** was created in Providence on 20 March 1977, with Morgan W. Lewis Jr. as president. By the beginning of the year 2000, the state had more than 3,214 members living in five **wards** and two branches.

SOURCE

1999–2000 Church Almanac. Salt Lake City: Deseret News, 1998. 236–37.

ROBERT L. MARROTT

RICH, BEN E. Benjamin Erastus Rich, a prominent missionary and long-time **mission president**, was born to **pioneers** Charles C. and Sarah Pea Rich on 7 November 1855 in Salt Lake City. He was one of his father's 51 children. He married Dianna Farr, daughter of pioneer **Lorin Farr**. Called as a missionary to **Great Britain** (1881), he later supervised the emigration of European converts.

Between **missions** he bought and managed newspapers in **Idaho** and was deeply involved in western and national politics. **Elder** Rich presided over three separate missions, one of them twice, spending more than 20 years of his life as a mission president. He presided over the **Southern States Mission** in 1898 and again in 1903 when his successor died. He presided over the Middle States Mission until it was dissolved in 1903 and over the **Eastern States Mission** from 1908 until he died in office 13 September 1913 in **New York City**.

As a mission president he wrote voluminously. Among his best-known titles are *A Friendly Discussion* and *Mr. Durrant of Salt Lake City*. Also published were nationally noted debates, including the *Bunner-Rich Debate* and another debate with Reverend Richard Harthey.

Rich presided at a highly volatile time and assisted in changing the **public image** of the Church through his association with high-profile figures such as **Theodore Roosevelt**. President Rich was charismatic, highly influential, and courageous in standing against injustices.

SOURCES

Anderson, Ted S. *The Southern States Mission and the Administration of Ben E. Rich, 1898–1908.* Provo, Utah: Brigham Young University, 1976.

Jenson, Andrew. *Latter-day Saint Biographical Encyclopedia.* 4 vols. 1901–36. Reprint, Salt Lake City: Western Epics, 1971. Vol. 3.

Romney, Thomas C. *The Gospel in Action.* Salt Lake City: Deseret Sunday School Union Board, 1949.

DAVID F. BOONE

RICH, CHARLES. Charles Coulson Rich was born 21 August 1809 at Campbell County, **Kentucky**, and spent most of his boyhood in **Indiana** before the family moved to Tazewell County, **Illinois**, in 1829. Tall of frame, Rich was an energetic, successful farmer. Latter-day Saint **missionaries** found the Riches in 1831, and the following year Charles was baptized. Like many early converts, his life became one of constant movement. He preached as a missionary; traveled to **Kirtland** to meet the **Prophet Joseph Smith**; moved to **Missouri**, where he participated in several military conflicts (including the Battle of Crooked River); and then sought new refuge in Illinois—sharing in many of the trials and toughening experiences of the Church during its early years.

The 1840s were a decade of expanded responsibility for Rich, who settled in **Nauvoo**, Illinois. He served on the **high council** and the city council and was a brigadier general in the **Nauvoo Legion**. During the **exodus**, starting in 1846 after the death of William Huntington, he presided over the branch at **Mount Pisgah** and was in charge of one of the companies that moved westward to the **Salt Lake Valley** in 1847. In 1849 he was called to be an **apostle**.

Charles Rich was a pioneer, missionary, politician, and family man. Along with Amasa M. Lyman, he was a founder of San Bernardino, California, in the 1850s. He had preached the gospel after his conversion, but as an apostle his missionary responsibilities increased in the early 1860s when, with **Amasa M. Lyman** and **George Q. Cannon**, he presided over the missions in **England** and on the Continent. After his return from **Europe**, he was assigned to lead the colonization of Bear Lake Valley, Idaho, and for the remainder of his life that area was his primary residence. In both California and Idaho he became a political leader, and for several years he attended the **Utah** territorial legislature. His marriage to Sarah DeArmon Pea in 1837 was followed by five **plural marriages** and eventually a total of 51 children.

A natural leader who inspired confidence and provided an example of remarkable ability combined with unshakable commitment, Rich died on 17 November 1883 in Paris, Bear Lake, Idaho.

Sources

Arrington, Leonard J. *Charles C. Rich: Mormon General and Western Frontiersman.* Provo, Utah: Brigham Young University Press, 1974.

Evans, John Henry. *Charles Coulson Rich: Pioneer Builder of the West.* New York: Macmillan, 1936.

Leonard J. Arrington

RICHARDS, FRANKLIN D. Franklin Dewey Richards, compiler of the **Pearl of Great Price** and president of the **Quorum** of the Twelve **Apostles**, was born 2 April 1821 in Richmond, **Massachusetts**. He was baptized in June 1838 and at age 17 he left home to join his 15-year-old brother, George, who had been baptized a few months earlier and had gone to **Missouri**. When Franklin reached Missouri, he learned of the tragedy at **Haun's Mill**, where a vicious mob had slain nearly a score of innocent people. Their bodies had been placed in a well, which served as their grave. Upon reaching Haun's Mill, he was horrified to learn that George was among the dead. During the years ahead, Franklin lost another brother as a result of the rigors of the **Mormon Battalion** trek, and two of his children died from privations suffered during the **exodus** from **Nauvoo** to **Winter Quarters**.

Undaunted by these losses and spurred by a testimony of the divinity of Mormonism, Franklin Richards served four **missions** to **Great Britain**, three times as president. He arranged passage for more than 30,000 **Saints** going to **Zion** and helped establish the **Perpetual Emigrating Fund**. He was called to the Quorum of the Twelve on 12 February 1849.

Feeling the importance of acquainting Church members in Britain—who at the time outnumbered those in the **United States**—with some of the **revelations** given to **Joseph Smith**, Elder Richards published a pamphlet called *Pearl of Great Price* in 1851. It contained the books of **Moses** and **Abraham**, writings of Joseph Smith, a poem ("Oh Say, What Is Truth?"), excerpts from the **Doctrine and Covenants**, and the 13 Articles of Faith. In 1880, nearly 30 years later, the Pearl of Great Price became one of the **standard works** of the Church. Richards also served as **Church historian** and president of the state genealogical and historical societies. On 13 September 1889, he became president of the Quorum of the Twelve and served in that calling until his death on 9 December 1899 in Ogden, Utah.

SOURCES

Cowley, Matthias F. *Prophets and Patriarchs.* Chattanooga, Tenn.: Ben E. Rich, 1902. 237.

Flake, Lawrence R. *Prophets and Apostles of the Last Dispensation.* Provo, Utah: Religious Studies Center, Brigham Young University, 2001. 333–35.

Jenson, Andrew. *Latter-day Saint Biographical Encyclopedia.* 4 vols. 1901–36. Reprint, Salt Lake City: Western Epics, 1971. 1:115.

LAWRENCE R. FLAKE

RICHARDS, FRANKLIN S. Franklin Snyder Richards (1849–1934), an attorney, served for 50 years as the first general counsel of the Church. He held this office during a period of intense persecutions in the 1880s, through **Utah statehood**, and during the Church's transition to a more accepted religion.

Born to **apostle Franklin D. Richards** and Jane Snyder Richards on 20 June 1849, he was one of the first children born in **Salt Lake City**. In

1869 **Brigham Young** asked him to study law and become clerk of the Weber County Probate Court. He established himself as a skilled attorney and in 1879 was retained by the Church to help probate the late Brigham Young's estate. He continued as general counsel for the Church until his death on 4 September 1934 in Salt Lake City.

Richards defended against the **polygamy** prosecutions of the 1880s up to the Supreme Court. He lobbied Congress on behalf of Church interests and played a role in securing Utah statehood in 1896. Richards and his wife, Emily Tanner, supported **women's** rights and were instrumental in placing suffrage in the state's initial 1894 constitution.

Richards later helped establish the Corporation of the **Presiding Bishopric** in 1916 and the Corporation of the **First Presidency** in 1923.

SOURCE

Driggs, Kenneth. "'Lawyers of Their Own to Defend Them'": The Legal Career of Franklin Snyder Richards." *Journal of Mormon History* 21 (Fall 1995): 84–125.

KENNETH DRIGGS

RICHARDS, GEORGE F. George Franklin Richards was born 23 February 1861 in Farmington, **Utah**, to **Elder Franklin D. Richards** and Nanny Longstroth. George was ordained an **elder** at age 15. He was a **counselor** in the Tooele **Stake** presidency for 16 years and became a **patriarch** at age 32. He was ordained an apostle on 9 April 1906, served on the **YMMIA** general board for nine years, and was president of the **European Mission** during the difficult years of **World War I** (1916–19). In 1921 he became president of the **Salt Lake Temple** and served as acting **patriarch to the Church** for five years; in 1945 he became president of the Quorum of the Twelve.

Brother Richards and his wife, Alice Robinson, were the parents of ten daughters and five sons. One of those sons, LeGrand, became a member of the Quorum of the Twelve two years after his father's passing, making three generations of apostles in that family. George F. Richards possessed a sense of honor, mellowness, and sweetness of disposition and was revered for his kindness and his dedication to the gospel. He died 8 August 1950 in Salt Lake City.

SOURCES

Flake, Lawrence R. *Prophets and Apostles of the Last Dispensation.* Provo, Utah: Religious Studies Center, Brigham Young University, 2001. 341–44.

Hinckley, Bryant S. "George Franklin Richards." *Improvement Era* 35 (April 1932): 327.

Richards, LeGrand. *Just to Illustrate.* Salt Lake City: Bookcraft, 1961.

Smith, Joseph Fielding. "President George F. Richards: A Tribute." *Relief Society Magazine* 37 (October 1950): 661–62.

LAWRENCE R. FLAKE

RICHARDS, LEGRAND. Third in a direct line of **apostles,** Elder LeGrand Richards had a grandfather (**Franklin D. Richards**) and a father (**George F. Richards**) who were also members of the **Quorum** of the Twelve. Born 6 February 1886 in Farmington, **Utah,** Elder Richards began his full-time Church service in 1905 as he accepted a **mission** call to the **Netherlands.** In 1914, at the age of only 27, he returned to his former mission field in Holland as president. In 1926 he served a short mission to the eastern states, and in 1931 he was called by President **Heber J. Grant** to move to **California** and serve as president of the Hollywood **Stake.** After three years in California, he again accepted a call as **mission president**—this time to the southern states. A year after returning to **Salt Lake City,** while serving as **bishop** of the University **Ward,** he received a call to become **presiding bishop** of the Church. On 10 April 1952, after 14 years in that office, he was called to the Quorum of the Twelve, where he rendered outstanding service for more than three decades.

Elder Richards became well-known throughout the Church as the author of *A Marvelous Work and a Wonder,* a missionary book that he published without monetary remuneration. It has sold more than three million copies and has helped in the conversion of thousands of people. His unbounded energy despite advancing years caused his fellow apostle **Harold B. Lee** to refer to Elder Richards himself as "a marvelous work and a wonder."

When Elder Richards died at Salt Lake City on 11 January 1983, he had lived one month short of 97 years.

SOURCES

Avant, Gerry. "Love Characterized Elder Richards' Life." *Church News,* 23 January 1983, 3.

Flake, Lawrence R. *Prophets and Apostles of the Last Dispensation.* Provo, Utah: Religious Studies Center, Brigham Young University, 2001. 489–91.

Walker, Joseph. "Beloved Apostle: Will Become Longest-Lived General Authority." *Church News,* 12 June 1982, 8.

LAWRENCE R. FLAKE

RICHARDS, STEPHEN L. Stephen L Richards served as first counselor to President David O. McKay (1951–59), **apostle** (1917–59), lawyer, educator, corporation executive, husband, and father. He nobly carried forward the Richards family legacy of faith, begun by his grandfather, **Willard Richards**, who offered his own life for the **Prophet Joseph Smith's** "on that sultry summer day" in **Carthage Jail** when Joseph and **Hyrum Smith** were martyred ("Appreciation," 497).

Stephen was born 18 June 1879 in Mendon, Cache County, **Utah**, to parents of remarkable faith, culture, and refinement (*Leaders*, 33). On 21 February 1900, he married Irene Smith Merrill—a woman of superior intellect, testimony, and artistic temperament. For a short time the newly married couple lived in **Idaho**, where he was a rancher and public school principal.

In 1904 Stephen L graduated cum laude from the University of Chicago law school. He and his family moved to the **Salt Lake Valley**, where he was known by some as one of the "ablest young [men] practicing before the Utah bar" (*Leaders*, 39). Throughout his life he was known for his wisdom as an eminent businessman, being involved in numerous Utah commercial, educational, and civic institutions. He loved nature with its green valleys, high mountains, fresh lakes, and pines (Flake, 105).

As companions in the superintendency of the **Sunday School** general board in 1909, Brother Richards and David O. McKay formed a lasting friendship. President McKay later said of Stephen: "Friends[hip] . . . like faith, is a gift of God. Stephen L's friendship is genuine—it is pure gold" (quoted in Flake, 106).

For 42 years as a **general authority**, Elder Richards made a significant contribution in many ways, serving as chairman of the Church **Radio, Publicity, and Mission Literature Committee** (1935–51); directing the missionary program (1951–59); handling matters of legal delicacy with leaders of government and industry; powerfully and persuasively advocating home and family; and acting as a mentor to **Gordon B. Hinckley**. Elder Hinckley said of Stephen L Richards, "I have partaken of his unfailing courtesy. . . . I have marveled at his matchless wisdom, his incisive mind, his persuasive expression. . . . His love of God was the polar star of his life, and his desire to help his fellow men his chief ambition. . . . [He was] a prince among men in the vineyard of the Lord" ("President," 489). President Richards died 19 May 1959 in **Salt Lake City**.

SOURCES

Anderson, Joseph. *Prophets I Have Known*. Salt Lake City: Deseret Book, 1973. 145–46.

Flake, Lawrence R. *Prophets and Apostles of the Last Dispensation*. Provo, Utah: Religious Studies Center, Brigham Young University, 2001. 209–211.

Hinckley, Gordon B. "An Appreciation of Stephen L Richards." *Improvement Era* 54 (July 1951): 496–99.

"President Stephen L Richards 1879–1959." *Improvement Era* 62 (June 1959): 417, 489.

"Stephen L Richards." *Our Leaders*. Arr. Doyle L. Green. Salt Lake City: Deseret Book, 1951. 31–46.

JOHN M. R. COVEY

RICHARDS, WILLARD. Willard Richards was born 24 June 1804 in Hopkinson, **Massachusetts**, the last of 11 children born to Joseph and Rhoda Richards. At age four Willard fell and suffered a head injury, which caused some lifelong paralysis and muscle tremor. Limited physical capabilities prompted him to turn his attention to book learning. He obtained a teacher's certificate at age 16 and taught school. He did additional studies in mechanics, science, and music, and he performed as a clarinetist with the Massachusetts Militia Band.

After his sister died, Willard began a study of medicine, including herbal remedies. At age 30 he spent two months at the Thomson Infirmary in Boston and became an agent for Thomson's Patent Rights herbal medicine. He practiced medicine and became known as Dr. Willard Richards.

As a teenager he had applied to join his parents' Congregational faith but was rejected. Not until the summer of 1836, when his cousins Brigham and **Joseph Young** visited the Holliston area as missionaries, did Richards show interest in organized religion again. They taught him about the **Book of Mormon** and the restored gospel. He was baptized on 31 December 1836.

Richards was called on a mission to **New York** and New England with **Brigham Young**, and later served a mission in the British Isles with Heber C. Kimball. In Britain he was ordained as a member of the **Quorum** of the Twelve **Apostles** in 1840 (D&C 118:6). He also met and married Jennetta (whose name was also Richards) while he was in England.

Elder Richards settled with his wife and son in **Nauvoo**, where he served as land agent, member of the city council, and editor of *Times and Seasons*. In 1841 he was called by the **Prophet Joseph Smith** to be his personal secretary. In December 1842 he was called as the **Church historian** and recorder, a position he held for the rest of his life, and was with the Prophet at **Carthage Jail** when Joseph and **Hyrum Smith** were killed. As a personal secretary and Church historian, **Elder** Richards was responsible for keeping the Prophet's diary and was involved in the development of the history of the Church, which was later edited by **B. H. Roberts** and published as the *History of The Church of Jesus Christ of Latter-day Saints.*

Elder Richards's wife, Jennetta, died at Nauvoo. He and the rest of his family spent the winter of 1847 in **Winter Quarters,** and he was with the first company of **Saints** who entered the **Salt Lake Valley.** When the First Presidency was reorganized in the winter of 1847 and sustained by the body of the Church about three weeks later at the Kanesville Tabernacle, which had been built for the occasion, he was called as second counselor to President Brigham Young. He also served as territorial secretary and founding editor of the *Deseret News.* He died in Salt Lake City 11 March 1854 at the age of 49.

SOURCE

Noall, Claire. *Intimate Disciple: A Portrait of Willard Richards.* 1951.

H. DEAN GARRETT

RICHMOND, MISSOURI. See RAY COUNTY, MISSOURI.

RICHMOND JAIL. After the Saints at **Far West** surrendered to the **Missouri** State Militia, 53 Latter-day Saint men were held for trial before Judge Austin A. King's Court of Inquiry (*Correspondence,* 97). Most of these men were imprisoned in the unfinished Richmond Courthouse. Joseph Smith, Hyrum Smith, Sidney Rigdon, Parley P. Pratt, Lyman Wight, Amasa Lyman, and George Q. Robinson were chained together in an unfinished cabin next to the courthouse because the jail was full. King's court lasted from 12 to 28 November 1838 (Pratt, 209–10). During this period, the Latter-day Saints were supervised by "guards . . . composed . . . of the most noisy foul-mouthed, vulgar, disgraceful rabble that ever defiled the earth" (Pratt, 210). Chained together, the Latter-day Saints listened to these vulgarities night after night until the situation became unbearable (Jessee, 368). One night Joseph Smith arose and spoke "in a voice of thunder": "Silence, ye fiends of the infernal pit. In the name of **Jesus Christ** I rebuke you, and command you to be still; I will not live another minute and hear such language. Cease such talk, or you or I die this instant" (Pratt, 211). The guards remained quiet until the guard was changed.

Eventually all but 10 men were excused by King's court. Joseph Smith and five others were sent to **Liberty Jail**, and **Parley P. Pratt**, Luman Gibbs, Darwin Chase, Norman Shearer, and Morris Phelps remained in Richmond prison to await their trial for treason, murder, and larceny (Smith, 3:212). Soon Darwin Chase and Norman Shearer were released; however, on 24 April 1839, King Follett was jailed with the others (Pratt, 234; Cannon, 180).

In May 1839, after more than six months of confinement at Richmond, the prisoners received a change of venue and were moved to Columbia, where after several more months of tedious confinement, two of the remaining four prisoners made their escape on 4 July 1839. King Follett was recaptured and remained in Columbia prison until October 1839 (Cannon, 180). During his confinement Luman Gibbs apostatized and acted as a spy for the prison guards at Richmond. After the escape he was acquitted on account of his cooperation with his jailers (Pratt, 234–37).

SOURCES

Cannon, Donald Q. "The King Follett Discourse: Joseph Smith's Greatest Sermon in Historical Perspective." *BYU Studies* 18 (Winter 1978): 179–92.

Document Containing the Correspondence, Orders &c. in Relation to the Disturbances with the Mormons. Published by Order of the General Assembly. Fayette, Mo.: Boon's Lick Democrat, 1841.

Jessee, Dean C., ed. *The Personal Writings of Joseph Smith.* Salt Lake City: Deseret Book, 1984.

Pratt, Parley P. *Autobiography of Parley P. Pratt.* Edited by Parley P. Pratt Jr. Salt Lake City: Deseret Book, 1985.

Smith, Joseph. *History of The Church of Jesus Christ of Latter-day Saints.* Edited by B. H. Roberts. 2d ed. rev. 7 vols. Salt Lake City: The Church of Jesus Christ of Latter-day Saints, 1932–51. 3:212.

CLARK V. JOHNSON

RICKS COLLEGE. Ricks College (later BYU–Idaho), owned and operated by The Church of Jesus Christ of Latter-day Saints, is an accredited, two-year, degree-granting institution of higher education located in the town of **Rexburg, Idaho**—an agricultural community of the upper Snake River Valley near Yellowstone and Grand Teton National parks. The main campus is situated on a 255-acre plot south of town and constitutes the largest private two-year college in **America**, with an enrollment in 1999 of more than 8,600 full-time students from 40 countries and all 50 states. It grants associate degrees in arts and sciences, as well as certificates and degrees in specialty programs, and prepares students to pursue baccalaureate degrees at universities and four-year colleges by offering a variety of general education courses.

The history of Ricks College is one of survival and is a tribute to the tenacity and optimism of its founders, leaders, teachers, and students in the face of perils and difficult eras. **Railroad** entrepreneur Thomas E. Ricks, for whom Ricks College was named, was called by the **First Presidency** to colonize the upper Snake River Valley in 1882. On 15 March 1883 a townsite was dedicated and officially named Rexburg ("Rex" was the German ancestral name of the Ricks family). **Anti-Mormon** sentiment was prevalent in the area at the time, and Latter-day Saints, faced with the prospect of sending their children to a school administered by antagonists, set up their own educational institution, as the Church was encouraging the stakes to do. Bannock **Stake** Academy was established as an elementary school housed in the Rexburg First **Ward** chapel on 12 November 1888. Three teachers were appointed to provide basics in education and spiritual growth.

Between 1898 and 1903 the name of the school was changed three times—first to the Fremont Stake Academy, next to Smith Academy, and then to Ricks Academy in honor of Thomas Ricks. On 25 June 1900 President **George Q. Cannon** of the First Presidency laid the cornerstone for a new academy building. Named after the school's first principal, the **Jacob Spori** Building was dedicated on 12 November 1906 and was for many years the school's main facility (as well as landmark), containing housing administrative offices, a library, and classrooms. In 1915 college classes were taught for the first time at the school, and eventually the elementary and high school curriculums were suspended. Shortly after George S. Romney was appointed principal of Ricks Academy in 1917, the school was granted state certification (allowing its graduates to teach in the state of Idaho) and became Ricks Normal College, with Principal Romney as its first president. In 1923 the school was given the name Ricks College.

The economic conditions of the 1920s and 1930s that so adversely affected America also took their toll on Rexburg and Ricks College. During the depression it was feared that the school would be closed. The Church had offered it to the state of Idaho but was turned down. The threat of closure had plagued the school almost since its inception— Bannock Stake Academy's founding principal, Jacob Spori, had given up part of his salary to help cover mounting debts and forestall extinction. But with the general easing of economic hardship toward the end of **World War II**, as well as self-sacrifice on the part of school administrators and faculty, the Church decided to keep Ricks College as part of the **Church Educational System**.

Under the presidency of John L. Clarke (1944–71) the college greatly expanded but not without facing continuing ups and downs. By 1949 the Church had authorized the addition of a third and fourth year to the college curriculum, and in the spring of 1950 the school's first bachelor's degrees were granted. In 1956, however, the upper-division courses were discontinued by action of the Church Board of **Education**, and the school became a two-year institution again. Faculty, students, and members of the Rexburg community received another blow in 1957 when they learned that the Church was considering moving Ricks College to **Idaho Falls**, a larger town thirty miles south of Rexburg and the site of an LDS **temple**. After significant lobbying on the part of college supporters, and careful review of the issues by Church leaders during a four-year period, Ricks College stayed in Rexburg. During President Clarke's exceptional tenure, student enrollment increased from 200 students to more than 5,300, and additional buildings were constructed.

After President Clarke's retirement, Ricks College was presided over by men who cemented a close relationship with Church leaders and the Church Education System; most either became, or already were, general authorities of the Church. Future **apostle Henry B. Eyring** served as president from 1971–78 and guided the school's transition from the status of a regional two-year college to the nation's largest private junior college. He was succeeded by Bruce C. Hafen (1978–85), a future member of the First Quorum of the Seventy, who oversaw the construction of the school's Fine Arts Center, Livestock Center, Outdoor Learning Center, and Viking Stadium. Under future Seventy's Quorum member Joe J. Christiansen (1985–89), Ricks reached its enrollment capacity as set by the Church Board of Education. Under the direction of Steven D. Bennion (1989–97), two new academic divisions of the college were created, the use of computers by students and faculty was increased, and ground was broken for the **John Taylor** building to house the religion and humanities departments. Seventy's Quorum member David A. Bednar (1997–) presided over the dedication of the John Taylor Building and the construction of the new **Spencer W. Kimball** Student and Administrative Services Building.

As declared in its mission statement, Ricks College (BYU–Idaho) is dedicated to building testimonies of the restored gospel of Jesus Christ; providing high-quality education for students of diverse interests and abilities; preparing students for further education and employment; and maintaining a wholesome academic, social, and spiritual environment. In the year 2000 the First Presidency announced that Ricks College would become a four-year school known as Brigham Young University–Idaho.

SOURCES

Crowder, David L. *The Spirit of Ricks: A History of Ricks College.* Rexburg, Idaho: Ricks College Press, 1997.

Jolley, JoAnn. "Rexburg and Ricks College." *Ensign* 14 (January 1984): 21–27.

ANDREW C. SKINNER

RIDGES, JOSEPH. Joseph Harris Ridges, the builder of the **Tabernacle organ** in **Salt Lake City**, was born 25 (or 27) April 1827 in Hampshire, **England**. He was trained in organ building as a youth in Southampton, **England**, and built his first organ in **Australia**, where he was converted to the restored gospel. Having come to the attention of **Brigham Young**, he moved to Salt Lake City, where he was asked to design an organ suitable for the tabernacle. When the tabernacle was opened for use in 1867, Ridges's organ was one-third complete. It was finished in 1877 with 2,638 pipes. Through the years, the organ has been rebuilt, electrified, and enlarged to 10,814 pipes. Joseph Ridges died 7 March 1914 in Salt Lake City.

SOURCES

Church History in the Fulness of Times. Salt Lake City: The Church of Jesus Christ of Latter-day Saints, 1989. 399–400.

Mullen, Robert. *The Latter-day Saints: The Mormons Yesterday and Today.* Garden City, N.Y.: Doubleday, 1966.

GERALD L. HOMER

RIGDON, SIDNEY. Sidney Rigdon, a key figure in the early Church, was a powerful, persuasive orator, a scribe for **Joseph Smith's** revision of the Bible, and first counselor in the **First Presidency**. He was born 19 February 1793 in St. Clair Township, Alleghany County, **Pennsylvania**. He married Phebe Brook on 12 June 1820 and they became the parents of 11 children. He was a tanner by trade.

A popular Baptist preacher in Pittsburgh, Pennsylvania, Sidney moved to Mentor, **Ohio**, where he left the Baptist faith altogether and joined Alexander Campbell's movement, which later became known as the Disciples of Christ or **Campbellites**. While living in Mentor, Sidney and Phebe were introduced to the LDS Church by **Parley P. Pratt**. Parley had been an earlier associate of Sidney's and was traveling through Ohio on his way to preach the gospel to the **Lamanites** in Missouri. Initially Sidney was quite skeptical of the new religious ideas preached to him. When he read the **Book of Mormon**, however, he saw the truth, and he and his wife were baptized on 14 November 1830.

Feeling compelled to meet the founder of his new religion, he traveled to **Fayette, New York**, to find Joseph Smith. His life would never be the same thereafter. He was soon called by revelation to assist Joseph as scribe in the revision of the Bible (D&C 35). He helped Joseph and the New York **Saints** gather to the **Kirtland, Ohio**, area and was called to travel with Joseph to **Jackson County, Missouri**, in 1831 (D&C 52). On 2 August he dedicated **Independence, Missouri**, as the land of **Zion**, pronouncing "this land consecrated and dedicated to the Lord for a possession and inheritance for the Saints" (D&C 58). In March 1832 in Kirtland, Ohio, Sidney was ordained to the presidency of the high priesthood as first counselor—a position he held until 1844.

He shared many sacred and wonderful revelations with Joseph—including the vision of the degrees of glory (D&C 76)—and helped organize the first edition of Joseph's revelations, known as the "**The Book of Commandments**." In 1833 he was called as "spokesman" for Joseph and the Church and was known as a "defender of the truth." Rigdon was promised that he would be "mighty in expounding all scriptures" (D&C 100). At the dedication of the **Kirtland Temple** 27 March 1836 he spoke for more than two hours and held the large audience spellbound. It was said of him by his contemporaries that when he spoke, "his action was graceful, his language copious, fluent in utterance, with articulation clear and musical" (Chase, 24).

Joseph and Sidney were often together during the most severe times of persecution. In March 1832 in **Hiram, Ohio**, Sidney was hauled from his home, tied behind a horse, and dragged along the frozen ground. He was rendered unconscious and sustained severe injuries to his head. When Joseph first saw him bloodied on the ground, he thought he was dead. Sidney was delirious for two days and suffered ill health the remainder of his life. Again at the hands of unruly and unjust men,

Sidney, with Joseph and others, was jailed in 1838 at Liberty, Missouri, for about three months in the dead of winter.

In 1834 Rigdon assisted in recruiting volunteers for **Zion's Camp** and, while the Prophet was in Missouri with the camp, he had charge of affairs in Kirtland, including the construction of the temple. He was a leading teacher at the Kirtland **School of the Elders** and helped arrange the revelations for publication in the 1835 edition of the **Doctrine and Covenants**. Under the Prophet's direction, Sidney helped compose and deliver some of the doctrinally rich **Lectures on Faith**.

In the wake of the failure of the **Kirtland Safety Society** and threats from apostates, Rigdon, along with Joseph Smith and other Saints, fled to **Far West, Missouri**, in 1838. There Rigdon delivered two famous volatile speeches, the "Salt Sermon" and the Independence Day oration, both of which stirred up fears and controversy in Missouri and helped contribute to the **extermination order** and the siege at Far West.

Rigdon made many trips with the Prophet to fulfill **missions** and Church business, including a proselyting mission to Upper **Canada** in 1833, trips to **Massachusetts** twice, and a visit to **Washington, D.C.**, in 1839 to seek redress of losses suffered in Missouri.

He took an active part in the founding of **Nauvoo**. He was elected to the Nauvoo City Council and served also as city attorney and postmaster. Despite his many appointments, however, he was nearly silent during this time and often sick. He was accused of being associated with **John C. Bennett** and other enemies of the Church in their evil plans to displace Joseph Smith, but this he always denied. He did not endorse the principle of **plural marriage**, although he never came out in open opposition to it. Joseph Smith eventually lost confidence in Rigdon and in 1843 wished to reject him as a counselor but, because of the intercession of **Hyrum Smith**, retained him in office.

Early in 1844, when Joseph Smith became a candidate for president of the **United States**, Rigdon was nominated as his running mate. As persecution mounted against the leaders of the Church, Sidney removed to Pittsburgh to distance himself from Joseph and the Church and to campaign. He was there when news arrived of Joseph Smith's murder. He hastened to Nauvoo to offer himself as a "guardian of the Church." His claims were duly considered, but at a memorable meeting in Nauvoo on 8 August 1844, in which many Church members miraculously saw Joseph's face in Brigham Young's visage, he was rejected as guardian, and the Twelve **Apostles** were sustained as the head of the Church. He undertook to establish a rival leadership and in September 1844 was excommunicated. He left with a few disciples for Pennsylvania, where they organized the short-lived Church of Christ. In 1863 he made another effort, founding the Church of Jesus Christ of the Children of Zion, which continued into the 1880s. From 1847 to his death 14 July 1876, Rigdon resided in Friendship, New York, usually in a state of emotional imbalance and unhappiness.

SOURCES

Backman, Milton V., Jr. *The Heavens Resound: A History of the Latter-day Saints in Ohio, 1830–1838.* Salt Lake City: Deseret Book, 1983.

Chase, Daryl. "Sidney Rigdon—Early Mormon." Master's thesis, University of Chicago, 1931.

Encyclopedia of Mormonism. Edited by Daniel H. Ludlow. 4 vols. New York: Macmillan, 1992.

Jenson, Andrew. *Latter-day Saint Biographical Encyclopedia.* 4 vols. 1901–36. Reprint, Salt Lake City: Western Epics, 1971. 1:31.

McKiernan, F. Mark. *The Voice of One Crying in the Wilderness: Sidney Rigdon, Religious Reformer 1793–1876.* Lawrence, Kansas: Coronado Press, 1971.

Roberts, B. H. *The Rise and Fall of Nauvoo.* Salt Lake City: Bookcraft, 1965.

Van Wagoner, Richard S. *Sidney Rigdon: A Portrait of Religious Excess.* Salt Lake City: Signature Books, 1994.

CRAIG K. MANSCILL

RIVERBOATS. Between 1830 and 1869, riverboats played key roles in transporting Latter-day Saint converts, missionaries, and agents. Rivers were **America**'s first interstate travel-ways, particularly the **Ohio**, **Mississippi**, and **Missouri Rivers**. When **Saints** first moved from **Kirtland** to **Jackson County** in 1831, they traveled by river steamers. Between 1840 and 1845, 4,000 European converts disembarked from sailing ships at **New Orleans** and reached **Nauvoo** aboard Mississippi steamers, including the Church's *Maid of Iowa*. After the Nauvoo **exodus** in 1846, Latter-day Saint immigrants went up river from New Orleans to **St. Louis** in one to two weeks, then up the Missouri River to outfitting points near present-day Omaha, **Nebraska**—another one- to two-week passage.

Between 1840 and 1855, 81 organized LDS companies traveled on steamers with such names as the *Julia Chouteau, Robert Campbell, Pride of the West, Arabia, Omaha,* and *West Wind.* Of the 45 steamboats identified as being used by the Saints, 44 were side-wheelers and 1 a stern-wheeler. By 1855 LDS emigrants disembarked in ports in the eastern United States and moved west by **railroad,** but they still used Missouri riverboats to reach the outfitting camps. Poor travelers went as deck passengers, those with money as cabin passengers. River steamers provided cheap transportation but not safety. In 1852 the *Saluda* blew up at Lexington, **Missouri**, killing about two dozen Saints out of 90 going upriver to join wagon trains headed for **Utah**.

SOURCE

Sonne, Conway B. *Saints on the Seas: A Maritime History of Mormon Migration, 1830–1890.* Salt Lake City: University of Utah Press, 1983. 89–112.

WILLIAM G. HARTLEY

RLDS. See REORGANIZED CHURCH OF JESUS CHRIST OF LATTER DAY SAINTS.

ROBERTS, B. H. Brigham Henry Roberts, the Church's most inclusive historian, as well as one of its most articulate defenders and effective doctrinal expositors, was born in Warrington, Lancashire, **England**, 13 March 1857.

He emigrated to **America** at age 9, crossed the plains to the **Great Basin**, and was reunited with his convert mother who had emigrated the year before. He then became a silver miner and a blacksmith, as well as the valedictorian of the University of Deseret. He married and abruptly went on a **mission** to the northern states. From that point on, his life was intertwined with the Church. He became a journalist-editor, an orator, and acting mission president in the southern states. He also accepted a lifetime calling as a member of the First Council of the **Seventy**. An outspoken Democrat, he was prominent in the Enabling Convention that led to Utah's **statehood** and was elected to the National House of Representatives in 1898. Due to a bitter press campaign, he was not seated on grounds of his practice of **plural marriage** (he had three wives).

He served as a **chaplain** in **World War I** and was president of the **Eastern States Mission** from 1923 to 1927. As assistant Church historian, in 1930 he completed *A Comprehensive History of The Church of Jesus Christ of Latter-day Saints,* a six-volume treatise that had begun as a series of articles in *Americana Magazine.* He also edited for publication the seven-volume *History of The Church of Jesus Christ of Latter-day Saints.* His historical writing demonstrates a bent for fairness and frankness in dealing with the turbulent history of the Church.

In his theological writing, Roberts confronted sensitive and controversial topics. His most impressive piece, published as *Mormon Doctrine of Deity*, developed from a debate with a Catholic priest, Van der Donkt. Here Roberts demonstrated a grasp of the main western philosophical and theological traditions and defended the distinctions of what he called the New Dispensation. He attempted to show not only the divinity but the deity of **Jesus Christ** as the full **revelation** of the nature of God.

Throughout his mature life he was a dedicated student and analyst of the **Book of Mormon**, struggling with both the modern and ancient contexts of the book. This is shown in his *New Witnesses for God* and his posthumously published *Studies in the Book of Mormon*. By his death at age 76, he had written more than 1,000 articles and printed sermons, **pamphlets**, and tracts, as well as 30 books. His last expansive summary of doctrinal writing, interlaced with biblical and Book of Mormon texts, was in manuscript form at his death, titled *The Truth, the Way, the Life*. With commentary by specialists in various fields, it has since been published.

After a long struggle with diabetes, Roberts died 27 September 1933 in Salt Lake City. Through all his writings, he affirmed that Mormonism is a world movement, not an encrusted sect, that it is open to all truth, and that in its second century would pervade more of the world than it did its first.

SOURCES

Madsen, Truman G. *Defender of the Faith: The B. H. Roberts Story.* Salt Lake City: Bookcraft, 1980.

Roberts, Brigham H. *The Truth, the Way, the Life.* Edited by John W. Welch. Provo, Utah: BYU Studies, 1994.

TRUMAN G. MADSEN

ROBERTSON, LEROY J. Leroy Jasper Robertson, one of the most prominent American composers of the twentieth century, was born 21 December 1896 in Fountain Green, **Utah**. He distinguished himself as a composer in virtually every musical form, winning several prestigious composition prizes for his best works. With academic degrees from the New England Conservatory and the University of Southern **California**, he headed both the **Brigham Young University** and **University of Utah music** departments. For 36 years he was a member of the general Church Music Committee. Aside from eight **hymns** in the 1985 LDS hymnbook,

Oratorio from the Book of Mormon is likely his best known work among the **Saints**. Leroy Robertson died 25 July 1971 in **Salt Lake City**.

SOURCES

Davidson, Karen Lynn. *Our Latter-day Hymns: The Stories and the Messages*. Salt Lake City: Deseret Book, 1988. 431–32.

Wilson, Marian R. *Leroy Robertson: Music Giant from the Rockies*. Salt Lake City: Blue Ribbon Publications, 1996.

GERALD L. HOMER

ROBIDOUX, ANTOINE. Antoine Robidoux, an **explorer** and fur trader who worked in the **Utah** area before the coming of the **Mormon pioneers**, was an important influence on the settlement of the West. He was one of the first American fur traders out of Taos (in what is now **New Mexico**), possibly as early as 1822. Robidoux explored and trapped all over the West and established two trading posts, one on the Gunnison River in **Colorado** around 1828. The other, known as Fort Robidoux, was established in 1832 on the Uintah River in Utah. This post served as a rendezvous point for trappers until 1844, when it was destroyed by the **Ute Indians**. His glowing descriptions of **California** influenced the arrival of some of the state's first overland emigration parties. Robidoux also served as an interpreter and guide with General Kearny in the **war** with **Mexico**.

SOURCES

Hill, Joseph J. "Antoine Robidoux, Kingpin in the Colorado River Fur Trade, 1824–1844." *Colorado Magazine* 7 (July 1830): 125–32.

Malone, Dumas, ed. *Dictionary of American Biography*. 21 vols. New York: Charles Scribner's Sons, 1835. 16:32.

Wallace, William S. "Antoine Robidoux." *The Mountain Men and the Fur Trade of the Far West*. Edited by LeRoy Hafen. 10 vols. Glendale, Calif.: Arthur H. Clark, 1966–72. 8:261–73.

FRED R. GOWANS AND LINDA WHITE

ROBINSON, EBENEZER. Ebenezer Robinson, a prominent editor and printer in early Latter-day Saint history, was born in 1816 at Floyd, **New York**. He learned the printing trade as a youth, became employed in the **Kirtland, Ohio**, Latter-day Saint printing firm of F. G. Williams & Co. in May 1835, and was soon converted to Mormonism. In the ensuing years, Robinson's name was associated with Church printing in **Ohio**,

Missouri, and **Illinois**. Principally, he is known for coediting the *Times and Seasons* periodical in **Nauvoo, Illinois**, with **Don Carlos Smith**. As the printers prospered, Smith and Robinson agreed in December 1840 to divide the business—Don Carlos was to take the *Times and Seasons* and handbill printing, and Ebenezer was to take the book and fancy job printing, the stereotype foundry, and the bookbindery. When Don Carlos Smith died in August 1841, Ebenezer became sole proprietor of the establishment until he sold it to the Church in February 1842. After the **martyrdom** of **Joseph Smith**, Robinson affiliated for a short time with **Sidney Rigdon**. In 1863 he joined the **RLDS Church** and in 1888 he became a follower of **David Whitmer**. He died in 1891.

SOURCE

Jesse, Dean C., ed. *The Papers of Joseph Smith*. Salt Lake City: Deseret Book, 1989. 509.

MacArthur Lee Jones

ROBISON, LOUISE Y. Louise Yates Robison, the seventh general president of the **Relief Society**, was born in Scipio, **Utah**, 27 May 1866. She was the daughter of English converts and the wife of Joseph Lyman Robison. Shy and self-effacing, Louise had little formal education and material wealth. Yet she was promised in her **patriarchal blessing** that her voice would be heard throughout the world. With strong faith in the Lord, Louise overcame her shyness and addressed Relief Societies in the **United States**, **England**, **Europe**, and **Hawaii**, as well as the International Council of Women in Paris, **France**.

Sustained in October 1928 on the eve of the **great depression**, Louise understood the financial struggles of families. She established the **Mormon** Handicraft Shop to provide an outlet for women to market their home crafts. She also initiated the Singing Mothers Chorus. The Relief Society emphasized compassionate service and officially adopted the colors of blue and gold. Released from her 11-year service in 1939, Louise died 30 March 1946 in San Francisco, California.

SOURCES

Louise Yates Robison Family Scrapbook. Compiled by Gladys Robison Winter. LDS Church Archives, Salt Lake City.

Derr, Jill Mulvay, and Susan Oman. "These Three Women." *Ensign* 8 (February 1978): 67–69.

Derr, Jill Mulvay, Janath Russell Cannon, and Maureen Ursenbach Beecher. *Women of Covenant: The Story of the Relief Society.* Salt Lake City: Deseret Book, 1992. 248–76.

Peterson, Janet, and LaRene Gaunt. "Louise Yates Robison." *Elect Ladies: Presidents of the Relief Society.* Salt Lake City: Deseret Book, 1990. 111–25.

JANET PETERSON

ROCKWELL, ORRIN PORTER. Orrin Porter Rockwell was one of the most colorful figures in Latter-day Saint Church history and perhaps its first folk hero. Born in Belcher, Hampshire County, Massachusetts, on 28 June 1813, he was a bodyguard to both **Joseph Smith** and **Brigham Young** and was driven from **Missouri** in the 1830s. He accompanied Joseph Smith to **Washington, D.C.,** in 1839–40 and spent nine months in a Missouri prison for allegedly shooting Governor **Lilburn W. Boggs.** His participation in the **Utah War,** his role as sheriff of **Salt Lake City,** and his ability to track by night added to his fame.

Porter could neither read nor write, so the documents that describe his life were written by others. The primary sources of information about his life include the *History of the Church* and an autobiographical statement in his petition for redress following his expulsion from Missouri.

Often portrayed as a man of violence, his notorious life provoked many yarns. Some of these stories may be based on truth, but they were often embellished by the teller. One account was of Joseph Smith promising Rockwell great strength if he would never allow his hair to be cut.

Rockwell died in his bed on 9 June 1878 in Salt Lake City after returning from a play.

SOURCES

Johnson, Clark V., ed. *Mormon Redress Petitions: Documents of the 1833–1838 Missouri Conflict.* Provo, Utah: Religious Studies Center, Brigham Young University, 1992. 525–28.

Schindler, Harold. *Orrin Porter Rockwell, Man of God, Son of Thunder.* Salt Lake City: University of Utah Press, 1966.

CLARK V. JOHNSON

ROCKY MOUNTAIN PROPHECY. On 26 April 1834 the Prophet **Joseph Smith** called all who held the priesthood to gather into a small log school house in **Kirtland** for instruction. **Wilford Woodruff** quoted the Prophet as stating: "There will be tens of thousands of Latter-day

Saints who will be gathered in the Rocky Mountains, and there they will open the door for the establishing of the Gospel among the **Lamanites**, . . . they will there build temples to the Most High" (CR, 57).

On 6 August 1842 at Montrose, Iowa, Joseph Smith prophesied that "the Saints would continue to suffer much affliction and would be driven to the Rocky Mountains, many would apostatize, others would be put to death by [their] persecutors or lose their lives in consequence of exposure or disease, and some of [them would] live to go and assist in making settlements and build cities and see the Saints become a mighty people in the midst of the Rocky Mountains" (Smith, 5:85).

Brigham Young stated that Joseph Smith comprehended the move of the Saints to the Rocky Mountains and sat for many hours discussing the area with Brigham and others. He further testified that the prophecy had been made known to the Saints long before they left **Nauvoo** (*JD*, 4:41; 11:16; 3:257–58).

SOURCES

Christian, Lewis Clark. "A Study of Mormon Knowledge of The American Far West Prior to the Exodus (1830–February, 1846)." Master's thesis, Brigham Young University, 1972.

Esplin, Ronald K. "'A Place Prepared': Joseph, Brigham and the Quest for Promised Refuge in the West." *Journal of Mormon History* 9 (1982): 85–111.

Journal of Discourses [JD]. 26 vols. London: Latter-day Saints' Book Depot, 1854–86. 3:257–58, 4:41; 11:16.

Smith, Joseph. *History of The Church of Jesus Christ of Latter-day Saints.* Edited by B. H. Roberts. 2d ed. rev. 7 vols. Salt Lake City: The Church of Jesus Christ of Latter-day Saints, 1932–51.

Woodruff, Wilford. Conference Report (April 1898): 57.

CALVIN R. STEPHENS

ROGERS, AURELIA SPENCER. Aurelia Read Spencer Rogers, founder of the **Primary** Association, was born 4 October 1834 in Deep River, **Connecticut**. Her father was a Baptist minister until he and his **family** joined the Church in 1841. Soon afterwards, in quick succession, Aurelia's mother passed away, and her father was called on a two-year **mission** to **England**. Aurelia and her siblings remained in **Nauvoo** with relatives and friends and then went to **Utah** with an early **pioneer** company. In 1851 Aurelia married Thomas Rogers and moved to Farmington, Utah.

In 1878 Aurelia became concerned with the unruly behavior of the little boys in Farmington. She voiced her concern to **Eliza R. Snow**, suggesting that there be a structured organization for boys and girls. Eliza R. Snow petitioned President **John Taylor**, and he authorized the establishment of the Primary organization. The first **ward** Primary was organized 11 August 1878 with Aurelia as president. In those early Primary **meetings**, the children were taught singing and given gospel instruction. Topics of discussion included obedience, faith in God, prayer, punctuality, and good manners.

In addition to being her ward Primary president, in 1880 Aurelia was called as the **stake** Primary president for the Farmington Stake. Aurelia and Thomas had 12 children, 5 of whom died in infancy. She passed away 19 August 1922 in Farmington.

SOURCES

Ashton, Wendell J. *Theirs Is the Kingdom.* Salt Lake City: Bookcraft, 1945.

Barrett, Ivan J. *Heroic Mormon Women: True Stories from the Lives of 16 Amazing Women in Church History.* American Fork, Utah: Covenant Communications, 1991.

Rogers, Aurelia S. *Life Sketches of Orson Spencer and Others and History of Primary Work.* Salt Lake City: Geo. Q. Cannon & Sons, 1898.

CATHERINE BRITSCH FRANTZ

ROLLINS, MARY ELIZABETH. In 1833 Mary Elizabeth Rollins risked her life to preserve pages of the **Book of Commandments**. She was born 9 April 1818 in Lima, Livingston, **New York**. After reading passages in the **Book of Mormon**, she requested baptism in October 1830 at **Kirtland, Ohio**.

In 1833, while residing in **Independence, Missouri**, Mary and her sister Caroline witnessed the destruction of the Latter-day Saint printing press and heard a mobber exclaim, "Here are the Mormon Commandments." She and her sister took the "Mormon Commandments" and ran to a nearby cornfield to hide. "[We] laid the papers on the ground, and hid them with our persons," Mary wrote ("Mary Elizabeth," 203). Although mobbers searched for the sisters, their hiding place was not detected.

On 11 August 1835, Mary married Adam Lightner, a non-Mormon. This union led **Joseph Smith** to say to Mary, "If [you] attempt to leave the Church [you will] have plenty of sorrow" ("Mary Elizabeth," 203). Mary did not heed the prophetic warning. For two decades she struggled to feed and clothe her children. She was a widow for 28 years. It was not until 1863 that she journeyed west and reunited with the **Saints**. Mary settled in Minersville, Beaver, **Utah**, where she died 17 December 1913 at age 95.

SOURCES

Lightner, Mary. "Mary Elizabeth Rollins Lightner." *Utah Genealogical and Historical Magazine* 17 (July 1926): 193–205, 250–60.

Lightner, Mary Elizabeth. "Address at Brigham Young University." Typescript. Archives and Manuscripts, Brigham Young University Library, Provo, Utah. 14 April 1905.

SUSAN EASTON BLACK

ROMANIA. Mischa Markow entered what is now Romania in July 1899 and preached the gospel there, baptizing several people and establishing branches at Temesvar and Kronstadt (now Brasov). Markow remained in Romania until June 1900, when he was arrested, tried, jailed for a few days, and then banished. Missionaries continued to work in these branches until their departure at the beginning of **World War I**. Political conditions severely limited Church activity until after the fall of the Communist government in 1989. In 1990 **Elder Russell M. Nelson** and Elder Hans B. Ringger met with Romanian leaders, and, as a result, the Church began to provide humanitarian aid. Romania was part of the **Austria** Vienna East **Mission** from July 1987 until June 1991, when it became part of the **Hungary** Budapest Mission. The Romania Bucharest Mission was created 1 July 1993. As of 2000 there were 1,545 members in the country residing in 2 districts and 17 branches.

SOURCES

Hungary Budapest Mission History. LDS Church Archives, Salt Lake City, 1991.

History of the Saints in Romania. Helene Bernhardt. LDS Church Archives, Salt Lake City.

1999–2000 Church Almanac. Salt Lake City: Deseret News, 1996. 380.

JEFFREY L. ANDERSON

ROMNEY, GEORGE. George Wilcken Romney, a well-known public servant and local Church leader, was born in the Latter-day Saint **Mexican colony** of Dublan on 8 July 1907 and died in Bloomfield Hills, **Michigan**, on 26 July 1995. After growing up in Mexico, **California, Idaho**, and Utah, he served a **mission** to **Great Britain** from 1926 to 1928. After his mission he worked as a lobbyist in **Washington, D.C.**, and married Lenore LaFount in the **Salt Lake Temple** in 1931. They moved to Detroit in 1939, and he headed the Automobile Manufacturers Association and then joined Nash-Kelvinator (later American Motors) in 1948, where he was CEO from 1954 to 1962. Meanwhile, he was called as the first president of the Detroit Michigan **Stake**, where he served from 1952 to 1963.

Elected governor of Michigan in 1962, he served until 1969, when he joined the cabinet of President Richard Nixon as Secretary of Housing and Urban Development; he resigned in 1972. He made an unsuccessful bid for the Republican presidential nomination in 1967 and 1968, a candidacy which brought national attention to Church standards. After leaving public life, he remained active in civic affairs, promoting bipartisan federal support for voluntary community action and founding VOLUNTEER, the National Center for Citizen Involvement.

SOURCES

"George Romney, Achiever." *Salt Lake Tribune,* 28 July 1995. A22.

Lythgoe, Dennis L. "The 1968 Presidential Decline of George Romney: Mormonism or Politics?" *BYU Studies* 11 (Spring 1971): 219–40.

Mollenhoff, Clark R. *George Romney: Mormon in Politics.* New York: Meredith, 1968.

JOHN THOMAS

ROMNEY, MARION G.

ROMNEY, MARION G. Marion George Romney, **counselor** to two presidents of the Church, was born 19 September 1897 in Colonia Juárez, **Mexico.** He was 14 years old when the Latter-day Saint settlers fled from that country. During this forced exodus, the **family** was robbed of their last 20 pesos by members of the rebel army, who pointed their guns into Marion's frightened face. This experience, as well as many others, verified the truth of a statement in Brother Romney's **patriarchal blessing:** "The **angels** of your choice have been over you and watched over you for your good" (quoted in Kimball, 26). Little could Marion imagine that 50 years later he would return to Mexico as an **apostle,** assigned to administer the affairs of the Spanish-speaking **missions** of the Church.

As a young man, Marion lived with his **family** in **Los Angeles, California,** and then in **Rexburg, Idaho,** where his father became the president of **Ricks College** (later BYU–Idaho). After serving in the army and completing a three-year mission to **Australia,** Brother Romney married Ida Jensen and graduated from the **University of Utah** with a law degree. He practiced law for 11 years in **Salt Lake City,** where he served terms as assistant county attorney and also district and city attorney. In 1935 he was elected to the state legislature. He served in the Church as a **bishop** and a **stake president**. While attending **general conference** in April 1941, he was stunned to hear President **J. Reuben Clark** explain from the pulpit that the **First Presidency** had found it necessary to call five men to assist the Twelve. His name was the first read. "I didn't hear any others at the time," he recalls (quoted in Heslop, 5). Ten years later he became a member of the **Quorum** of the Twelve Apostles, and 20 years after that he was called with President **N. Eldon Tanner** to serve as a counselor to the new president of the Church, **Harold B. Lee**. President Lee stated: "I have had the witness as to the men who should be called to be my counselors. . . . They've been called by the direction and guidance of the Spirit of the Lord" (quoted in "President Harold B. Lee," 20). Upon President Lee's death in December 1973, President **Spencer W. Kimball** retained President Romney as second and later first counselor in the First Presidency. When President Kimball died, Elder Romney returned to the Quorum of the Twelve as its president, where he served until his death on 20 May 1988 in **Salt Lake City**.

SOURCES

Flake, Lawrence R. *Prophets and Apostles of the Last Dispensation.* Provo, Utah: Religious Studies Center, Brigham Young University, 2001. 229–32.

Heslop, J. M. "President Romney—Prayer, Work." *Church News,* 15 December 1973, 5ff.

Kimball, Spencer W. "President Marion G. Romney: A Symbol of Righteousness." *Ensign* 2 (November 1972): 20–27.

Lee, Harold B. "Marion G. Romney of the Quorum of the Twelve." *Improvement Era* 65 (October 1962): 740.

"President Harold B. Lee Ordained Eleventh President of the Church." *Ensign* 2 (August 1972): 19–21.

"President Marion G. Romney: All Is Holy Where This Man Kneels." *Ensign* 18 (July 1988): 73–78.

LAWRENCE R. FLAKE

ROOSEVELT, THEODORE.

Theodore Roosevelt, 26th president of the **United States** and friend of the **Mormons**, was born 27 October 1858 in **New York City**. He graduated from Harvard University in 1880 and married Alice Hathaway Lee the same year. She died in childbirth four years later, and in 1886 Roosevelt married Edith Kermit Caron. Before he became president in 1901, he served in many public offices, including assistant secretary of the navy, governor of **New York**, and vice president of the United States.

Roosevelt came into contact with the Latter-day Saints in 1900 at **Rexburg, Idaho**, when he was campaigning for vice president. When **Ben E. Rich**, a prominent Church member, introduced Roosevelt, he predicted that the candidate would one day become president of the United States. The prediction made an impression on Roosevelt, which led to a lifelong friendship between the two that proved beneficial to the Church.

For example, in 1902 Roosevelt, now president of the United States, was in a parade in Chattanooga, **Tennessee**, where Rich was serving as **mission president**. When Roosevelt saw Rich in the crowd, he stopped the parade, walked over to the curb, shook hands with Rich, and asked him how he was doing in the **mission** field. After a brief visit, Roosevelt said: "I think now by this recognition, you will have more friends in the South" (quoted in Rich, 26).

When Latter-day Saint **apostle Reed Smoot**'s seat in the Senate was being challenged (1903–07), the Church sent Rich and Elder **John Henry Smith** to call privately on President Roosevelt. After the two assured Roosevelt that **Elder** Smoot had never been a polygamist, the president gave his full support to Senator Smoot. President **Joseph F. Smith** once claimed that "without Theodore Roosevelt's active support, Smoot probably would have lost" his seat in the Senate (quoted in Rich, 25–26).

Roosevelt also publicly defended the Latter-day Saints in 1911 after several of the nation's prominent magazines published bitter articles against the Church. In an open letter, printed by *Collier's* magazine, Roosevelt refuted many falsehoods published in the periodicals and praised the Saints for their high moral standards.

Theodore Roosevelt did more than any president before him to help alleviate the public animosity toward the Latter-day Saints. He died of a blood clot 6 January 1919 in Sagamore Hill, New York.

SOURCES

Merrill, M. R. "Theodore Roosevelt and Reed Smoot." *Western Political Quarterly* 4 (September 1951): 440–53.

Pringle, Henry F. *Theodore Roosevelt: A Biography.* New York: Harcourt, 1931.

Rich, Benjamin L. *Ben E. Rich: An Appreciation by His Son.* Salt Lake City: n.p. 1950.

Roosevelt, Theodore. "Mr. Roosevelt to the Mormons." *Collier's* (15 April 1911): 28, 36.

———. *Theodore Roosevelt: An Autobiography.* New York: Scribner, 1920.

ARNOLD K. GARR

RUNAWAY OFFICIALS. A group of men appointed by President Millard Fillmore to serve in several offices during the Utah territorial government became known as the "runaway officials" when they left their offices and returned to Washington, D.C. Arriving in Utah on 17 August 1851, this group consisted of Chief Justice Lemuel D. Brandebury, Associate Judge Perry E. Brocchus, territorial secretary Broughton D. Harris, and sub-Indian agent Henry R. Day.

These federally appointed officials were to serve along with locally appointed Latter-day Saint officials to run the newly created territorial government of Utah under Brigham Young, who served as territorial governor. Conflict soon arose, however, as Broughton Harris objected to the manner in which a census had been conducted and thereafter refused to release $25,000 allocated by the United States to aid in establishing the territorial government. Another conflict arose on 8 September, when Judge Perry Brocchus asked permission from Brigham Young to address the Saints in general conference. At first he thanked and praised the Saints for the hospitality they had shown him and the industry they exhibited in their new land. Brocchus then proceeded to condemn the Saints for supposed anti-government sentiment and the "immorality" of the Latter-day Saint women concerning polygamy. His harsh sentiment was then counteracted by Brigham Young, who sharply rebuked him.

These conflicts ended on 28 September, when the officials "ran away" from their offices and eventually made their way back to Washington, D.C., with reports of how the Latter-day Saints had taken over the territory, ruling it with debauchery. Although the Saints managed to counteract with their own side of the story, and President Fillmore replaced these officials with others, the incident of the runaway officials began to strain relations between the Saints and the U.S. government, which led to more serious conflict in the future.

SOURCES

Arrington, Leonard J., and Davis Bitton. *The Mormon Experience: A History of the Latter-day Saints.* New York: Vintage Books, 1980. 163–64.

Church History in the Fulness of Times. Salt Lake City: The Church of Jesus Christ of Latter-day Saints, 1989. 354–55.

Gibbons, Francis M. *Brigham Young: American Moses, Prophet of God.* Salt Lake City: Deseret Book, 1981. 168–72.

DANIEL E. BISHOP

RUSSIA. In 1843 Joseph Smith appointed Orson Hyde and George J. Adams to serve as the first missionaries to the Russian empire, but they were unable to complete their mission due to disruptions caused by the **martyrdom** of the **Prophet** a year later. Dedicated for preaching the restored gospel in 1903 by Elder **Francis M. Lyman**, Russia waited nearly 90 more years for the Church's establishment.

Andrei Anastasion, an emigrant convert, labored from 1925 to 1980 over his translation of the **Book of Mormon**. During the 1980s Elder **Russell M. Nelson** of the Quorum of the Twelve **Apostles**, Elder Hans B. Ringger of the Seventy, and President Dennis B. Neuenschwander, then **Austria** Vienna East mission president and later of the **Seventy**, visited Russia repeatedly to pave the way for the introduction of the Church into this region.

Under the direction of Steven R. Mecham, president of the **Finland** Helsinki Mission, six Finnish Russian-speaking couples and a handful of full-time missionaries labored in Leningrad and Vyborg. The first Russian branch was organized in Leningrad on 11 February 1990, followed by Vyborg on 25 March 1990.

By the time the Finland Helsinki East mission—the first Soviet Union mission (Russia and **Estonia**)—was organized in July 1990 under Gary L. Browning, 80 members had been baptized in Leningrad and 26 in Vyborg. Missionaries began serving in Moscow in October 1990. In May 1991 the LDS Russian Religious Association was registered, providing legal recognition for the Church throughout Russia.

When the Finland Helsinki East Mission became the Russia St. Petersburg and Russia Moscow **Missions** in February 1992, membership totaled 433, with 27 missionaries in St. Petersburg and Vyborg. In Moscow and neighboring Zelenograd, 24 missionaries served with 186 members.

Soon additional Russian missions were created: Russia Samara in July 1993, Russia Rostov-on-the-Don and Russia Novosibirsk in July 1994, Russia Yekaterinburg in July 1995, and Russia Moscow South in July 1997, making a total of seven missions. In the year 2000 the Church in Russia embraced more than 11,092 members and more than 650 missionaries.

SOURCES

Browning, Gary. *Russia and the Restored Gospel.* Salt Lake City: Deseret Book, 1997. xv–xxi, 339–41.

Smith, Joseph. *History of The Church of Jesus Christ of Latter-day Saints.* Edited by B. H. Roberts. 2d ed. rev. 7 vols. Salt Lake City: The Church of Jesus Christ of Latter-day Saints, 1932–51.

GARY BROWNING

RYDER, SYMONDS. Symonds Ryder, a controversial figure in Church history, was born 20 November 1792 in Hartford, **Vermont**. He served in many prominent positions in the community of **Hiram, Ohio**, where he lived most of his life. After hearing the **Prophet Joseph Smith** bear his **testimony** and following a prophecy by a Mormon girl about an earthquake in China, Symonds was **baptized** in early June 1831 and **ordained** an **elder** on 6 June of that year. Shortly afterward, Symonds was called to the ministry, replacing Heman Basset (D&C 52:37). Upon receiving his letter of official commission to preach, however, his name was spelled R-i-d-e-r instead of R-y-d-e-r. Symonds concluded that those who erred in spelling his name could also err in spiritual matters. This and other misgivings about the Church and its leadership led to his apostasy after only three months. He attacked the Church in the *Ohio Star* and helped lead a mob in tarring and feathering Joseph Smith and **Sidney Rigdon** at the **Johnson Farm**. Symonds eventually returned to the Campbellite ministry and died 1 August 1870 in Hiram at the age of 77.

SOURCES

Black, Susan Easton. *Who's Who in the Doctrine and Covenants*. Salt Lake City: Bookcraft, 1997. 256–59.

Brewster, Hoyt W. *Doctrine and Covenants Encyclopedia*. Salt Lake City: Bookcraft, 1988. 481–82.

MATTHEW O. RICHARDSON

SMITH, JOSEPH. Many artists have depicted the first leader of Church, including Pino Drago with this 1987 portrait of Joseph Smith.

SABBATH DAY. The institution of the Sabbath dates from the earth's creation, when God "rested" on the seventh day (Gen. 1:1, 31; 2:1–2). The word *Sabbath* seems to be affiliated with the Hebrew word *shavat* (a verb), which means to *stop, cease,* or *desist.* Thus *Sabbath* (a noun) reminds the faithful that on this day they should follow the pattern God established by "ceasing" from their weekly labors to worship him.

God reminded his people at Mount Sinai that he had "blessed and sanctified" the seventh day, making it a day wherein "thou shalt not do any work" (Ex. 20:8–11). **Moses** taught that the Sabbath was to be observed as "a perpetual covenant" and as "a sign between [the Lord] and the children of **Israel** for ever" (Ex. 31:16–17). The importance of the Sabbath manifests itself throughout Holy Writ (Ex. 20:8–11; 31:16–17; Isa. 58:13–14; Jer. 17:19–27; Ezek. 20:20–24; 22:8; 44:24; Neh. 10:31; 13:15–22; Acts 20:7; Rev. 1:10; Jarom 1:5; Mosiah 13:16–19; 18:23; D&C 59:9–13). Such admonitions regarding the Sabbath continue to the present day (Hinckley, 69).

Elder Mark E. Petersen of the Quorum of the Twelve **Apostles** emphasized the keeping of the Sabbath: "Our observance or non-observance of the Sabbath is an unerring measure of our attitude toward the Lord personally and toward his suffering in Gethsemane, his death on the cross, and his resurrection from the dead. It is a sign of whether we are Christians in very deed, or whether our conversion is so shallow that commemoration of his atoning sacrifice means little or nothing to us" (49). Today the Christian Sabbath typically occurs on Sunday, in commemoration of the resurrection of the Savior on the first day of the week (Acts 20:7; Rev. 1:10).

SOURCES

The Anchor Bible Dictionary. Edited by D. N. Freedman. 6 vols. New York: Doubleday, 1992. 5:851.
Hinckley, Gordon B. "Look to the Future." *Ensign* 27 (November 1997): 67–69.

McKay, David O. *Gospel Ideals*. Salt Lake City: Deseret News Press, 1953. 397–98.
Petersen, Mark E. "The Sabbath Day." *Ensign* 5 (May 1975): 47–49.

DAVID M. WHITCHURCH

SACRAMENT. In April 1830 the Lord revealed anew the purposes and procedures relating to the administration of the sacrament (D&C 20). Although little is known about specific sacrament services during the early history of the Church, these **meetings**, nevertheless, have always been a vital part of worship services in the Church. On **6 April** 1830, the first sacrament meeting in this dispensation took place in the log home of **Peter Whitmer**. Sacrament meetings were held on the main floor of the **Kirtland Temple** (D&C 95:16; 110:heading), and there will be a great sacrament meeting held one day at **Adam-ondi-Ahman** in preparation for the Savior's second coming (McConkie). Section 20 of the **Doctrine and Covenants** states that bread and wine serve as the emblems of the flesh and blood of Christ. In August 1830, however, the Lord revealed that "it mattereth not what ye shall eat or what ye shall drink when ye partake of the sacrament, if it so be that ye do it with an eye single to my glory" (D&C 27:2). Water is now used instead of wine, even though the Church did not adopt this new custom exclusively at first. On 8 March 1831 the Lord revealed that nonmembers should not be excluded from sacrament meetings, since the practice of doing such was beginning to creep into the Church (D&C 46).

From time to time, the **First Presidency** has issued guidelines, as deemed necessary, to improve the quality of the sacrament service. In 1877 the practice of administering the sacrament to children going to **Sunday School** was instituted. In 1932 instructions detailing the procurement of bread and instructions regarding the dress and grooming of those administering the sacrament were put forth. In 1942 a policy was initiated that standardized the frequency of sacrament meetings: "There has gradually crept into the Church a growing tendency for various subsidiary and auxiliary organizations to take over the time of the Sacrament meeting. This has in some areas grown to such proportions that the **Bishop** has difficulty in finding a Sunday on which he can hold a regular sacrament meeting. This situation does not accord with the revelations of the Lord and therefore is not right. . . . There should be one Sabbath Sacrament meeting each week in every ward" (Clark, 6:166). In 1946 instructions were given with regards to a divergence of opinion relating to the use of music during the administration of the sacrament. The First

Presidency and the Twelve unanimously recommended that "the ideal condition is to have absolute quiet during the passing of the sacrament, and that we look with disfavor upon vocal solos, duets, group singing, or instrumental music during the administration of this sacred **ordinance**" (Clark, 6:252). The evolution of the use of various types of vessels for the sacrament service of the Church is also noteworthy: "Early custom in the Church used a large metal goblet, later several glasses or metal goblets, then to individual small glass cups, then this changed to individual metal cups, then to individual small disposable paper cups. . . . The above evolutionary development may not have been uniform for all areas of the Church" (Clark, 4:269).

SOURCES

Clark, James R., comp. *Messages of the First Presidency of The Church of Jesus Christ of Latter-day Saints.* 6 vols. Salt Lake City: Bookcraft, 1965–75. 4:269; 6:166, 252.

McConkie, Bruce R. *The Millennial Messiah.* Salt Lake City: Deseret Book, 1982. 587.

Smith, Joseph Fielding. *Church History and Modern Revelation.* 2 vols. Salt Lake City: Council of the Twelve Apostles, 1953. 1:132.

C. ROBERT LINE

SACRAMENT MEETINGS. See MEETINGS.

SACRED GROVE.

The Sacred Grove is a place of reverence and a source of faith for many Latter-day Saints. A Church history site near **Palmyra, New York**, that commemorates **Joseph Smith's First Vision**, the grove is located in a wooded area on the west end of the **Joseph Smith Sr.** farm in **Manchester, New York**. The family made arrangements to purchase the property in 1820. In that year 14-year-old Joseph retired to a wooded area in order to seek divine guidance concerning which church he should join. At this time **God the Father** and **Jesus Christ** appeared to the boy and told him that he "must join none of [the churches], for they were all wrong" (JS-H 19). This vision was the first great event of the **restoration** of the gospel in the latter days.

The exact location of the vision is unknown, but the traditional site is about one-fourth mile west of the **Joseph Smith Sr. homes**, which are located on the family farm. Although the Smiths were unable to make payments on the property and lost title to the farm in 1825, they continued to work the land as renters until the spring of 1829, when they moved to their old log house in Palmyra township. The farm was owned and maintained by non-**Mormons** until 1907, when Elder **George Albert Smith** purchased it and later deeded it to the Church. In 1915 **Willard Bean** and his wife, Rebecca, were called as missionaries to live on the farm. Since that time thousands of people throughout the world visit the farm and the Sacred Grove every year. In 1999 the grove was visited by more than 50,000 people.

SOURCES

Enders, Donald L. "Palmyra, New York." *Historical Atlas of Mormonism*. Edited by S. Kent Brown et al. New York: Simon and Schuster, 1994. 10–11.

———. "Sacred Grove." *Encyclopedia of Mormonism*. Edited by Daniel H. Ludlow. 4 vols. New York: Macmillan, 1992. 1247–48.

ARNOLD K. GARR

SAGWITCH. Sagwitch, a chieftain of the Northwestern **Shoshone** tribe in the nineteenth century, led his entire band into the Church on 5 May 1873. Sagwitch's people claimed as their homeland the Box Elder, **Cache**, and Bear Lake Valleys of northern **Utah**, and a portion of southeastern **Idaho**. Born in 1822, Sagwitch grew up in the era of the fur traders and trappers. Soon after the **Latter-day Saints** made their entry into Utah in 1847, he established a relationship with them that endured until his death 40 years later in 1887. On 29 January 1863, federal troops attacked Sagwitch's people in their winter encampment near present-day Preston, Idaho. Nearly 300 Shoshone men, women, and children were killed in what has become known as the **Bear River Massacre**. Sagwitch, although wounded, survived. His leadership was crucial in regrouping what remained of his people.

In 1873, after experiencing a number of dreams or **visions**, Sagwitch petitioned George Washington Hill to teach the gospel to his people. Hill did so and baptized Sagwitch and his band, numbering 101 members. Three days later Sagwitch was **ordained** an **elder**, and on 22 February 1875 he entered the **Endowment House** in **Salt Lake City**, where he received **temple ordinances** and was sealed to his wife for time and eternity by Elder **Wilford Woodruff**. This was the second sealing of a Native American couple in this dispensation.

In 1880, Sagwitch's people moved to **Washakie**, a Church-sponsored farm in Box Elder County, Utah. The Shoshone residents of Washakie, including Sagwitch, donated thousands of hours in labor to the construction of the **Logan Temple**.

Sagwitch's descendants include grandson **Moroni Timbimboo**, the Church's first Native American **bishop**.

SOURCES

Christensen, Scott R. *Sagwitch: Shoshone Chieftain, Mormon Elder, 1822–1887.* Logan, Utah: Utah State University Press, 1999.

Madsen, Brigham D. *The Shoshoni Frontier and the Bear River Massacre.* Salt Lake City: University of Utah Press, 1985.

SCOTT R. CHRISTENSEN

SAINTS. The term *Saints* refers to members of The Church of Jesus Christ of Latter-day Saints. To become a member of the Church, one must have faith in **Christ**, repent, be baptized by proper authority, and receive the gift of the Holy Ghost by proper authority. These **ordinances** signify walking in a newness of life. **Doctrine and Covenants** 20:37 lists related requirements for becoming a member of the Church.

The word *saint* is from the Latin *sanctus,* which means "holy". A saint is someone who lives righteously. The section on *saint* in the *Oxford English Dictionary* takes up nearly five columns. Some religions use the word exclusively for a few honored dead.

SOURCE

The Compact Edition of the Oxford English Dictionary. 2 vols. London: Book Club Associates, 1979. 2:2623.

ROBERT L. MARROTT

SALEM, MASSACHUSETTS. The **revelation** recorded in section 111 of the **Doctrine and Covenants** was received in Salem, **Massachusetts**, on 6 August 1836. At that time the Church was heavily in debt, and money was desperately needed. When Jonathan Burgess reported that there was treasure in Salem, Church leaders readily believed him. Leaving **Kirtland, Ohio**, on 25 July 1836, they traveled by way of **New York City** and arrived in Salem on 4 August 1836. In this prosperous seaport **Joseph Smith** was on familiar ground. Years earlier he had stayed at the home of a relative there, recovering from a serious leg operation. Joseph Smith and the others rented a house on Union Street, hoping it contained the treasure they sought. They found nothing. On 6 August 1836, **Sydney Rigdon** and **Oliver Cowdery** visited the East India Marine Society Museum. Joseph Smith remained alone in the rented house and received a revelation that admonished them to seek other treasures besides money—treasures such as converts and names of ancestors. **Erastus Snow** arrived in Salem as a missionary in 1841, and by May of the following year he had baptized 90 members in the **branch** there.

SOURCES

Cannon, Donald Q. "Joseph Smith in Salem." *The Doctrine and Covenants.* Edited by Robert L. Millet and Kent P. Jackson. Vol. 1 of Studies in Scripture series. Sandy, Utah: Randall Book, 1984. 432–37.

Godfrey, Kenneth W. "More Treasures Than One: Section 111." *Hearken O Ye People.* Salt Lake City: Randall Book, 1984. 191–204.

DONALD Q. CANNON

SALMON RIVER MISSION. In April 1855, 27 missionaries from **Utah** were called by LDS Church leaders to establish a settlement among the nomadic Bannock and **Shoshone Indians** of **Idaho** (then part of **Oregon** Territory). The **mission's** purpose was to proselyte to the natives and teach them to settle permanently and raise grain. The missionaries' settlement was called **Fort Limhi** (later spelled Lemhi), after a **Book of Mormon** king, and was located along the Lemhi River about two miles north of Tendoy, Idaho. Thomas S. Smith presided over this first LDS colonizing attempt in Idaho.

In June 1855, the settlement site was chosen and a corral and stockade were constructed quickly. Crops were planted and irrigation began. Curious and friendly natives began to visit regularly. Additional settlers arrived later. **Brigham Young** and an entourage including **Ute** Chief Arapeen visited the settlement in May 1857. Numerous natives were baptized, but the settlers were unsuccessful in persuading the natives to abandon their roving nature and take up farming.

On 25 February 1858 natives unexpectedly drove off the settlers' cattle, killed two missionaries, and wounded five others. Messengers were dispatched to **Salt Lake City** to alert Church officials to the mission's precarious situation. The officials instructed the missionaries to return to Utah immediately and sent relief companies to accelerate the move.

By 28 March 1858 the colonizers had abandoned the settlement. En route to Utah some of the missionaries were again attacked by natives, and another missionary was killed.

SOURCES

"Manuscript History of Salmon River Mission." LDS Church Historical Department, Salt Lake City.

Moore, David. "Salmon River Mission Journal, 1855–1858." LDS Church Historical
    Department, Salt Lake City.

JAY G. BURRUP

SALT LAKE CITY, UTAH. Salt Lake City, established in 1847,
became the capital of **Utah** and the headquarters of The Church of Jesus
Christ of Latter-day Saints, which built its central offices and a temple in
the downtown area.

Drawing on **Joseph Smith's** plan for the city of **Zion** and on the
gridiron system of many American cities, the **Saints** began in 1847 to plat
the city with wide streets and large lots. In the downtown area, the pressure of business enterprise led to abutting buildings, and in other areas
subdividers often left less room for streets and built houses closer
together. The city grew because of such factors as Latter-day Saints gathering to Zion, commerce on the overland route, mining in the Wasatch
and Oquirrh Mountains, manufacturing, governmental activities, and
Church administration.

Until the late 1880s, Latter-day Saints dominated the elective posts
of mayor, aldermen, and councilors. In 1888 Latter-day Saints elected
several prominent non-Mormons as councilors. In 1890 the anti-Mormon
Liberal Party captured control of the city government.

After the Latter-day Saints divided into national political parties in
1891, city government began to look much like that of other cities. In
1905, however, voters turned control to the anti-Mormon **American
Party**. After 1911 the city operated under a commission system until
January 1980, when voters inaugurated a strong mayor system.

Salt Lake faced its share of problems. Because the city did not
provide various services, small businesses expecting a profit offered
streetcars, electric lights, and telephones. City residents coughed their
way into the twentieth century, surrounded by air pollution, poorly paved
streets, inadequate water supplies, a poor sewer system, and inadequate
public health services. In the early twentieth century, however, club
women worked with the civic organizations to reduce smoke pollution,
pave streets, install water and sewer systems, and beautify the city.

Since 1930, Salt Lake City has experienced swings in fortune. During
the great depression it suffered unemployment and deprivation far worse
than that endured by the rest of the nation. **World War II** revived the city
as a major center of war industry.

Following the **war**, the heavy reliance on mining and military operations continued into the 1970s, when Salt Lake had emerged as a major financial, service, commercial, high-tech, and educational center.

SOURCES

Alexander, Thomas G., and James B. Allen. *Mormons and Gentiles: A History of Salt Lake City.* Boulder, Colo.: Pruett, 1984.
McCormick, John S. *Salt Lake City: The Gathering Place.* Woodland Hills, Calif.: Windsor, 1980.

THOMAS G. ALEXANDER

SALT LAKE STAKE. Salt Lake Stake was formally organized 3 October 1847 with about 2,000 members and initially presided over by John Smith and counselors Charles C. Rich and John Young. Albert Carrington served as clerk of the high council and stake historian. Considered the Great Basin's "mother stake," from which the Weber Stake was created in 1851 and the Davis, Morgan, Summit, and Tooele Stakes were organized in 1877, it still had 51 wards before the Jordan and Granite Stakes were divided from it in 1900.

The united order was established in all wards of the stake in 1874. The Assembly Hall on Temple Square was constructed (1877–80) to serve as the stake's tabernacle. A stake academy, established in 1886, evolved in the early twentieth century to become LDS Business College.

As stake demographics changed dramatically during the 1960s to 1990s, branches and wards were established to better accommodate the cultural transition of immigrants from Japan, southeast Asia, Central and South America, eastern Europe, and Mexico.

By the end of the twentieth century, there were nearly 200 stakes in the area once included within the original boundaries of Salt Lake Stake.

SOURCES

"*Manuscript History of Salt Lake Stake.*" LDS Church Historical Department, Salt Lake City.
The Story of Salt Lake Stake, The Church of Jesus Christ of Latter-day Saints: 150 Years of History, 1847–1997. Salt Lake City: Salt Lake Stake, 1997.

JAY G. BURRUP

SALT LAKE TABERNACLE. See TABERNACLE, SALT LAKE.

SALT LAKE TEMPLE. The Salt Lake Temple, dedicated in 1893, was the first temple the pioneers began to build after they reached Utah. It is located on a 10-acre plot known as **Temple Square** in downtown **Salt Lake City**. **Brigham Young** chose the site on 28 July 1847, only a few days after his arrival in the Great Basin. He later described how on that occasion he had seen a vision of the temple with its six spires. **Truman O. Angell** became the temple's chief architect, and a groundbreaking ceremony was held on 14 February 1853. Soon thereafter, the cornerstones were laid at impressive services conducted during the Church's annual conference on 6 April 1853. During the next four decades, work on the "Great Temple" was delayed many times, due to the coming of **Johnston's Army** and problems in getting the huge granite blocks from the quarry to Temple Square. But beginning in the late 1880s, the Church's full resources were consecrated to the completion of the temple—a temple that Latter-day prophets declare fulfills Isaiah's prophecy: "And it shall come to pass in the last days, that the mountain of the Lord's house shall be established in the top of the mountains, and shall be exalted above the hills; and all nations shall flow unto it" (Isa. 2:2).

Thousands of Saints gathered in the streets and on the "Temple Block" for the capstone-laying ceremony on 6 April 1892. A year later to the day, amidst great celebration, President **Wilford Woodruff** dedicated the temple. The 31 dedicatory services extended over a period of nearly three weeks.

When completed, the temple's interior design included a basement, with a font for **baptisms for the dead**, and rooms to be used for the **endowment** ceremony. The endowment ordinance rooms are also found on the next floor, in addition to sealing rooms and the Holy of Holies. Rooms used by Church officers are located on the next floor. Finally, the top main floor consists primarily of a large assembly room used for monthly **general authority** meetings and other special gatherings.

The temple's exterior design includes six separate spires and many symbolic stones, such as moon, sun, and star stones, suggesting the three degrees of glory. Atop the east central spire is the statue of the **angel Moroni** blowing his trumpet to herald the Restoration and proclamation of the "everlasting gospel" to the nations of the earth in anticipation of the Savior's second coming. These symbolic stones and architectural representations are meant to reinforce the spiritual teachings revealed through the **ordinances** performed within the temple.

During the 1960s the temple was thoroughly renovated. An addition along the temple's north side provided more sealing rooms and the annex was greatly enlarged. All these facilities gave the temple a total of 253,015 square feet, making it the largest in the Church.

Brigham Young wanted the temple to stand as a witness to the dedication and industry of the nineteenth century Latter-day Saint **pioneers**. The temple is a magnificent monument to their faith, but more importantly, it remains a sacred place of prayer, meditation, and the administering of saving ordinances.

SOURCES

Cowan, Richard O. *Temples to Dot the Earth.* Springville, Utah: Cedar Fort, 1997.

Hamilton, C. Mark. *The Salt Lake Temple: A Monument to a People.* Salt Lake City: University Services Corp., 1983.

Hanks, Marion D. "Salt Lake Temple." *Encyclopedia of Mormonism.* Edited by Daniel H. Ludlow. 4 vols. New York: Macmillan, 1992. 3:1252–54.

Holzapfel, Richard Neitzel. *Every Stone a Sermon: The Magnificent Story of the Construction and Dedication of the Salt Lake Temple.* Salt Lake City: Bookcraft, 1992.

———. "Every Window, Every Spire Speaks of the Things of God." *Ensign* 23 (March 1993): 7–21.

Raynor, Wallace Alan. *The Everlasting Spires: A Story of the Salt Lake Temple.* Salt Lake City: Deseret Book, 1965.

RICHARD NEITZEL HOLZAPFEL

SALT LAKE THEATRE. **Brigham Young** appointed Hiram B. Clawson as construction manager and manager of the Salt Lake Theatre, with **William H. Folsom** as architect and E. L. T. Harrison as the building's interior designer. Dubbed the "Cathedral of the Desert," the theatre's construction began in 1861 and was sufficiently completed by March 1862, when opening ceremonies and a dedication were held. The Grecian Doric theatre measured 80 by 144 feet with a roof span of 85 feet. It was located on the northwest corner of State Street and First South Street in **Salt Lake City**, facing south. Total cost of the building was $100,000, which was funded in part from the sale of U.S. Army surplus material following the removal of the army from **Utah** at the beginning of the American **Civil War**.

The theatre was built on a foundation of red sandstone quarried from Red Butte Canyon, and timber came from Big Cottonwood Canyon, southeast of Salt Lake City. The walls were made of 385,000 bricks, plastered in a chalky white color. The spacious stage was 62 feet deep and 40 feet wide, and the theatre included dressing rooms, offices, a green room, an orchestra pit, and a work area. Originally lighted by 385 oil lamps, the theatre switched to gas lamps early in the 1870s and eventually to electric lights. Seating capacity was 1,500 on four levels: parquete, first circle, second circle, and third circle. For a time the parquet level had removable benches so dances and other functions could be held there. Permanent seating was added later.

Samuel Bowles said of the structure: "The building is itself a rare triumph of art and enterprise [and] it ranks . . . in capacity and elegance of structure and finish, along with the opera houses and academies of music of Boston, **New York**, Philadelphia, Chicago, and Cincinnati" (Arrington, 211).

The Salt Lake Theatre was razed in October 1928. The **Daughters of Utah Pioneers** museum facade, located on north Main Street in Salt Lake City, is a replication of the Salt Lake Theatre.

SOURCES

Arrington, Leonard J. *Great Basin Kingdom: Economic History of the Latter-day Saints, 1830–1900*. Cambridge, Mass.: Harvard University Press, 1958. 211–13.

Lindsay, John S. *The Mormons and the Theatre; or, The History of Theatricals in Utah*. Salt Lake City: n.p., 1905.

Maughan, Ila Fisher. *Pioneer Theatre in the Desert*. Salt Lake City: Deseret Book, 1961.

Pyper, George D. *The Romance of the Old Playhouse*. Salt Lake City: Deseret News, 1937.

Whitney, Horace G. "The Story of the Salt Lake Theatre." *Improvement Era* 18 (April 1915): 509–616; 18 (May 1915): 580–592, 686–695, 790–804.

CRAIG FULLER

SALT LAKE TRIBUNE. The *Salt Lake Tribune,* Utah's largest newspaper, was founded to oppose the Church. A group of excommunicated Church members, the **Godbeites**, who challenged **Brigham Young's** economic and religious practices, founded the *Mormon Tribune* in 1871, later changing its name to the *Salt Lake Tribune.* In 1873 three **Kansans** bought the *Tribune* and issued a "declaration of a no-holds-barred conflict with the [C]hurch" (Malmquist, 33). Over the years, this conflict was exemplified by attacks on Church leaders such as **John Taylor, George Q. Cannon**, and **Joseph F. Smith**. In 1901 mining magnate **Thomas Kearns** and his partner, David Keith, purchased the *Tribune.* Although not a profitable investment, Kearns was able to use the publication to attack **polygamy**, Senator **Reed Smoot**, and the Church, while promoting his own political agenda. In 1952 the *Tribune* and the *Deseret*

News entered into an agency agreement combining their printing, circulation, business, and advertising departments.

SOURCES

Bennion, Sherilyn Cox. "The *Salt Lake Tribune*." *Utah History Encyclopedia*. Edited by Allan Kent Powell. Salt Lake City: University of Utah Press, 1994. 485–86.

Malmquist, O. N. *The First 100 Years: A History of the Salt Lake Tribune, 1871–1971*. Salt Lake City: Utah State Historical Society, 1971.

KRISTIN B. GERDY

SALT LAKE VALLEY. The Salt Lake Valley provided a home and a place of refuge for the **Saints** in the mid-nineteenth century. Its high mountain walls formed a protective circle around the new Church headquarters, allowing the Saints to flourish and to advance the work of **gathering** Israel and building up the kingdom.

Long the domain of **Native Americans**, the Salt Lake Valley drew the attention of trappers and **explorers** from the 1830s to the 1840s. Their reports of the area informed Church leaders, who were studying potential settlement sites in the West. Before his death, the **Prophet Joseph Smith** had spoken of the Rocky Mountains as a future gathering place. Aware of Joseph's intentions, **Brigham Young** and other leaders focused their search for a refuge among the western mountains, settling on the Salt Lake Valley as the principal destination. An advance company of **pioneers**, led by Brigham Young, arrived in the valley in July 1847. Days later in a camp council, Brigham Young asserted, "I knew this spot as soon as I saw it," and assured that "we have come here according to the suggestion and direction of Joseph Smith" (quoted in Bennett, 230). More than 20 years later, **George A. Smith** explained that Brigham had seen the valley in **vision** and testified that "the God of Heaven by His inspiration led our Prophet right here" (*JD,* 13:86).

The pioneers found an arid but fertile land situated on the easternmost edge of the **Great Basin**. The valley stretched 25 miles north and south and 17 miles east and west. It was framed on the east by the soaring Wasatch Mountains and on the west by the compact Oquirrh Mountains. A narrow cleft on the south led to **Utah** Valley, while the broad opening to the northwest revealed the Great Salt Lake, from which the valley took its name.

Confident that the valley had been ordained of **God** as the new gathering place, the Saints set to work building **Zion** and gathering Israel. In their eyes, this new mountain home was a literal fulfillment of the prophecy declaring "in the last days, that the mountain of the Lord's house shall be established in the top of the mountains" (Isa. 2:2).

SOURCES

Alexander, Thomas G., and James B. Allen. *Mormons and Gentiles: A History of Salt Lake City.* Boulder, Colo.: Pruett, 1984.

Bennett, Richard E. *We'll Find the Place: The Mormon Exodus, 1846–1848.* Salt Lake City: Deseret Book, 1997.

Berrett, LaMar C. "Salt Lake Valley." *Encyclopedia of Mormonism.* Edited by Daniel H. Ludlow. 4 vols. New York: Macmillan, 1992. 3:1255–56.

Journal of Discourses [JD]. 26 vols. London: Latter-day Saints' Book Depot, 1854–86. Vol. 13.

JENNIFER L. LUND

SALT SERMON. During a **meeting** held June 1838 at the public square at **Far West, Missouri, Sidney Rigdon** used as a text for his discourse the words from St. Matthew: "If the salt have lost his savour, . . . it is thenceforth good for nothing, but to be cast out, and to be trodden under foot of men" (Matt. 5:13). While the verse has generally been interpreted to mean that the true believers in Jesus are expected to so live as to be an influence for good in the world, Rigdon's application of the **scripture** on the occasion was used in a much different context. At the time, several former Church leaders had become disaffected from the Church, including Oliver and Marcellus Cowdery, David, John, and **Jacob Whitmer, Lyman E. Johnson, William E. McLellin, Frederick G. Williams,** and **W. W. Phelps.** In spite of their disaffection, however, they remained in Far West and used their influence to undermine Church leaders, particularly the **First Presidency.** Rigdon saw the dissenters as having "lost their savour" and believed that they should therefore "be cast out and trodden under the feet of men." The implication was that these men must either leave Far West or suffer repercussion. Within a matter of a few days, seven of the dissenters left **Caldwell County.** The other two, W. W. Phelps and Frederick G. Williams, made restitution and remained in the Latter-day Saint community.

SOURCE

Baugh, Alexander L. "A Call to Arms: 1838 Mormon Defense of Northern Missouri." Ph.D. diss., Brigham Young University, 1996.

ALEXANDER L. BAUGH

SALUDA DISASTER. See **RIVERBOATS.**

SALVATION FOR THE DEAD. See **DEAD, REDEEMING THE.**

SAMOA. The first Latter-day Saints to enter Samoa were Samuela Manoa and Kimo Pelia, who were sent as missionaries from **Hawaii** by **Walter Murray Gibson** in 1863. After Gibson apostatized and was excommunicated in 1864, these faithful **elders** were evidently forgotten by later Church authorities in Hawaii. They enjoyed a measure of success, however.

After Pelia's death, Manoa eventually wrote to Hawaii for help. Finally, on 21 June 1888, he was joined in Samoa by Joseph and Florence Dean. Soon Manoa, his wife, and 35 others were baptized or **rebaptized.** Dean reordained Manoa an **elder.** Within months additional elders and couples arrived to extend the work throughout the islands. LDS **missionary work** has continued in the Samoas since that time.

In 1900 the island of Tutuila (and six nearby islands) became a territory of the **United States,** called American Samoa, and the remaining islands were brought under German control until 1914, when they came under British control. Western Samoa became independent in 1962. The two Samoas are about the size of **Rhode Island** and have a combined population of 287,000 (Samoa, 225,000; American Samoa, 62,000; est. 1998). Of this population, 25% are Latter-day Saints (58,477 in Samoa; 12,833 in American Samoa). The Samoas were the first countries in the world to be covered by **stakes** (although there is presently a **district**). By the year 2000 the Samoas consisted of 1 **mission,** 20 stakes, 1 district, 137 **wards,** and 27 **branches.**

Samoan Church history, rich in interest and color, includes gathering places such as Sauniatu and Mapusaga; chapel schools (beginning in 1892); the founding of missionary work in **Tonga** in 1891 and the refounding of the mission in French Polynesia in 1892; visits of unusual spiritual efficacy from Elder **David O. McKay** (later President McKay) in 1921 and 1955; the development of three residential schools at Pesega (Upolu Island), Viola (Savai'i Island), and Mapusaga (American Samoa); years of struggle during **World War II;** successful **building-missionary** work resulting in many beautiful, modern chapels during the 1950s and 1960s; and the creation of the Apia Stake, Samoa's first, on 18 March 1962. The dedication of the Apia Samoa **Temple** at the Church complex in Pesega on 5 and 6 August 1983 was the crowning historical event in Samoan Church history.

SOURCES

Britsch, R. Lanier. *Unto the Islands of the Sea: A History of the Latter-day Saints in the Pacific.* Salt Lake City: Deseret Book, 1986. 348–428.

1999–2000 Church Almanac. Salt Lake City: Deseret News, 1998. 267–68, 408–9, 443–44.

R. LANIER BRITSCH

SAMPSON-DAVIS, PRISCILLA. Priscilla Sampson-Davis, an early **pioneer** of the Church in **Ghana**, was born 4 May 1927 in Kumasi, Ghana. She was an unbaptized convert for 14 years before she was able to join the Church. From her early childhood, she sought to learn about God and to serve **Jesus Christ**.

At age 15, Priscilla had a **vision** in which she saw the Savior carrying his cross. Jesus stopped before her, with sweat and blood running down his face. He told Priscilla that he loved her and that it was for her he was carrying the cross. He then asked her for a handkerchief to wipe the blood and sweat from his eyes. Priscilla replied that she would do as he asked. For years Priscilla sought to find the meaning of the Savior's request.

In 1963, while Priscilla and her husband, John, were living in the **Netherlands**, she obtained a copy of the **Book of Mormon** and received a testimony that it was true. Upon returning to Ghana the following year, she met **Joseph W. B. Johnson**, who had also become converted through the Book of Mormon, and joined his congregation.

Eventually the missionaries arrived in Ghana, and Priscilla was soon baptized. Because the Church was so new, **literature** was not translated into their African dialect of Fante. Having spent her adult life teaching school, she felt a need to help illiterate Church members, most of whom were sisters and many of whom had become less active because of their inability to read and understand English.

About two years after joining the Church, Priscilla had a second vision. She saw herself in a Church meeting, when a glorified being appeared and asked her why many in the congregation had their heads down and were not singing. She told him that they were discouraged because they could not read or sing the English **hymns**. He asked her to help them.

When the vision ended, she began translating "Redeemer of Israel" into the Fante language. She eventually translated all of the hymns and the missionary materials. Then, under assignment, she translated the Book of Mormon, the **Doctrine and Covenants**, and the **Pearl of Great Price**.

After completing these translations, Sister Sampson-Davis felt at peace. She observed, "I see a relationship between giving a handkerchief to Jesus so he could see and translating so that the people of Ghana can see" (quoted in LeBaron, 50).

SOURCES

LeBaron, E. Dale, ed. *"All Are Alike unto God."* Orem, Utah: Granite Publishing, 1998. 43–50.

Oral histories of early Church converts collected by E. Dale LeBaron. Copies at BYU Library, Provo, Utah; LDS Church Historical Library, Salt Lake City, Utah.

E. DALE LEBARON

SAN BERNARDINO, CALIFORNIA.

SAN BERNARDINO, CALIFORNIA. In the 1850s San Bernardino was the largest Latter-day **Saint** colony outside of **Utah**, as well as the largest Anglo-American settlement in southern **California**. Established both to reclaim Latter-day Saints who were tempted by the gold rush and as a possible entryway for Church members immigrating to **Utah** from the **Pacific**, it flourished through a level of cooperation notable even among Church communities. In 1851 more than 400 colonists traveled from Utah down the **Mormon Corridor** to the mouth of Cajon Pass, where on 6 July 1851 they organized the San Bernardino **Stake**, the first in California. Each **family** helped defray the large initial cost of purchasing the Spanish rancho as the place for establishing the Latter-day Saint city. Other accomplishments of mutual efforts included building a large fort and residing in it for more than two years, building roads, and developing extensive farmlands. Members of the **wards** also made substantial contributions to **tithing**, the **Perpetual Emigrating Fund**, and missionary efforts.

After colony leaders **Amasa M. Lyman** and **Charles C. Rich** directed their people to commence building individual homes, more than a hundred sprang up along wide streets laid out in the summer of 1854. The colonists established the most advanced school system to that point in California, including adult **education**, a public library, and considerable organized musical activity. Church members from a wide variety of backgrounds, including African-Americans, Hispanics, Polynesians, **Native Americans**, **Jews**, Europeans, Canadians, and many from the southern **United States** mingled with the dominant population from the northern states in notable harmony within the San Bernardino Stake.

San Bernardino settlers led out in lumber and flour production in the California southland, also improving beef and dairy cattle breeds and establishing an efficient irrigation system. In these and other ways the Latter-day Saint community set a significant example for other citizens of the California southland. In 1857, after only six years, the colony was essentially disbanded at the time of the **Utah War**, chiefly because **Brigham Young** desired Latter-day Saints to reside closer to **Salt Lake City**. At least 2000 Church members sacrificed impressively to heed the **prophet's** wishes and show their own faithfulness.

SOURCES

Cowan, Richard O., and William E. Homer. *California Saints: A 150-Year Legacy in the Golden State*. Provo, Utah. Religious Studies Center, Brigham Young University, 1996.

Lyman, Edward Leo. *San Bernardino: The Rise and Fall of a California Community*. Salt Lake City: Signature Books, 1996.

EDWARD LEO LYMAN

SAN DIEGO, CALIFORNIA.

The second largest city in **California**, San Diego is located only a few miles north of the border with **Mexico**. San Diego Bay was discovered in 1542 by Juan Rodriguez Cabrillo, who claimed the area for Spain. A military outpost and the first of California's famed Franciscan missions were established here in 1769.

The first Latter-day Saints in San Diego were members of the **Mormon Battalion**, who arrived 29 January 1847 at the end of their epic march. While stationed in the area during the next several months, Battalion members dug wells, produced bricks, erected the first courthouse, and completed other projects benefiting the community.

After the last Battalion soldiers left in 1848, there were no known Latter-day Saints in the area for nearly four decades. By 1886 a Church member located there, and a **branch** was formed in 1898. The Church had its own pavilion at the California Pacific International Exposition, a **world's fair** held in Balboa Park during 1935 and 1936. The San Diego **Stake** was organized in 1941. Rapid growth, particularly during and following **World War II**, was reflected in the formation of several additional stakes. The Mormon Battalion Memorial **Visitor Center** opened at Old Town in 1972. The **San Diego California Temple** was dedicated in 1993.

SOURCE

Cowan, Richard O. and William E. Homer. *California Saints: A 150-Year Legacy in the Golden State.* Provo, Utah: Religious Studies Center, Brigham Young University, 1996.

RICHARD O. COWAN

SAN DIEGO CALIFORNIA TEMPLE.

The San Diego California Temple, the third **temple** in **California**, was dedicated by President **Gordon B. Hinckley** in 1993. (The **Los Angeles Temple** had been dedicated in 1956 and the **Oakland Temple** in 1964.) Situated on a seven-acre site next to the I-5 Freeway, the **San Diego** Temple is a well-known landmark in the suburb of La Jolla. The 82,447 square foot temple measures 165 by 194 feet. Its twin towers rise 190 feet, and the east spire is surmounted by a fourteen-foot gold-leafed statue of the **angel Moroni**. Gleaming white marble chips were blown into the temple's exterior plaster to give the structure a glistening appearance. A unique feature of this building is the atrium garden. To direct attention heavenward, architects provided large windows as sources of light. This temple serves not only the **Saints** in Southern California but also those across the nearby border in **Mexico**.

SOURCES

Cowan, Richard O. *Temples to Dot the Earth.* Springville, Utah: Cedar Fort, 1997. 184–87.

Cowan, Richard O., and William E. Homer. *California Saints: A 150-Year Legacy in the Golden State.* Provo, Utah: Religious Studies Center, Brigham Young University, 1996. 396–99.

RICHARD O. COWAN

SANDWICH ISLANDS. See HAWAII.

SAN FRANCISCO, CALIFORNIA.

San Francisco, the first Latter-day Saint settlement in the West, was the home of more than 230 **Saints** who arrived from **New York City** by boat on 31 July 1846—a full year before the first Saints reached the **Salt Lake Valley**. These Saints, arriving just three weeks after the flag of the **United States** was raised, made up **California's** first large group of settlers from the United States. The previously Mexican village of Yerba Buena had just nine permanent buildings, and the Saints held the city's first English-language church services in one of them. Over the next year and a half, using communal labor, they erected more than 100 permanent structures, including California's first public school. As they built, their leader, 27-year-old **Samuel Brannan**, prophesied their city would become the "Great Emporium of the **Pacific** and eventually the world" (Cowan and Homer, 101).

When **gold** was discovered in the Sierra foothills in January 1848, the Saints left the new city en masse. Newly arrived Chinese settlers squatted on their abandoned buildings, transforming their city into San Francisco's Chinatown. Many of the Saints never returned, and the city's Latter-day Saint majority became a small minority.

In 1851, **Parley P. Pratt** made San Francisco his headquarters for presiding over "the Islands and Coasts of the Pacific" (Cowan and Homer, 185). Another **apostle**, **Charles C. Rich**, came to organize a **stake**, but Church members were scattered over vast areas, making any kind of central organization impossible.

From 1857 until 1892 the Church had no presence in California, but after it returned, rapid **growth** caused the San Francisco stake to be organized in 1927. Today, this stake is a strong mix of ethnic peoples from around the world and from every socio-economic class. Early Church history sites in the city are commemorated with plaques, and Mormon **pioneer** memorabilia reside in several museums. A major street bears Brannan's name, and several of the streets and alleys in and around Chinatown bear the names of other early Mormon pioneers.

SOURCE

Cowan, Richard O., and William E. Homer. *California Saints: A 150-Year Legacy in the Golden State.* Provo, Utah: Religious Studies Center, Brigham Young University, 1996.

WILLIAM E. HOMER

SANTA FE TRAIL. The 780-mile Santa Fe Trail was an important international trade route between **Missouri** and **New Mexico** following Mexican independence from **Spain** in 1821. It divided at the Cimarron Crossing of the **Arkansas** River. One route, which assured adequate water for travelers, followed the Arkansas into southeastern **Colorado**, then southwest across Raton Pass and on to Santa Fe, New Mexico. The shorter route crossed the dry Cimarron Desert. Traders brought wagons loaded with eastern manufactured goods to exchange for mules, furs, gold, and silver in the Mexican frontier settlements. During the Mexican-American War (1846–48), the Army of the West, including the **Mormon Battalion**, followed the trail to invade New Mexico. After the **war**, the trail connected the **United States** to its southwest territories and was used in transporting all types of commercial and military freight. Stagecoach lines, fur trappers, some emigrants, and gold seekers heading for **California** and Colorado also traveled the route. After the railroad reached Santa Fe in 1880, the trail saw little use.

SOURCES

Connor, Seymour V. *Broadcloth and Britches: The Santa Fe Trail*. College Station, Tex.: Texas A. & M. University Press, 1977.

Gregg, Josiah. *Commerce of the Prairies*. Edited by Max L. Moorhead. Norman, Okla.: University of Oklahoma Press, 1954.

Inman, Henry. *The Old Santa Fe Trail: The Story of a Great Highway*. Minneapolis: Ross and Haines, 1966.

VIVIAN LINFORD TALBOT AND FRED R. GOWANS

SÃO PAULO, BRAZIL. São Paulo is the largest city in **South America** (with a population of 18 million in 1998) and the economic and commercial center of **Brazil**. It was chosen in 1935 as the first Brazilian **Mission** headquarters by Rulon S. Howells, first president of the mission. After missionary efforts were focused on the Portuguese-speaking population, São Paulo became the center of the Church in Brazil. Because of its role as the economic power of Brazil, the city's population grew, and the Church began to have success there. **Branches** developed, and in 1966 the first **stake** in South America was organized with **Walter Spät** as president. A second stake was organized in 1968. The first **temple** in South America was built in the city and dedicated in 1978. Along with the temple, the Church administrative center of Brazil was established in a nearby building. In 1997 a large **Missionary Training Center** was constructed. In 1998 city boundaries included four missions and more than 20 stakes. São Paulo continues to be a strong influence and center of the Church in Brazil.

SOURCES

Brigham, Janet. "The São Paulo Temple: Story of Sacrifice and Learning." *Ensign* 8 (October 1978): 858–60.

Grover, Mark L. "Mormonism in Brazil: Religion and Dependency in Latin America." Ph.D. diss., Indiana University, 1985.

MARK L. GROVER

SÃO PAULO BRAZIL TEMPLE. The São Paulo Brazil Temple, the first **LDS temple** to be built in **South America**, was announced 1 March 1975. The cornerstone was laid 9 March 1977, and the temple was dedicated by President **Spencer W. Kimball** 31 October 1978. This temple contains two ordinance rooms with capacity for 84 patrons, four sealing rooms, and other facilities, totaling 76 rooms. A separate four-story building to lodge patrons and serve as a missionary training center was dedicated in 1979.

Members throughout South America made great personal sacrifices in connection with the temple. Many sold their valuables and reduced their monthly household expenses to contribute to the construction and later to attend the temple regularly.

At first the temple district included all South America, with the exception of **Venezuela**. At the time of the dedication, there were 208,000 members living in the area. Twenty years after the dedication, most countries in the original district had their own temple (in operation or announced), and **Brazil** alone had around 700,000 members and three more temples under construction in the cities of Recife, Campinas, and Porto Alegre.

SOURCE

"Este é o Templo de São Paulo" ("This Is the São Paulo Temple"). *A Liahona* (November 1978): 2–13.

MARCUS H. MARTINS

SASKATCHEWAN, CANADA. A home **Sunday School** was first organized in Moose Jaw, Saskatchewan, in 1929, where Valentine Kenectol and Gordon Whyte were the earliest converts. Brother Whyte later moved 40 miles east to Regina, becoming the original **branch president** there in 1934. Military activity swelled membership during **WWII**, creating **branches** in Saskatoon (to the north) in 1944 and Moose Jaw in 1945.

Dan Morse was the initial president of the Saskatchewan District, created 12 June 1959. The North and South Saskatchewan Districts were created 10 years later. The Saskatoon Saskatchewan Stake was organized 5 November 1978 with Noel W. Burt as president; it covered the entire province, with the exception of the Fort Qu'Appelle District, which was organized 12 March 1978 and included the southern Native Canadian Church units. In 1998 President **Gordon B. Hinckley** visited Regina and announced a **temple** to be built in that city, which was dedicated 14 November 1999. At the beginning of the year 2000, Saskatchewan had 4,794 members and one stake with 18 **wards** and branches.

SOURCES

Gardner, Marvin K. "Taking the Church Anywhere." *Ensign* 11 (June 1981): 38–44.

Tagg, Melvin S. *A History of the Mormon Church in Canada.* Lethbridge, Alta.: Lethbridge Herald, 1968. 274–81.

JOHN P. LIVINGSTONE

SATAN. Latter-day Saint history is replete with examples of Satan's attempts to prevent the **Restoration** and expansion of the Church. Satan attempted to destroy **Joseph Smith** the **Prophet** in the **Sacred Grove** with such a power that Joseph said "it seemed to me for a time as if I were doomed to sudden destruction"(JS–H 1:15). This was not an isolated incident, for Joseph later explained, "the nearer a person approaches the Lord, a greater power will be manifested to prevent the accomplishment of His purposes" (quoted in Whitney, 146).

Between the time of the **First Vision** and the appearance of the angel **Moroni**, Joseph lamented that Satan had influenced so many people to revile against the Restoration (JS–H 1:20, 22). During this time Satan also tempted Joseph Smith to commit sin, which would have rendered him unfit to further God's work on earth. Satan was frustrated in those attempts, however, because the young prophet explained that he was not guilty of any serious sins (JS–H 1:28).

Satan next sought to prevent the translation of the **gold plates** by tempting Joseph to use the plates for personal gain. Again Satan was unsuccessful, and the angel Moroni allowed Joseph to see a vision of the "prince of darkness, surrounded by his innumerable train of associates," so that he would "know hereafter the two powers and never be influenced or overcome by that wicked one" (quoted in Cowdery, 393). Satan then influenced wicked men to attempt to take the plates by force (JS–H 1:60). Again unsuccessful, he devised a cunning plan to discredit the translated account of the **Book of Mormon** as the word of God by tempting wicked men to alter the text.

Still unsuccessful, Satan now attempted to stop the expansion and growth of the Church by external persecution and internal apostasy (Smith, 69–71). When these efforts were partially successful, the Lord sent **Heber C. Kimball**, **Orson Hyde**, and other Church missionaries to

England in 1837 to obtain new converts to strengthen the Church. After arriving in England, the elders experienced an attack by Satan similar to that made against the young Joseph Smith in the Sacred Grove. Throughout one night, **Elder** Kimball explained, "I witnessed a scene of satanic power and influence which I shall never forget" (quoted in Whitney, 143–46). He and his associates were attacked by legions of evil spirits with their leaders, who came toward them like armies rushing to battle. The missionaries, with the help of the Lord, were able to withstand the attack. The incident made such an impression on the mind of Elder Kimball that upon returning home, he asked Joseph Smith what it all meant. The Prophet explained that "at that time you were nigh unto the Lord; there was only a veil between you and Him, but you could not see Him. When I heard of it, it gave me great joy, for I then knew that the words of God had taken root in that land. It was this that caused the devil to make a struggle to kill you" (quoted in Whitney, 146).

Satan was unsuccessful in destroying the Church in those early days, but he has continued to oppose its growth by persecution from without and by tempting individual members to sin and apostatize.

SOURCES

Cowdery, Oliver. "Rise of the Church." *Times and Seasons* 2 (May 1841): 391–97.

Smith, Joseph Fielding. *Essentials in Church History.* Salt Lake City: Deseret Book, 1979.

Whitney, Orson F. *Life of Heber C. Kimball.* Salt Lake City: Juvenile Instructor Office, 1888.

LaMar E. Garrard

SATELLITE COMMUNICATIONS. With the perfection of **satellite communications**, the Church had a new means of reaching out to members around the world. Nine earth stations (downlinks) purchased by the Church were first used for the broadcast of **general conference** in April 1979, allowing Saints in Boston, Philadelphia, and **New York** to receive it live. In March 1980 Bonneville Satellite secured its access to this technology by agreeing to lease a transponder on Westar 1. The April 1980 **conference**, which celebrated the Church's sesquicentennial, used two satellites to present a synchronized program originating in two different locations. During the next few years, Church downlinks were installed at stake centers in the **United States** and **Canada**.

In April 1989 conference sessions were transmitted to **Europe** via PanAmSat. In March 1992 a **Relief Society** sesquicentennial program was sent by satellite to Europe, **Africa, Asia**, and the **Pacific**. This was followed by a broadcast of Sunday morning's session of the April 1992 conference to **England, France**, and **Germany**. Since 1993 regular satellite transmissions of conference have been received in Europe, where the Church now has more than 150 satellite downlinks in 13 countries.

Conference sessions were first sent by satellite to 12 countries in Central and **South America** in October 1998.

SOURCES

Brown, Thomas E. Letter to author, 6 November 1998. (Brown is the director of Satellite and Support Services for The Church of Jesus Christ of Latter-day Saints.)

Christensen, Bruce L. "Satellite Communications System." *Encyclopedia of Mormonism.* Edited by Daniel H. Ludlow. 4 vols. New York: Macmillan, 1992. 3:1261.

ROBERT L. HALES

SAUDI ARABIA. See MIDDLE EAST and MUSLIMS.

SCANDINAVIA. In 1849 President **Brigham Young** called **Erastus Snow** and Peter O. Hansen to open the Scandinavian Mission. Hansen arrived first; **Elders** Snow, John E. Forsgren, and George Dykes joined him in Copenhagen 14 June 1850. Forsgren went to **Sweden**, baptized his brother Peter on 26 July 1850 (the first convert baptism in the region), and was banished in September. Hans J. Peterson began preaching in Risør, **Norway**, in September 1851, though legal obstruction soon ensued there also. Snow sent two converts to teach in **Iceland** at the end of 1851. Preaching began in **Finland** in 1875, and a branch was organized in Larsmo, but harassment from Russian officials disrupted **missionary work**, leaving the few members generally isolated until 1946.

Scandinavia's first branch was organized in Copenhagen 15 September 1850. Despite legal difficulties, branches were formed in Oesterrisoer, Norway, 16 July 1852, and in Skönabäck, Sweden, 24 April 1853. Most members of the branch organized in Iceland 19 June 1853 soon emigrated. **Stakes** followed much later—the first was organized in Stockholm in April 1975.

The May 1851 Danish edition of the **Book of Mormon** was the first non-English version of the book. The **periodical** *Skandinaviens Stjerne* commenced in October that year, and a Danish translation of the **Doctrine and Covenants** was printed in February 1852. A Swedish version of the Book of Mormon came in 1878, but editions in Norwegian and Finnish did not appear until the 1950s. The Swedish-language periodical *Nordstjärnan* commenced publication in 1877. Other contemporary Church magazines include *Stjernen* (Danish), *Lys Over Norge* (Norwegian), and *Valkeus* (Finnish).

Emigration, which commenced in 1852, shaped the Church in Scandinavia and **America**. Nearly half of the 46,000 converts from 1850 to 1905 emigrated, mostly from **Denmark**. By 1974 some 29,000 members, plus many young children, had gone to **Zion** (Mulder, 107; Jensen, 46–47). Two **apostles**, **Anthon Lund** and **John A**. **Widtsoe**, were born in Scandinavia, and many other Church leaders, authors, and artists have had Scandinavian ancestry.

Social hardships and wartime isolation challenged the **Saints** in Scandinavia. Government opposition and war so depleted the missionary force that Elder Widtsoe and **Reed Smoot** visited regional capitals in 1923 to improve conditions. **Missions** and building programs expanded after **World War II**. The 1985 dedication of the Stockholm Sweden Temple and the 1999 announcement of a **temple** in Copenhagen cemented the Church's regional presence. Finnish Saints spearheaded missionary work across the Baltic in the late 1980s, and groups from **Russia** and the Baltic republics began visiting the Swedish temple several times a year.

SOURCES

Jensen, Richard L. "The Friendly Invasion." *Ensign* 4 (July 1974): 46–47.

Jenson, Andrew. *History of the Scandinavian Mission*. Salt Lake City: Deseret News, 1927.

Mulder, William E. *Homeward to Zion: The Mormon Migration from Scandinavia*. Minneapolis: University of Minnesota Press, 1957.

JOHN THOMAS

SCHAERRER, NEIL D. Neil Dean Schaerrer was the first **Young Men's** general president called after responsibility for youth was transferred from the presiding bishopric to the **Priesthood** Department in 1977. He was born 12 April 1930 in Payson, **Utah**, and was a missionary in **Switzerland** (1950–53) before serving as president of the **Austria** Vienna **Mission** (1972–75). He married Jane Coon in 1953. They were the parents of four children. Schaerrer was an attorney by profession. He died 18 January 1985 in **Salt Lake City** at age 54.

The new Young Men organization was correlated with **Young Women** and sought to streamline its programs for countries where the Church was rapidly expanding. President Schaerrer and his **counselors**, Graham W. Doxey and Quinn Gunn McKay, oversaw three areas: **Aaronic Priesthood** class instruction and leadership training; Young Men activities, including Scouting; and combined Young Men–Young Women activities. Acting under the direction of **Elder Marion D. Hanks**, managing director of youth, the presidency gave local counselors and committees greater supervisory roles over youth. Schaerrer was released in October 1979.

SOURCES

"Neil D. Schaerrer Dies, Church Official, Attorney." *Deseret News*, 20 January 1985. B–4.

"Youth Programs Are Refined." *Church News*, 21 May 1977. 4, 12.

JED L. WOODWORTH

SCHETTLER, PAUL. Paul Schettler, a **mission president** and multilingual interpreter, was born 13 August 1827 in Prussia. He emigrated to the **United States** in 1858. He accepted the gospel in **New York City** and was baptized there by **George Q. Cannon** on 9 February 1860. Soon thereafter he joined the **Saints** in **Utah** and began his life of service in the kingdom.

In 1861, when he had only been a member of the Church for four years, Brother Schettler was called to be a mission president in The **Netherlands**. From Amsterdam he was transferred to **Switzerland**, where he served until his release in 1864.

He served as the treasurer for **Salt Lake City** for 20 years, from 1864 to 1884. It was during this period that he joined President **George A. Smith** on a dedicatory mission to **Palestine** (1872–73), wherein he served as both interpreter and cashier because he spoke six languages and had an excellent talent for handling finances. Brother Schettler died in Salt Lake City on 3 November 1884.

SOURCES

Jenson, Andrew. *Latter-day Saint Biographical Encyclopedia.* 4 vols. 1901–36. Reprint, Salt Lake City: Western Epics, 1971. 4:357–58.

Journal of Discourses. 26 vols. London: Latter-day Saints' Book Depot, 1854–86. 16:101.

BLAIR G. VAN DYKE

SCHISMATIC GROUPS. From its earliest days, The Church of Jesus Christ of Latter-day Saints has had individuals and small groups apostatize and begin their own churches, either in opposition to or based upon some aspects of the **restoration** of the gospel through the **Prophet Joseph Smith**. The earliest known schism from the Church was Wycam Clark's Pure Church of Christ in 1831. Other offshoots prior to the death of Joseph Smith in 1844 included **George Hinkle's** Church of Jesus Christ, the Bride the Lamb's Wife, and groups founded by former Church members Isaac Russell, Gladden Bishop, and **Warren Parrish**. The Parrish group, known as The Church of Christ, drew away more than 30 prominent Church members in **Kirtland**, caused serious problems for Joseph Smith and the faithful Saints in **Ohio**, and took control of the **Kirtland Temple**. The final splinter group to emerge before the death of Joseph Smith was begun in Nauvoo by three sets of brothers—the Laws, the Fosters, and the Higbees. This group was responsible for the *Nauvoo Expositor*, a newspaper opposing Joseph Smith. The destruction of this paper by **Nauvoo** city officials was a contributing factor to the death of the Prophet.

After the **martyrdom** of Joseph Smith, there was some confusion among the general membership of the Church as to who would take Joseph's place. While most of the Saints followed the **Quorum** of the Twelve **Apostles**, a new type of schism appeared: dissidents that based their beliefs on some of the teachings of Joseph Smith but believed someone other than the Twelve should direct the Church. Some, like **Sidney Rigdon** and **James J. Strang**, sought to be Joseph Smith's successor immediately following his death. The Church of Christ (Temple Lot), led by Granville Hedrick, moved to Missouri from Illinois after the Martyrdom and purchased part of the original **temple** lot.

Others sustained the Quorum of the Twelve as the Church leadership and followed them for a time. They later left the Church and solicited a following for their own denominations. Prominent among this latter group were **Lyman Wight**, who had been a member of the Twelve; **Alpheus Cutler**, a member of the Nauvoo **high council**; **George Miller**, who had been a **bishop** in Nauvoo; and **William Smith**, the Prophet's brother.

Schismatic groups continued to appear after the Saints settled in the **Salt Lake Valley**. The **Morrisites** and **Godbeites** were Church offshoots during **Brigham Young's** administration. After the **Manifesto (1890)**, many factions emerged in opposition to the Church's discontinuation of the practice of **plural marriage**. These groups are typically referred to as **fundamentalists**.

Taking into account the break-offs from the break-offs, the number of divergent groups that originated with the teachings of Joseph Smith is more than one hundred and growing, with new groups still appearing from time to time. A few of these more recent offshoots have proven to be dangerous, to the extent of murdering people from rival factions.

Most schisms lasted only a few years, but some have persisted to the present. The largest of the schismatic groups is the **Reorganized Church of Jesus Christ of Latter Day Saints**, with its headquarters in **Independence, Missouri**. It has between two and three hundred thousand members.

SOURCES

Carter, Kate B., ed. "Denominations That Base Their Beliefs on the Teachings of Joseph Smith." *Our Pioneer Heritage.* 20 vols. Salt Lake City: Daughters of Utah Pioneers, 1958–77. 5:325–92.

Rich, Russell R. *Little Known Schisms of the Restoration.* 3d ed. Provo, Utah: Brigham Young University, 1967.

———. *Those Who Would Be Leaders.* 2d ed. Provo, Utah: Brigham Young University, 1967.

Shields, Steven L. *Divergent Paths of the Restoration.* 3d ed. Bountiful, Utah: Restoration Research, 1982.

RICHARD G. MOORE

SCHOOL IN ZION. During the summer of 1833, about 60 **Elders** in **Missouri** were organized into the School in Zion. It was modeled after the **School of the Prophets** in **Kirtland**, and members "prayed, preached, and prophesied, and exercised . . . the gifts of the Holy Spirit" (Pratt, 93–94). The school's teacher, **Parley P. Pratt**, said, "The Lord gave me great wisdom, and enabled me to teach and edify the elders"(Pratt, 94).

In a **revelation** to **Joseph Smith** in Kirtland, **Ohio**, the Lord noted that he was "pleased that there should be a school in **Zion**" and that he was also pleased with Parley P. Pratt, its teacher (D&C 97:3). He commanded Elder Pratt to continue with the school until he received "other commandments" (D&C 97:4).

SOURCE

Pratt, Parley P. *Autobiography of Parley P. Pratt.* Edited by Parley P. Pratt Jr. Salt Lake City: Deseret Book, 1985.

CLARK V. JOHNSON

SCHOOL OF THE ELDERS. Distinguished from the **School of the Prophets** held in **Joseph Smith's** home above the **Whitney store**, the

School of the Elders existed during at least two time periods. The School of the Elders, or "the school in **Zion**" (D&C 97:3–5), began in 1833 under the direction of **Parley P. Pratt**. Organized by **revelation**, this school had as its main focus the missionary preparation of the brethren living in **Jackson County, Missouri. Elder** Pratt wrote: "This class, to the number of about sixty, met for instruction once a week. The place of meeting was in the open air, under some tall trees, in a retired place in the wilderness, where we prayed, preached and prophesied, and exercised ourselves in the gifts of the Holy Spirit" (Pratt, 93–94).

The School of the Elders in **Kirtland, Ohio**, was organized in November 1834 and held in the lower story of the printing office located on the lot west of the **temple**. Although many secular subjects were studied (grammar, writing, government, **literature**, philosophy, etc.) the school had as its main purpose activities relating to missionary preparation. Additionally, seven lectures on theology were delivered to the school during the winter of 1834 and 1835 and eventually published in the first edition of the **Doctrine and Covenants** under the title *Lectures on Faith*. **Sidney Rigdon** was one of the main instructors, with Joseph Smith presiding. In 1836 this school was reorganized under the name School of the Prophets.

SOURCES

Backman, Milton V. *The Heavens Resound.* Salt Lake City: Deseret Book, 1983. 268–70.

Journal History of the Church. Salt Lake City: The Church of Jesus Christ of Latter-day Saints, Historical Department, 1830–1972. 1:417–18; 2:169–70.

Peterson, Orlen Curtis. "A History of the Schools and Educational Programs of The Church of Jesus Christ of Latter-day Saints in Ohio and Missouri, 1831–1839." Master's thesis, Brigham Young University, 1972. 34–41.

Pratt, Parley P. *Autobiography of Parley P. Pratt.* Edited by Parley P. Pratt Jr. Salt Lake City: Deseret Book, 1985.

C. ROBERT LINE

SCHOOL OF THE PROPHETS. The first School of the **Prophets** was established 24 January 1833 in the **Newel K. Whitney Store** in **Kirtland, Ohio**, for the purpose of preparing missionaries to teach the gospel. The school was established by **revelation** "for their instruction in all things that are expedient for them, even for all the officers of the church, or in other words, those who are called to the ministry in the church" (D&C 88:127). In this revelation the curriculum, textbooks, and operation of the school are outlined by the Lord. The curriculum was very broad as those involved were instructed to seek wisdom "out of the best books" and to seek learning not only by study but also by faith (D&C 88:118).

First and foremost they were to study the doctrine of the kingdom so they could "be instructed more perfectly in theory, in principle, in doctrine, in the law of the gospel." But in addition they were to expand their mind by studying (using modern terminology) astronomy, agriculture, geology, history, current events, international affairs, history, and geography. The Lord indicated they were to study "the best books" (D&C 88:78–80, 118).

This was not an ordinary group because its members were to sanctify themselves by purifying their hearts and cleansing their hands and their feet so the Lord could make them clean (D&C 88:74). There were as many as 21 members in the original school, known as the "first elders."

Two significant events occurred during the school. The **counselors** in the **First Presidency** received the keys of the kingdom, under the Prophet's direction, as promised in D&C 90:6–7, and at this same time a **vision** of the Father and Son occurred, which was seen by many present.

Similar schools were held in **Missouri** (1833), later in Kirtland (1834–35), and **Utah** (beginning in 1867 and continuing on into the 1880s). It was at the **School of the Elders** in Kirtland (1834–35) that the *Lectures on Faith* were first given (Peterson, 40).

SOURCES

Anderson, Karl Ricks. *Joseph Smith's Kirtland.* Salt Lake City: Deseret Book, 1989. 115–19.

Backman, Milton V., Jr. *The Heavens Resound.* Salt Lake City: Deseret Book, 1983. 264–70.

McConkie, Bruce R. *Mormon Doctrine.* 2d ed. Salt Lake City: Bookcraft, 1966.

Peterson, Orlen Curtis. "A History of the Schools and Educational Programs of The Church of Jesus Christ of Latter-day Saints in Ohio and Missouri, 1831–32." Master's thesis, Brigham Young University, 1972.

KEITH W. PERKINS

SCHOOLS. See EDUCATION.

SCHREINER, ALEXANDER.

Alexander Schreiner, a **tabernacle** organist for 53 years (1924–77), was born 31 July 1901 in Nürnberg, **Germany.** He emigrated with his family to **Salt Lake City** in 1912.

Due to his impressive accomplishments, Schreiner was invited to study with John J. McClellan, who was then the tabernacle organist. Upon graduating from high school, he worked as a theater organist for silent movies from 1918 through 1925. His earnings enabled him to serve a 30-month **mission** in southern **California** and afterwards to continue his study of classical organ in **Europe** with Louis Vierne and Charles Marie Widor.

Upon his return from Europe, Schreiner resumed regular duties as a tabernacle organist. In 1930 he was appointed university organist and lecturer at the University of California at Los Angeles (UCLA), a position he held until May 1939. He earned bachelor of arts and doctoral degrees from the **University of Utah**, studying under **Leroy J. Robertson**, and was awarded four honorary doctorates. He became widely known for articles, compositions, arrangements, recordings, radio performances, and concert tours. He wrote musical settings for nine of the hymns in the 1985 LDS hymnbook. He died in Salt Lake City on 15 September 1987 at age 86.

SOURCES

Davidson, Karen Lynn. *Our Latter-day Hymns: The Stories and the Messages.* Salt Lake City: Deseret Book, 1988. 435–36.
"News of the Church." *Ensign* 17 (November 1987): 106.

GERALD L. HOMER

SCIENCE AND SCIENTISTS. Both formally educated and self-taught scientists were among early generations of prominent Latter-day Saints. **Orson Pratt**, for example, was self-taught in mathematics and astronomy. Three members of the Quorum of the Twelve **Apostles** in the early part of the twentieth century were scientists: **James E. Talmage** (geology), **Joseph F. Merrill** (physics), and **John A. Widtsoe** (chemistry). In 2000 two members of the Quorum of the Twelve also had scientific backgrounds: **Russell M. Nelson** (medicine) and **Richard G. Scott** (nuclear engineering).

Harvey Fletcher (physics) was a director of the Bell Laboratories and later a dean at **Brigham Young University**, and **Henry Eyring** (chemistry), dean at the **University of Utah**, was the recipient of numerous international and national awards and honors, including the National Medal of Science, for his scientific contributions. These two exceptionally gifted scientists became the earliest Church members in the National Academy of Science, the most prestigious scientific organization in **America**.

Other Latter-day Saints of the twentieth century who have achieved international scientific prominence, as well as membership in the National Academy of Science, include Nobel laureate Paul D. Boyer, University of **California**–Los Angeles (biochemistry); Arthur Hasler, University of **Wisconsin**–Madison (population biology, evolution, and ecology); Philip F. Low, formerly at Purdue University (agronomy); and J. Edwin Seegmiller, University of California–San Diego (medical physiology and metabolism).

The Church has employed scientific technology in many programs. For example, **satellite communications** allow members all over the world to participate in **conferences** originating from **Salt Lake City**, and the Church **Family History** Program uses computer technology to achieve a recognized worldwide database of individual names and **family** associations.

Church members who are involved in the day-to-day practice of science commonly confront areas of apparent conflict between science and religion, yet their faith can remain strong, because they know that learning is continually expanding and ultimate truth will resolve all troubling issues. Concerning these matters, **Brigham Young** said that "our religion will not clash with or contradict the facts of science in any particular" (*JD*, 14:115–17). The Lord has revealed in divine **scriptures** this helpful information: "In that day when the Lord shall come, he shall reveal all things—Things which have passed, and hidden things which no man knew, things of the earth, by which it was made, and the purpose and the end thereof—Things most precious, things that are above, and things that are beneath, things that are in the earth, and upon the earth, and in heaven" (D&C 101:32–34). These verses indicate that we presently have an incomplete knowledge of his creation but that the Lord has promised to make these things known in his own time.

Latter-day Saints with scientific training can see harmony in scientific and divine paths to understanding and truth. To study God's creations, along with the study of scripture, is to have access to a greater understanding and appreciation of his work.

SOURCES

Eyring, Henry. *The Faith of a Scientist*. Salt Lake City: Bookcraft, 1967.

Haglund, Richard F., and Erich Robert Paul. "Resources for the Study of Science, Technology, and Mormon Culture." *Mormon Americana*. Edited by David J. Whittaker. Provo, Utah: BYU Studies, 1995.

Hardy, Kenneth R. "Social Origins of American Scientists and Scholars." *Science* 185 (9 August, 1974): 497–506.

Journal of Discourses [JD]. 26 vols. London: Latter-day Saints' Book Depot, 1854–86.

Paul, Erich Robert. *Science, Religion, and Mormon Cosmology.* Chicago: University of Illinois Press, 1992.

Widtsoe, John A. *Evidences and Reconciliations.* 3 vols. Salt Lake City: Bookcraft, 1943.

MORRIS S. PETERSEN

SCOTLAND. In partial fulfillment of Elder **Heber C. Kimball's** prediction that the spread of the fulness of the gospel in Britain would grow out of the Church's first foreign **mission** in **Canada**, Alexander Wright and Samuel Mulliner set sail for **Liverpool, England,** on 4 November 1839. Both had emigrated from Scotland to Canada, where they found the gospel only a few years earlier. On a wet Friday, 20 December, they arrived in Glasgow. The next day they traveled to Edinburgh, and after spending a few days with Mulliner at his parents' home, Wright went on to Marnock in Banffshire to share the gospel with friends and relatives.

The first converts in Scotland were baptized on 14 January 1840 in the River Clyde near the village of Bishopton. On the eve of Elder **Orson Pratt's** arrival in Scotland on 3 May, 20 people were baptized, making a total of 80 converts. Laboring mainly in Edinburgh, Elder Pratt saw the **conference** in that city grow to more than 200 members. The first decade brought growth from one branch with 80 members to 50 branches with 3,250 members. By 1855 conferences were established in Edinburgh, Dundee, Glasgow, and Kilmarnock. By the end of the century, 5,000 Scottish **Saints** had emigrated to **Zion,** leaving only 338 members in Scotland when **David O. McKay** arrived to serve his mission in the land of his forefathers.

Not until the 1950s and 60s did the Church see a resurgence of substantial growth in Scotland. The first **stake** in the country was organized by President David O. McKay in Glasgow on 26 August 1962. Further stakes were organized at Dundee in 1975 and at Aberdeen, Edinburgh, and Paisley in 1980. By the year 2000, Church membership in Scotland numbered 25,791, with Saints organized in 5 stakes and 1 mission, comprising 50 **wards** and branches.

SOURCES

Jenson, Andrew. *Encyclopedic History of The Church of Jesus Christ of Latter-day Saints.* Salt Lake City: Deseret News, 1941. 782–83.

1999–2000 Church Almanac. Salt Lake City: Deseret News, 1998. 401–2.

ROBERT RICHARDSON

SCOTT, RICHARD G. Richard Gordon Scott, **apostle**, missionary, and nuclear engineer, was born 7 November 1928 in Pocatello, Idaho, to Kenneth L. and Mary Whittle Scott. He graduated in mechanical engineering from George Washington University in 1950. After his graduation, he served a mission to **Uruguay**. He married Jeanene Watkins on 18 July 1953 in the **Manti Temple**. They became the parents of seven children, five of whom are living.

In 1955, Brother Scott received the equivalent of a doctorate in nuclear engineering at Oakridge, **Tennessee**. He served for twelve years under Admiral Rickover in designing, testing, and manufacturing nuclear fuel for the Navy nuclear program.

Brother Scott was called to preside over the **Argentina** North Mission in 1965. He was a **regional representative** and sustained as a member of the First **Quorum** of the **Seventy** on 2 April 1977. He was sustained to the presidency of the First Quorum of Seventy on 1 October 1983.

Elder Scott was sustained a member of the Quorum of the Twelve Apostles on 1 October 1988 and **ordained** an apostle 6 October 1988, at age 59. Sister Scott died of cancer 15 May 1995 in Salt Lake City, at the age of 65.

SOURCES

Gardner, Marvin K., "Elder Richard G. Scott: The Real Power Comes from the Lord." *Ensign* (January 1989): 6–11.
1999–2000 Church Almanac. Salt Lake City: Deseret News, 1998. 21.

MATTHEW O. RICHARDSON

SCOUTING. See **BOY SCOUTS**.

SCRIPTURES. See **STANDARD WORKS**.

SCULPTORS. Latter-day Saint sculptors have contributed significant statuary to the Church, and several have received national and international acclaim. The first LDS sculptors were stone and wood carvers who produced decorative sculpture in the mid-1800s. They include Ralph Ramsay (1852–1905), who created the eagle for the original **Eagle Gate** in **Salt Lake City**, and William C. Ward (nineteenth century), who carved the lions for **Brigham Young's Lion House** and assisted with the architecture of the **Salt Lake Temple**.

Among the first and most influential sculptors to complete commissions for the Church was Cyrus E. Dallin (1861–1944). Although born and reared in **Utah**, Dallin was not a member of the Church. His commissions from the Church include the statue of the angel **Moroni** atop the Salt Lake Temple and the *Brigham Young Monument* at the intersection of Main Street and South Temple in Salt Lake City. Dallin spent most of his distinguished career in Boston, where he created some of New England's most significant monuments.

A grandson of Brigham Young, **Mahonri M. Young** (1877–1957) was an LDS artist who attained international renown as a sculptor and painter. Although he lived most of his life in **New York City**, Young maintained strong ties with the Church and his native Utah. His best-known works for the Church are the *Joseph and Hyrum Smith* statues and the *Seagull Monument* on **Temple Square**, the *This Is the Place Monument* in Salt Lake City, and the *Brigham Young* statue on the **Brigham Young University** campus.

Torleif S. Knaphus (1881–1965) joined the Church in his native **Denmark** and immigrated to Utah. His works for the Church include the *Handcart Pioneer Monument* on Temple Square, the *Hill Cumorah Monument,* and the statuary for the **Cardston Alberta**, **Idaho Falls Idaho,** and **Mesa Arizona** Temples.

Perhaps the most prolific LDS sculptor was **Avard T. Fairbanks** (1897–1987), who is internationally known for his monumental sculpture. Among his numerous religious works are the *Winter Quarters Monument* in **Florence**, **Nebraska**, the angel Moroni statues on the **Washington D.C.**, Seattle Washington, South Jordan Utah, and **Mexico City Mexico Temples**, the friezes and garden statuary of the **Hawaii Temple** (done in collaboration with his brother, J. Leo Fairbanks), the *Restoration of the Aaronic Priesthood* Monument and the *Three Witnesses Monument* on Temple Square, the *Mortal Moroni Monument* on the **Manti Temple** grounds, the *American Family Monument* in **Provo**, **Utah**, and *Joseph Smith's Vision* on the BYU campus.

The number of successful LDS sculptors has grown significantly since the 1940s. Dennis Smith and other successful LDS sculptors did impressive work in the last half of the twentieth century.

SOURCES

Greenthal, Kathryn et al. *American Figurative Sculpture in the Museum of Fine Arts, Boston.* Boston: Museum of Fine Arts, 1986.

Olpin, Robert S. *Dictionary of Utah Art.* Salt Lake City: Salt Lake Arts Council, 1980.

Swanson, Vern G., Robert S. Olpin, and William C. Seifrit. *Utah Painting and Sculpture.* Salt Lake City: Gibbs-Smith, 1997.

DANIEL J. FAIRBANKS

SEAGULL MONUMENT. The spring after the **Saints'** arrival in the **Salt Lake Valley**, hordes of crickets descended from the hills and began devouring the newly sprouted grain. The **pioneers** prayed for deliverance, and their answer came in the arrival of great flocks of seagulls that devoured the crickets. In 1912 the Church commissioned **Mahonri M. Young** (1877–1957) to create a monument on **Temple Square** to celebrate this miracle.

Topping a tall granite column is the gilt bronze sculpture of seagulls. Bronze bas relief plaques arranged clockwise on the base tell the story. The east plaque shows the entry of the pioneers into the valley. Next the pioneers are depicted kneeling in prayer and welcoming the seagulls sent by the Lord to save their crops. Then the Saints are harvesting their miraculously saved wheat. The final plaque tells the story in text form.

The artist, a grandson of **Brigham Young**, studied in **New York** and Paris. His work is in more than 50 museums, including the Metropolitan Museum of Art in **New York City** and the rotunda of the National Capitol Building.

SOURCE

Oman, Richard G., and Robert O. Davis. *Images of Faith; Art of the Latter-day Saints.* Salt Lake City: Deseret Book, 1995.

RICHARD G. OMAN

SEAGULLS, MIRACLE OF. The 1847 **pioneers** desperately needed a bounteous harvest in 1848. By May 1848 crops looked promising but suffered from drought, frost, and loose livestock. In addition to these problems, starting 22 May "great numbers of large, black crickets . . . came swarming from the foot hills literally by millions" (Roberts, 331). "**Mormon** crickets," technically *Anabus simplex,* are thumb-sized crickets that lack wings and eat voraciously. By 4 June efforts to drown, burn, beat, and scare them had done little good. Some discouraged **Saints** wanted to head for **California**. Then help arrived. On 9 June valley leaders reported: "The seagulls have come in large flocks from the lake and sweep the crickets as they go; it seems the hand of the Lord is in our favor" (quoted in Hartley, 230). For about three weeks, gulls ate crickets, drank, regurgitated indigestible parts, and ate more, making pioneers believe the birds' mission was to save crops, not just to feed.

For many the gull attack was a **miracle**. A **First Presidency** assessment of the 1848 harvest noted crickets but not gulls: "The brethren were not sufficiently numerous to fight the crickets, irrigate the crops, and fence the farms of their extensive planting, consequently they suffered heavy losses" (quoted in Hartley, 236). Clearly, seagulls helped save crops and buoy up spirits. Utahns have adopted laws protecting seagulls. After 1848, cricket infestations and gull attacks on crickets and grasshoppers in the West have been common. Deservedly, the miracle of the gulls is a popular faith-promoting story among Latter-day Saints. The **Seagull Monument**, sculpted by **Mahonri M. Young**, was erected on **Temple Square** on 13 September 1913.

SOURCES

Hartley, William G. "Mormons, Crickets and Gulls: A New Look at an Old Story." *Utah Historical Quarterly* 38 (Summer 1970): 224–39.

Roberts, B. H. *A Comprehensive History of The Church of Jesus Christ of Latter-day Saints, Century One.* 6 vols. Salt Lake City: The Church of Jesus Christ of Latter-day Saints, 1930. 3:331–33.

WILLIAM G. HARTLEY

SEALING ORDINANCE. See TEMPLES AND TEMPLE WORK.

SECOND GREAT AWAKENING. See GREAT AWAKENING.

SECOND MANIFESTO. See MANIFESTO, SECOND.

SECURITY PROGRAM. See WELFARE PROGRAM.

SEER. In ancient times the Lord called, and endowed with power, men to act as seers. Such an office was not necessarily synonymous with "**prophet**" or "revelator." The **Book of Mormon** teaches "that a seer is greater than a prophet. . . . A seer is a revelator and a prophet also; and a gift which is greater can no man have except he should possess the power of God, which no man can" (Mosiah 8:15–16). In a **revelation** given in late 1830 concerning the ancient **patriarch** Enoch, the Prophet **Joseph Smith** learned that a seer is one who sees things "not visible to the natural eye" (Moses 6:36). Thus, a seer "can know of things which are past, and also of things which are to come, and by them shall all things be revealed" (Mosiah 8:17).

With the **restoration** of the ancient order of things in this **dispensation of the fulness of times**, when all things from previous dispensations will be reinstituted (Eph. 1:10), Joseph Smith, as presiding officer over the whole Church, was appointed by the Lord to be a "**prophet, seer, and revelator**" (D&C 107:91–92; 124:125). In the Church today, the 15 men who make up the Council of the **First Presidency** and the **Quorum** of the Twelve **Apostles** are called and then sustained by the general membership of the Church as prophets, seers, and revelators. As was declared in ancient times, where there is no **vision** of the kind possessed by seers, "the people perish" (Prov. 29:18).

Andrew C. Skinner

SEER STONES. Seer stones assisted **Joseph Smith** in receiving **revelations** and translating **scriptures** and worked according to the **Prophet's** faith, worthiness, and mental effort (*CHC,* 1:128–33). **David Whitmer** explained that such stones only worked when the Prophet had humbled himself before the Lord and when he was free of contention or worldliness (*CHC,* 1:130–31). According to **Elder Orson Pratt,** Joseph Smith's use of such physical instruments declined as he gained more experience in translating.

SOURCES

McConkie, Bruce R. *Mormon Doctrine.* 2d ed. Salt Lake City: Bookcraft, 1979. 818–19.

Roberts, B. H. *A Comprehensive History of The Church of Jesus Christ of Latter-day Saints, Century One.* 6 vols. Salt Lake City: The Church of Jesus Christ of Latter-day Saints, 1930. 1:128–33.

Turley, Richard E., Jr. "Seer Stones." *Encyclopedia of Mormonism.* Edited by Daniel H. Ludlow. 4 vols. New York: Macmillan, 1992. 3:1293.

Lisa Kurki

SEGO LILY. A small plant with delicate white blossoms and small bulbs, the sego lily (*Calochortus*) became **Utah's** state flower in 1911. **Mormon pioneers** observed **Indians** gathering and eating the bulb and adopted the tribal term "sego" for it. Many subsisted partly on sego bulbs during the winter of 1848 to 1849, though few relished this food, which was tiny, difficult to dig, and bland. Subsequent generations romanticized the plant as a symbol of peace and chastity, writing poetry to commemorate it. In 1913 the **Relief Society** designated the flower as its official emblem because of "its usefulness in sustaining life in the early pioneer settlements" (*Handbook,* 1).

SOURCES

Cannon, Brian Q. "The Sego Lily, Utah's State Flower." *Utah Historical Quarterly* 63 (Winter 1995): 70–84.

Relief Society Handbook. Salt Lake City: Corporation of the President of The Church of Jesus Christ of Latter-day Saints, 1988.

BRIAN Q. CANNON

SEIXAS, JOSHUA. A teacher in the **Kirtland** Hebrew School from 26 January to 29 March 1836, Joshua Seixas was born 4 June 1802 in **New York City**. He taught at Oberlin College in 1835. **Lorenzo Snow**, not yet a member of the Church, was enrolled in Joshua Seixas's Hebrew class at Oberlin. He wrote to his sister **Eliza R. Snow**, speaking favorably of Professor Seixas. Eliza, who was then living with the **Smith family**, brought this information to the attention of the **Prophet Joseph Smith**. Joseph Smith then sent **Orson Hyde** and **William E. McLellin** to procure Joshua Seixas's services as the Hebrew teacher in the Kirtland school in early January 1836. According to the agreement, Seixas would be paid $320 to teach 40 students for seven weeks. After 29 March 1836, there seems to have been little formal study of Hebrew in the Kirtland school. Seixas then went to New York City, where he continued teaching Hebrew.

SOURCES

Crawley, Peter. *A Descriptive Bibliography of the Mormon Church.* Provo, Utah: Brigham Young University, 1997. 62.

Ogden, D. Kelly. "The Kirtland Hebrew School (1835–36)." In *Ohio.* Edited by Milton V. Backman Jr. Regional Studies in Latter-day Saint Church History series. Provo, Utah: Brigham Young University, 1990. 69–80.

Snow, Leroi C. "Who Was Professor Joshua Seixas?" *Improvement Era* 39 (February 1936): 67–71.

BRIAN M. HAUGLID

SEMINARIES. Since 1912, the Church seminary program, a part of the **Church Educational System** (CES), has provided weekday religious instruction for hundreds of thousands of Latter-day Saint youth in the ninth through twelfth grades. Its purpose is to help students to come unto **Christ** (Moro. 10:32) and to balance secular secondary education with daily religious study. It features year-long courses in Old Testament, New Testament, **Book of Mormon,** and **Doctrine and Covenants**–Church history.

The forerunners of the seminary program were the Church's **academies**—which, beginning in 1875, provided secondary education, including religious instruction—and the **Religion Classes,** established in 1890 to provide a weekday program for elementary-aged children. At the beginning of the twentieth century, Church leaders noticed that the youth were drifting away from Church standards. To combat this trend, the Church experimented with a religion class adjacent to Granite High School in **Salt Lake City** during the 1912–13 school year. Students were released from high school to attend a religion class taught by Thomas J. Yates, which proved effective and was quickly adopted in other communities with a high ratio of LDS youth. This was the beginning of the seminary program.

Three types of seminary were developed to meet the needs of students throughout the world: (1) Released-time seminaries operate during the regular school day usually in Church-owned facilities adjacent to junior and senior high schools. The constitutionality of released-time religious education was tested as early as 1929 and upheld in the courts. (2) Early-morning seminaries, developed during the early 1950s, provide weekday religious instruction in areas where local public school laws do not grant released-time or where LDS populations do not warrant a released-time seminary program. Generally, these classes meet in the morning before public school begins and are taught by local Church volunteers. (3) Home-study seminaries are provided to meet the needs of LDS youth living where distance or other problems make participation in a daily class impossible or inadvisable. Home-study classes generally meet once a week and are usually taught by a local Church volunteer. Curriculum is provided for students to study daily when not in class.

A milestone for the seminary program was reached in 1970 when the Church Board of Education determined that it would be offered internationally and that Church Educational curriculum would be translated into 16 languages.

Under the Church Board of Education, seminaries are governed by administrators at the general level and regionally by area or country directors, all of whom are full-time CES employees. The directors are in turn assisted by seminary coordinators, principals, and instructors. In 1999 there were 373,887 students enrolled in seminary.

SOURCES

Bennion, Milton Lynn. *Mormonism and Education.* Salt Lake City: Deseret Book, 1939.

Berrett, William E. *A Miracle in Weekday Religious Education.* Salt Lake City: Salt Lake Printing Center, 1988.

Christensen, Joe J. "Seminaries." *Encyclopedia of Mormonism.* Edited by Daniel H. Ludlow. 4 vols. New York: Macmillan, 1992. 1295–96.

Monnett, John Daniel. "The Mormon Church and Its Private School System in Utah: The Emergence of the Academies, 1880–1892." Ph.D. diss., University of Utah, 1984.

Quinn, D. Michael. "Utah's Educational Innovation: LDS Religion Classes, 1890–1929." *Utah Historical Quarterly* 43 (Fall 1975): 379–89.

CRAIG K. MANSCILL

SENECA INDIANS. See LAMANITES and LAMANITE MISSION OF 1830–1831.

SENIOR AARONIC PROGRAM. See PROSPECTIVE ELDERS.

SERBIA. During the 1970s and 1980s, the gospel was taken to only two republics in the former Socialist Federal Republic of Yugoslavia: **Croatia** and Serbia. The Church's presence and missionaries in Serbia were extensions of the proselyting efforts in Croatia. Some members were converted elsewhere in **Europe**, and others were baptized in Serbia. In 1988 a small branch was organized in Belgrade.

The breakup of Yugoslavia after 1991 limited both membership growth and the activities of couples and young adult missionaries in Serbia. They were evacuated from time to time during the civil strife in the 1990s but returned when conditions improved. The Serbian **District** came under the **Austria** Vienna and **Hungary** Budapest **Missions** and, after 1996, the Austria Vienna South Mission.

The Serbian Saints commonly use the Croatian translation of the Book of Mormon. Recognition of the Church in Serbia had been tentative, even though it owned a branch building in Beograd. By the end of 1998 about 200 members were organized into three branches.

SOURCES

Mehr, Kahlile. *Frontier in the East.* Manuscript history, Yugoslavia and Croatia.

1999–2000 Church Almanac. Salt Lake City: Deseret News, 1998. 409.

EDWIN B. MORRELL

SERVICEMEN AND WOMEN. See MILITARY.

SESSIONS, J. WYLEY. James Wyley Sessions, a **pioneer** of the Church's **institute** of religion program, was born 11 December 1885 in Marion, Cassia County, **Idaho**. The son of Harvey Sessions and Alice Bryson, he presided over the South African **Mission** from 1921 to 1926.

Upon returning from **South Africa**, Brother Sessions and his wife, Magdalen, were called by the **First Presidency** to organize the Church's first institute program in Moscow, Idaho. Fifty-seven students were enrolled the first year. By 1928, the first institute building had been built in Moscow, and institute programs soon followed at colleges and universities in **Logan, Utah**; Pocatello, Idaho; and **Salt Lake City**.

Brother Sessions subsequently served briefly as director of the **Missionary Home** in Salt Lake City (1936) and as the first head of **Brigham Young University's** Division of Religion (1939–47). He left BYU in 1947 to pursue business and real estate development interests. He died in **Los Angeles** on 21 April 1977.

SOURCES

Berrett, William E. *A Miracle in Weekday Religious Education.* Salt Lake City: Salt Lake Printing Center, 1988.

Cowan, Richard O. *Teaching the Word: Religious Education at Brigham Young University.* Provo, Utah: Religious Education, Brigham Young University, 1998.

GERALD L. HOMER

SETTING APART. *Setting apart* is a **priesthood ordinance** that authorizes a person to serve in a Church position (D&C 42:11). It occurs after the individual has been called and sustained. Modern terminology distinguishes between *ordaining* to a priesthood office and *setting apart* to other Church positions. Responsibilities inherent in the priesthood or Church membership do not require setting apart. **Elder Spencer W. Kimball** said, "The setting apart may be taken literally; it is a setting apart from sin, apart from the carnal; apart from everything which is crude, low, vicious, cheap, or vulgar; *set apart* from the world to a higher plane of thought and activity" (Kimball, 57).

SOURCES

Kimball, Spencer W. Conference Report (October 1958): 53–57.
Packer, Boyd K. *The Things of the Soul.* Salt Lake City: Bookcraft, 1996. 153–54.

Smith, Joseph Fielding. *Doctrines of Salvation.* Compiled by Bruce R. McConkie. 3 vols. Salt Lake City: Bookcraft, 1954–56. 3:106–7.

RICHARD E. TURLEY JR.

SEVENTIES HALL. In 1843 the nearly 500 **seventies** in **Nauvoo, Illinois**, saw a need for a meeting hall to be used for furthering **education** and preparing missionaries. **Edward Hunter** donated almost an acre of land to the seventies for the construction of the building. In the fall of 1843, **John D. Lee** was appointed as head of the committee to construct the Seventies Hall. The two-story brick building was to be 40 feet long and 28 feet wide, and the seventies were asked to volunteer their time to construct the building. During construction a tornado leveled the unfinished building. At the suggestion of **Brigham Young** they relaid the bricks, this time making the walls one brick thicker.

The building was first used on 27 July 1844 for selection of candidates for the August election. It housed a library and a museum of "curiosities" brought to Nauvoo by returning missionaries. As the **Saints** left for the West, the building was sold and used as a Presbyterian meetinghouse. Later it became a school, and by 1897 it had been torn down. **Nauvoo Restoration, Inc.**, bought the land in 1962 and rebuilt a replica of the Seventies Hall.

SOURCE

Holzapfel, Richard Neitzel, and T. Jeffrey Cottle. *Old Mormon Nauvoo and Southeastern Iowa: Historic Photographs and Guide.* 2d ed. Santa Anna, Calif.: Fieldbrook Productions, 1991. 131–32.

MIKE TRAPP

SEVENTY. A **priesthood** body known since antiquity, the seventy in modern times hold an office in the **Melchizedek** Priesthood and are charged with the responsibility "to be especial witnesses [of **Jesus Christ**] unto the Gentiles and in all the world" (D&C 107:25). This ministry is grounded in ancient precedent, when Jesus sent his seventy disciples to preach the gospel (Luke 10:1–12, 17–20).

Since the restoration of this priesthood office in 1835, the organizational role of the seventy has been the most fluid in Church government. Joseph Smith inaugurated the first **Quorum** of Seventy on 28 February 1835 (*HC*, 2:201–12). As other seventies quorums were formed, members of the original quorum were moved into these new units. The seven presidents of the original quorum presided over these other quorums as well and were known as the First Council of the Seventy. These seven men were sustained as general authorities. After arriving in the West, members of each quorum settled in various locales, making quorum meetings virtually impossible.

In 1904, with 146 quorums that by now had been tied to local **stakes**, President Joseph F. Smith designated the seventies as "minute men" whose chief role was to be missionaries "to all the nations of the earth" (CR, 3). In 1912 seventies began to form the backbone of local missionary work, starting in the Granite Stake of **Salt Lake City**, thus opening an era when seventies served as **stake missionaries**.

On 3 October 1975 President **Spencer W. Kimball** began the process of organizing the First Quorum of Seventy as a body of general authorities. This was completed the following year when the **Assistants to the Twelve** were absorbed into that quorum. By doing so, President Kimball opened the organization of the seventy to dynamic change. On 4 October 1986, all other seventies quorums in the Church were discontinued. Depending on age, members of these quorums affiliated with local **elders** or **high priest** quorums. In April 1989, the First Presidency organized the Second Quorum of the Seventy as a body of general authorities, calling into its number those who would serve for a period of approximately five years. These two quorums minister "under the direction of the Twelve [**Apostles**] . . . in building up the church . . . in all nations" (D&C 107:34).

In a move that would establish "a pattern under which the Church may grow to any size," President **Gordon B. Hinckley** announced in 1997 the formation of the third, fourth, and fifth quorums of the Seventy, which would consist of Area Authorities, to be known as **area authority seventies**. Members of these three quorums work under the direction of general authorities and serve in the areas where they live. Their responsibilities including serving as counselors in area presidencies, largely mirror those of the members of other Quorums of the Seventy who are general authorities, (Hinckley, 4–5).

SOURCES

Brown, S. Kent. "The Seventy in Scripture." *By Study and Also by Faith*. 2 vols. Edited by John M. Lundquist and Stephen D. Ricks. Salt Lake City: Deseret Book and FARMS, 1990. 1:25–45.

Hinckley, Gordon B. Conference Report (April 1997): 4–5.

Parrish, Alan K. "Seventy." *Encyclopedia of Mormonism*. Edited by Daniel H. Ludlow. 4 vols. New York: Macmillan, 1992. 3:1300–1305.

Smith, Joseph. *History of The Church of Jesus Christ of Latter-day Saints [HC]*. Edited by B. H. Roberts. 2d ed. rev. 7 vols. Salt Lake City: The Church of Jesus Christ of Latter-day Saints, 1932–51.

Smith, Joseph F. Conference Report (October 1904): 1–6.

S. KENT BROWN

SEVENTY'S COURSE IN THEOLOGY, THE. Elder B. H. Roberts (1857–1933) articulated and modeled his views on the appropriate relationship between faith and reason in Christian discipleship in *The Seventy's Course in Theology*. A member of the First Council of Seventy, Elder Roberts sought to equip the seventies with a mature Latter-day Saint theology. From 1907 to 1912, all of the Church's seventies followed this course of study, which consisted of five yearbooks. The first yearbook includes a history of the seventies and an overview of the standard works; the second gives a dispensational history of the world; the third covers the doctrine of deity; the fourth describes the doctrine of the Atonement; and the fifth examines the nature of the Holy Ghost and the doctrine of divine immanence. Throughout the course of study, Elder Roberts attempts to clearly explicate revealed truths and to corroborate them by means of philosophical argument and scientific evidence.

SOURCES

Madsen, Truman G. *Defender of the Faith: The B. H. Roberts Story*. Salt Lake City: Bookcraft, 1980.

Roberts, B. H. *The Seventy's Course in Theology*. 5 vols. Salt Lake City: Deseret News, 1907. Reprint ed., 5 vols. in 1. Prominent Works in Mormon History series. Orem, Utah: Grandin Book, 1994.

DAVID L. PAULSEN

SHAKERS. A name given in consequence of the group's unusual dancing in their worship services, the Shakers belong to the United Society of Believers in Christ's Second Appearing. The Believers were formally organized by Ann Lee (Mother Ann) in England in 1772.

Because of continued persecution, the group immigrated to Watervliet, New York, in 1774 and established their first of many communal villages. One of these villages was called North Union (today Shaker Heights), Ohio. It was this community that had several encounters with the Latter-day Saints. The first contact was when missionaries came through on their way to the Lamanite Mission.

The most dramatic encounter came after **Leman Copley**, a former Believer, sought for and obtained a **revelation** through the **Prophet Joseph Smith**. The revelation (D&C 49) said that the Shakers "desire to know the truth in part, but not all" (v. 2). Most of the revelation challenges the group's basic beliefs. While the Latter-day Saints believe that all people must believe on **Jesus Christ**, repent, and be baptized (vv. 12–13), the Shakers taught that no outward ordinances were necessary. The LDS Church teaches that **marriage** is **ordained** of God (vv. 15–17), whereas the Shakers believed celibacy was a higher law. D&C 49:18–21 explains that meat is "ordained for the use of man," but Shakers ate no pork, and many ate no meat. Joseph Smith's revelation also affirmed that Jesus Christ will not come as a woman (vv. 22–23), while Shakers believed Mother Ann was the second appearing of Christ.

In addition to **Leman Copley**, **Jesse Gause**, once a member of the **First Presidency**, had also been a Shaker.

Although at the end of the twentieth century a number of former Shaker sites were open to visitors, the only active Shaker community was located in Sabbathday Lake, **Maine**. The group's numbers diminished until in 1999 there were only seven members.

SOURCES

Doctrine and Covenants Student Manual. Salt Lake City: The Church of Jesus Christ of Latter-day Saints, 1981. 104–7.

A Summary View of the Millennial Church; or, United Society of Believers. Albany: C. Van Benthuysen, 1848.

Perkins, Keith W. "The Ministry to the Shakers (D&C 49, 51, 54)." *The Doctrine and Covenants.* Vol. 1 of Studies in Scripture series. Edited by Robert L. Millet and Kent P. Jackson. Salt Lake City: Randall Book, 1984.

KEITH W. PERKINS

SHARON, VERMONT. Joseph Smith was born 23 December 1805 in the township (a geographical unit larger than a village) of Sharon, Vermont. In 1804 the Prophet's maternal grandfather, **Solomon Mack**, had purchased the 100-acre farm on which Joseph was born. Solomon had rented his cabin and part of the farm to **Joseph Smith Sr.**, the Prophet's father. The Smith family lived there from 1804 to 1807 and then moved to nearby Royalton, Vermont. After they left, Solomon Mack returned to his farm in Sharon until he sold it in 1811.

In 1905, **Junius F. Wells** purchased the 100-acre farm plus adjacent property in behalf of the Church. That same year, the Church constructed a memorial cottage and erected a 38½-foot polished granite monument to commemorate the birth of Joseph Smith. Each foot of the granite shaft represents one year of the Prophet's life. This memorial project was one of the first efforts the Church made to identify and preserve sites in the East that are significant to Church history.

The memorial building was torn down in 1959; it was replaced by a **visitors' center** and a director's building, which were built in 1961. The number of visitors to the site increased so much over the next three decades that it became advisable to build a camping facility to accommodate tourists. On 27 June 1998 Camp Joseph was dedicated. It included a lodge, a pavilion, and 15 log cabins. The Joseph Smith Memorial Historical Site has become a popular tourist spot which, by the end of the twentieth century, attracted more than 55,000 people annually.

SOURCE

Berrett, LaMar C., ed. *New England and Eastern Canada.* Vol. 1 of *Sacred Places.* Salt Lake City: Bookcraft, 1999. 97–108.

ARNOLD K. GARR

SHARP, JOHN. Commonly known as the Railroad **Bishop**, John Sharp was a self-made man in the Horace Greeley tradition. He was born into a poor coal-mining **family** on 9 November 1820 in Devon Iron Works, Clackmannon, **Scotland**. Sharp followed his father's footsteps, entering the mines at age eight. He was still working there when he was converted to Mormonism in 1847.

In 1850 Sharp immigrated to **Utah**. He quickly gained the respect and confidence of **Brigham Young**. He began his career hauling rocks and later moved into freighting. In 1869 he subcontracted with Brigham Young to construct a portion of the Union Pacific **Railroad** through Weber Canyon. Later that same year he represented Brigham Young in the driving of the golden spike at the completion of the transcontinental railroad. More importantly, Sharp had Young's power of attorney during the settlement of payments of the Union Pacific to the Church.

As a result of his success with Union Pacific officials, he became an officer in the Utah Central and Utah Southern Railroads. Even more, he was asked to be a director of the Union Pacific Railroad and served in that capacity until his death. Sharp was also a director of **Deseret Telegraph, Deseret National Bank, ZCMI,** and other business ventures.

In 1856 Sharp was called as the first bishop of the Salt Lake Twentieth

Ward. He held this position for almost 20 years. He also served the Church as an assistant trustee-in-trust. Politically, he was active in local and territorial politics, serving as a city councilman, legislator, and territorial chairman of the **People's Party**. He died on 23 December 1891 in Salt Lake City.

SOURCES

Allen, James B. "'Good Guys' vs. 'Good Guys': Rudger Clawson, John Sharp, and Civil Disobedience in Nineteenth-Century Utah." *Utah Historical Quarterly* 48 (Spring 1980): 148–74.

Foster, Craig L. "John Sharp and T. B. H. Stenhouse: Two Scottish Converts Who Chose Separate Paths." *John Whitmer Historical Association Journal* 17 (1997): 81–93.

CRAIG L. FOSTER

SHARP, THOMAS C. Thomas Coke Sharp was an attorney, journalist, and judge who was known for his anti-Mormon activities. He was born at Mt. Holly, **New Jersey**, on 25 September 1818, the son of a Methodist minister. After studying law in Pennsylvania, he arrived in **Hancock County, Illinois**, in 1840, shortly after Latter-day Saints began settling in **Nauvoo**. His plans for practicing law were changed when in Warsaw, Illinois, he purchased a newspaper, which he soon renamed the *Warsaw Signal*. It became the voice for **anti-Mormonism** in Hancock County. Thomas was one of five who stood trial for the murder of **Joseph Smith** in **Carthage Jail**. All were acquitted, even though their guilt was widely acknowledged. Thomas died in Carthage, Illinois, 9 April 1894.

SOURCE

Jessee, Dean C. *The Papers of Joseph Smith.* Vol. 2. Salt Lake City: Deseret Book, 1992. 590.

MIKE TRAPP

SHIPP, ELLIS REYNOLDS. Pioneer doctor Ellis Shipp combined medicine with motherhood. Born in Davis County, Iowa, on 20 January 1847, Ellis came to **Utah** in 1852. Her grandfather William Hawley was known for his bone-setting skill. When Ellis was 14 her mother died, and in 1865 **Brigham Young** invited her to live at the **Beehive House**. In 1866 she married Milford Bard Shipp, a store clerk 11 years her senior. Shipp soon married three other wives, and they all lived together in a small house.

In 1873 Brigham Young encouraged women to study medicine, and in 1875, 29-year-old Ellis Shipp, now the mother of 5 children, 3 of whom were living, enrolled in the Women's Medical College of **Pennsylvania**. Although pregnant, she completed her course and graduated in 1878.

In **Salt Lake City** Shipp worked at the **Deseret Hospital** and opened a school for obstetrics and nursing. She delivered an estimated 5,000 babies and bore 10 herself. Shipp pursued postgraduate studies in Philadelphia and **Michigan**, and from 1888 to 1891 she helped publish a medical magazine, *Salt Lake Sanitarian*. She also served on the general board of the **Relief Society** from 1898 to 1907. She died 31 January 1939 in Salt Lake City.

SOURCES

Arrington, Chris Rigby. "Pioneer Midwives." *Mormon Sisters*. Edited by Claudia L. Bushman. Cambridge: Emmeline Press, 1976.

Bennion, Sherilyn Cox. *Equal to the Occasion: Women Editors of the Nineteenth-Century West*. Reno: University of Nevada Press, 1990.

Casterline, Gail Farr. "Ellis R. Shipp." *Sister Saints*. Edited by Vicky Burgess-Olson. Provo, Utah: Brigham Young University Press, 1978.

Noall, Claire. *Guardians of the Hearth*. Bountiful, Utah: Horizon, 1974.

Shipp, Ellis Reynolds. *The Early Autobiography and Diary of Ellis Reynolds Shipp*. Edited by Ellis Shipp Musser. Salt Lake City: Deseret News, 1962.

Skalla, Judy. "Beloved Healer." *The Women Who Made the West*. Edited by Western Writers of America. Garden City, N.Y.: Doubleday, 1980.

CLAUDIA BUSHMAN

SHIPS. Although the story of the Mormons crossing the plains is generally well known, even among the **Saints** the story of how they reached the plains is often neglected. This is certainly true with regard to the history of Latter-day Saint maritime immigration history.

In 1840 the first company of Saints left **Liverpool, England**, on the ship *Britannia* to gather to **Zion**. On this voyage there were 40 Church members, led by **Elder** John Moon. This launched a successful LDS maritime immigration movement that continued until the end of the nineteenth century, when Church leaders began encouraging the Saints to build Zion where they lived. Between 1840 and 1890, nearly 90,000 Latter-day Saint converts left their foreign homelands and crossed the oceans on about 550 known voyages.

From 1840 to 1867, all but one voyage was made by sailing vessels. These voyages were often tedious and fraught with much seasickness. About 80% of the voyages were made from the port of Liverpool, due to its position at the center of several railroad arteries and the Mersey River, which provided an easy launch for vessels on the Atlantic. Between 1840 and 1855, almost all the voyages from Liverpool were bound for **New Orleans**. Voyage by sail during this period often took two months or more, depending on sailing conditions. When yellow fever and cholera became serious threats on the **Mississippi River**, **Brigham Young** advised the Saints to use the eastern ports of Philadelphia, Boston, or **New York**. Voyages to these ports averaged about five weeks and thus reduced the time crossing the Atlantic.

From 1855 to 1890, New York became the port of choice for Saints crossing the Atlantic. Philadelphia and Boston were occasionally used, however, and three ships arrived in **Quebec** in 1841. Saints who crossed the Pacific during this period used the port of **San Francisco** or San Pedro. By 1867 the Saints began to use steamships to cross the oceans. This had a great effect on immigration because the time from Liverpool to New York was reduced from about five weeks to an average of 10 to 12 days. This also made things much easier for LDS passengers and Church immigration agents, because now they had a more reliable schedule.

The Saints still had challenges beyond the usual seasickness. For example, many immigrant accounts relate the terror of crossing the oceans in severe storms. Yet they were aided by their faith, and each respective vessel was dedicated by the **priesthood**, ensuring them of a safe voyage. Furthermore, the priesthood was also employed to rebuke the winds and waves in the needed hour. These miraculous events led to the conversion of many non-LDS passengers, including some sailors and captains who were impressed with the Mormons' hygiene and order. It is remarkable that only one vessel wrecked carrying an LDS company across the Pacific and that none sank carrying the sea-going Saints over the Atlantic. Perhaps the psalmist said it best when he declared, "They that go down to the sea in ships . . . see the works of the Lord and his wonders in the deep" (Ps. 107:23–24).

SOURCE

Sonne, Conway B. *Saints On the Seas: A Maritime History of Mormon Migration, 1830–1890.* Salt Lake City: University of Utah Press, 1983.

FRED E. WOODS

SHOSHONI INDIANS. The Shoshonis were an **Indian** tribe living in the **Utah** area when the **Mormon pioneers** arrived. They were a Numatic-speaking people of the Uto-Aztecan linguistic group. Their territory was a triangular area encompassing central **Nevada**, northern Utah, central and eastern **Idaho**, and southwestern **Wyoming**. This area included the semidesert of eastern Nevada, the Snake and Salmon Rivers of Idaho, the Great Salt Lake and Bear Lake of Utah, and part of Yellowstone Park in Wyoming.

In 1847 Latter-day Saints moved into the valley of the Great Salt Lake—Shoshoni country. **Brigham Young** instituted policies of taking the "principles of the gospel" to their red brothers and encouraged feeding Indians rather than fighting them. In 1855 Latter-day Saint missionaries were sent to Shoshoni and Bannock Indians on the Salmon River. Also in 1857, Brigham Young visited the **Fort Lemhi Mission** and soon thereafter began sending more families there. With the increasing hostility of Indians, however, the mission was closed in 1858. By 1860, as numbers of Latter-day Saint colonists increased, the Shoshoni were forced to change their way of life. The Indians began to beg, forcing settlers to provide provisions, and with the advent of the Civil War, they raided the Overland Trail and Cache Valley. The result was the **Bear River Massacre** in January 1863, killing most of the Shoshoni band of the northern Utah area. In 1866 the governor of Idaho advised the Indian Commissioner to establish a reservation in southern Idaho. The Treaty of Fort Bridger, 3 July 1868, created the **Fort Hall** Reservation.

Sources

Calloway, Colin C. "Snake Frontiers: The Eastern Shoshones in the Eighteenth Century." *Annals of Wyoming* 63 (Summer 1991): 82–92.

Chief Pocatello: The "White Plum." Salt Lake City: University of Utah Press, 1986.

Coates, Lawrence G. "Mormons and Social Change among the Shoshoni, 1853–1900." *Idaho Yesterdays* 15 (Winter 1972): 2–11.

Crowder, David L. "Nineteenth-Century Indian-White Conflict in Southern Idaho." *Idaho Yesterdays* 23 (Spring 1979): 13–18.

Heaton, John W. "No Place to Pitch Their Teepees: Shoshoni Adaptation to Mormon Settlers in Cache Valley, 1855–70." *Utah Historical Quarterly* 63 (Spring 1995): 158–71.

Madsen, Brigham D. "Shoshoni-Bannock Marauders on the Oregon Trail, 1859–1863." *Utah Historical Quarterly* 35 (1967): 3–30.

Nash, John D. "The Salmon River Mission of 1855: A Reappraisal." *Idaho Yesterdays* 11 (Spring 1967): 22–31.

Stewart, Omer C. "The Shoshoni: Their History and Social Organization." *Idaho Yesterdays* 9 (Fall 1965): 2–5, 28.

Fred R. Gowans and Lyn Clayton

SHUMWAY, NAOMI M. Naomi Maxfield Shumway served from 1974 to 1980 as the sixth general **Primary** president. Born 3 October 1922 in **Provo, Utah**, she married Roden Grant Shumway. She was a teacher in various Church **auxiliaries** and was called to the Primary general board in 1963. She became Primary general president 11 years later. During her administration, the Primary celebrated its centennial with parades, fairs, and plays. She strived to make the Primary program fit the needs of the increasingly worldwide Church. Primary, which for a century had been held on a weekday afternoon, was moved to Sunday with the consolidated meeting schedule in early 1980. The new manuals emphasized the study of the scriptures and the **Articles of Faith.**

SOURCES

Madsen, Carol Cornwall, and Susan Staker Oman. *Sisters and Little Saints: One Hundred Years of Primary.* Salt Lake City: Deseret Book, 1978.

Peterson, Janet, and LaRene Gaunt. *The Children's Friends: Presidents of the Primary and Their Lives of Service.* Salt Lake City: Deseret Book, 1996. 103–19.

JANET PETERSON

SICK, BLESSING THE. See HEALINGS.

SIERRA LEONE. With a population of more than five million people, Sierra Leone is located on the west coast of **Africa**. Its inhabitants speak English and tribal languages, and in 1999, 60% were **Muslim**, 30% followed traditional religions, and 10% were Christian.

Among the earliest converts to the Church from Sierra Leone was Michael Samura, who was baptized in **Holland** in 1981 and later returned to Freetown, Sierra Leone. Christian George, also baptized outside the country, returned to preside over Sierra Leone's first official Church **meeting**, held 18 January 1988 at Goderich. Elizabeth Bangura and Monica Orleans joined the Church in **Ghana** in January 1988 and then returned to Sierra Leone, where they formed a study group in Freetown. Sierra Leone was included in the **Liberia** Monrovia **Mission**, which was created 1 March 1988. The first missionaries arrived in May 1988. On 11 June 1988, the first 14 converts were baptized in Sierra Leone, and the Goderich **Branch** was organized 7 August of the same year with Brother Samura as a **counselor** in the branch presidency. A year later Abu H. Conteh was called as the first full-time missionary from Sierra Leone, and he was assigned to serve in his own land.

In December 1990 the Freetown **District** was created, with Michael Samura as president. The following year a **seminary** program was started.

Due to civil **war** in Liberia, the Church dissolved the Liberia Monrovia Mission on 22 April 1991, and Sierra Leone became part of the Ghana Accra Mission. In the late 1990s Sierra Leone also experienced destructive civil war which resulted in missionary work being halted, and the 3,564 members in 16 branches and 3 districts at the dawn of the twenty-first century had little outside support.

SOURCES

Middleton, John, ed. *Encyclopedia of Africa South of the Sahara.* 4 vols. New York: Macmillan Library Reference USA, 1997. 4:77–88.

1999–2000 Church Almanac. Salt Lake City: Deseret News, 1998. 383–84.

Oral histories of early Church converts collected by E. Dale LeBaron. Copies at BYU Library, Provo, Utah; LDS Church Historical Library, Salt Lake City, Utah.

E. DALE LEBARON

SIGMA GAMMA CHI. A spiritually based Latter-day Saint fraternity, Sigma Gamma Chi functioned as an adjunct to **institutes of religion**. When the Church's coeducational **Lambda Delta Sigma** became a sorority in 1967, Sigma Gamma Chi was created for men, absorbing **Delta Phi Kappa**, the returned missionary fraternity, in 1978. In 1999 the fraternity included 105 chapters and 15,000 members. It provided social, spiritual, service, academic, leadership, and brotherhood activities. In 2000 Sigma Gamma Chi was absorbed by a new organization called Institute Men's Association, designed to serve all single young adults ages 18 to 30.

SOURCE

Church Education System. *Sigma Gamma Chi Reference Manual.* Salt Lake City: The Church of Jesus Christ of Latter-day Saints, 1995.

"New Institute Associations Will Reach More Young Adults." *Ensign* (June 2000), 70–71.

WILLIAM G. HARTLEY

SILK INDUSTRY. See TEXTILES.

SINGAPORE. Since the founding of Latter-day Saint **missionary work** in Singapore, this country has been the hub from which hundreds of missionaries have been sent to serve in other nations of South and Southeast **Asia. Elder Gordon B. Hinckley** first met there with several expatriate LDS families in 1963. On 19 March 1968, Keith E. Garner, president of the Southern Far East Mission in **Hong Kong**, took four elders to Singapore to begin proselyting activities. A month later, on 14 April 1969, Elder **Ezra Taft Benson** dedicated Singapore for the preaching of the gospel. In October 1969 **G. Carlos Smith** founded the Southeast Asia **Mission** (name changed to Singapore Mission in 1974) at Singapore, with responsibility for a number of countries in South and Southeast Asia.

As the number of missionaries grew rapidly and the presence of the white-shirted elders became common, opposition arose. In March 1970, 29 elders were expelled. Between that time and 1988, when the government eased its visa policy regarding LDS missionaries, only one proselyting elder was allowed in Singapore at any time. Local elders and sisters took over the missionary responsibility and continued to help the Church grow.

By the mid-1990s, seven **branches** were in the Republic of Singapore, with almost 1,700 members. Although this was a small number in comparison with Singapore's population of almost 3.5 million (76% Chinese, 15% Malayan, 6.4% Indian), it was a large enough body of well-educated English-speaking **Saints** to support a **stake**. Singapore Stake was organized 26 February 1995 with Woo Hoi Seng as president, and it had five **wards** and two branches by the year 2000, with 2,099 members. In 1997 Su Kiong Tan, former **district** president, was called as an **area authority seventy**.

SOURCES

Britsch, R. Lanier. *From the East: The History of the Latter-day Saints in Asia, 1851–1996.* Salt Lake City: Deseret Book, 1998. 452–70.

Pang, Beng Ling. *A History of The Church of Jesus Christ of Latter-day Saints in Singapore: Journey to Stakehood, 1964–1997.* Singapore: C. O. S. Printers, 1997.

R. LANIER BRITSCH

SINGLE ADULTS. The Church places a high value on the role and importance of **marriage** and **family**, yet a large percentage of adults in the Church are single. In 1992 approximately 30% of Church members older than 18 were single, including divorced, widowed, and never-married individuals.

Church **single adult** programs are often divided by age, with the Young Single Adult group aged 18 to 30 and the Single Adult group aged 31 and above. Beginning in the 1970s, local Church units sponsored a variety of programs for singles, ranging from instruction in Church **meetings** or weekday **institute** classes to other activities, such as social and recreational events, service projects, **family home evening**, and **confer-ences**. In areas of the Church where there is a high concentration of singles, **wards** or **branches** for singles have been formed, allowing single adults more opportunities for interaction, involvement, and service in the Church.

SOURCES

"The Family: A Proclamation to the World." *Ensign* 25 (November 1995): 102.

Hunter, Howard W. "The Church Is for All People." *Ensign* 19 (June 1989): 75–77.

Young, Lawrence A. "Single Adults." *Encyclopedia of Mormonism.* Edited by Daniel H. Ludlow. 4 vols. New York: Macmillan, 1992. 3:1316–19.

CYNTHIA DOXEY

SLAVERY. The volatile issue of slavery began to affect the Church when members started settling in **Missouri** in 1831 and eventually contributed to the expulsion of the **Saints** from the state in 1838 and 1839. The **Missouri Compromise** of 1820 had defined the north-south boundary separating slave-holding from non-slave-holding states and admitted Missouri to the Union as a slave state. Latter-day Saints migrating to the state from the antislavery northeast were viewed with deep distrust. By 1832 it was rumored that Church members were inciting slaves to rise up against their masters. The state already had a small, unwelcome pop-ulation of free **blacks**, officially limited in size by the Missouri Compro-mise, and a confrontation was triggered when the July 1833 issue of the Church's *Evening and the Morning Star* carried a piece entitled "**Free People of Color.**" Designed to warn blacks of laws pertaining to their status in the state, the article was interpreted by many Missourians as threatening the slave system, which was at the heart of their whole social structure. The result was constant opposition and violence against the Saints in Missouri, which lasted until their final expulsion. During that period, Church members declared unequivocally that they had no inten-tion of interfering with slavery, believing such interference to be both unlawful and unjust (though they may have believed, as did the **Prophet Joseph Smith**, that slavery was a curse and an iniquity). Many Missourians could not or would not accept their intentions as real.

The Prophet Joseph Smith was intimately acquainted with the slavery issue. Regarding the American **Civil War** (1861–65), which he prophesied in 1832 would commence in **South Carolina** (D&C 87:1), he noted in 1843 that it would "probably arise through the slave question"

(D&C 130:13). The slavery issue also played a role in the 1844 **presidential campaign of Joseph Smith**. While the Prophet's platform called for the abolition of slavery, it also advocated that compensation be paid to slave owners by the federal government.

Even after the Church became established in its **Utah** mountain refuge, it again became embroiled in the slavery issue. After passage of the Kansas-Nebraska Act in 1854, allowing people of newly created territories to decide for themselves the issue of slavery, antislavery **Republicans** tried to use **anti-Mormon** sentiment "to prohibit in the Territories those **twin relics of barbarism—Polygamy** and Slavery" in the elections of 1856 (Allen, 305). Church leaders from Joseph Smith on have spoken against slavery.

SOURCE

Allen, James B., and Glen M. Leonard. *The Story of the Latter-day Saints.* 2d ed. Salt Lake City: Deseret Book, 1992. 61–62, 93–100, 114–115, 202, 299–300, 305.

ANDREW C. SKINNER

SLOVAKIA. Located in the eastern region of Czechoslovakia, the Slovaks were not proselyted by missionaries from the Czechoslovak **Mission** during the 1930s or the late 1940s. The two peoples had been separated by religion (Slovaks were devoted Roman Catholics in contrast to the anticlerical Czech Roman Catholics, Hussites, and other Protestants) and by political history (Slovaks united with the Czechs only after 1918, separated under the Nazis [1939–45], reunited [1945–92]; and peacefully and democratically separated in 1993).

Valerie Ruzena Frantiska Zizkova, a Czech member who had lived in Slovakia for decades, and other Slovaks joined the Church while they were in exile. The first missionaries from the Czechoslovak Prague Mission began serving in Slovakia in 1991. In that year Peter and Hanka Vaclav were converted to the Church. On 24 January 1993, the first branch was organized in Trencin, and the **Book of Mormon, Pearl of Great Price, Doctrine and Covenants**, and *Liahona* were made available to the Slovaks in Czech. They also received monthly **First Presidency** messages and **visiting teaching** messages in Slovak.

The independent Slovak government did not honor the Czechs' 1991 recognition of the Church, but missionaries were allowed to stay in the country by means of tourist visas and to proselyte. It is anticipated that the government will grant Latter-day **Saints** some association status without formally recognizing the Church.

Despite these circumstances, by the end of 1998 there were about 100 members of record in three branches in Western Slovakia.

SOURCES

Mehr, Kahlile. *Frontier in the East.* Manuscript history, Czechoslovakia and the Czech Republic.
1999–2000 Church Almanac. Salt Lake City: Deseret News, 1998. 385.

EDWIN B. MORRELL

SLOVENIA. The Church presence and missionaries in Slovenia were extensions of the proselyting efforts in **Croatia**, since both were republics in Yugoslavia. The civil **war** following Slovenia's declaration of independence involved the Slovenes only briefly; its economy even before the 1990s was the strongest among these republics.

During the 1980s, one Austrian sister resided in Ljubljana. The first missionaries to serve continually in Slovenia arrived in 1989, and formal recognition was quickly achieved in 1991. They used the Croatian **Book of Mormon**. The Slovene **District** was under the **Austria** Vienna Mission and, after 1996, under the Austria Vienna South Mission.

As of 1998 there were 200 members organized into three branches in Slovenia.

SOURCES

Mehr, Kahlile. *Frontier in the East.* Manuscript history, Yugoslavia and Slovenia.
1999–2000 Church Almanac. Salt Lake City: Deseret News, 1998. 385–86.

EDWIN B. MORRELL

SMITH, ALEXANDER HALE. Alexander Hale Smith, the third living son of the **Prophet Joseph Smith** and **Emma Hale**, was born 2 June 1838 in **Far West, Missouri**. He turned six during June 1844, the month his father and uncle **Hyrum Smith** were martyred.

Alexander grew up loving frontier life. He married Elizabeth Agnes Kendall on 23 June 1861, and they had four sons and five daughters.

On 25 May 1862, Alexander became a member of the **Reorganized Church of Jesus Christ of Latter Day Saints** when he was baptized and confirmed by his older brother **Joseph Smith III**, president of the RLDS

Church. He became one of the RLDS Quorum of the Twelve in 1873, the quorum's president from 1890 to 1897, and a counselor to Joseph III in the church's presidency, as well as presiding patriarch in 1897. Released from the presidency in 1902, Alexander continued as presiding patriarch until his death at **Nauvoo, Illinois**, 12 August 1909.

SOURCES

Death Certificate of Alexander Smith.

The History of the Reorganized Church of Jesus Christ of Latter Day Saints. 2d ed. rev. 8 vols. Edited by the Board of Publication. Independence, Mo.: Herald, 1967–76.

Smith Family genealogical records in author's possession.

BUDDY YOUNGREEN

SMITH, ALVIN. Alvin Smith fully supported Joseph during the early years of Joseph's prophetic calling before Alvin's untimely death 19 November 1823 in **Palmyra, New York.** Born 11 February 1798 or 1799 in Tunbridge, **Vermont,** Alvin worked hard as a youth to relieve his **family** of its financial burdens and to provide his parents with a comfortable home. On his deathbed following an overdose of calomel for "bilious colic," Alvin admonished Joseph: "Be a good boy, and do everything that lies in your power to obtain the [Nephite] Record" (Smith, 87). On 21 January 1836 in the **Kirtland Temple**, Joseph saw a vision of Alvin in the celestial kingdom, at which time the **Prophet** learned that all those "who have died without a knowledge of this gospel, who would have received it if they had been permitted to tarry, shall be heirs of the celestial **kingdom of God**" (D&C 137:7).

SOURCE

Smith, Lucy Mack. *History of Joseph Smith.* Salt Lake City: Stevens and Wallis, 1945.

ANDREW H. HEDGES

SMITH, ASAEL. Asael Smith, the paternal grandfather of the **Prophet Joseph Smith** and the father of **Joseph Smith Sr.**, the first **patriarch to the Church**, was at the head of one of the greatest lineages of prophetic souls ever to minister among men. He was a devout religious man with a strong character, and he felt that all men in **America** should have free and equal religious liberty. Asael was born in **Topsfield, Massachusetts**, on 7 March 1744, the second and youngest son of Samuel Smith Jr. and Priscilla Gould. The greater part of his life was spent in Topsfield, where he followed his father's example by joining the patriot forces as a Revolutionary soldier. Six days after the **Declaration of Independence** was signed, he enrolled in a patriot company that marched to **Canada**. At age 23, he married **Mary Duty**, and they had eleven children: seven boys and four girls. Seeking inexpensive virgin land, Asael moved his family to **Tunbridge, Vermont**, where for the next 30 years he farmed and served in many civic positions. At Tunbridge, Asael's second son, Joseph, married **Lucy Mack**, who on 23 December 1805 at **Sharon, Vermont**, gave birth to Joseph Smith Jr.

Earlier, Asael had a premonition that one of his descendants would be a great teacher and leader of men. He said, "It has borne in upon my soul that one of my descendants will promulgate a work to revolutionize the world of religious faith" (McGavin, 9). Asael lived to see the dawn of the fulfillment of his words. Just before his death in Stockholm, New York, on 30 October 1830, a **Book of Mormon** (then recently published) was presented to him. He accepted it, "read it nearly through," and solemnly warned his attendants to "give heed to the book, for it was true and, its coming forth heralded a renewal of gospel light" (Cannon, 27). In addition Asael declared that his grandson, Joseph Smith Jr., "was the very Prophet that he had long known would come in his **family**" (Smith, 2:443).

With the exception of Jesse, Asael's children were all favorable toward the Church. Joseph, Asael Jr., Silas, and John all embraced the Church and were prominent in its counsels.

SOURCES

Bushman, Richard L., *Joseph Smith and the Beginnings of Mormonism*. Chicago: University of Illinois Press, 1984. 20–29.

Cannon, George Q. *Life of Joseph Smith the Prophet*. Salt Lake City: Deseret Book, 1986.

McGavin, Cecil E. *The Family of Joseph Smith*. Salt Lake City: Bookcraft, 1963. 9–21.

Smith, Joseph. *History of The Church of Jesus Christ of Latter-day Saints*. Edited by B. H. Roberts. 2d ed. rev. 7 vols. Salt Lake City: The Church of Jesus Christ of Latter-day Saints, 1932–51.

CRAIG K. MANSCILL

SMITH, BARBARA B. Barbara Bradshaw Smith, the tenth general president of the **Relief Society**, was born 26 January 1922 in **Salt Lake City, Utah**. Her service from 3 October 1974 until 7 April 1984 witnessed many advancements and achievements, including the creation of the Relief Society **Monument** to **Women at Nauvoo, Illinois**, in 1978. She led the Relief Society during a period of sweeping changes as the women's liberation movement gained the political spotlight. She was one of the main Church spokespersons against the proposed **Equal Rights Amendment** (ERA) in the **United States** and appeared on national television to explain the Church's opposition to the ERA.

During Barbara Smith's administration, the annual **meetings** for women, preceding each fall **general conference**, were instituted. She helped establish the resource center in the Relief Society Building, which provided help to local Relief Society leaders and to an increasingly diverse membership. The Sarah Granger Kimball home was restored in Nauvoo, Illinois, as part of an effort to commemorate the beginnings of the Relief Society. Nationally recognized as an important women's leader, she served as a member of the White House Advisory Committee during President Jimmy Carter's administration. Following her release as general president of Relief Society, she continued participating in community service endeavors and labored with her husband, Douglas H. Smith, a member of the Seventy, in behalf of the Church, including a three-year assignment in **Hong Kong**.

SOURCES

Bitton, Davis. "Smith, Barbara Bradshaw." *Historical Dictionary of Mormonism.* Metuchen, N.J.: Scarecrow Press, 1994. 211–12.

Derr, Jill Mulvay, Janath Russell Cannon, and Maureen Ursenbach Beecher. *Women of Covenant: The Story of Relief Society.* Salt Lake City: Deseret Book, 1992. 347–383.

RICHARD NEITZEL HOLZAPFEL

SMITH, BATHSHEBA WILSON.

SMITH, BATHSHEBA WILSON. Bathsheba Wilson Bigler, a general president of the **Relief Society** from 1901 to 1910, was born 3 May 1822 in Shinnston, **West Virginia**. She was converted to the Church in her home state. Witnessing her baptism was Elder **George A. Smith**, whom she married in **Nauvoo** in 1841. While George served **missions** for the Church, she wrote encouraging letters describing her life and the growth of their children. She was the youngest woman present at the first **meeting** of the Female Relief Society and became president of the organization in 1901. A faithful **temple** worker, she coordinated the work for **women** in the **Salt Lake Temple** for a time and acted as proxy for many of the dead. She died 20 September 1910 in **Salt Lake City**.

SOURCES

Derr, Jill Mulvay, Janath Russell Cannon, and Maureen Ursenbach Beecher. *Women of Covenant: The Story of Relief Society.* Salt Lake City: Deseret Book, 1992.

Peterson, Janet, and LaRene Gaunt. *Elect Ladies.* Salt Lake City: Deseret Book, 1990.

AUDREY M. GODFREY

SMITH, CATHERINE (SALISBURY). See SMITH FAMILY.

SMITH, DAVID ASAEL.

SMITH, DAVID ASAEL. President Joseph F. Smith gave his son David, born 24 May 1879 in **Salt Lake City**, the middle name of Asael in honor of his great-great-grandfather **Asael Smith**, who prophesied that one of his descendants "would promulgate a work to revolutionize the world of religious faith" (Smith, 25). The Prophet **Joseph Smith** began that work, and David A. Smith devoted his life to continuing it.

At age 28 he was called as a **counselor** to **presiding bishop Charles W. Nibley.** He served in the presiding bishopric for more than three decades. After his release he presided over the Canadian **Mission** for six years. Following his mission, he coordinated the missionary work on **Temple Square**. He was committed to the **Tabernacle Choir** and served as the president of that organization for 30 years. The father of seven sons and two daughters, **Bishop** Smith died **6 April** 1952 at Salt Lake City.

SOURCES

Flake, Lawrence R. *Mighty Men of Zion.* Salt Lake City: Karl D. Butler, 1974. 498.

Smith, Joseph Fielding. *Essentials of Church History.* Salt Lake City: Deseret Book, 1974.

Zobell, Albert L. "David A. Smith Passes." *Improvement Era* 55 (June 1952): 382, 385.

LAWRENCE R. FLAKE

SMITH, DAVID H.

SMITH, DAVID H. David Hyrum Smith, posthumous son of the **Prophet Joseph Smith** and the last child of Emma Hale, was born 17 November 1844 in **Nauvoo, Illinois**. He became a noted artist, musician, and writer. His book of poems, *Hesperis,* was published in 1875.

On 27 October 1861, David was baptized and confirmed into the **Reorganized Church of Jesus Christ of Latter Day Saints**. Demonstrating devotion to that organization in **missionary work** and musical talent, he was composer and lyricist for several of the church's hymns. He married Clara Charlotte Hartshorn 10 May 1870, and the couple had one son.

On 10 April 1873, David became counselor to his older brother **Joseph Smith III** in the RLDS Church presidency. In 1877, having been diagnosed with "brain fever," David was committed to the "hospital for

the Insane" at Elgin, Illinois. In 1885 he was officially released from all
church callings. He died at the hospital, 29 August 1904.

SOURCES

Death Certificate of David H. Smith.
The History of the Reorganized Church of Jesus Christ of Latter Day Saints. Edited by
    the Board of Publication. 2d ed. rev. 8 vols. Independence, Mo.: Herald, 1967–76.
Smith Family genealogical records. Manuscript in author's possession.

BUDDY YOUNGREEN

SMITH, DON CARLOS. Don Carlos Smith, the youngest brother of
the **Prophet Joseph Smith**, was born 25 March 1816 in Norwich,
Vermont—the tenth child and eighth son of **Joseph Smith Sr.** and **Lucy
Mack Smith.** Fair-haired and strong, he grew to be six feet four inches
tall. Don Carlos married Agnes Coolbrith 30 July 1835, in **Kirtland.** The
couple had three daughters: Agnes, Sophronia, and Josephine Donna
(Ina), who became **California's** first poet laureate, known as Ina
Coolbrith.

Don Carlos spent long hours with Joseph and **Oliver Cowdery,**
learning the trade of printer. From the few references to him, it is apparent he was a sober, responsible young man, never running from obligations or danger. In his short lifetime, his accomplishments included
becoming editor of *Times and Seasons,* a member of the **Nauvoo** City
Council, president of the **high priests quorums** in **Kirtland** and Nauvoo,
brigadier general in the **Nauvoo Legion**, lieutenant colonel in the
Hancock County Militia, and member of the board of regents of the
University of Nauvoo.

Joseph said of him, "He was a lovely, a good natured, a kind-hearted
and a virtuous and a faithful, upright child; and where his soul goes, let
mine go also" (*HC*, 5:127). Don Carlos died in Nauvoo, Illinois, 7 August
1841, at age 25.

SOURCES

Proctor, Scott, and Maurine Proctor, ed. *History of Joseph Smith by His Mother.* Edited
    by Preston Nibley. Rev. ed. Salt Lake City: Bookcraft, 1997.
Smith, Joseph. *History of The Church of Jesus Christ of Latter-day Saints.* Edited by
    B. H. Roberts. 2d ed. rev. 7 vols. Salt Like City: The Church of Jesus Christ of
    Latter-day Saints, 1932–51. 4:393–99; 5:127.
Smith, Lucy Mack. *History of Joseph Smith by His Mother.* Edited by Preston Nibley.
    Revised edition edited by Scot Facer and Maurine Jensen Proctor. Salt Lake City:
    Bookcraft, 1996.

HORTENSE C. SMITH

SMITH, ELDRED G. Eldred Gee Smith, the great-great-grandson of **Joseph Smith Sr.**, served as **patriarch to the Church**. Born 9 January 1907, Eldred was educated at the **University of Utah** and served in the Swiss-German Mission for three years. After his marriage to Jean Audrey Ness in 1932, he served in numerous Church callings, including high councilor and **bishop**. During **World War II**, Brother Smith was an engineer on the secret Manhattan Atomic Energy Project, in which the atom bomb was developed. He was sustained as patriarch to the Church on 10 April 1947 and went on to give thousands of **patriarchal blessings** to members of the Church all over the world, including some in the German language. He was given **emeritus general authority** status on 6 October 1979 when the **First Presidency** discontinued the office of patriarch to the Church.

SOURCES

Flake, Lawrence R. *Mighty Men of Zion*. Salt Lake City: Karl D. Butler, 1979.
Rea, Dorothy O. "Jeanne Audrey Ness Smith." *Church News*, 4 July 1964, 6.

LAWRENCE R. FLAKE

SMITH, EMMA HALE. Emma Hale, wife of the **Prophet Joseph Smith**, was the founding president of the **Relief Society**. The seventh child of Isaac and Elizabeth Lewis Hale, Emma was born 10 July 1804 in **Harmony, Pennsylvania**. She became a tall young woman with dark hair and eyes and a quick wit. She could manage a canoe and was a skilled horseback rider. Interested in religion, she sang in her church choir. She was also exceptionally bright and studied for one year at a girls' school.

In 1825 she met Joseph Smith, who boarded at her parent's home while he worked for **Josiah Stowell** in nearby **South Bainbridge, New York**. She and Joseph were married 18 January 1827, and they eventually became the parents of nine children. The newlyweds moved in with Joseph's **family** in **Manchester, New York**, and Emma went with her husband the evening of 21 September 1827 when he obtained the **gold plates**. She remained at the foot of the **Hill Cumorah** and prayed as he climbed to the crest to meet with **Moroni**.

Emma and Joseph remained in Manchester for only a short time before moving back to Harmony. While they were living on a small piece of land purchased from her family, Emma was one of the Prophet's scribes as he translated the **Book of Mormon** plates by the "gift and power of God through the **Urim and Thummim**." She was also the subject of a revelation, now canonized as section 25 of the **Doctrine and Covenants**. The Lord told Emma through Joseph that she was to select **hymns**, comfort her husband, expound **scriptures**, and exhort the **Saints** to good works. If she did so she was promised that her life would be preserved.

She moved with her husband to **Kirtland, Ohio**, in the winter of 1831. There Emma received a **patriarchal blessing** under the hands of **Joseph Smith Sr.**, which told her she would bear additional children (her first three had died), receive power to instruct other **women**, be watched over by **angels**, and be saved in the **kingdom of God**. After receiving this blessing, she bore six children, four of whom lived to adulthood. In Kirtland, her selection of hymns was published in 1835 as the Church's first hymnal.

During the winter of 1838, Emma and Joseph traveled by wagon to **Missouri**, where she lived until her husband was arrested and incarcerated in the **Liberty Jail**. With her family and other fleeing Saints she traveled the 200 miles to Illinois, often on foot. She carried concealed under her skirt the manuscript of her husband's translation of the **Bible**. After Joseph was allowed to escape from prison, they settled in **Nauvoo**. Escaping the fever and ague herself, she nursed back to health many sick Saints who lived in tents in her dooryard. In 1842 she was called and sustained as president of the Female Relief Society of Nauvoo, an organization for Latter-day Saint women. She presided over **meetings** and dispensed instruction, thus fulfilling the promise found in her patriarchal blessing.

After the **martyrdom** of her husband, Emma remained in Nauvoo, taking in boarders and caring for a number of her relatives, including her mother-in-law **Lucy Mack Smith**. Five months after Joseph's death, in November of 1844, she gave birth at age 40 to her last child, a boy, whom she named David Hyrum. Emma believed in **education** and hired teachers to instruct her children. Joseph III, her oldest living child, was justice of the peace in Nauvoo, and her youngest, David, became a poet and artist of some note.

During the fall of 1846, she lived in Fulton City, **Iowa**, but soon returned to Nauvoo. On 23 December 1847, Emma married **Lewis A. Bidamon** and began caring for a number of his relatives, along with her own family. She and Bidamon were married for more than 30 years. Bidamon constructed a wheelchair for Lucy Mack Smith, who was living with Emma and who suffered from arthritis. The last year of her life Lucy was unable to lift or bend her arms, and Emma fed her all of her meals. Lucy died in Emma's home.

In 1860 Emma traveled with her son **Joseph Smith III** to Amboy, Iowa, where he accepted the presidency of the **Reorganized Church of Jesus Christ of Latter Day Saints**. By unanimous vote she became a member of that church as well. After the conference she returned to Nauvoo.

Shortly before Emma's death, she declared that she saw the Savior. Her last words were, "Joseph! Yes, yes, I'm coming" (Newell and Avery, 304). She died 30 April 1879 in Nauvoo, Illinois.

SOURCES

Newell, Linda King, and Valeen Tippetts Avery. *Mormon Enigma: Emma Hale Smith: Prophet's Wife, "Elect Lady," Polygamy's Foe.* New York: Doubleday, 1984.

Terry, Keith, and Ann Terry. *Emma.* Santa Barbara: Butterfly Publishing, 1979.

Youngreen, Buddy. *Reflections of Emma.* Orem, Utah: Grandin Book, 1982.

KENNETH W. GODFREY

SMITH, G. CARLOS. George Carlos Smith was general superintendent in the **Young Men's Mutual Improvement Association**, as well as **stake** and **mission** leader. He was born 23 August 1910 in **Salt Lake City**. At age 39 he was called as president of the Big Cottonwood **Utah** Stake, and seven years later (1956) he became president of the Holladay Utah Stake. Later he served as the second and then first assistant superintendent in the Young Men's Mutual Improvement Association. He also presided over the Central States Mission. After his mission he served as the general superintendent in the Young Men's Mutual Improvement Association from 1967 to 1969.

In 1969 Brother Smith was called as the first president of the Southeast **Asia** Mission. In addition to his Church duties and earning a living, he raised five children with his wife, LaVon Peterson Smith. He died 29 March 1987 in Salt Lake City.

SOURCES

Britsch, R. Lanier. "The Church in Asia." *Encyclopedia of Mormonism.* Edited by Daniel H. Ludlow. 4 vols. New York: Macmillan, 1992. 1:75–81.

Conference Report. October 1949, April 1956, October 1958, October 1961, October 1967, April 1969.

Encyclopedia of Mormonism. Edited by Daniel H. Ludlow. 4 vols. New York: Macmillan, 1992. Appendix 1.

TIMOTHY W. BOTHELL

SMITH, GEORGE A. George Albert Smith, the youngest of the Twelve **Apostles** in this dispensation, was called into the **Quorum** of the Twelve at the age of 21. He served the Church in many different capacities: **temple** builder, member of **Zion's Camp**, **missionary**, vanguard **pioneer**, colonizer, territorial legislator, Church historian, and member of the **First Presidency**. He was ordained an apostle at **Far West, Missouri**, on 26 April 1839, and called by **Brigham Young** to the First Presidency in 1868, where he served for seven years until his death 1 September 1875 in **Salt Lake City**.

George was born 26 June 1817 at Potsdam, St. Lawrence County, New York, to John Smith and Clarissa Loomis Lyman. **John Smith** was a younger brother of **Joseph Smith Sr.**, making the **Prophet Joseph Smith** George's first cousin.

At age 16, George fell in with the recruits of Zion's Camp and marched 1,800 miles round trip for the cause of **Zion**. The Prophet Joseph Smith selected him to be his personal arm-bearer and bodyguard. George's reminiscences of Zion's Camp are one of the better sources the Church has of the march.

As an apostle he was called with his brethren in 1839 to labor in **England**. When he returned to **Nauvoo**, he married Bathsheba Bigler, a southern belle from Virginia, on 25 July 1841. He was included in the vanguard **pioneer trek of 1847** with Brigham Young and was later called to settle southern **Utah**, the town of St. George being named in his honor. Beginning in 1854 he served as Church historian and recorder and made his contribution by completing the "History of Joseph Smith" and directing the compilation of the "History of Brigham Young."

George A. Smith was known for his wonderful sense of humor. On one occasion while speaking in the Tabernacle on a hot afternoon, he took off his wig to wipe his brow, to the delight of all those present.

As a member of the First Presidency, President Smith was assigned to go to the **Holy Land** to rededicate it. On the Mount of Olives he prayed that Palestine might become fertile and that the promises to Abraham and the prophets would be fulfilled.

His great devotion to the Church led the Prophet Joseph Smith to say, "George A., I love you as I do my own life." George replied, "I hope Brother Joseph, that my whole life and actions will ever prove my feelings and affection toward you" (Pusey, 47). George A. Smith's valiant life was a tribute to that hope.

SOURCES

Allen, James B., Ronald K. Esplin, and David J. Whittaker. *Men with a Mission*

1837–1841: The Quorum of the Twelve Apostles in the British Isles. Salt Lake City Utah: Deseret Book, 1992. 8–9, 56.

Jenson, Andrew. *Latter-day Saint Biographical Encyclopedia.* 4 vols. 1901–36. Reprint, Salt Lake City: Western Epics, 1971. 1:38–40.

Pusey, Merlo J. *Builders of the Kingdom: George A. Smith, John Henry Smith, George Albert Smith,* Provo, Utah: Brigham Young University Press, 1981. 9, 66, 80, 110.

CRAIG K. MANSCILL

SMITH, GEORGE ALBERT. George Albert Smith, the eighth president of the Church (1945–51), was born in **Salt Lake City** on 4 April 1870, the son of John Henry and Sarah Farr Smith. **John Henry Smith** served as an **apostle** for 30 years and as counselor to **Joseph F. Smith**. George's grandfather, **George A. Smith**, after whom he was named, was an apostle and **counselor** to **Brigham Young**. His great-grandfather, **John Smith**, an uncle to the Prophet Joseph Smith, was the third **patriarch to the Church**.

At age 12 George went to **Provo**, where he spent a year at the **Brigham Young Academy** under the tutelage of **Karl G. Maeser**, who deeply affected his life. He returned home the next year when his father was called on a **mission**. As the oldest son, George matured rapidly with the responsibilities of helping lead and sustain the family. He took a job in the **ZCMI** clothing factory and quickly earned respect and promotions.

When he was 13 years old, George Albert received a remarkable **patriarchal blessing** from **Zebedee Coltrin**. He was told: "Thou shalt become a mighty prophet in the midst of the sons of **Zion**. Thou shalt become a mighty apostle in the church and **kingdom of God** upon the earth, for none of thy father's family shall have more power with God than thou shalt have, for none shall excel thee." Those promises were clearly fulfilled in his later Church service.

When his father returned from his mission, George enrolled in the **University of Deseret**. During the summer he worked on a railroad surveying job, but the glare of the desert sun permanently damaged his eyes, forcing him to drop out of school. His eyesight caused him pain and problems for the rest of his life.

George Albert married Lucy Emily Woodruff, a granddaughter of **Wilford Woodruff**, in 1892. A week after his marriage, George was called to the **Southern States Mission**, where he served as mission secretary to President **J. Golden Kimball**. His wife joined him, and they served together in the mission office until 1894. George and Lucy eventually had three children.

His call to the apostleship came in 1903 when George Albert was 33 years old. He served with his father in the **Quorum of the Twelve** for eight years. George Albert entered the new calling wholeheartedly. He traveled extensively, participating in as many as 10 meetings a week for extended periods. But his hard work aggravated his already frail health, requiring periods of convalescence in **California** and **St. George**. He gradually recovered but struggled throughout the rest of his life with health problems.

During one of those recovery periods in St. George, in a dream he saw his grandfather George A., who challenged him: "I would like to know what you have done with my name." After having his whole life flash before him, he was able to reply that he had never done anything of which his grandfather need be ashamed. It was a powerful lesson that George Albert later shared frequently in teaching others to respect their heritage and live their lives as they should.

Some of Elder Smith's greatest service was to the youth of the Church. He was involved in the leadership of the **Young Men's Mutual Improvement Association** as a board member from 1904 to 1921 and then as general superintendent until 1935. During that time he led the effort to incorporate the **Boy Scout** program into the Church. He later served on the national advisory board of the Boy Scouts of America, and received scouting's highest honors—the Silver Beaver and Silver Buffalo awards.

Elder Smith served as president of the **British Mission** from 1919 to 1921, during the critical period when **Europe** was recovering from **World War I**. He made great strides in building friendships and reestablishing missionary work in Europe.

He was also keenly interested in preserving **historic sites**. He participated in the centennial service of Joseph Smith's birth in December 1905 and was instrumental in the Church's acquiring the **Smith family farm** in **Manchester, New York**. He also organized the "Utah **Pioneer** Trails and Landmarks Association," which erected more than 100 monuments. On the occasion of the 1947 Pioneer **Centennial**, he unveiled the majestic *"This Is the Place" Monument*.

George Albert Smith succeeded **Heber J. Grant** as president of the Church; he was ordained and set apart on 21 May 1945 at age 75. As president, he focused on rebuilding efforts in Europe at the end of **World War II**, sending many supplies from Utah for relief efforts. Missionary work was revitalized and expanded; work among **Native Americans** received new emphasis. Microfilming of genealogical records accelerated. The **Idaho** Falls Idaho **Temple** was completed and dedicated.

On 4 April 1951, his eighty-first birthday, President George Albert Smith died in Salt Lake City. He was eulogized as a loving, faithful servant. His successor, **David O. McKay**, said he "lived as nearly as it is humanly possible for a man to live a Christ-like life."

SOURCES

Ellsworth, S. George, "Smith, George Albert." *Encyclopedia of Mormonism.* Edited by Daniel H. Ludlow. 4 vols. New York: Macmillan, 1992. 3:1326–29.

Gibbons, Francis M., *George Albert Smith: Kind and Caring Christian, Prophet of God.* Salt Lake City: Deseret Book, 1990.

Jenson, Andrew. *Latter-day Saint Biographical Encyclopedia.* 4 vols. 1901–36. Reprint, Salt Lake City: Western Epics, 1971. 3:776ff.

DAVID KENISON

SMITH, HYRUM. Hyrum Smith, beloved brother of the **Prophet Joseph Smith**, was the **assistant president** of the Church when the two were martyred in **Carthage, Illinois**. Hyrum was born to **Joseph Smith Sr.** and **Lucy Mack Smith** on 9 February 1800 in **Tunbridge, Vermont**. He immediately believed the spiritual events relayed by his brother Joseph and stood by his side throughout life with unparalleled devotion and loyalty. Extensively involved in the early events of the **Restoration**, Hyrum was called in 1829 as one of the **Eight Witnesses**; less than a year later he became one of the six original members of the Church.

In 1826 he married Jerusha Barden, and they had six children before her untimely death in 1837. Only months later, at the suggestion of the Prophet, he married an English convert named **Mary Fielding**. Mary bore him a son, Joseph F. (Fielding) in November 1838 and a daughter, Martha, in May 1841. Their son Joseph became the sixth president of the Church.

Hyrum was one of the noble and great ones, chosen in the beginning and reserved to come forth in the last days to help lay the foundation of the great latter-day work (D&C 138:53–56). He served for a short time in 1837 as the assistant **counselor** in the **First Presidency**. On 7 November 1837 he was called as the second counselor to Joseph Smith. In 1841 he replaced **Oliver Cowdery**, who had lost his calling through transgression, as the assistant president of the Church. In this calling he was elevated above the counselors in the First Presidency and was the acting president of the Church in Joseph's absence. Hyrum was called by the

Lord to be a **prophet, seer, and revelator** unto the Church (D&C 124:94) and signed letters as a president of the Church. After Father Smith's death, Hyrum was called as the **patriarch to the Church** and gave hundreds of **patriarchal blessings** to the **Saints in Nauvoo.**

Throughout their lives, Joseph and Hyrum were never separated for more than six months at a time, and seldom, if ever, did Joseph do anything of import without consulting his elder brother. Joseph wrote that Hyrum had the meekness and humility of **Christ** and that he loved him with a love that was stronger than death (*HC,* 2:338). Rarely have there ever been brothers who were more of one mind, heart, and purpose. Truly in "life they were not divided and in death they were not separated" (D&C 135:3). Hyrum voluntarily followed Joseph to Carthage, where the two brothers sealed their testimonies with their own blood—"the best blood of the nineteenth century" (D&C 135:6). It has been proclaimed that Hyrum's name shall "be had in honorable remembrance from generation to generation, forever and ever" (D&C 124:96).

SOURCES

Corbett, Pearson H. *Hyrum Smith: Patriarch.* Salt Lake City: Deseret Book, 1976.

Smith, Joseph. *History of The Church of Jesus Christ of Latter-day Saints [HC].* Edited by B. H. Roberts. 2d ed. rev. 7 vols. Salt Lake City: The Church of Jesus Christ of Latter-day Saints, 1932–51.

Smith, Joseph Fielding. *Life of Joseph F. Smith: Sixth President of The Church of Jesus Christ of Latter-day Saints.* Salt Lake City: Deseret Book, 1938.

JOSEPH FIELDING MCCONKIE

SMITH, HYRUM GIBBS. During the 20 years Hyrum Gibbs Smith served as **patriarch to the Church,** he gave nearly 22,000 blessings to **Saints** all over the world. Born 8 July 1879 in South Jordan, **Utah,** and named after his great-grandfather, the brother of the **Prophet Joseph Smith, Elder** Smith followed his grandfather **John Smith** directly to this calling on 9 May 1912. During most of his two decades as **patriarch,** he also served on the general board of the YMMIA or as director of the **Genealogical Society of Utah.** Elder Smith died 4 February 1932 in Salt Lake City at the early age of 52.

SOURCES

Flake, Lawrence R. *Mighty Men of Zion.* Salt Lake City: Karl D. Butler, 1974. 311.

"Hyrum Gibbs Smith." *Improvement Era* 35 (March 1932): 847–48.

LAWRENCE R. FLAKE

SMITH, HYRUM MACK. Hyrum Mack Smith, born 21 March 1872 in Salt Lake City, was taught to live worthy of all three of his names—he was named Hyrum for his grandfather, the martyred **patriarch**; Mack for his great-grandmother, **Lucy Mack Smith**; and Smith for his noble fore-bears, including his own father, President **Joseph F. Smith**. At age 29 **Elder** Smith was called to the **Quorum** of the Twelve **Apostles** on 24 October 1901. As an apostle he presided over the **European Mission**. Elder Smith died suddenly at the age of only 45 on 23 January 1918 in Salt Lake City, preceding his father in death by ten months.

SOURCES

Cowley, Matthias F. *Prophets and Patriarchs.* Chattanooga, Tenn.: Ben E. Rich, 1902. 318.

Flake, Lawrence R. *Prophets and Apostles of the Last Dispensation.* Provo, Utah: Religious Studies Center, Brigham Young University, 2001. 421–33.

LAWRENCE R. FLAKE

SMITH, JEDEDIAH. Jedediah Smith, born in 1799, was one of the most celebrated **explorers** in western history. He was captain of a trap-ping brigade across the Continental Divide in 1824 and rediscovered **South Pass**. By 1826 he became the principal figure in the Smith-Jackson-Sublette Fur Company, and in an adventurous search for beaver he blazed a trail from present-day **Utah** to **California**. His return trip took him across the **Nevada** and Utah deserts to what he called his "home of the wilderness," the vicinity of the Great Salt Lake. In 1827 he made a second similar trip to California. At the time of his death in 1831, his journeys had given him an unequaled knowledge of the territory that the Saints would settle.

SOURCES

Carter, Harvey L. "Jedediah Smith." *The Mountain Men and the Fur Trade of the Far West.* Edited by LeRoy Hafen. 10 vols. Glendale, Calif.: Arthur H. Clark, 1966–72. 331–48.

Morgan, Dale L. *Jedediah Smith and the Opening of the West.* Indianapolis: Bobbs-Merrill, 1853.

FRED R. GOWANS AND KERRY OMAN

SMITH, JESSE N. Jesse Nathaniel Smith, a noted colonizer and Church leader in the **pioneer** West, was born 2 December 1834 at

Stockholm, St. Lawrence County, New York, to Silas and Mary Aikens Smith. Jesse was a cousin of the Prophet Joseph Smith. His family joined the Saints and moved to Ohio, Missouri, Illinois, and finally west. His widowed mother was determined to raise her sons in the Church. The family was assigned to the Iron Mission and settled in Parowan. Jesse was county clerk and elected to the territorial legislature. He was also elected mayor, served as city clerk, city councilman, city magistrate, probate judge, deputy U.S. marshal, and county and district attorney. He also served the Church as president of the Scandinavian Mission (1860–64 and 1868–70), where he supervised emigration, the printing of the Swedish hymnbook, and the publication of a Scandinavian edition of the Doctrine and Covenants. In 1878 he was called to preside over the Eastern Arizona Stake and later the Snowflake Stake. While in Arizona he continued his Church and political service until his death 5 June 1906 in Snowflake.

─────────

SOURCES

Romney, Thomas C. *The Gospel in Action*. Salt Lake City: Deseret Sunday School Union Boards, 1949.

Smith, Oliver, ed. *Six Decades in the Early West: Journals of Jesse N. Smith*. Edited by Oliver R. Smith. 3d ed. Provo, Utah: Jesse N. Smith Family Association, 1970.

DAVID F. BOONE

SMITH, JOHN (1781). John Smith, the uncle of Joseph Smith the Prophet, was patriarch to the Church, assistant counselor in the First Presidency, and a great pioneer leader. John was born 16 July 1781 in Derryfield, New Hampshire, to Asael and Mary Duty Smith. He married Clarissa Lyman on 11 September 1815. They had four children, three of whom lived to adulthood. One of their sons, George A., eventually served as a counselor in the First Presidency of the Church.

In 1830 John's brother, Joseph Smith Sr., who was the father of the Prophet, visited John and other members of the Smith family in upstate New York and taught them about the restored gospel. John was baptized two years later in an icy stream on 9 January 1832, even though he was deathly ill with consumption. The neighbors, who gathered to watch the event, thought the baptism would kill John, but his health improved, and he lived another 22 years.

In 1833 John moved to Kirtland, Ohio, where he was called to the stake high council the following year. On 3 September 1837 he was sustained as assistant counselor in the First Presidency to his nephew Joseph

Smith. "Uncle John," as he was called by the Saints, served as a **stake president** in four different locations—**Adam-ondi-Ahman, Missouri** (1838); Zarahemla, **Iowa** (1839); **Nauvoo, Illinois** (1844); and **Salt Lake City** (1847–48). When he was called as stake president in Salt Lake, he was both ecclesiastical and civic leader in the valley, inasmuch as the stake was the only government in the pioneer community at the time. He served as patriarch to the Church from 1849 to 1854. He gave 5,560 patriarchal blessings before he died on 23 May 1854 in Salt Lake City.

SOURCES

Bates, Irene M. "Uncle John Smith, 1781–1854: Patriarchal Bridge." *Dialogue* 20 (Fall 1987): 78–89.

Cook, Lyndon. *The Revelations of the Prophet Joseph Smith*. Provo, Utah: Seventy's Mission Bookstore, 1981. 208.

1991–92 Church Almanac. Salt Lake City: Deseret News, 1990. 46, 176.

ARNOLD K. GARR

SMITH, JOHN (1832). John Smith, **patriarch to the Church** and son of Hyrum and Jerusha Barden Smith, was born 22 September 1832 in **Kirtland, Ohio**. When he was five years old, his mother gathered her five children, including an 11-day-old baby, to her bedside and said, "Tell your father when he comes home that the Lord has taken your mother and left you for him to take care of" (quoted in Smith, 41). She died that day, 13 October 1837. Seven years later, his father and uncle were slain by a bloodthirsty mob at **Carthage, Illinois**. He became patriarch to the Church on 18 February 1855.

When he was 15, John drove a wagon to the **Salt Lake Valley**. In 1860 he returned to **Winter Quarters** and led 350 **Saints** to **Utah**. Following a mission to **Scandinavia**, he was presiding officer on a ship of 973 immigrating Saints. During the 56 years he held the office of patriarch to the Church, nearly 20,000 Saints received their blessings from him. He died 6 November 1911 at **Salt Lake City**.

SOURCES

Flake, Lawrence R. *Prophets and Apostles of the Last Dispensation*. Provo, Utah: Religious Studies Center, Brigham Young University, 2001. 311–13.

Smith, Joseph Fielding. *Life of Joseph F. Smith*. Salt Lake City: Deseret Book, 1938. 41.

LAWRENCE R. FLAKE

SMITH, JOHN HENRY. John Henry Smith, an **apostle** for 30 years and a **counselor** in the **First Presidency**, was born 18 September 1848 in **Kanesville, Iowa**, and came to the **Salt Lake Valley** with his family and early **pioneers** in 1849. John's father, **George A. Smith**, was also an apostle and served as a counselor to **Brigham Young**; one of John's sons, **George Albert Smith**, became president of the Church.

John's mother died when he was not yet three years old, so he was reared by his mother's sister, a plural wife of his father. John attended school in **Provo** and **Salt Lake City**, obtaining a reasonable **education** for the time. He worked for a while as a telegraph operator and labored to build **railroads** through Utah. He married Sarah Farr on 20 October 1866; they had 11 children. He later married Josephine Groesbeck on 4 April 1877; she bore eight children.

John Henry's civic involvement began in 1872 when he served as a clerk for the Utah territorial legislature and constitutional convention. In 1874 he was called to serve a **mission** to **Europe**. He labored mostly in **Great Britain** but also visited several European countries. His mission was cut short by word that his father was very ill; he arrived home in August 1875 in time to spend two weeks at his father's bedside before his death.

John Henry went back to work at the railroad and was soon called as a **bishop**. His political involvement started in earnest in 1876 when he was elected to the city council and later to the territorial legislature.

John Henry Smith was ordained an apostle 27 October 1880 at age 32 by **Wilford Woodruff**. As a member of the **Quorum** of the Twelve, he served as president of the **British Mission** from 1882 to 1885 and also traveled extensively throughout Europe. On his return to Utah, his political activities continued; he was involved in efforts to organize the **Republican Party** in Utah and was president of the constitutional convention in 1895 that prepared for Utah's **statehood**.

John Henry was sustained as second counselor to President **Joseph F. Smith** on 7 April 1910, at age 61. He died 13 October 1911, at Salt Lake City at age 63.

SOURCES

Bickmore, Jean, ed. *Church, State, and Politics: The Diaries of John Henry Smith.* Significant Mormon Diaries series, no. 4. Salt Lake City: Signature Book, 1990.

Jenson, Andrew. *Latter-day Saint Biographical Encyclopedia.* 4 vols. 1901–36. Reprint, Salt Lake City: Western Epics, 1971. 1:141ff.

1999–2000 Church Almanac. Salt Lake City: Deseret News, 1998. 53.

DAVID KENISON

SMITH, JOSEPH, JR. As the first **prophet, seer, and revelator** of this dispensation, Joseph Smith was the founder of The Church of Jesus Christ of Latter-day Saints and translator of the **Book of Mormon**. The son of **Joseph Smith Sr.** and **Lucy Mack Smith**, Joseph was born 23 December 1805 in **Sharon**, Windsor County, **Vermont**. He resided in Vermont until 1811, when he and his **family** moved to West Lebanon, **New Hampshire**. There young Joseph contracted typhus and bravely endured surgery to remedy the life-threatening side effects of the illness. The Smiths moved from New Hampshire back to Vermont before settling in **Palmyra, New York**, in 1816.

By 1818 Father Smith had purchased a hundred acres in Manchester. Through back-breaking labor he and his sons turned the wooded acreage into a productive farm. On this farm in the spring of 1820, 14-year-old Joseph Smith Jr. saw in vision **God the Father** and his Son, **Jesus Christ**. Although the young man advocated the truthfulness of this vision, a local minister declared, "It was all of the devil" (JS–H 1:21). Some villagers in Palmyra echoed the minister's sentiments.

Joseph's refusal to deny his vision led to mockery and persecution. Compounding his personal difficulties was a tendency to fall "into many foolish errors, and display the weakness of youth, and the foibles of human nature" (JS–H 1:28). Feeling remorseful for his errors, on 21 September 1823 Joseph prayed to the Lord "for forgiveness of all [his] sins and follies" (JS–H 1:29). In answer to his supplication, "a messenger sent from the presence of God" appeared to him and said that God had a work for Joseph to do (JS–H 1:33). The work would entail translating an ancient book written upon **gold plates**. As the messenger, the angel **Moroni**, conversed with Joseph, "the place where the plates were deposited" was shown him in vision (JS–H 1:42).

Four years later, on 22 September 1827, eight months after Joseph had married **Emma Hale**, he received the plates from the angel and was given specific instructions to protect them. Keeping them safe proved difficult. A birch log, hearth stones, floor boards, flax, and a barrel of beans all concealed the plates at different times from Palmyra residents who wanted to seize and sell them.

To avoid the mounting curiosity and threats of violence, Joseph moved to **Harmony, Pennsylvania**, near his father-in-law, **Isaac Hale**. During his two years in Harmony, he translated most of the Book of Mormon from the ancient plates. **Oliver Cowdery**, a schoolteacher, was the principal scribe for the translation. During the months of translation, Joseph and his scribe received the **Aaronic Priesthood** from **John the**

Baptist on 15 May 1829 near the **Susquehanna River** and, shortly thereafter, the **Melchizedek Priesthood** from the ancient **apostles Peter,
James, and John**.

Soon after their priesthood ordinations, Joseph and Oliver left
Harmony, Pennsylvania. They resided for a brief time in the **Peter
Whitmer Sr.** cabin in **Fayette, New York**. There Joseph worked long
hours to complete the translation of the plates. The completed manu-
script, known as the Book of Mormon, was published in Palmyra, New
York, by E. B. Grandin in March 1830.

Although the publication was greeted with some skepticism, believers
claimed the Book of Mormon to be the word of God. About 50 of the
faithful met on **6 April** 1830 at the Peter **Whitmer Farm** for the official
organization of the Church. Joseph was acknowledged as "a seer, a translator, a prophet, an apostle of Jesus Christ, an **elder** of the church" (D&C
21:1).

News of the organization and the Book of Mormon was spread by
missionaries of the fledgling Church. In addition to work being done in
New York, four missionaries were sent to the western frontier to share
the news with native Americans. By October 1830 these missionaries had
arrived in **Kirtland, Ohio**, where more than a hundred believers were
baptized. Some of the new converts prayed to the Lord, asking for Joseph
Smith to come to their village.

In February 1831 Joseph arrived in Kirtland. He remained in the
community until September 1831, when he moved to the **John Johnson**
home in **Hiram, Ohio**. In this home Joseph pursued his translation of the
Bible, until 24 March 1832, when violence erupted. Angry men with
painted faces broke into the home, pulled Joseph from his bed, and tarred
and feathered him. Joseph survived the painful ordeal but soon left Hiram
for Kirtland.

During this time, the Latter-day Saints in **Independence, Missouri,**
were encountering further persecution and were eventually expelled from
Jackson County. In the spring of 1834 Joseph marched from Kirtland to
Missouri with a quasimilitary force called **Zion's Camp** to help his
followers reclaim their homes and possessions lost to mobocracy; however, the excursion failed to meet this objective.

On 27 March 1836, the Prophet dedicated the **Kirtland Temple**. One
week later, on 3 April, he and Oliver Cowdery were privileged to see "the
Lord standing upon the breastwork of the pulpit" in the **temple** and
heard the Savior say, "I have accepted this house" (D&C 110:2, 7).

Ancient prophets **Moses**, **Elias**, and **Elijah** restored additional priesthood keys to Joseph and Oliver on that occasion (D&C 110:11–16).

The glory of that April day was never forgotten nor obscured by the persecution that followed in 1837. Persecution caused Joseph much suffering in Ohio and later in Missouri. In Missouri the persecution accelerated to an **extermination order** against faithful Latter-day Saints, issued by the governor of Missouri, **Lilburn W. Boggs**. The **Haun's Mill** massacre and the fall of **Far West, Missouri**, followed. The betrayal and imprisonment of Joseph in Independence, **Richmond**, and **Liberty** also stemmed from the governor's order.

From the Liberty prison Joseph cried, "O God, where art thou? And where is the pavilion that covereth thy hiding place?" (D&C 121:1). The Lord comforted his Prophet: "My son, peace be unto thy soul; thine adversity and thine afflictions shall be but a small moment; . . . fear not what man can do, for God shall be with you forever and ever" (D&C 121:7; 122:9).

On 11 April 1839 Joseph was allowed to escape from his imprisonment to safety in **Quincy, Illinois**. Safe from the atrocities of Missouri, the Prophet directed his followers to settle in Commerce, a small community located along the **Mississippi River**. Commerce, renamed **Nauvoo**, became a haven for the faithful and a refuge from persecution for a season. With hammers, shovels, and trowels the Latter-day Saints worked alongside Joseph to build the city of Nauvoo, including another temple. He thus contributed not only his physical strength but also his gospel understanding to his followers. "Ah what pleasure this gave me," wrote Wandle Mace. "[The Prophet] would unravel the **scriptures** and explain doctrine as no other man could. What had been mystery he made so plain it was no longer mystery" (Mace, 94). **Brigham Young** added, "[Joseph] took heaven figuratively speaking, and brought it down to earth; and he took the earth, brought it up, and opened up, in plainness and simplicity, the things of God" (JD, 5:332).

Joseph, acknowledged as a prophet by his followers and as founder of Nauvoo by friend and foe alike, wanted no plaudits, even though his services as mayor of Nauvoo and lieutenant general of the **Nauvoo Legion** were laudatory. He wanted only to serve the Lord and live in peace. In the winter of 1843–44, however, ridicule, arrest warrants, and evil speaking accelerated as apostates among the Latter-day Saints united with the mob element to malign the character of the Prophet. By June they had published the *Nauvoo Expositor,* in which Joseph was branded a base seducer, liar, and murderer. He denounced these slanderous lies, and the city council ordered the cessation of the **periodical** and the destruction of its press.

When angry owners of the *Expositor* discovered that the newspaper was not only stopped but their property destroyed, they sought legal redress from a judge in Carthage, Illinois—the county seat. The subsequent arrest warrants against Joseph and **Hyrum Smith** led Joseph to say to his brother, "There is no mercy—no mercy here. Just as sure as we fall into their hands we are dead men" (*HC*, 6:545). Attempting to escape from judicial proceedings, Joseph and Hyrum crossed the Mississippi River to the territory of **Iowa** on 23 June 1844.

Ill-informed friends crossed from Nauvoo to Iowa to encourage the brothers to return to **Illinois** and arraignment in Carthage. "If my life is of no value to my friends it is of none to myself," lamented Joseph. "I am going like a lamb to the slaughter, but I am calm as a summer's morning" (*D&C* 135:4; *HC*, 6:549, 555). Joseph and Hyrum returned to Illinois and went to Carthage, where accusations stemming from the *Expositor* turned into accusations of treason, and the brothers were imprisoned in **Carthage Jail**.

The lawless element in Carthage bragged that the Smith brothers would not leave the town alive. A mob marching from nearby Warsaw to Carthage on 27 June 1844 sang: "Where now is the Prophet Joseph? Where now is the Prophet Joseph? Safe in Carthage jail!" (Roberts, 2:281). From the east bedroom in the second story of the jail, Joseph, Hyrum, and two members of the Quorum of the Twelve Apostles, **John Taylor** and **Willard Richards**, watched the mob arrive. Around 5 o'clock in the afternoon, Elder Richards saw a hundred or more men running around the corner of the jail. Elder Taylor described them as "an armed mob—painted black" (*D&C* 135:1). They easily overpowered the jailer, rushed up the stairs, and began shooting into the room. Despite their initial attempts to protect themselves, those in the bedroom were no match for the mob.

Hyrum was the first to fall. Bending over the body of his lifeless brother, Joseph cried out, "Oh dear, brother Hyrum!" (*HC*, 6:618). As the Prophet moved toward the window, two bullets hit him from the doorway and two struck him from outside. As he fell from the window to the ground below, he exclaimed, "*O Lord my God!*" (*D&C* 135:1).

The mob had finished its murderous plot, and Joseph, the Mormon prophet, lay dead outside the jail. "[He] left a fame and name that cannot be slain," wrote John Taylor. "He lived great, and he died great in the eyes of God and his people; and like most of the Lord's anointed in ancient times, has sealed his mission and his works with his own blood" (*D&C*

135:3). Concerning Joseph Smith's place in American history, **Josiah Quincy**, who had met the Prophet and who later became mayor of Boston, wrote: "It is by no means improbable that some future text-book, for the use of generations yet unborn, will contain a question something like this: What historical American of the nineteenth century has exerted the most powerful influence upon the destinies of his countrymen? And it is by no means impossible that the answer to that interrogatory may be thus written: Joseph Smith, the Mormon Prophet" (Quincy, 376).

SOURCES

Bushman, Richard L. *Joseph Smith and the Beginnings of Mormonism.* Chicago: University of Illinois Press, 1984.

Hill, Donna. *Joseph Smith the First Mormon.* Garden City, N.Y.: Doubleday, 1977.

Journal of Discourses [JD]. 26 vols. London: Latter-day Saints' Book Depot, 1854–86.

Mace, Wandle. "Autobiography." Typescript. Special Collections, Brigham Young University Library, Provo, Utah.

Porter, Larry C. "A Study of the Origins of The Church of Jesus Christ of Latter-day Saints in the States of New York and Pennsylvania, 1816–1831." Ph.D. diss., Brigham Young University, August 1971.

Quincy, Josiah. *Figures of the Past from the Leaves of Old Journals.* 5th ed. Boston: Roberts Brothers, 1883.

Roberts, B. H. *A Comprehensive History of The Church of Jesus Christ of Latter-day Saints, Century One.* 6 vols. Salt Lake City: The Church of Jesus Christ of Latter-day Saints, 1930.

Smith, Joseph. *History of The Church of Jesus Christ of Latter-day Saints [HC].* Edited by B. H. Roberts. 2d ed. rev. 7 vols. Salt Lake City: The Church of Jesus Christ of Latter-day Saints, 1932–51.

Smith, Lucy Mack. *History of Joseph Smith by His Mother.* Edited by Preston Nibley. Salt Lake City: Bookcraft, 1958.

SUSAN EASTON BLACK

SMITH, JOSEPH, SR. Joseph Smith Sr., father of the **Prophet Joseph Smith** and son of Asael and **Mary Duty Smith**, was born 12 July 1771, in **Topsfield, Massachusetts**. Dissatisfied with the religious dogma and practice of his day, he received inspired dreams and **visions**, which helped shape Joseph Jr.'s confidence in divine **revelation**. In one such vision, he was shown that an apostasy had occurred; in another, he saw himself and his family permitted to eat fruit from the tree of life.

Joseph married Lucy Mack 14 January 1796 in **Tunbridge, Vermont**. They became the parents of 11 children. Following three years of crop failure in Vermont, they moved to **Palmyra, New York**, in 1816, where the events of the **Restoration** began to unfold.

From the moment of the **First Vision** to his own death, "Father Smith," as he was called by the early **Saints**, was one of the Prophet Joseph's sturdiest supporters. He was the first person to receive Joseph's testimony that he had seen the angel **Moroni**, and later he became one of the Eight **Witnesses of the Book of Mormon**. He was the subject of one of the great revelations in the **Doctrine and Covenants** (section 4), was present at the **organization of the Church**, and was baptized on the day it was established, **6 April** 1830. His ordination as the first **patriarch** marked the **restoration** of the calling of "evangelical ministers" (or patriarchs) again on the earth. In February 1834 he was **ordained** a member of the first **high council**, in **Kirtland, Ohio**; and in 1837 he was sustained as an assistant **counselor** to the Prophet Joseph Smith (*HC*, 2:509).

While imbued with a missionary zeal which took him on several missions, Father Smith is best remembered as an inspired patriarch. Hundreds of the early **Saints** received blessings that spoke with prophetic accuracy and gave faith and encouragement to the first generations of Latter-day Saints. In addition, he had the perfect temperament to be the father of a prophet: he was kind and gentle, had perfect confidence in truth, possessed the faith and strength to endure persecution and poverty, and demonstrated a love of all humanity. Father Smith died 14 September 1840 in **Nauvoo, Illinois**, at age 69.

SOURCES

McConkie, Mark L. *The Father of the Prophet.* Salt Lake City: Bookcraft, 1993.

Smith, Joseph. *History of The Church of Jesus Christ of Latter-day Saints (HC).* Edited by B. H. Roberts. 2d ed. rev. 7 vols. Salt Lake City: The Church of Jesus Christ of Latter-day Saints, 1932–51.

Smith, Lucy Mack. *History of Joseph Smith by His Mother.* Edited by Preston Nibley. Salt Lake City: Bookcraft, 1958.

MARK L. MCCONKIE

SMITH, JOSEPH, III. The oldest surviving son of **Joseph Smith Jr.** and **Emma Hale Smith**, Joseph Smith III became prophet-president of the **Reorganized Church of Jesus Christ of Latter Day Saints** in 1860. Born 6 November 1832 in **Kirtland, Ohio**, Joseph remained in **Nauvoo, Illinois**, after the death of his father in 1844. He studied law in Canton, Illinois, and served for a time as justice of the peace in Nauvoo.

After the founders of the Reorganization invited him as son of the **martyred Prophet** to lead their movement, Joseph III spent 54 years as president promoting what became the second largest church in the

Latter-day Saint tradition. He concentrated on finding and bringing into the Reorganized church people who had been members while his father was alive but who had not followed **Brigham Young** west. Smith also traveled to **Utah** in 1876, 1885, 1887–88, and 1889. While there, he interacted with members of The Church of Jesus Christ of Latter-day Saints as son of the Prophet, missionary for the Reorganization, **antipolygamy** activist, and cousin of prominent leaders in the LDS Church.

Widowed twice, Joseph married Emmeline Griswold in 1856, Bertha Madison in 1869, and Ada Clark in 1898. He was the father of 17 children. He died 10 December 1914 in **Independence, Missouri**.

SOURCES

Howard, Richard P., ed. *The Memoirs of President Joseph Smith III (1832–1914)*. Independence, Mo.: Herald, 1979.

Launius, Roger D. *Father Figure: Joseph Smith III and the Creation of the Reorganized Church*. Independence, Mo.: Herald, 1990.

———. *Joseph Smith III: Pragmatic Prophet*. Urbana: University of Illinois Press, 1988.

LACHLAN MACKAY

SMITH, JOSEPH F. (1838). Joseph Fielding Smith, son of Hyrum and **Mary Fielding Smith**, was the sixth president of The Church of Jesus Christ of Latter-day Saints. He presided over the Church during a period of intense **anti-Mormon** sentiment both locally and nationally (1901–18).

President Smith was the last latter-day **prophet** to have personally known **Joseph Smith**. **Wilford Woodruff** said that he looked more like the Prophet Joseph than any living man and prophesied that he would one day lead the Church. President Smith possessed a great understanding of the gospel and had the ability to proclaim these doctrines boldly, poetically, and without equivocation. This ability came not by way of formal education but by years of association and refinement by the Spirit. Though he never wrote a book, he is one of the most often quoted of our Latter-day Saint leaders.

From birth Joseph F. Smith was a seed cast on rocky soil. He was born in Far West, Missouri, on 13 November 1838, the most strife-torn year in the Church's history. Only a few days after his birth he was almost suffocated when a mattress was thrown over him by an angry mob ransacking the home in which he was born. When he had reached the tender age of five, his father, Hyrum, leaned from his saddle, picked him up, hugged him, and rode off with his brother to **Carthage** and **martyrdom**. At eight years of age he was chased by hostile **Indians** at **Winter**

Quarters. By his tenth year he was a seasoned teamster, having driven his mother's covered wagon across the plains and through the Rockies to the **Salt Lake Valley.** His mother died before he turned 14. At 15 his formal education ended when he was expelled from school. The schoolmaster had taken out a leather strap to use on his younger sister, Martha. When Joseph objected, the teacher turned his wrath on him. The gangly youth proceeded to give the schoolmaster a good licking. Not knowing what to do with him, the Brethren sent Joseph on a **mission.** Though only 15, he was **ordained** an **elder** and sent to **Hawaii.** During his four-year mission to the islands, the fierce winds of sorrow and hardship caused the roots of his testimony to deepen. A dream in which he found himself in the presence of the great leaders of this dispensation, including his father, Hyrum, and his uncle the Prophet Joseph, inspired him in his labors. He knew he had been approved of and blessed by the great leaders of the **Restoration.**

In 1859, at the age of 21, Joseph married Levira A. Smith and shortly thereafter left for a three-year mission to **Great Britain.** Upon his return he served a special mission to Hawaii, relative to the **Walter Gibson** matter, and the following year became employed by the **Church historian's office.** Actively involved in politics, he was shortly elected to the territorial house of representatives and served seven consecutive terms on the **Salt Lake City** council.

On 5 May 1866 Joseph married Julina Lambson in accordance with the laws of **plural marriage.** Over the next 18 years he married Sarah Richards, Edna Lambson, Alice Kimball, and Mary Schwartz. He was a devoted husband and a loving father to his 43 children and five adopted children. President Smith's lifeline was his **family.** He often stated that "the richest of all my earthly joys is in my precious children" (*Life,* 4).

While working for the Church historian's office, Joseph was attending a meeting when President **Brigham Young** abruptly said he felt inspired to call him as an **apostle.** He was ordained an apostle and a **counselor** to the **First Presidency** on 1 July 1866 at the age of 27. This ordination was announced to the Church nine months later when there became a vacancy in the **Quorum.**

Elder Smith continued his missionary labors, being called twice to preside over the **European Mission.** In 1878 he accompanied **Orson Pratt** to the eastern **United States,** visiting **historical sites,** and interviewing former Church leaders such as **William McLellin** and **David Whitmer.** Following the death of President Young, he was set apart as the second counselor to President **John Taylor** and later held the same position under President Wilford Woodruff.

Elder Smith served for two years as the primary lobbyist for the Church in **Washington, D.C.**, combating intense **antipolygamy** sentiment. Because as a polygamist he was subject to arrest, he was often in exile between 1884 and 1891. He served as first counselor to President **Lorenzo Snow** before succeeding him as the president of the Church on 10 October 1901 at the age of 62.

During Joseph F. Smith's 17 years as president, the Church was attacked mercilessly by the press and at the pulpit. Its doctrines were distorted, ridiculed, and falsified, and the conduct of Church members was condemned. In defending the Church, President Smith was compelled to give laborious testimony before the U.S. Senate during the Reed **Smoot case.** This prompted him to issue an official statement, the **Second Manifesto**, reaffirming the Church's position in forbidding plural marriages.

President Smith did much to ease the strain between the Church and the government. During his presidency much of the animosity toward the Church subsided, while the Saints began to be seen as devoted American citizens. Under his direction the Church freed itself from debt, established a bureau of information on **Temple Square**, and purchased historical sites in **Vermont**, **Missouri**, and **Illinois**. The Church Administration Building was completed, and the **seminary** and **Boy Scout** programs were established in the Church. An official doctrinal exposition on "The Father and the Son" was given, along with important pronouncements on **war** and **evolution.**

During the final years of President Smith's life the veil became very thin on a number of occasions, and marvelous **visions** were manifest to him. One of the most remarkable and instructive is now known to Latter-day Saints as the **vision of the redemption of the dead** (D&C 138), which was added to the canon of **scripture** at **general conference** in April 1976. President Smith died 19 November 1918 in Salt Lake City at the age of 80.

SOURCES

Gibbons, Francis M. *Joseph F. Smith: Patriarch and Preacher, Prophet of God.* Salt Lake City: Deseret Book, 1984.

Smith, Hyrum M., III, and Scott G. Kenney. *From Prophet to Son: Advice of Joseph F. Smith to His Missionary Sons.* Salt Lake City: Deseret Book, 1981.

Smith, Joseph Fielding. *Life of Joseph F. Smith: Sixth President of The Church of Jesus Christ of Latter-day Saints.* Salt Lake City: Deseret News Press, 1938.

JOSEPH FIELDING MCCONKIE

SMITH, JOSEPH F. (1899). Joseph Fielding Smith, patriarch to the Church and university professor, was born 30 January 1899 in Salt Lake City to Elder Hyrum M. and Ida Elizabeth Smith. He served a **mission** to the Hawaiian Islands in 1920 and graduated from the **University of Utah** in 1924. Continuing his education at several prestigious institutions, including Oxford, he taught speech at seven other major universities, returning eventually to the University of **Utah.** Being in the direct line of **Joseph Smith Sr., Hyrum Smith, Joseph F. Smith,** and **Hyrum M. Smith,** he was ordained **patriarch to the Church** 8 October 1942. Facing daunting personal difficulties, **Elder** Smith offered to be released from his calling if the Brethren felt it best for the Lord's work. After much prayer, the **First Presidency** regretfully released him on 6 October 1946. He died 29 August 1964 in Salt Lake City.

SOURCES

Flake, Lawrence R. *Mighty Men of Zion.* Salt Lake City: Karl D. Butler, 1974. 313.
"Patriarch to the Church: Released from Duties." *Improvement Era* 49 (November 1946): 685, 708.

LAWRENCE R. FLAKE

SMITH, JOSEPH FIELDING. Joseph Fielding Smith, the tenth president of The Church of Jesus Christ of Latter-day Saints, was born in **Salt Lake City** on 19 July 1876, the son of **Joseph F. Smith** (sixth president of the Church) and Julina Lambson. During the impressionable years of Joseph's youth, the Church was under constant attack by ministers of other faiths, treated with malicious contempt by the media, and hounded by self-seeking politicians because of its practice of **plural marriage.** Its leaders, including Joseph's father and many of his relatives, were forced into exile. Many Latter-day Saints fled the **United States** in search of religious freedom. Federal legislation disincorporated the Church as a legal entity, escheated Church property, and took the right to vote from Latter-day Saint polygamists. Because Joseph's father was both a polygamist and prominent leader in the Church, the Smith home was constantly raided by U.S. marshals. Frequently the young Joseph Fielding was interrogated and threatened.

At age 21 Joseph Fielding married Louie Emily Shurtliff. A year later he was called as a missionary to **England,** where he spent the next two years. Following their reunion in the spring of 1901, the couple had two daughters. Complications associated with a third pregnancy claimed

Louie's life in March of 1908. That November Joseph Fielding married Ethel Georgina Reynolds, with whom he had five sons and four daughters. Thus, he was the father of 11 children. He always enjoyed spending time with his **family**. Ethel died in August 1937 of a cerebral hemorrhage. In April 1938 Joseph Fielding married for the third time, taking as his bride Jessie Ella Evans, a well-known contralto soloist in the **Tabernacle Choir**. For 33 years she traveled with him throughout the world on Church assignments. She died 3 August 1971.

As a young man, Joseph Fielding worked in the Church historian's office and was appointed an assistant Church historian in April 1906. He was called as an **apostle** on 7 April 1910 at age 33; no younger man was called to that office throughout the rest of the twentieth century. In conjunction with his call to the apostleship, he was appointed **Church historian** in 1921 and served in that capacity for nearly 50 years. At age 93 he succeeded **David O. McKay** as president of the Church.

By both name and heritage, Joseph Fielding Smith linked the Latter-day Saint people to their original roots. His father was the son of **Hyrum Smith**, brother to the Church's founder, **Joseph Smith**, who was martyred with the **Prophet** in **Carthage, Illinois**.

No one in the history of the Church has done more to encourage genealogical research and the writing of family histories than Joseph Fielding Smith. For 60 years he was a moving force behind the Genealogical Society of Utah, serving as its president for half that time. He was the first editor and business manager of the *Utah Genealogical and Historical Magazine*. While preparing this periodical's first issue in January 1910, Joseph and his family were quarantined because one of his daughters had contracted scarlet fever. Demonstrating his characteristic tenacity and creativity, he completed the manuscript at home, treated it with an antiseptic, and placed it in a box by his gate. From there the manuscript was taken to the printer and the galley proofs prepared. These were then sent to him for approval. After his final editing, he fumigated them and again placed them by the gate for delivery to the printer.

Joseph Fielding Smith is best remembered as a gospel scholar. He wrote 18 volumes on doctrinal themes and spent countless hours answering letters on gospel questions and writing articles for Church publications on doctrinal subjects. When he spoke, and no one spoke more often in the general conferences of the Church, he always used the scriptures, which he declared to be the standard by which every man's doctrine should be measured. "It makes no difference what is written or what anyone has said," he declared, "if what has been said is in conflict with what the Lord has revealed, we can set it aside. My words, and the teachings of any other member of the Church, high or low, if they do not square with the revelations, we need not accept them" (*Doctrines*, 3:203).

A tireless defender of the faith, Joseph Fielding Smith was an avowed opponent of the theory of **evolution**. He was unyielding in his testimony that we are the children of a divine Father. He held the declaration of Moses that we are created in the image and likeness of God to be literal (Gen. 1:27).

He served as an apostle for 60 years before becoming president of the Church in January 1970. He served in this capacity until his death in Salt Lake City on 2 July 1972. To that point he had traveled more miles, attended more meetings, preached more sermons, performed more ordinances, and written more voluminously about gospel truths than any other man in the Church. Stern at the pulpit, he was known to be kind and gentle in his personal associations. Where others sought to give credibility to the theology of Mormonism with **Bible** texts, he sought to do so with the revelations and teachings of the Prophet Joseph Smith. None have been more loyal to the Church's founder. His compilation entitled *Teachings of the Prophet Joseph Smith*, published by **Deseret Book Company** in 1936, is one of the most quoted books in the Church.

SOURCES

Arrington, Leonard J. *Presidents of the Church.* Salt Lake City: Deseret Book, 1986. 315–41.

Gibbons, Francis M. *Joseph Fielding Smith: Gospel Scholar, Prophet of God.* Salt Lake City: Deseret Book, 1992.

McConkie, Joseph F. *True and Faithful: The Story of Joseph Fielding Smith.* Salt Lake City: Bookcraft, 1971.

Smith, Joseph Fielding. *Doctrines of Salvation.* Compiled by Bruce R. McConkie. 3 vols. Salt Lake City: Bookcraft, 1954–56.

Smith, Joseph Fielding, Jr., and John J. Stewart. *The Life of Joseph Fielding Smith.* Salt Lake City: Deseret Book, 1972.

JOSEPH FIELDING MCCONKIE

SMITH, LOT. Lot Smith was a committed Latter-day Saint **pioneer,** soldier, **Indian** fighter, and stockman known chiefly for his exploits during the **Utah War.** He was born at Williamstown, **New York,** on 15 May 1830 and joined the Church at an early age. At 16, he joined the **Mormon Battalion** as its youngest member and made the historic trek to **California.** He mined for gold for a time before rejoining his **family** in

Farmington, **Utah**. He served one term as county sheriff and became an officer in the **Nauvoo Legion**.

During the Utah War, Major Smith and other officers led their raiders in a campaign of harassment to hinder the advance of the U.S. Army. Lot and his band caused great damage by burning three government supply trains totaling 74 large freight wagons. He also "borrowed" 1,400 head of cattle, which were returned the following year. A $1,000 reward was offered for his capture.

In 1876 Lot led a colonizing mission to the Little Colorado River country of northern **Arizona**, where he was later called to preside over the **stake** as well as over its **united order**. He took up ranching and raised fine horses and cattle. He died 21 June 1892 in Tuba City, Arizona, after being shot by an Indian with whom he had a disagreement over grazing rights.

SOURCES

Flake, Dennis D. "A Study of Mormon Resistance During the Utah War, 1857–58." Master's thesis, Brigham Young University, 1975. 57–73, 124.

Peterson, Charles S. "A Mighty Man Was Brother Lot: A Portrait of Lot Smith, Mormon Frontiersman." *Western Historical Quarterly* 1 (October 1970): 393–414.

DENNIS D. FLAKE

SMITH, LUCY MACK.

Lucy Mack Smith, mother of the **Prophet Joseph Smith Jr.** and wife of the **patriarch Joseph Smith Sr.**, was a courageous defender of the faith. The youngest of eight children, she was born in Gilsum, **New Hampshire**, 8 July 1775 to Solomon Mack and Lydia Gates. In 1796 she married Joseph Smith and became the mother of eight sons and three daughters. In addition to raising their children, she industriously earned money by selling ginger cakes, root beer, eggs, and oil cloth floor covers, which she painted. She often managed the **family**'s finances in her husband's absence, once offering her gold beads as payment for a debt.

From the moment her 14-year-old son Joseph came home in 1820 and told his parents about his **first vision**, his **mission** also became theirs. Lucy dedicated her life to serving the cause of the Savior. Her leadership abilities qualified her to shepherd the members of the **Fayette, New York, Branch** on their journey to **Kirtland, Ohio**, in 1831. She rationed the food and cautioned mothers to be watchful of their children. She settled difficulties and earned the respect of the captain and crew by dispensing wise counsel and ministering to the sick on board ship as they sailed across Lake Erie from Buffalo, New York, to Fairport Harbor, Ohio. Lucy's testimony of the truthfulness of the gospel became the hallmark of her life. Unafraid, she bore her testimony to people on the wharf at Buffalo Harbor from the ship that carried the Fayette **Saints** to Kirtland. She also bore testimony to her brothers and sisters and to a minister. When called upon to speak, the Prophet's mother rehearsed events in the history of the Church she had witnessed, and she dictated this testimony for publication.

After the organization of the **Relief Society** in 1842 at **Nauvoo, Illinois,** Lucy counseled the members to cherish, comfort, and look after one another and also to gain instruction. She continued to be an inspiration to Church members who thought of what she had endured in losing her husband and all but one of her sons, including Joseph and Hyrum in the Martyrdom and Samuel from the exertion of going to their aid. She was the epitome of a beloved mother and faithful servant in the kingdom.

The last years of Lucy's life were spent in the home of her daughter-in-law **Emma Smith** and Emma's second husband, **Lewis Bidamon.** Emma treated her with great care and love until her death in May 1855 or 1856 on the family farm east of **Nauvoo.**

SOURCES

Smith, Ethel R. "The Prophet's Mother." *Relief Society Magazine* 15 (June 1930): 319–23.

Smith, Lucy Mack. *The Revised and Enhanced History of Joseph Smith by His Mother.* Edited by Preston Nibley. Salt Lake City: Bookcraft, 1958.

AUDREY M. GODFREY

SMITH, LUCY (MILLIKEN). See SMITH FAMILY.

SMITH, MARY DUTY.

Mary Duty Smith, grandmother of **Joseph Smith Jr.** and progenitor of three other Church presidents, was born 11 October 1743 in Windham, **New Hampshire.** She married **Asael Smith** in 1767. Together they reared eleven children, five of whom were born before the outbreak of the **Revolutionary War.** At age 86, she received a copy of the **Book of Mormon,** which she accepted as **scripture,** from her son **Joseph Smith Sr.** Six years later Mary traveled 500 miles from Stockholm, **New York**, to gather with the **Saints** in **Kirtland, Ohio**, where she was joyously reunited with her **family**. She died two weeks later, 27 May 1836.

SOURCES

Anderson, Richard Lloyd. *Joseph Smith's New England Heritage.* Salt Lake City: Deseret Book, 1971.

Smith, Lucy. *Biographical Sketches of Joseph Smith the Prophet and His Progenitors for Many Generations.* Lamoni, Iowa: Reorganized Church of Jesus Christ of Latter Day Saints, 1912.

JULIE HUNSAKER

SMITH, MARY FIELDING. Mary Fielding Smith, wife of **Hyrum Smith** and mother of **Joseph F. Smith**, was born to John and Rachel Fielding on 21 July 1801 in Bedfordshire, **England**. She joined her brother Joseph and sister Mercy in **Canada** in 1834. The three were soon introduced to the Church, and in May 1836 were baptized. After joining the **Saints** in **Kirtland**, she met the recent widower Hyrum Smith, to whom she was married, becoming the stepmother of his children. Hyrum and Mary had two children: Joseph F., the future sixth president of the Church, and Martha. Mary's faith was strengthened through trying times in Kirtland, **Far West**, **Nauvoo**, and **Carthage**. She courageously responded to her husband's murder in Carthage by gathering her **family** and crossing the plains with her widowed sister, Mercy, and her brother Joseph and his family. When in distress, she relied on the Lord to guide her to her lost cattle and to heal her oxen. She died in **Salt Lake City** on 21 September 1852, four years after reaching the valley. Remembered for her refinement, courage, and tenderness, Mary was "a saint if ever one lived on this troubled earth. She was a heroine in her own right by reason of her greatness of spirit and soul" (Pearson Corbett, 444).

SOURCES

Arrington, Leonard J., and Susan Arrington Madsen. *Mothers of the Prophets.* Salt Lake City: Deseret Book, 1987. 89–107.

Corbett, Don Cecil. *Mary Fielding Smith: Daughter of Britain.* Salt Lake City: Deseret Book, 1970.

Corbett, Pearson H. *Hyrum Smith: Patriarch.* Salt Lake City: Deseret Book, 1976.

JOSEPH FIELDING MCCONKIE

SMITH, NICHOLAS G. Nicholas Groesbeck Smith spent all his adult life in Church service, eventually serving in two different **general authority** callings. After fulfilling a calling as **bishop**, he spent 13 years on the general board of the **Mutual Improvement Association**. From 1913 to 1921 he was president of the **South Africa** Mission. **Elder** Smith served as acting **patriarch to the Church** from 1932 to 1934. He was then called to preside over the **California** Mission (1934–36). After becoming an **assistant to the Twelve** in 1941, Elder Smith also served as the president of the Northwestern States Mission.

Nicholas G. Smith was born 20 June 1881 in **Salt Lake City, Utah**, the son of **apostle John Henry Smith** and Josephine Groesbeck. He married Florence Gay in 1906, and they had four children. He died in Salt Lake City 27 October 1945.

SOURCE

Jenson, Andrew. *Latter-day Saint Biographical Encyclopedia*. 4 vols. 1901–36. Reprint, Salt Lake City: Western Epics, 1971. 4:167.

MARY JANE WOODGER

SMITH, SAMUEL H. Samuel Harrison Smith was a witness to the **Book of Mormon**, one of the charter members of the Church, a prominent missionary, and the younger brother of the **Prophet Joseph Smith**. Samuel was born 13 March 1808 in Tunbridge, **Vermont**. When he was a boy he moved with his family to **Palmyra, New York**, where he joined the Presbyterian church with his mother and brother Hyrum. When Samuel heard of the visions of his brother Joseph, he became one of his earliest followers and was baptized in May 1829.

Called to be one of the Eight **Witnesses of the Book of Mormon** and one of the six original members of the Church, Samuel was also one of the first missionaries for the Church in this dispensation. His proselyting efforts in western New York eventually led to the conversion of **Brigham Young** and **Heber C. Kimball**. Samuel was ordained an **elder** 9 June 1830 and a **high priest** 3 June the following year. On 25 January 1832 he and **Orson Hyde** were called on a **mission** (D&C 75:13). This arduous mission lasted almost a year and took them to the states of **Ohio, New York, Pennsylvania, Connecticut, Rhode Island, Massachusetts**, and **Maine**. When the **Kirtland Stake** was organized on 17 February 1834, Samuel was called to the **high council**. He married Mary Bailey on

13 August the same year. In 1840 he moved to **Nauvoo** where he was an alderman, a **bishop**, and a member of the **Nauvoo Legion**.

In January 1841 Samuel's wife died and left him with four children. On 3 May of that year he married Levira Clark, with whom he had three children. In 1844, Samuel received word that his brothers, Joseph and Hyrum, had been imprisoned in **Carthage**. He rode as fast as he could to be with them and was chased by a mob. Although he escaped, Samuel died a month later, on 30 July, in Nauvoo, Illinois, from a fever he contracted during the episode.

SOURCES

Black, Susan Easton. *Who's Who in the Doctrine and Covenants.* Salt Lake City: Bookcraft, 1997. 295–97.

Cook, Lyndon W. *The Revelations of the Prophet Joseph Smith.* Provo, Utah: Seventy's Mission Bookstore, 1981. 34.

Jarman, Dean. "The Life and Contributions of Samuel Harrison Smith." Master's thesis, Brigham Young University, 1961.

ARNOLD K. GARR

SMITH, SOPHRONIA (STODDARD MCCLEARY). See SMITH FAMILY.

SMITH, SYLVESTER. Sylvester Smith, known for his contentious spirit during **Zion's Camp**, served in the Church as a missionary in 1832, as a member of the **Kirtland high council** between 17 February 1835 and 13 January 1836, and as one of the original presidents of the Quorum of the **Seventy** between 28 February 1835 and 6 April 1837. Born 15 October 1805 in Suffolk, **New York**, Sylvester had joined the Church by June 1831 and was called to preach the gospel with Gideon Carter 25 January 1832 (D&C 75:34). He assisted in laying the foundation stones for the **Kirtland Temple** 23 July 1833.

In 1834 Sylvester was a member of Zion's Camp, where he refused to share food with other members of the camp and disagreed with the **Prophet** on several fronts. When he returned to Kirtland, Sylvester charged the Prophet with abusing his authority during the march of Zion's Camp. Joseph was exonerated of the charges by each of two councils headed by **Bishop Newel K. Whitney**, after which Sylvester publicly acknowledged his error. Sylvester also served as Joseph's scribe, attended the **School of the Prophets**, studied Hebrew under **Joshua**

Seixas, was present at the Kirtland Temple dedication, and was a charter member of the **Kirtland Safety Society**. By 1838 he had left the Church.

SOURCES

Black, Susan Easton. *Who's Who in the Doctrine and Covenants.* Salt Lake City: Bookcraft, 1997. 298–99.

Jenson, Andrew. *Latter-day Saint Biographical Encyclopedia.* 4 vols. 1901–36. Reprint, Salt Lake City: Western Epics, 1971. 1:191.

Smith, Joseph. *History of The Church of Jesus Christ of Latter-day Saints.* Edited by B. H. Roberts. 2d ed. rev. 7 vols. Salt Lake City: The Church of Jesus Christ of Latter-day Saints, 1932–51.

ANDREW H. HEDGES

SMITH, WILLIAM B. William B. Smith, brother of the **Prophet Joseph Smith**, was one of the original members of the **Quorum** of Twelve **Apostles** but later fell away from the Church. Born 13 March 1811 in Royalton, Windsor County, **Vermont**, he was the fifth son of **Joseph Smith Sr.** and **Lucy Mack**. On 9 June 1830, shortly after the Church was organized, William was baptized in Seneca Lake by **David Whitmer**. He served **missions** in **New York**, **Ohio**, and **Pennsylvania** before he was **ordained** an **Elder**. He was ordained a **high priest** by **Sidney Rigdon** in June 1833. William went with **Zion's Camp** in 1834, after which he was ordained an apostle.

William frequently rebelled against his brother Joseph. During one meeting, in an uncontrollable rage, he tried to throw Joseph from the house. The Prophet was injured and could not sit or rise without help for some time. William was forgiven for his actions and called on a mission with the Twelve to **England**, but he failed to go. In 1841 he journeyed east to gather funds for the Nauvoo Temple, but he kept the funds for his own use. In 1842 he was elected to the **Illinois** House of Representatives (1842–48). He was excommunicated on 12 October 1845 for misuse of Church funds and publishing slanderous statements against the Church. William affiliated with the apostate **James J. Strang**. He later petitioned his nephew **Joseph Smith III**, then president of the **Reorganized Church of Jesus Christ of Latter Day Saints**, to appoint him as the presiding patriarch. His request was not granted. William died 13 November 1894 in Osterdock, **Iowa**.

SOURCES

Black, Susan Easton. *Who's Who in the Doctrine and Covenants.* Salt Lake City: Bookcraft, 1997. 300–3.

Jenson, Andrew. *Latter-day Saint Biographical Encyclopedia.* 4 vols. 1901–36. Reprint, Salt Lake City: Western Epics, 1971. 1:86–87.

Smith, Lucy Mack. *History of Joseph Smith by His Mother.* Edited by Preston Nibley. Salt Lake City: Bookcraft, 1958. 342–44.

BRIAN L. SMITH

SMITH FAMILY (DESCENDANTS OF JOSEPH SR.).

The family of **Joseph Smith Sr.** and **Lucy Mack Smith** is sometimes called "The First Family of the **Restoration**." The Smiths moved from **New York** to **Ohio** and made the journey to **Missouri** as a group. They settled in **Illinois** and were devoted to securing each other's welfare. They felt the heavy hand of persecution as a family but remained convinced that Joseph Jr. told the truth when he said that God and **angels** had visited him and called him to the work.

Joseph Smith Sr. and Lucy Mack were married in 1797, and within a year they had a baby boy who died shortly after birth and was not given a name. Alvin was born a year later while the family resided in **Vermont**. He grew up to become a devoted, obedient son who believed that Joseph had seen heavenly **visions**. Alvin died in November 1823, and in 1836 Joseph saw him dwelling in the celestial kingdom (D&C 137:6–7).

Approximately two years after Alvin's birth, the Smiths had another son, whom they christened Hyrum. He, too, was devoted to the family and, as an adult, farmed near his parents. He married Jerusha Barden, who bore him six children. Following Jerusha's early death, he married **Mary Fielding**, who became the mother and grandmother of two Church presidents. After serving as **assistant president** and **patriarch** to the Church, he was murdered with his brother Joseph in **Carthage Jail** on 27 June 1844.

While the Smiths were residing in Tunbridge, Vermont, their first daughter, Sophronia, was born (1803). She was 17 when Joseph had his **first vision**, and she lost friends when word spread that her brother claimed to have seen God. She married Calvin W. Stoddard while the family was living in New York and became the mother of two children. She assisted in building the **Kirtland Temple**, and after her husband's death she married William McLeary. Later she lived with her daughter, Marie, in Colchester, Illinois, where she died 28 August 1876.

By 1805 Joseph and Lucy were residing in **Sharon, Vermont**, where Joseph Jr. was born on 23 December. He married **Emma Hale**, who bore eight children, three dying in infancy as well as one stillborn child. Joseph suffered **martyrdom** for his teachings, but time has only increased his fame. He is now recognized by millions as a **prophet, seer, and revelator**.

In Tunbridge, in 1808, Lucy gave birth to **Samuel H. Smith**, her sixth child. Samuel is known as the Church's first missionary and one of the **Eight Witnesses**, who saw the **gold plates** from which the **Book of Mormon** was translated. He married Mary Bailey, and they had four children. After Mary's death he married Levira Clark, who later traveled with the **Saints** to the **Great Basin**. He died 31 July 1844, just a month after his two older brothers.

Ephraim, a sixth son, was born two years after Samuel but lived only 11 days, dying 13 March 1810. A year later a seventh son, William, was born in Royalton, Vermont. William became a member of the first **Quorum** of Twelve **Apostles** and served briefly as patriarch to the Church. William's wives, Caroline Amanda Grant, Roxey Ann Grant, and Eliza Elise Sanborn, bore him a total of eight children. He died in 1893, outliving his brothers by almost 50 years.

Two years after William was born, the Smith's second daughter, Catherine, was born. She grew to be a tall young woman of deep faith. Baptized by **David Whitmer**, she and her sister saved the plates by hiding them in their bed and pretending to be asleep. She married William Salisbury and was the mother of eight children. Catherine accompanied the bodies of Joseph and Hyrum back to Nauvoo on 28 June 1844. After suffering through poverty and other hardships, she died in 1900 and was buried in Webster, Illinois.

Don Carlos, the eighth son of Joseph and Lucy, was born in 1816, just before the family moved to **Palmyra, New York**. He edited the Church's *Elders' Journal* in **Kirtland, Ohio**, and the *Times and Seasons* in **Nauvoo, Illinois**. A faithful missionary, he also served as a brigadier general in the **Nauvoo Legion**. Don Carlos married Agnes Coolbrith, and one of his daughters became the poet laureate of **California**. He died in 1841 at the age of 25 and was buried at Nauvoo.

The eleventh and last child of Joseph and Lucy was born in Palmyra, New York, in 1824. Named after her mother, Lucy grew to be above average in height. In 1840 she married Arthur Milliken, her brother the Prophet performing the ceremony. She became the mother of nine children and spent much of her life in Colchester, Illinois, where she died at age 61.

SOURCES

Gunn, Stanley R. *Oliver Cowdery.* Salt Lake City: Bookcraft, 1962.

Jarman, Dean. "The Life and Contributions of Samuel Harrison Smith." Master's thesis, Brigham Young University, 1961.

McGavin, Cecil E. *The Family of Joseph Smith.* Salt Lake City: Bookcraft, 1963.

Rudd, Calvin P. "William Smith: Brother of the Prophet Joseph Smith." Master's thesis, Brigham Young University, 1973.

Stoker, Kevin. "The First Family of the Restoration." *Church News,* 7 January 1989.

Kenneth W. Godfrey

SMITH INSTITUTE FOR CHURCH HISTORY. See JOSEPH FIELDING SMITH INSTITUTE FOR LATTER-DAY SAINT HISTORY.

SMOOT, ABRAHAM O. Abraham Owen Smoot—born 17 February 1815 in Owenton (now Owen) County, **Kentucky**—was a church, civic, academy, and business leader of **Provo, Utah**, for nearly three decades. He was baptized into the Church in 1835 and the next year began missionary service. In 1836 he met **Joseph Smith** in **Kirtland**. He was with the Saints during their expulsions from **Missouri** in 1838 and from **Nauvoo** in 1846. Smoot had given three and a half years of missionary service before he led the "4th Hundred" company of Saints (fifth overall) into the Salt Lake Valley in September 1847. He served a mission to England in 1851–52 and from there led the first company of Saints to emigrate under the **Perpetual Emigrating Fund** Company. In 1880 he served a three-month mission to the **Sandwich Islands**. He also labored as mayor and bishop in **Salt Lake City**, eventually settling in Sugarhouse.

In 1868, **Brigham Young** called Smoot to Provo, where he served as president of the Utah Stake (all of Utah Valley) for 27 years until his death. He was elected mayor of Provo City in 1868, serving for 13 years. For many years he was also a member of the Utah territorial legislature.

In 1875 when the **Brigham Young Academy** was founded, President Young called Smoot as the first president of the board of trustees, a position he held for 20 years. Brigham Young told President Smoot to strengthen the school with his influence and to encourage others to patronize it. Smoot was instrumental in erecting the new Academy Building, dedicated in 1892. His personal credit secured construction funds. He also raised money for the building of the historic Provo **Tabernacle**, constructed from 1882 to 1898. A. O. Smoot was a prominent business leader in Provo. He was a long-time president of the Timpanogos Manufacturing Company (later Provo Woolen Mills

Company), the Provo Co-operative Institution, the First National Bank of Provo, the Utah County Savings Bank, and the Provo Lumber, Manufacturing, and Building Company. He died 6 March 1895 in Provo. The entire **First Presidency** of the Church spoke at his funeral.

SOURCES

Elliott, Berlin C. "Abraham Owen Smoot, Pioneer Mormon Leader." Master's thesis, Brigham Young University, 1955.

Nixon, Loretta D., and L. Douglas Smoot. *Abraham Owen Smoot.* Provo, Utah: A. O. Smoot Family Organization, 1994.

Smoot, A. O. "Early Experiences of A. O. Smoot." *Early Scenes in Church History.* Faith-Promoting Series, vol. 8. Salt Lake City: Juvenile Instructor Office, 1882. Reprint, Salt Lake City: Bookcraft, 1968. 17–18.

L. DOUGLAS SMOOT

SMOOT, MARY ELLEN. Mary Ellen Wood Smoot began her service as thirteenth general president of the **Relief Society** in April 1997. The fifth of six daughters, Sister Smoot was born 19 August 1933 in **Ogden, Utah,** and reared in Clearfield, Utah. She attended Utah State University and married Stanley M. Smoot in the **Salt Lake Temple** in 1952. They became the parents of seven children. Before her service as general president of the Relief Society, she and her husband were directors of Church Hosting (1993–97). She served with her husband as he presided over the **Ohio** Columbus **Mission** (1983–86) and also served on the editorial board of the *Friend* magazine, as a ward Relief Society president, and as a member of a Church curriculum writing committee. She wrote a history of Centerville, Utah, and helped to organize the Centerville Historical Society. As general president of the Relief Society she concentrated her efforts on the needs of sisters throughout the world, including the Relief Society literacy program, and focused on promoting family-centered values.

SOURCE

"Mary Ellen Wood Smoot: Relief Society General President." *Ensign* 27 (May 1997): 108.

CYNTHIA DOXEY AND LLOYD D. NEWELL

SMOOT, REED. One of the most influential Church figures of the twentieth century, Reed Smoot was the only **apostle**–U.S. senator in Latter-day Saint history—a position he held for 30 years. He was instrumental in legitimizing the Latter-day Saint presence in the world, particularly in the **United States,** at a crucial juncture in the Church's history. He was born 10 January 1862 in **Salt Lake City** to prominent Mormon **pioneer Abraham O. Smoot** and Anne Kristine Mauritsen Smoot, a Norwegian immigrant.

After graduating from **Brigham Young Academy** at age 17, Reed went on to become one of **Provo's** leading citizens and most successful businessmen. He was involved in banking, mining, and mercantile interests and also served as manager of the Provo Woolen Mills. He married his sweetheart, Alpha Mae (Allie) Eldredge, daughter of Horace S. Eldredge of the First Council of the **Seventy,** in 1884. In 1895, he was called into the Utah **Stake** presidency. In 1900 President Snow called him to serve as a member of the Quorum of the Twelve Apostles, filling a vacancy created by the death of **Franklin D. Richards.** Two years later Elder Smoot was elected as a Republican senator for **Utah,** a position he held until his defeat in the Roosevelt landslide of 1932.

Soon after his election in 1903, his senate seat was contested on religious grounds. Thus began a four-year ordeal for Smoot and the Church. Eventually Smoot and the Church were vindicated, but more importantly, the event brought the Church out of its nineteenth-century obscurity and allowed it to begin integration into the American mainstream. Smoot's continued and growing influence in **Washington, D.C.,** gave the Church much-needed stature and public approval. He single-handedly fought to reestablish the Church's missionary program in **Europe** after **World War I,** when European governments adopted policies of denying visas to missionaries. By the 1920s Smoot was one of the most powerful and well-respected senators in Washington, D.C. He had access to the city's highest circles, which enabled him to frequently escort Church presidents and **general authorities** to the White House, helping to ease the bias and prejudice that had accrued against the Church since its inception. During his last term in Washington, his wife, Allie, passed away, and he married Alice Sheets, mother-in-law of **J. Willard Marriott** of the Marriott Hotel chain.

After his defeat in the election of 1932, Smoot spent the remainder of his years fulfilling his apostolic duties. During his time in Washington, he had frequently been absent from Church headquarters and was now able to return to full-time service. He died 9 February 1941 in St. Petersburg, **Florida,** at the home of his stepson.

Sources

Heath, Harvard S. "Reed Smoot: The First Modern Mormon." Ph.D. diss., Brigham Young University, 1990.

————, ed. *In the World: The Diaries of Reed Smoot.* Salt Lake City: Signature Books, 1997.

Merrill, Milton R. *Reed Smoot: Apostle in Politics.* Logan, Utah: Utah State University Press, 1990.

HARVARD HEATH

SMOOT CASE. From 1904 to 1906, the U.S. Senate Committee on Privileges and Elections held a 30-month inquiry to consider whether **Reed Smoot**, a Latter-day Saint **apostle**, should be allowed to hold the seat to which he had been elected by the **Utah** state legislature in 1903. When the hearings were complete, the committee actually voted to oust Smoot, but after three more months of deliberation, the full Senate reversed the committee ruling and voted to seat him in February 1907. Smoot went on to become a powerbroker in the Senate and the **Republican Party**, as well as an able defender of the Church. The hearings themselves necessitated adjustments in the Church's administration of policies regarding Utah politics and industry and in its treatment of polygamists.

Smoot's right to hold office was challenged on two grounds: first, that he and other Church leaders continued to teach **plural marriage**, even if he did not practice it; and second, that the **First Presidency** and the **Quorum of the Twelve Apostles**, not the republic, would have first claim on his loyalties. The committee subpoenaed Church leaders, including President **Joseph F. Smith**, to explain their views on plural marriage and the Church's relationship to public authority and civil society. Before testifying before the Senate, President Smith published a statement distancing the Church from party politics. When he returned from the tense hearings, President Smith announced the **Second Manifesto** at the April 1904 **general conference**, stating that practicing or performing plural marriage were grounds for excommunication; **Matthias Cowley** and **John W. Taylor**, two apostles who had performed plural marriages after 1890, eventually resigned from the Quorum of the Twelve in the midst of national condemnation. The Church also divested itself of controlling interests in several businesses to demonstrate that it was not a regional economic monopolist.

Though Smoot was opposed by a wide coalition of church and women's organizations, as well as prominent senators, he successfully retained his seat because his personal behavior was unimpeachable and because powerful public officials, including President **Theodore Roosevelt**, eventually came to his defense. His "victory" did not end anti-**Mormon** attention to plural marriage, but it helped improve the Church's public image in the United States, an image Smoot cultivated at home and abroad in the following decades.

SOURCES

Alexander, Thomas G. *Mormonism in Transition.* Urbana: University of Illinois Press, 1986.

Cowan, Richard O. *The Latter-day Saint Century.* Salt Lake City: Bookcraft, 1999.

U.S. Senate. Committee on Privileges and Elections. In the Matter of Protests Against the Right of Hon. Reed Smoot, a Senator from the State of Utah, to Hold His Seat. 4 vols. Washington, D.C., 1904–1906.

JOHN THOMAS

SNEDERFLER, JIRI. Jiri Snederfler embraced the gospel as a teenager and remained a faithful member in Czechoslovakia under Communist rule for 40 years, serving as **district** president from 1972 to 1990. He was born 24 April 1932 in Plzen, Czechoslovakia. He was baptized in that city in 1949 and fulfilled his military commitment in a labor battalion. Thereafter he continued to serve quietly in the Church, even though it had been banned in 1950 by Communist authorities. For many years he and other members were interrogated by the police.

He married Olga Kozáková, who was baptized in Prague. They settled in that city, where he worked as a water resource engineer. In 1972 he was called as the district president. He continued with other **priest-hood** leaders to visit lone members, participating with the **Saints** in private meetings in their apartments in Prague, Brno, and Plezn. He faithfully trained local leaders and accounted for their **tithing**.

The Snederflers hosted neighboring **mission** leaders, as well as **general authorities** and officers, during their occasional visits and sustained the significant member-missionary conversions centered in Brno. They were blessed through friendly work colleagues to be able to visit the general authorities in **Salt Lake City**. Snederfler led out in the translation of the **temple** ceremonies. His persistence in seeking recognition for the Church was successful soon after the fall of the Communist regime.

From 1991 to 1995, the Snederflers served as the Freiberg Temple president and matron.

SOURCES

Gardner, Marvin K. "Jiri and Olga Snederfler: A Closer Look at Two Czech Pioneers." *Liahona* (English) 21 (September 1997): 16–24.

Mehr, Kahlile. "Czech Saints: A Brighter Day." *Liahona* (English) 21 (September 1997): 10–15.

———. "Frontier in the East." Manuscript history, Czechoslovakia and on the Czech Republic.

EDWIN B. MORRELL

SNOW, ELIZA R. A poet and charismatic leader of **women**, Eliza Roxcy Snow was one of the most celebrated Latter-day Saint women of the nineteenth century. Through her **poetry** she rallied the Latter-day Saint people, chronicled their history, chided their enemies, and expounded **scripture** and doctrine. Many of her **hymn** texts including "O My Father" and "How Great the Wisdom and the Love," remain in the Latter-day Saint hymnal. As second general president of the **Relief Society** (1867–1887), she helped define the active role women continue to play in the Church as leaders and teachers in Relief Society, **Young Women**, and **Primary**.

Born in Becket, Berkshire County, **Massachusetts**, 21 January 1804, Eliza was the second of seven children of Oliver and Rosetta Pettibone Snow. The family moved to the **Western Reserve** in 1806. The precocious girl, who sometimes wrote school lessons in rhyme, later worked as secretary in the office of her father, a justice of the peace. Trained by her mother in domestic arts, she earned income as a seamstress. She was also a schoolteacher. Between 1826 and 1832 she published more than 20 poems over various pen names in Ravenna, **Ohio**'s *Western Courier* and *Ohio Star.*

Eliza's Baptist parents welcomed into their Mantua, Ohio, home a variety of religious believers. She and other family members affiliated briefly with the Disciples of Christ. **Joseph Smith** visited the Snow home in 1831 and baptized Eliza's mother and sister Leonora before year's end. Eliza hesitated, deliberated, became fully committed, and was baptized 5 April 1835. She moved in December to **Kirtland, Ohio**, where she donated much-needed cash to the **temple**, lived with Joseph and **Emma Smith**, taught in their family school, and composed two hymns for Emma's new hymnal. Eliza's brother Lorenzo was baptized at Kirtland in June 1836. In 1838 the Snow family joined the **Saints'** migration to **Missouri**, permanently leaving Ohio to settle for nine months at **Adam-ondi-Ahman** until persecution forced the Saints to flee to **Illinois**.

In **Nauvoo** Eliza gained distinction as "Zion's Poetess," a title given her by Joseph Smith, and the city's periodicals regularly featured her hymns and occasional poetry. In 1842 she was appointed secretary of the

Female Relief Society of Nauvoo. She penned the minutes of the 1842–44 meetings, during which Joseph Smith designated the society's "constitution and law." She later brought the precious record to **Utah**.

Initially repelled by polygamy, she came to esteem it a divine principle and became a plural wife of Joseph Smith 29 June 1842. She later acknowledged him "the choice of my heart and the crown of my life" (Derr, 87). Following her parents' disaffection with the Church and removal from Nauvoo, she lived in the Smith household from August 1842 to February 1843, teaching again in the family school.

After the **Prophet's martyrdom**, Eliza became a plural wife of **Brigham Young** 3 October 1844. She left Nauvoo 4 March 1846 with the Saints trekking west under President Young's direction and arrived in the **Salt Lake Valley** 2 October 1847. Her two trail diaries (1846–1849) contain vivid descriptions, friendship poems, and "songs for the Camp of Israel." They also report informal gatherings where Eliza and other women exercised gifts of tongues, prophecy, and healing and received in times of suffering "rich seasons of refreshing from above" (*Personal Writings*, 29).

In **Salt Lake City**, Utah, childless Eliza Snow became a prominent member of Brigham Young's family, moving in 1855 into a small upstairs room in the **Lion House**, where she resided until her death. She continued to publish her poetry in Latter-day Saint **periodicals**. The first of her two volumes of *Poems, Religious, Historical, and Political* appeared in 1856, the second in 1877. Several of her poems affirm a woman's place in Latter-day Saint theology. Her hymn "O My Father" testifies simply of Father and **Mother in Heaven**. Other poems emphasize obedience and witness that righteous women receive the ministrations of the Holy Spirit and will ultimately be exalted, become joint heirs with **Christ**, and obtain "The power of reigning and the right to reign" (Snow, 2:178).

Called by Brigham Young in 1866 to help **bishops** reorganize Relief Societies in local **wards** and to "instruct the sisters," Eliza traveled from ward to ward, citing precedents and instructions from the Nauvoo minutes. She encouraged sisters to attend society **meetings**, sustain **priesthood** leaders, and support Brigham Young's program for economic self-sufficiency by establishing cooperatives, storing grain, raising silk, and obtaining medical training. Though not officially set apart as general president of the Relief Society until June 1880, she had essentially functioned in that capacity since 1867.

Because she was instrumental in the organization of **Retrenchment** Associations for Young Ladies (1869) and Primary Associations (1878) for children and helped oversee their work as well as that of the Relief Society, she became known as the "presidentess" of Latter-day Saint women's organizations. She also directed temple **ordinance** work in the **Endowment House** for many years.

Her ministry awakened a generation of Latter-day Saint women to new temporal and spiritual responsibilities. She counseled her sisters: "In your lives seek to refine and elevate, that you may be prepared to come into the presence of holy beings, and associate with Gods, we do not know our own abilities until they are brought into exercise" (quoted in Derr, 113). After Brigham Young's death, Eliza returned to using Joseph Smith's name, calling herself Eliza R. Snow Smith from 1880 on. She died 5 December 1887 in Salt Lake City and was buried in Brigham Young's family cemetery.

SOURCES

Beecher, Maureen Ursenbach, ed. *The Personal Writings of Eliza Roxcy Snow.* Salt Lake City: University of Utah Press, 1995.

Derr, Jill Mulvay. "The Significance of 'O My Father' in the Personal Journey of Eliza R. Snow." *BYU Studies* 36, 1 (1996–97): 85–126.

Snow, Eliza R. *Poems, Religious, Historical and Political.* 2 vols. Liverpool: F. D. Richards, 1856; Salt Lake City: LDS Printing and Publishing Establishment, 1877.

JILL MULVAY DERR

SNOW, ERASTUS. Erastus Snow, a missionary, **pioneer**, and **apostle** of the early Church, was born in St. Johnsbury, **Vermont**, 9 November 1818. He was baptized 3 February 1833 and began preaching soon thereafter. He attended the **Kirtland School of the Elders**, participated in the **endowment** in Kirtland in 1836, and was called to the Second **Quorum** of the **Seventy**. He served several **missions** to the eastern states before his marriage to Artemesia Beman in December 1838.

Snow aided **Joseph Smith's** unsuccessful escape attempt from **Liberty Jail** and helped secure the change of venue that eventually led to the prisoners' escape. He again preached in the East, living mainly in Philadelphia and **Salem** from 1840 to 1843. He was endowed in **Nauvoo** in December 1845 and left the city on 6 February 1846. He and **Orson Pratt** were the first explorers to enter the **Salt Lake Valley** in 1847.

After another mission to the East in 1848, Erastus Snow was ordained an apostle on 12 February 1849 and called to open the **Scandinavian** mission that October. After his return in 1852, he directed migration at **St. Louis**, organizing a stake there in 1854. In 1861 he was sent to colonize southern **Utah**, where he ministered among the **Saints**. Because of his work in colonizing **Arizona**, the community of Snowflake, Arizona, was named for him and William Jordan Flake. Snow made a second trip to **Europe** in 1873. Government action against polygamists forced him into exile during his last years. He died 27 May 1888 in **Salt Lake City**.

SOURCES

Jenson, Andrew. *Latter-day Saint Biographical Encyclopedia.* 4 vols. 1901–36. Reprint, Salt Lake City: Western Epics, 1971. 1:103–15.

Larson, Andrew Karl. *Erastus Snow: The Life of a Missionary and Pioneer for the Early Mormon Church.* Salt Lake City: University of Utah Press, 1971.

JOHN THOMAS

SNOW, LORENZO. Lorenzo Snow, the fifth president of the Church, is known particularly for his reemphasis of **tithing** and for his famous couplet "As man now is, God once was; as God now is, man may be" (quoted Williams, 2). The fifth of seven children, he was born 3 April 1814 in Mantua, **Ohio**, to Oliver and Rosetta Pettibone Snow. His parents were cultured, educated people from the east whose ancestors had come to **America** to escape religious persecution. In 1831 his mother and sister Leonora joined the Church.

Raised on a farm, Lorenzo learned to work hard but also developed a love of reading. At the age of 21 he had been attracted to and joined the military. He realized that to reach his military ambitions he would need a college education. In September 1835, just five months after his sister **Eliza R. Snow** joined the Church, he started out for Oberlin College in Ohio. On his way he providentially met **apostle David W. Patten** and was deeply impressed with his reasoning about God's purposes for his children on earth. Lorenzo was disenchanted with what he learned concerning religion at Oberlin, and soon Eliza convinced him to come to **Kirtland** and study Hebrew. Lorenzo was influenced by his association with the Church members. He was particularly stirred by the counsel of **Joseph Smith Sr.**, who said to him, "You will become as great as you can possibly wish—even as great as **God**, and you cannot wish to be greater" (Smith, 10). This and other experiences eventually led to Lorenzo's baptism on 23 June 1836 by **John Boynton**, one of the latter-day original Twelve Apostles.

A short time after his baptism, Lorenzo became concerned that he did not have a knowledge or spiritual witness of the truth of this work. He went to a secluded place and prayed earnestly when the following occurred: "I had no sooner opened my lips in an effort to pray, than I heard a sound, just above my head, like the rustling of silken robes, and immediately the Spirit of God descended upon me, completely enveloping my whole person, filling me, from the crown of my head to the soles of my feet, and O, the joy and happiness I felt! . . . I then received a perfect knowledge that God lives, that **Jesus Christ** is the Son of God, and of the restoration of the holy **Priesthood**, and the fullness of the Gospel" (Smith, 8).

Over the next several years (1837–39), Lorenzo served short-term **missions** to **Ohio, Missouri, Illinois**, and **Kentucky**. He served a mission in **Great Britain** (1840–43), during which time he presented a copy of the **Book of Mormon** to Queen Victoria and published the **pamphlet** *The Only Way to Be Saved.* Just prior to his leaving for his mission to Great Britain, Lorenzo indicated the Spirit communicated to him the understanding of man's potential to become like God. He shared this insight with **Brigham Young** when he arrived in **England**. Brigham advised him to lay the matter on the shelf until he heard the **Prophet** teach it, which he did. Upon returning from England it was Brigham Young who informed Lorenzo that the Prophet **Joseph Smith** had been teaching the doctrine to the people.

Following Joseph Smith's counsel on **marriage**, in 1845 Lorenzo married four wives and in later years would marry five additional wives. He would become the father of 41 children.

Lorenzo arrived in the **Salt Lake Valley** with his family in the summer of 1848. On 12 February 1849, he was called to the **Quorum** of the Twelve Apostles, and by October he was appointed to serve a mission to **Italy** and other European nations (1849–52). During this mission he published the pamphlet *The Voice of Joseph.*

Upon returning to the Salt Lake Valley he organized the **Polysophical Society** for the cultural and social development of the **Saints**. In 1853 Brigham Young called Elder Snow to preside over the **Saints** in present-day Box Elder County in northern Utah, where he named the chief settlement **Brigham City**. Elder Snow was called with others in 1864 to go to the Sandwich Islands (**Hawaii**) to resolve problems arising from the apostasy of **Walter Murray Gibson**. After drowning off the Island of Maui, Elder Snow was miraculously restored to life.

He served as president of the **Utah** Territorial Legislative Council (1872–82) and participated in the second dedication of the **Holy Land** in March 1873 with **George A. Smith**. Lorenzo was called and sustained as an additional **counselor** to Brigham Young in April 1873. Following this calling, he began earnestly to establish the united order in Brigham City. His success in this endeavor was unequaled among all the communities of the Saints. Of this effort Brigham Young said, "Brother Snow who has had charge of you, has set the best example for the literal building up of the **kingdom of God** of any of our presiding Elders" (Romney, 334).

Elder Snow served a short-term mission to the **Indians** in **Wyoming** (1885). Within months of his return he was arrested for practicing **plural marriage** and served an 11-month prison sentence (1886–87). He later offered the public dedicatory prayer for the **Manti Temple** on 21 May 1888. Following the death of President **John Taylor** in 1889, Elder Snow became the president of the Quorum of the Twelve. During this time he raised a young girl from the dead.

After the dedication of the **Salt Lake Temple** in 1893, he was set apart as its president at age 79. He served in this capacity until the death of President **Wilford Woodruff** in September 1898. Upon receiving news of the president's death, Elder Snow went to the Salt Lake Temple to petition the Lord for direction. The Savior appeared and instructed him to proceed immediately to reorganize the **First Presidency**. Heretofore, there had been a period of as much as three years (during which time the apostles presided) following the death of one president, before his successor was sustained.

President Snow inherited the pressing problems of the Church's financial debt, which had come in part because of the years of persecution and legal expenses arising from **antipolygamy** legislation. He prayerfully sought a solution to the Church's financial problems and was directed by the Lord to take a trip to **St. George, Utah**. While addressing the Saints on 18 May 1899 he was inspired by revelation to announce: "The time has now come for every Latter-day Saint . . . to do the will of the Lord and to pay his tithing in full. That is the word of the Lord to you" (Snow, 155). He sounded this same message throughout the **stakes** of the Church. The Saints responded, and within a few years the Church's debt was paid.

President Snow placed great emphasis on missionary work during his three years as prophet. In 1899 the Church, under his direction, sent out 1,059 missionaries, a record that would not be surpassed until 1919. On 10 October 1901, four days after **general conference**, Lorenzo Snow died of pneumonia in **Salt Lake City**.

SOURCES

Gibbons, Francis M. *Lorenzo Snow: Spiritual Giant, Prophet of God.* Salt Lake City: Deseret Book, 1982.

Romney, Thomas C. *The Life of Lorenzo Snow.* Salt Lake City: Deseret Book, 1955.

Smith, Eliza R. Snow. *Biography and Family Record of Lorenzo Snow.* Salt Lake City: Deseret News, 1884.

Snow, Lorenzo. *The Teachings of Lorenzo Snow.* Compiled by Clyde J. Williams. Salt Lake City: Bookcraft, 1984.

CLYDE J. WILLIAMS

SNOW COLLEGE. Snow College began as one of 33 **academies** founded by the Church between 1875 and 1910. It was established because of a lack of public education and to compete with non-LDS academies. Located in Ephraim, Sanpete County, **Utah**, Snow College was founded 3 November 1888 as the Sanpete Stake Academy. The academy's name changed several times from Snow Academy (1902)—in honor of **Lorenzo** and **Erastus Snow**—to Snow Normal College (1917), to Snow College (1923). The name changes represented the gradual changes in curriculum from elementary to college subjects. In 1932, the **Church** turned the school over to the state of Utah.

SOURCES

Bennion, M. Lynn. *Mormonism and Education.* Salt Lake City: Department of Education of The Church of Jesus Christ of Latter-day Saints, 1939. 147–74.

Jenson, Andrew. *Encyclopedic History of The Church of Jesus Christ of Latter-day Saints.* Salt Lake City: Deseret News, 1941. 801.

J. MICHAEL HUNTER

SNOWFLAKE, ARIZONA. Snowflake is a Latter-day Saint **pioneer** community located in Navajo County, Arizona, on Silver Creek. It was established in July 1878 by the arrival of the William Jordan Flake family, who had previously settled in "Old Taylor" on the Little Colorado River. The move was deemed necessary when it was discovered that earthen irrigation dams were not dependable. James Stinson, who had farmed the region for several years prior to the arrival of the **Mormons**, sold his holdings to Flake for $11,000 in livestock.

Snowflake was named for **Elder Erastus Snow**, who supervised Church colonization in Arizona, and for Flake, who settled the town. Snowflake was the site of a united order, and many of the early settlers were southern converts. In 1888 a Church academy was constructed, but it closed temporarily because of financial concerns. After resumption of operations, it was destroyed by fire in 1910. The facility was rebuilt and continued operation until 1924, when state schools replaced the need for Church **academies**.

Snowflake was part of the Little Colorado **Stake** (1879) until 1887, when the Eastern Arizona and Snowflake Stakes were organized. As of 1999 there were more than 5,000 Latter-day Saints living in the community. In April 2000 plans were announced to build a temple in Snowflake.

SOURCES

Erickson, Bess, ed. *Snowflake Stake, 1887–1987: 100 years of Faith and Service.* Snowflake, Ariz.: Snowflake, 1987.

Jenson, Andrew. *Encyclopedic History of The Church of Jesus Christ of Latter-day Saints.* Salt Lake City: Deseret News, 1941.

DAVID F. BOONE

SOCIAL HALL. The Social Hall was constructed in 1852 by **Brigham Young** in **Salt Lake City** as a place for amusement. It was located on the east side of State Street between South Temple and First South Streets. It contained two halls, the upper for drama and dancing, and the lower for dinners and parties. Over the years, the Social Hall served a variety of other uses. Several sessions of the **Utah** territorial legislature met there, as did several different schools. The building was demolished in 1922. A historical marker and museum now occupy the site.

SOURCES

Mortensen, A. R. "Social Hall Was Center of Entertainment for Pioneer Utah." *Salt Lake Tribune Home Magazine,* 5 May 1957, 27.

W. RANDALL DIXON

SOCIAL HISTORY. Latter-day **Saint** society has taken on distinctive qualities over time as beliefs and historical experience have given it shape and direction. Careful observers have long seen areas settled by Latter-day Saints as uniquely coherent and tightly knit—notably different from the more highly individualistic and liberal society of the **United States**.

Several forces have given this shape to Latter-day Saint society. The doctrine of **gathering** asked all converts to migrate to areas where they could live with other Saints. The **Prophet Joseph Smith** urged them, once gathered, to live in towns rather than on their lands, enhancing opportunities for social interaction. He taught also that cooperation was superior to individual enterprise and more conducive to a healthy society, founding economic and other programs to help build a more cohesive society among his followers.

Already by the mid-1840s some distinctive elements were becoming evident. A series of persecutions caused the Saints to look inward, avoiding association with those not of their faith, whom they came to call **Gentiles**. Also, in **Nauvoo**, **Joseph Smith** and close associates taught privately the doctrine of **celestial marriage** and the **law of adoption** (through which Church members were "adopted" into the families of leading Church officials), both institutions extending the reach of the **family** as the fundamental unit of society.

In **Illinois**, the large concentration of Latter-day Saints favored the further development of distinctive social institutions. The division of the city of Nauvoo into political "**wards**" began the process, later fully developed in **Utah**, of dividing the entire body of the faithful into geographically-defined congregations called "wards," each headed by a **bishop**. The Latter-day Saint ward was to become a social institution of great importance—perhaps the most powerful single instrument of the Saints' social organization. In the nineteenth century the towns of Mormon-settled areas were often composed of a single ward, making the overlay of secular and religious life particularly pronounced and powerful. But whether in rural towns or urban centers, the ward remained the center of social and cultural life for committed Latter-day Saints for more than a century, with a social function not unlike that of preindustrial villages. Beginning in the 1960s, Church leaders initiated changes some thought would diminish the ward's role at the center of Latter-day Saint neighborhoods and communities. A consolidated meeting schedule greatly reduced the amount of time spent at the **meetinghouse**. A more focused definition of Church purposes, "to proclaim the gospel, perfect the Saints, and redeem the dead," called into question the relevance of Church-sponsored cultural and social activities that do not contribute directly to those aims.

Church leaders evidently saw in this new initiative gains that in their judgment would outweigh the losses. Latter-day Saints were encouraged to devote more time to community service, providing more contact with non-Mormons, who would see the fruits of the gospel and want to learn more.

SOURCES

Arrington, Leonard J., and Davis Bitton. *The Mormon Experience.* New York: Alfred A. Knopf, 1979.

Bitton, Davis. "Early Mormon Lifestyles; or the Saints as Human Beings." *The Restoration Movement: Essays in Mormon History.* Edited by F. Mark Mckiernan et al. Independence, Mo.: Herald House, 1979.

May, Dean L. *Three Frontiers: Family, Land, and Society in the American West: 1850–1900.* New York: Cambridge University Press, 1994.

Walker, Ronald W. and Doris Dant, eds. *Nearly Everything Imaginable: The Everyday Life of Utah's Mormon Pioneers.* Provo, Utah: Brigham Young University Press, 1999.

DEAN L. MAY

SOCIAL SERVICES. In 1916 Church leaders organized a Social Advisory Committee to address moral and recreation issues of the time. This organization was a forerunner to LDS social services. As the Church grew in membership, so did the number and kinds of problems and the need for assistance. In 1919 the **Relief Society** Social Service Department was organized and licensed to perform adoptions and foster care services. It also helped post–**World War I** Church members with health, economic, and family problems.

Indian Student Placement Service was started in 1947 to provide educational opportunities for Native American children. In 1956 the Relief Society Social Service Department evolved into the Youth Rehabilitation Program, later to be become the Youth Services Department of the Church. In 1969 this program was combined with Indian Student Placement to become Unified Social Services, which in 1973 was incorporated as LDS Social Services.

This organization serves Church members in the **United States, Canada, England, Australia,** and **New Zealand.** Services include counseling with young women who have become pregnant out of wedlock, adoption of infants, limited placement of children in foster care, consultation with local Church leaders, and therapy for families and individuals referred by their bishops. Members are helped to pursue a life consistent with gospel principles.

SOURCES

Clement, C. Ross. "Social Services." *Encyclopedia of Mormonism.* Edited by Daniel H. Ludlow. 4 vols. New York: Macmillan, 1992. 3:1386–97.

History of Relief Society 1842–1966. Salt Lake City: General Board of Relief Society, 1966. 42, 64, 80, 92–94.

LDS Social Services. Pamphlet. Salt Lake City: LDS Social Services, 1994.

C. ROSS CLEMENT

SOLEMN ASSEMBLIES. Originating in Old Testament times, solemn assemblies provide opportunities for Church members to sustain their leaders, participate in **temple** dedications, and receive instruction from presiding authorities. In this dispensation the Church has continued to hold solemn assemblies to commemorate sacred occasions, such as the sustaining of a new **First Presidency** after a prophet's death or the dedicating of a temple. Members of the Church sustain the new presidency at a **general conference**, whether viewed live in **Salt Lake City** or as a broadcast or recording anywhere throughout the world. Temple dedications are held at the temple and nearby buildings, where worthy **Saints** are able to participate. For example, on 27 March 1836 the **Prophet Joseph Smith** gathered the Saints to the **Kirtland Temple** and a nearby schoolhouse to sustain their leaders. Those in attendance received an outpouring of the Spirit as the Prophet dedicated the temple and as Church leaders bore testimony of the gospel. Presiding authorities may also call solemn assemblies when **priesthood** leaders of a particular area gather to receive counsel and encouragement.

SOURCES

Haight, David B. "Solemn Assemblies." *Ensign* 24 (November 1994): 14–17.

McConkie, Bruce R. *Mormon Doctrine*. 2d ed. Salt Lake City: Bookcraft, 1979. 739.

Turley, Richard E., Jr. "Solemn Assemblies." *Encyclopedia of Mormonism*. Edited by Daniel H. Ludlow. 4 vols. New York: Macmillan, 1992. 3:1390–91.

LISA KURKI

SOLOMON ISLANDS. The Solomon Islands, located in the **Pacific**, east of **Papua New Guinea**, (including Guadalcanal of **World War II** fame), have a predominately Melanesian population of approximately 400,000, most of whom are Christians. The first converts were Imo Ta'asi, baptized at **Brigham Young University** in 1986, and Peter Joseph Salaka—baptized in **England**. Missionary work was opened in 1995. Eddie Misi, who was the first convert baptized in the islands, also became the first branch president when the Honaira Branch was organized in 1996. At the beginning of the year 2000, there were 148 Latter-day Saints in one **branch**.

SOURCE

1999–2000 Church Almanac. Salt Lake City: Deseret News, 1998. 386.

EMILY C. ZEIGLER

SOMALIA. Somalia covers more than 246,000 square miles and is Africa's easternmost country. Before gaining its independence in 1960, the country's northern section was ruled by **Great Britain** and its southern section by **Italy**. The population speaks Somali, a language that had not been written until 1972. Most of the people of Somalia are Sunni **Muslims**.

In 1992, when Somalia and its neighboring countries were suffering from a severe drought, the Church sent a million pounds of food and relief supplies. Coupled with civil **war**, this drought caused some Somalians to flee to **Kenya**, where many were introduced to the gospel and became members of the Church.

In 1998 Somalia had fewer than 100 members, and there was no official Church group. When President **Gordon B. Hinckley** visited Nairobi, Kenya, on 17 February 1998, several Somalian Saints traveled to see the **prophet**.

SOURCES

"Deadly Drought: LDS Humanitarian Relief Supplies Help Sustain Life in Africa." *Church News*, 26 September 1992, 6.

Middleton, John, ed. *Encyclopedia of Africa South of the Sahara*. 4 vols. New York: Macmillan Library Reference USA, 1997. 4:119–30.

1999–2000 Church Almanac. Salt Lake City: Deseret News, 1998. 386–87.

E. DALE LEBARON

SONS OF UTAH PIONEERS. The Sons of Utah **Pioneers**, organized 29 March 1933, was established to preserve the heritage of Utah's early settlers. The name was changed to The National Society of the Sons of Utah Pioneers in 1953, and the organization was incorporated by the Utah State Department of Business Regulation 11 January 1988. While its purposes and objectives have been compatible with The Church of Jesus Christ of Latter-day Saints, it is not sanctioned by the Church.

The mission of the Society is to honor the pioneers who entered the **Utah** Territory prior to the Transcontinental **Railroad** on 10 May 1869. To this end the Society publishes a quarterly **periodical** entitled *Pioneer,* maintains an historical Pioneer Village Museum at Lagoon; sponsors yearly historical treks; and participates in researching and erecting monuments, marking trails and sites, preserving historical buildings, and recognizing significant contributions to the preservation of Utah's pioneer heritage.

SOURCE

Youngberg, Florence. "National Society of the Sons of Utah Pioneers." *Utah History Encyclopedia*. Salt Lake City: University of Utah Press, 1994. 512.

J. ELLIOT CAMERON

SOUTH AFRICA. European explorers began arriving in South **Africa** in the 1500s and Dutch and English settlers soon followed. In 1853, three Latter-day **Saint** missionaries arrived in Cape Town and began **missionary work** on the African continent. On 16 August 1853, the first **branch** was organized at Mowbray, Cape Town. By August 1855 the South African **mission** consisted of three **conferences**, six branches, and 126 members.

The Church closed the mission from 1865 to 1903 because of government restrictions and difficulties with the language. During this time, many of the members immigrated to **Utah**, but a small nuclei remained in the country and maintained a presence of the Church. In 1903, President Warren H. Lyon reopened the mission. The first **meetinghouse** was built in 1916 by adding onto the mission home located in Mowbray. The Church grew slowly because many members emigrated to **America** and the area was isolated from Church headquarters. **World War I** and **World War II** also had a negative impact on the growth of the Church. By the 1950s the South African government had restricted the number of missionaries from the United States. Because South Africa was a member of the British Commonwealth, however, missionaries from **Canada** and other Commonwealth countries, along with local missionaries, continued to proselyte in the country. This effort was reinforced in 1954 when President **David O. McKay** became the first **general authority** to visit South Africa. He was followed by **Elder Harold B. Lee** in 1958 and Elder **Hugh B. Brown** in 1961. Other general authorities visited and the Church continued its growth and development.

The Transvaal Stake, the first **stake** in Johannesburg, was organized on 22 March 1970. The **Book of Mormon** was translated into the Afrikaans language in 1972. The **revelation** received through President Spencer W. Kimball in June 1978, granting the **priesthood** to all worthy male members of the Church, had a tremendous impact on the Church in South Africa. Missionary work commenced among all the people of

South Africa, and the Johannesburg South Africa **Temple** was dedicated in 1985. At the beginning of the year 2000 there were nine stakes and 29,220 members.

SOURCES

1999–2000 Church Almanac. Salt Lake City: Deseret News, 1998. 386–87.
Wright, Evan P. *A History of the South African Mission.* 3 vols. N.p. N.d.

H. DEAN GARRETT

SOUTH AMERICA. Latter-day Saints have been interested in South America almost from the beginning of the **Restoration**. In 1833, **Joseph Smith** prophesied to a small group of **priesthood** bearers gathered in **Kirtland, Ohio**: "Brethren . . . you know no more concerning the destinies of this Church and kingdom than a babe upon its mother's lap. You don't comprehend it. It is only a little handfull of Priesthood you see here tonight, but this Church will fill North and South America—it will fill the world." He continued to prophesy that from a stronghold in the Rocky Mountains the Saints would "open the door for the establishing of the Gospel among the **Lamanites**" (Woodruff, 57). Then in 1844, the **Prophet** declared that "the whole of **America** is **Zion** itself from north to south" (*TPJS*, 362).

Elder **Joseph Fielding Smith** linked an Old Testament prophecy to the Americas when he suggested that Isaiah's declaration of "Woe to the land shadowing with wings" (Isa. 18:1) would be better translated, "Hail to the land in the shape of wings" (*Signs*, 51). President **Spencer W. Kimball** tied all these thoughts together as he reminded the Saints in **Brazil** and **Argentina** that "Zion was all of North and South America, like the wide, spreading wings of a great eagle, the one being North and the other South America" (4).

South America needed to be prepared for the preaching of the gospel and the establishment of the Church. Elder **Ezra Taft Benson** saw the hand of the Lord in this process: "In the decade prior to the restoration of the gospel, many countries of South America fought wars of independence to free themselves from European rule." Their independence was further protected by the inspired 1823 proclamation of the United States known as the Monroe Doctrine, declaring that there should be no further colonization in the Americas by the European powers (31). Finally, the divinely inspired Constitution of the United States (D&C 101:80) became the pattern for the written constitutions in most other American countries.

The Church's first contact with South America came in 1851. Elder **Parley P. Pratt** was appointed to preside over the "islands and coasts" of the **Pacific**, with headquarters at **San Francisco**. From there he sailed to Valparaiso, **Chile**, arriving 8 November. Even though South America had already gained independence from **Europe**, revolutions continued in many areas, including Chile. These conditions diverted the people's attention from an interest in religion. Furthermore, despite diligent efforts, **Elder** Pratt did not succeed in learning Spanish. On 2 March 1852, he left Chile for home, lamenting that he had to depart "without a sufficiency of the language to turn the keys of the Gospel as yet to these nations" (Pratt, 371, 397).

The next contact did not come for three quarters of a century. In 1925 two German families residing in Argentina wrote to the **First Presidency**, asking for missionaries to come and establish the Church. In response, Elder **Melvin J. Ballard** of the Council of the Twelve, together with Elders **Rey L. Pratt** and **Rulon S. Wells** of the First Council of the **Seventy**, were sent to Buenos Aires. On Christmas Day, in the beautiful Tres de Febrero Park, Elder Ballard dedicated South America for the preaching of the gospel. For nearly eight months he and his two **general authority** missionary companions "walked the streets of Buenos Aires giving out two hundred to five hundred handbills every day but Sunday, inviting the people to learn the message of the Restoration" (Ballard, 13).

As Elder Melvin J. Ballard was addressing a small congregation during a testimony meeting in Buenos Aires on 4 July 1926, he felt prompted to share a prophetic **vision** about the future in South America: "The work of the Lord will grow slowly for a time here just as an oak grows slowly from an acorn. It will not shoot up in a day as does the sunflower that grows quickly and then dies. But thousands will join the Church here. It will be divided into more than one mission and will be one of the strongest in the Church. The work here is the smallest that it will ever be. The day will come when the Lamanites in this land will be given a chance. The South American Mission will be a power in the Church" (quoted in Ballard, 13).

One aspect of Elder Ballard's prophecy was fulfilled in 1935 when the original mission was divided to form the separate Argentine and Brazilian **missions**. The work in both countries had begun among German immigrants; with the coming of **World War II**, however, both governments discouraged the use of German in public meetings, so the missionaries shifted their emphasis to the larger Spanish- or Portuguese-speaking majorities. This change opened the way for greater growth. In 1936 there were only 329 members in South America, but by 1945 there were 1,200—even though no missionaries arrived during World War II.

The postwar decades witnessed an acceleration of Church growth. In 1956 the first missionaries were sent to countries along the western coast of South America; significantly, this is where those of Lamanite heritage are found in greater numbers. On 1 May 1966 Elder Spencer W. Kimball, then a member of the Quorum of the Twelve **Apostles**, organized the first **stake** in South America at São Paulo, Brazil. The second was organized in Buenos Aires, Argentina, on 20 November of that same year.

It is interesting to compare the Church's growth worldwide during its first 75 years with the growth in South America during a comparable period. In 1905 the Church had a membership of 322,779; at the beginning of the year 2000, after three-quarters of a century of growth, South America had 2,464,785. In 1905 the Church had four temples, all in Utah; by the year 2000 there were 13 temples announced or completed in South America. In 1905 there were 55 stakes, all in the Intermountain West; at the beginning of the year 2000 there were 560 stakes in South America.

South America could never become a power in the Church without being "endowed with power from on high" (D&C 95:8). President **Wilford Woodruff** prophesied that temples would "appear all over this land of Joseph,—North and South America" (*JD*, 19:230). The fulfillment of this prophecy for South America began with the dedication of the temple in São Paulo on 30 October 1978. Three more **temples** were dedicated during the coming decade: Santiago, Chile, in 1983, and Lima, **Peru**, and Buenos Aires, Argentina, in 1986. Eight more were announced during the 1990s: Cochabamba, **Bolivia**; Recife, Campinas, and Porto Alegre, Brazil; Bogotá, **Colombia**; Caracas, **Venezuela**; Guayaquil, **Ecuador**; and Montevideo, **Uruguay**. In the year 2000 a temple was announced for Asuncion, **Paraguay**.

As prophecies have been fulfilled, South America has become a land of power in the Church.

SOURCES

Ballard, M. Russell. "The Kingdom Rolls Forth in South America." *Ensign* 16 (May 1986): 12–15.

Benson, Ezra Taft. "A Witness and a Warning." *Ensign* 9 (November 1979): 31–33.

Journal of Discourses [JD]. 26 vols. London: Latter-day Saints' Book Depot, 1854–86. 19:223–30.

Kimball, Spencer W. Conference Report (April 1975): 3–9.

Peterson, John D. "History of the Mormon Missionary Movement in South America to 1940." Master's thesis, University of Utah, 1962.

Pratt, Parley P. *Autobiography of Parley P. Pratt.* Edited by Parley P. Pratt Jr. Salt Lake City: Deseret Book, 1966. 371–403.

Smith, Joseph. *Teachings of the Prophet Joseph Smith (TPJS).* Selected by Joseph Fielding Smith. Salt Lake City: Deseret Book, 1963.

Smith, Joseph Fielding. *The Signs of the Times.* Salt Lake City: Deseret Book, 1964.

Tuttle, A. Theodore. "South America . . . Land of Prophecy and Promise." *Improvement Era* 66 (May 1963): 352–96.

Woodruff, Wilford. Conference Report (April 1898): 57.

CARLOS E. AGÜERO

SOUTH BAINBRIDGE, NEW YORK. South Bainbridge, originally a village in the township of Bainbridge, Chenango County, **New York**, is now known as the village of Afton in the township of Afton (formed from Bainbridge township in 1857). **Joseph Smith Jr.** first became acquainted with the village in October–November 1825 at the time of his employment with **Josiah Stowell**. The Stowells lived on a farm 3.2 miles southwest of that community. On 20 March 1826, Joseph Smith was in court at South Bainbridge on the complaint of Peter G. Bridgeman, a nephew of Stowell's wife, who charged Joseph with being "a disorderly person." Stowell was among those called as witnesses and gave testimony supportive of Joseph Smith. The trial was conducted by Justice of the Peace Albert Neely and resulted in the acquittal of the defendant (Madsen, 91).

Joseph Smith and **Emma Hale** were married in South Bainbridge by Justice of the Peace Zachariah Tarbell on 18 January 1827. Stowell took the couple in his wagon to Manchester, New York, where they could farm with Joseph's parents during the 1827 season.

Following the **organization of the Church** in April 1830, the **Prophet** and others proselyted a number of families in the Chenango and Broome County areas. At an unspecified time, Josiah Stowell was among those baptized. Before joining the Latter-day Saints he had served as a deacon in the local Presbyterian congregation. His conversion stirred strong feelings of sectarian antagonism toward the Prophet and other Latter-day Saints in the neighborhood.

A significant baptismal service was held at the **Joseph Knight Sr.** farm in **Colesville**, Broome County, on Monday, 28 June 1830. The Prophet was arrested on that occasion by Constable Ebenezer Hatch and taken to South Bainbridge, where he was held in custody. Joseph was arraigned before Justice of the Peace Joseph P. Chamberlain on a warrant charging him with being a "disorderly person," and, as Joseph said, "Setting the country in an uproar by preaching the **Book of Mormon**" (Smith, 1:88). Joseph Knight Sr. secured the legal services of James Davidson and John S. Reid to defend the Prophet. Josiah Stowell was called as a witness by the prosecution but again gave testimony in favor of Joseph Smith, leading to the Prophet's acquittal. He was likewise acquitted following a second arrest in Colesville, Broome County.

SOURCES

Chamberlain, Joseph P. Justice's bill submitted to Chenango County, for the period 1 June–August 1830. In custody of Chenango County Historian's Office, Norwich, New York.

Hatch, Ebenezer. Constable's bill submitted to Chenango County, 4 July 1830. In custody of the Chenango County Historian's Office, Norwich, New York.

Madsen, Gordon A. "Joseph Smith's 1826 Trial: The Legal Setting." *BYU Studies* 30 (Spring 1990): 91–108.

Porter, Larry C. "A Study of the Origins of The Church of Jesus Christ of Latter-day Saints in the States of New York and Pennsylvania, 1816–1831." Ph.D. diss., Brigham Young University, 1971. 172–81, 186–94, 198–204.

Smith, Joseph. *History of The Church of Jesus Christ of Latter-day Saints.* Edited by B. H. Roberts. 2d ed. rev. 7 vols. Salt Lake City: The Church of Jesus Christ of Latter-day Saints, 1932–51. 1:81–96; 6:392–97.

LARRY C. PORTER

SOUTH CAROLINA. The first member in South Carolina is believed to have been Emmanual Masters Murphy, who was converted in **Tennessee** in the mid-1830s and moved to South Carolina. When **Elder** Lysander Davis arrived about two years later, he found that the Murphys had a group of neighbors and friends prepared for the gospel.

Davis was jailed, and many succeeding missionaries were mobbed, beaten, and threatened. Later, Elder A. H. Olpin was so severely beaten he lost sanity and was committed to an asylum. **Mission president** Ephraim H. Nye visited to make arrangements for Olpin's return home, and while in the asylum he had a severe heart attack and died the next day, 15 May 1903.

Despite opposition, membership in the state increased. Many of the early converts emigrated west, while others stayed behind to help strengthen the Church. Among them were the Catawba **Indians** (1885). Most of the tribe was converted, and they erected a **meetinghouse** on their reservation. Chief Samuel Taylor Blue visited **Salt Lake City** and spoke in the **tabernacle** during general conference 9 April 1950.

In 1947 the first **stake** was created in Columbia, which included the entire state. On 16–17 October 1999 the Church dedicated a **temple** in Columbia, South Carolina. By the year 2000, the state had 27,399 members living in 55 **wards** and **branches**.

SOURCES

Berrett, LaMar C. "History of the Southern States Mission, 1831–1861." Master's thesis, Brigham Young University, 1960.

Jenson, Andrew. *Encyclopedic History of The Church of Jesus Christ of Latter-day Saints.* Salt Lake City: Deseret News, 1941.

1999–2000 Church Almanac. Salt Lake City: Deseret News, 1998. 237–39.

DAVID F. BOONE

SOUTH CAROLINA PROPHECY. See WAR, PROPHECY ON.

SOUTH DAKOTA. In the 1840s, Church leaders considered Dakota Territory as a possible refuge for the **Saints**. A year after **Joseph Smith's martyrdom**, a group of Saints led by **James Emmett** established a settlement at Fort Vermillion in June 1845. The following year they were summoned to join the Saints in moving west. Most of the group heeded the call and abandoned the fort.

Missionary work in South Dakota began 5 June 1883, when **Elder** Charles N. Nielsen arrived at Big Stone, Dakota Territory. The Dakotas were placed in the Colorado Mission in 1900. **Sunday Schools** and **branches** gradually started to form within the state in the ensuing years. After several name changes, the area became known in 1974 as the South Dakota Rapid City Mission. By the year 2000 South Dakota had 8,077 members living in two **stakes** and 33 **wards** and branches.

SOURCES

Kruckenberg, R. Janet. "The Church in the Dakotas." *Church News,* 30 November 1996, 8–10.

1999–2000 Church Almanac. Salt Lake City: Deseret News, 1998. 239–40.

KAREN REED

SOUTHERN STATES MISSION. The Southern States Mission, which has had a significant impact on Latter-day Saint history, has at one time or another included the following states: **Alabama, Arkansas,**

Florida, Georgia, Kansas, Kentucky, Louisiana, Maryland, North and South Carolina, Ohio, Tennessee, Texas, Virginia, and West Virginia. As early as 1831, the gospel was introduced into the Southern United States, but many converts emigrated west.

The mission was organized in 1876 following the Civil War, with Henry G. Boyle as president. Boyle, himself a southerner, asked Church leaders for assistance in proselyting efforts, and seven missionaries were sent.

With the Church's emphasis on the Lamanites, concerted efforts were made to introduce the gospel among the Catawbas of South Carolina (1883), the Cherokee of North Carolina (1887), and other southern tribes. Significant success was realized with whole communities joining the Church, providing local leadership and chapels.

Andrew Jenson identified the Southern States as having more persecution toward the missionaries and members than any other Latter-day Saint mission. There were whippings, threats, and even deaths. Rarely did a monthly report fail to mention the mistreatment of individuals or damage of property. Between 1870 and the turn of the century, five full-time missionaries were killed: Joseph Standing in Georgia (1879), John H. Gibbs and William S. Berry in south-central Tennessee (1884), Alma Richards in Mississippi (1888), and John Dempsey in West Virginia (1900). Several local members were likewise killed, and numerous other attempts were made on the lives of the Saints.

The immense emigration of Southern Saints makes it difficult to measure the early growth of the Church in the South. Southern converts, however, contributed greatly to Latter-day Saint colonization, education, and missionary work.

At the beginning of the year 2000, there were 11 temples in operation or announced, 127 stakes, 23 missions, and approximately 575,00 members within the confines of the historic Southern States Mission.

SOURCES

Berrett, LaMar C. "History of the Southern States Mission, 1831–1861." Master's thesis, Brigham Young University, 1960.

Jenson, Andrew. *Encyclopedic History of The Church of Jesus Christ of Latter-day Saints.* Salt Lake City: Deseret News, 1941.

1999–2000 Church Almanac. Salt Lake City: Deseret News, 1998.

DAVID F. BOONE

SOUTH KOREA. See KOREA.

SOUTH PASS. South Pass is a low-lying pass on the continental divide (7,412 feet) situated at the southern end of the Wind River Mountains and the Oregon Buttes. This pass has great historical significance—it was the gateway through which the **Mormon pioneers** crossed to get to their new home in the mountain West.

In 1842 Lt. **John Charles Frémont** of the U.S. Army Topographical Corps was assigned to lead an expedition to South Pass to document the trail that led to the Oregon country. He surveyed what was to become known as the "**Oregon Trail**" from Independence to South Pass, and his report illustrated the possibility of traveling westward with easy passage through South Pass. The Latter-day Saints, under the direction of **Brigham Young**, read Frémont's popular government publication, and when trekking west in 1847, they used South Pass as their way over the continental divide. Afterward they parted from the main Oregon Trail to head towards **Fort Bridger** and on to the valley of the Great Salt Lake. In the South Pass area, the Willie **Handcart** Site is commemorated with graves of the many handcart pioneers who died there in a fall snowstorm in 1856.

South Pass has been the way west for trappers, explorers, missionaries, freight carriers, overland stages, military units, and emigrants. Between 1843 and 1860, more than 300,000 westward travelers crossed South Pass on their way to the **Great Basin, Oregon**, and **California**. Of the nearly 70,000 Mormon pioneers coming west between 1847 and 1869, most crossed over South Pass. In 1856 Brigham Young received a four-year U.S. mail contract between **Independence, Missouri**, and **Salt Lake City**. He constructed two of the stations in the South Pass area—Rocky Ridge and Sweet Water.

Sources

"Historic South Pass." *Wind River Mountaineer* 7 (1991): 4–28.

Munkres, Robert L. "Wyoming's Trails: A Centennial Appreciation." *Annals of Wyoming* 62 (Summer 1990): 74–89.

Ronda, James P. "Before Covered Wagons: The Early Years of the Oregon Trail." *Idaho Yesterdays* 37 (Fall 1993): 5–15.

FRED R. GOWANS AND LYN CLAYTON

SOVIET UNION. See **RUSSIA**.

SPAFFORD, BELLE S. The three decades of Belle Smith Spafford's administration as general **Relief Society** president (1945–74) saw sweeping changes in the world and in the status of women. Belle was a steady guide as a Relief Society president and also as a national and international leader of women. Born 8 October 1895 in **Salt Lake City** and named Marion Isabelle Sims Smith, she was known as Belle. Her lifelong interest in social work began while she was a student at the **University of Utah** and **Brigham Young University**. She and her husband, Willis Earl Spafford, had two children. Called to the Relief Society general board in 1935, Belle was editor of the *Relief Society Magazine* for eight years. In 1942 Amy Brown Lyman requested that Belle serve as her **counselor** in the general presidency.

Belle was called as the ninth general president of the Relief Society in 1945, at the end of **World War II**. At the time, Relief Society had 100,000 members that were concentrated in the western United States. When Belle was released 29 years later, the Relief Society, with nearly a million sisters, was spread throughout 65 countries. Social, political, and economic changes offered unprecedented challenges to women.

Belle was a member of the National Council of Women for 42 years, serving as vice president and then as president (1968–70). She was the first Latter-day Saint to hold that position. She was also a delegate to the International Council of Women.

As Relief Society president, Belle focused on social services, guiding programs for adoption, youth guidance, and abused children. She supervised construction of the Relief Society Building, which was dedicated in 1956. Belle served under six Church presidents before her release in October 1974. She died 2 February 1982 in Salt Lake City.

SOURCES

Belle Spafford Oral History. LDS Church Archives, Salt Lake City.

Derr, Jill Mulvay et al. *Women of Covenant: The Story of the Relief Society.* Salt Lake City: Deseret Book, 1992. 304–38.

Peterson, Janet, and LaRene Gaunt. "Belle S. Spafford." *Elect Ladies: Presidents of the Relief Society.* Salt Lake City: Deseret Book, 1990. 145–63.

JANET PETERSON

SPAIN. Spain is located on the Iberian Peninsula in southwestern **Europe** and has a rich heritage of different peoples, languages, and religions, including Christians, **Jews**, and **Muslims**. Four different languages still exist in the country: Spanish, Catalan, Basque, and Galician. Since Catholicism is the official religion in Spain, other churches were not recognized until 1967, when the "Religious Liberty Law" was enacted (Ventura, 6–11).

The LDS Church in Spain began with servicemen located on U.S. Air Force bases, and by 1966 two **branches** functioned under the direction of the French Mission. Through the instrumentality of **Elders Howard W. Hunter** and **Gordon B. Hinckley**, the Church was officially recognized on 22 October 1968, and the Spain Madrid Mission was formed in 1970. Four other Spanish **missions** followed. The first **stake** was created in Madrid in 1982, and several new stakes have been formed since, with a total of 7 stakes and 30,439 members by the year 2000.

In June 1998 the **Mormon Tabernacle Choir** gave three concerts in Spain, including an invited concert at the basilica in El Escorial. President Gordon B. Hinckley presided at the dedication of the Madrid Spain **Temple** and its adjacent buildings in March 1999.

SOURCES

1999–2000 Church Almanac. Salt Lake City: Deseret News, 1998. 388–89.
Ventura, Betty. "The Saints in Spain." *Ensign* 5 (April 1975): 6–11.

CYNTHIA DOXEY

SPANISH-AMERICAN MISSION. From 1936 to 1967 the Spanish-American Mission was the only "foreign" **mission** within the boundaries of the United States. When revolutions swept **Mexico** during the years following 1910, LDS missionaries were withdrawn from that country. The Mexican Mission was not dissolved, but began working with Spanish-speaking people in the southwestern United States. **Rey L. Pratt** continued to preside over the mission from headquarters in **Los Angeles, California**, and later El Paso, **Texas**; he visited the **Saints** in Mexico as often as conditions there permitted. In the 1930s missionaries returned to Mexico, so a separate mission was created to supervise the work north of the border. The Spanish-American Mission was officially organized by **Elder Reed Smoot** at a meeting in Los Angeles 28 June 1936. At first the mission covered the states of California, **Arizona**, **Colorado**, **New Mexico**, Texas, and **Louisiana**, but in 1950 its territory was reduced to Texas and New Mexico. This mission continued until 1967 when proselyting in Spanish was taken over by the regular English-speaking missions serving the area. In future years many mission presidents in Latin America were chosen from those who had served in the Spanish-American Mission.

RICHARD O. COWAN

SPANISH-AMERICAN WAR. The Spanish-American War was a brief conflict between the United States and **Spain**, centered on the issue of the liberation of Cuba. Battles took place in the **Philippines** and Cuba. During the course of the **war**, the United States gained possession of **Guam**, **Puerto Rico**, and the Philippine Islands. The conflict also led to the construction of the Panama Canal.

This engagement marked the beginning of a new era in Church members' support of **United States** military efforts. Unlike the **Mormon Battalion**, which served as a separate unit in the **Mexican War**, groups of Church members who fought in the Spanish-American War were integrated with units from other parts of the country. Saints also formed the bulk of two artillery units. **Utah** had gained **statehood** two years earlier, and its citizens, largely Latter-day Saints, were anxious to show their patriotism. They served with distinction, 13 paying the supreme sacrifice with their lives.

The first federally commissioned Latter-day Saint **chaplain** served during this campaign, marking the beginning of a long and distinguished history of LDS chaplains serving with the military. The Latter-day Saint Servicemen's Group program, which would continue through all of the following century, had its origin in this military undertaking. Also, the first LDS officers were trained at **West Point** Military Academy to serve in a major conflict. The Spanish-American War was the last conflict for many years fought with an all-volunteer force.

SOURCES

Boone, Joseph F. *The Roles of The Church of Jesus Christ of Latter-day Saints in Relation to the United States Military 1900–1975.* Ph.D. diss., Brigham Young University, 1975.

Call, Lowell. *Latter-day Servicemen in the Philippine Islands: A Historical Study of the Religious Activities and Influences Resulting in the Official Organization of The Church of Jesus Christ of Latter-day Saints in the Philippines.* Master's thesis, Brigham Young University, 1955.

JOSEPH F. BOONE

SPANISH TRAIL. The longest, most arduously winding trail in **America** (approximately 1,200 miles), the Spanish Trail began in 1776 with the Escalante Expedition's attempt to link **Spain's New Mexico** and **California** colonies. It was more a general route (with various main and branch routes) than a distinct pathway between Santa Fe and **Los Angeles**, arching through **Utah** between Moab and **St. George**. It formed a key route in Hispanic-**Indian** trade of goods, horses, and Indian slaves. American fur trappers and traders of the Far Southwest utilized it, as did Mormon and later government explorers. Its western segments became the "**Mormon Corridor**."

SOURCES

Arrington, Leonard J. *Great Basin Kingdom.* Cambridge, Mass.: Harvard University Press, 1958.

Hafen, LeRoy R., and Ann W. Hafen. *The Old Spanish Trail, Santa Fe to Los Angeles.* Glendale, Calif.: Arthur H. Clark, 1954.

FRED R. GOWANS AND S. MATTHEW DESPAIN

SPÄT, WALTER. Walter Spät was the first president of the São Paulo **Brazil** Stake—the first **stake** in **South America**. He played a critical role in the development of the Church in Brazil. He was born 4 April 1919 in Stimptach, **Germany**, and his **family** immigrated to Brazil four years later. A skilled artist, he became a furniture maker by trade and owned a highly respected factory. In 1950 he and his wife, Edith, joined the Church in **São Paulo**. He served in a variety of positions, such as **branch** president, **district** president, and **counselor** in the Brazilian **Mission**. He was called as a **stake president** in 1966 and served for more than 10 years. After his release, he served as a **regional representative** and in the São Paulo Brazil **Temple** presidency. He died 15 May 1989.

SOURCES

Durham, G. Homer. "Estados Unidos da Brasil." *Improvement Era* 69 (June 1966): 470–71.

Grover, Mark L. "Mormonism in Brazil: Religion and Dependency in Latin America." Ph.D. diss., Indiana University, 1985.

Longo, Nuesa. "Walter Spät and the First South American Stake." *Ensign* 20 (June 1990): 32–33.

MARK L. GROVER

SPAULDING THEORY. The claim that **Joseph Smith** used the writings of Solomon Spaulding (1761–1816) as the source for the **Book of Mormon** has come to be known as the "Spaulding Theory." This idea was first introduced in 1834 in **Eber D. Howe's** *Mormonism Unvailed.*

Proponents of the Spaulding Theory had to explain how Joseph Smith could have access to the writings of Spaulding, who died when

Joseph was only about 10 years old. An unsubstantiated claim was that the **Smith family** and Spaulding's uncle knew each other in **Vermont**. Others suggested the more popular idea that **Sidney Rigdon** had access to the manuscript in **Pennsylvania** and later gave it to Joseph Smith. There is no evidence that Sidney Rigdon had the manuscript, and there are many testimonies that show Rigdon did not even meet Joseph Smith until after the Book of Mormon was published.

In 1834 Howe published testimonies from Spaulding's friends and **family** members claiming that most of the main incidents in the Book of Mormon originated with Solomon Spaulding; that proper names found in the Book of Mormon, such as *Nephi, Lehi, Nephites,* **Lamanites**, and even brief mention of *Laban, Zarahemla,* and **Moroni**, were the exact names found in Spaulding's manuscript; and that Spaulding wrote in a scriptural style, often using phrases such as "and it came to pass," which appear frequently in the Book of Mormon.

For 50 years the Spaulding manuscript was lost, so these allegations could not be verified. But the rediscovery of the original Spaulding manuscript in 1884 proved them false. Spaulding's characters were not **Jews** from Jerusalem but Romans from Rome. There was not a single proper name from the Book of Mormon in the Spaulding manuscript, Spaulding did not write in a scriptural style, and he never used Book of Mormon phrases such as "and it came to pass."

After the 1884 discovery of the Spaulding manuscript, critics of the Book of Mormon added several elements to the Spaulding theory. Some claimed that the manuscript that was found was not the manuscript in question or that it was only an early version and that Spaulding later revised the manuscript to include Book of Mormon names and phrases. Despite its untenable premises and the questionable motives of its first proponents, the theory has persisted, with some variations, and continues to be used by a few critics of the Book of Mormon.

SOURCE

Jackson, Kent P., ed. *Manuscript Found: The Complete Original "Spaulding Manuscript."* Provo, Utah: Religious Studies Center, Brigham Young University, 1996.

REX C. REEVE JR.

SPENCER, ORSON. Orson Spencer, one of the great missionaries of the Church, was born in West Stockbridge, Massachusetts, on 14 March 1802. At age 12 he contracted a life-threatening fever sore that left him with a limp. He entered the Lenox Academy at age 15, then studied at Union College, graduating with honors in 1824. He taught school, joined the Baptist church, and entered the Theological College, graduating in 1829 as valedictorian. He served as pastor of three Baptist churches. During this time he married Catharine Curtis on 13 April 1830. They had eight children.

Spencer was baptized into the Church in 1841. He served as an alderman until the **Saints** were driven from **Nauvoo**. His wife died on the way to **Winter Quarters**, leaving him with six children under age 13. In the fall of 1846, he was called to serve a mission in **Great Britain**, and left his children in the care of his oldest daughter. He presided over the **British Mission** and was editor of the *Millennial Star*. Meanwhile, his children traveled across the plains and lived in a dugout in the **Salt Lake Valley**. While in Great Britain, Spencer married Martha Knight, with whom he had four children. He later married Ann Dibble, Margaret Miller, Jane T. Davis, and Mary Hill.

After being reunited with his children in the Salt Lake Valley, Spencer was appointed the first chancellor of the **University of Deseret**, a lifelong position, and served in the first legislative council of **Utah**.

He served a mission in Prussia, then another in Cincinnati, **Ohio**, in 1853. After Cincinnati, he was transferred to **St. Louis** and served as editor of the *St. Louis Luminary*. He then served a mission to the Cherokee Nation, where he became ill. He returned to St. Louis, Missouri, and his condition deteriorated. He died there on 15 October 1855.

SOURCES

Garrett, H. Dean, "Orson Spencer." *Utah History Encyclopedia.* Edited by Allan Kent Powell, Es. Salt Lake City: University of Utah Press. 1994. 525.

Rogers, Aurelia S. *Life Sketches of Orson Spencer and Others.* Salt Lake City: George Q. Cannon & Sons, 1898.

Spencer, Seymour H. *Life Summary of Orson Spencer.* Salt Lake City: Mercury, 1964.

H. DEAN GARRETT

SPERRY, SIDNEY B. Sidney Branton Sperry, prolific writer, professor, and university administrator, was born 26 December 1895 in Salt Lake City. His interest in the **Book of Mormon**, his awareness of **Joseph Smith**'s attitude about Hebrew studies, and his amazement as a youth at "scholarly" attacks on **LDS** scriptures stimulated him to become a scholar able to defend the faith. Sperry's education included a degree in chemistry and mathematics and a master's in Old Testament and Hebrew from the **University of Utah**, and a doctorate in Old Testament Language and Literature from the University of **Chicago**.

In 1932 he joined the faculty at **Brigham Young University** where he taught for nearly 40 years, influencing thousands in his campus classes, community lectures, and Bible-land tours. Through his classes, and scores of books and articles, he taught about origins, purposes, interpretations, and applications of the scriptures. He developed substantive concepts and refined them as developments warranted.

As director of the Division of Religion (1954–59) at BYU, Sperry felt the need for full-time teachers in Church history, doctrine, and the scriptures. He encouraged, helped, and eventually hired many. An annual symposium in his name has been held at BYU since 1973. Brother Sperry died 4 September 1977 in **Provo, Utah**.

ELLIS T. RASMUSSEN

"SPIRIT OF GOD, THE." "The Spirit of God" is one of the most popular Latter-day Saint **hymns**. It is sung at virtually all solemn occasions and is one of the few hymns to have appeared in every LDS hymnbook in all languages. **William Wines Phelps** wrote the text in 1835, apparently for the dedication of the **Kirtland Temple**, where it was sung by a large choir, probably to the military-band style tune still associated with it (most likely a march from the **War** of 1812 era). The vivid apocalyptic text celebrates the **Restoration**, the Second Coming, and the joining of earthly **Saints** with "the armies of heaven" in shouting "Hosanna to God and the Lamb" (a phrase shouted by the congregation at **temple** dedications).

SOURCES

Davidson, Karen Lynn. *Our Latter-day Hymns: The Stories and the Messages.* Salt Lake City: Deseret Book, 1988.

Hicks, Michael. *Mormonism and Music: A History.* Urbana: University of Illinois Press, 1989.

MICHAEL HICKS

SPOKEN WORD, MUSIC AND THE. See **MUSIC AND THE SPOKEN WORD**.

SPORI, JACOB. Jacob Spori was a prominent educator and missionary, born 26 March 1847 in Oberwyl, **Switzerland**. Throughout his life he demonstrated a talent and love for learning, and he acquired multiple degrees. According to his daughter, Jacob learned to speak nine languages and could read thirteen. Following his **marriage** to Magdalena Roschi, he was appointed principal of his former high school, held several government offices, and was elected to a seat on the Reformed Church's Synod Council. During this same period, Spori sustained a spiritual crisis wherein he resigned his seat on the synod. This led to a loss of his position as principal.

Early in 1877 Spori was introduced to the restored gospel and was baptized a member of the Church. In 1879 he immigrated to **Utah**, leaving his wife and children in Switzerland because they had not joined the Church and wished to remain behind to receive an inheritance. Late in 1884 Spori returned to Switzerland as a missionary. Shortly after his arrival, he baptized his wife. The following week he left to open the Turkish **Mission**. In 1886 he traveled to **Palestine**, where he baptized the first convert to the restored Church in the **Holy Land**, Johan **Georg Grau**.

After his mission release in 1888, Jacob returned to **America**, this time taking his **family** with him. They settled in **Rexburg, Idaho**, where Jacob participated in organizing the Bannock Stake Academy (later **Ricks College** and later still, BYU–Idaho). To his surprise he was appointed the first principal. After three years of dedicated and difficult service, he received an honorable release to resolve his financial difficulties. He turned his attention to numerous endeavors, one of which was digging a canal to bring water to the Snake River Valley. The canal was eventually named after him. He died 27 September 1903 in Montpelier, Idaho.

SOURCES

Christianson, James R. "In Search of the Sensational." *Hearken, O Ye People: Discourses on the Doctrine and Covenants*. Sandy, Utah: Randall Book, 38–41.

Stowell, Elizabeth S. "The History of Jacob Spori, by His Daughter." Manuscript. Ricks College Library. 1–14. 17 November 1926.

DAVID M. WHITCHURCH

SPORTS. See ATHLETES AND SPORTS.

SRI LANKA.

The nation of Sri Lanka, formerly known as Ceylon, is located on a large island off the southern tip of **India**. Although Latter-day **Saint** missionaries visited briefly in 1853, missionaries were not there on a permanent basis until Elder Stanley C. Kimball and his wife were assigned in 1977. Two years later, **Elder James E. Faust** dedicated Sri Lanka for the preaching of the gospel. At the beginning of the year 2000, there were 280 members and two **branches**.

Source

Vermillion, Douglas L. "Gospel Splendor in Sri Lanka." *Ensign*, 25 (August 1995): 78–79.

Richard O. Cowan

ST. GEORGE, UTAH. The city of St. George was founded in 1861 in the southwestern corner of the state (Washington County) and is at an elevation of 2,500 feet—2,000 feet lower than the communities of the **Great Basin**. Therefore, it is much drier (approximately 8 inches of precipitation annually) and much warmer (up to 117° F in the summer). This "**Cotton Mission**" was intended to support the raising of semitropical crops—cotton, grapes, tobacco, sugar cane, and even silk worms. Some 300 families were called initially by President **Brigham Young** and his counselor, **George A. Smith**. The city, which President Young named in honor of his counselor, became a headquarters for a whole southern strategy, including the Virgin, Muddy, and Little Colorado River basins, and eventually the Latter-day Saint **colonies** in northern **Mexico**.

Apostles Orson Pratt and **Erastus Snow** led the initial effort and supervised the communities already in Dixie (a nickname quickly adopted for the hot area). Elder Snow remained there more than two decades, encouraging the **Saints** to stay at the unrewarding task of living in the harsh desert. Under **Elder** Snow's leadership, great structures were built in the city—the **St. George Tabernacle**, the **St. George Temple**, the Opera House, the Courthouse, and the Cotton Mill in nearby Washington. Brigham Young, who maintained a winter residence in the city from 1870 to 1877, supported the major construction projects as a subsidy to underwrite the community, while the citizens struggled, against frequent flash floods, to build dams and canals for their small irrigated fields. Thereby subsistence agriculture took hold, though the yields were small and life was bleak. Gradually alfalfa farming and cattle ranching, better adapted to the terrain, replaced cotton and cane. Here President **Lorenzo Snow** launched a reemphasis on **tithing** in 1899, eventually enabling the Church to pay its debts.

Isolation characterized St. George until at least 1930, when Highway 91 was completed down the Black Ridge from Cedar City. The railroad was never able to conquer that pass, a problem that contributed to the isolation and economic limitations in Dixie. As automobiles arrived, the tourism industry emerged, partly because nearby Zion National Park also became accessible. Motels, restaurants, movie-making, and the presence of **Dixie College** (after 1911) brought increased attention to the city, but its population remained under 5,000 until after **World War II**. Then air conditioning, the I-15 Interstate highway (1972), and the retirement wave that transformed the American Southwest, brought new possibilities. St. George became the haven for second home owners, retirees, convention attendees, and students at the new Dixie College campus (1963). The city's population multiplied tenfold in the second half of the twentieth century.

The Bloomington and Green Valley housing developments set a new standard of quality and luxury; scores of condominium and planned-housing developments have been built since. A series of water reclamation projects enabled much of this growth, and additional projects were being planned in the late 1990s. As of 1998 there were nine **stakes** in the city, with five more in neighboring communities.

SOURCES

Alder, Douglas D., and Karl F. Brooks. *A History of Washington County: From Isolation to Destination*. Salt Lake City: Utah Historical Society, 1996.

Bradshaw, Hazel, ed. *Under Dixie Sun*. Panguitch, Utah: Daughters of Utah Pioneers, 950.

Larson, Andrew Karl. *I Was Called to Dixie*. St. George, Utah: Andrew Karl Larson, 1961.

Logue, Larry. *Sermon in the Desert*. Chicago: Illinois University Press, 1988.

DOUGLAS D. ALDER

ST. GEORGE TABERNACLE.

ST. GEORGE TABERNACLE. The **St. George** Tabernacle, which is heralded widely as one of the finest buildings constructed by **Mormon pioneers,** has a fascinating origin. By establishing a public works project, **Brigham Young** proposed to subsidize the so-called "**Cotton Mission**," which was near failure in face of the desert heat and flash floods. He wrote to the local leader, **apostle Erastus Snow**, instructing him to build a "commodius well-furnished **meetinghouse**, one large enough to comfortably seat at least 2,000 persons, and that will not only be useful, but also an ornament to your city" (Larson, 118).

Soon plans designed in **Salt Lake City** by **W. H. Folsom** arrived, and construction began in March of 1863. The building site was the northeast corner of the city square. The plans detailed a heroic building with a modest tone in pure New England style, somewhat akin to the **Kirtland Temple**. Native materials were used—red sandstone, timber from Pine Valley and Mount Trumble, and native limestone.

There were few seasoned craftsmen, but they quickly trained their brethren to be quarry men, mill workers, stone masons, and finish carpenters. Thus, a strong contingent of some 100 workers learned trades which were later crucial to the construction of the **St. George Temple** and other major civic structures. They labored for seven years and were paid with tithing scrip.

Miles Romney, the superintendent of construction, fashioned two elegant spiral staircases to the balcony. In 1992 the interior of the tabernacle was authentically restored to its original condition. It stands today, a monument to Mormon pioneer genius.

————

SOURCES

Alder, Douglas D., and Karl Brooks. The *History of Washington County.* Salt Lake City: Utah Historical Society, 1996. 54–66.

Hamilton, C. Mark. *Nineteenth Century Mormon Architecture and City Planning.* New York: Oxford University Press, 1995.

Larson, Andrew Karl. *I Was Called to Dixie.* St. George, Utah: Andrew Karl Larson, 1961.

DOUGLAS D. ALDER

ST. GEORGE TEMPLE. The St. George Utah Temple, dedicated 6 April 1877, was the first **temple** completed in the West and used in the last dispensation for complete temple ordinances.

Building the temple was a monumental task full of trials and hardships. The **Saints** had to quarry volcanic rock and transport it by ox team, then pound the rocks into the swampy ground to provide a firm foundation, using a cannon as a pile driver. Acquiring lumber was another major undertaking. Some was hauled from Pine Valley and the Kaibab forest, but most came from Mt. Trumbull in **Arizona**, about 75 miles away. The baptismal font and statues of 12 oxen to support it were cast in **Salt Lake City** and transported partway by train and then by ox team.

Sorely needed help came when the **general authorities** issued **mission** calls to a hundred or more families, and Saints throughout the Church donated funds and wagonloads of produce for the temple project.

Upon completion of the temple, **general conference** was held there in April 1877. The temple's dedication has long been considered the greatest event in southern **Utah's** history. The first **endowments** for the dead were given in the St. George Temple.

Elder Wilford Woodruff, who was serving as the temple's first president, reported that the signers of the **Declaration of Independence** appeared to him in the temple and said, "You have had the use of the **Endowment House** for a number of years, and yet nothing has ever been done for us. We laid the foundation of the government you now enjoy . . . and were faithful to God" (*JD,* 19:229). In response to this request, Elder Woodruff entered the temple 21 August 1877 and was baptized by John D. T. McAllister for 100 prominent men, including the signers of the Declaration of Independence.

From 1937 to 1938 the temple was closed for remodeling—separate rooms with murals on their walls were provided for presenting the endowment. Then in 1974 and 1975 the temple was once again extensively remodeled, this time to use films.

SOURCES

DeMille, Janice F. *The St. George Temple: First 100 Years.* Hurricane, Utah: Homestead, 1977.

Young, Brigham. *Journal of Discourses [JD].* 26 vols. London: Latter-day Saints' Book Depot, 1854–86. Vol. 19.

JANICE F. DEMILLE

ST. KITTS AND NEVIS. St. Kitts and Nevis is a nation in the Eastern Caribbean Leeward Islands. It has an English-speaking population of approximately 40,000, most of whom are Protestant. The capital is Basseterre, located on St. Kitts. In July of 1984, Elders Douglas Myers and Robert J. Molina arrived on St. Kitts. The St. Kitts-Nevis **Branch** was organized on 10 September 1985, with **Elder** Reuel Lambourn as its first president. The first convert on the island was Dianna Ermintude Johnson, baptized 2 February 1985. Terry Lewellyn Hanley became St. Kitts's first native branch president in early 1996. Hurricane Georges struck the islands in the autumn of 1998, damaging 85% of the homes, but no members' lives were lost. At the beginning of the year 2000, about 95 members of the Church attended the one branch in the country.

SOURCE

1999–2000 Church Almanac. Salt Lake City: Deseret News, 1998. 383.

TODD KRUEGER

ST. LOUIS, MISSOURI. During most of the nineteenth century, St. Louis was the hub of trade and culture for the vast Mississippi River drainage area. It was founded by the French in 1764, and by the time the Latter-day Saints first reached St. Louis in 1831, it was a young giant destined to become the "Fourth City" of the U.S. by the late 1800s.

Throughout the Missouri and Illinois periods of the Church, up to the coming of the railroad to Utah in 1869 and beyond, St. Louis became an oasis of tolerance and security for the LDS people.

The history of the Latter-day Saints in St. Louis can be divided into several periods. The colony stage lasted from 1833 to 1843. During this time there was no official Church presence in the city; rather, many Saints sought work or refuge here from Missouri persecution.

The branch period existed from 1844 to 1847. Early in 1844 the first formal branch of the Church was organized in St. Louis. This was followed by the district stage, which lasted from 1847 to 1854. At this time the growing branch was divided into six congregations, which at one time totaled about 3,000 members.

Next came the stake period, from 1854 to 1857. A stake was organized 4 November 1854, becoming the 16th stake in the Church. It commenced with at least 15 branches in Missouri, Illinois, and Iowa, combining to include about 1,320 members. The stake grew to at least 30 branches in Missouri, Illinois, Iowa, Indiana, Ohio, and Kansas Territory, totaling more than 2,000 members—not counting the hundreds of Saints who left the stake to go on to Utah.

This important and promising stake was disorganized in 1857 when **Brigham Young** called all Saints to Utah to defend the Church during the **Utah War**. On 1 June 1958, the second St. Louis stake was organized and has flourished. The St. Louis Missouri Temple was dedicated 1 through 5 June 1997 by President Gordon B. Hinckley.

Sources

Carter, Kate B., comp. *The Mormons in St. Louis.* Salt Lake City: Daughters of Utah Pioneers, 1962.

Kimball, Stanley B. "The Saints and St. Louis, 1831–57: An Oasis of tolerance and Security." *BYU Studies* 13 (Summer 1973): 489–519.

Salmon, Louise Linton. "St. Louis in the Story of the Church." *Improvement Era* (November 1954): 788–89, 830–31.

Stanley B. Kimball

ST. MAARTEN/ST. MARTIN. This 38-square-mile island is divided into two sides—Dutch (Saint Maarten) and French (Saint Martin). At the beginning of the year 2000, there were 138 Latter-day Saints organized into one **branch** on the island.

EMILY C. ZEIGLER

ST. VINCENT AND THE GRENADINES. St. Vincent and the Grenadines is a parliamentary democracy located in the eastern Caribbean. Most of the population of 120,000 are English-speaking and belong to the Methodist, Anglican, or Roman Catholic Churches. The Kingstown **Branch**, located in the nation's capital, was organized 22 October 1980. Ebenezer Joshua, a former prime minister of St. Vincent, joined the Church and served in the branch presidency. When Brother Joshua died in 1991, 30 to 40 thousand people, including top government officials, viewed or attended his televised funeral in the Kingstown meetinghouse and learned the basic tenets of the Church. At the beginning of the year 2000, there were 342 members living in one branch.

SOURCE

1999–2000 Church Almanac. Salt Lake City: Deseret News, 1998. 383.

TODD KRUEGER

STAKE. A stake is a unit of local Church organization designed to have jurisdiction over a group of about five or more **wards**. In **mission areas** the first units are **districts**, which are made up of **branches** until enough branches grow large enough to become wards so that a stake can be created. Stake officers, all unpaid, include a three-man stake presidency, 12-member **high council** (and alternates as needed), **auxiliary** presidents, clerks, and a stake **patriarch**. Stake presidencies initiate the selection of ward bishoprics and **Melchizedek Priesthood quorum** presidencies and group leaders, conduct regular **stake conferences** and high council and stake council meetings, preside at annual ward conferences, conduct **temple** recommend interviews, and report to and receive directions from Church **general authorities** and officers. Stake high councils exist to be courts to settle "important difficulties" and to be **disciplinary councils** (D&C 102; 107). Stakes are established to serve as a defense and refuge from calamities to come in the last days (D&C 115).

In 1834 the Church's first stakes were established in **Kirtland, Ohio,** and **Missouri**—Missouri was termed "**Zion**," and Kirtland and subsequent stakes were "stakes of Zion." The **First Presidency** served as the Kirtland Stake presidency. In pioneer **Utah**, some general authorities residing in colonizing areas served those areas as **stake presidents**. The **priesthood** reorganization of 1877 restructured and properly organized stakes, and over the next several decades many innovative programs originally produced at the stake level (recreational, cultural, and social activities as well as teaching) were adopted Churchwide.

Seventies **quorums** became stake entities in the 1880s and remained so until they were discontinued in 1986. In the 1880s many stakes built **tabernacles**, which were forerunners of modern stake centers. Stakes operated **academies** (high schools) from the late 1880s until the 1920s. Stake missionary work began in the 1920s. Stake welfare projects have been the backbone of the Church's **welfare program** since 1937. Quarterly stake conferences became standard from 1877 until the 1980s.

At Brigham Young's death in 1877, the Church had 19 stakes. In 1930 the 100-year-old Church had approximately 100 stakes. In 1994 the Church established its 2000th stake. The first stakes created in major regions outside of LDS-dominated locations were **Los Angeles** (1923), **New York** (1934), **New Zealand** (1958), **England** (1961), **Holland** (the first non-English-speaking stake, 1961), **Germany** (1961), **Mexico** (1961), **Brazil** (1966), and **Japan** (1970).

SOURCES

Hartley, William G. "The Priesthood Reorganization of 1877: Brigham Young's Last Achievement." *BYU Studies* 20 (Fall 1979): 3–36.

Hilton, Lynn M., ed. *The Story of the Salt Lake Stake: 125-Year History, 1847–1972.* Salt Lake City: Salt Lake Stake, 1972.

Widtsoe, John A. *Priesthood and Church Government.* Salt Lake City: Deseret Book, 1954. 286–300.

WILLIAM G. HARTLEY

STAKE CONFERENCE. Stake conference is a **meeting** in which members residing within specific geographical boundaries gather to sustain officers and receive opportunities "to worship the Lord, to feast upon the word of Christ, and to be built up in faith and testimony" (Kimball, 100).

Adhering to counsel given to "meet in conference once in three months, or from time to time. . . . to do whatever church business is necessary" (D&C 20:61–62), about 30 members, along with many others, gathered in the first conference of the Church on Wednesday, 9 June 1830, in **Fayette, New York**. The first conference to organize a stake was held Monday, 17 February 1834, in **Kirtland, Ohio**, (see D&C 102).

Over the years, Saturday and Sunday meetings, sometimes presided over by **general authorities**, have included general sessions, leadership training sessions for **priesthood** and **auxiliary** leaders, and sometimes a meeting for all adults. In 1979 stake conferences, which had been held quarterly, began to be held semiannually.

SOURCES

Journal History. *The Church of Jesus Christ of Latter-day Saints*. 9 June 1830. 1–2; 17 February 1834. 1–2. LDS Church Archives, Salt Lake City.

Kimball, Spencer W. "Living the Gospel in the Home." *Ensign* 8 (May 1978): 100–101.

"Stake Conferences to Be Semi-Annual." *Church News*, 1 April 1978, 4.

LARRY R. SKIDMORE

STAKE MISSIONARIES.

STAKE MISSIONARIES. The calling of **stake** missionaries represents a key part of the Church's efforts to share the gospel. During the early years of the twentieth century, "**home missionaries**" were assigned to activate Church members as well as to contact nonmembers living in the area. By 1912 in the **Salt Lake Stake**, for example, the local seventies **quorum** had organized a stake mission and assumed the responsibility to distribute tracts, loan Church books, speak in **meetings**, make visits, hold "gospel conversations," and baptize converts.

As Church members began moving into predominately non-Mormon areas such as the Pacific Coast, and as non-Mormons began moving into the traditionally Latter-day Saint Intermountain West, the **Saints** took advantage of opportunities to share the gospel with their new neighbors. During the early 1930s, hundreds were baptized through such efforts in **California, Arizona**, and the **Salt Lake Valley**. In 1936 Church leaders directed that a mission be organized in every stake, and the First Council of the **Seventy** was given supervision of these **missions**.

In 1970, as part of **priesthood correlation**, the work of the stake mission was more closely integrated with the **ward** organization. Stake missionaries increasingly were assigned to find individuals for the full-time missionaries to teach and then to fellowship those who were baptized.

SOURCES

Church News, 26 December 1970, 5.

Cowan, Richard O. *The Latter-day Saint Century.* Salt Lake City: Bookcraft, 1999. 164–65, 312, 314.

Humpfrey, A. Glen. "Missionaries to the Saints." *BYU Studies* 17 (Autumn 1976): 74–100.

Paul Edwards Damron

STAKE PRESIDENT. The first **stake** of the Church, known as the **Kirtland** Stake, was organized on 14 February 1834. **Joseph Smith Jr.**, **Sidney Rigdon**, and **Frederick G. Williams** were acknowledged as presidents. In July of 1834, a stake was organized in **Clay County, Missouri**, and from that time until now, stakes have been presided over by a president with two **counselors**.

The stake president presides over the **Melchizedek Priesthood** and, since 1956, serves as president of the **high priests quorum**. He is also responsible for keeping stake records and histories related to the stake and holds **disciplinary councils** as needed. Stake presidents are to sign **temple** recommends and make sure people do not go to the temple unworthily. They are also to carefully select missionaries who will not discredit the Church. The **First Presidency** has said that they should preside over the **Saints** and regard stake members as their own **family**.

Sources

Cameron, Kim S. "Stake President, Stake Presidency." *Encyclopedia of Mormonism.* Edited by Daniel H. Ludlow. 4 vols. New York: Macmillan, 1992. 3:1414–15.

Clark, James R., comp. *Messages of the First Presidency of The Church of Jesus Christ of Latter-day Saints.* 6 vols. Salt Lake City: Bookcraft, 1965–75. 1:115; 2:287–88; 3:17; 4:11–12, 35; 5:342; 6:14.

Stanley A. Johnson

STAMPS. The world of stamps has begun to take notice of **Utah** and the **Mormons**. Stamp collecting may be the biggest hobby in the world; certainly it is one of the biggest. A popular way to collect stamps is to build a collection based on one topic—such as Utah and the Mormons. There is a small but growing collection of at least 77 such stamps, post cards, cancellations, First Day Covers, and First Day Cachets issued between 1944 and 1997 by ten countries: **United States, Brazil, England, Nicaragua, Rarotonga, Sweden, Samoa, St. Vincent, Tahiti**, and **Tonga**.

Four Latter-day Saints are featured in the collection: **Joseph** and **Hyrum Smith**, **Philo Farnsworth** (inventor of TV), and Rarotongan missionary Elder Osborne J. P. Widtsoe. Six **temples** are pictured: **Nauvoo**, **Salt Lake**, Samoa, Sweden, Tahiti, and Tonga. Other subjects include the **seagull**, the **sego lily**, the Utah state flag, the **centennial**, the sesquicentennial celebration of the pioneers' arrival in Utah, the **Mormon Tabernacle Choir**, chapels in Rarotonga and Samoa, **ZCMI**, the transcontinental **railroad**, the **exodus** from **Nauvoo**, and the **Mormon trails** of 1846–47.

Sources

Kimball, Stanley B. "Mormon Stamps Grow in Number." *Church News*, 15 January 1994, 11.

———. "Stamp Sampler." *Ensign* 16 (February 1986): 60.

Stanley B. Kimball

STANDARD WORKS. The books accepted as scripture, or standard works, of The Church of Jesus Christ of Latter-day Saints include the **Bible**, the **Book of Mormon**, the **Doctrine and Covenants**, and the **Pearl of Great Price**. *Standard works* implies *canon*—an authoritative standard against which all other writings or utterances are measured. Latter-day Saints believe in a distinctive canon of authoritative scriptures, but it is not closed to new additions (A of F 9).

The earliest official acknowledgment of canon came with the establishment of the Church on **6 April** 1830, when both the Bible and the Book of Mormon were recognized as the word of God (D&C 20:8–11). Perhaps because those two books preceded the establishment of the Church, they did not need to be canonized by a vote of the Saints.

Doctrine and Covenants 20 (called the Articles and Covenants of the Church) was canonized by the vote of assembled members as early as June 1830. In 1833 the collected revelations received by **Joseph Smith** were published in the **Book of Commandments**. A later, updated compilation, renamed the Doctrine and Covenants, was published in 1835. That collection of revelations was received as authoritative by the common consent of the Church the same year.

The Pearl of Great Price, first published as a **British Mission** booklet in 1851, was canonized at the October **general conference** in 1880 and thus added to the standard works. A new edition of the Doctrine and Covenants was canonized at the same time. Since then, additions to the Doctrine and Covenants (**Official Declarations 1 and 2** and Sections 137 and 138) have been canonized independently as they were added to the scriptures.

SOURCE

"Scripture." *Encyclopedia of Mormonism*. Edited by Daniel H. Ludlow. 4 vols. New York: Macmillan, 1992. 3:1277–83.

KENT P. JACKSON

STANDING, JOSEPH. Joseph Standing, a missionary martyr, was born 5 October 1854 in **Salt Lake City** to parents who had accepted the gospel in **Great Britain**. In 1875 Standing was called to serve in the **Southern States Mission**.

On a second **mission** (1879), Standing was joined by **Rudger Clawson**, and in July he began to travel through north **Georgia** to a conference. **Elder** Standing had a foreboding dream, which caused them both considerable anxiety.

The events of the dream soon began to unfold. To avoid conflict, the elders stayed with nonmember families because of mob threats against the **Saints**. On 21 July 1879, as the missionaries were preparing to leave the area, they were accosted by a mob of 12 men. The missionaries were ordered into a remote area and threatened with death if they returned. Standing may have believed they were to be shot, because he suddenly jumped to his feet and shouted for the mob to surrender. After being shot in the face by one of the gunmen, Standing fell wounded and unconscious.

Clawson's life was saved when he folded his arms and said, "Shoot!" His calmness quieted passions, and he was permitted to seek help for his wounded companion at a nearby farm. When he returned he found Standing's body riddled with bullets.

The identity of the mobbers was known, but they left the area and were ultimately acquitted. Clawson borrowed money to transport Standing's body to Salt Lake City, where an estimated 10,000 Latter-day Saints gathered for a memorial at which President **John Taylor** and Counselor **George Q. Cannon** spoke. He was buried in the Salt Lake City cemetery.

SOURCES

Jenson, Andrew. *Latter-day Saint Biographical Encyclopedia*. 4 vols. 1901–36. Reprint, Salt Lake City: Western Epics, 1971. 3:719–21.

Nicholson, John. *The Martyrdom of Joseph Standing*. Salt Lake City: Deseret News, 1886.

David F. Boone

STAPLEY, DELBERT L. While attending the October **general conference** in 1950, **stake president** Delbert Stapley stepped out of an elevator in the lobby of **Hotel Utah** and met President **George Albert Smith**, who said, "You are just the man I'm looking for" (quoted in "Delbert L. Stapley," 998). Without even retiring to the privacy of an office, the **prophet** called the stunned Arizonian to be a member of the **Quorum** of the Twelve **Apostles**.

Delbert Leon Stapley was born in Mesa, Arizona, 11 December 1896 into a family of nine children. He loved sports but turned down an offer to enter a career in professional baseball because he knew it would require playing on the Sabbath. He went on a **mission** to the southern states at the early age of 18. His work in his father's hardware shop led him to an expansive retail business career. Active in civic affairs, Brother Stapley was a city councilman and president of the Lion's Club, and he was active in the Better Business Bureau and **Boy Scouts** of **America**. As a member of the Quorum of the Twelve (1950–78), he had charge of the missions in the eastern United States and **Canada**. He died 19 August 1978 in **Salt Lake City** at age 81.

Sources

Avant, Gerry. "Stapleys Reflect on 60 Happy Years of Loving Marriage." *Church News*, 21 January 1978, 4.
"Delbert L. Stapley of the Council of the Twelve." *Improvement Era* 69 (November 1966): 998–99.
Flake, Lawrence R. *Prophets and Apostles of the Last Dispensation*. Provo, Utah: Religious Studies Center, Brigham Young University, 2001. 485–87.
Kimball, Spencer W. "Delbert L. Stapley." *Improvement Era* 65 (February 1962): 91–95, 112–14.

Lawrence R. Flake

STATE OF DESERET. See **DESERET, STATE OF**.

STATEHOOD, UTAH. Between 1849 and 1896, Utahns applied for statehood seven times before securing admission into the Union. The Northwest Ordinance of 1787 and the admission of other territories established the procedure for admission. Briefly, a territory needed a population large enough to warrant one representative in Congress, members of Congress and the president had to approve the admission, and the territorial citizens had to agree to any terms Congress might dictate.

Although the Latter-day Saint settlers petitioned for both statehood and territorial status in 1849, they hoped to secure admission as the **State of Deseret**. The committee that drafted the constitution modeled it on the 1846 **Iowa** constitution. Instead of admitting the State of Deseret, Congress designated **Utah** as a territory in 1850.

Like many territories, Utah experienced reductions in size. Utah lost land to **Nevada** (1861, 1862, and 1866), **Colorado** and **Nebraska** (1861), and **Wyoming** (1868). Utah retained its size after 1868, and it ranks eleventh in area among the 50 states.

In a sense, Congress acted as a territorial schoolmaster until citizens conformed to national norms. **Polygamy** and "theocracy" (Church involvement in politics), formed the principal barriers to Utah's admission to the Union. Before Congress would agree to admit Utah, the Latter-day Saint people had to formally abandon both. They also had to convince Congress and the American people that they had sincerely forsaken these practices. Although the Morrill Act of 1862 prohibited the practice of plural marriage and the 1887 Utah constitution likewise prohibited it, Church members continued its practice, and the Church continued to dictate in Utah politics through the **People's Party**.

After 1849 Utahns drafted six more constitutions. The constitutions of 1856 and 1862 used the Iowa constitution as a model. The constitutions of 1872, 1882, and 1887 borrowed most heavily from the 1864 Nevada constitution. The 1895 convention drew on numerous constitutions, especially those of **Washington**, **Idaho**, **Montana**, **California**, **New York**, Colorado, and Wyoming.

Many changes led to congressional approval of an enabling act in 1894: cooperation between Mormons and non-Mormons in business, negotiations with national leaders of both parties, the **Manifesto (1890)**, the dissolution of the People's and **Liberal Parties**, the division of the people into the two national political parties, and interreligious cooperation in politics. The constitutional convention met between March and May of 1895; Utahns ratified the constitution in November, and President **Grover Cleveland** declared Utah's admission to the Union on 4 January 1896.

SOURCES

Alexander, Thomas G. "Utah's Constitution: A Reflection of the Territorial Experience." *Utah Historical Quarterly* 64 (Summer 1996): 264–81.

Bernstein, Jerome. "A History of the Constitutional Conventions of the Territory of Utah from 1849 to 1895." Master's thesis, Utah State University, 1961.

Crawley, Peter. *The Constitution of the State of Deseret.* Provo, Utah: Friends of the Harold B. Lee Library, 1982.

Hickman, Martin B. "The Utah Constitution: Retrospect and Prospect." Interim Report of the Constitutional Revision Commission Submitted to the Governor and the Legislature of the State of Utah. Edited by Neal A. Maxwell and Edward W. Clyde. Salt Lake City: Constitutional Revision Commission, 1971.

Lyman, Edward Leo. *Political Deliverance: The Mormon Quest for Utah Statehood.* Urbana: University of Illinois Press, 1986.

White, Jean B. *Charter for Statehood: The Story of Utah's State Constitution.* Salt Lake City: University of Utah Press, 1996.

THOMAS G. ALEXANDER

STEGNER, WALLACE. Wallace Stegner, born 18 February 1909 at Lake Mills, Iowa, is best known among Latter-day Saints for his two books on themes related to their history and culture. After spending his early youth in **Canada**, he moved with his **family** to **Salt Lake City**, where he attended East High School and graduated from the **University of Utah**. He received a Ph.D. from the University of Iowa, and after teaching briefly at the Universities of Utah, **Wisconsin**, and Harvard, he became a professor at Stanford University from 1945 to 1971. Recognized as one of the West's premier literary figures, Stegner received a Pulitzer Prize in 1971 for his *Angle of Repose.* Four years later his book *The Spectator Bird* was given the National Book Award. Stegner died 12 April 1993 in Santa Fe, **New Mexico**.

His *Mormon Country* tells of the "empire" **Brigham Young** created, which encompassed Utah and parts of several western states. Stegner skillfully and credibly describes the geography, the settlers, the **pioneers**, and the **patriarchs**. His other book about Latter-day Saints, *Gathering to Zion*, relates the heroic history of the Latter-day Saint flight from **Nauvoo**, the **Saints'** brief sojourn in **Winter Quarters**, and the thousand-mile journey from the banks of the **Missouri River** to the shores of the Great Salt Lake. His treatment of the Saints' migration and settlement of the **Great Basin** is sympathetic, if not entirely faith promoting. Several of his other novels also have Latter-day Saint settings, scenes, and characters.

SOURCES

Benson, Jackson J. *Wallace Stegner, His Life and Work.* New York: Viking Press, 1996.

Lamar, Howard R. *The Readers' Encyclopedia of the American West.* New York: Harper & Row, 1977.

Rankin, Charles E. *Wallace Stegner.* Albuquerque: University of New Mexico, 1996.

KENNETH W. GODFREY

STENHOUSE, T. B. H. Thomas Brown Holmes Stenhouse, who became a prominent journalist and author, was born 21 February 1824 in Dalkeith, Scotland. After joining the Church at age 21, he married Fanny Warn. In 1850 he helped **Lorenzo Snow** open the Italian **mission**. In 1855 Stenhouse and his **family** moved to **New York** and eventually to **Utah**, where he worked as a reporter for the *Deseret News*. Stenhouse entered the practice of plural marriage when he married Belinda Pratt and continued his newspaper work by founding and publishing the *Salt Lake Telegraph*.

In the late 1860s, Stenhouse opposed **Brigham Young**'s involvement in the management of the *Telegraph* and began associating with the **Godbeites**. Furthermore, **Zina Young**, Brigham Young's daughter, romantically spurned him. Both Stenhouse and his wife Fanny apostatized from the Church, and Belinda Pratt and Stenhouse divorced. Following his apostasy, Stenhouse wrote *The Rocky Mountain Saints,* one of the first comprehensive histories of the Latter-day **Saints**, which contributed to a negative image of nineteenth-century Mormonism. Stenhouse died on 7 March 1882 in **San Francisco, California**.

SOURCES

Stenhouse, Fanny. *Tell It All: The Tyranny of Mormonism; or, An Englishwoman in Utah.* Reprint, Sussex, England: Centaur Press, 1971.

Stenhouse, T. B. H. *The Rocky Mountain Saints.* New York: D. Appleton and Company, 1873.

Walker, Ronald W. "The Stenhouses and the Making of a Mormon Image." *Journal of Mormon History* 1 (1974): 51–72.

CATHERINE BRITSCH FRANTZ

STEPHENS, EVAN. Evan Stephens, a folk hero during his lifetime, conducted the **Mormon Tabernacle Choir** for 26 years (1890–1916). Born 28 June 1854 in Pencader, Wales, he became a successful composer, conductor, instrumentalist, tenor soloist, poet, and defender of the Latter-day Saint religion. Beginning in 1883, Stephens taught music at the **University of Deseret** in **Salt Lake City** for 17 years, instructing as many as 3,000 choral, vocal, opera, and organ students in a year. Intensely loyal to God, his Church, and his friends, Stephens's work honored God and celebrated Utah's beauty, as he sought to correct misconceptions among non-Mormons about the Latter-day Saints.

Friend to musicians Sousa, Paderewskik, Nordica, Gilmore, Melba, and Schumann-Heink, Stephens brought the Mormon Tabernacle Choir into national prominence. He wrote 88 hymns as well as numerous anthems, cantatas, operas, vocal solos, duets, trios, and quartets, and he led his choirs in winning honors from the Chicago World's Fair in 1893 to the National Eisteddfod at Leranton, **Pennsylvania**, in 1928. Evan Stephens died 27 October 1930 in **Salt Lake City**.

SOURCES

Pyper, George D. "Concerning Evan Stephens." *Instructor* (April 1931): 198–201.
Stephens, Evan. "Going Home to Willard." *Improvement Era* 19 (October 1916): 1088–93.

RHETT STEPHENS JAMES

STEVENSON, EDWARD. Edward Stevenson, a **pioneer**, missionary, and member of the First Council of **Seventy**, was born 1 May 1820 at Gibraltar (a British colony). He emigrated with his **family** in 1827 and located at Brooklyn and Albany, **New York**. Later, living in Pontiac, **Michigan**, Edward joined the Church.

He married Nancy Areta Porter 7 April 1845 at **Nauvoo, Illinois**, and they were endowed in the **Nauvoo Temple** 2 February 1846. They lived in **Montrose, Iowa**, and traveled to **Winter Quarters** in 1846. He was captain of the third ten in the artillery company led by **Charles C. Rich** and arrived in **Salt Lake City** 2 October 1847.

On 28 August 1852 Edward was called on a **mission** to Gibraltar. On 23 January 1854 he organized a **branch** of the Church there, which consisted of 10 members. Edward served nine other missions and was captain of four emigrating companies. In 1870 he went to **Kirtland, Ohio**, and brought **Martin Harris** to Salt Lake City, where Edward rebaptized him in the **Endowment House** 17 September 1870.

Edward was called as a member of the First Council of Seventy on 7 October 1894. **Elder** Stevenson had 27 children by four of his seven wives. He died 27 January 1897 in Salt Lake City.

SOURCE

Flake, Lawrence R. *Mighty Men of Zion: General Authorities of the Last Dispensation.* Salt Lake City: Karl D. Butler, 1974. 433–4.

JOSEPH GRANT STEVENSON

STOOF, REINHOLD. Karl Bruno Reinhold Stoof, the second president of the South American **Mission**, served between 1926 and 1935. He was born 12 January 1887 in **Germany**. A schoolteacher, he joined the Church in 1907. After participating in **World War I**, he served a mission in Germany. He migrated to **Utah** in 1923 and worked as an editor of the German language newspaper *Der Beobachter.* In 1926 he and his wife, Ella Hirte, were sent to Buenos Aires, **Argentina**, where he succeeded **apostle Melvin J. Ballard** as president of the South American Mission. He felt strongly that his call was to the German population of **South America** and consequently sent the first missionaries to **Brazil** to work in the southern German colonies. He died in 1957.

SOURCES

Grover, Mark L. "The Mormon Church and German Immigrants in Southern Brazil: Religion and Language." *Jahrbuch Fur Geschichte Von Staat, Wirschaft und Gesellschaft: Lateinamerikas* 26 (1989): 295–308.

——. "Mormonism in Brazil: Religion and Dependency in Latin America." Ph.D. diss., Indiana University, 1985.

"Três Gerações a Serviço do Senhor." *A Liahona* 34 (December 1981): 4–5.

MARK L. GROVER

STOUT, HOSEA. Hosea Stout—soldier, policeman, **pioneer**, colonizer, and government official—was born 18 September 1810 in Pleasant Hill, **Kentucky**. He was the eighth of twelve children. Because his parents were unable to care for such a large **family**, he was placed in a **Shaker** home for four years. Hosea's mother died when he was 14, and he was left in the care of a family friend, Ed Harvey.

Hosea moved to **Caldwell County, Missouri**, in 1837, and the following year he married Samantha Peck and joined the **Mormon** Church. After the **Saints** were expelled from Missouri, Hosea settled in **Nauvoo, Illinois**, where he served as acting brigadier general in the **Nauvoo Legion** and captain of the city's police force, a position he also held at **Winter Quarters** for one year.

A member of the **Heber C. Kimball** Company, Hosea arrived in the **Salt Lake Valley** in 1848. In October of 1852, Stout left his wife and children to serve as one of the first missionaries to **China**. Embarking in **San Francisco**, Stout arrived in China 47 days later. After more than two months of proselyting without an interested investigator, Stout and his companions returned to **America**. Only then did he learn that his wife, Louisa, and their infant child had both died the day he embarked for China.

Almost completely self-taught in law, Stout became a prominent attorney in **Utah**, eventually serving as speaker of the territorial house of representatives (1856–57). He was also appointed a regent of the **University of Deseret** (1857).

In 1861 the Church called Brother Stout to colonize **St. George**. He lived in Southern Utah for five years, during which time he served as U.S. District Attorney (1862–66). In 1866, Stout returned to **Salt Lake City**, where he served on the Salt Lake **Stake high council**. He died in Holladay, Salt Lake County, Utah, 2 March 1889 at age 78.

SOURCES

Brooks, Juanita, ed. *On the Mormon Frontier: The Diary of Hosea Stout.* 2 vols. Salt Lake City: University of Utah Press, 1964.

Stout, Wayne. *Hosea Stout, Utah's Pioneer Statesman.* Salt Lake City: Wayne Stout, 1953.

JAMES A. CARVER

STOWELL, JOSIAH. Josiah Stowell (sometimes spelled Stoal) was born in Winchester, **New Hampshire**, 22 March 1770, and later resided at his farm on the **Susquehanna River**, about 3.2 miles southwest of the village of **South Bainbridge** (now Afton). This village was part of the township of Bainbridge (now Afton), Chenango County, **New York**. In October 1825 Stowell was engaged in digging for reported Spanish treasure in the Ouaquaga (Ouaquagua) Mountains of **Harmony**, Susquehanna County, **Pennsylvania**. Hearing that **Joseph Smith Jr.** of **Manchester**, Ontario County, New York, had the ability to "discern things invisible to the natural eye," Mr. Stowell visited Joseph and employed him.

The men lodged at the home of **Isaac Hale** in Harmony. According to Hale, they dug from early November to about 17 November 1825, when successive failures caused them to withdraw to the Stowell farm. While at the Hale home, Joseph Smith had met Isaac's daughter, Emma. He continued to court her while he was employed in New York by Josiah Stowell and **Joseph Knight Sr.** After Joseph and Emma were married at South Bainbridge on 18 January 1827, Stowell gave the newlyweds a ride to Manchester, where they resided with Joseph's parents.

Stowell and Knight were both houseguests of the Smiths at Manchester on 21–22 September 1827, when Joseph Smith went to the **Hill Cumorah** and obtained the **gold plates** from **Moroni**. Stowell joined the Church in 1830 but did not go west with the **Saints** when they moved to **Ohio** in 1831. Josiah Stowell continued to express his belief in the **Prophet** and the **Book of Mormon** as indicated in a letter written by his son, Josiah Stowell Jr., to John S. Fullmer in February 1843. He also dictated a letter to the Prophet in **Nauvoo** on 19 December 1843 and told him of his desire "to come to **Zion** the next season"; however, conditions prevented his doing so. Josiah Stowell died in Smithboro, Tioga County, New York, on May 12, 1844. He is buried in the Smithboro Cemetery.

SOURCES

Porter, Larry C. "A Study of the Origins of The Church of Jesus Christ of Latter-day Saints in the States of New York and Pennsylvania, 1816–1831." Ph.D. diss., Brigham Young University, 1971. 121–32, 207–10.

Stowell, Josiah, Jr. Letter to John S. Fullmer. Chemung, Chemung County, New York, 17 February 1843. LDS Church Archives, Salt Lake City.

LARRY C. PORTER

STRANG, JAMES J. James Jesse Strang was a persuasive writer and speaker who challenged the authority of the Twelve **Apostles** after the death of **Joseph Smith**. Born 21 March 1813 in Scipio, Cayuga County, **New York**, Strang taught school and practiced law before Joseph Smith baptized him in **Nauvoo** in February 1844. Strang claimed that Joseph had appointed him as his successor in a letter written 18 June 1844, that an angel had anointed him to lead the Church, and that he had found and translated an ancient record entitled "The Book of the Law of the Lord." About three thousand people left the Church and followed Strang, including **William Smith**, **John E. Page**, **William Marks**, and **George J. Adams**. After moving his church from Voree, **Wisconsin**, to Beaver Island in Lake **Michigan**, Strang, who had been crowned a "king" by his followers, was shot and killed by disaffected members of his group on 9 July 1856.

SOURCES

Bennett, Richard E. *We'll Find the Place: The Mormon Exodus, 1846–1848.* Salt Lake City: Deseret Book, 1997. 12–18.

Black, Susan Easton, comp. *Membership of The Church of Jesus Christ of Latter-day Saints, 1830–1848.* 50 vols. Provo, Utah: Religious Studies Center, Brigham Young University, 1984–88. 4:66–67.

Quaife, Milo M. *The Kingdom of Saint James: A Narrative of the Mormons.* New Haven: Yale University Press, 1930.

ANDREW H. HEDGES

SUCCESSION IN THE PRESIDENCY. When the president of the Church dies, the process by which another man takes his place is called *succession.* Today, succession principles are defined and understood, and the transition from president to president is so orderly and smooth that the process has even been described as "automatic." But from the beginning of the Church, it was not always so clearly understood nor smoothly accomplished.

During the early years of Church history, the principles of succession were in embryo stage, developing "line upon line." Even **Joseph Smith** contemplated several possibilities before there emerged in his mind an inspired understanding that succession was to be "apostolic."

By the time of his death, some important principles had been revealed. In March 1835 the Lord declared that the Twelve **Apostles** "form a **quorum**, equal in authority and power to the three presidents," or **First Presidency** (D&C 107:23–24). Another **revelation** in July 1837 declared that the same "keys" that Joseph Smith held were also given to the Twelve (D&C 112:15–18). And in 1844, in what is known as the Prophet's "last charge" to the Twelve, Joseph informed them that all the keys were now on their shoulders and that they must succeed him and "roll forth" the work.

Upon his death, of course, there was "profound shock, disbelief, and confusion" but not as much confusion as some suggest (Esplin, 321). After the Twelve had a chance to gather, reflect, and remember, they knew that they were Joseph's successors. And further, they knew that **Brigham Young**, their senior member and quorum president, should be the new **president**. The **Saints** were not left in the dark, either. In the official funeral address for Joseph Smith and his brother Hyrum on 29 June 1844, **Elder W. W. Phelps** preached clearly to the 10,000 or so assembled Saints in the east grove: "Remember, beloved friends, that while he [Joseph] lived here upon the earth, he conferred all the keys and blessings of the **priesthood**, and the **Endowment**, upon the Apostles" (quoted in Van Wagoner, 11). Elder Phelps went on to say: "The priesthood remains unharmed" and "when the 'Twelve' return, they will wear the 'mantle' and step into the 'shoes' of the 'prophet, priest and king' of **Israel**; and then with the same power, the same God, and the same spirit . . . [they will] roll on the work until all Israel is gathered and the wicked swept from the earth" (quoted in Van Wagoner, 11).

So, regardless of how many so-called claimants had come on the scene, at the special Church conference in **Nauvoo, Illinois**, 8 August 1844, it was "truly manifested" and voted by the assembled Saints that President Brigham Young and the rest of the Twelve Apostles were the legitimate successors to Joseph. In fact, when Brigham Young spoke on that occasion, many testified that both his voice and appearance resembled those of Joseph Smith. **Wilford Woodruff**, who attended the meeting, later stated, "There was a reason for this in the mind of God; it convinced the people. They saw and heard for themselves, and it was by the power of God" (*JD*, 15:81). From that day to this, through several inspired clarifications, the law of succession in the Church is in place. The senior apostle, one who has served in the quorum or subsequently in the First Presidency for the longest continuous time, will preside as the Church's president, **prophet, seer, and revelator**.

SOURCES

Arrington, Leonard J. *Brigham Young: American Moses*. New York: Alfred A. Knopf, 1985. 113–16.

Durham, Reed C., Jr., and Steven H. Heath. *Succession in the Church*. Salt Lake City: Bookcraft, 1970.

Esplin, Ronald K. "Joseph, Brigham and the Twelve: A Succession of Continuity." *BYU Studies* 21 (Summer 1981): 301–41.

Hickman, Martin B. "Succession in the Presidency." *Encyclopedia of Mormonism*. Edited by Daniel H. Ludlow. 4 vols. New York: Macmillan, 1992. 3:1420–21.

Jorgensen, Lynne Watkins. "The Mantle of the Prophet Joseph Passes to Brother Brigham: A Collective Spiritual Witness." *BYU Studies* 36 (1996–97): 125–204.

Journal of Discourses [JD]. 26 vols. London: Latter-day Saints' Book Depot, 1854–86.

Quinn, D. Michael. "The Mormon Succession Crisis of 1844." *BYU Studies* 16 (Winter 1976): 187–233.

Van Wagoner, Richard, and Steven C. Walker. "The Joseph/Hyrum Smith Funeral Sermon." *BYU Studies* 23 (Winter 1983): 3–18.

REED DURHAM

SUDAN. See **MIDDLE EAST** and **MUSLIMS**.

SUGAR CREEK, IOWA. Sugar Creek was the **Iowa** staging campsite for **Brigham Young's** advance company of **Saints** who left **Illinois** for the West during February 1846. It was located across the **Mississippi River** from **Nauvoo**, seven miles west of present **Montrose, Iowa**. The site covered at least half of a square mile, with plenty of timber and water.

First to cross the river was Charles Shumway on 4 February. For three weeks, while temperatures steadily plummeted until they reached 12 below zero, wagons ferried across, often dodging ice, and then by 25 February scores of pioneers crossed on the iced-over river. Campers, protected by tents and covered wagons, suffered from the cold. Around some evening campfires the Nauvoo Band played and young people danced. In total some 500 wagons and 3,000 Saints collected there, many not properly supplied.

Brigham Young organized this "Camp of Israel" into companies of hundreds, fifties, and tens (wagons) and developed camp and travel rules. He sent ahead a vanguard to prepare roads and campsites. On 1 March the Camp of Israel pulled out, beginning a difficult three-and-a-half month trek across southern Iowa to the **Missouri River**. Later, in April through June, this campsite was reused constantly as a staging area for for several thousand Saints leaving the Nauvoo area.

Sources

Nibley, Preston. *Exodus to Greatness.* Salt Lake City: Deseret News, 1947.

Watson, Elden J., comp. *Manuscript History of Brigham Young, 1846–1847.* Salt Lake City: Elden J. Watson, 1971. 1–56.

William G. Hartley

SUGAR INDUSTRY. The Church and many of its members have been heavily involved in the sugar industry since the mid-nineteenth century. In 1849 **Brigham Young** delegated **John Taylor**, who was sent on a **mission** to **France**, to investigate industries that might benefit the **Mormons** in their new mountain retreat. A group of missionaries led by **Elder** Taylor visited a French sugar beet factory and reported to the **First Presidency** that a similar industry could be established in the **Great Basin**. Pleased at the prospect of supplying sugar locally to the Latter-day Saints, Brigham Young instructed the missionaries to raise funds and obtain beet seed, equipment, and personnel to provide the establishment of a sugar industry. John Taylor organized the Deseret Manufacturing Company and purchased beet seed in France and sugar beet processing equipment from a company in **Liverpool, England**. Experimental runs, however, produced only a small quantity of inedible molasses. In the spring of 1853, Public Works erected a factory building on the Church farm four miles south of **Salt Lake City**, in a district that became known as Sugar House. The factory ceased operations three years later because of the inability to boil the sugar syrups into crystals.

Arthur Stayner, a Latter-day Saint horticulturist, experimented in the 1880s with growing sorghum, sugar cane, and sugar beets in the territory. In 1886 a small company was organized to manufacture sugar from sorghum. The main result of this activity was the formation in 1889 of the Utah Sugar Company and a pronouncement from President **Wilford Woodruff** that it was "the mind and will of the Lord" that a sugar beet industry be established (quoted in *Kingdom,* 387). Church authorities stressed that economic self-sufficiency would result for the territory. With the help of the First Presidency and other **general authorities**, Church leaders raised funds locally and then in the East. A contract was given to E. H. Dyer and Company to build and equip the first beet sugar processing plant in the Intermountain West. The city of Lehi provided attractive financial inducements, along with water rights for the new sugar company to be built in that community.

James Gardner, who had served as a missionary in Hawaii and learned the art of boiling sugar, teamed up with Edward F. Dyer, who had come to Lehi to help operate his father's (E. H. Dyer) sugar beet plant. On 15 October 1891, they produced the first crystallized white sugar in the Intermountain West, the first from U.S.-manufactured sugar equipment, and the first using entirely American workmen. They also began a cooperation between Mormons and **Gentiles** that became the backbone of beet-sugar industry development throughout the **United States** and **Canada**. During a visit to the new sugar factory later that fall, the aged President Wilford Woodruff asked Gardner to take him where they were sacking sugar. After a time of watching, he said to Gardner: "This is one of the happiest experiences of my life, to sit here and see that sugar flow into the sacks. . . . I have seen the time when our people hungered for sugar and couldn't get it at any price. . . . And now right here before my eyes, I see refined white sugar being made by the carload—*our sugar!* It is the realization of the time that I have dreamed and prayed about" (quoted in Taylor, 91–92).

In the first several decades of the twentieth century, sugar beets proved to be the best cash crop for farmers. In many valleys in the West, and as far east as **South Dakota**, Latter-day Saint farmers with their irrigating skills managed to grow sugar beets expertly. As irrigated land became available in new areas, Latter-day Saint farmers tended to migrate, expanding the sugar industry.

On 23 January 1903, President **Joseph F. Smith** and his **counselor John R. Winder** met with Thomas R. Cutler and Horace G. Whitney (of the Utah Sugar Company) and others to organize the Idaho Sugar Company. The Church subscribed, under the name of Joseph F. Smith and Associates, to 7½% of the issued stock for $56,625.

On 21 May 1907, a merger plan was approved by the owners of Utah Sugar Company, Idaho Sugar Company, and Western Idaho Sugar

Company. On 31 July, Utah-Idaho Sugar Company was incorporated in the state of Utah, with general authorities of the Church, including members of the First Presidency, serving as officers. Several additional factories were built throughout the western United States.

The Church maintained its financial interest in Utah Sugar and its successors until 1979. During times of critical financial troubles for Utah-Idaho Sugar, especially after the stock market crash in 1929, the Church felt impelled to finance the sugar company for the benefit of the farmers.

The progress of the sugar industry in the last hundred years has been the result of Mormons and non-Mormons working together to make the industry successful. Perhaps one-ninth of the entire workforce in the sugar industry in the United States and Canada has been members of the Church. More than one-third of the sugar factories in North America were started by Latter-day Saints, and Saints have provided most of the beet-sugar industry's significant developments. Latter-day Saint leadership in the sugar industry has carried forth from the time of the Lehi factory in the 1890s to the present day.

SOURCES

Arrington, Leonard J. *Beet Sugar in the West: A History of the Utah-Idaho Sugar Company, 1891–1966.* Seattle: University of Washington Press, 1966.

———. *Great Basin Kingdom: An Economic History of the Latter-day Saints, 1830–1900.* Cambridge, Mass.: Harvard University Press, 1958. 116.

———. *Harold F. Silver: Western Inventor, Businessman, and Civic Leader.* Logan, Utah: Utah State University Press, 1992.

Bachman, J. R. *Story of the Amalgamated Sugar Company 1897–1961.* Caldwell, Idaho: Caxton, 1962.

"Practicing Pure Religion: Latter-day Saint Welfare and Humanitarian Service." Salt Lake City: Church Museum of History and Art, 1999.

Taylor, Fred G. *A Saga of Sugar.* Salt Lake City: Utah-Idaho Sugar Company, 1944.

BARNARD STEWART SILVER

SUNDAY SCHOOLS. The basic aim of Latter-day Saint Sunday School has always been to foster faith in **Jesus Christ** and his restored gospel through scripture and song. In the nineteenth century, when adult **Bible** literacy was widespread, participants were mostly children and young adults; at the turn of the century classes for adults were added to curb the decline in Bible literacy. **Priesthood** leaders called men and women to instruct classes, usually held on Sunday morning and lasting anywhere from 30 minutes to 2 hours. In 1980, classes were standardized at 40 minutes and held contiguous with other Sunday **meetings**.

The foundations of twentieth-century Sunday Schools were laid in the nineteenth century. The first Sunday School in **Utah** was organized in 1849 by **Richard Ballantyne**, a Scottish emigrant convert who was disturbed by the sight of children playing on the Sabbath day. His school opened with 50 children, ages 8 to 14, reciting scripture in his remodeled home in **Salt Lake City**. As Ballantyne's success spread, **bishops** in Salt Lake **Stake** and neighboring stakes organized similar schools. These schools operated independently until **Brigham Young** organized the supervisory Parent Sunday School Union (1867)—later changed to the Deseret Sunday School Union (1872)—under the superintendency of **Elder George Q. Cannon**. Elder Cannon published the *Juvenile Instructor*, a semimonthly publication started in 1866. By the winter of 1875, Brigham Young was urging each ward to organize a Sunday school. President **John Taylor** furthered his aims by calling missionaries to help local leaders establish Sunday School libraries and promote subscriptions to the *Juvenile Instructor*. A Sunday School for every ward and a reference library of materials were goals that remained through the twentieth century.

Emphasis on scripture-based lessons also took form in the nineteenth century. Students in Utah's early Sunday Schools recited from the scriptures and John Jacques's *Catechism for Children* (1854), a collection of gospel questions and answers using scriptures as proof texts. Jacques's *Catechism* proved so popular that it was translated into five languages and supplemented by official question-answer publications. To foster basic literacy, the youth studied the alphabet and moral lessons from the first and second *Deseret Sunday School Reader* (1879, 1880). Movement away from catechism began in the 1880s as the **Saints'** interest in day schools and access to printed media spread. By 1893, the standard works (including the **Pearl of Great Price**, canonized in 1880) and sophisticated explications of them had almost entirely replaced catechistic works as recommended texts. The course of twentieth-century instruction was further marked by the first publication of lesson outlines (1889), designed to help teachers organize instruction around the **scriptures**. Under correlation, lesson outlines were translated into many languages and from the 1970s on sought to eliminate culturally dependent commentary by quoting more from a common idiom—the scriptures.

As with scripture, music has remained essential to the Sunday School curriculum. Children in the earliest schools sang mostly hymns familiar to adult Saints until songs written specifically for children were printed in the *Juvenile Instructor* and then distributed on two-sided music cards in the 1870s. The Deseret Sunday School Union published its first songbook in 1884. In the twentieth century, new songs were added and older ones dropped from a children's songbook used by both the Sunday School and **Primary**. Some of the oldest pieces, such as "Joseph Smith's First Prayer," bound generations of children and adults together in faith. As lyrics were translated into various languages, music became vital for unifying an increasingly diversified Church population.

SOURCES

Deseret Sunday School Union. *Guide for the Officers and Teachers of Sunday Schools in the Various Stakes of Zion*. Salt Lake City: Deseret Sunday School Union, 1893.
———. *Jubilee History of Latter-day Saints Sunday Schools, 1849–1899*. Salt Lake City: Deseret Sunday School Union, 1900.
General Handbook of Instructions. Salt Lake City: The Church of Jesus Christ of Latter-day Saints, 1989.

JED L. WOODWORTH

SURINAME.

The Republic of Suriname, previously known as Dutch Guiana, is located on the north coast of **South America**. Its population consists predominantly of descendants of Africans, East Indians, and Indonesians, with a small **Native American** population. John and Beverly Limburg began proselyting there in October 1988. The first baptisms took place on Easter Sunday in 1989. On 24 February 1990 **Elder M. Russell Ballard** of the **Quorum** of the Twelve **Apostles** dedicated Suriname for preaching the gospel. In 1991 the first local leaders were called and a **branch** organized. Elder Paul Levie served as president of the branch, and Selma Armaketo as the first **Relief Society** president. The branch has continued to grow with some additional activity in rural areas of the country. In 1997 a missionary couple and eight elders served in Suriname. At the beginning of the year 2000, Suriname had 454 members organized into one branch.

SOURCE

1999–2000 Church Almanac. Salt Lake City: Deseret News, 1998.

MARK L. STAKER

SUSQUEHANNA RIVER.

Flowing through south central **New York** and northeastern **Pennsylvania**, the Susquehanna River was the scene of significant events in the **Restoration**. The name is derived from **Native American** words *susque* (crooked) and *hannah* (river). Emma Hale was raised near the Susquehanna River in the home of her parents, Isaac and Elizabeth Hale. **Joseph Smith Jr.** worked in the area beginning in 1825 and established his first home there after marrying Emma Hale in 1827. Here, he began translation of the **Book of Mormon** with the help of **Emma Smith**, **Martin Harris**, and **Oliver Cowdery** as scribes. Not more than a quarter of a mile from the Susquehanna, Joseph and Emma buried their firstborn infant son, Alvin Smith. On 15 May 1829 **John the Baptist** stood on the banks of the river and conferred the **Aaronic Priesthood** upon Joseph and Oliver, who then baptized one another. Also near this crooked waterway, Jesus' ancient apostles **Peter, James and John** conferred the **Melchizedek Priesthood** upon Joseph and Oliver.

W. SIDNEY YOUNG

SUSTAINING. To *sustain* means to uphold or support. Members of the **Church** participate in sustaining through a formal procedure known as common consent, as well as through informal acts reflective of Christian living. A member formally commits to sustaining by raising the right hand in approval of proposed priesthood ordinations, Church callings, principles, and/or policies. This commitment is a covenant to sustain the Church proposal without reservation. "To sustain," according to **Elder Loren C. Dunn**, "is to make the action binding on ourselves and to commit ourselves to support those people whom we have sustained . . . both in public and in private." The informal act of sustaining is demonstrated as members support and encourage others in righteous living and exercise charity toward all mankind. When members of the Church sustain, whether formally or informally, they pledge their full support and faith to bring about God's will and design.

SOURCES

Dunn, Loren C. "We Are Called of God." *Ensign* 2 (July 1972): 43.
Lee, Harold B. Conference Report (April 1970): 103.

MATTHEW O. RICHARDSON

SWAZILAND. Swaziland, known as the "**Switzerland** of **Africa**" for its scenic beauty, is located in southern Africa near the Indian Ocean. It is the continent's second smallest country. Its official languages are English and Siswati, and in 1999 its population was 57% Christian, with the remaining 43% of indigenous beliefs.

One of the first Swazis to join the Church was Robert Dlamini. He was baptized in 1979 while studying mining management in Cardiff, **Wales**, and returned home as an **elder**. Unaware that there had been other Church members in his land for several years, he waited a decade before meeting another Latter-day Saint in Swaziland.

The establishment of the Church in this country occurred through a group of non-African Latter-day Saints living in Swaziland in 1984. They included the families of Herman Van Thiel Berghuijs, George Gardner, and John Scott. On 5 November 1985, Brother Gardner became president of the newly organized Mbabane **Branch**. Two years later the Church gained government recognition, and the first missionaries arrived.

Paulo Cipriano Zandamela, a Mozambican who had been baptized 31 July 1988, became the first missionary called from Swaziland. The first Swazi to become a full-time missionary was Sister Fikile Dlamini. In February 1990 Elder **Neal A. Maxwell** dedicated Swaziland for the preaching of the gospel. On 18 July 1993 the country's first **meetinghouse** was dedicated.

When President **Gordon B. Hinckley** spoke at a Johannesburg regional **conference** in 1996, and again in 1998, members from Swaziland traveled to attend. By the beginning of the year 2000, there were 798 members living in one **ward** and two **branches**.

Sources

Cook, Darwin, and Maurine Cook. "New Day Dawning in 2 Small African Mountain Kingdoms." *Church News,* 10 March 1990, 3.

1999–2000 Church Almanac. Salt Lake City, Deseret News, 1998. 390–91.

Sheffield, Sheridan R. "Members Never Strangers Living Away from Homeland." *Church News,* 9 February 1991, 8.

"Sweet Is the Work in Swaziland." *Ensign* 22 (March 1992): 76–77.

E. Dale LeBaron

SWEDEN. John E. Forsgren was converted to the gospel in **America** and returned to preach in his native land of Sweden in 1850. The first baptism in **Scandinavia** was that of Peter Forsgren, John's brother, on 26 July 1850. On 24 April 1853, a branch was organized in Skonaback, and other groups were soon established despite legal and extralegal persecution. In 1878 a Swedish translation of the **Book of Mormon** was published, and convert baptisms swelled noticeably in the late 1800s as restrictions relaxed. Nearly half of the Swedish converts emigrated to the

Great Basin between 1852 and 1905, and significant numbers again left for America after **World War II**.

In 1905 the Swedish Mission was created from the Scandinavian Mission. Local Saints led the Church during both world **wars** and endured waves of official opposition before and after **World War I**. The missionary force increased noticeably after World War II, and building missionaries finished a **meetinghouse** in Gubbangen in 1961. The first **stake** was organized in Stockholm on 20 April 1975, eight months after the city hosted a Nordic **area conference**. On 2 July 1985, President **Gordon B. Hinckley** dedicated a **temple** outside Stockholm in Vasterhaninge, which served Scandinavia as well as much of **Russia** and the Baltic republics. As of the year 2000, Sweden was home to 4 stakes, 50 **wards** and **branches**, and 8,587 members of the Church.

SOURCES

Jenson, Andrew. *History of the Scandinavian Mission.* Salt Lake City: Deseret News, 1927.

Johansson, Carl-Erik. "History of the Swedish Mission 1905–1973." Master's thesis, Brigham Young University, 1973.

Van Orden, Bruce. *Building Zion: The Latter-day Saints in Europe.* Salt Lake City: Deseret Book, 1996.

JOHN THOMAS

SWISS TEMPLE. The Bern Switzerland Temple was the first Latter-day Saint temple built in **Europe** and also the first to use modern audio-visual technology to present portions of the endowment. President **David O. McKay** and Swiss-Austrian **Mission president** Samuel Bringhurst selected the Zollikofen site in 1952, and groundbreaking took place 5 August 1953. Edward O. Anderson and a local architectural firm finalized building plans for the temple, whose modern design covered some 35,000 square feet and used a new two-room arrangement for the presentation of the endowment.

President McKay said that **revelation** helped solve the problem of presenting temple **ordinances** in many languages with relatively few temple workers ("Temple," 3). He assigned Church staff member **Gordon B. Hinckley** to supervise production of the needed audio-visual materials, and Brother Hinckley personally delivered them to **Switzerland** and trained workers to use them.

On 11–15 September 1955, **Saints** from across Europe gathered for 10 dedicatory sessions conducted in seven different languages. The

Tabernacle Choir interrupted its European tour to sing at the services. Endowment sessions began the day after the dedication so that members could participate before their long journeys home. In 1992 President Gordon B. Hinckley returned to rededicate the temple after it was remodeled.

SOURCES

Cowan, Richard O. *Temples to Dot the Earth.* Salt Lake City: Bookcraft, 1989.
Dew, Sheri L. *Go Forward with Faith: The Biography of Gordon B. Hinckley.* Salt Lake City: Deseret Book, 1996.
"Temple Building Principles As Historically Established by the Restored Church." Typescript. Church Historical Department, 1974.

JOHN THOMAS

SWITZERLAND. Thomas B. H. Stenhouse began proselyting in multilingual Switzerland on 24 November 1850 in French-speaking Geneva. **Elder Lorenzo Snow** of the Twelve called Stenhouse to serve in Switzerland while they were laboring together in **Italy.** Elder Snow joined him in February 1851 and dedicated Switzerland for the preaching of the gospel. Geneva's first 20 converts became a branch in the spring of 1852. Lausanne was the site of the second branch where Serge Ballif, a former minister, published *Le Reflector,* the Church's first periodical in the country.

On 14 February 1853, Stenhouse, Ballif, and Frederick Roulet preached in German-speaking Basel. An advertisement for Elder **John Taylor's** German translation of the **Book of Mormon** preceded them.

At the first conference in Geneva, held 25 December 1853, 144 had been baptized, 20 had been excommunicated, and 4 had emigrated. Emigration took many converts for the next century. Growth was slowed by persecutions and imprisonments, and in August 1914 and September 1938 world wars forced the evacuation of LDS missionaries.

The first **temple in Europe** was dedicated by President **David O. McKay** in Zollikofen, Switzerland, 11 September 1955; this temple was the first to offer the temple **endowment** in various languages with a media presentation. On 28 October 1961, the first **stake** in Switzerland was established in Zurich with Wilhelm Frederick Lauener as president. The first person to serve as a **general authority** from the country was Hans B. Ringger, who was called into the First Quorum of the **Seventy** in 1985.

On 3 May 1981, Peter Lauener, Wilhelm's son, was called to preside over the Bern Stake. The first French-speaking stake was organized in Geneva on 20 June 1982 with Denis Bonny as president.

By the end of the twentieth century one organized Church unit was located in the Italian-speaking canton of Ticino—the Lugano Branch, served by the Italy Milan Mission. No **missionary work** or organized branches were in Romansch-speaking Switzerland. As of the year 2000 the country's LDS population was 7,043, residing in 3 stakes and 40 **wards** and **branches**.

SOURCES

Kirby, Dale Z. "History of The Church of Jesus Christ of Latter-day Saints in Switzerland." Master's thesis, Brigham Young University, 1971.

1997–1998 Church Almanac. Salt Lake City: Deseret News, 1996. 392.

DALE Z. KIRBY

SYRIA. Syria has been the setting for many significant events in modern Middle Eastern Latter-day Saint history. **Missionary work** in the **Middle East** formally began in the northern part of the Ottoman Empire in 1884. Finding little interest among Europeans and Turks in Istanbul, the missionaries moved inland and succeeded in establishing branches of the Church in the Armenian Christian communities of central **Turkey** and northern Syria. Eventually Aleppo, Syria, became one of the two largest branches in the mission and the location of mission headquarters from 1907 to 1909 and from 1921 to 1929. Missionaries also sought to establish the Church in other cities in Syria (Hama, Homs, and Damascus) but met with limited success.

When the Turkish Mission was closed in 1909 due to political turmoil, Church members remained without outside leadership and assistance for 12 years, until after the end of **World War I** and the dissolution of the Ottoman Empire. In 1921 the mission was reopened by **Joseph Booth**, former president of the mission, and renamed the Armenian Mission, with headquarters in Aleppo. Booth returned to find the mission in total disarray and ravaged by **war**: the number of Church members was depleted by death, emigration, and deportation, and those who remained were scattered, lonely, sick, and hungry. As a result, rather than pursuing normal ecclesiastical and missionary activities, Booth focused his efforts on dealing with problems of disease, poverty, illiteracy, and unemployment among Church members.

In December 1921, Booth arranged with the French authorities (who controlled Syria in the postwar mandate period) to evacuate LDS Church members from Aintab, Turkey, to Aleppo, Syria, where they could be given proper care and protection. This exodus was subsequently viewed by the Armenian **Saints** as a miraculous event in Church history—a sign of God's mercy and love for them—and was memorialized in plays, poems, and stories. After gathering the Armenian members to Aleppo and establishing a communal home for them in the Khan Jabria quarter, Booth sought tirelessly for the next seven years to alleviate their suffering and improve their lives: teaching them new skills like reading, writing, and carpentry; organizing cooperatives to produce rugs and other goods and market them overseas; soliciting clothing and food donations from Church members in **Utah**; and arranging for emigration to **Europe** and **North America**. The numerous descendants of these Armenian emigrants from Syria and Turkey have made important contributions to the Church and to the communities in which they have settled.

The mission home was moved from Aleppo to Haifa, **Palestine**, in February 1928. In December of that year, President Booth died of cardiac arrest and overexertion while working with the members in Aleppo. He is buried in the Protestant cemetery there alongside another Latter-day Saint missionary, Emil J. Huber, who died of typhoid in 1908. With Booth's death the mission was closed and not reopened until August 1933, when Badwagan Piranian arrived to preside over the renamed Palestine-Syrian Mission. Groups of expatriate Church members have held services intermittently in Syria since that time, and an expatriate branch was organized in Damascus in 1997.

SOURCES

"Correspondence, 1932–1955." Near East Mission. LDS Church Archives, Salt Lake City.

"History." Palestine-Syrian Mission. LDS Church Archives, Salt Lake City.

Lindsay, Rao H. "A History of the Missionary Activities of The Church of Jesus Christ of Latter-day Saints in the Near East, 1884–1929." Master's thesis, Brigham Young University, 1958.

"Manuscript History." Turkish Mission. LDS Church Archives, Salt Lake City.

"Papers of Joseph Wilford Booth." Special Collections and Manuscripts. Brigham Young University Library, Provo, Utah.

JAMES A. TORONTO

HIERO NO
TAHITI

TE EKALESIA A
IESU MESIA
I TE FEIA MO'A I TE
MAU MAHANA
HOPEA NEI

TEMPLE DE
TAHITI

ÉGLISE DE
JÉSUS·CHRIST
DES SAINTS
DES DERNIERS
JOURS

TEMPLES. Latter-day Saints build chapels for weekly worship services but reserve their temples, such as the Papeete Tahiti Temple, for special ordinance work for the living and the dead.

TABERNACLE, SALT LAKE. The Salt Lake Tabernacle, a large, dome-shaped building on **Temple Square**, has been home to the **Mormon Tabernacle Choir** since 1867. Constructed from 1863 to 1867, it is the oldest building on Temple Square. It has a capacity of seating more than 6,000 and serves as a gathering place for many concerts, well-known speakers, and performing artists. Built with pioneer ingenuity and resourcefulness, the Tabernacle is also renowned for its exceptional acoustic qualities.

Under **Brigham Young's** direction, Church architect **William H. Folsom** prepared preliminary plans for the Tabernacle. The design was for a structure 150 feet wide and 250 feet long with semicircular ends. The cornerstone was laid on 26 July 1864, and then began the construction of 44 sandstone piers to support the roof. In 1865 Brigham Young appointed an experienced bridge builder, **Henry Grow**, to oversee construction and to build unprecedented, huge trusses that spanned the entire width of the building. **Truman O. Angell**, appointed Church architect in 1867, designed the exterior cornice and interior woodwork. He was also responsible for the design of a balcony, which not only significantly increased the building's seating capacity but also improved its acoustics.

In 1890 a baptismal font was installed. The rostrum area underwent extensive remodeling in 1882, 1933, and 1977. The shingle roof was replaced with aluminum in 1947, and in 1968 a basement was added. Recognized for its engineering skill and architectural achievement, the Tabernacle was designated a National Historic Landmark in 1970.

At the 1967 April general conference of the Church, **apostle** and long-time choir announcer **Richard L. Evans** expressed his feelings about this beloved structure on its 100th anniversary: "We have performed in many of the great concert halls of **Europe** and **America**, and have talked in many auditoriums around the world, and find nothing to exceed this building in uniqueness of structure, in remarkable versatility, in its most pleasing and responsive acoustic qualities, in its simplicity and beauty and spirit. There have been some who would change it, some who have thought to 'improve' it, so they say, even as to some of its basic essentials; but it satisfies my soul, and I thank God for the minds that conceived it, for the inspiration given them to do so, for the hands that fashioned it in their poverty and loving care and skill and devotion" (Evans, 221).

The Salt Lake Tabernacle was home to the Church's general conferences from 1867 until 1999, when the meetings were moved to the Conference Center across the street.

SOURCES

Anderson, Paul L. "Salt Lake City Tabernacle." *Encyclopedia of Mormonism.* Edited by Daniel H. Ludlow. 4 vols. New York: Macmillan, 1992. 2:1433–34.

Evans, Richard L., Jr. *Richard L. Evans, the Man and the Message.* Salt Lake City: Bookcraft, 1973.

LLOYD D. NEWELL

TABERNACLE CHOIR. Known as the official choir of the Church, the Mormon Tabernacle Choir is named for its home in the historic **Tabernacle** on **Temple Square** in **Salt Lake City**. The choir is composed of more than 300 carefully selected and well-trained vocalists. They come from all walks of life and serve without pay, demonstrating great commitment in their service to the Church as they rehearse and perform more than 150 days each year. In addition to singing for LDS **general conferences** and other Church and civic functions, the Tabernacle Choir tours extensively and is heard and seen on its weekly radio and TV program, *Music and the Spoken Word,* carried internationally by some 600 stations. The Tabernacle Choir is known and beloved worldwide for more than 150 recordings and numerous films and videotapes.

Well before the Tabernacle was built, a small choir sang at the first general conference of the Church in the **Salt Lake Valley** on 22 August 1847. The quality of singing in the choir was greatly enhanced by the arrival of a group of 85 Welsh converts in 1849. Their leader, John Parry, was invited by **Brigham Young** to organize a choir for the next general conference, and this choir formed the nucleus from which the Tabernacle Choir grew. In 1869, **George Careless** became the conductor and organized the first large choir, made up of 304 members.

Subsequent musical directors include Ebenezer Beesley (1888–89),

Evan Stephens (1889–1916), Anthony C. Lund (1916–35), **J. Spencer Cornwall** (1935–57), **Richard P. Condie** (1957–74), Jay Welch (1974), Jerold Ottley (1975–99), and Craig Jessop (beginning 2000).

Sometimes called America's Choir and designated as "one of America's greatest treasures" by U.S. president George Bush, the choir has performed at four presidential inaugurals—those of George Bush (1989), Ronald Reagan (1981), Richard M. Nixon (1969), and Lyndon B. Johnson (1965)—and at other important national occasions, including the bicentennial celebration of the **Constitution of the United States** (1987); the American Bicentenary in **Washington, D.C.** (4 July 1976); nationwide radio memorial services for John F. Kennedy (24 November 1963) and Franklin D. Roosevelt (12 April 1945); and the first worldwide television satellite broadcast, transmitted from Mt. Rushmore (1962).

The choir has performed extensively in major concert halls throughout the **United States** and **Canada** and other parts of the world. Beginning with its first European tour in 1955, multiple international tours have taken the choir to **Europe** (1955, 1973, 1998), **Central America** (1968, 1972), the Far East (1979), **Brazil** (1981), **Scandinavia** (1982), **Japan** (1985), **Australia** and **New Zealand** (1988), Central Europe and the former **Soviet Union** (1991), and **Israel** (1993). The choir has also performed at 13 **world's fairs** and expositions.

Five gold and two platinum records have been awarded the choir, and the recording of "Battle Hymn of the Republic" with the Philadelphia Orchestra won a Grammy Award in 1959. The choir's first radio broadcast took place 15 July 1929, making *Music and the Spoken Word* the longest continuous network broadcast in the world. The choir has also been awarded the Peabody Award for service to American broadcasting (1944, 1962).

SOURCES

Calman, Charles J., and William I. Kaufman. *The Mormon Tabernacle Choir.* New York: Harper & Row, 1979.

Cornwall, J. Spencer. *A Century of Singing: The Salt Lake Mormon Tabernacle Choir.* Salt Lake City: Deseret Book, 1958.

Dayley, K. Newell. "Mormon Tabernacle Choir." *Encyclopedia of Mormonism.* Edited by Daniel H. Ludlow. 4 vols. New York: Macmillan, 1992. 2:950–52.

Miller, Roger L. "Mormon Tabernacle Choir." *Utah History Encyclopedia.* Edited by Allan Kent Powell. Salt Lake City: University of Utah Press, 1994. 378–80.

LLOYD D. NEWELL

TABERNACLE CHOIR BROADCAST. See *MUSIC AND THE SPOKEN WORD.*

TABERNACLE ORGAN. The world-renowned organ in the **Salt Lake Tabernacle** is an artistic masterpiece. Its imposing appearance and magnificent sound have made it an important attraction on **Temple Square** for decades. In 1994 the Organ Historical Society recognized the **Tabernacle** organ as "an instrument of exceptional historic merit" (certificate).

Pioneer organ builder **Joseph Ridges** installed the first organ in the Tabernacle in 1867. The instrument was later enlarged by Niels Johnson (1885) and rebuilt and further enlarged by the Kimball Organ Company (1901) and the Austin Organ Company (in several stages from 1915 to 1940). In the late 1940s, the organ was again rebuilt by the Aeolian-Skinner Organ Company under the direction of G. Donald Harrison. After nearly 40 years of service, the Aeolian-Skinner organ was renovated by Schoenstein & Company of **San Francisco**. The organ is recognized as one of the finest examples of a tonal style known as American Classic. The present organ, though much enlarged, retains Ridges's original case and large gilded front pipes made from **Utah** timber, as well as some original Ridges pipes inside the case. At the end of the twentieth century the organ contained 11,623 pipes organized into 147 voices (tone colors) and 206 ranks (rows of pipes) controlled from a console with five keyboards and a 32-note pedalboard. The pipes, made of wood, zinc, and various alloys of tin and lead, range in speaking length from 32 feet to three-quarters of an inch.

Recitals are presented daily by the Tabernacle organists.

SOURCES

Bethards, Jack M. "Tabernacle Organ." *Encyclopedia of Mormonism.* Edited by Daniel H. Ludlow. 4 vols. New York: Macmillan, 1992. 4:1434–36.

Organ Historical Society. Certificate of Citation, 1994.

Owen, Barbara. *The Mormon Tabernacle Organ: An American Classic.* The American Classic Organ Symposium, Salt Lake City: The Church of Jesus Christ of Latter-day Saints, 1990.

LLOYD D. NEWELL AND JOHN LONGHURST

TABERNACLES. Although the Israelites' tabernacle became a model for the temple they would ultimately build (see Ex. 25:8–9), Latter-day

Saint tabernacles are "merely large assembly rooms or halls" where Saints gather for **conferences** and other large meetings (Jenson, 859). The first tabernacle to appear in Latter-day Saint history was the "Log Tabernacle" of Pottawattamie County, **Iowa**, which was built while the **Saints** waited to move west. Here **Brigham Young** was sustained as second president of the Church on 27 December 1847. Later, tabernacles appeared in several Latter-day Saint communities in the West. Larger and more elaborate than regular **meetinghouses**, these structures have become historic sites in cities such as **Salt Lake**, **Brigham City**, **Logan**, **Ogden**, **Provo**, and **St. George**.

SOURCES

Jenson, Andrew. *Encyclopedic History of The Church of Jesus Christ of Latter-day Saints.* Salt Lake City: Deseret News, 1941. 850–61.

LISA KURKI

TAHITI. See FRENCH POLYNESIA.

TAI KWOK YUEN. Tai Kwok Yuen , the first Chinese **general authority**, was born 30 June 1941 in **Hong Kong**. Tai received his degree in chemical engineering from the University of Sydney in **Australia** and later pursued graduate studies at the University of Hong Kong. He married to Hui Hua Lai, and they became the parents of three children.

Elder Tai joined the Church on 9 June 1959 in Hong Kong at the age of 17. His Church callings have included **branch** president, high councilor, and **regional representative**. In 1989, while living in **Los Angeles, California**, he was called to preside over the Hong Kong mission. Following his release, he was called to the Second Quorum of the **Seventy** with an assignment to serve as the second counselor in the **Asia Area** presidency, headquartered in Hong Kong. In 1995 he was called as president of the area, where he actively worked to expand the Church's influence throughout South and Southeast Asia. He was released in October 1997.

SOURCES

Britsch, R. Lanier. *From the East: The History of the Latter-day Saints in Asia, 1851–1996.* Salt Lake City: Deseret Book, 1998. 289.

1997–1998 Church Almanac. Salt Lake City: Deseret News, 1996. 37.

JEFFREY RINGER

TAIWAN. Important in its own right, Taiwan is also a key base for taking the gospel to all of **China**. For 16 years the Church in Taiwan was an extension of the **mission** in **Hong Kong**. Missionaries were first assigned to the area in 1956. At this time Taiwan was in transition following the fall of China to the communists and the resulting influx of refugees. **Elder Mark E. Peterson**, the first **general authority** to visit Taiwan, dedicated the land for missionary work on 1 June 1959. When Elder **Gordon B. Hinckley** visited the mission in April 1960, there were not quite 500 members.

Taiwan became an independent mission in 1971, headquartered in Taipei with Malan Jackson as its first president. In 1976 a second mission, Taiwan Kaohsiung, was organized; a third mission headquartered in Taichung was added in 1979. By this time total Church membership was more than 8,000.

Other significant developments include the calling of local Chinese missionaries (28 by 1971), acquiring property for chapels and missionary quarters, the translation of gospel **literature**, and the preparation of systematic lesson plans and teaching aids. In December 1965 the first Chinese edition of the **Book of Mormon** was published. Translating this and other LDS **scriptures** was a special challenge for those involved. Through the 1970s a commendable **seminary** and **institute** program was developed, reflecting the strong testimony of the members and the value placed on literacy and **education** in Chinese culture.

The first all-Taiwan **area conference** took place in Taipei on 14 August 1975 with President **Spencer W. Kimball** presiding. More than 2,500 members and friends and 12 general authorities met in the Sun Yat-sen Memorial Hall. The first **stake** in the history of China—the Taiwan Taipei Stake—was organized by Elder Hinckley on 22 April 1976, with Chang I-Ch'ing as president.

The period between 1983 and 1984 was a historic time in the development of the Church in Taiwan. The first **temple** constructed in the Chinese realm was dedicated on 26 August 1984 by President Gordon B. Hinckley; the number of Church-built chapels doubled, and a fine seven-story building was purchased to house the mission headquarters, translation services, physical facilities, finances, and other functions. **Mission president** Paul Hyer oversaw these developments and later returned as **temple president**. In 1993 Wang Wei, the first Chinese to preside over a temple, was called. At the beginning of the year 2000 Taiwan had 26,805 members, 6 stakes, and 71 **wards** and **branches**.

SOURCE

Britsch, Lanier R. *From the East: The History of the Latter-day Saints in Asia, 1851–1996.* Salt Lake City: Deseret Book, 1998.

PAUL HYER

TALMAGE, JAMES E. The contributions of James E. Talmage to Church doctrine, practice, and policy rank him among the few **general authorities** who have substantially influenced and formulated Latter-day Saint theology. His *Articles of Faith* and *Jesus the Christ* remain among the few books published under the name of the Church rather than under the individual author. He was one of the Church's most gifted theologians, writing with clarity and power. As a respected geologist, he traveled widely throughout **Europe** and the **United States**, delivering papers in his area of speciality. He was also sent as a Church emissary to address numerous **conferences** on religion in general and Mormonism in particular.

Talmage was born 21 September 1862 in Hungerford, Berkshire, **England**, to James Joyce and Susannah Praeter Talmage. Soon after the **family** joined the Church, they emigrated to **Utah** in 1876, settling in Mapleton and **Provo**. Young James immediately enrolled at the **Brigham Young Academy** under the tutelage of **Karl G. Maeser**. Within a year he rose to the top of his class. His excellence as a scholar was soon recognized and rewarded with a teaching contract at the academy before his 17th birthday. Wishing to seek additional education, Talmage journeyed east in 1882 to enroll at Lehigh University in Bethlehem, **Pennsylvania**. After receiving his diploma there, he remained an additional year to study at Johns Hopkins University in Baltimore.

Upon his return to Utah, he resumed teaching at Brigham Young Academy and at the LDS college in **Salt Lake City**. He married May Booth in 1888 and was selected as president of the **University of Utah** in 1894. He remained in **education** and geology work until his call to the Quorum of the Twelve **Apostles** in 1911, when he filled the position vacated by the death of John Henry Smith. **Elder** Talmage became the fiftieth apostle of the Church in his fiftieth year. From 1924 to 1928, Elder Talmage presided over the **European Mission**, imparting a stature and prestige desperately needed at a time of rising **anti-Mormon** activities in Europe.

In addition to *Articles of Faith* and *Jesus the Christ,* Talmage wrote *The Vitality of Mormonism, The Story and Philosophy of Mormonism, The House of the Lord,* and *The Great Apostasy.* The **First Presidency** assigned him to revise the formats of a number of the **standard works** of the Church. In 1920 he corrected some minor errors in the **Book of Mormon,** the **Doctrine and Covenants,** and the **Pearl of Great Price.** In addition to the standard works, Talmage and **Joseph Fielding Smith** were assigned to rework and rewrite the *Ready References* for publication as an aid for scripture study. He wrote numerous **pamphlets** on a variety of topics. Throughout his career Talmage sought to reconcile science and religion through a number of lectures delivered to both **Mormon** and non-Mormon audiences. Talmage contributed substantially to our knowledge of the geology of Utah, researching and presenting papers at conventions all over the world.

With the advent of **radio** in the 1920s, Church leaders asked Talmage to deliver a number of addresses through this new mode of communication. It was during a series of these addresses that Talmage developed a severe streptococcus infection, from which he never recovered. He died 27 July 1933 in Salt Lake City.

SOURCES

Rowley, Dennis. "Inner Dialogue: James Talmage's Choice of Science as a Career, 1876–84." *Dialogue* 17 (Summer 1984): 112–30.

Talmage, James E. *The House of the Lord: A Study of Holy Sanctuaries Ancient and Modern.* Reprint of 1912 first edition with a new foreword by Harvard S. Heath. Salt Lake City: Signature Books, 1998.

Talmage, John R. *The Talmage Story: Life of James E. Talmage—Educator, Scientist, Apostle.* Salt Lake City: Bookcraft, 1972.

HARVARD HEATH

TANNER, ANNIE CLARK. In her autobiography, *A Mormon Mother* (1941), Annie Clark Tanner set the loneliness of one woman's **plural marriage** relationship against a backdrop of her wrestle with modernization.

Annie was born 24 September 1864 in Farmington, **Utah,** the second child of the second wife of Ezra T. Clark. In 1883 she became the second of six women who married educator **Joseph M. Tanner.** The memoir follows her relationship with Tanner from courtship through his death in 1927, painting him as emotionally and physically distant, leaving her to raise their 10 children alone.

Annie Clark Tanner died in Palo Alto, California, on 24 January 1942.

SOURCES

Embry, Jessie L. *Mormon Polygamous Families: Life in the Principle*. Salt Lake City: University of Utah Press, 1987.

Tanner, Annie Clark. *A Mormon Mother*. Salt Lake City: Deseret News Press, 1941.

JED L. WOODWORTH

TANNER, JOHN. An early Saint who blessed the Church with his monetary wealth and service, John Tanner was born 15 August 1778 in Hopkinton, **Rhode Island**, to Joshua and Thankful Tefft Tanner.

When he was 13 his **family** moved to Greenwich, **New York**. He married Tabitha Bentley, who bore a son, Elisha, on 23 March 1801. Following Tabitha's death, John married Lydia Stewart in the fall of 1801. From this union, 12 children were born—nine sons and three daughters.

In 1818 John moved to Bolton, near Lake George, New York. Through farming, dairying, stock-raising, and selling timber and other merchandise, he assembled a large estate. Lydia's death (31 May 1825) left John with a large family. He married Elizabeth Beswick 3 November 1825, and they had eight children.

Jared and Simeon Carter, who were serving as missionaries for the Church, contacted the Tanner family in September 1832. On 16 September Jared asked John if he thought his severely afflicted leg could be healed. He answered, "The Lord can heal it" (quoted in *Family*, 48). Jared laid his right hand on John Tanner's shoulder and commanded him in the name of the Lord to arise and walk, which he did.

The next day John Tanner and most of his family were baptized. When he joined the Church he made a commitment to be helpful and to sustain the **Prophet**. To do this he prepared to join the members at **Kirtland, Ohio**. He left Bolton on Christmas 1834, providing six wagons for his family and 10 more for other members.

They arrived in Kirtland around 20 January 1835. The following day John and his son Sidney met with the Prophet and the **high council**, lending **Joseph Smith** $2,000 to pay off the mortgage on the **temple** property and lending the high council $13,000. He also contributed to the temple-building fund and signed a $30,000 note for merchandise to help the **Saints** move to Kirtland.

John Tanner was one of few who came into the Church with great wealth, but he left Kirtland, Ohio, in April 1838 in a borrowed wagon to join the Saints in **Missouri**, having committed all of his resources to the Church.

His dedication to the Church continued through the trials of Missouri, **Illinois**, and during the exodus from **Nauvoo**. A few months before the **Martyrdom**, John returned the $2,000 note signed in Kirtland as a gift to the Prophet and was blessed by Joseph that he and his posterity would never beg for bread.

He and his family provided food and aid to the departing Saints both at Nauvoo (1846) and **Winter Quarters** (1847–48). He left Winter Quarters about 1 July 1848, arriving in **Utah** 29 October. They settled in South Cottonwood.

John Tanner died 13 April 1850 in Cottonwood, Salt Lake County, Utah. His wife, Elizabeth, joined Elders Lyman and Rich (1851) to establish the San Bernardino Mission. She died 8 June 1890 at Payson, Utah.

SOURCES

Tanner, George S. *John Tanner and His Family*. Salt Lake City: John Tanner Family Association, 1974.

Tanner, Maurice. *Descendants of John Tanner*. Salt Lake City: John Tanner Family Association, 1942.

WILMER W. TANNER

TANNER, JOSEPH M. Joseph Marion Tanner, husband of **Annie Clark Tanner** and other plural wives, was one of the most gifted teachers and writers in the Church in the late nineteenth and early twentieth centuries. Born in Payson, **Utah**, 26 March 1859, Tanner was a student and teacher at the **Brigham Young Academy** of **Provo** before serving a mission to **Europe** and the **Middle East** (1884–87), where he and **Jacob Spori** introduced the gospel in **Turkey** and organized the first Latter-day Saint congregations in **Palestine**.

After his mission Tanner served as principal of the **Brigham Young College** of Logan before leading a group of the first Latter-day Saint students to enroll at Harvard University in Boston in 1891. He studied law at Harvard until ill health forced his return to **Utah** in 1894. He was president of the Utah State Agricultural College from 1896 to 1900, and in 1901 he succeeded **Karl G. Maeser** as superintendent of Church schools.

In 1906 Tanner retired from the field of education, moved to

Canada, and took up farming near **Cardston, Alberta**. Over the next 15 years he wrote extensively for the *Improvement Era*. He died 19 August 1927 in Lethbridge, Alberta.

SOURCES

Tanner, J. M., to Charles W. Eliot. 14 April 1891. Joseph Marion Tanner Student Folder, Harvard University Archives, Cambridge, Massachusetts.

Ward, Margery W. *A Life Divided: The Biography of Joseph Marion Tanner, 1859–1927.* Salt Lake City: Publishers Press, 1980.

JED L. WOODWORTH

TANNER, N. ELDON. Nathan Eldon Tanner, a counselor to four presidents of the Church, was born 9 May 1898 in **Salt Lake City**. He was the first of eight children born to Nathan William Tanner and Sarah Edna Brown Tanner. His **family** settled in a tiny community called Aetna near **Cardston, Alberta, Canada**. In 1919 he accepted a teaching position and became the principal of a three-room school at Hill spring. There he fell in love with Sara Isabelle Merrill, one of the other teachers at the school, and they were married 20 December 1919. In 1929 his family moved to Cardston, where he served as principal of the public school and on the town council. In 1935 he was elected to the Alberta legislature and chosen as house speaker over a body of 63 members.

In 1936 he was appointed minister of lands and mines in the province of Alberta, where he helped develop the natural resources of Canada. He earned the nickname "Mr. Integrity" and helped Alberta become the first province free of public debt. After serving for 16 years in the government, he became president of Merrill Petroleum and director of the Toronto Dominion Bank of Canada. In 1954 the government asked him to oversee the construction of a $350 million 2,000-mile pipeline across Canada from Alberta to Montreal. It was completed in less than four years and was considered a project as significant as the transcontinental railroad.

President Tanner served as the first president of the Calgary **Stake** from 1953 to 1960. He was called as an **assistant to the Twelve** on 8 October 1960, ordained an **apostle** on 11 October 1962, and set apart as a second counselor in the First Presidency on 4 October 1963. President Tanner served as second counselor to Presidents **David O. McKay** (1963–70) and **Joseph Fielding Smith** (1970–72) and as first counselor to Presidents **Harold B. Lee** (1972–73) and **Spencer W. Kimball** (1973–82). Known for his business acumen and great integrity, which became his hallmark nationally and internationally, he served on boards of trustees for many businesses and universities. On 28 March 1979, the Salt Lake Chamber of Commerce awarded him the title "A Giant in Our City." He died 27 November 1982 in Salt Lake City.

SOURCES

"N. Eldon Tanner." *Church News,* 4 December 1982, 2.
"N. Eldon Tanner Dies." *Ensign* 13 (January 1983): 6–13.

BRIAN L. SMITH

TANZANIA. Tanzania is a republic of more than 30 million people located on the east coast of **Africa**. Its official languages are Swahili and English, and in 1999 its major religions were Christianity (45%), Islam (35%), and tribal beliefs (20%).

D. E. Tapie Rohm Jr. and his **family**, Church members from **Los Angeles, California**, visited Dar es Salaam, Tanzania, from 1988–89, while Brother Rohm was employed as a Fulbright scholar. They were among the first to hold Church **meetings** in the country.

One of the first Tanzanians to join the Church was Robert Israel Muhile. While working and studying in Cairo, **Egypt**, Robert attended his first Latter-day Saint Church meeting on Christmas Day 1990. He was taught by missionaries and was soon baptized. In May 1991, after being ordained an **elder**, he returned to Tanzania. Being isolated from the Church, Robert gained permission from the **Kenya** Nairobi **Mission** president to hold his own personal **sacrament** meeting each Sabbath. When Elder Lervae and Sister Joyce Cahoon were assigned to open the work in Dar es Salaam, Robert acted as a translator so they could teach the gospel to Swahili-speaking people.

In July 1991 Tanzania was included, along with Kenya and **Uganda**, in the Kenya Nairobi Mission. Several **Saints** from Tanzania traveled to Nairobi, Kenya, on 17 February 1998 to hear President **Gordon B. Hinckley** speak. By the beginning of the year 2000 there were 406 members living in 3 branches.

SOURCES

Hart, John L. "Nations Will 'Never Be Same' after Lengthy African Trip." *Church News,* 28 February 1998, 3.
LeBaron, E. Dale. "Pioneers in East Africa." *Ensign* 24 (October 1994): 20–24.
McDonald, Hiram. "Church Is Growing in East Africa: Kenya Mission Branches into Three Nations." *Church News,* 6 September 1997, 6.

Middleton, John, ed. *Encyclopedia of Africa South of the Sahara.* 4 vols. New York: Macmillan Library Reference USA, 1997. 4:209–16.

1999–2000 Church Almanac. Salt Lake City: Deseret News, 1998. 394–95.

Oral histories of early Church converts collected by E. Dale LeBaron. Copies at BYU Library, Provo, Utah; LDS Church Historical Library, Salt Lake City, Utah.

E. DALE LEBARON

TAYLOR, ELMINA SHEPHARD. Elmina Shephard Taylor was the first general president of the Young Ladies **Mutual Improvement Association** (**Young Women**). She was born 12 September 1830 in Middlefield, **New York.** Converting to the Church in upstate New York, Elmina and her husband, George Hamilton Taylor, joined the **Utah Saints** in 1859. When President **John Taylor** organized the three general auxiliary presidencies in June 1880, he called Elmina to serve as the president of the YLMIA. One of her challenges was to bring unity and uniformity to the organization, since the earlier ward retrenchment associations had each planned their own programs. The YLMIA published the *Young Woman's Journal*, designated Tuesdays as Mutual night, printed courses of study, and established traveling libraries. Elmina died in office 6 December 1904 in **Salt Lake City.**

SOURCES

A Century of Sisterhood: Chronological Collage, 1869–1969. Salt Lake City: YWMIA, 1969.

Gates, Susa Young. *History of the Young Ladies Mutual Improvement Association.* Salt Lake City: Deseret News, 1911.

Peterson, Janet, and LaRene Gaunt. *Keepers of the Flame: General Presidents of the Young Women.* Salt Lake City: Deseret Book, 1993.

JANET PETERSON

TAYLOR, JOHN. John Taylor, the third president of the Church, was born in Milnthorpe, **England**, 1 November 1808. As a boy he showed unusual spiritual qualities, sometimes hearing sweet, angelic music as if rendered by a heavenly choir. John's parents, James and Agnes, had him baptized as an infant into the Church of England and saw that he was trained in its catechism. Finding the cold forms of this church uncongenial with his spiritual temperament, however, he joined the Methodist church at age 16 and soon became an exhorter. Once while on assignment, he stopped in the middle of the road and, turning to his companion, said he had a strong impression to go to **America** and preach the gospel.

In 1832, after acquiring skills as a wood turner, he booked passage to **Canada**. During the Atlantic crossing, his ship encountered a terrible storm. John went topside, and despite the violent winds and turbulence, he was perfectly calm, convinced he would arrive safely.

John settled in Toronto, Canada, where he opened a turner shop and became active in the local Methodist Church. An attractive member, Leonora Cannon, accepted his proposal only after having a vivid dream which confirmed the propriety of it. They were married 28 January 1833. Three years later, 9 May 1836, they were converted to the **Mormon** Church and baptized by **Parley P. Pratt**.

Soon after, John traveled to **Kirtland, Ohio**, to meet **Joseph Smith**. Despite the furor against Joseph caused by the failure of the **Kirtland Safety Society**, John received confirmation of his prophetic status and openly defended him in the **temple**. On the way home, while with friends at Niagara Falls, John spoke in **tongues** and had the spiritual impression he would be called as an **apostle**. A few months later, he received a letter from Joseph Smith advising that he had been called to the Twelve.

At the **Prophet's** direction, the Taylors soon moved to **Missouri**. There on 6 October 1838, John was sustained an apostle. On 19 December 1838, he was ordained and set apart as a member of the Twelve. That same day a report was filed in the Missouri legislature, seeking **redress** for the losses suffered by the **Saints**. A similar report was later submitted to the U.S. Congress. John Taylor was a chief author of both reports. While neither brought the requested relief, they showed his writing skill and foreshadowed his role as a prominent Church author and editor.

Settling in **Montrose, Iowa**, after the expulsion from Missouri, John left with **Wilford Woodruff** on 8 August 1839 for their mission to England. In **New York**, John lived with Parley P. Pratt as he awaited passage to England. Embarking 19 December 1839 on the packet ship *Oxford*, John arrived in **Liverpool, England**, 23 days later. During 18 months in Great Britain, John helped convert many, including his brother-in-law, George Cannon, and George's wife, Ann Quayle, as well as their three children, among whom was 12-year-old **George Quayle Cannon**, who later became John Taylor's counselor in the **First Presidency**.

Back in **Nauvoo**, John was active in Church and civic affairs, including service as an editor of the *Times and Seasons* and the *Nauvoo Neighbor*. This was the beginning of a notable career as an editor of

Church **periodicals**. While in **Europe** in the early 1850s, he helped establish a French language paper, *L'Etoile du Deseret*, and a German language paper, *Zions Panier*. Later, while living in **New York City**, Elder Taylor was editor of *The Mormon*, a paper founded to counter adverse publicity resulting from the public announcement that the Church practiced **plural marriage**. Elder Taylor's most significant contributions to Church literature were his authorship of *The Government of God* and *The Mediation and Atonement*, often regarded as Latter-day Saint classics.

The public announcement about plural marriage had special meaning for John Taylor, since after he returned from **England**, he had followed the direction of Joseph Smith and had married Leonora's cousin Elizabeth Kaighin as a plural wife. Later he married five other wives: Jane Ballantyne, Mary Ann Oakley, Sophia Whitaker, Harriet Whitaker, and Margaret Young. Despite the demands of plural marriage, the Taylor family lived in harmony.

In 1844 when Joseph Smith began his **presidential campaign**, John Taylor was appointed manager with **Willard Richards** as his assistant. These two members of the Twelve had remained in Nauvoo while others of their **quorum** were campaigning. They were with Joseph and **Hyrum** in **Carthage Jail** on 27 June 1844 when the Smiths were martyred. Elder Taylor was hit with five balls, one of which might have killed him had it not been stopped by a watch in his vest pocket.

After the expulsion from Nauvoo, the Taylor family joined the **exodus**. John had a brief detour when at the **Missouri River** he and **Elders** Parley P. Pratt and **Orson Hyde** were sent to England to straighten out problems among the local leaders. When he and Elder Pratt returned, they brought valuable scientific instruments needed by the **Brigham Young** Company for the trek west. Elder Taylor led a company, which arrived in the **Salt Lake Valley** 3 October 1847.

Except for his mission to Europe and his years in New York, Elder Taylor remained in the West the rest of his life, active in building up the Church and its people.

When Brigham Young died on 29 August 1877, John Taylor became the leader of the Church. At first he led in his capacity as president of the Twelve, since the reorganization of the First Presidency was delayed. He was sustained officially as the third president of the Church at a solemn assembly on 10 October 1880.

The 1880s were years of trial for President Taylor and the Church. Because the **antipolygamy** laws had been upheld in 1879 and because other restrictive laws against the **Saints** were passed later, President

Taylor and other leaders had to live **underground**, being forced to move from place to place to avoid detection. In addition to his advancing age, lack of both exercise and a suitable diet hastened his death, which occurred on 25 July 1887 while he was a guest in the home of Thomas F. Roueche in Kaysville, **Utah**. Memorial services were held in the **Salt Lake Tabernacle**. He was interred in the **Salt Lake City** Cemetery. Mourning friends believed that what was begun by enemies in Carthage was finished in Utah.

SOURCES

Gibbons, Francis M. *John Taylor: Mormon Philosopher, Prophet of God.* Salt Lake City: Deseret Book, 1985.

Roberts, B. H. *The Life of John Taylor.* Salt Lake City: Bookcraft, 1963.

FRANCIS M. GIBBONS

TAYLOR, JOHN W. John Whittaker Taylor, a member of the **Quorum of the Twelve Apostles,** was the son of President **John Taylor.** Born 15 May 1858 in **Provo, Utah,** John served missions in the western and southern **United States,** as well as **Canada** and **Mexico,** baptizing more than 250 converts. As a representative of the Church, he spoke with the president of the United States (**Grover Cleveland**), President Porfirio Diaz of Mexico, and Premier John M. McDonald of Canada. Unfortunately, he could not align himself with the presidency of the Church and other members of the Twelve concerning the cessation of the practice of **plural marriage.** In October 1905 he resigned from the Quorum of the Twelve and on 29 March 1911 was excommunicated from the Church. He died 10 October 1916 in **Salt Lake City**.

SOURCES

Flake, Lawrence R. *Prophets and Apostles of the Last Dispensation.* Provo, Utah: Religious Studies Center, Brigham Young University, 2001. 407–9.

"John W. Taylor." Salt Lake City: *Improvement Era* 20 (November 1916): 93.

Lives of Our Leaders. Salt Lake City: Deseret News, 1901. 175.

LAWRENCE R. FLAKE

TEA. See WORD OF WISDOM.

TEACHER. Those who hold the office of teacher in the **Aaronic Priesthood** are to watch over the Church constantly; strengthen members; eliminate iniquity, hard feelings, lying, backbiting, and evil speaking; insure that the Church holds regular meetings; take the lead in meetings in the absence of a higher authority; and see that members perform their duties (D&C 20). A teachers **quorum**, led by a president from its own ranks, can have up to 24 members (D&C 107:62–63, 86).

During the nineteenth century, almost all ordained teachers were adults. The first in this dispensation were **Hiram Page**, 30, and **Christian Whitmer**, 32. From 1830 on, ordained teachers visited in members' homes (much as do today's **home teachers**), settled disputes, helped the needy, obtained needed resources, and handled some cases of Church discipline. In pioneer **Utah** a **ward's** basic officers were bishoprics and teachers—then called block teachers or ward teachers. During the **Brigham Young** period, almost all believing adult males held the **Melchizedek Priesthood**, so teachers quorums had to be filled by those men serving as *acting* teachers.

In 1908 the Church called for young men ages 15 through 17 to be the ordained teachers, solving the *acting* and *ordained* teacher duality by designating the monthly visiting work as "ward teaching," a ward calling not linked to any particular priesthood office. A teacher's duties did not include **sacrament** preparation until 1933. **Women** and custodians commonly did that task before then. By the end of the twentieth century, ordained teachers were boys ages 14 and 15, whose main work was to do home teaching, prepare the sacrament table, usher at **meetings**, and help with **deacons'** work when needed.

SOURCES

"Aaronic Priesthood Suggestions." *Improvement Era* 33 (March 1930): 349.

"Assignments for Ordained Teachers." *Improvement Era* 36 (December 1833): 868.

Hartley, William G. "From Men to Boys: LDS Aaronic Priesthood Offices, 1829–1996." *Journal of Mormon History* 22 (Spring 1996): 80–136.

Palmer, Lee A. *Aaronic Priesthood through the Centuries.* Salt Lake City: Deseret Book, 1964.

WILLIAM G. HARTLEY

TEACHER TRAINING. Formal training of Church lay teachers began with an evening lecture series by **Karl G. Maeser** to **Sunday School** workers in June 1892. Later that year a Sunday School Teacher Training class was held at **Brigham Young Academy**. Ultimately, **stakes** sent men and **women** there for a 20-week course to prepare them to train teachers locally. With Church **growth**, it became necessary to conduct teacher training solely on a stake and **ward** basis with manuals from head-quarters. In 1962 the Teacher Development Program, taught during Sunday School in 11-week courses, was managed first by Sunday School, then by **priesthood** leaders under Church correlation. In 1994 simplification reduced the course materials to a 20-page booklet reviewing effective teaching and shortened the course to eight weeks. This allowed the rendering of teacher training into multiple languages, simultaneously reducing the amount of material to be translated. At the October 1999 **general conference, Elder Dallin H. Oaks** announced initiatives in teaching, including a new 10-page booklet that emphasized every Church leader's role as a teacher; separate quarterly teacher improvement meetings for teachers of children, youth, and adult classes; and a 12-lesson course to be taught once a year in Sunday School.

Sources

Clark, James R., comp. *Messages of the First Presidency of The Church of Jesus Christ of Latter-day Saints.* 6 vols. Salt Lake City: Bookcraft, 1965–75. 5:184.

Hedquist, Steven A. "The Teacher Training Program Administered by the Sunday School of The Church of Jesus Christ of Latter-day Saints." Master's thesis, Brigham Young University, 1976.

Monson, Thomas S. Conference Report (October 1970): 107–8.

John P. Livingstone

TEASDALE, GEORGE. "Thus saith the Lord to the Twelve, and to the **Priesthood** and people of my Church: Let my servants George Teasdale and **Heber J. Grant** be appointed to fill the vacancies in the Twelve . . . for I have a great work to perform" (Clark, 348). So spoke the Lord in a **revelation** given to President **John Taylor** on the morning of 13 October 1882. George Teasdale, a native of Britain, had joined the Church 30 years before in London after having his interest kindled by an **anti-Mormon** tract published by the Church of England. Born in London 8 December 1831 and educated at the University of London, he taught school and was a member of both the Salt Lake Dramatical Association and the **Tabernacle Choir.**

Teasdale's extensive missionary service included two separate assignments to his homeland, once as president of the **European Mission.** He also went on a colonizing assignment to **Mexico** and served **missions** to the **Indian** territory and the southern states. His career in the mercantile business included supervision of **Brigham Young**'s store, the general **tithing** store, and **ZCMI.** As a member of the **Quorum** of the Twelve

Apostles, he traveled widely among the **stakes** of the Church, and his simplicity and sincerity endeared him to the **Saints**. Elder Teasdale died 9 June 1907 in Salt Lake City at age 75, after serving 24 years as an apostle.

SOURCES

Cowley, Matthias F., comp. *Prophets and Patriarchs.* Chattanooga, Tenn.: Ben E. Rich, 1902. 260–68.

Flake, Lawrence R. *Prophets and Apostles of the Last Dispensation.* Provo, Utah: Religious Studies Center, Brigham Young University, 2001. 403–5.

Lives of Our Leaders. Salt Lake City: Deseret News, 1901. 141.

LAWRENCE R. FLAKE

TEICHERT, MINERVA. Minerva Bernetta Kohlhepp Teichert (1888–1976) was a gifted Latter-day **Saint** artist who captured the essence of her faith and the beauties of the earth with an inimitable style and insight. Carefully trained in the finest art schools in the East, Minerva produced paintings that were exhibited across the world in **temples**, meeting halls, museums, LDS universities, institutions, private collections, public offices and famous buildings. Her illustrations are featured in commercial publications as well as Church literature, magazines, training manuals, and organizational resource centers. Her paintings include *Indian Captives at Night* (1936), *Madonna at Dawn* (1935), *Not Alone* (1920), *Miracle of the Gulls* (1935), *Christ with Mary and Martha* (1941), *Rescue of the Lost Lamb* (1940), and *Queen Esther* (1939). These works represent her focus on the American **Indian** and the ministry of **Jesus Christ**. Minerva's critically acclaimed **Book of Mormon** murals have been exhibited in several museums. In 1997, a massive undertaking to restore and appropriately frame these murals culminated in an exhibit at the Museum of Art at Brigham Young University. At the end of the twentieth century, public interest in Minerva's painting was increasing dramatically.

Minerva Kohlhepp was born 28 August 1888 in **Ogden, Utah**. From the time she was 13 years old, she helped her parents and siblings financially, as well as supporting herself as a painter, schoolteacher, and costumed western entertainer, doing rope tricks and Indian war dances in **New York**. In 1917 she married Herman Adolphe Teichert, and the couple was sealed after Herman's conversion to the Church in 1933. They reared five children and worked together in ranching and a dairy business in Cokeville, **Wyoming**.

Although Minerva always insisted that her children were her

masterpiece, a rival might be the stunning 60x27x24-foot wrap-around mural in the World Room of the **Manti Temple**. Teichert was 60 when, with the help of a young apprentice, Frank Stevens, she completed the project in 27 days over a seven-week period.

Her deep love of the Lord manifested itself in her paintings, her family, the Church classes she taught, and her influence with people. Minerva Teichert firmly declared that not only was her talent a gift from God but it was a commission to paint scriptural stories so that busy people could easily understand the word of God. She died 3 May 1976 in **Provo, Utah**.

SOURCE

Cannon, Elaine. *Minerva!* Salt Lake City: Bookcraft, 1997.

ELAINE CANNON

TELEGRAPH. See DESERET TELEGRAPH.

TELEVISION. See BROADCASTING.

TEMPERANCE MOVEMENT. The growth of temperance sentiment and the organization of temperance societies in the **United States** in the 1820s and 1830s were understandable responses to excessive drinking among Americans. Temperance fervor was notable in the state of **Ohio**, including the area of **Kirtland**, where many Latter-day Saints lived in the 1830s. The Kirtland Temperance Society, organized in 1830, had more than 160 members. Few Church members likely belonged to the Temperance Society, even though they agreed with its objectives. One significant result of temperance agitation in Kirtland was the closure of the Kirtland distillery just four weeks before **Joseph Smith** received the **Word of Wisdom** (D&C 89).

This **revelation**, received in February 1833, was among other things an inspired temperance statement. With its reception and, more particularly, its stipulation prohibiting the drinking of alcoholic beverages, believing Latter-day Saints had their own temperance guide—a meaningful and enduring one because of the prophetic authority that underlay it.

SOURCES

Arrington, Leonard J. "An Economic Interpretation of the 'Word of Wisdom.'" *BYU Studies* 1 (Winter 1959): 37–49.

Peterson, Paul H. "An Historical Analysis of the Word of Wisdom." Master's thesis, Brigham Young University, 1972.

PAUL H. PETERSON

TEMPLE DEDICATORY PRAYERS. Temple dedicatory prayers are inspired petitions and supplications that consecrate temples to the Lord before the commencement of **ordinance** work. These formal prayers contain the highest aspirations and explanations of the doctrines of exaltation. They are often an expression of the commitment of those who seek to be worthy of entering the sacred temple. Each prayer ultimately dedicates the building and the people to the Lord.

The oldest dedicatory prayer found in **scripture** is that of Solomon's Temple (1 Kgs. 8:22–54). No other such prayers are recorded in the biblical text. On 27 March 1836, the first temple of this dispensation was dedicated in **Kirtland, Ohio**. That prayer was given by direct revelation to **Joseph Smith** and was read by him at the dedication. The prayer is now canonized and published as section 109 in the **Doctrine & Covenants**. It has served as a model for all subsequent prayers. All dedicatory prayers since that of the Kirtland Temple have been written by someone holding apostolic authority. During dedication ceremonies the same prayer is repeated in subsequent sessions to accommodate all who wish to attend.

Once dedicated, the temple becomes officially "The House of the Lord" and a place where he can reveal himself to the people (Ex. 25:8, 22). At temple dedications many gifts of the spirit, including **visions**, have been witnessed by those in attendance. As people continue to attend the temple and sanctify themselves, they are promised inspiration and blessings from the Lord.

Common themes of latter-day dedicatory prayers include references to sanctifying and protecting the building and the **Saints**; **missionary work** among the living and the dead; and mention of Church leaders past and present, **priesthood** covenants, and local historical events past, present, and future. Each temple prayer collectively expresses the Latter-day Saints' testimony that life beyond the grave is real and that everyone can help to accomplish the divine work of God.

By November 1999, 65 temples had been dedicated in this last dispensation. President **Gordon B. Hinckley** set as a goal for the Church to have 100 temples by the year 2000. He has dedicated more temples than all other leaders combined in this dispensation.

SOURCES

Cowan, Richard O. *Temples to Dot the Earth*. Salt Lake City: Bookcraft, 1989.

Haycock, D. Arthur. "LDS Temple Dedications." *Encyclopedia of Mormonism*. Edited by Daniel H. Ludlow. 4 vols. New York: Macmillan, 1992. 4:1455–56.

Hinckley, Gordon B. "This Peaceful House of God." *Ensign* 23 (May 1993): 72–75.

BRIAN L. SMITH

TEMPLE GARMENT. See GARMENT.

TEMPLE MARRIAGE. See MARRIAGE.

TEMPLE PRESIDENT AND MATRON. Every operating **temple** is presided over by a president and a matron (husband and wife) appointed by the **First Presidency**, usually for three years. The president and his **counselors** are **high priests**. The matron's two assistants are usually the wives of the president's counselors. The president, assisted by the matron, sets the spiritual tone and is administratively responsible for all temple activities.

The principal work of the temple is performing and recording sacred **ordinances** and covenants of the gospel of **Jesus Christ** that are essential for the salvation of the living and the deceased. These ordinances can be performed only in a temple. Since the ordinances are equally necessary for men and **women**, the matron's role is absolutely essential, for without her the work could not be provided for women.

The president and his counselors set apart the necessary personnel to operate the temple facilities. In addition to ordinances, the president must see that everything necessary for the function of the temple is provided.

ROBERT J. MATTHEWS

TEMPLEREADY. TempleReady is a computer program which, by checking the Ordinance Index, assists LDS Church members in determining whether **temple ordinances** have already been performed for individuals they are interested in. It allows users to type names directly into it or to import names from a diskette from a **genealogy** program, such as **Personal Ancestral File**. TempleReady is not a database of names.

The program not only determines what ordinances may be done for deceased individuals but also checks the Ordinance Index and displays information if temple ordinances have been performed for a particular person. After LDS Church members have used this program, temple submission disks may then be taken or mailed to a Latter-day Saint temple for proxy ordinances. TempleReady also prints reports showing the status of temple work for the names entered.

Kip Sperry

TEMPLE RECOMMEND. An LDS **temple** recommend is a written verification of a member's good standing and an authorization allowing its holder to enter and worship in any operating LDS temple. A valid temple recommend is issued by an authorized **priesthood** officer (usually a member of a bishopric or **branch** presidency) after a worthiness interview has been conducted. The recommend is countersigned by the Church member as well as a member of that person's **stake**, **district**, or **mission presidency**, who conducts a second interview. Church officers are charged with the responsibility of ensuring that no unworthy person enters the temple.

Latter-day Saints have always regarded their temples as possessing the highest degree of sanctity and holiness; they are the Lord's houses. In a **revelation** given to **Joseph Smith** in 1833, the Lord said that if his people would build a house unto him, and would not allow any unclean thing to come into it so that it remained undefiled, his glory would rest upon it, and the pure in heart who entered it would "see God" (D&C 97:15–16). In 1836 at the dedication of the **Kirtland Temple**, the first in this final dispensation, the **Prophet** Joseph Smith prayed that the temple would be "sanctified and consecrated to be holy," so that the Lord's "holy presence [could] be continually" in his house (D&C 109:12, 20). All other temples have been similarly dedicated. Therefore, all members of the Church, eight years of age or older, must possess a valid recommend to enter any LDS temple and participate in sacred **ordinances**. The recommend certifies that the bearer is striving to live with exactness the principles of honesty, integrity, chastity, virtue, and loyalty to the Church and its leaders.

The modern practice of issuing certificates of worthiness to enter the house of the Lord follows an ancient pattern of ensuring covenant worthiness among those associated with the temple in Jerusalem. The prophet Ezekiel declared: "Thus saith the Lord God; No stranger, uncircumcised in heart, nor uncircumcised in flesh, shall enter into my sanctuary, of any stranger that is among the children of Israel" (Ezek. 44:9). In this dispensation, the criteria for determining worthiness developed over time, reflecting the shifts in concern over practices and emphasis of certain gospel principles in daily living. Similarly, written authorizations permitting entrance to the temple evolved over time. There was no centrally produced recommend form until about 1922, when the Church published the first recommend book, which included 12 instructional items as well as space for the applicant to answer seven specific questions. Up to that point, authorizations were first oral, determined by personal acquaintance and observation by Church leaders, and then handwritten. Once the Church was well established in Utah, some **bishops** had recommend forms printed locally. Most letters of recommendation were countersigned by the president of the Church until 1891, when President **Wilford Woodruff** delegated responsibility to determine worthiness to bishops and **stake presidents**.

SOURCE

Kimball, Edward L. "The History of LDS Temple Admission Standards." *Journal of Mormon History* 24 (Spring 1998): 135–76.

ANDREW C. SKINNER

TEMPLES AND TEMPLE WORK. In contrast to the Church's thousands of chapels, which house regular worship services and are open to the public, temples are buildings where sacred **priesthood ordinances** are solemnized, and they are open only to those judged worthy by their local ecclesiastical leaders. In these holy sanctuaries, instructions and blessings are received that Latter-day Saints regard as necessary for exaltation in the highest degree of the celestial kingdom. From the beginning, worshippers have felt the need to get out of the world and into sacred places, where they can turn their thoughts to more spiritual and eternal values. To this end, they erect temples.

Ancient peoples thought of temples as places where heaven and earth came together, places of contact between **God** and man. The portable tabernacle constructed by **Moses** served this function (Ex. 25:8, 22). Old Testament sanctuaries were also where prescribed sacrifices and other holy ordinances took place (D&C 124:38).

Latter-day Restoration of Temple Service

In 1831, just one year after the **organization of the Church**, a revelation directed **Joseph Smith** and other **elders** to travel to western Missouri (D&C 52:3–5). Here the Lord revealed that a temple should be built at the future "center place" of **Zion**, or the **New Jerusalem**, located at **Independence**, **Jackson County**, Missouri, (D&C 57:1–3, 84:2–4). Joseph Smith placed a cornerstone on 3 August 1831, but the Saints' expulsion from the area two years later prevented any further construction on the anticipated temple.

Meanwhile, late in 1832, the Lord directed the Saints to "establish a house" at **Kirtland, Ohio** (D&C 88:119), and in June of the following year revealed the basic plan for the new temple. It was to be used for general worship and instruction (D&C 95:13–17). Construction began with the placement of cornerstones on 23 July 1833 and went forward in the face of severe difficulties. Dedication of the **Kirtland Temple** on 27 March 1836 was the high point of a season of unusually rich spiritual outpourings. One week later, on 3 April 1836, the Savior, Moses, **Elias**, and **Elijah** appeared in the temple, the latter restoring the sealing powers by which ordinances performed on earth are bound in heaven (D&C 110; Matt. 16:19).

When the faithful were forced to flee from **Ohio** early in 1838, they gathered with the Saints at **Far West** in northern Missouri. Here a revelation directed that another temple be built, again for general worship (D&C 115:8). Once more cornerstones were laid, but the Saints' exodus following Governor **Lilburn Boggs's extermination order** thwarted any further construction.

As the Saints established a new city at **Nauvoo, Illinois**, the Lord revealed such basic temple ordinances as **baptism for the dead**, the **endowment**, and the sealing, or eternal **marriage**, of couples. His directive to build the **Nauvoo Temple** indicated it was to be a place of revelation as well as the setting for sacred ordinances (D&C 124:27–30). Hence, both functions of ancient temples were restored. Despite the **martyrdom** of the **Prophet** Joseph Smith and beginnings of the **pioneers'** westward exodus, temple construction was pushed forward. When individuals used some of the partially completed rooms for eating, sleeping, and even recreation, a need was felt to reserve the temple for more sacred purposes. This may have been the origin of requiring **temple recommends** for admission. The temple was completed and dedicated in 1846, after most of the Saints had left the area.

Within four days of the pioneers' arrival in the **Salt Lake Valley**,

Brigham Young identified the site for the future temple. Construction of the **Salt Lake Temple** took 40 years, during which time three others were completed. At the time of the **St. George Temple** dedication in 1877, vicarious endowments for the dead were inaugurated. This was the last temple built with two large auditoriums, one above the other, designed for general **meetings**. The next three temples—**Logan** (1884), **Manti** (1888), and Salt Lake (1893)—replaced the lower hall with specific rooms designed for presenting the endowment and other ordinances. Because the Kirtland and Nauvoo Temples had been lost, at the end of the nineteenth century the Church had only four operating temples—all in **Utah**.

Four additional temples were added during the first half of the 20th century in **Hawaii**, **Alberta**, **Arizona**, and **Idaho**. These omitted the upper **solemn assembly** room and retained only the facilities specifically for ordinances.

Expansion of Temple Building

The number of temples doubled during the third quarter of the 20th century. The **Los Angeles Temple** (1956) was the largest built to that point.

Meanwhile, Church leaders continued to encourage Saints to remain in their homelands and build up the Church there. A new interpretation was given to the "**gathering**" with the decision to build temples overseas. The **Swiss Temple** (1955) employed a new audio-visual method of presenting the endowment instructions; under the direction of President **David O. McKay**, this new process was developed by **Gordon B. Hinckley**, then an employee at Church headquarters. Temples at **Oakland**, **Ogden**, **Provo**, and **Washington, D.C.**, provided multiple presentation rooms to allow more than one group to receive the endowment at once.

During the concluding decades of the century the pace of temple construction accelerated substantially. In 1980 an unprecedented number of seven new temples at once was announced, with nine more the following year. In all, 26 temples were dedicated during the 1980s, including one at **Freiberg**, Germany (1985), then behind the "Iron Curtain." For the first time, there were temples on every continent. Near the end of the decade, the milestone of 100 million cumulative endowments for the dead was passed.

Even before becoming president of the Church (1995), Gordon B. Hinckley, as a **counselor** in the **First Presidency**, set the record of having dedicated more temples than any other person in the present dispensation. In 1997 he disclosed plans to build smaller temples for the benefit of Saints in isolated areas. The next year he announced the goal of dedicating at least thirty such temples by the end of the year 2000. At the end of 1999 there were 68 temples in service, ahead of the pace needed to achieve President Hinckley's goal of 100 operating temples by the end of the year 2000.

With the explosion in temple building worldwide have come corresponding advances in genealogy or **family history**. The introduction of microfilming during the late 1930s enabled records from all over the world to be gathered into the **Family History Library** in Salt Lake City. Beginning in the 1960s, computers have accelerated the organizing and making available of genealogical information. These developments enabled more than three thousand local **Family History Centers**™ to be established around the world. In 1999 the Church created a family history web page, which immediately became one of the most popular sites on the Internet.

SOURCES

Cowan, Richard O. *Temples to Dot the Earth.* Springville, Utah: Cedar Fort, 1997.
Lundwall, N. B. *Temples of the Most High.* Salt Lake City: Bookcraft, 1947.

RICHARD O. COWAN

TEMPLE SQUARE. Salt Lake City was organized around a 10-acre block known today as Temple Square, bounded by West Temple, North Temple, Main, and South Temple Streets. It was not only the religious and social center of the community but also the geographical focal point of **Deseret** and its capital. At the southeast corner of Temple Square, surveyors established the Great Salt Lake "Base and Meridian." The survey point was used as the base reference point for survey work done in the region.

During more than 150 years of history, efforts have been made to beautify and improve Temple Square. As a result, many structures were razed or moved, including three outdoor meeting places known as boweries during the nineteenth century. Other important nonextant buildings once located on Temple Square include the adobe **Tabernacle** (dedicated 1852), the **Endowment House** (dedicated 1855), and the Bureau of Information (dedicated 1902). An old **pioneer** log home placed on Temple Square in 1915 was moved in the 1980s to the block west of Temple Square.

Today on Temple Square, visitors find the famous Tabernacle (dedicated 1875); the beautiful Assembly Hall (dedicated 1882); the magnificent **Salt Lake Temple** (dedicated 1893) and its annex (completed 1966); the North Visitors' center (dedicated 1963), which houses a replica of the 11-foot *Christus* by Danish sculptor Bertel Thorvaldsen; and the South Visitors' center (dedicated 1978). Additionally, there are some important monuments and markers, including the Base and Meridian marker (dedicated 1932); **Relief Society** Memorial Campanile with the **Nauvoo** bell (dedicated 1966); **Seagull Monument** (dedicated 1913); **Handcart** Pioneer Monument (1947); **Aaronic Priesthood** Monument (dedicated 1958); **Joseph Smith** and **Hyrum Smith** statues, originally made for the niches of the Salt Lake Temple and later placed on the grounds in 1911; **Three Witnesses** Monument (dedicated 1927); a small bronze and granite sundial donated by **Young Women** of the Church in 1940; and the flagpole with scriptures (dedicated 1968). During the Christmas season, workers place thousands of lights in the trees and bushes on Temple Square—creating one of the most beautiful Christmas displays in North **America**. In 1999, Salt Lake City sold the block-long portion of Main Street between North Temple and South Temple Streets to the Church, and the Church turned the area into a pedestrian mall connecting Temple Square to the block east. Although the Church's annual and semiannual **general conference** meetings moved from the Tabernacle on Temple Square to the **Conference Center** in April 2000, Temple Square still remains a place of historical and spiritual significance and is visited by some 5 million people each year.

SOURCE

Rasmus, Carol J. "Temple Square." *Encyclopedia of Mormonism.* Edited by Daniel H. Ludlow. 4 vols. New York: Macmillan, 1992. 4:1465–68.

RICHARD NEITZEL HOLZAPFEL

TEMPLE SQUARE CHORALE AND TRAINING SCHOOL.

Organized in 1999, the **Temple Square** Chorale replaced the **Mormon** Youth Chorus and, together with the Training School, is designed to prepare singers to join the Mormon **Tabernacle Choir**, enhance the quality of the Tabernacle Choir's performances, and serve as a valuable **music-education** experience. Church members between the ages of 25 and 55 who are interested in singing with the Tabernacle Choir are eligible to audition and serve in the chorale and training school. The chorale is composed of both new applicants and selected, experienced members of the Tabernacle Choir who rotate through the chorale's school until all have had the experience. Singers who successfully complete service with the chorale become eligible to audition for the Tabernacle Choir. The Chorale and Training School, originally under the direction of Mack Wilberg, runs two 11-week cycles each year.

The Mormon Tabernacle Choir, Temple Square Chorale and Training School, and the **Orchestra at Temple Square** were originally united under the direction of a Church-service president, Wendell Smoot, and a full-time professional music director, Craig Jessop.

LLOYD D. NEWELL

TEMPLE WORK. See TEMPLES AND TEMPLE WORK.

TENNESSEE. **Missionary work** began in Tennessee as early as 1834. **Elder David W. Patten** was one of the earliest missionaries and was followed by **Wilford Woodruff**, **Abraham O. Smoot**, and **Warren Parrish**. Significant success and growth were experienced there from an early date, and new converts were encouraged to emigrate from their homes and join larger bodies of Latter-day Saints in **Ohio**, **Missouri**, **Illinois**, and later **Utah**.

Tennessee was the site of intense persecution against missionaries and members during the 1870s and 1880s. The most significant example was at Cane Creek, Lewis County. In what later became known as the **Cane Creek Massacre** (Mormon Massacre to locals), two missionaries, two local members who attempted to defend them, and one of the mob were killed. The mother of the two local martyrs was severely wounded—sustaining an injury from which she never fully recovered.

Tennessee was included in the **Southern States Mission** at its organization in 1876, headquarters being first in Nashville and later transferred to Chattanooga (1882). Church population in the year 2000 reached 31,104 in nine **stakes**. In the year 2000 two temples were dedicated in Tennessee—Memphis on 23 April and Nashville on 21 May.

SOURCES

Berrett, LaMar C. "History of the Southern States Mission, 1831–1861." Master's thesis, Brigham Young University, 1960.

Jenson, Andrew. *Encyclopedic History of The Church of Jesus Christ of Latter-day Saints.* Salt Lake City: Deseret News, 1941.

1999–2000 Church Almanac. Salt Lake City: Deseret News, 1998. 240–41.

David F. Boone

TENORIO, HORACIO A. Within six years of his baptism, Horacio Antonio Tenorio was serving as a **stake president** in Mexico City, and in 1989 he became the first native Mexican to serve as a **general authority**. Horacio was born 6 March 1936 in Mexico City, **Mexico**. There he attended a business college and received graduate training in purchasing, but he left his profitable job for ethical reasons after he and his wife, Maria Teresa, were baptized in 1969. A year after his baptism he was called as a **branch** president and in 1971 as a **bishop**. In 1974 he was called to be a counselor in the stake presidency, and the next year he became the president of the Mexico City Mexico Satellite Stake as the Church saw rapid expansion in Mexico (from 5 stakes to 55 over the following decade). Brother Tenorio also served as a **regional representative** and as president of the Mexico Torreon Mission before he was sustained to the Second **Quorum** of the **Seventy** on 1 April 1989. He was released 1 October 1994.

SOURCES

"Call Is in Keeping with Ancient Promise." *Church News,* 1 July 1989. 6, 12.

1999–2000 Church Almanac. Salt Lake City: Deseret News, 1998. 81.

Richard D. McClellan

TEST OATH. See **ANTIPOLYGAMY MOVEMENT.**

TEXAS. The earliest missionaries in Texas apparently arrived in 1843 from **Nauvoo, Illinois**. Most early proselyting occurred in eastern Texas. In 1844 the **Prophet Joseph Smith** recommended Texas as a possible **gathering** place for the **Saints** prior to his selection of the **Great Basin**.

After the Prophet's death, **Lyman Wight** and **George Miller** took groups of Latter-day Saints to Texas, claiming to have the permission of the Prophet. The settlement established by these Saints was south of the present city of Austin. Subsequently, Miller left Wight and established another colony north of Austin and in late 1849 he left Texas and joined the Strangites. Some of these individuals later returned to the main body of the Church.

In 1901 a Latter-day Saint settlement was colonized by southern converts at Kelsey, Texas. At its height, more than 400 Saints inhabited the townsite, which was patterned after the Latter-day Saint plan of the nineteenth century.

Church growth in Texas began slowly but increased significantly during the twentieth century. A unique Spanish-speaking mission was headquartered at El Paso in 1915, and at San Antonio in 1953–69, after which time this work was amalgamated with the English-speaking missions of the area. The first **stake** was organized at El Paso in 1952, and stakes were also established at Dallas and Houston the following year. In 1984 a **temple** was dedicated in Dallas. Construction began in 1998 on a temple in Houston, and in the April 2000 **general conference President Gordon B. Hinckley** announced another temple, to be built in Lubbock. In the year 2000 there were 210,892 members living in 42 stakes and 441 **wards** and **branches**. Texas has seven missions headquartered in Dallas, Houston, McAllen, Fort Worth, and San Antonio.

SOURCES

Berrett, LaMar C. "History of the Southern States Mission, 1831–1861." Master's thesis, Brigham Young University, 1960.

Jenson, Andrew. *Encyclopedic History of The Church of Jesus Christ of Latter-day Saints.* Salt Lake City: Deseret News, 1941.

1999–2000 Church Almanac. Salt Lake City: Deseret News, 1998. 241–44.

DAVID F. BOONE

TEXTILES. The roots of Latter-day Saint textiles began as early as 1833, when members in **Missouri** encouraged new converts to bring merino and other fine wool sheep with them to improve the poor quality of wool then being raised on the western frontier. Wool and flax (to make linen) were then commonly produced in New England, and members continued to produce them as they gathered west. When the **Saints** were driven from Missouri, **anti-Mormons** frequently shot their sheep, resulting in heavy losses.

About the same time, sericulture (raising silk worms) experienced a brief revival in the **United States**. In **Kirtland, Ohio**, the **periodical** *Northern Times* published a series on sericulture, and its editors produced a volume of the *Ohio Farmer* on raising silk. Ohio was one of the four leading states producing silk in the nineteenth century (**Illinois** and **Missouri** were also in this group). Developing sericulture was suggested in **Nauvoo, Illinois,** as a solution for poor, unemployed immigrants from **Europe's** textile mills, although the exodus from Nauvoo postponed those plans.

As the Saints fled west, they relied heavily on wool production, occasionally getting "wool" from buffalo or even dogs. Wool was always the major fiber produced by Latter-day Saints and the most economically successful. Early years in the West were marked by particularly limited clothing supplies. Antagonistic outsiders noted many individuals dressed in rags, with some of the better-dressed Saints wearing reworked grain sacks. As **Utah's** economy developed, Church leaders emphasized home production as a means of strengthening community cohesion and development. They encouraged members to take better care of their flocks and produce more wool, but wool was not perceived as suitable for some articles of clothing, and early attempts were made to diversify textile production. Flax was again grown in small quantities. **Ellis Reynolds** produced a sampler on homegrown linen in 1853, but flax was difficult to prepare properly in low dew levels and was rarely grown except to produce linseed oil. **Brigham Young** acknowledged in 1874 that flax could not be grown successfully in the Intermountain West.

In the early 1860s, Brigham Young began importing silkworm eggs from France through **Louis Bertrand**, whom he placed in charge of his cocoonery for a short time. In 1875, Brigham Young called his wife Zina on a special mission to promote sericulture in Utah Territory. Until that time most of the silk raised by Latter-day Saints was used to make ribbons or lace by women such as Eliza Ursenbach, who had been a lace maker for Queen Victoria. In 1880 the Deseret Silk Association was founded to promote sericulture among the women and children of the Church. Sericulture increased throughout the United States as associations promoted it everywhere. **California** became one of the leading producers of silk. Rising trade between **Japan** and the **United States** brought in large quantities of inexpensive silk that precipitated a decline in American production. By 1905, the Utah state legislature stopped funding the state's silk commission, and the following year the county silk associations dissolved. Three years later, most other states began dismantling their commissions promoting sericulture. Despite the abandonment of formal support for silk, many older Latter-day Saint women viewed raising silkworms as a religious obligation and raised enough for their own thread or other uses. Sericulture died with these women, leaving behind a few mulberry trees as a memento of their faith.

Before the earliest efforts to raise silk, many pioneers gathering from southern states brought cottonseed to the West. Cotton was first grown in Davis County, north of **Salt Lake**, in 1851. Production spread in small regions of **Ogden**, Tooele, and **Utah Counties**. When Augustus Hardy returned from his mission to the **Indians** in the southwest, he mentioned a climate suitable for cotton and returned south with cottonseed from southern converts. This resulted in the establishment of the **Cotton Mission**, where more than one thousand individuals were called to grow cotton and other crops in the longer seasons of southern Utah. The **Civil War** dramatically raised the price of cotton, making early efforts more profitable. With the end of the war, however, cotton production in Utah's Dixie faltered. Though cotton production was again bolstered during the cooperative efforts of the united order movement in the 1870s, after the era of the cooperative efforts, production slowly declined and growers turned to fruits and vegetables, which were more productive.

The cotton mill in **Washington County**, which had always produced both cotton and woolen textiles, closed in 1910. There were also woolen mills in **Provo**, **Brigham City**, and the **Salt Lake Valley**. During the 1870s, cooperative herds of thousands of sheep filled the grazing lands of central Utah. In regions such as Mt. Pleasant, sheep farmers became successful as Utah produced more sheep than any state in the West, and in the surrounding states it was generally Latter-day Saints who raised large herds of sheep.

SOURCES

Barret, Ivan Junius. "History of the Cotton Mission and Cotton Culture in Utah." Master's thesis, Brigham Young University, 1947.

Hanson, Brooks Kent. "A Geographical Analysis of the Emergence and Subsequent Disappearance of the Cotton Industry in the Virgin River Basin (1856–1910)." Master's thesis, Brigham Young University, 1967.

Potter, Margaret Schow. "The History of Sericulture in Utah." Master's thesis, Oregon State College, 1949.

Reid, Hyrum Lorenzo. "Early History of Utah's Dixie." Master's thesis, Brigham Young University, 1931.

MARK L. STAKER

THAILAND. In August 1852 President **Brigham Young** called four **elders** to open missionary work in Siam, now known as Thailand. Two years later Elam Luddington reached Bangkok by boat, alone. His only baptisms were those of the ship captain and his wife. No further formal missionary efforts were attempted by the Church until the 1960s.

Latter-day Saint educators and military personnel began holding Church **meetings** in Thailand in 1961. Missionaries were moved in from the Southern Far East **Mission** on 2 February 1968. Elder **Gordon B. Hinckley** dedicated the country for the preaching of the gospel on 1 November 1968. On 1 November 1969, Thailand became part of the new Southeast **Asia** Mission, and on 19 July 1973 it became a separate mission with Paul D. Morris as president.

Relations with Thailand's immigration office became troubled in 1972. For 20 years missionaries were limited to numbers under 100, and visas were issued for only brief periods. In 1992 the government created a new visa policy for LDS missionaries that allowed 100 missionaries to remain for 2 years with only one renewal. Growth expanded rapidly after that action.

The **Book of Mormon** was published in Thai in 1976. Bangkok Thailand **Stake** was organized 18 June 1995 with 5 **wards** and 3 **branches**. By the year 2000, membership was 10,808 with 1 stake, 5 districts, and 29 wards and branches.

SOURCE

Britsch, R. Lanier. *From the East: The History of the Latter-day Saints in Asia, 1851–1996.* Salt Lake City: Deseret Book, 1998. 374–407.

R. LANIER BRITSCH

THATCHER, MOSES.

Moses Thatcher, a prominent businessman, politician, and Church leader, was born 2 February 1842 at Springfield, Sagamon County, **Illinois**, to Hezekiah and Alley Thatcher. Only a few months after his birth, his **family** joined the Church. He crossed the plains while still a child and resided in **Salt Lake City** for a short time before moving with his family to **California** and the gold fields. When he was 15, Moses was ordained an **elder** and called on a **mission**. His labors lasted only a few months before the California **Saints** were called back to Utah in preparation for the coming of **Johnston's Army**.

After the **Utah War**, Moses and his family moved to **Logan, Utah**, where they acquired a large farm and constructed a mill and a mercantile establishment. One winter he attended the **University of Deseret** in Salt Lake City, where he met Lettie Farr, whom he married. In 1865 he was called on a two-year mission to **Great Britain**, where he served as the Birmingham **Conference** president.

After his mission, Moses became the superintendent of construction for the Utah and Northern **Railroad**, served on the board of directors of several banks, and was also the director of **Cache Valley's** Zion's Board of Trade. In the 1870s **John Taylor** asked him to travel throughout the territory organizing boards of trade. While Moses was engaged in this activity, President Taylor called him to be an **apostle**.

Soon afterward he was called as the first president of the mission in Mexico City. He visited **Mexico** more than 30 times, supervising missionary work and colonization. He also served in the Church's **YMMIA** presidency and was known as an exceptional public speaker.

Thatcher was active in the **Democratic Party**, and in 1896 he refused to sign the Church's **Political Manifesto**, which required Church clearance for ecclesiastical leaders to run for political office. He was therefore dropped from the Quorum of the Twelve, but later, after a week-long trial before the Salt Lake **Stake** presidency and **high council**, he retained his Church membership by accepting the Political Manifesto.

After an unsuccessful bid for a U.S. Senate seat, Thatcher returned to his business affairs and directed his large land holdings in Mexico. He died at Logan, Utah, on 21 August 1909 and was buried in the Logan cemetery.

Sources

Godfrey, Kenneth W. "Moses Thatcher in the Dock: His Trials, the Aftermath, and His Last Days." *Journal of Mormon History* 24 (Spring 1998): 54–88.

Lyman, Edward Leo. "The Alienation of an Apostle from His Quorum: The Moses Thatcher Case." *Dialogue* 15 (Winter 1982): 44–58.

Kenneth W. Godfrey

THAYRE, EZRA. Ezra Thayre was an early Latter-day Saint Church **agent** appointed to purchase the **French Farm**, on which land the **Kirtland Temple** was built. Thayre was born 14 October 1791 in Randolph, Windsor, **Vermont**. He joined the Church in 1830 and was soon called on a series of **missions** (D&C 33:1–2; 52:22; 75:31). Even though one of these mission calls was revoked (D&C 56:5, 8–10), his service as a Church agent in **Ohio** and as a **high counselor** in **Adam-ondi-Ahman** are commendable. By 1840 Thayre was living in Rochester, New

York. By 1860 he had affiliated with the **RLDS** Church in **Michigan**. His death date is unknown.

SOURCES

Black, Susan Easton. *Early Members of the Reorganized Church of Jesus Christ of Latter Day Saints*. 6 vols. Provo, Utah: Brigham Young University, 1993. 5:77.

———. *Who's Who in the Doctrine and Covenants*. Salt Lake City: Bookcraft, 1997. 318–21.

Cannon, Donald Q., and Lyndon W. Cook, eds. *Far West Record: Minutes of The Church of Jesus Christ of Latter-day Saints, 1830–1844*. Salt Lake City: Deseret Book, 1983. 16.

SUSAN EASTON BLACK

"THIS IS THE PLACE" MONUMENT. At the mouth of Emigration Canyon, the *"This Is the Place" Monument* marks where the **Mormon pioneers** entered the **Salt Lake Valley** on 24 July 1847, when **Brigham Young** proclaimed this was the right place.

In 1937 a state commission (composed of representatives from different religions) spearheaded a commemoration of this significant event. **Mahonri M. Young**, a grandson of Brigham Young, was commissioned to sculpt a monument to be unveiled at the **centennial celebration**. Utah granite was used to make a base 206 feet long with a 60-foot high center pylon. Although this monument primarily commemorates the arrival of the Mormon pioneers and the founding of Utah, there is a broader representation of western **exploration**.

At the north end of the base is a group sculpture of fur trappers, the first explorers of the American West. At the south end of the base is a depiction of the Spanish explorers. On the back side of the monument there are sculptures of six significant men of the West and a plaque honoring the **Donner Party**, who blazed a trail the Mormon pioneers followed when they could.

In the front at the base of the pylon are **Orson Pratt**, standing, and **Erastus Snow** on horseback. These two men were the first Mormon pioneers to enter the valley, on 21 July 1847. The horsemen depicted in bas-reliefs on the north and south sides of the center pylon represent the exploring party of nine that entered the valley on 22 July. On the front of the base section are bas-reliefs showing the Mormon pioneers traveling along the trail. At the top of the pylon stand the figures of Church leaders Brigham Young, **Heber C. Kimball**, and **Wilford Woodruff**.

The monument was dedicated 24 July 1947 by Church president

George Albert Smith. On 29 June 1996, after extensive refurbishing, the monument was rededicated by President **Gordon B. Hinckley.**

SOURCES

Kimball, James L., Jr. "'This Is the Place' Monument." *Encyclopedia of Mormonism.* Edited by Daniel H. Ludlow. 4 vols. New York: Macmillan, 1992. 4:1476–77.

Lloyd, R. Scott. "'Strikingly Beautiful' Monument Rededicated; Tabernacle Choir Sings." *Church News,* 6 July 1996, 3–4.

This Is the Place Monument and Mural. Salt Lake City: Regency Investments, 1996.

VENEESE C. NELSON

THOMPSON, OHIO. Thompson, Ohio, which is east of **Kirtland,** is home of the **Leman Copley family.** The **law of consecration** and stewardship was first implemented here when the **Colesville Saints** moved from **New York** in May 1831 and settled on Copley's 759-acre farm (D&C 51). The Saints were given stewardship over the land, but this lasted only a few weeks. After the failure of the mission to the **Shakers,** Copley—a former Shaker and one of the missionaries to them—broke his covenant and ordered the Saints off his land. The Thompson Saints were then called to **Missouri** (D&C 54).

SOURCE

Anderson, Karl R., and Perkins, Keith W. "Thompson/Madison." *A Walk through the Sacred Land of "The Ohio:" A Personal Guidebook through the Land.* Provo, Utah: Keith W. Perkins, 1995.

KEITH W. PERKINS

THOUGHT, HISTORY OF MORMON. See **INTELLECTUAL HISTORY.**

THREE DEGREES OF GLORY. See **VISION OF THE THREE DEGREES OF GLORY.**

THREE WITNESSES. See **WITNESSES OF THE BOOK MORMON.**

TIMBIMBOO, MORONI. Moroni Timbimboo, a member of the Northwestern **Shoshoni** nation, served as the first **Native American**

bishop in the Church. **Elder George Albert Smith** ordained Timbimboo bishop of **Washakie Ward** in Box Elder County, **Utah**, on 22 January 1939. He served until 4 March 1945.

Moroni, a grandson of Chief **Sagwitch**, was born to Yeager and Yampitch Wongan Timbimboo on 1 August 1888 at Washakie, a Church-sponsored farming community. He married Amy Hootchew (1893–1999) on 21 March 1910. The following year their **marriage** was solemnized in the **Logan Temple**. They became the parents of nine children.

In 1935 he filled a short-term **mission** to the North Central States Mission, working among the Indians on the Fort Peck Reservation at Wolf Point, **Montana**. He died 25 April 1975 in **Ogden**, Utah, and is buried in the Clearfield, Utah, cemetery.

SOURCES

Jenson, Andrew. "Washakie Ward Manuscript History, 1847–1930." Manuscript. LDS Church Archives, Salt Lake City.
"Service Is a Way of Life for First Indian Bishop." *Church News,* 28 March 1970, 11.

SCOTT R. CHRISTENSEN

TIMES AND SEASONS. *Times and Seasons,* a major source of information on early Latter-day Saint thought, was published at **Nauvoo** 1840–1846. During the spring of 1839, Elias Smith and Hyrum Clark retrieved from a muddy grave in **Far West, Missouri,** the press and type that had been used in the publication of *The Elders' Journal.* (The equipment had been buried there for safety when the **Saints** were driven out.) Various editors then used the machinery to publish *Times and Seasons,* which became the Church's journalistic voice during the **Nauvoo, Illinois,** era. The **periodical** was first issued as "a monthly religious paper, in **pamphlet** form" (Smith, 4:23) in November 1839 by **Don Carlos Smith** and **Ebenezer Robinson.** Following its first year, *Times and Seasons* became a semimonthly publication.

In December 1840, the firm Robinson & Smith, Publishers, was dissolved, and Don Carlos Smith became the editor, taking on Robert B. Thompson as a partner during the spring of 1841. Following the deaths of Smith on 7 August and of Thompson on 27 August 1841, Ebenezer Robinson once again became the editor and this time the sole manager as well. When the **Quorum** of the Twelve **Apostles** determined either to take over the periodical or start a competing paper at the end of 1841, Robinson reluctantly sold the periodical to the Church (Smith, 4:463).

Thereafter it was edited by the **Prophet Joseph Smith** (volume 3, from the eighth number on) and then by **John Taylor** (volumes 4–6).

Altogether, 131 issues of *Times and Seasons* were produced. "Each number of the paper consisted of 16 large octavo pages, the printing matter on each page measuring 4¼ by 8 inches" (Jenson, 875). Its final edition came off the press on 15 February 1846, a few days after the **exodus** from Nauvoo had begun.

SOURCES

Jenson, Andrew. *Encyclopedic History of The Church of Jesus Christ of Latter-day Saints.* Salt Lake City: Deseret News, 1941. 875–876.

Smith, Joseph. *History of The Church of Jesus Christ of Latter-day Saints.* Edited by B. H. Roberts. 2d ed. rev. 7 vols. Salt Lake City: The Church of Jesus Christ of Latter-day Saints, 1932–51.

RICHARD D. McCLELLAN

TINGEY, MARTHA HORNE. Martha Jane Horne Tingey served the young women of the Church for 49 years as a counselor and then the second president of the Young Ladies' **Mutual Improvement Association** (**Young Women**). Known as Mattie, she was born 15 October 1857 in **Salt Lake City** and later married Joseph S. Tingey. Called as the YLMIA president in 1905, Mattie initiated the **Beehive** and **Gleaner** programs, yearly slogans, and roadshows. She chose gold and green as the Mutual colors (and started the popular Gold and Green Balls), introduced camping to the young women's program, and celebrated the **MIA** golden jubilee. The YLMIA also operated the **Beehive House** as a home for girls. Beginning her YLMIA service as a single 22-year-old, Mattie was released in 1929 at age 72. She died 11 March 1938 in Salt Lake City.

SOURCES

A Century of Sisterhood: Chronological Collage, 1869–1969. Salt Lake City: YWMIA, 1969.

Gates, Susa Young. *History of the Young Ladies' Mutual Improvement Association.* Salt Lake City: Deseret News, 1911.

Peterson, Janet, and LaRene Gaunt. *Keepers of the Flame: General Presidents of the Young Women.* Salt Lake City: Deseret Book, 1993.

JANET PETERSON

TITHING. By 1838 it was clear that many Church members were not responding well to the **law of consecration**. On 8 July 1838, **Joseph**

Smith received a revelation in **Far West, Missouri,** outlining the law of tithing. Under it, the **bishop** was to receive each individual's surplus property and, from then on, one-tenth of that person's increase. This was to be "a standing law unto them forever" (D&C 119:1–4).

During the **Nauvoo** period and through **pioneer** times, a bishop both received tithing from the members of his congregation and disbursed it to those in need. After the Church was established in **Utah,** commodities were placed in the local **bishop's storehouse** or the central Tithing Office, pending distribution. The small amount of cash received could be used for the poor or sent in to the **presiding bishop** for general Church use. Workers on the **temple, tabernacle,** or other Church buildings, as well as teamsters going east to pick up immigrating **Saints,** were paid in goods from the tithing stores.

In Nauvoo, and again in 1849, an innovation was added: labor tithing. Every man was expected to put in one work day in ten on ward projects or in the public works program. Throughout the pioneer period, this plan provided the work force for roads, bridges, fences, dams, ditches, and public buildings. As it became more practical to contract out such work, the practice faded away.

In the nineteenth century, handling tithing was one of the main tasks of a bishop. At least once a year it was his duty to meet with every **family** head to determine what the correct tithing should be. Since the mandated definition was one tenth of all increase, it was deemed proper that the tithe could be in kind. This often involved paying tithing in the form of commodities. For example, if a man harvested ten bushels of carrots, one bushel was tithing. If his herd increased by ten cows, he paid one cow.

In the 1880s, revenue from tithing declined because members were reluctant to contribute when the federal government was confiscating Church property and money under **antipolygamy** legislation, plunging the Church deep into debt. It was not until May 1899, when President **Lorenzo Snow,** by revelation, chastised the Saints in **St. George, Utah,** for neglecting the law of tithing that a reformation began and Church membership headed toward paying a full tithe. Because of this renewed emphasis, **Joseph F. Smith** was able to announce that the Church was free from debt in April 1907.

By the beginning of the twentieth century, most people had started paying their bills in cash, and the Church had a desperate need for money rather than perishable goods. The general handbook of 1913 said "cash is always acceptable" as well as other things not in kind, although "not strictly a proper kind of payment" (6–7).

In the late twentieth century, commodities are still accepted as payment of tithing. Now, however, we generally speak of income, not increase, and a person's tithe is set generally at one-tenth of the money he or she has received.

SOURCES

Arrington, Leonard J., Dean L. May, and Feramorz Y. Fox. *Building the City of God: Community and Cooperation among the Mormons.* Salt Lake City: Deseret Book, 1976.

Circular of Instructions. No. 12. Salt Lake City: The Church of Jesus Christ of Latter-day Saints, 1913. 6–7.

DALE BEECHER

TOBACCO. See WORD OF WISDOM.

TOGO.

TOGO. Formerly known as Togo Land, this **African** nation was a colony of Germany and then of France before gaining its independence in 1960. Togo is bounded on the west by **Ghana**. Approximately one-ninth of its nearly 4,000,000 inhabitants are Christians, but most are animists (believing that natural objects as well as beings possess souls). At the beginning of the year 2000, there were 122 Latter-day Saints living in one **branch** in Togo.

RICHARD O. COWAN

TOKYO TEMPLE.

TOKYO TEMPLE. The Tokyo Japan Temple, dedicated 27–29 October 1980 by President **Spencer W. Kimball,** was the first temple to be built in a non-Christian nation. Church architect Emil B. Fetzer and Masao Shiina gave the temple a modern design, with a structure measuring 103 by 134 feet and one spire reaching 178.5 feet into the air. Described as the most earthquake-proof building in Tokyo at the time, it is made of structural steel and reinforced concrete and faced with 289 panels of precast stone, giving it the appearance of light gray granite. This 18th operating temple of the Church contains two ordinance rooms and five sealing rooms. Used by 48,627 members at the time of dedication, it now serves the members of 25 **stakes** in **Japan.**

At the dedication, **Elder Gordon B. Hinckley**, then a member of the **Quorum of the Twelve Apostles,** promised, "This nation will be blessed because this temple stands on its soil. This people will be blessed because of its presence." He also stated: "This land is called the land of the Rising

Sun. I have felt this is the land of the rising Church. This is a place where the Church has a tremendous future" ("Dedication," 3).

SOURCES

"Dedication of Temple Called Historic Event." *Church News*, 8 November 1980, 3.
1997–98 Church Almanac. Salt Lake City: Deseret News, 1996. 465.
"Tremendous Future for Church in Japan." *Church News*, 8 November 1980, 10.

MAREN M. MOURITSEN

TONGA. The kingdom of Tonga is a constitutional monarchy in the South **Pacific** consisting of 150 islands. Its first Christian mission was established in 1826 during violent civil unrest. By 1853 the islands were united under the undisputed authority of Taufa'ahau Tupou I, who freed the commoners from bondage to the chiefs (1862) and established a constitution (1875).

The first Latter-day Saint missionaries to Tonga were sent from the Samoan **Mission**, arriving 15 July 1891. After six difficult years and very little success, the missionaries were withdrawn. Missionaries were later sent back to Tonga, first to Vava'u (1909), then to Tongatapu (1911).

The Tongan Mission was established in 1916, but it was immediately threatened by the passage of the Passport Act, which forbade the entry of foreign missionaries. Thanks to the efforts of President Vernon Coombs and the few devoted local **Saints**, the Act was repealed in 1924. A Church high school, Makeke, was established the following year.

By 1941 Church membership exceeded 2,000. Except for **mission president** Emil E. Dunn, foreign missionaries were withdrawn from Tonga during **World War II**, giving native Tongans greater opportunity for Church leadership. The **Book of Mormon** was published in the Tongan language in 1946. In 1953 **Elder LeGrand Richards** dedicated a new Church School, Liahona, and in 1956 an extensive chapel-building program was launched throughout the islands. In 1958, 35 Tongan Saints traveled to **New Zealand** on the first of many excursions to the temple there.

By the early 1960s, missionary work began to flourish, and in 1968 the first **stake** in Tonga was organized under the direction of Elders **Howard W. Hunter** and **Thomas S. Monson**. Saineha High School, located in Nejafu Vava'u, was dedicated in 1978. By the time the Nuku'alofa Tonga Temple was dedicated by President **Spencer W. Kimball** in 1983, there were 11 stakes, and the Tongan Mission was averaging well more than 1,000 converts per year. Large numbers of Tongan Saints have emigrated to New Zealand, **Australia**, and the **United States**. Worthy Tongan youth serve in missions around the world. At the beginning of the twenty-first century, there were 16 stakes and 44,819 members of record in Tonga.

SOURCES

Britsch, R. Lanier. *Unto the Islands of the Sea: A History of the Latter-day Saints in the Pacific.* Salt Lake City: Deseret Book, 1986.

Cummings, David W. *Mighty Missionary of the Pacific.* Salt Lake City: Bookcraft, 1961.

Shumway, Eric B., ed. and trans. *Tongan Saints: Legacy of Faith.* Laie, Hawaii: Institute for Polynesian Studies, 1989.

ERIC SHUMWAY

TONGUES, SPEAKING IN. The Savior's parting commission to his **apostles** before he ascended into heaven was for them to go "into all the world, and preach the gospel to every creature" (Mark 16:15). He promised that signs would follow those who believed, including that of speaking in tongues (Mark 16:17). Within weeks, during Pentecost, the Holy Ghost rested upon his disciples insomuch that "every man heard them speak in his own language" (Acts 2:6). This phenomenon of speaking in tongues is an identifiable gift of the Spirit associated with the Church of **Jesus Christ** (Moro. 10:15–16, 19; D&C 46:24–25; 1 Cor. 12:10, 28, 30; Omni 1:25; Alma 9:21). It is of such importance that the Savior himself warned against those who might reject or deny its authenticity (3 Ne. 29:6; Moro. 9:7–8). In some instances speaking in tongues may be experienced without an interpreter. Paul taught that these were special circumstances intended for the benefit of the individual (1 Cor. 14:2, 28). He directed that the use of tongues should be orderly, edifying, and, when in public, accompanied by an interpreter (1 Cor. 14:9, 11–13, 26–28).

Joseph Smith provided important instruction regarding the use of this divine gift. First, "We wish you . . . to be careful, lest in this you be deceived. **Satan** will no doubt trouble you about the gift of tongues" (Smith, 25). Second, "The devil can speak in tongues. . . . Let no one speak in tongues unless he interpret, except by the consent of the one who is placed to preside" (Smith, 162). Third, the gift of tongues is intended "for the benefit of the servants of God to preach to unbelievers" (Smith, 195). Fourth, "I lay this down for a rule, that if anything is taught by the gift of tongues, it is not to be received for doctrine" (Smith, 229). And fifth, "If persons are very anxious to display their intelligence, let them speak to such in their own tongues. . . . When [the gifts of God] are applied to that which God does not intend, they prove an injury, a snare and a curse instead of a blessing" (Smith, 247).

One of the first instances of speaking in tongues in this dispensation took place in **New York** during the spring of 1832. While engaged in **family** prayer at the **Heber C. Kimball** home, the recently converted **Brigham Young** began to speak in tongues (Arrington, 32). Throughout the nineteenth century, many members of the Church also experienced this gift. In **New Zealand** in 1921 **Elder David O. McKay** admonished a predominantly Maori congregation to pray for the gift of interpretation because he could not speak their language. He recorded that many in the audience were blessed with this gift (Middlemiss, 53–54). In 1923 the **First Presidency** wrote a letter discouraging the practice of speaking in tongues in **meetings** where all present spoke the same language (Alexander, 293–95). Many missionaries are convinced that they are recipients of this gift as they quickly learn a new language.

SOURCES

Alexander, Thomas G. *Mormonism in Transition: A History of the Latter-day Saints, 1890–1930.* Urbana: University of Illinois Press, 1986.

Arrington, Leonard J. *Brigham Young: American Moses.* New York: Alfred A. Knopf, 1985.

McConkie, Bruce R. *Mormon Doctrine.* 2d ed. Salt Lake City: Bookcraft, 1966. 799–801.

McKay, David O. *Cherished Experiences from the Writings of David O. McKay.* Compiled by Clare Middlemiss. Salt Lake City: Deseret Book, 1976.

Smith, Joseph. *Teachings of the Prophet Joseph Smith.* Selected by Joseph Fielding Smith. Salt Lake City: Deseret Book, 1977.

DAVID M. WHITCHURCH

TOPSFIELD, MASSACHUSETTS.

TOPSFIELD, MASSACHUSETTS. Home of five generations of **Joseph Smith's** ancestors, Topsfield, **Massachusetts**, was founded in 1641. The founders of Topsfield immigrated from Toppesfield, **England**, which had been named for Topp, a Saxon chieftain who crossed the North Sea ca. 550 A.D. Topsfield, Massachusetts, today is a picturesque New England village, a bedroom community for Boston commuters.

The early settlers of Topsfield, Massachusetts, earned a living as farmers or craftsmen. Religion played a great role in their lives, as they faithfully followed the tenets of Puritanism.

The ancestors of Joseph Smith who resided in Topsfield include Robert Smith, Samuel Smith I, Samuel Smith II, **Asael Smith**, and **Joseph**

Smith Sr. They lived there between 1626 and 1791. From their collective experience in Topsfield, these ancestors of the **Prophet** developed three basic values: patriotism, religiosity, and socioeconomic success. These values were passed along to Joseph Smith Jr. Physical evidence of the early Smiths is confined to a marker in the Pine Grove Cemetery, erected by **George A. Smith** in 1873.

SOURCES

Cannon, Donald Q. "Topsfield, Massachusetts: Ancestral Home of the Prophet Joseph Smith." *BYU Studies* 14 (Fall 1973): 56–76.

Dow, George Francis. *History of Topsfield, Massachusetts.* Topsfield, Mass.: Topsfield Historical Society, 1940.

DONALD Q. CANNON

TORONTO, WALLACE F. Wallace Felt Toronto, a grandson of the first Italian convert, became a pioneering missionary leader among the Slavic people. He served three **missions** among the Czechs and continued as their **mission president** in absentia for another 25 years.

Born 9 December 1907 in **Salt Lake City**, Wallace was called to the German Mission. In 1929 he joined the first elders transferred to open the Czechoslovak Mission under Authur Gaeth. When released, Wallace studied at the **University of Utah** and soon married Martha Sharp.

In 1936 he was called to preside over the Czech Mission. New cities were opened, and conversions continued. The Nazi occupation of Czech lands in 1938 and 1939 led to the evacuation of all missionaries. During the **war**, Wallace became director of the Utah Red Cross.

In 1946 Wallace and his **family** returned to Prague. With a larger missionary force, the Church expanded even after the February 1948 Communist coup. But by 1950 the missionaries were expelled, and the registration of the Church was canceled. Faithful **Saints** were now left without the opportunity even to hold **branch meetings**.

At home Wallace taught **seminary**, served on the **Young Men's MIA** board, and became executive secretary of the **Utah** Cancer Society. Through cryptic letters, he kept in touch with the Saints in Czechoslovakia. In 1964 President McKay assigned the Torontos to visit the Czech Saints as tourists. In 1965 he was asked to return alone to meet with the ministry officials. He did so, but only after he was arrested following his interview on television during the huge national sports festival. His request for Church recognition was rejected, and he was deported at the German border. Wallace Toronto remained president of the Czech Mission until his death from cancer on 10 January 1968 in Salt Lake City.

SOURCES

Anderson, Martha [Sharp] Toronto. *A Cherry Tree behind the Iron Curtain: . . . Autobiography.* Salt Lake City: Martha Toronto Anderson, 1977.
Mehr, Kahlile. "Frontier in the East." Manuscript history, Czechoslovakia.
1999–2000 Church Almanac. Salt Lake City: Deseret News, 1998. 308.

EDWIN B. MORRELL

TRANSKEI. See SOUTH AFRICA.

TREASURE HUNTING AND MAGIC. In the early 1800s, folk belief and even folk magic were part of the total religious experience of many Americans. For such people (and they hailed from all sectors of society), practices such as stone divination, use of divining rods, and treasure seeking—activities that today would be regarded as superstitious aberrations—were thought to be harmonious with traditional patterns of Christian living and worship. Many early members of the Church, including **Joseph Smith** and his **family**, participated in folk magic practices. In **Lucy Mack Smith's** history, the **Prophet's** mother honestly declared that such pursuits were early on a part of her family's quest for religious truth.

Of all the so-called magical activities Joseph was involved with, he was remembered most by neighbors for treasure seeking. Reputably, Joseph was able to find or locate treasure, generally with the aid of a divining rod or seerstone. In 1825 Joseph was hired by **Josiah Stowell** to help find a supposed Spanish treasure. Nothing came of the venture, and in 1826 Stowell's nephew, likely persuaded that Joseph was taking advantage of his uncle, brought charges against Joseph for being a "disorderly person." The limited extant evidence indicates that Joseph truthfully testified of his treasure-seeking activities and that Stowell expressed confidence in Joseph's veracity. The misdemeanor trial ultimately resulted in Joseph's being acquitted.

As Joseph matured in his religious seeking and experience, and as he gradually refined his spiritual gifts and assumed the stature of a prophet, there was a corresponding decline in his involvement with what historian Richard Bushman called "vernacular magic." After the **organization of the Church** in 1830, he rarely commented on such activities, though, understandably, degrees of magical pursuits persisted for some years among a minority of Church members as an adjunct to their more conventional religious practices.

Historians both in and out of the Church who have closely studied the rise of Mormonism in the larger context of American religion and culture agree that the involvement of Church members in practices common to thousands is hardly crucial to the Church's claims to divine origins. President **Gordon B. Hinckley** reached a similar conclusion, stating in the October 1987 **general conference**: "I have no doubt there was folk magic practiced in those days," but adding that the evidence of such "is no evidence whatever that the Church came of such superstition" (Hinckley, 66).

SOURCES

Anderson, Richard Lloyd. "The Mature Joseph Smith and Treasure Searching." *BYU Studies* 24 (Fall 1984): 489–560.

Bushman, Richard L. *Joseph Smith and the Beginnings of Mormonism.* Chicago: University of Illinois Press, 1984. 64–80.

———. "Treasure-seeking Then and Now." *Sunstone* 11 (September 1987): 5–6.

Hinckley, Gordon B. Conference Report (October 1987): 64–68.

Madsen, Gordon A. "Joseph Smith's 1826 Trial: The Legal Setting." *BYU Studies* 30 (Spring 1990): 91–108.

PAUL H. PETERSON AND BRIAN L. SMITH

TREJO, MELITON G. Meliton Gonzalez Trejo, who translated the **Book of Mormon** into Spanish, was born 10 March 1843 at Garganto-la-Olla in western **Spain**. After receiving a liberal education, he became an officer in the royal army. He often thought deeply about religion but found no answers to his questions. One day when he overheard a comment about a group of "**Saints**" in the Rocky Mountains led by a **prophet**, he felt a determination to become better acquainted with them. While the army was stationed in the **Philippines**, Meliton became seriously ill. One night he had a "sacred dream" that prompted him to leave the military and to sail for **America**. He reached **Salt Lake City** in 1874, met **Brigham Young**, and was taught the gospel. Having a great desire to translate the Book of Mormon into Spanish, he was assigned to assist **Daniel W. Jones**, who was then struggling to accomplish that very task. Together they prepared a **pamphlet** containing selected Book of Mormon quotations, which would be distributed in 1876 by the first group of missionaries in **Mexico**. His complete translation of the book was published at Mexico City in 1886. Meanwhile, in 1884 he married Emily Jones, and they became the parents of 10 children. He later taught Spanish in Salt Lake

City, lived in the **Mexican colonies**, and farmed at St. David in south-eastern **Arizona**. He died 29 April 1917 in Wilcox, Arizona.

SOURCE

Duke, K. E. "Meliton Gonzalez Trejo." *Improvement Era* 59 (October 1956): 714–15, 753.

RICHARD O. COWAN

TRINIDAD AND TOBAGO. The Republic of Trinidad and Tobago is located on the southernmost Caribbean Islands. In 1974 Liz Anne Rogers, a Trinidadian by birth, was baptized in **England**. Two years later she returned to Trinidad and requested that missionaries be sent to the republic. The **Venezuela** Caracas **Mission** sent missionaries, and Lucy Josephine Payne was the first person baptized in Trinidad, 2 June 1977.

On 22 February 1990, **Elder M. Russell Ballard** dedicated Trinidad and Tobago for the preaching of the gospel. In 1991 the Trinidad Tobago Mission was created.

By the year 2000 there were six **branches** of the Church on the two islands, with about 1,581 members in the **district**.

SOURCES

Borde, Jean A. B. *History of the Saints in Trinidad and Tobago*. N. p.:Jean A. Borde, 1995.
"Services in 3 South American Nations and Island Republic." *Church News,* 10 March 1990, 3.

DAVID R. CROCKETT

TRUMBO, ISAAC. Though Isaac Trumbo's role in Latter-day Saint history was relatively brief, it was also pivotal. The U.S. Congress had disenfranchised the Church and threatened to cancel citizenship for those who practiced **plural marriage**. At his San Francisco home, Trumbo, his friend Alexander Badlam, and California senator Leland Stanford decided to lobby Congress on the Church's behalf. They helped convince Congress to reverse itself and grant **Utah** statehood. Later, President **Wilford Woodruff** spent his final days with Trumbo and died in his home, which still stands in San Francisco at the corner of Octavia and Sutter Streets.

SOURCE

Cowan, Richard O., and William E. Homer. *California Saints.* Provo, Utah: Brigham Young University, 1996.

WILLIAM E. HOMER

TRUSTEE-IN-TRUST. The trustee-in-trust of The Church of Jesus Christ of Latter-day Saints is the individual legally entrusted to hold real, financial, and personal assets of the Church. The position of trustee-in-trust was established 30 January 1841 at a **general conference** of the Church. At that conference, President **Joseph Smith** was appointed trustee-in-trust and was authorized to receive, manage, and convey real and personal property for the benefit of the Church. In 1848, President **Brigham Young** was appointed by a general conference vote as trustee-in-trust, a position that became legally recognized in 1851 when the territorial legislature granted the charter incorporating The Church of Jesus Christ of Latter-day Saints. The charter authorized the corporation to elect one trustee-in-trust to acquire and manage real and personal property of the Church. With the exception of three brief periods, the president of the Church has held the position of trustee-in-trust.

SOURCE

Arrington, Leonard J. *Great Basin Kingdom: An Economic History of the Latter-day Saints, 1830–1900*. Cambridge, Mass.: Harvard University Press, 1958.

L. DWIGHT ISRAELSEN

TUCKER, POMEROY. Pomeroy Tucker was a newspaper editor, public servant, and author of the **anti-Mormon** book *Origin, Rise and Progress of Mormonism*. Born 10 August 1802 in **Palmyra**, **New York**, and apprenticed at the *Palmyra Herald* office, he later purchased the business, which he sold to Egbert Grandin in 1828. He assisted in arranging the contract for printing the **Book of Mormon** and served as foreman of Grandin's shop while the book was at press.

Tucker and Grandin married sisters. Pomeroy and Lucy Rogers raised six children. He was a devout Democrat, and Masonry was his religion. He served as Palmyra town supervisor, postmaster, and **Erie Canal** collector, as well as on numerous civic and political committees. He was a talented and respected editorialist in western New York.

The growing national resentment of Mormonism led Tucker to write his anti-Mormon work in 1867, based on his professed acquaintance with the **Joseph Smith Sr. family** and his presumed awareness of the origin events of the Church. Tucker died in Palmyra, 30 June 1870.

SOURCES

"Death of Pomeroy Tucker." *Palmyra Courier,* 8 July 1870. Copy, Church Historical Archives, Salt Lake City.

Pettengill, C. N. "Light in the Valley: Memorial Sermon Delivered at the Funeral of
   Pomeroy Tucker, Palmyra, Wayne County, New York." Troy, N.Y.: Times Steam,
   1870. Special Collections, Brigham Young University Library, Provo, Utah.

DONALD L. ENDERS

TUNISIA. See MIDDLE EAST and MUSLIMS.

TUNBRIDGE, VERMONT. Tunbridge is a township settled after the
Revolutionary War in central Vermont, near Royalton, comprising
several smaller villages. Organized as a township in 1786, Tunbridge fig-
ured prominently in Latter-day Saint Church history because Joseph
Smith's ancestors, both the Macks and the Smiths, lived there. The Asael
Smith and Joseph Smith Sr. farms are located in this township. Four of
Joseph Smith's siblings were born on the farm operated by Joseph Smith
Sr. The Solomon Mack and Stephen Mack farms were also located in
Tunbridge Township. The Smiths and the Macks were both prominent in
the business and civic life of this area. According to local historical tra-
dition, Joseph Smith Sr. first met Lucy Mack in Tunbridge (Tunbridge
Center), where she was working in her brother Stephen's store. The struc-
ture was still standing in 1999.

SOURCE

Berrett, LaMar C., ed. *New England and Eastern Canada*. Vol. 1 of *Sacred Places*. Salt
   Lake City: Bookcraft, 1999. 111–22.

DONALD Q. CANNON

TURKEY. The first missionary labors of the Church in the modern
Middle East were initiated in Turkey, the heartland of the Ottoman
Empire, in 1884. The ensuing years of mission history were marked by
constant interruptions and by the suffering of members and missionaries
as the fledgling Church attempted to cope with the political and economic turbulence of the times.

   Jacob Spori, the first full-time Latter-day Saint missionary in
the Middle East, arrived in Istanbul on 31 December 1884 to open the
Turkish Mission. Less than a week later, on 4 January, he baptized the first
converts to the Church—an Armenian man, Hagop Vartooguian, and his
family. Finding little interest among Turks or Europeans in Istanbul, the
missionaries moved inland and began to establish branches of the Church

in the Armenian Christian communities of central and southern Turkey: Zara, Sivas, Maras, and Gaziantep (Aintab). Aintab eventually became one of the largest branches in the mission, and, until 1907 when the mission headquarters was moved to Aleppo, **Syria**, it was a center of Church activity and administration. In 1890 a Latter-day Saint missionary, Edgar D. Simmons, died of smallpox and was buried in Aintab. The membership of the Turkish Mission was comprised mainly of Armenians from central Turkey and northern Syria, but also a few European and Arab converts in other parts of the mission, including **Palestine, Greece, Egypt**, and **Lebanon**.

The mission was closed in 1896 when political conflict in Turkey threatened the members and missionaries, but it was reopened in 1897. President Ferdinand Hintze finally received permission from the Ottoman government in 1899 to publish the first Latter-day Saint literature, and missionary tracts and 28 sections of the **Doctrine and Covenants** were printed in several languages. Another milestone was achieved in 1906 when Hintze succeeded in having the first Turkish language/Armenian script **Book of Mormon** published in Boston. The mission was closed again in 1909 due to increasing political turmoil in Turkey.

When **Joseph Booth**, president of the newly named Armenian Mission, returned to Turkey in 1921 following **World War I**, he found that many of the members had been killed or deported during the war and that those who had managed to survive were suffering from poverty, disease, and hunger. In December 1921, Booth arranged with the French authorities (who controlled southern Turkey and Syria in the postwar period) to evacuate Latter-day Saint members of the Church from Aintab to Aleppo, where they could be given proper care and protection. After this exodus, which subsequently was celebrated by the Armenian **Saints** as one of the great events in Church history, only a few scattered members were left in Turkey, and the Church shifted the focus of its activities to Syria, Lebanon, and Palestine. Since the closure of the Near East Mission in 1951, Church branches with mostly expatriate members have been organized intermittently in Turkey at Istanbul, Ankara, Adana, Izmir, and Sinop. At the end of 1997 there were about 200 members.

Sources

"Correspondence, 1932–1955." Near East Mission. LDS Church Archives, Salt Lake City.

"History." Palestine-Syrian Mission. LDS Church Archives, Salt Lake City.

Lindsay, Rao H. "A History of the Missionary Activities of The Church of Jesus Christ of Latter-day Saints in the Near East, 1884–1929." Master's thesis, Brigham Young University, 1958.

"Manuscript History." Turkish Mission. LDS Church Archives, Salt Lake City.

"Papers of Joseph Wilford Booth." Special Collections and Manuscripts. Brigham Young University Library, Provo, Utah.

JAMES A. TORONTO

TURLEY, THEODORE. Theodore Turley, missionary, **pioneer**, and colonizer, was born 10 April 1801 in Birmingham, **England**. He joined the Church in **Canada** in 1837 and migrated to **Missouri**, where he served on the **high council** of **Zion**, became a **Seventy**, helped carry petitions from **Joseph Smith** and other prisoners to state officers, endured physical abuse from Church critics, and sacrificed time and resources to assist the **Saints** in removing from the state. He built the first home erected by a Latter-day Saint in **Nauvoo** before accompanying members of the Quorum of the Twelve **Apostles** on a **mission** to **England** during 1839 and 1840.

Returning from his mission as leader of a large company of Saints, he settled in Nauvoo, where he held important positions in city government and the **Nauvoo Legion**. He lost several members of his **family** in the **Winter Quarters** region before finally reaching **Utah** in 1849. He helped colonize **San Bernardino, California**, eventually returning to Utah, where he spent the final years of his life. Theodore Turley died in Beaver, Utah, 12 August 1871.

SOURCES

Turley, Nancy Romans, ed. *The Theodore Turley Family Book.* N.p.: Theodore Turley Family Organization, 1977.

Turley, Richard E., Jr. "Theodore Turley: A Biography." *Theodore Turley Family Newsletter* 1–12 (1994–98).

RICHARD E. TURLEY JR.

TUTTLE, A. THEODORE. A member of the First Council of the **Seventy**, Albert Theodore Tuttle was born 2 March 1919 in **Manti, Utah**. His mother, who had dedicated him to the Lord before his birth, helped him prepare, memorize, and deliver 2½-minute talks, learning to project his voice "clear to the back row."

As a youth he learned the value of hard work, high character, relationships, and service, and he held leadership positions at **Snow College** and **Brigham Young University**. After serving in the Northern States **Mission,** "financed by faith," he returned to BYU, marrying Marné Whitaker in 1943. He was promptly enlisted in the Marine Corps and trained as an officer. He fought in the terrible battle of Iwo Jima and returned in 1946 to meet his 13-month-old son. Three more sons and three daughters joined the **family** as he taught **seminary** in **Idaho** and **Utah,** served as **institute** director in **Nevada,** and became assistant administrator of seminaries and institutes.

Elder Tuttle was sustained a member of the First Council of the Seventy in 1958 and three years later was assigned to supervise the seven **missions** in **South America.** In October 1976 he became a member of the First **Quorum** of the Seventy, serving as a president of that Quorum from 1976 until 1980. He died 28 November 1986 in **Salt Lake City.**

SOURCES

Flake, Lawrence R. *Mighty Men of Zion.* Salt Lake City: Karl D. Butler, 1974. 457–58.
1999–2000 Church Almanac. Salt Lake City: Deseret News, 1998. 70.

DAVID TUTTLE

TUVALU. Originally named the Ellice Islands, Tuvalu was brought under British colonialism in 1892. It is a small country made up of nine coral islands, eight of which are inhabited. It gained independence from **Great Britain** on 1 January 1976. In 1985 **Elder** Glenn and Sister Shirley Cornwall were the first missionaries sent to Tuvalu's principal island, Funafuti. At a former **World War II** battle spot on the beach at Betio, Tarawa, **Kiribati,** Elder L. Tom Perry dedicated four countries, including Tuvalu and three provinces of **France,** on 10 August 1996. At the beginning of the year 2000 there were 88 members in one branch on Funafuti.

SOURCES

"Elder Perry Creates First Kiribati Stake, Dedicates Islands." *Church News,* 21 September 1996, 3.
Fiji-Suva Mission Historical Report. LDS Church Archives, Salt Lake City.
Micronesia-Guam Mission Historical Report. LDS Church Archives, Salt Lake City.

W. JAMES JACOB

TWELVE APOSTLES. See APOSTLES.

"TWIN RELICS OF BARBARISM". At its national convention in 1856, the newly-created **Republican Party** referred to slavery and polygamy as the "twin relics of barbarism." Filling its ranks with Protestants from the northern states who opposed the expansion of slavery into the territories, early **Republicans**, who were antagonistic toward **Mormons**, pointed to the **Saints** in **Utah** as an example of what terrible things could happen when the citizens of a territory were allowed to govern themselves. Vowing to end both "relics of barbarism" if placed in power, the Republicans struck powerful blows at each in 1862, when **Abraham Lincoln** issued the Emancipation Proclamation and signed the first antipolygamy bill, the **Morrill Act**, into law. Subsequent Republican presidents followed Lincoln's lead over the years until **Benjamin Harrison's** presidency, when **Wilford Woodruff** issued the **Manifesto (1890)**, ending the solemnizing of plural marriages.

ANDREW H. HEDGES

TYLER, DANIEL. Author, missionary, and **pioneer**, Daniel Tyler was born 23 November 1816 in Semproneous, Cayuga, **New York**. On 16 January 1833, he joined the Church and journeyed to **Kirtland, Ohio**, where he met **Joseph Smith**. Years later he gave a description of the Prophet that was published in the *Juvenile Instructor*. Tyler experienced the mobbings of **Missouri** and **Illinois**.

In January 1839 he signed a "covenant" with 214 others to help the poor remove from the state of Missouri (Smith, 3:251, 253). The day following his marriage to Ruth Welton, they were forced to leave **Nauvoo**. Arriving at **Council Bluffs, Iowa**, he enlisted in the **Mormon Battalion** on 16 July 1846. Tyler's book, *A Concise History of the Mormon Battalion in the Mexican War 1846–47*, published during President **John Taylor's** administration, has become the standard account of the battalion's march to **California** during the **Mexican War**. Following a year's service to his country, he arrived in **Salt Lake City** 16 October 1847.

Tyler served a mission to **Mississippi** and later was president of the Swiss-German Mission (1854–56), where he launched the *Der Darsteller* in 1855. On his way home, he brought a company of 454 **Saints** with him, landing in New York 27 March 1856. Journeying across the **United States**, they joined with the Edward Martin **handcart** company, with Tyler as assistant leader.

Tyler made his home in Beaver, **Utah**. There he worked as a teacher, telegraph operator, attorney, and justice of the peace. He served as second

counselor in the **stake** presidency until he was **ordained** a **patriarch**. He died 7 November 1905 in Beaver, Utah.

SOURCES

Jenson, Andrew. *Latter-day Saint Biographical Encyclopedia.* 4 vols. 1901–36. Reprint, Salt Lake City: Western Epics, 1971.

Smith, Joseph *History of The Church of Jesus Christ of Latter-day Saints.* Edited by B. H. Roberts. 2d ed. rev. 7 vols. Salt Lake City: The Church of Jesus Christ of Latter-day Saints, 1932–51.

"Tyler History: The Family of Dan and Tillie." Manuscript. Photocopy in possession of the author. 1969.

CLARK V. JOHNSON

RULES

THAT SHOULD BE OBSERVED BY MEMBERS OF THE

UNITED ORDER.

RULE 1. We will not take the name of the Deity in vain, nor speak lightly of His character or of sacred things.

RULE 2. We will pray with our families morning and evening, and also attend to secret Prayer.

RULE 3. We will observe and keep the Word of Wisdom according to the Spirit and meaning thereof.

RULE 4. We will treat our families with due kindness and affection, and set before them an example worthy of imitation; in our families and intercourse with all persons, we will refrain from being contentious or quarrelsome, and we will cease to speak evil of each other, and will cultivate a spirit of charity towards all. We consider it our duty to keep from acting selfishly or from covetous motives, and will seek the interest of each other and the salvation of all mankind.

RULE 5. We will observe personal cleanliness, and preserve ourselves in all chastity by refraining from adultery, whoredom and lust. We will also discountenance and refrain from all vulgar and obscene language or conduct.

RULE 6. We will observe the Sabbath day to keep it holy, in accordance with the revelations.

RULE 7. That which is not committed to our care we will not appropriate to our own use.

RULE 8. That which we borrow we will return according to promise, and that which we find we will not appropriate to our own use, but seek to return it to its proper owner.

RULE 9. We will, as soon as possible, cancel all individual indebtedness contracted prior to our uniting with the Order, and when once fully identified with said Order, will contract no debts contrary to the wishes of the Board of Directors.

RULE 10. We will patronize our brethren who are in the Order.

RULE 11. In our apparel and deportment we will not pattern after nor encourage foolish and extravagant fashions, and cease to import or buy from abroad any article which can be reasonably dispensed with, or which can be produced by combination of home labor. We will foster and encourage the producing and manufacturing of all articles needful for our consumption as fast as our circumstances will permit.

RULE 12. We will be simple in our dress and manner of living, using proper economy and prudence in the management of all entrusted to our care.

RULE 13. We will combine our labor for mutual benefit, sustain with our faith, prayers and works, those whom we have elected to take the management of the different departments of the Order, and be subject to them in their official capacity, refraining from a spirit of fault-finding.

RULE 14. We will honestly and diligently labor, and devote ourselves and all we have to the Order and the building up of the Kingdom of God.

UNITED ORDERS. The "Rules That Should Be Observed by Members of the United Order" reveal the Latter-day Saints' efforts to unite during the 1870s and 1880s.

UGANDA. Uganda is located in east central **Africa** and has a population of 20 million, two-thirds being Christian. The country has a military government, and its official language is English. Perhaps the first Ugandan to join the Church was Edward Ojuka, who was baptized in 1982 while attending a university in Perth, **Australia**. As early as the 1960s, expatriate Latter-day Saints held Church **meetings** in Uganda. In March 1990 Guy Denton, his wife, Peggy, and their six children arrived in the country on a three-year assignment with a USAID program. The first baptism in Uganda was that of Mugisa James Collins on 25 August 1990, performed by Brother Denton in Lake Victoria. In December 1990, the first full-time missionary couples arrived in Uganda.

In March 1991 Uganda granted the Church official status, and on 23 October of that year **Elder James E. Faust** of the **Quorum** of the Twelve **Apostles** dedicated the land for the preaching of the gospel. In July 1991 the **Kenya** Nairobi **Mission** was created, which included Uganda as well as Kenya and **Tanzania**. Ugandan ambassador H. E. Ethith Grace Ssempala, a Latter-day Saint, was hosted in October 1997 by the **First Presidency**. By the year 2000 there were 2,375 members in two **districts** in Uganda.

SOURCES

Clark, Gretchen Knecht. "Missionary Efforts Spur Growth in Uganda, Africa." *Ensign* 26 (July 1996): 78–79.

LeBaron, E. Dale. "Pioneers in East Africa." *Ensign* 24 (October 1994): 20–25.

Middleton, John, ed. *Encyclopedia of Africa South of the Sahara.* 4 vols. New York: Macmillan Library Reference USA, 1997. 4:299–309.

1999–2000 Church Almanac. Salt Lake City: Deseret News, 1998. 397–98.

Oral histories of early Church converts collected by E. Dale LeBaron. Copies at BYU Library, Provo, Utah; LDS Church Historical Library, Salt Lake City, Utah.

E. DALE LEBARON

UINTAH BASIN. Located in eastern **Utah**, south of the Uintah mountain range, the Uintah (or Uinta) Basin is a fertile, well-watered region, about 125 miles long and 90 miles wide, temperate in the summer but subject to harsh, cold winters. Notable cities include Vernal, Roosevelt, and Duchesne. White settlers were in the area as early as 1850, taking advantage of the cooler climate for livestock grazing. An **Indian** reservation was created in the Uintah Basin in 1861. The first **ward** in the Basin, the Uintah Ward, was created in 1877. The area called Ashley Valley, later Vernal, on the eastern end of the Basin, was settled by Church members beginning in 1878. A ward was formed there in 1883, and the Uintah Stake with headquarters in Vernal was created in 1886. The Uintah Basin was opened for homesteading in 1905, and the population expanded rapidly. The Uintah Stake was divided and the Duchesne Stake created in 1910. The Roosevelt Stake followed in 1920.

The Uintah Stake **Tabernacle** was dedicated by President **Joseph F. Smith** on 24 August 1907. After serving the needs of the members in the Basin for decades, the building fell into disrepair and was not occupied for some 20 years. On 13 February 1994, the First Presidency announced that the tabernacle would be remodeled to serve as a **temple**. The **Vernal Temple**, the Church's fifty-first, was dedicated by President **Gordon B. Hinckley** on 2 November 1997. Church membership in the Uintah Basin had grown to nine stakes by the time of the temple dedication.

SOURCES

"Construction Begins on Vernal Utah Temple." *Ensign* 25 (August 1995): 76.

Jenson, Andrew. *Encyclopedic History of The Church of Jesus Christ of Latter-day Saints.* Salt Lake City: Deseret News, 1941. 199–200, 895–96.

Smart, William H. Conference Report (April 1907): 62.

DAVID KENISON

UKRAINE. Missionary work began in Kiev on 7 October 1990, as **Elders** Ivan Stratov and Brian Bradbury arrived in the Ukrainian capital, accompanied by **mission president** Dennis B. Neuenschwander of the **Austria** Vienna East Mission. At this time, Ukraine was a part of the Union of Soviet Socialist Republics (USSR), but the "Law on the Freedom of Conscience and Religious Organizations" had just been adopted in Moscow. On 1 December 1991, the citizens of Ukraine voted overwhelmingly to proclaim independence from the USSR.

The first citizen of Ukraine to accept the restored gospel was Valery

Stravichenko, who was baptized 25 November 1990 by **Elder** Ivan Stratov in the icy Dneper River at Kiev. Brother Stavichenko, the first ordained elder and **branch** president in Ukraine, led the first excursion of 22 Latter-day Saints from the former Soviet Union to the Freiburg **Germany Temple** on 22–29 November 1992.

Ukraine was dedicated for the preaching of the gospel by Elder **Boyd K. Packer** of the Quorum of the Twelve **Apostles** on 12 September 1991. The Ukraine Kiev Mission was officially opened by announcement of the **First Presidency** on 3 February 1992, with Howard L. Biddulph already heading the Austria Vienna East Mission. On 1 July 1993, a division of the mission created the Ukraine Donetsk Mission under President Leo Merrill.

The decision to erect the Kiev Ukraine Temple, the first in the former Soviet Union, was announced by the First Presidency in the summer of 1998. By the beginning of the year 2000 there were 6,369 members of the Church in Ukraine organized into 59 branches.

SOURCES

Biddulph, Howard L. *The Morning Breaks: Stories of Conversion and Faith in the Former Soviet Union.* Salt Lake City: Deseret Book, 1996.

1999–2000 Church Almanac. Salt Lake City: Deseret News, 1998. 398.

"Temple to Be Erected in Kiev Ukraine." *Church News,* 8 August 1998. 3.

HOWARD L. BIDDULPH

UNDERGROUND. The Latter-day Saint underground was an informal system during the late 1880s designed to protect polygamous families from federal arrests. Following the passage of extensive **antipolygamy** legislation, including the Edmunds Act (1882) and the Edmunds-Tucker Act (1887), the federal government began a judicial crusade—a "roundup" of all suspected polygamists—creating an atmosphere of incredible tension and disruption in Latter-day Saint life. Latter-day Saint polygamists went on the "underground"—a complicated system of hide-outs, code names, and subterfuge designed to protect polygamists from arrest, prevent women from being forced to testify against their husbands, and keep families from being torn apart.

SOURCES

Embry, Jessie. *Mormon Polygamous Families.* Salt Lake City: University of Utah Press, 1987.

Jensen, Kimberly James. "Between Two Fires: Women on the 'Underground' of Mormon Polygamy." Master's thesis, Brigham Young University, 1981.

MARTHA SONNTAG BRADLEY

UNIFIED MAGAZINE. See LIAHONA MAGAZINE.

UNIONISM. In **Nauvoo** and **pioneer Utah** (**Deseret**), worker guilds, often associated with Church-sponsored cooperatives, were encouraged by Church leaders. With the coming of the **railroads**, however, Utah's businesses increasingly became more secularized, profit-oriented, and focused on cost and wage cutting. On the other hand, Utah's workers increasingly associated with the national labor unions, and their demands for shorter hours, higher wages, and union shops often resulted in strikes, violence, and other forms of labor strife.

Church leaders consequently discouraged members from joining these unions with their perceived "Gentile ways." Where union shops existed that required membership, **Mormons** who were obedient to Church leaders were denied employment.

A survey of the public pronouncements by Church **general authorities** on the subject, as well as editorials of the Church-owned *Deseret News* from 1870 to 1959, shows a persistent negative reaction to unionism, especially union security, which was seen as a denial of the "right of free-agency."

This attitude was also reflected in a 1959 survey, which showed that local Church leaders (**stake presidents** and **bishops**) and some of the most active Church members, who were mostly white-collar and middle-class, opposed unionism. On the other hand, some of the least active Church members, generally blue-collar, were more likely to support it. This dichotomy tended to separate Latter-day Saint working-class union members from Church activity.

With the Church's attempts to reactivate these members and with its international growth since the 1960s, its leaders have been relatively silent on labor issues, leaving the question of union membership and activity by Latter-day Saint workers to individual preference and c-onscience.

SOURCES

Davies, J. Kenneth. *Deseret's Sons of Toil*. Salt Lake City: Olympus, 1977.

———. "The Development of a Labor Philosophy within The Church of Jesus Christ of Latter-day Saints." Ph.D. diss., University of Southern California, 1959.

Wirthlin, Richard, and Bruce D. Merill. "The L.D.S. Church as a Significant Political Group in Utah; 'Right to Work.'" *Dialogue* (Summer 1968): 129–33.

J. KENNETH DAVIES

UNIT. The term *unit* may refer to any local Church entity including **branches**, **wards**, **districts**, **stakes**, or **missions**. *Unit* may also be a general designation of any small group that is not officially organized as one of these bodies. In earlier years when **seventies quorums** were organized in most stakes, *unit* referred to a group of seventies in a stake where there were not enough seventies to constitute a quorum.

RICHARD O. COWAN

UNITED ARAB EMIRATES (DUBAI, ABU DHABI). See MIDDLE EAST and MUSLIMS.

UNITED BRETHREN. The United Brethren was a group of more than 600 people who, in their search for truth, had broken off from the Wesleyan Methodists. **Elder Wilford Woodruff** was introduced to them in Herefordshire, **England**, on 5 March 1840. They readily accepted the gospel, which he preached to them. After 30 days he had baptized 160 members and 48 of their preachers.

With these baptisms the Church also gained 42 locations already licensed for preaching, including the Gadfield Elm chapel. The preachers in the United Brethren used a printed Preacher's Plan of visits to each of their congregations weekly. After converting all of their preachers to the Church, it was easy to continue the weekly visits, now preaching only LDS doctrine to all the congregations. This opened the door for more than 1,800 souls to be baptized, including all but one of the United Brethren.

SOURCES

Allen, James B., Ronald K. Esplin, and David J. Whittaker. *Men with a Mission: The Quorum of the Twelve Apostles in the British Isles, 1837–1841.* Salt Lake City: Deseret Book, 1992.

Bloxham, V. Ben, James R. Moss, and Larry C. Porter, eds. *Truth Will Prevail: The Rise of The Church of Jesus Christ of Latter-day Saints in the British Isles, 1837–1997.* Cambridge: Cambridge University Press, 1987.

LeBaron, E. Dale. "Sacrifice Brings Forth the Blessings of Heaven." In *British Isles*. Edited by Donald Q. Cannon. Regional Studies in Latter-day Saint Church History series. Provo, Utah: Brigham Young University, 1990. 151–76.

DAVID COOK

UNITED FIRM. See UNITED ORDER.

UNITED KINGDOM. See ENGLAND, IRELAND, SCOTLAND, and WALES.

UNITED ORDER. The term *united order* has been used in Latter-day Saint history in at least three distinct ways: 1) As another name for the law of **consecration** and stewardship (D&C 42:30–42; 48; 51), which some of the **Saints** attempted to live during the early 1830s. 2) As the name for a group of Church leaders who assisted the bishop in managing the law of consecration. This group was organized in the spring of 1832 as a "board of directors for the supervision of business affairs" in **Ohio** and **Missouri** (Arrington, 31). This group formed a "United Order" or "United Firm" to hold property jointly and organize a storehouse for the benefit of the poor (D&C 78:3–4, 82:11–12). The order was dissolved in 1834 (D&C 104). 3) As the name of a series of cooperative ventures in **Utah** and surrounding areas during the 1870s. With the success of the **cooperative movement** of the 1860s, **Brigham Young** promoted the concept of united orders beginning in 1874. This was done not only to lessen the impact of the previous year's nationwide economic panic but also to promote moral reform and emphasize the principles of consecration. Anticipating that there might be some reluctance to move away from the prevailing capitalistic economy, President Young instructed **bishops** not to push their members further than they were willing to go toward cooperative living. This resulted in a "bewildering variety" of organizational forms (May, 578).

In the urban centers of northern Utah these united orders typically sponsored specific business enterprises. In the more isolated communities in southern Utah they sometimes included a more thorough restructuring of society. At **Orderville**, for example, all ate in a community dining hall, wore similar, locally produced clothing, and pooled their resources to operate an array of communally owned enterprises. Most of the orders lasted only briefly, but Orderville continued until the middle

1880s, when it was disbanded amid the pressures of the **antipolygamy** "raids." Though short-lived, the united order movement helped to shield the Saints from economic fluctuations, facilitated important building projects such as the first four Utah **temples**, and inculcated the ideals of industry and cooperative effort that would influence the **welfare program** of the following century.

SOURCES

Arrington, Leonard J., Feramorz Y. Fox, and Dean L. May. *Building the City of God.* Salt Lake City: Deseret Book, 1976.

Israelsen, L. Dwight. "United Orders." *Encyclopedia of Mormonism.* Edited by Daniel H. Ludlow. 4 vols. New York: Macmillan, 1992.

May, Dean L. "The United Order Movement." *Utah History Encyclopedia.* Edited by Allan Kent Powell. Salt Lake City: University of Utah Press, 1994. 576–99.

RICHARD O. COWAN

UNITED STATES OF AMERICA. See AMERICA.

UNIVERSALISTS. The fundamental doctrine of the Universalist Church was that "it is the purpose of God, through the grace revealed in our Lord **Jesus Christ**, to save every member of the human race from sin" (Ahlstrom, 482). John Murray established the first Universalist church in **America** in 1779 in Gloucester, **Massachusetts**. The movement grew quickly during the early nineteenth century; by 1819 the Universalists were publishing a weekly paper, and by 1841 the sect claimed to have more than 500 ministers. By 1869 they supported several colleges and seminaries. **Joseph Smith Sr.** was involved with the Universalists as a young man. This sect, particularly popular in frontier regions of America during the nineteenth century, is also mentioned frequently in the **journals** and diaries of early Latter-day Saints living and proselyting in **Missouri** and other midwestern states. The Universalists merged with the Unitarians in 1961.

SOURCE

Ahlstrom, Sidney E. *A Religious History of the American People.* New Haven, Conn.: Yale University Press, 1972. 481–83.

ANDREW H. HEDGES

UNIVERSITY OF DESERET. See **UNIVERSITY OF UTAH.**

UNIVERSITY OF NAUVOO. The origins of the "University of the City of **Nauvoo**" have a basis in latter-day **revelations**, which contain many references to the value of **education**. Authorization for the school was part of the **Nauvoo Charter** signed by Governor Thomas Carlin of **Illinois**, 16 December 1840. The Nauvoo City Council passed an ordinance creating the university on 3 February 1841. The board of trustees included many of the prominent men of the city. The first president was James Kelley, who had a master's degree from Trinity College in Dublin, **Ireland**. The faculty included **Orson Pratt**, **Orson Spencer**, **Sidney Rigdon**, Gustavus Hills, and John Pack. Orson Pratt taught mathematics, English, astronomy, and philosophy. The university offered classes and granted degrees, but its life was cut short when the **Saints** were forced to leave Nauvoo.

SOURCES

Cannon, Donald Q. "Joseph Smith and the University of Nauvoo." *Joseph Smith: The Prophet, the Man.* Provo, Utah: Religious Studies Center, Brigham Young University, 1993. 285–300.

"University of the City of Nauvoo." *Times and Seasons* 3 (15 December 1841): 630–31.

DONALD Q. CANNON

UNIVERSITY OF THE CHURCH OF JESUS CHRIST OF LATTER-DAY SAINTS. In the early 1890s, the short-lived University of The Church of Jesus Christ of Latter-day Saints in **Salt Lake City** was the highest institution of learning in the Church school system. A board of 26 trustees, including seven **apostles** and the entire **First Presidency**, founded Young University on 1 June 1891. The institution's name was officially changed to the University of The Church of Jesus Christ of Latter-day Saints (commonly called the Church University) at the April 1892 conference. Church leaders called **Willard Young**, **Brigham Young's** son, to serve as president and gave **James E. Talmage** charge of the science department.

During the Church University's first and only school year (1893–94), financial stringency curbed curriculum to classes in chemistry and theology. In competition for students, **University of Utah** officials asked the First Presidency to close the Church University and in return agreed to install Talmage as president of the University of Utah. The First

Presidency accepted the proposition and issued a statement on 18 August 1894, officially closing the Church University. This decision allowed Brigham Young Academy (later **Brigham Young University**) to reassert its place atop the Church school system. Talmage's theological lectures at the Church University were later published under the title *Articles of Faith* (1899).

SOURCES

Quinn, D. Michael. "The Brief Career of Young University at Salt Lake City." *Utah Historical Quarterly* 41 (Winter 1973): 69–89.

Woodworth, Jed L. "Refusing to Die: Financial Crises at Brigham Young Academy, 1877–1897." *BYU Studies* 38 (1999): 70–123.

JED L. WOODWORTH

UNIVERSITY OF UTAH. Though not sponsored by the Church, the University of Utah has nevertheless played a major role in Latter-day Saint education. Founded as the University of Deseret in 1850, it was the only institution of higher learning in Latter-day Saint country. An examination of early catalogues reveals a curriculum essentially on the high school level, and the number of students had still not reached 200 by the end of the century. In 1894 the school's name was officially changed from the University of Deseret to the University of Utah.

By the late twentieth century, the university served between 20,000 and 30,000 students and boasted a law school, a medical school, and graduate schools of social work, health sciences, architecture, mines and engineering, education, and business. Its College of Engineering was noted for significant advances in medical application and computer-generated imagery. Under Dean **Henry Eyring** and his successors, the College of Science granted many advanced degrees and produced significant research. Thousands of teachers and administrators received credentials for working in public schools. A healthy research park allows close cooperation between the university and many private businesses and research institutions. For the benefit of students and adding to the cultural life of the community are programs in music, dance, theater, and art as well as the Utah Museum of Natural History and the Utah Museum of Fine Arts.

Like other state universities, the University of Utah does not sponsor or promote a specific religion. Hiring practices, having to meet guidelines of the funding agencies, require a national search to fill most vacancies in the administration and faculty. This leads to a reduction in the number of LDS faculty. To counterbalance the bias of a secular campus, the Church established an institute of religion in the mid-1930s. Led by educator **Lowell L. Bennion**, the institute offered religious instruction, individual counseling, and social interaction. An expanded institute faculty continues to provide an off-campus haven for interested Latter-day Saint students, including social activities sponsored by **Lambda Delta Sigma** and the **Latter-day Saint Student Association**.

The University of Utah has provided college training to many **general authorities** and countless local Church leaders. **Elders James E. Talmage** and **John A. Widtsoe** served as presidents of the university. Elder **Neal A. Maxwell** was administrative vice president. Because the student body is more than half Latter-day Saint, reflecting the population of the state, the University continues to be a major educator of young Latter-day Saints.

SOURCES

Chamberlin, Ralph V. *Life Sciences at the University of Utah.* Salt Lake City: University of Utah, 1950.

———. *University of Utah: A History of Its First One Hundred Years.* Salt Lake City: University of Utah Press, 1960.

Haglund, Elizabeth, ed. *Remembering the University of Utah.* Salt Lake City: University of Utah Press, 1981.

Hodson, Paul W. *Crisis on Campus: The Exciting Years of Campus Development at the University of Utah.* Salt Lake City: Keeban Corporation, 1987.

DAVIS BITTON

UPPER CANADA. See ONTARIO, CANADA.

URIM AND THUMMIM. Prior to **Joseph Smith**, little was known about the Urim and Thummim. The primary sources of information about this device are a few Old Testament references, complemented by a handful of rabbinical and early Christian commentaries (see Ex. 28:30; Lev. 8:8; Deut. 33:8; Num. 27:21; 1 Sam. 28:6; Ezra 2:63; Neh. 7:65). Most early writers concluded that the Urim and Thummim was a device used by the high priest to communicate with God. The words *Urim* and *Thummim*, translated from the Hebrew, possibly mean "light" and "perfection," respectively.

The Urim and Thummim played an integral role in the translation of the **Book of Mormon** (JS–H 1:42, 62). Joseph Smith received them with the **gold plates** on 22 September 1827, along with the charge to "preserve them" until such time as **Moroni** "should call for them" (JS–H 1:59). Joseph describes the Urim and Thummim as "two transparent stones set in the rim of a [silver] bow" (*HC*, 4:537; JS–H 1:35). Modern revelation teaches that the Urim and Thummim Joseph Smith used was the same one given to the brother of Jared by the Lord (see D&C 17:1; Ether 3:6–16, 23). It differed from that had by **Moses** or **Abraham**.

The Book of Mormon uses the term *interpreters*, first mentioned at the time of King Mosiah (Mosiah 8:13). Presumably, all the record keepers following Mosiah also had them (Mosiah 8:19–20; 28:20; Alma 37:21), and "whosoever is commanded to look in them, the same is called seer" (Mosiah 8:13; JS–H 1:35). While Abraham was still living in Mesopotamia, the Lord showed him the stars and order of the heavens through a Urim and Thummim (Abr. 3:1–5).

The **Doctrine and Covenants** teaches that God resides on a great Urim and Thummim and that this earth, in its sanctified state, will also be a Urim and Thummim, whose inhabitants will have the capacity to learn of "things pertaining to . . . all kingdoms of a lower order" (D&C 130:9). Further, celestial inhabitants will receive a "white stone" (Urim and Thummim) that will reveal "things pertaining to a higher order of kingdoms" (Rev. 2:17; D&C 130:10–11).

SOURCES

Encyclopedia Judaica. 17 vols. Jerusalem: Keter, 1974. 16:8–9.

Hoskisson, Paul Y. "Urim and Thummim." *Encyclopedia of Mormonism.* Edited by Daniel H. Ludlow. 4 vols. New York: Macmillan, 1992. 4:1499–1500.

Peterson, H. Donl. "Translation and Publication of the Book of Abraham." *Encyclopedia of Mormonism.* Edited by Daniel H. Ludlow. 4 vols. New York: Macmillan, 1992. 1:134.

Smith, Joseph. *History of The Church of Jesus Christ of Latter-day Saints [HC].* Edited by B. H. Roberts. 2d ed. rev. 7 vols. Salt Lake City: The Church of Jesus Christ of Latter-day Saints, 1932–51. 1:60–61.

Smith, Joseph Fielding. *Doctrines of Salvation.* Compiled by Bruce R. McConkie. 3 vols. Salt Lake City: Bookcraft, 1954–56. 3:223–24.

Turley, Richard E., Jr. "Seer Stones." *Encyclopedia of Mormonism.* Edited by Daniel H. Ludlow. 4 vols. New York: Macmillan, 1992. 3:1293.

Ungar, Merrill F. *The New Unger's Bible Dictionary.* Edited by R. K. Harrison. Chicago: Moody Press, 1988. 1319–20.

DAVID M. WHITCHURCH

URUGUAY. The Uruguay **Mission** officially opened in August 1947 with Frederick S. Williams as president. The first **sacrament meeting**, held in La Florida Hotel, had only six people in attendance. Among those were Avelino Juan and Maria Esther Rodriguez, the first converts. The first chapel in **South America** was also built in Montevideo; the cornerstone was laid by President **David O. McKay** in 1954 and the building dedicated by **Elder Mark E. Peterson**. Uruguay's first **stake** was organized in Montevideo in 1967, with Vicente Rubio as president. In 1999 the Church began construction on a **temple** in Montevideo. At the beginning of the year 2000, Uruguay, the second country in the world to be completely covered by stakes, had an LDS population of more than 73,194 members living in 15 stakes and 176 **wards** and **branches**.

SOURCES

Hart, John L. "A Half-Century of Modern Church Expansion: 1947–97." *Church News,* 17 September 1997. 8.

"Mission Created in Uruguay Flourishes among a Prepared People." *Church News,* 27 September 1997. 9.

Williams, Frederick S. *From Acorn to Oak Tree: A Personal History of the Establishment and First Quarter Development of the South American Missions.* Fullerton, Calif.: Et Cetera, 1987.

CLARK V. JOHNSON

UTAH. Utah was organized as a territory in 1850 and achieved statehood in 1896. In the 1990s it had the largest majority of a single religion (70% LDS) of any state in the Union.

Utah's first inhabitants were Native American. Anthropologists believe Paleo-Indians lived in the area from 11,000 B.C. to about 6,500 B.C.; archaic peoples dwelled there until about the time of Christ. From about 375 B.C. to about A.D. 1300, the Anasazi inhabited the southern portion of the state, and the Fremont lived in central and northern Utah. About A.D. 1100, Numic peoples—the **Ute**, **Shoshone**, **Paiute**, and Gosiute—began to move into Utah from the southwest. The Diné, or **Navajo**, reached Utah's San Juan region in about 1620.

In the late eighteenth and early nineteenth centuries, mountain men, explorers, and overland migrants began passing through Utah, establishing forts and reporting on the geography and resources. Explorations in 1765 by Juan Maria Antonio Rivera and in 1776 by Fathers Francisco Atanasio Domingues and Silvestre Velez de Escalante originated in Spanish Santa Fe. Fur trappers and traders penetrated Utah in the 1820s, 30s, and 40s from Taos, St. Louis, and British forts in present-day **Washington** and **Montana**. Trappers established forts in the **Uintah Basin** during the 1830s, and **Miles Goodyear** built a post at the confluence of the Weber and Ogden Rivers in 1845. Overland migrants began passing through southern and central Utah over the Old **Spanish Trail** in 1829. In 1841 parties began crossing northern Utah on the way to **California**. **John C. Frémont's** expedition (1843–44) revealed a great deal of information on the Bear River and **Salt Lake Valley**.

As religious persecution and civil war raged in **Hancock County, Illinois**, Latter-day Saints began planning to move west. In preparation for their trek, they studied the reports of Frémont and the mountain men, and at some point **Brigham Young** was inspired to settle in the Salt Lake Valley.

On 23 July 1847, the advance parties headed by **Orson Pratt, Erastus Snow, Willard Richards**, and **George A. Smith** began plowing, planting, and irrigating at the site of **Salt Lake City**. On 26 July the Saints began laying out the city, as **explorers** began searching for places for likely settlements. Church members settled more than 500 communities in Utah, often on land previously occupied by **Indians**.

In 1850 Congress established Utah territory. Under the territorial system, the national government exercised plenary power over local government. Territorial citizens elected their city and county officers, members of the territorial legislature, and a delegate to Congress. The president appointed the territorial executive and judicial officers with the consent of the Senate.

The first set of appointees consisted of about half local people, including Brigham Young as governor, and half outsiders. In 1857, because of erroneous reports of a rebellion in Utah, **James Buchanan** removed Young, appointed **Alfred Cumming** of **Georgia** as governor, and sent an army of 2,500 to escort Cumming. Wary of the approaching army, Young declared martial law and mounted delaying tactics that forced the army to winter near **Fort Bridger**. Tragically, in September 1857, while the territory remained under martial law, units of the Iron County militia, assisted by local Paiutes, massacred a party of immigrants from **Arkansas** and neighboring areas at **Mountain Meadows**.

Negotiations conducted by **Thomas L. Kane**, Lazarus W. Powell, and Ben McCullough led to a resolution by which the army established **Camp Floyd** in Cedar Valley, and Cumming assumed the governorship at Salt Lake City.

The Latter-day Saints' practice of **plural marriage**, together with their control of local government and the economy, caused national opposition to local autonomy in Utah. Congress passed the **Morrill** (1862),

Poland (1874), **Edmunds** (1882), and **Edmunds-Tucker** (1887) Acts to punish polygamists and undermine the economic and political power of the LDS Church.

These laws had the desired effect. The **Manifesto (1890)** began the end of plural marriage, Latter-day Saints cooperated with non-Mormons in business ventures, the two peoples joined together in organizing national political parties, and in 1896 Utah entered the Union.

In the meantime, Utah's economy and population had begun to change. The discovery of minerals in the Oquirrh and Wasatch Mountains in the 1860s, the completion of the transcontinental **railroad** in 1869, the opening of coal mines in Carbon and Emery Counties, and the development of mineral deposits at such places as the **San** Francisco Mountains and Silver Reef attracted Protestants, Catholics, Orthodox Christians, and Jews to Utah. Utah became more racially diverse as Chinese, Japanese, African Americans, and Hispanics moved in. With this diversity, conflicts and discrimination plagued Utah throughout its history.

Like many of the other states in the Intermountain West during the Progressive Era from the 1890s through 1920, Utahns addressed problems caused by environmental abuse, large business organizations, and monopolistic public utilities. The legislature passed laws regulating utilities, mandating worker's compensation, providing pensions for widows, and implementing other programs to try to make the commerce and industry more humane.

, During the 1920s the economy stagnated. Utahns tried prohibition, and they participated with other western states in negotiating a compact to divide the waters of the **Colorado** River.

Utah suffered from the effects of the **great depression** of the 1930s more than most other states. Its unemployment rate skyrocketed to nearly 36%. In attempting to mitigate this economic disaster, Utahns participated in public works programs while the Church helped members through the **welfare program**.

Activities of the federal government became increasingly important during the **great depression, World War II**, and the Cold War. During World War II, the federal government constructed a large number of defense installations, especially in Wasatch Front cities, and populations burgeoned. The Cold War and American involvement in **Korea** and **Vietnam** kept these installations operating.

The national government owns approximately two-thirds of Utah's real estate. Most is managed by the Bureau of Land Management, but some lies in military reservations. Additional lands are managed by the Forest Service, the National Park Service, and the Bureau of Reclamation.

During the 1980s and 90s, Utah's economy diversified. The unemployment rate remained consistent between 3 and 4%, and per-family income exceeded the national average. Church members have contributed to the improvement of the quality of life by involvement in the communities where they live, participation in public service programs, and construction of churches and **temples**. By the year 2000, Utah had 1,604,686 Church members, 458 **stakes**, and 11 temples.

SOURCES

Alexander, Thomas G. *Utah: The Right Place.* 2d ed. Layton, Utah: Gibbs Smith, 1996.

Arrington, Leonard J. *Great Basin Kingdom: An Economic History of the Latter-day Saints, 1830–1900.* Cambridge, Mass.: Harvard University Press, 1958.

May, Dean L. *Utah: A People's History.* Salt Lake City: University of Utah Press, 1987.

THOMAS G. ALEXANDER

UTAH GENEALOGICAL AND HISTORICAL MAGAZINE. The

Utah Genealogical and Historical Magazine, which was published quarterly from 1910 to 1940 by the **Genealogical Society of Utah**, provided genealogical instruction and historical information to subscribers. Articles focused on such topics as news of the Society, printed pedigrees and biographies, local histories, specific research sources and methodologies for more serious genealogists, genealogy lessons to be used in local Church meetings, and the process of submission of ancestral names for temple ordinances. Other articles were often written by **general authorities** to describe and clarify doctrines associated with **temple** and genealogy work.

By 1940 the **First Presidency** assigned responsibility for individual genealogical activities to local **priesthood** leaders, diminishing the need for a separate publication from the Society. After that point, other Church **magazines** (the *Instructor* and the *Improvement Era*) published articles on genealogy and temple work, as well as statements from Church leaders, and the *Utah Genealogical and Historical Magazine* was discontinued.

SOURCES

Allen, James B., and Glen M. Leonard. *The Story of the Latter-day Saints.* 2d ed. Salt Lake City: Deseret Book, 1992.

Cowan, Richard. *The Latter-day Saint Century.* Salt Lake City: Bookcraft, 1999.

Wright, Raymond S., III. "Utah Genealogical and Historical Magazine." *Encyclopedia of Mormonism.* Edited by Daniel H. Ludlow. 4 vols. New York: Macmillan, 1992.

CYNTHIA DOXEY

UTAH-IDAHO SUGAR COMPANY. See SUGAR INDUSTRY.

UTAH STATE HISTORICAL SOCIETY. Founded in 1897, the Utah State Historical Society became a state agency in 1917. It was relatively inactive until 1928, when its board appointed J. Cecil Alter secretary-treasurer and editor-in-chief. That year, Alter edited the first volume of the *Utah Historical Quarterly,* which, except for five years during the Depression, has been published continually since then.

The society hired its first staff in the 1930s and its first professional director, A. Russell Mortensen, in 1950. Mortensen, who headed the society until 1961, arranged in 1957 to move the organization's offices from the state capitol to the historic Kearns Mansion. He also started the state archives program and directed the creation of a research library. Today, the society's collections of published works, manuscripts, and photographs are among its greatest strengths. Among its collections are many valuable sources for LDS history.

In 1968 the legislature changed the society's official name to the Division of State History and separated the state archives from the society. The next year the federal government began funding state historic preservation programs, and the society began to assist in preservation efforts in a variety of ways.

The society moved to the historic Rio Grande Depot in 1980; thereafter the depot's grand lobby housed **Utah** history exhibits, seen by thousands of visitors each year.

SOURCES

Leonard, Glen M., "The Utah State Historical Society, 1897–1972." *Utah Historical Quarterly* 40 (Fall 1972): 300–34.

Topping, Gary, "One Hundred Years at the Utah State Historical Society." *Utah Historical Quarterly* 65 (Summer 1997): 200–302.

MAX J. EVANS

UTAH WAR. Also referred to as Buchanan's Blunder, the **Utah** Expedition, or the coming of **Johnston's Army**, the Utah War was essentially a national disapproval of Latter-day Saint polygamy and polit-ical influence. Ever since **Orson Pratt's** public announcement of **plural marriage** in 1852, the **public image** of the Latter-day Saints had deterio-rated. Furthermore, reports coming back from various federal appointees in the territory of Utah, most particularly from Judge **W. W. Drummond**, fueled an active misperception that **Brigham Young**, as both territorial governor and **prophet**-leader, was wielding theocratic and dictatorial power over a zealous, disloyal, rebellious, and misguided people. Adding to this volatile mix the **Republican's** attack on the Democratic doctrine of popular sovereignty, and their charges that **James Buchanan** (elected 1856) was soft on ending the "**twin relics of barbarism**—polygamy and **slavery**," it is little wonder that Buchanan felt compelled to act.

In April 1857, President Buchanan mobilized an army of 2,500 infantry, artillery, and dragoons under the eventual command of General Albert Sidney Johnston to replace Brigham Young with **Alfred Cumming** as territorial governor and reestablish law and order in Utah Territory.

News of the advancing force reached Brigham Young on 24 July 1857 and caused widespread consternation and disbelief, bordering on panic. Battered, beaten, and driven out of their homes in **Missouri** and **Illinois** not many years before, the Latter-day Saints believed they had been led by the hand of **God** to their new **Zion** in the valleys of the **Great Basin**, where they could worship as American citizens without further fear of **persecution**. Their only options were to meet the army without a fight, resist militarily, negotiate, or abandon their settlements and find refuge in **Vancouver Island, Mexico**, or some other distant locale. In the end, they chose a mixture of all four.

Declaring martial law in mid-September 1857, Brigham Young mobi-lized the **Nauvoo Legion** (the Latter-day Saint militia) to counter the approaching force by resorting to such guerrilla tactics as blocking moun-tain passes, stampeding animals, burning wagons—every stalling tactic short of bloodshed and open combat—in hopes that public opinion might somehow shift against Buchanan's decree. Seventy-four supply wagons, enough to outfit the entire army for three months, were destroyed and 1,400 of the army's 2,000 cattle were captured by such "Mormon raiders" as **Lot Smith** and **Orrin Porter Rockwell**. These actions forced the army to retreat in embarrassment to a burned-out **Fort Bridger**, shiver through a cold winter in improvised shelter at their hastily built headquarters named Camp Scott, and await further instructions and reinforcements.

Though public opinion was shifting against Buchanan, spring might well have witnessed widespread bloodshed had it not been for the efforts of **Thomas L. Kane.** A long-time friend of both the Latter-day Saints and of Democratic administrations, Kane proposed to broker a personal solution to the impasse. With the tacit support of a beleaguered president, Kane sailed at his own expense to **California** via **Panama,** and then overland by horse, arriving in **Salt Lake City** 25 February 1858. Viewed as a godsend by most Latter-day Saint leaders, Kane gained their trust and continued east to Fort Bridger, where he successfully arbitrated terms for a peaceful solution. Cumming would replace Young as governor, the army would be allowed into the territory but would have to establish camp 40 miles south of Salt Lake (**Camp Floyd**), and the Latter-day Saints would receive a presidential pardon. When the army finally marched into the valley on 26 June 1858, Salt Lake City, a community of more than 30,000 residents, was virtually abandoned (its residents scattered southward) and ready to be torched. Church records had been buried and the **Salt Lake Temple** foundation had been covered over. Still, the Saints received Governor Cumming amicably and the crisis was defused. The army remained in Utah three years, until the outbreak of the **Civil War.**

In retrospect, Buchanan's blunder was in "reacting without inquiry to alarmist reports" about the Latter-day Saint people, in dispatching a very costly military expedition hampered by poor communications and coordination, and in caving in to political pressures (Poll, 33). For their part, the Saints underestimated the groundswell of public disapprobation for plural marriage and failed at communicating more effectively Latter-day Saint loyalties towards **America.** In the end, the war helped postpone Utah **statehood** another 40 years, caused unnecessary government expense, and led to hysteria that contributed, in part, to the tragedy of the **Mountain Meadows Massacre** of September 1857. For his part, Thomas L. Kane won the undying gratitude of the Latter-day Saints.

SOURCES

Furniss, Norman. *The Mormon Conflict, 1850–1859.* New Haven, Connecticut: Yale University Press, 1969.

Poll, Richard D., and William P. MacKinnon. "Causes of the Utah War Reconsidered." *Journal of Mormon History* 20:2 (Fall 1994): 16–44.

RICHARD E. BENNETT

UTE INDIANS.

UTE INDIANS. Formerly occupying most of **Colorado** as well as much of **Utah** and northern **New Mexico,** the Ute Indians presently live on reservations in southwestern Colorado and northeastern Utah, numbering approximately 7,500. Historically the Utes had brief encounters with the Spaniards, fur trappers, and traders. In 1847 the **Mormons** arrived in the **Great Basin** and began settling on the Utes' homeland. With the increased encroachment of the Latter-day Saints on the Utes' land, friendly relations became unstable. This brought about a series of minor raids which escalated into two major confrontations known as the **Walker War** and the **Black Hawk War**.

Organized efforts to proselyte the Utes commenced with the establishment of the Southern Indian **Mission** in 1854. During the 1850s and 1860s, a number of Ute children were brought into Latter-day Saint homes to be raised and educated. Some missionary work was conducted among the Utes after 1905, when part of the Uintah Reservation was opened up to the non-Indians. Proselyting efforts were started again in 1949, when the Uintah Basin Mission was established.

SOURCES

Conetah, Fred A. *A History of the Northern Ute People.* Salt Lake City: University of Utah, 1982.

Lyman, June, and Norma Denver, comps. *Ute People: An Historical Study.* Edited by Floyd A. O'Neil and John D. Sylvester. Salt Lake City: University of Utah, 1970.

FRED R. GOWANS AND V. ROBERT WESTOVER

HEAR, O ye Heavens, and give ear, O earth, and rejoice ye inhabitants thereof, for the Lord he is God, and beside him there is none else; and great is his wisdom; marvelous are his ways; and the extent of his doings, none can find out; his purposes fail not, neither are there any who can stay his hand: from eternity to eternity, he is the same, and his years never fail.

I the Lord am merciful and gracious unto them who fear me, and delight to honor them who serve me in righteousness, and in truth; great shall be their reward, and eternal shall be their glory; and unto them will I reveal all mysteries; yea, all the hidden mysteries of my Kingdom from days of old; and for ages to come will I make known unto them the good pleasure of my will concerning all things; yea, even the wonders of eternity shall they know, and things to come will I show them, even the things of many generations; their wisdom shall be great, and their understanding reach to Heaven; before them the wisdom of the wise shall perish, and the understanding of the prudent shall come to nought; for by my Spirit will I enlighten them, and by my power will I make known unto them the secrets of my will; yea, even those things which eye has not seen, nor ear heard, nor yet entered into the heart of man.

We, Joseph and Sidney, being in the Spirit on the sixteenth of February, in the year of our Lord, one thousand eight hundred and thirty two, and through the power of the Spirit, our eyes were opened, and our understandings were enlightened, so as to see and understand the things of God; even things which were from the biginning before the world was, which was ordained of the Father, through his only begotten Son, who was in the bosom of the Father, even from the beginning, of whom we bear record, and the record which we bear is the fulness of the Gospel of Jesus Christ, which is in the Son whom we saw and with whom we conversed in the Heavenly Vision; for as we sat doing the work of translation, which the Lord had appointed unto us, we came to the twenty ninth verse of the fifth chapter of John, which was given unto us thus: speaking of the resurrection of the dead who should hear the voice of the Son of man, and shall come forth; they who have done good in the resurrection of the just, and they who have done evil in the resurrection of the unjust. Now this caused us to marvel, for it was given us of the Spirit; and while we meditated upon these things, the Lord touched the eyes of our understandings, and they were opened, and the glory of the Lord shone round about; and we beheld the glory of the Son, on the right hand of the Father, and received of his fulness; and saw the holy angels, and they who are sanctified before his throne, worshiping God and the Lamb forever and ever. And now after the many testimonies which have been given of him, this is the testimony, last of all, which we give of him, that he lives; for we saw him, even on the right hand of God; and we heard the voice bearing record that he is the only begotten of the Father; that by him, and through him, and of him, the worlds are made, and were created; and the inhabitants thereof are begotten sons and daughters unto God. This we saw also and bear record, that an angel of God, who was in authority in the presence of God, who rebelled against the only begotten Son, (whom the Father loved, and who was in the bosom of the Father,) and was thrust down from the presence of God and the Son, and was called Perdition; for the Heavens wept over him; for he was Lucifer, even the son of the morning; and we beheld and lo, he is fallen! is fallen! even the son of the morning. And while we were yet in the Spirit, the Lord commanded us that we should write the Vision; for behold satan, that old serpant, even the devil, who rebelled against God, and sought to take kingdoms of our God, and of his Christt; who _____ r with the saints of God, and encompasses them about: A_____ he eternal sufferings of those

VISION. Joseph Smith's vision of the three degrees of glory, recorded as Doctrine and Covenants 76, was first published in *The Evening and the Morning Star* in July 1832.

VAN BUREN, MARTIN. Martin Van Buren, the eighth president of the United States, alienated **Joseph Smith** and the **Mormons** with his insensitive attitude and comments. Van Buren was born 5 December 1782 in Kinderhook, **New York**. He practiced law and was admitted to the New York State bar in 1803. In 1807 he married Hannah Hoe, who died of tuberculosis 12 years later. Before Van Buren became president in 1837, he served as U.S. senator, governor of New York, secretary of state, and vice president of the United States.

He encountered the Latter-day Saints on 29 November 1839, when Joseph Smith and **Elias Higbee** called on him to seek help from the federal government in obtaining redress for the property lost and afflictions suffered by the **Saints** during the **Missouri** persecutions. The first meeting in history between a Latter-day Saint **prophet** and a U.S. president was memorable but frustrating. Van Buren asked Joseph Smith what the difference was between Mormonism and other religions of the day. The Prophet replied that the "mode of baptism, and the gift of the Holy Ghost by the laying on of hands" were the basic differences (Smith, 42). When the conversation changed from religion to the subject of Latter-day Saints being compensated for property lost in Missouri, Van Buren showed little sympathy, so Joseph and Elias spent the next two months trying to gain support from various senators and representatives.

Finally, in early February, the Prophet and Higbee met with Van Buren one last time. Joseph Smith reported that during this interview the president treated them disrespectfully, saying: "Gentlemen, your cause is just, but I can do nothing for you. . . . If I take up for you I shall lose the vote of Missouri" (Smith, 80). His position might be partially excused because of the prevailing doctrine of states' rights. Nevertheless, it infuriated Joseph Smith, who wrote: "On my way home I did not fail to proclaim the iniquity and insolence of Martin Van Buren, toward myself and an injured people . . . and may he never be elected again to any office of trust or power" (Smith, 89). This prophecy came true. Van Buren lost the election of 1840 to William Henry Harrison. He also lost as the nominee of the Free Soil Party in the presidential election of 1848. Martin Van Buren died 24 July 1862 in his hometown of Kinderhook.

SOURCES

Garr, Arnold K. "Joseph Smith: Candidate for President of the United States." In *Illinois*. Edited by H. Dean Garrett. Regional Studies in Latter-day Saint Church History series. Provo, Utah: Brigham Young University, 1992. 151–68.

Lynch, Dennis T. *An Epoch and a Man: Martin Van Buren and His Times.* New York: H. Liveright, 1929.

Smith, Joseph. *History of The Church of Jesus Christ of Latter-day Saints.* Edited by B. H. Roberts. 2d ed. rev. 7 vols. Salt Lake City: The Church of Jesus Christ of Latter-day Saints, 1932–51. 4:42, 80, 88.

ARNOLD K. GARR

VANCOUVER ISLAND, CANADA.

In a letter published 1 November 1845, **Brigham Young** named Vancouver Island as a possible place of western settlement for the Latter-day Saints. This influenced British Latter-day Saints to petition Queen Victoria to support their settling on the island (McCue, 4). The petition was ignored, and no Latter-day Saints lived on the island until the 1875 arrival of William Francis and Maria Judson Copley, who settled near Shawnigan Lake. In 1887 Anthony Maitland Stenhouse, a member of the **British Columbia** legislative assembly, resigned his seat to become the first LDS convert on the island. Stenhouse then moved to an LDS community in southern Alberta.

Missionary work began on the island on 13 May 1903, when seven **elders**, led by President Nephi Pratt of the Northwestern States Mission, arrived in Victoria. The first **Sunday School** was organized in 1918 with 21 members. Independent branches were organized in Victoria and Nanaimo in 1946. After a **branch** was established at Port Alberni, the Vancouver Island **District** was created as part of the Western Canadian Mission in 1959.

The Victoria British Columbia Stake was organized by Elder **Boyd K. Packer** of the **Quorum of the Twelve Apostles** on 9 February 1975, with Howard L. Biddulph as the first **stake president**. On 12 March 1984, the northern units of the **stake** were organized into the Courtenay District of the **Canada** Vancouver Mission by Elder Dean L. Larsen of the presidency of the **Seventy**. The Nanaimo British Columbia Stake was organized on 10 October 1997 by Elder D. Todd Christofferson of the First Quorum of the Seventy. This second stake also included the units of the former Courtenay District.

SOURCES

McCue, Robert J. "The Church of Jesus Christ of Latter-day Saints and Vancouver Island: The Establishment and Growth of the Mormon Community." *B. C. Studies* (Summer 1979).

1999–2000 Church Almanac. Salt Lake City: Deseret News, 1998. 290–91.

"The Saints on Vancouver Island." *Church News,* 16 August 1998, 6–7.

HOWARD L. BIDDULPH

VANDENBERG, JOHN H. John Henry Vandenberg, a **presiding bishop, assistant to the Twelve,** and **Seventy,** was born 18 December 1904 in **Ogden, Utah,** to Dirk Vandenberg and Maria Alkema. He attended Weber Academy and then was called on a mission to **Holland** in 1925. He married Ariena Stok 18 June 1930, and they became the parents of two daughters. He was involved in several business enterprises in Denver, **Colorado,** including the livestock and textile industries. Before he became a **general authority,** he served as a **stake president**'s counselor in both the Denver and Ensign Stake in **Salt Lake City.** He was sustained as presiding bishop of the Church on 30 September 1961 and served in that office until 6 April 1972. He then became an assistant to the Twelve from 1972 to 1976 and a member of the First **Quorum** of Seventy from 1976 to 1978, when he was named an **emeritus general authority.** Elder Vandenberg died 3 June 1992 in Sandy, Utah, at age 87.

SOURCES

"John H. Vandenberg." *Improvement Era.* November 1967. 61.

1999–2000 Church Almanac. Salt Lake City: Deseret News, 1998. 85.

ARNOLD K. GARR

VANDEWEGHE, COLLEEN HUTCHINS. See HUTCHINS, COLLEEN.

VANUATU. Vanuatu, a Melanesian island nation formerly known as the New Hebrides and jointly colonized by the British and French Empires under a condominium government, gained its name and its independence in 1980. The name Vanuatu simply means "Our Land." Under the colonial government there were actually two governments, along with two heads of state, two government headquarters, two hospitals, two immigration services, two police forces, two currencies, and a duplication of services in almost all areas.

On 15 July 1973, **Fiji-Suva Mission president** Ebbie L. Davis and **Elder** John H. Groberg of the **Seventy** flew to the New Hebrides to organize the first **branch** of the Church in Port Vila. There had been members of the Church in the New Hebrides for more than 15 years; most of these early members were Tongans or Fijians who were working in the New Hebrides. Lanipota Fehoko, a member from **Tonga**, was made the first branch president.

Elders Mokofisi and Malohifo'ou, transferred from Tonga, were the first missionaries sent to Port Vila on 12 January 1975. The first chapel in Port Vila was dedicated by President Arthur F. Kay of the Seventy on 23 May 1989.

Vanuatu was dedicated for the preaching of the gospel by Elder L. **Tom Perry** on 10 August 1996. At a former **World War II** battle spot on the beach at Betio, Tarawa, **Kiribati**, Elder Perry dedicated a total of four countries (one being Vanuatu) and three provinces of **France** for the preaching of the gospel. By the year 2000 the country had 1,121 members living in 8 branches.

SOURCES

Britsch, R. Lanier. *Unto the Islands of the Sea: A History of the Latter-day Saints in the Pacific.* Salt Lake City: Deseret Book, 1986. 514–15.

"Elder Perry Creates First Kiribati Stake, Dedicates Islands." *Church News,* 21 September 1996. 3.

Fiji-Suva Mission Historical Report. Archives, Historical Department, The Church of Jesus Christ of Latter-day Saints, Salt Lake City.

1999–2000 Church Almanac. Salt Lake City: Deseret News, 1998. 405.

W. JAMES JACOB

VAN VLIET, STEWART. From the time he first met the Latter-day Saints at the beginning of the **Utah War**, Stewart Van Vliet became their friend and advocate. He was born 21 July 1815 in New York, and at age 21 he entered **West Point** and became an officer in the U.S. Army. Representing the Quartermaster Corps, Captain Van Vliet arrived in **Salt Lake City** on 7 September 1857, intending to secure food and forage for the approaching **Johnston's Army**. His request was denied, but he was impressed with the Latter-day Saint people and determined to help bring about a peaceful solution to the conflict. He vowed that if the government made **war** against the Saints, he would withdraw from the army rather than shed the blood of American citizens. His influence in **Washington, D.C.**, helped bring an end to the matter.

SOURCES

Flake, Dennis D. "A Study of Mormon Resistance during the Utah War." Master's thesis, Brigham Young University, 1979. 38–43.

Rich, Russell R. *Ensign to the Nations.* Provo, Utah: Brigham Young University, 1972. 245–48.

Smith, Joseph Fielding. *Essentials in Church History.* Salt Lake City: Deseret Press, 1971. 410–11.

DENNIS D. FLAKE

VENEZUELA. Elder **Marion G. Romney** organized the first **branch** of the Church in Venezuela on 2 November 1966, with Carl C. Wilcox as president. Church **meetings** had been held at the home of Brother Wilcox prior to the branch's official organization. The branch consisted of 45 members, most of whom were expatriates working in Venezuela.

Soon after the branch's organization, the first four missionaries were sent to the area from the **Costa Rica** Mission. Work advanced to the point that the Colombia-Venezuela Mission was created in 1968 and the Venezuela Mission was formed on 1 July 1971, with approximately 1,200 members.

President **Gordon B. Hinckley** announced plans for a **temple** in Caracas, Venezuela, in 1995, and in 1998 it was reassigned to be one of the smaller temples. The Church began construction on the temple in January 1999. By the beginning of the year 2000 there were 89,484 members living in 16 **stakes** and 219 **wards** and **branches** throughout Venezuela.

SOURCES

Echeverri, Mario G. "Venezuela." *Ensign* 7 (February 1977): 30–33.

"Five New Temples Are Announced." *Church News,* 11 October 1997. 3.

"From around the World." *Church News,* 4 November 1995. 12.

1999–2000 Church Almanac. Salt Lake City: Deseret News, 1998. 405–6.

KYLE R. WALKER AND FRANCISCO GERARDO GIMENEZ

VERMONT. Admitted as the fourteenth state of the Union on 4 March 1791, Vermont was the birthplace of **Joseph Smith, Brigham Young,**

Hyrum Smith, Oliver Cowdery, Heber C. Kimball, and Erastus Snow. Altogether, the Green Mountain State, as it is nicknamed, was the birthplace to more than a dozen **general authorities**.

In 1831 Jared Carter became the first Latter-day Saint missionary to preach the gospel in Vermont. He baptized 27 people and organized a **branch** in Benson. A year later Jared and his brother, Simeon, baptized more than a hundred people in the state. Missionary work continued until the **martyrdom** of the Prophet Joseph in 1844. Two years later, when the **pioneers** migrated to the Rocky Mountains, most of the faithful **Saints** in Vermont joined them. During the next half century very little missionary activity took place in the state. In 1893 the **Eastern States Mission** was reopened, and Vermont was within its jurisdiction.

On 23 December 1905, the Church dedicated a monument to Joseph Smith in **Sharon, Vermont**, the birthplace of the prophet. It is a polished granite shaft that stands 38½ feet tall, one foot for each year of Joseph Smith's life. In 1927 Vermont became part of the Canadian **Mission**, and in 1937 the state was included in the newly created New England States Mission. The first **stake** in Vermont was organized at Montpelier on 11 April 1976. By the beginning of the year 2000, the state had 3,759 members living in one stake and 12 **wards** and branches. By the end of the twentieth century, more than 55,000 tourists each year visited Joseph Smith's birthplace and other Church history sites in the state.

SOURCES

Cowan, Richard O. "Yankee Saints: The Church in New England during the Twentieth Century." In *New England.* Edited by Donald Q. Cannon. Regional Studies in Latter-day Saint Church History series. Provo, Utah: Brigham Young University, 1988. 101–18.

Berrett, LaMar C., ed. *New England and Eastern Canada.* Vol. 1 of *Sacred Places.* Salt Lake City: Bookcraft, 1999. 87–132.

1999–2000 Deseret News Church Almanac. Salt Lake City: Deseret News, 1998. 258–59.

ARNOLD K. GARR

VERNAL UTAH TEMPLE. The Vernal Utah Temple is the 51st operating temple in the Church and the first Latter-day Saint **temple** built from an existing structure. Following an extensive renovation of the Uintah Stake Tabernacle, it became the 10th temple in the state of **Utah**. The Uintah Stake Tabernacle was built between 1899 and 1907, becoming the most prominent building in all eastern Utah. The building was simple in design and character and was built from locally available materials and donated labor. It was built with a rough-cut sandstone foundation and handmade brick and had stone arches over the doors and windows. It had a single octagonal tower. The interior had painted wood trim (grained to look like oak), a raised rostrum, and a horseshoe gallery on the two sides and the rear of the space. The building was closed by the **Church** in 1984. From then until February 1994, when the temple was announced, the future of the building was uncertain.

The temple includes an area of new construction adjacent to the old building. A basement was excavated for the baptismal font, and a new tower, with a statue of **Moroni**, was added to the building. The temple has two ordinance rooms and three sealing rooms. The popularity of the building was attested by the more than 120,000 visitors during the two-week open house, and more than 20,000 participants in the 11 dedication sessions. The temple was dedicated 2 November 1997 by **President Gordon B. Hinckley**.

SOURCE

Jackson, Roger P. "The Building of the Vernal Utah Temple." *Utah Preservation* 2 (1998): 11–18.

ROGER P. JACKSON

VIETNAM. Vietnam was first introduced to the Church through **war** as Latter-day Saint service groups were organized in that nation, starting in the early 1960s. On 30 October 1966, **Elder Gordon B. Hinckley** dedicated Vietnam for missionary work. A year later the Church was recognized by the Saigon government. In 1968 there were 60 groups serving more than 5,500 American **Saints**, mostly in the military. By 1973 most were withdrawn. Full-time missionaries served in Saigon from 6 April 1973 until they were evacuated on 5 April 1975. Before the fall of Saigon to the Communists on 30 April 1975, there were approximately 250 Vietnamese Saints in the Saigon **Branch**. An estimated 100 escaped before the collapse, and most of the 150 who were left behind eventually found their way to **America**, though some remained.

In the 1990s the Church provided humanitarian assistance to Vietnam, and on 6 January 1993 it began sending nonproselyting missionaries. On 28 February 1996, Vietnamese ambassador Le Van Bang visited the **First Presidency** and spoke at **Brigham Young University**. In the spring of 1996, while visiting Hanoi, President Hinckley gave an addendum to his 1967 dedicatory prayer. At the end of the twentieth century there were about 100 expatriate Saints living in Hanoi and Ho Chi Minh City, and the Church had yet to establish legal recognition.

SOURCES

Bradshaw, William S., and Marjorie Bradshaw. "Escape from Vietnam: An Interview with Nguyen Van The." *Dialogue* 13 (Spring 1980): 23–39.

Britsch, R. Lanier. *From the East: History of the Latter-day Saints in Asia, 1851–1996.* Salt Lake City: Deseret Book, 1998. 417–51.

RAY C. HILLAM

VIEW OF THE HEBREWS. A book published in 1823 and 1825 by the Reverend Ethan Smith, *View of the Hebrews* has been cited by some anti-Mormon writers as a possible source of the Book of Mormon. Since 1903 some critics who rejected Joseph Smith's statement of the origin of the Book of Mormon have claimed that the Prophet got it from *View of the Hebrews,* or that at the very least he got the main ideas from reading that book. They claim, for example, that Joseph got the idea that the American Indians were Israelites from *View of the Hebrews.* But even in this similarity, the Book of Mormon is different in bringing Lehi's family to the Americas by boat, where Reverend Smith argues the Tribes of Israel were driven north and crossed over a land bridge in the Bering Straits. *View of the Hebrews* was out of print for more than 170 years until 1996, when the Brigham Young University Religious Studies Center reprinted it so today's readers can see that, though it has a few similarities to the Book of Mormon, there are major differences between the two works.

SOURCE

Smith, Ethan. *View of the Hebrews.* 2d ed. 1825. Edited by Charles D. Tate Jr. Provo, Utah: Religious Studies Center, Brigham Young University, 1996.

CHARLES TATE

VIRGINIA. In 1837 Elder Jedediah M. Grant and later his brother Joshua were legendary missionaries in Virginia. Remembered later for his power of oratory and persuasive logic, Elder Grant often used the Prophecy on War (D&C 87) as his text. Early success in Patrick, Montgomery, Wythe, and Nelson Counties set a pattern for further Church growth. Those converted in Virginia who contributed significantly to the

Church's history include Henry G. Boyle, later president of the **Southern States Mission**, and David H. Peery, **Civil War** veteran and western educator.

At the **martyrdom** of **Joseph Smith** (1844), most missionary efforts ceased, and members generally gathered to Church settlements in the West. Following the Civil War, missionary efforts resumed (1870). Six years later Virginia was included in the Southern States Mission, where it continued with only a brief interruption (1902–3) until 1929, when Virginia was included in the East Central States Mission.

Substantial Church growth was fueled in the twentieth century by major population influxes supported by government, military, and industrial operations. In 1957 the first **stake** was organized. By the year 2000 Virginia had two **missions**, 17 stakes, and a Church population of 66,622.

SOURCES

Berrett, LaMar C. "History of the Southern States Mission, 1831–1861." Master's thesis, Brigham Young University, 1960.

Jenson, Andrew. *Encyclopedic History of The Church of Jesus Christ of Latter-day Saints.* Salt Lake City: Deseret News, 1941.

1999–2000 Church Almanac. Salt Lake City: Deseret News, 1998. 241–44.

DAVID F. BOONE

VIRGIN ISLANDS, BRITISH. The British Virgin Islands, which are less developed than the U.S. **Virgin Islands**, have a population of about 20,000, primarily of African descent. At the beginning of the year 2000, there were 11 Latter-day Saints there in one **branch**.

RICHARD O. COWAN

VIRGIN ISLANDS, U.S. Located 70 miles east of **Puerto Rico**, the U.S. Virgin Islands consist of St. Thomas, St. John, St. Croix, and many tiny islands. The residents hold U.S. citizenship.

In 1969 Earl and Celia Keele moved to St. Thomas from **Nevada** with their two children. They held **Sunday School** in their home and received leadership from the **branch** in Puerto Rico. Later, James and Carolyn Boykin also moved to the island. Debra Rybacki met with the **family** and in January 1976 was the first person baptized in the Virgin Islands. The first full-time missionaries to the islands labored there in 1978.

In the year 2000 there were 289 members and 2 branches in the Virgin Islands.

SOURCES

Millett, Richard L. "The Work Spreads to the Other Islands of the Caribbean." Manuscript.

1999–2000 Church Almanac. Salt Lake City: Deseret News, 1998. 407.

DAVID R. CROCKETT

VISION, FIRST. See FIRST VISION.

VISION OF THE REDEMPTION OF THE DEAD.

On Thursday, 3 October 1918, President **Joseph F. Smith** sat pondering on the **scriptures**, particularly 1 Peter 3:18–20 and 4:6, and reflecting on the Savior's infinite atonement. He saw in vision "an innumerable company of the spirits of the just" (D&C 138:12) in the postmortal spirit world as the crucified Lord entered therein. President Smith watched as the Master entered the spirit world and "preached to them the everlasting gospel" (v. 18).

President Smith beheld that the Redeemer did not go in person to the wicked but organized his righteous servants to carry "the light of the gospel to them that were in darkness" (v. 30; compare vv. 20–22, 36–37). He saw that "the dead who repent will be redeemed, through obedience to the ordinances of the house of God." President Smith also confirmed the doctrine that faithful **Saints** who die continue to preach and labor in the postmortal spirit world (v. 57).

The vision of the redemption of the dead was dictated by President Smith to his son, **Elder Joseph Fielding Smith**, who read it to the **First Presidency**, the Twelve, and the **Church Patriarch** on 31 October 1918. After President Smith's death on 19 November, it appeared in the *Deseret News* and in every official Church magazine. It was published also in chapter 24 of *Gospel Doctrine*, a collection of President Smith's sermons and writings.

At the April 1976 conference of the Church, the assembled Saints approved the First Presidency's proposal that this vision be added to the standard works and placed in the **Pearl of Great Price**. In June of 1979, by administrative decision, the vision was shifted to the **Doctrine and Covenants** and became section 138. This **vision**, a grand illustration of the principle of the expanding canon in a living Church, represents "a complete and comprehensive confirmation of the established doctrine of the Church where salvation for the dead is concerned" (McConkie, 11).

SOURCES

Ehat, Andrew F., and Lyndon W. Cook, comps. and eds. *The Words of Joseph Smith.* Provo, Utah: Religious Studies Center, Brigham Young University, 1980. 370–71.

McConkie, Bruce R. "A New Commandment: Save Thyself and Thy Kindred!" *Ensign* 6 (August 1976): 7–11.

ROBERT L. MILLET

VISION OF THE THREE DEGREES OF GLORY. One of the great **revelations** of all times, the vision of the three degrees of glory was received by **Joseph Smith** and **Sidney Rigdon** on 16 February 1832. After holding a series of conferences in the **Kirtland** area, Joseph Smith and Sidney Rigdon returned to the task of working on the **Joseph Smith Translation of the Bible** at the **John Johnson** home in **Hiram, Ohio**. They reviewed John 5:29 concerning the resurrection of the just and the unjust, and as they meditated upon this subject, the heavens were opened and they saw a **vision** concerning life after resurrection from the dead. **Elder Philo Dibble** and several men were present in the room when the vision opened to the **Prophet** and Rigdon. It appears that the vision lasted more than an hour. Dibble reported that he felt the influence of the Spirit but did not see the vision, and he witnessed the effect of the vision on the Prophet: "Joseph wore black clothes, but at this time seemed to be dressed in an element of glorious white, and his face shone as if it were transparent" (Andrus and Andrus, 76). He also indicated that Joseph and Sidney discussed with one another what they saw during the heavenly manifestation. No one else in the room saw the glories. The vision was recorded by Sidney Rigdon and is found in section 76 of the **Doctrine and Covenants** ("Recollections," 302–4).

The vision is actually a series of visions. Joseph Smith and Sidney Rigdon recorded first seeing the Son of **God** sitting on the right hand of God with holy angels worshiping him. They bore solemn testimony of **Jesus Christ** and his role as the Son of God (20–24). A vision of **Satan** and his role in the pre-earth life as well as his attack on the **kingdom of God** in this life were also recorded, along with the qualifications of those who will become sons of perdition (25–48). They then saw three visions describing the celestial, terrestrial, and telestial kingdoms, including information about the kinds of people who inherit each of these kingdoms. There followed a comparison of the three glories and how each would be administered (86–106). An invitation was issued for all to come to the knowledge contained in these visions (107–19).

The information in this vision departed significantly from the beliefs of the Protestant world of the 1800s and has had a significant impact on the Saints' knowledge of life after death.

SOURCES

Andrus, Hyrum L., and Helen Mae Andrus. *They Knew the Prophet.* Salt Lake City: Deseret Book, 1999.

Cannon, Donald Q. "Doctrine and Covenants: Section 76." *Encyclopedia of Mormonism.* Edited by Daniel H. Ludlow. 4 vols. New York: Macmillan, 1992. 1:413–14.

Dahl, Larry. "The Visions of the Glories (D&C 76)." *The Doctrine and Covenants.* Studies in Scripture series, vol. 1. Edited by Robert L. Millet and Kent P. Jackson. Sandy, Utah: Randall Book, 1984. 22–308.

"Recollection of the Prophet Joseph Smith." *Juvenile Instructor* 27 (May 1892): 302–4.

Smith, Joseph. *History of The Church of Jesus Christ of Latter-day Saints.* Edited by B. H. Roberts. 2d ed. rev. 7 vols. Salt Lake City: The Church of Jesus Christ of Latter-day Saints, 1932–51. 245.

Smith, Joseph Fielding. *Church History and Modern Revelation.* 2 vols. Salt Lake City: Deseret Book, 1953. 2:50.

Woodford, Robert J. "The Historical Development of the Doctrine and Covenants." Ph.D. diss., Brigham Young University, 1974. 926–72.

H. DEAN GARRETT

VISIONS. Visions are a form of **revelation**, given to the visual senses, in which God discloses information concerning himself or his divine purposes. Visions lift, bless, call, or teach individuals and groups. Visions are visual experiences in which anything past, present, or future can be made known. Personal visitations from God, **angels**, or departed spirits who have been commissioned to impart relevant information are also referred to as visions.

During the Old Testament period, numerous visions were given to **prophets**. For instance, many ancient prophets such as **Moses**, Abraham, Nephi, and the brother of Jared were given significant visions (Moses 1:8, 27–29; Abr. 3; 1 Ne. 11–14; Ether 3:25–26). In fact, some prophets also related visions in which they saw Deity. Moses, for example, had a vision when he saw the Lord "face to face" (Moses 1:2). In the New Testament period, Stephen, Saul, and John had visions of the Savior (Acts 7:55–56; Acts 9:1–7; Rev. 1:13–18). Peter received a vision teaching the necessity of preaching the gospel to the Gentiles (Acts 10:9–16).

In modern times the Prophet **Joseph Smith** received many visions to aid in restoring the gospel and the Church organization upon the earth. He communicated with the Father and the Son in the **First Vision** (JS–H 1:14–20). Three years later the angel **Moroni** appeared and told him about the **gold plates** of the **Book of Mormon** (JS–H 1:30–54). **John the Baptist** restored the **Aaronic Priesthood** (D&C 13), and shortly afterward **Peter, James, and John** restored the **Melchizedek Priesthood** (D&C 27:12–13; 128:20). Joseph Smith and **Sidney Rigdon** saw a **vision of the three degrees of glory** (D&C 76), and one week following the **Kirtland Temple** dedication, the Prophet and **Oliver Cowdery** were visited by the Savior, Moses, **Elias**, and **Elijah** (D&C 110). President **Lorenzo Snow** was visited by **Jesus Christ** in the **Salt Lake Temple** (Snow). President **Joseph F. Smith** received a **vision of the redemption of the dead** (D&C 138). Numerous other visions and personal visitations are also recorded in Church history, including additional appearances of **God the Father**. Concerning the probability of visions in the last days before the second coming, the Old Testament prophet Joel wrote, "And it shall come to pass afterward, that I will pour out my spirit upon all flesh; and your sons and your daughters shall prophesy, your old men shall dream dreams, your young men shall see visions" (Joel 2:28).

SOURCES

Bergin, Allen E. "Visions."*Encyclopedia of Mormonism*. Edited by Daniel H. Ludlow. 4 vols. New York: Macmillan, 1992.

McConkie, Bruce R. *Mormon Doctrine*. 2d ed. Salt Lake City: Bookcraft, 1966.

Snow, LeRoi C. "An Experience of My Father's." *Improvement Era* 36 (September 1933): 677, 679.

BRIAN M. HAUGLID

VISITING TEACHING. Organized under the auspices of **Relief Society**, visiting teaching provides one way to develop and maintain a feeling of sisterhood and fellowship among the women in a **ward**. The local Relief Society president usually assigns companionships of two women to regularly visit other women in the ward, deliver a spiritual thought, assess the needs of the **family**, and then report back to the president. She can then inform the **bishop** if the family needs his assistance.

The history of visiting teaching goes back to 1843, when there was a "necessity committee" appointed to visit and bring relief to the poor and suffering. Since that time, visiting teaching has also included the sharing of an inspirational message with the women. In 1987 visiting teaching messages became available in the Church's **international magazines** and the *Ensign*.

SOURCES

"A Circle of Support: The New Visiting Teaching Messages." *Ensign* 17 (January 1987): 32.

History of Relief Society—1842–1966. Salt Lake City: Relief Society General Board Association, 1967. 68.

Kimball, Spencer W. *The Teachings of Spencer W. Kimball*. Edited by Edward L. Kimball. Salt Lake City: Bookcraft, 1982.

CYNTHIA DOXEY

VISITORS' CENTERS. Visitors' centers, earlier known as bureaus of information, are buildings located adjacent to **temples** or historical sites. The first was established at **Salt Lake City's Temple Square** in 1903, and others followed as the Church purchased key historic sites during the early twentieth century.

In addition to permanent structures, the Church has constructed temporary visitors' centers for temple open houses, as well as pavilions at fairs or expositions in cities around the world. Experience at the **New York** World's Fair pavilion in 1964 and 1965 enabled the Church to transform its existing visitors' centers into more effective teaching tools.

Open to the public free of charge, these centers include displays and literature providing information about the Church and the specific site. Visitors may walk through the surrounding grounds at their leisure or take guided tours. Each center is staffed with volunteer couples or sister missionaries. Arrangements can be made for missionaries to visit those who desire further information.

In the 1990s most visitors' centers were remodeled to emphasize three themes: families are forever, our Heavenly Father's plan for our salvation, and most importantly, Jesus the Christ is the Savior of all mankind. Replicas of the *Christus*, a statue by Danish sculptor Bertel Thorvaldsen, have been placed in many centers to represent this central doctrine.

Under the direction of the Missionary Department, the Church managed visitors' centers at 29 sites in 1999. The best known and most frequently visited site is Temple Square in Salt Lake City, which receives

more than five million visitors annually. It is the most visited attraction in
Utah.

SOURCES

Jacobsen, Florence Smith. "Christus Statue." *Encyclopedia of Mormonism*. Edited by
Daniel H. Ludlow. 4 vols. New York: Macmillan, 1992. 1:273–74.

Peterson, Gerald Joseph. "History of Mormon Exhibits in World Expositions."
Master's thesis, Brigham Young University, Provo, Utah, 1974.

Seastrand, Gareth W. "Visitors' Centers." *Encyclopedia of Mormonism*. Edited by
Daniel H. Ludlow. 4 vols. New York: Macmillan, 1992. 4:1517–18.

W. JEFFREY MARSH

VOICE OF WARNING. Titled after the phrase "voice of warning" in
Doctrine and Covenants 1:4, the 216-page *Voice of Warning* was written
in 1837 by **Parley P. Pratt** as a missionary tract introducing the history
and doctrine of the Church. It was the first missionary tract giving a
comprehensive exposition of the tenets of Mormonism and was the most
effective and widely distributed missionary tract in the nineteenth
century. Subtitled "containing a declaration of the faith and doctrine of
the Church," this tract explains the **Restoration** and coming forth of the
Book of Mormon as a fulfillment of biblical prophecies. It also reviews
the prophetically foretold signs of the times and the events of the Second
Coming and the Millennium. **Elder** Pratt's descriptions of Latter-day Saint
doctrine, his exposition of biblical passages, and many of his expressions
became standard formulae in future apologetic works.

DAVID ROLPH SEELY

Welfare Services. On 10 September 1982 United States president Ronald Reagan tours a Church cannery with Gordon B. Hinckley of the First Presidency to see the Church's welfare program in action.

WALDENSIANS. During the period of the first LDS mission in **Italy** (1850–67), **missionaries** concentrated their proselyting efforts and found their greatest measure of success among the Waldensians, a Protestant community living in the Cottian Alps southwest of Turin. Tracing the roots of their movement to a religious reformer named Peter Waldo (d. 1217), the Waldensians were branded as heretics for challenging the doctrinal and ecclesiastical authority of the Catholic Church, and over time they were forced to take refuge in the mountain valleys of Piedmont to escape persecution.

Contrary to the high expectations of the LDS missionaries, who viewed the Waldensians as a remnant of Israel with doctrines and history similar to their own, proselyting labors of more than nearly two decades yielded only about 180 converts. The insular nature of Waldensian religious society, opposition from local pastors, and the impoverished living conditions of the people worked against the missionaries' efforts. The mission was disbanded by 1867 because many members (approximately 70 total) had immigrated to **Utah** and the rest had either apostatized or been excommunicated. Though few in number, the Waldensian converts who made the **pioneer** trek from Italy to **Zion** (among whom are the Beus, Cardon, Malan, Bertoch, Pons, and Chatelain families) left a legacy of faith, sacrifice, and industry.

SOURCES

Stokoe, Diane. "The Mormon Waldensians." Master's thesis, Brigham Young University, 1985.

Tourn, Giorgio. *I Valdesi: La Singolare Vicenda di un Popolo-Chiesa (1170–1976)*. Torino, Italy: Claudiana, 1977.

———, et al. *You Are My Witnesses: The Waldensians across 800 Years*. Torino, Italy: Claudiana, 1989.

Watts, George B. *The Waldenses in the New World*. Durham, NC: Duke University Press, 1941.

JAMES A. TORONTO

WALES. Missionaries crossed the border from **England** to Wales as early as 1840, but the gospel was not preached to Welsh speakers until late 1843, when William Henshaw was sent to the Merthyr Tydfil area. There were nearly 500 Welsh converts when Captain **Dan Jones** was assigned to preside over members and missionaries in Wales in December 1845. Many **pamphlets** and a monthly periodical, *Prophwyd y Jubili* (*Prophet of the Jubilee*), together with a small missionary force resulted in an increasing number of convert baptisms in Wales—about 500 during 1846, nearly 1,000 during 1847, and more than 1,700 during 1848.

When Dan Jones departed for **America** with about 330 Welsh converts in early 1849, William Phillips, Abel Evans, and John Davis began to preside over the LDS Church in Wales. Church membership there peaked at more than 5,000 in 1852. In August of 1852, Dan Jones returned for his second **mission** and experienced success similar to that of his first mission.

More than 500 Welsh converts went with Captain Jones to America in April 1856, and at this point the Latter-day Saint presence in Wales began a sharp decline. The periodical ceased publication in April 1862, and for many years membership consisted of only a handful of members and missionaries. The Church experienced a resurgence in the twentieth century. There were 1,500 members in 1950, and the first **stake** was organized 12 January 1975 in Merthyr Tydfil. By the year 2000 there were 7,097 members living in two stakes with 20 wards and branches.

SOURCES

Dennis, Ronald D. *The Call of Zion: The Story of the First Welsh Mormon Emigration.* Provo, Utah: Religious Studies Center, Brigham Young University, 1988.

———. *Welsh Mormon Writings from 1844 to 1862: A Historical Bibliography.* Provo, Utah: Religious Studies Center, Brigham Young University, 1988.

———, ed. and trans. *Prophet of the Jubilee.* Provo, Utah: Religious Studies Center, Brigham Young University, 1997.

1999–2000 Church Almanac. Salt Lake City: Deseret News, 1998. 402–3.

RONALD D. DENNIS

WALKARA. One of the most notable Indian leaders of the American West was Walkara (also Walker, Wakara), a **Ute** war chief who was brave, fierce, proud, strong, brutal, moody, vain, and shrewd—a man who lived his life passionately and to the full. He was the epitome of the native chieftain, and although massive European encroachment ultimately subdued him, he died proud and untamed.

Walkara was born in the first decade of the nineteenth century at the base of the Wasatch Range in the **Utah** area. Before the arrival of the **Mormons** in 1847, he became famous throughout the West as an audaciously successful trader of stolen horses and slaves, but his fortunes steadily declined after 1850 until his death in January 1855.

First accommodating but ultimately enraged by Latter-day Saint expansion into the limited oases of the central Wasatch, Walkara more than once sought to remove the problem by intimidation and by war. Finally, in May 1854, he was forced to capitulate. Upon Walkara's death in 1855, **Brigham Young**, his most tenacious foe, respectfully eulogized him as having been a "brave and shrewd man equaled by few and excelled by none of his race in the Rocky Mountains" (Brigham Young manuscript).

SOURCES

Bailey, Paul. *Walkara, Hawk of the Mountains.* Los Angeles: Westernlore Press, 1954.

Brigham Young Manuscript History. LDS Church Archives, Salt Lake City. 29 January 1855, 3.

Christy, Howard A. "Open Hand and Mailed Fist: Mormon-Indian Relations in Utah, 1847–52." *Utah Historical Quarterly* 46 (Summer 1978): 216–35.

———. "The Walker War: Defense and Conciliation as Strategy." *Utah Historical Quarterly* 47 (Fall 1979): 395–420.

Larson, Gustive O. "Walkara's Half Century." *Eastern Humanities Review* 6 (Summer 1952): 235–59.

HOWARD CHRISTY

WALKER, CHIEF. See WALKARA.

WALKER, JOSEPH. Known for exploring the **Salt Lake Valley** before the coming of the **Mormon pioneers**, Joseph Reddeford Walker was born 13 December 1798 in Roane County, **Tennessee**. His close contact with adventure-seeking men would influence his entire life. He is said to have been about six feet tall, muscular, dark complected, and courageous. In 1833 Walker passed along the northern shore of the Great Salt Lake and down the Humboldt en route to **California**. During the expedition, Walker encountered Yosemite, the giant Redwood (Sequoia) trees, and the northernmost snow-free pass across the Sierra Nevada. He was at the **Fur Trade Rendezvous** of 1834 and 1835, where he met the first company of emigrants in the Green River Valley. Later Walker went into business with **Jim Bridger** and Louis Vasquez. He sold horses and sheep along the Old **Spanish Trail**. Walker saved the Edwin Bryant company from the pitfalls of the Hastings Cutoff and years later was asked to recommend a railroad route to the Pacific Coast. He has been memorialized with such places as Walker Lake, Walker River, Walker Pass, Walker Creek, Walker Post Office, and Walker Mining District. He died in California 13 November 1872.

SOURCES

Conner, Daniel Ellis. *A Confederate in the Colorado Gold Fields.* Norman, Okla.: University of Oklahoma Press, 1970.

———. *Joseph Reddeford Walker and the Arizona Adventure.* Norman, Okla.: University of Oklahoma Press, 1968.

Hafen, LeRoy R., ed. *The Mountain Men and the Fur Trade of the Far West.* Edited by LeRoy Hafen. 10 vols. Glendale, Calif.: Arthur H. Clark, 1966–72.

FRED R. GOWANS AND VERN GORZITZE

WALKER WAR. In 1853 **Ute Indians**, having previously threatened **war** if the **Mormons** persisted in banning the Indian slave trade, revolted along the central valleys of the Wasatch. Hostilities commenced on 18 July when a settler killed a Ute in a dispute over the trade of fish for flour. An offer of reconciliation was rebuffed, and later in the day a militiaman was killed in retaliation.

Governor **Brigham Young** ordered settlers all along the Wasatch to retrench and then offer conciliation, but angry militiamen had already marched, and a series of bloody exchanges followed.

Throughout the war Governor Young extended the olive branch. In October he entreated: "Brethren we must have peace. We must cease our hostilities and seek by every possible means to reach the Indians with a peaceful message" (quoted in Christy, 413). In December he offered total amnesty, and in May 1854 President Young and Chief **Walkara** (Walker) finally met in friendship, thus ending the war.

SOURCE

Christy, Howard A. "The Walker War: Defense and Conciliation as Strategy." *Utah Historical Quarterly* 47 (fall 1979): 395–419.

HOWARD CHRISTY

WAR. The position of the Church on the complex issue of war is guided by doctrine and principles found in **scripture** and articulated by living

prophets. Fundamental principles were presented in a revelation given through the Prophet **Joseph Smith** 6 August 1833 (**Doctrine and Covenants** 98). Therein the Lord declared that the **Saints** were to "renounce war and proclaim peace" (v. 16). He described a policy of what might be called "defensive war," exhorting his covenant people to bear patiently the attacks inflicted upon them by their enemies (v. 23–27) and "not go out unto battle" unless the Lord commands it (v. 33). Anciently the Lord justified his people going out to battle only after they had raised "a standard of peace" three times (v. 32–36). The Lord promised great rewards to those who follow his desires and instructions regarding warfare, where readiness to forgive far outweighs readiness to go to war (v. 24–26, 39–43).

Similar insights come from the **Book of Mormon**. Captain Moroni counseled the Nephites to "defend themselves against their enemies, even to the shedding of blood if it were necessary," but never to launch an offensive war (Alma 48:14; see also 43:45–47). On his title of liberty Moroni acknowledged that there are certain things worth defending by taking up arms: God, true religion, freedom, peace, and family (Alma 46:12).

In this final dispensation, wars and rumors of wars are part of the signs of the times, incident to the end of the world and the Second Coming of Christ (JS–M 1:23–31). The Prophet Joseph Smith's **Civil War** Prophecy, uttered in 1832 (see **War, Prophecy on**), foretold of increasing conflict and destruction from that time onward, until the Lord made "a full end of all nations" (D&C 87:6).

During the twentieth century Church leaders spoke about the tragedy of war and condemned its use to further the ambitions of states. At the outbreak of **World War I** President **Joseph F. Smith** exhorted Church members serving in the armed forces to keep cruelty, hate, and murder out of their hearts, even during battle. Less than a week after the United States entered **World War II**, the **First Presidency's** Christmas message echoed similar sentiments, insisting that only adherence to the gospel of **Jesus Christ** would bring peace to the world. President **J. Reuben Clark** of the First Presidency was particularly emphatic in his denunciation of war, declaring that "nothing is more unrighteous, more unholy, more ungodly than man-declared mass slaughter of his fellow man for an unrighteous cause" (Clark, 11). At the same time, Church leaders also mentioned that citizens should support the country to which they owed their allegiance and that leaders of warring nations held the blame and not individual citizens or soldiers.

In tangible ways the First Presidency promoted peace and relief of suffering from war. In 1915, for example, they encouraged Church members to contribute to the **Zion's** Emergency Fund to aid needy Church members in **Europe**. In the wake of World War II, the Church shipped food, clothing, and other supplies to war-torn countries outside the United States. War has deeply affected the Church around the world, including the curtailing or, in some cases, halting of construction projects, program activities, and **missionary work** in many countries.

SOURCES

Allen, James B. *The Story of the Latter-day Saints.* 2d ed. Salt Lake City: Deseret Book, 1992. 493–94, 536–40.

Clark, J. Reuben. Conference Report (October 1939).

Cowan, Richard O. *The Latter-day Saint Century.* Salt Lake City: Bookcraft, 1999. 43–45, 116–29.

Roy, Denny, Grant P. Skabelund, and Ray C. Hillam, eds. *A Time to Kill: Reflections on War.* Salt Lake City: Signature Books, 1992.

ANDREW C. SKINNER

WAR, PROPHECY ON.

WAR, PROPHECY ON. On 25 December 1832 **Joseph Smith** prophesied that the approaching **wars** of the last days would commence with a rebellion in **South Carolina**. This rebellion, he said, would lead to a great division between the northern and southern states, would involve **Great Britain** as well as other countries, and would terminate in the death and misery of many souls (D&C 87:1–8). On 2 April 1843 the Prophet emphasized that he had learned in the 1832 **revelation** that the cause of the war would likely be the issue of slavery (D&C 130:12–13). Since those fateful days when Joseph Smith's prophecy began to be fulfilled (with the secession of South Carolina from the Union on 20 December 1860, followed by Confederate forces firing on Fort Sumter on 12 April 1861), "the world has seen as a result of warfare the death and misery of many souls" (Benson, 4). Joseph Smith's Civil War prophecy, given in 1832, was published to the world in 1851 as **Doctrine and Covenants** 87. It has been regarded by many as a validation of Joseph Smith's prophetic calling (see also **Prophecies**).

SOURCES

Benson, Ezra Taft. "Joseph Smith: Prophet to Our Generation." *Ensign* 24 (March 1994): 2–5.

Smith, Joseph Fielding, comp. *Teachings of the Prophet Joseph Smith.* Salt Lake City: Deseret Book, 1970. 160, 286–87.

ANDREW C. SKINNER

WARD. The Latter-day Saint ward is the local ecclesiastical unit of the Church, equivalent to a Protestant congregation or a Roman Catholic parish. **Joseph Smith** initiated the name in **Nauvoo**, where he envisioned a community uniting economic, political, and spiritual elements, much as in ancient **Israel**. When Joseph designed Nauvoo as a planned community, he divided it into 10 units called wards, appointing a lay **bishop** to preside over each. Initially the bishop's primary responsibilities were temporal—visiting each **family** to alleviate hunger and issuing work assignments on community projects such as the construction of a **temple**. Religious meetings were not held in each ward; instead, they were conducted outdoors for the whole community or in homes during cold weather.

Once the first major community was organized in **Salt Lake City** in 1847, **Brigham Young** implemented the ward organization as it had been established in Nauvoo. The capital city was divided into several wards with laymen, called as bishops, appointed to focus on the temporal needs. As other sites were quickly established, a bishop was called to preside over each, and a ward was created. In these small villages, wards were the center of both temporal and religious activities, and they also maintained ward schools. Larger communities such as **Provo**, **Logan**, **Ogden**, and **St. George** had more than one ward. These wards soon added ecclesiastical and educational functions as well as the collection of tithes to their responsibilities.

During this **pioneer** period, wards were rather informal in their organization. The Twelve **Apostles** were assigned to establish a permanent residence in a specific region, each visiting the wards personally and instructing the bishops and members. Printed instructions did not appear until 1893, and the first **handbooks** weren't printed until 1913.

Auxiliary organizations—the **Sunday School**, the **Relief Society**, the **Young Women**'s and **Young Men**'s Mutual Improvement Societies, and **Primary**—emerged during Brigham Young's presidency, but their systematic attachment to wards was only finalized when centralized leadership boards were established to instruct local ward members about conducting such activities in each ward. A strategy gradually emerged to encourage adult members to accept responsibility in one of the many activities in the wards—visiting, teaching, performing, presiding, etc. The activities attempted to involve each child and youth as well. A policy developed to keep the wards rather small, somewhere between 300 and 600 members, so that each person knew everyone else and felt a strong sense of spiritual and social community. When wards grew beyond that number they were divided, and a new ward was established. The communal spirit of the village was embodied in the ward. Bishops of each ward recognized the ecclesiastical and financial jurisdiction of **stake** and general Church leaders.

As membership in the Church spread beyond the **Great Basin** and as **missions** matured, wards and stakes were established widely. At first they took root in **California, Arizona, Idaho,** and **Alberta, Canada,** and other western regions, but gradually they spread throughout the **United States** and **Canada.** Since the 1950s they have been organized throughout the world. With the formation of these wards, local lay members have taken on responsibility for the ecclesiastical and temporal affairs of the Church in their area—a job that had previously been done in missions and branches and often by missionaries. Many of these newer wards did not inherit the pioneer communalism, but they usually developed a close fellowship among members, well beyond being just a congregation.

There are some demographic differences in wards. In the core area of the Church, wards have access to seasoned members, often fifth- or sixth-generation Latter-day Saints. Outside the Great Basin, members are much more scattered, and many are recent converts. Beyond North America, wards are often small with very few seasoned leaders and usually cover a large geographical area. Members do not choose which ward to attend but are assigned to a ward on the basis of the geographic location of their homes. Thus, local economic and social conditions are reflected in the wards. With each passing decade they gain greater stability, and they, too, are already spawning new wards as the older ones are divided. Specialized wards have been created for language minorities and single adults. At the beginning of the year 2000, there were a total of 17,699 LDS wards (2,542 stakes) throughout the world. Most were in the United States and Canada, but there were 5,582 in Latin **America** (including the Caribbean), 603 in **Europe,** 774 in **Asia** (including the **Philippines**), 188 in **Africa,** and 637 in the **Pacific.**

SOURCES

Alder, Douglas D. "The Mormon Ward: Congregation or Community?" *Journal of Mormon History* 5 (1978): 61–78.

Shipps, Jan, Cheryll L. May, and Dean L. May. "Sugarhouse Ward: The Latter-day Saint Congregation." *American Congregations,* Vol. 1. *Portraits of Twelve Religious Communities.* Edited by James P. Wind and James W. Lewis. Chicago: University of Chicago Press, 1994. 293–348.

Tabor, Susan Buhler. *Mormon Lives: A Year in the Elkton Ward.* Urbana: University of Illinois Press, 1993.

DOUGLAS D. ALDER

WARD TEACHING. See HOME TEACHING.

WARNER, FRANK W. Frank W. Warner was one of the first Native American missionaries for the Church, serving three separate **missions** among American **Indians** before his death in 1919. A member of the Northwestern **Shoshone** tribe, Warner was born about 1861 to **Sagwitch** and Tan-tapai-cci. He was first known as Pisappíh "Red Oquirrh" Timbimboo ("To mark or write on the rocks"). As a two-year-old victim of the **Bear River Massacre** on 29 January 1863, he somehow survived after receiving seven bullet wounds.

A few years later he was adopted by the Amos Warner **family** and renamed Frank W. Warner. He received a formal education at **Brigham Young College** in **Logan**, **Utah**, and worked most of his life as an educator. President **John Taylor** called Warner as a missionary in October 1880 to work with his own people, the Shoshone, at the **Washakie** settlement in Box Elder County, **Utah**. Warner also served in the Northwestern States Mission, 1914–15, working among the Sioux and Assiniboin Indians at Fort Peck, **Montana**. He served a third mission, also at Fort Peck, in 1917.

Warner died during the Spanish Influenza epidemic of 1919 in Parker, **Idaho**.

SOURCES

Christensen, Scott R. *Sagwitch: Shoshone Chieftain, Mormon Elder, 1822–1887*. Logan, Utah: Utah State University Press, 1999.

Warner, Frank W. "Missionary journal, November 1914–January 1915." Manuscript. LDS Church Archives, Salt Lake City.

SCOTT R. CHRISTENSEN

WARSAW SIGNAL. See SHARP, THOMAS.

WASHAKIE, CHIEF. An important **Native American** chief who joined the Church, Washakie was born about 1798 in **Montana**. He spent his early life among a band of Lemhi **Shoshoni** after his father Paseego, a Flathead, was killed by Blackfoot attackers. Washakie's mother was probably Shoshone. He also spent several years with the Bannock people. The name Washakie is interpreted as either "a rawhide rattle" or "shoots straight." In 1840 Osborne Russell, a trapper, noted that Washakie was a well-known and feared young warrior, an emerging leader. Apparently, by 1849 Washakie had assumed leadership of the Eastern Shoshone.

During the 1850s the chief became a firm friend of **Brigham Young** and the **Mormons**. In a letter to Young dated 17 August 1856, Washakie stated that his heart felt bad when he had to fight and lamented the long-standing hostility between his tribe and the **Utes** he distrusted. Because of the Shoshone tribe's relatively small numbers, they frequently engaged in hostile disputes with other tribes regarding hunting ground boundaries.

At the **Fort Bridger** Treaty Council of 1868, the Wind River Indian Reservation in western **Wyoming** was created. Washakie settled there peaceably, despite his distaste for having to share its boundaries with the Arapaho, traditional Shoshone enemies. U.S. president Chester A. Arthur visited Chief Washakie at his reservation home in 1883.

Washakie converted to Mormonism and was baptized by Amos R. Wright on 25 September 1880 on the Wind River Reservation. According to Wright's records, 310 members of Washakie's tribe were also baptized in September and October of that year. Chief Washakie died on 23 February 1900 and was accorded full U.S. military honors at his burial in the Ft. Washakie cemetery.

SOURCES

Hebard, Grace Raymond. *Washakie: An Account of Indian Resistance of the Covered Wagon and Union Pacific Railroad Invasions of Their Territory.* Cleveland: Arthur H. Clark, 1930.

Trenholm, Virginia Cole and Maurine Carley. *The Shoshonis: Sentinels of the Rockies.* Norman, Okla.: University of Oklahoma Press, 1964.

Wright, Amos R. "Record book: Indians baptized, confirmed, etc. [July 1877–October 1880]." LDS Church Archives, Salt Lake City. This document is an enclosure to a letter dated 18 November 1880 that Wright sent to LDS Church president John Taylor.

JAY G. BURRUP

WASHAKIE (SETTLEMENT). The town of Washakie, located in Box Elder County, **Utah**, was founded in 1880 by the Church as a home for **Shoshoni Native American** converts to Mormonism. The Church established a **mission** among the Shoshone in northern Utah in 1873 after Chief **Sagwitch** petitioned for the baptism of his people. Attempts were made to establish a farming community for the Shoshone at Franklin, **Idaho**, in 1874 and near Corinne, Utah, in 1875. In 1876, missionaries and Shoshone converts established a settlement in Box Elder

County that they named Lemuel's Garden. Difficulties with irrigation systems caused them to petition President **John Taylor** in 1879 for another location. He offered them the **Brigham City** Cooperative farm near Portage. In 1880 most residents relocated there and named the new town Washakie. The Washakie **Ward** was formed in 1880, with Native Americans filling most posts in the organization. **Moroni Timbimboo** was **ordained bishop** of Washakie Ward in 1939, becoming the first Native American in the Church to hold that position. Eventually most residents moved to other communities in Utah, Idaho, and **Wyoming**. Washakie Ward was disbanded in 1960, and its replacement, the Washakie **Branch**, was dissolved in 1966. The Washakie townsite is now a privately owned ranch.

Sources

Christensen, Scott R. *Sagwitch: Shoshone Chieftain, Mormon Elder, 1822–1887*. Logan, Utah: Utah State University Press, 1999.

"Washakie: Description of the Lamanitish City in Malad Valley." *The Utah Journal*, 1 December 1883.

"Washakie Lives On—Mostly in Memories." *Deseret News*, 31 January 1966, B1.

Scott R. Christensen

WASHINGS AND ANOINTINGS. In Old Testament times, **Moses** was commanded to perform ritual washings and anointings upon those who were preparing to enter the **tabernacle** (Ex. 29:4–7; 30:17–21). These **ordinances** were symbolic of cleansing oneself of sin and remaining clean from the pollutions of the world. Once cleansed, a person was prepared to make deep and meaningful covenants with the Lord and to participate in sacred ordinances. Further detail of these Old Testament ordinances is not given due to their sacred nature (Smith, 794).

In 1836 the **Kirtland Temple** was dedicated, and newly revealed ordinances were performed therein. The ordinances of washings and anointings (including the washing of feet) were introduced on 21 January 1836 (*HC*, 2:379). These ordinances were revealed to the **Prophet** as part of the **restoration** of all things. Later it was revealed to **Joseph Smith** that the **Nauvoo Temple** should be built "that those ordinances might be revealed which had been hid from before the world was" (D&C 124:38), again emphasizing the eternal nature of such ordinances. The full **endowment** was not given to the **Saints** until 1842 in **Nauvoo**.

Today washings and anointings are administered in holy **temples** by men to other men and by women to other women. They are preparatory to the sacred covenants made in the holy endowment.

SOURCES

Cowan, Richard O. *Temples to Dot the Earth.* Salt Lake City: Bookcraft, 1989. 12–13.

Smith, Joseph. *History of The Church of Jesus Christ of Latter-day Saints [HC].* Edited by B. H. Roberts. 2d ed. rev. 7 vols. Salt Lake City: The Church of Jesus Christ of Latter-day Saints, 1932–51.

Smith, Joseph Fielding. "Was Temple Work Done in the Days of the Old Prophets?" *Improvement Era* 58 (November 1955): 794.

BRIAN L. SMITH

WASHINGTON, D.C. The capital of the **United States,** named for **George Washington,** has always played an important role in the history of The Church of Jesus Christ of Latter-day Saints. From **Joseph Smith's** visit to President **Martin Van Buren** following the persecution in **Missouri** to the opening of a **temple** in 1974, the position of the city as the seat of federal power has been important to the history of the Saints.

During the nineteenth century, numerous Latter-day Saint leaders visited the capital to seek federal support for the move west and for **statehood,** although the Church and the federal government were at odds over a variety of issues from 1857 until 1907. Territorial politics were significant, but the main issue was **plural marriage.** The **Manifesto (1890)** thawed relationships somewhat, but the U.S. House still refused to seat representative **B. H. Roberts.** The seating of Reed Smoot after lengthy hearings on his election to the Senate finally brought Latter-day Saint influence to the national capital.

Senator Smoot established a branch in Washington, D.C., and he became both the spiritual and political spokesman for the Church. Many member families and students migrated for employment and educational opportunities. Senator Smoot, federal trade commissioner Edgar Brossard, consumer advocate Esther Peterson, and many other Latter-day Saints have served the nation with considerable distinction. In 1933 the Saints completed a beautiful chapel on 16th Street that gave the Church a visible presence in the city. During the **great depression,** numerous Utahns moved into government and military service. Consequently, the Washington **Stake** was organized in 1940 with **Ezra Taft Benson** as the first **stake president. World War II** accelerated Church **growth** in the area. Such members as Edgar Brossard and J. **Willard Marriott** planned for a temple on the East Coast, and this dream became a reality in 1974. The **Washington D.C. Temple** became a gathering point for all members east of the **Mississippi River**. Although the magnificent chapel downtown was sold in 1975, the LDS Church has maintained a positive and respected position in Washington, D.C. The relationship with the federal government has evolved from one of antagonism and prejudice to one of participation and influence. At the beginning of the year 2000, Washington, D.C., had 1,660 Church members, five **branches**, and one **district**.

SOURCE

Burke, Lee H. *History of the Washington, D.C., LDS Ward.* Salt Lake City: Publishers Press, 1991.

F. ROSS PETERSON

WASHINGTON D.C. TEMPLE. The Washington D.C. Temple is the first North American **temple** built east of the **Mississippi River** since the days of **Kirtland** and **Nauvoo** and the third largest in the Church, with 160,000 square feet of floor space. During the early 1970s, the **Saints** in the eastern **United States** and **Canada** were the largest group of Church members not living within a day's drive of a temple. In 1968 plans were announced to construct the temple on a wooded hill, giving it a feeling of isolation from nearby urban bustle. The temple's majestic presence makes it a monument to the **Restoration**. Its six-tower design makes this structure easily identifiable as a Latter-day Saint Temple, being a modern adaptation of the widely recognized **Salt Lake Temple**. The building's vertical lines express mankind's relationship with God. The exterior is covered with **Alabama** marble, with vertical bands every few feet cut to a thickness of only ⅝ inch. These "marble windows" admit a soft amber light during the day and allow the temple to glow when illuminated within at night. An 18-foot statue of the angel **Moroni** stands atop the 280-foot east center tower, both statue and tower the tallest of any temple. The interior includes six 120-seat ordinance rooms and a large solemn assembly room on the upper floor. More than 750,000 people attended the seven-week open house, including members of the diplomatic corps representing many nations. The temple was dedicated by President **Spencer W. Kimball** on 19 November 1974. This temple also served Latter-day Saints in **South America** until the construction of temples there.

SOURCE

Cowan, Richard O. *Temples to Dot the Earth.* Springville, Utah: Cedar Fort, 1997. 174–78.

RICHARD O. COWAN

WASHINGTON, GEORGE. Latter-day Saint **apostles** and **prophets** have taught that George Washington was not only the "Father of His Country" but also an instrument in the Lord's hands to help prepare the way for the **restoration** of the gospel in this last **dispensation**. Washington was born 22 February 1732 on his family plantation in Westmoreland County, **Virginia**. A surveyor and planter by profession, he married Martha Dandridge Curtis on 6 January 1759. Before he became president of the United States in 1789, he served as commander-in-chief of the Continental Army during the American Revolution and as president of the Constitutional Convention in 1787. After serving two terms as president of the United States, Washington retired to his Mount Vernon plantation, where he died 14 December 1799.

Brigham Young taught that the Lord "moved upon Washington to fight and conquer [during the American Revolution] in the same way He moved upon ancient and modern **prophets**, each being inspired to accomplish [a] particular work" (*JD*, 7:13). **George Q. Cannon** maintained: "George Washington, Thomas Jefferson, John Adams, Benjamin Franklin, and all the fathers of the Republic were inspired to do the work which they did. . . . This **church** and kingdom could not have been established on earth if their work had not been performed" (*JD*, 14:55). **Wilford Woodruff** declared: "Every one of those men that signed the **Declaration of Independence**, with General [George] Washington, called upon me, as an apostle of the Lord **Jesus Christ**, in the **temple** at **St. George**, two consecutive nights, and demanded at my hands that I should go forth and attend to the ordinances of the House of God for them" (Woodruff). On this occasion George Washington was ordained a **high priest** by proxy (Benson, 604).Wilford Woodruff further proclaimed that Washington and the others who appeared to him were "the best spirits the God of Heaven could find on the face of the earth" (Woodruff).

SOURCES

Benson, Ezra Taft. *The Teachings of Ezra Taft Benson*. Salt Lake City: Bookcraft, 1988.

Flexner, James Thomas. *Washington: The Indispensable Man*. Boston: Little, Brown and Company, 1974.

Journal of Discourses [JD]. 26 vols. London: Latter-day Saints' Book Depot, 1854–86. Vols. 7 and 14.

Woodruff, Wilford. Conference Report (April 1898): 89.

ARNOLD K. GARR

WASHINGTON STATE. Latter-day Saints first arrived in Washington in 1854, when four **elders** from the **California Mission**, Alfred Bybee,

Clark Faben, Silas Harris, and John Hughes, were sent to labor in the Washington Territory. Elder Hughes converted a small group of people, and a **branch** was organized on the Lewis River. Washington became part of the Northwestern States Mission when it was organized on 26 July 1897. Spokane held its first **Sunday School** class 9 September 1906, but its first branch was not organized until 10 years later on 12 March 1916.

In 1930 the Church was growing well in Washington, with 1,855 members in eight branches. With **World War II**, many new members found their way to the state to work in the defense industries. The first **stake** was organized in Seattle on 31 July 1938, and membership reached the 5,000 mark in 1940.

At each of the next 10-year marks, it has been easy to see the steady increase in Church membership. By 1960 there were 11,000 members, increasing to 67,203 in 1970 and 138,000 in 1980. At the beginning of the year 2000 Washington had 226,411 members and 52 stakes with 470 **wards** and branches. The Seattle Washington **Temple** was dedicated 17–21 November 1980, the Spokane Washington Temple was dedicated 21 August 1999, and in April 2000 the construction of a temple in the Tri-Cities area (Pasco, Richland, and Kennewick) was announced.

———

SOURCES

Arrington, Leonard J. "History of the Church in the Pacific Northwest." *Task Papers in LDS History.* No. 18. Salt Lake City, Church Historical Department, 1975.

"First Presidency Announces Temples for Spokane, Detroit." *Church News,* 29 August 1998, 3.

Horne, J. Arthur. *Latter-day Saints in the Great Northwest.* Seattle: Graphic Arts Press, 1968.

Jenson, Andrew. *Encyclopedic History of The Church of Jesus Christ of Latter-day Saints.* Salt Lake City: Deseret News, 1941.

1999–2000 Church Almanac. Salt Lake City: Deseret News, 1998.

THOMAS L. STINEBAUGH

WATT, GEORGE D. George D. Watt, the first shorthand reporter for Latter-day Saint **general conference**, was born 12 May 1812 in **Manchester, England**. He was baptized by **Heber C. Kimball** on 30 July 1837 in Preston, England. After a mission to **Scotland**, where he learned Pitman shorthand, he immigrated to **Nauvoo, Illinois**. He taught shorthand in Nauvoo but did not use this skill until the trial for the accused murderers of **Joseph Smith**.

Watt served a mission to Britain from 1846 to 1851. Upon his return he began using his shorthand skills in recording the Brethren's speeches. The **First Presidency** gave him permission to publish the *Journal of Discourses,* a semimonthly publication that ran from 1854 to 1886 and contained sermons of Church leaders. These issues were later bound into 26 volumes. Watt was also a member of the committee that created the **Deseret Alphabet.** In the late 1860s, he wrote a series of stories for the *Juvenile Instructor* known as "The Little George Stories." Watt participated in and promoted raising silkworms and making silk products. He later left **Salt Lake City** and moved to Kaysville, where he died 24 October 1881.

SOURCES

Stringham, Ida Watt, and Dora Dutson Flack. *England's First Mormon Convert: The Biography of George Darling Watt.* N.p.: n.d.

Watt, Ronald G. "Sailing the Old Ship Zion: The Life of George D. Watt." *BYU Studies* 18 (Fall 1977): 48–65.

RONALD G. WATT

WATTS, STAN. Stanley Howard Watts, a member of the Basketball Hall of Fame, was an outstanding college basketball coach and faithful member of the LDS Church. Born 30 August 1911 in Murray, **Utah,** to William Eugene and Ethel Gertrude Watts, Stan attended Weber College and **Brigham Young University.** He married Emily Kelly on 21 August 1939 and they had four children. He coached at Millard High School, **Dixie College,** and Jordan High School before he began coaching at Brigham Young University. Watts was the head basketball coach at BYU from 1949 to 1972. During those 23 years he compiled a record of 372 wins and 254 losses. His teams won eight conference titles and two National Invitational Tournament (NIT) championships (1951 and 1966). Watts was president of the National Association of Basketball Coaches in 1969 and 1970 and was elected to the Basketball Hall of Fame 6 March 1986. He died 6 April 2000 in **Provo, Utah.**

SOURCES

Call, Jeff. "Legendary Y. Coach Dies at 88." *Deseret News.* 7 April 2000. D1, 4.

Obituary. *Deseret News,* 9 April 2000. B9

ARNOLD K. GARR

WAYNE SENTINEL. Egbert B. Grandin purchased the *Wayne Sentinel* (**Palmyra, New York**) from Pomeroy Tucker and **John H. Gilbert** in 1827.

Grandin edited the paper from1 1827 to 1832 (with Theron R. Strong in 1832). Commencing in mid-August 1829, he began printing the **Book of Mormon**, at the instigation of **Joseph Smith Jr.**, in the *Wayne Sentinel* printing office on the third story and west bay of the newly constructed "Thayer & Grandin's Row." On 26 March 1830 the first copies were available to the public in Grandin's Palmyra bookstore. Pomeroy Tucker declared, "The largest printing job ever done in [Wayne County], was the first edition of Jo Smith's 'book of Mormon,' or the 'Golden Bible'" (Follett, 64). **Abner Cole**, under the pseudonym of "Obediah Dogberry, Jun.," was editor of a local paper called the *Reflector*. He used the *Sentinel* office on weekends to publish his sheet from 2 September 1829 to 19 March 1831. Cole unlawfully printed some extracts from the copyrighted text of the Book of Mormon and also published numerous satirical commentaries on Mormonism in his newspaper.

SOURCES

Follett, Frederick. *History of the Press of Western New-York*. Rochester, N.Y.: Jerome & Brother, Daily American Office, 1847. 64.

Hamilton, Milton W. *The Country Printer: New York State, 1785–1830*. Port Washington, L.I., N.Y.: Ira J. Friedman, 1964. 275, 303–4.

Porter, Larry C. "The Book of Mormon: Historical Setting for Its Translation and Publication." *Joseph Smith, The Prophet, The Man*. Edited by Susan Easton Black and Charles D. Tate Jr. Provo, Utah: Religious Studies Center, Brigham Young University, 1993.

LARRY C. PORTER

WEBER, JOHN H. Mountain man John H. Weber helped open the American West for settlement as he engaged in the fur trade. Born in Altona, **Denmark**, in 1779, he went to sea as a young boy, serving as captain of passenger ships before coming to **America** in 1807. After settling in **Missouri** for several years, he joined the William Ashley–Andrew Henry fur trade venture as a brigade leader and possibly as a partner. Between 1824 and 1827 his trade took him to many well-known Rocky Mountain sites, including several in present-day northern **Utah**. He spent the remainder of his life in **Illinois** and **Iowa**, where he died in 1859. In recognition of his leadership, his colleagues named Weber Canyon and Weber River after him.

SOURCES

Hafen, LeRoy R. "John H. Weber." *The Mountain Men and the Fur Trade of the Far*

West. Edited by LeRoy Hafen. 10 vols. Glendale, Calif.: Arthur H. Clark, 1966–72. 379–84.

Morgan, Dale L. *Jedediah Smith and the Opening of the West.* Lincoln: University of Nebraska Press, 1964.

————, ed. *The West of William H. Ashley.* Denver, Colo.: Old West, 1964.

Fred R. Gowans and Vivian Linford Talbot

WEBER STATE UNIVERSITY. Originally organized as the Weber Stake Academy, the school now known as Weber State University first opened its doors 7 January 1889 in **Ogden, Utah.** Louis W. Shurtliff, president of the **stake** that encompassed all of Weber County, became the driving force behind the academy's creation. Louis Moench was chosen as the first principal of the school, and for the next decade and a half his educational philosophy formed the foundation of the fledgling institution. During its first decade, the Academy struggled financially to survive, and it endured only through the individual sacrifice of members of the stake board of education who mortgaged their homes to support the school. The school was called Weber Stake Academy from 1889 until 1908, when the name was changed to Weber Academy. In 1918 the name became Weber Normal College, and in 1922 the name was changed to Weber College. **David O. McKay** was principal of the academy from 1902 to 1908, and he maintained a lifelong interest in the school.

During the 1920s, the Church began to evaluate the college's position in terms of educational expenses, and during the depths of the depression, Weber, Dixie, and **Snow Colleges** were transferred to **Utah** state ownership. Weber became part of the state system on 1 July 1933, and all of Weber's facilities on Jefferson Avenue in Ogden became state property. By 1950 Weber had begun to change locations to Ogden's east bench. In 1962 it became a four-year institution, and in 1963 it changed its name to Weber State College. In 1964 Weber graduated its first four-year class. A quarter of a century later, on 1 January 1991, Weber State College became Weber State University. During 1998, 1,809 individuals received bachelor's degrees.

Source

Sadler, Richard W. *Weber State College, A Centennial History.* Salt Lake City: Publishers Press, 1988.

Richard W. Sadler

WEEKS, WILLIAM. William Weeks, architect of the **Nauvoo Temple**, was one of the outstanding early Latter-day **Saint** architects and builders. In addition to drawing various sets of plans for the Nauvoo Temple under the direction of the Prophet Joseph Smith, he became general superintendent of the temple's construction. His skills were also used in planning the **Nauvoo Legion** arsenal, the Masonic (Cultural) Hall, the **Nauvoo House**, and his own brick home.

Born in Martha's Vineyard, **Massachusetts**, on 11 April 1813, William Weeks was raised in a family of builders. After uniting with Latter-day Saints, he married Caroline M. Allen on 11 June 1839. Caroline gave birth to 11 children, 7 of whom died in infancy.

Following his exodus from **Nauvoo**, Weeks did not utilize his architectural skills on any major projects. Shortly after arriving in the **Great Basin** in September 1847, he returned to the midwestern **United States**. He made a second trip across the plains in the early 1850s, settled temporarily in **Provo**, and then moved to **San Bernardino, California**. In 1857, when the Latter-day Saints abandoned that community because of the coming of **Johnston's Army**, Weeks moved elsewhere in southern California and operated a dairy farm. He died in **Los Angeles** 8 March 1900 outside the Church.

SOURCES

Arrington, J. Earl. "William Weeks, Architect of the Nauvoo Temple." *BYU Studies* 19 (Spring 1979): 336–59.

MILTON V. BACKMAN Jr.

WELFARE PROGRAM. During the 1930s, Church members suffered from a shortage of money for buying food and clothing. Unemployment was high, but the curse of idleness seemed to be the main problem facing members. **Elder Harold B. Lee** said on a number of occasions that it was idleness that brought about the development of the Church welfare program. In 1936, "one of the main concerns of the **First Presidency** was the increasing number of Church members receiving relief through public funds" (Rudd, 39). The First Presidency felt it necessary to move forward more quickly in addressing the problems of unemployment and idleness.

In 1935, Pioneer Stake president Harold B. Lee, acting under the direction of the First Presidency, adapted a local program to meet the needs of the entire Church. In the April 1936 **general conference**, President **Heber J. Grant** publicly announced the establishment of a centrally directed welfare program called the "Church Security Plan." On

18 April 1936, Harold B. Lee was called as the managing director of the new program, and Elder **Melvin J. Ballard** was named by the First Presidency as the chairman of the welfare program.

Elder **Albert E. Bowen** of the **Quorum** of the Twelve **Apostles** had stated that "among other things the Presidency urged the importance of and the necessity for a revival in observance of the law of **tithing** and of **fast offerings** . . . as a means of providing revenue in the manner established by the Lord for the needs of the poor and for the incidental spiritual benefit to all who conform" (quoted in Rudd, 41).

The long-term objective of the welfare program of the Church, as stated by President **J. Reuben Clark Jr.**, is "the building of character in the members of the Church, givers and receivers, rescuing all that is finest down deep inside of them, and bringing to flower and fruitage the latent richness of the spirit, which after all is the mission and purpose and reason for being of this Church" (quoted in Rudd, 44–45).

The First Presidency also stated that the "primary purpose was to set up, in so far as it might be possible, a system under which the curse of idleness would be done away with, the evils of a dole abolished, and independence, industry, thrift and self-respect be once more established among our people. The aim of the Church is to help the people to help themselves. Work is to be re-enthroned as the ruling principle of the lives of our Church membership" (CR, 3).

SOURCES

Blumell, Bruce D., and Garth L. Mangum. *The Mormons' War on Poverty: A History of LDS Welfare, 1830–1990.* Salt Lake City: University of Utah Press, 1993.

Conference Report [CR] (October 1936): 3.

Rudd, Glen L. *Pure Religion: The Story of Church Welfare Since 1930.* Salt Lake City: The Church of Jesus Christ of Latter-day Saints, 1995. 39–45.

GLEN L. RUDD

WELFARE SERVICES MISSIONARIES. By 1970, Latter-day Saint leaders had become increasingly concerned about those coming into the Church throughout the world who had great temporal as well as spiritual needs. As a result, the first two "medical missionaries" were called in 1971. Later such missionaries—many of whom were nurses—were called health missionaries, then health services missionaries.

Agricultural missionaries were added in 1973 to give technical, practical assistance to farmers and gardeners. Educational and vocational missionaries were also called. Eventually they were gathered together under the umbrella term of welfare missionaries. At the end of the twentieth century they were called missionaries with an additional assignment in welfare, or Welfare Services Missionaries. The assignment included support to local leaders in seeking out and caring for the poor and needy. These missionaries helped Church members meet challenges such as poverty, disease, illiteracy, malnutrition, and inadequate sanitation. This was done by teaching and helping to implement welfare/gospel principles such as self-reliance.

SOURCES

Cowan, Richard O. *The Latter-day Saint Century.* Salt Lake City: Bookcraft, 1999.

Mangum, Garth L. "Welfare Services." *Encyclopedia of Mormonism.* Edited by Daniel H. Ludlow. 4 vols. New York: Macmillan, 1992. 4:1554–58.

MARY ELLEN EDMUNDS

WELFARE SQUARE. In 1937, the Church obtained approximately 10 acres of property on the west side of **Salt Lake City**, and this site became the central operation of the general Church **welfare program**. In 1938, eight buildings that had been condemned by the city were demolished, and the materials were used to erect several buildings on Welfare Square. The first edifice to be built was the root cellar, large enough to hold 50 railroad cars of potatoes and other commodities. The cannery was built immediately thereafter and was used as a storehouse until the Bishops' Storehouse was built in early 1939. In 1940, a small milk-processing plant was added.

On 6 March 1940, excavation began on the grain elevator, which holds 118,000 bushels of grain. Approximately 640 men worked on the project and contributed 70,000 volunteer hours of labor. The towering structure, which is 178 feet high, is clearly visible throughout the **Salt Lake Valley** and has become the symbol of the welfare program of the Church.

In 1960, a new milk-processing plant replaced the original one, and a new cannery was added three years later. In 1975, a new Bishops' Storehouse was constructed. In 1998, plans were made for a modern milk-processing plant and cannery to enlarge and refurbish the entire area known as Welfare Square.

SOURCE

Rudd, Glen L. *Pure Religion: The Story of Church Welfare Since 1930.* Salt Lake City: The Church of Jesus Christ of Latter-day Saints, 1995. 65–80, 95, 99, 110–12.

GLEN L. RUDD

WELLS, DANIEL H. Daniel Hanmer Wells was a counselor to Brigham Young, a military leader, and a mayor. He was born 27 October 1814 in Trenton, New Jersey. As a sympathetic non-Mormon landowner in Commerce, Illinois, he divided 80 acres of his property into lots, which he sold to the homeless Latter-day Saint refugees from Missouri at low prices and with easy terms. Known as "Squire Wells," he was active in public affairs in Nauvoo for years before joining the Church. When his friends Joseph and Hyrum Smith were martyred, this good man's sense of justice was outraged. Two years later, in 1846, Squire Wells's anger was kindled again when lawless mobs, in direct violation of a pact, fired upon the Saints who remained in Nauvoo. At this time he decided to ally himself with what he felt to be right, and he joined the Church 9 August 1846. His wife opposed this decision so firmly that she refused to leave Nauvoo with him, and there he bade her and his only child farewell.

Reaching the Salt Lake Valley in 1848, he continued to play a prominent part in public life, serving as lieutenant general of the territorial militia, mayor of Salt Lake City for 10 years (1866–76), and territorial legislator for many terms. In 1857 President Brigham Young chose Elder Wells as his second counselor and ordained him an apostle 4 January 1857.

Elder Wells served faithfully in the First Presidency for 20 years, including a brief term as European Mission president (1864–65), until the death of Brigham Young. Then for the next 14 years, until his own death, he served as a counselor to the Twelve Apostles. During his service as a general authority, Brother Wells suffered a great deal of persecution, all of which he met with an uncanny coolness and dignity. While mayor of Salt Lake City, he encountered an unruly mob, including some armed U.S. marshals, who attempted to interfere with the election of 1874. They attacked Brother Wells, tore his coat, and shouted, "Shoot him! Shoot him!" During these insults he calmly stood on the balcony of City Hall and read the official order to disperse. Late in life he served as president of the Manti Temple. Elder Wells died in Salt Lake City 24 March 1891 at age 76.

SOURCES

Cowley, Matthias F. *Prophets and Patriarchs.* Chattanooga, Tenn.: Ben E. Rich, 1902. 147–51.

Flake, Lawrence R. *Prophets and Apostles of the Last Dispensation.* Provo, Utah: Religious Studies Center, Brigham Young University, 2001. 255–57.

LAWRENCE R. FLAKE

WELLS, EMMELINE B. Emmeline Blanche Woodward Harris Whitney Wells was a well-known women's advocate and a general president of the Relief Society. In 1928, in celebration of the one hundredth anniversary of her birth, the women of **Utah** presented to the Utah State Capitol a marble bust of Wells, which bore the inscription, "A Fine Soul Who Served Us." This was a fitting tribute to this outstanding Latter-day Saint woman, who declared early in her adult life, "I desire to do all in my power to help elevate the condition of my own people especially women" (Diary), and who spent 40 years devoted to that goal.

Born 29 February 1828 in Petersham, **Massachusetts**, Emmeline Woodward joined the Church in 1842. She married James Harris in 1843 and traveled to **Nauvoo** the next year, where she lost her newborn son, was deserted by her husband, and married **Newel K. Whitney**. Two daughters were born of this union. After Whitney's death in 1850, Emmeline married **Daniel H. Wells**, with whom she had three more daughters, two of whom died as young women.

Through her 37-year editorship of the *Woman's Exponent*, an independent Latter-day Saint woman's paper, she defended the Church against its detractors and advocated **women's suffrage** and the equality of women and men. In 1879 she represented the women of Utah at the annual Woman Suffrage Convention in **Washington, D.C.**, the first of many conventions she attended. She was a charter member of the National and International Councils of Women and personal friend of Susan B. Anthony and other national women's leaders. She also headed the Utah Woman Suffrage Association in its successful drive to put women's suffrage in the Utah State Constitution.

At age 82, after serving as general secretary for 20 years, she was called as general **Relief Society** president. During her tenure, the Relief Society adopted a uniform pattern of lessons, a social service program, and an official publication, the *Relief Society Magazine*. She met four U.S. presidents, including Woodrow Wilson, who visited her in her **Salt Lake** home to express gratitude for the sale of Relief Society wheat to the government during **World War I**.

She was heralded on her 82d birthday celebration as a woman who had "traveled tens of thousands of miles to render service in defense of her Church and sex and enjoys the respect . . . of the leading women, not only of America, but of the world" ("Noble," 4).

Emmeline Wells died 25 April 1921 in Salt Lake City, three weeks after her release from the Relief Society presidency

SOURCES

Madsen, Carol Cornwall. "Emmeline B. Wells: A Mormon Woman in Victorian America." Ph.D. diss., University of Utah, 1985.

———. "Emmeline B. Wells: Romantic Rebel." *Supporting Saints: Life Stories of Nineteenth-Century Mormons*. Edited by Donald Q. Cannon and David J. Whittaker. Provo, Utah: Religious Studies Center, Brigham Young University, 1985. 305–42.

"A Noble Woman." *Deseret Evening News*, 5 March 1910, 4.

Richards, Mary Stovall, and Carol Cornwall Madsen. "Emmeline B. Wells." *Encyclopedia of Mormonism*. Edited by Daniel H. Ludlow. 4 vols. New York: Macmillan, 1992. 1559–60.

Wells, Emmeline B. Diary. Typescript. 4 January 1878.

CAROL CORNWALL MADSEN

WELLS, JUNIUS F. Junius Free Wells, the founder of the **Young Men's Mutual Improvement Association**, was born 1 June 1854 in **Salt Lake City**. He was the son of **Daniel H. Wells** and Hannah C. Free. Junius served several **missions** for the Church, including two to the **British Isles** and others in the **United States**. Following Junius's studies at the **University of Deseret, Brigham Young** asked him to organize the Young Men's Mutual Improvement Association in 1875, for which he was the first general superintendent. He established *The Contributor*—a periodical dedicated to the young men and women of the Church—a few years later in 1879. Beginning in 1905, he was commissioned by the Church to erect several important monuments, including the memorial at **Joseph Smith's** birthplace in **Vermont** (1905), the **Oliver Cowdery** monument in **Richmond, Missouri** (1911), and the **Hyrum Smith** monument in Salt Lake City (1918). He also served as an assistant **Church historian** from 1921 until his death in 1930. In this capacity he arranged the purchase of the George Edward Anderson glass plate negative collection of Latter-day Saint **historical sites**. Junius married Helena Middleton Fobes on 17 June 1879. He died in Salt Lake City on 15 April 1930.

SOURCES

"Junius F. Wells." *Deseret News*, 15 April 1930. 1.

Smith, Paul Thomas. "Junius F. Wells." *Encyclopedia of Mormonism*. Edited by Daniel H. Ludlow. 4 vols. New York: Macmillan, 1992. 4:1560–61.

RICHARD NEITZEL HOLZAPFEL

WELLS, RULON S. Rulon Seymour Wells served as a member of the First Council of the **Seventy** for almost 50 years. He was born in **Salt Lake City** 7 July 1854, the son of Louisa Free and **Daniel H. Wells**. He was called on a **mission** to **Europe** 22 October 1875 and was ordained a seventy at age 21 by **Brigham Young**. He served for two years among the German and Swiss people. He married Josephine Eliza Beatie in 1883; they were the parents of seven children. **Elder** Wells was sustained to the presidency of the Seventy on 5 April 1893 at age 38 and served as a member of the First Council of the Seventy until his death. He also served as president of the **British Mission** from 1896 to 1898.

Elder Wells spoke German fluently; that ability was important when he accompanied Elder **Melvin J. Ballard** of the Twelve and Elder **Rey L. Pratt** of the Seventy to **Argentina** in 1925. There were only four members of the Church in **South America** at the time. Within a week of their arrival, six new converts, German-speaking immigrants, were baptized. Missionary work continued among the German-speaking immigrants in South America to establish the foundation for later **growth**. Elder Ballard dedicated South America for the preaching of the gospel during that visit. Elder Wells died 7 May 1941 in Salt Lake City at age 86.

SOURCES

Jenson, Andrew. *Latter-day Saint Biographical Encyclopedia.* 4 vols. 1901–36. Reprint, Salt Lake City: Western Epics, 1971. 1:212–14.

1999–2000 Church Almanac. Salt Lake City: Deseret News, 1998. 66–67.

DAVID KENISON

WELLS, SHARLENE. On 15 September 1984 Sharlene Wells received international attention when she became the second Latter-day Saint woman to be crowned Miss **America** (the first being **Colleen Hutchins** in 1952). The high moral principles she espoused were noted by the press, and she was often acclaimed for living her Church's standards. For instance, *USA Today* called her "squeaky clean," and *Time* magazine called her "promotional heaven." Sharlene was born 16 March 1964 to Robert E. (of the First **Quorum** of the **Seventy**) and Helen Wells in Asuncion, **Paraguay**. She married Robert A. Hawkes and as of 1999 was living in Centerville, **Utah**, where she was a full-time mother raising their four children. She occasionally free-lanced as a broadcaster for *ESPN* sports network.

SOURCE

Dew, Sheri L. *Sharlene Wells, Miss America.* Salt Lake City: Deseret Book, 1985.

MARY JANE WOODGER

WENTWORTH LETTER. John Wentworth was the editor and manager of the *Chicago Democrat.* He wrote to **Joseph Smith** for information concerning the rise and beliefs of Mormonism so he could share it with a friend, Mr. Bastow, who was then writing a history of **New Hampshire**. Joseph Smith's response is the Wentworth Letter, which **B. H. Roberts** describes as "one of the choicest documents in our Church literature" (1:55n). It was published in the Church's **Nauvoo** newspaper, *Times and Seasons,* on 1 March 1842.

The letter has three main areas of interest. First, it contains a narrative history of the progress of and persecutions against The Church of Jesus Christ of Latter-day Saints from its beginnings until 1842. Roberts states that this is the earliest published history of the Church written by Joseph Smith (Smith, 535n).

Second, the letter gives a summary of **Book of Mormon** history. Joseph Smith describes the Book of Mormon plates: "These records were engraven on plates which had the appearance of gold, each plate was six inches wide and eight inches long and not quite so thick as common tin . . . with three rings running through the whole. The volume was something near six inches in thickness, a part of which was sealed" (Smith, 537).

Third, the Wentworth Letter provides a listing of 13 beliefs of the Latter-day Saints, now known as the **Articles of Faith**, relative to issues of religious interest and debate during that period. This list does not contain all the beliefs of the Church, nor is it comparable to an all-inclusive creed. In 1880 the Articles of Faith were sustained and canonized as **scripture** and are published as the concluding section of the **Pearl of Great Price**.

SOURCES

Roberts, B. H. *A Comprehensive History of The Church of Jesus Christ of Latter-day Saints, Century One.* 6 vols. Salt Lake City: The Church of Jesus Christ of Latter-day Saints, 1930. 1:55n, 167; 2:130–31.

Smith, Joseph. *History of The Church of Jesus Christ of Latter-day Saints.* Edited by

B. H. Roberts. 2d ed. rev. 7 vols. Salt Lake City: The Church of Jesus Christ of Latter-day Saints, 1932–51. 4:535–41.

ROBERT L. MARROTT

WESTERN RESERVE. The Western Reserve comprised four million acres and included such towns as **Kirtland** and Cleveland. It was that portion of northeastern **Ohio** that lay between the 41st parallel and Lake Erie and extended west 125 miles from the **Pennsylvania** border. This area had originally been assigned to **Connecticut** by Charles I early in the colonial period as part of a land grant stretching, in theory, "from sea to sea." Unlike other eastern states, which between 1781 and 1802 ceded to the federal government the western lands given them in similar colonial grants, Connecticut retained the right to sell this portion of its western lands. Lush vegetation and fair prices brought an influx of adventuresome **pioneers** to the area, many of whom were zealous in their religious affiliations. Owing to the religious climate, Mormonism spread quickly in the Western Reserve, gaining many important converts there, such as **Sidney Rigdon**, **Newel K. Whitney**, **Edward Partridge**, and Lorenzo and **Eliza R. Snow**.

SOURCE

Backman, Milton V. Jr. *The Heavens Resound: A History of the Latter-day Saints in Ohio, 1830–1838*. Salt Lake City: Deseret Book, 1983. 22–23.

ANDREW H. HEDGES

WESTERN SAMOA. See **SAMOA**.

WEST INDIES. West Indies is a common name given to the islands of the Caribbean Sea. In 1853 missionaries were sent to the region and labored in **Jamaica**. They experienced some success but were eventually driven from the islands by mobs.

During the twentieth century, the gospel has spread throughout the West Indies with great success. Church **meetings** were held in expatriate member homes in **Puerto Rico** as early as 1940. Gardner H. Russell, who later became a member of the **Seventy**, held meetings with his **family** and LDS servicemen starting in 1947. For the next 20 years, servicemen met together and started spreading the gospel through member-missionary work. After the revelation on the **priesthood** in 1978, other islands were opened. Since that time tens of thousands of people have embraced the restored gospel in the **Dominican Republic**, resulting in the construction of a **temple** in that nation.

Church growth has moved forward at slower paces in **Haiti**, Jamaica, **Barbados**, and the smaller islands in the West Indies. Anti-Mormon opposition and misunderstanding has been common, resulting at times in restrictions on missionary numbers. But on each of the islands, a core of faithful members has kept the Church progressing, and through their examples, Latter-day Saints have gained their neighbors' respect.

By the onset of the year 2000 there were 110,073 members in the West Indies, residing in 16 **stakes** and 290 **wards** and **branches**.

SOURCES

Millett, Richard L. Manuscript. History of the Church in the Caribbean.

1999–2000 Church Almanac. Salt Lake City: Deseret News, 1998. 546–47.

Russell, Gardner. "Chronology—The Church of Jesus Christ of Latter-day Saints in Puerto Rico from 1940 to 1970." Manuscript.

"Temple to Be Built in the Caribbean." *Church News,* 4 December 1993. 3.

DAVID R. CROCKETT

WEST POINT, NEW YORK. The **United States** Military Academy, commonly called West Point, has a Latter-day Saint dimension to its history. Founded in 1802, West Point is the oldest military service academy and has been attended by a number of Mormons. The first Latter-day Saint to attend West Point was Willard Young, son of President **Brigham Young**. Willard enrolled in 1871 and was commissioned in 1875. He had a distinguished military career in the Corps of Engineers. Another member of the Young **family**, Richard W. Young, was the first Latter-day Saint graduate of West Point to be promoted to the rank of general. A grandson of Brigham Young, he saw action in the **Spanish American War** and **World War** I. He was promoted to brigadier general in 1918.

Other LDS graduates of West Point who were promoted to general include Briant H. Wells, Robert M. Cannon, Reese M. Howell, William Styer, Joseph Odell, George W. Coolidge, Jacob Reynolds, Royden E. Beebe Jr., Charles G. Dunn, and Brent Scowcroft. General Scowcroft went on to serve in the Air Force and also as national security advisor to President George Bush.

The number of Latter-day Saint cadets at West Point has gradually increased over the years. From 1871 to 1946 a total of 81 attended, but in

1998 alone there were 81 LDS cadets at the academy. In 1998 LDS cadets met in the West Point **Branch** with other members from the academy such as officers and staff and their families. Members from the nearby town of Highland Falls also attended this branch, meeting in buildings and rooms provided by the Army on the reservation at West Point.

SOURCES

Annual Report of the Association of Graduates of the United States Military Academy at West Point, New York. Saginaw, Michigan: Seeman and Peters, 1890–1998.

Fleming, Thomas J. *West Point: The Men and the Times of the United States Military Academy.* New York: William Morrow, 1969.

Jessee, Dean C. *Letters of Brigham Young to His Sons.* Salt Lake City: Deseret Book, 1974.

DONALD Q. CANNON

WEST VIRGINIA. The earliest Latter-day Saint missionaries in what later became West Virginia arrived in 1832 and included several who would eventually become **apostles**. **Luke S. Johnson** and **William McLellin** entered the area from across the **Ohio** River; others, including the **Prophet Joseph Smith**, visited the area on Church business. Significant success led to an immigration of converts to **Far West, Missouri,** and others later joined the **Saints** in the Rocky Mountains. One notable convert, **Bathsheba Smith,** later served as general president of the **Relief Society**.

West Virginia was created from **Virginia** in 1861, and missionary efforts continued under the auspices of the **Southern States Mission** after 1876. Before the turn of the century, the state was absorbed into the **Eastern States Mission** (1897), Middle States Mission (1902), and back to the Eastern States Mission, where it remained until smaller **missions** were created.

Prior to 1900 persecution was prevalent, culminating with the murder of **Elder** John Dempsey by a local minister. Gradual success in the twentieth century increased until the first **stake** (Charleston) was organized in 1970. By the year 2000 there were 12,290 members living in West Virginia in two stakes and 36 **wards** and **branches**.

SOURCES

Berrett, LaMar C. "History of the Southern States Mission, 1831–1861." Master's thesis, Brigham Young University, 1960.

Jenson, Andrew. *Encyclopedic History of The Church of Jesus Christ of Latter-day Saints.* Salt Lake City: Deseret News, 1941.

1999–2000 Church Almanac. Salt Lake City: Deseret News, 1998. 241–44.

DAVID F. BOONE

WHITLOCK, HARVEY. Harvey Whitlock was an early Church member whose name appears in the **Doctrine and Covenants** and who eventually apostatized. Born in **Massachusetts** in 1809, Whitlock joined the Church sometime prior to June 1831. At a **conference** of the Church in **Kirtland** on 3 June 1831, he was **ordained** a **high priest** by **Joseph Smith**, becoming one of the first high priests in this dispensation. On this occasion he was overcome by **Satan**, and Joseph cast the evil spirit out of him.

On 7 June 1831, he and **David Whitmer** were called to preach the gospel in **Missouri** (D&C 52:25). Whitlock was among the **Saints** expelled from **Jackson County** in 1833. He attended conferences and labored as a missionary until 1834, when he was disfellowshipped from the Church. In September 1835 he wrote to Joseph Smith expressing remorse for his departure. The **Prophet** wrote back expressing his joy at Harvey's repentant spirit and promising him forgiveness if he would return.

Harvey Whitlock was rebaptized and ordained a high priest on 30 January 1836 in Kirtland, and he remained in the Church until he was excommunicated in 1838. By 1840 he was living in Cedar County, **Iowa**, and by 1850 he had come west to **Salt Lake City**. He was a doctor and accumulated some land but was arrested in 1851 for theft. In 1858 he was rebaptized again, but once again he denied the faith. He moved to **California** in 1864 and joined the Reorganized church, serving a mission for them in 1866. Harvey Whitlock died in 1874 at Bishop Creek, California.

SOURCES

Black, Susan Easton. *Who's Who in the Doctrine and Covenants.* Salt Lake City: Bookcraft, 1997. 326–27.

Brewster, Hoyt W. *Doctrine and Covenants Encyclopedia.* Salt Lake City: Bookcraft, 1997. 630–31.

Smith, Joseph. *History of The Church of Jesus Christ of Latter-day Saints.* Edited by B. H. Roberts. 2d ed. rev. 7 vols. Salt Lake City: The Church of Jesus Christ of Latter-day Saints, 1932–51. 2:313–16.

GUY L. DORIUS

WHITMER, CHRISTIAN. Christian Whitmer, one of the Eight Witnesses of the Book of Mormon, was born 18 January 1798 in Pennsylvania. He moved with his parents to Fayette, New York, in the early 1800s. In 1825, he married Anna Schott; the couple was childless. Before his conversion to Mormonism, Christian served as a local militia officer and was elected a town constable. He was also a skilled shoemaker. Shortly after the organization of the Church in 1830, Christian and Anna were baptized. By 1831 he moved to Kirtland, and then in 1832 he relocated to the Whitmer settlement in Jackson County, Missouri. Mobocrats in the area expelled Christian and other Church members in late 1833. Christian moved to Liberty, Clay County, Missouri, where he served in a bishopric and presided over the elders. Christian was a member of the first Missouri high council. After suffering for years with a growth on his leg, he died 27 November 1835 at Liberty, Missouri. Oliver Cowdery, his brother-in-law, confirmed that Christian "proclaimed to [his] last moments, the certainty of [his] former testimony." Cowdery concluded, "The testament is in force *after* the death of the testator" (*Messenger and Advocate*).

SOURCES

Anderson, Richard L. *Investigating the Book of Mormon Witnesses.* Salt Lake City: Deseret Book, 1981.

Anderson, Richard L., and Scott H. Faulring. *The Book of Mormon Witnesses: A Resource Guide.* Provo, Utah: Richard L. Anderson and Scott H. Faulring, 1998.

Cowdery, Oliver. "The Closing Year." *Messenger and Advocate* 3 (December 1836): 426.

SCOTT H. FAULRING

WHITMER, DAVID. David Whitmer was one of the Three Witnesses of the Book of Mormon and an early leader in the Church. The son of Peter Whitmer and Mary Musselman, he was born 7 January 1805 near Harrisburg, Dauphin County, Pennsylvania, and then moved with his family to Fayette County, New York, about 1809. David learned of the Restoration in 1829 from Oliver Cowdery, a family friend. David became acquainted with Joseph Smith in the summer of 1829, when Joseph and Oliver Cowdery were invited to come to the Whitmer farm to live while completing the translation of the Book of Mormon. In the summer of 1829 a series of spiritual experiences convinced Whitmer that Joseph

Smith was a **prophet** and that his work was divine. In June 1829 Joseph received a revelation for David Whitmer (D&C 14), who became one of the **Three Witnesses** that same month.

At the organization of the Church **6 April** 1830, Whitmer was ordained an elder. He married Julia Ann Jolly 9 January 1831, and they were the parents of two children. The new couple moved to **Kirtland, Ohio**, where in June 1831 David was called to serve a **mission** to western **Missouri** with **Harvey Whitlock**. On 25 October 1831 Whitmer was ordained a **high priest**. In 1832 he moved to **Jackson County, Missouri**. On 7 July 1834 Whitmer was temporarily designated as a successor to Joseph Smith and set apart as "president of the Church in Missouri." In the summer of 1834 he was called to return to Kirtland to help complete the **temple** and to participate in its dedication. Whitmer stayed in Kirtland until 1837, actively engaged in numerous Church-related activities, including the selection of the Twelve **Apostles**, acting as sales agent for the Literary Firm, serving as a member of the Kirtland **high council**, and participating in a committee to draft rules to govern worship in the House of the Lord.

By 1837 Whitmer privately and publicly disapproved of Joseph Smith's leadership and expressed sympathy with other dissenting Latter-day Saints at Kirtland. The Kirtland high council brought charges against him in May 1837 for conduct unbecoming a high official in the Church. The court concluded that it did not have authority to try Whitmer, and the case was dismissed. He returned to western Missouri in the summer of 1837 and there broadcast his growing opposition against the **First Presidency**. In February 1838 Whitmer was rejected by the Missouri **Saints** as a Church leader in Missouri, and in April 1838 he was excommunicated at **Far West** for apostasy.

After separating from the Church, Whitmer and his family located at **Richmond, Missouri**. There he opened a livery and feed stable business. Whitmer became a respected and valued citizen at Richmond, where he served on the city council and was mayor (1867–1868). During the 1860s, 1870s, and 1880s, Whitmer entertained scores of visitors who wished to question him about his testimony of the Book of Mormon, which he never denied. In 1887, he wrote and published a 75-page **pamphlet** titled *An Address to All Believers in Christ*, an appeal for Christians to join Mormonism and for the scattered believers of the original faith to unite. Whitmer died on 25 January 1888 and was buried at Richmond.

SOURCES

Anderson, Richard Lloyd. *Investigating the Book of Mormon Witnesses.* Salt Lake City: Deseret Book, 1981. 67–92.

LYNDON W. COOK

WHITMER, JACOB. Jacob Whitmer was one of the Eight **Witnesses of the Book of Mormon**. He was born 27 January 1800 in **Pennsylvania** and moved with his parents to **Fayette, New York**, in the early 1800s. In 1825 he married Elizabeth Schott; they had nine children. Baptized with his wife on 11 April 1830, Jacob moved to **Kirtland** and then to the Whitmer settlement in **Jackson County, Missouri**, in 1831. After the **Saints'** expulsion from Jackson County in 1833, Jacob served on the Missouri **high council**. In 1837 he was a member of the building committee for the anticipated temple at **Far West**, Missouri. After his brothers John and David were excommunicated in 1838, Jacob left Latter-day Saint society and settled in Richmond, **Ray County**, Missouri. Jacob was a shoemaker and farmer. He died 21 April 1856 and is buried near his parents and **Oliver Cowdery** in the Richmond pioneer cemetery. His son, John C. Whitmer, later verified, "My father, Jacob Whitmer, was always faithful and true to his testimony to the Book of Mormon, and confirmed it on his death bed" (Anderson, 129).

SOURCES

Anderson, Richard L. *Investigating the Book of Mormon Witnesses.* Salt Lake City: Deseret Book, 1981.
Anderson, Richard L., and Scott H. Faulring. *The Book of Mormon Witnesses: A Resource Guide.* Provo, Utah: Richard L. Anderson and Scott H. Faulring, 1998.

SCOTT H. FAULRING

WHITMER, JOHN. John Whitmer was one of the Eight **Witnesses of the Book of Mormon** plates and was appointed to act as Church historian. He was born 27 August 1802 in **Fayette, New York**, the third son of Peter and Mary Whitmer. He served as a scribe for the **Prophet Joseph Smith** in translating the **Book of Mormon**. **Oliver Cowdery** baptized him in Seneca Lake in June 1829.

In November 1831 John Whitmer and Oliver Cowdery were called to transport the manuscript of the **Book of Commandments** to **Independence, Missouri**, for publication. During the conflict in **Jackson County**, he and five others offered themselves to be whipped or killed if the mobs would leave the rest of the **Saints** alone. John was ordained 3 July 1834 as one of the assistant presidents of the Church in **Missouri**. Less than two years later, he was present at the dedication of the **Kirtland Temple** and received his blessings and anointings.

The **high council** in **Far West, Missouri**, excommunicated John from the Church 10 March 1838 for conduct unbecoming of a Chrisitian. He remained in Far West until his death 11 July 1878. Though he never reunited with the Church, John remained true to his testimony of the Book of Mormon plates.

SOURCES

Black, Susan Easton. *Who's Who in the Doctrine and Covenants*. Salt Lake City: Bookcraft, 1997. 331–34.

Jenson, Andrew. *Latter-day Saint Biographical Encyclopedia*. 4 vols. 1901–36. Reprint, Salt Lake City: Western Epics, 1971. 4:251.

Perkins, Keith W. "The Whitmers." *Ensign* 19 (February 1989): 34–42.

CRAIG J. OSTLER

WHITMER, MARY. Mary Musselman Whitmer, affectionately known by members of the Church as "Mother Whitmer," was born in Strausburg, **Pennsylvania**, on 27 August 1778. She married **Peter Whitmer Sr.**, with whom she had eight children. All five sons recorded their names in the **Book of Mormon** as **witnesses** of the authenticity of the "gold plates." Two daughters (Catherine and Elizabeth Ann) married two other witnesses (**Hyrum Page** and **Oliver Cowdery**, respectively). One daughter (Nancy) died in infancy. Mary opened her small one-and-a-half-story log home to **Joseph Smith**, his wife, Emma, and his scribe, Oliver Cowdery, to continue the translation of the Book of Mormon. One evening, perhaps as a compensation for being burdened by additional household duties, she was shown the Book of Mormon plates. The messenger who showed her the plates admonished her to be patient and promised her great blessings. Mary Whitmer bears the distinction of being the only woman shown the plates. On **6 April 1830**, Mary's log home became the location for the **organization of the Church**. Mary and her husband were baptized in Seneca Lake by Oliver Cowdery 18 April

1830. Mother Whitmer died January 1856 and is buried next to her husband in the old Richmond graveyard, **Ray County, Missouri.**

SOURCES

Bushman, Richard L. *Joseph Smith and the Beginnings of Mormonism.* Chicago: University of Illinois Press, 1984. 79–113.

Jenson, Andrew. *Latter-day Saint Biographical Encyclopedia.* 4 vols. 1901–36. Reprint, Salt Lake City: Western Epics, 1971.

Porter, Larry C. *A Study of the Origins of The Church of Jesus Christ of Latter-day Saints in the States of New York and Pennsylvania, 1816–1831.* Provo, Utah: Joseph Fielding Smith Institute for Latter-day Saint History and BYU Studies, 2000.

W. SIDNEY YOUNG

WHITMER, PETER, JR. Peter Whitmer Jr. was one of the **Eight Witnesses of the Book of Mormon** plates and was called on the **Lamanite Mission of 1830 and 1831.** He was born 27 September 1809 in **Fayette, New York,** the fifth son of Peter and Mary Whitmer. He assisted the **Prophet Joseph Smith** in translating the **Book of Mormon.** **Oliver Cowdery** baptized him in Seneca Lake in June 1829.

In September 1830 he was called by **revelation** to accompany Oliver Cowdery to preach the gospel among the **Lamanites** (D&C 30). Later Parley P. Pratt and **Ziba Petersen** were called to be their companions (D&C 32). Preaching along the way, the missionaries stopped in **Kirtland, Ohio,** and Peter bore testimony, as a witness of the **gold plates**, to the truthfulness of the Book of Mormon. After arriving in **Jackson County, Missouri,** Peter was employed as a tailor and waited in **Independence** for the Prophet Joseph Smith, who arrived the following July.

Peter suffered the 1833 persecutions of the **Saints** in Jackson County. After being consumptive for several years, he died in Liberty, **Missouri,** 22 September 1836, a faithful member of the Church.

SOURCES

Black, Susan Easton. *Who's Who in the Doctrine and Covenants.* Salt Lake City: Bookcraft, 1997. 334–36.

Jenson, Andrew. *Latter-day Saint Biographical Encyclopedia.* 4 vols. 1901–36. Reprint, Salt Lake City: Western Epics, 1971. 1:277.

CRAIG J. OSTLER

WHITMER, PETER, SR. Peter Whitmer Sr., titled "Father Whitmer" by the **Prophet Joseph Smith,** was the father of five **witnesses of the**

Book of Mormon (Christian, Jacob, John, Peter Jr., and David Whitmer) and the father-in-law of two other witnesses (Oliver Cowdery and Hiram Page). Peter's wife, Mary Whitmer, was the only woman to be shown the gold plates.

Peter was born 14 April 1773 in Harrisburg, Pennsylvania, and married Mary Musselman, with whom he had eight children. The Whitmers were Presbyterian Germans living near Harrisburg, Pennsylvania. In 1809 the family moved to western New York, where Peter purchased a 100-acre farm and log home three miles south of Waterloo in Seneca County, Fayette Township. The Whitmer Farm was the site of the completion of the Book of Mormon translation and the organization of the Church. Oliver Cowdery baptized Peter and Mary in Seneca Lake 18 April 1830. The following year the family moved to Kirtland, Ohio, and in 1832 to Jackson County, Missouri. Father Whitmer died 12 August 1854 in Richmond, Ray County, Missouri. He is buried in the old Richmond graveyard.

SOURCES

Bushman, Richard L. *Joseph Smith and the Beginnings of Mormonism.* Chicago: University of Illinois Press, 1984. 79–113.

Jenson, Andrew. *Latter-day Saint Biographical Encyclopedia.* 4 vols. 1901–36. Reprint, Salt Lake City: Western Epics, 1971.

Porter, Larry C. "A Study of the Origins of The Church of Jesus Christ of Latter-day Saints in the States of New York and Pennsylvania, 1816–1831." Ph.D. diss., Brigham Young University, 1971.

W. SIDNEY YOUNG

WHITMER FARM. The Whitmer Farm was the site for much of the Book of Mormon translation and the organization of the Church. Located in the Finger Lake Region of western New York, the farm is situated in Fayette Township, Seneca County, approximately six miles northwest of the village of Fayette and about 28 miles southeast of Palmyra between Seneca and Cayuga Lakes. Peter Whitmer Sr. purchased the 100-acre parcel of land from Samuel and Rebecca Miller on 14 April 1819. A 20-by-30-foot, one-and-one-half-story log home was constructed as the family lived on the farm. In June 1829 Joseph Smith and his wife, Emma, along with Oliver Cowdery, resided with the Whitmers to complete the translation of the Book of Mormon. The Three Witnesses were shown the plates in a wooded area on the farm in June 1829. On 6 April 1830, approximately 50 to 60 believers crowded inside the Whitmer log home to witness the Church's organization. Three

general conferences were held at the farm between June 1830 and January 1831. Twenty **revelations** were received here. The farm was sold in 1831 when the Whitmers moved to **Kirtland, Ohio.**

In 1926 **Elder B. H. Roberts** purchased 120 acres of land at the site of the Whitmer farm in behalf of the Church. For years many Latter-day Saints assumed that the home that was already on the property was where the Church had been organized, but during 1946 and 1947 William L. Powell, caretaker of the land, uncovered the foundation of the old log home where the meeting had actually taken place. In preparation for the Church's sesquicentennial (1980), the reconstruction of the log home was completed, with a **visitors' center** nearby and a chapel for the Fayette, New York **Branch**. Via **satellite** transmission from the log home, President **Spencer W. Kimball** spoke and dedicated the Whitmer farm complex while presiding over the Church's 150th annual general conference 6 April 1980.

SOURCES

Porter, Larry C. "Organizational Origins of The Church of Jesus Christ, 6 April 1830." In *New York*. Edited by Larry Porter, Milton V. Backman Jr., and Susan Easton Black. Regional Studies in Latter-day Saint Church History series. Provo, Utah: Brigham Young University, 1992.

———. "A Study of the Origins of The Church of Jesus Christ of Latter-day Saints in the States of New York and Pennsylvania, 1816–1831." Ph.D. diss., Brigham Young University. 1971.

W. SIDNEY YOUNG

WHITMER HISTORICAL ASSOCIATION. See JOHN WHITMER HISTORICAL ASSOCIATION.

WHITNEY, HELEN MAR. Helen Mar Whitney is best known for her series of reminiscences published in the *Woman's Exponent* from May 1880 to August 1886. With this series she has provided one of the most detailed accounts of early Church history from a woman's perspective. Born 22 August 1828 in Mendon, New York, to Heber C. Kimball and Vilate Murray Kimball, Helen grew up among prominent Latter-day Saint leaders such as Joseph Smith, Brigham Young, Newel K. Whitney, Eliza R. Snow, and Emmeline B. Wells. She was a plural wife of the Prophet Joseph Smith and a public defender of the doctrine of plural marriage. On 3 February 1846, she married Horace K. Whitney, son of Bishop Newel K. and Elizabeth Whitney, in the Nauvoo Temple before journeying with the Saints to Winter Quarters and, finally, to Salt Lake City. She bore eleven children, seven of whom lived to adulthood. Helen Mar died in Salt Lake City on 15 November 1896. Her series of reminiscences, which include excerpts from the diaries and letters of her father, mother, and husband, provide details of the day-to-day lives of many early Saints.

SOURCE

Holzapfel, Jeni Broberg, and Richard Neitzel Holzapfel. *A Woman's View: Helen Mar Whitney's Reminiscences of Early Church History.* Provo, Utah: Religious Studies Center, Brigham Young University, 1997.

LISA KURKI

WHITNEY, NEWEL K. Newel Kimball Whitney, a **presiding bishop** of the Church, was born 5 February 1795 in Marlborough, **Vermont.** By the age of 19 he was a merchant living in Plattsburg, **New York.**

Newel moved to Painesville, **Ohio,** where he became a business partner with **Algernon Sydney Gilbert.** They later established a business in **Kirtland.** While living in Kirtland, Newel married Elizabeth Ann Smith 20 October 1822. In November 1830 they were converted to the gospel and baptized by **Sidney Rigdon.**

On 4 December 1831 Whitney was called as a **bishop** over the Ohio area (D&C 72). Unable to see himself in this position, Whitney "shrank from the responsibility." The Prophet answered: "Go and ask the Lord about it." Newel did so and heard a voice from heaven say: "Thy strength is in me" (Whitney, CR, 47–48). With this comforting confirmation, he accepted the call. Whitney also participated in the **School of the Prophets** held in his Kirtland store.

Whitney left Kirtland in the fall of 1838, eventually settling at **Quincy, Illinois,** and then **Nauvoo.** In May 1842 he was one of a select few to receive the endowment from Joseph Smith. When the Nauvoo Stake was organized 5 October 1839, Whitney served as bishop of the Middle Ward. At the October 1844 **general conference,** Whitney was sustained as the first bishop of the Church. At **Winter Quarters** 6 April 1847 he was sustained as presiding bishop of the Church, which position he held until his death in **Salt Lake City** 23 September 1850.

SOURCES

Jenson, Andrew. *Latter-day Saint Biographical Encyclopedia.* 4 vols. 1901–36. Reprint, Salt Lake City: Western Epics, 1971. 1:222–27.

Poulsen. Larry N. "The Life and Contributions of Newel Kimball Whitney." Master's thesis, Brigham Young University, 1966.

Whitney, Orson F. "Newel K. Whitney." *Contributor.* Salt Lake City: Deseret News,
    1885. 123–32.
———. Conference Report [CR] (April 1919): 47–48.

CALVIN R. STEPHENS

WHITNEY, ORSON F. Called as a member of the **Quorum** of the
Twelve **Apostles** in 1906, Orson Ferguson Whitney was a gifted speaker
and orator, a prolific writer and poet, and a renowned educator and
scholar. His grandfathers, **bishop Newel K. Whitney** and apostle **Heber
C. Kimball**, served in the leading councils of the Church. Born 1 July
1855 in **Salt Lake City** to Horace Kimball Whitney and **Helen Mar
Kimball**, Orson served a **mission** in the eastern **United States**. While on
that mission, he had a remarkable dream in which he was a witness to
the Savior's agony in Gethsemane. It was the turning point of his life, and
he traced all of his future success to that singular event. Three months
after returning from his mission, he was called as **bishop** of the Salt Lake
Eighteenth **Ward**, a position he held for 28 years, until he was called to
the Council of the Twelve. He married Zina Beal Smoot, and she bore
nine children. His second wife, May Wells, gave birth to two children.

   Among **Elder** Whitney's literary achievements are hundreds of
books, **pamphlets**, and articles. Most noteworthy are his books *The Life of
Heber C. Kimball, Through Memory's Halls: The Life Story of Orson F.
Whitney,* and the four-volume *History of Utah*, as well as a book-length
poem, "Elias: An Epic of the Ages." He died 16 May 1931 in Salt Lake
City.

SOURCES

Flake, Dennis D. "Orson F. Whitney's Philosophy of Education." Ph.D. diss., Brigham
    Young University, 1989.
Flake, Lawrence R. *Prophets and Apostles of the Last Dispensation.* Provo, Utah:
    Religious Studies Center, Brigham Young University, 2001. 435–37.
Whitney, Orson F. *Through Memory's Halls: The Life Story of Orson F. Whitney.*
    Independence, Mo.: Zion's Printing and Publishing, 1930. 82–83.

DENNIS D. FLAKE

WHITNEY STORE. The **Newel K. Whitney** store was the first
mercantile store in **Kirtland**, dating from 1826. After being in business
alone for a few years, Newel K. Whitney was joined by **A. Sidney Gilbert**,
until the latter was called to **Missouri**. This store was the center of

Church life from 1831 to 1834. A number of **revelations** mention the store and its owners (D&C 63:42–46; 64:26; 104:39–42; 117:1). **Joseph Smith III** was born there as well.

Some of the most sacred events of early Church history took place on the second floor of the store. Seventeen revelations were received there, including the **Prophecy on War** (D&C 87), the Olive Leaf (D&C 88), the **Word of Wisdom** (D&C 89), and Doctrine and Covenants 93. During the winter of 1833 it was also the location of the first **School of the Prophets**. The highlight of the revelations received in the store was 18 March 1833, when members of the School of the Prophets beheld a vision of the Father and the Son. At this time **Sidney Rigdon** and **Frederick G. Williams** were given the keys of the kingdom in connection with **Joseph Smith** (D&C 90:6–9). In 1984 the store was restored to its original 1830s appearance and became a Church **historical site**. In 1988 the store was awarded a president's Historic Preservation Award in recognition of its excellent restoration.

SOURCES

Anderson, Karl Ricks. *Joseph Smith's Kirtland.* Salt Lake City: Deseret Book, 1989.

Backman, Milton V., Jr. *The Heavens Resound.* Salt Lake City: Deseret Book, 1983.

"House of Revelation." *Ensign* 23 (January 1993): 30–37.

"Whitney Store Wins Major U.S. Preservation Award." *Ensign* 19 (January 1989): 76–77.

KEITH W. PERKINS

WIDTSOE, JOHN A. At age six, John Andreas Widtsoe, a future educator and apostle, dropped a rose onto his father's casket as a token of his pledge to pursue the educational ideals his schoolmaster father had not attained because of an early death. That pledge led John to distinction at **Brigham Young College**, graduation from Harvard University, and master's and Ph.D. degrees at one of the world's highest rated universities— Goettingen in **Germany**. His international acclaim in soil chemistry, irrigation, and dry farming led to his being director of the Utah Experiment Station, president of the Utah State Agricultural College (now Utah State University), and principal of agriculture at **Brigham Young University**; he eventually became the president of the **University of Utah**. His scientific training and his absolute devotion to the Church made him a uniquely qualified voice on issues of science and religion.

John was born 31 January 1872 in Norway to John A. Widtsoe and Anna Karine Daarden. About the time John's father died, his mother joined the Church and was therefore ostracized from society. When John was 11 years old, his mother took the family to America hoping for better opportunities for her two sons.

On 17 March 1921, just a few weeks after his 49th birthday, John Widtsoe was called into the **Quorum** of the Twelve Apostles. In the Quorum he gave 31 years of distinguished service to the Church. Prior to that call he had served in the **Young Men's Mutual Improvement Association** and on the board of the **Genealogical Society of Utah**. He had written several books and instruction manuals for the Church and dozens of articles for the *Improvement Era.*

While an apostle, he also served the federal government on the Hoover Commission, charged with management of the Colorado River. He spent two years in **Washington, D.C.**, reorganizing the Federal Bureau of Reclamation.

Elder Widtsoe's unusual abilities led him to important assignments as an apostle. He continued to write many Church manuals and books on doctrine and the teachings of Church leaders. He was a major voice in the development of genealogical and **temple** work. He played a key role in Church education and served twice as commissioner. He assisted **Reed Smoot**, apostle and U.S. senator, with securing Church recognition and getting **missionaries** back into the nations of **Europe** following **World War I**. He was president of the **European Mission** for six years, during which the Church gained a more positive image in the press and the gospel was spread to the Slovak people with the creation of a mission in **Czechoslovakia**. When he returned he was assigned to head a committee to consider Church publicity, which led in 1935 to the creation of the Church Radio, Publicity, and Mission Literature Committee, with recently returned missionary **Gordon B. Hinckley** hired as its executive secretary.

Elder Widtsoe was also made the editor of the *Improvement Era* and was sent to the University of Southern California on a special one-year assignment to teach Mormonism for university credit. While there he promoted the spread of **institutes** of religion. As editor of the *Improvement Era* for 17 years, he directed its growth from a magazine primarily for the youth to the voice of the whole Church. He wrote hundreds of editorials, special articles, book critiques, and answers to difficult doctrinal and historical questions under the title "Evidences and Reconciliations"; selections from these writings were later compiled into three volumes bearing that title.

John A. Widtsoe married Leah Dunford, the eldest daughter of **Susa**

Young Gates, the daughter of Brigham Young and Lucy Bigelow. His association with these three women made him an important bridge between the first generation of Saints and the modern Church. He died 29 November 1952 in Salt Lake City.

SOURCES

Josephson, Marba C. "John A. Widtsoe—1872–1952." *Improvement Era* 56 (January 1953): 19–20, 58–61.

ALAN K. PARRISH

WIGHT, LYMAN. Lyman Wight, an early apostle in the Church, was born 9 May 1796 at Fairfield, New York. He joined the Church in Kirtland, Ohio, being baptized and ordained an elder in November of 1830. In June 1832, Joseph Smith ordained him the first high priest in the Church. He then ordained Joseph to that same office.

Having a military background, Lyman played a vital role in the defense of the Saints in Missouri and was second in command to Joseph in Zion's Camp. He was responsible for the Saints' protection in Jackson County and also in their northern Missouri settlements. Eventually, he was imprisoned with Joseph Smith and other Church leaders in Liberty Jail.

As the Saints established themselves in Nauvoo, Lyman was ordained a member of the Quorum of the Twelve Apostles 8 April 1841. Along with others of the Twelve, he campaigned for Joseph Smith in his run for the presidency in 1844.

With the death of the Prophet, Lyman proceeded with plans to move to Texas and establish a mission there. He had been charged with this responsibility by Joseph before the Prophet's death. Once removed from the body of the Saints, he apostatized and was excommunicated from the Church 12 February 1849. He died in Dexter, Medina County, Texas, 31 March 1858.

SOURCES

Booth, Major C.C. "Lyman Wight in Early Texas," *Improvement Era* 57 (January 1954): 26–28.

Wightman, Philip C. "The Life and Contributions of Lyman Wight." Master's thesis, Brigham Young University, 1971.

PHILLIP C. WIGHTMAN

WILKINSON, ERNEST L. Ernest Leroy Wilkinson was one of the most successful leaders in the history of Church education. He was born

4 May 1899 into a poor but devoted Latter-day **Saint family** in **Ogden, Utah.** Raised in a rough-and-tumble neighborhood, the diminutive (he was only five feet tall) yet pugnacious Wilkinson graduated from **Weber Academy** (then a Church school) in 1914 and earned a B.A. from **Brigham Young University.** After he married Alice Ludlow, the couple moved to **Washington, D.C.**, where he earned a law degree from George Washington University. He then graduated from Harvard with a doctor of juridical science degree in 1927.

Wilkinson worked for Charles Evans Hughes (later chief justice of the Supreme Court) before forming his own law firm in 1935. A persuasive lawyer, Wilkinson redrafted the **Indian** Claims Commission Act and, after 13 years of work, successfully brought suit against the government on behalf of the Ute Indian tribes for lost compensation. This consolidated judgment, awarded in 1950, totaled $32,000,000—one of the largest judgments ever entered against the U.S. government.

In 1950 President **George Albert Smith** invited Wilkinson to become president of Brigham Young University. His inauguration in October 1951, coupled with **David O. McKay**'s succession to the presidency of the Church in April 1951, bode well for the future of the small **Provo** Church school. An educator by profession, President McKay shared Wilkinson's vision of building a great Church university. With the help of scores of others along the way, this dynamic tandem transformed BYU into **America**'s largest Church-sponsored university.

Refusing a salary for several years, Wilkinson accepted his second career with abundant relish. During his 20-year term as president (save for a short leave when he ran an unsuccessful campaign for U.S. senator in 1964), Wilkinson increased student enrollment from 4,000 to 25,000, created a master plan with more than 300 university buildings, and in the process built one of America's most beautiful college campuses. Academic excellence was also strengthened with a better-trained and better-paid faculty, higher admission standards, and improved graduate programs. Meanwhile the school devotedly maintained Church standards of conduct and behavior. Wilkinson's self-admitted greatest accomplishment was the creation of a widespread network of student **wards** and **stakes** on campus.

Wilkinson also served simultaneously as administrator and chancellor of the unified **Church Educational System** from 1953 to 1964. Though his vision of a network of Church-sponsored junior colleges never materialized, he helped lay the groundwork for the remarkable expansion of Church **seminaries** and **institutes** worldwide. On the day of his resignation in 1971, the Church announced the fulfillment of one of his most cherished dreams—the establishment of the **J. Reuben Clark** Law School.

An intensely private man and father of five, Wilkinson died 6 April 1978 in **Salt Lake City**. As a lawyer, Church leader, philanthropist, and university builder, he left an indelible impression upon modern Church history.

SOURCES

Deem, Woodruff J., and Glenn V. Bird. *Ernest L. Wilkinson—Indian Advocate and University President.* Provo, Utah: Alice L. Wilkinson, 1982. 290.

Wilkinson, Ernest L., ed. *Brigham Young University: The First One Hundred Years.* 4 vols. Provo, Utah: Brigham Young University Press, 1975–76.

RICHARD E. BENNETT

WILLIAMS, CLARISSA SMITH. Clarissa Smith Williams, the sixth general **Relief Society** president, was the first native Utahn to fill the office. Daughter of the **apostle George A. Smith** and Susan West, Clarissa was born 21 April 1859 in **Salt Lake City**. She married William Newjent Williams, a successful businessman, with whom she had 11 children. A charismatic leader and gracious hostess, Clarissa drew people from all walks of life to her home and office. Having served in the Relief Society as a general board member, treasurer, and **counselor**, she was called as general president in April 1921. During her seven-year administration, Clarissa focused on health, maternity, and child **welfare** services, desiring to improve the standard of living for women. Clarissa was released in October 1928, and she died in Salt Lake City 8 March 1930.

SOURCES

Derr, Jill Mulvay, Janath Russell Cannon, and Maureen Ursenbach Beecher. *Women of Covenant: The Story of the Relief Society.* Salt Lake City: Deseret Book, 1992. 228–29.

Peterson, Janet, and LaRene Gaunt. *Elect Ladies: Presidents of the Relief Society.* Salt Lake City: Deseret Book, 1990. 97–109.

JANET PETERSON

WILLIAMS, FREDERICK G. Frederick Granger Williams was second **counselor** to **Joseph Smith** from 18 March 1833 to 7 September 1837. He was born 28 October 1787 in Suffield, Hartford, **Connecticut**.

He fought the British during the **War** of 1812 before gaining employment as a boat navigator on Lake Erie. By 1816, Williams was practicing medicine and teaching school in **Ohio**.

Williams met Latter-day Saint missionaries **Parley P. Pratt**, **Ziba Peterson**, **Oliver Cowdery**, and **Peter Whitmer Jr.** in **Kirtland, Ohio**, in 1830. After his baptism in October 1830, he accompanied the missionaries on the **Lamanite mission** of 1830 and 1831. He served as a scribe and a counselor to Joseph Smith and was also a trustee of the **School of the Prophets**, editor of the *Northern Times,* paymaster of **Zion's Camp**, and president of the **Kirtland Safety Society**. When the bank failed in 1837, Williams briefly turned against the **Prophet**. He was dropped from the **First Presidency** in November 1837. **Family** tradition and historical records disagree over whether he also lost his membership. The answer may be found in the Prophet's writing of 5 August 1838: "Frederick G. Williams . . . had recently been re-baptized" (Smith, 55).

Williams was numbered among the **Saints** who suffered from the effects of the **extermination order** in **Missouri**. He claimed that the suffering "reduced and left [him] and [his] family in a state of poverty, with a delicate state of health" (Johnson, 377). He fled from mobocracy in Missouri to **Quincy, Illinois**, where his health continued to deteriorate. One night, while Williams was visiting with the Prophet, Joseph said to him, "Brother Frederick, I don't like to see you leave. You are going home to die." He answered, "I am already a dead man" (Williams, 126–27). He died 25 (or 10) October 1842 in Quincy from a lung hemorrhage at age 55.

SOURCES

Johnson, Clark V., ed. *Mormon Redress Petitions: Documents of the 1833–1838 Missouri Conflict.* Provo, Utah: Religious Studies Center, Brigham Young University, 1992. 377.

Smith, Joseph. *History of The Church of Jesus Christ of Latter-day Saints.* Edited by B. H. Roberts. 2d ed. rev. 7 vols. Salt Lake City: The Church of Jesus Christ of Latter-day Saints, 1932–51. 3:55.

Williams, Nancy Clement. *After 100 Years! Meet Frederick Granger Williams.* Independence, Mo.: Zion's Printing & Publishing Company, 1951.

SUSAN EASTON BLACK

WINDER, BARBARA W. Barbara Woodhead Winder, born 9 May 1931 in Midvale, **Utah**, was general president of the **Relief Society** from 1984 to 1990. Before she became president she served on the Relief Society general board and as the national president of **Lambda Delta Sigma**. She also served with her husband, Richard W. Winder, when he presided over the **California San Diego Mission** (1982–84) and the Czechoslovakia Mission (1990–93). Under her direction, the Relief Society program was simplified to accommodate women worldwide. The changes included smaller stake Relief Society boards and more flexibility in **visiting teaching**. The general presidencies of the Primary and Young Women were moved into the Relief Society Building with the Relief Society general presidency during her administration.

SOURCE

"Barbara W. Winder: Relief Society General President." *Ensign* 14 (May 1984): 97.

CYNTHIA DOXEY

WINDER, JOHN R. John Rex Winder, a **counselor** in the **First Presidency**, was born 11 December 1821 in Biddenham, **London**. He was introduced to the Church when he found a small scrap of paper lying on the floor of the cobbler's shop where he worked. The paper had only the words "Latter-day Saints" written on it. His curiosity led him to a missionary meeting, where he heard **Elder Orson Spencer** preach. He and his wife soon joined the Church and immigrated to **Zion**. In **Utah** he distinguished himself as a captain and later a lieutenant colonel in the **Nauvoo Legion**. He was involved in the guarding of Echo Canyon against **Johnston's Army** and in various **Indian** campaigns, including the **Black Hawk War**. Over the years he held more than a score of prominent governmental and business positions.

In 1887 President **John Taylor** called Brother Winder to serve as second counselor in the **presiding bishopric**. In 1892 while **Bishop** Winder was serving in that position, Church leaders decided they would try to finish the construction of the **Salt Lake Temple** by the next April. They gave Bishop Winder the responsibility and credit for seeing that the 250-man crew met this deadline. After the dedication 6 April 1893, he was called to the First Presidency by **Joseph F. Smith** on 17 October 1901: "To think that one who had sprung from the source I had, without any **education** . . . slow to speech, feeling as though I could pass through the floor whenever I am called upon to speak to the people—was it possible that President Smith could choose me for his counselor?" (quoted in Anderson, 624). President Winder served in this office until his death on 27 March 1910 in Salt Lake City.

SOURCES

Anderson, Edward H. "President John R. Winder." *Improvement Era* 13 (May 1910): 617–27.

Flake, Lawrence R. *Prophets and Apostles of the Last Dispensation.* Provo, Utah: Religious Studies Center, Brigham Young University, 2001. 187–89.

Jenson, Andrew. *Latter-day Saint Biographical Encyclopedia.* 4 vols. 1901–36. Reprint, Salt Lake City: Western Epics, 1971. 1:244.

LAWRENCE R. FLAKE

WINTER QUARTERS. Winter Quarters, sometimes called Mormonism's "second Sacred Grove" and America's "other Valley Forge," was Nebraska's first city. This Latter-day Saint winter quarters on the west bank of the Missouri River was not a part of Brigham Young's original plans for exodus. Because of bad weather, inadequate provisions, and overcrowded wagon trains, the Latter-day Saints finally reached Council Bluffs on their way west from Nauvoo, Illinois, exhausted, relatively disorganized, and too late to send even an express company to the Rockies that year. With the U.S. Army's request for a 500-man Mormon Battalion to march to California in the Mexican War, Brigham Young negotiated rights to settle his people on Indian lands west of the Missouri River, allowing for a faster departure for the Rockies the following spring.

Beginning in October 1846, Winter Quarters sprang up almost overnight—"like Jonah's gourd"—near Cutler's Park in grid-like fashion, with large city streets and a central council house. By December approximately 5,000 Latter-day Saints had hunkered down for the winter in hastily erected log cabins, huts, tents, and hovels. Some even lived in caves on the river banks. Farms and gardens were planted to the south of the city, while their cattle herds grazed in the rush bottoms north of the settlement. Across the river in and about Council Bluffs, Iowa, an equal number took winter refuge in tiny family encampments like Miller's Hollow, Pigeon Creek, and 30 other gatherings that later combined to create the town of Kanesville.

With so many husbands and fathers away with the Battalion or off working in Missouri or elsewhere, Church leaders divided the city into 22 wards and called bishops to provide for the temporal and spiritual needs of from 200 to 300 members each. High councils were established on both sides of the river. Socials, picnics, and even balls were frequently held, and Church services were convened in the council house or in the outdoors. Willard Richards's octagon house, or "potato heap," doubled as a post office and as a sacred center where Brigham Young solemnized several celestial marriages "in the wilderness." Schools and women's groups thrived throughout the community. A flour mill (a remnant of which still stands) was erected during the winter of 1846 and 1847 on Turkey Creek on the city's north end.

Winter Quarters will, however, be best remembered for the trial of faith experienced there by so many Latter-day Saints. Due to their weakened and malnourished condition, as well as inadequate shelter from the cold winter weather, disease in the form of malaria and scurvy began to decimate their numbers. Between October 1846 and May 1848, as many as 1,000 perished on both sides of the river, and several were buried in unmarked graves. Yet defections were uncommon—faith remained strong, and most retained loyalty to Brigham Young and his exodus mission. Said the Latter-day Saint leader: "We are willing to take our full share of trouble, trials, losses and crosses, hardships and fatigues, warning and watching, for the kingdom of heaven's sake; and we feel to say: Come, calm or strife, turmoil or peace, life or death, in the name of Israel's God we mean to conquer or die trying" (Journal History).

By early spring of 1847, the vanguard company of **pioneers** had left Winter Quarters for the Great **Salt Lake Valley**. Brigham Young and others returned to Winter Quarters in October 1847. Brigham Young was sustained as president of the Church on the east side of the river in the log tabernacle at Kanesville on 27 December 1847. As per agreement with the Office of Indian Affairs, Winter Quarters was evacuated in the summer of 1848 as the Saints either moved west or found other temporary shelter east of the river.

By the early 1850s, the new town of Florence sprang up on the approximate site of old Winter Quarters and became a favored jumping-off place for scores of later Latter-day Saint wagon trains bound for the West. Later, with the establishment of the Union Pacific terminus in Nebraska, Omaha began its eclipse of Council Bluffs, Iowa, as a transportation hub and commercial center. Today Florence is a busy northside suburb of Omaha, Nebraska's largest city. In June 1999 the Church announced plans to build the Omaha Nebraska Temple. In October of the same year the name was changed to the Winter Quarters Temple. Construction began on the temple in November 1999.

SOURCES

Bennett, Richard E. *Mormons at the Missouri, 1846–1852: "And Should We Die. . . ."* Norman: University of Oklahoma Press, 1987.

Journal History, 16 April 1847. LDS Church Archives, Salt Lake City.

Shumway, Ernest Widtsoe. "History of Winter Quarters, Nebraska 1846–1848." Master's thesis, Brigham Young University, 1953.

RICHARD E. BENNETT

WINTER QUARTERS MONUMENT. After being driven out of Nauvoo, the Saints spent the winter of 1846 and 1847 at Winter Quarters, their settlement on the western banks of the Missouri River near what became Omaha, Nebraska. Hundreds of Saints died there and were buried in the cemetery.

In 1935 the Church graced the Winter Quarters cemetery with a superb sculptural setting of markers, entrance gates, plaques, and a figure grouping. The visual centerpiece is a heroic-sized bronze sculpture of a pioneer father and mother looking down into the shallow grave of their dead baby. The father shelters the mother with his great cloak as he holds the shovel he has just used to dig the grave. On the back of the granite pedestal (stone from the same quarry as that used for the Salt Lake Temple) is a bronze dedicatory plaque with a Latter-day Saint wagon train. The artist, Avard Fairbanks (1897–1987), has three of his great-grandparents buried in this cemetery.

For the pioneer sesquicentennial of 1997, the Church built a pioneer museum and visitors' center next to this site.

SOURCE

Fairbanks, Eugene F. *A Sculptor's Testimony in Bronze and Stone.* Salt Lake City: Publishers Press, 1994.

RICHARD G. OMAN

WIRTHLIN, JOSEPH B. Apostle, missionary, and businessman, Joseph Bitner Wirthlin was born 11 June 1917 in Salt Lake City to Joseph Leopold and Madeline Bitner Wirthlin. His father, Joseph L. Wirthlin, served as the presiding bishop from 1952 to 1961.

Elder Wirthlin served in the German-Austrian/Swiss-Austrian Mission before the outbreak of World War II. In 1941 he graduated from the University of Utah in business administration. He married Elisa Young Rogers 26 May 1941 in the Salt Lake Temple, and they became the parents of eight children. Brother Wirthlin operated a family meat business. He was the president of the Utah Grocers Association and the Utah Meat Surveyors Association.

Brother Wirthlin served as a counselor in the Sunday School general presidency from 1971 to 1975. He was sustained as an assistant to the Twelve on 4 April 1975 and as a member of the First Quorum of the Seventy on 1 October 1976. He became a member of the presidency of the First Quorum of the Seventy on 28 August 1986. As a general

authority, Elder Wirthlin served as **area** supervisor for the European areas, executive administrator for the southeastern **United States** and the Caribbean Islands, executive administrator for **Brazil**, and president of the European area. Elder Wirthlin was sustained to the Quorum of the Twelve Apostles 4 October 1986 and **ordained** an apostle 9 October 1986 at age 69.

SOURCES

1999–2000 Church Almanac. Salt Lake City: Deseret Book, 1998. 21.

Searle, Don L. "Elder Joseph B. Wirthlin: Finding Happiness Serving the Lord." *Ensign* 16 (December 1986): 8–13.

MATTHEW O. RICHARDSON

WIRTHLIN, JOSEPH L. Joseph Leopold Wirthlin, who became a **presiding bishop** of the Church, was born 14 August 1893 in **Salt Lake City** to Joseph Wirthlin and Emma Hillstead. He grew up tending sheep and followed his father's profession in the livestock and meat business. He and his wife, Madeline Bitner, were the parents of five children, including a son, Joseph B., who was called to the **Quorum** of the Twelve **Apostles**. Joseph L. Wirthlin served as a **bishop** and then as president of the Bonneville **Stake**. In 1938 he was called as second **counselor** to **LeGrand Richards**, seventh presiding bishop of the Church. Eight years later he became first counselor, and in 1952 he was sustained as the presiding bishop of the Church. In that position, he especially loved his work as director of the ranching interests of the Church, and he took every occasion to visit those enterprises and enjoy the nostalgia of his boyhood days. As presiding bishop he also served on the Church Budget Committee, and in 1961, after his release, he became secretary-treasurer of Deseret Holding Corporation, which managed Church properties. Bishop Wirthlin died in Salt Lake City 25 January 1963.

SOURCES

Flake, Lawrence R. *Prophets and Apostles of the Last Dispensation.* Provo, Utah: Religious Studies Center, Brigham Young University, 2001. 543–46.

Grant, Carter E. "Joseph L. Wirthlin: Retiring Presiding Bishop." *Improvement Era* 64 (December 1961): 908.

Hinckley, Bryant S. "Joseph L. Wirthlin: Eighth Presiding Bishop of the Church." *Improvement Era* 56 (March 1953): 146–49, 170–75.

LAWRENCE R. FLAKE

WISCONSIN. Church members contributed to the development of nineteenth-century Wisconsin, and the territory, in turn, helped the Church by providing resources for building **Nauvoo**. Wisconsin later provided the venue for proliferation of **schismatic groups** following the **Prophet's martyrdom**.

Church members were in Wisconsin by 1835, where they organized a **branch** with more than 100 members by 1838; founded or participated in the development of communities at Burlington, Blanchardville (Zarahemla), Roaring Creek, Jenkynsville, La Crosse, and Black River Falls; and raised the first grain and built the first mills in several parts of the territory. During 1844, seven branches of the Church functioned in this area.

The Black River Falls Branch, administered by Elder **Lyman Wight** and **Bishop George Miller**, supplied lumber used to build the **Nauvoo Temple**, the **Nauvoo House**, and a number of homes. After the Prophet's death, Wisconsin members either joined the westward migration or organized alternative groups (Strangites, RLDS, and others). During 1847 and 1848, **Oliver Cowdery** practiced law in Elkhorn and was a Democratic candidate for the first state legislature. Defeated, he left Wisconsin to rejoin the Church. Wisconsin had no LDS congregations from 1844 to 1876. The first **stake** was organized in 1963, and by the year 2000, there were 19,282 members in 5 stakes with 57 **wards** and branches.

SOURCES

Clark, David L. "The Mormons of the Wisconsin Territory: 1835–1848," BYU Studies 37 (Spring 1998): 57–85.

———. "Moses Smith: Wisconsin's First Mormon." *Journal of Mormon History* 21 (1995): 155–70.

———. "Oliver Cowdery in Wisconsin: The Final Years." *Mormon Heritage Magazine* 2 (1995): 17–20.

DAVID L. CLARK

WITNESSES OF THE BOOK OF MORMON. Every copy of the **Book of Mormon** includes the Testimony of Three Witnesses, describing their experience of seeing an **angel** who displayed the original **gold plates** and hearing the voice of God both declare the translation correct and command the three to certify its truth. The book also includes the Testimony of Eight Witnesses, reporting their lifting the plates and examining the engravings under natural circumstances.

Oliver Cowdery, **Martin Harris**, and **David Whitmer** were the Three

Witnesses. They were generally accepted as honest, independent, and professionally capable. They respectively pursued the occupations of law, farming, and business and lived to 1850, 1875, and 1888. They never modified their written declaration. Because of intense curiosity about their experience, more than 200 reports of interviews with them are found in letters, **journals**, or newspaper articles. They freely answered questions about the supernatural event, and all three reiterated their joint testimony just before death.

The Three Witnesses made distinctive contributions to bring forth the Book of Mormon. They later served **missions** and held leadership positions in the Church. During the depression year of 1837, however, they quarreled with the **Prophet** on administrative and doctrinal matters, which resulted in their excommunication. Oliver Cowdery and Martin Harris returned to the Church; David Whitmer did not. Yet not one of them deviated from his testimony that he had seen the plates and the angel.

Similarly, most of the Eight Witnesses contributed to the translation and printing of the Book of Mormon and gave much time to Church service. They were: **Christian Whitmer, Jacob Whitmer, Peter Whitmer Jr., John Whitmer, Hiram Page, Joseph Smith Sr., Hyrum Smith**, and **Samuel H. Smith**. Three of this group (Jacob Whitmer, John Whitmer, and Hiram Page) left the Church in 1838, but all eight continued to assert that they had handled the ancient metallic record.

Both sets of witnesses drew up their statements "with words of soberness." The **apostles** of Christ told of double verification of the resurrection: "And we are his witnesses of these things; and so is also the Holy Ghost, whom God hath given to them that obey him" (Acts 5:32). The Book of Mormon repeats this promise—its truth is made known through earthly witnesses and the witness of the Holy Ghost, all of which "shall stand against the world at the last day" (Ether 5:4; 2 Ne. 27:14).

SOURCES

Anderson, Richard Lloyd. *Investigating the Book of Mormon Witnesses.* Salt Lake City: Deseret Book, 1981.

———. "Personal Writings of the Book of Mormon Witnesses." *Book of Mormon Authorship Revisited.* Edited by Noel B. Reynolds. Provo, Utah: Foundation for Ancient Research and Mormon Studies, 1997. 39–60.

Cook, Lyndon W. *David Whitmer Interviews.* Orem, Utah: Grandin Book, 1991.

RICHARD LLOYD ANDERSON

WOMAN'S EXPONENT. From June 1872 to February 1914, the *Woman's Exponent*, an independent, 8-page, semi-monthly newspaper, was the public voice of Latter-day Saint women. Founded and named by Edward L. Sloan, editor of the Salt Lake *Herald*, it joined the growing number of women's publications that reached a broad readership through their exchange programs. Edited first by Louisa Greene Richards (1872–77) and then by **Emmeline B. Wells** (1877–1914), it offered its readers articles, poems, stories, letters, reports of women's organizations and activities, and editorials on "every subject as it arises in which the women of **Utah** . . . are specially interested" (*Exponent* 1, 4). But its primary objective was to refute and correct **anti-Mormon** misrepresentations, particularly about Latter-day Saint women. Its advocacy of **woman suffrage** (Utah women were given the vote in 1870) connected it with national women's leaders and helped to weaken the wall of misunderstanding that had isolated Latter-day Saint women from their eastern counterparts.

Though not an official publication of the Church, the *Exponent* reported the activities of Latter-day Saint women's organizations and supported home industries. With the surrender of the practice of plural marriage in 1890 and the enfranchisement of women at statehood, the *Exponent* focused even more on **Relief Society** and other Church activities, with a special emphasis on publishing life sketches of Latter-day Saint women.

Reflecting 42 years of LDS women's thoughts and experience during a volatile period for the Church, the *Woman's Exponent* is an important source of Latter-day Saint women's history. It is a valuable record of women's work and has fulfilled its editor's promise that it "will furnish good material for future historians" (*Exponent* 40, 4).

SOURCES

Bennion, Sherilyn Cox. "The *Woman's Exponent*: Forty-Two Years of Speaking for Women." *Utah Historical Quarterly* 44 (Summer 1976): 222–39.

Madsen, Carol Cornwall. "Remember the Women of Zion: A Study of the Editorial Content of the *Woman's Exponent*." Master's thesis, University of Utah, 1977.

Thomas, Shirley W. "*Woman's Exponent*." *Encyclopedia of Mormonism*. Edited by Daniel H. Ludlow. 4 vols. New York: Macmillan, 1992. 4:1571–72.

Woman's Exponent 1 (1 June 1871): 4.

Woman's Exponent 40 (July 1911): 4.

CAROL CORNWALL MADSEN

WOMAN SUFFRAGE. The question of suffrage for **women** appeared early in **Utah's** history. Under the provisional government of **Deseret**, women were permitted to vote, but after the **United States** organized the **territory of Utah**, the privilege was withdrawn. Utah women were eager for the privilege to be restored.

In January 1870, when a proposed congressional bill threatened the practice of **polygamy**, a group of women from the Fifteenth **Ward** of **Salt Lake City** met and resolved to hold a rally to show their support for plural marriage and at the same time demand voting rights from the territorial governor. **Brigham Young**, meanwhile, called together leading members of the Utah legislature and advised them to grant suffrage to women. A bill to that effect was introduced by **George Q. Cannon** on 9 February 1870, and passed unanimously. The acting territorial governor, S. A. Mann, signed the measure on 12 February, and nine days later, on 21 February, Utah women were permitted to vote in a municipal election. They were the first in the **United States** to have the privilege; the **Wyoming** legislature had previously approved the right for women to vote, but Utah women voted in two elections before Wyoming women had that opportunity.

There were further setbacks. The **Edmunds Act of 1882** abolished voting for polygamists, and the **Edmunds-Tucker Act of 1887** canceled voting privileges for all Utah women. The Woman Suffrage Association of Utah was soon formed and began to lobby for a return of this right. The 1890 **Manifesto** by **Wilford Woodruff** abolishing plural marriage paved the way for a full suffrage provision in the Utah constitution when **statehood** was approved in 1895.

Utah women prominent in the fight for suffrage included **Emmeline B. Wells**, **Sarah M. Kimball**, and Emily S. Richards.

SOURCES

Carter, Kate B., "Woman Suffrage—1870." *Our Pioneer Heritage.* Salt Lake City: Daughters of Utah Pioneers, 1971. 14:8ff.

Madsen, Carol Cornwall, "Emmeline B. Wells: 'Am I Not a Woman and a Sister?'" *BYU Studies* 22 (1982): 161ff.

———. "Woman Suffrage." *Encyclopedia of Mormonism.* Edited by Daniel H. Ludlow. 4 vols. New York: Macmillan, 1992. 4:1572–73.

———, ed., *Battle for the Ballot: Essays on Woman Suffrage in Utah, 1870–1896.* Logan, Utah: Utah State University, 1997.

DAVID KENISON

WOMEN, ROLE OF. Elder **John A. Widtsoe** observed that "the place of woman in the Church is to walk beside the man, not in front of him nor behind him. In the Church there is full equality between man and woman" (Widtsoe, 305). Much of the world does not understand such a divine plan. Throughout history, women have struggled to prove their equality with men. Traditionally, societies placed women in an inferior position, granting them fewer rights and a lower social status.

Women's lives have centered on their homes, and they have depended on their husbands for the necessities of life. Because Latter-day Saints emphasize the importance of the mother being in the home, some have assumed that Latter-day Saint women are subservient to their husbands. Early Church members were more concerned with survival than role distinction. The woman worked alongside the man, sharing the hardships and sorrows, the spiritual insights and growth, and the blessings of community and **family**. They worked together to govern that which God had entrusted to their care. As homes and lives were given for the sake of the gospel, the women's faith and spiritual strength helped sustain the Church in those tenuous first years. Spiritual gifts such as blessing the sick were practiced by both men and women in the developing Church.

As early as March 1842, when **Joseph Smith** organized the **Relief Society**, women were given the opportunity to explore possibilities, to lead, and to serve. Joseph Smith declared that "the Church was never perfectly organized until the women were thus organized" (Kimball, "Autobiography," 51). The experience they gained in their own organization gave the women confidence to lead out in other areas. The Relief Society is still influencing women's lives as the largest women's organization in the world.

Brigham Young encouraged women of the Church to broaden their abilities. As early as 1869, he stated: "We have sisters here who, if they had the privilege of studying, would make just as good mathematicians or accountants as any man; and we think they ought to have the privilege to study these branches of knowledge that they may develop the powers with which they are endowed. We believe that women are useful, not only to sweep houses, wash dishes, make beds, and raise babies, but that they should stand behind the counter, study law or physic [medicine], or become good book-keepers and be able to do the business in any counting house, and all this to enlarge their sphere of usefulness for the benefit of society at large. In following these things they but answer the design of their creation" (Young, 61). Nevertheless, he cautioned his daughter, **Susa Young Gates**: "Use all your gifts to build up righteousness in the earth. Never use them to acquire name or fame. Never rob your home, nor your children. If you were to become the greatest woman in this world, and your name should be known in every land and clime, and you would fail in your duty as wife and mother, you would wake up on the morning of the first resurrection and find you had failed in everything; but anything you can do after you have satisfied the claims of husband and family will redound to your own honor and to the glory of God" (Gates, 307–8).

Many who followed that counsel provide significant role models for today's women. For example, **Eliza R. Snow** pursued her literary talents and blessed the Church with her organizational skills. At the age of 17, Emma Lucy Gates traveled to **Europe** to study **music** and eventually returned to **Utah** to establish her own opera company. **Ellis Reynolds Shipp** aptly managed a career as a mother and medical doctor. **Martha Hughes Cannon** added political service to her medical profession, becoming the first woman state senator in the **United States**.

During the second half of the nineteenth century, the practice of **plural marriage** attracted rampant criticism and persecution. When the practice was first introduced in the 1840s, many women were indignant, but as they came to understand the principle, they caught the vision and willingly became polygamous wives. In January 1870, women filled the **Salt Lake Tabernacle** to oppose **antipolygamy** legislation. The movement quickly spread to all the Latter-day Saint settlements.

This excitement carried over to the matter of women's right to vote. The Utah Legislative Assembly passed a bill to enfranchise women (without the right to hold office) on February 12, 1870. Only one other territory, **Wyoming**, granted women the right to vote before Utah. In 1882, the U.S. Congress passed the **Edmunds Act**, which withdrew polygamists' right to vote, and in 1887 the **Edmunds-Tucker Act** repealed **woman suffrage** in Utah. The role of women further changed when President **Wilford Woodruff** announced the 1890 **Manifesto**, stopping the practice of plural marriage. **Statehood** was now a possibility. When Utah became a state in 1896, full voting rights were returned to women. Utah women were involved not only in the woman suffrage movement but in other issues important to them and their families.

With more and more women being lured from their primary responsibilities of wife, mother, and homemaker, the **First Presidency** issued the **Proclamation on the Family**, declaring that "gender is an essential characteristic of individual premortal, mortal, and eternal identity and purpose," and reemphasizing the prime place of women in the home.

Women who are well-grounded in the gospel will understand the importance of what President **Gordon B. Hinckley** told the women of the Church regarding their eternal role: "You, my beloved associates, are where you are in the balance of the sexes because God your Eternal Father, who loves you, put you there" (Hinckley, 90).

In 1999 the general leaders of the Relief Society issued a special declaration proclaiming: "We are beloved spirit daughters of God, and our lives have meaning, purpose, and direction. . . . [we] dedicate ourselves to strengthening marriages, families, and homes, . . . find nobility in motherhood and joy in womanhood," and we "sustain the priesthood as the authority of God on earth" (Relief Society Declaration). Concerning women's ultimate destiny, **James E. Talmage** stated: "Woman shall yet come to her own, exercising her rights and her privileges as a sanctified investiture which none shall dare profane. Then shall woman reign by Divine right, a queen in the resplendent realm of her glorified state, even as exalted man shall stand, priest and king unto the Most High God. Mortal eye cannot see nor mind comprehend the beauty, glory, and majesty of a righteous woman made perfect in the celestial **kingdom of God**" (Talmage, 602–3).

Sources

Beck, Martha Nibley. "Women, Roles of." *Encyclopedia of Mormonism*. Edited by Daniel H. Ludlow. 4 vols. New York: Macmillan, 1992. 4:1574–75.

Burgess-Olson, Vicky, ed. *Sister Saints*. Provo, Utah: Brigham Young University Press, 1978.

"The Family: A Proclamation to the World." *Ensign* 25 (November 1995): 102.

Gates, Susa Young, and Leah D. Widtsoe. *The Life Story of Brigham Young*. New York: Macmillan, 1931. 307–8.

Hanks, Marion D. "Magic Aplenty." *Woman*. Salt Lake City: Deseret Book, 1980. 99–122.

Hinckley, Gordon B. "If Thou Art Faithful." *Ensign* 14 (November 1984): 89–92.

Journal of Discourses. 26 vols. London: Latter-day Saints' Book Depot, 1854–86. 13:56–62.

Kimball, Camilla. "A Woman's Preparation." *Ensign* 7 (March 1977): 58–59.

Kimball, Sarah M. "Auto-Biography." *Woman's Exponent* 12 (1 September 1883): 51.

Smith, Barbara B. "New Lamps for Old." *Ensign* 6 (April 1976): 67–69.

Talmage, James E. "The Eternity of Sex." *Young Woman's Journal* 25 (1914): 600–4.

Widtsoe, John A. "What Is the Place of Woman in the Church?" *Evidences and Reconciliations*. Salt Lake City: Bookcraft, 1960. 305–9.

Veneese C. Nelson

WOOD, WILFORD C.

Perhaps best known for his purchase of several Church history sites and artifacts, Wilford C. Wood owned such items as the original uncut sheets of the 1830 edition of the **Book of Mormon**; the **John Taylor** home and original **temple** site in **Nauvoo, Illinois**; the jail in Liberty, **Missouri**; and the **Newel K. Whitney Store** in Kirtland, Ohio. Born 22 May 1893 in South Bountiful, **Utah**, Wood began purchasing important Church history sites after returning from his mission to the Northern States in 1918. At this time there was little interest in preserving such areas, but Wood's admiration for the **Prophet Joseph Smith** and his appreciation for the Church's early history led him to purchase many of these sites with his own funds (Dockstader, 4). Over several years he secured property at **Adam-ondi-Ahman** and along the **Susquehannah River**, as well as many acres of the original **Martin Harris Farm**. Wood later sold most of these sites to the Church and set up the Wilford C. Wood Museum in Bountiful, Utah, to allow the **Saints** to view the items he collected.

In addition to his purchase of historical lands and items, between 1934 and 1947 Wood preserved several significant Church events on film, which his family donated to the Church after his death. Wood also owned an original edition of the **Book of Commandments** and a first edition of the **Doctrine and Covenants**, containing the *Lectures on Faith*. He reprinted these books, along with an 1830 edition of the Book of Mormon and several historical photographs, in an attempt to "place the reader . . . in the shoes of the men who founded the Mormon faith" (Wood, foreword). Wood served for several years on the board of Utah Trails and Landmarks Association and on the Church's historical committee. He died 17 January 1968 in **Salt Lake City** at age 74.

SOURCES

Allen, James B., and Glen M. Leonard. *The Story of the Latter-day Saints*. 2d ed. Salt Lake City: Deseret Book, 1992. 531.

"Church Receives Historical Films." *Church News*, 7 January 1978. 14.

Dockstader, Julie A. "Foresight Preserves Historical Legacy." *Church News*, 1 June 1991. 4.

Wood, Wilford C. *Joseph Smith Begins His Work*. Vol. 2. Salt Lake City: Wilford C. Wood, 1962.

LISA KURKI

WOODRUFF, ABRAHAM O. Abraham Owen Woodruff was born 23 November 1872 in **Salt Lake City**. The son of President **Wilford Woodruff**, he departed for the Swiss-German **Mission** in 1893 at the age of 20. He was called to the **Quorum** of the Twelve **Apostles** on 7 October

1897 at age 24. As an apostle he was the chief colonizer and spiritual leader of the Latter-day Saints who settled in the Big Horn Basin of **Wyoming**. Accompanied by his wife and four children, **Elder** Woodruff traveled to **Mexico** in 1904 to visit the Latter-day Saint settlements there. His wife contracted smallpox and died. Two weeks later, 20 June 1904, Elder Woodruff died at age 31, having been stricken with the disease while caring for her.

SOURCES

Flake, Lawrence R. *Prophets and Apostles of the Last Dispensation.* Provo, Utah: Religious Studies Center, Brigham Young University, 2001. 423–25.

"In Memoriam." *Improvement Era* 7 (August 1904): 743–46.

LAWRENCE R. FLAKE

WOODRUFF, WILFORD. Wilford Woodruff was born in Farmington (now Avon), **Connecticut**, 1 March 1807 to Aphek and Beulah Thompson Woodruff. He lived to serve as president of The Church of Jesus Christ of Latter-day Saints (1889–98) and to move the Church on to a new path which would lead to statehood for **Utah** and greater recognition for the Latter-day Saint people.

Wilford received his early education in local schools and at the Farmington Academy. Although he grew up in a family of community leaders who were pillars of the Congregational Church, he, his father, his uncle Ozem, and others of his family left that church after Connecticut disestablished Congregationalism in 1818.

Concerned about religion and salvation, Wilford began searching for primitive Christianity. In Connecticut, he joined with a group of like-minded seekers in studying the gospel and adopting biblical beliefs and practices. After moving to Richland, **New York**, to farm with his brother Azmon, he heard preaching by Latter-day Saint missionaries Zera Pulsipher and Elijah Cheney. He was converted by their message and accepted **baptism** on 31 December 1833. Responding to a call to join **Zion's Camp**, he participated with **Joseph Smith** and others in the 1834 expedition to recover the Saints' property in **Jackson County, Missouri**.

After working as a laborer in Missouri for a time, Wilford accepted a call to begin a series of **missions** that marked him as one of the most successful missionaries in the nineteenth-century Church. He served a proselyting mission to **Arkansas, Tennessee**, and **Kentucky** from 1835 to 1836. He returned to **Kirtland** in 1836, where he enjoyed spiritual experiences in the newly dedicated temple and married Phoebe Whittemore Carter (1807–85) in 1837. He also received calls to the Second (1836) and then the First **Quorum of the Seventy** (1837). In 1838 he served a mission in Southeastern **Canada** and **New England**. He labored principally in **Maine**, and especially in the **Fox Islands**. Though he served primarily with **Jonathan Hale** and Milton Holmes, he also proselyted with his wife, Phoebe. In Illinois when the Saints fled from the mob violence in northern Missouri, he farmed there and worked with other Church leaders as Latter-day Saint refugees flooded **Mississippi River** towns in western **Illinois**.

After his call to the **Quorum of the Twelve** in 1838, Elder Woodruff learned that Joseph Smith had received a revelation assigning the Twelve to take up a mission to **Great Britain**. Elder Woodruff returned to Far West, Missouri, with Brigham Young and other members of the Twelve, where he and George A. Smith were ordained apostles. In fulfillment of revelation (D&C 118), the Twelve left on their mission 26 April 1839 from the temple site at Far West, Missouri. On this mission to the United Kingdom (1839–41), Elder Woodruff baptized hundreds of people in Staffordshire, Herefordshire, and Gloucestershire, including several congregations of United Brethren, an offshoot of the Methodists.

Joseph Smith increasingly relied on the Twelve to assist in leading the Church. Elder Woodruff returned to Nauvoo from England and constructed a house. He also served as business manager for the *Times and Seasons*, which later became a Church newspaper. While campaigning for Joseph Smith's candidacy for the presidency of the United States and proselyting for the Church in New England, Elder Woodruff and others in the Twelve learned of the murder of the Prophet and his brother Hyrum. They returned to Nauvoo, where the members of the Church assembled on 8 August 1844 and gave the Twelve the sustaining vote to lead the Church.

The Twelve called Elder Woodruff to assume the presidency of the mission in Great Britain, and he left in the fall of 1844 for Liverpool. In Britain, he directed the Church's proselyting efforts as he worked to promote harmony in the face of contrary efforts by some Church members and by followers of **Sidney Rigdon**.

By November 1845, Elder Woodruff had learned of the mob violence in Hancock County, Illinois, and realized he would have to return to assist the other leaders in moving west. He reached Nauvoo on 13 April 1846 to find that the **Saints** had begun to depart. He sold his house and purchased equipment to move himself and his family. On 30 April and

1 May 1846, Wilford Woodruff assisted **Orson Hyde** in dedicating the **Nauvoo Temple**. Elder Woodruff began his journey from Nauvoo across **Iowa** and eventually to **Winter Quarters** on the Missouri.

Following teachings by Joseph Smith, Elder Woodruff entered **plural marriage**. He married Mary Ann Jackson (1846), Mary Carolyn Barton (1846), Mary Giles Meeks Webster (1852), Emma Smith, niece of Abraham O. Smoot (1853), Sarah Brown (1853), Sarah Delight Stocking (1857), and Eudora Lovina Young (1877).

As a religious leader, farmer, horticulturist, rancher, educator, leader of voluntary organizations, and politician, Elder Woodruff helped to build communities in the West and to govern the LDS Church. He served as founding president of the Universal Scientific Society, a voluntary study group that met in **Salt Lake City** in 1854 and 1855. He also served as an officer in the Deseret Theological Institute and the Deseret Typographical Society, and he belonged to the **Polysophical Society**. He served as president of the Deseret Horticultural Society and of the Apiary Society. He conducted surveys of primary schools in **Utah** towns and served as a member of the territorial legislature and the board of regents of the University of Deseret. As Church historian, he collected documents and established archives for Latter-day Saint records.

Elder Woodruff was a founding director of the Deseret Agricultural and Manufacturing Society (1856–61), and he served as president from 1862 until 1877. In this capacity he corresponded with authorities and scientists outside Utah, helped to import large quantities of plants and animals, and supervised and conducted experiments in various types of agriculture.

Deeply spiritual, he received numerous revelations which provided guidance in marriage relationships, personal salvation, and sacred ordinances. He played the role of facilitator and moderator, particularly in the **reformation** of 1856 to 1857. President Brigham Young called Elder Woodruff to preside over the St. George Temple and direct the ordinances there. In this assignment Woodruff redirected temple work by authorizing vicarious work, including the endowment, for deceased men and women. Most notably, he and Lucy Bigelow Young directed vicarious work for a large group of deceased political, literary, and scientific leaders.

During the 1880s and 1890s, he played a central role in the leadership of the Church. He became president of the Quorum of the Twelve in 1880, and in that capacity led the Church following the 1887 death of John Taylor. He was sustained as president of the Church on 7 April 1889 and served until his death on 2 September 1898. This service coincided with a time of crisis for the Church. Harried by the federal campaign to imprison Church leaders who had married polygamously, President Woodruff and other Church leaders hid out from U.S. marshals during part of the 1880s. While on the **underground**, President Woodruff lived in northern **Arizona** and southern Utah, especially in the **St. George** area. During this time, the enforcement of the **Edmunds Act** of 1882 and **Edmunds-Tucker Act** of 1887 led to the confiscation of much of the Church's secular property and the imprisonment of more than 1,000 Latter-day Saint men and a smaller number of women for practicing plural marriage.

President Woodruff and other Church officials worked to secure recognition from the national political parties and relieve the burden from the Church, negotiating with the national **Democratic Party** and **Republican Party**. After it became apparent that the federal government would begin to confiscate even the Church's religious properties, including its **temples**, President Woodruff made the Church's problems a matter of prayer and consultation. He consulted with political and business leaders, and he received a revelation directing the abandonment of plural marriage. He presented the revelation to his counselors and the Twelve on 24 and 25 September 1890, and the Saints sustained the **Manifesto** in **conference** on 6 October.

Throughout his presidency he worked for accommodation with the remainder of American society, developing productive relationships with national business and political leaders. He authorized the dissolution of the Latter-day Saint **People's Party** in 1891 and urged Church members to join the two national political parties. He presided over the completion of the **Salt Lake Temple**, which he dedicated in 1893. He clarified the law of adoption, urging members to seal themselves to their ancestors rather than to prominent Church leaders. He also received and announced a revelation concerning the performance of vicarious temple work for unrelated people, and he organized the **Genealogical Society of Utah**.

President Woodruff died 2 September 1898 in **San Francisco, California**, while visiting a non-Mormon friend, **Isaac Trumbo**.

Sources

Alexander, Thomas G. *Things in Heaven and Earth: The Life and Times of Wilford Woodruff, a Mormon Prophet.* Salt Lake City: Signature Books, 1991.

Cowley, Matthias F. *Wilford Woodruff: History of His Life and Labors.* Salt Lake City: Bookcraft, 1964.

Gibbons, Francis M. *Wilford Woodruff: Wondrous Worker, Prophet of God.* Salt Lake City: Deseret Book, 1988.

Woodruff, Wilford. *Wilford Woodruff's Journal, 1833–1898.* Typescript. 9 vols. Edited by Scott G. Kenney. Midvale, Utah: Signature Books, 1983.

THOMAS G. ALEXANDER

WOOL INDUSTRY. See TEXTILES.

WORD OF WISDOM. Section 89 of the **Doctrine and Covenants,** commonly called the Word of Wisdom, is a **revelation** that gives counsel pertaining to proper and improper, or healthy and unhealthy, diet and drink. The revelation was given to **Joseph Smith** in **Kirtland, Ohio,** on 27 February 1833. The historical record indicates that the use of tobacco by some members of the **School of the Prophets** led Joseph to inquire of the Lord about the propriety of it.

The revelation contains proscriptions, prescriptions, and promises. The proscriptions prohibit wine, strong drink, tobacco, and hot drinks, which were defined early as tea and coffee. The prescriptions enjoin the frequent use of herbs (including vegetables), fruits, and grains and the limited use of meat. The promises indicate that **Saints** who obey the precepts in the revelation will receive health, strength, wisdom, and "great treasures of knowledge," and escape the destroying angel "who shall pass by them, as the children of **Israel,** and not slay them" (D&C 89:21).

For the most part, Church leaders have chosen to emphasize the proscriptive portion of the revelation. Such an emphasis may reflect, in part, the unfortunate social and moral consequences that often accompany excessive drinking and smoking. This is the only portion of the revelation that has become a criteria for fellowship or worthiness. When modern Church members report to ecclesiastical authorities that they observe the Word of Wisdom, they are, in almost all cases, reporting that they abstain from using alcohol, tobacco, tea, and coffee.

The Word of Wisdom was given as inspired counsel rather than as a commandment (D&C 89:2). President **Joseph F. Smith** indicated one reason the Lord did not initially give it as a commandment was that it would have brought a good many Church members, who were addicted to some of the prohibited items, under condemnation.

In general, observance of the Word of Wisdom throughout the nineteenth century implied moderation rather than complete abstinence. Beginning with the administrations of Joseph F. Smith and **Heber J. Grant** in the twentieth century, compliance came to be understood as total abstinence from alcohol, tobacco, tea, and coffee. From his ordination to the apostleship in the early 1880s until his death in 1945, President Grant spoke often and vigorously about the need for complete compliance. It was during President Grant's administration that the Word of Wisdom became perhaps the best-known social practice of the Latter-day Saints.

In later years health benefits attributable to obedience to the Word of Wisdom have become more apparent. In the 1950s medical experts first postulated a correlation between lung cancer and smoking. Since that time, other diseases have been linked with tobacco use. Additional studies have found that Latter-day Saints, in addition to having a substantially lower risk for various diseases, also have an increased life expectancy. Some would say these desirable results are likely due not only to the avoidance of tobacco and liquor but also to the tendency of some Church members to adhere to the prescriptive portions of the revelation.

SOURCES

Alexander, Thomas G. *Mormonism in Transition*. Urbana: University of Illinois Press, 1986. 258–71.

Lyon, Joseph Lynn. "Word of Wisdom." *Encyclopedia of Mormonism*. Edited by Daniel H. Ludlow. 4 vols. New York: Macmillan, 1992. 4:1584–85.

Peterson, Paul H. "An Historical Analysis of the Word of Wisdom." Master's thesis, Brigham Young University, 1972.

PAUL H. PETERSON

WORLD'S FAIRS. The concept of international expositions or world's fairs was first developed in **England** in the mid-nineteenth century. Prince Albert's vision of bringing together the world's best exhibits of human industry, **art**, and natural resources was realized at the Great Exhibition of London in 1851. Although the Church did not have formal representation at the fair, missionaries there contacted people and answered questions.

The Church was also indirectly involved in later fairs. At some late nineteenth-century international expositions, exhibits representing **Utah** introduced fair visitors to Mormonism. The Church was formally invited by the Smithsonian Institute to contribute an exhibit at the Alaska-Yukon-Pacific Exposition held in Seattle in 1909. The exhibit focused on the influence of the Latter-day Saints in building up the West, but no **missionary work** was done because this was part of a larger governmental exhibit.

The Church's first truly independent and mission-oriented exhibit was at the "Century of Progress" Exposition held in Chicago during 1933–34. Nearly two and one-half million people visited the Church's attractive exhibit in the Hall of Religions. Performances by the **Mormon Tabernacle Choir** and lectures by prominent Church leaders, including **Elders John A. Widtsoe** and **James E. Talmage**, brought much favorable publicity.

Because of the success in Chicago, the Church expanded its participation in world's fairs from a small display area to its own separate building or pavilion. This was done for the first time at the **California**-Pacific International Exposition in **San Diego** in 1935–36. The Church sponsored an extensive exhibit in a pavilion shaped like the **Salt Lake Tabernacle** at the 1939–40 Golden Gate International Exposition on Treasure Island in **San Francisco** Bay. The missionaries' organ recitals and presentations on Mormonism made a favorable impression on more than a million visitors.

At the 1964–65 World's Fair in **New York City**, the Church's pavilion housed the largest and most sophisticated exhibit yet. Nearly six million people from every state and many countries around the world visited this pavilion, most seeing the new film *Man's Search for Happiness*. Not only did this pavilion have a major effect on missionary work but it also shaped future exhibits and Church **public communications** efforts. Many of the materials developed for New York were subsequently used at Church exhibits at world's fairs in Montreal and Toronto, **Canada**; San Antonio, **Texas**; Osaka, **Japan**; and Spokane, **Washington**, eventually becoming part of a permanent **visitors' center** on **Temple Square**. Participation in these fairs and expositions made friends for the Church, introduced people to its message, dispelled misconceptions, and developed technologies that could be used in proclaiming the gospel to the world.

SOURCES

Peterson, Gerald Joseph. "History of Mormon Exhibits in World Expositions." Master's thesis, Brigham Young University, 1974.

Top, Brent L. "The Miracle of the Mormon Pavilion: The Church at the 1964–65 New York World's Fair." In *New York*. Edited by Larry C. Porter, Milton V. Backman Jr., and Susan Easton Black. Regional Studies in Latter-day Saint Church History series. Provo, Utah: Brigham Young University, 1992.

———. "Tabernacle on Treasure Island: The LDS Church's Involvement at the 1939–40 Golden Gate International Exposition." In *California*. Edited by David F. Boone, et al. Regional Studies in Latter-day Saint Church History series. Provo, Utah: Brigham Young University, 1998.

BRENT L. TOP

WORLD WAR I. World War I began in August 1914 when **Germany** and **Austria-Hungary** (the Central Powers) declared war on **Serbia**, **Russia**, and **France**. Great Britain quickly joined the latter, forming the nucleus of the Allied Powers. American president Woodrow Wilson immediately declared impartiality and the **United States** did not become involved in the conflict until three years later (Matloff, 358). LDS Church leaders encouraged Church members to support their own governments; however, missionaries were immediately evacuated from Europe. Units of the Church continued to function under local leaders, and Church membership in Germany actually increased during the war years, from approximately 7,500 to 8,000.

The United States officially entered the conflict by declaring war on Germany on 6 April 1917 while the Church's April **general conference** was in session. President **Joseph F. Smith** reminded those who might be entering military service that they should "go forth in the spirit of defending the liberties of mankind rather than for the purpose of destroying the enemy" (Smith, 3).

Church members generally adopted the attitude that the war was being fought for the noble purposes of preserving democracy, liberty, and peace. They supported the war effort in a number of ways. Enlistments far exceeded the quota assigned to Utah. Six of President Joseph F. Smith's sons donned the uniform of their country. Utahns contributed generously to the Red Cross and purchased $9.4 million worth of war bonds (their quota was $6.5 million). The Church itself purchased $850,000 worth of bonds. The **Relief Society** also helped with commodities for war-torn Europe. The American press praised these efforts, helping to dispel some **anti-Mormon** sentiment in the country.

World War I ended the eleventh hour of the eleventh day of the eleventh month, 1918. More than 8.5 million men in uniform from every nation that fought were killed, including 544 Utahns and 75 German Saints.

SOURCES

Allen, James B., and Glen M. Leonard. *The Story of the Latter-day Saints.* 2d ed. Salt Lake City: Deseret Book, 1992. 493–94.

Cowan, Richard O. *The Latter-day Saint Century.* Salt Lake City: Bookcraft, 1999. 60–62.

Matloff, Maurice, ed. *American Military History.* Washington, D.C.: Office of the Chief of Military History, United States Army, 1973. 358–404.

Smith, Joseph F. Conference Report (April 1917): 3.

ANDREW C. SKINNER

WORLD WAR II. World War II affected every indiviudal regardless of age, race, or religion. Latter-day Saints were not immune to the changes wrought by the world-wide conflict. Church programs were hindered, **missionary work** was disrupted, communication between Church head-quarters and local congregations was impeded, construction on Church buildings was slowed, and men from both sides of the conflict were pressed into military service. LDS soliders and civilians were faced with violence, tyranny, and moral dilemmas on a daily basis. These hardships prompted new efforts by Church leaders to minister to servicemen, strengthen local teaching and leadership, and supply humanitarian relief. The war also called forth an important 1942 statement of the Church's views on **war** and military service (Clark, 148–62).

A speedy and at times miraculous evacuation of foreign missionaries began in **Europe** on 24 August 1939 and continued as hostilities spread. In 1942 Church leaders agreed not to call draft-eligible American men on missions, significantly shrinking the number of missionaries serving, especially outside North **America**. The loss of full-time missionaries was redressed in part by local efforts.

In **Germany**, 14,000 Saints continued Church work under the extra-ordinary problems of Nazi rule, and some Saints, such as **Helmuth Hübener** and Heinrich Worbs, died because of their opposition to Hitler's regime. In North America, the war effort diverted time from Church pro-grams, restricted travel and attendance at **general conference**, delayed building construction (such as the **Idaho** Falls **Temple**), and closed the **Tabernacle** to some public events from 1942 until 1945.

Church leaders appointed **Hugh B. Brown** as servicemen's coordina-tor in 1940 and formed a military relations committee in 1942. These measures boosted the number of U.S. military chaplains and reached sol-diers through preservice training, Church **literature**, and contacts with local congregations, thereby helping LDS soldiers live and teach Church standards. American servicemen introduced the gospel into the **Philippines**, helped reopen the work in **Japan**, and assisted local Saints in Europe. Many LDS soldiers of other nationalities also taught the gospel, some as prisoners of war. The Servicemen's Committee reported that 5,714 soldiers were killed, wounded, or missing in action during hostilities (Cowan, 192).

At war's end, **apostles** were sent to direct temporal relief efforts, revive the morale of isolated congregations, and reorganize Church government and missionary work. **Ezra Taft Benson** headed the **European Mission** and **Matthew Cowley** supervised the **Pacific** Mission.

SOURCES

Boone, David F. "The Worldwide Evacuation of Latter-day Saint Missionaries at the Beginning of World War II." Master's thesis, Brigham Young University, 1981.

Clark, James R., comp. *Messages of the First Presidency of The Church of Jesus Christ of Latter-day Saints.* 6 vols. Salt Lake City: Bookcraft, 1965–75. 6:148–62.

Cowan, Richard O. *The Latter-day Saint Century.* Salt Lake City: Bookcraft, 1999.

JOHN THOMAS

WYOMING. By the time **Brigham Young's** wagon train crossed Wyoming's eastern border in late May 1847, two other groups of Latter-day Saints had already entered the territory. Early in 1846, six men stopped at **Fort Laramie** en route to the **Salt Lake Valley** to explore and make a map. In July of that year, a group of **Mississippi Saints** stopped near Fort Laramie before wintering in **Colorado** and then traveled with members of the **Mormon Battalion's** sick detachments to join Brigham Young's company the following spring.

Brigham Young's wagon train prepared the way for later companies by building ferries at the crossing of the **Platte River** near Casper and on the Green River and by leaving men to run them. By the end of 1847, more than 2,000 **Mormons** had crossed Wyoming into **Utah**. Although there were hardships, many emigrants later traversed Wyoming safely by wagon train and **handcarts**. In 1857, however, the Martin and Willie Handcart companies encountered severe snows on the Sweetwater River, and some 200 people perished before rescuers arrived from Utah.

The earliest Latter-day Saint settlement in Wyoming was established at **Fort Supply** (near **Fort Bridger**) in 1853. In 1855 the Church purchased Fort Bridger. These holdings were abandoned and burned before **Johnston's Army** encamped at Fort Bridger in 1858, preparing to fight the Latter-day Saints.

Subsequently, Church influence in Wyoming increased. In 1862, at the request of **Abraham Lincoln**, Brigham Young sent 120 men into Wyoming to guard transcontinental telegraph and mail routes until they were relieved by government troops. Between 1875 and the end of the century, colonies were established in Star Valley and the Big Horn Basin, irrigation canals were dug, and members of the Church moved into other areas. The first **stake** was organized in Star Valley on 14 August 1892.

The Church has continued to maintain strong visibility in Wyoming.

Before the sesquicentennial commemoration of the **Mormon Trail**, many pioneer sites were improved through activities sponsored by the Riverton Wyoming Stake. Church authorities dedicated some of these sites, and monuments were erected. Among Wyoming's contributions to the artistic heritage of the Church are the famous Cody Chapel Mural painted by Edward Grigware and the **Book of Mormon** paintings by **Minerva Teichert**. The **institute of religion** at the University of Wyoming in Laramie, dedicated by **Heber J. Grant** in 1936, was the third institute building erected by the Church. At the beginning of the year 2000, Wyoming had 54,425 members living in 16 stakes and 143 **wards** and **branches**.

SOURCES

Contant, Charles Griffin. *History of Wyoming and the Far West.* New York: Argonaut Press, 1966. 341–395.

Larson, Taft Alfred. *History of Wyoming.* 2d ed. Lincoln: University of Nebraska Press, 1978. 164, 224, 304.

1997–1998 Church Almanac. Salt Lake City: Deseret News, 1996. 278–80.

LOWELL A. BANGERTER

YOUNG, BRIGHAM. The second president of the Church as he appeared on 10 December 1850, just a few years after he had established Utah as the main gathering place for the Saints.

YEAR'S SUPPLY. In the April 1937 **general conference**, President J. Reuben Clark Jr. urged the **Saints** to live righteously, avoid debt, live within their incomes, and "let every head of every household see to it that he has on hand enough food and clothing, and, where possible, fuel also, for at least a year ahead" (Clark, 26).

Since **President Clark** made that statement, "Church leaders have never given an exact formula for what members should store but have suggested that they store that which would keep a person alive in case there was nothing else to eat" (*Providing*, 7). These necessities might include "water, wheat or other grains (corn, rice), legumes, salt, honey or sugar, powdered milk, and cooking oil" (*Providing*, 7).

SOURCES

Clark, J. Reuben, Jr. Conference Report (April 1937): 26.

Providing in the Lord's Way: A Leader's Guide to Welfare. Salt Lake City: The Church of Jesus Christ of Latter-day Saints, 1990. 7.

GLEN L. RUDD

YEMEN. See **MIDDLE EAST** and **MUSLIMS.**

YERBA BUENA, CALIFORNIA. See **SAN FRANCISCO, CALIFORNIA.**

YLMIA. See **YOUNG WOMEN.**

YMMIA. See **YOUNG MEN.**

YOUNG, ANN ELIZA. The most widely publicized case of a plural wife suing for divorce took place in 1875 when Ann Eliza Webb Young petitioned the court for a divorce from **Brigham Young** on the grounds of neglect, cruel treatment, and desertion. Justice James B. McKean fined Brigham Young $3,000 in court fees and ordered him to pay Ann Eliza $500 a month maintenance. On the advice of his lawyers, President Young refused to pay the money to Ann Eliza pending appeal. The vindictive judge fined the **prophet** $25 and sentenced him to a day in prison. The litigation continued for more than two years and was heard by five different judges. During this time Brigham Young's alimony debt increased to $18,000. Finally, in the spirit of compromise, Judge Michael Schaefer reduced the debt to $3,600. President Young paid the amount, and the case was dismissed in April 1877.

Ann Eliza Webb was born in **Nauvoo, Illinois**, on 13 September 1844 to Chauncey G. and Eliza Churchill Webb. At age 24 she married Brigham Young (age 68) in the **Endowment House** on 7 April 1869. After the divorce hearings, she toured **America** lecturing against Mormonism.

SOURCES

Allen, James B., and Glen M. Leonard. *The Story of the Latter-day Saints.* 2d ed. Salt Lake City: Deseret Book. 1992.

Young, Ann Eliza Webb. *Wife No. 19; or, The Story of a Life in Bondage, Being a Complete Exposé of Mormonism, and Revealing the Sorrows, Sacrifices and Sufferings of Women in Polygamy.* Hartford: Dustin, Gilman & Co., 1875.

MARY JANE WOODGER

YOUNG, BRIGHAM. Prophet, second president of The Church of Jesus Christ of Latter-day Saints, **pioneer**, colonizer, and organizer, Brigham Young was the ninth of eleven children born to Revolutionary War veteran John Young and his wife, Abigail (Nabby) Howe. His birth on 1 June 1801 in Whitingham, Vermont, came after the family had left **Massachusetts** seeking to improve its fortune. John and Nabby brought the teachings of the Methodist Episcopal faith into their home.

The family was again uprooted in 1804, relocating in Sherburne, Chenango County, **New York**. Following a succession of moves, they settled on a homestead in the vicinity of Genoa or in the town of Aurelius, Cayuga County, New York, in 1813. Here Nabby succumbed to consumption (tuberculosis), and she died on 11 June 1815. Brigham Young later reminisced, "Of my mother—she that bore me—I can say, no better woman ever lived in the world than she was. . . . My mother, while she lived, taught her children all the time to honour the name of the Father and the Son, and to reverence the holy Book" (*JD,* 6:290). John then took the family to the area of Tyrone and the "Sugar Hill" district of Steuben (now Schuyler) County, New York.

The merger of John's family with the widow Hannah Dennis Brown's through their marriage in 1817 signaled the need for sixteen-year-old Brigham to make his own way. He recalled that his father said to him, "You can now have your time; go and provide for yourself" (*JD,* 10:360). Through his apprenticeship to John C. Jeffries of Auburn, New York, Brigham learned the trades of carpenter, joiner, painter, and glazier. While he was employed manufacturing furniture, buckets, and pails south of Bucksville (later Port Byron), Brigham courted Miriam Angeline Works from the town of Aurelius, Cayuga County. They were married on 5 October 1824. The couple lived first at Haydenville and then at Port Byron, where their first child, Elizabeth, was born 26 September 1825.

After a brief sojourn at Oswego, Oswego County in 1828, Brigham moved that same year to **Mendon**, Monroe County, New York. His residence was on the farm of his father, John Young, who had relocated from Tyrone. Brigham established his woodworking trade there complete with a combination house and a shop with a water-powered turning lathe (Fisher, 434–47).

In Mendon, Brigham was introduced to the Church by family members. In April 1830 his brother **Phinehas H. Young**, a Reformed Methodist preacher, stopped at Tomlinson's Inn on his way home to nearby Victor. He was approached by **Samuel H. Smith**, the brother of **Joseph Smith Jr.**, who was performing missionary service in the area. Handing Phinehas a copy of the **Book of Mormon** he stated, "There is a book, sir, I wish you to read," and then stipulated, "If you will read this book with a prayerful heart, and ask God to give you a witness, you will know of the truth of this work" ("Manuscript History," vol. 1, "Addenda," 2–3). That book and another placed by Samuel during June 1830 in the home of **John P. Greene** and Rhoda Young Greene began to make the rounds in the family.

With the aid of Latter-day Saint missionaries from Bradford and Tioga counties in **Pennsylvania**, most of the John Young family was baptized there or in the Mendon area. Brigham Young was baptized on 15 April 1832 at Mendon nearly two years after the family's first contact with the Church by Eleazer Miller from the Columbia Branch in Bradford County, Pennsylvania (*JD,* 9:219). Commenting on his conversion, Brigham Young affirmed, "When I saw a man without eloquence, or talents for public speaking, who could only say, 'I know, by the power of the Holy Ghost, that the Book of Mormon is true, that Joseph Smith is a Prophet of the Lord,' the Holy Ghost proceeding from that individual illuminated my understanding . . . and I knew for myself that the testimony of the man was true" (*JD,* 1:90).

With his baptism and simultaneous **confirmation** and ordination as an **elder,** Brigham Young came alive. He stated, "I wanted to thunder and roar out the Gospel to the nations. It burned in my bones like fire pent up" (*JD,* 1:313). He immediately began preaching in the surrounding area and over a period of several months taught the gospel in the communities of Hector, Avon, Warsaw, Henrietta, Reding (or Reading), Hornby, and Patten.

His wife, Miriam, who had been baptized about three weeks after her husband, passed away from consumption on 8 September 1832. She was buried in the Tomlinson Corners Cemetery on the Boughton Hill Road in Mendon. Brigham and his two daughters, Elizabeth and Vilate, moved in with Heber C. and Vilate Kimball for a year and a half.

With his brother **Joseph Young** and **Heber C. Kimball,** Brigham journeyed to **Kirtland, Ohio,** where they met Joseph Smith for the first time during September and October 1832. Brigham declared that he "received the sure testimony by the Spirit of prophecy" that Joseph was "a true prophet," ("Manuscript History," 1:11). Joseph Smith recorded their visit, commenting "Joseph Young is a great man, but Brigham is a greater, and the time will come when he will preside over the whole Church" (Jessee, 1:386, n. 2).

Brigham Young continued to labor as a missionary both locally and in Upper **Canada** (**Ontario** Province) until the Young and Kimball families migrated to Kirtland in 1833, where he applied his craftsmanship in helping to build the new **temple.** He married Mary Ann Angell on 18 February 1834.

When the Lord called for the "strength of his house" to restore the **Missouri** Saints to their **Jackson County** homes in 1834 (D&C 103), Brigham and Joseph Young enlisted and undertook the long march of **Zion's Camp.** Upon their return to Kirtland, Brigham was one of nine members of Zion's Camp who were called to fill the ranks of the original **Quorum** of the Twelve **Apostles** on 14 February 1835.

During the dark days associated with the demise of the **Kirtland Safety Society** Bank, Brigham stoutly defended the Prophet against his detractors. When the opposition sought to replace Joseph Smith with **David Whitmer** as president of the Church, Elder Young declared, "I rose up and told them in a plain and forcible manner that Joseph was a prophet, and I knew it; and that they might rail at and slander him as much as they pleased, they could not destroy the appointment of the Prophet of God" (Tullidge, 82–83).

The "fury of the mob" drove Brigham Young from Kirtland on 22 December 1837. The Prophet was also forced to flee with **Sidney Rigdon** on 12 January 1838. Brigham Young, in Dublin, **Indiana**, was able to secure material assistance for Joseph Smith in his flight to **Far West, Missouri,** and chose to join the Prophet en route.

When Joseph Smith was incarcerated in **Liberty Jail** at the time of the **extermination order** of Governor **Lilburn W. Boggs,** the Prophet called upon Brigham Young and Heber C. Kimball of the Twelve to organize the exodus of the troubled **Saints** from the state of Missouri. On 26 April 1839, in accordance with the revelation that the apostles should depart on an overseas mission from the Far West temple site (D&C 118:4–5), Brigham Young and other members of the Twelve returned to that location, from the safety of **Quincy, Illinois,** and, at grave danger to themselves, carried out their business on the **temple** site. This assignment ultimately took nine of the Twelve Apostles to the British Isles under the personal leadership of Brigham Young during 1840 and 1841.

Following their return, Brigham Young assumed a major responsibility for the business affairs of the Church in Nauvoo. He, together with **Willard Richards** and Heber C. Kimball, was among a select group of men designated as the first recipients of the Lord's **endowment** at the hands of the Prophet, 4 May 1842 in Joseph's **Red Brick Store.** Brigham Young later directed the endowment of some 5,615 Saints in the **Nauvoo Temple** before the western exodus in 1846.

Joseph Smith felt the urgency of convening the Quorum of the Twelve and bestowing upon them all of the keys required to conduct the business of the kingdom, should anything happen to him. The best evidence suggests that this investiture took place in a series of instructive meetings occurring between 23 March and 4 April 1844. The **martyrdom** of the Prophet and his brother **Hyrum Smith** in the **Carthage Jail** took place only a short time later, on 27 June 1844.

Brigham Young and others of the Twelve were on political missions for the **presidential campaign of Joseph Smith** at the time of the Prophet's death. Upon their return to Nauvoo they found Sidney Rigdon advancing his claims as "guardian" of the Church; however, on 8 August the Saints sustained Brigham Young and the Twelve Apostles as their leaders. While Brigham spoke to the congregation, many reported that he was transfigured before them. It appeared to them that the mantle, form, and even voice of the Prophet Joseph came upon President Young.

When circumstances in Illinois became intolerable because of mobocracy and failed protection from the state, President Young led the unprecedented exodus of pioneers to the Rocky Mountains. On 27 December 1847 in Kanesville, Iowa, Brigham Young, Willard Richards, and Heber C. Kimball were sustained as the new **First Presidency**. As governor of **Utah** Territory (1850–58), he established policies affecting its citizens, including **native Americans**. Through his leadership new industries were established, public buildings constructed, roads and irrigation canals laid out, and local government organized. He supervised the establishment of more than 350 **colonies** throughout the **Great Basin**, and in his travels to these communities he preached several hundred sermons. His down-to-earth counsel endeared him to his followers. He also dictated or wrote more than 30,000 letters.

In August 1852, President Young had Orson Pratt publicly announce in general conference the practice of **plural marriage**. President Young married more than two dozen wives and had at least 57 children (Arrington, 420–21). During the conflict with the U.S. government known as the **Utah War** (1857–58), he played an integral part in the amicable settlement of the hostility.

His name is likewise associated with the notable expansion of the worldwide missionary effort of the Church. A viable program of **immigration** was instituted for the tens of thousands of converts who were transplanted to the **Great Basin** in response to the doctrine of **gathering**. He launched the construction of four **temples** and numerous other houses of worship. Assistance in the construction of the transcontinental telegraph system and the implementation of the **Deseret Telegraph** were under his domain. Similarly, the building of the transcontinental **railroad** and the erection of other railway systems within the territory were greatly facilitated by this man of vision. Church **auxiliaries** were either regenerated (the **Relief Society**) or inaugurated (**Sunday School, Young Women**, and **Young Men**) for the first time. Focusing on **education**, he founded the University of Deseret (now **University of Utah**) in **Salt Lake City**, Brigham Young Academy (now **Brigham Young University**) in **Provo**, **Brigham Young College** in **Logan**, and other institutions of learning. His foresight was also demonstrated in undertaking certain measures to secure the economic independence of his people. Recognizing the need for a redefinition of organizational guidelines governing the **priesthood**, he instituted significant changes at both the general and local levels.

In life Brigham Young testified, "Joseph Smith has laid the foundation of the **kingdom of God** in the last days; others will rear the superstructure" (*JD*, 6:364–65). After a lifetime of shoring up the framework and adding to the structure established by the Prophet Joseph Smith, President Young died in Salt Lake City on Wednesday, 29 August 1877. His final words in mortality were of his earthly mentor: "Joseph! Joseph! Joseph!" (Arrington, 399).

SOURCES

Allen, James B., Ronald K. Esplin, and David J. Whittaker. *Men with a Mission: The Quorum of the Twelve Apostles in the British Isles, 1837–1841.* Salt Lake City: Deseret Book, 1992.

Arrington, Leonard J. *Brigham Young: American Moses.* New York: Alfred A. Knopf, 1985.

Black, Susan Easton, and Larry C. Porter. *Lion of the Lord: Essays on the Life and Service of Brigham Young.* Salt Lake City: Deseret Book, 1995.

Esplin, Ronald K. "The Emergence of Brigham Young and the Twelve to Mormon Leadership, 1830–1841." Ph.D. diss., Brigham Young University, 1981.

———. "Joseph, Brigham and the Twelve: A Succession of Continuity." *BYU Studies* 21 (Summer 1981): 3.

Fisher, J. Sheldon. "Brigham Young as a Mendon Craftsman: A Study in Historical Archaeology." *New York History* 61 (October 1980): 4.

Gates, Susa Young, and Leah D. Widtsoe. *The Life Story of Brigham Young.* New York: Macmillan, 1930.

Jessee, Dean C. *The Papers of Joseph Smith.* Vol. 1. Salt Lake City: Deseret Book, 1989.

Journal of Discourses [JD]. 26 vols. London: Latter-day Saints' Book Depot, 1854–86.

"Manuscript History of Brigham Young, 1844–1846." 4 vols. LDS Church Archives, Salt Lake City.

Palmer, Richard F., and Karl D. Butler. *Brigham Young: The New York Years.* Provo, Utah: Charles Redd Center for Western Studies, 1982.

Tullidge, Edward W. *Life of Brigham Young.* New York: n.p., 1876.

Young, S. Dilworth. *"Here Is Brigham": Brigham Young–the Years to 1844.* Salt Lake City: Bookcraft, 1964.

LEONARD J. ARRINGTON AND LARRY C. PORTER

YOUNG, BRIGHAM, JR. Named after his father, one of the most valiant men in the history of the Church, Brigham Young Jr. served as president of the **Quorum** of the Twelve **Apostles.** Born with a twin sister 18 December 1836 in **Kirtland, Ohio,** Brigham grew up in **Nauvoo, Winter Quarters,** and **Salt Lake City.** He gained a lifelong reputation of having "an indomitable spirit, a merriment which was as infectious as June sunshine" (Jenson, 123). He helped in colonizing **Cache Valley,** southern **Utah, New Mexico, Arizona,** and **Mexico.** A member of the

Nauvoo Legion, he participated in **Indian** battles, the Echo Canyon War, and the rescue of the Willie and Martin **Handcart** Companies.

Brigham's missionary service included four assignments in **Great Britain,** two of them as **mission president.** Traveling extensively, he visited many countries, including **Russia.** Elder Young was **ordained** an apostle 4 February 1864 at age 27, but because there were no vacancies in the quorum, he did not become a member of the Twelve until 9 October 1868. Elder Young served nearly 40 years as an apostle of the Lord. Four and a half of those years he labored as an additional **counselor** to President **Brigham Young.** After the death of his father, 29 August 1877, Brigham Young Jr. returned to the Quorum of the Twelve. He became the president of that body on 17 October 1901, serving until his death on 11 April 1903 in Salt Lake City at age 66.

SOURCES

Flake, Lawrence R. *Prophets and Apostles of the Last Dispensation.* Provo, Utah: Religious Studies Center, Brigham Young University, 2001. 289–91.

Jenson, Andrew. *Latter-day Saint Biographical Encyclopedia.* 4 vols. 1901–36. Reprint, Salt Lake City: Western Epics, 1971. 1:123.

LAWRENCE R. FLAKE

YOUNG, DWAN J. Dwan Jacobsen Young, born 1 May 1931 in Salt Lake City, was general president of the **Primary** from April 1980 until April 1988. She and her husband, Thomas Young Jr., became the parents of five children. Sister Young's Primary service was characterized by adaptation to the new consolidated meeting schedule, implemented only one month before she became president. The Primary developed a new Children's Songbook, created lessons that emphasized the **Articles of Faith,** and added Achievement Day Activities, laying the foundation for the organization to function successfully in a worldwide Church. Following her presidency, Dwan assisted her husband as he presided over the **Canada** Calgary Mission.

SOURCE

"New Primary Presidency Sustained." *Ensign* 10 (May 1980): 106.

CYNTHIA DOXEY

YOUNG, JOHN W. John Willard Young, a **counselor** in the **First Presidency** and **railroad** builder, was born in **Nauvoo, Illinois,** on

1 October 1844 to **Brigham Young** and Mary Ann Angell. While yet a boy, John was ordained an **apostle** by his father. This ordination was confirmed by President Young when John was 19. Although John never became a member of the **Quorum** of the Twelve, he honored his sacred office of apostle while serving as president of the Salt Lake **Stake**, as a missionary in **England**, and as an additional counselor to Brigham Young from 8 April 1873 to 7 October 1876. At that time he became first counselor in the **First Presidency**, serving in that capacity until his father's death 29 August 1877. For the next 14 years, until 6 October 1891, he and his father's former second counselor, **Daniel H. Wells**, were sustained as "Counselors to the Twelve Apostles."

Like his father, John W. Young was an empire builder. Among his undertakings were four railroads, Utah's first streetcar line, the Deseret Museum and Menagerie, the consolidation of several large shipbuilding companies, and other schemes involving hundreds of millions of dollars. When Brother Young died in New York City on 11 February 1924, he was eulogized as one who loved and bore testimony of the restored gospel.

SOURCES

"The Death of John W. Young." *Improvement Era* 27 (April 1924): 582.

Flake, Lawrence R. *Prophets and Apostles of the Last Dispensation*. Provo, Utah: Religious Studies Center, Brigham Young University, 2001. 177–79.

Jenson, Andrew. *Latter-day Saint Biographical Encyclopedia*. 4 vols. 1901–36. Reprint, Salt Lake City: Western Epics, 1971. 1:42.

LAWRENCE R. FLAKE

YOUNG, JOSEPH. One of the original seven presidents of the First Quorum of **Seventy**, Joseph Young was born 7 April 1797 in Hopkinton, Massachusetts, to John Young and Abigail Howe. Before he joined the Church, Joseph was a Methodist minister in **Canada**. On one occasion he was startled to see among the congregation his younger brother from **New York**, **Brigham Young**. Reminiscent of Andrew's words to Peter in the New Testament, "We have found the Messiah," Brigham said, "Joseph, I have found the Gospel. Come with me" (quoted in Young, 950). The Spirit bore witness that the words of his brother were true, and Joseph Young became a lifelong missionary for the Lord's true Church.

Joseph Young served as a member of **Zion's Camp**. At the conclusion of that courageous undertaking, the **Prophet Joseph Smith** declared that Brigham would be one of the **apostles** and said, "Brother Joseph the Lord has made you president of the seventies" (quoted in Whitney, 444). His son Seymour and his grandson Levi Edgar Young followed his noble example of faithfulness and were, like him, designated by the Lord to serve in the **First Council of Seventy**. All three men became senior members of that council, giving a total of 140 years of dedicated service. Joseph Young died 16 July 1881 in **Salt Lake City** at age 84.

SOURCES

Flake, Lawrence R. *Mighty Men of Zion.* Salt Lake City: Karl D. Butler, 1974. 385.

Whitney, Orson F. *History of Utah.* 4 vols. Salt Lake City: George Q. Cannon and Sons, 1904. Vol. 4.

Young, Levi Edgar. "Advice to Teachers." *Improvement Era* 62 (December 1959): 950–51.

LAWRENCE R. FLAKE

YOUNG, MAHONRI M. Artist and sculptor Mahonri Mackintosh Young was born 9 August 1877 in **Salt Lake City, Utah**. He left school in the ninth grade, studied art with James Harwood, and became a sketch artist for the *Salt Lake Herald* and the *Salt Lake Tribune* before studying at the New York Art Students' League in 1899. He studied in Paris from 1901 to 1905, then began his career in Utah as one of America's first sculptural realists. After leaving Utah in 1910, he spent most of his career in **New York**.

Although not a practicing **Mormon**, as a grandson of **Brigham Young** Mahonri developed a strong sense of his Latter-day Saint heritage. Latter-day Saint religious leaders and themes provided subjects for his work.

His enduring works of Utah and Mormonism include statues of **Joseph** and **Hyrum Smith** and the *Sea Gull Monument,* displayed on Salt Lake's **Temple Square**; the **Brigham Young** statue in the Capitol Rotunda in **Washington, D.C.**; and his best known piece, the *"This Is the Place" Monument* at the mouth of **Emigration Canyon**, unveiled 24 July 1947 for the Utah **Centennial**.

At the time of his death 2 November 1957, Mahonri Young was regarded as one of America's greatest and most versatile artists, with works displayed in more than 50 museums and galleries in the United States and **Europe**.

SOURCES

Hinton, Wayne K. "A Biographical History of Mahonri M. Young, a Western American Artist." Ph.D. diss., Brigham Young University, 1974.

Toone, Thomas E. *Mahonri Young: His Life and Art.* Salt Lake City: Signature, 1997.

————. "Mahonri Young: His Life and Sculpture." Ph.D. diss., Pennsylvania State University, 1982.

WAYNE HINTON

YOUNG, PHINEHAS. Phinehas (sometimes spelled Phineas) Howe Young, the older brother of **Brigham Young**, is best known for taking the restored gospel of **Jesus Christ** to Brigham. Born 16 February 1799 in the town of Hopkinton, Middlesex County, **Massachusetts**, he was the seventh child of John Young and Abigail Howe.

Much like other early Church members, Phinehas was a 'seeker' of truth from the **Bible** and religious philosophers. This quest for knowledge brought him into contact with the first missionary of the Church, **Joseph Smith's** younger brother Samuel. While doing **missionary work** in the summer of 1830, Samuel sold a copy of the **Book of Mormon** to Phinehas, who immediately read it and, after careful study, declared that he believed the book to be true. It was this copy, as well as another copy left with his sister Rhoda, that introduced the Young **family** to Mormonism. Phinehas and his father, John, were baptized 5 April 1832 in **Pennsylvania**, a week before his brother Brigham.

Phinehas remained true to his testimony throughout his life. He was an active **pioneer** and settler when the **Saints** moved west and served **missions** to both **Canada** and **England**. His Church service ended only with his death on 10 October 1879 in **Salt Lake City**.

SOURCES

England, Eugene. *Brother Brigham*. Salt Lake City: Bookcraft, 1980. 9–13.

Gibbons, Francis M. *Brigham Young: Modern Moses, Prophet of God*. Salt Lake City: Deseret Book, 1981. 12–18.

DANIEL E. BISHOP

YOUNG, S. DILWORTH. When Seymour Dilworth Young entered the First Council of the **Seventy**, he became part of a great **family** tradition. His uncle **Levi Edgar Young**, his grandfather **Seymour B. Young**, and his great-grandfather **Joseph Young** were all members of the First Council of the Seventy. On his mother's side he also had a distinguished heritage, for she was a granddaughter of **Brigham Young** and a great-granddaughter of **Edward Partridge**, first **bishop** of the Church.

Dilworth was born in **Salt Lake City**, 7 September 1897. Following his service in **France** during **World War I**, he went on a **mission** to the central states, where he served for 26 of 33 months as secretary to the **mission president, Samuel O. Bennion.** He was serving as an executive with the **Boy Scouts** of America when he was called to the First Council of the Seventy on 6 April 1945. Two years later, he was assigned to preside over the New England Mission with headquarters in Cambridge, **Massachusetts.** He was given emeritus status on 30 September 1979, ending 33 years as a **general authority. Elder** Young had a remarkable talent for writing both prose and poetry and is remembered for his exercise of this gift. He died in Salt Lake City on 9 July 1981 at age 83.

SOURCES

Flake, Lawrence R. *Mighty Men of Zion.* Salt Lake City: Karl D. Butler, 1974. 453.
"Funeral Rites for S. Dilworth Young." *Church News,* 18 July 1981, 3.

LAWRENCE R. FLAKE

YOUNG, STEVE.

Steve Young, one of the best-known LDS athletes at the end of the twentieth century, was born 11 October 1961 in **Salt Lake City** and reared in **Connecticut**. He burst onto the national football scene in 1983. After a successful senior season as quarterback of the **Brigham Young University** football team, he was runner-up in balloting for the Heisman Trophy and was a consensus first-team All-American. The Los Angeles Express of the fledgling United States Football League drafted Steve No. 1 in 1984 and signed him to a $40 million contract. The USFL soon folded, and Steve went to the Tampa Bay Buccaneers for two seasons. He was later traded to the San Francisco 49ers, where he backed up Joe Montana before assuming the quarterback position and leading the 49ers to the Super Bowl championship in 1994. He was named the National Football League's Most Valuable Player in 1992 and 1994. He retired from professional football in 2000.

VAL HALE

YOUNG, ZINA D.

Zina Diantha Young, an original member of the **Relief Society** in **Nauvoo**, became its third general president in 1888 at the age of 67. She had served as first counselor under **Eliza R. Snow,** beginning in 1866. Young's presidency was marked by instituting annual dues and officially incorporating the auxiliary. She became the official representative of the Relief Society to the National Council of Women.

She also represented the Church in the National **Woman's Suffrage** Association and the World Congress of Women held in Chicago in 1893.

Zina was born 31 January 1821 in Watertown, New York, and baptized in 1835 by **Hyrum Smith**. She was first married to Henry Jacobs in 1841. Later, she was sealed to **Joseph Smith**, and after his death she married **Brigham Young** in 1846, traveling to **Utah** in 1848. Throughout her life she was affectionately known among the **Saints** as "Aunt Zina." Church members gave her this title because of her extensive travels to far-flung Latter-day Saint settlements, her warm personality, and her spiritual gifts, which included healing and speaking in tongues. The mother of three children, Zina was also involved extensively in mid-wifery, teaching, and sewing. She died 28 August 1901 in **Salt Lake City**.

SOURCES

Derr, Jill Mulvay, Janath Russell Cannon, and Maureen Ursenbach Beecher. *Women of the Covenant: The Story of Relief Society*. Salt Lake City: Deseret Book, 1992.

Higbee, Marilyn. "A Weary Traveler: The 1848–1850 Diary of Zina D. Young." Honors project, Brigham Young University, 1992.

MARY JANE WOODGER

YOUNG MEN. On 6 June 1875 **Brigham Young** asked his counselor **Daniel H. Wells** to have his son **Junius F. Wells** "organize the young men." President Young wanted that new organization to provide an opportunity for the young men of the Church to serve, learn public speaking, and bear testimony. Junius responded with promptness and on 10 June at 7:00 P.M. he organized the First **Ward** Young Men's **Mutual Improvement Association** (YMMIA) at the Thirteenth Ward **meeting-house** in **Salt Lake City**. One of the original 18 young men registered was **Heber J. Grant**, later seventh president of the Church.

Through the summer and fall, additional ward YMMIA organizations were created. Junius was called on another **mission** in November, but **John Henry Smith**, Milton H. Hardy, and B. Morris Young (son of Brigham Young) were called to continue establishing YMMIA groups. They were the earliest of many "Mutual Improvement" missionaries called between 1877 and 1905. The first **general conference** of the association took place 8 April 1876 with 57 groups and 1,200 members. A decrease in loitering and misbehavior by young men throughout the territory was noted as associations multiplied. The program was further prospered by its concurrence with aggressive **stake** rejuvenation and reorganization efforts immediately before Brigham Young's death.

In 1880 a general superintendency made up of members of the Twelve was created with Heber J. Grant as secretary. From 1887 to 1918 the president of the Church was the general YMMIA president. A general board was established during the first decade of the twentieth century to form policies, write lessons, and visit associations.

Junius Wells privately published the *Contributor* for young men from 1879 to 1892, when **Abraham H.** Cannon became publisher until his untimely death in 1896. In 1897 the *Improvement Era* **magazine** began publishing under the general board of the YMMIA.

Early **meetings** of the YMMIA were filled with testimony bearing. Later, theology, **science**, history, **literature**, **athletics**, **dance**, **drama**, **music**, and public speaking activities were promoted. Study classes were added. Membership initially ranged in age from approximately 14 to between 40 and 50. Weekly meetings were instigated in 1889. In 1900 opening exercises were started with division into junior and senior classes, which featured lesson manuals the following year. Conjoint meetings of the YMMIA and YWMIA began on Sunday evenings in 1900 also. In 1908 a more social emphasis was taken as priesthood **quorums** assumed more responsibility for spiritual development as requested by the **First Presidency**. Tuesday was designated as **MIA** night for many years. **Boy Scouts** was inaugurated in 1911 with national chartering in 1913.

Wartime saw targeted antismoking and antidrinking campaigns, as well as age-grouping redefinition reflecting draft eligibility. Afterwards, sports tournaments, speech, music, and dance festivals were held Churchwide, burgeoning in the 1950s and then decentralizing in 1971 because of ever-increasing Church **growth**.

In 1972, the new titles **Aaronic Priesthood MIA** and **Melchizedek Priesthood** MIA signaled a change from auxiliary to **priesthood** organization. When the **presiding bishopric** assumed general responsibility in 1974, the suffix MIA was dropped. Three years later the name "Young Men" was adopted when stewardship was transferred to the Priesthood Department.

SOURCES

Hartley, William. "The Priesthood Reform Movement, 1908–1922." *BYU Studies* 13 (Winter 1973): 137–56.

Roberts, B. H. *A Comprehensive History of The Church of Jesus Christ of Latter-day Saints, Century One.* 6 vols. Salt Lake City: The Church of Jesus Christ of Latter-day Saints, 1930.

Strong, Leon M. "A History of the Young Men's Mutual Improvement Association 1875–1938." Master's thesis, Brigham Young University, 1939.

Williams, John Kent. "A History of the Young Men's Mutual Improvement Association 1939 to 1974." Master's thesis, Brigham Young University, 1976.

JOHN P. LIVINGSTONE

YOUNG UNIVERSITY. See UNIVERSITY OF THE CHURCH OF JESUS CHRIST OF LATTER-DAY SAINTS, THE.

YOUNG WOMAN'S JOURNAL. The *Young Woman's Journal* was introduced in 1889 by editor **Susa Young Gates** as the official organ of the Young Ladies' National **Mutual Improvement Association** (**Young Women**). Devoted to the YLNMIA's purpose of encouraging teenage girls to focus on spiritual rather than worldly things, the *Journal*, with its circulation of 15,000, included religious articles, talks from **general authorities**, and YLNMIA lessons. The *Journal* also featured recipes, sewing patterns, short stories, and features on homemaking, marriage, and fashion. In 1929 the *Journal* merged with the *Improvement Era*, which had been published by the **Young Men's** Mutual Improvement Association, creating a publication to serve both associations.

SOURCES

Arrington, Leonard J. "Persons for All Seasons: Women in Mormon History." *BYU Studies* 20 (Fall 1979): 39–58.

Roberts, B. H. *A Comprehensive History of The Church of Jesus Christ of Latter-day Saints, Century One.* 6 vols. Salt Lake City: The Church of Jesus Christ of Latter-day Saints, 1930. 5:484.

KRISTIN B. GERDY

YOUNG WOMEN. Developed for Latter-day Saint young **women** ages 12 to 18, the Young Women's program was first established by **Brigham Young** for his daughters. Originally titled the Young Ladies' Department of the Cooperative **Retrenchment** Association, the name was quickly shortened to the Young Ladies' Retrenchment Association. At the organization's first meeting on 28 November 1869, Brigham Young stated his vision of the Church's newest society: "I have long had it in my mind to organize the young ladies of **Zion** into an association so that they might assist the older members of the Church, their fathers and mothers, in propagating, teaching, and practicing the principles I have been so long teaching. There is need for the young daughters of Israel to get a living testimony of the truth. . . . For this purpose I desire to establish this organization and want my **family** to lead out in the great work." President Young continued, "I want you to vote to retrench in your dress, in your tables, in your speech, wherein you have been guilty of silly, extravagant speeches and light mindedness of thought. Retrench in everything that is not good and beautiful . . . to live so that you may be truly happy in this life and the life to come" (quoted in Peterson, xi).

Eliza R. Snow was given the responsibility of organizing the association, and Ella Young Empey was elected president. In 1870 the first **ward** association was established, and within the year organizations had spread throughout **Utah**. A change in name to the Young Ladies' National **Mutual Improvement Association** occurred in 1877.

On 19 June 1880, **Elmina Shephard Taylor** was called as the association's first general president. During her presidency, the organization created the *Young Woman's Journal* (1889), designated Tuesday night as Mutual night (1893), installed Annual Day (a Church-wide day of sports), and made traveling **MIA** libraries (1898) available.

When **Martha Horne Tingey** became president, the organization's name was again changed, this time to the Young Ladies' Mutual Improvement Association. During Sister Tingey's presidency (1905–29), the Young Women's program instituted field days and summer camp programs.

In 1912 the original two class divisions of senior and junior became the **Beehive** Girls and the Senior Girls. The Senior Girls were then divided into Seniors and Advanced Seniors before a Junior class was added. Subsequently, the Senior Girls became the Junior Gleaners (1924) and finally the Laurels (1959). Under the presidency of **Bertha Stone Reeder**, the Young Women age groups were realigned in 1950. The twelve- and thirteen-year-olds were called Beehives; fourteen- and fifteen-year-olds, MIA Maids; and sixteen- and seventeen-year-olds, Laurels.

By mid-twentieth century, the Young Women's program published lesson manuals that were distributed Churchwide, replaced previous slogans with scripture themes, and sponsored dance, music, and speech festivals; art programs; and sports events. Above all, the organization emphasized strengthening one's testimony, living a righteous life, and striving to be like Christ.

Under **Ruth Hardy Funk**, the name of the organization was changed in 1972 to Young Women. In addition, the program instituted a structured, individualized program of initiatives and goals called the Personal Progress Program. Under the direction of **Ardeth Greene Kapp**, the general presidency established the system of Young Women's Values. As companion programs, Personal Progress and the Young Women Values focused on implementing seven values—each associated with a color—into the lives of the young women: faith (white), divine nature (red), individual worth (blue), knowledge (green), choice and accountability (orange), good works (yellow), and integrity (purple). Each group (Beehive, MIA Maid, and Laurel) had a motto and a **scripture** that were incorporated into their lessons and activities. To obtain achievement awards in each of these groups, a young woman had to accomplish two initiatives or goals in each value area every year. The capstone Young Women's Recognition Award and Medallion was earned and presented when these goals had been accomplished over the six years.

SOURCES

M.I.A. Handbook. Salt Lake City: The Church of Jesus Christ of Latter-day Saints, 1928.

Peterson, Janet, and LaRene Gaunt. *Keepers of the Flame.* Salt Lake City: Deseret Book, 1993.

MAREN M. MOURITSEN

YOUTH ACTIVITIES. From the early days of the **Young Women's** Retrenchment Society and the **Young Men's** organization, activities have played a vital role in the Church's youth programs. In the early twentieth century, activities included involvement in community affairs (Mutual Improvement League), "**stake** conventions," and joint youth leadership week. Young men's participation was encouraged in summer scout activities and self-improvement courses, while the young women enjoyed "junior" festivals, reading courses, and their own summer camps.

As the Church progressed and grew, more extensive programs were initiated. Besides regular Sunday **meetings**, the youth held weekly activities to teach gospel principles. Other activities which fostered personal growth included art festivals, **conferences**, sport days, dances, and roadshows.

Although many of the earlier activities are no longer implemented, weekly meetings are still held for both the young men and young women, focusing on spiritual development, personal growth, and service. All of these activities emphasize teaching principles of the gospel, building testimonies, strengthening the youth, forming lasting friendships, and teaching the importance of good citizenship.

SOURCES

M.I.A. Handbook. Salt Lake City: The Church of Jesus Christ of Latter-day Saints, 1928.

Peterson, Janet, and LaRene Gaunt. *Keepers of the Flame.* Salt Lake City: Deseret Book, 1993.

MAREN M. MOURITSEN

YUKON TERRITORY, CANADA. Since the gold rush days of the Klondike in the 1890s, **Canada's** vast northwestern territory of the Yukon has held a spell over the adventurous and the prospector. More recently opened to settlement with the completion of the **Alaska** Highway in 1942, Yukon's major cities are Dawson Creek and Whitehorse. With the coldest winter temperatures ever recorded in the western hemisphere (−82 degrees Fahrenheit), the Yukon has a population of only 30,000.

The Church has grown in proportion to the settlement. The first **branch** was established at Whitehorse in 1963, and by the year 2000 it had 204 members scattered over a territory larger than most **stakes** in the Church. At the end of the twentieth century, the recently completed Anchorage Alaska **Temple** served faithful Church members in the Yukon Territory.

RICHARD E. BENNETT

YWMIA. See YOUNG WOMEN.

Y. X. COMPANY. The **Brigham Young** Express and Carrying Company, often called the Y. X. Company, was organized in **Salt Lake City** in early 1857 to carry mail and freight from the East to **Utah** and to assist emigrating **Saints.** Operations were suspended indefinitely after just five months when the federal government canceled the mail contract and the Saints retrenched in anticipation of federal troops being sent to Utah to quell rumored rebellion.

SOURCE

Arrington, Leonard J. *Great Basin Kingdom: An Economic History of the Latter-day Saints, 1830–1900.* Lincoln: University of Nebraska Press, 1966. 162–70.

JED L. WOODWORTH

ZCMI. In an effort to create a network of wholesale warehouses, Brigham Young established Zion's Cooperative Mercantile Institute (ZCMI) in 1869 as part of the Church's movement toward self-sufficiency.

ZAIRE. See DEMOCRATIC REPUBLIC OF CONGO.

ZAMBIA. The Republic of Zambia in south central **Africa** has a population that speaks English and local dialects. Prior to its independence from **Great Britain** in 1964, the country was known as Northern Rhodesia. Most of its citizens are Christian.

The Church was first established in Zambia in 1950, when President Evan P. Wright of the **South Africa Mission** organized a group for the few Latter-day Saint families living in northern Zambia. The following year missionaries were sent to help strengthen and build the group. Church growth was relatively slow, although in 1965 a **branch** was organized and a chapel dedicated. Soon after Zambia gained its independence, the government refused to issue visas for Latter-day Saint missionaries. Gradually the Latter-day Saint families moved back to South Africa, and the branch dissolved. Sometime later the chapel was sold to the government to be used as a school.

In 1991 the mission headquartered in **Zimbabwe** began reestablishing contact with members of the Church who were living in Zambia. The Church was formally registered with the government 10 July 1992, and four days later a branch of about 50 members was organized in Lusaka, with Johnson Makombe as president and his wife, Noria, as **Relief Society** president. On 10 August of that year, Elder **Russell M. Nelson** dedicated Zambia for the preaching of the gospel. A **seminary** program began in 1995, and by the year 2000 the country had 711 Church members in 3 branches.

SOURCES

Middleton, John, ed. *Encyclopedia of Africa South of the Sahara.* 4 vols. New York: Macmillan Library Reference USA, 1997. 4:409–17.

Mostert, Mary, and Gerry Avant. "Prayers of Dedication Offered on 4 Nations in Central, Southern Africa." *Church News,* 26 September 1992. 3.

1999–2000 Church Almanac. Salt Lake City: Deseret News, 1998. 409–10.

Oral histories of early Church converts collected by E. Dale LeBaron. Copies at BYU Library, Provo, Utah; LDS Church Historical Library, Salt Lake City, Utah.

E. DALE LEBARON

ZANE, CHARLES S. Charles S. Zane, chief justice of the **Utah** Territorial Supreme Court (1884–88; 1889–94), was born 2 March 1831 in Cumberland County, **New Jersey**. He presided over the trials for unlawful cohabitation of hundreds of Latter-day Saints.

Zane practiced law and served as a judge in **Illinois** before President Chester Arthur appointed him to the Utah bench. In Utah he earned a reputation for fairness in secular matters and for severity in sentencing polygamists who refused to obey the law.

After the **Manifesto (1890)** Zane worked with other Utahns to heal the breach between the **Mormon** and non-Mormon communities. Utahns rewarded these efforts by electing him the first chief justice of the Utah State Supreme Court in 1895. He died in 1915.

SOURCES

Alexander, Thomas G. "Charles S. Zane, Apostle of the New Era." *Utah Historical Quarterly* 34 (Fall 1966): 290–314.

Zane, Charles S. Autobiography. Typescript. Special Collections, Harold B. Library, Brigham Young University, Provo, Utah.

———. Diaries. Illinois State Historical Society, Springfield, Ill.

Zane, John M. "A Rare Judicial Service, Charles S. Zane." *Journal of the Illinois State Historical Society* 19 (April–July 1926): 31–48.

THOMAS G. ALEXANDER

ZARAHEMLA, IOWA. See LEE COUNTY, IOWA.

ZCMI. When Zion's Cooperative Mercantile Institution (ZCMI) was organized in March 1868, it officially began **Brigham Young's** economic boycott of non-Mormon businesses in **Utah** Territory. In line with Young's belief in the importance of self-sufficiency and home manufacture, ZCMI cooperatives were established during the next few years in hundreds of Latter-day Saint settlements, creating a network centered in the **Salt Lake City** ZCMI wholesale warehouse. ZCMI sales that first year totaled 1.5

million dollars. Goods sold ranged from **clothing**, fabric, homemade brooms, and straw hats to wagons, machinery, sewing machines, overalls, boots, and shoes made at ZCMI-owned and operated factories. The first section of the familiar ZCMI cast-iron store front was built in 1876. By 1880 this impressive three-story, brick-and-iron facade stretched across three bays along Salt Lake City's Main Street.

In the twentieth century, ZCMI continued to grow, expanding to shopping malls throughout the Wasatch Front, including the Cottonwood, Valley Fair, and University Malls, as well as other shopping centers in **Ogden** and **Logan**. In October 1999 the Church sold its 14 ZCMI stores to May Department Store Company, a St. Louis-based operation. It was announced that the stores would be renamed Meier and Frank.

SOURCES

Bradley, Martha Sonntag. *ZCMI: America's First Department Store*. Salt Lake City: ZCMI, 1990.

MARTHA SONNTAG BRADLEY

ZELPH. **Joseph Smith** identified the remains of this ancient American warrior during the march of **Zion's Camp** in 1834. The group crossed the Illinois River three miles east of present-day Griggsville, En route to **Missouri**. As they camped near the ferry on 2 June, some of the men went to visit several ancient burial mounds. On one of the mounds, now designated as Naples-Russell Mound Number 8, they discovered three stone altars and unearthed a skeleton with an arrow in its ribcage.

On the following day, Joseph Smith visited the mound and identified the skeletal remains as belonging to Zelph, a warrior and a white Lamanite. According to **Wilford Woodruff**, the **Prophet** Joseph Smith had a vision concerning Zelph. Six members of Zion's Camp recorded the experience in their diaries: **George A. Smith**, **Levi Hancock**, Reuben McBride, **Heber C. Kimball**, Moses Martin, and Wilford Woodruff. On 4 June 1834 Joseph Smith wrote to his wife, Emma, that they had been "wandering over the plains of the Nephites" (quoted in Cannon, 31).

SOURCES

Cannon, Donald Q. "Zelph Revisited." In *Illinois*. Edited by H. Dean Garrett. Regional Studies in Latter-day Saint Church History series. Provo, Utah: Brigham Young University, 1995. 97–111.

Godfrey, Kenneth W. "The Zelph Story." *BYU Studies* 29 (Spring 1989): 31–56.

DONALD Q. CANNON

ZIMBABWE. The nation once known as Rhodesia in southern **Africa** declared its independence from **Great Britain** in 1965, and its white government struggled to retain power until 1980, when the Republic of Zimbabwe was proclaimed. The country's official languages are English and the tribal dialects of Shona and Ndebele. About 25% of the population is Christian, and approximately half follow a mixture of Christianity and indigenous beliefs.

Although missionaries arrived in Rhodesia in the early 1930s, the work was not successful, and for many years the country received only brief visits from **elders** serving in **South Africa**. In 1950 President Evan P. Wright of the South Africa **Mission** sent eight missionaries to Salisbury (Harare) and Bulawayo. They baptized Hugh Hodgkiss, the first convert in the country, on 1 February 1951.

The Church began to grow steadily in numbers and strength, and by 1979 there were 739 members within a **district** of four **branches.** Following the takeover of the Zimbabwe government in 1980, most Latter-day Saints moved to South Africa or overseas.

The first black Zimbabwean to join the Church was Ernest Sibanda, who was baptized in December 1979. Missionary work accelerated among the **blacks,** and when the Zimbabwe Harare Mission was created on 1 July 1987 with Joseph Hamstead as president, there were more than 1,000 members. In 1981 Peter Chaya became the first Zimbabwean of African descent to serve a full-time mission. Many have followed since. For several years the Zimbabwe government refused to issue visas to foreign missionaries, so during that time the missionary force came primarily from within the country.

On 25 October 1991, Elder **James E. Faust** of the **Quorum** of the Twelve **Apostles** dedicated Zimbabwe for the preaching of the gospel. Many converts came into the Church with a desire to share their faith. One couple, Brother and Sister Chikunguwo from the Muturi region, set a goal at the time of their baptism to share the gospel with 100 friends and relatives during the first year of their membership. They exceeded their goal, with 149 people joining the Church. Like hundreds of other Saints in Zimbabwe, they sacrificed greatly to travel hundreds of miles to receive their **temple ordinances** in the Johannesburg South Africa Temple.

President **Gordon B. Hinckley** and Elder **Jeffrey R. Holland** of the Quorum of the Twelve Apostles spoke to almost 1,500 members of the Church in Harare on 18 February 1998. At the beginning of the year 2000 there were 8,287 Latter-day Saints in Zimbabwe living in one **stake** and 25 **wards** and branches scattered over more than 150,803 square miles.

SOURCES

LeBaron, E. Dale, ed. *All Are Alike unto God.* Orem, Utah: Granite Publishing, 1998. 116–38. 116–38.

Middleton, John, ed. *Encyclopedia of Africa South of the Sahara.* 4 vols. New York: Macmillan Library Reference USA, 1997. 4:421–30.

1999–2000 Church Almanac. Salt Lake City: Deseret News, 1998. 410.

Oral histories of early Church converts collected by E. Dale LeBaron. Copies at BYU Library, Provo, Utah; LDS Church Historical Library, Salt Lake City, Utah.

E. DALE LEBARON

ZION. In the **Book of Mormon,** we encounter a concept of Zion that is broader than Jerusalem or the Holy Mount. Zion is a holy community, a fortification of the **Saints** against evil; it is God's church and kingdom (1 Ne. 13:37; 2 Ne. 10:11–13; 26:29–31; 28:20–21, 24). In addition, Zion is a specific location, a sacred site. For example, the **scriptures** of the **Restoration** affirm that Zion would begin to be built up in the land of **America** and that the Lord would watch over it and hold it in his hand (3 Ne. 16:16–18; D&C 6:6; 11:6; 28:9; 57:1–3; 63:25; Ehat and Cook, 353, 415).

As he began work on what is now called the **Joseph Smith Translation of the Bible,** the **Prophet** learned by revelation in December 1830 of the ancient city of Zion established by Enoch: "And the Lord called his people Zion, because they were of one heart and one mind, and dwelt in righteousness; and there was no poor among them" (Moses 7:18; JST Gen. 7:23). This great historical discovery was pivotal in the quest for a society of Zion among the Latter-day Saints. Enoch's Zion was a glorious success and thus became the pattern, the scriptural prototype. Within a short time, the Lord began to reveal through **Joseph Smith** how to establish a like community of faith in the last days, and how to build a latter-day Zion upon the same foundational principles of consecration and stewardship (see D&C 42:29–42; 51:1–5; 70:1–14; 72:1–4; 83:1–6). In 1831 the Lord revealed that **Independence, Jackson County, Missouri,** was the center place of Zion. During the next several years, the term *Zion* was almost synonymous with Missouri for the Saints.

In time, however, Zion came to refer not only to a specific location—whether Jackson County, **Kirtland**, **Nauvoo**, or **Salt Lake City**—but to a state of being, a state of righteousness. Zion is "the pure in heart" (D&C 97:21), or the place where the pure in heart gather. "Who are Zion?" President **Brigham Young** asked. "The pure in heart are Zion; they have Zion within them. Purify yourselves, sanctify the Lord God in your hearts, and have the Zion of God within you, and then you will rejoice more and more" (*JD*, 8:198; see also 2:253; 8:205).

It was never intended that there ultimately be only one location to which all Saints were to gather; rather, the Lord foresaw that the people of the covenant throughout the earth would gather to the **stakes** of Zion (D&C 101:17–21), for therein is their safety. Thus the work of purifying our lives and thereby building Zion will continue. "We ought to have the building up of Zion as our greatest object," Joseph Smith taught in 1839 (Smith, 160). Truly, as President **Spencer W. Kimball** observed, Zion is "the highest order of **priesthood** society" (Kimball, 125).

SOURCES

Ehat, Andrew F., and Lyndon W. Cook, comps. and eds. *The Words of Joseph Smith.* Provo, Utah: Religious Studies Center, Brigham Young University, 1980. 353, 415.

Journal of Discourses [JD]. 26 vols. London: Latter-day Saints' Book Depot, 1854–86.

Kimball, Spencer W. Conference Report (October 1977): 121–26.

Smith, Joseph. *Teachings of the Prophet Joseph Smith.* Selected by Joseph Fielding Smith. Salt Lake City: Deseret Book, 1976.

ROBERT L. MILLET

ZION'S BANK. On 6 August 1873, Zion's Savings Bank and Trust Company was established with a capital stock of $200,000. The bank was created as an offshoot of **Deseret National Bank**, taking over its savings department. **Brigham Young** was elected the bank's first president. As a part of the Church's business enterprises, the bank financed a number of Church-sponsored projects.

By the turn of the century, the bank's policies had become more secularized, but the Church continued to have controlling interest. By 1918 deposits had grown to $9 million. On 22 April 1960, majority control of the bank was sold to Keystone Insurance and Investment Co. In 1965 the company's name was changed to Zions Bancorp.

SOURCES

Arrington, Leonard J. *Great Basin Kingdom: Economic History of the Latter-day Saints, 1830–1900.* Lincoln: University of Nebraska Press, 1958. 316–17.

Bliss, Jonathan. *Merchants and Miners in Utah: The Walker Brothers and Their Bank.* Salt Lake City: Western Epics, 1983.

Knudson, Max B. "Zions Still Pushing Frontier; Bank of '90s Building Big Presence in the West." *Deseret News,* 29 November 1998. M1.

CRAIG L. FOSTER

ZION'S CAMP. During May and June of 1834, a group of 229 Latter-day Saints called **Zion's Camp** marched the thousand miles from **Kirtland, Ohio**, and other areas toward **Jackson County, Missouri**. The formation of Zion's Camp was commanded by a **revelation** (D&C 103) and consisted of volunteers recruited by the **Prophet Joseph Smith** and others to work with the Missouri state militia in restoring property taken by the mob in Jackson County.

Fully aware of the inherent danger of this effort, members of the camp left their homes and families at great sacrifice. The average age of group members was 29, the youngest being 16 and the oldest 79. Included in Zion's Camp were eleven women and seven children. They marched an average of 35 miles a day through difficult conditions created by humidity, heavy spring rains, and inadequate supplies. Complaints and contention grew as camp members suffered, prompting Joseph to warn of a scourge if they did not humble themselves.

The well-armed group attempted to conceal their identity, but news of a Latter-day Saint invasion force caused the citizens of Jackson County to prepare for hostilities. Aware of this reality and fearing a civil war in Jackson County, Governor Dunklin of Missouri withdrew the promised militia support. Zion's Camp would have to face its enemies without government support. In anticipation of the coming conflict, a band of approximately 300 men gathered at **Fishing River**, across from the encamped Mormons, in nearby Clay County to prevent the Latter-day Saints from entering Jackson County. A violent storm arose and scattered the mob, preventing a confrontation. The next day the Prophet Joseph Smith received a revelation (D&C 105) disbanding Zion's Camp and explaining that the Saints had to wait and prepare before returning to

Jackson County. The Lord informed Zion's Camp that the effort had been for a trial of their faith. In fulfillment of the warning pronounced earlier in the march, a scourge of cholera then struck the camp, leaving at least 13 dead (Backman 194).

The chastening process proved difficult as members of the camp faced the consequences of their own failings. The Prophet Joseph placed the experience in perspective: "God did not want you to fight. He could not organize his kingdom with twelve men to open the gospel door to the nations of the earth . . . unless he took them from a body of men who had offered their lives, and who had made as great a sacrifice as did Abraham" (Smith, 2:182n). In February of 1835, nine of the original **apostles** and all of the **seventies** were veterans of Zion's Camp. While the camp failed to achieve its original objective, the experience prepared the Church leaders who would direct the great western Latter-day Saint exodus of 1847.

SOURCES

Allen, James B., and Glen M. Leonard. *The Story of the Latter-day Saints.* 2d ed. Salt Lake City: Deseret Book, 1992.

Backman, Milton V. *The Heavens Resound: A History of the Latter-day Saints in Ohio 1830–1838.* Salt Lake City: Deseret Book, 1983.

Church Educational System. *Church History in the Fulness of Times.* Salt Lake City: The Church of Jesus Christ of Latter-day Saints, 1989.

Smith, Joseph. *History of The Church of Jesus Christ of Latter-day Saints.* Edited by B. H. Roberts. 2d ed. rev. 7 vols. Salt Lake City: The Church of Jesus Christ of Latter-day Saints, 1932–51.

JOHN M. BECK AND DENNIS A. WRIGHT

ZION'S CENTRAL BOARD OF TRADE. See UNITED ORDER.

ZION'S COOPERATIVE MERCANTILE INSTITUTION. See ZCMI.

ZION'S PRINTING AND PUBLISHING COMPANY.

Owned and operated by the LDS Church for almost half a century, **Zion's** Printing and Publishing Company was established at **Independence, Missouri**, on 18 October 1907. Its purpose was to print literature, including the periodical *Liahona the Elders' Journal,* for all the missions of North **America**. In 1915 the Church constructed its own building to house the printing plant, and after 1916 all the editors of the *Liahona* became employees of the company. During its 44-year history, Zion's printed millions of tracts, pamphlets and books, including missionary editions of the **Book of Mormon**. The Church discontinued the company in 1951, and many of its functions were taken over by the **Deseret News** Press in **Salt Lake City**.

SOURCES

Garr, Arnold K. "A History of *Liahona the Elders' Journal,* a Magazine Published for the Mormon Missions of America, 1903–1945." Ph.D. diss., Brigham Young University, 1986. 81–82, 102.

Roberts, B. H. *A Comprehensive History of The Church of Jesus Christ of Latter-day Saints, Century One.* 6 vols. Salt Lake City: The Church of Jesus Christ of Latter-day Saints, 1930. 6:431.

ARNOLD K. GARR

ZION'S SECURITIES CORPORATION. See BUSINESSES.

CHRONOLOGY

1801   *1 June*—**Brigham Young** born in Whitingham, **Vermont.**

1805   *23 December*—**Joseph Smith Jr.** born in **Sharon, Vermont.**

1807   *1 March*—**Wilford Woodruff** born in Farmington (now Avon), **Connecticut.**

1808   *1 November*—**John Taylor** born in Milnthorpe, **England.**

1814   *3 April*—**Lorenzo Snow** born in Mantua, **Ohio.**

1820   *Early spring*—**First Vision.**

1823   *21–22 September*—**Moroni** visited **Joseph Smith** and showed him **gold plates** buried in **Hill Cumorah.**

1827   *18 January*—**Joseph Smith** married **Emma Hale** in **South Bainbridge, New York.**

        22 September—**Moroni** gave the **gold plates** to **Joseph Smith.**

1828   *February*—**Martin Harris** showed **Book of Mormon** characters to **Charles Anthon** and **Samuel L. Mitchill.**

        June–July—**Martin Harris** lost 116 pages of **Book of Mormon** manuscript.

1829   *7 April*—**Joseph Smith** resumed translation of the **Book of Mormon** with **Oliver Cowdery** as scribe.

        15 May—**John the Baptist** bestowed the **Aaronic Priesthood** on **Joseph Smith** and **Oliver Cowdery** in **Harmony, Pennsylvania.**

        May or June—**Peter, James, and John** conferred the Melchizedek Priesthood upon Joseph Smith and Oliver Cowdery.

        June—Translation of the **Book of Mormon** completed; **witnesses** saw the **gold plates.**

        11 June—Copyright secured for the **Book of Mormon.**

        August—Printing of the **Book of Mormon** began in the **Grandin Printing Shop, Palmyra, New York.**

1830   *26 March*—**Book of Mormon** published in **Palmyra, New York.**

        April–June—**Samuel Smith** went on early **missions** in Western New York.

        6 April—**Organization of the Church** at **Whitmer Farm** in **Fayette, New York.**

        June—**Book of Moses,** chapter 1, revealed to **Joseph Smith** in **Harmony, Pennsylvania.**

        9 June—First **conference** held at **Whitmer Farm; Articles and Covenants** accepted (D&C 20; 22).

September–October—**Missionaries** called to **Lamanite mission.**

October–November—About 130 individuals converted in **Kirtland, Ohio,** and vicinity.

December—**Sidney Rigdon** appointed as scribe for the **New Translation** of the **Bible** (D&C 35:20).

1831   *January–May*—Members from **New York branches** moved to **Ohio.**

1 February—**Joseph Smith** arrived at the Newel K. **Whitney Store** in **Kirtland, Ohio.**

4 February—**Edward Partridge** became first **bishop.**

9 February—**Joseph Smith** received "the law of the Church," including the **law of consecration** (D&C 42).

Spring— **Parley P. Pratt, Leman Copley,** and **Sidney Rigdon** visited **Shakers** near **Cleveland, Ohio.**

3–6 June—First **high priests** ordained.

20 July—Site revealed to **Joseph Smith** for center of **Zion** in **Independence, Missouri** (D&C 57).

2 August—**Zion** dedicated by **Sidney Rigdon.**

3 August—**Joseph Smith** dedicated the **temple** site at **Independence, Missouri.**

1–2 November—Decision made at conference in **Hiram, Ohio,** to print **Book of Commandments.**

1832   *25 January*—**Joseph Smith** sustained as president of the high priesthood, in **Amherst, Ohio.**

16 February—**Joseph Smith** and **Sidney Rigdon** received **vision of the three degrees of glory** (D&C 76), in **Hiram, Ohio.**

24 March—**Joseph Smith** and **Sidney Rigdon** beaten and tarred and feathered at John **Johnson Farm** in **Hiram, Ohio.**

1 June—*The Evening and the Morning Star* began publication at **Independence, Missouri.**

25 December—**Joseph Smith** received the **prophecy on war** (D&C 87).

1833   *22 January*—**School of the Prophets** organized in **Whitney Store** at **Kirtland, Ohio.**

27 February—**Word of Wisdom** revealed (D&C 89).

18 March—**First Presidency** organized with **Sidney Rigdon** and **Frederick G. Williams** (replacing **Jesse Gause**) as counselors to **Joseph Smith.**

2 July—First draft of **Joseph Smith Translation of the Bible** completed.

20 July—**Independence, Missouri, Printing Office** destroyed; **Edward Partridge** tarred and feathered by mob.

23 July—**Kirtland Temple** cornerstones laid; **Saints** made treaty with mob, agreeing to leave **Jackson County, Missouri.**

Late summer—**School of the Elders** organized by **Parley P. Pratt** in **Jackson County, Missouri.**

7 November—**Saints** driven from **Jackson County, Missouri**.

18 December—**Joseph Smith Sr.** became first **patriarch** to the Church.

1834   *17 February*—First **stake** and **high council** organized in **Kirtland, Ohio**.

3 May—Church adopted the designation "Latter-day Saints" (see **Church, Names of**).

8 May—**Zion's Camp** began its march from **Ohio** to **Missouri**.

October—*Messenger and Advocate* began publication in **Kirtland, Ohio**.

November—**School of the Elders** organized in **Kirtland**.

5 December—**Oliver Cowdery** named **assistant president** of the Church in **Kirtland, Ohio**.

1835   *14 February*—**Quorum** of the Twelve **Apostles** organized at **Kirtland**.

28 February—Original **Quorum** of **Seventy** organized.

28 March—**Revelation** on **priesthood** received (D&C 107).

6 July—Church members purchased **Egyptian** mummies and **papyri** from **Michael Chandler**.

17 August—**Doctrine and Covenants** accepted by the **Saints** as a **standard work**.

Fall—**Emma Smith** compiled **hymns** for publication.

1836   *27 March*—**Kirtland Temple** dedicated (D&C 109).

3 April—**Jesus Christ, Moses, Elias**, and **Elijah** appeared to **Joseph Smith** and **Oliver Cowdery** in the **Kirtland Temple** (D&C 110).

9 May—**John Taylor** and wife, Lenora, baptized near Toronto, **Canada**.

29 June—Group of citizens at Liberty, Missouri, passed a resolution to expel the **Saints** from **Clay County**.

2 November—Articles of agreement drawn up for **Kirtland Safety Society**.

1837   *2 January*—**Kirtland Safety Society** antibanking company formed.

13 June—**Heber C. Kimball** and others left **Ohio** for **England**, the first **missionary** effort to extend beyond North **America**.

30 July—First converts baptized in Great Britain.

October—*Elder's Journal* began publication in **Kirtland, Ohio**.

December—**Martin Harris** excommunicated.

1838   *12 January*—**Joseph Smith** fled persecution in **Kirtland, Ohio**.

14 March—**Far West, Missouri**, established as new Church headquarters.

12 April—**Oliver Cowdery** excommunicated.

13 April—**David Whitmer** excommunicated.

26 April—**Name of the Church** specified as "The Church of **Jesus Christ** of Latter-day **Saints**" (D&C 115:4).

19 May—**Adam-ondi-Ahman** selected for settlement in **Daviess County, Missouri**.

4 July—**Far West** Temple cornerstones laid.

6 July—Exodus of most **Saints** from **Kirtland, Ohio.**

8 July—**Joseph Smith** received **revelation** on **tithing** (D&C 119).

6 August—**Gallatin Election Day** fight.

25 October—**Battle** of **Crooked River; David W. Patten** killed.

27 October—**Lilburn W. Boggs** issued **extermination order,** driving the **Saints** from **Missouri.**

30 October—**Haun's Mill Massacre.**

31 October—**Joseph Smith** and other leaders arrested by **Missouri** State Militia.

9 November—**Joseph Smith** and others imprisoned in **Richmond, Ray County, Missouri.**

13 November—**Joseph F. Smith** born in **Far West, Missouri.**

1 December—**Joseph Smith** and others moved to **Liberty Jail.**

1839   *Winter–Spring*—Most **Saints** fled from **Missouri.**

February—Exiled **Saints** arriving in **Quincy, Illinois,** assisted by local citizens.

20–25 March—**Joseph Smith** wrote epistle to **Saints** from **Liberty Jail** (D&C 121–23).

April—**Saints** decided to settle at **Commerce** (later **Nauvoo**), **Illinois,** and soon began purchasing land.

26 April—**Apostles** gathered at **Far West** temple site in fulfillment of commandment respecting overseas mission (D&C 118).

29 October–4 March—**Joseph Smith** went to **Washington, D.C.,** with **redress petitions.**

November—***Times and Seasons*** began publication in **Nauvoo.**

1840   *27 May*—***Millennial Star,*** first LDS **periodical** produced outside North **America** began publication in **Manchester, England,** with **Parley P. Pratt** as editor.

15 August—**Baptism for the dead** announced in **Nauvoo.**

14 September—**Patriarch Joseph Smith Sr.** died.

16 December—**Nauvoo Charter** signed by **Illinois** governor Thomas Carlin.

1841   *19 January*—**Joseph Smith** received **revelation** to build **Nauvoo Temple** and **Nauvoo House; Hyrum Smith** called as **assistant president of the Church** and to succeed his father as **patriarch** (D&C 124).

February—First **wards** organized at **Nauvoo.**

24 October—**Holy Land** dedicated by **Orson Hyde.**

1842   *1 March*—First segment of the **book of Abraham** and **Wentworth letter,** including the **Articles of Faith,** published in *Times and Seasons.*

17 March—Female **Relief Society** of **Nauvoo** organized.

4 May—First full **endowments** given on second floor of the **Prophet's Red Brick Store,** in **Nauvoo.**

6 August—Rocky Mountain prophecy given by Joseph Smith.

10 October—Lorenzo Snow presented copies of the Book of Mormon to Queen Victoria of England.

1843   *May*—Missionaries called to first non-English-speaking mission in the Church, island of Tubuai (now in French Polynesia).

12 July—Revelation on celestial marriage (including plural marriage) recorded (D&C 132).

1844   *29 January*—Presidential campaign of Joseph Smith began.

11 March—Council of Fifty organized.

7 April—King Follett Discourse given by Joseph Smith.

7 June—Only issue of *Nauvoo Expositor* published; three days later the press was declared a nuisance and destroyed by the Nauvoo City Council.

27 June—Joseph and Hyrum Smith killed at Carthage Jail.

8 August—Leadership of the Church under the Twelve Apostles approved by the majority of the Saints in Nauvoo.

1845   *January*—Nauvoo Charter repealed by Illinois legislature.

6 April—Apostles issued proclamation to all the world.

3 May—*Nauvoo Neighbor* began publication.

10 December–7 February 1846—Saints completed more than 5,000 endowments in the Nauvoo Temple.

1846   *4 February*—Saints began their evacuation from Nauvoo; other Saints left New York City for California on ship *Brooklyn,* under the leadership of Samuel Brannan.

24 April—Saints encamped at Garden Grove, Iowa.

30 April—Nauvoo Temple privately dedicated by Orson Hyde.

14 June—Saints encamped at Council Bluffs.

July—Thomas Kane visited the Saints on the Missouri River; U.S. Army enlisted approximately 500 volunteers for the Mormon Battalion.

31 July—Ship *Brooklyn* arrived in San Francisco bay.

13 August—Mormon Battalion began its 2,000-mile march from Fort Leavenworth to San Diego, California.

10–17 September—Battle of Nauvoo.

23 September—Saints encamped at Winter Quarters.

1847   *14 January*—Brigham Young received revelation regarding organization of Saints for journey west (D&C 136).

29 January—Mormon Battalion completed trek at San Diego, California.

5 April—Pioneer trek began with first company leaving Winter Quarters under the direction of Brigham Young.

16 July—Mormon Battalion disbanded at Los Angeles.

21–24 July—First pioneers arrived in the Salt Lake Valley.

28 July—Site selected for the Salt Lake Temple.

27 *December*—Brigham Young, Heber C. Kimball, and Willard Richards sustained as new First Presidency at Kanesville, Iowa.

1848 *24 January*—Saints at Sutter's Mill in California when gold was discovered.

May–June—Miracle of the seagulls in Salt Lake Valley.

9 October—Arsonists burned Nauvoo Temple.

November—Oliver Cowdery rebaptized near Kanesville/Council Bluffs, Iowa.

1849 *March*—Icarians settled in Nauvoo, Illinois.

5 March—Provisional state of Deseret created.

October—Perpetual Emigrating Fund Company established.

9 December—First Sunday School organized in Rocky Mountains by Richard Ballantyne.

1850 *28 February*—University of Deseret (later University of Utah) founded.

3 March—Oliver Cowdery died in Richmond, Missouri.

15 June—*Deseret News* began publication in Salt Lake City.

9 September—Territory of Utah created by Congress; Brigham Young appointed governor 11 days later.

1851 *June*—Saints settled San Bernardino, California.

11 July—Franklin D. Richards published pamphlet entitled *The Pearl of Great Price* in Liverpool, England.

1 November—First issue of *Journal of Discourses* published in Liverpool, England.

8 November—Parley P. Pratt, the first missionary to South America, arrived in Chile.

1852 *8 April*—Preparation of Deseret Alphabet begun.

28–29 August—Plural marriage publicly announced at special conference, in which 106 missionaries were called to carry the gospel to various parts of the world.

1853 *6 April*—Cornerstones laid for Salt Lake Temple.

July—Walker War began.

1855 *5 May*—Endowment House dedicated in Salt Lake City.

1856 *26 September*—First handcart company arrived in the Salt Lake Valley.

October–November—Willie and Martin Handcart Companies rescued from early winter storms in Wyoming; more than 200 had died.

22 November—Heber J. Grant born in Salt Lake City.

1856– Mormon Reformation.
1857

1857 *13 May*—Parley P. Pratt murdered in Arkansas.

28 May—U.S. President James Buchanan sent 2,500 troops to Utah under Albert Sidney Johnston, beginning the Utah War.

24 July—**Brigham Young** informed of oncoming **Johnston's Army**.

5 August–15 September—**Brigham Young** declared martial law for **Utah** Territory and forbade **Johnston's Army** to enter the **Salt Lake Valley**.

11 September—**Mountain Meadows Massacre**.

October—Mormon raiding parties in **Wyoming** slowed progress of **Johnston's Army**.

1858   *May*—**Saints** in northern **Utah** evacuated their settlements in response to army's approach.

11 June—Peaceful resolution to **Utah War**, largely due to negotiating of **Thomas L. Kane**.

26 June—**Johnston's Army** passed through **Salt Lake City** en route to Cedar Valley.

July—**Saints** returned to their homes.

1859   *10–17 July*—**Horace Greeley** interviewed **Brigham Young** during visit to **Salt Lake City**.

1860   *3 April*—First **Pony Express** rider reached **Salt Lake City**.

24 September—Last **handcart** company arrived in **Salt Lake City**.

1861   *23 April*—First wagon trains sent from **Salt Lake Valley** with supplies to help bring immigrating **Saints** to Utah.

18 October—**Telegraph** line reached **Salt Lake City**.

1862   *6 March*—**Salt Lake Theatre** dedicated.

8 July—U.S. president **Abraham Lincoln** signed the **Morrill Act**, the first federal **anti-polygamy legislation**.

1864   *26 July*—Cornerstone laid for **Salt Lake Tabernacle**.

1865   *9 April*—Beginning of four-year **Black Hawk War**.

1866   *1 January*—*Juvenile Instructor* began publication.

1867   *6 October*—First **general conference** in the new **Tabernacle**.

8 December—**Relief Society** reestablished with **Eliza R. Snow** as president.

1868   *25 September*—Last wagon train of **pioneers** entered the **Salt Lake Valley**.

1869   *1 March*—**ZCMI** opened for business.

10 May—Transcontinental **Railroad** completed at Promontory Point, **Utah**.

25 June—First **Saints** to immigrate completely by **railroad** from the East arrived in the **Salt Lake Valley**.

28 November—**Young Women** program initiated under the title Young Ladies' Retrenchment Association.

December—**Godbeite** movement began.

1870   *1 January*—First issue of *Mormon Tribune* (later the *Salt Lake Tribune*).

February—**Liberal Party** organized, which represented **anti-Mormon** interests in **Utah** Territory; it was opposed by the **People's Party**, representing the Church's point of view.

12 February—**Woman suffrage** granted by **Utah** Territorial legislature.

4 April—**George Albert Smith** born in **Salt Lake City**.

30 August—**Martin Harris** arrived in **Salt Lake City** and testified at **general conference**.

1872   *2 January–25 April*—**Brigham Young** placed under house arrest for bigamy; never brought to trial.

June—*Woman's Exponent* began publication.

1873   *8 September*—**David O. McKay** born in Huntsville, **Utah**.

1874   *Winter*—**United orders** inaugurated.

23 June—**Poland Act** became law, forcing **Mormon** polygamists to be tried by federal courts.

1875   *10 June*—**Young Men's Mutual Improvement Association** organized.

10 July—**Martin Harris** died in Clarkston, **Utah**.

9 October—**Salt Lake Tabernacle** dedicated.

16 October—**Brigham Young Academy** founded in **Provo, Utah**.

1876   New edition of **Doctrine and Covenants** prepared under **Orson Pratt's** direction with 24 new sections.

14 July—**Sidney Rigdon** died at Friendship, New York.

19 July—**Joseph Fielding Smith** born in **Salt Lake City**.

1877   *23 March*—**John D. Lee** executed for his participation in **Mountain Meadows Massacre**.

6 April—Dedication of **St. George Temple**.

11 July—**First Presidency** circular letter outlined Church organization.

29 August—**Brigham Young** died.

4 September—**Twelve Apostles** sustained as leaders of the Church under **John Taylor**.

1878   *25 August*—**Primary** organized.

1879   *6 January*—U.S. Supreme Court upheld the constitutionality of **antipolygamy legislation** in the **George Reynolds** case.

4 October—The *Contributor* began publication.

1880   *6 April*—Year of **Jubilee** declared.

10 October—**First Presidency** reorganized with **John Taylor** as president; **Pearl of Great Price** accepted by the **Saints** as a **standard work**.

1882   *8 January*—**Assembly Hall** on **Temple Square** dedicated.

22 March—**Edmunds Act** signed into law.

17 July—**Deseret Hospital** opened by the **Relief Society**.

1883   *14 April*—**John Taylor** received **revelation** on the **seventies**.

1884   *17 May*—**Logan Temple** dedicated.

1885	*1 February*—After delivering his last speech in the **Tabernacle, John Taylor** went into hiding because of **antipolygamy movement**.
	3 February—**Idaho test oath** prohibited **Mormons** from voting.
1887	*3 March*—**Edmunds-Tucker Act** became law without signature of **Grover Cleveland**.
	25 July—**John Taylor** died in hiding; **Twelve Apostles** lead the Church for nearly two years.
	30 July—Federal government disenfranchised the Church, and confiscated Church property.
	November—The Church began renting **Temple Square** and other confiscated property from the government.
1888	*25 January*—**David Whitmer**, the last of the Three **Witnesses**, died in Richmond, Missouri.
	17 May—**Manti Temple** dedicated in a private session. It was publicly dedicated 21–23 May.
1889	*6 April*—First **Relief Society** conference.
	7 April—**Wilford Woodruff** sustained as president of the Church.
	October—*Young Woman's Journal* began publication.
	November—**Endowment House** razed.
1890	*6 October*—The **Saints** sustained President Wilford Woodruff's **Manifesto** stopping the performance of new **plural marriages**.
1891	*March*—**Relief Society** became a charter organization of the National Council of Women.
1893	*4 January*—U.S. president **Benjamin Harrison** granted amnesty to polygamists.
	6 April—Dedication of **Salt Lake Temple**.
	8 September—**Tabernacle Choir** performed at Chicago **World's Fair**.
1894	*April*—"**Law of adoption**" ended.
	13 November—**Genealogical Society of Utah** organized.
1895	*28 March*—**Spencer W. Kimball** born in **Salt Lake City**.
1896	*4 January*—**Utah** became a state.
	6 April—**Political manifesto** issued publicly.
	5 November—**Fast day** changed from first Thursday to first Sunday of the month.
1897	*November*—*Improvement Era* began publication.
1898	*2 September*—**Wilford Woodruff** died.
	13 September—**Lorenzo Snow** ordained and set apart as president of the Church.
	April—**Conference Reports** began regular twice-yearly publication.
1899	*Articles of Faith,* by **James E. Talmage**, published.
	28 March—**Harold B. Lee** born in Clifton, **Idaho**.

17 *May*—**Lorenzo Snow** received **revelation** on **tithing** in St. George, **Utah.**

4 *August*—**Ezra Taft Benson** born in Whitney, **Idaho.**

1900   25 *January*—U.S. House of Representatives denied **B. H. Roberts** his seat.

1901   12 *August*—**Apostle Heber J. Grant** dedicated **Japan** for the preaching of the gospel.

10 *October*—**Lorenzo Snow** died.

17 *October*—**Joseph F. Smith** ordained and set apart as president of the Church.

1902   First volume of *History of the Church,* edited by **B. H. Roberts,** published; new edition of **Pearl of Great Price** prepared under the direction of **James E. Talmage.**

January—*Children's Friend* first published.

4 *August*—Bureau of Information opened on **Temple Square.**

1903   15 *October*—Brigham Young **Academy** became **Brigham Young University.**

5 *November*—Church purchased **Carthage Jail.**

1904   *March*—Hearings opened in U.S. Senate concerning **Reed Smoot's** right to hold the seat to which he had been elected (see **Smoot Case**).

5 *April*—**Second Manifesto** on plural marriage issued by **Joseph F. Smith.**

April 14—Church repurchased 25 acres of the land originally bought in 1831 at **Independence, Missouri.**

1905   1 *January*—**Dr. William H. Groves's** Latter-day Saint **Hospital** opened.

28 *October*—**Apostles John W. Taylor** and **Matthias F. Cowley** resigned from the **Quorum** of Twelve on disagreement over **plural marriage.**

23 *December*—Church dedicated **Joseph Smith** memorial cottage and monument in **Vermont.**

1906   **Sunday School** initiated first class for adults.

Summer—**Joseph F. Smith** became first Church president to visit **Europe.**

1907   Church established **Zions Printing and Publishing Company** in **Independence, Missouri.**

10 *January*—**Joseph F. Smith** announced that the Church was finally out of debt after financial problems stemming from **antipolygamy movement.**

February—**Reed Smoot** retained his seat in the Senate after lengthy hearings of the **Smoot Case.**

June—**George Albert Smith** purchased 100-acre Smith Farm in **Manchester, New York,** for the Church.

14 *November*—**Howard W. Hunter** born in Boise, **Idaho.**

7 *December*—**Charles W. Nibley** became **presiding bishop** and began implementing several financial changes, including a shift to an all-cash policy in collecting **tithing.**

1908   *8 April*—General **Priesthood** Committee created; it specified ages for ordination to **priesthood** offices.

1909   Weekly **ward priesthood** meetings inaugurated.

Church acquired property at **Far West, Missouri.**

November—**First Presidency proclamation** entitled "Origin of Man" published in the *Improvement Era.*

1910   *January*—*Utah Genealogical and Historical Magazine* began publication.

23 June—**Gordon B. Hinckley** born in **Salt Lake City.**

1911   Church opened **Hotel Utah.**

Church adopted **Boy Scout** program.

15 April—*Collier's* magazine published a letter from U.S. president **Theodore Roosevelt** refuting false charges made against the Church.

26 October—First **stake missionaries** called in Granite **Utah Stake.**

1912   Exodus from **Mexican colonies** during Mexican revolution.

James E. Talmage published *The House of the Lord.*

Fall—First **seminary** opened at Granite High School, **Salt Lake City.**

8 November—**Correlation Committee,** headed by **David O. McKay,** was established by **First Presidency** to prevent duplication in auxiliary programs.

1913   Church established Maori Agricultural College in **New Zealand.**

1915   *January*—*Relief Society Magazine* began publication.

September—**James E. Talmage** published *Jesus the Christ.*

1916   *30 June*—**Official declaration** of the First Presidency issued on the identities of **God** and **Jesus,** titled "The Father and the Son."

1917   *6 April*—United States entered **World War I,** which began in 1914.

2 October—Church Administration Building completed.

1918   *May*—**Relief Society** sold stored wheat to the U.S. government to alleviate **war** shortages.

3 October—**Joseph F. Smith** received **vision of the redemption of the dead** (D&C 138).

11 November—Armistice ended **World War I.**

19 November—**Joseph F. Smith** died.

23 November—**Heber J. Grant** ordained and set apart as president of the Church.

1919   Church membership reached half a million (see **Growth**).

27 November—**Heber J. Grant** dedicated **Hawaii** Temple.

1920   Church decided to close its **academies.**

1921   *Essentials in Church History,* by **Joseph Fielding Smith,** published.

M-Men and **Gleaner** programs established for young adults.

24 December—**David O.** McKay concludes 56,000-mile tour of the **missions** of the world.

1922   *May*—**Primary Children's Hospital** opened.

6 May—First use of the radio for Church purposes with **broadcast** of message by **Heber J. Grant.**

1923   Church purchased part of the **Hill Cumorah.**

26 August—**Cardston Alberta Temple** dedicated.

1924   Church purchased radio station KZN and changed call letters to **KSL;** in October **general conference** broadcast by **radio** for first time.

1925   **Missionary Home** opened in **Salt Lake City.**

25 December—**South America** dedicated for **missionary** work by **Melvin J. Ballard.**

1926   *Fall*—First **institute** of religion initiated at University of **Idaho.**

25 September—Peter **Whitmer Farm** in **Fayette, New York,** acquired by the Church.

1927   *23 October*—**Arizona** Temple at Mesa dedicated.

1928   Large portion of the **Hill Cumorah** purchased by the Church.

100th **stake** organized at Lehi, **Utah.**

Adult **Sunday School** class named Gospel Doctrine.

1929   *15 July*—**Tabernacle Choir** began weekly network **broadcasting.**

24 July—**Czechoslovakia** Mission opened, the first in Eastern **Europe.**

29 October—Stock Market crash precipitated **great depression.**

1930   *6 April*—Church celebrated centennial; B. H. Roberts's *Comprehensive History of the Church* officially published for this occasion.

1931   All Church junior colleges, except **Ricks,** transferred to states.

6 April—*Church News* introduced by *Deseret News.*

1932   *2 April*—Church began reemphasis on living the **Word of Wisdom,** launching a campaign against the use of tobacco.

1933   *1 June*—Church opened a large exhibit at the Chicago **World's Fair.**

26 July—First **historic marker** in **Nauvoo, Illinois,** placed by the **Relief Society.**

Fall—Program launched to reactivate men later designated as **prospective elders.**

1935   Church had its own exhibit building at the **California**–Pacific International Exposition.

20 April—**Harold B. Lee** appointed to formulate **Welfare Program.**

21 July—**Hill Cumorah** Monument dedicated by **Heber J. Grant.**

22 August—**Gordon B. Hinckley** appointed executive secretary of newly formed **Radio, Publicity, and Mission Literature Committee.**

1936   *April*—Supervision of **stake missions** given to the First Council of the Seventy, and missions were soon organized in every stake.

7 April—**Welfare Program** introduced under the title Church Security Program.

20 September—**Winter Quarters Monument** dedicated at **Florence, Nebraska.**

1937   **J. Reuben Clark Jr.** challenged **Saints** to store a **year's supply** of food, clothing, and, where possible, fuel.

Missionary Handbook first published.

Church purchased 88 acres of the **Martin Harris Farm.**

January—**Aaronic Priesthood** ages set at deacon, 12; teacher, 15; priest, 17.

20 February—**Wilford Wood** purchased a portion of the **Nauvoo Temple** lot for the Church.

July—First **Hill Cumorah Pageant** performed.

1938   Church Security Program renamed **Welfare Program.**

General Church Board of Education formed, composed of **general authorities,** to replace local boards.

8 August—**J. Reuben Clark Jr.** delivered address entitled "The Charted Course of the Church in Education."

14 August—First **Deseret Industries** opened.

November—**Nauvoo Temple** sealing records became first genealogical records microfilmed by the Church.

1939   Smaller-scale **Tabernacle** opened as Church pavilion at **San Francisco World's Fair.**

19 June—**Liberty Jail** purchased for the Church by **Wilford Wood.**

24 August—**First Presidency** began evacuating missionaries from **Europe.**

1 September—**World War II** began with German invasion of **Poland.**

1940   **Missionaries** evacuated from the **South Pacific.**

1941   Membership records centralized in **presiding bishop's** office.

10 millionth **endowment** performed for the dead.

6 April—First **Assistants to the Twelve** called.

May—**Hugh B. Brown** appointed as the LDS **Servicemen's** Coordinator.

7 December—Attack on Pearl Harbor brought United States into **World War II.**

1942   *October*—LDS **Servicemen's** Committee organized with **Harold B. Lee** as chair.

1944   *July*—Church Committee on Publications organized with **Joseph Fielding Smith** as chair.

November—**Genealogical Society of Utah** changed its name to Genealogical Society of the Church of Jesus Christ of Latter-day Saints.

1945   *14 May*—**Heber J. Grant** died.

21 May—**George Albert Smith** ordained and set apart as eighth president of the Church.

14 August—Japanese surrender ended **World War II.**

September—Church began calling new **mission presidents** and reopening **missions** closed during **World War II.**

23 September—**Idaho Falls Temple** dedicated by **George Albert Smith.**

3 November—**George Albert Smith** met with U.S. president Harry S Truman to discuss shipment of Church welfare supplies to **Europe.**

1946   Missionary work resumed in **South Pacific** under the direction of **Matthew Cowley.**

January—Church began shipping supplies to **Europe** to relieve suffering.

4 February—**Ezra Taft Benson** began his postwar tour of **Europe,** reopening the area for **missionary work.**

May—**George Albert Smith** visited **Mexico** and helped reunify disaffected Church members.

1947   Church membership reached one million (see **Growth**).

24 July—**This Is the Place Monument** dedicated during **pioneer centennial.**

1949   *October*—First time **general conference** publicly **broadcast** on television.

1950   **Indian Student placement** program implemented.

LeGrand Richards's book *A Marvelous Work and a Wonder* published.

September—Early-morning **seminary** inaugurated in southern **California.**

1951   *4 April*—**George Albert Smith** died.

9 April—**David O. McKay** sustained as president of the Church.

20 July—**Seventies** and many married men were asked to serve **missions** because of missionary shortages during the **Korean War.**

1952   Church published first official proselyting outline for **missionaries.**

2 March—New **Primary Children's Hospital** dedicated.

5 April—**Priesthood** session of **general conference** first carried to buildings outside of **Temple Square** (by direct telephone wire).

25 November—**Ezra Taft Benson** appointed U.S. Secretary of Agriculture (served 1953–61).

31 December—**Primary** program incorporated Cub scouts.

1953   *25 March*—Church announced that **missionaries** would now report their missions to **stake presidencies,** not to **general authorities.**

1954   *31 August*—Ages for advancement in the **Aaronic Priesthood** set at deacon, 12; teacher, 14; priest, 16.

1955   *11 September*—**Swiss Temple** became first in Europe; films introduced to provide the **endowment** in various languages.

26 September—Church College of Hawaii (later **Brigham Young University–Hawaii Campus**) opened.

1956   *8 January*—First student **wards** and **stakes** at **Brigham Young University**.

        3 October—**Relief Society** Building dedicated.

1957   *April*—Videotape first used to record and rebroadcast **general conference**.

        October—**General conference** canceled because of flu epidemic.

1958   *18 May*—**New Zealand Stake**, in Auckland, became the first outside North **America** and **Hawaii**.

        20 May—**New Zealand Temple**, the first in southern hemisphere, dedicated **by David O. McKay**.

1960   *27 March*—First **stake** in Europe organized at **Manchester, England**.

1961   First use of computers to provide names for **temple** ordinances.

        12 March—**Netherlands Stake** in The Hague became the first non-English-speaking stake in the Church.

        26 June–5 July—Uniform system for teaching investigators introduced as the Church's standard teaching plan at **mission presidents'** conference in **Salt Lake City**.

        30 September—Priesthood **Correlation** program instituted.

        3 December—First Spanish-speaking **stake** established in Mexico City.

        4 December—Missionary Language Institute opened at **Brigham Young University** in **Provo, Utah**, with Ernest J. Wilkins serving as director (see **Missionary Training Centers**).

1962   *March*—Age for male **missionaries** lowered from 20 to 19.

        23 July—**Tabernacle Choir** participated in its first **satellite** broadcast.

        27 July—**Nauvoo Restoration, Inc.**, founded.

        10 October—Church purchased short-wave **radio** station WRUL and began **broadcasting** to countries outside the United States.

1963   Missionary Language Institute changed to Language Training Mission (see **Missionary Training Centers**).

        Church membership reached 2 million (see **Growth**).

        12 October—**Polynesian Cultural Center** dedicated in **Laie, Hawaii**.

        December—Construction of **Granite Mountain Record Vault** completed.

1964   *January*—**Ward priesthood** executive committees and **correlation** councils are formed; **home teaching** program replaced **ward** teaching.

        April—Church hosted a pavilion at **New York World's Fair**.

        16 November—**Oakland Temple** dedicated.

1965   *January*—**Family home evening** program initiated.

        February—Government of **Italy** allowed **missionaries** to proselyte after the mission had been closed since 1862.

1966   Home-study program initiated for **seminary** students.

        1 May—First **stake** in **South America** organized at **São Paulo, Brazil**.

        August—New **Visitors Center** opened on **Temple Square**.

1967   Church **auxiliaries** unified calendars and age groupings.

29 September—First **regional representatives** called.

November—Church received a portion of the **book of Abraham** papyrus from the **New York** Metropolitan Museum of Art.

1968　　**Belle Spafford**, president of the **Relief Society**, was elected president of the National Council of **Women**.

1969　　*3 January*—**First Presidency** announced that all non-English-speaking **missionaries** would receive two months' language training before entering the field.

3–8 August—World Conference on Records hosted in **Salt Lake City**.

1970　　Monday nights designated for **family home evening**.

18 January—**David O. McKay** died; 500th **stake** organized in Fallon, **Nevada**.

23 January—**Joseph Fielding Smith** ordained and set apart as tenth president of the Church.

15 March—First **stake** in **Asia** organized at Tokyo, Japan.

22 March—First **stake** in **Africa** organized at Transvaal, **South Africa**.

1971　　*January*—Church **periodicals** consolidated into the *Ensign, New Era,* and *Friend.*

July—Health **missionary** program began; it was later expanded to **Welfare Services missionary** program.

27–29 August—First **area conference** held in **Manchester, England**.

November—All LDS women automatically enrolled in the **Relief Society**; payment of dues discontinued.

1972　　**Public Communications Department** organized.

14 January—**Church Historian's Office** became Church **Historical Department**.

2 July—**Joseph Fielding Smith** died.

7 July—**Harold B. Lee** ordained and set apart as 11th president of the Church.

Fall—Gospel Doctrine classes began studying **standard works** rather than prepared manuals.

4 November—New 28-story **Church Office Building** opened.

1973　　*February*—Agricultural **missionary** program began with missionaries sent to **South America**.

7 April—Welfare Services Department announced, correlating health services, social services, and the **Welfare Program**.

26 December—**Harold B. Lee** died.

30 December—**Spencer W. Kimball** ordained and set apart as 12th president of the Church.

1974　　*14 January*—**Stake** names changed to reflect headquarters city and state or country.

23 March—Church acquired **Brigham Young**'s winter home in **St. George, Utah**, and Jacob Hamblin's home in Santa Clara, **Utah**.

4 April—**Spencer W. Kimball** delivered his maxim "Lengthen your stride" at **regional representatives** seminar.

20 June—**Mission** names changed to reflect headquarters city and state or country.

23 June—**Aaronic Priesthood** MIA changed to **Aaronic Priesthood** and **Young Women**.

1 September—Church College of **Hawaii** renamed **Brigham Young University–Hawaii Campus**.

6 September—Church announced divestiture of its 15 **hospitals**; actual transfer took place the following March.

3 October—**Seventies** quorums and **stake mission** leadership combined.

19 November—**Washington Temple** dedicated.

1975   *3 May*—**Regions** and **stakes** incorporated into **areas**; **area** supervisors announced.

27 June—Churchwide **auxiliary** conferences discontinued.

24 July—**Church Office Building** dedicated.

3 October—**Spencer W. Kimball** announced organization of First **Quorum** of the **Seventy**.

1976   *3 April*—Two **revelations** (later D&C 137 and 138) added to **Pearl of Great Price**.

25 June—**Extermination Order** of 1838 rescinded by **Missouri** governor Christopher S. Bond.

27 September—New Language Training Mission complex dedicated in **Provo, Utah** (see **Missionary Training Centers**).

1 October—**Assistants to the Twelve** and members of the First Council of the **Seventy** became members of the First **Quorum** of the Seventy.

1977   *1 January*—**General conferences** shortened from three to two days.

14 May—**Aaronic Priesthood** program adopted title **Young Men**.

22 May—Church **Activities Committee** organized.

1978   Name extraction program introduced.

31 March—Quarterly **stake conferences** became semiannual.

1 June—**Revelation** received to extend **priesthood** to all worthy males; made public on 9 June (see **Official Declaration 2**).

1 July—**Spencer W. Kimball** dedicated **Relief Society** Monument to Women at **Nauvoo, Illinois**.

9 September—All training of missionaries consolidated at new **Missionary Training Center** in **Provo, Utah**.

30 September—**Emeritus** status announced for **general authorities** over age 70.

30 October—**São Paulo Temple** dedicated.

1979   *18 February*—1,000th stake organized at **Nauvoo, Illinois,** by **Ezra Taft Benson.**

August–September—Church published a new edition of the King James Version of the **Bible** with study aids.

6 October—**Patriarch to the Church Eldred Gee Smith** granted **emeritus** status; no successor was appointed.

1980   *2 March*—Consolidated meeting plan began for **Saints** in **Canada** and the United States.

6 April—Church **sesquicentennial** commemorated with telecast from the **Whitmer Farm** and Salt Lake **Tabernacle.**

1981   Installation of extensive **satellite** system for the Church.

18 March—Formation of **Missionary, Priesthood,** and **Temple** and **Genealogy** Executive Councils.

23 July—**Gordon B. Hinckley** called as additional counselor in the **First Presidency.**

26 September—The Church published new editions of the **Book of Mormon, Doctrine and Covenants,** and **Pearl of Great Price.**

1982   Church membership passed five million (see **Growth**).

2 April—Church announced it would fund 96% of the cost of **meetinghouse** construction; 4% would continue to be drawn from local contributions.

3 October—"Another Testament of **Jesus Christ**" added to the title of the **Book of Mormon.**

30 October—Partially restored **Grandin Print Shop** in **Palmyra, New York,** opened as a **historic site** with a **visitors' center.**

1983   **Stake** welfare properties placed under general Church control.

1984   **Whitney Store** restored as **historic site** in **Kirtland, Ohio.**

April—**Personal Ancestral File** software released.

4 April—**Museum of Church History and Art** dedicated in **Salt Lake City.**

7 April—First **general authorities** called to serve with a five-year, rather than lifetime, appointment.

24 June—**Area** presidencies organized.

1985   Special fasts raised $11 million for famine victims.

29–30 June—**Freiberg Temple** dedicated in East Germany, behind the Iron Curtain.

2 August—New edition of the **hymnal** published.

23 October—Genealogical Library dedicated (see **Family History Library**).

5 November—**Spencer W. Kimball** died.

10 November—**Ezra Taft Benson** ordained and set apart as 13th president of the Church.

1986   *4 October*—**Seventies** quorums discontinued in **stakes**.

1987   Genealogy Program renamed **Family History**.

        23 January—Mark Hofmann imprisoned, responsible for two deaths and several **forgeries of historic documents**.

1988   *15 May*—First **stake** in **West Africa** organized at Aba, **Nigeria**.

        Mid-August—100 millionth **endowment** performed for the dead.

1989   *1 April*—Second **Quorum** of the **Seventy** organized.

        16 May—BYU **Jerusalem Center** dedicated by **Howard W. Hunter**.

        25 November—Church announced discontinuance of **stake** and **ward** budget assessments; budgets to be funded entirely by **tithing**.

1990   *2 April*—**FamilySearch**™ database became available at **Family History** Centers throughout the Church.

        November—Cost for funding **missionaries** equalized for all fields of labor.

1991   *Encyclopedia of Mormonism* published.

        1 May—500,000th **missionary** called.

        24 June—**Russia** granted formal recognition to the Church.

1992   **Relief Society** sponsored Gospel Literacy program.

        26 December–6 January 1993—**Tabernacle Choir** toured the **Holy Land**.

1993   **TempleReady** software released.

        25 April—**San Diego Temple** dedicated.

        27 June—**Joseph Smith Memorial Building** dedicated.

1994   *30 May*—**Ezra Taft Benson** died.

        5 June—**Howard W. Hunter** ordained and set apart as 14th president of the Church.

        11 December—2,000th **stake** of the Church organized, at **Mexico** City.

1995   *3 March*—**Howard W. Hunter** died.

        12 March—**Gordon B. Hinckley** ordained and set apart as 15th president of the Church, with **Thomas S. Monson** and **James E. Faust** as counselors.

        1 April—The position of **regional representative** discontinued; position of area authority announced (see **area authority seventy**).

        23 September—**Proclamation on the Family** first presented at General **Relief Society** Meeting.

1996   *18 January*—Church announced that **general authorities** would be withdrawn from boards of corporate **businesses**.

        28 February—More than half of 9.4 million **Saints** now lived outside the United States.

        7 April—*60 Minutes* interview of Gordon B. Hinckley by Mike Wallace telecast.

        26–27 May—**Hong Kong Temple** dedicated.

27–28 May—**Gordon B. Hinckley** became first Church president to visit mainland **China**.

9 December—Church website initiated at lds.org.

1997   *5 April*—**Area** authorities, now **area authority seventies**, grouped into Third, Fourth, and Fifth **Quorums** of the **Seventy**.

21 April–22 July—Re-creation of **pioneer trek of 1847**.

24 July—**Pioneer** sesquicentennial celebrated.

4 October—**Gordon B. Hinckley** announced the building of smaller **temples**.

November—Church membership reached 10 million.

November 2—**Vernal Utah Temple** dedicated, the first to be created from an existing building.

1998   *4 January*—**Melchizedek Priesthood** and **Relief Society** began coordinated study of the teachings of latter-day prophets.

26 March—**Grandin Print Shop** dedicated.

27 March—Replica of **Smith family** log home dedicated in **Palmyra**, New **York**.

April—**Gordon B. Hinckley** announced that 30 smaller **temples** would be built, with a goal of 100 functioning temples by the end of the year 2000.

26 April—**Gordon B. Hinckley** addressed a large gathering at Madison Square Garden in **New York City**.

26–27 July—Monticello **Utah Temple** became the first of the smaller **temples** dedicated.

8 September—**Gordon B. Hinckley** interviewed on the nationwide television show *Larry King Live*.

1999   *4 April*—Plans announced to rebuild **Nauvoo Temple**.

24 May—Church launched www.FamilySearch.com on the Internet.

2000   *Early March*—100 millionth copy of the **Book of Mormon** distributed.

2–3 April—First **general conference** held in the **Conference Center**.

6 April—Dedication of the **Palmyra** Temple.

21 June—Church announced that **Ricks College** would become a four-year institution and be renamed Brigham Young University–Idaho.

1 October—100th temple dedicted in Boston, Massachusetts.

CONTRIBUTORS

Linda Hunter Adams
Carlos E. Agüero
Douglas D. Alder
Thomas G. Alexander
Gary L. Allen
James B. Allen
Grant Allen Anderson
Jeffrey L. Anderson
Karl Ricks Anderson
Paul L. Anderson
Richard Lloyd Anderson
Leonard J. Arrington
Keith Atkinson
Kim C Averett
Milton V. Backman Jr.
Will Bagley
Kenneth W. Baldridge
Lowell A. Bangerter
Brent A. Barlow
Ronald O. Barney
Alexander L. Baugh
John M. Beck
Dale Beecher
Kenneth H. Beesley
Richard E. Bennett
Reed A. Benson
Joseph C. Bentley
Barbara J. Bernauer
LaMar C. Berrett
Richard Berrett
Howard L. Biddulph
Daniel E. Bishop
M. Guy Bishop
Davis Bitton
JoAn Bitton
Susan Easton Black
Albert Jay Blair
John Bluth

David F. Boone
Joseph F. Boone
Timothy W. Bothell
Randy Bott
Jonathan T. Bowns
M. Gerald Bradford
Mary Lythgoe Bradford
Martha Sonntag Bradley
Scott Bradshaw
Rodney H. Brady
Hoyt W. Brewster Jr.
Newell G. Bringhurst
JoAnn M. Britsch
R. Lanier Britsch
Karl F. Brooks
S. Kent Brown
Gary Browning
Jay H. Buckley
R. William Burnett
An Burvenich
Jay G. Burrup
Lester Bush
Claudia Bushman
Richard L. Bushman
Kenneth Rey Call
J. Elliot Cameron
Brian Q. Cannon
Donald Q. Cannon
Edwin Q. Cannon Jr.
Elaine Cannon
Kenneth L. Cannon
Lorena Cannon
Patrick Cannon
Laura D. L. Card
Lyndia Carter
James A. Carver
Dong Sull Choi
Bruce L. Christensen

Clinton D. Christensen
Scott R. Christensen
Howard Christy
Lewis R. Church
David L. Clark
Lyn Clayton
C. Ross Clement
Marjorie Draper Conder
David Cook
Lyndon W. Cook
T. Jeffrey Cottle
John M. R. Covey
Richard O. Cowan
Richard H. Cracroft
Peter Crawley
David R. Crockett
Larry E. Dahl
Paul Edwards Damron
James V. D'Arc
J. Kenneth Davies
Garold N. Davis
Wilfried Decoo
Janice F. DeMille
Ronald D. Dennis
Jill Mulvay Derr
S. Matthew Despain
Francisco Xavier Dias
W. Randall Dixon
Guy L. Dorius
Cynthia Doxey
Kenneth Driggs
Cole Durham
Reed Durham
Mary Ellen Edmunds
Jessie L. Embry
Chad Emmett
Donald L. Enders
David Ericson

Ronald K. Esplin
Max J. Evans
Harden R. Eyring
Henry J. Eyring
Daniel J. Fairbanks
Scott H. Faulring
Jan Felix
Dennis D. Flake
Elaine McMeen Flake
Lawrence R. Flake
Craig L. Foster
Catherine Britsch Frantz
Robert C. Freeman
Camille Fronk
Craig Fuller
David B. Galbraith
Marvin K. Gardner
Arnold K. Garr
LaMar E. Garrard
H. Dean Garrett
Kristin B. Gerdy
Sara Lee Gibb
Francis M. Gibbons
Gary Gillespie
Francisco Gerardo
  Gimenez
Jamie L. Glenn
Audrey M. Godfrey
Kenneth W. Godfrey
Kristen L. Goodman
Fred R. Gowans
Arnold H. Green
C. Wilfred Griggs
Mark L. Grover
John Hajicek
Val Hale
Robert L. Hales
C. Mark Hamilton
Steven C. Harper
Jonathan Hart
William G. Hartley
Brian M. Hauglid
Harvard Heath
Andrew H. Hedges
Michael Hicks
Ray C. Hillam
Larry A. Hiller
Wayne Hinton

Gail Holmes
Richard Neitzel Holzapfel
Gerald L. Homer
William E. Homer
Douglas A. Hooper
Paul Y. Hoskisson
Jason Wayne Hughes
Sydney Marie Hughes
LeAnne Hull
Julie Hunsaker
J. Michael Hunter
Paul Hyer
L. Dwight Israelsen
Kent P. Jackson
Rebecca Jackson
Richard H. Jackson
Richard W. Jackson
Roger P. Jackson
W. James Jacob
Rhett Stephens James
MacArthur Lee Jones
Mario Javier Jiménez
  Sandí
Clark V. Johnson
Stanley A. Johnson
James R. Kearl
Alan F. Keele
Roger R. Keller
David Kenison
Edward L. Kimball
Stanley B. Kimball
Dale Z. Kirby
Sterling Knapp
Eleanor Knowles
Todd Krueger
Jozsef Kucskar
Lisa Kurki
Eduardo Lamartine
Michael N. Landon
Connie R. Lankford
Roger D. Launius
E. Dale LeBaron
Janet Lee
Glen M. Leonard
Constance L. Lieber
C. Robert Line
John P. Livingstone
John Longhurst

Daniel H. Ludlow
Jennifer L. Lund
Edward Leo Lyman
Lachlan Mackay
Ann N. Madsen
Carol Cornwall Madsen
Truman G. Madsen
David Magleby
Michael Manookin
Craig K. Manscill
Robert L. Marrott
W. Jeffrey Marsh
Marcus H. Martins
Robert J. Matthews
Cory H. Maxwell
Dean L. May
Ralph M. McAffee
Richard D. McClellan
Richard L. McClellan
Joseph Fielding
  McConkie
Mark L. McConkie
Byron R. Merrill
Charles Metten
Robert L. Millet
Michael F. Moody
Richard G. Moore
Edwin B. Morrell
Dale C. Mouritsen
Maren M. Mouritsen
Veneese C. Nelson
Lloyd D. Newell
Dallin D. Oaks
Terrance D. Olson
Kerry Oman
Richard G. Oman
Craig J. Ostler
Kenneth W. Packer
Spencer J. Palmer
Max H Parkin
Alan K. Parrish
David L. Paulsen
Virginia H. Pearce
Keith W. Perkins
Lee Tom Perry
Morris S. Petersen
Roger K. Petersen
Erlend D. Peterson

F. Ross Peterson
Janet Peterson
John A. Peterson
Paul H. Peterson
Richard G. Peterson
R. Douglas Phillips
Vaughn R. Pickell
Gordon Pollock
Larry C. Porter
David H. Pratt
Andrea G. Radke
Carolyn J. Rasmus
Ellis T. Rasmussen
Russell C. Rasmussen
Karen Reed
Rex C. Reeve Jr.
Michael D. Rhodes
A. LeGrand Richards
Matthew O. Richardson
Robert Richardson
Jeffrey Ringer
Richard C. Roberts
Elwin C. Robison
Ronald E. Romig
David R. Rowberry
Glenn N. Rowe
Glen L. Rudd
Jack L. Rushton
Richard W. Sadler
Gilbert W. Scharffs

Mark A. Scherer
David Rolph Seely
Jan Shipps
Eric B. Shumway
John Sillito
Barnard Stewart Silver
Larry R. Skidmore
Andrew C. Skinner
Royal Skousen
Barbara McKay Smith
Brian L. Smith
Hortense C. Smith
L. Douglas Smoot
Kip Sperry
Mark L. Staker
Calvin R. Stephens
Joseph Grant Stevenson
Thomas L. Stinebaugh
Gaye Strathearn
Glen R. Stubbs
Vivian Linford Talbot
Wilmer W. Tanner
Charles Tate
John Thomas
Clark T. Thorstenson
Jay M. Todd
Brent L. Top
James A. Toronto
Mike Trapp
F. LaMond Tullis

Richard E. Turley Jr.
David Tuttle
Blair G. Van Dyke
Dell Van Orden
Kyle R. Walker
Ronald G. Watt
John W. Welch
A. Bryan Weston
V. Robert Westover
Relva L. Whetten
David M. Whitchurch
Linda White
David J. Whittaker
Philip C. Wightman
Alan L. Wilkins
Rachel Wilkins
Matthew P. Willden
Clyde J. Williams
Keith J. Wilson
William A. Wilson
James Wirshborn
Mary Jane Woodger
Fred E. Woods
Jed L. Woodworth
Dennis A. Wright
Norman E. Wright
Raymond S. Wright
W. Sidney Young
Buddy Youngreen
Emily C. Zeigler

PHOTOGRAPHIC CREDITS

All images are used by permission.

Frontispiece
Capstone-laying ceremony for the Salt Lake Temple, 6 April 1892, C. L. Joy; courtesy of LDS Church Archives, Salt Lake City, Utah.

Page xiv
Gibbon Street Chapel, Brisbane, Australia, ca. 1904; courtesy of Elva Mitchell, Sydney, Australia.

Page 70
Book of Mormon project in Sierra Leone, West Africa, ca. 1988–89, Robert W. Stum; courtesy of LDS Church Archives, Salt Lake City, Utah.

Page 162
Joseph F. Smith and party at Cardston, Alberta, Canada, 27 July 1913, Henson Photo; courtesy of LDS Church Archives, Salt Lake City, Utah.

Page 272
Deseret Alphabet publication of 1 and 2 Nephi; courtesy of R. Q. Shupe, San Juan Capistrano, California.

Page 312
The Evening and the Morning Star, March 1833; courtesy of Special Collections–Manuscripts, Harold B. Lee Library, Brigham Young University, Provo, Utah.

Page 354
A book of Abraham facsimile from the *Times and Seasons,* 1 March 1842; courtesy of R. Q. Shupe, San Juan Capistrano, California.

Page 406
Temple Square, Salt Lake City, Utah, 6 April 1906, Shipler Photography; courtesy of Utah State Historical Society, Salt Lake City, Utah (#2094).

Page 454
Handcart Pioneers, oil on canvas, 1908, Danquart A. Weggeland; courtesy of Museum of Church History and Art, Salt Lake City, Utah.

Page 530
Elder Horace Hayes, R. Lanier Britsch, and Randy Booth introducing BYU Young

Ambassadors to India prime minister Indira Gandhi, January 1982; courtesy of R. Lanier Britsch.

Page 562

Mutual Improvement Association officers in Japan, 1916; courtesy of LDS Church Archives, Salt Lake City, Utah.

Page 598

West pulpits, Kirtland Temple, 1836; courtesy of Historic American Building Survey, United States Library of Congress, Washington D.C.

Page 634

Little Soldier, ca. 1867, Charles W. Carter; courtesy of LDS Church Archives, Salt Lake City, Utah.

Page 690

Angel Moroni statue, Salt Lake Temple, 6 April 1892, Charles R. Savage; courtesy of LDS Church Archives, Salt Lake City, Utah.

Page 814

Edward Hunter's home, Nauvoo, Illinois; courtesy of Manuscripts Division, J. Willard Marriott Library, University of Utah.

Page 860

First Presidency Letter, 8 June 1978; courtesy of Special Collections–Manuscripts, Harold B. Lee Library, Brigham Young University, Provo, Utah.

Page 882

Proclamation on the Family, 23 September 1995; courtesy of The Church of Jesus Christ of Latter-day Saints, Salt Lake City, Utah.

Page 972

Catching Quails, tempera on canvas, 1880s, C. C. A. Christensen, ©Brigham Young University Museum of Art; courtesy of Brigham Young University Museum of Art, Provo, Utah.

Page 978

1880 Relief Society Banner; courtesy of Museum of Church History and Art, Salt Lake City, Utah.

Page 1048

Monday 24 June 1844, Beyond the Events, oil on canvas, 1987, Pino Drago; courtesy of Museum of Church History and Art, Salt Lake City, Utah.

Page 1210

Papeete Tahiti Temple; courtesy of LDS Church Archives, Salt Lake City, Utah.

Page 1266

Rules of the united order; courtesy of LDS Church Archives, Salt Lake City, Utah.

Page 1286

The Vision, from *The Evening and the Morning Star,* July 1832; courtesy of Special

Collections–Manuscripts, Harold B. Lee Library, Brigham Young University, Provo, Utah.

Page 1302

Ronald Reagan and Gordon B. Hinckley, 10 September 1982; courtesy of LDS Church Archives, Salt Lake City, Utah.

Page 1372

Brigham Young, 10 December 1850, Marsena Cannon; courtesy of LDS Church Archives, Salt Lake City, Utah.

Page 1392

Town clock store with ZCMI sign, ca. 1869, Charles W. Carter; courtesy of LDS Church Archives, Salt Lake City, Utah.

INDEX